GRE®
All the Verbal

GRE® is a registered trademark of Educational Testing Service (ETS), which is not affiliated with Kaplan and was not involved in the production of, and does not endorse, this product.

GRE All the Verbal

Retail ISBN: 978-1-5062-8182-7
Course ISBN: 978-1-5062-8184-1
Retail eISBN: 978-1-5062-8183-4
Course eISBN: 978-1-5062-8185-8

Copyright © 2023 Kaplan, Inc.

10 9 8 7 6 5 4 3 2 1

All rights reserved. The text of this publication, or any part thereof, may not be reproduced in any manner whatsoever without written permission from the publisher.

GRE® is a registered trademark of Educational Testing Service (ETS), which is not affiliated with Kaplan and was not involved in the production of, and does not endorse, this product.

INSTRUCTIONAL GUIDE SERIES

1 GRE All the Quant

2 GRE All the Verbal

3 5 lb. Book of GRE® Practice Problems

SUPPLEMENTAL MATERIALS

500 Essential Words:
GRE® Vocabulary Flash Cards

500 Advanced Words:
GRE® Vocabulary Flash Cards

May 2, 2023

Hello! Welcome to **GRE® All the Verbal.**

I hope this book provides just the guidance you need to get the most out of your GRE studies. **If you have any questions or feedback, please do not hesitate to contact us at gre@manhattanprep.com or 212-721-7400.** Also: We try to keep all of our books free of errors, but if you think we've goofed, please visit manhattanprep.com/GRE/errata.

All of our Manhattan Prep books are based on the continuing experiences of both our instructors and our students. The primary vision for this edition of the book was developed by Chris Gentry and Whitney Garner. The primary authors of this edition of the book were Manhattan Prep instructors Chris Gentry and Ryan Starr, and the primary editors were Whitney Garner and Logan Smeallie. Project management, design, and quality assurance were led by Deepika Devan, Mario Gambino, Marie Gugnishev, and Helen Tan.

Finally, we are indebted to all of the Manhattan Prep students who have given us excellent feedback over the years. This book wouldn't be half of what it is without their voice.

And now that you are one of our students too, please chime in! I look forward to hearing from you. Thanks again and best of luck preparing for the GRE!

Sincerely,

Stacey Koprince
Director of Content and Curriculum
Manhattan Prep

www.manhattanprep.com/gre   623 Broadway, New York, NY 10012   Tel: 212-721-7400

TABLE OF CONTENTS

Introduction 1
    Your GRE Journey 3
    The GRE Exam 3
    Off the Deep End: What GRE Verbal Can Look Like 5
    Verbal Question Formats in Detail 6
    Timing 12
    How to Use This Book 13

UNIT ONE: Words and Sentences **15**

Chapter 1: GRE Vocabulary 17
    Learning Vocabulary Words in This Book 19
    Studying Vocabulary Effectively 19
    Two Options for Vocabulary Study 21
    Other Study Techniques 24
    When to Use Roots 24
    Specialized Vocabulary in Reading Comprehension Passages 26
    Using Social Networks to Buttress Your Vocabulary Studies 26
    Vocabulary Challenge 27
    Answers and Explanations 28

Chapter 2: GRE Sentences 29
    Complex Sentences 31
    Unpacking GRE Sentences 32
    Principles for Unpacking Sentences 33
    Link to Real Ideas 35
    Vocabulary Challenge 36
    Problem Set 37
    Answers and Explanations 38

Chapter 3: Text Completion and Sentence Equivalence 41
    One-Blank Text Completion 43
    The Three-Step Process for Text Completions 44
    Direction Markers 50
    Drill: Sentence Analysis 53

 vii

Sentence Equivalence. 55
Sentence Analysis in Sentence Equivalence 56
Answer Choice Analysis. 58
When to Use (and NOT to Use) Answer Choice Analysis 61
Drill: Answer Choice Analysis. 63
What If I Don't Know the Words?. 66
Why It Is Important to Learn Words in Context 67
Traps in TC and SE 68
Text Completion and Sentence Equivalence Recap 69
Vocabulary Challenge 69
Problem Set (Text Completion). 70
Problem Set (Sentence Equivalence) 75
Answers and Explanations 91

UNIT TWO: Paragraphs and Passages **109**

Chapter 4: GRE Paragraphs 111
Making Connections. 113
Signals and Pronouns 115
Components of Paragraphs 117
The Main Idea (and Archetypes) 119
The Big Picture 122
Don't Just Read, Do Something! 123
A Note-Taking Exercise (Sample Notes) 124
Common Notations 124
Vocabulary Challenge 125
Problem Set 126
Answers and Explanations 127

Chapter 5: Short Passages in Reading Comprehension 129
Two Types of Passages 131
Scanning Ahead 132
Strategy for General Questions 133
Strategy for Specific Questions 134
Common Wrong Answer Categories 137
Summary of Strategies for Answer Choice Eliminations 138
Comprehensive Strategies for All Reading Comprehension 139
Vocabulary Challenge 139
A Short Introduction to the Problem Set 140

viii

    Problem Set 141

    Answers and Explanations 145

Chapter 6: Argument-Based Reading Comprehension. 153

    Recognizing Argument-Based Passages 155

    Components of Argument-Based Passages 156

    Identifying the Components of an Argument 157

    Strategy for ABP Questions. 158

    Taking Notes 160

    Useful Focal Points for All Question Types 162

    Question Types 165

    Vocabulary Challenge 178

    Problem Set 179

    Answers and Explanations 184

Chapter 7: Multi-Blank Text Completion 199

    Two- and Three-Blank Text Completions 201

    Start with the Easier (or Easiest) Blank 202

    Tricky Aspects of Multi-Blank Text Completion. 206

    More on Traps in Text Completion. 210

    Vocabulary Challenge 212

    Problem Set 213

    Answers and Explanations 222

Chapter 8: Long Passages in Reading Comprehension. 237

    Long Passages 239

    Two Extremes and a Balanced Approach 240

    Principles of Active Reading 241

    The Headline List 245

    Practice on Non-GRE Material 247

    A Review of Strategies for RC Questions 248

    Pulling It All Together 251

    Vocabulary Challenge. 252

    Problem Set 253

    Answers and Explanations 257

Chapter 9: Reading Comprehension Problem Set 265

    Problem Set 269

    Answers and Explanations 278

Chapter 10: Essays 299
    Essays in a Nutshell 301
    Analyze an Issue 303
    Analyze an Argument 310
    Style Points 319
    Analyze an Issue Sample Essays 320
    Analyze an Argument Sample Essays 324
    Notes on Preparation 327
    Vocabulary Challenge 327
    Answers and Explanations 328

Introduction

In This Chapter...

- Your GRE Journey
- The GRE Exam
- Off the Deep End: What GRE Verbal Can Look Like
- Verbal Question Formats in Detail
- Timing
- How to Use This Book

Introduction

Your GRE Journey

We know that you're looking to succeed on the GRE so that you can go to graduate school and do the things you want to do in life. We also know that you're not frequently taking standardized tests asking you to answer multiple choice questions after reading long passages of text you're not interested in (or at least not recently).

In order to succeed, you will need to get (back) into an academic mindset, reading dense material, confronting difficult vocabulary, and answering analytical questions, all within short time limits. In other words, it's going to take hard work on your part to get a top GRE score. That's why we've put together this set of books that will take you from the basics all the way up to the material you need to master for a near-perfect score (or whatever *your* goal score may be).

In this chapter, you will learn the format of the test, with more information specific to question formats in the Verbal section of the test. You'll also see study planning advice to help you place elements of this book (and possibly the class syllabus) into a context more relevant to your personal needs.

You've taken the first step. Now it's time to get to work!

The GRE Exam

Exam Structure

The GRE has six scored sections. You will get a 10-minute break between the third and fourth sections and a 1-minute break between the other sections. The Analytical Writing section, also known as the Essay section, is always first.

The remaining sections can be seen in any order and will include:

- Two Verbal Reasoning sections, each of which has 20 problems to answer in 30 minutes
- Two Quantitative Reasoning (Math) sections, each of which has 20 problems to answer in 35 minutes
- Either an unscored section or a research section (or both or neither. . .more on this in a bit)

Introduction

Section #	Section Type	# Problems	Time	Scored?
1	Essay	2 essays	30 minutes each	Yes
2	Math or Verbal	Approx. 20	30–35 minutes	Maybe
3	Math or Verbal	Approx. 20	30–35 minutes	Maybe
10-Minute Break				
4	Math or Verbal	Approx. 20	30–35 minutes	Maybe
5	Math or Verbal	Approx. 20	35–35 minutes	Maybe
6	Math or Verbal	Approx. 20	30–35 minutes	Maybe
Last	Research Section	Varies	Varies	No

You will definitely have at least two Verbal and at least two Math sections. You *may or may not* have a third Verbal or a third Math section. These four or five sections can come in any order. For example, you could see:

- Math 1, Verbal 1, Math 2, Verbal 2, Math 3
- Verbal 1, Verbal 2, Math 1, Verbal 3, Math 2
- Math 1, Verbal 1, Verbal 2, Math 2 (no fifth section)

If you do see a total of three Verbal sections, then one of those sections won't count towards your score—but you won't know which one. Likewise, if you see a total of three Math sections, one of the three won't count towards your score, but you won't know which one. It is *not* necessarily the case that the first four multiple-choice sections will be the scored sections. As a result, complete all of the sections to the best of your ability.

At the end of the test, you may be asked to do a research section. If so, they will tell you in advance that this section is unscored and it will be the very last section you see.

Finally, it's possible that you will not be given any unscored section at all. In this case, you will receive just four multiple-choice sections (two Math and two Verbal) and all four will count.

Navigating the Problems in a Section

The GRE offers you the ability to move freely around the problems in a single section. You can go forward and backward one-by-one and can even jump directly to any problem from the "review list" screen. You can also mark a problem for later review. The review list screen provides a snapshot of which problems you have answered, which ones you have marked, and which ones are incomplete.

If you finish a section early, double-check the review list for completion. Do answer every problem—there's no penalty for getting something wrong. You'll get a chance to practice with the review list when you take practice exams.

Introduction

The majority of GRE test-takers are pressed for time in at least some of the sections. You may find that you have time to go back to just one or two problems—or you may not have time to go back to any of them. With these points in mind, here's what we recommend:

1. In general, do the problems in the order in which they appear.
2. When you encounter a pretty-hard-but-not-impossible problem, do your best to eliminate answer choices that you know are wrong. Then choose one of the remaining answers and keep going. (What you've just done is called "educated guessing".)
3. If it's an impossible one, don't try to eliminate answers first—just put in a random guess and move on.
4. When you encounter an "I could do this but it's going to take extra time" problem, put in a random guess *for now* but mark the problem for later review. Do this on a maximum of 3 problems in the section. (If it turns out that you don't have time to get back to it, at least you've made a guess.)
5. Aim to save at least a minute at the end of the section to review the review list. Scan down: Did you leave any problems blank? If so, click into them and put in a random guess.
6. If you still have more time left, jump into one of your "marked for later" problems.

Avoid repeatedly clicking forward and backward through all of the problems, searching for "easy" ones. This will eat up valuable time. Instead, be disciplined about making the call to move on when you hit a problem that's just too hard. (And how do you know that, quickly and confidently? Via your studies. Part of the value in prioritizing your studies as you go is knowing when you want to bail on a problem during the test.)

Getting good at navigating the test sections will take a lot of practice. Use the above advice on practice exams *and* when doing timed problem sets (even when you're doing timed sets out of a book and not on a computer screen).

Off the Deep End: What GRE Verbal Can Look Like

> *The tokens given by the aristocrat, while nugatory, still served as a reminder that the power of the Crown continued to be held in some esteem even in such mercurial political times.*

Welcome to the marvelous world of GRE Verbal, where you too will find forbiddingly dense and frustratingly constructed, sentences, paragraphs, and passages the norm rather than the exception. The GRE both works within and directly tests formal, sometimes nearly archaic, phrasings and structures to mimic the challenges of difficult academic writing. (And yes, the phrasing of those two sentences was deliberate. This is similar to the writing style used on the GRE.)

Hopefully, the above introduction serves as a demonstration that a need exists to "learn to read for the GRE." Therefore, test takers need to follow a reading process that will address these challenges at the outset and build a study process that reinforces the necessary mental habits to implement that reading process.

Or, put in less GRE-ish terms, yes, you do actually want to study Verbal. It's not a situation of "well, I'll just try my best," hoping that repetition of problems will make you better. There is a method to the madness, and that is why this book exists!

Introduction

Why Is GRE Verbal So Challenging?

There are several specific, concrete reasons for why GRE Verbal is so challenging.

- The content is demanding. GRE Verbal questions focus on specific and often unfamiliar topics in sciences, social science, history, and other humanities (literature, art, music). You might be neither knowledgeable nor enthusiastic about these fields.
- You have to read on the screen, which is physically stressful on the human eye.
- You have to read quickly, regardless of how dense the material is. Some verbal questions need to be answered in one minute; that is not a lot of time!
- You have to stay engaged, even if you do not feel you understand, or maybe even just don't *like,* a sentence or passage. So even in those situations, you need strategies to continue to work productively through the section.

Thus, this book! The following sections will address specific Verbal question formats and timing guidelines.

Verbal Question Formats in Detail

The 20 questions in each Verbal section can be broken down by format as follows:

- Reading Comprehension questions (≈ 10)
- Text Completion questions (≈ 6)
- Sentence Equivalence questions (≈ 4)

Before going into these Verbal question types further, let's go back to the beginning of the exam: the Analytical Writing section, also known as the Essay (although it's really two essays).

The Essays

The Analytical Writing section consists of two separately timed 30-minute tasks: Analyze an Issue and Analyze an Argument. As you can imagine, the 30-minute time limit implies that you aren't aiming to write an essay that would garner a Pulitzer Prize nomination but rather to complete the tasks adequately and according to the directions. Each essay is scored separately, but your reported essay score is the average of the two, rounded up to the next half-point increment on a 0–6 scale.

Issue Task: This essay prompt will present a claim, generally one that is vague enough to be interpreted in a variety of ways and discussed from numerous perspectives. Your job as a test-taker is to write a response discussing the extent to which you agree or disagree and support your position. Don't sit on the fence—pick a side!

Argument Task: This essay prompt will be an argument comprised of both a claim (or claims) and evidence. Your job is to dispassionately discuss the argument's structural flaws and merits (well, mostly the flaws). Don't agree or disagree with the argument—simply evaluate its logic.

Check out the official GRE website (www.ets.org/gre) for example essay prompts and sample essays with scores.

Introduction

Multiple-Choice Questions

In this book and in *The Official Guide to the GRE® General Test*, you will see letters at the beginning of the answer choices for multiple choice questions (A, B, C, and so on). When you're taking a test on a computer, however, there will be no answer letters, just boxes or open bubbles that you will select with your mouse.

Although the real test won't show letters on the screen, there's an important reason why you want to imagine that there are letters there: As you solve problems, you'll eliminate wrong answers before selecting the correct one—but you can't cross off answers on the screen.

Write down A, B, C, D, E (or however many letters are needed for that problem) on your scratch paper to keep track of your answer-choice eliminations as you go. The answer letters shown in this book will help you get into the habit of doing this, even though you will not see answer letters on the screen when you take the test.

Reading Comprehension Questions

Reading Comprehension (RC) questions will be associated with four or five passages that vary in length from one paragraph to several. A passage typically has between one and four questions associated with it, and longer passages typically have more questions.

Most Reading Comprehension problems will have five answer choices from which you'll choose one answer. For these, use the letters A, B, C, D, and E to keep track of your eliminations. There are also two other possible RC formats, Select One or More and Select-in-Passage.

Select One or More Answer Choices

Some RC problems will give you three statements about a passage and ask you to "select all that apply." Either one, two, or all three can be correct (there is no "none of the above" option). There is no partial credit; you must indicate all of the correct choices and none of the incorrect choices. Use the letters A, B, and C to keep track of your eliminations on these problems.

On your screen, the answer choice boxes for "Select One or More" will always be *squares*, while the standard "pick just one" multiple-choice problems will always use *circles*. The squares are a good visual reminder that you may need to select more than one choice on these problems, just as you might check more than one box on a checklist.

> *Strategy Tip:*
>
> On **Select One or More Answer Choices**, consider each choice independently! You cannot use the process of elimination in the same way as you do on normal multiple-choice questions.

Select-in-Passage

For the question type Select-in-Passage, you are given an assignment such as "Select the sentence in the passage that explains why the experiment's results were discovered to be invalid." Clicking anywhere on the sentence in the passage will highlight it. (As with any GRE question, you will have to click "Confirm" to submit your answer, so don't worry about accidentally selecting the wrong sentence due to a slip of the mouse.)

Introduction

> *Strategy Tip:*
>
> Because **Select-in-Passage** questions don't have a consistent number of sentences or paragraphs, use numbers rather than letters to keep track of your eliminations.
>
> If you have a single paragraph, number each sentence. If you have multiple paragraphs, start by numbering each paragraph. Once you've narrowed down to one paragraph, number the sentences in that paragraph.

Now give these new question types a try.

The sample questions below are based on this passage:

Physicist Robert Oppenheimer, director of the fateful Manhattan Project, said, "It is a profound and necessary truth that the deep things in science are not found because they are useful; they are found because it was possible to find them." In a later address at MIT, Oppenheimer presented the thesis that scientists could be held only very nominally responsible for the consequences of their research and discovery. Oppenheimer asserted that ethics, philosophy, and politics have very little to do with the day-to-day work of the scientist and that scientists could not rationally be expected to predict all the effects of their work. Yet, in a talk in 1945 to the Association of Los Alamos Scientists, Oppenheimer offered some reasons why the Manhattan Project scientists built the atomic bomb; the justifications included "fear that Nazi Germany would build it first" and "hope that it would shorten the war."

For question #1, consider each of the three choices separately and select all that apply.

1. The passage implies that Robert Oppenheimer would most likely have agreed with which of the following views:

    A Some scientists take military goals into account in their work.
    B Deep things in science are not useful.
    C The everyday work of a scientist is only minimally involved with ethics.

2. Select the sentence in which the writer implies that Oppenheimer has not been consistent in his view that scientists have little consideration for the effects of their work.

   (Here, you would highlight the appropriate sentence with your mouse. There are four sentences, so there are four options.)

To answer the first question, Oppenheimer is quoted in the last sentence as saying that one of the reasons the bomb was built was the scientists' "hope that it would shorten the war." Thus, Oppenheimer would likely agree with the view that "some scientists take military goals into account in their work." Choice (B) is a trap answer using familiar language from the passage. According to the passage, Oppenheimer says that the possible usefulness of scientific discoveries is not why scientists make discoveries; he does not say that the discoveries aren't useful. The passage quotes Oppenheimer as saying that ethics has *very* "little to do with the day-to-day work of the scientist," which is a good match for "only minimally involved with ethics." So for the Select One or More, you would select choices (A) and (C), but not choice (B).

Introduction

> *Strategy Tip:*
>
> On Select One or More Answer Choices, write A B C on your paper and mark each choice with a check, an *X*, or a symbol such as ~ if you're not sure. This should keep you from crossing out all three choices.

For the second question, the correct sentence is the final sentence:

"Yet, in a talk in 1945 to the Association of Los Alamos Scientists, Oppenheimer offered some reasons why the Manhattan Project scientists built the atomic bomb; the justifications included 'fear that Nazi Germany would build it first' and 'hope that it would shorten the war.'"

The word *yet* is a good clue that this sentence is about to express a view contrary to the views expressed in the rest of the passage. On the test, you would click this sentence in the text of the passage with the computer mouse, highlighting it. (If you clicked on a sentence by mistake, you can just click on the sentence you actually intended to change the highlight.)

The chapters on Reading Comprehension in this book contain more detail on solving both the more standard multiple choice RC questions and these more unique ones.

Text Completion Questions

Text Completion (TC) questions will consist of anywhere from one to three blanks spread across one to five sentences. When TCs have one blank, you will have five words or phrases to choose from for that blank, so use answer letters A, B, C, D, and E to keep track of your eliminations.

When TCs have two or three blanks, each blank will have three options, and you will select words or short phrases for each blank independently. There is no partial credit; the selection for every blank in the problem must be correct in order to get that question right. Use answer letters A through F for two-blank TCs and answer letters A through I for three-blank TCs.

Try the following two-blank example:

Leaders are not always expected to (i) _____ the same rules as are those they lead; leaders are often looked up to for a surety and presumption that would be viewed as (ii) _____ in most others.

	Blank (i)		Blank (ii)
A	decree	D	hubris
B	proscribe	E	avarice
C	conform to	F	anachronism

In the first blank, you need a word similar to *follow*. In the second blank, you need a word similar to *arrogance*. The correct answers are *conform to* and *hubris*.

> *Strategy Tip:*
>
> In **Text Completion** questions, do NOT look at the answer choices until you've decided for yourself what kind of word needs to go in each blank. Then, review the choices and eliminate those that are not matches.

9

Introduction

Now try an example with three blanks:

For Kant, the fact of having a right and having the (i) _____ to enforce it via coercion cannot be separated, and he asserts that this marriage of rights and coercion is compatible with the freedom of everyone. This is not at all peculiar from the standpoint of modern political thought—what good is a right if its violation triggers no enforcement (be it punishment or (ii) _____)? The necessity of coercion is not at all in conflict with the freedom of everyone, because this coercion only comes into play when someone has (iii) _____ someone else.

	Blank (i)
A	technique
B	license
C	prohibition

	Blank (ii)
D	amortization
E	reward
F	restitution

	Blank (iii)
G	questioned the hypothesis of
H	violated the rights of
I	granted civil liberties to

In the first sentence, use the clue "he asserts that this marriage of rights and coercion is compatible with the freedom of everyone" to help fill in the first blank. Kant believes that *coercion* is "married to" rights and is compatible with freedom for all. So you want something in the first blank like *right* or *power*. Kant believes that rights are meaningless without enforcement. Only the choice *license* can work (while a *license* can be physical, like a driver's license, the word *license* can also mean *right*).

The second blank is part of the phrase "punishment or _____," which you are told is the *enforcement* resulting from the violation of a right. So the blank should be something, other than punishment, that constitutes enforcement against someone who violates a right. (More simply, it should be something bad.) Only *restitution* works. *Restitution* is compensating the victim in some way (perhaps monetarily or by returning stolen goods).

The final sentence says, "coercion only comes into play when someone has _____ someone else." Throughout the text, *coercion* means "enforcement against someone who has violated the rights of someone else." The meaning is the same here. The answer is *violated the rights of*.

The complete and correct answer is this combination:

	Blank (i)		Blank (ii)		Blank (iii)
B	license	F	restitution	H	violated the rights of

There are a total of 3 × 3 × 3, or 27 possible ways to answer a three-blank Text Completion question—and only one of those 27 ways is correct. In theory, these are tough odds. In practice, you will often have certainty about some of the blanks, so your guessing odds are almost never this difficult. Just follow the basic process: Come up with your own filler for each blank, and match to the answer choices. If you're confused by this example, don't worry! The chapters on Text Completion and Sentence Equivalence in this book cover all of this in detail.

> *Strategy Tip:*
>
> On **Text Completion** questions, the GRE will give you a clue to the correct answer in the text. Look for textual evidence for each answer choice you select.

Sentence Equivalence Questions

For this question type, you are given one sentence with a single blank. This looks very much like a one-blank Text Completion question, but the assignment has a twist. This time, instead of five choices, there are six, and instead of choosing one answer, you need to pick two that fit the blank and are alike in meaning. Use answer letters A through F to keep track of your eliminations.

Of the Verbal question types, this one depends the most on vocabulary and also yields the most to strategy.

No partial credit is given on Sentence Equivalence; both correct answers must be selected, and no incorrect answers may be selected. When you pick 2 of 6 choices, there are 15 possible combinations of choices, and only 1 is correct. However, this is not nearly as daunting as it sounds.

If you have six choices, but the two correct ones must be similar in meaning, then you have, at most, three possible *pairs* of choices. There may be fewer, since not all choices are guaranteed to have a partner. If you know the meaning of the words in the answer choices and can match up the pairs, you can seriously narrow down your options.

Here is a sample set of answer choices. The square boxes indicate that you are to select more than one answer.

- [A] tractable
- [B] taciturn
- [C] arbitrary
- [D] tantamount
- [E] reticent
- [F] amenable

The question is deliberately omitted here in order to illustrate how much you can do with the choices alone, assuming you have learned these words during your vocabulary studies.

Tractable and *amenable* are synonyms (*tractable, amenable* people will do whatever you want them to do). *Taciturn* and *reticent* are synonyms (both mean "not talkative").

Arbitrary (based on one's own will) and *tantamount* (equivalent) are not similar in meaning and cannot be a pair. Therefore, the *only* possible correct answer pairs are choices (A) and (F) or choices (B) and (E). You have improved your chances from 1 in 15 to a 50/50 shot without even reading the question!

Of course, in approaching a Sentence Equivalence question, you do want to analyze the sentence in the same way you would in Text Completion—read for a textual clue that tells you what type of word *must* go in the blank. Then, look for a matching pair.

Introduction

> *Strategy Tip:*
>
> In **Sentence Equivalence** questions, if you're sure that a word in the choices does *not* have a partner, cross it out!

The sentence for the previous answer choice options could read as follows:

Though the dinner guests were quite _____, the hostess did her best to keep the conversation active and engaging.

Since the hostess needed to work "to keep the conversation active and engaging" due to the nature of her dinner guests, you can infer that the guests were not talkative. Thus, choice (B) and choice (E) are the best pairing.

Try this example of a complete problem:

> While athletes usually expect to achieve their greatest feats in their teens or twenties, opera singers don't reach the _____ of their vocal powers until middle age.
>
> A harmony
> B zenith
> C acme
> D terminus
> E nadir
> F cessation

Those with strong vocabularies might go straight to the choices to make pairs. *Zenith* and *acme* are synonyms, meaning "high point, peak." *Terminus* and *cessation* are synonyms meaning "end." *Nadir* is a low point, and *harmony* is present here as a trap answer reminding you of opera singers. Cross off choices (A) and (E), since they do not have partners. Then, go back to the sentence, knowing that your only options are a pair meaning "peak" and a pair meaning "end."

Since the sentence discusses the various career points when two groups of professionals "achieve their greatest feats," the correct answer pair is choice (B) and choice (C).

Now that you have a few examples of the question formats, let's examine the timing goals for each question type. (The Essays are omitted from the following chart, as they are not scored as a section, but rather as a single response to a single prompt. Your timing goal for the Essays is direct: 30 minutes to write each essay.)

Timing

One of the most pressing challenges on GRE Verbal is the timing. Spending enough time to answer the questions accurately but not so much that you lose points because you run out of time requires practice and planning.

Use the following chart as a guideline for how much time to spend answering a question. There are two things to note. First, the following are timing recommendations for standard (1x) GRE timing. If you have timing accommodations (1.5x or 2x), adjust your goals accordingly. Second, these recommendations are for time spent attempting the problem—time yourself while attempting problems, but don't time yourself when reviewing problems.

Introduction

Question Type	Time Spent Reading	Time Spent in Answer Choices	Total Time
Text Completion	45 to 60 seconds	10 seconds per blank	55–90 seconds
Sentence Equivalence	45 to 60 seconds	20 seconds	65–80 seconds
Reading Comprehension	1.5 to 3.5 minutes, depending on passage length	30–60 seconds per question	2 to 6 minutes, depending on number of questions and length of passage

You probably already notice a challenge: Reading Comprehension timing varies extensively. This is an awkward necessity due to the fact that the length of passages varies, as does the number of questions per passage. Your exact timing will vary according to your strengths, and you must take into account that your timing needs to pace you through a whole section.

While you will need to be flexible in your timing allocations for Reading Comprehension, here is a general guideline: Spend about half of your total time reading the passage and about half of your total time evaluating the answer choices for each question. The table below illustrates a typical timing breakdown for each likely length of a Reading Comprehension passage.

# of Questions	Time Spent Reading	Time Spent on Answer Choices	Total Time
1	1 minute 30 seconds	45 seconds	2 minutes, 15 seconds
2	2 minutes	45 seconds	3 minutes, 30 seconds
3	3 minutes	45 seconds	5 minutes, 15 seconds
4	3 minutes	45 seconds	6 minutes
5 (very rare)	3 minutes	45 seconds	6 minutes, 45 seconds

These timing benchmarks are rough, especially because more questions doesn't necessarily mean a longer passage. You will see one long passage with up to four questions, but the other passages could be very short, even if they have two or three questions attached. Additionally, different question types take differing amounts of time. More detailed timing suggestions are in the coming chapters that cover each type of question you will see.

How to Use This Book

If you're using this book as part of a course, you will have a syllabus to guide you. If you are not, however, we want to offer you some additional guidance.

This book is *not* a novel, a news story, or an article on a topic that interests you; it isn't meant to be dug into and read cover to cover. However, this book also isn't meant to be used as an encyclopedia, only flipping to specific sections for reference or to look up a topic. Our recommendation is to instead see this book as a balance between the two.

Introduction

The organization of material is intended to build skills in order from the briefest units of verbal text (vocabulary) to the lengthiest (long passages). Don't confuse "brief" with easy or introductory, however. The material in the first chapters on words and sentences will set you up for some of the most advanced study and test taking strategies in the entire book. Skipping these earlier sections completely is likely to artificially limit your progress in the later sections.

That said, we understand that your needs may not lie in the order this book presents the material. Rather than skipping around, though, consider instead changing your pace as you move through the book. Dig more deeply into areas of weakness and be ready to skim or briefly reference areas of strength. If you find yourself struggling with later chapters, return to earlier sections to reinforce the micro-skills that build better performance in longer problem types.

Top Tips for Studying GRE Verbal

Regardless of how you feel about your verbal abilities and which areas are strengths and weaknesses, all students benefit from doing the following three things:

1. **Practice vocabulary early and often.**
   - Before you do anything else, read Chapter 1: GRE Vocabulary, and choose your favorite method(s) for learning and practicing new words.
   - Commit to consistent (daily) practice. Even if you don't have time to sit down and study anything else that day, find five minutes for your flashcards or stories.
2. **Give yourself mental variety.**
   - Everyone needs a break sometimes—even if it's just studying a different component of the test.
   - Keep in mind, you can move backward to old material or forward to new material as you wish.
3. **Periodically test yourself.**
   - Periodically challenge yourself to *do* something. Whether this is a full practice test or a single problem, make regular attempts to apply your skills.
   - Use practice tests as assessments and reassessments. Your abilities will change, and you need periodic "checks" on your actual abilities versus your perception of them.

Final Notes

Keep in mind that, while some of your study materials may be on paper (including the Educational Testing Service's most recent source of official GRE problems, *The Official Guide to the GRE® General Test*), your exam will be administered on a computer. Because this is a computer-based test, you will *not* be able to underline portions of reading passages or otherwise physically mark up problems. Get used to this now. Use separate scratch paper to solve the problems in these books.

And use your available online resources. Create a free account on the Manhattan Prep website to gain access to a plethora of online resources, including a vocabulary tracker/organizer, Interact lessons, and a full practice test!

UNIT ONE

Words and Sentences

This unit provides you with a comprehensive approach to the study of the most fundamental building blocks of GRE Verbal problems: words and sentences. Included are practical techniques for developing vocabulary and grasping the meaning of complex sentences. Finally, this unit introduces two question types: Text Completions and Sentence Equivalence.

In This Unit ...

- Chapter 1: GRE Vocabulary
- Chapter 2: GRE Sentences
- Chapter 3: Text Completion and Sentence Equivalence

CHAPTER 1
GRE Vocabulary

In This Chapter ...

- Learning Vocabulary Words in This Book
- Studying Vocabulary Effectively
- Two Options for Vocabulary Study
- Other Study Techniques
- When to Use Roots
- Specialized Vocabulary in Reading Comprehension Passages
- Using Social Networks to Buttress Your Vocabulary Studies
- Vocabulary Challenge
- Answers and Explanations

CHAPTER 1 GRE Vocabulary

GRE Vocabulary is one of the, if not the, first stumbling blocks students face when preparing for the Verbal section of this test. In this chapter, you will learn methods to study vocabulary that are effective and time-efficient.

Learning Vocabulary Words in This Book

Each chapter in this book will feature a few GRE vocabulary words mixed into the text. Six will be introduced at the start of the chapter; look for them as you read! They might appear in different forms— for example, from this chapter's list, "assiduous" could appear as "assiduously."

At the end of the chapter, you'll have a chance to write your own predicted definition based on the context in which they appeared, and then you'll be given the official definition.

Each chapter's list contains three words labeled (E) for essential and three words labeled (A) for advanced. The essential words are essential for everyone; study the advanced words if you are aiming for an especially high verbal score. (You can also find all of these words in our GRE Flash Cards, if you have purchased them.)

Here are your Chapter 1 vocabulary words, listed in the order in which they appear in the chapter:

assiduous (A)

engender (A)

bombastic (A)

inchoate (E)

judicious (E)

buttress (E)

Studying Vocabulary Effectively

The tokens given by the aristocrat, while nugatory, still served as a reminder that the power of the Crown continued to be held in some esteem even in such mercurial political times.

In that introductory sentence there are a few words that are probably unfamiliar to most English speakers; the most likely culprits are *nugatory* and *mercurial*. Can you name synonyms for these words immediately and confidently? If not—if you find yourself mentally saying "well, mercurial is kind of like when..."—then you need to study this vocabulary!

The study of vocabulary for the GRE, unsurprisingly, begins with the definition. (The following are some of the definitions published in dictionary.com.)

Unit One: **Words and Sentences**

> Nugatory (adj.): of no real value; trifling; worthless
>
> Mercurial (adj.): changeable, volatile, fickle, flighty, or erratic

Great! Now what?

Many students want to know *how many* words they have to learn in order to get a high score on the GRE, as though the GRE were a pure vocabulary quiz. It would be far simpler if the GRE tested you by giving you a list of words and asking you to write out the definition for each. You could memorize the dictionary definitions of 1,000 vocabulary words and regurgitate them up as quickly as possible on test day. Memorizing 500 new words (much less 1,000) in the weeks before the exam would be a substantial feat, but the GRE wants more.

The GRE is *actually* testing whether you've been reading college-level and academic writing (in English) for years, assiduously looking up all the words you didn't know in *The Scarlet Letter* and *The Great Gatsby* or researching the technical language from scientific papers when you didn't understand the meaning. And then, if you've been out of school, you've continued reading college-level material ever since. In other words, the GRE is testing whether you know these "big" words *in context:* not merely memorized, but internalized over years of study.

Simulating that level of verbal knowledge (when you haven't actually been doing the things listed above) takes some work. It can be done, but it's very important to *learn*—not just memorize—vocabulary words.

Many students make the mistake of memorizing dictionary definitions of words without really understanding those definitions or being able to comfortably use those words in sentences. Memorizing by itself is not learning; it is not flexible. If you've learned *torpid*, you can make a connection to *torpor*. If you've learned *anthropology* and *engender*, you can make some reasonable assumptions about *anthropogenesis*.

For sources of difficult material, try *The Economist, Scientific American, Smithsonian, Foreign, MIT Technology Review*, or any of the articles posted on aldaily.com (that's Arts and Letters Daily). These are also the same resources recommended for improving your reading comprehension; you can do both at the same time!

If you've ever learned a foreign language, think about the words that were easiest to learn. When you're in class, most of the words you learn (*stove, tire, classroom, grandmother*) seem equally important. But when you are actually in a foreign country, trying to speak that language, it is *very, very easy* to learn and remember words and phrases like *bathroom,* "What is the price?" and "Where is the hotel?" That is, the easiest things to learn are things that you *really wanted to know* at the time so you looked them up; the emotion or urgency of the situation told your brain that it was important to learn that word, and you did.

Similarly, if you are reading something interesting and come across a word you don't know, look up the word and consider its usage in the sentence you were just puzzling over—that's almost as good as learning the word *bathroom* when you really need to use one! It's easier to retain a new word when there's a "hole" in your knowledge that you just cannot wait to fill.

If you look up unknown words right away, you are creating an immediate, real connection between that word and some external source. You create immediate associations to the meaning of that word. It is these associations that engender the learning process! If you make this a daily habit and supplement it with tools for later review (like the flashcards we will discuss in the next section), your vocabulary studies will be immensely effective.

20

Finally, don't hesitate to look up or ask someone about the words you *thought* you knew but that seem to be used in novel ways. (Did you notice what just happened there? As a noun, a *novel* is a book-length work of fiction, but as an adjective, *novel* means "new, original.")

For another example, consider the use of "informed by" in the following sentence: "Her historical analysis of family dynamics in the antebellum South is informed by an academic background in feminist theory." Clearly, an "academic background in feminist theory" can't talk—"informed by" means "influenced by" in this context. Or the use of "qualified" in the sentence, "Dr. Wong could give only qualified approval to the theory, as the available data was limited in scope." ("Qualified" here means "limited, conditional, holding back.")

If you read a definition of a word—on a flashcard, in a test prep book, or anywhere else—and it doesn't make sense to you, look up the word in several online dictionaries (thefreedictionary.com, m-w.com, and dictionary.com), ask someone, and/or Google the word to see how other people are using it.

Combine the mindset of immediate gratification—"I will look up the definition of any new or unusual word *now*"—to the more long-term strategies for vocabulary studies discussed in the following sections, and you'll have great success!

Two Options for Vocabulary Study

There are two options that many people find effective: building flashcards and writing stories.

Option 1: Flashcards

Flashcards are possibly the most 'old-school' of memorization aids. Most people *want* to use them, but few want to actually *make* them and commit to studying them consistently. While flashcards allow for quick quizzing (once created), the standard "word on front, definition on back" versions slow down the process of learning the words in the first place. And even less effective are pre-made decks: With zero effort in their creation, you drastically increase the number of times you'll have to flip through each card to even start learning the word.

As mentioned before, emotion, interest, and need are huge drivers of learning and memorizing new vocabulary. To capitalize on that, you want a flashcard that allows for creativity and personalization. A good flashcard certainly has the word on the front and the definition on the back, but a great flashcard has more. A great flashcard should include multiple mnemonic devices to aid memorization: a sample sentence, a picture, a rhyme, or a reference to a person or memory connected to that word.

Do you remember what *mercurial* means? If not, that's proof that reading the definition of a word isn't enough to learn that word; if it was, then you'd know *mercurial* from the definition provided just a few pages ago. How many times do you think you'd need to review that card before really knowing the word? You might be okay if this is one of only a few words you need to learn, but this card is going to be in a deck of hundreds of new words. Learning in this way is going to be slow.

But what if, instead, you decided that you wanted to create a great flashcard for *mercurial*. You looked it up and saw that it was based on the Roman god Mercury, who is often depicted with a winged helmet. You connected wings with the idea of flying or flight, and then connected that to the word flighty (easily changeable or irresponsible). To help remind you, you didn't just write the words, you sketched an image of Mercury's helmet, wings and all. How many times do you think you'll need to see this card to remember?

Honestly, you might know the word already given the research and creativity you used to make the card in the first place! Plain, boring flashcards just can't compare to richly customized flashcards.

Here is a sample flashcard that you can use as a model for making your own.

---

torpid

(adj)

Also *torpor* (noun)

Definition:

Slow, sluggish, lazy

Usage: After a massive family dinner, Ani felt too **torpid** to even get up off the couch. "My **torpor** has turned me into a tired turtle," she said slowly.

You can find a word's synonyms by using the "Thesaurus" tab on dictionary.com, although make sure you click on a synonym and verify that it really is similar in meaning—many thesauruses will give more than 20 synonyms for a single word, but most of them won't be that closely related (and some will be quite obscure). Make sure to look at the etymologies of any words you don't know. This is how you learn the roots of words like *mercurial*!

Now that you're *making* great flashcards, what do you *do* with them? If you're most people, it looks something like this:

> Okay, here's my enormous stack of flashcards. How many is this? 500? Okay, let's start. *Synoptic* ... Hmm, I don't know, I'll look at the answer. Oh, right, okay ... Next. *Turpitude*. Hmm ... I'll flip and read. Oh that's right. Next. *Platitude* ... Hmm ...

You see where this is going: nowhere and slowly.

There's not much motivation to remember the words because your brain knows deep down that the information is already written on the flashcard, and you'll be seeing that flashcard again (and again and again). Brains are efficient but not great at memorizing—imagine if you remembered everything you saw, did, ate, etc., in just a single day! Your brain dumps well over 99 percent of the information it is presented with. You need to give it a very good reason to hang on to that specific vocabulary word.

The other problem with this approach is that you have no idea when you're done, and it rarely feels like you're making any progress. Instead, use this method:

1. Pull out a small stack of cards, perhaps 10.
2. Go through the stack one word at a time. When you get one right, *take it out of the stack* and lay it aside.
3. As you continue, the stack will get smaller and smaller. It will become easier and easier to remember the words that are left.

Now you're done. You did a set. Move on to another set if you like.

Because this exercise has an end (as opposed to just cycling through your flashcards over and over again), you get to feel a sense of accomplishment when you're finished.

Depending on your timeline and goal score, you might decide to do this once or twice per day. In fact, if you are working a full-time job and have a hard time studying on weeknights, make a vow that you can do this one thing *every* day, no matter what (if you're really tired, you can make it a 5–6 card set rather than 10, but do at least a little vocab every single day).

Option 2: Stories

A second option is to build a story with vocabulary words. Each day is a new addition to the story, and each week is the start of a new story! To use this method, take ten vocabulary words you wish to learn that day. (Ten is merely a suggested number, but keep the number of words you use reasonable.)

Take those ten words and use as many as you can to build that day's portion of the story. Any of the words that you cannot use get held over to the next day, and you will add new words to the held-over words to create a new list of ten.

Imagine that while studying, you encountered the following dense bits of text (the first you read earlier, but the other two are new):

> Example 1: *The tokens given by the aristocrat, while nugatory, still served as a reminder that the power of the Crown continued to be held in some esteem even in such mercurial political times.*

> Example 2: *Architectural cognoscenti such as Koolhaas recognized Hadid's talents early and encouraged their development. By 1977, only a few years after their initial encounter, she had perfected her heteromorphic style, inspired equally by such disparate styles as Malevich's sparse constructivism and the flowing calligraphy of her native Arabic.*

> Example 3: *The Biblical portrayal of flagitious times preceding the great deluge stands in stark contrast to the ancient Greek representation of the antediluvian past as a Golden Age from which humanity has slowly descended into godless chaos.*

Ouch. Those examples are very convoluted, and if you have concerns about how complicated they are, don't worry; you will address that in later chapters. For now, let's consider only the vocab.

Let's assume these are the words you didn't know: *nugatory, mercurial, cognoscenti, heteromorphic, disparate, flagitious, deluge, antediluvian*. Now, you create your story.

There are a few guidelines when creating stories. First, attempt to make each sentence as GRE-like as possible. This means incorporating more than one vocabulary word into each sentence. Second, give enough context in each sentence so that you are reminded of the meaning of the word from the story alone. Finally, be kind to yourself! This is a difficult exercise.

A Sample Story:

> *The town's citizenry had so many **disparate** interests, many of which were so different from each other, that any attempts to satisfy all of the various desires were bound to be **nugatory**. The **cognoscenti** of the town, comprised of those individuals with the most expertise in governance, knew that the **heteromorphic** demands of the townspeople were unfortunately **mercurial**, changing in a moment from one wish to another. Because of the **deluge** of unending demands, there seemed no way to reduce the immense stress of the job ...*

That is the beginning of a story, and it could serve as a starting point for a week's worth of vocabulary words. Note that the words *antediluvian* and *flagitious* did not make it into the story: that's ok! Those words can be reattempted the next day, with a new set.

Other Study Techniques

Whack-a-word: Whack-a-Mole is an arcade game in which you have to hit a bunch of mechanical creatures with a mallet before the time runs out. Play whack-a-word by spreading out a huge pile of flash cards on a table, bed, or floor, and then trying to remove words from the pile by defining them before looking at the back of the card. If you get a word wrong, put it aside in a "to review" pile. If you end up with words you don't know anything about, make a stack and try creating a story to help learn the words. Once you've learned those words better, spread them all back out and play whack-a-word one more time. Whack-a-word is also fun with a friend. Take turns defining words and removing them from the spread, working together to clear the space as quickly as possible.

Chat with a study buddy: Another fun technique is to find a study partner and agree to email or text each other every day using a certain number of GRE words in your messages (three seems about right—if you make the task too daunting, it might be too hard to stick with the plan).

When to Use Roots

Your online syllabus includes a targeted Root List. In this context, the word *root* is the etymological origin of a portion of the word (not a part of a plant). Some portion of the word is "rooted" in another word, usually an ancient Latin or Greek word.

Take judicious advantage of roots. Many words are easily decomposed into roots and can be understood more clearly in terms of them. But some words now have misleading roots or derivations! During the exam itself, you have to be very careful when you resort to root analysis to guess an unknown word's meaning. The GRE often uses words with surprising meanings, or at least, meanings that might be surprising for a test-taker relying solely on roots. For instance, *baleful* does not mean "full of hay bales"—it means "threatening or menacing." Although a *scribe* is a person whose job is to copy by hand, *proscribe* doesn't seem to be about writing—it means prohibit or condemn.

Ironically, even those words that stray furthest from the apparent meaning of their roots can be better learned with knowledge of the roots: if you learn that a word *doesn't* relate very logically to its roots, that surprise can be helpful in itself.

Many words have strange and memorable relationships with their etymological roots. For instance, the word *desultory* means "lacking in method or purpose; disappointing." That's not so interesting, but if you know that the word comes from a Latin word describing circus riders who *jumped from* horse to horse (*de* = from, *sult* = jump), then you might remember the word *desultory* better.

And maybe *proscribe* didn't *seem* to be about writing before, but it is still based off of the same root as a scribe (as in *script, scribble, scripture,* etc.) Why the same root? Because, in ancient times, *to proscribe* was to publish a record of someone's punishment—to condemn or sentence that person publicly. The trick, or rather discipline, is to acknowledge that learning vocabulary through roots is a supplement to your normal vocabulary practice (flashcards? stories? something else?), and not a replacement for it.

Here are a few more favorites (more information like this appears in *500 Essential Words* and *500 Advanced Words GRE® Vocabulary Flash Cards* sets from Manhattan Prep):

Amortize (gradually pay off a debt, or gradually write off an asset) contains the root *mort*, meaning death. **Amortization** is when a financial obligation dies a long, slow death.

Anachronism (something that is not in its correct historical time; a mistake in chronology, such as by assigning a person or event to the wrong time period)—the prefix *ana* means "against," and *chron* means "time." This is one word you can work out entirely with a knowledge of roots: **anachronistic** means "against time."

Legerdemain (sleight-of-hand, trickery, deception) comes from Middle French, meaning "light of hand." The modern French word for hand is *main*, which is related to the root in the English *manual* (relating to hands, as in *manual labor*) and *manumit* (free from slavery, untie the hands).

Malediction (a curse) has the prefix *mal* (meaning "bad"). The root *dict* comes from *dicere* (to say) and also appears in *dictator, dictionary,* and *indict* (connect to a crime), as well as in **malediction**'s antonym, *benediction* (blessing).

Not all words have a cool story or a helpful derivation. For instance, *pulchritude* means "beauty." The reason that seems so weird—"you're so pulchritudinous," really doesn't sound like a compliment—is that the Latin root *pulcher*, meaning "beautiful," doesn't occur in any other English words.

So recognize that roots are just one of many helpful tools. One good way to proceed is to go through the Root List in the Appendix and focus on roots that actually look familiar to you and like something you'd be able to spot in the future; for instance, *circum* (meaning "around") appears in *circumference*, and it's pretty hard to miss the root in *circumnavigate, circumcise, circumambulate,* and *circumlocution*. So you might make a flash card for this and other roots that seem most useful to you.

Unit One: **Words and Sentences**

Specialized Vocabulary in Reading Comprehension Passages

Although knowledge of GRE vocabulary will play a role in your success on Reading Comprehension passages, the GRE will never test you on vocabulary that is unique to the topic of the passage. For example, in a passage about the human brain, the GRE might use the term dendrites—but the GRE would not expect you to know this vocabulary.

When using a term such as "dendrites" that is exclusive to a specialized field, the GRE will define that term within the passage. This is how you determine whether an unknown word in a reading comprehension passage is worth adding to your word list: Does the test itself define the word there in the passage? If the definition is in the passage, then the test-writers do not expect you to know the word, and you do not need to add it to your vocabulary studies.

You will notice this most commonly for words that are particular to specific academic fields, especially technical fields, although this can occur in passages on any topic.

What do you do in the moment, if you see a word in a reading comprehension passage that you do not know? Search inside the same sentence or the following sentence for either an outright definition or context clues that would allow to make your own partial definition. Jot an abbreviation of the word, with your abbreviated definition, on your paper, and move on! Remember, if the test expected you to know the word, the passage would not have given you the definition.

Using Social Networks to Buttress Your Vocabulary Studies

If you have a robust social network, you can use that community as a support group for your studies! Let people know you're studying for the GRE and ask for help with vocabulary: You can make a game out of it. Post a word, and the person who builds the most creative or memorable sentence with that word "wins." That's merely one option: Use anything that will help you remember the vocabulary you are studying.

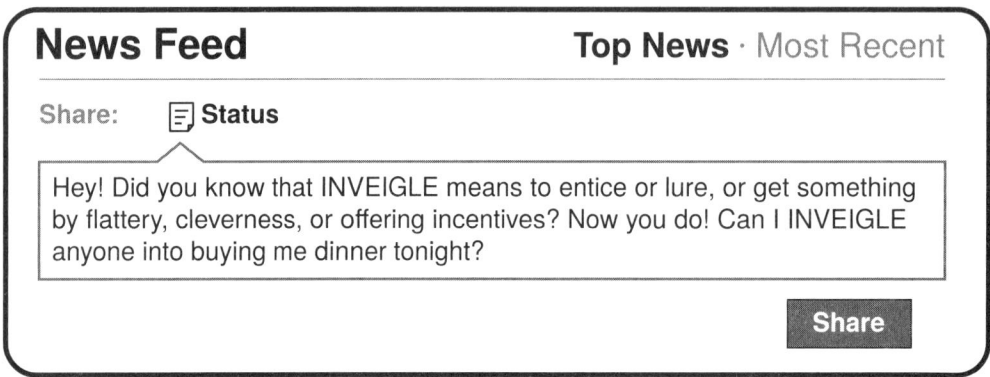

If you post a word and its definition as your status update, it only takes one peculiar comment from a friend (some people have way too much time on their hands) to help you remember the word forever.

Manhattan Prep maintains several social media accounts, and we were pleased to see that one of our followers posted the word *deleterious* (meaning "harmful or damaging") in a status update: "Does anyone actually use that word?"

Another friend wrote back:

> *Deleterious* is used quite a bit in genetics. For example, "Epigenetic silencing of transposable elements may reduce *deleterious* effects on neighboring gene expression in the genome."

The original poster replied, "I looked for examples of this word's use in a sentence. It seems that *deleterious effects* is indeed the way it is most often used."

Now that's how to learn *deleterious*!

Feel free to find, follow, and contribute to any of Manhattan Prep's social networking accounts!

Vocabulary Challenge

> Did you spot these vocabulary words? If not, go back and find them in context! (The word may be in a different form than listed here— "digressing" instead of "digress," for example.) Write your own definitions based on the evidence in the chapter.

1. assiduous (*adj.*), p. 20
2. engender (*v*), p. 20
3. bombastic (*adj.*), p. 24
4. inchoate (*adj.*), p. 24
5. judicious (*adj.*), p. 24
6. buttress (*v*), p. 26

Unit One: **Words and Sentences**

Answers and Explanations

Vocabulary Challenge

1. assiduous (*adj.*): careful, diligent, and persistent in attention or application

2. engender (*v*): to give rise to, create, or cause

3. bombastic (*adj.*): overblown, pompous, inflated, or pretentious

4. inchoate (*adj.*): incipient, still developing or incomplete

5. judicious (*adj.*): demonstrating sound judgement

6. buttress (*v*): to support, strengthen, or shore up

CHAPTER 2
GRE Sentences

In This Chapter...

- Complex Sentences
- Unpacking GRE Sentences
- Principles for Unpacking Sentences
- Link to Real Ideas
- Vocabulary Challenge
- Problem Set
- Answers and Explanations

CHAPTER 2 GRE Sentences

Chapter 1: GRE Vocabulary was all about understanding the meaning of new and difficult words. That said, vocabulary, or challenging word choice within a sentence, is merely the first level of GRE reading. Those complex words get packed into dense and complex sentences that get packed into dense and complex paragraphs that get packed into dense and complex passages. In this chapter, you will learn how to deal with this next level of complexity: the complex sentence.

Here are your Chapter 2 vocabulary words:

> pellucid (A)
> daunt (E)
> vex (A)
> inculcate (A)
> opaque (E)
> eclectic (E)

Complex Sentences

Consider the following example:

> *Despite assurances to the contrary by governments around the world, the development of space as an arena of warfare is nearly certain, as military success often depends on not ceding the "high ground," of which outer space might be considered the supreme example.*

With the possible exception of the word *ceding*, which roughly means "giving up," most of the words used in this sentence are probably familiar to you. (Also, if you were unsure of the word "ceding," don't accept our assertion that "*ceding* = roughly like giving up." Add *ceding* to your vocabulary list and verify that you understand the specifics of its definition!

Now that you do know what *ceding* means, did this sentence become immediately pellucid? Probably not! Why? Because GRE writers are outstanding at packing a paragraph's worth of information into a single sentence. This isn't great for easy reading, but it is great for testing whether you can quickly and correctly interpret dense (academic) writing.

That only begs the question...what can you do to become more effective at understanding such dauntingly dense writing? The next sections will introduce you to "unpacking" sentences.

Unit One: **Words and Sentences**

Unpacking GRE Sentences

GRE students often feel vexed that the test feels like it's speaking a different language. All the words are English, but arranged in a way that no longer feels like English! They no longer feel like English because, in a sense, they aren't English anymore, at least, not English as it's colloquially spoken.

Let's return to the example sentence:

> *Despite assurances to the contrary by governments around the world, the development of space as an arena of warfare is nearly certain, as military success often depends on not ceding the "high ground," of which outer space might be considered the supreme example.*

Even if you are one of the few who read this sentence and grasped it without issue, exam pressure makes it harder to maintain clarity when the structure of a sentence gets increasingly dense. In fact, the abstract and technical language makes reading sentences such as this one a challenge even outside an exam setting.

How do you make sense of this sentence given how much information is packed into it? Maybe you rephrase it or put it into your own words. Sounds like a good idea in theory, but in practice it often fails to help. Consider the following rephrasing:

Rephrase	Is it Effective?
Despite promises by governments that it isn't true, the development of space as an area of warfare is going to happen, because military success requires not giving up the high ground, and outer space is the ultimate example of high ground.	This is a pure translation: Words have been substituted, but there has been no effort to unpack the dense elements of the original. This translation has not transformed either the verbiage or presentation choices.

Instead of simply swapping out hard vocabulary words and cutting a bit of text here and there, this sentence needs to be more fully unpacked. As you read the two examples of "unpacking" below, consider how much information was contained in the original sentence. It's as if the GRE writers have managed to pack an entire paragraph of information into that single sentence.

Unpacking	Is it Effective?
"High ground" is the military concept of being higher up than your opponent (so easier to win). Outer space is the best of the best "high ground." Therefore space will almost certainly become important to world militaries. Governments around the world say that won't happen—but it will.	This is much more effective! Much of the word choice is the same, but the order of presentation is reversed (last sentence first, first sentence last). This attempt requires more analysis of the intended connections between the statements presented, while at the same time breaking those statements into more manageable chunks; note that one original sentence is now four.
Governments say this isn't true. BUT Space will be a war-place. (Yeah, that's not a word.) WHY? Because being up there would be the highest of "high ground" you could get to.	This is another version of unpacking, and it may be one that resonates more with you. It condenses the entire sentence into two extremely short elements that express the oppositional tension in the sentence: what governments say vs. what will actually happen.

And before you ask, no, you would not write down a complete unpacking on test day. The exercise of putting this down pen-to-paper is crucial during your studies, but you would never have the time to literally write these thoughts down to this extent during the exam. This is a study process to inculcate *mental* habits that you will carry through to test day.

So this begs yet another question…how do you learn to effectively unpack sentences yourself?

Principles for Unpacking Sentences

Hopefully the previous discussion convinced you that paraphrasing by substituting less-abstract words isn't a great way to get past dense sentences. So how do you unpack a sentence?

First, don't just give up on a sentence if it seems too opaque or complex: You do not need to digest the entirety of a long sentence in one bite! Since a dense GRE sentence is really several sentences in disguise, it may be useful to read ahead to later in the sentence to gain context and then come back to the first portion. However you manage it, the earlier you can understand some portion of the sentence, the easier the rest of the sentence will be. Reconsider the sentence from the previous section:

Despite assurances to the contrary by governments around the world, the development of space as an arena of warfare is nearly certain, as military success often depends on not ceding the "high ground," of which outer space might be considered the supreme example.

To push your unpacking skills beyond mere translation, here are five principles that can be applied to your unpacking attempts. You do not need to apply all five for every sentence: Use as many or as few as will do the job!

Five Principles to Unpack sentences

1. **Grab a concrete concept first.**

    I know what outer space is, so I'll start there.

2. **Define something that concept is or does.**

    outer space = high ground

3. **Put only *one* simple thought in a sentence.**

    Military success often depends on having the high ground. Space is the ultimate high ground.

4. **Link each subsequent sentence to the previous one. (In this statement, "subsequent" and "previous" refer to the order of sentences in your unpacking, not necessarily the order presented in the original sentence.)**

    Space is the ultimate high ground, and military success often depends on having the high ground. Because of this, governments will seek to militarize space. They say they won't, but they will.

5. **Simplify or "quote off" details.**

    "arena of warfare" = militarization

And this is how the efficient unpacking from the previous section was created! Done habitually during your studies, this process becomes automatic, and will allow you to work through GRE Verbal problems on the test much more successfully.

Unit One: **Words and Sentences**

Unpacking the sentence makes the concepts much more accessible than merely paraphrasing or pushing through and hoping you figure it out later. Here's a dense sentence to practice your unpacking skills. Use as many of the five principles mentioned previously as you feel are useful.

> *Most exobiologists—scientists who search for life on other planets or moons—agree that carbon probably provides the backbone of any extraterrestrial biological molecules, just as it does of terrestrial ones, since carbon is unique among the elements in its ability to form long, stable chains of atoms.*

Once you've unpacked the sentence yourself, consider the following options:

Rephrase	Is it Effective?
"Exobiologists" = scientists who search for aliens. They agree that carbon is unique. It can form long, stable chains. Because carbon is unique in this respect, it probably is the building block of any alien biological molecules. In this way, alien biological molecules might be similar to biological molecules on earth.	Yes. Note that the long, single sentence given initially has been broken into multiple smaller sentences (principle 3 of unpacking dense sentences). Exobiologists are now scientists who search for aliens (principle 5), extraterrestrial is now alien, and terrestrial is now "on Earth." (principles 1 and 2). Finally, transitions such as "because" and "in this way" link sentences together in the unpacked version (principle 4).
Scientists (alien hunters) agree this is true, because carbon is unique. ("this" = carbon forms the basis of both alien and earth biological molecules)	This is merely an example of an exceedingly brief unpacking that takes advantage of principle 5 to massively shorten the text you might write. This version is not preferred over the above version, it is merely one other example.

Here is one more example of a possible unpacking of the "exobiologists" sentence, this time arranged in order of principle, from first to fifth. Note that this example is not the same as the previous two. There is no single correct way to unpack a dense sentence. Ultimately, success is determined by your increased understanding of the test writer's intent.

1. **Grab a concrete concept first.**

    The scientists are the main actors in this sentence.

2. **Define something that concept does.**

    The scientists are agreeing.

3. **Put only *one* simple thought in a sentence.**

    The scientists agree that carbon is important.

4. **Link each subsequent sentence to the previous one.**

    <u>They</u> agree on <u>that</u> because carbon makes chains of atoms.

5. **Simplify or "quote off" details.**

    "Exobiologists" are the specific scientists being discussed.

Correspondingly, the unpacking could look like this on your paper:

> The EB scientists agree that carbon is important.
> They agree on that because carbon makes chains of atoms.
> Carbon already uses that trait to make life on Earth.
> It probably does the same thing for life elsewhere.

This unpacking has the same major points, but was created from a different starting point. As long as you begin with something you can understand, you can unpack even the most complex sentences. At the end, no single concept or sentence within your unpacking should be too complex for you to hold in your mind.

Eventually, your pen-on-paper unpacking will become more and more brief, until your test day unpacking (if you unpack on paper at all!) might look like this:

> sci agree this is true
> because
> carbon is unique

Link to Real Ideas

For some of the more abstract concepts, translating the sentence visually or even taking graphical notes can ease the transition to understanding. If even finding the concrete concept is challenging at the start of a sentence, try to grab something and imagine what it might literally look like. Finding that visual representation can make the process much simpler.

In your mind, you might imagine any of the ideas from the exobiologist sentence in the following manner:

Words	Real Ideas
. . . exobiologists—scientists . . .	smart folks in white coats
. . . who search for life on other planets or moons . . .	who peer through telescopes looking for little green men
. . . carbon probably provides the backbone of extraterrestrial biological molecules . . .	carbon: charcoal, key element in living things
	backbone: like a spine to a little molecule
. . . any extraterrestrial biological molecules, just as it does of terrestrial ones . . .	extraterrestrial: little green men (aliens)
	terrestrial: from Earth; humans, not aliens
. . . its ability to form long, stable chains of atoms.	a literal chain but made up of carbon

Do *not* write the real ideas down (except as an exercise during your studies, as needed). The process should happen quickly in your head so that you find a concrete idea you're comfortable starting with. Moreover, as you read further in a passage, do this less. In fact, if you do it too much along the way, you might introduce too many outside ideas and lose track of what is actually written in the passage. However, making the sentence real can help you make sense of a difficult sentence, so practice this technique.

You can also break down the sentence visually for certain types of sentences, especially science sentences or any sentence describing a multistep process. In these sentences, a T-chart, diagram, or picture can be an effective note-taking method.

Unit One: **Words and Sentences**

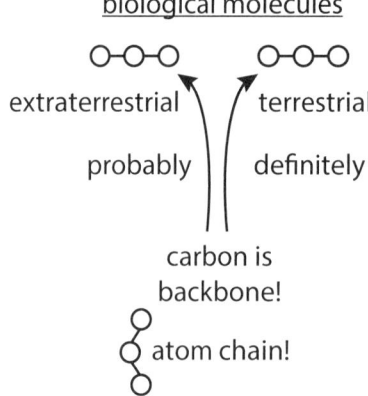

Practice an eclectic mix of methods so you can choose what will be most effective for each sentence you study.

Vocabulary Challenge

> Did you spot these vocabulary words? If not, go back and find them in context! (The word may be in a different form than listed here—"digressing" instead of "digress," for example.) Write your own definitions based on the evidence in the chapter.

1. pellucid (*adj.*), p. 31
2. daunt (*v*), p. 31
3. vex (*v*), p. 32
4. inculcate (*v*), p. 33
5. opaque (*adj.*), p. 33
6. eclectic (*adj.*), p. 36

Problem Set

> In problems 1–6, **unpack** each complex sentence. Find a concrete idea to start, and form a sentence with just a portion of the information in the sentence. Then create a second sentence that adds some additional information to the first. Keep going until you have unpacked all of the detail in the sentence (this might take five or so sentences). Write the sentences down as you work.

Unpacking

These unpacked sentences are examples of the process. Your versions will likely differ. Again, only write down unpacked sentences when absolutely necessary during the GRE, and even when necessary, use as much abbreviation as you can. This exercise is meant to develop your mental muscles so you can take apart complex academic language on test day, without resorting to pen and paper.

1. Various popular works of art have been influenced by syncretic religious traditions such as Candomblé, Santería, and voodoo, but few such works treat these traditions with appropriate intelligence or sensitivity.

2. The rise of Athenian democracy in ancient times can be considered a reaction to class conflict.

3. The simplistic classification of living things as plant, animal, or "other" has been drastically revised by biologists in reaction to the discovery of microorganisms that do not fit previous taxonomic schemes.

4. Neither Chinese nor Japanese verbs, for instance, change form at all to indicate the number or person of the subject; however, personal pronouns in both subject and object roles are regularly omitted in both speech and writing, leaving the meaning to be inferred from contextual clues.

5. Since the success of modern digital surveillance does not obviate the need for intelligence gathered via old-fashioned human interaction, agencies charged with counterterrorism responsibilities must devote significant effort to planting and/or cultivating "assets"—that is, spies—within terrorist organizations that threaten the country.

6. Students learning to fly fixed-wing aircraft are taught to use mnemonic devices, such as the landing checklist GUMPS (gas, undercarriage, mixture, propeller, switches), that remain constant even when not every element of the device is relevant, as in the case of planes with non-retractable landing gear.

Unit One: **Words and Sentences**

Answers and Explanations

Vocabulary Challenge

1. pellucid (*adj.*): transparent; clear, easy to understand

2. daunt (*v*): discourage, dishearten, lessen the courage of

3. vex (*v*): annoy or bother; puzzle or distress

4. inculcate (*v*): to teach, impress, or implant by frequent repetition

5. opaque (*adj.*): not transparent; dark, dull, unclear, or stupid

6. eclectic (*adj.*): various; selecting the best of everything or from many diverse sources

Problem Set

1.

Original Sentence	Unpacked Rephrase
Various popular works of art have been influenced by syncretic religious traditions such as Candomblé, Santeria, and voodoo, but few such works treat these traditions with appropriate intelligence or sensitivity.	There are blended (syncretic) religious traditions: C, S, and V.
	Some popular art was influenced by / is based on those traditions.
	But not very much of that art (few such works) really honors those traditions as much as the author thinks they should.

2.

Original Sentence	Unpacked Rephrase
The rise of Athenian democracy in ancient times can be considered a reaction to class conflict.	There was class conflict: People from upper and lower were fighting each other in ancient times?
	People created the Athenian democracy in response.

3.

Original Sentence	Unpacked Rephrase
The simplistic classification of living things as plant, animal, or "other" has been drastically revised by biologists in reaction to the discovery of microorganisms that do not fit previous taxonomic schemes.	Biologists found some new microorganisms.
	These MOs don't really fit into any categories (*taxonomic schemes*) that already existed.
	Biologists used to just call things *plant, animal, or "other."* but because of these new MOs, that simple classification had to be totally updated.

Chapter 2: GRE Sentences

4.	Original Sentence	Unpacked Rephrase
	Neither Chinese nor Japanese verbs, for instance, change form at all to indicate the number or person of the subject; however, personal pronouns in both subject and object roles are regularly omitted in both speech and writing, leaving the meaning to be inferred from contextual clues.	C and J verbs don't change form for subject-verb agreement (like they do in English, e.g., she sings vs. they sing). And it seems like they don't even really use pronouns to help. The only way to get at the meaning of a sentence is to use other context clues.

5.	Original Sentence	Unpacked Rephrase
	Since the success of modern digital surveillance does not obviate the need for intelligence gathered via old-fashioned human interaction, agencies charged with counterterrorism responsibilities must devote significant effort to planting and/or cultivating "assets"—that is, spies—within terrorist organizations that threaten the country.	Even though you can spy with computers and tech now, you still need to have humans out there getting information too (*does not obviate the need for . . .*). So if you're trying to fight terrorists, you still have to spend the time and effort to get your human spies into those terrorist groups.

6.	Original Sentence	Unpacked Rephrase
	Students learning to fly fixed-wing aircraft are taught to use mnemonic devices, such as the landing checklist GUMPS (gas, undercarriage, mixture, propeller, switches), that remain constant even when not every element of the device is relevant, as in the case of planes with non-retractable landing gear.	When people learn to fly planes, they learn memory tricks. One example is GUMPS. They learn these memory tricks even though some of the pieces aren't always relevant—not sure why they mentioned the specific case of landing gear. So this might mean that students learn GUMPS, even though some of the letters won't always apply? Maybe you don't always care about propeller, for example?

CHAPTER 3

Text Completion and Sentence Equivalence

In This Chapter...

- One-Blank Text Completion
- The Three-Step Process for Text Completions
- Direction Markers
- Drill: Sentence Analysis
- Sentence Equivalence
- Sentence Analysis in Sentence Equivalence
- Answer Choice Analysis
- When to Use (and NOT to Use) Answer Choice Analysis
- Drill: Answer Choice Analysis
- What If I Don't Know the Words?
- Why It Is Important to Learn Words in Context
- Traps in TC and SE

Unit One: **Words and Sentences**

- Text Completion and Sentence Equivalence Recap
- Vocabulary Challenge
- Problem Set (Text Completion)
- Problem Set (Sentence Equivalence)
- Answers and Explanations

CHAPTER 3 Text Completion and Sentence Equivalence

The sentence-deconstruction strategies discussed in Chapter 2: GRE Sentences will be immediately useful on Text Completion and Sentence Equivalence questions. Text Completion questions on the GRE are sentences or paragraphs with one, two, or three blanks for which you must select the appropriate word or words. In this chapter, you will learn methods to answer one-blank Text Completion and the closely related Sentence Equivalence; a discussion of two- and three-blank Text Completion questions can be found in Chapter 7: Multi-Blank Text Completion.

Here are your Chapter 3 vocabulary words:

> tortuous (A)
> recondite (A)
> embellish (E)
> paragon (A)
> satiate (E)
> augment (E)

One-Blank Text Completion

One-blank Text Completion (TC) questions always appear at the very beginning of a GRE Verbal section, and they always consist of a single sentence. The following example shows how one-blank Text Completion questions are laid out:

If the student had been less _____, she would not have been expelled from her grade school.

A	indefatigable
B	persevering
C	delinquent
D	playful
E	indigent

On the real test, you won't see the letters A, B, C, D, and E; each word will just be in its own box.

43

Unit One: **Words and Sentences**

All one-blank Text Completions have exactly five answer choices, of which exactly one is correct. The answer choices for a given blank will always be the same part of speech. Your task is to find the choice that best fits the meaning of the sentence as a whole. Once you've found the answer that best fits the meaning of the sentence, select it by clicking on the box in which it appears; the test will record this selection by highlighting the entire box. Under standard timing conditions, the whole process would ideally take about 1 minute on average per problem.

On your scratch paper, write down the letters A, B, C, D, and E to keep track of which answers you think are wrong, which ones you think might be right, and which words you don't know (more on this later).

A lot of test-takers regard Text Completion as difficult because of the high-level vocabulary that often appears in the answer choices. However, the GRE's goal in these questions is not primarily to test your lexicon. Rather, the goal of these questions is to test whether you can extract crucial bits of meaning from the written parts of the sentence to inform what should go in the blank.

Therefore, the best approach to Text Completion questions will be to deconstruct the sentence and **predict an answer** before looking at the choices. Many test-takers plug in the choices one by one, rereading the sentence and stopping when it sounds good. The problems with this approach are twofold. First, the sentences are often too tortuous to make quick sense of even if you read words into the blank, leaving you in a position to have to analyze the sentence anyway. Second, the GRE deliberately chooses tempting words for the wrong answers, words that can improperly color your understanding of the sentence or seem superficially to be a good fit for the sentence but that don't actually suit its intended meaning.

The Three-Step Process for Text Completions

You can approach every Text Completion question with the same three-step process:

1. Read only the sentence.
2. Use proof from the sentence to make a prediction.
3. Compare your prediction to each answer choice.

Here's the sentence from earlier in the chapter:

If the student had been less _____, she would not have been expelled from her grade school.

A	indefatigable
B	persevering
C	delinquent
D	playful
E	indigent

1. Read only the sentence.

The answer choices will distract you if you read them before you've made sense of the sentence. The sentence is the truth, but four of the five answer choices are lies. Don't read the lies until you're solid on the truth.

When you first read the sentence, note the structure of the sentence. One-blank Text Completion sentences will often be broken into two parts with a comma or semicolon in the middle. One part of the sentence will have the blank in it, and the best information about what goes in the blank will almost always come from the other part of the sentence. This sentence is separated into two parts by the comma near the middle, and the blank is in the first part.

2. Use proof from the sentence to make a prediction.

This is the crux of the process for Text Completion. One-blank TC questions always provide proof of the correct answer in the sentence. The proof is what forces the contents of the blank to be perfectly predictable, and Text Completion and Sentence Equivalence questions are designed to test whether you're able use the proof in the sentences to correctly determine the meaning of the blank. After all, the GRE is a standardized test, and as such, every question has to have exactly one objectively right answer or combination of answers. There's no subjectivity to the answers, and you won't need to rely on any specialized outside knowledge to get these questions correct—except, of course, for vocabulary. And while the vocabulary can be challenging, it's worth knowing that in the most difficult of these questions, you're more likely to run into trouble with convoluted sentence structures than with recondite vocabulary.

So how do you find the proof in a sentence? There are two main ways: by unpacking the sentence into several simple sentences (as discussed in Chapter 2: GRE Sentences) or by parsing the sentence into *content clues* and *direction markers*. The sentence above will be used to demonstrate both of these approaches.

Unpacking the sentence

First, take some time to consider how *you* might rewrite the sentence into a few simple sentences. Here's one possible rewrite:

> The student was expelled from her school.
> Therefore, she most likely broke rules.
> She could have *not* been expelled from her school...
> ...but only if she'd been less <u>something</u>.

When you've unpacked the sentence, the next step is to think about what would make the most sense in place of the *something*. If her being expelled from school is a good indication that the student must have broken some rules, then she could have avoided being expelled if she'd been less rule-breaky. Does it matter that "rule-breaky" isn't a real word? Not at all! The goal is not to predict the exact word that will show up in the answer choices, but to come away from the sentence with as clear an idea as possible of the *meaning* of the correct answer.

There are a few things worth explicitly noting in the unpacked version of the sentence above. To start, you may have noticed that the first simple sentence expresses what actually happened in the situation (that is, the concrete truth of the situation) rather than reflecting what the sentence specifically stated. The sentence only says that she would *not* have been expelled *if* something had been different; however, that necessarily implies that she was expelled, and acknowledging this concrete truth is more helpful in understanding the sentence's meaning than is sticking strictly to what the sentence says. When unpacking a sentence, **grab a concrete concept first**.

It's also worth noting that the first simple sentence above came from the second part of the original sentence. In unpacking one-blank Text Completion questions, it will almost always be beneficial to start from the part of the sentence that *doesn't* contain the blank. It's generally true that if the blank is in the first part of the sentence, the proof for the right answer will be in the second part of the sentence (and vice versa). Moreover, the part of the sentence *without* the blank is likely to contain the concrete truth that serves as the best starting point to understanding the meaning of the sentence; the part of the sentence *with* the blank, by contrast, is necessarily incomplete.

Next, the second simple sentence (*Therefore, she most likely broke rules*) is not expressed anywhere in the original sentence. For many, this is the most dangerous part of extracting meaning from the sentences in the GRE.

Unit One: **Words and Sentences**

Can you know *for sure* from the original sentence that the student broke any rules? No. The student could have been unfairly expelled because the school administrators didn't like her shoes, or she could have been framed by another student for some expulsion-worthy infraction.

On the other hand, *some* information must be added to the sentence to make sense of the first part of the sentence and ultimately to make a prediction for the blank. When adding information to the sentence, **aim for the simplest story possible**. In this case, the truth of the situation is that the student was expelled, and expulsion is generally used as a punishment for wrongdoing. Scenarios such as those outlined above, while technically possible, are less likely to have led to the student's expulsion and will not be the interpretations that determine the meaning of the missing word.

Parse the sentence

You can also parse the sentence into *content clues* and *direction markers*. Content clues are the elements of the story that are relevant to the blank, and direction markers are the words, phrases, and punctuation marks used to relate parts of the sentence to each other. Start by stripping a sentence of all its reversal words—words that indicate an opposite or a negation, such as *not* or *however*. Next, use content clues from the simplified sentence to predict for the blank. Finally, add the reversal words back in one by one, updating your prediction each time. Here's an example of how that process would play out in the sentence above:

Content and direction clues	Prediction and analysis
If **the student** had been ____, **she** would have been **expelled** from her grade school.	**Badly behaved:** The word that goes into the blank is describing the student, meaning that the sentence *must* provide content clues about the student. Because the blank appears in the first half of the sentence, the second part of the sentence is likely to contain information about the student that will serve as the proof for the blank. In this version of the sentence, the only direction marker is *If*, indicating that there will be a causal relationship between the first and second parts of the sentence. Given this relationship and the content clues in the second part of the sentence, whatever goes in the blank must be something that would reasonably cause the student to be expelled: bad behavior.
*If the student had been ____, she would **not** have been expelled from her grade school.*	**Well behaved:** Add the reversal markers back in one at a time, ideally starting with any reversal markers in the part of the sentence that doesn't contain the blank. In the original sentence, the *not* in the second part of the sentence was a reversal marker. Adding the marker back in is like flipping a switch in the sentence: What goes in the blank must be the opposite of what it was before.
*If the student had been **less** ____, she would not have been expelled from her grade school.*	**Badly behaved:** Adding the last reversal marker (*less*) back to the sentence effectively nullifies the reversal above, much as two negatives cancel to a positive.

Chapter 3: **Text Completion and Sentence Equivalence**

You might have noticed that this approach has a lot in common with the first approach. While the process of parsing a sentence focuses more explicitly and carefully on direction markers, making the first prediction still requires some unpacking of the sentence. Similarly, while unpacking the sentence doesn't necessarily require you to strip out reversal markers, the process usually begins with stating what *is* the case, even when the sentence itself focuses on what's *not* the case.

Perhaps most importantly, both approaches leave you with a similar prediction for the blank. Write down this prediction as well as letters for answers (A) through (E).

rule-breaky / badly behaved

A
B
C
D
E

3. Compare your prediction to each answer choice.

With a prediction in hand, it's time to head to the answer choices. Here they are again:

| indefatigable |
| persevering |
| delinquent |
| playful |
| indigent |

Compare each answer choice to your prediction to see how well they match. It's usually helpful to think of less familiar words in more common terms:

indefatigable = ?
persevering = never giving up
delinquent = troublesome
playful
indigent = ?

Finally, as you proceed down the answers, mark down one of the following next to your "A B C D E": Good (✓), Bad (✗), Sort Of (∼), or Unknown (?). Your paper might look like this:

rule-breaky / badly behaved

A ?
B ✗
C ✓
D ∼
E ?

The correct answer is in fact (C), since *delinquent* means "troublesome" or even "criminal." But even if you didn't know what *delinquent* means, you might have a shot at getting this problem right through process of elimination, especially if you know the definitions of the other words and trust that the GRE will *always* give you an answer that fits the clues in the sentence.

47

Unit One: **Words and Sentences**

All told, this process should eventually take an average of 1 minute per question. However, as you're first learning to analyze sentences, the process will likely take considerably longer. That's okay: Analyzing sentences well is the key to success on Text Completion and Sentence Equivalence, and it will get faster (and more accurate) with practice.

Also, you can come up with a plausible and interesting story around some of the wrong answer choices, but the story would be less directly based on the evidence in the sentence. For example, "If the student had been less *playful*, she wouldn't have been expelled" might make sense if the student was constantly playing games during serious lessons. Notice that building a connection between being *playful* and getting expelled requires the addition of extra, unproven story elements (specifically, that the expulsion happened because of the student's behavior during lessons and that playing during lessons is an expellable offense). You might find that this sort of story-building happens automatically in your mind when you consider certain answer choices. This is why it's so important to unpack and interpret the sentence as straightforwardly as possible and to make a prediction before looking at the answers: The GRE has trap answers waiting for those inclined to embellishment. Stick to the story in the sentence, and when possible, recycle words and phrases from the sentence to make your predictions.

> *Strategy Tip:*
>
> **Always predict answers when you practice Text Completion questions.**
> Proactively practicing sentence analysis is the best way to get faster and more accurate at TC.

Practice the whole three-step process on the following sentence:

Despite his extreme _____, he failed to secure the prestigious university's coveted diploma.

inhibition
depression
lucubration
magnanimity
character

First, read **only** the sentence. Again, it's divided into two parts by a comma and the blank appears in the first part.

Now unpack or parse the sentence to find the proof and make a prediction. What's the concrete truth? The protagonist of this sentence *failed to secure the prestigious university's coveted diploma*. This happened *despite* some truth about the student, so whatever was true about the student *should* have been helpful in securing the diploma. What sort of things are helpful in getting a diploma? The most straightforward story would be *studying* or *intelligence*, and either would make a sensible prediction.

48

Chapter 3: **Text Completion and Sentence Equivalence**

Finally, compare *studying* or *intelligence* with every answer choice:

studying *or* intelligence

A ✗

B ✗

C ?

D ?

E ~

This can be a tough spot to be in. If you don't know the meaning of *lucubration* and *magnanimity*, the choice you make depends on whether any of the words you *do* know is a close match for your prediction (and the sentence as a whole). *Character* kind of works for the sentence, but it's a very general word, and the GRE is likely to give you a word that more specifically fits the story in the sentence. If you don't know the meaning of the words *lucubration* and *magnanimity*, your final consideration is this: Does *lucubration* feel like it could mean studying or intelligence, or does *magnanimity* seem like it might be a better match? You might feel that a word like *lucubration* would denote an action whereas *magnanimity* seems more like a character trait, for instance, and choose accordingly. Or you might have absolutely no idea. In either case, make a choice and move on. As it happens, *lucubration*, meaning intense or laborious study, is a straightforward match for the prediction *studying*, so it's the best choice: Despite his intense studying, he failed. (Of course, it's also helpful to know that *magnanimity* means "generosity.")

Be a little flexible as you make your match. You might not have predicted the exact contours of the right answer, but that's okay. In fact, it was better that you didn't waste time trying to make an extremely precise prediction. And if you have question marks on your scratch paper because you lack some vocabulary knowledge (e.g., *lucubration, magnanimity*), make the most of the words you do know and move on. Spending time staring at words you don't know won't make them suddenly surrender their meaning.

Just decide whether the answer choices you do know keep the sentence's story simple; if those words don't work, choose one of the words whose definition you don't know. The right answer won't always be a word you know, but it must always be a good fit for the sentence.

Unpack or parse the following sentence, and make an explicit prediction for the blank:

In the past decade, the coffee chain has dramatically expanded all across the country, leading one commentator to describe the franchise as _____.

This sentence has two major parts, with the blank in the second part. Read and then unpack the sentence, starting from a concrete truth:

A coffee chain has expanded. It's now all across the country. This has led a commentator to describe it as <u>something</u>.

All you know about the coffee chain is that it's everywhere in the country, and as that concrete fact must have led to the commentator's description, the most straightforward prediction would be something like <u>everywhere</u> or <u>nationwide</u>.

 49

Unit One: **Words and Sentences**

Alternatively, you can parse the sentence into content clues and direction markers:

The first part of the sentence *leads* to the second part (that is, "leading" functions as a causal direction marker). There are no reversal markers to strip out. In terms of content clues, the word in the blank is being used to describe "the franchise," which itself is a reference to the coffee chain mentioned in the first part of the sentence. Look here for descriptions of the coffee chain that will serve as content clues for the blank. The only thing mentioned is that the chain has "expanded all across the country." Keep the prediction simple and straightforward: everywhere or having dramatically expanded.

Having dramatically expanded may seem like an awkward prediction, but recycling words or phrases from the sentence is a good idea. It will ensure that your prediction doesn't stray too far from the proof in the sentence. And in general, your prediction should feel boring, recycling words or ideas already in the sentence. Notice how uninteresting these fill-ins feel:

> In the past decade, the coffee chain has dramatically expanded all across the country, leading one commentator to describe the franchise as everywhere.

> In the past decade, the coffee chain has dramatically expanded all across the country, leading one commentator to describe the franchise as having dramatically expanded.

These would be redundant ways to end the sentence in real life, and as such it's easy to imagine a more colorful description than *everywhere*. For instance, it can be tempting to add a negative or positive spin to your prediction (*a dangerous monopoly, a paragon of capitalism,* etc.). However, the GRE will always go with the boring, redundant answer. It's testing your ability to match evidence in the sentence to a word in the answer choices, not your ability to write an exciting narrative.

If this were a real question and there were answer choices, you'd now be in a position to find a match. In this case, the answer would probably be something like *ubiquitous*, a GRE favorite meaning "being everywhere."

Direction Markers

As mentioned previously in the chapter, direction markers are words, phrases, or punctuation marks that indicate how the parts of a sentence are related to each other. They tend to fall into three general categories: straight-ahead markers, reversal markers, and causal markers.

Consider the different direction markers in each of the versions of the sentence below, and make a prediction for each:

> **Version 1:** In keeping with her reputation for _____, the politician asserted that in a time of crisis it was important to speak honestly.

> **Version 2:** Despite her reputation for _____, the politician asserted that in a time of crisis it was important to speak honestly.

> **Version 3:** Due to her reputation for _____, many expected that in a time of crisis, the politician would speak honestly.

In all versions, the blank describes the politician's reputation and the second part of the sentence sees the politician speaking honestly. However, the direction markers change, leading to opposing predictions:

> **Version 1:** In this version, the marker *in keeping with* is a straight-ahead marker. Since her assertion that honesty is important was **in keeping with** the politician's reputation, she must have a reputation for honesty.

Version 2: By contrast, this version starts out with *despite*, a reversal marker. If asserting the importance of honesty is something the politician does **despite** her reputation, she must have a reputation for not being honest.

Version 3: This is the most complicated version. **Due to** is a causal marker, meaning that the politician's reputation for something created an expectation that she would speak honestly. Thus, she must have had a reputation for honesty. Notice that while this prediction is the same as the prediction for Version 1, the sentence in this case had an added element: people's expectations. Causal markers tend to function in the same way as straight-ahead markers, but they also invite more complicated sentence structures and require more inferential analysis.

Be redundant. Don't hesitate to recycle the word *honest*. And very importantly, watch for reversals and unpack or parse the sentence carefully around them.

Try another:

For all his studying, his performance on the test was _____.

This one relies on a somewhat uncommon idiom. *For all* means "despite." It's another reversal signal. Studying usually leads to a *good* test performance, so the sentence wants a word that upends the expected result: Despite his studying, his performance was ***not*** *good.* If you predicted the opposite, make a flashcard for the idiom *for all*. Direction marker idioms are as important to learn as any other vocabulary.

Although he has a reputation for talking too much, others at the party didn't find him especially _____.

Did you say something like *talkative*? Or did you go for *not talkative*? Notice that you have a bit of proof ("a reputation for talking too much" and a signal word that reverses direction: "Although").

But you also have another reversal signal—the *not* in "didn't."

As mentioned earlier, reversing yourself twice (much like turning 180 degrees twice) is like not reversing yourself at all. In your blank, you just want another word for "talking too much."

Although he has a reputation for talking too much, others at the party didn't find him especially talkative.

Here are some common signal words, phrases, and structures, grouped into the three very general categories mentioned above. Pay attention to the reversals, especially when you have more than one of them.

Unit One: **Words and Sentences**

Straight-Ahead	Reversal	Causal
; (semicolon)	Although	As
: (colon)	Anything but	As a result
Also	Belied	Because
And	But	Consequently
Besides	Contrast	Due to
Furthermore	Despite	Hence
Given	Even though	If
In addition	Even with	Since
In fact	For all	So
In light of	However	Therefore
Indeed	Instead	Thus
Just as	In spite of	
Moreover	Nevertheless	
Not only . . . but also . . .	Not	
So . . . as to be . . .	Notwithstanding	
So . . . that . . .	On the contrary	
Such	On the other hand	
X, Y, and Z (items in a list)	Rather than	
	Still	
	Surprise	
	Though	
	Yet	

Drill: Sentence Analysis

> Analyze each sentence for the proof, and then make a prediction for the blank.

1. The camp established by the aid workers provided a _____ for the refugees, many of whom had traveled for weeks to get there.

2. While others had given only accolades, the iconoclastic critic greeted the book's publication with a lengthy _____.

3. Though many have impugned her conclusions, the studies on which she based her analysis are beyond _____.

4. The ancient poem's value was more _____ than literary; the highly literal work made no attempt at lyricism and ended by warning the reader never to lie.

5. For all the clamor about bipartisanship, in the end, the actual votes _____ to factional loyalties.

6. The notion that digital media should last forever is untenable, considering the warehouses full of computer tape drives and other media that have been _____ by newer technologies.

7. Chad was capricious in his youth, but as an adult he was downright _____.

8. The _____ position he adopted on the issue belied his reputation for equivocation.

Unit One: **Words and Sentences**

Answers and Explanations

1. This sentence states that *aid workers* are providing something for *refugees*, who have traveled for a long time to get there. In the absence of contradictory information, it's safe to infer that aid workers would be helping the refugees in some way. Therefore, a good prediction would be **refuge** or **sanctuary**.

2. The blank is in the second half of the sentence, so the proof for it is likely in the first part, which starts with the *While*. In terms of content, both parts of the sentence focus on the critical reception of a book. The first part mentions *accolades* received by the book, but the *While* means that the second part will highlight a negative critical response. A good prediction would be something like **condemnation**.

3. The blank—in the second part of the sentence—is describing *the studies* that informed a certain analysis. The first part of the sentence also focuses on this analysis (referenced here as *her conclusions*). It's stated that her conclusions have been *impugned*, a decidedly negative reaction. However, the first part also contains the reversal marker *Though*. So if the first part highlights a negative aspect of her analysis, the second part must be highlighting a positive aspect of it. Be careful. Though the overall impact of the second part of the sentence should be positive say something good about the studies, the blank appears just after a second reversal marker: *beyond*. To convey the fact that the studies are good in some way, the sentence must say that they are *beyond* something bad. A good prediction would be **impugning**. (As a note, though, if it were on the test, this sentence would almost certainly be completed with the expression *beyond* **reproach**).

4. The blank is talking about the poem, stating that it's *more* something *than literary*. Already, you know the poem is *not* very literary, but look to the second part of the sentence for more content clues. Apparently, the poem *made no attempt at lyricism* (further confirmation that it's not literary) and ended with a moral: Never lie. Sticking to the evidence in the sentence, a good fill-in would be **moralistic** or **didactic**.

5. The blank is in the second part of the sentence and is connected to *votes* and *factional loyalties*. Look to the first part of the sentence for a concrete truth. All it says is that there was *clamor about bipartisanship*. That concrete truth is bundled with the reversal marker *For all*. So the second part of the sentence should indicate that the voting was the opposite of *bipartisan*—that is, the votes were partisan. Since *factional loyalties* describe a partisan environment, a good prediction would be **conformed** or **bowed**.

6. The word in the blank will be something that happened to *computer tape drives and other media* as a result of *newer technologies*. The first part of the sentence focuses on the *notion that digital media should last forever*, though it says this notion is *untenable* in light of the second part of the sentence, with *untenable* serving as a de facto reversal marker. Thus, the second part of the sentence should serve to highlight the fact that digital media do not last forever. A good prediction would be **replaced**. GRE-type words that might appear here would be *supplanted* or *superseded*.

7. The blank is describing how Chad was as an adult. The first part of the sentence contains the concrete truth that *Chad was capricious* when he was young. The reversal marker *but* connects the two parts of the sentence, which would ordinarily mean that the word in the blank would have to contradict *capricious*. However, the *downright* subverts this expectation in a subtle way: Rather than an opposite for *capricious*, the downright forces the word in the blank to be a more extreme version of *capricious*. Thus, a good prediction might be something like **volatile** or **tempestuous**.

8. The blank describes the person's *position*. The concrete truth in this sentence is that the person in question has a *reputation for equivocation*, meaning that he doesn't generally communicate in a forthright way. Complicating things further is the reversal marker *belied*, which means "contradicted" or "gave a false impression of." So a good prediction would go in the opposite direction of *equivocation*—something like **clearly communicated** or **firm**.

54

Chapter 3: **Text Completion and Sentence Equivalence**

Sentence Equivalence

Sentence Equivalence (SE) questions on the GRE are very similar to one-blank Text Completion questions. Here's what ETS says about this question type:

> *Like Text Completion questions, Sentence Equivalence questions test the ability to reach a conclusion about how a passage should be completed on the basis of partial information, but to a greater extent they focus on the meaning of the completed whole. Sentence Equivalence questions consist of a single sentence with just one blank, and they ask you to find two choices that both lead to a complete, coherent sentence and that produce sentences that mean the same thing.*

Essentially, the only difference between Sentence Equivalence and Text Completion is that rather than picking the single best answer for the blank, you will have to pick *two* answers that give the sentence an equivalent meaning. Consider the following example:

> The judge dismissed Steffen's lawsuit, ruling that since Steffen had been the first to _____ the contract, the company he was suing was no longer obligated to uphold the provisions of the original agreement.

- [A] forswear
- [B] transmute
- [C] breach
- [D] abrogate
- [E] vituperate
- [F] slake

Throughout the exam (in math, too), the GRE uses square checkboxes, not circles, to indicate questions that can have more than one correct answer; in this case, you'll choose two answers. Sentence Equivalence problems will always have six answer choices, so use the answer letters A through F to keep track of your work on your scratch paper.

To get credit for a Sentence Equivalence question, you must select **both** correct answers. There is no partial credit. In the previous question, the correct answer is *breach* and *abrogate*, which both mean "fail to do what is required by."

Although the idea of two correct answers is an interesting test-making twist, it doesn't necessarily make the questions any harder for you. In fact, it opens up the strategic tool of Answer Choice Analysis, which will be explained in this chapter.

All of the skills you have already learned for Text Completion still apply here. You will still unpack or parse the sentence and come up with a prediction for the blank, and you'll still look to add as little as possible to the story.

There are two main methods of attack for a Sentence Equivalence question, both of which will be reviewed in the pages that follow:

1. Sentence Analysis
2. Answer Choice Analysis

Unit One: **Words and Sentences**

Sentence Analysis in Sentence Equivalence

Like Text Completion questions, Sentence Equivalence questions ask you to fill in a blank based on the information contained in the text around it.

The sentences are not anything like sentences pulled from a newspaper, with a few words blanked out. In such a real-life case, you might not be able to fill in the missing word, since a lot of the necessary context would be contained in other sentences, not in the sentence in question.

On the GRE, all of that necessary context has to be provided in the one sentence you're reading. In fact, as discussed with regards to Text Completion, the GRE has to go further: The test makers have to write sentences containing definitive proof for the words that have to fit in the blank. If that weren't the case, the problem would not have two objectively correct answers and four objectively incorrect answers.

The basic process for Sentence Equivalence is the same as it is for Text Completion. As a reminder, here are the three steps:

1. Read only the sentence.

Don't let yourself get distracted by trap answer choices.

2. Use proof from the sentence to make a prediction.

The same sentence-deconstruction tools work, and just as for Text Completion, you should write down your prediction and aim to recycle text from the sentence whenever possible.

3. Compare your prediction to each answer choice.

If you're approaching Sentence Equivalence using sentence analysis, this is the only step in the process that differs from the one-blank Text Completion process. In Sentence Equivalence, you need to find exactly *two* good matches for your prediction, not just one. However, it's important to note that both words might not feel like an equally apt fit. Often only one of the correct answer choices will fit your prediction perfectly, while the other correct answer will be correct by association: It'll be the closest synonym for the first correct answer.

Here's an example problem with some admittedly tough vocabulary:

The village's water supply had been _____ by toxic industrial byproducts that had seeped into groundwater.

|A| adumbrated
|B| contaminated
|C| abashed
|D| adulterated
|E| truncated
|F| abridged

The blank is about something that happened to the water supply. What do you know about that supply? You know that *toxic* substances seeped into it—that's a very strong and very negative word. There is no reversal marker to send the meaning in the opposite of the expected direction. If you had to pick a single word as proof for the blank, *toxic* would be that word.

Chapter 3: **Text Completion and Sentence Equivalence**

So your fill-in could be *made toxic* or something similar, like *contaminated*.

Finally, look for two matches among the answer. The correct answers are *contaminated* and *adulterated*. *Contaminated* is a perfect fit for the sentence and is in line with the prediction above. *Adulterated* is the best match for *contaminated* among the answer choices, though it's more often used for a new substance that cheapens or degrades what it's added to. Note that among the incorrect answers, *truncated* and *abridged* both mean roughly the same thing ("shortened"), *adumbrated* means "outlined or sketched lightly," and *abashed* means "made to feel shame."

Try another hard one:

> Unlike the more genial researchers, who often went out together after work, the _____ Dr. Spicer believed that socializing was nothing more than a distraction, and thus made few friends at the lab.
>
> A sedulous
> B baneful
> C standoffish
> D partisan
> E glacial
> F assiduous

The blank is describing Dr. Spicer. A key reversal marker is the word *Unlike*, which sets up a comparison between *the more genial researchers* and *the _____ Dr. Spicer*.

Since the two are *unlike*, the blank should be something that means "*not* genial," in contrast to the *genial* folks. You could use *not genial* itself as your prediction, or you could put down *unfriendly*, as using more common words can make your prediction more immediately comprehensible and thus easier to use effectively.

The answers are *standoffish* and *glacial*. Both words can mean "emotionally cold and distant." (*Glacial* can also mean "slow, physically cold, or pertaining to glaciers.") Both are a good enough match to *not genial* or *unfriendly* to be the winners.

Rounding out the vocabulary lesson, *sedulous* and *assiduous* mean "hardworking or persistent," *baneful* means "harmful," and *partisan* means "biased, in favor of only one's own side or party."

Unit One: **Words and Sentences**

Answer Choice Analysis

When ETS introduced the Sentence Equivalence format, most people's natural response was, "So we pick a pair of synonyms, right?" ETS officials insist that the two correct answers don't have to be precise synonyms:

> *Do not simply look among the answer choices for two words that mean the same thing. This can be misleading for two reasons. First, the answer choices may contain pairs of words that mean the same thing but do not fit coherently into the sentence, and thus do not constitute a correct answer. Second, the pair of words that do constitute the correct answer may not mean exactly the same thing, since all that matters is that the resultant sentences mean the same thing.*

Hmm. When the two correct answers are inserted into the sentence, do the resulting sentences mean the same thing? Sounds like those words would have to be pretty close, right?

What seems to be going on is that the GRE is being overly respectful of the English language. To quote the famous science-fiction writer, Theodore Sturgeon, "There are no synonyms." In other words, subtleties of meaning technically separate any two words you find listed in any individual entry in a thesaurus. *Deluge* and *flood* don't mean the exact same thing (a *deluge* is, by definition, a severe flood). The GRE wants to acknowledge that the two words you pick will likely differ in terms of some nuance.

However, unless you are trying to write some very stylish and precise prose, the difference between *deluge* and *flood* doesn't really matter. And for Sentence Equivalence on the GRE, that difference definitely won't matter. In fact, in almost every real Sentence Equivalence problem we've seen, the two correct answers are pretty close to being 100 percent synonymous. (We can only think of <u>one</u> official counterexample, a question whose correct answer is *susceptibility* and *characteristic*.)

Consider this example:

> Many people at the dinner party were inordinately interested in questioning the _____ new guest, who refused to reveal his profession or even where he used to live.
>
> A acerbic
> B mysterious
> C insightful
> D trenchant
> E intrepid
> F inscrutable

Look for the proof. The blank describes the new guest, who *refused to reveal* things about himself. If there were a word meaning "not self-revealing," you'd pick it. The word needs to be something like *secretive* or *mysterious*.

As it turns out, *mysterious* and *inscrutable* are the correct answers. *Inscrutable* means "not able to be scrutinized" and often indicates hiding emotions. It's not exactly the same thing as *mysterious*, but there's more overlap between their meanings than between *mysterious* and any other answer.

Most correct answer pairs are at least as closely related as these two. Think of the correct answers as **near-synonyms**. There is a second approach to Sentence Equivalence questions that takes advantage of this property of the answers: Answer Choice Analysis.

So far, you've used **Sentence Analysis** to answer questions, focusing first on the meaning of the given sentence and analyzing it closely to come up with your own prediction. **Answer Choice Analysis**, by contrast,

Chapter 3: **Text Completion and Sentence Equivalence**

involves ignoring the sentence completely and instead going straight to the answer choices, *sorting them into pairs of near-synonyms*. The right answer must be one of these pairs. And given that there are only six answer choices, there just can't be that many reasonable pairs.

While Sentence Analysis should still be the default approach to Sentence Equivalence, there can be circumstances in which the sentence doesn't yield its proof as readily as you might like. Answer Choice Analysis can work better in these cases (and if your vocabulary is strong, it can even work well as a primary approach).

On the surface, going straight to the answers might seem like a bad idea. Mathematically, your chance of randomly guessing the correct answer pair is 1 in 15. That's less than 7 percent. Those odds are so low that it seems like a waste of time to bother looking at the answers when you aren't following the sentence in the first place. But good Answer Choice Analysis can raise those chances *dramatically*. It can get you from 1 in 15 to 1 in 3 or 1 in 2. It even sometimes gets you to 1 in 1; that is, it gets you all the way to the right answer.

How? The correct answer will be two words that (mostly) mean the same thing. If you know what the six words mean, you can group them into near-synonym pairs. And given that there are six answer choices, at most you'll find three pairs.

Let's look at some examples. Many sets of Sentence Equivalence answer choices are "two by two"—that is, among the six choices there are two different pairs of synonyms, plus two "loose," unrelated words.

Typical two by two:

> horrible
> nice
> pleasant
> impoverished
> terrible
> dying

Horrible and *terrible* are a pair of synonyms. *Pleasant* and *nice* are a different pair of synonyms. *Impoverished* and *dying* are unrelated.

This leaves only two viable answers to consider: the two different pairs of synonyms. At this point, you have a 50 percent chance of guessing correctly. Notice also that the two pairs are antonyms of each other. While this doesn't always happen, it does happen very often, a sign to be meticulous with any reversal markers in the sentence itself.

Here is a weaker variant of a two by two:

> wicked
> healthful
> evil
> qualified
> gifted
> well-practiced

Wicked and *evil* are a pair. *Gifted* and *well-practiced* are sort of a pair—that is, *gifted* implies an ability that comes from within, whereas *well-practiced* implies an ability that comes from (obviously) practice. However, both are different paths to the same goal (being talented or skilled). They're a weak pair.

In the case that a set of choices provides a closely related pair and a less closely related pair, *the more closely related pair is more likely to be the answer*. However, make sure that the pair has some support in the sentence before you choose it.

 59

Unit One: **Words and Sentences**

Occasionally, three words will seem to match up (a *triplet*). In such cases, usually two are really synonyms and the third is off in terms of spin, strength, or usage. For instance, in the case of *excoriate*, *admonish*, and *castigate*, the real pair is *excoriate* and *castigate*—both mean "to criticize or scold very harshly," and *admonish* means "to scold mildly." Note that if all three triplets really were synonyms, they would necessarily all be wrong, since there can only be two correct answers. However, this doesn't happen often. Indeed, it more often happens that the two true synonyms in a triplet end up being the right answer, with the third word included as a trap answer for test-takers who understood the sentence but are unaware of the nuance difference among the three words.

Here's a set of answers with another false triplet:

> determined
> talkative
> hapless
> unsuccessful
> unlucky
> resolute

Determined and *resolute* are a pair. *Hapless*, *unsuccessful*, and *unlucky* seem to be a triplet. (*Talkative* is not related to the others.)

Hapless really does mean *unlucky* (*hap* is actually a rarely used Old English word for "luck" or "lot"). But a person can be *unsuccessful* without being *unlucky*. *Hapless* and *unlucky* are the true pair.

It is also possible to have just one pair, or three.

Only one pair:

> pale
> flexible
> hidden
> celebrated
> equitable
> fair

Equitable and *fair* are a pair. The other four words are unrelated. Answer Choice Analysis gets you all the way to the right answer!

Three pairs:

> candid
> latent
> ingenuous
> inimical
> dormant
> hostile

Candid and *ingenuous* are a pair. *Latent* and *dormant* are a pair. *Inimical* and *hostile* are a pair. Answer Choice Analysis gets you down to three choices.

Even in this last case, this is still a huge jump in your random-guessing chances, from about 7 percent to about 33 percent.

Chapter 3: **Text Completion and Sentence Equivalence**

When to Use (and NOT to Use) Answer Choice Analysis

When you use Answer Choice Analysis as your main tool for Sentence Equivalence questions, you proceed to the choices first, before even reading the sentence. For instance:

Blah blah blah blah blah blah blah blah blah blah blah blah blah _____, blah blah blah blah blah blah blah blah blah.

- A toadies
- B aesthetes
- C tyros
- D lackeys
- E anchorites
- F novices

As you examine the answers, attempt to make pairs: *toadies* and *lackeys* are subordinates who follow without question. *Tyros* and *novices* are both beginners. *Aesthetes* love or study beauty, and *anchorites* are recluses, especially religious hermits, and thus those two words are not related.

Therefore, the answer must be *toadies/lackeys* or *tyros/novices*. The only question you need to ask at this point is, "Does the sentence call for a *suck-up* or a *beginner*?" Here is the complete problem:

It may be true that everyone likes flattery, but a good manager is not unduly persuaded by it, and thus not taken in by _____, who use wheedling and fawning to get ahead.

- A toadies
- B aesthetes
- C tyros
- D lackeys
- E anchorites
- F novices

There is a lot of proof (such as *flattery* and *wheedling and fawning*) that the question is calling for *toadies* and *lackeys*.

Answer Choice Analysis is at its most effective when you know all of the words in the choices.

However, most test-takers don't have strong enough vocabularies to be able to complete Answer Choice Analysis consistently, especially when the words get really tough.

Moreover, most of the time this approach does *not* get you all the way to the right answer. You'll either need to lightly deconstruct the sentence or, if the sentence proves too inscrutable, to guess one of the pairs. That's unsatisfying.

So in general, start a Sentence Equivalence question by quickly scanning the answer choices. If the words are all familiar, Answer Choice Analysis is a viable option; keep it in mind as a backup plan, and then proceed to the sentence. For most, Sentence Analysis ought to be the first line of attack.

Unit One: **Words and Sentences**

But when should you break out this backup plan? When you read and reread the sentence, but you're not getting anything out of it. Maybe the topic or the structure is really confusing. Or under the pressure of time and the exam, you just can't get a handle on the original text. Or maybe you've understood a lot of the sentence, but you're still struggling to come up with a prediction for the blank. In this case, you might be starting to hit a state of *semantic satiation*. Have you ever repeated some word over and over, until it loses meaning and sounds like nonsense? That's semantic satiation.

Under exam pressure, even the glimmers of this state can lead to a downward spiral. As meaning slips from your grasp, you reread the sentence even more frantically, berating yourself for not getting it, falling even further into semantic satiation, distraction, and panic…

Stop it. Break out of the spiral. If you're familiar with the words in the answer choices, it's time to invoke Answer Choice Analysis. You'll make good progress toward the goal. If you come back to the sentence, you'll be refreshed and ready to take in its meaning. Moreover, it'll be an easier prospect to deal with the sentence at that point, as rather than coming up with the meaning of the sentence from scratch, you'll just have to decide between two or three meanings (depending on how many answer pairs you find). If you still can't decide, make a good guess and move on.

In fact, as you progress through the exam, you might proactively change it up for yourself. Go ahead and decide to attack the next Sentence Equivalence question with Answer Choice Analysis from the outset. That strategic decision will reassure you. It will remind you that you're in charge of the exam, not the other way around. However, that will only work if you've practiced Answer Choice Analysis before test day, so as you study Sentence Equivalence, make sure that you proactively alternate between Sentence Analysis and Answer Choice Analysis so that you hone both skills.

Chapter 3: **Text Completion and Sentence Equivalence**

Drill: Answer Choice Analysis

> For each set of choices, match up the pairs. Most, but not all, sets of choices consist of two pairs of near-synonyms and two other unrelated words. A few will have one or three sets of near-synonyms.

1. verbose
   turbid
   diffident
   prolix
   self-effacing
   pious

2. amicable
   pithy
   scholarly
   arcane
   succinct
   esoteric

3. distend
   traduce
   alienate
   flatter
   slander
   complement

4. auxiliary
   cardinal
   principal
   ordinal
   collateral
   prefatory

5. hawkish
   cogent
   turgid
   eloquent
   bombastic
   intelligible

Unit One: **Words and Sentences**

6. pellucid
   transparent
   rustic
   sedulous
   assiduous
   earthy

7. eclecticism
   aberrance
   deviation
   idiosyncrasy
   adulation
   eccentricity

8. bevy
   modicum
   paucity
   excess
   surfeit
   bunch

9. disclosure
   epitome
   scruple
   apothegm
   contumely
   maxim

10. pique
    slake
    quench
    succor
    fructify
    stimulate

Chapter 3: **Text Completion and Sentence Equivalence**

Answers and Explanations

1. Two pairs: **Verbose** and **prolix** are a pair, each meaning "talkative." **Diffident** (lacking confidence) and **self-effacing** (putting oneself down) are a pair; they are not perfect synonyms, but they are close enough for Sentence Equivalence questions on the GRE. *Pious* and *turbid* have no relationship.

2. Two pairs: **Pithy** and **succinct** both mean "short and to the point." **Arcane** and **esoteric** both mean "obscure or specialized, known to only a few" (about information). *Amicable* and *scholarly* are not related.

3. One pair: **Traduce** and **slander** are a pair, meaning "tell malicious lies about." *Complement* and *flatter* are a TRAP—*complement* (to complete, to make up a whole with) is *not* the same word as *compliment* (to say something nice about). *Distend* and *alienate* are also unrelated. If these were the answer choices in a real question, *traduce* and *slander* would be the correct answer.

4. Two pairs: **Auxiliary** and **collateral** mean "secondary, off to the side." **Cardinal** and **principal** (first, main) are actually synonyms with each other *and* antonyms with *auxiliary* and *collateral*. *Ordinal* and *prefatory* are not related, though watch out for an association trap: *Cardinal* and *ordinal* are both used to designate kinds of numbers and so may initially seem as though they form a pair.

5. Two pairs: **Turgid** and **bombastic** are a pair. *Bombastic* means "pompous, overinflated" and is used to describe speech. While *turgid* can simply mean "swollen," when it is applied to speech, it has the same meaning of "overinflated, showing off." **Eloquent** and **cogent** are a weak pair—*eloquent* means "beautiful and articulate" (about speech), and *cogent* means "compellingly persuasive." *Intelligible* and *hawkish* are not related.

6. Three pairs: **Pellucid** and **transparent** are a pair (see-through), as are **rustic** and **earthy** (primitive, of the earth, undeveloped) and **assiduous** and **sedulous** (hardworking).

7. Two pairs: **Aberrance** and **deviation** are a pair (being different from the normal). *Eclecticism, idiosyncrasy,* and *eccentricity* may all seem similar. However, **idiosyncrasy** and **eccentricity** (harmless personal oddness) are a true pair. *Eclecticism* (having mixed, wide-ranging tastes) is unrelated to *adulation* (excessive admiration).

8. Two or three pairs: **Bevy** and **bunch** are a pair, as are **surfeit** and **excess**. **Modicum** and **paucity** are questionable as a pair because they differ in spin—*modicum* means "a little," and *paucity* means "not enough." It's the subtle but key difference between *having a little* and *having little*.

9. One pair: **Apothegm** and **maxim** are a pair (proverb; pithy statement). *Disclosure, epitome, scruple,* and *contumely* are unrelated.

10. Two pairs: **Pique** and **stimulate** are a pair. **Slake** and **quench** (satisfy, especially of thirst) are a pair. *Succor* (provide comfort or relief) might seem related to the second pair, but one *succors* a person, and one *slakes* or *quenches* a desire. *Fructify* (make productive) is unrelated.

Unit One: Words and Sentences

What If I Don't Know the Words?

It almost seems as though Sentence Equivalence on the GRE was designed to prevent lucky guesses. On a standard choose-one multiple-choice question with choices (A) through (E), a test taker has a 1 in 5 chance of randomly guessing the correct answer. On a Sentence Equivalence, however, there are six answers total and you must choose two. A random guess here has only a 1 in 15 chance of being correct.

If you know *one* of the correct choices and randomly guess on the other, your chance of getting the question correct is 1 in 5. Thus, it is very important that you *assiduously augment* your vocabulary.

That said, even a little Answer Choice Analysis can help you make a good guess, increasing your odds of success. Many Sentence Equivalence questions match the two-by-two format. That is, the answer choices contain two pairs of synonyms or near-synonyms and two other loose words.

So if you can find a single pair of synonyms in the choices, there is about a 50 percent chance that that pair is correct (it is only *about* 50 percent, since not all sets of choices follow a two-by-two format). Here is an example:

- [A] agog
- [B] akimbo
- [C] obeisant
- [D] dyspeptic
- [E] kowtowing
- [F] crotchety

If you were able to pick out that *dyspeptic* and *crotchety* were a pair—or that *obeisant* and *kowtowing* were—then test that pair in the sentence and pick it if it seems to be a good match. (As will be the case in most questions, the two remaining words, *agog* and *akimbo*, have no relationship.)

If the pair that you are able to find is not a fit for the sentence, cross off both words. You now have a 1/6 chance of guessing correctly.

If you cannot find a synonym pair, you are unlikely to get the question correct. Accept that fact and don't waste time. Your strategy here is simply to make a guess and move on. Save time for questions that you will be able to answer later.

Although the GRE allows you to move around within a section and come back to questions you previously left blank or wish to reconsider, keep in mind that **if you don't know the words, you probably won't do any better by attempting the question twice**. You'll only waste time and lower your chance of getting other questions correct. (One caveat: Every now and then, a word you didn't know when you attempted an earlier question will come up in a passage later in the section. Keep your eyes open!)

To be clear, though, if you don't know the words, **do not leave the question blank**. There's no penalty for choosing the wrong answer on the GRE, and there's no advantage whatsoever to leaving a question blank—if you do, you're *guaranteed* to get it wrong. Make your best guess on the question and move on. Don't waste time deliberating over it, and don't mark it for review. That extra time will be better spent on Reading Comprehension or other vocabulary questions that you are able to answer more effectively.

Chapter 3: Text Completion and Sentence Equivalence

Why It Is Important to Learn Words in Context

ETS tells you not only to check that the two answers you select for a question create sentences that mean the same thing, but also to make sure that each one "produces a sentence that is logically, grammatically, and stylistically coherent."

Hmm. Asking test-takers to check that the completed sentences are grammatically coherent implies that some of the choices will create sentences that are not. Here's an example:

Education advocates argued that the free school lunch program was vital to creating a school environment _____ to learning.

- A conducive
- B inimical
- C substantial
- D appropriate
- E beneficial
- F hostile

"Education advocates" are certainly in favor of learning; your fill-in might be something like *helpful*.

Looking at the choices, *conducive*, *appropriate*, and *beneficial* all seem to be matches.

However, if you place each word into the sentence, one choice creates an incorrect idiom. *Conducive to* and *beneficial to* work, but *appropriate to* is not a correct idiom—instead, you would say "appropriate *for* learning." The Idioms list in your online syllabus contains several examples of these idiomatic expressions.

Thus, it is important not only to memorize dictionary definitions of words, but also to be able to use those words in context, in a grammatically correct way.

Here's another example:

He's a _____ fellow, always grandstanding and deploying his formidable lexicon for oratorical effect.

- A declamatory
- B grandiloquent
- C didactic
- D florid
- E titanic
- F cabalistic

The blank describes what kind of *fellow* he is, and the content clue is *grandstanding and deploying his formidable lexicon for oratorical effect*. That is, he speaks in a pompous way, as though showing off his vocabulary for an audience.

Unit One: **Words and Sentences**

The word *florid* seems appropriate—it means "flowery" and often applies to words, as in *florid poetry*. But wait! *Florid* applies to writing, speech, decor, etc., not to the people who produce those things. (Actually, you can apply *florid* to people, but in that context it means "flushed, ruddy," as in having rosy cheeks, which is not appropriate here.)

The answer is **declamatory** and **grandiloquent**, both of which describe pompous orators (that is, people who make speeches) or the speech of such people.

Memorizing that *florid* means "flowery" is better than nothing, but it doesn't really tell you what kinds of things can be described by that word or how to use it metaphorically. Once again, it is important to learn words in context.

There are several ways to do this. Manhattan Prep's *GRE® Vocabulary Flash Cards* provide example sentences for all 1,000 words. Many online dictionaries provide quotes from literature in which the word being defined is used in context. In some cases, it is fruitful to simply Google a word to see how different writers are using it.

Whatever your process, your goal is to be able to do two things for any given word: first, to define it in a concise and straightforward way and, second, to be able to use it in a sentence in a descriptive way (such that someone reading the sentence would understand what it meant from the context).

You want to be comfortable when seeing a word used in any legitimate way. For instance, you would understand if the word *darkness* were used metaphorically (*While she at first resisted going on antidepressants, she ultimately decided that she would do anything that might lift the darkness*) or if the word *enthusiastic* were used sarcastically (*As enthusiastic as I am about unnecessary surgery, I will have to decline your offer to appear on an extreme makeover reality show*).

To perform with excellence on the GRE, you want to know your new words inside and out. You want to be *flexible* in how you use and interpret those words. The online resources associated with this book provide more guidance for formidably fortifying your lexicon.

Traps in TC and SE

Here is a list of common trap answer types and other twists the GRE can use to make Text Completion and Sentence Equivalence questions easier to miss. As you practice, keep your eye out for these traps and make an explicit note of any that you fall into. By paying specific attention to which traps you're vulnerable to as you study, you'll be better prepared to dodge those same traps on test day. Also, bear in mind that this list is not comprehensive; be on the lookout for other traps along the way.

- **Double reversal markers,** which create **opposite traps**
- **Story traps,** which tempt you to add unproven elements to the story of the sentence
- **Unfamiliar style/content,** which can confuse you and cause you to abandon your process
- **Familiar content,** which can lead to picking answers based on what you know to be generally true rather than what's actually written in the sentence
- **Idiom traps,** which are answer choices that form part of a common phrase with a word near the blank and therefore artificially feel like a good fit
- **Red herring clues,** which, while in the sentence, are not related by content to the blank
- **Blanks in tough spots,** which require careful unpacking or parsing of the sentence

- **Theme traps,** where wrong answer choices are thematically related to elements of the sentence but not logical fits for the blank
- **Spin traps,** in which a wrong answer has a nearly apt dictionary definition but the wrong connotation (positive or negative)
- **Close but not close enough traps,** where wrong answers have the right spin but are incorrect in degree, detail, or fit
- **Vocab traps,** where the GRE takes advantage of visual similarities between words to trick you into thinking one word has a similar meaning to another

Text Completion and Sentence Equivalence Recap

This is the three-step process for Text Completion and Sentence Equivalence:

1. Read only the sentence.
2. Use proof from the sentence to make a prediction for the blank.
3. Compare your prediction to each answer choice.

For Sentence Equivalence, if a quick glance at the answer reveals only familiar words, you have the additional option of using Answer Choice Analysis:

1. Group the answer choices into pairs of near-synonyms. Eliminate any answers that don't form a pair.
2. Consider which pair's meaning best fits the sentence.

Practice both of these approaches as you study TC and SE, with a special focus on predicting answers.

Vocabulary Challenge

> Did you spot these vocabulary words? If not, go back and find them in context! (The word may be in a different form than listed here— "digressing" instead of "digress," for example.) Write your own definitions based on the evidence in the chapter.

1. tortuous (*adj.*), p. 44
2. recondite (*adj.*), p. 45
3. embellish (*v*), p. 48
4. paragon (*n*), p. 50
5. satiate (*v*), p. 62
6. augment (*adj.*), p. 66

Unit One: **Words and Sentences**

Problem Set (Text Completion)

As you do these questions, look for the proof before going to the answer choices, write down your own prediction in your scratch work, write out the letters A B C D E, and use process of elimination. Try to identify the traps mentioned in this chapter. Also, make a list of vocabulary words to look up later.

If your current vocabulary is extremely limited, here's another idea: Go through the following questions looking at the answer choices only, without reading the sentences. Make flash cards for all of the words you can't precisely define (look words up on Google, dictionary.com, m-w.com, thefreedictionary.com, etc.). Learn all of the words, and *then* come back later to try these questions.

1. Although it appeared to be _____ after its stagnation and eventual cancellation in 1989, *Doctor Who* returned to the BBC in 2005, becoming the longest-running science-fiction show in history.

A	lackluster
B	ascendant
C	unflagging
D	defunct
E	sated

2. _____ against China's record on environmental protection has become a ubiquitous pastime at energy summits, especially among those already inclined to invective on such topics.

A	Inveigling
B	Speculating
C	Needling
D	Ranting
E	Lauding

3. In 1345, the brothers of Queen Blanche of Namur, Louis and Robert, were appointed _____ to her spouse, conveying upon them the protection of King Magnus Eriksson in exchange for their homage and fealty.

A	protégés
B	vassals
C	vanguards
D	precursors
E	partisans

Chapter 3: **Text Completion and Sentence Equivalence**

4. Social critic Neil Postman identified what he saw as a sort of intellectual _____ when he wrote, "What Orwell feared were those who would ban books. What Huxley feared was that there would be no reason to ban a book, for there would be no one who wanted to read one."

A	pondering
B	mulishness
C	degeneration
D	cerebration
D	banishment

5. The doctor's presentation went into great detail about the supposed _____ of the treatment, but failed to discuss any way of obviating damage to auxiliary structures.

A	diagnosis
B	mien
C	prognosis
D	costs
E	benefits

6. It takes only a smattering of dry shrub for an errant spark to touch off a full-blown _____.

A	wasteland
B	renewal
C	scintilla
D	emergency
E	conflagration

7. While it would be a relief if the announcement were _____, many shareholders have doubts, based on the prevarications that have marked the CEO's long tenure at the company.

A	libelous
B	credible
C	nullified
D	unverified
E	forestalled

8. In determining sentencing, the judge will take into account whether the defendant acted on _____ motives or, as the prosecution alleges, acted primarily to protect himself and his profits.

A	altruistic
B	hidden
C	pathological
D	lucrative
E	violent

Unit One: Words and Sentences

9. During years of mismanagement by the Socialist Party, Burma drifted into economic _____ and isolation, a far cry from the power and influence exerted by the country at the peak of the Toungoo Dynasty in the 16th century.

A	monotony
B	opulence
C	nonchalance
D	feebleness
E	recriminations

10. As the new government revealed itself to be far more authoritarian than the people ever could have guessed, and curfews and roadblocks threatened the _____ of citizens, the public houses began to fill with whispers of a possible coup d'état.

A	insolence
B	epitome
C	belligerence
D	recidivism
E	autonomy

11. He is the most hubristic individual his colleagues have ever met, never missing an opportunity to _____ his own accomplishments.

A	flout
B	augment
C	dictate
D	downplay
E	vaun

12. The negotiator's _____ was so incomprehensible to the Royal delegation, accustomed to speaking only in formal Queen's English, that the parties struggled to complete the negotiation.

A	fortitude
B	patois
C	equanimity
D	diffidence
E	consternation

13. Traditional upper-class _____ such as fox hunting and cricket have largely given way to more egalitarian amusements over the course of the last century.

A	stereotypes
B	diversions
C	vocations
D	canards
E	professions

Chapter 3: **Text Completion and Sentence Equivalence**

14. Professor Honeycutt was known as a probing questioner of her students; she always wanted to get to the _____ of any intellectual matter.

A	emotions
B	academics
C	pith
D	periphery
E	examination

15. After Bismarck's cunning leadership helped the Prussians overcome years of infighting, they were able to turn the aggression outward, becoming known across Europe for their _____.

A	ennui
B	extravagance
C	opulence
D	covetousness
E	truculence

16. The idea, espoused by such heavyweights as Peter Singer, that each sentient being deserves fair treatment on par with human beings clashes with the ecological insight that _____ some members of a species is occasionally necessary to prevent the devastating effects of overpopulation.

A	protecting
B	culling
C	murdering
D	reintroducing
E	depleting

17. After renouncing the advantages of his noble birth, he wandered from village to village as a _____; along with the other members of his religious order, he maintained that this reliance on alms was the life best suited to one who wished to see both the miserliness and the generosity of humanity.

A	abettor
B	mendicant
C	rube
D	anachronism
E	malefactor

Unit One: Words and Sentences

18. A crotchet of many grammarians is that the serial comma is _____ addendum to a perfectly clear sentence structure; obviously, they're wrong, as the serial comma is critical to understanding the sentence's meaning, cadence, and grammatical delineations.

A	an unnecessary
B	a proper
C	a misunderstood
D	a dogmatic
E	an inspired

19. In contrast to American social conventions regarding neighborly relations, in which families and individuals often interact on a familiar basis, residential _____ does not necessarily imply intimacy (or even amity) among the English.

A	commodiousness
B	amiability
C	reciprocity
D	proximity
E	cordiality

20. It is quite dangerous to _____ unnecessarily through the city these days, when explosions shake the buildings to their foundations without letup; it is best to conduct only essential errands, and to do so with haste.

A	bop
B	saunter
C	circumambulate
D	sidle
E	reconnoiter

Chapter 3: **Text Completion and Sentence Equivalence**

Problem Set (Sentence Equivalence)

In this set, try to practice both approaches to Sentence Equivalence: Sentence Analysis and Answer Choice Analysis. Write out A B C D E F on your scratch paper, and remember to choose two answers that are near-synonyms. As in the Text Completion set, make sure to add unfamiliar words to your vocab list after you attempt the questions, and try to identify any traps.

> *Directions*
>
> For the questions in this set, select the two answer choices that, when used to complete the sentence, fit the meaning of the sentence as a whole and produce completed sentences that are alike in meaning.

1. The children's story—seemingly a simple tale of animals gathering for a picnic in the forest—took a _____ turn at the end, admonishing readers to always be honest.

    - [A] magnanimous
    - [B] beneficent
    - [C] didactic
    - [D] garrulous
    - [E] moralistic
    - [F] futile

2. Floodwaters had already breached the library's walls, but hopeful volunteers in hip boots worked tirelessly to _____ the damage.

    - [A] mitigate
    - [B] exacerbate
    - [C] abase
    - [D] bolster
    - [E] forestall
    - [F] flummox

3. The candidate campaigned on a platform of willingness to cooperate with the members of other political parties, yet many commentators were nevertheless surprised that she indeed turned out to be less _____ than her predecessor.

    - [A] irate
    - [B] divisive
    - [C] impulsive
    - [D] wily
    - [E] infuriated
    - [F] combative

Unit One: **Words and Sentences**

4. When Sven got angry, whether it was during an argument with his family or just with a coworker, it proved almost impossible to _____ him and thereby return him to his normal demeanor.

    A   condemn
    B   pacify
    C   judge
    D   incense
    E   mollify
    F   influence

5. The graduate student's experiment yielded results as surprising as they were promising; her next step was to pursue additional data that would _____ her findings.

    A   undergird
    B   buttress
    C   gainsay
    D   undermine
    E   eschew
    F   lecture

6. There is no fundamental difference between a person who quietly _____ a bigoted viewpoint to a friend and one who spews chauvinist vitriol on television.

    A   eschews
    B   espouses
    C   professes
    D   denies
    E   reneges
    F   substantiates

7. A 1957 lawsuit against the U.S. Department of Agriculture regarding aerial pesticide spraying was the _____ for Rachel Carson to begin the writing of her environmentalist manifesto *Silent Spring*, though she had become concerned about and started researching the practice years earlier.

    A   stimulus
    B   conspiracy
    C   atrocity
    D   impetus
    E   catastrophe
    F   climate

Chapter 3: **Text Completion and Sentence Equivalence**

8. A commentator with a more _____ worldview would not find it so easy to divide up the nation into good guys and bad guys.

   - [A] belligerent
   - [B] subtle
   - [C] philosophical
   - [D] aberrant
   - [E] peaceful
   - [F] nuanced

9. James Joyce's *Finnegan's Wake*, written in a stream-of-consciousness style full of convoluted puns and obscure allusions, has a deserved reputation for linguistic _____.

   - [A] elaborateness
   - [B] opacity
   - [C] meaninglessness
   - [D] informality
   - [E] uniqueness
   - [F] inscrutability

10. The financial situation in many European nations is _____ enough that even a small incident could lead to catastrophe.

    - [A] drab
    - [B] unstable
    - [C] illegitimate
    - [D] unsafe
    - [E] precarious
    - [F] churlish

11. While the argument for global warming may not be _____ by the record low temperatures reported this year, this data does not undermine the overall trend of steadily higher global temperatures.

    - [A] bolstered
    - [B] fortified
    - [C] subverted
    - [D] defined
    - [E] supplanted
    - [F] undercut

Unit One: **Words and Sentences**

12. The debate coach expected some gravitas from her team, arguing that pithy quips and gibes, while sometimes effective, had no place in a _____ argument.

    - [A] polite
    - [B] shallow
    - [C] competitive
    - [D] serious
    - [E] cantankerous
    - [F] sober

13. Last year it was discovered that *South Park* writers _____ part of its *Inception* spoof from a similar *College Humor* sketch.

    - [A] amalgamated
    - [B] filched
    - [C] indulged
    - [D] combined
    - [E] poached
    - [F] assumed

14. Some critics view Abstract Expressionism, which is characterized by geometric shapes and swaths of color, as a _____ of realist painting.

    - [A] rejection
    - [B] manifestation
    - [C] renunciation
    - [D] memento
    - [E] commemoration
    - [F] vindication

15. The first spy of the nascent United States, Nathan Hale, was captured by the British when he attempted to _____ British-controlled New York City to track enemy troop movements.

    - [A] thwart
    - [B] penetrate
    - [C] infiltrate
    - [D] permeate
    - [E] research
    - [F] conquer

Chapter 3: **Text Completion and Sentence Equivalence**

16. Romantic comedies of the 1950s were characterized more by _____ than by the straightforward vulgarity that characterizes dialogue in today's rom-coms.

    - [A] conversation
    - [B] blatancy
    - [C] insinuation
    - [D] illusion
    - [E] innuendo
    - [F] rapport

17. Inflation isn't dead, only _____; as the economy turns around, the purchasing power of the dollar is likely to fall again.

    - [A] paralyzed
    - [B] dormant
    - [C] immobile
    - [D] itinerant
    - [E] problematic
    - [F] quiescent

18. Some boxers talk about trying to access their more _____ selves in order to counter the fact that civilized people generally don't punch each other in the face.

    - [A] seething
    - [B] barbaric
    - [C] irate
    - [D] insidious
    - [E] nefarious
    - [F] primitive

19. Many people assume that creative work is less _____ than manual labor, but they underestimate the difficulty of being entirely self-motivated (as well as writing one's own paychecks).

    - [A] inventive
    - [B] collaborative
    - [C] serious
    - [D] arduous
    - [E] taxing
    - [F] grave

Unit One: **Words and Sentences**

20. The education debate is only getting more _____ as politicians demonize teachers unions and every special interest group jumps into the fray.

    - [A] vehement
    - [B] overt
    - [C] heated
    - [D] problematic
    - [E] tired
    - [F] unavoidable

21. While many individual religions insist on the primacy of their particular deity, syncretism advocates the _____ of multiple religious beliefs, attempting to reconcile even opposing principles and practices.

    - [A] exclusion
    - [B] marriage
    - [C] commingling
    - [D] division
    - [E] transgression
    - [F] schism

22. The ambassador was invested with _____ power by her government and hence did not hesitate to draft and finalize the agreement unilaterally, without first consulting even the president.

    - [A] tertiary
    - [B] consummate
    - [C] enigmatic
    - [D] tyrannical
    - [E] complete
    - [F] dictatorial

23. Sometimes it seems that today's politicians will exploit any opportunity to _____ their views to the world, no matter how sordid or partisan.

    - [A] declaim
    - [B] invoke
    - [C] disparage
    - [D] parrot
    - [E] adduce
    - [F] trumpet

Chapter 3: **Text Completion and Sentence Equivalence**

24. The many scattered chapters of the organization decided that a mandatory national _____ would be the best way to bring leadership together and reconcile what had become a haphazard and often chaotic set of bylaws and regulations.

    A introduction
    B acclamation
    C intervention
    D colloquium
    E symposium
    F mediation

25. Though it seems implausible that one could be a great writer without some experience of life, many famous authors have led a(n) _____ existence.

    A idiosyncratic
    B cloistered
    C hermetic
    D enigmatic
    E sheltered
    F cryptic

26. Though she wasn't particularly well-known as a humanitarian, her deep sense of responsibility for those who were suffering was real, and was belied by an outward appearance of _____ .

    A concern
    B sagacity
    C mirth
    D felicity
    E nonchalance
    F indifference

27. Excessive patriotism is ineluctably _____, as the elevation of one country to the rank of preeminent on Earth necessarily requires some amount of demonization of other people.

    A minatory
    B xenophobic
    C unethical
    D bigoted
    E nationalistic
    F truculent

Unit One: **Words and Sentences**

28. One possible explanation for the mandatory debauchery of most bachelor parties is that if the husband-to-be is able to practice _____ in those circumstances, he must be ready for the self-restraint attendant to marriage.

    - [A] forbearance
    - [B] gentility
    - [C] fiat
    - [D] tenacity
    - [E] temperance
    - [F] autonomy

29. Jon Stewart's "Rally to Restore Sanity" was purportedly organized to prove that it was possible to discuss politics humorously but civilly, without _____ those on the other side of the fence.

    - [A] bespeaking
    - [B] eulogizing
    - [C] lampooning
    - [D] vilifying
    - [E] caricaturing
    - [F] maligning

30. Though occasionally used in practice, very few forms of corporal punishment have been _____ by the military, due less to the prescriptions of the Geneva Conventions than to the overwhelmingly negative popular response to reports of abuse.

    - [A] upbraided
    - [B] sanctioned
    - [C] endorsed
    - [D] considered
    - [E] rejected
    - [F] rebuked

31. The budget debate progressed well for the first few months, in spite of all the ardent and sometimes bitter squabbling, but slowly descended into a _____ of competing interests and claims.

    - [A] quagmire
    - [B] covenant
    - [C] feud
    - [D] morass
    - [E] quarrel
    - [F] accord

32. The difference between similes and metaphors is subtle, but for the poet who takes his or her work seriously, it is absolutely _____.

   A frivolous
   B superfluous
   C dispensable
   D crucial
   E trifling
   F requisite

33. It is _____ reasoning to ascribe to Keynesian economics a recommendation that the limit on how much debt the government can incur should be perpetually raised, when Keynes states clearly that deficit spending must be done responsibly.

   A indigenous
   B corrupt
   C venial
   D fallacious
   E specious
   F axiomatic

34. In many ways, teenage rebellion can be seen as the effect of a communication gap between an older generation's calcified language and the protean _____ of the new generation.

   A argot
   B defiance
   C prolixity
   D insubordination
   E verbosity
   F jargon

35. His cantankerous reputation was cemented by years of _____ at every conceivable opportunity.

   A imputing
   B grousing
   C assaulting
   D carping
   E convulsing
   F imbibing

Unit One: **Words and Sentences**

36. The police were called when people in the neighborhood witnessed a small _____ in progress outside of a bar.

    - [A] fracas
    - [B] discourse
    - [C] altercation
    - [D] battle
    - [E] colloquy
    - [F] mutiny

37. Given her sheltered upbringing and the limited breadth of experience imposed on her by economic circumstance, her work reflected a surprisingly _____ sensibility.

    - [A] shallow
    - [B] eclectic
    - [C] profound
    - [D] multifarious
    - [E] callow
    - [F] facile

38. Many people expect documentary filmmakers to be dispassionate and objective, but Michael Moore has a reputation for never missing a chance to _____ against those with whom he disagrees.

    - [A] rail
    - [B] advertise
    - [C] fulminate
    - [D] censure
    - [E] strain
    - [F] aspirate

39. The movie critic was best remembered for the way she used the language of food to describe films, for example, how she praised Iñarritu's action sequences by comparing them to _____ empanada.

    - [A] an insipid
    - [B] a spectacular
    - [C] a brilliant
    - [D] a piquant
    - [E] a zesty
    - [F] an astonishing

Chapter 3: **Text Completion and Sentence Equivalence**

40. Every few years, someone manages to survive a skydive with a parachute that doesn't open, often with only a few broken bones, some _____ , and a gash or two.

    A torpor
    B trauma
    C bruises
    D finesse
    E lesions
    F contusions

41. As official _____ to this country, she was called upon to answer questions about the Japanese government's position on various issues.

    A envoy
    B tyro
    C emissary
    D neophyte
    E ascetic
    F libertine

42. While the group's street protests had had an aggressive, uncompromising tenor, once admitted to the halls of power to begin formal lobbying, its leaders wisely chose to _____ the stridency of their rhetoric.

    A metamorphose
    B gild
    C wane
    D palliate
    E succor
    F damp

43. The women's rights movement has been mostly _____ in the Middle East, but it is likely that activists will be newly galvanized by the political upheavals currently sweeping the region.

    A dogged
    B stagnant
    C interminable
    D lissome
    E abeyant
    F tenacious

Unit One: **Words and Sentences**

44. Debate rages on between proponents and detractors of corporal punishment and the death penalty, though even the most ardent supporter agrees that punishments must be _____ and the justice system evenhanded and thorough.

    A meet
    B clement
    C delimited
    D apposite
    E tantamount
    F merciful

45. Peer-reviewed journals are a sacred cow of most scientific rationalists, but studies have shown that the premise of impartiality is _____, as results are always colored by the personal proclivities and suppositions of the experimenters.

    A inane
    B prejudicial
    C fatuous
    D chimerical
    E unachievable
    F vexing

46. The description of the restaurant as a garden of _____ delights is fair enough, as Chef Marcel conjures up a menu of texture and taste that calls into question one's preconceived notions of what constitutes a meal.

    A salubrious
    B epicurean
    C carnal
    D voluptuous
    E terrestrial
    F gustatory

47. Most of the book drones on for chapter after chapter, each one providing yet another example of her thesis, the _____ of which can be found in précis form in the tome's first few pages, and which is recapitulated from that point on.

    A gist
    B adage
    C pith
    D stub
    E nimbus
    F aphorism

86

Chapter 3: **Text Completion and Sentence Equivalence**

48. In order to ascertain the efficacy of the new exam vis-à-vis the old one, it will be necessary not only to collect, but also to _____ detailed score reports of test-takers from both groups, as only by studying the differences and similarities in results can proper inferences be drawn.

    A aggregate
    B deduce
    C collate
    D juxtapose
    E agglomerate
    F glean

49. In World War I, trenches were dug so that the soldiers could avoid the near constant _____ from the other side of the line of battle, but not even a trench could protect a battalion from grenades or aerial bombardment.

    A volleys
    B provocations
    C fervency
    D imprecations
    E goading
    F salvos

50. Cary Grant's reputation as a _____ ladies man extended beyond the silver screen to his real life, where he was known to never let a woman pull out her own chair, in keeping with the custom of gentlemen at that time.

    A consummate
    B genteel
    C debonair
    D waggish
    E courtly
    F cosmopolitan

51. Focusing primarily on self-awareness, empathy, and honest self-expression, the communication process known as "nonviolent communication" states that the attempt to find parity in a relationship is a fallacious principle, as any notion of fairness is entirely _____.

    A subjective
    B introverted
    C pragmatic
    D utilitarian
    E illicit
    F personal

87

Unit One: **Words and Sentences**

52. Education has become a kind of albatross in American politics, in that a speech with any hint of _____ is actually more pernicious to a politician's reputation than one with numerous signs of ignorance, or even outright stupidity.

    [A] bromide
    [B] erudition
    [C] patrimony
    [D] condescension
    [E] cerebrality
    [F] bloviation

53. Laurent Cantet's *Time Out* tells the true story of a man so obsessed with retaining the _____ of plenitude after he is discharged from his employment that he doesn't even tell his wife and his kids about his termination.

    [A] corollaries
    [B] paradigms
    [C] semblance
    [D] prepossessions
    [E] veneer
    [F] consequences

54. What people fail to remember about Don Juan is that his astronomical number of amatory adventures were due more to his _____ approach to seduction than to any surfeit of charisma or skillfulness.

    [A] sumptuous
    [B] lurid
    [C] covert
    [D] indiscriminate
    [E] blanket
    [F] hedonistic

55. Even the most far-reaching campaign finance reform proposals will fail to _____ the influence of money, which doesn't just buy speedboats and golf weekends in the Bahamas, but directly relates to a politician's capacity to run for office.

    [A] quash
    [B] graft
    [C] pander
    [D] check
    [E] importune
    [F] indemnify

56. In their landmark study of Victorian literature's relationship to feminism, Gilbert and Gubar _____ the many ways in which 19th-century women writers created characters that fit into archetypes of "angel" and "monster."

- [A] delineate
- [B] interpolate
- [C] debunk
- [D] limn
- [E] explode
- [F] castigate

57. While it's inarguably prejudiced to imply that there is some kind of innate _____ in certain countries, it's more reasonable to say that certain cultures are more willing to prioritize relaxation and a sense of moderation between work and play.

- [A] obtundity
- [B] enfeeblement
- [C] enervation
- [D] indolence
- [E] seemliness
- [F] lethargy

58. Autodidacts may argue that the enforced lucubration of a standard education is _____ , but while some people are able to learn without outside guidance and strictures, most people learn better when accountable to others.

- [A] slack
- [B] prudent
- [C] lax
- [D] extraneous
- [E] unnecessary
- [F] sagacious

59. The best of Sigur Ros's music evokes _____ landscape, as if the music had transported one to some twilit avenue in a long since abandoned city.

- [A] a dusky
- [B] an urban
- [C] a crepuscular
- [D] a precipitous
- [E] an avuncular
- [F] a civic

Unit One: **Words and Sentences**

60. Some historians argue that at least in so far as the broad strokes are concerned, cataclysmic events such as the Great Depression are _____ , due to what some have termed "the inertia of history."

   A ineluctable
   B incontrovertible
   C interminable
   D inviolate
   E inexorable
   F ineffable

Chapter 3: **Text Completion and Sentence Equivalence**

Answers and Explanations

Vocabulary Challenge

1. tortuous (*adj.*): winding; containing numerous twists, turns, or bends

2. recondite (*adj.*): related to or something abstruse or little understood

3. embellish (*v*): to enhance by adding details, often fanciful or invented

4. paragon (*n*): a model of excellence or virtue

5. satiate (*v*): to satisfy fully; or, to satisfy overmuch or to excess

6. augment (*adj.*): to enlarge, make greater, more intense, or more numerous

Solutions: Problem Set (Text Completion)

1. defunct: The blank in the sentence is describing the show *Doctor Who*, and the immediate proof offered is that the show stagnated and was canceled in 1989, so a good prediction would be dead or over.

A *lackluster* (dull) show might be canceled, but it doesn't make sense that *Doctor Who* appeared to be dull *after* it was canceled. A canceled show is unlikely to appear in a positive light, such as *ascendant* (upwardly moving) or *unflagging* (not tiring; steady and unrelenting). *Sated* (fully satisfied, maybe too much) wouldn't be used to describe a television show.

2. Ranting: The blank will be filled by an action ("pastime") undertaken "against China's record on environmental protection." The second part of the sentence, which is connected to the first by the straight-ahead marker "especially," describes the people participating in the mystery pastime: "those already inclined to invective." "Invective" means "harsh criticism," so the word that goes in the blank must be something to do with criticism.

Inveigling (winning over by flattery) doesn't fit, but a similar word *inveighing* (speaking with hostility) would have fit. This is a vocab trap. *Speculating* (guessing at) is too neutral, and *lauding* (praising) is too positive. *Needling* (teasing or provoking) is close, but would likely be done to someone or to some group—not "against China's record." Plus, *ranting* is a better match with "invective."

3. vassals: The queen's brothers "were appointed something to her spouse," the king. The word for the blank will be a noun; in such cases, part of the sentence will usually give a definition for that noun. The second part of the sentence states that the brothers received "the protection of King Magnus Eriksson in exchange for their homage (publicly expressed respect) and fealty (loyalty)." Look for an answer that reflects this exchange.

Protégés are like apprentices; *vanguards* are leaders of movement in a certain direction, including militarily; *precursors* are forerunners, people who come before others; and *partisans* are dedicated (and perhaps biased) supporters. Several of these are roles that a King or Queen might appoint, but they don't match the exchange of protection for loyalty. *Vassal* (someone who earns something, but has obligations to a leader) fits the exchange aptly.

4. degeneration: The blank appears in the first part of the sentence and is connected to something "intellectual." The first part of the sentence offers no hints as to what word would work, so the proof must be in Postman's quote. Look there for content clues that relate to something intellectual. Only the talk about books is salient to intellectual concerns, and more specifically, a society in which no one wants to read books anymore is suggestive of an intellectual weakening or decline.

Unit One: **Words and Sentences**

Pondering (thoughtful consideration) and *cerebration* (thinking about something) are near-synonyms to each other and are too positive in tone, and thus the opposite of what the blank requires. They're also theme traps. *Mulishness* (unreasonable stubbornness) is theoretically a reason someone wouldn't want to read a book, but stubbornness isn't alluded to specifically in the sentence. *Banishment* (condemnation to exile) is unrelated to the actual proof in the sentence.

5. benefits: Take care unpacking the sentence. The main reversal marker here is "but," meaning the two parts of the sentence contradict each other. However, the second part of the sentence also contains more subtle vocabulary reversal markers: "failed" and "obviate." Start concrete: The treatment causes "damage to auxiliary structures." If the doctor had discussed some way of "obviating damage" (that is, preventing damage), it would have been a good thing, but the doctor "failed to discuss" that—which is a bad thing. Since the "but" makes the two parts of the sentence opposites, the doctor must have gone "into great detail about supposed <u>good things</u> about the treatment."

Diagnosis (determination of disease) and *prognosis* (forecast of medical outcome; chances of recovery) both relate to the medical theme, but neither fits in the blank, as they aren't specifically positive things. *Mien* (appearance, bearing) is unrelated. *Costs* is the opposite of the blank, as the blank should discuss the positive aspects of the treatment.

6. conflagration: The blank is presented as a "full-blown" outcome of the ill-advised combination of "dry shrub" and "an errant spark." The most sensible prediction would be <u>fire</u>, particularly a big fire or a wildfire.

A *wasteland* might be what's left of the landscape after the *conflagration* sweeps through it, but it's not something that would be "touched off" directly by a spark. Similarly, a *renewal* of the landscape might follow in the years after the fire, but it won't be the immediate consequence of an errant spark. A *scintilla* is itself a spark, though it's almost exclusively used in a figurative way (for instance, *a scintilla of inspiration*)—not a good fit for the blank. *Emergency* is probably the toughest to eliminate. A situation in which a giant fire erupts is almost by definition an emergency. However, it's not a perfect fit. As discussed above, the content clues more strongly suggest a fire, and in one-blank Text Completions, the GRE is almost certain to give you a word that's apt to the content clues. If you didn't know the meaning of *conflagration* (a large and destructive fire), it could be especially hard to pass *emergency* up—and indeed, one of the hardest things you'll have to do in TC is pick a word you don't really know instead of a word you *do* know but that doesn't quite fit.

7. credible: The blank describes an "announcement," and it's something that would be "a relief" to shareholders. Whatever goes into the blank must be <u>something good</u>. The rest of the sentence provides opportunities to predict something more specific. It mentions that shareholders have "doubts" about the announcement and that those doubts are based on "prevarications" (lies) that have been common under the CEO's management. Therefore, a good prediction for the blank would be <u>truthful</u>.

Libelous (which deals with printed lies) is the opposite of what the blank demands. *Nullified* (invalidated or voided) and *forestalled* (prevented or delayed) don't fit the truth/lying theme in the sentence, and *unverified* (unconfirmed) would likely only add to the shareholders' doubts.

8. altruistic: The missing word describes the motives that a defendant acted on, and it's part of a larger *whether … or …* structure, which generally functions as a reversal marker. The prosecution claims that the defendant acted "to protect himself and his profits," and the judge is choosing between this explanation *or* a contrary explanation. The word in the blank should offer that contrary explanation, so a good prediction would be <u>not self-interested</u>.

You can stretch *hidden* into an answer for the blank, especially since "hidden motives" makes sense in the context of a courtroom. But this doesn't contradict the prosecution's characterization of the defendant's motives, at least not nearly as directly as *altruistic* (unselfish, giving). *Pathological* (related to physical or mental disease) introduces a theme of illness that's not mentioned in the sentence. *Lucrative* (producing large profit) has proof in the sentence ("his profits"), but it's the opposite of the word needed. *Violent* is a theme trap relating to a trial, but there is no evidence of violent action.

9. feebleness: You know that Burma was being mismanaged, so look for the word in the blank to be something bad. "A far cry" serves as a reversal marker, revealing that the missing word and "isolation" are contrasted with "power and influence." Just as isolation and influence are (somewhat) counterpoints, you can expect the blank to be a counterpoint to power: something like not power or weakness.

Monotony (lack of variety, tedious repetition) is negative, but no proof in the sentence supports this meaning. *Opulence* (wealth, abundance) is opposite of the desired meaning. Both *nonchalance* (casual lack of concern) and *recriminations* (counteraccusations) don't make sense following *economic*.

10. autonomy: What would an authoritarian government threaten with "curfews and roadblocks"? Most likely, something like free movement.

Belligerence (aggressiveness) might describe these citizens' behavior, but it does not describe something that is "threatened" that they might lose. Likewise, *insolence* (rude and disrespectful behavior) does not work in the blank. The remaining choices, *epitome* (a perfect example of something) and *recidivism* (tendency to relapse to previous behavior, often criminal), are not indicated by clues in the sentence.

11. vaunt: "Hubristic" means "arrogant"—a hubristic person would never decline an opportunity for bragging about his accomplishments.

Flout (blatantly disregard) is closer to the opposite of the prediction, but its similarity to *flaunt* makes this a potential vocabulary trap. *Augment* (make or become greater in size) is not quite right, as a hubristic would be inclined to brag about their accomplishments more, but may not necessarily have more or better accomplishments. *Dictate* can be stretched to sort of fit, but it's usually used in a more technical context. *Downplay* accomplishments is directly opposite of what a hubristic person would do. *Vaunt*, meaning to boast or praise, fits perfectly.

12. patois: Since the negotiators find the negotiator "incomprehensible," there must be something in the negotiator's speech that is confusing them. The proof in the sentence pertains to the dialect that the delegation employed: "formal Queen's English." Therefore, the word in the blank should meet this comparison head-on, making dialect a good prediction.

The Royal visitors would not find any of the other characteristics—*fortitude* (courage, resilience), *equanimity* (composure, mental calmness), *diffidence* (hesitance or resistance to speak), *consternation* (amazement or dismay that leads to confusion)—"incomprehensible," nor do any of these relate to the clue about styles of speech. *Patois* (the dialect of a region's common people) fits the evidence well.

13. diversions: The blank describes how the upper class sees things "such as fox hunting and cricket." There's also another piece of proof later in the comparison to "more egalitarian amusements." The blank must mean something like amusements.

Vocations and *professions* both contradict the idea of these activities as "amusements." Fox hunting and cricket are not examples of *canards*, which are unfounded rumors or stories, or of *stereotypes*. Stereotypes is, however, a theme trap; while fox hunting and cricket may be seen as stereotypical activities of the upper class, they are not themselves *stereotypes*.

14. pith: A "probing questioner" probably wants to get to the bottom of things. The semi-colon and "always" serve as straight-ahead direction markers. Professor Honeycutt is looking for the <u>central point</u> of a matter.

Emotions certainly might be revealed under probing questioning, but they also might not, depending on the questions. *Periphery* (the outside edges) is the opposite of where a probing questioner hopes to arrive. *Examination* and *academics* are traps that go with the scholastic theme, but they aren't supported by the sentence. *Pith* (the essence of something) is exactly what a probing questioner would likely be looking for—at the very least, it is more likely that Professor Honeycutt is seeking *pith* generally than *emotions* specifically.

15. truculence: The blank is a word describing how Europe viewed the Prussians after they "were able to turn the aggression outward." As such, <u>aggression</u> makes sense as a prediction for the blank.

Ennui (listlessness arising from boredom) is nearly the opposite of aggression. *Covetousness* (envious desire to possess something) could work if you imagine that the purpose of the Prussians' aggression is to acquire the lands and property around them, but there is no such evidence. An answer for which you have to make extra context assumptions is a story trap. *Extravagance* and *opulence* (both mean lavishness) are too close in meaning to each other to be correct, and they have nothing to do with "aggression." *Truculence*, which is similar to belligerence, fits nicely.

16. culling: The discussion is about doing something to "some members of a species…to prevent the devastating effects of overpopulation." The word should oppose "overpopulation," so something like <u>removing</u> or <u>getting rid of</u> would work in the blank. Such a grim prospect would definitely "clash" with the idea outlined in the first part of the sentence.

Protecting and *reintroducing* are both theme traps (due to their association with species) and opposite traps—they do not clash with the idea of fair treatment of sentient beings. *Depleting* can apply to a resource, but not to individual "members." *Murdering* and *culling* are both types of killing, but *culling* is the better option since it is a technical term for killing individual members to avoid overpopulation. (Bonus: If you understand this sentence, you've got a handle on one of the key debates among environmentalists.)

17. mendicant: The character "renounced the advantages of his noble birth," with "renouncing" serving as a reversal marker. This part of the sentence reveals that the blank should oppose those advantages. In the second part of the sentence, "this reliance" indicates a direct callback to something mentioned earlier in the sentence. Because it appears as part of the phrase "this reliance on alms" (which is to say a reliance on charity), there's sufficient proof to predict a word like <u>beggar</u> for the blank. A *mendicant* is indeed a beggar; even better, it often carries a religious connotation, a particularly good fit for something undertaken by a "religious order."

The other choices all introduce meanings that the rest of the sentence doesn't suggest. Both *abettor* (a person who supports an action, typically wrongdoing) and *malefactor* (evildoer) introduce the unsupported idea that the character was immoral in some way. *Rube* (unsophisticated or naïve person) only works if certain extra assumptions are made, and there are no clues suggesting an *anachronism* (person or object out of its proper time).

18. an unnecessary: The blank is connected to "the serial comma" and its relationship to a "sentence structure." The sentence does start with a minor clue ("crotchet"); however, you'd be forgiven if that word is totally unfamiliar to you. Luckily, there are more clues to be found in the second part of the sentence, which starts by indicating a reversal ("obviously, they're wrong") and goes on to describe the serial comma as "critical." The blank should therefore be something like <u>not critical</u>.

Among the incorrect answers, *a proper* and *an inspired* are both too positive for the blank. *A misunderstood* doesn't fully oppose the "critical" role the author assigns to serial commas. *A dogmatic* (marked by absolute adherence to rules or principles) likewise has no basis in the proof. (By the way, did you look up "crotchet"? Remember to add any unfamiliar words you encounter to your vocabulary list.)

19. proximity: The reversal marker "In contrast to" at the beginning of the sentence indicates that the two parts of the sentence will contradict. The main contrast drawn is between neighborly individuals interacting "on a familiar basis" in America and the fact that there's no guarantee of "intimacy (or even amity)" in England. This contrast only works if the description in the last part of the sentence is also about "neighborly relations," and since "residential" immediately precedes the blank, the word in the blank must be something like closeness to properly mirror "neighborly relations." *Proximity* is the only answer that comes close. (Pun 100% intended.)

The other answer choices all deal with comfort or friendliness, and their association with "neighborly" and "amity" makes them theme traps: *commodiousness* (spaciousness), *amiability* (friendliness), *reciprocity* (relationship with mutual exchange of favors or benefits), and *cordiality* (amity). Amiability and cordiality in particular are the opposite of the correct fill-in, since the passage states that amity is "not necessarily implied," meaning it is potentially not present at all.

20. saunter: The blank describes something dangerous to do "through the city," and it's later contrasted with "only essential errands" and "with haste." It certainly sounds dangerous to conduct non-essential errands…but a more likely prediction is to move without haste.

All five of the answer choices describe movements or related activities, but *saunter*, to stroll without haste, offers the best fit for the clues. Both *bop* (move or travel energetically) and *sidle* (walk timidly or sideways) carry a strange spin and don't effectively contrast "haste." *Circumambulate* means "walk all the way around," which would entail avoiding the city rather than going "through" it. *Reconnoiter* (make a military observation of a place) carries a militaristic spin that makes it a good theme trap but doesn't fit the evidence about doing this action "unnecessarily," or the comparison to errands.

Solutions: Problem Set (Sentence Equivalence)

1. didactic; moralistic: The children's story was "seemingly" simple—which means it was not actually simple. Instead, the story took some kind of "turn"—meaning that it changed in some way—and admonished "readers to always be honest." That is, it took a turn by talking about morals or prescribing correct behavior. A good prediction would be moralistic, and *didactic*, which means intended to teach, is a near enough synonym to work.

Magnanimous (generous) and *beneficent* (good, or doing good) are an incorrect pair. *Garrulous* (overly talkative, wordy) and *futile* (ineffective, useless) have no relationship to each other or the sentence.

2. mitigate; forestall: That "floodwaters had already breached the library's walls" sounds very bad—the water is already inside. The direction marker "but" tells you that the sentence is going to change direction, and indeed, the volunteers are "hopeful." So you're looking for something good in the blank—although it doesn't seem like they're going to cure the problem entirely. A good fill-in would be something like limit.

Exacerbate (make more severe, aggravate), *abase* (reduce in prestige, humiliate), *bolster* (support, boost), and *flummox* (confuse) do not contain any pairs. *Exacerbate* would also constitute an opposite trap, since the goal is to improve the flooding problem. *Mitigate* (to make less severe) and *forestall* (to prevent) are not precise synonyms, but they both fit the blank and create equivalent narratives of the volunteers' work.

Unit One: **Words and Sentences**

3. divisive; combative: The first part of the sentence gives you the concrete truth that the candidate is interested in cooperation, but the second part of the sentence is full of direction markers: "yet," "nevertheless," "surprised," "indeed," and "less." A case with this many markers can be difficult to untangle, but luckily the "indeed" alone offers a lot of help. As part of the phrase "she indeed turned out to be," "indeed" confirms that what was expected actually happened: The candidate *did* cooperate with others. Still, watch out for the direction marker "less" just before the blank. If the candidate is indeed cooperative, the thing she would be *less of* is <u>uncooperative</u>.

Irate and *infuriated,* both of which mean angry, are an incorrect pair and together represent a story trap—an angry person is probably less willing to cooperate, but the fit isn't as direct as *divisive* and *combative*, both of which directly imply a difficulty working with others. *Impulsive* (moved or swayed by emotional or involuntary urges) and *wily* (crafty or cunning) have no relationship.

4. pacify; mollify: This sentence provides the clues that when Sven "got angry," returning him "to his normal demeanor" was "almost impossible." His normal demeanor must be something like *not angry*, so you're looking for something like the verb <u>calm</u> in the blank.

Condemn (censure; sentence), *judge* (form an opinion about), *incense* (infuriate), and *influence* (determine or guide) do not contain any strong pairs. Even if you do consider *condemn* and *judge* a close enough pair, there's no reason to believe that judging Sven would "return him to his normal demeanor."

5. undergird; buttress: The blank is a verb that denoting the effect that additional data will have on the student's findings. Those results "were promising" (but "surprising," indicating some uncertainty about the apparent conclusion). The semicolon is a straight-ahead direction marker. Thus, her next step would likely be to <u>verify</u> or <u>corroborate</u> the findings.

Gainsay (deny or prove false) and *undermine* (weaken or subvert secretly) are an opposite trap. *Eschew* (shun, avoid, or abstain from) and *lecture* (speak at length) are unrelated to each other or to the sentence (though *lecture* is a theme trap). *Undergird* and *buttress* both mean something like "to support," so they fit the sentence nicely.

6. espouses; professes: This sentence originally posits that there is "no fundamental difference" between two things, but the overall point is that the two things might appear different on the surface. The "between … and …" structure contrasts the first person who speaks quietly to a friend, and the second person who "spews" on television. They're both focused on different ways of communicating the same thing, so a good prediction would be <u>communicates</u>.

Denies and *reneges* (renounces or denies) are an incorrect pair. *Eschews* is also pretty close to that pair. *Substantiates* (to support or verify) goes beyond simple communication and also fails to fit the context (in that *substantiation* is something more apt to the courtroom than to a quiet conversation between friends).

7. stimulus; impetus: Prior to 1957, Rachel Carson was already concerned about "aerial pesticide spraying" and had begun researching it, but the lawsuit caused her "to begin the writing" of her book. A good fill-in would therefore be <u>cause</u>.

Atrocity (extremely wicked or cruel act) and *catastrophe* (disaster) have similar spins, but they don't match the prediction and are not really a pair—an *atrocity* usually has to be perpetrated by another person, but a *catastrophe* generally isn't. *Climate* (the general weather conditions in an area over a long period) and *conspiracy* (a secret plan by two or more people to do something unlawful) have no relationship, though *climate* represents a theme trap.

Chapter 3: **Text Completion and Sentence Equivalence**

8. subtle; nuanced: The blank pertains to a "worldview," and the concrete truth in this sentence is that the commentator's worldview makes it "easy" to split people into good and bad categories. This is a very simplistic take on the world. Someone with a more complex worldview would be unlikely to break things down so simplistically.

Belligerent (aggressive), *philosophical* (devoted to the study of knowledge), *aberrant* (atypical), and *peaceful* (tranquil) have no relationship.

9. opacity; inscrutability: Joyce's book is described as "stream-of-consciousness," with "convoluted puns and obscure allusions." The adjectives "convoluted" and "obscure" are the most important parts of this sentence. They tell you that the novel is likely hard to understand. The final bit of proof—that the novel's reputation is "deserved"—tells you that the blank will agree with the preceding characterization. A good prediction would be difficulty or incomprehensibility.

The novel is not necessarily *meaningless*, its meaning is simply hard to decipher. Similarly the novel is not necessarily *unique*—even if this style is unusual, there may be others like it. The novel may well be *elaborate* (complex and intricate) or *informal* (relaxed in style), but neither word has a strong pair. *Opacity* (not transparent) and *inscrutability* (difficult to understand) match each other well when applied to a novel, and both fit the prediction.

10. unstable; precarious: The situation in Europe is described as something enough that even a small incident might lead to a catastrophe. This means that everything is on the brink of disaster. You could fill in the blank with something like shaky.

Drab (dull, colorless, or cheerless), *illegitimate* (not authorized by the law), *unsafe* (not safe; dangerous), and *churlish* (uncivil, boorish, or vulgar) all have the correct negative tone, but none have strong pairs.

11. bolstered; fortified: All you need to notice is the contrast between "warming" and "record low temperatures," as well as the signal word "While." Record low temperatures would not directly help an argument about global warming, so a good fill-in would be helped.

Subverted (undermined, in terms of power or authority), and *undercut* (weakened) form a pair, but they constitute an opposite trap. *Defined* (described exactly) and *supplanted* (replaced, substituted for) have no close relationship to each other.

12. serious; sober: The debate coach values "gravitas" (seriousness) and argues that "quips" (witty remarks) and "gibes" (taunts) don't belong in a certain kind of argument. *Serious* and *sober* is the only pair that works.

Polite could work, but it has no pair and it doesn't follow as well from "gravitas." *Shallow*, *competitive*, and *cantankerous* (disagreeable or difficult to deal with) have no relationship, though *competitive* constitutes a theme trap due to its connection to debate.

13. filched; poached: The most important word here is the adjective "similar." If both *South Park* and *College Humor* created a similar spoof, then one of them may have derived the sketch from the other. The fact that something was "discovered" about the *South Park* writers implies that they're the ones responsible, and that there may have been some wrongdoing. Copied would be a good prediction.

Amalgamated and *combined* are an incorrect pair. *Indulged* (allowed oneself to enjoy) and *assumed* (supposed without proof) have no relationship. *Assumed* can mean "took or began to have (power or responsibility)" or even "took on or adopted (an appearance, manner, or identity)," but you wouldn't use *assume* in the context of taking any other kind of item, such as a comedy spoof. This is a close but not close enough trap. *Filched*

Unit One: **Words and Sentences**

and *poached* both mean "stolen," which is a bit more severe than the prediction of copied but nonetheless fits the sentence effectively.

14. rejection; renunciation: Abstract Expressionism is described as "characterized by geometric shapes and swaths of color." Clearly, this is very different from "realist painting." A good fill-in would thus be something like *repudiation*, which means a rejection or a refusal to deal with something.

Memento (an object serving as a reminder) and *commemoration* (a service or celebration serving to remember a person or event) are an incorrect (and imperfect) pair. *Manifestation* (the action or fact of showing an abstract idea; symptom or sign) and *vindication* (exoneration, acquittal) have no relationship, and they indicate a similarity between Abstract Expressionism and realist painting, rather than a contrast.

15. penetrate; infiltrate: You are told that Nathan Hale was a spy working for the United States and that he was captured by the British. That means he must have been involved in some kind of espionage in "British-controlled" New York. A good fill-in would be sneak into or possibly observe.

Thwart (prevent someone from accomplishing something) and *conquer* (take control of by military force) are vaguely related, but are not quite a pair. *Conquer* is also a theme trap. *Permeate* (spread throughout; pervade) and *research* have no relationship to each other, though they're both individually close but not close enough traps. *Research* in particular is something Hale may have been doing, but *penetrate* and *infiltrate* both mean something like "to force into something." Their similarity makes them the correct pair.

16. insinuation; innuendo: The phrase "more by … than …" implies a contrast between the two elements. The second element here is "straightforward vulgarity," so look for a word that means non-straightforward language or non-vulgar language. *Insinuation* and *innuendo* both match the prediction.

Conversation (an informal verbal exchange) and *rapport* (a harmonious relationship) are not quite a pair. *Blatancy* (obviousness) and *illusion* (something that looks or seems different from what it is) are almost opposites.

17. dormant; quiescent: The blank is there to describe "inflation" in a way that contrasts the notion that inflation is entirely "dead." You're told that in the future, "the purchasing power of the dollar is likely to fall," a literal description of inflation. So while inflation isn't dead, the sentence avers that it may come back at any time. A good fill-in would be something like dormant (there aren't a lot of simple words that get across this meaning).

Paralyzed (unable to move or act) and *immobile* do form a pair, but they also represent a close but not close enough trap: While they both indicate a sort of inactivity, they don't capture the idea that inflation could return "as the economy turns around." *Itinerant* (traveling from place to place) and *problematic* (presenting a difficulty) have no relationship. *Dormant* and *quiescent* both correctly imply inflation is in a state of rest but might someday awaken.

18. barbaric; primitive: It's a concrete truth that boxers "punch each other in the face," which according to the sentence isn't "civilized." If they need to "counter" this civilized tendency, then they must access a part of themselves that is not civilized.

Seething and *irate* are an incorrect pair, both meaning "angry," but they are a story trap—if you convince yourself that angry people find it easier to punch each other in the face, these could kind of work. But compared to the correct answers, they're not as perfect a counterpoint to "civilized." *Insidious* (seductive but harmful; treacherous, deceitful) and *nefarious* (wicked or criminal) are likewise an incorrect story-trap pair.

19. arduous; taxing: The concrete truth in this sentence is that people "underestimate the difficulty of being entirely self-motivated," and the reversal marker "but" means that this concrete truth is contradicted in the first part of the sentence. People must assume that creative work is relatively easy, but given the reversal marker "less" just before the blank, a good fill-in would be difficult.

Serious and *grave* are an incorrect (albeit tempting) pair. The proof in the sentence is not about the seriousness of creative work but rather about its difficulty. *Inventive* and *collaborative* are words that you might associate with creativity, but they are not a pair and again do not fit the contrast related to difficulty.

20. vehement; heated: The concrete truth is that "politicians demonize teachers unions" and others are jumping "into the fray." Both "demonize" and "fray" characterize the debate as intense and antagonistic, both of which could serve as good predictions (though the correct answers are closer in meaning to the former.)

Overt (done openly) and *unavoidable* (impossible to ignore) are not quite a pair and aren't supported by the sentence. *Problematic* and *tired* have no relationship, so even if *problematic* might work for the sentence, it can't be chosen. *Vehement* and *heated*, both meaning something like "passionate and forceful" do form a strong pair in addition to fitting the sentence.

21. marriage; commingling: This sentence begins with the marker "While" before describing religions that "insist on the primacy of their particular deity." "Syncretism" on the other hand relates to "multiple religious beliefs," and attempts to "reconcile even opposing principles and practices." Because of that concrete truth about syncretism and the reversal marker at the opening, there's good reason to believe that syncretism is in favor of multiple religious beliefs. The prediction should be something like reconciliation or mixing.

Division and *schism*, which often refers to a division within something like a religious organization, are an opposite trap. *Exclusion* (deliberate act of omission) and *transgression* (act that violates a rule or duty) have no relationship. *Schism* and *transgression* are also individual theme traps due to their religious connotations.

22. consummate; complete: The blank is about the ambassador's power. You have a straight-ahead marker ("hence") and an important clue is that, due to this power, she is performing some of her functions "unilaterally." A good prediction would be something like unilateral or total.

Tyrannical and *dictatorial* are a pair that goes too far, introducing a negative spin (exercising total power in a cruel or unjust way) that isn't supported by any proof in the sentence. *Tertiary* (third-ranking) and *enigmatic* (mysterious) have no relationship.

23. declaim; trumpet: The blank focuses on what politicians do with "their views to the world." There is not much direct evidence about what this action might be, but a reasonable prediction might be announce or spread. The fact that their views are later characterized as "sordid" and "partisan"—the kinds of views one would think *shouldn't* be broadcast to the world—but connected to the rest of the sentence with the reversal marker "no matter" is further confirmation that indeed the politicians are somehow putting these ideas out into the world.

Invoke (reference something in support of an argument) and *adduce* (reference something as evidence) are an incorrect pair. *Disparage* (belittle or discredit) and *parrot* (repeat mindlessly) have no relationship. *Declaim* and *trumpet* both aptly mean something like "to speak confidently and proudly."

24. colloquium; symposium: The concrete truth in this sentence is that the organization, which has "many scattered chapters," has somehow acquired a "haphazard and often chaotic set of bylaws and regulations." Thus, it wants to "bring leadership together" in order to reconcile all these rules. A good prediction would be meeting or conference.

Unit One: **Words and Sentences**

Intervention and *mediation* are a close but incorrect pair—while both might help, they don't reflect the proof ("bring leadership together") as well as *colloquium* and *symposium*. *Introduction* and *acclamation* (loud demonstration of approval or welcome) have no relationship.

25. cloistered; sheltered: The marker "Though" tells you that the first part of the sentence is going to be contradicted by the second part. Be careful as you unpack the rest of the first part, though, as it's replete with reversal markers. The situation that seems implausible is becoming a great writer without life experience, but the second part of the sentence must contradict this, so the "many famous authors" in question should in fact have a lack of life experience. It may be difficult to put this concept into one word, but "a <u>not-full-of-experience</u> existence" is a perfectly fine made-up prediction.

Enigmatic and *cryptic* (having hidden meaning; mysterious) are an incorrect pair. *Idiosyncratic* (unique to an individual; eccentric, quirky) and *hermetic* (completely sealed) have no relationship. Careful with *hermetic*, though. It's both a vocabulary trap due to its similarity to *hermitic* (which might have worked for the blank) and a close but not close enough trap due to its inappropriateness to the context (it's usually used for containers). *Cloistered* (kept away from the outside world) and *sheltered* (kept *safe* from the outside world) both correctly imply that these authors would not have had many worldly experiences.

26. nonchalance; indifference: In this sentence, the key is the word "belied," which functions as a kind of reversal marker. *Belie* means "to misrepresent or disguise," suggesting that whatever goes in the blank should contrast the underlying concrete truth: She feels a "deep sense of responsibility." A good fill-in for the blank would be <u>not caring</u>.

Mirth and *felicity* are a trap pair, both meaning something like "happiness" and thus contradicting "suffering." However, the blank must relate to the subject of the sentence ("her deep sense of responsibility"), as that is what's "belied" by her outward appearance. *Concern* and *sagacity* (keen judgment) have no relationship, and *concern* is the opposite of the prediction.

27. xenophobic; bigoted: The blank here is defined by the second half of the sentence. The "patriotism" that the blank describes is defined as "the elevation of one country to the rank of preeminent on Earth," a process that the author claims requires the "demonization of other people." The word "ineluctably," meaning "inescapably," serves as a straight-ahead marker, so the blank should reflect this demonization. A good fill-in would be <u>prejudiced</u>.

Minatory and *truculent* are not quite a pair (the former means "threatening," while the latter means "aggressively defiant"), and even if you take them as a pair they don't quite fit, as the sentence does not describe particular actions taken against "other people," more so the opinions of those people. *Unethical* and *nationalistic* both arguably fit the sentence, but neither has a pair word as strong as the pair *xenophobic* and *bigoted*, both of which specifically relate to prejudiced opinions against groups of people.

28. forbearance; temperance: It's important to know the word "debauchery" (meaning "excessive indulgence in sensual pleasures") to solve this question. The sentence describes a husband-to-be who will *not* be engaging in debauchery at the bachelor party, as debauchery is implicitly contradictory to "self-restraint." So you need a word that describes someone who exhibits some amount of <u>restraint</u>.

Fiat (authoritative decree) and *autonomy* (the right to self-government; independence) are not quite a pair and would be incorrect anyway. *Gentility* (the state of belonging to polite society; refinement of manner) and *tenacity* (the quality of being persistent or stubborn) have no relationship.

29. vilifying; maligning: The rally here is described as discussing politics "civilly, without" doing the thing in the blank. Since "without" functions as a reversal marker and the blank is connected to "those on the other side of the fence," a good recycled prediction for the blank would be being uncivil to.

Lampooning and *caricaturing* make an incorrect pair, both meaning "mocking or ridiculing." The sentence mentions that the rally was "humorous." This means that *lampooning* and *caricaturing*, both of which imply a kind of humorous teasing, would be welcome at the rally, so not a great fit for the blank. They're also not particularly uncivil. *Bespeaking* (suggesting; ordering or reserving something in advance) and *eulogizing* (to praise highly, especially at a memorial service) have no relationship, and the latter is the opposite of what you want here.

30. sanctioned; endorsed: The blank focuses on how the military has handled "corporal punishment," a phrase meaning punishment involving physical force. The first part of the sentence tells you that such punishments are "occasionally used in practice," but the reversal marker "though" indicates that the blank will somehow contradict this. The second half of this sentence contains the concrete truth that "reports of abuse" (a reference to corporal punishment) receive an "overwhelmingly negative popular response." This means that despite using them on occasion, the military would be unlikely to condone or formally adopt these forms of abuse.

Upbraided and *rebuked* (both meaning criticized or scolded) form an incorrect pair—if the military has criticized "few" forms of corporal punishment, it might well *approve* of such punishment, a bad fit for the meaning of the sentence. These choices also constitute a theme trap due to their relationship with "punishment." *Rejected*, similarly, implies that the military may actually be using many of these punishments. It's possible that few such punishments have been *considered* by the military, but this has no clear pair, while *sanctioned* and *endorsed* both mean something like "approved of publicly."

31. quagmire; morass: The first part of the sentence, which describes how the budget debate "progressed well" is very important: If you miss that, you might be tempted to choose the wrong words here. The part of the sentence with the blank, which starts with the reversal marker "but" and contains the negative content clues "descended" and "competing interests and claims," is describing a worsening situation. The negativity of that situation wouldn't be a good contrast for the *also* negative picture of "bitter squabbling" in the part of the sentence that immediately precedes the part with the blank. Instead, the part of the sentence with the blank must be contrasting the positivity of the first part of the sentence, meaning that the blank should be something contrary to "progressed well." A good prediction would be mess or muddle.

Feud and *quarrel* are an incorrect pair. While they correctly get across the negative spin you want for the blank, they don't address the idea of progressing badly. They constitute a theme trap for their similarity to "squabbling." *Covenant* and *accord* are an incorrect pair, both indicating an agreement. They are part of a red herring trap in that they both contrast the middle part of the sentence, a part that, as outlined above, has no bearing on what goes in the blank despite its proximity to the blank. *Quagmire* and *morass* both correctly mean something like "a complex and difficult situation."

32. crucial; requisite: This is a tough question, because the sentence gives you only "subtle" as a content clue. The blank should oppose it, but the opposite of "subtle" would be something like obvious, and there's no match for *obvious* among the answers. This is a good time to try Answer Choice Analysis.

Among the answers, there are three pairs:

- *frivolous* and *trifling* (having little value or importance)
- *superfluous* and *dispensable* (unnecessary)
- *crucial* and *requisite* (necessary)

Consider each pair's meaning in the context of the sentence. Which offers the best contrast to the subtleness of "the difference between similes and metaphors"? Add in the fact that the blank describes how this difference is perceived by "the poet who takes his or her work seriously," and the choice becomes clearer. A serious poet would consider the difference between these two poetic devices important, even if its subtleness can make the difference hard to distinguish. Only **crucial** and **requisite** work. *Frivolous* and *trifling* both contrast "seriously," and *superfluous* and *dispensable* have no connection to any of the content clues in the sentence.

33. fallacious; specious: This sentence leans heavily on content clues, so it's important that you understand all of it. You are given two statements about economics. Start with the more concrete one: "Keynes states clearly that deficit spending must be done responsibly." Then come back to the first part of the sentence. If Keynesian economics is ascribed a belief that the limit on government debt "should be perpetually raised," a belief that contrasts what Keynes actually states, then it must be the product of faulty reasoning.

Indigenous (native to or naturally occurring in a region), *corrupt*, *venial* (forgivable or pardonable), and *axiomatic* (self-evident or unquestionable) have no relationship. In addition, *axiomatic* is the opposite of what is needed for the blank.

34. argot; jargon: This sentence is describing rebellion as the effect of a "communication gap." On one side of the communication gap is "an older generation's calcified language"; on the other side is "the protean something of the new generation." Given that the gap is laid out in the descriptors here ("older generation's" vs. "of the new generation" and "calcified" vs. "protean"), the blank should probably just be language.

Defiance and *insubordination* are an incorrect pair, both meaning something like "disobedience." *Prolixity* and *verbosity* are another incorrect pair. They constitute a theme trap, as both words mean "wordiness," which might superficially feel like a good fit for a sentence about communication.

35. grousing; carping: "Cantankerous" means "bad-tempered and argumentative." Because there is no reversal marker here, you simply need a word that means those things. A good fill-in for the blank would be arguing or complaining.

Imputing (attributing or blaming), *assaulting* (physically attacking), *convulsing* (suffering violent involuntary contraction of the muscles), and *imbibing* (drinking) have no relationship. *Grousing* and *carping* on the other hand are very close both to each other, and to our prediction of complaining.

36. fracas; altercation: In this sentence, you need to figure out what kind of thing would result in the police being called—likely, some kind of crime or fight. Only the latter has matches in the answer choices.

Discourse and *colloquy* are an incorrect pair, both meaning "conversation." *Battle* may be close to what you want, but it implies a certain level of (often military) organization among the two opposing sides that's inappropriate to the bar setting and would rarely be remedied by calling the police. *Mutiny* (open rebellion against authorities) is not related to the others.

37. eclectic; multifarious: In this sentence, the word "surprisingly" acts as a reversal marker, so the part of the sentence with the blank contrasts the part before the comma. The woman had a "sheltered upbringing" and a "limited breadth of experience," so the blank should be the opposite of that. A good fill-in would be varied or worldly.

Shallow and *facile* are an incorrect pair, in that both can mean "superficial." *Profound* has the right spin, but it isn't such a good counterpoint to "limited breadth" (it would be a better counterpoint to "limited depth"). *Callow* (immature or inexperienced) has no relationship with the other choices, and it incorrectly agrees with "limited breadth of experience." *Eclectic* (derived from a wide range of sources) and *multifarious* (of many types) both fit the prediction of <u>varied</u>.

38. rail; fulminate: The word "but" is a signal to reverse course here, taking you in the opposite direction of the "dispassionate" and "objective" nature initially used to define documentary filmmakers. A good fill-in would be <u>speak out</u>.

Advertise (draw attention to publicly in order to promote sales), *censure* (express strong disapproval of), *strain* (make a strenuous effort), and *aspirate* (pronounce a sound in the exhalation of breath) have no relationship to each other. Note that *censure* forms a false triple with *rail* and *fulminate*; it is incorrect largely because it's unidiomatic to say "censure against" something. "Rail against" and "fulminate against" both work, and both imply speaking out or protesting.

39. a piquant; a zesty: There are two important portions of this sentence to focus on. First, the word "praised" implies that the critic's review will be positive. Second, the way she's described as using "the language of food to describe films" implies that, if possible, the correct answers should also use the language of food. So you want two words that are positive and that are also preferably in food-language.

A spectacular, a *brilliant*, and *an astonishing* form a sort of triple, at least inasmuch as they're all very positive words. However, there's no need to figure out which one doesn't fit with the other two: The two food words (*piquant* and *zesty*) reflect more of the proof in the sentence and therefore are better choices. *Insipid* (bland, tasteless, or flavorless) is a food word, but its negative spin makes it an opposite trap.

40. bruises; contusions: In this sentence, a short list of possible injuries after a skydiving accident is described. Two of the items are "broken bones" and "a gash," which means your blank should be a physical injury different from those two. A good fill-in would be <u>bruises</u>.

Torpor (a state of physical inactivity; apathy, lethargy) and *finesse* (skillful or adroit handling) are not physical injuries, so they don't fit with the other two items on the list provided. *Trauma* (physical injury; shock following a disturbing event or injury) and *lesions* (wounds, ulcers, tumors, etc.) are both things that someone might experience after a skydiving accident, but neither has a synonym pair.

41. envoy; emissary: The person in question is serving as "official" something for Japan to another country, and is "called upon to answer questions about the Japanese government's position." This role sounds like an <u>ambassador</u>.

Tyro and *neophyte* are an incorrect pair, both meaning "beginner." *Ascetic* (self-denying; austere) and *libertine* (one who is debauched or without moral restraint) are not synonyms, though both have something to do with self-control, in opposite ways.

42. palliate; damp: The blank is about both the leadership and the "stridency of their rhetoric"—you need the relationship between those two things. "While" is a reversal marker. In the first part of the sentence, the protests are "aggressive" and "uncompromising." Thus, in the second part, they should be softer and more in favor of compromising. "Stridency" means harshness and is on the same side as "aggressive" and "uncompromising," so the group must have chosen to <u>reduce</u> the stridency.

Wane means "decrease" and is an attractive trap answer. However, *wane* is an intransitive verb—that is, something (such as the moon) *wanes* on its own; you can't *wane* an object. Therefore, the word's usage does not fit in this sentence. *Metamorphose* (change) could work, but it doesn't indicate the direction of the change (increase or decrease), which the blank needs to do in order to show that the leaders "wisely" chose to do something. *Gild* (cover in gold; give a deceitfully pleasing appearance to) and *succor* (aid, assist, or relieve) have no relationship to each other or to the sentence.

Unit One: **Words and Sentences**

43. stagnant; abeyant: The key bit of proof that you're looking for here is that "activists will be newly galvanized." Because of the reversal signal "but," you need a blank that means the opposite of "galvanized." A good fill-in word would be dormant (implying that the movement is quiet but could rise again).

Dogged (stubbornly determined) and *tenacious* form an opposite-trap pair. *Interminable* (endless) and *lissome* (flexible or easily bent) have no relationship. *Stagnant* and *abeyant* both mean something like "temporarily stopped."

44. meet; apposite: The first half of this sentence sets up the topic, but the important information is in the second half. There, you're introduced to the hypothetical "most ardent supporter" of corporal punishment who agrees with detractors on at least one thing, for which "evenhanded and thorough" is a content clue. A good prediction for the blank would be fair. *Meet* (in this case meaning suitable) and *apposite* (appropriate) mostly fit that prediction, but you'll probably have to use some process of elimination before fully signing off on them.

Clement and *merciful* both add a positive spin that wouldn't be adopted by "the most ardent supporter" of corporal punishment and the death penalty. *Delimited* (having limits established; bounded) and *tantamount* (equivalent; virtually the same as) are not related. *Tantamount* may remind you of the idea of the punishment fitting the crime, but the sentence would need to establish *what* the punishments are tantamount to.

45. chimerical; unachievable: The portion of this sentence after the blank tells you that "results are always colored by...personal proclivities and suppositions." Meanwhile, the blank is describing "the premise of impartiality." Since being "colored by personal proclivities" directly clashes with "impartiality," the fact that results are "always" colored by these things would make impartiality impossible.

Inane and *fatuous* are an incorrect pair, both meaning "silly." While the "premise of impartiality" may not be accurate, that doesn't make it silly—this pair is a spin trap. *Prejudicial* (detrimental) and *vexing* (irksome; irritating) have no relationship.

46. epicurean; gustatory: Everything in this sentence relates to food, whether it's the "texture and taste" or the "notion of what constitutes a meal." The type of "delights" referred to in the blank must relate to food. A good fill-in would be culinary.

Carnal (relating to physical, especially sexual, activities) and *voluptuous* (characterized by luxury or sensual pleasure) are an incorrect pair, relating to sensuality rather than specifically food. *Salubrious* (promoting health or well-being) and *terrestrial* (of, on, or relating to the Earth) have no relationship.

47. gist; pith: The verb "drone" has a very specific meaning, implying that someone is going on at length in a dull or boring way. The implication is that the point could be made more efficiently. This sentence then tells you that a "précis" (summary) containing the thesis can be found in "the tome's first few pages." A good prediction would be something like succinct summary or essence.

Adage (a traditional expression of a common observation) and *aphorism* (a pithy expression of a common truth) form a good pair, but the pair is not appropriate to the context (that is, you can't meaningfully talk about the *adage* or *aphorism* of a thesis). *Stub* (a short part left after a larger part was broken off) and *nimbus* (a circle of light) have no relationship.

48. collate; juxtapose: The final portion of this sentence describes "studying the differences and similarities" between two different things. "Vis-à-vis" likewise means "in relation to." Clearly you'll be doing some form of comparison between the old and new exam, so a good fill-in word would be compare.

Aggregate, *agglomerate*, and *glean* are an incorrect triple, all meaning "gather." While gathering the data together is required in order to make a comparison, the sentence already said "not only to collect." All of these words are just fancy versions of "collect," which you don't need to repeat—the blank calls for something beyond simple collection. *Deduce*, which means "to arrive at a conclusion logically," doesn't match any other choice. In addition, it doesn't quite fit the context: you can reason logically *about* the score reports, but you wouldn't reason the score reports themselves. *Juxtapose* (place next to each other to compare) and *collate* (to place in order or compare) are not quite synonyms but both correctly result in comparing the score reports.

49. volleys; salvos: Most of what you need to know in this sentence comes from the few words before the blank: "trenches were dug so that soldiers could avoid" something. What would you avoid in a trench? Perhaps bullets? This is backed up by the second part of the sentence, which compares the trenches' successful protection against the blank with their unsuccessful protection against "aerial bombardment." A prediction borrowed from the passage could be non-aerial bombardment.

Provocations and *goading* are an incorrect pair—the sentence is not discussing being taunted or provoked by the enemy. *Fervency* (fervor; strong feeling of excitement) and *imprecations* (offensive words or phrases said in anger) have no relationship. *Volleys* and *salvos* both correctly represent a series of military gunfire.

50. genteel; courtly: The blank concerns "Cary Grant's reputation," a reputation that was earned both on screen and in real life. What else is mentioned about his reputation? A specific example is given (that he "never let a woman pull out her own chair"), and it's mentioned that his actions were in keeping with the "custom of gentlemen." A good prediction would be gentlemanly.

Debonair and *cosmopolitan* are an incorrect pair. These words mean "sophisticated," but they don't necessarily imply good manners or gentlemanly conduct. *Consummate* (complete or perfect) and *waggish* (humorous in a playful way) are words that could make sense in describing a "ladies man," but they have no relationship. *Genteel* and *courtly* fittingly both mean "polite."

51. subjective; personal: The blank pertains to "any notion of fairness" in a relationship. In the section just before the blank, the sentence states concretely that the attempt to find "parity," or fairness, is "fallacious," or logically incorrect. How could fairness be illogical? Given the focus on "self" behind the communication process in question, a good fill-in would be subjective or unachievable (these are fairly disparate predictions, but luckily, only the former has matches among the answers).

Pragmatic and *utilitarian* are a near-pair meaning "practical." This is almost the opposite of the evidence, as something "fallacious" likely wouldn't be very practical. *Introverted* (introspective) and *illicit* (unlawful) are not related.

52. erudition; cerebrality: The blank pertains to "a speech," and the sentence contrasts the speech that the blank describes with speeches that feature "ignorance" and "stupidity." Further, the first part of the sentence presents education as a liability (from the figurative interpretation of "albatross"). A good fill-in would be something the opposite of ignorance or stupidity, perhaps knowledge.

Bromide (commonplace or trite saying) and *bloviation* (talking at length in a pompous or boastful way) both have some relationship to speech, but they aren't really a pair, and neither relates to "education" or "ignorance." *Condescension* (patronizing attitude; disdain) is similar to *bloviation*, but neither reflects the anti-education message in the sentence or contrasts properly with "ignorance." *Patrimony* (inheritance from a father or other male ancestor) is unrelated to everything else. *Erudition* (learnedness) and *cerebrality* (intelligence) both appropriately oppose ignorance.

Unit One: **Words and Sentences**

53. semblance; veneer: In this sentence, you're told about a man who has been fired and doesn't tell his wife and kids. This somehow relates to "plenitude," which means "abundance" or "completeness." If you get fired and don't tell your family, it could be because you want to seem like you're still okay. A good fill-in word would be appearance.

Corollaries and *consequences* are an incorrect pair. *Paradigms* (things serving as an example or model) and *prepossessions* (attitudes or beliefs formed beforehand) have no relationship.

54. indiscriminate; blanket: The sentence tells you that Don Juan had "an astronomical number of amatory adventures," but that it was not because he had a "surfeit of charisma or skillfulness." If Don Juan didn't have any particular skills when it came to seduction, what else could account for that astronomical number? Perhaps if Don Juan wasn't very choosy. A good fill-in for the blank would be not choosy.

Sumptuous and *hedonistic* are an incorrect pair, meaning "luxurious" and "devoted to luxury or pleasure," respectively. While they both describe someone like Don Juan (and so are a theme trap), they don't explain how he had so many lovers. *Lurid* (gruesome, shocking) and *covert* (not openly done; veiled) have no relationship.

55. quash; check: The sentence indicates that "Even" major campaign finance reform will "fail" to do something to "the influence of money." This money "directly relates" to a politician being able to become a politician, so the influence of money must be pretty strong. Thus, the reform proposals will fail to eliminate or strongly reduce the influence.

Graft (join or unite), *pander* (cater to the lowest or most base desires), *importune* (harass with constant demands; annoy, irritate), and *indemnify* (protect against loss or damage) have no relationship. On the GRE, the choices for a given blank will always be of the same form of speech; here, they are verbs. Don't confuse the verb *graft* with the noun *graft*, which means "acquisition of money (or other valuable) in dishonest or questionable ways" and represents a theme trap here. Indeed, the GRE loves to use alternative definitions of common words, so don't be too hasty to write off *check* in this problem! Here *quash* (to put an end to) and *check* (to slow the progress of) both fit the evidence.

56. delineate; limn: There are no signals to reverse course in this sentence, so you simply need a word that fits the description of a book that explores the "many ways in which 19th-century women writers . . ." In other words, you can just fill in the blank with explore or present.

Debunk and *explode* are an incorrect pair, both meaning "disprove" in this context. *Interpolate* (insert between parts, pieces, or things) and *castigate* (criticize or punish severely) have no relationship. *Castigate* almost fits into a triple with the incorrect pair, but it's more of a criticism than an attempt to disprove something. Both *castigate* and the pair *debunk* and *explode* represent story traps. Gilbert and Gubar *might* have focused on disproving things in their study, but there's no evidence to directly support that expectation. This makes *delineate* and *limn*, both of which are fairly neutral and can mean "to describe in detail," a safer pair to choose.

57. indolence; lethargy: With the reversal marker "While," this sentence creates a contrast between a positive and negative view of the same fact. The positive view is the one that's more concretely established: Certain cultures prioritize "relaxation" and "moderation between work and play." The negative or "prejudiced" view of this same quality would be something like laziness.

Enfeeblement and *enervation* are an incorrect pair, meaning "weakening" or "weakness." Though they are close to what you want, they imply a taking away of energy, which is not the same as being innately lazy or inactive. *Obtundity* (lessening of intensity; dulling or deadening) and *seemliness* (conforming to standards of proper conduct) have no relationship.

Chapter 3: **Text Completion and Sentence Equivalence**

58. extraneous; unnecessary: The blank describes the opinion autodidacts hold regarding "standard education," and the reversal marker "but" reveals that this opinion will be contrary to the concrete truth revealed later. That truth is that "most people learn better when accountable to others," implying that autodidacts believe the opposite of this. They must have a negative opinion of standard education—perhaps that it is unhelpful or even misguided. Note that this prediction can be made by unpacking the sentence *without* understanding the word "autodidacts" or even if understanding its definition (people who teach themselves things) is useful.

Slack and *lax* are an incorrect pair meaning "loose." *Prudent* and *sagacious* are an incorrect (and opposite of our prediction) pair meaning "wise, having good judgement."

59. a dusky; a crepuscular: The only piece of real proof in this sentence comes in the second half, a "twilit avenue in a long since abandoned city." So you want a word that relates to "twilit" or "abandoned city," such as darkish or desolate.

Urban and *civic* are something of a pair here. Though they both reflect the sentence's reference to a "city," they fail to correctly account for the descriptor "abandoned," as *urban* is associated with the active character of a city and *civic* is associated with a city's functioning. *Precipitous* (extremely steep) and *avuncular* (relating to an uncle; kind to younger people) have no relationship. *Dusky* (dimly lit) and *crepuscular* (relating to twilight) are not exact synonyms, but both aptly fit the evidence of a twilit environment.

60. ineluctable; inexorable: The key phrase here is "the inertia of history." Inertia is resistance to change, so this phrase must mean that history is difficult to change. So your blank here should be something like difficult to change or unavoidable.

This question gives six words all with the prefix "in-" but not all six have similar meanings. *Incontrovertible* (not able to be denied or disputed), *interminable* (endless), *inviolate* (untouched or unspoiled), and *ineffable* (not able to be expressed in words) have no relationship. But *ineluctable* and *inexorable* both match the prediction of unavoidable.

UNIT TWO

Paragraphs and Passages

This unit provides you with a comprehensive approach to the study of the final building blocks of GRE Verbal problems: paragraphs and passages. Included are tools for analysis of relationships across long bodies of text. Finally, this unit introduces longer, multiple-blank Text Completions and the various Reading Comprehension types.

In This Unit...

- Chapter 4: GRE Paragraphs
- Chapter 5: Short Passages in Reading Comprehension
- Chapter 6: Argument-Based Reading Comprehension
- Chapter 7: Multi-Blank Text Completion
- Chapter 8: Long Passages in Reading Comprehension
- Chapter 9: Reading Comprehension Problem Set
- Chapter 10: Essays

CHAPTER 4
GRE Paragraphs

In This Chapter...

- Making Connections
- Signals and Pronouns
- Components of Paragraphs
- The Main Idea (and Archetypes)
- The Big Picture
- Don't Just Read, Do Something!
- A Note-Taking Exercise (Sample Notes)
- Common Notations
- Vocabulary Challenge
- Problem Set
- Answers and Explanations

CHAPTER 4 GRE Paragraphs

Previous chapters address the challenges of GRE Vocabulary and GRE Sentences. In this chapter, you will learn how to evaluate the relationships between sentences within a paragraph. (For the purposes of this book, a paragraph is any text that consists of two or more sentences.)

Here are your Chapter 4 vocabulary words:

> exhaustive (E)
> qualified (E)
> abreast (A)
> facilitate (E)
> disparate (A)
> precipitate (A)

Making Connections

Hopefully, the discussion of Sentences in Chapter 2: GRE Sentences convinced you of the value of unpacking sentences in GRE Verbal problems. The next layer of GRE complexity requires you to string those sentences together to make sense of the underlying meaning and purpose of each paragraph or passage.

Revisit the following example from Chapter 1:

> *The Biblical portrayal of flagitious times preceding the great deluge stands in stark contrast to the ancient Greek representation of the antediluvian past as a Golden Age from which humanity has slowly descended into godless chaos. Such observations can easily give rise to the notion that stories about the past are less faithful attempts at reconstruction than allegories, expressing both our cultural fears and hopes.*

How was the vocabulary? If you didn't know some of the words, look them up, make flash cards, and read the paragraph again.

Did simply knowing the words make it substantially easier to read? Probably not! Why? Because the sentence structure itself is dense, and you need to deal with that, too.

Unit Two: **Paragraphs and Passages**

Start by unpacking just the first sentence. Try it on your own before reading the rephrase below.

Sentence	Rephrase
The Biblical portrayal of flagitious times preceding the great deluge stands in stark contrast to the ancient Greek representation of the antediluvian past as a Golden Age from which humanity has slowly descended into godless chaos.	According to the Bible, the time before the great flood (deluge) was shameful and bad (flagitious). The Greeks also talked about the time before the great flood (antediluvian past), but said it was actually *good* before, but had gotten bad after. Wow, the Bible and the Greeks had exactly opposite views.

How did it go? Hopefully unpacking is feeling a little more efficient now that you've been practicing.

So what now? You'll continue through a paragraph, unpacking each sentence as you go. However, in order to understand the meaning or purpose of the paragraph as a whole, you'll also need to make connections between the sentences you're unpacking.

Take, for example, a pure unpacking of the second sentence without any attempt to connect it to the first.

Sentence	Rephrase
Such observations can easily give rise to the notion that stories about the past are less faithful attempts at reconstruction than allegories, expressing both our cultural fears and hopes.	There are observations. Something about how stories might be more symbolic (allegories) than actually trying to "reconstruct" a factual history. Because they're symbolic, these stories are more about the hopes and fears of the people writing them.

This sentence is a little bit more clear now (maybe), but without any connections to earlier sentences, it's difficult to build a complete story of the paragraph.

Chapter 4: **GRE Paragraphs**

You need connections to get the larger story. Consider the following unpacking of the second sentence, built by connecting back to the first.

Paragraph	Rephrase + Connections
The Biblical portrayal of flagitious times preceding the great deluge stands in stark contrast to the ancient Greek representation of the antediluvian past as a Golden Age from which humanity has slowly descended into godless chaos.	According to the Bible, the time before the great flood (deluge) was shameful and bad (flagitious). The Greeks also talked about the time before the great flood (antediluvian past), but said it was actually *good* before, but had gotten bad after. Wow, the Bible and the Greeks had exactly opposite views.
Such observations can easily give rise to the notion that stories about the past are less faithful attempts at reconstruction than allegories, expressing both our cultural fears and hopes.	Everything in the first sentence (such observations) leads people to think that (gives rise to the notion that) . . . . . . stories might be more symbolic than just trying to "reconstruct" a factual history. How else could you explain the two drastically different stories about the exact same time period? And if they're symbolic, they represent the hopes and fears of the people writing them.

Now the bigger story is becoming more clear; connections allow you to find deeper meaning during your initial read of a paragraph. For that reason, making connections as you read sentences is the subject of the rest of this chapter.

Signals and Pronouns

As paragraphs get longer or more complex, conventions of good writing thankfully encourage the use of specific types of words and phrases as signposts, directly connecting one part of a sentence or paragraph to another. You already saw many of these direction markers in Chapter 3: TC and SE, but if you have not reviewed that chapter recently, now would be a good time to look back.

Signal Words and Phrases

Signal words and phrases (direction markers) indicate relationships between different parts of text. Take, for example, this sentence from Chapter 3: TC and SE.

> *Despite her reputation for _____, the politician asserted that in a time of crisis it was important to speak honestly.*

The word *despite* is a signpost of contrast. The information before the comma is going to be in opposition to the information after the comma.

As you learn to recognize these signal words, you'll note additional subtleties in their meaning (see the differences among *in contrast*, *despite*, and *however* in the table below). The following are a number of such words and phrases alongside their relationship implications.

115

Unit Two: Paragraphs and Passages

Signal	Relationship
As for; Regarding; In reference to	Focus attention
Furthermore; Moreover; In addition; As well as; Also; Likewise; Too	Add to previous point
On one hand/on the other hand; While; Rather; Instead; In contrast; Alternatively	Provide contrast
Granted; It is true that; Certainly; Admittedly; Despite; Although	Provide conceding contrast (author unwillingly agrees)
But; However; Even so; All the same; Still; That said; Nevertheless; Nonetheless; Yet; Otherwise; Despite	Provide emphatic contrast (author asserts own position)
In any event; In any case	Dismiss previous point
Likewise; In the same way	Point out similarity
First, Second, etc.; To begin with; Next; Finally; Again	Structure the discussion
For example; In particular; For instance	Give example
In general; To a great extent; Broadly speaking	Generalize
In conclusion; In brief; Overall; Except for; Besides	Sum up, perhaps with exception
Therefore; Thus; As a result; So; Accordingly; Hence	Indicate logical result
Because; Since; As; Resulting from	Indicate logical cause
In other words; That is; Namely; So to speak	Restate for clarity
Apparently; At least; Can, Could, May, Might, Should; Possibly; Likely	Hedge or soften position
After all; Must, Have to; Always, Never, etc.	Strengthen position
Actually; In fact; Indeed; Yet; Surprisingly	Introduce surprise
Fortunately; Unfortunately; Luckily; So-called	Reveal author's attitude

Feel free to use this as a starter list for your studies; choose a few phrases and search for them in anything you read throughout the day. You can also practice using those same phrases in your own writing. While this list is long, it is not exhaustive; as you practice more GRE problems, add new signal phrases and words to your list as you encounter them.

Pronouns

Pronouns are used to refer to something indirectly; <u>they</u> take the place of nouns. In that sentence, *they* pointed back to *pronouns*.

Some pronouns are more obviously seen as "pronouns"—he, she, it, or they—and they point back to a specific noun or term earlier in the sentence or paragraph. Take, for example, the exobiologist sentence from earlier in the book: *carbon probably provides the backbone of any extraterrestrial biological molecules, just as <u>it</u> does of terrestrial ones.* The word *it* in that sentence refers to *carbon*.

But there are also pronouns that aren't so obvious! Did you notice the word *ones* at the end of the exobiologist sentence? *Ones* refers back to *biological molecules*: *carbon probably provides the backbone of any extraterrestrial biological molecules, just as it does of terrestrial [biological molecules].*

The main examples of these less obvious pronouns are *one*, *such*, *this*, *that*, *these*, and *those*. Although you might not think of these unique pronouns when you think about pronouns, the GRE does use them quite frequently! Add these pronouns to your list of signal words and phrases to practice. The faster you notice the signposts, the faster you make connections on test day.

And while many pronouns point back to a specific word or simple noun earlier in the text, they are also used to refer back to abstract ideas or even complete sentences. You encountered this scenario in the paragraph about the flood in the previous section: The *such* in *such observations* at the start of the second sentence referred back to the content of the *entire* previous sentence.

When you see *any* pronouns, either the more or the less familiar to you, pause and verify that you know exactly what <u>it</u> is referring to. The author is linking back to a previous idea.

Can you spot the pronoun(s) in the following paragraph? What do they refer back to?

> Most anemones, sea creatures that belong to the group Cnidarians, reproduce asexually through budding, longitudinal fission, or basal laceration. This trait is essentially a form of cloning that theoretically enables them to live forever absent predators and disease.

The more familiar pronoun *them* in the middle of the second sentence refers back to the *anemones*, but did you spot the subtle pronoun *this* at the start of the second sentence? The phrase *this trait* refers to the fact that *most anemones...reproduce asexually*. The second sentence is expanding upon that initial concept. The list of different types of asexual reproduction is meant to distract you from determining what the word *this* is actually referring to.

When you're unsure what a pronoun is pointing to, unpack the sentence to see what could be substituted for the pronoun. In the above example, the second sentence makes sense if you substitute the broader concept for the word *this*: the trait that most anemones have of reproducing asexually is essentially a form of cloning…

Components of Paragraphs

Before going any further, it is important to take a step back and look at the real goal for the GRE Verbal section: Can you identify the central message the author means to convey? In order to know what words fill in the blanks for TC and SE, you need to understand what the whole sentence is trying to say. Similarly, in order to answer any questions about a Reading Comprehension passage, you need to understand what the whole passage is trying to say.

You're already improving your vocabulary and applying the skills of unpacking sentences and identifying connections. Next is to bring it all together under one cohesive story. In other words, you're trying to understand **the author's main idea or primary purpose** behind writing any of the text you encounter on the test.

Unit Two: **Paragraphs and Passages**

Sometimes an understanding of that main idea might follow naturally from the steps you've taken so far. But on tougher passages, it can help to more formally understand what each sentence in a paragraph is *doing* to create that overarching idea.

Imagine parts of speech when working to understand the grammar of a sentence. Within a sentence, verbs tell you the action, nouns tell you who or what is doing the action, and adjectives and adverbs provide additional description. You don't always need to know the parts of speech in order to make sense of the sentence, but knowing how the parts fit together can help when sentences become particularly confusing.

In the same way, paragraphs and their storylines are created through the intentional use of the following specific components:

1. Conclusion
2. Premises
3. Point and Counterpoint
4. Background
5. Implications

Most paragraphs contain only a few of these components, but some might contain them all. They can come in any order, not necessarily the order above.

As the GRE adds more paragraphs to passages, these components can and will spread beyond the bounds of a single paragraph. For now, though, focus on learning to identify these component pieces within individual paragraphs. Multiple-paragraph passages will be addressed in Chapter 8: Long Passages in RC.

The Conclusion

Some paragraphs contain a clear position from the author: They are convinced of something, and they also want to convince you. These paragraphs contain a very active, opinionated author's point of view.

Not all GRE paragraphs will contain conclusions, but if they do, that conclusion will form the basis of the main idea and primary purpose.

When reading a GRE paragraph, strive to maintain an understanding of the point of view presented from each sentence. Is this sentence the author's own point of view, or some other point of view? If a sentence contains a strongly stated, active point of view from the author (e.g., the author argues, rejects, justifies, challenges, proposes, etc.), then you are probably reading a conclusion. Your next step would then be to identify any premises.

Premises

The premises in a paragraph are the assertions and opinions that support a conclusion. If there is a conclusion, there is at least one premise for that conclusion. They may be facts, opinions, or claims. If they are opinions or claims, they will not be the overall claim the author is making; rather, they will be some intermediate claim the author is using to support the overall claim (conclusion).

Points and Counterpoints

Counterpoints undermine or go against a stated position. Occasionally, a paragraph will present both sides of an issue, with evidence to support both. The author might themselves take one side, or merely present opposing sides. Regardless of whether the author takes a side, when you find competing positions, you have point and counterpoint components.

Background

The background is information presented without opinion or information that doesn't specifically work for or against a conclusion. The context and the basic facts about the topic are given in the background.

In some paragraphs, the author may simply wish to inform the reader of facts, rather than convince the reader of a debatable position. In these cases, the entire paragraph could be called background. These types of paragraphs are common in passages that you'll encounter later in the book, namely Chapter 6: Argument-Based RC and Chapter 8: Long Passages in RC.

Differentiating background from premise or counterpoint can be tricky! If a paragraph contains a conclusion, it is crucial to distinguish whether a given piece of information is working for or against the conclusion or whether the information is purely background.

Implications

Implications, if present, are the predicted consequences of other information or positions. In other words, the author has given you information, opinions, or both, and now wishes to enumerate potential results of that information. Implications are not always present, but when they are, they tend to be important.

As you continue your GRE Verbal studies, consider how the components of paragraphs impact your understanding of Verbal problems. This understanding can impact your ability to solve Reading Comprehension problems of all varieties, and can also play a role in your ability to solve the multi-blank Text Completion questions, as some of those problems contain multiple sentences.

As a final summation, here is a list of questions to ask as you read:

1. Is this the main belief or claim? If so, this is the conclusion.
2. Is this supporting evidence for the conclusion? If so, this is a premise.
3. Is this opposing evidence for the conclusion? If so, this is a counterpoint.
4. Is this neutral information that gives context to the conclusion? If so, this is background.
5. Is this a consequence of another fact or opinion? If so, this is an implication.

The Main Idea (and Archetypes)

As mentioned in the last section, your goal as you read on the GRE is to get into the head of the author and understand their big picture story: You need to understand the author's purpose for writing the text and the main idea that the text conveys.

In many ways, you can think of main idea and primary purpose as getting at the same idea. However, there is a subtle but important difference: The main idea is the *what* of the paragraph, while the primary purpose is the *why* of the paragraph. For example, the main idea might be "Elephant trunks are signs of an evolutionary adaptation," while the primary purpose might be "explain how elephants evolved trunks." The main idea is a declaration: This fact is true. The primary purpose is an action: Explain why this fact is true.

The Main Idea

The main idea is the *what* of the paragraph. What central concept does the author wish to convey? This main idea is sometimes directly stated in the paragraph; if there is a sentence in which the author asserts their own point of view, that sentence forms at least part of the main idea.

If the paragraph does not contain a point of view statement from the author, then an analysis of the paragraph components discussed in the previous section will reveal the main idea. Perhaps the author merely presents competing positions on an issue, but does not state an opinion of their own. In that case, the main idea is the existence of that debate. Or perhaps the author presents facts laying the background of an existing situation, and then poses questions regarding the future outcomes for that situation. In that case, the main idea is that this situation may lead to these various outcomes.

Notice that both of the examples in the previous paragraph arose directly from a recognition of the components in the paragraph: point and counterpoint, and background plus implications, respectively. While these components have many possible combinations, there are some that the GRE uses more often than others.

Passage Archetypes

Just as there are patterns in wrong answers (think back to Chapter 3: TC and SE), there are patterns in the passages themselves! Think of a film or TV genre that has predictable elements, like a superhero movie where you know the hero and villain will have a final showdown or a cooking show where you know something is going to go horribly wrong for one contestant right before the commercial break. Those patterns actually make the stories easier to understand and more fun to watch! If you pay attention, you might be able to achieve the same effect with GRE passages.

Many GRE passages follow one of the "archetypes" described below—a predictable pattern of information. These archetypes can occur within one paragraph, or across multiple paragraphs; accordingly, you will see this mentioned again in Chapter 8: Long Passages in RC. Note that the archetypes have nothing to do with the topic of the passage, but everything to do with the structure of the passage. Whatever topic you see (say, the Japanese textile industry in the 19th century . . .) will almost certainly be something you've never seen before. But if you're familiar with the GRE's favorite structures, you'll still have something to hold onto to better understand the passage.

We can understand the archetypes through their use of the elements of paragraphs discussed previously—Conclusion, Background, Premises, Points and Counterpoints, and Implications. The main idea gives the archetype its structure, and it defines the relationship between the other elements.

1. **Explanation of a concept**

    - **Main idea:** ___ is a concept/theory/subject that exists, and ___ is how it works/why people believe it.
    - **Background:** an introduction to the concept itself—maybe a historical theory, a scientific process, or artistic
    - **Premises:** facts that help to explain the concept
    - **Implications:** not always present, but might be a summary of why the concept is impactful or worthy of discussion

2. **Competing theories on a subject**
   - **Main idea:** One person or group thinks ____ about ____, but another person or group thinks ____.
   - **Background:** an introduction to the subject itself
   - **Premises:** the reasons why each side believes what it does about the subject
   - **Point and Counterpoint:** There are two opposing sides to the issue.
   - **Implications:** not always present, but might be the author's prediction of which side will "win" the debate, or what will happen next in the conflict

3. **A critic's opinion of a work**
   - **Main idea:** ____ is a subject people have opinions on, and one particular critic thinks ____ about it.
   - **Background:** an introduction to the subject itself
   - **Premises:** the reasons why the critic thinks what they do about the subject
   - **Implications:** not always present, but might be a summary of how people responded to the critic's opinion

4. **The author's opinion of a work**
   - **Conclusion:** ____ is a subject people have opinions on, and the author thinks ____ about it.
   - **Background:** an introduction to the subject itself
   - **Premises:** the reasons the author thinks what they do about the subject
   - **Implications:** not always present, but might be an outcome the author wishes to see based on their opinion

5. **A change in perception over time**
   - **Main idea:** People used to think ____. But then ____ happened, and now people think ____.
   - **Background:** the previous prevailing opinion
   - **Premises:** the reasons why opinions on the subject might be changing
   - **Implications:** This type of story typically has implications: What's the outcome of the change that occurred?

This should be qualified by a few caveats: This list of archetypes is not exhaustive—nor are these archetypes officially defined anywhere by the GRE. Not every passage is going to follow one of these archetypes, and not every example of an archetype will have every element of that archetype—just like not every superhero movie will have every type of scene you expect to see in a superhero movie. Some harder passages might combine multiple archetypes into one: For example, a paragraph might contain a change in perception over time and then supply the author's opinion of that (archetypes 5 and 4) or a critic's opinion of another critic's opinion (archetypes 3 and 2).

But despite all those caveats, if you look through official GRE reading comprehension passages, you'll start to see the threads of these archetypes repeating themselves. That familiarity will help you better orient yourself to new passages, especially those that are particularly difficult.

Unit Two: **Paragraphs and Passages**

The Big Picture

Let's expand on the discussion of the sample short paragraph at the beginning of the chapter and see how the previous section's discussion applies.

> *The Biblical portrayal of flagitious times preceding the great deluge stands in stark contrast to the ancient Greek representation of the antediluvian past as a Golden Age from which humanity has slowly descended into godless chaos. Such observations can easily give rise to the notion that stories about the past are less faithful attempts at reconstruction than allegories, expressing both our cultural fears and hopes.*

If needed, take a moment to revisit the sentence-by-sentence translation in the initial section of this chapter. Then, consider the purpose behind the paragraph author's choice of words to begin the second sentence: "such observations can . . . ." What does this word choice imply about the relationship between the first and second sentences?

The author intends to link the second sentence to the first: The first sentence contains facts while the second sentence states the implications the author would draw from those facts. As such, the first sentence would be characterized as background, and the second sentence would be characterized as implications. A possible main idea for this paragraph would be "the contrast in portrayals of the ancient past suggest that cultural characteristics influence these portrayals more than literal history," while the author's purpose would be to "derive implications of what stories of the ancient past reveal about the cultures that produced them."

Apply the discussion to another example, drawn from the Chapter 1: GRE Vocabulary. Read the paragraph, make your own characterizations of what components exist, and see if you can paraphrase the main idea.

> *Architectural cognoscenti such as Koolhaas recognized Hadid's talents early and encouraged their development. By 1977, only a few years after their initial encounter, she had perfected her heteromorphic style, inspired equally by such disparate styles as Malevich's sparse constructivism and the flowing calligraphy of her native Arabic.*

As always, take any time needed to review potential vocabulary issues: Who are *cognoscenti*? What is *heteromorphic*?

Once done with that task, consider the various transition choices: *such as*, *by 1977*. In this instance, the author of the passage indicates that Koolhaas is merely an example of the general sentiment regarding Hadid's talents. In this paragraph, *by 1977* indicates a continuation of the earlier sentence, expanding on the remarkable nature of Hadid's talents. And finally, *such disparate styles as* serves a similar purpose to the *such as* in the first sentence. Malevich's sparse constructivism and flowing calligraphy are only two examples of a larger statement regarding Hadid's inspirations. Since each sentence gives examples to illustrate facts regarding Hadid, both sentences are technically background. But in this particular example, although both sentences are background (merely stating factual elements regarding Hadid), you have an example of a potential for point of view analysis.

Point of View Analysis: A Supplement to Component Analysis

In the first sentence, the author references *cognoscenti such as Koolhaas* to establish an external point of view—how did the architectural community at large view Hadid? But in the second sentence, notice that there is no attribution to other groups or people; there are no cognoscenti telling the reader that Hadid had *perfected her heteromorphic style*. This is a clue to the author's view of Hadid. This point of view analysis can be particularly helpful when attempting Reading Comprehension questions of almost all varieties; if you can identify when the author begins speaking for themselves in a paragraph, you can become much more efficient when addressing the answer choices. For this example, a possible main idea could be that the author shares the architectural community's admiration for Hadid.

(As an aside, if you are not abreast of Zaha Hadid's work, take a few moments to look her up in the search engine of your choice: You will not be disappointed!)

Don't Just Read, Do Something!

If you are struggling with a paragraph, instead of passively reading, take notes. You can build your comprehension more quickly and effectively—*especially* when the paragraph is unfriendly—by using more than one learning method. Writing as you read activates a second learning process that facilitates comprehension. Now, what you write during the GRE must be different from other kinds of notes you have taken (e.g., during a college lecture). In college, you take notes in order to study from them later. In contrast, **you take notes during the GRE to precipitate comprehension right then and there**.

Identifying and writing down key elements of the paragraph will force you to read *actively* as opposed to passively. If you proactively write the translation as you read (in a massively-abbreviated fashion—more on this in a moment), your comprehension of unfriendly paragraphs will improve dramatically.

Of course, it is not possible to translate, pencil to paper, every sentence, paragraph, and passage on the GRE in the time given. And in fact, the Text Completion and Sentence Equivalence questions must be answered too quickly to allow note-taking: If you find yourself needing to take notes on one of these questions during the test, guess and move on!

But even if you could not, or would not, make notes for a particular paragraph, practicing a note-taking strategy during untimed review will improve your comprehension skills on the test, for all question types. Therefore, practice a writing strategy for every paragraph during untimed review, even if you would not write anything for a particular paragraph during the actual test. And when you *would* take notes on the test—for example, on a dense Reading Comprehension problem set—that process will be natural, smooth, and fast.

How would you take notes on these example paragraphs from the earlier pages?

> *The Biblical portrayal of flagitious times preceding the great deluge stands in stark contrast to the ancient Greek representation of the antediluvian past as a Golden Age from which humanity has slowly descended into godless chaos. Such observations can easily give rise to the notion that stories about the past are less faithful attempts at reconstruction than allegories, expressing both our cultural fears and hopes.*

Unit Two: **Paragraphs and Passages**

Architectural cognoscenti such as Koolhaas recognized Hadid's talents early and encouraged their development. By 1977, only a few years after their initial encounter, she had perfected her heteromorphic style, inspired equally by such disparate styles as Malevich's sparse constructivism and the flowing calligraphy of her native Arabic.

When you've made your notes on these two paragraphs, continue to the next section to see some sample notes. And after the sample notes for these paragraphs, you will see a few suggestions for common notations to save time when you find yourself taking notes during the test.

A Note-Taking Exercise (Sample Notes)

The Sentence	Possible Notes
The Biblical portrayal of flagitious times preceding the great deluge stands in stark contrast to the ancient Greek representation of the antediluvian past as a Golden Age from which humanity has slowly descended into godless chaos. Such observations can easily give rise to the notion that stories about the past are less faithful attempts at reconstruction than allegories, expressing both our cultural fears and hopes.	**B vs AG** (The Biblical portrayal is opposite that of the ancient Greeks.) **story → not lit. but alleg.** (This observation leads to the notion that the stories are not literal, but allegorical.)
Architectural cognoscenti such as Koolhaas recognized Hadid's talents early and encouraged their development. By 1977, only a few years after their initial encounter, she had perfected her heteromorphic style, inspired equally by such disparate styles as Malevich's sparse constructivism and the flowing calligraphy of her native Arabic.	**K = arch: H talent** (Koolhass is an example of architects who recognized Hadid's talents.) **(auth) H perf'd style** (This is the author speaking to the reader. Hadid perfected her style, and the author seems to really like Hadid's style.)

Common Notations

To create your translation on paper as quickly as possible, consider some following notation suggestions:

- Abbreviate long terms, particularly proper nouns.
- Use arrows (e.g., →) to indicate cause-effect relationships or changes over time.
- If a passage contains speakers, writers, points of view, arguments, and so on, keep them organized by using a colon to indicate who is providing a particular opinion. For example, if a passage says that historians believe that economic interests led to the outbreak of war, you might write: **H: econ int → war**.
- If you write down examples, mark them with parentheses or "Ex." For example: **Ex: Insects = inflexible (wasp)**.
- Create images. This may mean sketching a quick diagram of a planet with three moons in orbit or it may mean adding smiley and frowny faces to indicate the author's opinion.

You will have your own note-taking style. Regardless of the notations you use, practice them and keep them *consistent*. You do not want to use up precious focus during the GRE figuring out how to indicate that the passage presents a problem and a solution when you could have shorthand already in place for this common structure!

Vocabulary Challenge

> Did you spot these vocabulary words? If not, go back and find them in context! (The word may be in a different form than listed here—"digressing" instead of "digress," for example.) Write your own definitions based on the evidence in the chapter.

1. exhaustive (*adj.*), p. 116
2. qualified (*adj.*), p. 121
3. abreast (*adj.*), p. 123
4. facilitate (*v*), p. 123
5. disparate (*adj.*), p. 122
6. precipitate (*v*), p. 123

Unit Two: **Paragraphs and Passages**

Problem Set

1. Read the following passage and jot down any notes within 2.5–3 minutes (this is a bit more time than you'll want to spend on the actual exam). After answering the questions below the passage, compare your notes to the sample in the answer key. How well did your notes succeed in pushing you to read actively? How well did they capture the main idea of the passage without getting bloated with details?

Passage A: Arousal and Attraction

In 1974, psychologists Dutton and Aron discovered that subjects who had just crossed a precarious wire-suspension bridge reacted to an attractive interviewer differently than subjects who had instead crossed a low, solid bridge. Specifically, in response to a questionnaire that secretly measured sexual arousal, subjects from the wire-suspension bridge revealed significantly more sexual imagery than the others; moreover, a far greater fraction of wire-suspension subjects than of solid-bridge subjects contacted the interviewer afterward. Dutton and Aron explained their results in terms of misattribution. In their view, subjects crossing the wobbly bridge experienced physiological fear reactions, such as increased heart rate. Such reactions with ambiguous or suppressed causes are easily reinterpreted, in the presence of a potential partner, as sexual attraction. However, Foster and others later found that an unattractive interviewer is actually perceived as much less attractive by subjects physiologically aroused by fearful situations. Thus, the arousal is reinterpreted either as attraction or as repulsion, but in either case, the true cause is masked.

2. What is the main idea of this passage? Justify your choice.

3. Identify the other components of the passage, if present: conclusion, premises, point and counterpoint, background, and implications. Again, justify your assignments.

4. Read the following passage and take notes in 1.5 minutes. After answering the questions below the passage, compare your notes to the sample in the answer key and provide critiques.

Passage B: Animal Treatment

In the early nineteenth century, educated Britons came to accept the then-novel notion that animals must be treated humanely, as evidenced by the outlawing of certain forms of domestic animal abuse, as well as the founding of the Society for the Prevention of Cruelty to Animals in 1824. This trend may be regarded as part of a broader embrace of compassionate ideals, such as abolitionism and alleviation of poverty. For instance, in 1785 the Society for the Relief of Persons Imprisoned for Small Sums persuaded Parliament to restrict that archaic punishment, and similar societies focused on various issues of humane treatment emerged around this time. However, a deeper explanation should be traced to socioeconomic conditions related to ongoing industrialization. Those protesting cruelty to animals were city dwellers who viewed animals as pets rather than as livestock, despite the ubiquity of horse transport. In fact, nature was no longer considered menacing, since society's victory over wilderness was conspicuous. Animals were to some extent romanticized as emblems of a bucolic, pre-industrial age.

5. What is the main idea of this passage? Justify your choice.

6. Identify the other components of the passage, if present: conclusion, premises, point and counterpoint, background, and implications. Again, justify your assignments.

Chapter 4: GRE Paragraphs

Answers and Explanations

Vocabulary Challenge

1. exhaustive (*adj.*): comprehensive, thorough; exhausting a topic or subject, accounting for all possibilities

2. qualified (*adj.*): modified, limited, conditional on something else

3. abreast (adj.): side-by-side; keeping up with, staying aware of, or remaining equal in progress with

4. facilitate (*v*): make easier, help the progress of

5. disparate (*adj.*): distinct, different

6. precipitate (*v*): cause to happen suddenly; fling, plunge, or hurl down

Problem Set

1. **Read the following passage and jot down any notes within 2.5–3 minutes (this is a bit more time than you'll want to spend on the actual exam). After answering the questions below the passage, compare your notes to the sample in the answer key. How well did your notes succeed in pushing you to read actively? How well did they capture the main idea of the passage without getting bloated with details?**

    <u>Arousal and Attraction</u>—Sample Notes
    Psychs D+A:
    Wire bridge: aroused → attr
    Expl: misattrib physiol fear AS attractn
    BUT actually: attr OR repuls masks the cause ← main idea

2. **What is the main idea of this passage? Justify your choice.**

    The author draws a collective conclusion about the results of two separate sets of studies: that people experiencing a fearful situation are likely to unconsciously redirect that feeling of fear into a feeling of attraction toward another person and that this could manifest as either increased or decreased attraction to that person. Everything in the passage leads up to this final conclusion.

3. **Identify the other components of the passage, if present: conclusion, premises, point and counterpoint, background, and implications. Again, justify your assignments.**

    The paragraph is all background and support (premises), leading up to the conclusion at the end.

4. **Read the following passage and take notes in 1.5 minutes. After answering the questions below the passage, compare your notes to the sample in the answer key and provide critiques.**

    <u>Animal Treatment</u>—Sample Notes
    19th c: Educ B's: animal cruelty = bad
    Why: Part of broader embrace of compassn. Ex's
    Deeper Why: Industzn → city dwellers ← main idea
    Nature romantic

127

Unit Two: **Paragraphs and Passages**

5. What is the main idea of this passage? Justify your choice.

The author of this passage uses the direction marker "however" to indicate a relationship between the first few sentences and the last few sentences. The change in direction indicated by "however" combined with the opinionated "should" language in the same sentence indicates that this is the author's conclusion. A main idea statement for this passage could be the following: The push for humane animal treatment in nineteenth-century Britain was because of the socioeconomic conditions related to industrialization.

6. Identify the other components of the passage, if present: conclusion, premises, point and counterpoint, background, and implications. Again, justify your assignments.

The paragraph begins with background (all the text before the conclusion sentence), then states the conclusion (the deeper reason). That conclusion is followed by the premises (support for the deeper reason).

CHAPTER 5

Short Passages in Reading Comprehension

In This Chapter . . .

- Two Types of Passages
- Scanning Ahead
- Strategy for General Questions
- Strategy for Specific Questions
- Common Wrong Answer Categories
- Summary of Strategies for Answer Choice Eliminations
- Comprehensive Strategies for All Reading Comprehension
- Vocabulary Challenge
- A Short Introduction to the Problem Set
- Problem Set
- Answers and Explanations

CHAPTER 5 Short Passages in Reading Comprehension

While the skill of reading comprehension is something that you've been practicing throughout this book, what the GRE specifically calls *Reading Comprehension* (RC) is the family of questions that are based on specific passages. Those passages will be either content-based or argument-based. In this chapter, you will learn the initial strategies for content-based passages, and practice them on short passages—on the GRE, short passages are generally one paragraph.

Here are your Chapter 5 vocabulary words:

> perspicacious (A)
>
> harrowing (A)
>
> indeterminate (E)
>
> prudent (E)
>
> dubious (E)
>
> wanton (A)

Two Types of Passages

While *The Official Guide to the GRE® General Test* labels all Verbal questions that are neither TC nor SE as *Reading Comprehension*, there are actually two different types of passages used for RC.

Content-based passages (CBP) look like text you'd pull from a college textbook or some other reference material, and they typically discuss science, arts, history, or other academic topics. So far in this book, all of the practice paragraphs that you've been interpreting have been content-based.

Alternatively, **argument-based passages (ABP)** read more like short persuasive arguments that are based on real-world concepts, but often include fictional cities, companies, and other such details.

But the differences don't just stop at the topics you'll be reading about in each passage type. CBPs are longer and often multi-paragraph; even the single paragraph CBPs are quite lengthy. Difficult vocabulary is common, the text is dense (as you've seen already), and you will be tested on your ability to determine the meaning of words in context. ABPs, on the other hand, are typically short paragraphs consisting of only a couple of sentences. Vocabulary and jargon are less frequent, and you're more concerned with making sense of how the sentences work to build a cohesive argument or claim.

Unit Two: **Paragraphs and Passages**

Perhaps the most profound difference, though, is in the questions that you'll be asked about each type of passage. For CBPs, questions test whether you understood the passage by asking you to extract information from what you read. You'll see anywhere from one to five questions (although five-question passages are very rare) based on a single content-based passage, and topics include stating the main idea or correctly identifying details that were mentioned. The rest of this chapter will focus on the strategies for content-based questions.

ABPs, however, are always accompanied by a single question that tests your understanding of not only what you read but also the underlying types of arguments that can be made. These questions will expect you to bring in new, outside information in order to strengthen, weaken, or evaluate the argument in some specific way. The next chapter, Chapter 6: Argument-Based RC, will focus on the strategies to apply for argument-based questions.

The table below is a summary of the primary differences between the two types of passages and their questions. Anytime you encounter a passage on test day, your first goal is to determine its type.

Content-Based Passages (CBPs)	Argument-Based Passages (ABPs)
One or more lengthy paragraphs	Single (shorter) paragraph
Passages discuss science, social science, and business: content typical of textbooks and reference material.	Passages make persuasive arguments; the information included might be fictional.
One to five questions per passage	One question per passage
Questions typically ask you to pull information from the passage.	Questions typically ask you to add information to the passage.

Scanning Ahead

Because passages can have multiple questions, the test clearly identifies which question numbers accompany that passage in a banner at the top of the screen; for example, it might say *Questions 9 to 12 are based on the following passage*. This is true even when there is only a single question.

Before you begin reading, it is helpful to use the questions as a sort of pre-scan. By clicking through any accompanying questions to see what you will be asked to do, you can better direct your focus once you begin reading. This is not suggesting that you read the question and answer choices thoroughly, just that you skim the question stems and possibly jot down a few words for each. This is meant to supplement your understanding of the passage, *not* to take up so much time that you sacrifice your ability to fully read and unpack the text.

As you scan, you will encounter one of two types of questions: those asking for general (big picture) understanding and those asking for information about something specific. The following two sections will go through the process for handling each.

> *Strategy Tip:*
>
> For all passages, scan the questions, but not the answer choices, before reading the passage.

Additionally, make note of how many questions are associated with the passage. How long you have on the entire segment, both reading the passage and answering the questions, is dictated by how many questions there are. With an average time of approximately two minutes per question, you can spend approximately half of the total time to read. The Introduction of this book and a later section of this chapter list a more detailed breakdown of timing. For now, consider budgeting approximately one minute per question to read, but not more than four minutes. For example, if you see that the passage has three questions, you have about three minutes to read. The following table has approximate timing benchmarks for reading comprehension based on the number of questions for a passage:

# of Questions	Time Spent Reading	Time Spent in Answer Choices	Total Time
1	1 minute 30 seconds	45 seconds	2 minutes, 15 seconds
2	2 minutes	45 seconds	3 minutes, 30 seconds
3	3 minutes	45 seconds	5 minutes, 15 seconds
4	3 minutes	45 seconds	6 minutes
5 (rare)	3 minutes	45 seconds	6 minutes, 45 seconds

Short passages will likely have only one to three questions; long passages might have four (or, rarely, five) questions. In Chapter 8: Long Passages in RC, you will learn how to adapt your strategies to these longer passages.

Strategy for General Questions

The following is a step-by-step breakdown of the process for RC questions. After absorbing the components of the process, read on to see how this process applies to general questions.

1. **Scan the question(s).**

    - Whether there is only one question or several, this step is always valuable.
    - Jot notes from the question (but *not* the answer choices) to aid your reading.

2. **Read and deconstruct the passage.**

    - Always seek out the main idea.
    - Use the Chapter 4: Components of Paragraphs concepts to aid your analysis.

3. **Address each question in turn, predicting an answer if you can.**

    - Always anchor your prediction to the text.

4. **Eliminate and select.**

    - Keep track of your eliminations on your scratch paper as you go.
    - If you have a prediction, does an answer choice match it?
    - If you do not like any of the choices, focus on eliminating wrong answers.
    - Guess if needed. As best you can, match the tone of the answer choice to the tone of the text.

Recognizing and Answering General Questions

General questions follow the forms listed in the following table (the bold is for emphasis here and will not appear in actual questions):

Type of General Question	Common Phrasing
Main Idea	Which of the following best expresses **the main idea** of the passage?
Primary Purpose	The author's **primary purpose** is . . .
	The passage is **primarily concerned with** which of the following?

Your understanding of the paragraph from your initial read-through provides the key to answering general questions. The good news is that you're already reading for the main idea, assuming you're following the advice from Chapter 4. Because the answer will come from that initial read, the expectation is that you can answer most general questions in around 30 seconds.

Don't reread the passage. Instead, first predict the answer in your own words (step 3). This is the same as Text Completion and Sentence Equivalence: Predicting an answer can help you avoid trap answers and keep you engaged with your own interpretation of the text. It is also the same as TC and SE in that the goal isn't to predict the *exact* phrasing of the answer choice. Just predicting the general shape or theme will help you spot it more perspicaciously.

Once you have a prediction, dive right into the answer choices and start eliminating. Arming yourself with an effective interpretation of the paragraph will allow you to eliminate two or three choices quickly.

If you find yourself stuck with several answers left, you can apply a scoring system: On general questions, an answer choice that incorporates elements from more parts of the paragraph or passage is a better candidate, as it likely covers a greater overview of the whole passage.

If you're still unsure of your final answer after making some eliminations, be careful about going back and forth between answer choices. It is better to just pick something rather than spending the time that was budgeted for other questions. If you think a fresh look will help you decide, click the Mark for Review button and come back to it later if you have time.

> *Strategy Tip:*
> For general questions, articulate a prediction in your own words, and eliminate answers that do not match.

Strategy for Specific Questions

The step-by-step process for specific questions does not differ significantly from the process outlined in the previous section. However, your process for predicting an answer and eliminating wrong choices may have more nuance.

Recognizing and Answering Specific Questions

Specific questions follow the forms listed in the following table (the bold is for emphasis here and will not appear in actual questions):

Type of Specific Question	Common Phrasing
Specific Detail	*In the example discussed in the passage,* **what is true** *about poppy seeds in bread dough, once the dough has been thoroughly mixed?* *The passage* **states** *...*
Inference	*It can be* **inferred** *from the passage that ...* *The author* **suggests** *...*
Select a Sentence	**Select the sentence** *that, according to the author, would best explain the early nineteenth-century trends toward more humane treatment of animals.*
Specific Purpose	*The author references the work of Von Neumann primarily* **in order to** *...*
Word in Context	*In the context in which it appears, "abstruse" (line 27)* **most nearly means** *...*

Specific questions deal with details and inferences from specific elements within a paragraph, but in a variety of ways.

Two of the examples in the table (specific detail and inference) ask either what is true or what can be inferred. This is a common theme in most specific questions: You are instructed to find particular text and then *use* that text to prove a choice.

Everyday use of the word *inference* often refers to something that is suggested by facts, but is not definitively certain. For example, if you see someone carrying an umbrella outside, you would likely infer that the person is expecting rain that day. But on the GRE, you can only infer that the person has *some reason* to carry an umbrella. **Any GRE inference should stick so closely to stated text that it feels provable from the text.**

The next two examples in the table (select a sentence and specific purpose) are the logical inverse of the first two. These questions do not task you with using the information, but instead ask how the author of the passage used the information. These questions strongly benefit from the type of analysis presented in Chapter 4: GRE Paragraphs.

The final example (word in context) asks you to identify the intended meaning of a word in the sentence and could almost be considered Sentence Equivalence in Reading Comprehension form. Your goal will be to select a word that could replace the quoted word without changing the original meaning of the sentence. As such, synonyms for the word in the question are your prediction.

Using the Specifics of a Specific Question

Imagine that in your initial scan you read the question *Robinson raises the issue of cultural bias to do which of the following?* You have no idea who Robinson is or how cultural bias is discussed. Don't expect to predict an answer or even understand the question before reading the paragraph! Instead, make a note of what is being asked. You might jot down the following note on your paper:

> R: cult. bias why?

Unit Two: **Paragraphs and Passages**

When you reach the part of the passage that pertains to this question, do one thing: Make note of where in the passage this information is and make an effort to understand it within your work-in-progress interpretation. Do not stop reading to go answer the question! Many trap answers will seem tempting if you don't have the context of the entire paragraph. They're written that way intentionally, knowing some test takers will hunt for the relevant text and only skim the passage. If you think you can predict the answer partway through the passage, make a note of your prediction; then, continue reading the entire passage and working to understand the main idea. If the passage has multiple questions and you want to jump to this specific question to tackle first after you're done reading, that's fine. The order of the questions is up to you, but if you try to answer a question without the context of the entire passage, it will ultimately make the problem more harrowing and perhaps more frustrating.

Some specific questions won't provide enough detail for you to make a note. For example, the question "Which of the following can be inferred from the passage?" gives you no information about what to analyze while you read. When you see questions like that, anticipate that you'll spend more time on process of elimination with the answer choices and that the question may take a little longer than average.

To answer these frustratingly indeterminate questions, first eliminate any answer choices that are opposed to or not mentioned in the passage. Of the remaining answers, you *will* need to return to the passage. Find key words in the answer choices that help you find the relevant part of the passage. Use your notes as a search tool, if necessary.

> *Strategy Tip:*
>
> For specific questions, use key words from the question or answer choices to find relevant parts of the passage.

In order to find the relevant parts of the passage, you may need to find a synonym for the key words in the question. For example, if the question addresses *natural disasters*, you may need to find a sentence that addresses *natural hazards or similar*. In a question with no key words, e.g., *Which of the following can be inferred from the passage?*, your only option for key words will be key words from each choice.

Once you find the key words in the passage, analyze the surrounding sentence or sentences to predict an answer to the question. Almost all specific questions can be proven from one or two sentences; a small handful require more than two proof sentences. You may have to revisit the text or, in longer passages, take a few notes to figure out what the sentences mean. That is expected because, after all, the goal was not to master those details while reading. If you are working on a question with context clues, such as the original example *Robinson raises the issue of cultural bias . . .* , do not look at the answer choices until you boil down the relevant sentence or sentences into a synopsis—work to keep it to just a few words. (If you took notes as described in Chapter 4: Don't Just Read, Do Something!, this part of the process will be easier.)

Then you can bring that synopsis back to the answer choices and hold it in your head as you eliminate choices and seek out a match.

> *Strategy Tip:*
>
> For specific questions, craft a synopsis from one or two proof sentences and compare the choices to it.

Chapter 5: **Short Passages in Reading Comprehension**

If you struggle to summarize the relevant text or you cannot find relevant text at all, then you know that the question is hard. The remaining sections of this chapter will offer you some additional strategies to use when you encounter these situations. If you still have multiple choices remaining after prudent eliminations, it is time to guess. No one question is more important than the others, so pick an answer and move on, perhaps marking the question to return to should you have more time.

Common Wrong Answer Categories

Wrong answers on Reading Comprehension questions tend to fall into one or more of five broad categories. You do not need to categorize wrong answers as you eliminate them in timed attempts. On the test, do not spend time pondering the category of an answer choice that you know is blatantly wrong. But take the time to categorize as many wrong answers as you can during untimed review: You will find that the test writers repeat these archetypes very often, sometimes even in wrong answers within the same question. And if you become adept at this categorization, the wrongness of the wrong choices becomes more apparent, more quickly, on the actual test.

As another benefit to this analysis, you might recognize a pattern in your own dubious answer selections. For example, you might discover upon review that you frequently choose Direct Contradiction answers. With this realization, you can incorporate one more double check into your process to look for that particular sort of error.

1. **One Word Wrong**
   - Just one word (or maybe two) is incorrect; this includes extreme words
   - Very common in general questions

2. **Out of Scope**
   - Introduces an unsupported assertion that has no evidence in the passage
   - Might be "real-world plausible" (that is, the answer might be true, or at least believable, in the real world)—however, if the answer is not supported in the passage, it is out of scope

3. **Direct Contradiction**
   - States the exact opposite of something asserted in the passage
   - Paradoxically attractive because it relates to the passage closely; if you miss one contrast or switchback in the trail, you can easily think a direct contradiction is the right answer

4. **Mix-Up**
   - Scrambles together different words or phrases from the passage, but the meaning of the choice does not reflect what the passage said
   - Tries to trap the student who simply matches language, not meaning

5. **True but Irrelevant**
   - True according to the passage, but does not answer the given question
   - May be too narrow or simply unrelated

Unit Two: **Paragraphs and Passages**

Summary of Strategies for Answer Choice Eliminations

In the correct answer choice, every word must be completely true and within the scope of the passage. If you cannot justify *every* word in the answer choice, eliminate it. For example, consider the following answer choices:

(A) The colonists resented the king for taxing them without representation.
(B) England's policy of taxation without representation caused resentment among the colonists.

The difference in these two answer choices lies in the word *king* versus the word *England*. Although this seems like a small difference, it is the key to eliminating one of these answer choices. If the passage does not mention the *king* when it discusses the colonists' resentment, then the word *king* cannot be justified, and the answer choice can be eliminated.

> *Strategy Tip:*
> Justify *every* word in the answer choice.

Extreme words, such as *all* and *never*, tend to broaden the scope of an answer choice too much or make it too extreme. The GRE typically uses moderate language and ideas. Avoid wantonly selecting answer choices that sound confident, but go too far. Occasionally you are justified in picking an extreme choice, but the passage must back you up 100 percent.

> *Strategy Tip:*
> Only choose an answer with an extreme word if the passage itself uses similarly extreme language.

Many Reading Comprehension questions ask you to infer something from the passage. An inference is an informed deduction. Reading Comprehension inferences rarely go far beyond what is stated in the passage. In general, infer so little that the inference seems obvious.

It is often surprising how simplistic GRE inferences are. If an answer choice answers the question and can be confirmed by language in the passage, it will be the correct one. Conversely, eliminate answer choices that require any logical stretch or leap. When you read *The passage suggests …* or *The passage implies …*, rephrase that language: *The passage states just a little differently …* You must be able to prove the answer, just as if the question asked you to look it up in the passage.

> *Strategy Tip:*
> As you work through answer choices, keep inferences close to the text.

Comprehensive Strategies for All Reading Comprehension

You now have seven effective strategies to use on Reading Comprehension questions on the GRE. Practice them frequently.

For general questions:

1. Articulate the main idea in your own words and eliminate answers. If you are stuck between two answer choices, use a scoring system to find the one that covers more of the breadth of the whole passage.

For specific questions:

2. Match key words in specific questions to key words (or synonyms) in the passage.
3. Defend your answer choice with one or two proof sentences.

For all questions:

4. Justify *every* word in your answer choice.
5. Justify *extreme* words in answer choices.
6. Choose an answer choice that infers as *little* as possible.

And do not forget:

7. Preview the questions before reading the passage.

Vocabulary Challenge

> Did you spot these vocabulary words? If not, go back and find them in context! (The word may be in a different form than listed here— "digressing" instead of "digress," for example.) Write your own definitions based on the evidence in the chapter.

1. perspicacious (*adj.*), p. 134
2. harrowing (*adj.*), p. 136
3. indeterminate (*adj.*), p. 136
4. prudent (*adj.*), p. 137
5. dubious (*adj.*), p. 137
6. wanton (*adj.*), p. 138

Unit Two: **Paragraphs and Passages**

A Short Introduction to the Problem Set

As you will see in this chapter's problem set, content-based Reading Comprehension questions can be presented in one of three formats: Select One, Select One or More, and Select-in-Passage.

Select One is the standard, five-answer multiple choice question for which you pick one answer. In that format, you can expect to see both general and specific questions. Jot down A through E on your scratch paper for these problems.

Select One or More questions offer three answer choices, multiple of which might be correct; jot down A through C on your scratch paper.

Select-in-Passage questions ask you to click the sentence in the passage that matches a certain description. If you're given one paragraph, number each sentence in that paragraph to keep track of your answer eliminations. (For example, if there are six sentences, jot down 1 through 6.) If you are given multiple paragraphs, first number each paragraph; when you have narrowed down to a single paragraph, number each sentence.

Both Select One or More and Select-in-Passage will typically be specific questions. For full descriptions of the two types, return to the Introduction: Verbal Question Formats in Detail. Ensure you can quickly recognize the format and the applicable strategies.

In the following problem set, you will first revisit two passages you've already seen, and attempt GRE questions on them for the first time. Then, you will apply the strategies you've learned to a completely new passage and question set.

For the purpose of practice and exposure to different question types, this chapter will review many questions on some passages. However, on the GRE, a short passage will typically have only one to three questions associated with it; even a long passage will typically have a maximum of four questions associated with it.

Preview the questions for the passage, then read that passage. As you read, take notes if you wish. Aim for approximately 30 seconds or so for general questions and about one minute for specific questions (though some may take you longer). When you're done, review the problems and analyze the answer choices in order to learn how to get better next time.

Chapter 5: **Short Passages in Reading Comprehension**

Problem Set

> The next two passages are revisited from the problem set in Chapter 4: GRE Paragraphs. Review the passages and attempt the questions that follow, using the 4-step process.

Passage A: Arousal and Attraction

In 1974, psychologists Dutton and Aron discovered that male subjects who had just crossed a precarious wire-suspension bridge reacted to an attractive female interviewer differently than subjects who had instead crossed a low, solid bridge. Specifically, in response to a questionnaire that secretly measured sexual arousal, subjects from the wire-suspension bridge revealed significantly more sexual imagery than the others; moreover, a far greater fraction of wire-suspension subjects than of solid-bridge subjects contacted the interviewer afterward. Dutton and Aron explained their results in terms of misattribution. In their view, subjects crossing the wobbly bridge experienced physiological fear reactions, such as increased heart rate. Such reactions with ambiguous or suppressed causes are easily reinterpreted, in the presence of a potential partner, as sexual attraction. However, Foster and others later found that an unattractive interviewer is actually perceived as much less attractive by subjects physiologically aroused by fearful situations. Thus, the arousal is reinterpreted either as attraction or as repulsion, but in either case, the true cause is masked.

1. Based on the passage, which of the following could be reasonably assumed about passengers of a particularly turbulent flight?

    Select all that apply.

    [A] They would be likely to misattribute the cause of a sexual attraction they felt to a fellow passenger during a lull in turbulence.

    [B] They would be likely to misattribute the cause of a sexual attraction they felt to a fellow passenger a few days after the flight.

    [C] They would be more likely to find themselves viscerally disgusted by a baggage handler at their arrival gate whom they typically would have found merely unappealing.

> Review the following passages and attempt the questions that follow.

Passage B: Animal Treatment

In the early nineteenth century, educated Britons came to accept the then-novel notion that animals must be treated humanely, as evidenced by the outlawing of certain forms of domestic animal abuse, as well as the founding of the Society for the Prevention of Cruelty to Animals in 1824. This trend may be regarded as part of a broader embrace of compassionate ideals, such as abolitionism and alleviation of poverty. For instance, in 1785 the Society for the Relief of Persons Imprisoned for Small Sums persuaded Parliament to restrict that archaic punishment, and similar societies focused on various issues of humane treatment emerged around this time. However, a deeper explanation should be traced to socioeconomic conditions related to ongoing industrialization. Those protesting cruelty to animals were city dwellers who viewed animals as pets rather than as livestock, despite the ubiquity of horse transport. In fact, nature was no longer considered menacing, since society's victory over wilderness was conspicuous. Animals were to some extent romanticized as emblems of a bucolic, pre-industrial age.

Unit Two: **Paragraphs and Passages**

2. Based on the passage, which of the following is true about the first few decades of the nineteenth century?

    Select all that apply.

    [A] England was entering a more bucolic age of industry.

    [B] English society was becoming more compassionate towards some oppressed animals and humans.

    [C] Some viewed industrialization as a victory over wilderness.

3. Select the sentence that, according to the author, would best explain the early nineteenth-century trend towards more humane treatment of animals.

> The following problem set consists of a passage followed by a series of questions. On the GRE, you will typically see one to four questions associated with each passage. However, in this problem set, there are excessive questions so that you can gain more practice answering a variety of question types. (Remember that you can preview the questions!) As such, use the following modified timing guidelines:
>
> - **When reading passages**, spend approximately 1.5 minutes for medium-length passages and 2–3 minutes for longer passages. If a topic is more complex or detailed, spend less time on the details; just get the main ideas and major twists.
>
> - **When answering questions**, spend approximately 30 to 45 seconds on General questions and approximately 45 to 60 seconds on Specific questions. Expect to spend the full time on Select-One-or-More and EXCEPT questions; these will almost always take longer.
>
> Finally, if you'd like, answer only three or four of the questions the first time you do the passage. You can then save the passage for a second pass (with the remaining three or four questions) later on in your study.

Passage C: Japanese Swords

Historians have long recognized the traditional Japanese sword, or *nihonto*, as one of the finest cutting weapons ever produced, but it has even been considered a spiritual entity. The adage "the sword is the soul of the samurai" reflects the sword's psychic importance, not only to its wielder, but also to its creator, the master smith. Not classically regarded as artists, master smiths nevertheless exerted great care in the process of creating swords, no two of which were ever forged exactly the same way. Over hundreds of hours, two types of steel were repeatedly heated, hammered, and folded together into thousands of imperceptible layers, yielding both a razor-sharp, durable edge and a flexible, shock-absorbing blade. Commonly, though optionally, the smith physically signed the blade; moreover, each smith's secret forging techniques left an idiosyncratic structural signature. Each unique finished product reflected the smith's personal honor and devotion to the craft, and today, the Japanese sword is valued as much for its artistic merit as for its historical significance.

4. The primary purpose of the passage is to
   - (A) challenge the observation that the Japanese sword is highly admired by historians
   - (B) introduce new information about the forging of Japanese swords
   - (C) identify the Japanese sword as an ephemeral work of art
   - (D) argue that Japanese sword makers were motivated by honor
   - (E) explain the value attributed to the Japanese sword

5. Each of the following is mentioned in the passage EXCEPT
   - (A) every Japanese sword has a unique structure that can be traced back to a special forging process
   - (B) master smiths kept their forging methodologies secret
   - (C) the Japanese sword was considered by some to have a spiritual quality
   - (D) master smiths are now considered artists by major historians
   - (E) the Japanese sword is considered both a work of art and a historical artifact

6. What could be inferred from the mention of an individual smith's secret forging techniques mentioned in the passage?
   - (A) The Japanese sword is the most important handheld weapon in history.
   - (B) The skill of the samurai is what made the Japanese sword so special.
   - (C) If a sword had a physical signature, other swords with that signature could be attributed to that sword's creator.
   - (D) Master smiths were more concerned about the artistic merit of their blades than about the blades' practical qualities.
   - (E) The Japanese sword has more historical importance than artistic importance.

7. Which of the following can be inferred about the words "structural signature" in this passage?
   - (A) They indicate the inscription that the smith places on the blade during the forging process.
   - (B) They imply the particular characteristics of a blade created by a smith's unique forging process.
   - (C) They suggest that each blade can be traced back to a known master smith.
   - (D) They reflect the soul of the samurai who wielded the sword.
   - (E) They refer to the unique curved shape of the blade.

8. The author most likely describes the forging process in order to
   - (A) present an explanation for a change in perception
   - (B) determine the historical significance of Japanese swords
   - (C) explain why each Japanese sword is unique
   - (D) compare Japanese master smiths to classical artists
   - (E) review the complete process of making a Japanese sword

Unit Two: **Paragraphs and Passages**

9. Select the sentence in the passage that best indicates that the author believes traditional Japanese swords are works of art.

10. Which of the following statements about Japanese swords is supported by the passage?

    Select all that apply.

    |A| There is a way to determine the creator of a given sword other than his signature on the blade.
    |B| They have been viewed in terms other than the purely material.
    |C| They have not always received the artistic recognition that they deserve.

Chapter 5: **Short Passages in Reading Comprehension**

Answers and Explanations

Vocabulary Challenge

1. perspicacious (*adj.*): having penetrating insight or good discernment

2. harrowing (*adj.*): painfully disturbing or distressing

3. indeterminate (*adj.*): not fixed or determined, indefinite; vague

4. prudent (*adj.*): wise in practical matters, carefully providing for the future

5. dubious (*adj.*): doubtful, questionable, suspect

6. wanton (*adj.*): reckless, vicious, without regard for what is right

Problem Set

> The first two passages are repeated from the Chapter 4: GRE Paragraphs problem set. If desired, refer to the Chapter 4 problem set explanations for additional instruction on taking notes for each passage.

1. Based on the passage, which of the following could be reasonably assumed about passengers of a particularly turbulent flight? Select <u>all</u> that apply.

   - [A] They would be likely to misattribute the cause of a sexual attraction they felt to a fellow passenger during a lull in turbulence.

   - [B] They would be likely to misattribute the cause of a sexual attraction they felt to a fellow passenger a few days after the flight.

   - [C] They would be more likely to find themselves viscerally disgusted by a baggage handler at their arrival gate whom they typically would have found merely unappealing.

This is a Select One or More question that asks you to extrapolate from the bridge example to an example involving an airplane. Despite the seemingly out-of-context setting, this should still be treated as an inference question: A turbulent flight would be almost exactly like crossing a wobbly bridge. Which of the choices are closest to the statements in the text itself? Your prediction might be "they would react more extremely immediately after the flight, but not really know why."

   - [A] **CORRECT.** This example is analogous to the one given in the passage. A passenger on a turbulent flight would still likely be experiencing "physiological fear reactions" even during a lull in the turbulence. This physiological arousal can be "reinterpreted either as attraction or repulsion," so any feeling of attraction is likely to be caused by the fear reaction.

   - [B] The passage stresses the manner in which the researchers interviewed subjects *immediately* after crossing the bridge, when the "physiological fear reactions" were still fresh. A few days after a turbulent flight, passengers would be unlikely to continue to experience those reactions.

   - [C] **CORRECT.** This example is analogous to the one given in the passage. A passenger coming off of a turbulent flight would likely still be experiencing "physiological fear reactions" that can cause repulsion as easily as attraction. The passage states that an "unattractive interviewer is actually perceived as much less attractive by subjects physiologically aroused by fearful situations."

Unit Two: **Paragraphs and Passages**

2. Based on the passage, which of the following is true about the first few decades of the nineteenth century? Select all that apply.

|A| England was entering a more bucolic age of industry.

|B| English society was becoming more compassionate towards some oppressed animals and humans.

|C| Some viewed industrialization as a victory over wilderness.

This is a Select One or More question asking about the beginning of the nineteenth century. The passage mentions a few dates, all of which will be useful in determining what was true at the dawn of the nineteenth century. This is an inference question: The entire paragraph is about the early nineteenth century, so there is no single sentence you could point to for your answer. Examine the choices for key words, and compare those back to the paragraph.

|A| The last sentence says that in the nineteenth century, animals became emblems of a "bucolic, pre-industrial age." The point is that that bucolic age was coming to an end at this time. This answer choice mismatches the details: "bucolic" is associated with the "pre-industrial age", not an age of industry.

|B| **CORRECT.** The passage states that, in the early nineteenth century, some "forms of domestic animal abuse" were outlawed and society was also embracing "abolitionism and alleviation of poverty" (both of which are aimed at humans).

|C| **CORRECT.** The author's "deeper explanation" relates the trends to "ongoing industrialization," as city dwellers came to view animals more as pets. The passage then states that "nature was no longer menacing, since society's victory over wilderness was conspicuous." Society, in this context, is the city dwellers who are living a more industrialized life.

3. Select the sentence that, according to the author, would best explain the early nineteenth-century trend towards more humane treatment of animals.

This is a Select-in-Passage question. The second sentence states: "This trend may be regarded as part of a broader embrace of compassionate ideals, such as abolitionism and alleviation of poverty." While this sentence would be tempting to select, as it provides one possible explanation for the phenomenon discussed, the author does not subscribe to this explanation. The author presents a "deeper explanation" in the fourth sentence of the paragraph: "However, a deeper explanation should be traced to socioeconomic conditions related to ongoing industrialization." This is the correct answer.

Answers to Passage C: Japanese Swords

> Upon previewing the questions, here is an example of what you might jot down:
>
> 1. main idea
> 2.
> 3. Au agree
> 4. structural signature
> 5. forging process why describe?
> 6. swords = art where?
> 7. sword facts
>
> Questions 4, 5, and 6 are specific enough that you can look for the answer to those as you read the passage. The other will take more focus on the answer choices. Question 2 has no context, so don't bother writing anything about it during your preview.
>
> **Upon reading the passage, here is one example of a possible set of notes for this passage:**
>
> 1. H: J sword = 1 of best cutting weapons, but even spiritual ← main idea
>   —Soul of Samurai
>   —Impt to smith too
> 2. —Smiths careful, swords unique
>   —Forging = complex
>   —Physical + structural signat

4. **The primary purpose of the passage is to**

    (A) challenge the observation that the Japanese sword is highly admired by historians

    (B) introduce new information about the forging of Japanese swords

    (C) identify the Japanese sword as an ephemeral work of art

    (D) argue that Japanese sword makers were motivated by honor

    (E) explain the value attributed to the Japanese sword

Unit Two: Paragraphs and Passages

To identify the primary purpose of the passage, examine the passage as a whole: the correct choice will reflect the main idea. Avoid answer choices that address only limited sections of the passage. The main idea of the passage (*the Japanese sword has been considered not just a fine weapon but a spiritual entity*) is established in the first two sentences; the purpose of the passage is to explain and support that main idea. Your prediction should resemble this main idea statement.

- (A) The passage does not call into question the admiration that historians have for the Japanese sword.
- (B) The middle of the passage discusses forging techniques, but none of the information is presented as new. Moreover, these forging techniques are not the overall focus of the passage.
- (C) The Japanese sword is not identified as an ephemeral (passing) work of art in the passage.
- (D) Japanese sword makers were indeed motivated by honor, at least in part, according to the last sentence, but this is not the overall purpose of the passage, much of which describes the Japanese sword's physical properties and reasons for its importance.
- (E) **CORRECT.** The passage as a whole describes the immense value of the Japanese sword to both the samurai (the sword's owner) and the smith (its maker). The saying "the sword is the soul of the samurai" is referenced early to indicate this importance. Later portions of the passage detail the tremendous effort that is put into each sword, reflecting the importance of each one.

5. Each of the following is mentioned in the passage EXCEPT

- (A) every Japanese sword has a unique structure that can be traced back to a special forging process
- (B) master smiths kept their forging methodologies secret
- (C) the Japanese sword was considered by some to have a spiritual quality
- (D) master smiths are now considered artists by major historians
- (E) the Japanese sword is considered both a work of art and a historical artifact

With no context clues in the question, use the answer choices themselves for key words. For an EXCEPT question (almost always a Specific question), use the process of elimination to cross out those details mentioned in the passage. Eliminate any answer choices you can remember, then use key words to seek out the remaining choices to verify that 4 of the 5 are present in the passage. You will not be able to make a prediction on this question: this will be entirely process of elimination.

- (A) In the passage, this *unique signature* is referred to as a "structural signature" in the fifth sentence.
- (B) The fifth sentence mentions the "secret forging techniques" used by each smith.
- (C) The first sentence indicates that "the traditional Japanese sword…has even been considered a spiritual entity."
- (D) **CORRECT.** The time and effort master smiths devote to making a sword is discussed, and the passage does indicate that the Japanese sword is valued for its artistic merit. However, the passage does not state that major historians consider master smiths themselves to be artists. *Major* historians are not referenced in the passage. Moreover, who values the Japanese sword for its artistic merit is not mentioned.
- (E) In the last sentence, the passage indicates that "the Japanese sword is valued as much for its artistic merit as for its historical significance."

6. What could be inferred from the mention of an individual smith's secret forging techniques mentioned in the passage?

(A) The Japanese sword is the most important handheld weapon in history.

(B) The skill of the samurai is what made the Japanese sword so special.

(C) If a sword had a physical signature, other swords with that same signature could likely be attributed to that sword's creator.

(D) Master smiths were more concerned about the artistic merit of their blades than about the blades' practical qualities.

(E) The Japanese sword has more historical importance than artistic importance.

This specific detail question refers to the next-to-last sentence: "...each smith's secret forging techniques left an idiosyncratic structural signature." The answer will reflect this sentence.

(A) The opening sentence says: "Historians have long recognized the traditional Japanese sword…as one of the finest cutting weapons ever produced"; however, there is no indication that the Japanese sword is the *most* important handheld weapon in history.

(B) This passage does not discuss the skill of the samurai warrior.

(C) **CORRECT.** According to the passage, every master smith had a "structural signature" due to his own secret forging process. Therefore, if a physical signature is present on a blade, that blade's structural signature could then be associated with a master smith, whose *master* status implies the creation of numerous swords.

(D) The passage mentions that each sword "reflected the smith's personal honor and devotion to craft"; however, there is no claim that master smiths emphasized their swords' artistic merit at the expense of practical qualities.

(E) The final sentence indicates that the sword "is valued as much for it artistic merit as for its historical significance." According to the passage, the two attributes are essentially equally valued; the Japanese sword is not more valued for the historical aspect.

7. Which of the following can be inferred about the term "structural signature" in this passage?

(A) They indicate the inscription that the smith places on the blade during the forging process.

(B) They imply the particular characteristics of a blade created by a smith's unique forging process.

(C) They suggest that each blade can be traced back to a known master smith.

(D) They reflect the soul of the samurai who wielded the swords.

(E) They refer to the unique curved shape of the blade.

This question is a cross between a specific detail question and a word in context question. The correct answer will essentially rephrase the information in the sentence. The author states that "each smith's secret forging techniques left an idiosyncratic structural signature." The words *idiosyncratic* and *signature* imply the uniqueness of the smith's process. Be careful not to infer any additional information, particularly when the question refers to a specific sentence or phrase.

- (A) In the passage, such an inscription is referred to as a "physical signature," not a "structural signature."
- (B) **CORRECT.** The proof sentence indicates that each smith had his own process; the "structural signature" was unique to each smith (not necessarily to each individual blade).
- (C) This statement seems reasonable. However, the passage does not say whether all master smiths are currently "known." Certain swords with a "structural signature" may be of unknown origin.
- (D) The second sentence mentions the saying "the sword is the soul of the samurai," but does not say that the "structural signature" was the aspect of the sword reflecting the soul of the samurai who wielded it. The second paragraph explains that the sword "reflected the smith's personal honor and devotion to craft." This statement, however, does not justify the claim that the structural signature itself reflects the soul of the samurai who wielded it.
- (E) The passage does not discuss the shape of any Japanese blade.

8. **The author most likely describes the forging process in order to**

- (A) present an explanation for a change in perception
- (B) determine the historical significance of Japanese swords
- (C) explain why each Japanese sword is unique
- (D) compare Japanese master smiths to classical artists
- (E) review the complete process of making a Japanese sword

To answer this specific purpose question, pay attention to the emphasized content of the referenced sentence, in particular any reiterated points, and to the relationship that part has to other portions of the passage. Note that this sentence extends the discussion of how "no two of which were ever forged exactly the same way."

- (A) The final sentence mentions that Japanese swords are now appreciated more for their artistic merit, but no explanation as to why is provided.
- (B) The words "historical significance" close the passage, but the description of the forging process fails to explain or outline that significance.
- (C) **CORRECT.** The description of the forging process underscores the uniqueness of individual Japanese swords. One sentence mentions that "no two [swords] were ever forged in exactly the same way." Later, "structural signature" and "unique finished product" reinforce this point.
- (D) The passage explains that master smiths were not considered artists in the classical sense, and then goes on to point out the painstaking creation of each sword. This implicitly draws a parallel between the creation of the sword and classical artistry. However, the passage does not actually describe or discuss classical artists, nor does it set forth criteria for classical artists. There is no actual comparison to classical artists, despite the mention of "artistic merit." This answer choice goes too far beyond the passage.
- (E) Elements of the forging process are discussed, but the "complete" process of making a Japanese sword, such as making the handle, polishing the blade, etc., is not discussed in the paragraph.

Chapter 5: **Short Passages in Reading Comprehension**

9. Select the sentence in the passage that best indicates that the author believes traditional Japanese swords are works of art.

The passage first mentions the idea of art in the third sentence, but indicates that master smiths were *not* regarded as artists. After describing the meticulous forging process, the last sentence indicates that each sword is "unique" and is valued for its "artistic merit." The last sentence, then, best indicates that the author would consider these swords works of art.

The correct answer is the last sentence of the paragraph: "Each unique finished product reflected the smith's personal honor and devotion to the craft, and today, the Japanese sword is valued as much for its artistic merit as for its historical significance."

10. Which of the following statements about Japanese swords is supported by the passage? Select all that apply.

- [A] There is a way to determine the creator of a given sword other than his signature on the blade.
- [B] They have been viewed in terms other than the purely material.
- [C] They have not always received the artistic recognition that they deserve.

This is an inference question of the Select One or More variety. Since the question references the entire paragraph rather than pointing to a specific detail, no prediction is possible. Tackle each answer choice as its own question.

- [A] **CORRECT.** The second-to-last sentence says that "each smith's secret forging techniques left an idiosyncratic structural signature." This structural signature, then, could possibly be used to determine the creator of a given sword, even in the absence of a physical signature.

- [B] **CORRECT.** The first sentence tells you that the Japanese sword "has even been considered a spiritual entity." In other words, it has been viewed in terms other than the strictly material.

- [C] **CORRECT.** The last sentence tells you that "today, the Japanese sword is valued as much for its artistic merit as for its historical significance." Earlier in the passage, however, you were told that master smiths were "not classically regarded as artists." This means that those smiths viewed as artists today did not always receive the same recognition and neither did the swords they made.

CHAPTER 6

Argument-Based Reading Comprehension

In This Chapter ...

- Recognizing Argument-Based Passages
- Components of Argument-Based Passages
- Identifying the Components of an Argument
- Strategy for ABP Questions
- Taking Notes
- Useful Focal Points for All Question Types
- Question Types
- Vocabulary Challenge
- Problem Set
- Answers and Explanations

CHAPTER 6 Argument-Based Reading Comprehension

As discussed at the beginning of the previous chapter, some GRE passages are Argument-Based Passages (ABPs). ABPs consist of a brief argument, generally one to three sentences long, and a question relating to that argument. In this chapter, you will learn how to adjust your approach to RC for this passage type, and use that approach to answer various question types.

Here are your Chapter 6 vocabulary words:

>discrepancy (E)
>diverge (E)
>circumspect (A)
>germane (E)
>multifarious (A)
>circumscribe (A)

Recognizing Argument-Based Passages

Expect to see one to three ABPs per section, each accompanied by a single question. These individual questions should take about the same amount of time as similar questions on other RC passages. Though there aren't multiple questions to preview, still read the question before you read the passage, as it will tell you exactly what kind of ABP you're dealing with.

Similarly to the standard RC passages, arguments in ABPs are made up of premises, counterpoints, assumptions, and conclusions. Some arguments will also contain background information or context; this information helps you to understand the topic under discussion but is not actually part of the argument itself.

The Official Guide to the GRE® General Test does not differentiate between regular Reading Comprehension passages and Argument-Based Passages, but the difference is beneficial to your process. Your first job on any passage will be to categorize it.

How? Before you dive into the argument itself, read the question stem to determine what you've got.

Unit Two: **Paragraphs and Passages**

The following question types appear only on ABPs:

- Analyze Argument Structure: These questions will highlight a sentence or two in the passage and then ask you what purpose they're serving in the argument. Generally, when you see the word *argument*, think ABP.
- Strengthen and Weaken: If a question asks you to strengthen (support) or weaken (undermine) the argument, it's an ABP.
- Resolve a Paradox/Explain a Discrepancy: If the question asks you to resolve or explain something puzzling, then you've got an ABP.
- Find the Assumption: If a question asks you what is assumed by the argument or what the argument depends on, then you have a Find the Assumption ABP.

These question types appear only on RC passages:

- Main Idea, Tone, and Attitude: ABPs are generally too short to get across any kind of overall main point or tone.
- Look-Up Detail: Any question that begins "According to the passage" or asks what the author talked about in detail signals a regular RC passage.
- Author's Purpose: Some questions ask why the author mentioned a particular detail. If you see the language "in order to" in the question stem, then you know you've got a regular RC passage.
- Select-in-Passage or Select-One-or-More questions always signal a regular RC passage. ABP questions always ask you to choose exactly one answer choice from a listed set of five answers.

One question type can appear on both RC passages and ABPs. This chapter will focus on the presentation used for ABPs: a very brief paragraph followed by only one question.

- Inference: Any RC paragraph or passage can have a question that asks what is inferred, implied, or suggested—including ABPs. Here's the good news: The solution process for Inference is the same regardless of the passage type.

> *Strategy Tip:*
>
> For all RC questions, read the question stem itself to determine what type of question you have. If you have an ABP, jot down answer letters A through E to keep track of your eliminations.

Components of Argument-Based Passages

If you notice that the following discussion is eerily similar to what you read in Chapter 4: Components of Paragraphs, why yes…yes it is! Similar active reading habits are helpful across GRE Verbal, regardless of question type. If you already feel confident in breaking down paragraphs, merely skim the following paragraphs until the discussion of **assumptions**.

Premises provide support for the argument's conclusion. They may be facts, opinions, or claims. If they are opinions or claims, they will not be the overall claim the author is making; rather, they will be some intermediate claim the author is using to support the overall claim (conclusion). Some ABPs contain only premises: These paragraphs are used for questions that ask you to derive a conclusion or explanation based

Chapter 6: **Argument-Based Reading Comprehension**

on those facts. In these instances, the question will not refer to the paragraph as an argument, but rather use language that indicates all the information in the paragraph is factual (e.g., *If the facts above are true, which of the following…* or *Which of the following provides an explanation for the surprising result described above?*)

The main idea of the argument is the conclusion, which is logically supported by the premises (and assumptions). Conclusions are in the form of an opinion or a claim; they are not pure facts. All arguments contain conclusions, so if the question references an argument, there will be a conclusion.

Counterpoints (or counter-premises) undermine or go against the conclusion. Occasionally, an argument will present both sides of an argument, with evidence to support both. The passage will still come down one way or the other in terms of an overall conclusion, but some of the provided evidence will be used as premises and some as counter-premises (supporting a kind of counter-conclusion).

Assumptions are unstated pieces of information that the argument requires to function. This is where you may need to adapt your process in ABPs. Whenever the question asks you to Strengthen, Weaken, or Find an Assumption, that's a clue that the passage is not stating a crucial element to the author's argument. Ask yourself: *What is this argument missing?*

> *Strategy Tip:*
> For all questions that pertain to an argument, pause and consider what unstated assumptions the argument has made.

Assumptions are often a factor the author didn't consider, such as an alternative explanation for a certain outcome that occurred or an additional outcome that might occur from a certain choice. Other assumptions can involve shifts in terminology: There is an example of this type of assumption in the argument regarding Melissa's GRE improvement in the next section.

Here's a simple example to illustrate:

> While the plot of the movie was compelling, the acting was atrocious. Thus, the movie will not win an Oscar.
>
> **Conclusion**: Thus, the movie will not win an Oscar.
> **Supporting premise**: The acting was atrocious.
> **Counterpoint**: The plot of the movie was compelling.
> **Assumption**: Atrocious acting prevents a movie from winning an Oscar (any kind of Oscar).

The paragraph evaluation elements discussed in Chapter 4: GRE Paragraphs still apply to Argument Structure Passages. The first word in the above example, "while," is a signal word to aid your evaluation of the relationships between the sentences.

Identifying the Components of an Argument

In order to do well on Argument-Based Passage questions, you must be able to identify the parts of an argument as described in the previous section. Consider the following argument and try to find the different pieces.

> Studying regularly is one factor that has been shown to improve one's performance on the GRE. Melissa took the GRE and scored a 150 on the Verbal section. If she studies several times a week, Melissa can expect to improve her score.

Unit Two: **Paragraphs and Passages**

In analyzing an argument, look first for the conclusion, which is the main idea of the argument. The conclusion is often at the end of the paragraph, and may be its own full sentence, but it does not have to be either. In this instance, the conclusion is at the end of the paragraph, but it is not a full sentence.

Conclusion: ". . . Melissa can expect to improve her score."

Note that the conclusion is just that she'll improve her score: This is the author's prediction, based on other given statements.

After finding the conclusion, identify the roles that the other statements play.

Premise: "Studying regularly is one factor that has been shown to improve one's performance on the GRE." This sentence supports the conclusion that Melissa can expect to improve her score.

Premise: "If she studies several times a week . . ." Studying several times a week is a given statement, and it is one reason the author predicts that Melissa can expect to improve her score.

Background: "Melissa took the GRE and scored a 150 on the Verbal section." This is good context for the argument, but has no direct bearing on whether Melissa can expect to improve her score.

The next step in the evaluation is where ABPs diverge from other RC passages and paragraphs. You need to identify what the author *assumes*. Here, there are multiple assumptions. The argument assumes that studying "several times a week" is the same as studying "regularly." Maybe "regularly" means every day! (This is an example of a "term shift" assumption: The author assumes that the term means a certain thing but there is no evidence to prove that this is the exact, correct meaning.) In that case, studying several times a week may not be enough.

The argument also assumes that there are not other factors involved. Yes, studying regularly is one factor that can improve performance on the GRE. But what if those studies are not organized or guided in any way, or are done in the midst of distraction? Maybe those factors would counterbalance any benefit of the regularity of the studies.

One more note: The conclusion was very, very carefully phrased in each step of this analysis. The conclusion was circumspect in avoiding more declarative language such as *will improve*. The original conclusion was less assertive, merely stating that Melissa *can expect* to improve. Take care with your conclusion statements, and do not insert language the author did not actually use.

Strategy for ABP Questions

In much the same way you tackled problems in Chapter 5: Short Passages in RC, you'll use a four-step process for every ABP you encounter:

Step 1: Identify the question type
Step 2: Deconstruct the argument
Step 3: State the goal
Step 4: Work from wrong to right

Chapter 6: **Argument-Based Reading Comprehension**

An overview follows; later, you'll go through the process in detail for each question type.

Step 1: Identify the Question Type

The vast majority of question stems will allow you to categorize a question into one of the types discussed previously. However, if the question stem is not immediately helpful or the question type is difficult to identify, do not dwell on the issue. Go ahead to the next step; afterward, you can reexamine the question.

Step 2: Deconstruct the Argument

Look for the conclusion, premises, counterpoints, and background. The question type will help you anticipate what to expect from the paragraph. (For example, if you've identified the question type, you'll know whether to look for a conclusion when reading the paragraph.) You may want to take notes while deconstructing; a few potential note-taking strategies will be discussed later.

Step 3: State the Goal

First, you probably won't be able to predict the exact language of the correct choice. Rather, you'll have a particular goal that you're trying to accomplish for each question type. Do not leave your goal a generic "weaken the argument" prediction. Instead, restate the question in terms of the argument whenever possible. For example, in a paragraph about climate effects on lobster populations, "Which choice makes it more likely that the lobster population will increase?" is more useful than "Which choice strengthens the argument?"

Step 4: Work from Wrong to Right

As on any RC question, process of elimination rules the day. (And those who don't follow process of elimination will *rue* the day! Sorry. . .we'll see ourselves out.) As a general rule, cross definitely wrong answers off first, and then compare any remaining tempting answers. Certain question types have common traps in the wrong answers:

Wrong Answer Category	Description	Commonly Found in Question Type . . .
Opposite Direction	This answer choice is germane to the argument, but has the opposite impact on the conclusion than the question requested (e.g., a Weaken question, but an answer that makes the argument more convincing, or an explain question, but the answer makes the situation more surprising).	Strengthen Weaken Explain
Wrong Focal Point	This answer choice focuses on background statements or counterpoints. Although this choice directly addresses a component of the paragraph, it fails in comparison to the common correct choice, which focuses on the argument's conclusion.	Strengthen Weaken Assumption
Too Extreme / Beyond the Scope	This wrong answer commonly contains absolute or overly broad language compared to the language in the paragraph.	Inference

Unit Two: **Paragraphs and Passages**

Taking Notes

When dealing with Argument-Based Passages, you may wish to take some light notes as you do for regular Reading Comprehension passages. These notes will be even more abbreviated though, and they will focus on the flow of the information. What information leads to what conclusion, and what is the author assuming?

There are any number of ways to take notes; choose what you think would work best for your process. First, though, make sure you know what these notes are supposed to accomplish.

Your two main goals are as follows:

1. To classify each piece of information
2. To understand how the different pieces of information fit together

Option 1: Stream-of-Consciousness Notes

This option tends to work for people who jot down notes as they read. Read the first sentence (or part of a sentence), jot down a short note, and move on to the next sentence. At times, you may decide not to jot down a particular detail (e.g., background information may not be necessary to write down). Each new idea gets its own line.

When you're done, determine the conclusion if there is one. Place a C next to it (it's also a good idea to put a circle around the C). Put + (plus) signs next to any premises that support that conclusion. Put − (minus) signs next to any counterpoints that go against the conclusion.

Here's an example:

> Environmentalist: The national energy commission's current plan calls for the construction of six new nuclear power plants during the next decade. The commission argues that these plants are extremely safe and will have minimal environmental impact on their surrounding communities. However, all six nuclear power plants will be located far from densely populated areas. Clearly, the government is tacitly admitting that these plants do pose a serious health risk to humans.
>
> Which of the following, if true, most seriously weakens the environmentalist's claim of an unspoken government admission?

The left column shows sample notes. The right column, in italics, shows what someone may be thinking as they take these notes.

NEC plan: 6 NP next 10yr	*This is a fact, not a conclusion. I don't know yet whether it will support or go against the conclusion.*
NEC: v. safe, low enviro impact	*Okay, this group is claiming something.*
BUT NP not in pop areas	*Big contrast. Another fact.*
Gov admits NP = health risk	*Okay, this is the big claim.*

Now that you know what's going on, go back and add labels to each line:

   NEC plan: 6 NP next 10yr
− NEC: v. safe, low enviro impact
+ BUT NP not in pop areas
Ⓒ Gov admits NP = health risk

Chapter 6: **Argument-Based Reading Comprehension**

The first line is background information; these plants are going to be built. This fact doesn't work for or against the argument. The second line is information that goes against the conclusion. The author thinks these nuclear plants are bad, but the NEC thinks they will be safe. The third line is the author's sole premise and helps to support the author's conclusion. Since the NEC isn't placing any of these nuclear power plants in populated areas, the author concludes that the nuclear power plants must represent a health risk.

What does the author assume when drawing this conclusion?

One thing the author assumes is that there is no other reason why the nuclear power plants might be located in less populated areas. Perhaps the power plants need a lot of land and there isn't enough room in populated areas. If you think of that when reading the argument, you can add it to your notes:

[no other reason NP not in pop areas?]

Note the brackets; these can indicate that the argument itself doesn't mention this information. Rather, it's something you thought of yourself.

Option 2: The T-Diagram

This option tends to work for people who prefer to read the entire argument first and then jot down notes.

First, draw a large T on your scratch paper. Make it asymmetrical, leaving more room on the left side, which will be the "pro" side. In most arguments, you will have very little on the "con" side (to the right).

Step 1.

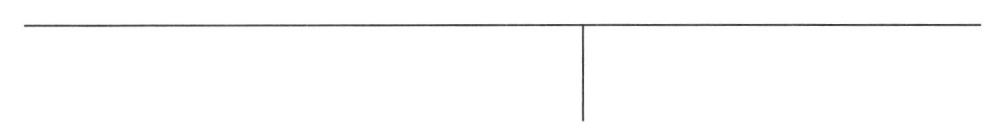

Second, read the argument and look for the conclusion. Once you find the conclusion, write it above the top line of the T, abbreviating heavily.

Step 2.

Third, add the rest of the argument information to the diagram. Write anything that supports the conclusion on the left side of the T ("pro" or "premise"), and write anything that goes against the conclusion on the right side of the T ("con" or "counterpoint").

Step 3.

Conclusion	
– Pro	– Con
– Pro	
– [Assumption]	

161

Finally, if you happened to think of any assumptions while reading, place them in brackets somewhere below the T. Make sure you can differentiate between information stated in the argument and your own thoughts when looking at your notes.

Here's how the environmentalist passage from above might look in T-diagram form:

plnts = ↑ hlth rsk	
plnts far frm pop areas	Comm: plnts safe, ↓ enviro impct
[No other reason for distance?]	

Note that this diagram contains different abbreviations from the first one. There is more than one way to write something down; use what works best for you.

How do I Know Whether My Notes are "Good"?

The above two options aren't the only ones. There are multifarious ways someone might choose to take notes. For example, some people are more visual and might feel most comfortable drawing or mapping out the information. You aren't obligated to follow one particular method; you can develop your own as long as you are accomplishing three goals:

1. If the argument does contain a conclusion, find and note it. The conclusion is the most important part of the argument.

2. If the argument contains any kind of *flow* of information (e.g., one thing leads to another or one thing goes against another), take note of how that information fits together.

3. Use simple and consistent ways to note important information. You don't need to designate the conclusion with a C, but you do need to designate the conclusion the same way every time. You don't want to spend time thinking about how to write something down or wondering what one of your abbreviations means.

If your notetaking style accomplishes those three goals at a minimum, then your process is good!

Useful Focal Points for All Question Types

Here are a few other approaches to try as you tackle the various question types in the next section.

Boundary Words in the Argument

For any question, it is helpful to focus your attention on the boundary words and phrases provided in the argument. These words and phrases specify what is being referred to, narrowing the scope of a premise or conclusion. For example:

Premise: The percentage of literate adults has increased.

The boundary word "percentage" circumscribes the scope of the premise. It restricts the meaning to percentage only, as opposed to the actual number of literate adults. For all you know, the actual number went down. The boundary word "adults" also limits the scope of the premise. It restricts the meaning to adults only, as opposed to the total population or children.

Here is another example:

> Conclusion: Controversial speech should be allowed, provided it does not incite major violence.

The sentences discusses an exception to the general rule that "Controversial speech should be allowed." The boundary word "major" limits the exception—controversial speech should *not* be allowed when it incites *major* violence, but the exception does not apply to speech that incites minor violence. Note that the argument doesn't define what constitutes major versus minor violence.

Boundary words and phrases are vital because they provide nuances to the argument, and these nuances will often be major factors in the answer choices. These details can single-handedly make some answer choices correct or incorrect. At the least, mentally note boundary words; if you write them down (recommended), you might underline them or capitalize them for emphasis. This will help you identify answer choices that try to trick you on the argument boundaries.

Extreme Words in the Argument

Another general strategy for all ABP questions involves extreme words and phrases in the body of the argument. Extreme words, such as *always*, *never*, *all*, and *none*, are the opposite of boundary words—they make the argument very broad or far-reaching.

Using extreme words opens up an argument unreasonably, making it very susceptible to strengthening or weakening. For example:

> Conclusion: Sugar is never healthy for anyone trying to lose weight.

The extreme word "never" unreasonably opens up this argument, placing no limitation on the claim that sugar is unhealthy. A more moderate conclusion would argue that sugar is often unhealthy or that excessive sugar is unhealthy. The extreme word "anyone" further opens up this argument. A more moderate conclusion might be that this claim applies to *most* people trying to lose weight. Note any extreme language used in premises or conclusions; any such words will likely be very useful in eliminating answer choices.

(The reason extreme words open an argument to attack is the same reason Too Extreme is one of the wrong answer traps listed earlier. Extreme words make a statement easier to question and harder to prove.)

Boundary Words in the Answer Choices

Boundary words in the answers are just as important as boundary words in the body of the argument, though for a different reason. A correct answer choice must be 100 percent correct. As long as you interpret the words legitimately, such a choice must be valid no matter which way you interpret it. This principle provides an approach to evaluating answer choices. When you see boundary words in an answer choice, ask yourself, "What is the most extreme example I can think of that would still fit the wording of this answer choice?" Then, using the conclusion and the question asked, see whether your extreme example allows you to eliminate that answer choice.

For example, an answer choice might say:

(D) Some teachers leave the profession entirely within three years of beginning their teaching careers.

You might choose to address one of two different boundaries here. The word "Some" refers to some number of teachers but does not specify the size of the group. The phrase "within three years" refers to a period of time but does not specify the exact length of time.

If you choose to address the word "Some," you could say that 1 percent of teachers leave within three years or that 99 percent of teachers do so. Either way, the statistics still fit the criterion that some teachers do this. Suppose the conclusion asserted that new teacher turnover is having a major impact on the industry. If only 1 percent of new teachers leave within three years, then new teacher turnover will probably not have much of an impact.

Alternatively, you could interpret "within three years" to mean that many teachers in this category leave after 1 day of teaching. You could also imagine that many teachers in this category leave after 2 years and 364 days of teaching. Again, either way, the statistics still fit the criterion that new teachers leave the profession within 3 years of beginning their careers. Depending upon the conclusion and the question, you would then try to disprove answer choices by using these extreme interpretations.

Process of Elimination

It is important to eliminate answer choices on your scratch paper. Do *not* just eliminate answer choices in your head. As you go through many different questions during the test, it can be very difficult to remember which answer choices you have ruled out. You do not want to find yourself reevaluating answers that you have already eliminated or—even worse—accidentally choosing an answer that you meant to eliminate. By the end of the Verbal section of the GRE, your scratch paper will be filled with columns or rows of "A–E" (and a bit of "A–C" and "A–F" for the various question types that have three or six options) with incorrect answer choices crossed out and correct answers circled. Study this way when practicing as well; don't write in your books, since you can't write on the problem itself during the real test.

Even if you believe you have found the correct answer, always check all of the answer choices on Verbal questions. You may find that another answer choice is better, forcing you to rethink your initial choice.

Chapter 6: **Argument-Based Reading Comprehension**

Question Types

The following chart contains the same information presented in the section Recognizing Argument-Based Passages. It is presented here in chart form for your convenience as you examine the example problems later in this section.

Question Type	Example	How to Recognize
Strengthen the Conclusion	Which of the following, if true, most strongly supports the scientists' hypothesis?	In the question stem: *strengthen*, *support*, or similar Will often (but not always) include the words *if true*
Weaken the Conclusion	Which of the following, if true, most seriously undermines the mayor's claim?	In the question stem: *weaken*, *undermine*, or similar May ask what *supports* the idea that something will *not* be successful Will often (but not always) include the words *if true*
Find the Assumption	Which of the following is an assumption on which the argument depends?	In the question stem: either the word *assumption* or some word indicating that the answer choice is needed (e.g., *relies*, *depends*, or *requires*)
Analyze the Argument Structure	In the argument above, the two portions in boldface play which of the following roles?	In the question stem: *role* or similar In the argument: boldface font
Resolve a Paradox/Explain a Discrepancy	Which of the following pieces of evidence, if true, would provide the best explanation for the discrepancy?	In the question stem: *paradox*, *discrepancy*, *resolve*, or similar
Inference (This type can exist in both types of passages.)	Which of the following conclusions can best be drawn from the information above?	In the question stem: *conclusion*, *assertion*, *infer*, or similar Occasionally "is most strongly supported" by the paragraph Will often contain words indicating the paragraph is purely factual (e.g., "information" above)

Unit Two: **Paragraphs and Passages**

Strengthen, Weaken, and Find the Assumption Analysis

On Strengthen, Weaken, and Find the Assumption questions, your analysis is so similar that each will be discussed in the following argument example. Then, you will see a new example of each question type presented as the GRE would present them.

Step 1: Identify the Question Type

Each of the following could be questions for the paragraph that will follow:

- Which of the following statements would most reinforce the assertion that Shuai will win the tournament this year?
- Which of the following, if true, most weakens the author's conclusion?
- In making the above argument, the author is assuming which of the following?

Step 2: Deconstruct the Argument

Your first task is to find the conclusion. Also take note of the premises offered to support the conclusion and think about the gaps in the argument. What is the author assuming must be true in order to draw that particular conclusion?

You may or may not be able to brainstorm any concerns you have with the conclusion made by the author; it's worth spending about 15 to 20 seconds to try. Consider this argument:

> Shuai is the number one tennis player in the country. She lost in the final match of last year's national tennis championship, but she will win the tournament this year. Last year, an injury she suffered in the second set of the final match hampered her serve style.

The conclusion is that Shuai will win the tennis tournament this year; that is the author's prediction. What premises are you offered? Shuai is the number one tennis player in the country. And yet, there is a counterpoint: Shuai lost the final match of last year's tournament. Finally, the author offers information to qualify the impact of that counterpoint. Shuai's loss was (presumably) due to injury, not her skill level.

Brainstorm some issues you think the author should address. For example, has Shuai undergone physical conditioning this year to make her less prone to injury? Or conversely, is last year's injury the type of injury that is likely to recur during the physical stress of a tournament? Perhaps Shuai was ranked tenth last year, and her current number one ranking reflects her improved skills?

Step 3: State the Goal

For Strengthen questions, the correct answer will be a new piece of information that makes the conclusion at least a little more likely to be valid or true. It could be inserted into the argument as a new premise supporting the conclusion. Perhaps the answer might state that Shuai has undergone a surgery during the offseason to prevent recurring injury. Note this doesn't *prove* the conclusion; it merely makes it more convincing.

Find the Assumption questions are similar, with a small twist: The information supplies a needed link between the premise and conclusion. In this case, the assumption answer choice might state that there the likelihood of winning a tournament is strongly connected to the player's rank.

Finally, Weaken answers will contain a new piece of information that would make the conclusion a little less likely. Perhaps the answer choice would present something similar to, but opposite of, the Strengthen answer: Shuai's injury was of a type that, if it has happened once, becomes increasing likely to happen again the more physical stress is placed on the body.

Step 4: Work from Wrong to Right

Use an A–E chart on your paper to keep track of the answers. Mark a letter next to a choice (S, W, or A, for Strengthen, Weaken, and Assumption, respectively) if you believe that answer supplies a potential correct choice for that question type. Mark irrelevant choices with a "?" to indicate that you question whether that choice has any relevance at all to the argument. And finally, if you happen to realize that an answer choice is actually one of the common wrong answers described in the earlier section (four step process), mark it with an "X". If you cannot determine what mark to place next to a choice, do not stress: leave the corresponding answer choice letter unmarked on your page, and move on the next choice.

Try the following sample problems.

Strengthen Example

> At QuestCorp, many employees have quit recently and taken jobs with a competitor. Shortly before the employees quit, QuestCorp lost its largest client. Clearly, the employees were no longer confident in QuestCorp's long-term viability.
>
> Which of the following, if true, most strengthens the claim that concerns about QuestCorp's viability caused the employees to quit?
>
> (A) Employees at QuestCorp's main competitor recently received a large and well-publicized raise.
> (B) QuestCorp's largest client accounted for 40 percent of sales and nearly 60 percent of the company's profits.
> (C) Many prospective hires who have interviewed with QuestCorp ultimately accepted jobs with other companies.
> (D) Shortly before QuestCorp lost its largest client, that client was part of a corporate merger.
> (E) QuestCorp lost the client because QuestCorp is shifting focus to other markets out of that client's industry.

Step 1: Identify the Question Type

The "most strengthens" clearly indicates that this is a Strengthen the Conclusion question.

Step 2: Deconstruct the Argument

The question stem provides the conclusion: Concerns about Q's viability caused employees to quit. One set of notes might look like this:

+ Q lost client, then emp's quit, went to compet
Ⓒ emp's lost conf in Q viab

Step 3: State the Goal

The author assumes that the employees weren't quitting for some other reason. One way to strengthen the argument would be to show that there was some significant negative consequence because the largest client left.

Unit Two: **Paragraphs and Passages**

Step 4: Work from Wrong to Right

Use a chart to categorize and eliminate answer choices.

(A) Weaken or ?. If the competitor is offering more money, then perhaps that's why the employees switched companies; if so, this choice weakens the argument. Note that this choice doesn't actually say that the competitor is now paying more money than QuestCorp, so perhaps this information is irrelevant. Either way, this choice does not strengthen the argument.

(B) Strengthen. The largest client accounted for a very large percentage of both sales and profits. This piece of information does strengthen the idea that some employees may have lost confidence in Quest-Corp's long-term viability.

(C) ?. The argument concludes something about QuestCorp employees, not people who interviewed with QuestCorp but ultimately accepted a job elsewhere.

(D) ?. While a corporate merger might explain why the client dropped QuestCorp, it does not indicate anything about whether QuestCorp's employees' perceptions of the company's long-term prospects.

(E) Weaken or ?. Arguably, this choice could weaken the argument, because QuestCorp's shift in focus could be to a market with better long-term potential. This choice does not state anything about the new market focus, however, so ultimately this could be considered a ? because there is not enough information to predict what impact this choice could have on either QuestCorp's growth or the employees perception of QuestCorp.

Note that choice A is one of the common wrong answer categories: Opposite Direction.

Answer choice (B) is correct.

Weaken Example

The national infrastructure for airport runways and air traffic control requires immediate expansion to accommodate the increase in private, smaller planes. To help fund this expansion, the Federal Aviation Authority (the FAA) has proposed a fee for all air travelers. However, this fee would be unfair, as it would impose costs on all travelers to benefit only the few who utilize the new private planes.

Which of the following, if true, would cast the most doubt on the claim that the proposed fee would be unfair?

(A) The existing national airport infrastructure benefits all air travelers.
(B) The fee, if imposed, will have a negligible effect on the overall volume of air travel.
(C) The expansion would reduce the number of delayed flights resulting from small private planes congesting runways.
(D) Travelers who use small private planes are almost uniformly wealthy or traveling on business.
(E) A substantial fee would need to be imposed in order to pay for the expansion costs.

Chapter 6: **Argument-Based Reading Comprehension**

Step 1: Identify the Question Type

The "cast the most doubt" and "if true" language indicate that this is a Weaken the Conclusion question.

Step 2: Deconstruct the Argument

The question stem indicates the conclusion: the proposed fee would be unfair. One set of notes might look like this:

Fee unfair	
Cost for all, benefits only for priv planes	

Step 3: State the Goal

The author assumes that the benefits will apply only to those flying in the private plans. One way to weaken the argument would be to show that there was some benefit for a greater group, or perhaps for all of the people who would be paying the fee.

Step 4: Work from Wrong to Right

Use an answer choice chart to categorize and eliminate answer choices.

(A) ?. The argument concerns a fee needed in order to expand the existing infrastructure. The status of the existing infrastructure is irrelevant to the argument.

(B) ?. A negligible impact is a very small impact. The fee, though, is intended to be used for infrastructure expansion. The argument makes no claim about what will happen with the overall volume of air travel.

(C) Weaken. This choice offers a benefit for all air travelers: if the expansion can reduce congestion, and therefore the number of delayed flights in general, then others besides the private plane travelers will benefit from the fee.

(D) ?. The wealth or employment status of the passengers does not address whether the fee benefits just these passengers versus all of the passengers.

(E) Strengthen or ?. The amount of the fee does not address whether the fee is unfair. If anything, you might argue that a very high fee is even more unfair, in which case this choice would strengthen the argument, not weaken it.

Note that choice E is one of the common wrong answer categories: Opposite Direction. Choice A is another common wrong answer category: its focus on the existing infrastructure only impacts the background information in the first sentence.

Answer choice (C) is the correct answer.

Unit Two: **Paragraphs and Passages**

Assumption Example

Many people who suffer from high blood pressure also have low levels of magnesium in their blood. Clearly, then, low magnesium levels contribute to high blood pressure.

Which of the following is an assumption made in the argument?

- (A) There is no connection between trace chemical elements in the blood and blood pressure levels.
- (B) Magnesium levels in the blood can contribute to various other health issues.
- (C) The people in question did not have high blood pressure before their magnesium levels dropped below normal levels.
- (D) Relatively minor changes in diet and lifestyle are enough to supplement magnesium intake.
- (E) The medical costs associated with treating high blood pressure are significantly greater than those associated with treating magnesium deficiencies.

Step 1: Identify the Question Type

The question requests an assumption made by the argument.

Step 2: Deconstruct the Argument

The signal word "clearly" indicates a position held by the author. The previous sentence offers a fact in support of that position.

```
low mag causes HBP
HBP = low mag in blood
```

Step 3: State the Goal

The author assumes causation: There is an association between high blood pressure and low magnesium levels, but that does not prove that low magnesium causes the high blood pressure. There may not be a definitive link between the two. For a Find the Assumption, your goal is to find an answer choice that establishes a link between the two, and in the causal order desired: Low magnesium leads to high blood pressure.

Step 4: Work from Wrong to Right

(A) Weaken. This choice would counter the connection between magnesium and blood pressure needed by the argument. Eliminate answer A.

(B) ?. Does the argument require an assessment of other health issues? There is no indication that those other health issues would cause high blood pressure. Eliminate answer B.

(C) Correct. This choice addresses a link between high blood pressure and low magnesium, and offers the needed causal order: In order for high blood pressure to be caused by magnesium levels, the high blood pressure cannot exist before the low magnesium levels.

(D) ?. Does the argument need information on how to rectify low magnesium? While this information might be promising to someone who has high blood pressure, it has no impact on whether that high blood pressure was actually caused by the low magnesium levels. Eliminate answer D.

(E) ?. Does the argument need a comparison of treatment costs? This might provide a reason to treat low magnesium levels as early as possible, but this would not change the fundamental question of whether it is low magnesium that causes the high blood pressure. Eliminate answer E.

Note that choice A is one of the common wrong answer categories: Opposite Direction. In Find the Assumption questions, a weaken choice is the opposite of supplying a link between premise and conclusion.

Answer choice (C) is the correct answer.

Analyze the Argument Structure

Analyze the Argument Structure questions ask you to describe the role of a part or parts of the argument; these portions will be shown in bold font. The arguments tend to be complex, often with an argument/counterargument structure. Be prepared with guessing strategies (discussed next).

Step 1: Identify the Question Type

The question type will be immediately apparent because of the boldface font in portions of the argument. The question will typically ask what *role* the bold portions play in the overall argument.

Step 2: Deconstruct the Argument

The boldface portions can play one of three primary roles:

1. (C): The statement in boldface is the author's *conclusion*.
2. (S): The statement in boldface is a premise that *supports* the author's conclusion.
3. (E): The statement in boldface is *something else* (this could be a statement counter to the conclusion or it could be merely background information).

Find the author's conclusion, then classify each statement according to the categories C, S, or E. These arguments tend to be longer than average; note that the correct choice will not categorize the entire argument, just the two statements in bold font. Do not go to the answer choices until you have found the conclusion and categorized the statements.

Step 3: State the Goal

Your goal is to categorize the boldface statements and then to find an answer choice that matches your categorization. Note also whether the boldface statements are both aligned with the author's conclusion (C and S above) or not aligned with the author's conclusion (C vs E, or S vs E).

Step 4: Work from Wrong to Right

The wrong answers will provide descriptions of the wrong combination of categories. For example, you might decide that the first boldface is a conclusion (C) while the second is support (S). One wrong answer might describe the combination C, E, in that order, while another is E, C. Both would be incorrect if you are looking for the combination C, S.

Unit Two: **Paragraphs and Passages**

Here is an example:

Mathematician: Recently, Zubin Ghosh made headlines when he was recognized to have solved the Hilbert Conjecture, postulated a hundred years ago. Ghosh posted his work on the Internet rather than submit it to established journals. In fact, **he has no job, let alone a university position**; he lives alone and has refused all acclaim. In reporting on Ghosh, the press unfortunately has reinforced the popular view that mathematicians are antisocial loners. **But mathematicians clearly form a tightly knit community**, frequently collaborating on important efforts; indeed, teams of researchers are working together to extend Ghosh's findings.

In the argument above, the two portions in boldface play which of the following roles?

(A) The first is an observation the author makes to illustrate a social pattern; the second is a generalization of that pattern.

(B) The first is evidence in favor of the popular view expressed in the argument; the second is a brief restatement of that view.

(C) The first is an example of a generalization that the author contradicts; the second is a reiteration of that generalization.

(D) The first is a counterexample to a generalization that the author asserts; the second is that generalization.

(E) The first is a judgment that counters the primary assertion expressed in the argument; the second is a circumstance on which that judgment is based.

Step 1: Identify the Question Type

The boldface font in the argument and the word "role" in the question stem indicate that this is an Analyze the Argument Structure question.

Step 2: Deconstruct the Argument

The author's conclusion is that mathematicians actually form a tightly knit community. The counterargument is that mathematicians are antisocial loners. Now, label each statement as either Conclusion (C), Support (S), or Something Else (E).

The first boldface represents an example that supports the *counter*argument; label this statement E. The second boldface represents the author's conclusion, C.

Step 3: State the Goal

You're looking for an answer that describes the first statement as an E and the second statement as a C. Note that these two statements are on opposite sides of the argument (the first goes with the counterargument and the second goes with the author's argument).

Step 4: Work from Wrong to Right

(A) This answer says that the author uses the first statement to illustrate a pattern. On the contrary, the author believes that the pattern described by the counterargument is not valid. Eliminate answer (A).

(B) The first portion of this answer is accurate: It supports the popular view, which goes against the view held by the author. The second half of this answer, though, is inaccurate. The second statement does not restate the popular view; rather, it provides the author's opposing view. Eliminate answer (B).

(C) The first portion of this answer is accurate: It supports an idea that the author contradicts. The second statement, though, is not "that generalization," or the popular view. Rather, the second statement reflects the author's opposing point of view. Eliminate answer (C).

Note that answers (A), (B), and (C) all describe the two statements as being on the same side of the fence. You're looking for the two statements to be on opposite sides of the fence.

(D) **CORRECT.** The author does assert something, and the first statement does go against that assertion; the first half of this answer is accurate. The second half of this choice refers to "that generalization," or the generalization that the author asserts. The author asserts their own conclusion, so the second half of this answer is also accurate. Leave this answer in.

(E) The first does counter the author's assertion, or conclusion, though note that this answer choice describes the first statement as a "judgment." It is not a judgment; rather, it's a fact or example. The second half of the choice says that the second boldface statement is based on the first statement; in fact, the second statement goes against the first one. Eliminate answer (E).

The correct answer is (D).

Alternative Approach for Argument Structure

If you have trouble with the above approach, or if you hit a very confusing or convoluted argument, you can try an alternative method for steps 2 through 4 that should help you to eliminate some answers (though you may not be able to eliminate all four wrong answers).

Step 2: Deconstruct the Argument

Read the passage and label each boldface statement as one of the following:

(F) Fact	A verifiable statement
(O) Opinion	A minor claim, or an opinion of someone other than the author
(C) Conclusion	The major claim of the author

In the case of the previous problem, the first statement represents a Fact while the second statement represents the Conclusion.

Step 3: State the Goal

You're looking for F followed by C.

Step 4: Work from Wrong to Right

When working through the answers, look for words that can indicate the type of statement:

(F) Fact	= "evidence" "circumstance" "finding"
(O) Opinion	= "judgment" "claim" "position" (taken by someone else)
(C) Conclusion	= "position" (taken by the argument) "assertion" (of the author)

Do *not* dive very deeply into the content of the answer choices; rather, focus on moving pretty quickly and eliminating answer choices that do not match the Fact/Opinion/Conclusion classification. In the case of the previous problem, you can confidently eliminate answer (E) because a judgment is not the same thing as a fact. Answer (A) is questionable; an observation can be a fact, but facts are more often described as evidence or examples. If you had to guess, avoid (A) on this one.

Unit Two: **Paragraphs and Passages**

With this alternative method, you can avoid getting bogged down in the messy details and make a good guess without spending too much time, but you might not be able to eliminate all of the wrong answers.

If you can figure out how to categorize only one of the two boldface statements, then assess the corresponding half of the answer choices. Eliminate whatever answer choices you can, choose immediately from among the remaining answer choices, and move on.

Inference

Inference questions for ABPs are very similar to Inference questions for regular Reading Comprehension passages; the ABP versions differ from regular RC mainly in the length of the paragraph. As with any Inference question, you need to find the answer that logically follows, or must be true, based upon the information given in the argument.

It's critical to make a distinction between conclusions given in an argument and conclusions (or inferences) given in answer choices. When an ABP provides a conclusion for you in the argument itself, that conclusion is pretty faulty. It's an arguable statement, or claim, that is only partially supported by the premises of the argument, and you can find lots of gaps in the argument.

By contrast, if you are asked to draw a conclusion or to infer something yourself, that conclusion must be able to be *proven* from the given premises. The conclusion will not require you to make any additional assumptions at all, even tiny ones. The correct answer to an Inference question is *not* a claim or an arguable statement, but must be verifiably true based on the information given in the argument.

Step 1: Identify the Question Type

The question stem may appear in a number of forms:

- If the statements above are true, which of the following must be true?
- Which of the following conclusions can best be drawn from the information above?
- The statements above, if true, best support which of the following assertions?
- Which of the following can properly be inferred from the statement above?
- (A full paragraph of text, ending with . . .) Students typically study five days a week. Therefore, _____ .

The last is an example of a Fill-in-the-Blank format. The word "Therefore" signals that the correct answer is the conclusion of the argument.

Step 2: Deconstruct the Argument

Inference questions do not contain a conclusion in the paragraph. The paragraph will contain only premises and these premises will be primarily factual (though some might be more on the opinion or claim side). As with the other question types, jot down some light notes. If you can brainstorm any possible conclusions, do so—but remember that you might not think of what the correct answer will actually say.

Consider the following simplified example:

Samantha and Isabel are the only two people in the dining room. They are both over 50 years old.

What can be safely inferred from these facts? That is, what absolutely *must* be true as a result?

Must be true: There is no one under 50 years old in the dining room.

This conclusion may not seem very meaningful or important in a real-world sense, but this is what the correct answer to an Inference question is like. Avoid grand conclusions in these problems. A correct answer might simply restate one or more of the premises, using synonyms. Sometimes, a correct answer might be a mathematical or logical deduction.

Step 3: State the Goal

You need to find the answer choice that must be true given some or all of the information found in the argument. (Note that the correct answer is not required to use *all* of the given information.)

Step 4: Work from Wrong to Right

Eliminate any answers that require additional assumptions or outside information in order to be true. The wrong answers will all include something that doesn't have to be true.

Consider the following example:

> In certain congested urban areas, commuters who use public transportation options, such as trains and subways, spend approximately 25 percent less time in transit, on average, to reach their destinations than commuters who travel by car. Even individuals who drive their entire commute in carpool lanes, which are typically the least congested sections of roadways, still spend more time, on average, than commuters who use trains and subways.
>
> The statements above, if true, best support which of the following assertions about commuting in the congested urban areas mentioned above?
>
> (A) Waiting in traffic accounts for approximately 25 percent of the commuting time for individuals who drive to their destinations.
> (B) Walking between a subway or train station and one's final destination does not, on average, take longer than walking between one's car and one's final destination.
> (C) Using carpool lanes does not, on average, reduce driving time by more than 25 percent.
> (D) Individuals who commute via public buses spend approximately 25 percent more time in transit than those who commute using public trains or subways.
> (E) Subways and trains are available in the majority of congested urban areas.

Step 1: Identify the Question Type

The word "assertion" coupled with the fact that the assertion is in the answer choices indicates that this is an Inference question.

Step 2: Deconstruct the Argument

One set of notes might look like this:

Pub trans (trn, sub): ~25% < t than ppl using car

Even true for carpool

Step 3: State the Goal

You're looking for something that must be true using at least some of the presented information. It might be tempting to conclude that people *should* use public transportation—but note that this doesn't have to be true. Don't introduce opinions or real-world logic.

Unit Two: **Paragraphs and Passages**

Step 4: Work from Wrong to Right

(A) While waiting in traffic probably does account for *some* of the commuting time, there's no reason why it must account for approximately 25 percent of that time. This might be an appropriate answer for a Strengthen question, but not for an Inference question. Eliminate answer (A).

(B) Careful! This one is tempting initially because it might cause someone to think, "Oh, wait, did they account for the time it takes to get from the subway to work or your house? Maybe this is it!" The difficulty here is that this length of time does not have to be similar to the length of time it takes to walk from the car to the final destination. The argument compares the overall commute time, not the time for smaller pieces of the commute. Eliminate answer (B).

(C) The argument does mention that "even" when someone uses a carpool lane, which should save time, it's still faster to take public transportation. Given that info, if public transportation also takes about 25 percent less time than using a car, then it actually must be the case that using a carpool lane does not (on average) save more than 25 percent of car commuting time. If it did, then carpooling might actually be faster than taking public transportation. Leave this answer in.

(D) The argument does not make a comparison between different forms of public transportation. Rather, it compares all of public transportation to all commuting by car. Eliminate answer (D).

(E) Tricky! Again, this one might make someone think, "Oh, they're assuming that public transportation is actually available." Note first that this argument is assuming nothing at all—it does not contain a conclusion and, by definition, only arguments containing conclusions also have assumptions. Next, the argument provides actual data for areas that do have public transportation, so that's the only concern. Finally, the argument never specifies that these areas must have subways and trains specifically (buses are also public transportation), nor does it specify that a "majority" of these areas have public transportation. In fact, the argument refers only to "certain congested urban areas."

Note that choice (E) is one of the common wrong answer categories: Too Extreme / Beyond the Scope. While it may not seem that a statement about the "majority" of congested urban areas, for a paragraph that only mentions "certain" congested areas, that is too extreme.

The correct answer is (C). Note that the correct answer addressed only one narrow part of the situation. It did not assume anything or go at all beyond the scope of the information given in the argument.

Resolve a Paradox

This question type poses two seemingly contradictory premises and asks you to find the answer choice that best reconciles them.

Step 1: Identify the Question Type

The question will often, though not always, indicate what the discrepancy is or provide a keyword pointing to the discrepancy in the argument. For example:

- Which of the following statements, if true, would best explain the sudden drop in temperature?
- Which of the following, if true, most helps to resolve the paradox described above?

Step 2: Deconstruct the Argument

Like Inference paragraphs, Paradox paragraphs do not contain a conclusion in the paragraph: it will contain only premises, and these premises will be primarily factual. Jot down some light notes, and articulate the paradox to yourself.

176

Chapter 6: **Argument-Based Reading Comprehension**

Consider the following simplified example:

> According to researchers, low dosages of aspirin taken daily can significantly reduce the risk of heart attack or stroke. Yet doctors have stopped recommending daily aspirin for most patients.

What? That doesn't make any sense! If aspirin is beneficial, why wouldn't doctors recommend it for patients?

There must be some other reason why they wouldn't want patients to take aspirin. Perhaps there are some other side effects that are worse than the possible benefits.

Step 3: State the Goal

Your goal is to find an answer that explains why the surprising facts given in the argument are not so paradoxical after all. The correct answer should resolve whatever paradox caused you to think, "Wait, that doesn't make sense!" If you insert the correct answer into the argument, someone who reads it would then say, "Oh, I see! Now it makes sense why they've stopped recommending aspirin."

Step 4: Work from Wrong to Right

As with all ABPs, read through each answer. Eliminate choices that do not explain or resolve the paradox. Often, some wrong answers on Resolve a Paradox questions will make the paradox even *more* confusing.

Consider the following example:

> In a recent poll, 71 percent of respondents reported that they cast votes in the most recent national election. Voting records show, however, that only 60 percent of eligible voters actually voted in that election.
>
> Which of the following pieces of evidence, if true, would provide the best explanation for the discrepancy?
>
> (A) The margin of error for the survey was plus or minus 5 percentage points.
> (B) Fifteen percent of the survey's respondents were living overseas at the time of the election.
> (C) Prior research has shown that people who actually do vote are also more likely to respond to polls than those who do not vote.
> (D) Some people who intend to vote are prevented from doing so by last-minute conflicts on election day or other complications.
> (E) Polls about voting behavior typically have margins of error within plus or minus 3 percentage points.

Step 1: Identify the Question Type

The word "discrepancy" in the question stem indicates that this is a Resolve the Paradox question.

Step 2: Deconstruct the Argument

> Poll: 71% of ppl said they voted
> Rec: 60% of eligible voters voted

Step 3: State the Goal

The goal is to find something that resolves the apparent discrepancy in these two numbers. First, the people who responded to the poll might not be the same group of people who were eligible to vote. Alternatively, there might be a reason why people said they voted when they actually didn't. Possibly there is some other reason to explain what happened.

Unit Two: **Paragraphs and Passages**

Step 4: Work from Wrong to Right

(A) This choice begins promisingly by discussing a margin of error. However, a margin of error of 5 percentage points will not close the 11-percentage point gap between the two statistics in the argument. Eliminate this choice.

(B) Fifteen percent is larger than the 11-point discrepancy in the argument. The percentage, however, applies to the percentage of respondents living overseas at the time of the election. If absentee ballots are allowed, then these people could still have voted. This choice doesn't definitively resolve the paradox, so eliminate it.

(C) If people who do vote are also more likely to respond to polls, then those people are overrepresented in the polling results. That is, they represent a greater proportion of the people answering the poll than they do of the overall population; this explains why a greater percentage of poll respondents said they had voted. Keep this answer in.

(D) This is probably true in the real world, but it does not explain the discrepancy in the statistics presented in the argument. The 60 percent figure represents people who actually did vote, not those who intended to vote but didn't. Eliminate this choice.

(E) This choice does not explain the discrepancy in the statistics presented in the argument; this poll might not have the same margin of error of "typical" polls. Even if you do adjust for a 3 percent margin of error, 11 percent still represents a substantial gap. Eliminate this choice.

The correct answer is (C). Incorrect choice (E), in this instance, is a common wrong answer category: Opposite Direction. If the typical margin of error is only 3 percent, then the existence of an 11 percentage point gap in these polls is more surprising, not less.

Vocabulary Challenge

> Did you spot these vocabulary words? If not, go back and find them in context! (The word may be in a different form than listed here—"digressing" instead of "digress," for example.) Write your own definitions based on the evidence in the chapter.

1. discrepancy (*n*), p. 156
2. diverge (*v*), p. 158
3. circumspect (*adj.*), p. 158
4. germane (*adj.*), p. 159
5. multifarious (*adj.*), p. 162
6. circumscribe (*v*), p. 163

Chapter 6: **Argument-Based Reading Comprehension**

Problem Set

> Use the four-step process taught for all ABPs, as well as any specific techniques recommended for that question type (e.g., the answer choice chart to track your eliminations). Consider all five answer choices before you make your final decision.

1. John was flying from San Francisco to New York with a connecting flight in Chicago on the same airline. Chicago's airport is one of the largest in the world, consisting of several small stand-alone terminals connected by trams. John's plane arrived on time. John was positive he would make his connecting flight 30 minutes later because _____ .

   Which of the following most logically completes the argument above?

   - (A) John's airline is known for always being on time
   - (B) a number of other passengers on John's first flight were also scheduled to take John's connecting flight
   - (C) at the airport in Chicago, airlines always fly into and out of the same terminal
   - (D) John knew there was another flight to New York scheduled for one hour after the connecting flight he was scheduled to take
   - (E) the airline generally closes the doors of a particular flight 10 minutes before it is scheduled to take off

2. Media Critic: Network executives have alleged that television viewership is decreasing due to the availability of television programs on other platforms, such as the internet, video-on-demand, and mobile devices. These executives claim that **declining viewership will cause advertising revenue to fall so far that networks will be unable to spend the large sums necessary to produce programs of the quality now available**. That development, in turn, will lead to a dearth of programming for the very devices that cannibalized television's audience. However, technology executives point to research that indicates that **users of these platforms increase the number of hours per week that they watch television** because they are exposed to new programs through these alternative platforms. This analysis demonstrates that networks can actually increase their revenue through higher advertising rates, due to larger audiences lured to television through other media.

   The portions in boldface play which of the following roles in the media critic's argument?

   - (A) The first is an inevitable trend that weighs against the critic's claim; the second is that claim.
   - (B) The first is a prediction that is challenged by the argument; the second is a finding upon which the argument depends.
   - (C) The first clarifies the reasoning behind the critic's claim; the second demonstrates why that claim is flawed.
   - (D) The first acknowledges a position that the technology executives accept as true; the second is a consequence of that position.
   - (E) The first opposes the critic's claim through an analogy; the second outlines a scenario in which that claim will not hold.

Unit Two: **Paragraphs and Passages**

3. In the last year, real estate prices, such as those for houses and condominiums, have gone up an average of 7 percent in the city of Galway but only 2 percent in the town of Tuam. On the other hand, average rents for apartments have risen 8 percent in Tuam over the last year but only 4 percent in Galway.

   Which of the following is an inference that can be reasonably drawn from the premises given above?

   (A) In the last year, the ratio of average apartment rents to average real estate prices has increased in Tuam but fallen in Galway.
   (B) Tuam has experienced a greater shift in demand toward the rental market than Galway has.
   (C) It has become easier for Galway real estate to be bought and sold, whereas it has become easier for Tuam real estate to be rented.
   (D) The supply of rental apartment units has decreased more in Tuam than in Galway.
   (E) The average amount spent on housing is higher in Galway than it is in Tuam.

4. Due to the increase in traffic accidents caused by deer in the state, the governor last year reintroduced a longer deer hunting season to encourage recreational hunting of the animals. The governor expected the longer hunting season to decrease the number of deer and therefore decrease the number of accidents. However, this year the number of accidents caused by deer has increased substantially since the reintroduction of the longer deer hunting season.

   Which of the following, if true, would best explain the increase in traffic accidents caused by deer?

   (A) Many recreational hunters hunt only once or twice per hunting season, regardless of the length of the season.
   (B) The deer in the state have become accustomed to living in close proximity to humans and are often easy prey for hunters as a result.
   (C) Most automobile accidents involving deer result from cars swerving to avoid deer, and they leave the deer in question unharmed.
   (D) The number of drivers in the state has been gradually increasing over the past several years.
   (E) A heavily used new highway was recently built directly through the state's largest forest, which is the primary habitat of the state's deer population.

Chapter 6: **Argument-Based Reading Comprehension**

5. Political Analyst: After a coalition of states operating under a repressive regime collapsed, some hoped that freedom would bolster the population of the largest state, Algan, but as a result of dislocation and insecurity, the Algan population continues to dwindle at the rate of 700,000 a year. The government proposes to address the problem with a wide range of financial incentives, along with investments in improved healthcare, road safety, and the like. These are positive measures, but **they have been tried before, to little avail**. A better plan to reverse the population decline is to improve Algan's governance in both the public and the private sphere. **If a greater part of the population participated in important decisions and shared in Algan's wealth, then larger families would result.** In addition, if corruption and greed among the elite were curbed, public health would improve, and average life expectancy would increase.

    The two boldfaced statements serve what function in the argument above?

    (A) The first is the main point of the analyst's argument; the second is a premise that supports the first.
    (B) The first is a premise that undermines an alternative to the analyst's proposal; the second is a premise that supports the analyst's main claim.
    (C) The first is a premise that contradicts the main point made by the analyst; the second is the main point of the argument.
    (D) The first is a premise that supports a proposal; the second is that proposal.
    (E) The first is a conclusion that the argument endorses; the second is a premise that opposes that conclusion.

6. Displayco is marketing a holographic display to supermarkets that shows three-dimensional images of certain packaged goods in the aisles. Displayco's marketing literature states that patrons at supermarkets will be strongly attracted to goods that are promoted in this way, resulting in higher profits for the supermarkets that purchase the displays. Consumer advocates, however, feel that the displays will be intrusive to supermarket patrons and may even increase minor accidents involving shopping carts.

    Which of the following, if true, most seriously weakens the position of the consumer advocates?

    (A) The holographic displays are expensive to install and maintain.
    (B) Many other venues, including shopping malls, are considering adopting holographic displays.
    (C) Accidents in supermarkets that are serious enough to cause injury are rare.
    (D) Supermarkets tend to be low-margin businesses that struggle to achieve profitability.
    (E) Studies in test markets have shown that supermarket patrons quickly become accustomed to holographic displays.

Unit Two: **Paragraphs and Passages**

7. Brand X designs and builds custom sneakers, one sneaker at a time. It recently announced plans to sell "The Gold Standard," a sneaker that will cost five times more to manufacture than any other sneaker that has ever been created.

   A prediction that The Gold Standard shoe line will be profitable would require which of the following assumptions?

   - (A) At least some consumers would be willing to spend enough money on sneakers to allow Brand X to charge prices for The Gold Standard that would exceed the cost to manufacture the sneaker.
   - (B) Of the last four new sneakers that Brand X has released, three have sold at a rate that was higher than projected.
   - (C) A rival brand recently declared bankruptcy and ceased manufacturing shoes.
   - (D) The market for The Gold Standard will not be more limited than the market for other Brand X shoes.
   - (E) The Gold Standard is made using canvas that is more than five times the cost of the canvas used in most sneakers.

8. With information readily available on the internet, consumers now often enter the automobile retail environment with certain models and detailed specifications in mind. In response to this trend, CarStore has decided to move toward a less aggressive sales approach. Despite the fact that members of its sales personnel have an average of 10 years of experience each, CarStore has implemented a mandatory training program for all sales personnel, because _____.

   - (A) the sales personnel in CarStore have historically specialized in aggressively selling automobiles and add-on features
   - (B) the sales personnel in CarStore do not themselves use the internet often for their own purposes
   - (C) CarStore has found that most consumers do not mind negotiating over price
   - (D) information found on the internet often does not reflect sales promotions at individual retail locations
   - (E) several retailers that compete directly with CarStore have adopted "customer-centered" sales approaches

Chapter 6: **Argument-Based Reading Comprehension**

9. Government restrictions have severely limited the amount of stem cell research that companies in the United States can conduct. Because of these restrictions, many U.S.-based scientists who specialize in the field of stem cell research have signed long-term contracts to work for foreign-based companies. Recently, the U.S. government has proposed lifting all restrictions on stem cell research.

    Which of the following statements can most properly be inferred from the information above?

    (A) Some foreign-based companies that conduct stem cell research work under fewer restrictions than some U.S.-based companies do.
    (B) Because U.S.-based scientists are under long-term contracts to foreign-based companies, there will be a significant influx of foreign professionals into the United States.
    (C) In all parts of the world, stem cell research is dependent on the financial backing of local government.
    (D) In the near future, U.S.-based companies will no longer be at the forefront of stem cell research.
    (E) If restrictions on stem cell research are lifted, many of the U.S.-based scientists will break their contracts and return to U.S.-based companies.

10. Traditionally, public school instructors have been compensated according to seniority. Recently, the existing salary system has been increasingly criticized as an approach to compensation that rewards lackadaisical teaching and punishes motivated, highly qualified instruction. Instead, educational experts argue that, to retain exceptional teachers and maintain quality instruction, teachers should receive salaries or bonuses based on performance rather than seniority.

    Which of the following, if true, most weakens the conclusion of the educational experts?

    (A) Some teachers express that financial compensation is not the only factor contributing to job satisfaction and teaching performance.
    (B) School districts will develop their own unique compensation structures that may differ greatly from those of other school districts.
    (C) Upon leaving the teaching profession, many young, effective teachers cite a lack of opportunity for more rapid financial advancement as a primary factor in the decision to change careers.
    (D) A merit-based system that bases compensation on teacher performance reduces collaboration, which is an integral component of quality instruction.
    (E) In school districts that have implemented pay for performance compensation structures, standardized test scores have dramatically increased.

Unit Two: **Paragraphs and Passages**

Answers and Explanations

Vocabulary challenge

1. discrepancy (*n*): difference or inconsistency

2. diverge (*v*): differ, deviate; branch off or turn aside, as from a path

3. circumspect (*adj.*): cautious, prudent; careful to consider the circumstances and consequences

4. germane (*adj.*): relevant and appropriate, on-topic

5. multifarious (*adj.*): diverse, having a lot of variety

6. circumscribe (*v*): strictly limit a role, range of activity, or area

Problem Set

1. **(C):**

    John was flying from San Francisco to New York with a connecting flight in Chicago on the same airline. Chicago's airport is one of the largest in the world, consisting of several small stand-alone terminals connected by trams. John's plane arrived on time. John was positive he would make his connecting flight 30 minutes later, because _____.

    Which of the following most logically completes the argument above?

    (A) John's airline is known for always being on time

    (B) a number of other passengers on John's first flight were also scheduled to take John's connecting flight

    (C) at the airport in Chicago, airlines always fly into and out of the same terminal

    (D) John knew there was another flight to New York scheduled for one hour after the connecting flight he was scheduled to take

    (E) the airline generally closes the doors of a particular flight 10 minutes before it is scheduled to take off

Step 1: Identify the Question Type

The blank in this Fill-in-the-Blank question is preceded by the word "because," most commonly signaling a Strengthen question, but you'll need to read the argument to be sure. The beginning of that sentence contains the conclusion, so this is indeed a Strengthen question.

Step 2: Deconstruct the Argument

The Chicago airport is busy and very large, consisting of several small stand-alone terminals. Despite this, John thinks he will make his connecting flight.

Step 3: State the Goal

The correct answer choice will make it a little more likely that John's conclusion is valid. The information needs to support the idea that he'll make the connecting flight despite the size of the airport.

Step 4: Work from Wrong to Right

- (A) ?. This is a general observation about the timeliness of John's airline, but it does not provide any new information—the argument already states that John's particular flight arrived on time. The fact that his connecting flight will probably depart on time might even weaken the argument.

- (B) ?. The argument doesn't give any reason to believe that the airline would delay John's second flight just to allow more passengers to catch the flight. Even if this situation might be conceivable in the real world, if more additional assumptions are needed to demonstrate relevance, look for a better choice.

- (C) **CORRECT.** Strengthen. Since John's connecting flight is on the same airline, John will not have to take a tram to another terminal in order to reach his connecting flight. The premises describe the individual terminals as "small." If he can walk to his next flight in a small terminal, then 30 minutes is likely enough time to make the connection.

- (D) ?. This choice is out of scope. The argument concludes that John will make his current flight; the later flight has no bearing on John's ability to catch the flight on which he is currently booked.

- (E) X. If anything, this choice weakens the idea that John will catch the connecting flight by shortening the length of time he has to get to the second flight's gate. He now has only 20 minutes, not 30.

2. (B):

Media Critic: Network executives have alleged that television viewership is decreasing due to the availability of television programs on other platforms, such as the internet, video-on-demand, and mobile devices. These executives claim that **declining viewership will cause advertising revenue to fall so far that networks will be unable to spend the large sums necessary to produce programs of the quality now available**. That development, in turn, will lead to a dearth of programming for the very devices that cannibalized television's audience. However, technology executives point to research that indicates that **users of these platforms increase the number of hours per week that they watch television** because they are exposed to new programs through these alternative platforms. This analysis demonstrates that networks can actually increase their revenue through higher advertising rates, due to larger audiences lured to television through other media.

The portions in boldface play which of the following roles in the media critic's argument?

- (A) The first is an inevitable trend that weighs against the critic's claim; the second is that claim.
- (B) The first is a prediction that is challenged by the argument; the second is a finding upon which the argument depends.
- (C) The first clarifies the reasoning behind the critic's claim; the second demonstrates why that claim is flawed.
- (D) The first acknowledges a position that the technology executives accept as true; the second is a consequence of that position.
- (E) The first opposes the critic's claim through an analogy; the second outlines a scenario in which that claim will not hold.

Step 1: Identify the Question Type

The boldface font indicates that this is an Analyze the Argument question. Note that the question stem references the "media critic's argument"—this is the conclusion you want.

Unit Two: **Paragraphs and Passages**

Step 2: Deconstruct the Argument

The first three sentences describe the network executives' argument: Alternative viewing platforms will cause fewer people to watch TV, resulting in lower advertising revenues. The networks then won't have enough money to continue producing high-quality programming, so everyone will lose, even the people who are watching on alternative viewing platforms.

The fourth sentence begins with the word "However." The argument goes on to indicate that technology executives have research that contradicts the network executives' view. The media critic then concludes that the networks can actually *increase* their advertising revenues.

Label each statement C for Conclusion, S for Support, or E for Something Else. (Refer to the Argument Structure questions for a review on this approach.) The first boldface portion opposes the critic's position by predicting smaller audiences; label it E. The second boldface lends support to the critic's conclusion by citing evidence that alternative media platforms lead their users to watch more television; label this one S.

Step 3: State the Goal

The correct answer will first describe an E and then an S. More specifically, it will describe a point of support for the executives' argument, but then a point of support for the media critic's argument.

Step 4: Work from Wrong to Right

(A) The first boldface statement does weigh against the critic's claim, but it is a prediction, rather than an inevitable trend. The second boldface statement is a premise supporting the claim; it is not the conclusion itself.

(B) **CORRECT.** The first boldface statement's prediction about shrinking audiences and falling revenue is counter to the critic's conclusion about a potential increase in network revenue is contrary to the. Also, the critic's argument does depend upon the second boldface statement's assertion that users of alternative devices actually watch more hours of television.

(C) The first boldface statement opposes the critic's claim, rather than clarifies it. The second boldface statement supports the critic's claim; it does not indicate that the critic's claim is flawed.

(D) The argument does not indicate whether the technology executives accept or deny the prediction of the network executives. (Given, though, that the technology executives think that people will watch more television, not less, it doesn't seem likely that the technology executives will agree with the network executives.) The second boldface statement contradicts the first one; it does not follow as a consequence.

(E) The first boldface statement offers a prediction, not an analogy. The second boldface statement is in agreement with, not in opposition to, the critic's claim.

Chapter 6: **Argument-Based Reading Comprehension**

3. **(A):**

   In the last year, real estate prices, such as those for houses and condominiums, have gone up an average of 7 percent in the city of Galway but only 2 percent in the town of Tuam. On the other hand, average rents for apartments have risen 8 percent in Tuam over the last year but only 4 percent in Galway.

   Which of the following is an inference that can be reasonably drawn from the premises given above?

   (A) In the last year, the ratio of average apartment rents to average real estate prices has increased in Tuam but fallen in Galway.

   (B) Tuam has experienced a greater shift in demand toward the rental market than Galway has.

   (C) It has become easier for Galway real estate to be bought and sold, whereas it has become easier for Tuam real estate to be rented.

   (D) The supply of rental apartment units has decreased more in Tuam than in Galway.

   (E) The average amount spent on housing is higher in Galway than it is in Tuam.

Step 1: Identify the Question Type

The word "inference" indicates that this is an Inference question. Expect to see only premises in the argument.

Step 2: Deconstruct the Argument

One set of notes might look like this:

   Past yr: RE $ > 7% in G but 2% in T
        Avg rent > 4% in G but 8% in T

Notice two things. First, the argument gives only percentages, not real numbers; you can't conclude anything that involves real numbers, including which town has higher rents or home prices. Second, rents are increasing at a faster rate in Tuam but home prices are increasing at a faster rate in Galway.

Step 3: State the Goal

What must be true according to the given information?

Unit Two: **Paragraphs and Passages**

Step 4: Work from Wrong to Right

- (A) **CORRECT.** While it isn't possible to conclude anything about real numbers, you can use percentages to determine something about ratios. In Tuam, rents have gone up at a faster rate (8 percent) than have real estate prices (2 percent). Thus, the ratio of average rents to average real estate prices must have grown in that city—the numerator has grown faster than the denominator. In contrast, Galway rents have gone up at a slower rate (4 percent) than real estate prices (7 percent). Thus, the ratio of average rents to average real estate prices has decreased in Galway.

- (B) It's conceivable that a shift in demand towards renting has driven the rise in rent prices in Tuam. But there are other potential explanations as well. (For instance, a decline in the supply of rental units could explain it.) Without more evidence, this can't be inferred.

- (C) Similarly, this might be true but does not have to be. The premises do not indicate whether Galway real estate is easier or harder to be bought and sold or whether Tuam real estate is easier or harder to be rented. The premises simply indicate the growth in prices and rents, which could be for any number of causes.

- (D) Again, it is not necessarily true that the supply of rental units has decreased more in Tuam than in Galway. Just like B and C, this is one possible explanation for the data in the passage. But there is no evidence for this explanation in particular.

- (E) The premises indicate nothing about the actual amounts of money spent in the two towns. You are given only percentage growth rates.

4. **(E):**

Due to the increase in traffic accidents caused by deer in the state, the governor last year reintroduced a longer deer hunting season to encourage recreational hunting of the animals. The governor expected the longer hunting season to decrease the number of deer and therefore decrease the number of accidents. However, this year the number of accidents caused by deer has increased substantially since the reintroduction of the longer deer hunting season.

Which of the following, if true, would best explain the increase in traffic accidents caused by deer?

- (A) Many recreational hunters hunt only once or twice per hunting season, regardless of the length of the season.
- (B) The deer in the state have become accustomed to living in close proximity to humans and are often easy prey for hunters as a result.
- (C) Most automobile accidents involving deer result from cars swerving to avoid deer, and they leave the deer in question unharmed.
- (D) The number of drivers in the state has been gradually increasing over the past several years.
- (E) A heavily used new highway was recently built directly through the state's largest forest, which is the primary habitat of the state's deer population.

Step 1: Identify the Question Type

The words "explain" and "if true" signal that this is a Resolve a Paradox question.

Chapter 6: Argument-Based Reading Comprehension

Step 2: Deconstruct the Argument

Attempting to decrease the number of deer in his state, a governor extended the recreational hunting season. However, despite extending the hunting season, the number of accidents caused by deer has not declined—instead, it has increased substantially.

Step 3: State the Goal

You need to find the answer choice that explains why the accidents have increased rather than decreased as expected. Perhaps another influence is bringing more deer into the region. Perhaps many accidents are caused by deer fleeing the hunters, in which case more hunting could actually lead to more accidents.

Step 4: Work from Wrong to Right

- (A) If the longer hunting season doesn't change the amount of times hunters go hunting, the policy might not be effective at reducing accidents. But, it doesn't explain why the number of accidents would *increase* instead.

- (B) If the deer are "easy prey," then the governor's extension of the hunting season should be *effective* in reducing the deer overpopulation. This does not explain the increase in traffic accidents.

- (C) Careful! This does explain how accidents occur but does not explain why there are more accidents this year, after the governor put in place a plan designed to reduce accidents.

- (D) This answer choice does help to explain why car accidents involving deer might be increasing. However, it does not explain a substantial increase in accidents from just last year to this year. Both the extent of the increase and the time frame serve to make this answer choice an unsatisfactory explanation. It's the closest answer so far, but keep reading.

- (E) **CORRECT.** A new highway system built directly through the deer's primary habitat provides a specific explanation as to why the number of accidents involving deer has increased. More people are driving in the area where deer primarily live. Since the highway was recently built, and would significantly change the amount of interactions between drivers and deer, this is the correct choice.

5. (B):

Political Analyst: After a coalition of states operating under a repressive regime collapsed, some hoped that freedom would bolster the population of the largest state, Algan, but as a result of dislocation and insecurity, the Algan population continues to dwindle at the rate of 700,000 a year. The government proposes to address the problem with a wide range of financial incentives, along with investments in improved healthcare, road safety, and the like. These are positive measures, but **they have been tried before, to little avail**. A better plan to reverse the population decline is to improve Algan's governance in both the public and the private sphere. **If a greater part of the population participated in important decisions and shared in Algan's wealth, then larger families would result.** In addition, if corruption and greed among the elite were curbed, public health would improve, and average life expectancy would increase.

Unit Two: **Paragraphs and Passages**

The two boldfaced statements serve what function in the argument above?

(A) The first is the main point of the analyst's argument; the second is a premise that supports the first.

(B) The first is a premise that undermines an alternative to the analyst's proposal; the second is a premise that supports the analyst's main claim.

(C) The first is a premise that contradicts the main point made by the analyst; the second is the main point of the argument.

(D) The first is a premise that supports a proposal; the second is that proposal.

(E) The first is a conclusion that the argument endorses; the second is a premise that opposes that conclusion.

Step 1: Identify the Question Type

The bold font indicates that this is an Analyze the Argument Structure question. Expect two opposing points of view in the argument. Use the CSE or FCO technique to label the two boldface statements.

Step 2: Deconstruct the Argument

The analyst recounts a proposal by the Algan government to increase the Algan population. The analyst dismisses the plan with the implication that, because the measures have not worked in the past, they will not work now. The analyst then offers a "better plan" (the analyst's conclusion) and offers two premises (the two if-then statements) in support of this better plan.

Step 3: State the Goal

The first boldface statement dismisses the government's plan; as such, it is in support of the analyst's conclusion. Label it with an S. The second boldface directly supports the analyst's proposal; it is also an S.

Step 4: Work from Wrong to Right

(A) The first statement is not itself the main point of the argument, which is to propose a new plan for the state. The second statement is a premise in support of the argument's proposal, not in support of the first statement.

(B) **CORRECT.** The first statement does undermine the alternative proposal made by the government. The second statement does support the analyst's conclusion by showing one way in which better governance might lead to a population increase.

(C) The first statement does not contradict the analyst's conclusion; rather, it undermines the government proposal. The second statement is not the conclusion itself; rather, it supports the conclusion by explaining why, in the analyst's opinion, the new plan would work.

(D) The first statement is a statement *against* the government's proposal, rather than a statement in *support* of a particular proposal. The second bolded statement is arguably part of the author's proposal, but it is not supported by the first bolded statement.

(E) The first statement is not by itself the analyst's conclusion. The second statement is indeed a premise, but it does not oppose the first statement.

Chapter 6: Argument-Based Reading Comprehension

6. (E):

Displayco is marketing a holographic display to supermarkets that shows three-dimensional images of certain packaged goods in the aisles. Displayco's marketing literature states that patrons at supermarkets will be strongly attracted to goods that are promoted in this way, resulting in higher profits for the supermarkets that purchase the displays. Consumer advocates, however, feel that the displays will be intrusive to supermarket patrons and may even increase minor accidents involving shopping carts.

Which of the following, if true, most seriously weakens the position of the consumer advocates?

(A) The holographic displays are expensive to install and maintain.

(B) Many other venues, including shopping malls, are considering adopting holographic displays.

(C) Accidents in supermarkets that are serious enough to cause injury are rare.

(D) Supermarkets tend to be low-margin businesses that struggle to achieve profitability.

(E) Studies in test markets have shown that supermarket patrons quickly become accustomed to holographic displays.

Step 1: Identify the Question Type

This is a Weaken the Conclusion question. Find the conclusion and look for an answer that makes this conclusion at least a little less likely to be valid. Note that the question stem specifically references the conclusion of the "consumer advocates."

Step 2: Deconstruct the Argument

One set of notes might look like this:

D: 3D goods → cust want → > profits
CA: bad, accident

The company, Displayco, points out the potential benefits of its new technology: increased profits for the stores. The advocates, though, point out a possible negative effect: shopping cart accidents. Note that the advocates don't deny that stores will increase their profits; rather, they offer other reasons for avoiding use of the technology. At the very least, then, the advocates assume their concerns outweigh the possible benefits of increased profits.

Step 3: State the Goal

Find an answer that makes the advocates' conclusion less likely to be valid, so an answer that decreases the chance of the displays being intrusive to patrons or causing shopping cart accidents.

Unit Two: **Paragraphs and Passages**

Step 4: Work from Wrong to Right

- (A) This answer choice may weaken Displayco's claim that the stores will have better profits, but it does not weaken the *advocates'* argument. This choice does not influence whether patrons will find the displays intrusive and distracting.

- (B) The potential adoption of holographic displays by other venues does not impact the concerns of consumer advocates that the displays will be intrusive and distracting. It could be the case that holographic displays will be intrusive and distracting in all of these other venues as well. Alternatively, the argument might not apply to other venues where there might not be potential for minor shopping cart accidents.

- (C) This seems true in the real world, so it can be tempting. But the consumer advocates' argument did not claim that the minor accidents would result in injury. Minor accidents can be bothersome to patrons without causing injury.

- (D) While this choice might help Displayco to convince supermarkets to use its product, you were asked to weaken the consumer advocates' concerns. The struggles of supermarkets to achieve profitability is not relevant to the consumer advocates' concerns.

- (E) **CORRECT.** If studies in test markets have shown that patrons quickly become accustomed to holographic displays, then patrons are much less likely to find the displays intrusive after an initial adjustment period. And if patrons become used to the displays, the displays are less likely to increase the frequency of minor shopping cart accidents. Note that this choice does not completely dismiss the advocates' concerns; rather, the concerns are diminished just a little bit.

7. **(A):**

Brand X designs and builds custom sneakers, one sneaker at a time. It recently announced plans to sell "The Gold Standard," a sneaker that will cost five times more to manufacture than any other sneaker that has ever been created.

A prediction that The Gold Standard shoe line will be profitable would require which of the following assumptions?

- (A) At least some consumers would be willing to spend enough money on sneakers to allow Brand X to charge prices for The Gold Standard that would exceed the cost to manufacture the sneaker.

- (B) Of the last four new sneakers that Brand X has released, three have sold at a rate that was higher than projected.

- (C) A rival brand recently declared bankruptcy and ceased manufacturing shoes.

- (D) The market for The Gold Standard will not be more limited than the market for other Brand X shoes.

- (E) The Gold Standard is made using canvas that is more than five times the cost of the canvas used in most sneakers.

Step 1: Identify the Question Type

The question stem asks you to "which of the following assumptions" is required to believe that The Gold Standard shoe line will be profitable. This is best categorized as a Find the Assumption question.

Chapter 6: **Argument-Based Reading Comprehension**

Step 2: Deconstruct the Argument

The passage states only that the costs of manufacturing this shoe are exceptionally high, and does not make a formal argument. In this case, the conclusion is sneakily buried in the question stem itself. The question asks you to analyze "A prediction that The Gold Standard shoe line will be profitable." That prediction is the conclusion.

Step 3: State the Goal

Find an assumption that helps to confirm that The Gold Standard is profitable. What's the missing link between the shoes' high production costs and the prediction that they will be profitable nonetheless? Typically, if costs are exceptionally high, the only way a profit can be made is if revenue is also exceptionally high.

Step 4: Work from Wrong to Right

- (A) **CORRECT.** This answer choice supplies the needed connection to reach the conclusion, namely, a confirmation that the company will receive a high amount of revenue to compensate for their high costs.

- (B) The results of past releases are not necessarily indicative of the case at hand. And while this info might increase your faith in Brand X, it is not required for the conclusion that Brand X has had successful sales in the past.

- (C) One can argue that this is good for Brand X, in that it will mean that there is one less competitor, or that this is bad for Brand X, in that it is indicative of a sagging sneaker market. In either case, there is no direct connection between this rival brand and the potential profitability of The Gold Standard.

- (D) It's possible for The Gold Standard to be profitable regardless of whether its market is larger or smaller than Brand X's other shoe lines. So, this is not a required assumption.

- (E) This helps to explain why the costs might be high, but it does not provide the needed link between high cost and revenue.

8. **(A):**

With information readily available on the internet, consumers now often enter the automobile retail environment with certain models and detailed specifications in mind. In response to this trend, CarStore has decided to move toward a less aggressive sales approach. Despite the fact that members of its sales personnel have an average of 10 years of experience each, CarStore has implemented a mandatory training program for all sales personnel, because _____.

- (A) the sales personnel in CarStore have historically specialized in aggressively selling automobiles and add-on features

- (B) the sales personnel in CarStore do not themselves use the internet when making their own purchase decisions

- (C) CarStore has found that most consumers do not mind negotiating over price

- (D) information found on the internet often does not reflect sales promotions at individual retail locations

- (E) several retailers that compete directly with CarStore have adopted "customer-centered" sales approaches

Unit Two: **Paragraphs and Passages**

Step 1: Identify the Question Type

The word "because" just before the blank signals a possible Strengthen question, but you'll have to read the argument to be sure. The "Despite X, CarStore has implemented Y, because [answer]" structure indicates that this is actually a somewhat less common type: Resolve a Paradox.

Step 2: Deconstruct the Argument

The argument describes CarStore's decision to move toward a less aggressive sales approach in response to consumers coming into the stores with all kinds of information they have already found on the internet. Surprisingly, despite the fact that its sales personnel are very experienced, CarStore is implementing a mandatory training program. Why?

Step 3: State the Goal

Find an answer that explains why CarStore would require its very experienced sales team to go through a mandatory training program.

Step 4: Work from Wrong to Right

- (A) **CORRECT.** If the sales personnel at CarStore have historically specialized in aggressive sales tactics and promoting add-on features, but CarStore wants to move to a less aggressive approach, then the sales team will need to learn new sales tactics. This explains the need for a mandatory retraining program.

- (B) Though it may be helpful for the sales personnel of CarStore to use the internet to research car details so that they can relate to many of their customers, this choice refers to the sales team using the internet to research their own purchases, not necessarily for cars. The mandatory training must have something to do with the job of selling cars, so this choice is not relevant enough to the situation.

- (C) If consumers do not mind negotiating over price, a less aggressive sales approach may not be necessary. This does not resolve the discrepancy, and can even be considered to make the discrepancy more severe.

- (D) Similarly to C, if information found on the internet is often incomplete, it might make it less necessary for CarStore to adopt new tactics in response to the proliferation of online information. Again, if anything this makes the discrepancy more severe.

- (E) What is a "customer-centered" sales approach? This choice might imply that competitors are already using the less aggressive approach, which might help explain why CarStore must adopt it as well. But it does not further explain why even experienced salespeople would need new training.

9. **(A):**

Government restrictions have severely limited the amount of stem cell research that companies in the United States can conduct. Because of these restrictions, many U.S.-based scientists who specialize in the field of stem cell research have signed long-term contracts to work for foreign-based companies. Recently, the U.S. government has proposed lifting all restrictions on stem cell research.

Chapter 6: **Argument-Based Reading Comprehension**

Which of the following statements can most properly be inferred from the information above?

(A) Some foreign-based companies that conduct stem cell research work under fewer restrictions than some U.S.-based companies do.

(B) Because U.S.-based scientists are under long-term contracts to foreign-based companies, there will be a significant influx of foreign professionals into the United States.

(C) In all parts of the world, stem cell research is dependent on the financial backing of local government.

(D) In the near future, U.S.-based companies will no longer be at the forefront of stem cell research.

(E) If restrictions on stem cell research are lifted, many of the U.S.-based scientists will break their contracts and return to U.S.-based companies.

Step 1: Identify the Question Type

The word "inferred" indicates that this is an Inference question type. There won't be a conclusion in the argument.

Step 2: Deconstruct the Argument

Two things have already occurred: the U.S. government has restricted stem cell research for companies in the United States, and U.S.-based scientists in this field have thus chosen to work instead for foreign-based companies. One thing has been proposed: the U.S. government is considering lifting the restrictions on this type of research.

(A) **CORRECT.** If U.S.-based scientists signed contracts with foreign-based companies *specifically because of restrictions* in the United States, then the new companies with which these scientists signed must operate under fewer restrictions. Therefore, at least some foreign companies must work under fewer restrictions than some American companies do.

(B) Even if a significant number of foreign professionals are displaced from their jobs because of the U.S.-based scientists working abroad, there's no guarantee that they would move to the United States to work. In general, avoid inferences that predict the future, unless that future outcome is virtually guaranteed based on the passage.

(C) This passage is about government restrictions in the United States; the source of the financial backing required for stem cell research is out of scope, and it is far too extreme to infer that any aspect of stem cell research is true in all parts of the world.

(D) You are not given any information regarding America's current or future position in terms of stem cell research. Though government restrictions and scientists switching companies could be issues related to a company's prosperity, you are given no information about America's position in stem cell research or how it has been impacted by restrictions.

(E) Though this is a reasonable expectation, it is impossible to conclude for certain that it will happen. Similar to other answers above, do not pick answers that predict a future outcome without specific evidence for it.

Unit Two: **Paragraphs and Passages**

10. **(D):**

    Traditionally, public school instructors have been compensated according to seniority. Recently, the existing salary system has been increasingly criticized as an approach to compensation that rewards lackadaisical teaching and punishes motivated, highly qualified instruction. Instead, educational experts argue that, to retain exceptional teachers and maintain quality instruction, teachers should receive salaries or bonuses based on performance rather than seniority.

    Which of the following, if true, most weakens the conclusion of the educational experts?

    (A) Some teachers express that financial compensation is not the only factor contributing to job satisfaction and teaching performance.

    (B) School districts will develop their own unique compensation structures that may differ greatly from those of other school districts.

    (C) Upon leaving the teaching profession, many young, effective teachers cite a lack of opportunity for more rapid financial advancement as a primary factor in the decision to change careers.

    (D) A merit-based system that bases compensation on teacher performance reduces collaboration, which is an integral component of quality instruction.

    (E) In school districts that have implemented pay for performance compensation structures, standardized test scores have dramatically increased.

Step 1: Identify the Question Type

The words "weaken" and "if true" indicate that this is a Weaken the Conclusion question. Look for the conclusion made by the "educational experts."

Step 2: Deconstruct the Argument

The argument is concerned with how public school teachers are compensated. According to the argument, educational experts claim that a system of teacher compensation based on performance rather than seniority would help to retain exceptional teachers and maintain quality instruction.

What are the experts assuming? Can "performance" actually be measured in a meaningful way? Should it be based on how much the students like the teacher? A fun but incompetent teacher might be beloved by students. A challenging teacher might receive lower teacher ratings even though their students learn more.

Step 3: State the Goal

The correct answer to this Weaken question will make the experts' conclusion at least a little less likely to be valid. Look for something that will make the performance-based salary system less likely to improve teacher retention and quality instruction.

Step 4: Work from Wrong to Right

(A) ?. The fact that other factors also contribute to job satisfaction and teaching performance neither weakens nor strengthens this argument. Either way, the teachers are getting paid; the issue is whether that pay should be based on performance or seniority.

(B) ?. Nothing in the argument indicates that one universal system of compensation must be adopted in order to implement this plan. It is very possible that several effective models of performance-based pay could be developed and implemented successfully.

(C) X. This choice indicates that many young, effective teachers are extremely frustrated by the traditional pay structure, in which financial advancement is directly tied to seniority. This bolsters the experts' argument: these young but effective teachers who are leaving the profession might stay longer if they had better opportunity for advancement based on performance.

(D) **CORRECT.** Weaken. This choice indicates that collaboration among teachers is integral to high-quality instruction and that a system of compensation based on teacher performance reduces collaboration. Thus, the effect of a merit-based system of pay might undermine quality instruction, which is one of the two stated goals of the educational experts.

(E) X. The educational experts' argument in favor of performance-based compensation is bolstered, not weakened, if standardized test scores have dramatically risen in school districts that have instituted such pay structures.

CHAPTER 7
Multi-Blank Text Completion

In This Chapter...

- Two- and Three-Blank Text Completions
- Start with the Easier (or Easiest) Blank
- Tricky Aspects of Multi-Blank Text Completion
- More on Traps in Text Completion
- Vocabulary Challenge
- Problem Set
- Answers and Explanations

Chapter 7 Multi-Blank Text Completion

Multi-blank Text Completion questions will build on your one-blank Text Completion skills, requiring you to adapt those skills to questions that often contain multiple sentences and less concrete truth. In this chapter, you will learn the similarities and differences between multi-blank Text Completion questions and their one-blank counterparts, as well as strategies to handle these more complicated questions effectively.

Here are your Chapter 7 vocabulary words:

>discrete (A)
>apposite (A)
>paucity (E)
>prohibitive (E)
>reticent (E)
>nettled (A)

Two- and Three-Blank Text Completions

Roughly half of the Text Completion questions that appear at the beginning of every GRE Verbal section will have more than one blank. Consider the following example:

>In the twentieth century, the United States witnessed a nearly (i) _____ ascent to ever greater wealth, leaving its leaders (ii) _____ of publicly acknowledging budgetary limitations.

Blank (i)		Blank (ii)	
A	portentous	D	chary
B	pertinacious	E	capable
C	unremitting	F	guilty

In sentences with multiple blanks, the blanks themselves and the answer choices are labeled with lowercase Roman numerals.

Below the sentence, the first column contains the choices—*portentous, pertinacious,* and *unremitting*—for the first blank. The second column contains the choices—*chary, capable,* and *guilty*—for the second blank.

Your choice for the first blank is independent of your choice for the second blank. That is, if you correctly choose *unremitting* for the first blank, you are not simultaneously choosing *guilty* for the second blank. You must instead make a discrete decision for the second blank. In addition, *there is no partial credit.* You must get both words right or you receive no credit for your response. Fortunately, this fact is somewhat offset by the fact that, for each blank, there are only three options rather than five.

Unit Two: **Paragraphs and Passages**

The baseline approach to multi-blank Text Completion, as it was for one-blank Text Completion, is to **use proof from the sentence to predict answers for the blank**. However, there are a few ways in which making predictions for multi-blank questions can play out differently:

- Two- and especially three-blank TC questions often consist of multiple sentences, and a blank that appears in one sentence can rely on proof from another sentence.
- Similarly, a prediction you're able make for one blank will often serve as proof for the other blank.
- Because there are often multiple sentences, pronouns (*this*, *these*, *that*, *it*, *they*, etc.) and transition words will be frequently used to reference ideas brought up in previous sentences. Think of these as additions to your list of direction markers. For more on these words and how they inform an understanding of paragraphs, see Chapter 4: Signals and Pronouns.
- The presence of multiple blanks leaves less room for concrete truth, making it sometimes difficult to come up with specific predictions for the blanks.

One more pleasant feature of two-blank and three-blank problems is that, while they may *seem* harder because they are generally longer, there are often more clues for you to use. Also, having multiple blanks means you get to choose which blank to tackle first. . .and some blanks are easier to predict for than others.

Start with the Easier (or Easiest) Blank

Don't force a prediction for the first blank simply because it comes first. Read the entire prompt first, consider all of the blanks, and figure out which one has the clearest proof. Write down your prediction for that blank, and use that prediction as extra proof for the harder blank(s).

An Example with Two Blanks

Take a look at this example:

> Even seasoned opera singers can be (i) _____ performing in Rome, where audiences traditionally view (ii) _____ performers as a birthright, passed down from heckler to heckler over generations.

Blank #2 is easier. Why? Compare the proof for each blank:

	Content Clues and Direction Markers	**Interpretation**
Blank (i)	*Even seasoned opera singers* *Performing in Rome*	The blank focuses on how *opera singers* can feel when performing in Rome, but the only thing you know about those opera singers so far is that they're *seasoned*. *Even* is a reversal marker in most cases, so the blank should in some way contradict *seasoned*, but *novices* probably doesn't seem like a great fit. Read on.
Blank (ii)	*a birthright, passed down from heckler to heckler over generations*	Whatever goes in this blank is seen as a *birthright* and is therefore linked to the *generations* of hecklers referenced in the last part of the sentence. This is significantly more concrete proof than was given for the first blank, and it supports a prediction like <u>heckling</u>.

This sentence offers more definitive proof for the second blank than for the first blank, so start your prediction process there. With that prediction in hand, making a prediction for the first blank becomes more feasible. The blank describes how opera singers feel about performing in Rome, and the only information you have about Rome is that performers get heckled there. Therefore, it's most likely the case that the opera singers are <u>nervous about</u> appearing there.

Your paper might now look like this: nervous about. . .heckling

On your paper, draw a grid to keep track of your take on the answer choices for both blanks:

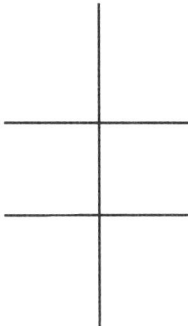

Or, if you prefer, write:

    A   D
    B   E
    C   F

Finally, compare your predictions to the answer choices and mark your paper:

Blank (i)			Blank (ii)	
A	intrepid about	D	extolling
B	daunted by	E	lionizing
C	tempered by	F	badgering

Here is an example of what a student might have written down for this question. In this scenario, the student wasn't sure about *tempered by* and didn't know exactly about *lionizing* but felt that it wasn't quite right.

    nervous about   heckling

    ✗ | ✗
    ✓ | ~
    ? | ✓

This student would pick *daunted by* and *badgering*, which are the correct responses.

Unit Two: **Paragraphs and Passages**

> *Strategy Tip:*
> Some blanks will be harder to predict for than others. Predict for easier blanks first, and you'll have more concrete proof to use to determine the harder blanks.

An Example with Three Blanks

Take a look at the following three-blank TC question and try to identify the easiest blank:

> Perceptions of the (i) _____ role of intellectual practices within modern life underlie the familiar stereotypes of the educated as self-appointed elites in ivory towers. This mischaracterization may be rooted in a (ii) _____ of the aims of academia, but it is unlikely to be (iii) _____ unless teachers take efforts to address it directly.

Blank (i)		Blank (ii)		Blank (iii)	
A	incongruous	D	dissemination	G	espoused
B	refractory	E	confounding	H	dispelled
C	salubrious	F	corroboration	I	promulgated

While this problem has three blanks instead of two and is made up of more than one sentence, the method is largely the same: Start with the easiest blank. The easiest blank is often the one surrounded by the most text—that is, the one that is farthest from the other two blanks and thus has the most potential proof located near it. Here, the first blank seems promising:

> Perceptions of the (i) _____ role of intellectual practices within modern life underlie the familiar stereotypes of the educated as self-appointed elites in ivory towers.

The blank describes the *role of intellectual practices*, which underlies stereotypes about *self-appointed elites in ivory towers*. So the word describing the role should be related to the idea that intellectuals are perceived as separate from the majority of those in *modern life*. A good prediction for Blank (i) would be disconnected.

The second sentence references this perception of intellectuals and then seeks to explain the root cause. It's clear from *This* that the narrator is calling back to the situation described in the first sentence, and *mischaracterization* makes it clear that the narrator of this sentence believes that the take on intellectuals presented there is incorrect. As *the aims of academia* is also a reference to intellectuals, the best prediction for Blank (ii) would be misunderstanding or mischaracterization. (You can recycle wording from elsewhere in the sentences where apposite.)

The last part of the problem has a couple of reversal markers in *unlikely* and *unless*. Break it down into individual parts, taking care with the markers and substituting actual nouns in for reference language:

> *If* teachers *don't* address it (the *mischaracterization*) directly . . .
>
> . . . the mischaracterization will continue . . . (reasonable inference)
>
> . . . *so* the mischaracterization is *unlikely* to be ended.

7

204

Chapter 7: **Multi-Blank Text Completion**

On your paper, you might have:

        disconnected   misunderstanding   ended

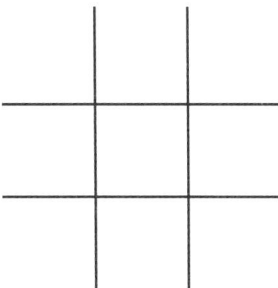

Or, if you prefer:

disconnected	misunderstanding	ended
A	D	G
B	E	H
C	F	I

Consider your choices and mark your paper appropriately:

Blank (i)

A	incongruous
B	refractory
C	salubrious

Blank (ii)

D	dissemination
E	confounding
F	corroboration

Blank (iii)

G	espoused
H	dispelled
I	promulgated

Your notes for this question might look like this:

disconnected	misunderstanding	ended
✓	✗	~
?	✓	✓
✗	✗	✗

The correct answer is *incongruous*, *confounding*, and *dispelled*.

Unit Two: **Paragraphs and Passages**

Tricky Aspects of Multi-Blank Text Completion

This section will cover a few ways the GRE can up the difficulty level further on multi-blank text completion. Many of these *can* occur on single-blank questions, but are more likely to occur in longer sentences or full paragraphs, and therefore more likely in multi-blank questions.

Phrases in the Blanks

Double-blank and triple-blank questions can sometimes have choices that are phrases rather than single words. These questions tend to be less about knowing difficult vocabulary words than about being able to work out the meaning of the sentence(s).

Try this question:

(i) _____ subject of the sermon, her words possessed a (ii) _____ quality few could fail to find utterly enchanting. It was only when her conclusion devolved into (iii) _____ that the congregation began to fantasize about returning to the comfort of home.

	Blank (i)		Blank (ii)		Blank (iii)
A	In spite of the insipid	D	euphonious	G	a fallacious slew of prevarications
B	Notwithstanding the salubrious	E	euphemistic	H	an unending string of digressions
C	Because of the inauspicious	F	eulogistic	I	a sanctified series of assignations

Attack the easiest blank first. That might be the last one, since it's the only blank in its sentence. And indeed, the sentence provides clues: The sermon's conclusion *devolved into* whatever goes in the blank, and *the congregation began to fantasize about returning to the comfort of home*. Both bits of proof tell you that the sermon went off track in some way, but it's unclear exactly how. Rather than add to the story, for now keep your prediction appropriately vague, along the lines of <u>something bad</u>.

Now that you have mentally completed the last sentence, it might help to paraphrase it before using the information to work backward and analyze the rest of the sentence: *It was only when the conclusion went bad that the people wanted to leave*. The phrase *It was only when* serves as a reversal, signaling that before things went bad, they must have been pretty good, which in turn means that the first sentence must be describing the sermon favorably. That's backed up by the *utterly enchanting* at the end of the sentence, though due to the reversal markers (in bold below), some untangling will still be useful here:

Her words possess <u>some kind</u> of quality.

Few could *fail* to find this quality enchanting.

If many could *fail* to find this quality enchanting, her words would possess a <u>bad</u> quality . . .

. . . so if *few* could *fail*, her words must possess a <u>good</u> quality.

The second blank should be something good; recycle the word <u>enchanting</u>.

Finally, come to the first blank. It's pretty hard to fill in this one without glancing at the answer choices, but at least try to figure out a general category of what you'll be looking for. Whatever goes in this blank is

Chapter 7: **Multi-Blank Text Completion**

about the *subject of the sermon*, and this whole part is followed by something nice about the words used in the sermon. These two parts of the sentence will go either in the same direction (that is, the *subject of the sermon* will also be *enchanting*) or in an opposite direction (that is, the *subject of the sermon* will be unenchanting even though the *words* themselves were *enchanting*).

You might have something like this on your paper:

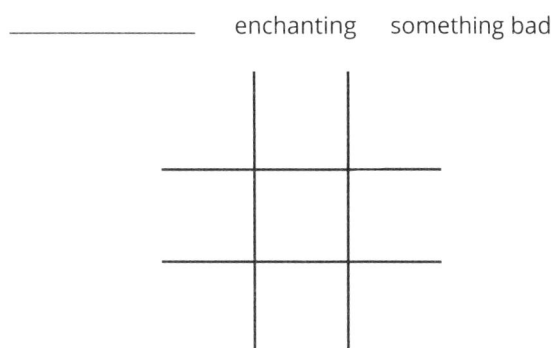

Now go to the choices, proceeding in order from the blank for which you have the clearest prediction to the blank for which you have the least clear prediction.

In Blank (ii), only *euphonious* works. The root *eu* means "good," but that's not too helpful here, since all three words use that root. However, *euphemistic* (substituting inoffensive words in for more explicit or hurtful ones) doesn't make sense, and *eulogistic* (full of praise, especially for a deceased person) also doesn't match the idea of *enchanting*. Bonus points if you recognized that *eulogistic* was a theme trap, as a *eulogy* is something that a sermonizer would likely deliver in other circumstances.

For Blank (iii), the third choice includes *sanctified*, a theme trap meaning "holy," and *assignations*, which are romantic meetups, so it's definitely out. However, the other two answer choices both offer something bad. At this point, rephrase each of those answer choices into simpler terms and consider which is a better fit for the content clues in the sentence. *A fallacious slew of prevarications* is basically a bunch of lies, and *an unending string of digressions* is a bunch of tangents. The question to resolve is which one would more likely lead people to *fantasize about returning to the comfort of home*. It can be helpful to imagine yourself in both situations and think of how you might react. A sermon that descends into a bunch of lies would probably provoke a more extreme or specific reaction than simply fantasizing about going home. On the other hand, a sermon that descends into a bunch of tangents would likely cause some impatience, which in turn could plausibly lead to fantasizing about going home. Go with *an unending string of digressions*.

The choices for Blank (i) require a bit more analysis in that they all contain direction markers. The first two choices contain the reversal markers *In spite of* and *Notwithstanding*, so for them to be right, they would have to contain a word that contrasts *euphonious*, the choice for Blank (ii). *In spite of the insipid* makes sense, as *insipid* is a good contrast for *euphonious* and *enchanting*. By contrast, *Notwithstanding the salubrious* doesn't work because *salubrious* (healthy) is a good thing, making it a poor contrast for the second part of the sentence. The third choice starts with *Because of*, a straight-ahead marker, but *inauspicious* (unfavorable) is a bad thing, making this choice incongruous with the second part of the sentence as well. Only *In spite of the insipid* works.

The answer is *In spite of the insipid, euphonious*, and *an unending string of digressions*.

Unit Two: **Paragraphs and Passages**

> *Strategy Tip:*
>
> When a blank won't yield to attempts at prediction, settle for a vague prediction (i.e., *something good / something bad*) and let the answer choices carry you the rest of the way.

Heavy Use of Markers

Take a look at this example:

> Although Paula claimed not to be (i) _____ that she was not selected for the scholarship, we nevertheless worried that our typically sanguine friend was not entirely (ii) _____ by the decision.

This sentence is just chock-full of switchbacks. Count the reversal signals: "Although . . . not . . . nevertheless . . . typically . . . not entirely . . ."

It's easy to lose your way in a thicket of reversals, especially under exam pressure. How many wrongs make a right?

The familiar process of chopping up the sentence and processing it in small chunks works well in these cases, even if there are multiple blanks. As always, start with the most concrete part of the story—a thing that actually happened. Then add one chunk of the sentence at a time to the story. Change complicated reversals and other signals to simple words, such as *but* and *so*.

As you go, emotionally punctuate each part of the story. Exaggerate the switchbacks in your mental voice, as if you were telling a story you really cared about. Finally, as you think about the whole, discard unnecessary elements so that you don't have to hold everything in your head at once.

For the previous example sentence, the breakdown might go like this:

> Our friend Paula is *typically* sanguine (optimistic).
>
> She was not selected for a scholarship.
>
> She was probably unhappy about this. (reasonable inference)
>
> She claimed NOT to be <u>something</u>.
>
> *But* we still worried that
>
> she was NOT entirely <u>something</u> by the decision.

Something like <u>unhappy</u> would be appropriate for the first blank and <u>pleased</u> would work for the second.

It looks like a lot of work, but with practice, your brain can generate this train of thought in seconds; by contrast, keeping the sentence in its original form makes it a lot harder to understand.

Now break down a few more challenging sentence types.

Not Enough Concrete Proof

Sometimes the GRE will construct sentences in such a way as to make predicting specific words for the blanks particularly difficult. This is most common in two-blank Text Completions, in which a paucity of proof is not necessarily prohibitive to success. In problems that don't give you enough information to predict specific answers, **predict the relationship between the blanks instead**. Consider the following example:

> No one expected Salazar to (i) _____, given his long track record of (ii) _____.

Despite the fact that this sentence is relatively simple, it's impossible to make a specific prediction for either of the blanks. For instance, the first blank could be fail if the second blank were success, but the correct pairing could just as easily be eat and fasting, speak and reticence, fly and not flying, or a thousand other things. In these cases, the best thing to do is to predict a relationship between the blanks. The second half of the sentence points to Salazar's long track record of something, and this track record is presented as a reason that *no one expected* something else. It makes sense that the two blanks would be opposites. And while that might not seem like a lot to go on, in such cases the GRE will provide only one set of opposites in the answer choices.

Unfamiliar Style or Content

The GRE uses uncommon constructions and unfamiliar topics in TC in much the same way that it does in Reading Comprehension. Consider the following example:

> That such a _____ of precedent would be countenanced was itself unprecedented in the court, a bastion of traditionalism.

The sentence starts with a *that* clause, a hallmark of a very academic writing style. If that sounds weird (and it probably does), add in *The fact* to make "The fact that such a _____ of precedent..."

Also, the content is about a legal matter. Add in the difficult vocabulary (*precedent, countenanced, bastion*), and it's no wonder that the sentence is forbidding.

In these cases, **swap in simpler words and phrases**.

The meaning of the sentence is something like, *The fact that such a _____ of previously established examples would be tolerated was a brand-new and surprising instance of a very traditional court going against tradition.*

A good prediction here would be something like *rejection*.

Red Herring Clues

A red herring is something that seems to offer a nice bit of proof but is actually only there to confuse you. Such traps occasionally appear on Text Completion questions, so be careful that all the proof you're using is *actually* proof.

(Fun fact: "Red herring" is an expression for something that seems like it's going to be important, but turns out to be just a distraction. The expression arose when criminals starred rubbing herring—a type of fish—on trails to distract the hunting dogs chasing after them. Okay, back to the GRE!)

> By (i) _____ observing social behavior, anthropologists (ii) _____ strict, though implicit, codes of conduct.

Unit Two: Paragraphs and Passages

Here, the word *strict*, despite its propinquity to the second blank, turns out to be less important to the meaning of that blank than *implicit*. Decoy answers for the second blank might be *follow* or *denounce*—that is, they might try to give you plausible options for how the *anthropologists* in question could react to *strict codes of conduct*. Such answers would represent story traps, however, as none of the proof elsewhere in the sentence provides any indication of how the *anthropologists* feel about *strict codes of conduct*.

By contrast, the *implicit* (hinted at or unspoken) nature of the behavior is more germane to the overall meaning of the sentence because the first part of the sentence deals with *observing social behavior*, a prospect that's definitely more complicated if the behavior is *implicit* (but has no clear relationship to the strictness of the behavior). Indeed, the implicit nature of this behavior would require assiduous observation to detect. A good prediction word for the first blank would be <u>assiduously</u>.

You may find that even with a solid prediction in hand for the first blank, the second blank is hard to make a specific prediction for. This will often be the case when the blanks represent verbs. Given the central role verbs play in sentences, it can be difficult to get a handle on a sentence's intended meaning when the sentence lacks a verb. In these cases, rely on the answer choices to help supply clarity to the sentence.

> *Strategy Tip:*
> When sentences get tricky, break them into smaller, easier to understand chunks—even if you end up needing *a lot* of chunks.
>
> If a sentence is still too abstruse to make specific predictions, **predict the relationship between the blanks** or **cheat off the answer choices**.

More on Traps in Text Completion

The previous section examined some aspects of Text Completion that can make it difficult to interpret the sentence's meaning and make predictions for the blanks. This section goes into more depth on some of the most common traps among answer choices. For a more exhaustive list of the traps that will appear in fill-in-the-blank questions on the GRE, see Chapter 3: Traps in TC and SE.

Theme Trap

This trap has already appeared in a few examples, but here it takes center stage. Give the following problem a try:

> The event horizon (or boundary) of a black hole represents both (i)_____ and intangibility; space travelers would pass through this literal "point of no return" so (ii)_____ that the precise moment at which their fate was sealed would almost certainly not be registered.

	Blank (i)		Blank (ii)
A	constellation	D	indiscernibly
B	irrevocability	E	universally
C	infallibility	F	cosmically

Which is the easier blank? Most would agree that the second blank is easier. A good part of the proof is that *the precise moment...would certainly not be registered*, and the lack of any signal to the contrary tells you that your prediction should agree with that proof. So you might fill in something like <u>without registering</u> (again, recycling language from the sentence itself).

Now turn to the first blank. It's directly connected to the *event horizon of a black hole*, and it's something different from *intangibility*. That's not a lot to go on. Luckily, the second part of the sentence contains a more complete description of the *event horizon*, referencing it as *this literal "point of no return"* and focusing on how a space travelers' fate would be sealed as they passed through. Because *intangibility* isn't related to this later information about the event horizon, it's likely that whatever goes in the first blank *is* related to that description. A good prediction might be <u>no return</u> or <u>unreturnability</u>. (It's totally fine to make up your own words when predicting an answer—as long as your prediction makes sense to you.)

Now match your predictions to the answer choices. Only *indiscernibly* fits *without registering* for Blank (ii), and only *irrevocability* fits *no return*, making this pair of answers correct.

A **theme trap** is an answer choice that shares a theme or field (such as medicine, sports, etc.) with the sentence. Since you naturally associate the trap word with the subject matter of the sentence, the choice sounds okay on its own and somehow seems to make sense in the sentence, even though it doesn't really fit with the proof for the blanks.

Notice the trap language in the choices: *constellation, universally, cosmically*. Like the sentence itself, these words all relate to space, but they have no actual relation to the meanings that the proof for the blanks demands. Be disciplined and follow the strategy every time, and you'll avoid traps like this.

Close But Not Close Enough Trap

Like theme traps, these appear in the answer choices, especially when the correct answer is a word that the GRE knows will be unfamiliar to most test-takers. Try this problem:

Marie was nettled by her sister's constant jocularity and preferred a(n) _____ approach to life.

A	miserable
B	indignant
C	waggish
D	staid
E	sycophantic

It may have been pretty straightforward for you to identify the proof (*nettled, jocularity,* and *preferred* all play a part) and see that Marie is against *constant jocularity*, or joking behavior. A safe prediction might be <u>serious</u>.

Now go through the answer choices. *Miserable* and *indignant* both have the negative inflection we're looking for, but they're not great matches for serious, and they might be too extreme. Just because Marie doesn't like her sister's constant joking, that doesn't mean she's *miserable* or *indignant* in her outlook on life. Perhaps you don't know what *waggish* or *staid* mean, and you don't totally remember *sycophantic* either, but you're sure it doesn't mean *serious*.

Unit Two: **Paragraphs and Passages**

So your paper might look like this:

serious

A ∼

B ∼

C ?

D ?

E ✗

The **close but not close enough trap** occurs when a wrong answer choice is in the ballpark of what you want but slightly off the mark in its meaning, connotation, degree, or usage. This trap is at its most dangerous when the trap answer is familiar and the correct answer is unfamiliar.

In the sentence above, while you may not love *miserable* or *indignant*, the total unfamiliarity of the words in answers (C) and (D) can make you loath to choose them. Overcome this reluctance. If your prediction is based on clear proof in the sentence, the GRE will give you an answer that fits it; you shouldn't have to stretch an answer to make it work. Here, as it turns out, the correct answer is *staid*, which means "serious; sedate by temperament or habits." This is a better counterpoint to *jocularity* than either *miserable* or *indignant*.

It takes confidence to pick a word you don't know! To build that confidence, when you review your work on TC questions, keep track of problems on which you fall for a close but not close enough trap and should have picked the unfamiliar word instead. Use those questions to calibrate your sensitivity to these traps and bolster your confidence in picking a mystery word.

> *Strategy Tip:*
>
> Even the most pernicious traps can be avoided by making proof-based predictions and sticking to them. Pay attention to these traps as you study Text Completion and Sentence Equivalence, and make a special note of it when you fall into one. Knowing which traps you're susceptible to can help obviate those traps in the future.

Vocabulary Challenge

> Did you spot these vocabulary words? If not, go back and find them in context! (The word may be in a different form than listed here— "digressing" instead of "digress," for example.) Write your own definitions based on the evidence in the chapter.

1. discrete (*adj.*), p. 201

2. apposite (*adj.*), p. 204

3. paucity (*n*), p. 209

4. prohibitive (*adj.*), p. 209

5. reticent (*adj.*), p. 209

6. nettle (*v*), p. 211

Chapter 7: **Multi-Blank Text Completion**

Problem Set

As you do these questions, look for the proof, and start from the easier (or easiest) blank. Write down your own predictions, write out the letters A B C or make a grid, and use process of elimination.

That said, specific predictions are often harder to come by in multi-blank Text Completions. If you find it difficult to come up with a fill-in for a blank, try to guess its spin or its relationship to other blanks in the problem, and then proceed to the answer choices. Eliminate answers that don't agree with the proof in the sentence; choose those with the strongest connections to the proof.

As always, look up any unfamiliar words as you review the questions and add them to your vocabulary list.

1. Richardson's (i) _____ handling of the (ii) _____ scandal successfully prevented what seemed poised to become the ruination of her coalition.

Blank (i)		Blank (ii)	
A	penitent	D	fretful
B	adroit	E	looming
C	heterogeneous	F	ecumenical

2. The (i) _____ forces were just barely held at bay by a loyalist battalion (ii) _____ by its allies' reinforcements.

Blank (i)		Blank (ii)	
A	revolting	D	obviated
B	outclassed	E	bolstered
C	fascistic	F	sapped

3. (i) _____ by circumstance, the entrepreneur once known for his overweening (ii) _____ was now seen by others as the possessor of a broken spirit and timid demeanor.

Blank (i)		Blank (ii)	
A	Unaffected	D	pretension
B	Humbled	E	liberality
C	Exalted	F	wealth

4. Though he had been largely successful in his attempts to adopt a more (i) _____ lifestyle, he was not above occasionally indulging his proclivities for (ii) _____ dishes.

Blank (i)		Blank (ii)	
A	truculent	D	odious
B	salutary	E	sodden
C	frugal	F	unwholesome

Unit Two: Paragraphs and Passages

5. The discovery that exposure to allergens through the mother's diet during the last trimester could lead to complications during the first year after birth (i) _____ the U.K. Department of Health to (ii) _____ dietary recommendations for expecting mothers.

Blank (i)		Blank (ii)	
A	prompted	D	intuit
B	instigated	E	codify
C	lulled	F	officiate

6. Fearful of being seen as (i) _____, the Bieber Appreciation Society took pains to include (ii) _____ voices in its monthly newsletter.

Blank (i)		Blank (ii)	
A	enthusiasts	D	tantamount
B	detractors	E	critical
C	toadies	F	conciliatory

7. The fact that bringing together criminals and their victims for a moderated conversation has been shown to vastly reduce rates of (i) _____ might be explained by the fact that those who commit crimes can only do so by convincing themselves their actions have no (ii) _____.

Blank (i)		Blank (ii)	
A	violence	D	inconsistencies
B	recidivism	E	aberrations
C	malfeasance	F	ramifications

8. The (i) _____ of monks and abbots in Eastern Christianity were typically of plain black modest cloth, indicating their spiritual indifference to matters of this world in favor of a commitment to a (ii) _____ mindset. In this regard, the contrast with the (iii) _____ garments of Buddhist monks is striking.

Blank (i)		Blank (ii)		Blank (iii)	
A	vestiges	D	mundane	G	iridescent
B	habiliments	E	dogmatic	H	drab
C	paragons	F	transcendent	I	flowing

9. In many criminal trials, it emerges that the defendant (i) _____ some kind of abuse as a child. However, these biographical revelations should not have any effect on how the jury apportions (ii) _____. An excuse is not a justification, and the criminal justice system wasn't constructed to help balance the (iii) _____ of someone's life.

Blank (i)		Blank (ii)		Blank (iii)	
A	appreciated	D	culpability	G	ledger
B	exploited	E	history	H	imprisonment
C	suffered	F	insanity	I	verdict

Chapter 7: Multi-Blank Text Completion

10. The university president argued that top universities should not (i) _____ education as an academic (ii) _____; discouraging our brightest students from pursuing teaching careers does a disservice to the next generation of students by (iii) _____ them of the opportunity to learn from the cream of the crop.

	Blank (i)		Blank (ii)		Blank (iii)
A	disdain	D	recommendation	G	denigrating
B	proscribe	E	tome	H	degenerating
C	circumvent	F	discipline	I	divesting

11. Seeing its only alternative to be a (i) _____ diplomacy unbecoming of political visionaries—as members of the so-called National Liberation Organization saw themselves in those days—the militant branch veered toward a policy of (ii) _____ aggression against its perceived rivals.

	Blank (i)		Blank (ii)
A	wheedling	D	supine
B	freewheeling	E	unremitting
C	verdant	F	superfluous

12. A (i) _____ ran through the crowd of protesters chanting slogans and threats when the queen made the sudden announcement—only a fortnight after vowing not to give in to the popular demands for her departure—that she would abdicate the throne, (ii) _____ a period of disorder and confusion.

	Blank (i)		Blank (ii)
A	frisson	D	marring
B	murmur	E	precipitating
C	panegyric	F	diluting

13. A perfectionist in all things, Joseph expected to immediately become a (i) _____ and was downtrodden indeed when he remained (ii) _____ despite his best efforts.

	Blank (i)		Blank (ii)
A	hack	D	novel
B	musician	E	inane
C	virtuoso	F	inept

14. (i) _____ is unlikely to be an asset to someone (ii) _____ by liars and fabulists.

	Blank (i)		Blank (ii)
A	Credulity	D	forsaken
B	Duplicity	E	brooked
C	Ingenuity	F	beset

Unit Two: **Paragraphs and Passages**

15. While she was known to all her friends as quite the (i) _____, legendary for humorous stories from her years spent driving a taxi, her private behavior belied this (ii) _____ image.

Blank (i)	
A	sage
B	prevaricator
C	raconteur

Blank (ii)	
D	belligerent
E	pedantic
F	genial

16. The common opinion at the court had it that her droll utterances as often as not (i) _____ attitudes unbecoming of a lady. This reputation cost her the attentions of some gentlemen, above all thanks to their fear of being bested by her (ii) _____.

Blank (i)	
A	eluded
B	derided
C	evinced

Blank (ii)	
D	subtlety
E	doggerel
F	repartee

17. While courage is anything but unimportant—and his character is indeed (i) _____—a cartoon mouse with a (ii) _____ for excessive violence is hardly an appropriate mascot for a children's charity.

Blank (i)	
A	mettlesome
B	impetuous
C	heady

Blank (ii)	
D	penchant
E	kinship
F	largess

18. The double-dealing ambassador's political (i) _____ and backpedaling looked all the worse when compared to the (ii) _____ straightforwardness of his Australian counterpart.

Blank (i)	
A	plutocracy
B	bugaboo
C	sleight of hand

Blank (ii)	
D	occlusive
E	ostensible
F	intransigent

19. The most (i) _____ puzzle was in determining how to deliver the antisense strand to the right place at the right moment, after the virus had penetrated the cell but before it had replicated and escaped to infect other cells. To accomplish this, the synthetic strand had to be potent enough to be effective and to resist rapid (ii) _____ inside the body, allowing it time to accomplish its task.

Blank (i)	
A	recalcitrant
B	pedestrian
C	monolithic

Blank (ii)	
D	desiccation
E	degradation
F	compunction

Chapter 7: **Multi-Blank Text Completion**

20. The Russo-Turkish War (i) _____ Albanians, placing before them the (ii) _____ prospect of a division of their lands among competing powers. This, above all, served to bring Albanian nationalism surging out of its former (iii) _____, culminating in a successful bid for independence only a few decades later.

	Blank (i)		Blank (ii)		Blank (iii)
A	rankled	D	evanescent	G	latency
B	enervated	E	pernicious	H	insularity
C	debased	F	transient	I	lucidity

21. Though she acknowledges that modern farming practices are more (i) _____ than traditional agriculture, she nonetheless argues that this difference represents no real (ii) _____. Perhaps more worrying, however, is her insistence that similar claims can be advanced regarding the treatment of farmers by an often (iii) _____ social hierarchy.

	Blank (i)		Blank (ii)		Blank (iii)
A	expensive	D	progress	G	iniquitous
B	efficient	E	disincentive	H	halcyon
C	polluting	F	countermand	I	stratified

22. The (i) _____ of the word *assassin* is (ii) _____ in philological circles, as the word comes from a sect of brutal killers believed to have smoked the drug hashish before going on a mission. The topic is equally attractive to historians, as the (iii) _____ of the sect, which dates to before the First Crusade in the 11th century, remains a mystery.

	Blank (i)		Blank (ii)		Blank (iii)
A	introduction	D	notorious	G	provenance
B	derivation	E	unheralded	H	legend
C	circumlocution	F	enigmatic	I	bane

23. Statistics often need to be (i) _____ for their real meaning: In the last decade, while both the population and the amount of meat eaten annually in the nation remained (ii) _____, the growing gap between rich and poor meant that the wealthy few were eating more meat than ever while the masses suffered from a (iii) _____ of foodstuffs of all kinds.

	Blank (i)		Blank (ii)		Blank (iii)
A	plumbed	D	plastic	G	deceleration
B	calculated	E	static	H	dearth
C	designed	F	demographic	I	glut

Unit Two: **Paragraphs and Passages**

24. Although Cage supported the expanded reliance on electronically produced (i) _____, most of his early music is surprisingly (ii) _____. His "Music for Marcel Duchamp," a prepared-piano work from 1947, never rises above mezzo-piano, offering instead (iii) _____ melody that maintains its softness throughout.

	Blank (i)		Blank (ii)		Blank (iii)
A	timbre	D	strident	G	a noisome
B	murmur	E	auspicious	H	an undulating
C	clangor	F	subdued	I	an erstwhile

25. The tokens given by the aristocrat, while (i) _____, still served as a reminder that the power of the Crown continued to be held in some esteem even in such (ii) _____ political times.

	Blank (i)		Blank (ii)
A	sardonic	D	mercurial
B	nugatory	E	jocund
C	sumptuous	F	magisterial

26. Having built up to a (i) _____, the shelling stopped as suddenly as it had begun; gazing at the drooping barrels of the artillery, one might be forgiven for thinking they were rendered (ii) _____ by the pathetic sight of their (iii) _____ targets.

	Blank (i)		Blank (ii)		Blank (iii)
A	pique	D	sidereal	G	ethereal
B	crescendo	E	doleful	H	affluent
C	euphony	F	erroneous	I	haggard

27. Despite having capably engineered and overseen the return of several stray dioceses that had broken away under his predecessor's (i) _____, the bishop had a modest quality that (ii) _____ the (iii) _____ of his position.

	Blank (i)		Blank (ii)		Blank (iii)
A	diligence	D	construed	G	tenuousness
B	epaulet	E	belied	H	audacity
C	laxity	F	derided	I	eminence

28. The (i) _____ of "surds"—irrational roots—with the Pythagoreans' faith that all phenomena in the universe could be expressed through harmonious ratios of whole numbers led the cult to (ii) _____ any mention of their existence to the uninitiated.

	Blank (i)		Blank (ii)
A	absurdity	D	condone
B	incongruity	E	proscribe
C	imperilment	F	palliate

Chapter 7: **Multi-Blank Text Completion**

29. Architectural (i) _____ such as Koolhaas recognized Hadid's talents early and encouraged their development. By 1977, only a few years after their initial encounter, she had perfected her (ii) _____ style, inspired equally by such disparate styles as Malevich's sparse constructivism and the flowing calligraphy of her native Arabic.

	Blank (i)		Blank (ii)
A	cognoscenti	D	fungible
B	fledglings	E	malleable
C	neophytes	F	heterogeneous

30. Aleister Crowley, despite being given to wildly fantastic claims—he insisted, for instance, that the founding book of his religion was dictated to him by a divine being who visited his hotel room wearing sunglasses and a trench coat—had his share of (i) _____ followers. It is hard to know whether these were spurred on or dissuaded by the (ii) _____ cast on him by the popular press, whose dubbing him "the wickedest man in the world" was, to be fair, hardly (iii) _____ given the relative harmlessness of his eccentricities.

	Blank (i)		Blank (ii)		Blank (iii)
A	sober	D	disadvantages	G	glib
B	sordid	E	gauntlets	H	peevish
C	skeptical	F	aspersions	I	condign

31. The Biblical portrayal of (i) _____ times preceding the great deluge stands in stark contrast to the ancient Greek representation of the (ii) _____ past as a Golden Age from which humanity has slowly descended into godless chaos. Such observations can easily give rise to the notion that stories about the past are less faithful attempts at reconstruction than (iii) _____, expressing both our cultural fears and hopes.

	Blank (i)		Blank (ii)		Blank (iii)
A	flagitious	D	proximate	G	allegories
B	dubious	E	antediluvian	H	equivocations
C	rustic	F	obscure	I	platitudes

32. Seeing digestive irregularity as perhaps the (i) _____ of preventable illness, such twelfth-century physicians as Moses Maimonides aimed the bulk of their (ii) _____ pamphlets at the prescription of prophylactic dietary regimens, offering advice that often appears risible to modern sensibilities.

	Blank (i)		Blank (ii)
A	most significant cause	D	maleficent
B	only panacea	E	didactic
C	sine qua non	F	tenable

Unit Two: Paragraphs and Passages

33. Not trusting his (i) _____ attire to impress the suave, sharply dressed executive, despite the latter's frequent professions of a fondness for rural life, Francis reduced himself to near (ii) _____ through costly new wardrobe acquisitions. If only he had known that the executive was secretly ashamed of her (iii) _____ showboating, which she only indulged to conceal her financial ruin.

	Blank (i)		Blank (ii)		Blank (iii)
A	rustic	D	penury	G	bombastic
B	natty	E	malaise	H	runic
C	exclusive	F	lethargy	I	sartorial

34. (i) _____ is generally unlikely to gain a reputation for reliability; Garth's poorly disguised excuses for his frequent absences, however, were improbably interpreted by his (ii) _____, hypochondriac employer as a sign of great foresight and (iii) _____.

	Blank (i)		Blank (ii)		Blank (iii)
A	An embezzler	D	casuistic	G	insipidity
B	A malingerer	E	imposing	H	sagacity
C	A pilferer	F	credulous	I	temerity

35. Perhaps unjustifiably, history has (i) _____ the movement's leader to the extent that his considerable moral shortcomings—his (ii) _____ misogyny, for example—are (iii) _____ and, if mentioned at all, are seen as little more than peccadilloes.

	Blank (i)		Blank (ii)		Blank (iii)
A	lionized	D	diffident	G	mere relics
B	extirpated	E	incorrigible	H	widely praised
C	impugned	F	reformed	I	rarely discussed

36. The new film chronicles exploitation and iniquity as the dark side of its overarching theme of (i) _____. The film succeeds in creating an immediately sympathetic protagonist, and it does well to showcase the elimination of all her longtime abusers in the end, granting the audience the (ii) _____ they've been awaiting for two hours. Despite the satisfying upheaval, however, the ponderous plot en route to this (iii) _____ leaves much to be desired.

	Blank (i)		Blank (ii)		Blank (iii)
A	fairness	D	catharsis	G	embellishment
B	slavery	E	revelation	H	denouement
C	injustice	F	inconclusiveness	I	platitude

Chapter 7: **Multi-Blank Text Completion**

37. Although (i) _____ is frequently used to give otherwise insubstantial work (ii) _____ of profundity, even Wallgot's most charitable readers were known to sneer at the breadth of his references.

	Blank (i)			Blank (ii)
A	stringency		D	an iota
B	insularity		E	a veneer
C	eclecticism		F	a medley

38. She rarely bothered to (i) _____ her lengthy tomes, but their surprising popularity with the public empowered her to avoid editorial complaints through (ii) _____ threats to sign a contract with a different publisher.

	Blank (i)			Blank (ii)
A	emend		D	impuissant
B	allay		E	preemptive
C	edify		F	toothsome

39. In future discounting, subjects place a lower value on events in the distant future than on (i) _____ ones, explaining the common tendency to (ii) _____ present pleasures even at the expense of a likely (iii) _____ of future detriments.

	Blank (i)			Blank (ii)			Blank (iii)
A	atavistic		D	avert		G	malady
B	remote		E	rescind		H	proliferation
C	proximate		F	protract		I	buttressing

40. She makes the facile claim that it is possible to deduce matters of fact from logic and, with just as little (i) _____ , aims to derive ethical and economic truths as well. The laws of logic, in her opinion, (ii) _____ her proclamation that "existence exists," which is very much like saying that the law of thermodynamics gave rise to the discovery that heat is hot.

	Blank (i)			Blank (ii)
A	syllogism		D	undergird
B	warrant		E	occlude
C	fallacy		F	galvanize

Unit Two: **Paragraphs and Passages**

Answers and Explanations

Vocabulary Challenge

1. discrete (*adj.*): separate, distinct, detached, existing as individual parts

2. apposite (*adj.*): highly appropriate, suitable, or relevant

3. paucity (*n*): scarcity, the state of being small in number

4. prohibitive (*adj.*): tending to forbid something, or serving to prevent something

5. reticent (*adj.*): not talking much; private (of a person), restrained, reserved

6. nettle (*v*): irritate, sting, or annoy

Problem Set

1. (i) adroit; (ii) looming: The first blank describes Richardson's "handling" of a situation, and the second blank describes a "scandal." Start, as always, with some concrete proof. There was something that "seemed poised to become the ruination" of Richardson's coalition (probably the scandal), but it was "successfully prevented" by "Richardson's handling." Well done, Richardson. The first blank needs to be a positive word, such as successful, so *adroit* (skilled, adept) fits well. Neither a *penitent* (sorry for sin) nor a *heterogeneous* (mixed; composed of differing parts) handling of the scandal is supported by proof in the sentence.

In predicting for the second blank, look for clues in the sentence that describe the scandal. All you know is that it "seemed poised" to ruin things—that is, it hadn't done so already. A word that means about to happen would make sense. *Looming* (taking shape as an impending event) is the most sensible match. Someone might be *fretful* (worried) over a scandal, but *fretful* doesn't make sense as a description of the scandal itself, and there are no indications in the sentence that the scandal was *ecumenical* (worldwide in scope).

2. (i) revolting; (ii) bolstered: The first blank describes "forces," and the second blank is connected to a "battalion." Given the thematic similarity between "forces" and "battalion," look to the word used to describe the battalion: "loyalist." If a loyalist battalion is holding some other forces at bay, those other forces must be rebels. You don't have any indication that the forces were *outclassed* (surpassed in quality) or *fascistic* (totalitarian, led by dictator). Don't be thrown off by the dual meaning of *revolting*—*revolting* can mean "disgusting," but it can also mean engaging in a literal revolt, such as against a government.

The second blank links the loyalist battalion to "its allies' reinforcements." Since allies and reinforcements are both good things to have when you're engaged in conflict, and since the loyalists have been able to hold the revolting forces at bay, the word must be something good, like helped. Only *bolstered* (supported) makes sense. *Obviated* (anticipated and made unnecessary) isn't supported by any proof in the sentence. *Sapped* (weakened, especially of energy) conflicts with the idea that allies would help the loyalists, making this an opposite trap.

3. (i) humbled; (ii) pretension: Both blanks in this sentence describe "the entrepreneur" in some way. The concrete truth in this sentence is that the entrepreneur is now "the possessor of a broken spirit and timid demeanor." This informs the second blank, which describes what the entrepreneur *was* known for before his spirit broke. The adjective "overweening" means "conceited" or "excessive," so a good prediction for the second blank might be confidence, albeit likely with a more negative spin. *Pretension* fits this.

Neither *liberality* (giving or spending freely; open-mindedness) nor *wealth* correctly oppose the idea of having a broken spirit or being timid.

Now move on to the first blank. It's in an awkward position in the sentence, so it's good to have as clear an idea as possible of what's going on in the rest of the sentence before working on this. Given how things turn out for the entrepreneur, a good prediction for this blank might be brought down or broken. The only answer that comes close is *humbled*. *Exalted* (held in high regard; in a state of extreme happiness) is the opposite of what the blank requires, and *unaffected* clashes with the meaning of the sentence: The entrepreneur has definitely been affected by circumstance, given the change in how he's perceived.

4. (i) salutary; (ii) unwholesome: The blanks in this sentence can be difficult to predict with certainty, as there aren't many concrete clues given in the sentence. When this happens in a two-blank TC question, settle for determining the relationship between the blanks rather than making a specific prediction. The reversal marker "though" offers a clue: The two parts of the sentence must contradict each other in some way. Since the first part describes something "successful," it would make sense if the word in the first blank, which describes the "lifestyle" he had been making efforts to adopt, were a good word, but it's not totally guaranteed—you'll need some information about the second blank before you can decide.

The second part of the sentence says that the person in question was "not above occasionally indulging" proclivities (inclinations or predilections) for some kind of dishes. Unpack it a little. If he *were* above indulging his proclivities, he wouldn't indulge them; since he's *not* above it, he must actually indulge these proclivities on occasion. Now, it can help to simplify the sentence a bit: Though he'd adopted some kind of lifestyle, he still sometimes indulged his liking for some kind of dishes. The two words need to be opposites.

Examine the answer choices. It's hard to imagine what kind of dishes could possibly be a counterpart to a *truculent* (ferocious, cruel, or savage) lifestyle, but regardless, none of the options for Blank (ii) is a good opposite. *Salutary* (conducive to health) does have a good counterpoint in the other blank: *unwholesome*. And *unwholesome* works to describe dishes, too, so this is looking like a pretty promising pair of answers. *Frugal* (thrifty) would work in Blank (i) if there were a word like "expensive" among the choices for the second blank, but neither *odious* (extremely repulsive) nor *sodden* (soaked) means anything like expensive.

5. (i) prompted; (ii) codify: Both blanks here represent verbs, which can make them particularly hard to predict. Unpack the sentence: There was a discovery, and this discovery did something to the "U.K. Department of Health." The discovery was that pregnancy complications are being caused and can be avoided. This is a health issue, so the Department of Health would definitely want to do something about. It's likely that the first blank means something like caused. Among the options for Blank (i), there are two that mean something like "caused": *prompted* and *instigated*. *Instigated* (urged, goaded, provoked, or incited) has a somewhat negative spin that means it's most often used before negative acts (instigate a fight, for instance). The more neutral *prompted* is a better fit, as it doesn't seem any urging or goading was necessary. *Lulled* (deceptively caused to feel safe) is the opposite of the reaction this sort of health discovery would elicit from the Department of Health.

The second blank will describe what the Department of Health was *prompted* to do by the discovery. Given that it would likely be important to get the word about this discovery out to "expectant mothers," a word like publish would make sense here. *Intuit* (understand or solve by instinct) isn't right, as there's no reason to intuit what has already been discovered. *Officiate* (act as an official in charge) wouldn't be used in this

Unit Two: **Paragraphs and Passages**

context, though it is a potential theme trap due to the Department of Health's official leadership status. Only *codify* (put into an explicit law or code) works.

6. (i) toadies; (ii) critical: The first blank describes "the Bieber Appreciation Society," which clearly exists to appreciate all things Bieber, and the second blank describes the "voices" that the society will soon include in its publication. These voices are going to be included specifically because the BAS has become "fearful" of being seen in a certain way, so the voices are probably meant to create the opposite impression. Therefore, the two blanks should be opposites.

Look at the options for the first blank. The answer choices are gentle, happily. There's no reason that the Bieber Appreciation Society would be "fearful" of being seen as *enthusiasts* (or they'd better consider a name change), and they're likely in no danger of being seen as *detractors* (people who criticize something)—this represents an opposite trap. Only *toadies* (servile followers) makes sense here, as it has a negative spin that fits "fearful" but that *enthusiasts* lacks.

In the second blank, *tantamount* (equivalent) doesn't make any sense, and *conciliatory* would be positive toward Bieber (so why would the Bieber Appreciation Society have trouble finding such voices?). Only *critical*, which in this context likely means "involving careful evaluation and judgment," works in offering a good contrast to *toadies* (because a toady is by definition uncritical).

7. (i) recidivism; (ii) ramifications: " Bringing together criminals and their victims" reduces the rates of something, and the second part of the sentence offers a potential explanation for why that reduction has been observed: The criminals convince themselves their actions have no something in order to commit the crimes in the first place. A good prediction for the second blank might be something like consequences or effect on others, as that would provide a good reason why making criminals face their victims might bring about a change. Both *inconsistencies* and *aberrations* mean something like "deviations from the norm," which doesn't work for this blank; *ramifications*, on the other hand, fits the "consequences" prediction.

The sentence doesn't give much to go on for the first blank except that it will probably be something bad. Unfortunately, all the options for Blank (i) are negative words, so a more subtle analysis will be needed. *Violence* could work, but nothing in the sentence suggests that these were necessarily violent criminals. *Recidivism* (a tendency to re-engage in crime or bad behavior) works really well here. If the criminals could only commit crimes when they believed their actions had no consequences, meeting the victims—the human consequences of their actions—would disabuse them of this belief, rendering them unable to commit more crimes. *Malfeasance* (crime or lesser wrongdoing) works better than *violence* in that criminals have by definition committed some kind of malfeasance; however, it doesn't fit as well as *recidivism*, which is specifically about *repeated* malfeasance.

8. (i) habiliments; (ii) transcendent; (iii) iridescent: The first blank is referring to something made of cloth, which is contrasted with the "garments of Buddhist monks." For this comparison to work, the first blank must mean something like garments. *Habiliments* (clothes associated with a particular profession or occasion) is the only choice that fits—*vestiges* (remaining traces of something) and *paragons* (the best exemplars of a usually good quality) are off the mark.

The contrast between the first sentence and the second sentence make the third blank the next easiest to predict for. Since the first sentence describes the Christian garments as being made of "plain black modest cloth," it would make sense if the garments of the Buddhist monks were not plain, bright and colorful, or immodest. *Iridescent* is a decent match for the second prediction. *Drab* (dull-colored) is an opposite trap, and *flowing* has no connection to the content clues in the first sentence.

The word in the second blank has nothing to do with clothing. Instead, it describes the "mindset" of the Eastern Christians. The only information in the sentences that touches on their mindset is the part about "their spiritual indifference to matters of this world." If they're indifferent to matters of this world, they're likely "in favor of a commitment to" something not of this world. *Mundane* (boring; relating to this world) is an opposite trap, and *dogmatic* (marked by absolute adherence to rules or principles) is a theme trap. *Transcendent* correctly indicates a focus on matters beyond the material plane.

9. (i) suffered; (ii) culpability; (iii) ledger: The first blank is a good place to start, as there aren't many words that could plausibly precede "some kind of abuse as a child." A prediction of suffered wouldn't go amiss, and indeed it's reflected in the answer choices. That said, there's not much in the way of content clues to support such a prediction, so look at the other answers for Blank (i) before you finalize the choice. *Appreciated* is pretty unlikely—nobody appreciates abuse. *Exploited* is a bit trickier, but the text never implies that the abuse was used to exploit anything.

For the second blank, you only need to know what a jury does: They apportion (assign) blame, which is a synonym of *culpability*. *History* doesn't make sense here, and *insanity* is a theme trap due to the frequency of insanity pleas in criminal trials.

The third blank is fairly hard to predict for, so go to the answer choices instead. The only option that can be "balanced" is *ledger* (a record of transactions, used here figuratively). You can't as clearly balance an *imprisonment* or a *verdict*, and neither word makes sense with the "of someone's life" that follows the blank. They're both theme traps.

10. (i) disdain; (ii) discipline; (iii) divesting: The concrete proof is that the "brightest students" are being discouraged from "pursuing teaching careers," something the sentence describes as a "disservice." This will help with the first blank, but it's still probably easier to predict for the third blank first, as there's much more concrete information in the second part of the sentence. If the brightest students aren't pursuing teaching careers, how does that affect the next generation of students? The next generation won't be learning from "the cream of the crop," a reference to the bright students who won't be pursuing teaching. A good prediction would be depriving. *Divesting* is a good synonym for "depriving." Don't fall for the traps of *denigrating* (defaming, belittling) and *degenerating* (deteriorating, declining), both of which fit with the overall negative theme but don't fit into the blank.

Back to the first part of the sentence now. The second part of the sentence has fully described a negative consequence of discouraging students from choosing to teach; therefore, it's justifiable to say that "top universities should not (i) discourage education as an academic (ii) pursuit." In Blank (i), *disdain* (look down on) is somewhat close in tone and effect to "discourage." *Proscribe* (ban) is much more extreme than "discourage," and *circumvent* (avoid via circuitous means) doesn't really fit. In Blank (ii) *discipline* (in this case, an area of study) is the closest match for the prediction pursuit in the context of academics. *Tome* (a large, usually academic book) is a theme trap, and *recommendation* is a story trap—you can sort of make it work, but the sentence isn't advocating for education to be recommended as a pursuit, just for it not to be discouraged.

11. (i) wheedling; (ii) unremitting: The first blank describes "diplomacy," and the second describes "aggression." Since the political organization is described as "militant," it would likely favor aggression against rivals, so check the answers for Blank (ii) to see if one of the words is consistent with that expectation. *Supine* (lying flat; passive) doesn't work to describe "aggression" and doesn't fit with "militant." *Unremitting* (not letting up) works in that it intensifies the aggression described. *Superfluous* (dispensable;

redundant; more than what's needed) adds a strange spin to the sentence, in that it implies that the organization is going to somehow act with more aggression than it's able to use.

Returning to the first blank, the kind of "diplomacy" that the blank describes is characterized as "unbecoming" and is presented as an "alternative" to the aggression described later in the sentence (the information between the dashes in this sentence is a red herring). Therefore, the diplomacy in question must offer a contrast to aggression. It might best be described as weak. *Wheedling* (persuade through flattery) is decidedly *not* an aggressive approach, so it might work, but consider the other answers before making a decision. *Freewheeling* (acting without concern for rules or consequences) is not indicated by any proof in the sentence and isn't as clear a counterpoint to "unremitting aggression." *Verdant* (green, covered in vegetation) is totally unrelated to diplomacy. *Wheedling* might be considered a bit of a story trap in other circumstances, compared to *freewheeling* and *verdant* it's definitely the safest bet.

12. (i) frisson; (ii) precipitating: Start from the concrete truth: There are people who have been demanding the queen's departure for at least a fortnight, and the queen has announced her abdication (giving up a throne) to a crowd of those people, acceding to their demands. Thus, the protesters to whom the first blank is connected are getting what they want. Thrill may work well for the first blank, and among the answer choices, *frisson* fits. *Murmur* is definitely possible, but its neutrality makes it a less than ideal fit for the clues in the sentence (especially "chanting threats" and "popular demands"). A *panegyric* (formal speech or composition in praise of someone or something) is not something that would "run through the crowd," and certainly not in praise of the very queen the crowd wishes to depose.

For the second blank, one might expect a period of disorder to either begin or end with the act of abdication—after all, there's clearly been some disorder in the weeks leading up to this abdication, but there's also likely to be more disorder in the wake of such a political upheaval. Among the answers, *precipitating* (causing to begin) is the only possibility. *Marring* (damaging, disfiguring) doesn't work and is inappropriate in the context of something negative (*marring* tends to happen to something that would've been good otherwise, like a beautiful day *marred* by clouds). Similarly, *diluting* (making weaker by adding other elements to it) isn't really a thing that could be done to "a period" of time.

13. (i) virtuoso; (ii) inept: The overall message of the sentence is that Joseph "expected" to become one thing but, disappointingly, "remained" something else. Since Joseph is a "perfectionist," he probably expected to become perfect, or at least good, and was disappointed when he remained something like unskilled or bad. *Virtuoso* (highly skilled, especially in music or art) and *inept* (lacking competency) match those predictions well. A perfectionist would certainly not expect to become a *hack* (a dull, unoriginal writer), and while he might have expected to become a *musician*, one of the choices in Blank (ii) would have to mean "non-musician" for this to work, as the two blanks are definitely opposites.

As for the answers that are offered for the second blank, *novel* (new) would've offered a decent contrast to *hack* in Blank (i), but the spin of that pair is the opposite of what the sentence calls for (the first blank should be something good and the second something bad). *Inane* (silly) might have worked with an appropriate option in the first blank (such as "genius"), but it doesn't work as a contrast to *virtuoso*.

14. (i) Credulity; (ii) beset: For the first blank, you are looking for something that is unhelpful to a person connected in some way to "liars and fabulists" (*fabulists* are just very creative liars), but there's not enough concrete proof to grab onto in this sentence to make a confident prediction for either blank. Look to the answer choices for help. In Blank (i), *ingenuity* (inventiveness or cleverness) is basically always an asset no matter the circumstances, and it has less connection to "liars and fabulists" than the other two options. *Credulity* (a willingness to believe people too easily) and *duplicity* (deceptiveness) are both relevant to "liars

Chapter 7: **Multi-Blank Text Completion**

and fabulists" clue. *Credulity* wouldn't be an asset to someone surrounded by liars, because a credulous person would be easy to take advantage of. *Duplicity* wouldn't be an asset for someone on some kind of crusade against liars and fabulists, as a duplicitous person would look like a hypocrite in such circumstances. See which of these options is offered in Blank (ii).

Forsaken (abandoned) doesn't match either of these needed meanings, so it can be eliminated it. It also carries an unhelpful spin suggesting that it would be preferable to be around liars (because you're usually *forsaken* by something positive). *Brooked* (tolerated) also isn't a great match for the predictions or for the context. But *beset* (surrounded or threatened persistently by) does match the prediction for what the blank would contain if *credulity* were chosen for the first blank.

15. (i) raconteur; (ii) genial: The first blank describes how a person "was known to all her friends." The concrete description of her in the sentence indicates that she was "legendary for humorous stories" from a certain set of life experiences. So she must be known as a storyteller or a funny person. A *raconteur* is someone who tells amusing stories, but there's no clear reason why her humorous stories would lead to her being known as a *sage* (wise or learned person) or a *prevaricator* (someone who tells false stories).

In the last part of the sentence, the reversal marker "belied" indicates that "her private behavior" is actually at odds with her public reputation. Someone who tells amusing stories would plausibly be considered *genial* (friendly and cheerful), but not *belligerent* (hostile and aggressive) or *pedantic* (overly concerned with small details or rules).

16. (i) evinced; (ii) repartee: The first sentence tells you that an opinion has formed about a lady's "droll utterances." That's not much to go on yet. Luckily, the second sentence immediately calls back to "the common opinion" by talking about "this reputation," and from this sentence you can confirm what you might have already suspected: The opinion about her is clearly negative, given that it has "cost" her something. Given that, the opinion at court must hold that her behavior *is* "unbecoming of a lady," so look for a word that means displayed. *Evinced* (demonstrated) works. Her utterances don't *deride* (ridicule) these attitudes, though that's a theme trap, nor *elude* (avoid) them, an opposite trap.

The second blank refers to some characteristic of the lady that gentlemen fear "being bested by," and since the only thing you know about the lady's character is that she makes droll (amusing and wry) utterances, they must be afraid of her drollness. *Repartee* (clever, quick, and witty banter) is the best fit—watch out, gentlemen. *Doggerel* (a comic poem) might work, but compared to *repartee*, it requires more assumptions to fit. *Subtlety* doesn't reflect any proof in the sentence.

17. (i) mettlesome; (ii) penchant: The dashes indicate that the first blank comes in a part of the sentence that is meant as an addendum to the first part of the sentence. There, you're told only that courage is important ("anything but" is a reversal marker), and the "indeed" just before the blank indicates that this cartoon mouse's character agrees with this principle. Therefore, the mouse must be courageous. *Mettlesome* does mean "courageous," and its positive spin fits well with this part of the sentence—it's only after this blank that negativity creeps into the sentence. As such, *impetuous* (impulsive or rash), which could be seen as an offshoot of courage but has a lightly negative spin, can't work. *Heady* (intoxicating; exhilarating) doesn't come close.

The second blank describes the mouse's relationship with "excessive violence." Whatever this relationship is, it's not a good look for a children's charity mascot. So the mouse may have a liking (or, if you're feeling fancy, a proclivity) for excessive violence. *Penchant* (a strong liking) is a perfect fit. *Kinship* (blood relationship) doesn't work—even if you interpret it figuratively, the correct idiom would have been "kinship with," not "kinship for." *Largess* (generosity) isn't a good fit.

227

Unit Two: Paragraphs and Passages

18. (i) sleight of hand; (ii) ostensible: The ambassador is "double-dealing" (duplicitous) and "backpedaling" (retreating from a position), so a good fit in the first blank would be something like <u>deceitfulness</u>. *Sleight of hand* (skillful deception) works. There is no indication that the ambassador had political *plutocracy* (government by the wealthy) or political *bugaboo* (something causing fear).

The tricky ambassador's "Australian counterpart" is straightforward and is compared favorably to the ambassador himself. So while it may prove difficult to predict an exact answer for the second blank, expect a positive adjective that can describe "straightforwardness." *Occlusive* (tending to close off) would conflict with being straightforward, and *intransigent* (uncompromising, obstinate) has too negative a spin. Only *ostensible* (seemingly true, but not necessarily true) is neither too negative nor at odds with any proof in the sentence. *Ostensible* works in a sentence about how politicians "looked," not necessarily about how they really were.

19. (i) recalcitrant; (ii) degradation: The first blank describes a puzzle that sounds quite <u>complicated</u>—delivering an "antisense strand," to the right place at just the right moment. Only *recalcitrant* (stubborn) is appropriate to describe a complicated puzzle; *pedestrian* (commonplace, uninspired) conflicts with the proof, and *monolithic* (large and indivisible) is not indicated by any piece of evidence and is usually used to describe groups.

The second blank is something that the strand must be strong enough to resist so that it has "time to accomplish its task." The strand needs time to work, so it needs to resist something like <u>destruction</u>. *Desiccation* (drying out) would *probably* be bad for the strand, but there is no indication in the sentence that drying out would prevent the strand from working, and *compunction* (uneasiness due to guilt) doesn't apply to strands. However, *degradation* (deterioration, breakdown) is something the strand would have to resist in order to work on the virus.

20. (i) rankled; (ii) pernicious; (iii) latency: The third blank is probably the easiest to predict for in this question, as it's the sole blank in a long sentence offering a lot of concrete proof to go on. There, the blank denotes the state "Albanian nationalism" had been in before it came "surging out." The blank should be something like <u>dormancy</u>. *Latency* (a state of being unexpressed) works here as a good counterpoint for the subsequent surging. *Insularity* (isolation) and *lucidity* (clarity) don't offer the same kind of counterpoint, though *insularity* is a theme trap because it's often associated with nationalism.

Back to the first blank. The war would have had some sort of <u>negative effect</u> on Albanians, given the prospects laid out in the second part of the sentence, but it's hard to make a very specific prediction. Worse still, all three answers are negative words, so the nuance of the words will be important. *Enervate* (weaken) doesn't quite fit, as the rest of the story describes an Albania that if anything has seen its resolve for independence strengthened. And while some aspects of the war might have *debased* (degraded) them, the prospect of division of their lands didn't do this. However, the war might have left the Albanians *rankled* (angered or resentful), given the strength and duration of the subsequent nationalistic surge.

Finally, expect another negative word in the second blank—a good prediction might be to recycle <u>rankling</u> for now. *Pernicious* (greatly destructive, deadly, injurious, or harmful) is a bit more extreme than *rankling*, but *evanescent* (fleeting; tending to vanish like vapor) and *transient* (quickly coming into and passing out of existence; transitory) aren't negative enough, and both have short-term meanings that conflict with the long time frame indicated by the decades-long struggle referenced in the second sentence.

Chapter 7: Multi-Blank Text Completion

21. (i) efficient; (ii) progress; (iii) iniquitous: The fact that the second sentence starts out with "Perhaps more worrying" is an indication that whatever was expressed in the main body of the preceding sentence was already somewhat worrying, and whatever's to come in the second sentence is also worrying. Start with Blank (iii), as it's in a longer sentence with fewer blanks. There's something worrying about "treatment of farmers by" some kind of "social hierarchy." The hierarchy in question must not be great for farmers, so look to the options for something negative. *Halcyon* (calm, peaceful) is positive, so that can be eliminated. *Stratified* (divided into classes) describes literally any hierarchy, but its tone isn't inherently negative, even if "social stratification" is commonly referenced as a problem in the real world. *Iniquitous* (unjust) offers the best fit.

Return to the first sentence now. The first sentence must be describing a worrying situation. It's broken down into two contrasting parts by the reversal marker "though" at the beginning. The second part of the first sentence is the worrying part (because it come right before the second sentence), so the first part must contain a bit of good news. Go into Blank (i) looking for a positive word. *Expensive* and *polluting* are both negative, leaving *efficient* as the only possible option.

Now that you know modern farming is more *efficient*, it's time to tackle the worrying part of the sentence. The reversal marker "no" just before the second blank means that, for this part of the sentence to be worrying, the word in the blank has to be a good thing. Predict something like improvement and head to the answers. *Progress* isn't always the same as improvement, but it's close, so keep it around. *Disincentive* (deterrent) and *countermand* (an order that revokes a previous order) aren't particularly positive, so go with *progress*.

22. (i) derivation; (ii) notorious; (iii) provenance: The first sentence comes in two parts linked with the straight-ahead marker "as." The second part of it contains concrete proof about where the word *assassin* comes from, so the first part should be about the same thing. A good prediction for the first blank would be origin. *Introduction* seems somewhat close to this prediction, but the proof in the sentence doesn't tell you anything about how the word was introduced to people. *Derivation* comes closer, as it specifically reflects the idea of tracing the origins and development of something. *Circumlocution* (roundabout or evasive speech; use of more words than necessary) represents a theme trap.

The second sentence states that "the topic is equally attractive to historians," and because historians and philologists are both academics, this would seem to merit a prediction of attractive for the second blank. However, there's no match for this among the words. Switch to process of elimination. Since the derivation is known, it follows that it isn't *enigmatic* (mysterious) or *unheralded* (unannounced, unsung); while *notorious* can sometimes have a negative connotation, it at least carries the denotation of "well known."

With the phrase "The topic," the second sentence is calling back to the topic of the first sentence: the derivation of the word *assassin*. However, while the derivation of the word is known, something about the sect presents a mystery. Because the sentence also discusses how the sect "dates to before the First Crusade in the 11th century," you can expect a word that means something like origin once again. *Provenance* is a synonym for origin or derivation. The *legend* of the sect must not be much of a mystery, given that it is summarized in this sentence, and the sentence indicates nothing about any *bane* (curse, affliction) that the sect might have been subject to.

23. (i) plumbed; (ii) static; (iii) dearth: The third blank is likely the easiest to predict for, as there's a lot of concrete information around it. There, a mention of the "growing gap between rich and poor" prefaces the part with the blank. The wealthy were "eating more meat than ever," so the masses—the poor side of the gap—must have suffered from a lack of foodstuffs. A *dearth* is exactly that: a lack. *Glut* (excessive supply) is an opposite trap, and *deceleration* (slowing down) could happen to the production or harvest of foodstuffs, but not to foodstuffs themselves.

The second blank is a bit trickier. The reversal marker "while" draws a contrast between this part of the sentence and latter part where the rich are eating more meat and the poor are eating less. The statistics about meat consumption must be contradicting that reality, and since the second blank is immediately preceded by "remained," a good prediction would be the same. *Plastic* (artificial; changeable) has some definitions that are unrelated and others that are somewhat opposite to this prediction. *Demographic* (related to structure of a population) is a theme trap. But *static* fits.

Finally, now that you know that the statistics about population and meat consumption obscured the growing gap, it would make sense to say that statistics need to be examined closely. *Plumbed*, which among other things means "explored fully," works. *Calculated* doesn't go far enough (the sentence is saying you need to do more than just calculate), and *designed* goes a bit too far (the sentence doesn't say people should design or invent statistics, just that they should study statistics thoughtfully).

24. (i) clangor; (ii) subdued; (iii) an undulating: The two parts of the first sentence should contradict each other, owing to the complementary reversal markers "although" and "surprisingly." Since both blanks describe the sound of Cage's music, you could go straight to the answer choices right away and see if there are any decent opposite pairs. Unfortunately, there are two pairs of opposites: *murmur* (a soft sound) contrasts *strident* (loud and harsh), and *clangor* (loud noise) contrasts *subdued* (soft and restrained). Concrete proof in the second sentence, which in the absence of other markers should be presumed to discuss Cage's early music in more detail, describes music that "maintains its softness throughout." Therefore, the pair to choose for the first two blanks is *clangor* and *subdued*. *Timbre* (the unique quality of a given instrument) and *auspicious* (promising or propitious) aren't a good pair, though *timbre* is a theme trap.

The third blank describes the melody of Cage's "Music for Marcel Duchamp." This music "never rises above mezzo-piano" (meaning a moderately low volume), and the melody "maintains its softness throughout." A good prediction for the blank would be gentle. Among the answers, only *undulating* (rising or falling smoothly in pitch, volume, or cadence) works in the last blank, particularly in the *pitch* sense. *Noisome* (noxious, harmful, or dangerous) and *erstwhile* (former) are unrelated to the sentence. Don't be distracted by the superficial similarity between *noisome* and "noise."

25. (i) nugatory; (ii) mercurial: The "while" in front of the first blank suggests that the description of the tokens that will go in the blank will contradict the surrounding description of the tokens. That description points to the fact that the tokens serve as a reminder of the Crown's power, so the blank should emphasize that the tokens may have no *real* power. Look for a word like powerless. *Nugatory* means "of no value," a decent fit, especially given that *sumptuous* (very costly, luxurious, or lavish) implies real value and *sardonic* (scornfully or derisively mocking) is unrelated.

The second blank is preceded by the reversal marker "even," so look for the blank to contrast what comes before the "even." There, it's stated that "the power of the Crown continued to be held in esteem," so these must be either changing political times or anti-monarchist political times. *Mercurial* (highly changeable or frequently changing) fits the first prediction. *Jocund* (cheerful, merry) political times are not indicated by any proof. *Magisterial* (having great authority; dictatorial) is a theme trap, and as it implies a strong government, it doesn't reflect the reversal called for by "even."

26. (i) crescendo; (ii) despondent; (iii) haggard: Before it suddenly stopped, the shelling had built up to something like a peak. *Crescendo* (climax; loudest point) is the choice that works best. *Pique* (a passing feeling of irritation at a perceived slight) sounds the same as *peak* (making it a vocabulary trap) but is unrelated to shelling. *Euphony* (a pleasing sound) doesn't match "shelling."

The second blank describes the "drooping barrels of the artillery," and specifically their reaction to a "pathetic sight." Both of these bits of proof support a prediction like sad, Only *doleful* (mournful) fits; *sidereal* (relating to the stars or constellations) and *erroneous* (wrong) are unrelated.

The third blank describes the "targets," who are elsewhere described as a sight so pathetic it leaves even artillery depressed. Look for a word that reflects this, like pathetic itself. The targets aren't likely to be *ethereal* (light, airy; heavenly, celestial) or *affluent* (rich), as these are both positive words. Instead, the targets are most likely *haggard* (worn out).

27. (i) laxity; (ii) belied; (iii) eminence: The first blank has the most concrete truth around it: The predecessor had some quality that allowed "several stray dioceses" to break away. A prediction like negligence or incompetence wouldn't go amiss. *Laxity* (looseness; leniency) is the only choice that comes close; *diligence* (perseverance; attentiveness) is the opposite of what is needed, and *epaulet* (a shoulder ornament typically worn on military uniforms) has no relationship.

The third blank will contain some characteristic of the bishop's position, but the rest of the sentence doesn't give much to go on except "modest." However, without the sentence's verb, which will be the answer for Blank (ii), it's hard to know what the third blank's relationship to "modesty" is. It's worth examining the answer choices to see if any might work as a plausible descriptor. There is no indication of *tenuousness* (uncertainty); it offers neither a clear relationship with "modesty" nor a description of the bishop's position that lines up with the sentence (if his position were tenuous, he might be about to lose that position). *Audacity* (recklessness, daring) works as a counterpoint to "modesty," but again, "the *audacity* of his position" doesn't quite fit, as a bishop's position isn't generally audacious and there's no proof to suggest that this one would be. *Eminence* (high rank, station, or status), on the other hand, would generally apply to a leader's position, and it's also a good counterpoint to modesty.

You can now turn to the second blank. You don't expect someone in a position of *eminence* to be "modest," so his modesty seems to disguise or contradict that *eminence*. *Belied*, the perennial GRE favorite, means exactly that. *Construed* (deduced; explained) is an opposite trap, and *derided* (mocked, ridiculed) doesn't work.

28. (i) incongruity; (ii) proscribe: Interpreting this sentence correctly will require some guesswork if you're not comfortable with the phrase "irrational roots," because the first blank describes the relationship between these roots and the belief that everything can be expressed "through harmonious ratios of whole numbers." The contrast of "irrational" and "harmonious" may lead you to predict contrast or even incompatibility for the first blank. It's difficult to be completely sure if you aren't familiar with surds, but you know whatever the blank is must be describing the relationship between surds and something harmonious. Check the answer choices. *Absurdity* (ridiculousness) and *imperilment* (endangerment) don't capture any clear relationship, but *incongruity* (lack of agreement) does, and in a way that makes sense.

For the second blank, if surds have *incongruity with* a tenet of the Pythagoreans' faith, the cult would likely be hesitant to mention them; they'd at the very least discourage any mention of surds to those outside the cult. *Condone* (accept, allow) does the opposite of what you need, and in addition to not fitting with the prediction, *palliate* (alleviate, diminish) also doesn't fit the context (you can't "palliate any mention" of something). *Proscribing* (forbidding) is more extreme than the prediction, but of these answer choices, it fits the best.

Unit Two: **Paragraphs and Passages**

29. (i) cognoscenti; (ii) heteromorphic: The first blank will be a word describing people such as Koolhaas, who recognized and encouraged the development of Hadid's nascent talents. This serves as the concrete proof for the blank: The word should indicate an ability to spot talent and foster it. Something like experts or mentors might work. *Cognoscenti* (people well informed about a subject) matches the first prediction. *Fledglings* (young, immature, or inexperienced people) and *neophytes* (beginners) are opposite traps—they might have been appropriate to describe Hadid at this point in the story, but not Koolhaas.

The second blank describes Hadid's style, which is further described as influenced by "disparate styles." Look for a word like eclectic. *Fungible* (replaceable) doesn't work, and while *malleable* (easily changed) could work, it contradicts the assertion that her style had been "perfected," which implies that her style is no longer developing. *Heterogeneous* (diverse in character or composition) does a better job of reflecting that her perfected style was a reflection of disparate influences.

30. (i) sober; (ii) aspersions; (iii) condign: The first blank is alone in a sentence full of proof, so it's likely an easy place to start. Acknowledge the truth between the dashes—that Crowley founded a religion and its angels have style—and then reread the sentence without that part. Crowley is "given to wildly fantastic claims," and "despite" that, he has some kind of followers. The blank must contrast the fantastic claims in some way, so a good prediction might be sensible. *Sober* (serious and sensible) is a good fit. *Sordid* (morally degraded or contemptible) is a theme trap, meant to appeal through its connection to Crowley's alleged wickedness. However, it doesn't offer a good counterpoint to fantastic claims. *Skeptical* is an opposite trap—if anything you'd expect people to be skeptical of wildly fantastic claims.

In Blank (ii), something is being "cast on him by the popular press," and it's not looking good: Crowley is being called wicked. Look for a word like criticisms or attacks. The negative coverage might be causing Crowley some *disadvantages* down the road, but it wouldn't typically be described as "casting" them on him. *Gauntlets* (open challenges) goes too far, as there's no evidence of anyone challenging him. Luckily, *aspersions* (attacks on someone's reputation) doesn't require any extra story to work.

The third blank connects the allegation of wickedness to Crowley's "relative harmlessness." This juxtaposition makes the allegation seem disproportionately harsh, but this shouldn't be your prediction: The reversal marker "hardly" before the blank makes merited or fair a better fit. Neither *glib* (fluent to the point of insincerity) nor *peevish* (discontented; ill-tempered) fits, though *peevish* represents an opposite trap. *Condign* (deserved or appropriate) fits, especially as it's most often used to describe punishments and other negative repercussions.

31. (i) flagitious; (ii) antediluvian; (iii) allegories: The first sentence makes a comparison between the "Biblical portrayal" of a period in the past and the "Greek representation" of what must be the same time (otherwise there'd be no common ground on which to base a comparison). Since the first part of the comparison specifies the time period (the "times preceding the great deluge"), choose something for Blank (ii) that means before the flood or distant. *Antediluvian* satisfies both predictions: It literally means "before the flood" but is therefore also used as a synonym for "ancient." *Proximate* is an opposite trap, and while *obscure* (hard to discover) almost works, in that all moments in the past are obscured by the veils of time, it's not as close to the concrete proof in the sentence as *antediluvian*.

The first blank is the other missing piece in the comparison between the two times: It contains the Biblical characterization of these times, which "stands in stark contrast" to the Greek representation of these times as a "Golden Age." The blank should be diametrically opposed to "Golden Age," so look for the word to be bad. Starkly bad. *Dubious* (warranting uncertainty or doubt) and *rustic* (rural; lacking refinement) don't match specific proof and aren't anywhere near as negative as *flagitious* (marked by vice).

Chapter 7: **Multi-Blank Text Completion**

For the third blank, look to the surrounding text for clues. The word should be something that contrasts "faithful attempts at reconstruction" but still expresses "cultural fears and hopes." It could be something like fictions, but it's probably best to just consider the answers. *Allegories* are fictional accounts with a moral or political meaning, and given the comparison between *flagitious* times and Golden Ages earlier in the problem, this is the best fit. *Equivocations* would make sense if we knew that the stories were intended to deceive or mislead, but it's hard to know their true intent, making this a story trap. There's no reason to believe these weren't good-faith attempts at expressing some cultural truth, even if allegorically. *Platitudes* (dull, trite statements or remarks) similarly introduces a connotation of banality not indicated by the text.

32. (i) most important cause; (ii) didactic: Start with the second blank in this case. It's a description of "pamphlets," which are otherwise noted in the sentence as offering prescriptions and advice. A good prediction would be advisory. *Maleficent* (malicious; intending or producing evil) is way off unless you make a lot of assumptions, and *tenable* (able to be held, maintained, or justified) doesn't quite work as a description of a pamphlet, though it might have worked for some of the advice contained within. *Didactic* (intended to instruct) works best.

The first blank contains phrases, but it's still worth trying to make a prediction before engaging with the answers. The blank is connecting "digestive irregularity" to "preventable illness." Whatever this connection is, it prompted medieval physicians to focus heavily on "prophylactic dietary regimens." It's reasonable to infer that these were meant to avert digestive problems, which in turn suggests that the physicians saw the prevention of those digestive problems as very important. That would make sense if digestive irregularity were a cause of preventable illness. *Most significant cause* is a good match. *Only panacea* (cure-all or remedy) doesn't work; Maimonides and the other physicians might have wanted a panacea for preventable illness, but they wouldn't say that digestive irregularity *was* the panacea. *Sine qua non* (an absolutely essential component) also doesn't quite fit, as its positive spin makes digestive irregularity seem like a desirable thing.

33. (i) georgic; (ii) penury; (iii) sartorial: The first blank describes Francis' attire, which Francis doesn't believe will impress the well dressed executive *despite* her "fondness for rural life." The best prediction would be rural. *Rustic* means exactly that, and has the added benefit of meaning "simply made," a good contrast to the sharpness of the executive's apparel. *Natty*, meaning "sharp and stylish," is an opposite trap. *Exclusive* would give his attire a unique and unobtainable air, which, while possibly true of his attire, isn't justified by the proof and is usually used in a positive sense.

Following the concrete truth forward, his discomfort with his *rustic* garb led Francis to some "costly new wardrobe acquisitions." It sounds like Francis spent a lot of money on clothes and in so doing "reduced himself to" something. The phrase negative spin of "reduced himself" and the concrete proof that he spent money support a prediction of poverty. *Penury* (destitution) is a more extreme synonym. *Malaise* (vague, general sense of unease or mental discomfort) and *lethargy* (state of sluggishness, inactivity, laziness, or indifference) are near-synonyms of each other, and neither follows from the proof "costly" as well as *penury* does.

The plot thickens in the second sentence. The suave executive was concealing her own "financial ruin" with some kind of "showboating." What kind of showboating makes sense? All you know about the executive is that she's suave, sharply dressed, and financially devastated. Given that showboating is usually done to flaunt something that others will find impressive and "suave showboating" seems like a mismatch, stylistic showboating makes the most sense. *Bombastic* (pompous; pretentious) and *runic* (mysterious or arcane) don't match this prediction and have no clear support from any of the proof in the sentence. *Bombastic* showboating makes sense in general, but there is more direct proof for the correct answer *sartorial* (relating to clothes or style), since she is known to be "sharply dressed."

34. (i) A malingerer; (ii) credulous; (iii) sagacity: The word in the first blank should be identified with unreliability, but all three options for Blank (i) are words for people who are unreliable in some way. Look to see which of the words identifies a kind of unreliability that has more proof in the sentence. To be *an embezzler*, Garth would need to steal money entrusted to him by his employer, and no proof suggests that he does. Indeed, there's no evidence that Garth has stolen anything, ruling out *a pilferer* as well. *A malingerer* (someone who fakes illness to elude duty or obligation) fits with Garth's "frequent absences" and his hypochondriac employer's seemingly positive reaction.

The second blank is a word that, alongside "hypochondriac," describes Garth's employer. The only other thing we know is that the employer seems inclined to believe Garth's ill-disguised lies. So the word should either be something akin to hypochondriac or gullible. The boss could maybe be *casuistic* (practicing clever but unsound reasoning) or *imposing* (grand and impressive in appearance), but *credulous* (prone to easily believing things) is the best fit for the proof and matches the second prediction.

The last blank is a word similar to "foresight," and only *sagacity* fits. *Insipidity* (boringness, dullness) and *temerity* (excessive confidence, audacity) both usually have negative connotation, and would require extra story elements to work.

35. (i) lionized; (ii) incorrigible; (iii) rarely discussed: The concrete proof in this sentence indicates that the leader had "considerable moral shortcomings" that are seen as "peccadilloes" (minor transgressions) if they're mentioned at all. Blank (iii) contains a phrase that should make sense as a lead-in to "if mentioned at all." A good prediction would be not usually mentioned. *Rarely discussed* is a good match. *Mere relics* is a theme trap with "history" but is incorrect, as *relics* are the parts of history that survive until latter days, whereas mentions of the leader's shortcomings seem to be increasingly uncommon. *Widely praised* offers superficial agreement with the correct answer for Blank (i) but doesn't agree with "if mentioned at all."

With Blank (iii) filled in, Blank (i) is easier to manage. It's a word that identifies history's treatment of this leader, and the concrete proof is that the leader's negative qualities are *rarely discussed* and excused when they are discussed. It seems history has been kind to this leader—too kind. A word like whitewashed would fit the proof well. *Lionized* (popularly approved or lauded) takes this idea and runs with it, whereas *extirpated* (removed completely) and *impugned* (called into question) contradict the proof in the sentence.

The second blank describes the leader's "misogyny," an example of one of his "considerable moral shortcomings." There's no other description of his misogyny in the sentence, rendering prediction difficult, though there's a chance that the word in the blank should have some overlap with considerable. There's no proof suggesting that his misogyny would be *diffident* (shy or timid) or *reformed* (corrected). *Incorrigible* (inveterate; irredeemable) requires less assumption than the other choices in that it suggests only that the misogyny likely went on for the duration of the leader's time in prominence. This corroborates the proposition that his moral shortcomings were "considerable."

36. (i) fairness; (ii) catharsis; (iii) denouement: The first blank identifies the "overarching theme" of the new film. Since this theme's "dark side" is "exploitation and iniquity," the theme itself may be a more positive version of these two ideas. Look for something like fairness or good treatment. The former is there, and as exploitation and iniquity are both by definition unfair, this must be the right answer. *Slavery* and *injustice* are both theme and opposite traps in that they agree with "exploitation and iniquity" rather than follow the content reversal marker "dark side."

The film showcases the elimination of all the sympathetic protagonist's abusers, a move that garners the approval of the sentence's narrator and grants the audience something they've awaited the entire time, in a "satisfying upheaval." Look for a word that means something like good ending or satisfaction—something positive. The audience hasn't been waiting for *inconclusiveness*, which contradicts the proof and is vaguely negative. Maybe it has been waiting for a *revelation*, but this adds to the story of the sentence rather than reflects it, as there's no indication of anything unknown or discovered. *Catharsis* (release from built-up emotions) is a good fit.

The final blank is preceded by "this," a pronoun calling back to something recently mentioned. This something is what the "ponderous plot" was leading up to, and as the previous sentence discussed the cathartic ending of the film, the blank should be something like conclusion. *Denouement*, the part of a narrative in which the plot resolves, is a perfect match for the context. A *platitude* (trite saying) wouldn't provide a "satisfying upheaval," and there is no indication that the conclusion of the film was an *embellishment* (an often untrue detail added to a story to make it more interesting).

37. (i) eclecticism; (ii) a veneer: The concrete truth in the sentence is after the comma, and it would benefit from some rephrasing: Wallgot makes such wide-ranging references that even his biggest fans think it's ridiculous. The first part of the sentence, which starts with the reversal marker "although," must contrast this concrete truth in some way, saying something like "Although making wide-ranging references can be a good thing. . ." So the first blank should be something like making wide-ranging references. *Stringency* (strictness) and *insularity* (the narrow point of view resulting from life in a closed off community) imply the opposite of wide-ranging, but *eclecticism* (drawing on a wide variety of sources) fits well.

With *eclecticism* in the first blank, there's more concrete truth for the second. This part of the sentence must be expressing something beneficial about eclecticism. Perhaps it gives insubstantial work an illusion of profundity. *An iota* (a minimal amount) could be tempting as it allows the eclecticism to "give" something to the work. But if even Wallgot's fans "sneered" at its references, it may be safer to assume that in truth the work still had no profundity at all. Keep it for the moment. *A medley* (a mixture), which represents a theme trap with *eclecticism*, has no support in the sentence. *A veneer* is a surface covering designed to make low-quality underlying materials appear more attractive that they actually are, which is to say *a veneer* is perfect for this sentence: Eclectic references won't give the book *actual* profundity, but they might seem substantial enough to disguise a lack of profundity.

38. (i) emend; (ii) preemptive: For the first blank, you are looking for something the writer *could* do to "her lengthy tomes" that would appease editors if she did it. Shorten seems like a reasonable prediction, as all you really know about the book is that it's long. However, none of the options for Blank (i) mean "shorten." Look for the answer that has the best connection to other proof in the sentence. Though it doesn't mean shorten, *emend* (make corrections to) is something that can be done to a text, and it would also help "avoid editorial complaints," giving it a connection to the proof in the sentence. *Allay* (alleviate; put to rest) is not something that can be done to a tome, and while many tomes may *edify* (instruct, especially morally) their readers, a tome can't *be* edified.

She may not be a fan of edits, but the author is popular with the public. This popularity gives her a certain amount of leverage with her editors, in that she can threaten to sign with another publisher whenever she wants to avoid their complaints. The second blank is a word describing these threats, but the sentence doesn't offer much characterization of the threats. See if one of the answers has a connection to

Unit Two: **Paragraphs and Passages**

the proof. *Impuissant* (powerless) clashes with the proof, as the ability to make these threats is one of the ways that the author has been "empowered" by her popularity. There's no proof for or against *toothsome* (tasty). On the other hand, *preemptive* (intended to prevent or forestall) is a great fit, as the threats are said help the author to "avoid editorial complaints."

39. (i) proximate; (ii) protract; (iii) proliferation: The first blank asks for a contrast with "distant future," so look for a word meaning not distant. *Proximate* means exactly that. *Atavistic* (manifesting or reverting to ancestral characteristics) seems to call more directly to the past; this seems like it could actually work as a counterpoint to "the distant future," but it adds a very particular spin (reversion or regression) that's not justified by the context.

The second blank is connected to "present pleasures," a callback to the *proximate* times that subjects are said to place a higher value on. This preference for present times means the second blank should be a word that's positive, like enjoy or appreciate. None of the words mean exactly that, but *avert* (avoid by turning away) and *rescind* (revoke) are both too negative to fit with the higher value the subjects place on present times. *Protract* (prolong) reflects the subjects' predilection for the present better.

The third blank is some kind of "expense" and is connected to "future detriments." The subjects place a low value on things in the distant future, so it's fair to infer they would *protract* present pleasures even if it meant incurring or accumulating future expenses. *Proliferation* (a rapid increase; a large number) fits the second prediction well. *Malady* (illness) makes no sense here, and while *buttressing* (reinforcing) has a tempting positive spin, it doesn't fit the context (*buttressing* is typically used for things you want to protect or fortify).

40. (i) warrant; (ii) undergird: It is clear from "facile claim" (superficial, lacking complexity) and the generally derisive tone of the sentence that the author does not think the "she" in question has argued her point well enough. That informs the first blank, which will be something that her argument has "little" of. A good prediction would be nuance or justification. *Warrant* fits the latter prediction. *Syllogism* (a common form of logical reasoning) is a theme trap, and *fallacy* (logical flaw) is both a theme trap and an opposite trap—if anything, the author of this sentence *does* think an error has been made.

The second sentence also equates two things: how the "laws of logic" affected her dubious proclamation and how the "law of thermodynamics" led to a dubious discovery. Given the parallel between these two parts of the sentence as well as evidence from the first sentence, the word in the blank should be something like led to. *Undergird* (provide the basis for) is a good match. *Occlude* (close, cover, or obstruct) doesn't fit at all. *Galvanize* (spur to action) might initially seem like a good fit, but it's not as good a match for "gave rise to" as *undergird*. *Galvanize* often implies a subtext of excitement or intrigue that isn't present in the passage.

CHAPTER 8

Long Passages in Reading Comprehension

In This Chapter...

- Long Passages
- Two Extremes and a Balanced Approach
- Principles of Active Reading
- The Headline List
- Practice on Non-GRE Material
- A Review of Strategies for RC Questions
- Pulling It All Together
- Vocabulary Challenge
- Problem Set
- Answers and Explanations

Chapter 8 Long Passages in Reading Comprehension

In this chapter, you will learn how to adapt the techniques you learned in Chapter 5: Short Passages in RC to longer RC passages with multiple paragraphs.

Here are your Chapter 8 vocabulary words:

>delineate (E)
>
>manifest (A)
>
>aloof (A)
>
>maxim (A)
>
>abate (E)
>
>abhor (E)

Long Passages

In Chapter 5: Short Passages in RC, you worked with short passages; these passages are generally one paragraph in length, and you will be able to see the entire passage on the screen without scrolling. Long passages, on the other hand, consist of approximately 450 to 475 words spread over three to five paragraphs and 75 to 85 lines on the computer screen; you will need to scroll up and down on the screen to read the whole passage. Most likely, you will see one long passage per GRE exam (one Verbal section will have a long passage, and one will not). Each long passage will likely have four questions. (If you see three Verbal sections, one will be an experimental section and may also have a long passage.)

Long passages present the same challenges as short passages, but with increased length and occasionally increased complexity. Further, because there are multiple associated questions, it is not typically advisable to guess on the entire passage. However, the individual questions associated with long passages will not be any harder, on average, than questions for shorter passages.

The next few sections will address strategies to manage your focus and attention as you read a long passage, including delineating an adjusted note-taking process for long passages.

Unit Two: **Paragraphs and Passages**

Two Extremes and a Balanced Approach

To respond to the challenges of long passages and timing constraints on the GRE, test takers use strategies that manifest as one of two extreme styles of reading: they become either scholars or hunters. Neither extreme will serve you well. As you read the following descriptions, ask yourself whether these are habits you've fallen into in the past, and if so, which is more common for you.

Scholars do a very careful first read-through, paying attention to details—applying the same level of focus to each paragraph in a long passage that they applied to the short passages. "After all," scholars worry, "I could be asked about any aspect of the passage—and if I skim over anything, how can I be sure that that one clause was not important—even critical—to my overall understanding?" And while that *is* a productive mindset for short passages and for argument-based reading comprehension, it is *not* productive for the long passages.

One problem with this method is that it takes far too much time. More importantly, if you read *too* slowly and pay *too* much attention to every detail, you lose sight of the big picture: the gist and structure of the whole passage. In fact, the big picture is what you absolutely need to take away from the first read, not the minutiae. Recall the lessons in Chapter 5: Short Passages in RC; if asked about a detail, you *will* look it up again.

At the other extreme is the **hunter**. Hunters avoid the first read-through altogether, reasoning that most questions require some kind of detailed lookup anyway—so why not just skip the initial reading and go right to the questions? As their name implies, hunters simply go hunting for the answer in a passage they never read completely. (Note that a hunter is not merely scanning the questions in advance and then reading the whole passage, which is advisable. Rather, a hunter goes directly to the questions, and tries to search for the answer to each question immediately, with no first read of the passage at all.)

Admittedly, this strategy does save time up-front, but it creates two problems that greatly outweigh that advantage. First, the extra time needed to analyze the question, search for the information without really knowing where to look, and then move through the choices with no prediction in mind completely erases any time you save by not reading. Second, and perhaps even more damaging, hunters usually have lower accuracy on the questions.

The middle ground between hunters and scholars is occupied by **big-picture readers** who take a balanced approach. While big-picture readers may quickly scan the questions in order to get some early clues about the passage, they don't try to answer the questions immediately. Rather, they next read the full passage with an eye toward structure. At the beginning of the passage, big-picture readers go slowly, ensuring a solid grasp of the expected structure. But they go quickly as their understanding of the main idea increases, keeping minor details at arm's length. They read *actively* but *efficiently*.

The goal of big-picture reading is to avoid finishing a passage and feeling that you just wasted your time—either because you got lost in the weeds or because you skimmed over the passage too aloofly to grasp any content.

If hunters spend too little time reading, and scholars spend too much time reading, then the balanced approach of big-picture readers is *just right*. (And yes, our favorite fairy tale is *Goldilocks and the Three Bears*. How did you guess?)

Chapter 8: **Long Passages in Reading Comprehension**

Principles of Active Reading

How do you become a big-picture reader on the GRE? By using the seven principles of active, efficient reading. These principles are meant to be used as needed to understand long, complex passages, and are not to be used as a sequential "must-do" list while reading the passage.

Seven Principles of Active Reading

1. Engage with the passage.
2. Understand the beginning.
3. Pick up the pace.
4. Pay attention to signals.
5. Link to what you already know.
6. Link to what you have just read.
7. Look for the simple story.

(Principles 5 and 6 may sound similar, but as you'll see, they incorporate different but complementary aspects of active reading.)

Keep in mind that these principles apply more directly to content-based passages than to argument-structure passages, which do not feature as much text, in terms of either length or detail. However if you are struggling to focus on a particular argument, these strategies can help there, too.

If some of these principles feel oddly familiar to you—if you have the distinct, deja-vu-like impression that you've read them before—you're somewhat correct! These are, largely speaking, not new. Your mental processes as you read do not change drastically across the Verbal section: These are merely expansions of discussions throughout this entire book.

Principle 1: Engage with the Passage.

First, your **emotional attitude** toward the passage impacts how well you can process and recall it. The maxim *engage with the passage* is based on a simple truth about your brain: You cannot learn something that you actively loathe or viscerally reject. Getting over your dread of the passage is not just a feel-good exercise; it is a prerequisite. You do not have to fall madly in love with medieval Flemish poetry or the chemistry of zinc, but you cannot effectively read the passage if you're antagonistic toward the content.

So what do you do if your mind keeps wandering because this just isn't something you're particularly interested in reading?

One quick and effective method is to **pretend that you really like this stuff**. Say to yourself, "This is great! I get to spend the next six minutes thinking about *sea urchins*!" However sarcastic you may be when you say that to yourself, who knows—you might actually like them, learn something along the way, and do well on the questions (the most important thing). This also works if you imagine that you're going to have a conversation with someone you really admire, but they'll only talk about this topic. Seek out interesting twists that you can surprise them with. ("Did you know sea urchins don't have a single bone in their entire body?!")

Another way to help yourself get into the passage psychologically is to **identify good guys and bad guys**. If the sea urchins are threatened by environmental damage, get a little angry on their behalf. Engaging your

Unit Two: **Paragraphs and Passages**

emotions strengthens your mind's ability to recall. That's why you remember really good events and really bad events much more easily than events where nothing exciting happened.

If you cannot stomach these steps, **simply acknowledge that you do not find the passage thrilling**. Allow yourself a moment of disappointment. Then hunker down and get back into it. Whatever you do, do not let yourself be pushed around by the passage. Love it or hate it, you have to *own* it. When you find yourself in this situation, pick and choose what you're going to focus on so you can still read with purpose. Typically, seek out these kinds of important moments in the passage:

1. **Beginnings of paragraphs.** The first or second sentence often functions as a topic sentence, indicating the content and/or purpose of the paragraph.

2. **Big surprises** or changes in direction.

3. **Big results**, answers, or payoffs.

Remember, you're not trying to grasp the whole passage deeply. Your energy and your focus are the most valuable assets you have on the GRE in general and on Reading Comprehension in particular. Allocate these assets carefully.

Principle 2: Understand the Beginning.

Give the first paragraph of a long passage the same care and detail that you give to short reading comprehension passages and argument-based passages. A full understanding of the first paragraph builds a conceptual framework that will allow you to move more quickly through the following paragraphs. If you fully understand the introductory paragraph, each following paragraph is now merely "How does this fit within the introductory framework?" You can move more quickly with the information if you only need to place that information within the context of what you already know.

All too often, GRE students satisfy themselves with an impressionistic sense of the beginning of a passage. However, **forming an impression is not the same as comprehending the passage**. Given the importance of the initial sentences, try to grasp 100 percent of the beginning of any passage (even if you only grasp 40 percent of the end). That is far better than comprehending 70 percent of the text throughout.

Stuck on an early sentence? Apply the unpacking techniques from Chapter 2: GRE Sentences. It can be tempting to read too quickly when the passage is long and time is short. However, taking the time to unpack the first couple of sentences will allow you to speed up more quickly as you get the main idea.

Imagine that the following is the first sentence from a passage. Practice unpacking using what you learned in Chapter 2: GRE Sentences.

In a diachronic investigation of possible behavioral changes resulting from accidental exposure in early childhood to environmental lead dust, two sample groups were tracked over decades.

A sample unpacking might look something like this:

1. There was lead dust in various environments.

2. Young kids in these environments were exposed to this dust by accident.

3. This exposure may have changed how the kids behaved.

4. This whole matter was investigated.

5. In this "d-something" investigation, two sample groups were tracked over time.

This unpacked "story" is easier to dive into and understand than the original sentence—even though the story contains nearly twice as many words. Also, note that the subject and verb of the original sentence do not appear until the end. This phenomenon is very common. Often, it is easiest to understand the outer "frame" of the original sentence *last*.

During untimed review, as you start to practice breaking down a sentence in this way, don't be discouraged by the amount of time it takes. The goal is not to actually write the five summary sentences down on test day but rather to train your mind to process text more deliberately and ultimately more efficiently. And if you find yourself needing more work on unpacking sentences, go back to the discussion and problem set in Chapter 2: GRE Sentences.

Principle 3: Pick up the pace.

As seen in the previous paragraphs, understanding the introduction fully can be very time-consuming. But what happens as you get further into a passage? Each new sentence can only do one of two things: continue the story as you already understand it or introduce a contradiction or surprise that you weren't expecting.

If information seems to be "more of the same," don't get lost in the details: You can speed up. However, if you run into a piece of information that is unexpected or provides a new point of view, slow down a bit to find clarity. How does this new information fit?

Yes, you must read the whole passage—but later parts are often support or background and won't need the same attention to detail as the earlier material.

Principle 4: Pay attention to signals.

Various language signals can help you link new material to text you have already read. Breaks within and between sentences, as well as between paragraphs, all indicate some transition of ideas. You'll have to be able to confidently pick up on those transitions. Signal words, such as *therefore* or *however*, can be used to figure out the structure of the passage and to help give you an idea of what to expect as you continue reading. For more on this, return to the sections on direction markers and signals in Chapter 3: TC and SC and Chapter 4: GRE Paragraphs.

Principle 5: Link to what you already know.

To both engage with the passage and select what to focus on, link what you're reading to concrete ideas or images. The more realistic you can make the text, the easier it will be to process.

Consider the *lead dust* example under principle 2. Were you able to imagine children coughing from lead dust?

When you are engaged with a passage, the words on the page typically activate preexisting knowledge in your head. This is a crucial part of comprehending what you are reading. Every word that you know in the English language is naturally tied to a web of memories and ideas. But if a word does *not* activate ideas when you read it, it might as well be *zzyrglbzrch*!

Normally, your brain wakes up these ideas and memories as a natural part of reading. However, under stress, your eyes can pass over words and even recognize them, but no ideas come to life in your brain. You are too distracted and overwhelmed, and the words on the page remain "just words."

In this case, try making the story real. That is, **actively *imagine* what the words are referring to**. Re-explain the original text to yourself. Visualize what it represents. Indulge in simplifications, even stereotypes. Make up examples, and use any other mental handles that you have.

Note that you are *not* bringing in outside knowledge to help you answer questions; this can lead you to falling for trap answers. You are bringing your outside knowledge together with your imagination in order to make the text on the screen seem more *real* and therefore more engaging.

Principle 6: Link to what you have just read.

As you read further, continue to ask yourself about the **meaning** and **purpose** of what you are reading. What does this sentence mean *in relation to everything else I have read*? Why is this sentence or paragraph here? What function does it serve in relation to the previous text? Often, you can answer these questions by considering the following:

1. Is the new sentence or paragraph **expected or surprising**?
2. Does it **support or oppose** earlier material?
3. Does it **answer or ask** a question?
4. Does this text serve as one of the **paragraph components** from Chapter 4: GRE Paragraphs?

Principle 7: Look for the simple story.

As you find the connections between sentences and paragraphs, you'll end up writing the **simple story**. Here are a few ways you can think about the passage to make it more manageable:

1. **Text it to me.** As you read, ask yourself this question: How would you retell all this stuff to an intelligent but bored teenager in just a couple of sentences? Can you use just 5–10 words to describe a paragraph? You will find yourself cutting out the trivia.
2. **Make a table of contents.** Use five words or fewer for the headline of each paragraph. As written, these headlines may not sound exactly like a story, but they outline the same narrative.
3. **Look for content and judgment.** The parts of a simple story can generally be classified as content or judgment, as follows:

    Content: the scientific, historical, or artistic subject matter of the passage
    a. Causes (effects, evidence, logical results)
    b. Processes (steps, means, ends)
    c. Categories (examples, generalities)

    Judgment: what the author and any other people believe about the Content
    a. Theories and hypotheses
    b. Evaluations and opinions
    c. Comparisons and contrasts
    d. Advantages and disadvantages

For example, a passage might be about the worldwide decline in the population of bees. In describing various theories, the passage might emphasize a distinction between the pessimistic theories shared by most scientists and the optimistic theory of one, Scientist X, who believes that the decline is taking place within a natural oscillation.

The simple story might go like this:

> The number of bees in the world is falling fast. There are a few possible explanations including pollution, climate change, and loss of habitat. Most scientists think this decline is a serious problem caused by human activity, but Scientist X thinks it's part of a natural cycle, and the bees will come back soon on their own.

Here, the main idea is the contrast between what most scientists believe about the bee decline and what Scientist X believes.

The Headline List

The discussion of notes in Chapter 4: GRE Paragraphs is particularly applicable to long passages. It is not reasonable to try to keep that much information solely in your head while you read. It is also not reasonable (or necessary) to make detailed notes on every paragraph. Just as there is a balanced approach to reading, there is a balanced approach to taking notes on long passages: a headline list.

You can think of a headline list as a sort of annotated table of contents, emphasizing the major points of each paragraph and adding supporting notes as needed.

The purpose of your headline list is twofold: to help you grasp the main ideas and to know where to look for certain details. If you've done your job well, you'll be able to answer all general questions without referring to the passage and you may not even need to refer to your notes.

When you hit a specific question, you will need to reread the relevant details in the passage; don't try to answer from memory. If you don't happen to remember where something was mentioned, use your headline list as a guide—this is precisely why you created it. Also, note that if you can answer a detailed question using just your notes, then you wrote too much down; this is an opportunity to improve and streamline your process on future passages.

Four Steps to Create Your Headline List

To create a headline list, follow these steps:

1. Identify the main idea of each paragraph.

Just as a headline summarizes the main idea of a newspaper article, most paragraphs in RC passages have one topic sentence. Generally, the topic sentence is the first or second sentence, although it can also be a combination of the two. As you read the first couple of sentences, identify the topic sentence and summarize it concisely on your scratch paper in the form of a headline (typically five words or fewer). If you cannot identify a topic sentence, then your headline should summarize the main idea or purpose of the paragraph in your own words. You may not be able to articulate this idea until after you've read the entire paragraph.

2. Note any big surprises and results you encounter.

As you read the rest of the paragraph, briefly summarize anything else that is very important or surprising in the paragraph. Often, this will consist of jotting down just a word or two: a note on what paragraph component(s) you see or a note on whose point(s) of view you see. You may not add anything to the original topic sentence if the paragraph fits neatly within the scope of that sentence.

3. Follow the same process for any subsequent paragraphs.

Let your note-taking abate some as you progress through the passage, but don't stop entirely. Taking notes can take you out of the flow, but forcing yourself to reinterpret what you just read in order to take the note can increase attention and understanding. For that reason, force yourself to stop periodically to add to your Headline List.

4. Once you have finished the passage, articulate the main idea.

The main idea is almost like a title for your headline list. It may be one of the headlines you've already written down; if so, label or mark it. If that is not the case, jot down the main idea at the bottom of your headline list before proceeding to the questions.

Try using the four steps discussed above to create a headline list for the following passage.

> Electroconvulsive therapy (ECT) is a controversial psychiatric treatment involving the induction of a seizure in a patient via the passage of electricity through the brain. While beneficial effects of electrically induced seizures are evident and predictable in most patients, a unified mechanism of action has not yet been established and remains the subject of numerous investigations. According to most, though not all, published studies, ECT has been shown to be effective against several conditions, such as severe depression, mania, and some acute psychotic states, that are resistant to other treatments. However, like many other medical procedures, ECT has its risks.
>
> Since the inception of ECT in 1938, the public has held a strongly negative conception of the procedure. Initially, doctors employed unmodified ECT. Patients were rendered instantly unconscious by the electrical current, but the strength of the muscle contractions from induced, uncontrolled motor seizures often led to compression fractures of the spine or damage to the teeth. In addition to the effect this physical trauma had on public sentiment, graphic examples of abuse were documented in nonfiction or loosely fictional books and movies, such as Ken Kesey's *One Flew Over the Cuckoo's Nest*, which portrayed ECT as punitive, cruel, overused, and violative of patients' legal rights. Indeed, the alternative term *electroshock* has a negative connotation, tainted by these depictions in the media.
>
> In comparison with its earlier incarnation, modern ECT is virtually unrecognizable. The treatment is modified by the muscle relaxant succinylcholine, which renders muscle contractions virtually nonexistent. Additionally, patients are given a general anesthetic. Thus, the patient is asleep and fully unaware during the procedure, and the only outward sign of a seizure may be the rhythmic movement of the patient's hand or foot. ECT is generally used in severely depressed patients for whom psychotherapy and medication prove ineffective. It may also be considered when there is an imminent risk of suicide, since antidepressants often require several weeks to show results. Exactly how ECT exerts its influence on behavior is not known, but repeated applications affect several important neurotransmitters in the brain, including serotonin, norepinephrine, and dopamine.
>
> The consensus view of the scientific and medical community is that ECT has been proven effective, but the procedure remains controversial. Though decades-old studies showing brain cell death have been refuted in recent research, many patients do report retrograde amnesia (of events prior to treatment) and/or anterograde amnesia (of events during or shortly after treatment). Patients have also reported that their short-term memories continue to be affected for months after ECT, though some doctors argue that this memory malfunction may reflect the type of amnesia sometimes associated with severe depression. A recent neuropsychological study at Duke University documents a significant decline in performance on memory tests, ironically accompanied at times by self-reports of improved memory function; however, the researchers recommended only that these potential detriments be weighed against the potential benefits of ECT in any particular case.

The following is a sample headline list. Your headline list certainly does not need to be identical, but check to see whether you feel you noted similar points in your list:

> 1. ECT controv psych treat: Electr into brain → seizure
>   —Beneficial, but mech not understood
>   **Effective for some conditions; has risks
> 2. Since 1938, public dislikes ECT
> 3. Modern ECT totally diff
> 4. ECT effective but still controv ← main idea

Paragraph one has a headline and some detail. (Try to use as much shorthand and as many abbreviations as possible on your own paper; you only need to understand them for the few minutes that you'll be working on that passage.)

The notes for paragraphs two through four are much more concise, consisting only of the headline of each body paragraph. In these paragraphs, the main idea was found in the first one or two sentences of the paragraph.

The main idea of this passage is contained in the first sentence of the last paragraph and is therefore marked in the notes: ECT has proven effective, but it remains controversial.

Practice on Non-GRE Material

Reading Comprehension may seem difficult to improve, especially in a short period of time. You can accelerate your progress by applying these principles to what you read *outside* of the GRE, as part of your daily life. Actively engage with the material, especially if you are not initially attracted to it. Look for the simple story. Link what you read to what you already know and to what you have just read. Unpack and/or make the story real if necessary. Pay attention to signals. And pick up the pace as you read, in order to avoid getting lost in details.

These principles work on a wide range of expository writing—a company's annual report, a book review in the newspaper, an article in your college alumni magazine. By applying these principles outside of a testing or test-prep environment, you will become much more comfortable with them.

Granted, some outside material is more GRE-like than other material. You can read major journals and newspapers, such as *The New Yorker, The Economist, The Wall Street Journal, The Atlantic,* and *The New York Times,* to become better informed about the world in general. However, these publications are somewhat *too* digestible. The paragraphs are too short, and neither the topics nor the writing itself is quite as boring as what you find on the GRE.

In this regard, university alumni magazines are good sources of articles that resemble Reading Comprehension passages in style and substance. (No offense to your alma maters!) Also, if you tend to abhor science passages, then read articles in *Scientific American* or similar publications that popularize the latest advances in science and technology. In this way, you can gain familiarity with science writing aimed at an educated but nonspecialized audience.

Unit Two: **Paragraphs and Passages**

There are also good online resources. For instance, the website aldaily.com (Arts and Letters Daily) is an excellent source of articles with high intellectual content. Reading Arts and Letters Daily is an excellent way to prepare for the Reading Comprehension portion of the exam while also filling your brain full of information that might come in handy for the GRE Issue Essay. Look up any words you don't know, and practice reading with an eye for the main idea, tone, and structure of an argument or article.

A Review of Strategies for RC Questions

As discussed in Chapter 5: Short Passages in RC, GRE Reading Comprehension questions come in a variety of forms, but they can be placed into two major categories:

1. General questions
2. Specific questions

The following sections will reiterate the discussion points from Chapter 5: Short Passages in RC, with small tweaks to the processes as needed to adjust to longer passages. If it has been a while since you've reviewed that section, do so before you proceed.

But fundamentally, the following material is not new and *is not meant to be*! In fact, it's crucial to develop robust strategies that are broadly applicable across multiple elements of the test. Ultimately, Reading Comprehension is Reading Comprehension, whether the passage is one paragraph or forty. (No, there are no forty-paragraph passages on the GRE. . .)

Regardless of whether the passage is long or short, the four-step process is the same:

1. Scan the question(s).
2. Read and deconstruct the passage.
3. Address each question in turn, predicting an answer if you can.
4. Eliminate and select.

The chart outlining timing approximations based on the number of questions in a passage is reproduced below:

# of Questions	Time Spent Reading	Time Spent in Answer Choices	Total Time
1	1 minute 30 seconds	45 seconds	2 minutes, 15 seconds
2	2 minutes	45 seconds	3 minutes, 30 seconds
3	3 minutes	45 seconds	5 minutes, 15 seconds
4	3 minutes	45 seconds	6 minutes
5 (very rare)	3 minutes	45 seconds	6 minutes, 45 seconds

Chapter 8: Long Passages in Reading Comprehension

Revisiting General Questions

General questions follow the forms listed in the following table (the GRE will not bold words in the question):

Type of General Question	Common Phrasing
Main Idea	Which of the following best expresses the **main idea** of the passage?
Primary Purpose	The author's **primary purpose** is . . . The passage is **primarily concerned with** which of the following?
Purpose of Paragraph	Which of the following best describes the **function of** the second **paragraph**?

For main idea or primary purpose questions, if you find yourself stuck with several answers left, apply a scoring system. Assign two points to answer choices that incorporate elements from the first paragraph, and one point for each element from another paragraph. The answer choice with the highest score incorporates the most references across the whole passage and is the best selection.

The third type, purpose of paragraph, appears only in passages with multiple paragraphs.

Purpose of paragraph questions test your ability to place a whole paragraph within the context of the passage. Your headline list will aid you in answering these. These questions are a middle-ground between primary purpose, which ask for the purpose of the whole passage, and specific purpose, which ask for the purpose of a single detail.

> **Strategy Tip:**
>
> For **general** questions, **articulate a prediction** in your own words, and eliminate answers that do not match.

Unit Two: Paragraphs and Passages

Revisiting Specific Questions

Specific questions follow the forms listed in the following table (the GRE will not bold words in the question):

Type of Specific Question	Common Phrasing
Specific Detail	In the example discussed in the passage, **what is true** about poppy seeds in bread dough, once the dough has been thoroughly mixed?
	The passage **states** . . .
Inference	It can be **inferred** from the passage that . . .
	The author **suggests** . . .
Select a Sentence	**Select the sentence** that, according to the author, would best explain the early nineteenth-century trends toward more humane treatment of animals.
Specific Purpose	The author references the work of Von Neumann primarily **in order to** . . .
Word in Context	In the context in which it appears, "abstruse" (line 27) **most nearly means** . . .
Author Agrees	With which of the following statements would the **author** of the passage be most likely to **agree**?

The only example new to this table, Author Agrees, asks for the author's opinion. While the answer could be the main idea, the GRE can also construct answer choices that are *not* the main idea but instead conform to a statement made somewhere in the passage. Regardless of whether the answer is main idea or a more narrow statement, the correct answer will closely conform to the text of the passage.

Using the Specifics of a Specific Question

When you reach the part of the passage that pertains to a specific question, make note of where in the passage this information is and make an effort to understand it within your work-in-progress interpretation. If the specific question contained no key words in the question for you to use, you'll have to use key words in the answer choices to find the relevant part of the passage.

> *Strategy Tip:*
>
> For **specific questions, use key words** from the question or answer choices to find relevant parts of the paragraph.

Once you find the key words, **boil down the relevant sentence or sentences into a synopsis**—five words of truth.

Then you can bring that synopsis back to the answer choices and hold it in your head as you eliminate the four "untruths," matching the correct answer to your synopsis.

> *Strategy Tip:*
>
> For **specific questions, craft a synopsis** from one or two proof sentences and compare the choices to that.

Chapter 8: **Long Passages in Reading Comprehension**

Pulling It All Together

You have learned and practiced strategies for Reading Comprehension throughout this guide. At this point, you may find it worthwhile to take some time to revisit a few discussions across various chapters:

1. **What to do as you read**
   - Chapter 4: Components of Paragraphs
   - Chapter 4: The Main Idea (and Archetypes)
   - Chapter 8: Principles of Active Reading
2. **How to take notes**
   - Chapter 4: Don't Just Read, Do Something!
   - Chapter 8: The Headline List
3. **Tackling the questions themselves**
   - Chapter 5: Comprehensive Strategies for All Reading Comprehension
   - Chapter 5: Summary of Strategies for Answer Choice Eliminations
   - Chapter 8: A Review of Strategies for RC Questions

As one last supplement to bullet 1, here is an abbreviated reproduction of the archetypes list from Chapter 4. After you finish the Problem Sets from Chapters 5, 8, and 9, consider how these passages fit these archetypes.

1. **Explanation of a concept**
2. **Competing opinions/theories on a subject**
3. **A critic's opinion of a subject/work**
4. **The author's opinion of a work**
5. **A change in perception over time**

Keep in mind that most passages are not *perfect* examples; that said, an understanding of how a passage approximates an archetype aids your understanding of the passage. Some harder passages might combine multiple archetypes into one: For example, Passage D: Ether's Existence is arguably both archetype 1 and archetype 5, because the passage presents explanations of nineteenth-century physics, but also how an experiment led to changes in scientific understanding.

Unit Two: **Paragraphs and Passages**

Vocabulary Challenge

> Did you spot these vocabulary words? If not, go back and find them in context! (The word may be in a different form than listed here— "digressing" instead of "digress," for example.) Write your own definitions based on the evidence in the chapter.

1. delineate (*v*), p. 239
2. manifest (*v*), p. 240
3. aloof (*adj.*), p. 240
4. maxim (*n*), p. 241
5. abate (*v*), p. 245
6. abhor (*v*), p. 247

Chapter 8: **Long Passages in Reading Comprehension**

Problem Set

> The following problem set consists of two passages followed by a series of questions on each passage. Just as on the real test, you can and should scan the questions before reading.
>
> The first passage has four accompanying questions. If you'd like to practice official timing for this passage and its questions, budget approximately 6 minutes total: 2–3 minutes to read the passage and approximately 45 seconds to complete each question.
>
> The second passage has additional questions so that you can gain more practice answering a variety of problem types. You can decide whether to answer only three or four of the questions initially. You can then save the passage for a second pass (with the remaining three or four questions) later on in your studies.

Passage D: Ether's Existence

In 1887, an ingenious experiment performed by Albert Michelson and Edward Morley severely undermined classical physics by failing to confirm the existence of ether, a ghostly massless medium that was thought to permeate the universe. Although the implications of this experimental failure were not completely evident for many years, they ultimately paved the way for Einstein's special theory of relativity.

Prior to the Michelson–Morley experiment, nineteenth-century physics conceived of light as a wave of electric and magnetic fields. These fields were governed by Maxwell's equations, which predicted that these waves would propagate at a particular speed c. The existence of ether was hypothesized in part to explain the propagation of light waves, which was believed to be impossible through empty space. Moreover, the ether provided the theoretical baseline for the speed of light predicted by Maxwell's equations: light was to travel at speed c, relative to the ether. Physical objects, such as planets, were also thought to glide frictionlessly through the unmoving ether.

The Michelson–Morley experiment relied on the concept that the Earth, which orbits the Sun, would be in motion relative to the fixed ether. Just as a person on a motorcycle experiences a "wind" caused by the cycle's motion relative to the air, the Earth would experience an "ethereal wind" caused by its motion through the ether. Such a wind would affect our measurements of the speed of light. If the speed of light is fixed with respect to the ether, but the Earth is moving through the ether, then to an observer on Earth, light must appear to move faster in a downwind direction than in an upwind direction.

In 1887, there were no clocks sufficiently precise to detect the speed differences that would result from an ethereal wind. Michelson and Morley surmounted this problem by using the wavelike properties of light itself to test for such speed differences. In their apparatus, known as an interferometer, a single beam of light is split in half. Mirrors guide each half of the beam along a separate trajectory before ultimately reuniting the two half-beams into a single beam. If one half-beam has moved more slowly than the other, the reunited beams will be out of phase with each other. In other words, peaks of the slower half-beam will not coincide exactly with peaks of the faster half-beam, resulting in an interference pattern in the reunited beam. However, this interference pattern failed to appear. No matter how they positioned the arms of the interferometer in relation to the theoretical ethereal wind, Michelson and Morley detected only a tiny degree of interference in the reunited light beam—far less than what was expected based on the motion of the Earth. This null result helped demolish the ether construct and replace it, in the end, with a far stranger view of time and space.

Unit Two: **Paragraphs and Passages**

1. Which of the following best describes the main purpose of the passage above?
    - (A) To discuss the difficulties faced by two scientists while designing an experiment
    - (B) To trace the changes occurring in nineteenth-century physics
    - (C) To argue for continued research in a particular field of experimental physics
    - (D) To explore the implications of the existence of ether on the properties of light
    - (E) To describe two scientists' experimental result and its significant implications for theoretical physics

2. The third paragraph of the passage plays which of the following roles?
    - (A) It foreshadows the difficulties Michelson and Morley would face when performing their experiment.
    - (B) It supports the author's view that Michelson and Morley's experiment was unappreciated in its time.
    - (C) It contrasts the views of Einstein with nineteenth-century physicists.
    - (D) It introduces an analogy to further explain the nineteenth-century understanding of ether's effect on the observed speed of light.
    - (E) It describes the theories of physics which governed scientific understanding in Michelson and Morley's time.

3. Select the sentence in the final two paragraphs that explains why Michelson and Morley had to depend on interference patterns to test their theory.

4. Which of the following would the author of the passage be likely to agree with?
Select all that apply.
    - [A] Michelson and Morley's experiment failed to produce meaningful results.
    - [B] The lack of precise stopwatches did not significantly impact Michelson and Morley's eventual results.
    - [C] Twentieth-century physics would not necessarily have progressed as quickly as it did without Michelson and Morley's experiment.

Passage E: Sweet Spot

Though most tennis players generally strive to strike the ball on the racket's vibration node, more commonly known as the "sweet spot," many players are unaware of the existence of a second, lesser-known location on the racket face, the center of percussion, that will also greatly diminish the strain on a player's arm when the ball is struck.

In order to understand the physics of this second sweet spot, it is helpful to consider what would happen to a tennis racket in the moments after impact with the ball if the player's hand were to vanish at the moment of impact. The impact of the ball would cause the racket to bounce backward, experiencing a translational motion away from the ball. The tendency of this motion would be to jerk all parts of the racket, including the end of its handle, backward, or away from the ball. Unless the ball happened to hit the racket precisely at the racket's center of mass, the racket would additionally experience a rotational motion around its center of mass—much as a penny that has been struck near its edge will start to spin. Whenever the ball hits the racket face, the effect of this rotational motion will be to jerk the end of the handle forward, toward the ball. Depending on where the ball strikes the racket face, one or the other of these motions will predominate.

However, there is one point of impact, known as the center of percussion, which causes neither motion to predominate; if a ball were to strike this point, the impact would not impart any motion to the end of the handle. The reason for this lack of motion is that the force on the upper part of the hand would be equal and opposite to the force on the lower part of the hand, resulting in no net force on the tennis player's hand or forearm. The center of percussion constitutes a second sweet spot because a tennis player's wrist typically is placed next to the end of the racket's handle. When the player strikes the ball at the center of percussion, their wrist is jerked neither forward nor backward, and they experience a relatively smooth, comfortable tennis stroke.

The manner in which a tennis player can detect the center of percussion on a given tennis racket follows from the nature of this second sweet spot. The center of percussion can be located via simple trial and error by holding the end of a tennis racket between your finger and thumb and throwing a ball onto the strings. If the handle jumps out of your hand, then the ball has missed the center of percussion.

5. The passage primarily focuses on

    (A) a proposal for an improvement to the design of tennis rackets
    (B) an examination of the differences between the two types of sweet spots
    (C) a definition of the translational and rotational forces acting on a tennis racket
    (D) a description of the ideal area in which to strike every ball
    (E) an explanation of a lesser-known area on a tennis racket that dampens unwanted vibration

6. According to the passage, all of the following are true of the forces acting upon a tennis racket striking a ball EXCEPT

    (A) the only way to eliminate the jolt that accompanies most strokes is to hit the ball on the center of percussion
    (B) the impact of the ball striking the racket can strain a tennis player's arm
    (C) there are at least two different forces acting upon the racket
    (D) the end of the handle of the racket will jerk forward after striking the ball unless the ball strikes the racket's center of mass
    (E) the racket will rebound after it strikes the ball

7. In the context of the author's argument, the second paragraph performs which of the following functions?

    (A) It establishes the main idea of the passage.
    (B) It provides an explanation of the mechanics of the phenomenon discussed in the passage.
    (C) It introduces a counterargument that elucidates the main idea of the passage.
    (D) It provides an example of the primary subject described in the passage.
    (E) It explains why the main idea of the passage would be useful for tennis players.

Unit Two: **Paragraphs and Passages**

8. The author mentions "a penny that has been struck near its edge" in order to
   - (A) show how the center of mass causes the racket to spin
   - (B) argue that a penny spins in the exact way that a tennis racket spins
   - (C) explain how translational motion works
   - (D) provide an illustration of a concept
   - (E) demonstrate that pennies and tennis rackets do not spin in the same way

9. Which of the following can be inferred from the passage?
   - (A) If a player holds a tennis racket anywhere other than the end of the handle, the player will experience a jolting sensation.
   - (B) The primary sweet spot is more effective at damping vibration than is the secondary sweet spot.
   - (C) Striking a tennis ball at a spot other than the center of percussion can result in a jarring feeling.
   - (D) Striking a tennis ball repeatedly at spots other than a sweet spot leads to a repetitive stress injury.
   - (E) If a player lets go of the racket at the moment of impact, the simultaneous forward and backward impetus causes the racket to drop straight to the ground.

10. Select the sentence in the second or third paragraph that describes the physics of the center of percussion's perceived sweetness.

11. It can be inferred that a tennis ball that strikes a racket's center of percussion will do which of the following?
    Select all that apply.
    - [A] Cause the racket to bounce backward
    - [B] Not cause the wrist to jerk
    - [C] Allow for a cleaner stroke than a ball striking a racket's primary sweet spot

Chapter 8: **Long Passages in Reading Comprehension**

Answers and Explanations

Vocabulary Challenge

1. delineate (*v*): mark the outline of; sketch; describe in detail

2. manifest (*v*): to show, make clear, or prove

3. aloof (*adj.*): distant physically or emotionally; reserved; indifferent

4. maxim (*n*): a general truth or fundamental principle, especially expressed as a proverb or saying

5. abate (*v*): reduce, diminish

6. abhor (*v*): detest, regard with disgust

Problem Set

Answers to Passage D: Ether's Existence

> **Upon previewing the questions, here is an example of what you might jot down:**
>
> 1. main purp
>
> 2. role par3
>
> 3. select: why interf. patt.
>
> 4. author agree
>
> Take a moment to consider when you might encounter the information needed for each question. The first and second are both about the big picture of the passage: the main idea and how the third paragraph fits into that context. These will both come from your first read. The third question is something you can look for as you read the passage: Keep an eye out for "interference patterns" as you read the third and fourth paragraphs. Unfortunately, the fourth question wants a general inference, so you will have to review the passage for every answer choice.
>
> **Here is one example of a possible set of notes for this passage:**
>
> 1. <u>MM undermine class. phys.</u> ← main idea pt1
>   <u>— led to Einstein Th. of Rel.</u> ← main idea pt2
>
> 2. prior MM, ether → speed of light
>
> 3. MM exp. relied on relative motion
>
> 4. no clocks, so MM used light wave. failure → new view of time and space

Unit Two: **Paragraphs and Passages**

1. **Which of the following best describes the main purpose of the passage above?**

   (A) To discuss the difficulties faced by two scientists while designing an experiment
   (B) To trace the changes occurring in nineteenth-century physics
   (C) To argue for continued research in a particular field of experimental physics
   (D) To explore the implications of the existence of ether on the properties of light
   (E) To describe two scientists' experiment that had significant implications for theoretical physics

   The main idea of this passage is contained in the first paragraph. In fact, rewriting those two sentences into a one-sentence summation would be the main idea. Michelson and Morley's experiment failed, but this failure ultimately led to Einstein's theory of relativity. The succeeding paragraphs, although interesting to the passage author, are background information regarding the previous theories of physicists and the intricacies involved in the experiment itself. The result of the experiments and the implications of that result are the main idea.

   (A) While much of the passage does discuss the intricacies of the experiment, this is too narrow. The main idea is focused on the larger implications of the result.
   (B) The passage does not provide a detailed chronology of changes in nineteenth-century physics.
   (C) "To argue" is stronger than the author's tone. Additionally, there are no mentions of further research needs.
   (D) As with choice (A), this choice is also too narrow. Although much of the passage does discuss the implications of ether on the properties of light, this discussion is not the result of the experiment or the implications of that result.
   (E) **CORRECT.** This choice is the only choice that addresses the result and implication of the experiment.

2. **The third paragraph of the passage plays which of the following roles?**

   (A) It foreshadows the difficulties Michelson and Morley would face when performing their experiment.
   (B) It supports the author's view that Michelson and Morley's experiment was unappreciated in its time.
   (C) It contrasts the views of Einstein with those of nineteenth-century physicists.
   (D) It introduces an analogy to further explain the nineteenth-century understanding of ether's effect on the observed speed of light.
   (E) It describes the theories of physics which governed scientific understanding in Michelson and Morley's time.

Chapter 8: Long Passages in Reading Comprehension

On purpose of paragraph questions, place the paragraph within the context of the main idea. Furthermore, look for the answer that effectively captures the entire paragraph and avoids making unjustified statements.

- (A) Although Michelson and Morley had difficulties to overcome, this paragraph does not contain any statements that would lead the reader to suspect the existence of those difficulties.
- (B) Although this is possibly a view of the author ("the implications of this experimental failure were not completely evident for many years"), it is not mentioned in the third paragraph.
- (C) Einstein's views are most clearly referenced in the first paragraph, not the third.
- (D) **CORRECT.** The person on a motorcycle is an analogy meant to illustrate scientists' understanding of how ether could affect measurements of the speed of light.
- (E) Although this paragraph does make an effort to describe the scientific understanding of Michelson and Morley's time, this answer choice fails when compared to choice (D). This choice does not acknowledge both the scientific understanding and the use of the analogy to illustrate that understanding.

3. **Select the sentence in the final two paragraphs that explains why Michelson and Morley had to depend on interference patterns to test their theory.**

Look to where "interference" is mentioned, and then try to work backward to figure out why Michelson and Morley needed it. The first sentence of the final paragraph states: "In 1887, there were no clocks sufficiently precise to detect the speed differences that would result from an ethereal wind." Because they couldn't time the light, Michelson and Morley had to depend on the interference patterns of split light beams.

The correct sentence is the first sentence of the final paragraph: "In 1887, there were no clocks sufficiently precise to detect the speed differences that would result from an ethereal wind."

4. **Which of the following would the author of the passage be likely to agree with? Select all that apply.**

- [A] Michelson and Morley's experiment failed to produce meaningful results.
- [B] The lack of precise stopwatches did not significantly impact Michelson and Morley's eventual results.
- [C] Twentieth-century physics would not necessarily have progressed as quickly as it did without Michelson and Morley's experiment.

Unit Two: **Paragraphs and Passages**

This is a very general Select One or More question, which could draw from information provided anywhere in the passage.

- [A] The passage indicates that the experiment "failed to confirm the existence of ether," but this does not mean that the experiment failed to produce any usable or meaningful results. In fact, the results of the experiment were far-reaching; the end of the first paragraph says that the implications "ultimately paved the way for Einstein's special theory of relativity."

- [B] **CORRECT.** The final paragraph states that Michelson and Morley *surmounted* the problem of not having precise enough clocks. That means that the lack of such clocks did not significantly impact their results.

- [C] **CORRECT.** According to the second sentence of the first paragraph, the results of the experiment "paved the way for Einstein's special theory of relativity." In other words, without the experiment, it is *possible* that physics would not have progressed as quickly.

Answers to Passage E: Sweet Spot

Upon previewing the questions, here is an example of what you might jot down:

5. main idea
6. EXCEPT: infer forces
7. purpose par2
8. why: "penny"
9. infer
10. sentence par2 / par3: physics → "sweet"
11. infer: tennis ball hits CP

Take a moment to consider when you might encounter the information needed for each question. Questions 5 and 7 are both about the big picture of the passage: the main idea and how the second paragraph fits into that context. Questions 8, 10, and 11 are specific enough that you can note where you see that information in your headline list. Unfortunately, questions 6 and 9 are extremely general, so you will have more work to find the correct answer.

Here is one example of a possible set of notes for this passage:

1. Tennis: hit ball on "sweet spot"
   <u>Many unaware: 2nd spot, CP, also ↓ arm strain</u> ← main idea

2. Motion without hand
   —Jerk handle back or fwd

3. If ball hits CP, no jerk—doesn't jerk wrist either

4. Find CP w/trial & error

Chapter 8: Long Passages in Reading Comprehension

5. The passage primarily focuses on

    (A) a proposal for an improvement to the design of tennis rackets
    (B) an examination of the differences between the two types of sweet spots
    (C) a definition of the translational and rotational forces acting on a tennis racket
    (D) a description of the ideal area in which to strike every ball
    (E) an explanation of a lesser-known area on a tennis racket that dampens unwanted vibration

The first paragraph introduces the main idea that there are two sweet spots on the face of a tennis racket: one well-known spot and another "lesser-known" spot. The rest of the passage discusses the existence of this less well-known spot.

   (A) Nothing in the passage suggests that the author is trying to propose an improvement to the design of tennis rackets.
   (B) The passage does mention both types of sweet spots in the first paragraph, but it does not focus on the differences between the two.
   (C) The second paragraph explains the types of forces acting on the racket, but this topic is too narrow to be the primary message of the overall passage. The passage as a whole focuses on the idea of sweet spots in general.
   (D) While the passage does mention one benefit of hitting the ball on a sweet spot, it does not claim that this is the "ideal area" to hit "every" ball. There may be other areas that convey other benefits. The word *every* is too extreme.
   (E) **CORRECT.** The passage introduces the notion of a "second, lesser-known" sweet spot and explains how it works.

6. According to the passage, all of the following are true of the forces acting upon a tennis racket striking a ball EXCEPT

    (A) the only way to eliminate the jolt that accompanies most strokes is to hit the ball on the center of percussion
    (B) the impact of the ball striking the racket can strain a tennis player's arm
    (C) there are at least two different forces acting upon the racket
    (D) the end of the handle of the racket will jerk forward after striking the ball unless the ball strikes the racket's center of mass
    (E) the racket will rebound after it strikes the ball

EXCEPT questions require you to validate the answer choices. Go through the choices one by one, using key words from each.

   (A) **CORRECT.** False. This choice contradicts information given in the first paragraph: The center of percussion is only one of two sweet spots that minimize vibration. The vibration node is the other sweet spot.
   (B) True. The first paragraph introduces the concept that the impact can "strain" the player's arm.
   (C) True. The second paragraph describes at least two different forces that act upon a tennis racket striking the ball: "translational," as described in the second and third sentences, and "rotational," as described in the fourth and fifth sentences.

261

Unit Two: **Paragraphs and Passages**

- (D) True. The fourth sentence of the second paragraph states that "unless the ball happened to hit the racket precisely at the racket's center of mass, the racket would additionally experience a rotational motion." The fifth sentence then reads, "whenever the ball hits the racket face, the effect of this rotational motion will be to jerk the end of the handle forward, toward the ball."
- (E) True. The second sentence of the second paragraph states that a racket will "bounce backward" after striking the ball; these words are synonyms for *rebound*.

7. **In the context of the author's argument, the second paragraph performs which of the following functions?**

   - (A) It establishes the main idea of the passage.
   - (B) It provides an explanation of the mechanics of the phenomenon discussed in the passage.
   - (C) It introduces a counterargument that elucidates the main idea of the passage.
   - (D) It provides an example of the primary subject described in the passage.
   - (E) It explains why the main idea of the passage would be useful for tennis players.

The purpose of the second paragraph is to introduce and explain, in great detail, the forces that act on a racket when striking a ball.

- (A) The main idea is established in the first paragraph: There is a second sweet spot that results in minimal vibration when a tennis racket strikes a ball.
- (B) **CORRECT.** This matches the function of the second paragraph, which explains the forces that occur when a racket strikes a ball.
- (C) The second paragraph introduces the forces that act on a racket when striking a ball. This follows from the main idea; it is not a counterargument.
- (D) While the second paragraph does provide an example, this is not an example of the center of percussion, which is the primary subject described in the passage. The example helps to explain the forces behind the center of percussion, but is not itself an example of a center of percussion.
- (E) The first and third paragraphs, not the second paragraph, make reference to why tennis players would want to know about the sweet spot: to minimize strain on the arm.

8. **The author mentions "a penny that has been struck near its edge" in order to**

   - (A) show how the center of mass causes the racket to spin
   - (B) argue that a penny spins in the exact way that a tennis racket spins
   - (C) explain how translational motion works
   - (D) provide an illustration of a concept
   - (E) demonstrate that pennies and tennis rackets do not spin in the same way

Chapter 8: **Long Passages in Reading Comprehension**

The passage says that "the racket would additionally experience a rotational motion around its center of mass—much as a penny that has been struck near its edge will start to spin." In other words, the motion of the penny is an example that closely mimics the situation with the tennis racket. The correct answer should match this specific purpose (provide an analogous example).

- (A) The center of mass does not cause the racket to spin; rather, a ball striking the racket causes it to spin.
- (B) The author does not present the information about the penny as an argument; rather, it is an example. In addition, the author implies, via the words "much as," that the penny and the racket spin in similar ways; this is not the same as saying that they spin in the "exact" same way.
- (C) This sentence is about rotational motion, not translational motion.
- (D) **CORRECT.** The example of the penny is an analogy for the rotational motion experienced by the tennis racket.
- (E) The example is intended to demonstrate a situation in which tennis rackets and pennies do spin in similar ways.

9. **Which of the following can be inferred from the passage?**

   - (A) If a player holds a tennis racket anywhere other than the end of the handle, the player will experience a jolting sensation.
   - (B) The primary sweet spot is more effective at damping vibration than is the secondary sweet spot.
   - (C) Striking a tennis ball at a spot other than the center of percussion can result in a jarring feeling.
   - (D) Striking a tennis ball repeatedly at spots other than a sweet spot leads to a repetitive stress injury.
   - (E) If a player lets go of the racket at the moment of impact, the simultaneous forward and backward impetus causes the racket to drop straight to the ground.

Because the question applies to the whole passage, examine the answer choices first. Base the inference only on information presented in the passage.

- (A) The passage does explain that holding the racket at the end of the handle and hitting the ball at a particular spot results in a comfortable stroke that reduces the strain on a player's arm. It does not address, however, what would happen if the player grasped the racket at a different point. It is possible that grasping the racket at another point would simply result in a different center of percussion.
- (B) The passage states that there is one commonly known sweet spot and a second, lesser-known sweet spot. However, the passage says nothing about the relative efficacy of these two sweet spots.
- (C) **CORRECT.** According to the passage, playing tennis can result in strain on a player's arm, and striking the ball at the center of percussion leads to a "smooth, comfortable stroke," or one which does not cause the same kind of damage as a regular stroke. Striking the ball at a spot other than the center of percussion, then, could lead to a jarring stroke, or one that could cause damage to a player's arm.
- (D) The passage mentions nothing about injuries due to repetitive stress (or any other cause); it merely talks about "strain." Be careful not to add additional information beyond what is presented in the passage.
- (E) The second paragraph obliquely addresses a situation in which a tennis player lets go of the racket at the moment of impact. However, this question does not specify the point at which the tennis ball struck the racket. If the ball did not strike a sweet spot, the racket may have some translational or rotational force transferred from the ball and so might not drop straight to the ground.

Unit Two: **Paragraphs and Passages**

10. Select the sentence in the second or third paragraph that describes the physics of the center of percussion's perceived sweetness.

The second paragraph of the passage explores what happens when a ball strikes a racket in general, but doesn't go into any detail about the sweet spot itself. The sentence you want will therefore be in the third paragraph.

The correct sentence is the second sentence of the third paragraph: "The reason for this lack of motion is that the force on the upper part of the hand would be equal and opposite to the force on the lower part of the hand, resulting in no net force on the tennis player's hand or forearm." The final sentence of this paragraph describes the effects of hitting this second sweet spot, but it does not describe the actual physics of the sweet spot.

11. It can be inferred that a tennis ball that strikes a racket's center of percussion will do which of the following? Select all that apply.

A	Cause the racket to bounce backward
B	Not cause the wrist to jerk
C	Allow for a cleaner stroke than a ball striking a racket's primary sweet spot

This is a Select One or More variation on a specific detail question. The answers are likely to be found in the first or third paragraphs, as the second explores a hypothetical situation and the fourth describes how to find the center of percussion.

A	The passage states that the ball would cause the racket to bounce backward in a hypothetical situation: if the player's hand were to vanish at the moment of impact. This part of the passage is not discussing what happens with a real stroke at the center of percussion.
B	**CORRECT.** The last sentence of the third paragraph says that a player who strikes the center of percussion will not have their wrist jerked "forward or backward."
C	The passage does state that when someone hits the center of percussion, the player will experience "a relatively smooth, comfortable tennis stroke." The passage never compares this situation, however, to what happens when the player hits the primary sweet spot. The passage doesn't indicate whether one is cleaner than the other or whether they're both the same.

8

264

CHAPTER 9

Reading Comprehension Problem Set

In This Chapter...

- Problem Set
- Answers and Explanations

Chapter 9 Reading Comprehension Problem Set

In this chapter, you will practice all the techniques you have learned for content-based reading comprehension.

Problem Set

The following problem set consists of passages accompanied by a series of questions for that passage. Just as on the real test, scan the questions before reading the passage.

On the GRE, you will typically see one to four questions associated with each passage. However, in this problem set, each passage has additional questions so that you can gain more practice answering a variety of problem types. As such, use the following modified timing guidelines:

- **When reading passages**, spend approximately 1.5 minutes for medium-length passages and 2–3 minutes for longer passages. If a topic is more detailed or complex, spend less time on the details; focus on the main ideas and major twists.
- **When answering questions**, spend approximately 30 to 45 seconds on general questions and approximately 45 to 60 seconds on specific questions. Expect to spend the full time on Select-One-or-More and EXCEPT questions; these will almost always take longer.

Finally, if you'd like, answer only three or four of the questions the first time you do a passage. You can then save the passage for a second pass (with the remaining three or four questions) later on in your studies.

Unit Two: **Paragraphs and Passages**

Passage F: Television's Inventor

In the early years of television, Vladimir Zworykin was considered the device's inventor, at least publicly. His loudest champion was his boss David Sarnoff, the president of RCA and the "father of television," as he was, and is, widely regarded. Modern historians agree that Philo Farnsworth, a self-educated prodigy who was the first to transmit live images, was television's technical inventor. But Farnsworth's contributions have gone relatively unnoticed, since it was Sarnoff, not Farnsworth, who put televisions into living rooms. More importantly, it was Sarnoff who successfully borrowed from the radio industry the paradigm of advertiser-funded programming, a paradigm still dominant today. In contrast, Farnsworth lacked business savvy and was unable to realize his dream of television as an educational tool.

Perhaps Sarnoff simply adapted his business ideas from other industries, such as newspapers, replacing the revenue from subscriptions and newsstand purchases with that of television set sales, but Sarnoff promoted himself as a visionary. Some critics argue that Sarnoff's construct has damaged programming content. Others contend that it merely created a democratic platform allowing audiences to choose the programming they desire.

1. The primary purpose of the passage is to

    (A) correct public misconceptions about Farnsworth's role in developing early television programs
    (B) debate the influence of television on popular culture
    (C) challenge the current public perception of Vladimir Zworykin
    (D) chronicle the events that led from the development of radio to the invention of the television
    (E) describe both Sarnoff's influence on the public perception of television's inception and the debate around the impact of Sarnoff's paradigm

2. It can be inferred from the second paragraph of the passage that

    (A) television shows produced by David Sarnoff and Vladimir Zworykin tended to earn negative reviews
    (B) educational programs cannot draw as large an audience as sports programs
    (C) a number of critics feel that Sarnoff's initial decision to earn television revenue through advertising has had a positive or neutral impact on content
    (D) educational programs that are aired in prime time, the hours during which the greatest number of viewers are watching television, are less likely to earn a profit than those that are aired during the daytime hours
    (E) in matters of programming, the audience's preferences should be more influential than those of the advertisers

3. According to the passage, the television industry, at its inception, earned revenue from

    (A) advertising only
    (B) advertising and the sale of television sets
    (C) advertising and subscriptions
    (D) subscriptions and the sale of television sets
    (E) advertising, subscriptions, and the sale of television sets

Chapter 9: **Reading Comprehension Problem Set**

4. Select the sentence that provides factual evidence that Sarnoff's talents were more imitative than innovative.

5. Which of the following statements is supported by the passage?
   Select all that apply.

A	The advertising-funded model of television has damaged programming content.
B	The contributions of television's technical inventor were overshadowed by the actions of those who popularized the medium.
C	There is no way to definitively prove who invented the first television.

Unit Two: **Paragraphs and Passages**

Passage G: Life on Mars

    Because of the proximity and likeness of Mars to Earth, scientists have long speculated about the possibility of life on Mars. Roughly three centuries ago, astronomers observed Martian polar ice caps, and later scientists discovered other similarities to Earth, including length of day and axial tilt. But in 1965, photos taken by the *Mariner 4* probe revealed a Mars without rivers, oceans, or signs of life. Moreover, in the 1990s, it was discovered that unlike Earth, Mars no longer possessed a substantial global magnetic field, allowing celestial radiation to reach the planet's surface and solar wind to eliminate much of Mars's atmosphere over the course of several billion years.

    More recent probes have investigated whether there was once liquid water on Mars. Some scientists believe that the presence of certain geological landforms definitively resolves this question. Others posit that wind erosion or carbon dioxide oceans may be responsible for these formations. Mars rovers *Opportunity* and *Spirit*, which landed on Mars in 2004, have both discovered geological evidence of past water activity. These findings substantially bolster claims that there was once life on Mars.

6. The author's stance on the possibility of life on Mars can best be described as

   (A) optimistic
   (B) open-minded
   (C) skeptical
   (D) simplistic
   (E) cynical

7. The passage is primarily concerned with which of the following?

   (A) Disproving a widely accepted theory
   (B) Initiating a debate about the possibility of life on Mars
   (C) Presenting evidence in support of a controversial claim
   (D) Describing the various discoveries made concerning the possibility of life on Mars
   (E) Detailing the findings of the Mars rovers *Opportunity* and *Spirit*

8. Each of the following is a discovery mentioned in the passage EXCEPT

   (A) Wind erosion and carbon dioxide oceans are responsible for certain geological landforms on Mars.
   (B) Mars does not have a substantial global magnetic field.
   (C) Mars had water activity at some point in the past.
   (D) The length of day on Mars is similar to that on Earth.
   (E) The axial tilt of Mars is similar to that of Earth.

9. In the first paragraph, the author most likely mentions the discovery of polar ice caps to suggest that

   (A) until recently Mars's polar ice caps were thought to consist largely of carbon dioxide
   (B) Martian polar ice caps are made almost entirely of water ice
   (C) Mars has multiple similarities to Earth, including the existence of polar ice caps
   (D) Mars has only a small fraction of the carbon dioxide found on Earth and Venus
   (E) conditions on the planet Mars were once very different than they are at present

10. Each of the following can be inferred from the passage EXCEPT

   (A) the presence of certain geological landforms is not definitive proof that there was once life on Mars
   (B) similarities to Earth bolster the idea that a planet might be or have been capable of supporting life
   (C) the absence of a substantial global magnetic field on Mars suggests that it would be difficult to sustain life on Mars
   (D) the presence of water activity on Mars is related to the possibility of life on Mars
   (E) the claim that there was once water on Mars has only marginal support from recent discoveries

11. It can be inferred from the passage that which of the following characteristics of a planet would imply that it might support life?
   Select all that apply.

   [A] A significant global magnetic field
   [B] Evidence of liquid carbon dioxide on the planet's surface
   [C] The average daily level of sunlight reaching the planet's surface

12. Select the sentence in the passage that provides the best evidence that, at the given time, life did not exist on Mars.

Unit Two: **Paragraphs and Passages**

Passage H: Fossils

Archaeological discoveries frequently undermine accepted ideas, giving rise to new theories. Recently, a set of 3.3-million-year-old fossils, the remains of the earliest well-preserved child ever found, were discovered in Ethiopia. Estimated to be 3 years old at death, the female child was of the *Australopithecus afarensis* species, a human ancestor that lived in Africa over 3 million years ago. "Her completeness, antiquity, and age at death make this find of unprecedented importance in the history of paleo-anthropology," said Zeresenay Alemseged, a noted paleo-anthropologist, opining that the discovery could reconfigure conceptions about early humans' capacities.

Previously, *afarensis* was believed to have abandoned arboreal habitats. However, while the new fossil's lower limbs support the view of an upright stance, its gorilla-like arms suggest that *afarensis* was still able to swing through trees, initiating a reexamination of long-held theories of early human development. Also, the presence of a hyoid bone, a rarely preserved larynx bone that supports throat muscles, has dramatically affected concepts of the origin of speech. Although primitive and more ape-like than human-like, this fossil hyoid is the first found in such an early human-related species.

13. The organization of the passage could best be described as

    A discussing a controversial scientific discovery

    B contrasting previous theories of development with current theories

    C illustrating a general contention with a specific example

    D arguing for the importance of a particular field of study

    E refuting a popular misconception

14. The passage quotes Zeresenay Alemseged in order to

    A provide evidence to qualify the main idea of the first paragraph

    B question the claims of other scientists

    C provide evidence to support the linguistic abilities of the *afarensis* species

    D provide corroboration for the significance of the find

    E provide a subjective opinion that is refuted in the second paragraph

15. Each of the following is cited as a factor in the importance of the discovery of the fossils EXCEPT

    A the fact that the remains were those of a child

    B the age of the fossils

    C the location of the discovery

    D the species of the fossils

    E the intact nature of the fossils

16. It can be inferred from the passage's description of the discovered fossil hyoid bone that

    A *Australopithecus afarensis* was capable of speech

    B the discovered hyoid bone is less primitive than the hyoid bone of apes

    C the hyoid bone is necessary for speech

    D the discovery of the hyoid bone necessitated the reexamination of prior theories

    E the hyoid bone was the most important fossil found at the site

Chapter 9: **Reading Comprehension Problem Set**

17. The impact of the discovery of the hyoid bone in the field of archaeology could be best compared to which one of the following examples in another field?

    (A) The discovery and analysis of cosmic rays lend support to a widely accepted theory of the origin of the universe.

    (B) The original manuscript of a deceased nineteenth-century author confirms ideas of the development of an important work of literature.

    (C) The continued prosperity of a state-run economy stirs debate in the discipline of macroeconomics.

    (D) Newly revealed journal entries by a prominent Civil War–era politician lead to a questioning of certain accepted historical interpretations about the conflict.

    (E) Research into the mapping of the human genome gives rise to nascent applications of individually tailored medicines.

18. Select the sentence that most distinctly undermines an accepted paleo-anthropological theory.

Unit Two: **Paragraphs and Passages**

Passage I: Chaos Theory

Around 1960, mathematician Edward Lorenz found unexpected behavior in apparently simple equations representing atmospheric air flows. Whenever he reran his model with the same inputs, different outputs resulted—although the model lacked any random elements. Lorenz realized that tiny rounding errors in his analog computer mushroomed over time, leading to erratic results. His findings marked a seminal moment in the development of chaos theory, which, despite its name, has little to do with randomness.

To understand how unpredictability can arise from deterministic equations, which do not involve chance outcomes, consider the non-chaotic system of two poppy seeds placed in a round bowl. As the seeds roll to the bowl's center, a position known as a point attractor, the distance between the seeds shrinks. If, instead, the bowl is flipped over, two seeds placed on top will roll away from each other. Such a system, while still not technically chaotic, enlarges initial differences in position.

Chaotic systems, such as a machine mixing bread dough, are characterized by both attraction and repulsion. As the dough is stretched, folded, and pressed back together, any poppy seeds sprinkled in are intermixed seemingly at random. But this randomness is illusory. In fact, the poppy seeds are captured by "strange attractors," staggeringly complex pathways whose tangles appear accidental but are in fact determined by the system's fundamental equations.

During the dough-kneading process, two poppy seeds positioned next to each other eventually go their separate ways. Any early divergence or measurement error is repeatedly amplified by the mixing until the position of any seed becomes effectively unpredictable. It is this "sensitive dependence on initial conditions" and not true randomness that generates unpredictability in chaotic systems, of which one example may be the Earth's weather. According to the popular interpretation of the "Butterfly Effect," a butterfly flapping its wings causes hurricanes. A better understanding is that the butterfly causes uncertainty about the precise state of the air. This microscopic uncertainty grows until it encompasses even hurricanes. Few meteorologists believe that we will ever be able to predict rain or shine for a particular day years in the future.

19. The main purpose of this passage is to

    (A) explore a common misconception about a type of complex physical system
    (B) trace the historical development of a scientific theory
    (C) distinguish a mathematical pattern from its opposite
    (D) describe the spread of a technical model from one field of study to others
    (E) contrast possible causes of weather phenomena

20. In the example discussed in the passage, what is true about poppy seeds in bread dough once the dough has been thoroughly mixed?

    (A) They have been individually stretched and folded over.
    (B) They are scattered in random clumps throughout the dough.
    (C) They are accidentally caught in tangled objects called "strange attractors."
    (D) They are bound to regularly dispersed patterns of point attractors.
    (E) They are in positions dictated by the underlying equations that govern the mixing process.

276

21. According to the passage, the rounding errors in Lorenz's model
    - (A) indicated that the model was programmed in a fundamentally faulty way
    - (B) were deliberately included to represent tiny fluctuations in atmospheric air currents
    - (C) were imperceptibly small at first, but tended to grow
    - (D) were at least partially expected, given the complexity of the actual atmosphere
    - (E) shrank to insignificant levels during each trial of the model

22. The passage mentions each of the following as an example or potential example of a chaotic or non-chaotic system EXCEPT
    - (A) a dough-mixing machine
    - (B) atmospheric weather patterns
    - (C) poppy seeds placed on top of an upside-down bowl
    - (D) poppy seeds placed in a right-side-up bowl
    - (E) fluctuating butterfly flight patterns

23. It can be inferred from the passage that which of the following pairs of items would most likely follow typical pathways within a chaotic system?
    - (A) Two particles ejected in random directions from the same decaying atomic nucleus
    - (B) Two stickers affixed to a balloon that expands and contracts over and over again
    - (C) Two avalanches sliding down opposite sides of the same mountain
    - (D) Two baseballs placed into a device designed to mix paint
    - (E) Two coins flipped into a large bowl

24. The author implies which of the following about weather systems?
    Select all that apply.
    - [A] They illustrate the same fundamental phenomenon as Lorenz's rounding errors.
    - [B] Experts agree unanimously that weather will never be predictable years in advance.
    - [C] They are governed mostly by seemingly trivial events, such as the flapping of a butterfly's wings.

25. Select the sentence in the second or third paragraph that illustrates why "chaos theory" might be called a misnomer.

Unit Two: **Paragraphs and Passages**

Answers and Explanations

Answers to Passage F: Television's Inventor

In the early years of television, Vladimir Zworykin was considered the device's inventor, at least publicly. His loudest champion was his boss David Sarnoff, the president of RCA and the "father of television," as he was, and is, widely regarded. Modern historians agree that Philo Farnsworth, a self-educated prodigy who was the first to transmit live images, was television's technical inventor. But Farnsworth's contributions have gone relatively unnoticed, since it was Sarnoff, not Farnsworth, who put televisions into living rooms. More importantly, it was Sarnoff who successfully borrowed from the radio industry the paradigm of advertiser-funded programming, a paradigm still dominant today. In contrast, Farnsworth lacked business savvy and was unable to realize his dream of television as an educational tool.

Perhaps Sarnoff simply adapted his business ideas from other industries, such as newspapers, replacing the revenue from subscriptions and newsstand purchases with that of television set sales, but Sarnoff promoted himself as a visionary. Some critics argue that Sarnoff's construct has damaged programming content. Others contend that it merely created a democratic platform allowing audiences to choose the programming they desire.

Upon previewing the questions, here is an example of what you might jot down:

1. Main Idea
2. Infer from P2
3. How TV get rev?
4. Select: talent = imitative
5. Infer

The first question will come from your initial read. As you read, try to see how paragraph two fits into the context of the passage, and note when you see the discussion of revenue from TV or talent that is imitative. The fifth question will require using the answer choices before finding proof.

Here is one example of a possible set of notes for this passage:

1. Early TV, Z seen as invntr
    —Champ by Sarn (father of TV)
    BUT now hist agree: F = TRUE invntr
    —S: launched: advrs pay
    —F: not biz savvy, wanted TV = educ
2. S: visionary or adopter?
    + or – effect?

Simple Story: Farnsworth really invented TV, but he didn't know how to turn it into a business. Sarnoff used the radio model to make television big business. People have differing feelings about his role.

Chapter 9: **Reading Comprehension Problem Set**

1. The primary purpose of the passage is to

   (A) correct public misconception about Farnsworth's role in developing early television programs
   (B) debate the influence of television on popular culture
   (C) challenge the current public perception of Vladimir Zworykin
   (D) chronicle the events that led from the development of radio to the invention of the television
   (E) describe both Sarnoff's influence on the public perception of television's inception and the debate around the impact of Sarnoff's paradigm

The main idea is that even though Sarnoff did not invent the television, he was responsible for introducing television to the public and establishing a dominant paradigm. This is foreshadowed when Sarnoff is called "the father of television."

   (A) Farnsworth's influence on the development of the television itself is only mentioned in the first paragraph; Farnsworth's role in developing programs is never mentioned.
   (B) The impact of television is not discussed until the second paragraph. Although this paragraph debates whether or not Sarnoff's influence was a positive one, it does not address the influence of television on popular culture.
   (C) Vladimir Zworykin is only mentioned briefly in the first paragraph, so he is not the primary subject of the passage. Furthermore, even though the passage mentions the initial public perception, it says nothing about the current public perception of Zworykin.
   (D) The passage discusses events that occurred after the invention; there is no mention of the events that led up to the invention of the television.
   (E) **CORRECT.** The passage does describe how Sarnoff made television popular; some critics think that his role was positive while others think that it was negative. Notice that this is the only answer choice that mentions Sarnoff. He is featured prominently in every paragraph, so any answer choice representing the point of the passage should not mention other people while ignoring him.

2. It can be inferred from the second paragraph of the passage that

   (A) television shows produced by David Sarnoff and Vladimir Zworykin tended to earn negative reviews
   (B) educational programs cannot draw as large an audience as sports programs
   (C) a number of critics feel that Sarnoff's initial decision to earn television revenue through advertising has had a positive or neutral impact on content
   (D) educational programs that are aired in prime time, the hours during which the greatest number of viewers are watching television, are less likely to earn a profit than those that are aired during the daytime hours
   (E) in matters of programming, the audience's preferences should be more influential than those of the advertisers

Unit Two: **Paragraphs and Passages**

The second paragraph states that some critics viewed Sarnoff's approach negatively and others thought his approach embodied a democratic concept. The correct inference must follow from at least one of those statements.

- (A) There is no information about the television programs Sarnoff and Zworykin produced; in fact, you have not been told that they produced television shows. The paragraph is about the advertising revenue construct Sarnoff implemented, not about the television shows he produced.
- (B) It is implied that ratings for educational programs are, in general, not strong, but that does not mean that any one particular educational program cannot have higher ratings than one particular sports program. Beware of answer choices that contain absolutes such as *cannot*.
- (C) **CORRECT.** The passage states that "[o]thers contend that it created a democratic platform." This sentence, following immediately after the negative implications of "[s]ome critics argue . . ." states that there are mixed feelings among critics. Some view Sarnoff's decision as negative, but others view it as at least neutral, if not positive.
- (D) The passage does not differentiate programming based on what time television shows air, nor does it mention profitability.
- (E) The word "should" implies a moral judgment, and the answer is therefore out of the scope of the passage. The second paragraph does not indicate a belief as to who should influence programming choices.

3. According to the passage, the television industry, at its inception, earned revenue from

- (A) advertising only
- (B) advertising and the sale of television sets
- (C) advertising and subscriptions
- (D) subscriptions and the sale of television sets
- (E) advertising, subscriptions, and the sale of television sets

In an attempt to trick you on a specific detail question such as this, the GRE will offer incomplete answers that incorporate language from throughout the passage but do not directly bear on the question at hand. Two sections in the passage discuss ways in which the television industry brought in revenue. The first paragraph mentions "advertiser-funded programming." The second paragraph states that Sarnoff borrowed from other business models by "replacing the revenue from subscriptions and newsstand purchases with that of television set sales."

- (A) This answer choice, with the word "only," would deny the revenue from television set sales.
- (B) **CORRECT.** Advertising and the sale of television sets are the two ways mentioned through which the industry could generate revenue.
- (C) Subscriptions are mentioned as a method for newspapers to earn revenue; the last paragraph states that television replaced this revenue with that earned by selling the sets themselves.
- (D) This choice does not mention advertising revenue; moreover, it incorrectly mentions subscription revenue.
- (E) This answer choice incorrectly mentions subscription revenue.

Chapter 9: **Reading Comprehension Problem Set**

4. **Select the sentence that provides factual evidence that Sarnoff's talents were more imitative than innovative.**

This question relates to Sarnoff's legacy as an imitator versus his legacy as an innovator. There are two plausible candidates. First, the second-to-last sentence of the first paragraph says that Sarnoff "successfully borrowed from the radio industry the paradigm of advertiser-funded programming." This sentence states a fact indicating that Sarnoff took a business model from another medium, which would be imitative rather than innovative.

The second possible answer is the first sentence of the second paragraph, which says, "Perhaps Sarnoff simply adapted his business ideas from other industries such as newspapers." However, the use of the word *perhaps* means that this is an idea of the author's, rather than a statement of fact. For this reason, this cannot be the answer.

The correct answer is the second-to-last sentence of the first paragraph: "More importantly, it was Sarnoff who successfully borrowed from the radio industry the paradigm of advertiser-funded programming, a paradigm still dominant today."

5. **Which of the following statements is supported by the passage? Select all that apply.**

   A The advertising-funded model of television has damaged programming content.

   B The contributions of television's technical inventor were overshadowed by the actions of those who popularized the medium.

   C There is no way to definitively prove who invented the first television.

Expect to need extra time on Select One or More inference questions. This one, annoyingly, does not provide any clues about where to look in the passage. Use the key words in each statement to determine where to examine the passage.

   A While the last sentence says that some critics "argue that Sarnoff's construct has damaged programming content," this is not stated as a fact, only a possible opinion. Always be careful to differentiate between opinions and facts on RC passages.

   B **CORRECT.** The first paragraph indicates that Farnsworth was the technical inventor of television. That paragraph also says that "Farnsworth's contributions have gone relatively unnoticed, since it was Sarnoff who put televisions into living rooms."

   C Though the passage describes the ways in which both Zworykin and Farnsworth have been described as the progenitors of television, and though it makes a case that there remains a lively debate over who deserves the credit, this does not mean that there is "no way" of determining who invented the first television. Always be wary of extreme language like this when dealing with RC questions.

Unit Two: **Paragraphs and Passages**

Answers to Passage G: Life on Mars

   Because of the proximity and likeness of Mars to Earth, scientists have long speculated about the possibility of life on Mars. Roughly three centuries ago, astronomers observed Martian polar ice caps, and later scientists discovered other similarities to Earth, including length of day and axial tilt. But in 1965, photos taken by the *Mariner 4* probe revealed a Mars without rivers, oceans, or signs of life. Moreover, in the 1990s, it was discovered that unlike Earth, Mars no longer possessed a substantial global magnetic field, allowing celestial radiation to reach the planet's surface and solar wind to eliminate much of Mars's atmosphere over the course of several billion years.

   More recent probes have investigated whether there was once liquid water on Mars. Some scientists believe that the presence of certain geological landforms definitively resolves this question. Others posit that wind erosion or carbon dioxide oceans may be responsible for these formations. Mars rovers *Opportunity* and *Spirit*, which landed on Mars in 2004, have both discovered geological evidence of past water activity. These findings substantially bolster claims that there was once life on Mars.

Upon previewing the questions, here is an example of what you might jot down:

6. Was life on mars?
7. Main idea
8. List discoveries
9. P1 why "polar ice caps"?
10. Infer
11. Infer: what supports life?
12. Select: proof no life on Mars

The first two questions will involve an understanding from your first read. While you read the first paragraph, consider why the author mentions the polar ice caps. As you build your headline list, note discoveries and any details about what supports life.

Here is one example of a possible set of notes for this passage:

1. S: Mars close, simil to Earth → poss life on M
   —Sims (polar ice, day, tilt)
   —Diffs (no water, no more mag field)

2. Rec. focus: was there water?
   —Evid: yes/no, now <u>more</u> support for life on M ← main idea

Simple Story: Debate about life on Mars. Positives and negatives, but the big deal was the discovery of water, increasing the chance that there was life on Mars.

Chapter 9: Reading Comprehension Problem Set

6. The author's stance on the possibility of life on Mars can best be described as

    (A) optimistic
    (B) open-minded
    (C) skeptical
    (D) simplistic
    (E) cynical

This passage is concerned with the possibility of life on Mars. It details the various discoveries that have been made over centuries. The main idea is that, although not definitively proven, recent evidence shows there may have been life on Mars. The correct answer will reflect the tone of that main idea.

   (A) The author is neither optimistic nor pessimistic about the possibility of life on Mars.
   (B) **CORRECT.** Open-minded reflects the main idea: It is not proven, but there is new evidence to be considered.
   (C) There is no indication that the author of the passage is skeptical. The main idea is not as negative as this choice.
   (D) The author considers several different factors in the determination of life on Mars. The author's stance could not appropriately be described as simplistic.
   (E) Again, the author is more objective in tone and could not accurately be characterized as cynical.

7. The passage is primarily concerned with which of the following?

    (A) Disproving a widely accepted theory
    (B) Initiating a debate about the possibility of life on Mars
    (C) Presenting evidence in support of a controversial claim
    (D) Describing the various discoveries made concerning the possibility of life on Mars
    (E) Detailing the findings of the Mars rovers *Opportunity* and *Spirit*

This passage is primarily concerned with the possibility of life on Mars. The two paragraphs discuss various discoveries that have been made over the past few centuries. The passage concludes that recent findings substantiate claims that there was once life on Mars. However, scientists are still not certain. In determining the purpose or main idea of the passage, avoid extreme words and be able to defend every word, matching your choice to your prediction.

   (A) This passage does not set out to *disprove* the theory that there is life on Mars. It is also too extreme to suggest that this is a "widely accepted theory."
   (B) This answer choice is tempting because it is relatively neutral. However, the passage does not seek to initiate a debate; it is more concerned with documenting findings that pertain to life on Mars. In other words, the passage presents the findings that frame a debate; it doesn't initiate the debate itself.
   (C) The passage presents evidence in support of and against the possibility of life on Mars. It is too limited to suggest that the passage is primarily concerned with presenting evidence "in support of" life on Mars.
   (D) **CORRECT.** This answer choice avoids extreme words and best summarizes the purpose of the passage.
   (E) This answer choice is too specific. The passage does mention the Mars rovers *Opportunity* and *Spirit*, but it is inaccurate to suggest that the passage is primarily concerned with these two rovers.

Unit Two: Paragraphs and Passages

8. **Each of the following is a discovery mentioned in the passage EXCEPT**

    (A) Wind erosion and carbon dioxide oceans are responsible for certain geological landforms on Mars.
    (B) Mars does not have a substantial global magnetic field.
    (C) Mars had water activity at some point in the past.
    (D) The length of day on Mars is similar to that on Earth.
    (E) The axial tilt of Mars is similar to that of Earth.

To address this specific detail question, point out specific evidence in the text to defend your answer choice. The passage discusses several discoveries; to answer this question, find the four choices which *are* discoveries specifically mentioned. A prediction for this question will not be possible, you must work from key words in the answer choices.

(A) **CORRECT.** The passage does make mention of wind erosion and carbon dioxide oceans, but the author states that these are other possible explanations for certain geological landforms on Mars. The text states that some scientists "posit" that wind erosion and carbon dioxide oceans may have had an effect, but that is a hypothesis, not a discovery.

(B) At the end of the first paragraph, the passage states that "in the 1990s, it was discovered that, unlike Earth, Mars no longer possessed a substantial global magnetic field."

(C) In the second paragraph, the author indicates that two rovers "both discovered geological evidence of past water activity."

(D) Certain similarities Mars has to Earth were discovered sometime between three centuries ago and 1965, including the length of day, as noted in the second sentence of the first paragraph.

(E) Certain similarities Mars has to Earth were discovered sometime between three centuries ago and 1965, including the axial tilt of Mars being similar to that of the Earth, as noted in the second sentence of the first paragraph.

9. **In the first paragraph, the author most likely mentions the discovery of polar ice caps to suggest that**

    (A) until recently Mars's polar ice caps were thought to consist largely of carbon dioxide
    (B) Martian polar ice caps are made almost entirely of water ice
    (C) Mars has many similarities to Earth, including the existence of polar ice caps
    (D) Mars has only a small fraction of the carbon dioxide found on Earth and Venus
    (E) conditions on the planet Mars were once very different than they are at present

Chapter 9: **Reading Comprehension Problem Set**

This is a specific purpose question that refers back to the second sentence in the first paragraph. The best approach is to determine, using surrounding sentences, what the author's purpose is in mentioning Mars's polar ice caps. The second part of the sentence, "later scientists discovered other similarities to Earth, including length of day and axial tilt," indicates that polar ice caps are introduced as an example of the similarity of Mars to Earth (note the use of the word *other*).

- (A) The passage does not mention the content of the polar ice caps, just that they were observed.
- (B) Again, you do not know, from the passage, the composition of Mars's polar ice caps.
- (C) **CORRECT.** As stated above, polar ice caps are introduced as one of several similarities of Mars to Earth.
- (D) The passage does not indicate the carbon dioxide content of Mars or Earth. It also does not mention Venus.
- (E) While you know from the rest of the passage that conditions on Mars were probably different from what they are now, the author does not mention polar ice caps in order to indicate this.

10. Each of the following can be inferred from the passage EXCEPT

- (A) the presence of certain geological landforms is not definitive proof that there was once life on Mars
- (B) similarities to Earth bolster the idea that a planet might be or have been capable of supporting life
- (C) the absence of a substantial global magnetic field on Mars suggests that it would be difficult to sustain life on Mars
- (D) the presence of water activity on Mars is related to the possibility of life on Mars
- (E) the claim that there was once water on Mars has only limited and indirect support from recent discoveries

An inference question, but an EXCEPT variation. A prediction will not be possible, although if you notice that a choice clearly contradicts the passage, that will be the correct choice. Find each inference that can be defended by going back to the text and does not go far beyond the language in the passage and eliminate those four choices.

- (A) In the second paragraph, the author states that while the presence of geological landforms may indicate the presence of water, it is also possible that these landforms were caused by wind erosion or carbon dioxide oceans.
- (B) The first paragraph describes three similarities between Mars and Earth (polar ice caps, length of day, and axial tilt). The passage then contrasts that evidence: "But" later photos showed a planet "without rivers, oceans, or signs of life." If this later evidence showed no signs of life, in contrast to earlier evidence showing similarities with Earth, then the similarities must support the possibility of life on Mars.
- (C) In the second paragraph, the absence of a substantial global magnetic field is presented as evidence of the lack of life on Mars. Again, note that this answer choice avoids extreme words by using the word *suggests*.
- (D) The first sentence in the second paragraph states that "more recent probes have investigated whether there was once liquid water on Mars." Given this purpose, it is clear that the existence of water is important in order to establish whether or not there was life on Mars.
- (E) **CORRECT.** According to the second paragraph, the "Mars rovers *Opportunity* and *Spirit* . . . have both discovered geological evidence of past water activity." As made clear by the subsequent sentence that "these findings substantially bolster claims," the evidence supporting the claim that there was once water on Mars is substantial. Thus, the passage contradicts the statement that this claim is supported by only marginal evidence.

Unit Two: **Paragraphs and Passages**

11. It can be inferred from the passage that which of the following characteristics of a planet would imply that it might support life?
Select all that apply.

- [A] A significant global magnetic field
- [B] Evidence of liquid carbon dioxide on the planet's surface
- [C] The average daily level of sunlight reaching the planet's surface

Most of the passage is about what aspects of Mars might or might not imply that it once supported life. Polar ice caps, length of day, and axial tilt are all mentioned to imply life may be possible. The lack of a magnetic field made it impossible, so a magnetic field must be necessary.

- [A] **CORRECT.** The passage says that "Mars no longer possessed a substantial global magnetic field," which led to the disappearance of Mars's atmosphere. This dissimilarity with Earth is used in the passage as evidence against life on Mars. Conversely, therefore, the existence of a global magnetic field would imply that it is possible a planet could support life.

- [B] The passage mentions "carbon dioxide oceans" as a possible cause for certain geological formations. Another possible (and contrasting) cause is liquid water. Since water activity is associated with possible life, and carbon dioxide oceans are mentioned in contrast, carbon dioxide is probably not evidence of life.

- [C] While your general knowledge of the importance of the sun might make it reasonable to assume that the sun would be important on other planets as well, the passage does not discuss this particular issue. The passage does mention "length of day" as a similarity between Mars and the Earth, but length of day does not necessarily mean hours of daylight. A day can also refer to the length of time it takes a planet to rotate on its own axis.

12. Select the sentence in the passage that provides the best evidence that, at the given time, life did not exist on Mars.

The correct answer probably will not be found in the second paragraph, which mostly provides evidence that there *was* life on Mars at one point. In the first paragraph, the third sentence says that in 1965, photos "revealed a Mars without rivers, oceans, or signs of life," providing evidence that life did not exist at that time. The next sentence indicates that the lack of a magnetic field caused some negative consequences incompatible with life. However, this sentence says that there is no longer such a magnetic field, indicating that the field did once exist.

The correct sentence is the third sentence of the first paragraph: "But in 1965, photos taken by the *Mariner 4* probe revealed a Mars without rivers, oceans, or signs of life."

Answers to Passage H: Fossils

Archaeological discoveries frequently undermine accepted ideas, giving rise to new theories. Recently, a set of 3.3-million-year-old fossils, the remains of the earliest well-preserved child ever found, were discovered in Ethiopia. Estimated to be 3 years old at death, the female child was of the *Australopithecus afarensis* species, a human ancestor that lived in Africa over 3 million years ago. "Her completeness, antiquity, and age at death make this find of unprecedented importance in the history of paleo-anthropology," said Zeresenay Alemseged, a noted paleo-anthropologist, opining that the discovery could reconfigure conceptions about early humans' capacities.

Previously, *afarensis* was believed to have abandoned arboreal habitats. However, while the new fossil's lower limbs support the view of an upright stance, its gorilla-like arms suggest that *afarensis* was still able to swing through trees, initiating a reexamination of long-held theories of early human development. Also, the presence of a hyoid bone, a rarely preserved larynx bone that supports throat muscles, has dramatically affected concepts of the origin of speech. Although primitive and more ape-like than human-like, this fossil hyoid is the first found in such an early human-related species.

> **Upon previewing the questions, here is an example of what you might jot down:**
>
> 13. Passage org
>
> 14. Why quote ZA?
>
> 15. Why discovery important?
>
> 16. infer: hyoid bone disc.
>
> 17. impact disc hyoid bone
>
> 18. select: undermine theory
>
> The first question is a twist on a main idea. The remaining questions all provide some context clues to help find the answers, and also set you up to know that the hyoid bone discovery must have been pretty important!
>
> **Here is one example of a possible set of notes for this passage:**
>
> 1. Arch: disc → undermine old, lead to new thry ← main idea
>   —e.g., child foss Eth
>
> 2. Before: thought af no longer in trees
>   BUT disc → reexam old thry
>   Also hy bone → ∆ thry
>
> **Simple Story:** New discoveries change old ideas and give rise to new theories. A detailed archaeological example illustrates this overall point. The discovery of a particular skeleton led researchers to reexamine theories about early human life.

13. The organization of the passage could best be described as

- (A) discussing a controversial scientific discovery
- (B) contrasting previous theories of human development with current theories
- (C) illustrating a general contention with a specific example
- (D) arguing for the importance of a particular field of study
- (E) refuting a popular misconception

Unit Two: **Paragraphs and Passages**

This question is a variation of a purpose of paragraph question. The correct choice will reflect the purpose of several components of the passage, in order of presentation in the passage. This passage begins by noting that "archaeological discoveries frequently undermine accepted ideas, giving rise to new theories." It supports this statement by relating the impact of one discovery in the field. Thus, your predicted answer will reference both the overall contention and the use of the example.

(A) This choice omits the phenomenon that the discovery is meant to illustrate: discoveries often give rise to new theories. Also, there is nothing controversial about the described discovery.

(B) The passage does not focus on the contrast between previous theories of human development and current theories. Rather, it discusses a singular discovery that affects previous theories. The passage would need to outline both previous and current theories of development and then contrast them. Instead, the passage focuses on how one example illustrates a way in which the field of archaeology evolves.

(C) **CORRECT.** The passage makes a general claim and uses a specific example to support that claim, just as this choice states.

(D) One might feel that the evolution of theories of human development is a worthwhile object of contemplation, but the *passage* does not argue for the importance of archaeology as a field of study. This answer choice misstates the organization of the passage.

(E) The passage does not indicate how popular the earlier theories of human development were. Also, the passage provides only one example of a single discovery and its importance. The language employed in the passage does not warrant describing the passage as a refutation of past theories.

14. The passage quotes Zeresenay Alemseged in order to

(A) provide evidence to qualify the main idea of the first paragraph
(B) question the claims of other scientists
(C) provide evidence to support the linguistic abilities of the *afarensis* species
(D) provide corroboration for the significance of the find
(E) provide a subjective opinion that is refuted in the second paragraph

This specific purpose question references the quotation in the first paragraph. That quote highlights the importance of the discovery and is followed by another similar reference. The quotation is used to emphasize the exceptional importance of this find; the correct answer for this Inference question will reflect this emphasis.

(A) The main idea of the first paragraph is that a new finding can call accepted archaeological theories into question. The rest of the paragraph provides an example of this phenomenon. The quotation emphasizes the importance of the discovery itself, not the example, nor does the quotation qualify or limit the main idea of the first paragraph.

(B) The passage does not discuss claims of other scientists.

(C) The discussion of the linguistic ability of the *afarensis* species is in the second paragraph and is unrelated to this quotation.

(D) **CORRECT.** The point of this paragraph is to illustrate that in archaeology, important factual discoveries lead to theoretical changes. The quotation corroborates the idea that this discovery is in fact a significant one.

(E) The quotation is offered as corroboration of the importance of the discovery and is not refuted at any point in the passage.

Chapter 9: **Reading Comprehension Problem Set**

15. **Each of the following is cited as a factor in the importance of the discovery of the fossils EXCEPT**

    (A) the fact that the remains were those of a child
    (B) the age of the fossils
    (C) the location of the discovery
    (D) the species of the fossils
    (E) the intact nature of the fossils

On EXCEPT questions, it is typically easier to eliminate incorrect answer choices until only one is left. No prediction will be possible.

(A) The fourth sentence of the first paragraph cites a quotation from a noted paleo-anthropologist that the find of the child fossils was of unprecedented importance due to the child's "age at death." Therefore, the fact that the remains were those of a child was of substantial significance.

(B) The "antiquity" (a synonym for *age*) of the fossils is mentioned in the fourth sentence of the first paragraph as a reason why the fossils were an important discovery.

(C) **CORRECT.** The location of the fossil discovery is mentioned in the first paragraph of the passage. However, the location is not provided as a reason why the fossils are significant.

(D) This choice is tricky. The second paragraph describes what was previously "believed" about *afarensis* and that this evidence "dramatically affected" certain theories about the development of speech in humans. The fossils were of a "human-related species," so the species itself was significant in influencing the theories about human speech.

(E) The fourth sentence of the first paragraph notes that the find was important due its "completeness." The intact nature of the fossils is another way of saying that the fossils are complete.

16. **It can be inferred from the passage's description of the discovered fossil hyoid bone that**

    (A) *Australopithecus afarensis* was capable of speech
    (B) the discovered hyoid bone is less primitive than the hyoid bone of apes
    (C) the hyoid bone is necessary for speech
    (D) the discovery of the hyoid bone necessitated the reexamination of prior theories
    (E) the hyoid bone was the most important fossil found at the site

289

Unit Two: **Paragraphs and Passages**

The passage provides the following information about the discovered hyoid bone: It is the oldest ever found, and it is "primitive and more ape-like than human-like." The passage also states that the discovery will impact theories about speech.

(A) The passage gives no information about the linguistic capacities of *Australopithecus afarensis*. The passage does not give enough information to infer that the species was capable of speech.

(B) The passage indicates that the discovered hyoid bone more closely resembles those of apes than humans. However, while the passage does generally relate to evolution, the discovered bone is not necessarily less primitive than that of an ape. It could be slightly different in an equally primitive way; not all differences in structure would make a bone more advanced.

(C) While it can be inferred that this bone has some effect on speech, the passage does not indicate that it is "necessary for speech." It is possible that a species could be capable of speech without a hyoid bone.

(D) **CORRECT.** The passage states that the discovery of the hyoid bone "has dramatically affected concepts of the origin of speech." Thus, it can be inferred that the discovery made the reexamination of prior theories necessary.

(E) The passage does not rank the importance of the fossils found; as a result, this choice is not necessarily true. It is possible that other fossils were of equal or greater importance.

17. **The impact of the discovery of the hyoid bone in the field of archaeology could be best compared to which one of the following examples in another field?**

(A) The discovery and analysis of cosmic rays lend support to a widely accepted theory of the origin of the universe.

(B) The original manuscript of a deceased nineteenth-century author confirms ideas of the development of an important work of literature.

(C) The continued prosperity of a state-run economy stirs debate in the discipline of macroeconomics.

(D) Newly revealed journal entries by a prominent Civil War–era politician lead to a questioning of certain accepted historical interpretations about the conflict.

(E) Research into the mapping of the human genome gives rise to nascent applications of individually tailored medicines.

When you are asked to choose which answer best parallels a part of a passage, be sure that you grasp the nature of the example in the passage before considering the answer choices. This is a variation on the specific purpose question type: Which answer choice contains a statement that would serve a similar purpose?

The passage indicates that the discovery of the hyoid bone "has dramatically affected concepts of the origin of speech." This evidence supports the passage's main point: New discoveries can undermine or call into question existing theories and give rise to new ones.

Chapter 9: **Reading Comprehension Problem Set**

The correct answer will describe a discovery that would have a nearly identical impact in another field.

(A) In this example, the discovery serves to support a widely accepted theory, as opposed to causing a reexamination of that theory.

(B) In this answer choice, the discovery serves to confirm earlier held ideas, as opposed to causing a reexamination of those ideas.

(C) There is no indication that an accepted theory is applicable and being called into question. Further, the "continued prosperity" is not a new discovery or change in the way that things used to be done or viewed.

(D) **CORRECT.** This answer choice correctly describes a discovery that causes a reexamination of earlier ideas. In this case, newly uncovered journal entries spur a reevaluation of certain historical ideas regarding an important conflict.

(E) In this answer, scientific advances in the field of biology give rise to new applications. It does not discuss a discovery that calls accepted ideas into question.

18. **Select the sentence that most distinctly undermines an accepted paleo-anthropological theory.**

This Select-in-Passage question asks for a specific example of the main idea: a new discovery that undermines or calls into question an accepted theory or idea.

The first sentence of the second paragraph describes a previously accepted theory about *afarensis*. The next sentence describes how this theory was undermined, and it is the correct answer: "its gorilla-like arms suggest that *afarensis* was still able to swing through trees, initiating a reexamination of long-held theories of human development." The example of the hyoid bone mentioned later never describes exactly what theory was undermined by its discovery.

The correct sentence is the second sentence of the second paragraph: "However, while the new fossil's lower limbs support the view of an upright stance, its gorilla-like arms suggest that *afarensis* was still able to swing through trees, initiating a reexamination of long-held theories of early human development."

Answers to Passage I: Chaos Theory

Around 1960, mathematician Edward Lorenz found unexpected behavior in apparently simple equations representing atmospheric air flows. Whenever he reran his model with the same inputs, different outputs resulted—although the model lacked any random elements. Lorenz realized that tiny rounding errors in his analog computer mushroomed over time, leading to erratic results. His findings marked a seminal moment in the development of chaos theory, which, despite its name, has little to do with randomness.

To understand how unpredictability can arise from deterministic equations, which do not involve chance outcomes, consider the non-chaotic system of two poppy seeds placed in a round bowl. As the seeds roll to the bowl's center, a position known as a point attractor, the distance between the seeds shrinks. If, instead, the bowl is flipped over, two seeds placed on top will roll away from each other. Such a system, while still not technically chaotic, enlarges initial differences in position.

Chaotic systems, such as a machine mixing bread dough, are characterized by both attraction and repulsion. As the dough is stretched, folded, and pressed back together, any poppy seeds sprinkled in are intermixed seemingly at random. But this randomness is illusory. In fact, the poppy seeds are captured by "strange attractors," staggeringly complex pathways whose tangles appear accidental but are in fact determined by the system's fundamental equations.

During the dough-kneading process, two poppy seeds positioned next to each other eventually go their separate ways. Any early divergence or measurement error is repeatedly amplified by the mixing

Unit Two: **Paragraphs and Passages**

until the position of any seed becomes effectively unpredictable. It is this "sensitive dependence on initial conditions" and not true randomness that generates unpredictability in chaotic systems, of which one example may be the Earth's weather. According to the popular interpretation of the "Butterfly Effect," a butterfly flapping its wings causes hurricanes. A better understanding is that the butterfly causes uncertainty about the precise state of the air. This microscopic uncertainty grows until it encompasses even hurricanes. Few meteorologists believe that we will ever be able to predict rain or shine for a particular day years in the future.

> **Upon previewing the questions, here is an example of what you might jot down:**
>
> 19. main idea
> 20. poppy after mixed
> 21. rounding errors
> 22. examples of systems
> 23. pairs in chaotic sys
> 24. author: weather systems
> 25. select P2–P3: why misnomer?
>
> The first question will come from your initial read. Many of the other questions offer specific items to keep an eye out for as you create your headline list.
>
> **Here is one example of a possible set of notes for this passage:**
>
> 1. 1960 L: unexp behav in air flow eqs
>
>   Reran model, diff results
>
>   tiny rounding errors blew up
>
>   help dev <u>chaos thry</u>—<u>little to do with randomness</u> ← main idea
>
> 2. Unpredict can come fr determ eqs
>   —non-chaotic: 2 poppy seeds in or on bowl
>
> 3. Dough mixing (chaos): seed movmnt <u>seems</u> random but is NOT
>
> 4. Seeds go sep ways → unpredict, not truly random
>   —weather, butterfly eff
>
> **Simple Story:** Lorenz discovered something about chaos theory (which is not really about randomness). Non-chaotic systems are predictable. Chaotic systems increase initial differences, so even though they are not actually random, they are hard to predict.

Chapter 9: **Reading Comprehension Problem Set**

19. **The main purpose of this passage is to**

- (A) explore a common misconception about a type of complex physical system
- (B) trace the historical development of a scientific theory
- (C) distinguish a mathematical pattern from its opposite
- (D) describe the spread of a technical model from one field of study to others
- (E) contrast possible causes of weather phenomena

The first paragraph introduces chaos theory by describing a historical moment in its development. The main idea comes at the end of the first paragraph: "chaos theory. . .has little to do with randomness." The next three paragraphs focus on further explaining this mystery with analogies involving poppy seeds and bread dough. Finally, as a minor addendum, the last paragraph mentions how this understanding of chaos theory might be applied to the weather, as a possible specific case of a chaotic system.

Taking all of these roles together, the main idea of the passage is an explanation of how chaotic systems *seem* to be random (a common misconception) but actually are governed by very complex equations.

- (A) **CORRECT.** The complicated aspects are the characteristic features of chaotic systems, such as "sensitive dependence on initial conditions and staggeringly complex pathways." The point of the passage is to explain such features.
- (B) The first paragraph, as an introduction, describes a particular milestone in the historical development of chaos theory. However, the passage does not go on to describe other developments of this theory over time.
- (C) Perhaps the behavior of chaotic systems could arguably be described as a "mathematical pattern." However, the passage does not discuss any category of systems that is categorized clearly as the *opposite* of chaotic systems. Certain non-chaotic systems are described in the second paragraph, but it is not clear whether these systems would be the opposite of chaotic systems, or whether *random* systems would be the opposite.
- (D) If chaos theory is the technical model mentioned in the answer choice, the passage never describes how that model spreads from one field of study to any other.
- (E) In the fourth paragraph, the "Butterfly Effect" is mentioned as a popular explanation for at least some hurricanes. However, no other causes of weather phenomena are ever discussed.

20. **In the example discussed in the passage, what is true about poppy seeds in bread dough once the dough has been thoroughly mixed?**

- (A) They have been individually stretched and folded over.
- (B) They are scattered in random clumps throughout the dough.
- (C) They are accidentally caught in tangled objects called "strange attractors."
- (D) They are bound to regularly dispersed patterns of point attractors.
- (E) They are in positions dictated by the underlying equations that govern the mixing process.

Unit Two: **Paragraphs and Passages**

The third paragraph contains this specific detail, describing what happens to these poppy seeds: they "are intermixed seemingly at random." But the positions of the seeds are not random, as the next sentences emphasize. Rather, the seeds "are captured by 'strange attractors,' staggeringly complex pathways whose tangles. . .are in fact totally determined by the system's fundamental equations." Thus, the positions of the seeds are themselves "determined by the system's fundamental equations."

- (A) The passage mentions nothing about any stretching or folding of the poppy seeds themselves; rather, the dough is stretched and folded.
- (B) The poppy seeds are scattered throughout the dough, but not in random clumps.
- (C) The poppy seeds are caught in strange attractors, but there is nothing *accidental* about their capture. Moreover, the strange attractors described in the passage are not physical objects but rather mathematical pathways.
- (D) Point attractors are not mentioned in relation to the dough-mixing process. Also, the poppy seeds, which have been "intermixed seemingly at random," are not placed at regular intervals.
- (E) **CORRECT.** The poppy seeds may seem to be scattered at random, but they follow the pathways of the strange attractors. These pathways, and thus the seeds' positions, have been "determined by the system's fundamental equations."

21. According to the passage, the rounding errors in Lorenz's model

- (A) indicated that the model was programmed in a fundamentally faulty way
- (B) were deliberately included to represent tiny fluctuations in atmospheric air currents
- (C) were imperceptibly small at first, but tended to grow
- (D) were at least partially expected, given the complexity of the actual atmosphere
- (E) shrank to insignificant levels during each trial of the model

Use the key words "rounding errors" and "Lorenz's model" to find the relevant text for this specific detail question. The reference to Lorenz leads to the first paragraph: "Lorenz realized that tiny rounding errors in his analog computer mushroomed over time, leading to erratic results." In other words, the rounding errors started out small but became larger.

- (A) Although these rounding errors are in fact *errors*, nothing in the passage indicates or implies that the model overall was built incorrectly.
- (B) The errors were not deliberately included in the model. The passage's first sentence states that Lorenz found "unexpected behavior" in his model. It may be argued that the role of these errors is similar to the role of "tiny fluctuations in atmospheric air currents"—that is, they both introduce uncertainty that grows over time. However, this answer choice claims incorrectly that the errors were inserted on purpose.
- (C) **CORRECT.** This answer choice corresponds very closely to the statement in the passage. Some synonyms have been used, but the meaning is the same: "were imperceptibly small at first" substitutes for "tiny," and "tended to grow" substitutes for "mushroomed over time."
- (D) The passage indicates that the behavior of the model was *unexpected*. Nothing in the passage indicates that Lorenz expected the errors at all.
- (E) The errors did not shrink, but rather "mushroomed over time."

Chapter 9: **Reading Comprehension Problem Set**

22. **The passage mentions each of the following as an example or potential example of a chaotic or non-chaotic system EXCEPT**

    (A) a dough-mixing machine
    (B) atmospheric weather patterns
    (C) poppy seeds placed on top of an upside-down bowl
    (D) poppy seeds placed in a right-side-up bowl
    (E) fluctuating butterfly flight patterns

    The passage mentions several examples of systems, both chaotic and non-chaotic, to illustrate the special characteristics of chaos. This question is an exercise in finding the references to key words contained in the four wrong answers.

    (A) A dough-mixing machine is first mentioned at the beginning of the third paragraph as an example of chaos in action: "Chaotic systems, such as a machine mixing bread dough . . ."

    (B) Atmospheric weather patterns as a system to be studied are mentioned in both the first and the last paragraphs. In the last paragraph, the passage states that the Earth's weather may be an example of a chaotic system.

    (C) Poppy seeds placed on an upside-down bowl are described in the second paragraph as an example of a non-chaotic system that creates divergence.

    (D) Poppy seeds placed in a bowl that is right-side-up are described in the second paragraph as an example of a non-chaotic system that creates convergence.

    (E) **CORRECT.** Butterfly flight patterns are not discussed as examples of systems themselves. According to the last paragraph, the "Butterfly Effect" is a popular metaphor with a common interpretation, but that is not the same as a literal chaotic system.

23. **It can be inferred from the passage that which of the following pairs of items would most likely follow typical pathways within a chaotic system?**

    (A) Two particles ejected in random directions from the same decaying atomic nucleus
    (B) Two stickers affixed to a balloon that expands and contracts over and over again
    (C) Two avalanches sliding down opposite sides of the same mountain
    (D) Two baseballs placed into a device designed to mix paint
    (E) Two coins flipped into a large bowl

    Stripped down to its essence, this inference question asks which of the five choices describes a system that is the most *chaotic,* according to the characteristics of chaos outlined in the passage. The most important proof sentence is at the beginning of the third paragraph: "Chaotic systems, such as a machine mixing bread dough, are characterized by both attraction and repulsion." Thus, look for the system that is the most analogous to the dough-mixing machine. Moreover, the system should contain both attractive and repulsive elements: In other words, the two items embedded within the system should sometimes come near each other and then separate again.

    At the beginning of the fourth paragraph, there is a superficially appealing, but ultimately distracting, sentence: "During the dough-kneading process, two poppy seeds positioned next to each other eventually go their separate ways." This sentence could lead you to think that the defining characteristic of chaotic systems is simply that two embedded items move away from each other. The question is asked in such a way as to focus your attention on the two items, so that you might then use this proof sentence alone and choose an incorrect answer. It is better to use the very first sentence of that

295

Unit Two: **Paragraphs and Passages**

paragraph that applies to *any* chaotic system for your prediction: "characterized by both attraction and repulsion."

- (A) The two particles ejected from a nucleus do diverge, but they do not approach each other again. Moreover, there is no implication of any activity analogous to mixing bread dough.
- (B) The stickers on the balloon separate and come together repeatedly. This behavior meets the criterion of "both attraction and repulsion." However, there is no mixing, and as a result, the system cannot be said to be analogous to a machine mixing dough.
- (C) As in answer choice (A), the two items in question (avalanches) separate but never draw near each other again. Likewise, there is no mixing in the system.
- (D) **CORRECT.** Two baseballs placed into a device designed to mix paint is analogous to two poppy seeds placed in bread dough being mixed by a machine: Parts of the system are separated, intermingled, and brought back together again in regular, though complex, ways, as determined by the laws of physics. The pathways of the two baseballs will diverge and converge repeatedly, as in any other chaotic system.
- (E) The two coins flipped into a bowl are closely analogous to the example in the second paragraph of the passage of two poppy seeds placed in a bowl and allowed to fall; this system is presented as non-chaotic.

24. **The author implies which of the following about weather systems? Select all that apply.**
    - [A] They illustrate the same fundamental phenomenon as Lorenz's rounding errors.
    - [B] Experts agree unanimously that weather will never be predictable years in advance.
    - [C] They are governed mostly by seemingly trivial events, such as the flapping of a butterfly's wings.

This is a Select One or More question of a specific detail variety. It is mostly relevant to the last paragraph of the passage, so take a little time to refresh your understanding of the few sentences devoted to weather systems.

- [A] **CORRECT.** Lorenz's rounding errors are actually found in the first paragraph: "Lorenz realized that tiny rounding errors. . .mushroomed over time." Similarly, from the final paragraph: "This microscopic uncertainty grows until it encompasses even hurricanes." These are both examples of chaotic systems.
- [B] The last sentence of the passage says: "Few meteorologists believe that we will ever be able to predict rain or shine for a particular day years in the future." The sentence does not indicate that meteorologists are unanimous in this opinion; in fact, "Few meteorologists" indicates that at least one actually believes that such predictions might be able to be made in the future.
- [C] While the passage indicates that the wings of a butterfly can affect weather systems, it does not say that this is the most important contributing factor. Likely, major climatic events are more important than seemingly trivial events, such as a butterfly taking flight.

25. **Select the sentence in the second or third paragraph that illustrates why "chaos theory" might be called a misnomer.**

Misnomer means that something has been given an incorrect or misleading name. The first paragraph states that chaos theory, despite its name, "has little to do with randomness." Look for a sentence in the second or third paragraph that illustrates this point.

Chapter 9: **Reading Comprehension Problem Set**

The final sentence of the third paragraph uses poppy seeds to show that even the bread-mixing machine, which appears to be mixing things at random (in a "chaotic" manner), is actually moving the seeds through "staggeringly complex pathways whose tangles appear accidental but are in fact determined by the system's fundamental equations." In other words, there's nothing chaotic at all, only a very complex organization. This is a perfect example of why "chaos theory" is a kind of misnomer. (The question's request for an illustration is a good clue that you want an example from the passage.)

Note that the second-to-last sentence of the third paragraph, "But this randomness is illusory," does indicate that chaos theory might be called a misnomer. This sentence, though, does not illustrate *why* this is so.

The correct sentence is the final sentence of the third paragraph: "In fact, the poppy seeds are captured by 'strange attractors,' staggeringly complex pathways whose tangles appear accidental but are in fact determined by the system's fundamental equations."

CHAPTER 10
Essays

In This Chapter...

- Essays in a Nutshell
- Analyze an Issue
- Analyze an Argument
- Style Points
- Analyze an Issue Sample Essays
- Analyze an Argument Sample Essays
- Notes on Preparation
- Vocabulary Challenge
- Answers and Explanations

CHAPTER 10 Essays

The first part of the exam will consist of two essays, technically called the Analytical Writing Assessment (AWA). Each essay is to be completed in 30 minutes, and you will see one of each of these types:

Analyze an Issue (30 minutes)—Discuss a general interest topic.
Analyze an Argument (30 minutes)—Analyze the argument presented.

These essay assignments can occur in either order, but always before any of the Math or Verbal sections. The essays do not factor into your main GRE score; they are scored on a separate 6-point scale in increments of 0.5 (0 is lowest, 6 is highest). In this chapter, you will learn strategies for practicing, planning, and executing your essay.

Here are your Chapter 10 vocabulary words:

> indefatigable (A)
> amalgamate (A)
> malleable (E)
> veracity (E)
> peddle (A)
> ubiquitous (E)

Essays in a Nutshell

For those who consider themselves already very good at essay writing and have limited study time, here's the gist:

The Issue essay is very much like every other five-or-so paragraph academic essay you've ever written. Some people have trouble thinking of examples for abstract topics, such as, "Is justice more important in a society than compassion?" But if you feel confident about that, it's likely you won't need much preparation.

The Argument essay requires you to analyze a flawed argument. While the prompt may indicate that you are asked for your own opinion, that opinion will always be the same: The argument/plan/recommendation contains flaws.

When you take practice tests, **do** write the essays, even if you don't need the practice or don't care about the essay score. The extra hour of writing tests your stamina and can tire you out before you reach the multiple-choice sections. Practicing the extra length will make you more indefatigable on test day.

Write a lot. No matter what the official rules say, longer essays get higher scores.

Pay attention to the specific instructions. While the essay prompts will broadly follow the themes mentioned above, each will have slightly different instructions. Responding to everything asked of you in the instructions is a key component of achieving a high score.

How Essays are Used by Graduate Schools

Graduate schools to which you send your GRE scores will be able to read your actual essays. Don't write anything you wouldn't want the admissions committee to read (avoid writing anything offensive or anything with a very political or self-exposing slant).

The schools are aware of the constraints you are under as you write. In the "Guide to the Use of Scores" that ETS offers to graduate school admissions departments, ETS writes, "A GRE essay response should be considered a rough first draft since examinees do not have sufficient time to revise their essays during the test. Examinees also do not have dictionaries or spell-checking or grammar-checking software available to them."

It is impossible to say broadly how much the essay counts in graduate school admissions; there are simply too many programs and too many schools. Some math and science programs may take little or no account of the essay, and some more writing-intensive graduate programs may consider the essays more carefully. Some schools may use the essays as a screening device (so a very low essay score might keep the rest of your application from being given a serious review). It's also reasonable to presume that your essays are more likely to be taken into account if your undergraduate schooling was done in a language other than English.

The admissions department at the particular graduate program to which you are applying is the best source of information about how the GRE essay will be used. If the admissions department is not forthcoming, you'll just have to do your best, which is a good policy anyway.

Most MBA programs do not weigh AWA scores highly at all. If you are applying to a program that does not heavily weight the AWA, do your best, make sure that the AWA score is respectable, but do not place much emphasis on this element of your GRE preparation! If, on the other hand, you are applying for a PhD or for a master's in a field other than business, ask your desired programs how they weigh the AWA section of the GRE, and adjust your preparation emphasis accordingly.

The Physical Mechanics of Essay Writing

Assuming that you are taking a computer-based GRE (true in the United States and most other countries), you will be typing your essays into a text box. There is no limit to how much text you can enter, but you can only see about 10 lines of what you've written before you have to scroll. The system feels like a clunky, old-fashioned word processing program. You will have "Cut" and "Paste" buttons, as well as an "Undo" button. There is no bold, italic, or underline. There is no tab/indent. The program does not offer any type of spell-check or grammar check.

You will have scratch paper (the same scratch paper you use for the rest of the exam) on which to plan your essay, but you can also outline in the text box (though be sure to delete any notes or outlines before submitting your essay).

Once you've completed an essay and clicked on "Submit," you cannot go back. If you complete an essay before the time expires, you can go immediately to the next section, but you do *not* get to use any extra time on other sections. If you do finish early, consider letting the clock run down and using that extra time to take a mental break. (If you do this, you must remain in your seat, as this is not an official break.)

There is no break after the essays; you will proceed to your first Math or Verbal section.

Essay Length

For each essay, use a five-paragraph structure as a baseline. Sometimes you'll write four paragraphs, sometimes you'll write six, but the basic structure is an intro and a conclusion sandwiching a few main examples or reasons, each in its own body paragraph.

Interestingly, Manhattan Prep's analysis of published GRE essays written by actual students and given real scores shows a very strong correlation between length and score. Let's be very clear: **Even when ETS says that essay length doesn't matter, it does.**

To ensure your essay is long enough, you will have to brainstorm and plan your essay very efficiently (3–4 minutes for the Issue, 2–3 minutes for the Argument) so that you can get started writing as soon as possible.

Write as much as you can in the time allotted!

Spelling and Grammar

On the GRE, while good spelling and grammar are better than poor spelling and grammar, the ideas you present are far more important.

According to ETS, "Scorers are trained to focus on the analytical logic of the essays more than on spelling, grammar, or syntax. The mechanics of writing are weighed in their ratings only to the extent that these impede clarity of meaning." In other words, as long as the grader can understand you, they are not supposed to count off for minor and infrequent spelling and grammar errors.

Scoring

Essays are scored from 0–6, and are reported separately from your Math and Verbal scores. Each essay is scored according to a publicly available Scoring Guide, which is slightly different between the two types. The Scoring Guides will be discussed more fully in the following sections.

Essays are scored by specially trained college and university faculty who will not see your name, gender, geographical location, or any other identifying information. Each of your essays will be read by one human grader and one *e-rater*®, described by ETS as "a computerized program developed by ETS that is capable of identifying essay features related to writing proficiency." If the human grader and the *e-rater*® disagree, another human grader reads the essay, and the two human scores are amalgamated to create your final score for that essay. Ultimately the scores on the two essays are averaged to create your final 0-6 essay score.

It goes without saying that any evidence of cheating, which includes using anyone else's work without citation, will get your GRE score (the entire thing, not just the essays) canceled and your fee forfeited.

Analyze an Issue

For the Analyze an Issue assignment, you will be presented with a statement or a claim. Your job is to agree or disagree with the statement, and then write a compelling essay to support the position you've taken.

The topic that you are given on the real test will be chosen from a list of topics available on the ETS website. Yes, that's right—you can view all of the possible topics ahead of time. There are dozens, so don't spend your time memorizing them, but do use them to get a sense of what you might see on test day.

In the issue essay, you are generally expected to **take a side**. Don't just say, "It depends." Instead, make sure you articulate a particular point of view. You can, and usually should, acknowledge that the other side has some merit, but do so in a way that doesn't hurt your own argument. If you do write a more modified thesis along the lines of "it depends," make sure you clearly explain *what* it depends on, so that your essay seems thoughtful and precise, rather than just indecisive.

Scoring Guide

According to *The Official Guide to the GRE®*, an essay that scores a 6 generally does the following:

- "Articulates a clear and insightful position on the issue in accordance with the assigned task
- "Develops the position fully with compelling reasons and/or persuasive examples
- "Sustains a well-focused, well-organized analysis, connecting ideas logically
- "Conveys ideas fluently and precisely, using effective vocabulary and sentence variety
- "Demonstrates superior facility with the conventions of standard written English (i.e., grammar, usage and mechanics), but may have minor errors"

As discussed in the previous section, a majority of the scoring rubric is based on the quality of your argument, not the quality of your writing. This section will discuss how to generate strong arguments for the Issue essay. A subsequent section will discuss tips for writing style on the GRE essay.

Essay Instructions

Pay attention to the specific instructions given with the essay as it may affect how much content you have to write about the other side of the argument. ETS lists six different possible ways you might be prompted to respond to a topic. Here they are, from *The Official Guide for the GRE® General Test*:

1. "Write a response in which you discuss the extent to which you agree or disagree with the statement, and explain your reasoning for the position you take. In developing and supporting your position, consider ways in which the statement might or might not hold true and explain how these considerations shape your position.

2. "Write a response in which you discuss the extent to which you agree or disagree with the recommendation, and explain your reasoning for the position you take. In developing and supporting your position, describe specific circumstances in which adopting the recommendation would or would not be advantageous and explain how these examples shape your position.

3. "Write a response in which you discuss the extent to which you agree or disagree with the claim. In developing and supporting your position, be sure to address the most compelling reasons and/or examples that could be used to challenge your position.

4. "Write a response in which you discuss which view more closely aligns with your own position, and explain your reasoning for the position you take. In developing and supporting your position, address both of the views presented above.

5. "Write a response in which you discuss the extent to which you agree or disagree with the claim and the reason on which that claim is based. (NOTE: For this prompt, the claim will be accompanied by a reason why the claim has been made. You'll need to give your opinion on both.)

6. "Write a response in which you discuss your views on the policy above, and explain your reasoning for the position you take. In developing and supporting your position, consider the possible consequences of implementing the policy and explain how these consequences shape your position."

Chapter 10: **Essays**

These instructions may seem quite different, but they really fall into three general categories:

1. Pick a side of the prompt and defend it, but explain when the other side might be true or more logical (#1, #2, #3, and #4 from above).
2. Pick a side of the prompt, and also make sure to discuss the reason the author gives in defense of that prompt (#5 from above).
3. Pick a side and discuss the consequences of your opinion (#6 from above).

In the end, you will *always* want to do the following, regardless of the Issue prompt you're given:

1. Take a point of view on the given issue.
2. Support your point of view using relevant and *specific* examples.
3. Acknowledge both sides of the issue and the specific instructions in the question.

Brainstorming

Spend 3–4 minutes brainstorming specific, real-world examples. Let your perspective be malleable: Try to think of examples on both sides of the issue. *Real-world* means some event or phenomenon that actually occurred, whether in history, in your own life, or even in a book that you read. Once you're done brainstorming, pick the side for which you have the best examples; plan for the strongest points on that side to each become a body paragraph and start writing.

Practice it with this topic:

> "The better a new idea is, the greater the opposition to that idea when it is first presented. Only later, usually once the person who had the idea is no longer around to enjoy its success, do we consider the thinker a genius."

First, make a T-chart, like this:

Why brainstorm both sides of an issue? It is often true that the side you don't believe is the easier side to write. Perhaps this is because when you believe in something strongly, it seems obvious to you, and it's harder to come up with concrete reasons or examples to support your opinion. By writing down "For" and "Against," you are setting yourself up to think in each direction. This is especially useful when you are trying to come up with counterexamples.

Write down one-word (or very short) tags for each possible reason or example. On this prompt, for instance, Galileo might pop to mind because he was persecuted for saying that the Earth moved around the Sun, but after his death, his ideas were vindicated, and he was considered a scientific hero. On the other hand, there are plenty of geniuses who were renowned during their own lifetimes (Einstein was quite famous in his own time). Jot these down on your T-chart—Galileo on the left, and Einstein on the right.

Unit Two: **Paragraphs and Passages**

A good way to get your brainstorming done quickly is to piggyback off examples you already have. Once you've thought of Galileo, can you think of other people like him who were persecuted for their ideas—ideas that are now considered correct? You might think of someone like Nelson Mandela, who spent 27 years in prison. But wait! He was hailed as a hero for so much of his life, and he was the first democratically elected president of South Africa. This is actually a pretty good example for the Against side. (This is why it's good to brainstorm both sides.)

Also on the Against side—once you've thought of Einstein, can you think of other famous geniuses? How about Stephen Hawking? If you run out of steam, think to yourself, "Hmm, Einstein and Stephen Hawking are both scientists. Can I think of the "Einstein" of some other field?" Perhaps someone like W. E. B. DuBois, who was considered a radical in his own time; however, after his death, his ideas were vindicated by the civil rights movement of the 1960s. Hmm, DuBois actually fits better on the "For" side. Is there someone else who was a social activist whose ideas were later vindicated? How about the early feminists, such as Elizabeth Cady Stanton and Lucretia Mott? See, you're on a roll!

Here, the example goes further than it needs to for the sake of demonstrating the brainstorming process. Stop as soon as you have three good ideas for one side.

For	Against
Galileo	Einstein, Hawking, Mandela

Your initial thought might have been that you wanted to argue for, but you've come up with three against examples. Go with it! Your goal is to write the best essay you can as quickly and as easily as possible. You've got what you need to do that, so start writing.

You may have noticed that the previous examples were drawn from history and current events. While personal examples are allowable, they don't tend to make for the most rigorous and persuasive essays. Personal examples can be considered a backup plan for when you get stuck in your brainstorming.

You are *not* required to use example after example in your essay. You are also perfectly welcome to use well-considered reasoning. Some topics lend themselves better to examples, while other topics lend themselves better to argumentation.

Here's another example topic.

> **"Every nation should require students to study at least one foreign language from the elementary school level through the university level."**

Your challenge here is to "divide up" your reasoning into discrete arguments so that your essay doesn't just ramble on without structure.

You might just start with the first thing that comes to mind. For instance, is it equally true in "every nation" that students should be required to study foreign language? Probably not. Jot this down in the Against column.

On the other hand, the world is becoming more connected. Most people who end up conducting international business, or emigrating to new lands, don't know from childhood that they're going to do so. As children, they're not in a position to decide whether to take foreign languages. It would be best to require foreign languages so that they're prepared for whatever happens in their adult lives. This would go in the left column.

One possible thesis might be, "While foreign language study has many benefits, both practical and intellectual, it is going too far to say that such study should be mandatory for every citizen of every nation. Other factors should be taken into account." Those broad factors mentioned (maybe whether the nation's primary language is already an international language, whether the nation's primary language is in danger of dying out, and whether the nation has more pressing concerns) could each become the foundations of one of the following body paragraphs. This thesis clearly takes a stance against the prompt, but it certainly isn't arguing that foreign language study is bad—it is taking a very reasonable, balanced approach.

When a topic is phrased in an extreme way ("everyone should do X"), **don't ignore practical issues**. In some nations, it would be difficult to even find foreign language teachers. Some nations barely have schools of any kind, so foreign language instruction hardly seems like a main priority. And who decides which languages are mandatory? Not all students are the same—maybe most students could be required to take foreign languages, but the few who are having trouble with basic skills that they will need for adult life ought to be waived from foreign language requirements so that they can focus on things they will really need.

Here is a sample T-chart containing some of these ideas:

For	Against
World is more int'l—students don't know what they'll need as adults, so prep them now.	Some nations need f.l. more than others.
	Some nations not practical—schools very basic, no f.l. teachers.
	Which f.l.? Who decides?
	Preserve culture, some nations' languages might die out.
	ALL PEOPLE EVERYWHERE? Too extreme.

It's totally okay to have an unbalanced T-chart. You *want* to use this to pick which side to write on. (Of course, there is no "right" answer to an Issue question, and your personal T-chart might have led you to argue in favor.)

This chart shows five arguments against. You probably won't have time to write an entire body paragraph about each one, and some ideas are really building off of other ones (for instance, it might be hard to write an entire paragraph on the idea "Who decides which foreign languages to take?"). So either pick your three or so strongest arguments, or else *group* your arguments into three or so groups.

Here is what a test-taker might jot on paper next to the chart:

F.l. good but shouldn't be mandatory for all.
  I. Diff countries, diff needs.
  II. Some nations must focus on survival—priorities!
  III. Not practical—some nations can't, what lang? Some want to preserve culture.
  IV. Individual students are diff.

You also want to make sure to **acknowledge the other side** (usually in the introduction, although sometimes in the course of the body paragraphs). This is very easy to do, since you have brainstormed both sides. Just take a point or two from the side you *didn't* pick, and say something like, "While a reasonable person might think X, actually Y is more important," or "While a reasonable person might think X, this is not the case *all of the time*." For instance, on the foreign language topic:

While a reasonable person might suggest that because children don't know whether they'll move to other nations or engage in international business as adults, we should prepare them for such experiences now. However, some people will stay in their home countries and work in jobs that don't require a second language. It makes sense to leave decisions about education in the hands of each nation and its school systems.

Acknowledging the other side is a great way to fill out your introduction or conclusion. Or, if you have a lot to say in rebuttal to an opposing point, you can write a body paragraph of the form "objection → your response → your argument."

In other words, *anticipate counterarguments and respond to them*. This is especially important if you have decided on what you know to be an unusual viewpoint. If your argument is that governments should not provide public schools, you absolutely must address the first thing that may pop into someone's mind: "But what about children whose parents can't afford to pay private school fees?"

Finally, a word about your thesis or main idea: While sometimes it makes sense to simply agree or disagree with the topic, feel free to take a balanced, in-between approach. The graders enjoy nuance. Just be very clear about what you mean. Still, *in between* doesn't mean vague or wishy-washy. For instance, if you want to say that foreign language instruction should be mandatory in some countries and not others, say exactly what should be the deciding factor. A good thesis (for someone who is more on the "for" side of the foreign language topic) might be:

Because foreign language instruction is increasingly important in our interconnected world, it should be a priority in school curricula. However, in some nations, foreign language instruction is simply not practical or even possible. Thus, foreign language instruction should be mandatory at all levels of schooling except in nations where such a requirement is impracticable or for individual students whose learning difficulties make the requirement unreasonable.

Note that this person isn't exactly arguing for the topic as written. But there's no question what the writer's position is. This is a detailed, balanced, and reasonable thesis.

If you do go beyond a simple "agree" or "disagree" thesis, avoid theses that are too extreme, but also those that are too soft and agreeable. An overly extreme thesis might be "*Foreign languages should not be made mandatory for any students, because students should never have to study something they don't want to. Children should always make their own decisions.*" This goes beyond what is required and is difficult to prove. An example of an overly soft or agreeable thesis might be "*Foreign languages can be valuable in certain pursuits. For example, foreign language study can help students become translators, foreign language teachers, or travel writers."* This statement is so mild that it is almost impossible to *disagree* with, and it doesn't confidently answer the instructions.

In sum, your thesis or main idea shouldn't be something so extreme that you can't defend it, but it also shouldn't be something so humdrum and obvious that a reasonable person couldn't take an opposite view. Don't oversimplify the topic. **Pick a thesis you would use to start an interesting, intelligent discussion among reasonable people.**

The brainstorming and planning process above might sound as though it would take a person *much* longer than the 3–4 minutes recommended at the beginning of the chapter. Keep in mind that the sample T-charts contain a bit more information than you would need to write down, since you'll only be writing for yourself. If you write "SH" for "Stephen Hawking," you only have to remember what your abbreviation means for a couple of minutes, so feel free to be brief.

You can write an essay outline, separate from your brainstorming, if you find it helpful. But consider labeling points from your T-chart "I," "II," and "III" to save time, as opposed to rewriting your notes in outline form. Alternatively, you can type your outline on the computer so that you have bits of it to reuse as you write your full essay. Whatever you do, practice your preferred approach so you can confidently implement in the time constraints of the test.

Practice with brainstorming will reveal that the same examples can often be used on a variety of prompts. There's nothing wrong with that! Many topics lend themselves to discussing climate change; for instance, the issue of whether technology/progress/new ideas can have a downside seems to be a common underlying theme. And, of course, write about what you know. If you were a philosophy major, or an environmental science major, etc., feel free to draw disproportionately on those types of examples.

When you practice brainstorming, give yourself plenty of time the first time through—maybe 10 minutes. The next time, cut it down to 8 minutes, then 6, 5, 4…With practice, you will be able to reliably brainstorm in 3–4 minutes or even faster.

Writing the Issue Essay

Structure

Here is a basic structure for the Issue essay:

Introduction: Briefly restate the issue with the goal of demonstrating to the grader that you understand the topic. *Do not simply repeat the prompt* (the grader knows what topic you are writing about). Then define terms (if needed), acknowledge complexity, and establish your "take" or thesis on the issue.

Body: Write two to four paragraphs, each illustrating one of your main points. Keep in mind: *Don't spend too much time making a single point or you will run out of time!*

Conclusion: Re-summarize your position, perhaps acknowledging the other side. An exemplary conclusion adds some final extra insight—a new window to the main idea you've been discussing all along.

Aim for three substantive sentences in your conclusion; these sentences can vary widely in length and content. A relevant quote would be a good way to fill out a conclusion.

A conclusion often ends with a final sentence that either generalizes the situation and makes it more universal or looks toward the future. For instance:

> As our world becomes more interconnected through technology and increasingly global outlooks, we must look for every possible way to prepare the next generation for a more international world—a world replete with possibilities, if we are willing to look beyond our already blurring national boundaries and engage with humanity at large.

Of course, many wind up right near the end of the 30 minutes when it comes down to writing a conclusion. So while a new insight would be nice, it may not realistically happen. Don't stress. In general, if you are running out of time or are stuck for a final concluding sentence, try something along the lines of "In order to have a better world in the future, we must do X."

Trouble Getting Started?

If you freeze when trying to start your introduction, write a different paragraph first! Just pick whichever example seems easiest to write and dive in. You can certainly cut and paste as needed. In the worst case, use a starter sentence to turn the engine over in your mind: "This is a dumb idea because…" or "This is a great idea because…" Just keep an eye on the clock and make sure you leave enough time for both an intro and a conclusion.

A Note on Proofreading

Very few test-takers will have time for significant proofreading. Keep in mind that the graders are aware of your time constraints. They are not judging your spelling or punctuation, except where it muddies your meaning. In fact, the most important part of proofreading on the GRE is to check that you responded to the specific instructions that were presented in the prompt. Beyond that, just try to put yourself in the shoes of the grader, and check that all of your points are stated clearly. Let the commas fall where they may!

Analyze an Argument

The Analyze an Argument task gives you 30 minutes to plan and write a critique of an argument presented in the form of a short passage. To score well, you need to do three things. First, analyze the line of reasoning in the argument (which will always be faulty). Then, explain the logical flaws and assumptions that underlie that reasoning. Finally, discuss what the author could add in order to make the conclusion of the argument more logically sound.

It is absolutely critical to realize you are *not* being asked to present your own views on the subject matter of the argument. You are being asked only to analyze how well the author made their argument.

Scoring Guide

According to *The Official Guide to the GRE®*, an Argument essay that scores a 6 will generally do the following:

- "Clearly identifies aspects of the argument relevant to the assigned task and examines them insightfully
- "Develops ideas cogently, organizes them logically, and connects them with clear transitions
- "Provides compelling and thorough support for its main points
- "Conveys ideas fluently and precisely, using effective vocabulary and sentence variety
- "Demonstrates superior facility with the conventions of standard written English (i.e., grammar, usage and mechanics), but may have minor errors"

These points are slightly different from the Issue Essay, but it is still true that the quality of your analysis is the most important factor in your score. This section will discuss how to build that analysis by finding the flaws in the arguments provided to you by the GRE, and the next section will focus on writing style tips.

Argument Essay Instructions

As with the Issue essay, you can find all possible prompts for the Argument essay on the ETS website. Also like the Issue essay, there are a variety of possible instructions you might receive. ETS lists eight possible sets of instructions that could accompany an Argument essay prompt. However, the eight of them are even less interesting than the six provided for the Issue essay! Not one of them demands anything that wouldn't be featured in any successful Argument essay on the given prompt:

1. Write a response in which you discuss what specific evidence is needed to evaluate the argument, and explain how the evidence would weaken or strengthen the argument.

2. Write a response in which you examine the stated and/or unstated assumptions of the argument. Be sure to explain how the argument depends on these assumptions and what the implications are if the assumptions prove unwarranted.

3. Write a response in which you discuss what questions would need to be answered in order to decide whether the recommendation and the argument on which it is based are reasonable. Be sure to explain how the answers to these questions would help to evaluate the recommendation.

4. Write a response in which you discuss what questions would need to be answered in order to decide whether the advice and the argument on which it is based are reasonable. Be sure to explain how the answers to these questions would help to evaluate the advice.

5. Write a response in which you discuss what questions would need to be answered to decide whether the recommendation is likely to have the predicted result. Be sure to explain how the answers to these questions would help to evaluate the recommendation.

6. Write a response in which you discuss what questions would need to be answered in order to decide whether the prediction and the argument on which it is based are reasonable. Be sure to explain how the answers to these questions would help to evaluate the prediction.

7. Write a response in which you discuss one or more alternative explanations that could rival the proposed explanation and explain how your explanation(s) can plausibly account for the facts presented in the argument.

8. Write a response in which you discuss what questions would need to be addressed in order to decide whether the conclusion and the argument on which it is based arc reasonable. Be sure to explain how the answers to the questions would help to evaluate the conclusion.

A well-written essay in which you locate logical flaws in the argument and then explain how they could be fixed will likely score highly. That said, do read the specific instructions and make sure that they are addressed, just to be on the safe side.

The Construction of Arguments

It may be helpful to quickly diagram an argument to reveal its structure, similar to the way you take notes for argument-based passages.

Unit Two: **Paragraphs and Passages**

When you diagram, the point is to put the conclusion at the top and the supporting arguments (premises) below in a logical way—the way they are being used to support the argument. Sometimes, the diagram will look a bit strange because the argument itself is a bit strange—and therein probably lies a flaw. Feel free to note your questions in parentheses as you go.

Try one:

> The town of Arcana should institute an 11pm curfew for teenagers in order to curb crime and improve academic performance. Many crimes are being committed by young people after dark, and a curfew would both make such crimes impossible and provide an extra legal offense with which to charge those who do break the law. Furthermore, many young people study less than one hour per night. An 11pm curfew would improve students' grades.

11PM curfew for teens will ↓ crime, ↑ GPA	
crimes after dark (same as "11PM"?)	teens study < 1 hr (start studying at 11 now?)
curfew → "impossible" to commit crimes + extra charge	
(if impossible, who would be charged?!)	

Feel free to make use of a two-column format, liberal use of arrows, etc.—whatever makes visual sense of the argument.

Once you've diagrammed (either on paper or mentally), it's time to brainstorm the flaws. How do you find them? Fortunately, most of the mistakes have been made before …

Argument Essay: Flaws to Watch Out For

The following is a list of common fallacies found in GRE arguments. After you read through the examples and try to find the flaws, practice finding some of them in real GRE arguments.

The list is quite long. You don't have to "get" every one, nor do you have to memorize the list. This is just to get you thinking about some of the kinds of things to look out for. You do not need to memorize the names for the flaws, nor should you actually use the names in your essay. Just deconstruct the argument, pointing out the sorts of things detailed in this list.

In a typical GRE argument, you can expect to find one to five of these flaws. It is also possible that some GRE arguments may possess flaws not listed—as with anything, there are an infinite number of ways to mess something up.

Fallacy Type	Explanation
Unjustified assumptions	The argument is based on a questionable assumption. That is, in order for the argument to be true, the author is depending on a premise that he or she didn't write down and hasn't proven. The argument's veracity cannot be validated unless the assumptions can be proved to be true.
Skill and will	The argument assumes that people have the ability (skill) to do something or the motivation (will) to do it, when this has not been proven to be the case. The recommendations that "Everyone should exercise two hours per day" and "Children should be offered green vegetables three times daily" run into problems regarding the ability of people to exercise that much (what about people who are already ill?) and the desire of children to eat the vegetables.
Extreme language	The argument (usually the conclusion) uses language so extreme that the premises cannot justify the conclusion. Extreme words to watch out for include the following: only, never, always, cannot, certainly.
Terms are too vague	Just as you are on the lookout for language that is too extreme, you're also on the lookout for language that is too vague.
Predicting the future	There's nothing wrong with trying to predict the future, of course; it's hard to run a government (or anything) without doing so. However, whenever an argument tries to predict the future, that's your opportunity to point out that the future could actually turn out some other way. Anyone who tries to predict the future is automatically introducing a level of uncertainty into his or her argument.
What's their motivation?	Whenever an argument is in the form of an advertisement or company announcement, you get to ask, "What's the speaker's motivation?" Is the speaker trying to peddle a medication, make a company look good, sell something, or get elected?
The troubled analogy	There's nothing wrong with a good analogy, of course, but analogies in GRE arguments are never good. Every time you make an analogy, you're saying that something is like something else—except that it isn't *exactly* like that, or you'd just be talking about the original topic. It's your job to find and exploit the dissimilarities.
Confusing signs of a thing for the thing itself:	Medical tests often report false positives, while failing to catch everyone who actually has the disease. The number of people who test positive for a disease is not identical to the number of people who have the disease. This effect is especially acute when people have an incentive (such as money) to over-report something or an incentive (such as fear or laziness) to under-report something. For instance, reports of crimes such as littering and jaywalking are extremely low, but that doesn't mean people aren't committing those crimes all the time. Reports of whiplash from car accidents may be inflated, since victims are often in a position to gain money from insurance companies. Reports of workplace harassment may be lower than actual incidents of harassment because workers fear losing their jobs or worsening the problem.

Unit Two: **Paragraphs and Passages**

Fallacy Type	Explanation
Short term vs. long term	Something that's good in the short term, under certain circumstances (antibiotics, for instance), may not be good for you in the long term. Something that is a good idea in the short term (working all night to rescue people in an emergency) might not even be possible in the long term.
	Similarly, something that's good or possible long term may not be good or possible short term. Eating a carrot a day may be beneficial for your eyesight over many years, but it won't help you pass your pilot's exam next week.
Sample isn't representative	If the GRE mentions a study, chances are that the sample is not representative. One in the argument pool refers to "French women in their eighties who were nursing-home residents." Wow, what a very specific group! It's your job to point out that what works for French female octogenarians might not work for non-French people, men, and people under 80.
Sample is too small	If a GRE argument mentions how many people were in a study, it's your job to say that the study should've been bigger. *A study of 120 elderly, hospital-bound patients* is a pretty small study.
No control group	A good study should have a control group—that is, a group of people who are as similar as possible in every way, and differ from the test group by only one variable.
	You can't just give people a new medicine and measure whether their condition improves; you have to get together a big enough group of people who meet certain conditions (such as having a particular illness at a particular stage), divide the people into two groups (balanced by gender, age, and a host of other factors), and give the drug to only one group. It's important to make sure that the people receiving the drug do not just get *better*, but *better than the other group*. After all, what if it's the sort of illness that goes away on its own? Maybe some outside force (the changing seasons?) will cause improvement in both groups. It's your job to point out when a study lacks a control group, and what impact this might have on the study's findings.
The ever-changing pool	Most groups of people have a rotating cast of members. If a civic club voted in favor of something yesterday and against it 20 years ago, you wouldn't automatically conclude that people in the club changed their minds over time; it's pretty likely that the club includes different people than it did back then.
Correlation does not equal causation	Just because two things are happening at the same time doesn't mean one causes the other. They might both be happening because of the same *other* cause, or they might be happening at the same time by complete coincidence.

Chapter 10: Essays

Fallacy Type	Explanation
Nothing is quantified	Sometimes, you can get away with failing to attach numbers to things. Most people would be happy to be healthier or richer, even if you can't measure that exactly. However, quantification (expressing things as numbers) becomes important when you try to argue something like "the eventual savings will outweigh the startup costs." Be on the lookout for this type of situation—you are trying to compare two things that *can* be quantified, but aren't.
How was it before?	It's hard to judge the present or predict the future without information about the past. When an argument does try to predict the future, make sure it has provided enough information about the previous state of things.
Alike doesn't mean identical	People who (or things that) are alike in some ways are undoubtedly different in others.
Percentages vs. real numbers (and other mathematical confusion)	If David pays 28 percent of his income in taxes and Marie pays 33 percent of her income in taxes, who pays more money to the government? Without knowing how much the two people make, it's impossible to say. Don't confuse percentages with actual numbers of dollars, people, etc. If any numbers are presented in an Argument topic, see whether they are being cited in a logical way.

Don't Forget to Strengthen the Argument: Just Flip the Flaw

Some sets of Argument essay instructions ask you to strengthen the argument. To discuss in your essay how the argument might be strengthened, just flip the flaw around. For instance:

Nothing is quantified?

This argument could be improved by quantifying X, Y, and Z ...

Possible alternative causes?

This argument could be improved by investigating and ruling out alternative causes such as ...

Correlation does not equal causation?

This argument could be improved by proving that X causes Y through a controlled study ...

No control group, nonrepresentative sample, too-small sample?

This argument could possibly be validated by a new study having the following qualities ...

Brainstorming the Argument Essay

Look back at the list of flaws, and try to find several that apply to the following argument:

> Invoice Regulators, Inc. (IRI) can make your company more profitable. IRI examines our client firms' outgoing invoices and vendor receipts to help clients recoup money owed and refunds due. One client, a family firm with a 100-year history, discovered $75,000 worth of uncashed checks in an employee's desk drawer, and others have also made large gains. 80 percent of our client firms have experienced an increase in sales during the quarter our services were acquired. Hire IRI to improve your firm's profitability.

Unit Two: Paragraphs and Passages

Here are some example flaws for this argument:

Correlation does not equal causation: So 80 percent of client firms had a sales increase around the time IRI was hired. So what? Firms often have sales increases; one thing didn't necessarily cause the other.

Alike doesn't mean identical/unjustified assumptions: The argument assumes that other businesses have outgoing invoices in the first place and that, quite frankly, the business owners are a bit incompetent. It does not seem likely that the "family firm with a 100-year history" and a drawer full of forgotten money is representative of other companies. There are **small sample/unrepresentative sample** issues here as well.

Short term vs. long term: The promise to "make your company more profitable" implies an ongoing financial improvement. The two cases cited seem temporary—the $75,000 is a one-shot deal, and the "increase in sales during the quarter" makes no mention of some improved, systemic way to enhance ongoing profitability.

Terms are too vague/nothing is quantified: Other clients have "made large gains." How large? Big enough to offset the cost (which was never mentioned) of IRI's services? What percent of clients experience the large gains?

What's their motivation? Obviously, this is an advertisement. But it doesn't hurt to point out that IRI clearly has its own financial interests in mind here.

There is also another big problem that isn't named in this chapter, but is specific to this argument:

Confusing sales with profitability: Here, the argument confuses increased profitability (which is at least temporarily achievable by cashing a drawer full of checks or chasing refunds) with sales. Perhaps IRI costs more than the sales increase and would thus hurt profitability.

Once you've identified the flaws, make a quick outline. If you have more than four or so flaws to write about, you may wish to group any that are very similar or simply omit the weakest.

Put your ideas in a logical order so that your argument is persuasive and so that you can write logical transitions from one idea to the next.

Here is one sample outline:

    the "checks in the drawer" client ≠ representative of other potential clients

        big mistake!
        one biz is insufficient evidence
        not all biz even have outgoing invoices

    claims of "other biz" are vague, nothing quantified
        gains big enough to outweigh costs of IRI? (what ARE costs of IRI?)

    claims of enhanced profitability even for existing clients are suspect

        sales ≠ profitability
        sales "in same quarter"—not even clear it's DUE TO IRI
        even if it were, correlation ≠ causation!

    "profitability" implies ongoing

If this seems like a lot to write before even getting started typing, don't worry—you would not need to write all this out on your paper. You'll be able to skip anything you know you'll remember, and you would abbreviate much more than shown here.

The following is an argument from a "debater" perspective (this isn't something you'd actually write down, since you're about to type the real essay, but your outline should reflect a coherent argument that you've formed mentally before you begin to write):

I. Just because hiring IRI has been profitable for some clients doesn't mean it would be profitable for others.

II. However, it's not even clear that IRI *has* been profitable for anyone, since there are no actual numbers to quantify most of the firms' gains, and the costs to hire IRI are not known.

III. The claims of profitability for existing clients are also suspect because IRI has confused sales with profitability, taking credit for something that is irrelevant to IRI's services and that possibly even began before IRI was hired.

IV. Profitability implies an ongoing financial improvement. IRI fails to define the period. A one-shot cash infusion is not the same thing as enhanced profitability.

These statements are the parts of the argument each body paragraph will make. Note how the order seems "right"—it goes from arguing that IRI won't be profit-enhancing for everyone to questioning whether it's profit enhancing for anyone at all. Statements II and III make the same point from different angles and clearly should come one after the other.

The outline/argument above leaves out the question "What's their motivation?" (the idea that, because the text is from an ad, the speaker is biased). This point seems way too obvious to write an entire paragraph about, although mentioning it would be perfectly appropriate in an introduction.

Note that there is no thesis written down. The thesis for an Argument essay will pretty much always be something like, "The argument rests on questionable assumptions, suffers from vaguely defined terms, and contains numerous logical flaws that make it impossible to validate the conclusion."

Spend 2–3 minutes on the entire process of diagramming, brainstorming flaws, and organizing your thoughts into a coherent and persuasive outline. However, for now, it would be reasonable to take a bit more time (say, 5 or 6 minutes), knowing that with practice you'll get better and faster at spotting flaws.

Similarly to the Issue essay, practice with brainstorming will speed up the process. You may find some flaws seem to occur more often than others. If you find yourself brainstorming or writing three "correlation does not equal causation" essays in a row, there's nothing wrong with that. The GRE writers implant the same flaws into their argument topics over and over.

Argument Essay Outline

I. Introduction: In the intro, summarize the argument at hand and give your "take." Do not repeat the argument; the grader is already very familiar with it.

> Candidates for office are often prompted to make unlikely promises to gain support. While it is clear that the people of Brownsville would like more jobs to be created, it is unlikely that the mayoral candidate's plan will bring about the intended effect.

You are then going to establish your "take," or thesis. Unlike in the Issue essay, where you were instructed to brainstorm both sides and construct a sophisticated, nuanced main idea, here your main idea is much easier. It's pretty much always going to say that the argument has some serious problems:

> While the mayor's goals may be admirable, his plan rests on a number of unjustified assumptions and fails to take into account other factors affecting job creation in a seaside resort town.

Notice that this paragraph begins with acknowledging some small positive—at least the mayor's intentions are good! This is a good way to add some nuance to your main idea.

II. Body: Explain one main point in each of two to four paragraphs.

Each of the flaws you decided to write about will become the main point of a body paragraph. Or if you decide to group more than one flaw into a paragraph, make sure that the two flaws are closely and logically related. For instance, "the sample size is too small" and "the sample is not representative" are good candidates to be grouped into a single paragraph. Generally, though, keep it to one main point per paragraph. GRE graders have given high scores to Argument essays that include as many as six body paragraphs—in such cases, many of the body paragraphs are quite short.

Arrange your main points in a logical way, and use **transitions** to segue from paragraph to paragraph. Transitions are usually located in the first sentence of a new body paragraph. For instance, if you have just written a paragraph about how a study's sample size was too small and not representative, you might begin the next paragraph with something like:

> Not only should it be apparent that a study based on a sample of 80 women is not necessarily applicable to humanity at large, it is also the case that, due to the lack of a control group, we are unable to evaluate the results of the study for even this extremely limited sample.

Here, the example segues from talking about the sample's size and makeup to talking about a problem related to working even within the small and limited sample. This is a logical progression of ideas; the use of such transitions throughout an essay creates a sense of coherence and fluency.

Don't forget to **improve the argument**. There are (at least) three possible ways to arrange your argument to incorporate this component:

1. Each time you mention a flaw, follow up with how to fix it. The "improve the argument" component would therefore be part of each body paragraph.

2. Write two or more body paragraphs about the argument's flaws, and follow up with one body paragraph on how to fix those flaws.

3. Use the body paragraphs entirely to discuss the flaws, and save the discussion of how to fix those flaws for the conclusion. This may be the best plan for anyone frequently stuck for a conclusion. Keeping the "improve the argument" component brief is also a good way to keep from sounding repetitive.

III. Conclusion: In the conclusion, summarize your critique. Restate your thesis or main idea in different words, and state or restate what would need to be done to improve the argument. Ending with ideas for improvement gives a nice, positive note at the end:

> The candidate for mayor who proposed bringing a big-box home improvement store to Brownsville may have been motivated by the admirable goal of creating jobs in an economically distressed area. However, the candidate failed to take into account job loss from local hardware stores that would likely

be run out of business, as well as the cost to the city of tax incentives that are likely to outweigh the store's economic boost. If we are to believe in the candidate's plan, and the candidate, further research and more rigorous quantification will be required.

Ideally, the conclusion will sum things up while offering some special perspective or insight. But try to avoid having your conclusion sound repetitive. If in doubt, keep it short.

Style Points

No, the GRE does not literally award "style points." But, as seen in the citations of the Scoring Guide, an effective and engaging writing style can help you achieve a high score. While the previous sections focused on how you might structure your arguments, this section offers tips for the nitty-gritty of writing your paragraphs and sentences.

General Style Tips

Tone: There's no specific rule against saying "I," but don't be too informal. Avoid conversational asides, and don't try to be funny. Keep the tone serious and academic. When you're referring to an argument and it's not clear who's talking, refer to that person as "the speaker."

Varied diction: Throughout the essay, you will say the same thing several times. Don't use the exact same words: Paraphrase yourself. If in the introduction, you wrote, "The most important virtue in a leader is a strong sense of ethics," in your conclusion, you might write, "A strong moral framework is paramount for a leader."

However, don't get excessive about it—if you're writing an essay about the environment, you're definitely going to have to use the word "environment" numerous times. It would be great if you could switch up "environment" every now and then with something like "global ecosystem," but don't get too distractingly creative (Mother Earth, the rotating blue orb we call home), and as long as the same exact word isn't too ubiquitous, you've done the job.

Varied sentence structure: Aim for a mix of long and short sentences. Throw in an occasional semicolon, hyphen, colon, or rhetorical question. For example:

> Is it the case that sacrifice is the noblest of all virtues? Even a cursory analysis ought to indicate that it is not; the greatest of all virtues can hardly be said to be the one with, typically, the least utilitarian value.

Make sure you know how to correctly use any punctuation you decide to include.

Vocabulary: Use GRE-type words in your writing, as long as you're sure you can use them correctly. Some good vocabulary words to think about are those about arguments themselves, since those will work in nearly any essay. Some examples are: *aver, extrapolate, contend, underpin, claim, hypothesize, rebuttal, postulate, propound,* and *concur*.

Transitions: A top-scoring essay has body paragraphs that lead logically into one another. You can create this chain of logic by arranging your examples or reasons in a progressive way and by using transition phrases and similar signals. The simplest transitions involve phrases such as "On the other hand…" or "Finally…" A more complex transition might take the following form:

> The obstacles toward international cooperation include not only [the stuff I discussed in my last paragraph], but also [the stuff I'm about to discuss in this paragraph].

Unit Two: **Paragraphs and Passages**

Debate Team Tactics for the Argument Essay

On the Issue Essay, the tips summarized above will get you where you need to go. For the Argument Essay, you might want a few more tricks up your sleeve.

It's possible to say something in a way that is not very persuasive, or in a way that is. Say you are trying to argue against the school superintendent's plan for year-round school:

1. The superintendent has not proven that her plan will achieve the goal of improving academic performance. However, it may serve the function of reducing crime.

2. While the superintendent's plan may indeed reduce crime, she has not proven that her plan will achieve the stated goal of improving academic performance.

Which version sounds worse for the superintendent? The second one, right? *If you have two opposing things to say, put the one that's on your side last.* This makes the one that isn't on your side seem less important. The order should be 1) concession, then 2) your assertion.

If you have a fairly weak point, use that point's weakness to your advantage to emphasize how strong your next point is. For instance, say you were only able to come up with three flaws for a particular argument, and one of them is pretty weak, but you can't toss it out because then you wouldn't have enough to write about. Put the weakest point in the middle (if that won't disrupt the flow of the argument), and use it to underscore the final, biggest point.

For instance, your second (weak) point may be that the company president is trying to predict the future, and no one can really predict the future. Your third (strong) point is that the company president is basing these predictions on an analogy with another company—and that company is completely different from the president's own company. Here's a snippet of that essay (the entire second paragraph and the beginning of the third), written in a persuasive way:

> The company president's argument is also weak because it attempts to predict the future, and to predict it absolutely. The president even goes so far as to say that the company will "certainly" meet its sales target. But what if the lead salesperson gets sick, or what if a nationwide crisis suddenly causes sales to plummet? The president's conclusion is dubious because it relies on an unwisely extreme assertion that simply cannot be validated.
>
> Even if we were to accept the presence of some uncertainty in predicting the future, the most grave flaw in the president's argument is its dependence on a highly questionable analogy . . .

The second paragraph isn't wonderful. But notice how it is set up to create a nice transition into the third, stronger paragraph. You do this all the time when you're arguing in real life: "But if that's not good enough for you, try this!"

Analyze an Issue Sample Essays

> **Every nation should require students to study at least one foreign language from the elementary school level through the university level.**
>
> Write a response in which you discuss the extent to which you agree or disagree with the recommendation, and explain your reasoning for the position you take. In developing and supporting your position, describe specific circumstances in which adopting the recommendation would or would not be advantageous and explain how these examples shape your position.

10

Foreign language study can be a valuable component of a balanced education. So, too, can poetry, economics, or public speaking. But students are individuals, and live in a wide variety of circumstances around the world. It is going too far to say that every nation should require its students to study foreign languages.

Different countries have different needs and circumstances. While many bemoan the lack of international outlook in the United States, it is reasonable to note that most Americans do just fine speaking only one language. Of course, universities, prep schools, and other institutions are still free to make foreign language instruction mandatory, as many do now. In Sweden, however, it is a sound policy to make foreign language mandatory for nearly everyone; Sweden has an excellent school system, free through the university level, and it is clear that Swedish is a minority language, and English has actually become the language of international business in Sweden and throughout Europe. Sweden currently mandates the teaching of English, as it should. If the government did not compel students to learn English, they would struggle to compete in the global job market.

While Sweden has one of the highest standards of living in the world, many nations simply have no ability to provide foreign language instruction, nor does it seem as though such instruction should be the top priority. In many countries, primary schools cost money, and many girls don't get to go to school at all, or must drop out due to lack of funds, early marriage, or their families' needing them to work. If female students in Afghanistan are to receive only a few years of education in their entire lives, it seems absurd to mandate that they learn foreign languages, as this would be a waste of their time and effort. Individual schools and teachers should be free to decide how to best use the limited time available.

Finally, not only are nations different from one another, but so are students. Many students have learning disabilities that make foreign language learning virtually impossible. Even those who don't have such disabilities have individual differences and interests that should be respected. A scientific prodigy who may go on to cure cancer or AIDS ought to be permitted to focus solely on science at least at certain levels of his or her education. For every hour spent learning a foreign language, there is an opportunity cost: something else not being mastered.

Of course, virtually everyone is in favor of a more global outlook, and virtually no one thinks that foreign language study is bad. However, making foreign language instruction mandatory in every nation, at every level of schooling, is unjustifiable. Different nations have different needs, and different individuals have their own capacities and goals. Foreign language study can truly open the world to those who partake, but there are many reasons not to mandate it.

Comments:

This is a moderately lengthy, argument-based essay that takes the somewhat obvious tack of disagreeing with an extreme topic.

The essay contains good transitions at the top of the third and fourth paragraphs, linking a discussion of Sweden to a discussion of poorer nations, and then linking differences among nations to differences among individuals. The examples progress in a logical way.

The language and ideas are clear, and the essay persuades by acknowledging common beliefs on the topic ("virtually everyone is in favor of a more global outlook, and virtually no one thinks that foreign language study is bad") and addressing those beliefs ("there are many reasons not to mandate it"). Also, the essay responds to the specific instruction to describe how the mandate would be advantageous (as in Sweden's case) or not advantageous (as in the case of the United States, learning-disabled children, etc.).

Unit Two: Paragraphs and Passages

The previous essay is not perfect, but even if it had contained several typos, misspellings, or grammar errors, it would likely receive a strong score of 5 to 6.

> **Strong beliefs prevent people from thinking clearly about issues.**
>
> Write a response in which you discuss the extent to which you agree or disagree with the claim. In developing and supporting your position, be sure to address the most compelling reasons and/or examples that could be used to challenge your position.

The phrase "strong beliefs" may bring to mind images of heroes, people who have fought valiantly for what they knew to be right, or it may bring to mind images of tyrants, people whose beliefs were so strong (if misguided) that they were able to commit atrocities without regard for others. Whether such figures fall on the right side of history or not, strong beliefs often brook no adjustment and permit no new information to be considered. However, some beliefs are strong for good reason—who is not possessed of a strong belief that the earth is round, for instance? Strong beliefs do prevent people from thinking clearly about issues when those beliefs are based on emotion, group loyalty, or tradition; however, strong beliefs need not cloud our thinking when those beliefs are a genuine product of a logical, ongoing search for truth that is open to revision and new evidence.

Seventeenth-century Italian astronomer Galileo Galilei alleged that the Earth moved around the Sun, rather than the reverse; for this heliocentric theory he was tried by the Catholic Church, convicted of heresy, and placed under house arrest for the rest of his life. Leaders of the Church held the strong belief that the Earth must be at the center of the universe. When presented with evidence that the orbits of the planets seemed to go every which way in this model (yet Galileo's model showed the planets moving, more sensibly, in ellipses), the Church did not admit this new evidence into its thinking. Of course, Galileo himself was possessed of strong beliefs, and although he was forced to publicly recant, he did not actually change his view. Yet Galileo's belief was not dogmatic; it was based on years of astronomical observation and careful calculations. Furthermore, Galileo, a Catholic, began with a geocentric worldview; his very heliocentric position was proof of his willingness to change his mind in the face of new evidence.

While Church leaders possessed strong beliefs that brooked no adjustment, Rene Descartes was a devout religious thinker whose strong beliefs did not cloud his thinking. The purpose of Descartes's famous "I think, therefore I exist" was to create a system of logic that would allow him to clear away that which he only thought he knew (but didn't actually know for sure) so he could logically build a case for his religious belief. Adopting a position of ultimate skepticism, Descartes asserted that all he really knew was that he existed. He then reasoned, logically, from that point. Whether one agrees with Descartes's conclusions, his "Meditations" is a masterwork of clear and rigorous thinking.

Just as Descartes was willing to toss aside all he thought he knew in pursuit of verifiable truth, thinkers on moral issues, such as slavery, have demonstrated that strong beliefs cloud our thinking if we don't admit of new evidence, but can be a force for good if we do. In the United States prior to the Civil War, pro-slavery forces argued that the great society of ancient Athens had been built on a framework of slavery. When presented with new information—such as that Greek slavery was very different from the slavery practiced in the United States or Sojourner Truth's poignant "Ain't I a Woman?" address, reprinted across the nation—many did not change their minds. Of course, some did, and the North had no shortage of outspoken abolitionists. The Civil War was a war of strong belief against strong belief; the side most willing to change its mind in the face of moral argument was, rightfully, the side that won.

All people are created equal, but all strong beliefs are not. Strong beliefs based on evidence and logic are strong beliefs that are nevertheless changeable, and need not muddy our thinking. It is dogmatism that is the enemy, not strength of conviction.

Comments:

This is a lengthy, example-based essay that gives a balanced, nuanced position on the topic. "Strong beliefs prevent people from thinking clearly about issues" is a fairly extreme statement, so a more nuanced thesis here is a good strategy. The introduction is long in order to give time to develop that thesis: "Strong beliefs do prevent people from thinking clearly about issues when those beliefs are based on emotion, group loyalty, or tradition; however, strong beliefs need not cloud our thinking when those beliefs are a genuine product of a logical, ongoing search for truth that is open to revision and new evidence."

The first body paragraph is sophisticated—it actually gives two intertwined examples by showing that the Church's strong belief was indefensible, but Galileo's strong belief was justifiable.

The second body paragraph is somewhat weaker, but there is a nice transition between the two paragraphs ("While Church leaders possessed strong beliefs that brooked no adjustment, Rene Descartes . . ."), and the writer balanced out an example about religious belief gone wrong with an example of religious belief the writer thinks falls on the other side of the thesis.

The third body paragraph is fine, although it doesn't seem to fit the topic as well as the first two; the writer makes no distinction between "new information" such as astronomical observation and "new information" in a moral sense. However, the slight shift in emphasis allows the writer to incorporate other examples recalled from his or her college course on pre–Civil War U.S. history.

The conclusion flows nicely from the third example (although this is not necessarily expected in an essay). It is brief and to the point and restates the thesis in different words.

Though this essay does not take an overarching stance for or against, it succeeds at explaining *why* the statement might sometimes be true, and other times untrue. It makes clear what the strongest arguments both for and against the prompt are, and provides an argument for when each side applies. This is an example that succeeds adequately in addressing the specific instructions, even without a declarative "for" or "against" thesis.

The writer's language and main ideas are clear. The second and third examples are not as strong as the first, but this essay's main strengths are its well-developed main idea and sophisticated attempt to validate a two-part thesis with relevant examples.

The previous essay is also not perfect, but would likely receive a strong score of 5.

Unit Two: **Paragraphs and Passages**

Analyze an Argument Sample Essays

> Invoice Regulators, Inc. (IRI) can make your company more profitable. IRI examines our client firms' outgoing invoices and vendor receipts to help clients recoup money owed and refunds due. One client, a family firm with a 100-year history, discovered $75,000 worth of uncashed checks in an employee's desk drawer, and others have also made large gains. Eighty percent of our client firms have experienced an increase in sales during the quarter our services were acquired. Hire IRI to improve your firm's profitability.
>
> Write a response in which you discuss what questions would need to be answered in order to decide whether the recommendation and the argument on which it is based are reasonable. Be sure to explain how the answers to these questions would help evaluate the recommendation.

One ought to consider the claims of any advertisement with skepticism, and the entreaty to acquire Invoice Regulators' services is no different. IRI offers to examine a firm's invoices and receipts, and asserts that these services will enhance profitability. The argument is dubious; it rests on a questionable analogy, suffers from a lack of quantification, confuses sales with profitability, and makes unwarranted claims of causality.

IRI's ad relates the peculiar story of a company employee who neglected to cash $75,000 in checks. We don't know anything else about this company, or whether what worked for that type of business would work for other types of businesses—some types of businesses, such as retail stores, collect money on the spot, so it is unclear whether IRI's services could enhance such firms' profitability. However, we need not even go that far—very few employees could forget $75,000 in a desk drawer, and very few firms would need outside assistance to notice that such a sum had gone missing. But are there any other businesses that have had similar lucky discoveries because of IRI's help? The argument fails to extend the analogy from this "family firm with a 100-year old history" to any other types of businesses, or even to more competently managed businesses of the same type.

One might object that IRI has made "large gains" for other clients. However, this claim is vague. What are "large gains"? What kind of companies were these, and would their results apply to other companies? This claim utterly lacks quantification, an argumentative offense made all the more egregious when we consider that "gains" are not the same as "profitability." For the gains to translate into profitability, we would need to know the cost of IRI's services and whether the gains outweigh the cost.

IRI goes on to claim that 80 percent of clients achieved an increase in sales. However, just because increased sales happened around the same time as hiring IRI does not mean that IRI is responsible for the sales. The ad never explains how reviewing invoices and receipts could have an effect on sales. Is there any evidence to directly link the increase in sales to IRI's intervention? In fact, the ad doesn't even say that the sales increase happened after IRI was hired—just "in the same quarter." Maybe the causal relationship actually runs the opposite way—perhaps it was the increased sales that gave the companies the funds to hire IRI in the first place.

IRI is soliciting new clients based on an advertisement that makes an extremely weak analogy from a single case study, fails to quantify gains made or costs incurred by clients, confuses sales and profit, and assumes a model of causality for which there is no evidence. To better evaluate IRI's argument, the readers would need to know whether IRI has helped businesses similar to their own and whether IRI's success at those companies could be reasonably predicted to be repeated, as well as the cost of IRI's services so that the two costs could be weighed. The ad would be further improved by the omission of the irrelevant claim about sales; perhaps the space could be better used to quantify other claims central to evaluating IRI's services.

Comments:

This is a fairly lengthy essay that comprehensively covers the errors made in the argument. The language is clear, and the main idea ("The argument is dubious; it rests on a questionable analogy, suffers from a lack of quantification, confuses sales with profitability, and makes unwarranted claims of causality") gives a good road map of the rest of the essay.

The transitions between paragraphs are nice, especially "One might object. . ." which astutely anticipates the objection that more than one company was mentioned, but then points out that the mention was so vague as to be useless.

The coverage of causality in the third body paragraph was good, especially the counterexample ("perhaps it was the increased sales that gave the companies the funds to hire IRI in the first place").

The conclusion thoroughly covers how the argument could be improved, including the omission of irrelevant claims.

Notice how each body paragraph presents at least one question that the author of the argument would need to address, as requested in the specific instructions.

This essay, while not perfect, would likely receive a strong score of 5-6, even if it had several typos or errors.

> The following appeared as a letter to the editor of National Issues magazine in the country of Ganadia.
>
> **Last month, National Issues ran an article about the decline—as measured by shrinking populations and the flight of young people—of small towns in Ganadia. Here in Lemmontown, a small resort town on the ocean, we are seeing just the opposite: Citizens from the neighboring towns of Armontown and Gurdy City are moving here at a record rate. Furthermore, greater than ever numbers of high school graduates in Lemmontown are choosing to stay in Lemmontown, as the building of new hotels has created a significant number of jobs. All along the eastern seaboard are similar stories. Small towns in Ganadia are not in decline.**
>
> Write a response in which you discuss one or more alternative explanations that could rival the proposed explanation, and explain how your explanation(s) can plausibly account for the facts presented in the argument.

A letter to the editor of *National Issues* magazine takes issue with the magazine's claim that small towns in Ganadia are declining. It seems that the writer is from a small town that is not declining. Of course, the magazine's contention was almost certainly that small towns, on average, are declining; a single counterexample does not disprove that claim. The arguments' other flaws stem from the same central problem: Lemmontown is just one town, and not necessarily a very representative one.

The writer explains that Lemmontown is a resort town on the ocean. Resort towns depend on income flowing in from visitors, and the seaside (or whatever else visitors are there to see) is an asset that most towns do not have. These atypical resort assets are directly cited as the driver behind the jobs that are keeping young people in Lemmontown. Non-resort towns would not likely experience a similar effect. To set the argument on more sound footing, the writer would need to demonstrate that Lemmontown is typical of other Ganadian towns.

Of course, the writer does mention two other towns: Armontown and Gurdy City. While the writer means to cite those towns as evidence that Lemmontown is doing well, he or she inadvertently weakens the argument by giving two counterexamples: both Armontown and Gurdy City are losing residents, in accordance with the trend cited by *National Issues*. In fact, of the three towns the writer references, two of them are losing people. To strengthen the argument, the writer would have to prove that there are more Lemmontowns (so to speak) than Armontowns and Gurdy Cities, or that Armontown and Gurdy City are not small towns.

Finally, the writer points out that "all along the eastern seaboard are similar stories." This assertion is vague. Are there enough stories of non-declining small towns to outweigh accounts of declining small towns? The claim lacks quantification. Also, the eastern seaboard is not necessarily representative of the rest of Ganadia. Perhaps the seaboard is full of thriving resort towns, but the bulk of Ganadia's small towns exist in the interior and on the west coast, where conditions are worse. To validate his or her claims, the writer would need to quantify the claim that eastern seaboard success stories are more numerous than accounts of small towns in decline.

The letter to the editor takes exception to a general claim by providing a specific exception. One anecdote does not make an argument. The argument as written fails to establish that Lemmontown's happy situation is representative of Ganadian towns at large.

Comments:

This is a moderately lengthy essay that effectively takes apart the writer's attempt to use an anecdote to disprove a general trend. "The arguments' other flaws stem from the same central problem" is an apt description and ties the essay into a coherent whole.

The essay follows the structure of detailing a problem in each body paragraph and then offering suggestions for improving the argument within the same paragraph. Thus, the conclusion is fairly short, which is fine.

The language is clear, and adequate transitions between body paragraphs are provided.

Notice that each paragraph succeeds in giving an alternative explanation for a given fact, as requested in the specific instructions.

This essay, while not perfect, would likely receive a strong score of 5–6.

Notes on Preparation

For more sample Issue and Argument essays, with comments provided by the people who grade the real GRE, check the ETS website or the *Official Guide* Analytical Writing chapter.

Now that you know the ins and outs of the GRE essays, here are some final notes on how to finish your preparation:

1. Read the GRE's official sample essays.

2. Brainstorm examples for a large number of topics from the published topic pool on the ETS website.

3. Write several practice essays under timed conditions, also using topics from the topic pool. Don't select the topics you most *want* to write about—just scroll down the list and do the first topic you land on, or ask someone else to assign you a topic. Write your practice essays on a computer, using only the functions available to you on the real exam (i.e., turn off spell check and grammar check).

4. Take several full-length Manhattan Prep GRE practice exams, and don't skip the essay section!

Vocabulary Challenge

> Did you spot these vocabulary words? If not, go back and find them in context! (The word may be in a different form than listed here— "digressing" instead of "digress," for example.) Write your own definitions based on the evidence in the chapter.

1. indefatigable (*adj.*), p. 301
2. amalgamate (*v*), p. 303
3. malleable (*adj.*), p. 305
4. veracity (*n*), p. 313
5. peddle (*v*), p. 313
6. ubiquitous (*adj.*), p. 319

Unit Two: **Paragraphs and Passages**

Answers and Explanations

Vocabulary Challenge

1. indefatigable (*adj.*): untiring, not able to become fatigued

2. amalgamate (*v*): blend, merge, or unite

3. malleable (*adj.*): able to be bent, shaped, or adapted

4. veracity (*n*): truthfulness, accuracy; habitual adherence to the truth

5. peddle (*v*): travel around while selling; sell illegally; give out or disseminate

6. ubiquitous (*adj.*): existing everywhere at the same time

NEED MORE THAN BOOKS? TRY INTERACT™ FOR GRE®!

Interact for GRE is an on-demand, adaptive learning experience made by Manhattan Prep's 99th-percentile GRE instructors. It's like having a GRE teacher with you anywhere you are. Interact adapts to your performance by providing you with prompts and delivering customized feedback based on your responses. This branching video technology makes Interact personalized to your skill level, so you'll never feel left behind.

GRE®
All The Quant

GRE® is a registered trademark of Educational Testing Service (ETS), which is not affiliated with Kaplan and was not involved in the production of, and does not endorse, this product.

GRE All The Quant

Retail ISBN: 978-1-5062-8178-0
Course ISBN: 978-1-5062-8180-3
Retail eISBN: 978-1-5062-8179-7
Course eISBN: 978-1-5062-8181-0

Copyright © 2023 Kaplan, Inc.

10 9 8 7 6 5 4 3 2 1

All rights reserved. The text of this publication, or any part thereof, may not be reproduced in any manner whatsoever without written permission from the publisher.

GRE® is a registered trademark of Educational Testing Service (ETS), which is not affiliated with Kaplan and was not involved in the production of, and does not endorse, this product.

INSTRUCTIONAL GUIDE SERIES

1 GRE All The Quant

2 GRE All The Verbal

3 5 lb. Book of GRE® Practice Problems

SUPPLEMENTAL MATERIALS

500 Essential Words:
GRE® Vocabulary Flash Cards

500 Advanced Words:
GRE® Vocabulary Flash Cards

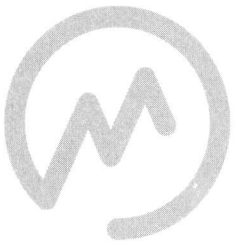

May 2, 2023

Hello! Welcome to **GRE® All The Quant.**

I hope this book provides just the guidance you need to get the most out of your GRE studies. **If you have any questions or feedback, please do not hesitate to contact us at gre@manhattanprep.com or 212-721-7400.** Also: We try to keep all of our books free of errors, but if you think we've goofed, please visit manhattanprep.com/GRE/errata.

All of our Manhattan Prep books are based on the continuing experiences of both our instructors and our students. The primary authors and editors of this edition of the book were Manhattan Prep instructors Dmitry Farber, Chris Gentry, Rina Goldfield, Tyler Johnson, Stacey Koprince, Logan Smeallie, and Ryan Starr. Project management, design, and quality assurance were led by Deepika Devan, Mario Gambino, Marie Gugnishev, and Helen Tan. I'd like to send particular thanks to Manhattan Prep instructors Whitney Garner and Emily Meredith Sledge for their additional content contributions to this edition.

Finally, we are indebted to all of the Manhattan Prep students who have given us excellent feedback over the years. This book wouldn't be half of what it is without their voice.

And now that *you* are one of our students too, please chime in! I look forward to hearing from you. Thanks again and best of luck preparing for the GRE!

Sincerely,

Stacey Koprince
Director of Content and Curriculum
Manhattan Prep

www.manhattanprep.com/gre   623 Broadway, New York, NY 10012   Tel: 212-721-7400

TABLE OF CONTENTS

Getting the Most Out of Your GRE Math Studies 1
    The GRE Exam 8
    Math Formats in Detail 11

UNIT ONE: Number Properties

Chapter 1: Develop Your Number Sense 17
    Integers and Their Digits 19
    Non-Integers and Their Digits 22
    Manipulating Integers. 25
    Factors 26
    Prime Numbers 27
    Positives, Negatives, and Zero 28
    Calculator Use 29
    Number Lines 30
    Check Your Skills Answer Key 32
    Problem Set 33
    Solutions 35

Chapter 2: Number Properties. 39
    Understanding the Unknown 41
    Positives and Negatives. 42
    Absolute Values 46
    Testing Positive and Negative Cases. 48
    Evens and Odds 50
    The Sum of Two Primes. 53
    Testing Odd and Even Cases 54
    Exponents 56
    Check Your Skills Answer Key 60
    Problem Set 67
    Solutions 69

Table of Contents

Chapter 3: Quantitative Comparison: Pick Numbers 71
    QC Structure 73
    Simplify and Pick Numbers 76
    Check Your Skills Answer Key 83
    Problem Set 84
    Solutions 86

UNIT TWO: Algebra

Chapter 4: Equations 93
    The Order of Operations (PEMDAS) 95
    Fraction Bars as Grouping Symbols 98
    Solving for a Variable with One Equation 99
    Solving Absolute Value Equations 105
    Check Your Skills Answer Key 107
    Problem Set 111
    Solutions 112

Chapter 5: Exponents and Roots 117
    Exponents and Roots Language 119
    Roots as Exponents 121
    Exponential Equations 121
    Same Bases 123
    Same Exponents 127
    Special Powers 129
    Special Bases 132
    Rules of Exponents 136
    Common Exponent Errors 137
    Exponents on QC 139
    Check Your Skills Answer Key 141
    Problem Set 145
    Solutions 147

Chapter 6: Formulas and Functions 151
    Plug In Formulas 153
    Strange Symbol Formulas 154
    Functions 157
    Check Your Skills Answer Key 161
    Problem Set 163
    Solutions 164

Table of Contents

Chapter 7: Inequalities and Systems of Equations 167
    Interpreting Inequalities 169
    Solving Inequalities 171
    Manipulating Compound Inequalities. 175
    Inequalities and Absolute Values 176
    Systems of Equations 177
    An Equation and an Inequality 182
    Seriously, Distribute! 183
    Two Inequalities 185
    Equations on QC. 187
    Check Your Skills Answer Key 189
    Problem Set 196
    Solutions 198

Chapter 8: QC Gameplan: Simplify. 201
    The Hidden Inequality. 203
    Relative Order 206
    Pick Numbers: Part Two 209
    Check Your Skills Answer Key 212
    Problem Set 213
    Solutions 214

UNIT THREE: Factors

Chapter 9: Divisibility 221
    Divisibility Terms. 223
    Divisibility Shortcuts. 227
    Factor Pair Method 229
    Prime Factor Tree 231
    Divisibility of Unknowns 235
    Combining Givens 239
    Divisibility and Addition/Subtraction 244
    Divisibility and Consecutive Integers 245
    Remainders 247
    Check Your Skills Answer Key 250
    Problem Set 256
    Solutions 258

Table of Contents

Chapter 10: Common Factors 263
    Distributing and Factoring 265
    Exponents and Factors 266
    Roots and Factors 269
    Fractions and Factors 273
    Check Your Skills Answer Key 280
    Problem Set 283
    Solutions 284

Chapter 11: Fractions 287
    Improper Fractions and Mixed Numbers 290
    Multiplying and Dividing Fractions. 292
    Adding and Subtracting Fractions 300
    NEVER Split the Denominator! 304
    Fractions and Equations 305
    Comparing Fractions 308
    Comparing Complex Fractions. 312
    Check Your Skills Answer Key 315
    Problem Set 320
    Solutions 322

Chapter 12: Quadratic Equations 327
    Equivalent Forms 329
    Solving Quadratic Equations 335
    Using FOIL with Square Roots 337
    One-Solution Quadratics 337
    The Three Special Products. 338
    Quadratics in QC. 340
    Quadratics and Fractions 343
    Check Your Skills Answer Key 345
    Problem Set 349
    Solutions 351

Chapter 13: QC Gameplan: Compare 357
    Compare, Don't Compute. 359
    Problem Set 367
    Solutions 368

Table of Contents

UNIT FOUR: Stories, Percents, Ratios, Stats, and Data

Chapter 14: Algebraic Translations 371
    Common Translations. 373
    Complex GRE Translations 376
    Common Translation Errors 382
    Hidden Constraints 384
    Check Your Skills Answer Key 387
    Problem Set 388
    Solutions 390

Chapter 15: Percents 397
    Percents as Fractions 399
    Percents as Word Problems 402
    Percent Change 403
    Percent of Original 404
    Successive Percents 408
    Pick 100 for Unspecified Amounts 409
    Check Your Skills Answer Key 411
    Problem Set 415
    Solutions 417

Chapter 16: Ratios 425
    Label A Ratio with Units 428
    Ratios and Fractions 429
    Proportions 430
    The Unknown Multiplier 431
    Multiple Ratios: Make a Common Term 433
    Ratios in QC 436
    Check Your Skills Answer Key 438
    Problem Set 440
    Solutions 442

Chapter 17: Fractions, Decimals, Percents, and Ratios 447
    Converting Forms 450
    Powers of 10: Shifting the Decimal 454
    Common FDP Equivalents 457
    When to Use Which Form 458
    Put It All Together 460

Table of Contents

Check Your Skills Answer Key 465
Problem Set 468
Solutions 470

Chapter 18: Statistics 475
Averages 477
Using the Average Formula. 478
Special Cases: Weighted Averages. 480
Median: The Middle Number. 482
Range 483
Quartiles and Percentiles. 483
Standard Deviation 484
The Normal Distribution 486
Check Your Skills Answer Key 489
Problem Set 492
Solutions 494

Chapter 19: Data Interpretation 501
The Basic DI Process 503
Types of Charts 504
Pie Charts. 504
Column Charts 509
Line Charts 514
Bar Charts 517
Tables 519
Other Diagrams 520
Check Your Skills Answer Key 523
Problem Set 530
Solutions 536

UNIT FIVE: Geometry

Chapter 20: Geometry on the GRE 545
Geometry Formulas 547
Using Geometry Equations 549
Check Your Skills Answer Key 558
Problem Set 560
Solutions 562

Table of Contents

Chapter 21: Triangles and Diagonals 567
- The Basic Properties of a Triangle 569
- Perimeter and Area 574
- Right Triangles 577
- Pythagorean Triples 578
- Isosceles Triangles and the 45–45–90 Triangle 581
- Equilateral Triangles and the 30–60–90 Triangle 582
- Diagonals of Other Polygons 584
- Check Your Skills Answer Key 587
- Problem Set 593
- Solutions 596

Chapter 22: Polygons 605
- Polygons and Interior Angles. 607
- Polygons and Perimeter 609
- Polygons and Area. 609
- 3 Dimensions: Surface Area 611
- 3 Dimensions: Volume 612
- 3 Dimensions: Diagonal of Cube. 613
- Quadrilaterals: An Overview 614
- Quadrilaterals 614
- Check Your Skills Answer Key 618
- Problem Set 621
- Solutions 623

Chapter 23: Circles and Cylinders 629
- The Basic Elements of a Circle 631
- Sectors 635
- Inscribed vs. Central Angles 637
- Inscribed Triangles 638
- Cylinders and Surface Area. 639
- Cylinders and Volume. 639
- Check Your Skills Answer Key 641
- Problem Set 642
- Solutions 645

Table of Contents

Chapter 24: Lines and Angles 651
    Line Segments 653
    Intersecting Lines 655
    Exterior Angles. 656
    Parallel Lines 657
    Check Your Skills Answer Key 659
    Problem Set 660
    Solutions 664

Chapter 25: The Coordinate Plane. 669
    Creating the Coordinate Plane. 671
    Knowing Just One Coordinate 676
    Knowing Ranges 678
    Reading a Graph 680
    Plotting a Relationship 683
    Lines in the Plane 686
    The Intercepts of a Line. 692
    The Intersection of Two Lines 692
    The Distance Between Two Points. 694
    Check Your Skills Answer Key 695
    Problem Set 700
    Solutions 702

Chapter 26: QC Geometry 711
    Shape Geometry. 713
    Variable Creation 723
    Word Geometry 724
    Pick Numbers 726
    Problem Set 729
    Solutions 732

UNIT SIX: Advanced Topics

Chapter 27: Rates 739
    Rate Formula. 741
    Basic Motion: The RTD Chart. 742
    Matching Units in the RTD Chart. 744
    Multiple Rates 747
    Average Rate: Don't Just Add and Divide 750

xiv

Working Together: Add the Rates 754
Population Problems 756
Check Your Skills Answer Key 758
Problem Set 763
Solutions 766

Chapter 28: Sequences and Patterns 775
Sequence Formulas 777
Logical Sequencing 780
Properties of Terms 781
Digit Problems 783
Evenly Spaced Sequences 785
Defining Evenly Spaced Sequences 786
Visualizing Evenly Spaced Sets 788
Properties of Evenly Spaced Sequences 789
Evenly Spaced Sets on QC 792
Check Your Skills Answer Key 793
Problem Set 797
Solutions 799

Chapter 29: Combinatorics 803
The Fundamental Counting Principle 805
Distinct Labels 807
Repeated Labels 810
Multiple Arrangements 813
Overlapping Sets 814
Check Your Skills Answer Key 817
Problem Set 820
Solutions 822

Chapter 30: Probability 827
Probability Outcomes 829
The Range of Probabilities 831
Combining Probabilities 831
The "1 − x" Probability Shortcut 837
Overlapping Sets and Probability 840
Check Your Skills Answer Key 841
Problem Set 844
Solutions 846

Table of Contents

Chapter 31: Optimization 851

    Optimization Constraints 853

    Algebraic Optimization 855

    Optimization in QC 857

    Optimizing Groups 858

    Overlapping Sets 859

    Geometry Optimization. 861

    Check Your Skills Answer Key 864

    Problem Set 867

    Solutions 869

Chapter 32: Advanced Concepts 873

    Making Up Numbers 875

    Substituting Properties 879

    Benchmarking 882

    Benchmarking Around B 884

    Interest Formulas: Simple and Compound 887

    Division Theory 888

    Sequencing. 891

    Geometry. 893

    Check Your Skills Answer Key 900

    Problem Set 904

    Solutions 907

Appendix: GRE Math Glossary 913

Getting the Most Out of Your GRE Math Studies

In This Chapter:

- The GRE Exam
- Math Formats in Detail

Getting the Most Out of Your GRE Math Studies

Congratulations! You've taken the first big step on your way to graduate school.

You may not have done a lot of math since high school, and any complex math you do today is likely done in a spreadsheet or some other advanced software. It's going to take hard work to get ready for the GRE Math section—but you can do it! This book will take you from the basics all the way up to the material you need to master for a top GRE Math score (or whatever your goal score may be).

In this chapter, you'll learn how to use this book to lift your GRE math skills as effectively and efficiently as possible. You'll also learn how the GRE works, including the types of math skills covered and the problem types used on the GRE.

Also: You have access to additional digital resources on the Manhattan Prep website. Create a free account to get a free, full-length practice test as well as guidance on making flash cards, memorizing hard vocabulary, setting up an effective study calendar, and more.

How to Use This Book

Your first task is to get into the right mindset to study for the GRE Quant section. This test is *not* about blindly applying a bunch of formulas, rules, and steps that you've memorized. Yes, you will have to relearn a bunch of math that you first learned in school, but you will also need to develop your *number sense*—that is, your ability to think in a logical way about quantitative concepts. This ability is crucial to success both in grad school and in the working world (not to mention your personal financial life). However, there's a decent chance you weren't taught how to think about math this way during your prior schooling.

This book will help you build that number sense right from the very first unit, Number Properties. This unit will also reintroduce you to a lot of math concepts you first learned when your age was measured in single digits. Don't remember exactly what a *digit* is? The first unit will remind you.

This book is organized to build from foundational topics to more advanced ones, so continue through the rest of the book in order. The later units will build on those number sense skills while adding more advanced formulas, rules, and strategies to your repertoire. (By the way, *Repertoire* is a good vocabulary word to know for the verbal portion of the GRE.)

This book covers everything that someone would need to get a perfect GRE Math score—but very few people actually need a perfect score. As you study, keep in mind that you *don't* have to know it all! Prioritize based on your strengths and weaknesses, of course, but don't necessarily try to master *all* of your weaknesses; you can let a few things go.

Getting the Most Out of Your GRE Math Studies

Also, for those weaknesses you do address, you don't have to address everything at once. When a particular topic or subtopic is driving you crazy, set it aside for now. Move on to other material and loop back around in a week or two. It may be the case that what you learn in the meantime will better prepare you to handle the problem or topic that's frustrating you today.

As you use this book, you may find yourself wanting to jump back to something you learned earlier…but you don't remember exactly where it was. The Table of Contents (ToC) is your friend. The ToC lists not just the unit and chapter names but also the names of every subheading in each chapter. Flip to the beginning of the book to scan the ToC to find what you need. (This little skill will also be extremely useful in grad school—start practicing now!)

If you are taking one of our classes…

Follow your course syllabus! It will give you reading assignments from the chapters and will tell you which problems to do for homework. Don't hesitate to talk to your instructor if you have questions, want advice about an issue, or are struggling with any particular assignment.

If you are just starting out…

Unless you are still in high school or you earned an undergraduate degree in math, you'll likely need to work carefully through this book right from the very beginning. Take your time in the first unit, in particular. Make flash cards, and think through your Takeaways. You're not just relearning foundational math; you're also developing your number sense. This early work will help you to push a lot further when you get to more advanced math later.

Don't feel that you have to master every single concept or solve every single problem. When a particular topic is driving you crazy, set it aside for now. Move on to other material and loop back around in a week or two. It may be the case that what you learn in the meantime will better prepare you to handle the problem or topic that's frustrating you today.

And feel free to move more quickly through material that is a strength for you. Even if you haven't done math on paper in a while (or at all!), you may find that certain concepts and skills come back to you more easily than others.

If you haven't already, create a free account on our website to get access to a free study syllabus containing additional resources (including a full-length practice test!) that will help you through your studies.

If you have already been studying for a while…

You may be able to work more quickly through some of the earlier sections of the book—but don't skip anything entirely. Do work through the first unit in order to develop your number sense, but you may find that you can work more quickly through the practice problems in this unit. Do make flash cards and think through your takeaways carefully as you learn.

You probably already have some idea of your strengths and weaknesses, so use that information to help prioritize your studies (more on this a little later in this chapter). However, don't get bogged down by your biggest weaknesses. When you find yourself stuck, set that topic aside for a week or two and loop back around later.

Finally, if you haven't already, create a free account on our website to get access to a free study syllabus containing additional resources (including a full-length practice test!) that will help you through your studies.

Getting the Most Out of Your GRE Math Studies

Don't Write in This Book

Because the GRE is computer based, you will not be able to write directly on the problems or diagrams given on screen. Instead, you're going to need to transcribe what you need from the screen to your scratch paper, including redrawing geometry figures. Get used to this now. Use separate scratch paper to solve the problems in this book.

Bonus: You'll avoid spoiling yourself when you want to retry certain problems.

Doing (And Redoing) Practice Problems

There are a lot of practice problems in this book! Here's how to get the most out of them.

Use problems to pretest and diagnose

When you're about to start a new chapter, consider first flipping to the end-of-chapter problem set and trying a few problems...yes, before you've read anything in the chapter.

Why? Learning science shows that you actually learn better when you quiz yourself on the material *before* you learn it. You'll almost certainly struggle and get stuff wrong, but you'll also see what you do and don't know. That creates curiosity and focus: When you read the chapter, your brain will be primed to figure out whatever it was that was giving you trouble. In addition, you'll be better positioned to remember what you're learning right now because it's resolving the "mystery" that you created for yourself when you struggled with those problems.

Finally, knowing something about your strengths and weaknesses will help you to prioritize as you work through the material in that chapter. Speed up when you're getting it (you might even skim or skip certain parts of the chapter) and spend that extra time on the material that's giving you more trouble.

In-chapter problems

You'll see Check Your Skills problems sprinkled throughout the chapters. Do these problems as you see them, immediately after you read the subsection leading up to the problems. Don't keep track of your time.

If you're skipping a subsection because you did well on the related end-of-chapter problems that you tried ahead of time, then also skip the Check Your Skills problems.

End-of-chapter problems

Every chapter contains an end-of-chapter problem set. If you pretested, try those problems again when you're done working through the chapter, and then try a few more. If you didn't pretest, do about half of the problems.

You don't need to set a timer, but pay attention to whether you feel like you're solving efficiently or whether you feel like this is taking some time. (You can also set a timer if you like or if you find that you don't remember afterward which problems took you longer.)

Pretty accurate and efficient? Check the solutions to see whether there's an even better/more efficient way to solve. (If so, try it out yourself!) Then, save the other half of the problems in this set to do closer to your test date and move on to the next chapter.

Struggling with either accuracy or efficiency? Don't read the solutions yet. Consider this an open-book test. Go back into the chapter to reread and relearn, and then come back and try *one of the same* problems again.

5

Getting the Most Out of Your GRE Math Studies

Can you push further now or is it still a struggle? Go back and look in the chapter or check the explanation to see whether that helps. If you're still stuck, set aside this topic area for three days (keep a list or log), and then come back and try again. Still stuck? Set it aside for two weeks, and then try again—or if it's a pretty discrete* topic, consider putting this on your "bail" list as one of the topics that you *aren't* planning to master.

*_Discrete_ is another great GRE vocabulary word. Look it up if you're not sure what it means. At the same time, look up the word *discreet* and compare the definitions.

Redo problems

If you're planning to do a thousand problems once each and never look at them again…then you're not going to get the most out of your studies. But it's also probably not a good idea to do every problem three times. There's a balance to be found here.

Keep a Redo Log. The first time you solve a problem, if you do so correctly *and* within a reasonable time *and*, if when reviewing, you don't find a better/faster way to do that same type of problem in future, you don't need to list that problem in your Redo Log.

Alternatively, if the problem is way too hard and/or it's in one of your "big weakness" categories, don't add it to the Redo Log either. It's not a good use of your study time. Just get something like it wrong faster in the future.

When you do add something to your Redo Log, include the date you want to try the problem again. Here are some guidelines:

Reason to Redo	To Do Today	Date to Redo
Got it wrong *and* don't want to just bail on similar in future	Review the topic or skill	Min: 3 days Max: 2 weeks
Got it right but took too long	Figure out how to solve more efficiently	Min: 1 week
Got it right but not confident	Nothing	Min: 1 week
Got it right but realize there's a better way	Solve it the better way	Min: 1 week

If you feel comfortable with spreadsheets, it's great to keep your log in Excel so that you can filter to find all of the problems that you slated to redo today.

Your log is going to get long. You're going to wonder how you can ever possibly do all of the new problems in your problem sets alongside all of the problems listed in your Redo Log.

The answer was actually already mentioned earlier in this chapter: You're *not* going to do every problem in each problem set (not right now, anyway). Save approximately half of the problems for your review period, the final few weeks before you take the official test. (You still might not do all of them then, but you can make that call when you get there.)

Getting the Most Out of Your GRE Math Studies

How to Use This Book with Other Resources

This book can't teach you everything you need to know for the GRE—for example, it doesn't address the Verbal or Analytical Writing (essay) sections at all. So you'll need to choose another resource to study for those sections. (We do have another book for those sections if you're interested.)

It's also a great idea to get *The Official Guide to the GRE General Test*, which is published by the test makers and contains real, past GRE test questions. You may want additional drill material beyond that—we've collected more than 1,500 math and verbal drill problems into our *5 lb. Book of GRE Practice Problems* (it literally weighs five pounds).

In general, start by learning the math and vocab content and analytical skills and strategies that cover the problems tested on the GRE—so start with this book and an equivalent book for the Verbal side of the test. Don't do all math and only then switch to verbal (or vice versa). Do some math today and some verbal tomorrow and then back to math again on the third day.

As you build your knowledge and skill base, use the *GRE 5 lb.* book for extra drills wherever you feel the need for more practice.

After a few weeks, take a practice test. You won't feel ready yet, but take it anyway. This will help you to get a feel for the timing and pacing you'll need when you get to the real test, and it will also provide you with a wealth of data on your strengths and weaknesses. That data will be crucial to helping you prioritize your studies.

Analyze that data in two ways:

Already studied:	• What worked and what didn't? • Of the things that didn't stick in my brain, which ones do I want to review now? • Which ones do I want to defer to later (and maybe never master them because I don't need them to get my goal score)?
Haven't studied yet:	• What are my strengths? When I get to it, move through this material more quickly or focus on the harder parts of this material. • Which weaknesses are opportunities (e.g., I was almost there or I understand the explanation)? Prioritize these areas (when I get there). • What are my biggest weaknesses? Defer these when they first come up in my studies. Later, decide whether to loop back around to them.

Depending on your overall study time frame—most people study for about three to six months—take practice tests approximately every three to five weeks. The official test makers offer both free and paid official practice tests, and test prep makers also offer tests (you can take one of ours for free, too!).

Getting the Most Out of Your GRE Math Studies

The GRE Exam

Exam Structure

The GRE has six scored sections. You will get a 10-minute break between the third and fourth sections and a 1-minute break between the other sections. The Analytical Writing section, also known as the Essay section, is always first.

The remaining sections can be seen in any order and will include:

- Two Verbal Reasoning sections, each of which typically has 20 problems to answer in 30 minutes
- Two Quantitative Reasoning (Math) sections, each of which typically has 20 problems to answer in 35 minutes
- Either an unscored section or a research section (or both or neither...more on this in a bit)

Section #	Section Type	# Problems	Time	Scored?
1	Essay	2 essays	30 minutes each	Yes
2	Math or Verbal	Approx. 20	30–35 minutes	Maybe
3	Math or Verbal	Approx. 20	30–35 minutes	Maybe
10-Minute Break				
4	Math or Verbal	Approx. 20	30–35 minutes	Maybe
5	Math or Verbal	Approx. 20	35–35 minutes	Maybe
(6)	Math or Verbal	Approx. 20	30–35 minutes	Maybe
(Last)	Research Section	Varies	Varies	No

You will definitely have at least two Verbal and at least two Math sections. You *may or may not* have a third Verbal or a third Math section. These four or five sections can come in any order. For example, you could see:

- Math 1, Verbal 1, Math 2, Verbal 2, Math 3
- Verbal 1, Verbal 2, Math 1, Verbal 3, Math 2
- Math 1, Verbal 1, Verbal 2, Math 2 (no fifth section)

If you do see a total of three Math sections, then one of those sections won't count toward your score—but you won't know which one. Likewise, if you see a total of three Verbal sections, one of the three won't count toward your score, but you won't know which one. It is *not* necessarily the case that the first four multiple-choice sections will be the scored sections. As a result, complete all of the sections to the best of your ability.

At the end of the test, you may be asked to do a research section. If so, they will tell you in advance that this section is unscored and it will be the very last section you see.

Finally, it's possible that you will not be given any unscored section at all. In this case, you will receive just four multiple-choice sections (two Math and two Verbal) and all four will count.

Using the Calculator

The GRE does provide an on-screen calculator, so memorizing times tables or square roots is less important than it used to be. However, if you have *nothing* memorized, having to pull up the calculator every time will slow you down too much. You'll still want to know your times tables up to at least 10×10 and both squares and square roots up to at least 10^2.

In addition, the calculator is not a cure-all; in many problems, the difficulty is in figuring out what numbers to put into the calculator in the first place. In some cases, using a calculator will actually be less helpful than doing the problem some other way. And the calculator itself is very limited: You can add, subtract, multiply, divide, or take a square root. That's it.

Take a look at this example:

> If x is the remainder when $(11)(7)$ is divided by 4 and y is the remainder when $(14)(6)$ is divided by 13, what is the value of $x + y$?

This problem is designed so that the calculator won't tell the whole story. Certainly, the calculator will tell you that $11 \times 7 = 77$. When you divide 77 by 4, however, the calculator yields an answer of 19.25. The remainder is not 0.25, because a remainder is always a whole number.

One option is to go back to your pencil and paper and find the largest multiple of 4 that is less than 77. Since 4 goes into 76, the remainder is 1 (there's one left over) when dividing 77 by 4.

In fact, since the problem asks only about the remainder, you don't even need to know how many times 4 goes into 76—just that it does go in! One way to mentally "jump" to 76 is to say that 4 goes into 40, so 4 also goes into 80…but that's a bit too big, so subtract 4 to get 76.

Likewise, $14 \times 6 = 84$. How many times does 13 go into a value that's less than 84 but as close as possible to 84? Start listing the multiples of 13:

$$13, 26, 39, 52, 65, 78$$

Bingo, 78 is it. How many are left over? That is, how many more numbers are there till you get to 84? A total of 6, so 6 is the remainder when 84 is divided by 13.

The questions asks for $x + y$ and $1 + 6 = 7$, so the answer is 7.

It is also possible to use the calculator to find a remainder, if you prefer. You'll learn how to do that later in this book.

Some people will want to use the calculator for the above math, and others will prefer to do the work on paper. Choose the best path for you. Your task is to study enough to know, before the test starts, when you want to do the work on paper and when you want to pull up the on-screen calculator.

9

Getting the Most Out of Your GRE Math Studies

Practice Using the Calculator!

The on-screen calculator can slow you down or lead to incorrect answers if you're not careful! Do plan to use it on test day—and practice first. You can use any calculator, including the one on your phone, but use only the operations that are allowed on the GRE calculator:

- Add
- Subtract
- Multiply
- Divide
- Square root

That's it. There's not even a button to square a value—you have to type in 32×32 to get the square of 32.

Navigating the Problems in a Section

The GRE offers you the ability to move freely around the problems in a single section. You can go forward and backward one by one and can even jump directly to any problem from the "review list" screen. You can also mark a problem for later review. The review list screen provides a snapshot of which problems you have answered, which ones you have marked, and which ones are incomplete.

If you finish a section early, double-check the review list for completion. Do answer every problem—there's no penalty for getting something wrong. You'll get a chance to practice with the review list when you take practice exams.

The majority of GRE test-takers are pressed for time in at least some of the sections. You may find that you have time to go back to just one or two problems—or you may not have time to go back to any of them. With these points in mind, here's what we recommend:

1. In general, do the problems in the order in which they appear.
2. When you encounter a pretty-hard-but-not-impossible problem, do your best to eliminate answer choices that you know are wrong. Then choose one of the remaining answers and keep going. (What you've just done is called educated guessing.)
3. If it's an impossible problem, don't try to eliminate answers first—just put in a random guess and move on.
4. When you encounter an "I could do this but it's going to take extra time" problem, put in a random guess *for now* but mark the problem for later review. Do this on a maximum of 3 problems in the section. (If it turns out that you don't have time to get back to the problem, at least you've made a guess.)
5. Aim to save at least a minute at the end of the section to review the review list. Scan down. Did you leave any problems blank? If so, click into them and put in a random guess.
6. If you still have more time left, jump into one of your "marked for later" problems.

Avoid repeatedly clicking forward and backward through all of the problems, searching for "easy" ones. This will eat up valuable time. Instead, be disciplined about making the call to move on when you hit a problem that's just too hard. (How do you know that quickly and confidently? Via your studies. Part of the value in prioritizing your studies as you go is knowing when you want to bail on a problem during the test.)

10

Getting good at navigating the test sections will take a lot of practice. Use the above advice on practice exams *and* when doing timed problem sets (even when you're doing timed sets out of a book and not on a computer screen).

Math Formats in Detail

The 20 problems in each Math section can be broken down by format as follows (all numbers are approximate):

- 7 Quantitative Comparison problems—These ask you to compare two quantities and pick one of four choices (A, B, C, or D).
- 10 Discrete Quant problems—Most of these are standard multiple-choice problems, asking you to pick one of five choices (A, B, C, D, or E). A few will ask you to pick one *or more* choices from a list. Others will ask you to "fill in the blank," essentially; these are called numeric entry.
- 3 Data Interpretation problems—All three problems will be related to a single set of data given in graph or table form. The formats of the problems themselves are the same as for Discrete Quant. Most are standard multiple-choice, and the rest ask you to pick one or more choices or to fill in the blank.

It's typically the case that the Quantitative Comparison problems will appear together at the beginning of each section and that the Data Interpretation problems will appear together starting around question 13.

Quantitative Comparison

The format of every Quantitative Comparison (QC) problem is the same. All QC problems contain a Quantity A and a Quantity B. Some also contain common information that applies to both quantities.

Your job is to, well, compare the two quantities (surprise!) and decide which one of the following four statements is true:

(A) Quantity A is *always* greater than Quantity B, in every possible case.

(B) Quantity B is *always* greater than Quantity A, in every possible case.

(C) Quantity A is *always* equal to Quantity B, in every possible case.

(D) *None* of the above is *always* true.

For example: Most of the time, Quantity A is greater, but in just one case, Quantity B is greater. As the GRE puts it, "The relationship cannot be determined from the information given." So the correct answer is (D).

Getting the Most Out of Your GRE Math Studies

On the actual GRE, these four choices are worded exactly as shown in the following example:

$$x \geq 0$$

Quantity A	**Quantity B**
x	x^2

(A) Quantity A is greater.

(B) Quantity B is greater.

(C) The two quantities are equal.

(D) The relationship cannot be determined from the information given.

When $x = 0$, then the two quantities are equal. Eliminate answers (A) and (B) since one quantity cannot *always* be greater than the other quantity.

If $x = 2$, then Quantity B is greater. Eliminate answer (C) since the two quantities cannot *always* be equal.

The answer is (D): The relationship can't be determined from the information given.

Select One or More Answer Choices

Discrete Quant and Data Interpretation problems can ask you to pick one *or more* choices. According to the *Official Guide to the GRE Revised General Test*, the official directions for "Select One or More Answer Choices" read as follows:

> **Directions**
>
> Select one or more answer choices according to the specific question directions.
>
> If the question does not specify how many answer choices to select, select all that apply.
>
> The correct answer may be just one of the choices or as many as all of the choices, depending on the question.
>
> No credit is given unless you select all of the correct choices and no others.
>
> If the question specifies how many answer choices to select, select exactly that number of choices.

There is no partial credit. If three of six choices are correct and you indicate two of the three, no credit is given. If you are told to indicate two choices and you indicate three, no credit is given. Read (and follow!) the directions carefully.

On your screen, the answer choice boxes for "Select One or More" will always be *squares*, while the standard "pick just one" multiple-choice problems will always use *circles*. The squares are a good visual reminder that you may need to select more than one choice on these problems, just as you might check more than one box on a checklist.

Also: Even when they ask you to select <u>all</u> that apply, it might be the case that only one answer needs to be selected!

Here's a sample problem:

If $ab = |a| \times |b|$ and $ab \neq 0$, which of the following could be true?

Indicate <u>all</u> that apply.

- [A] $a = b$
- [B] $a > 0$ and $b < 0$
- [C] $ab > 0$

This is a select-all problem, so only one, only two, or all three of the choices may be correct. The equation given in the question stem must be valid. Try some real numbers to test each answer choice.

For answer (A): If $a = 2$ and $b = 2$, then it's true that $ab = |a| \times |b|$, so answer choice (A) could be true and therefore is a correct answer.

Answer (B): If $a = 2$ and $b = -2$, then $ab = -4$ but $|a| \times |b| = 4$, which is not true. But could there be another set of numbers for which this answer is true? Examine the pattern. If a is positive and b is negative, then ab must be negative. But $|a| \times |b|$ must always be positive due to the absolute value symbols. Therefore, the left side of the equation would be negative and the right side would be positive, which is impossible. Choice (B) cannot be true, so eliminate this choice.

Answer (C): Based on the work done so far, the right side of the equation will always be positive, so the left side must also be positive. The left side is equal to ab, so it is true that ab could be positive. In fact, ab must be positive.

To answer this problem correctly, select answer (A) and answer (C). Do not select answer (B).

> **Strategy Tip**
>
> Fully process the statement given in the problem (simplify it or list the possible scenarios) before considering the answer choices. That is, don't just look at $ab = |a| \times |b|$ and move on. It's your job to draw inferences about that statement before plowing ahead. This will save you time in the long run!

Numeric Entry

Some Discrete Quant and Data Interpretation problems won't offer any answer choices at all. Instead, you'll type a number into a blank box on the screen—literally, you'll fill in the blank. This can feel more challenging, but the math principles being tested are the same as on the rest of the exam.

You'll be given one box if you are supposed to enter an integer (such as 12 or 0 or -3) or a decimal (such as 2.7 or -1.53). Click on the answer box and type your answer.

Getting the Most Out of Your GRE Math Studies

If you are supposed to enter a fraction, though, you'll be given two boxes. One box (the numerator) will be on top of a fraction line, while the other box (the denominator) will be underneath. Click on each box separately to enter the numerator and denominator. You do not have to simplify the fraction before you enter. For example, you can enter $\frac{2}{4}$; you don't have to simplify it to $\frac{1}{2}$.

Do pay attention to the directions. You may be asked to round your answer in a particular way, for example, or you may be asked to answer in minutes even though the problem provides some time measurements in hours.

Here's an example of a numeric entry problem:

If $x \Delta y = 2xy - (x - y)$, what is the value of $3 \Delta 4$?

This is a "weird symbol" function: The test writers made up a definition, or function, for a symbol that isn't a real math symbol. Essentially, they're asking you to follow directions. Substitute the asked-for values into the given function ($x = 3$ and $y = 4$) and simplify:

$$x \Delta y = 2xy - (x - y)$$
$$3 \Delta 4 = 2(3)(4) - (3 - 4)$$
$$3 \Delta 4 = 24 - (-1)$$
$$3 \Delta 4 = 25$$

The answer is 25, so you would type 25 into the box.

UNIT ONE

Number Properties

Understanding different types of numbers and how they interact is fundamental to doing well on the math sections of the GRE. In this unit, you will learn multiple methods used to categorize numbers as well as how to approach various question types that require using number sense, including the often-dreaded Quantitative Comparison question format.

In This Unit:

- Chapter 1: Develop Your Number Sense
- Chapter 2: Number Properties
- Chapter 3: Quantitative Comparison: Pick Numbers

CHAPTER 1
Develop Your Number Sense

In This Chapter:

- Integers and Their Digits
- Non-Integers and Their Digits
- Manipulating Integers
- Factors
- Prime Numbers
- Positives, Negatives, and Zero
- Calculator Use
- Number Lines
- Check Your Skills Answer Key
- Problem Set
- Solutions

CHAPTER 1 Develop Your Number Sense

Whether you use math in your current work or haven't seen an equation since 11th grade, you have already developed a number sense. You employ your number sense when you:

- Decide how much lettuce to buy at the grocery store
- Scale up a recipe in the kitchen
- Figure out how much money to put into the tip jar
- Send your share of the utility bill to your roommate
- Check your speed while driving

You need a well-developed number sense for the GRE as well—and you'll also be able to use that number sense in grad school and at work.

This book begins with a review of some core number concepts and terms. In this chapter, you will learn about different kinds of numbers, including integers, factors, and prime numbers, as well as the relationships among these kinds of numbers. You'll also learn how to use number lines and the calculator on the GRE. And you'll use all of these concepts as a foundation to address harder problems in subsequent chapters.

Integers and Their Digits

Integers

Integers are whole numbers: They are numbers that do not have any fractions or nonzero decimals attached. Some people think of them as counting numbers, that is, 1, 2, 3, and so on. Integers can be positive or negative. For instance, the negative counting numbers are all integers as well: −1, −2, −3, −4, and so on. Finally, there's one more important number that qualifies as an integer: 0.

Number lines offer a visualization of many number concepts, and you will find them throughout this book. They orient numbers in relation to one another, ordering them on a line that moves from left to right, from smaller numbers to bigger numbers. The most structured version of a number line will contain evenly spaced tick marks:

Unit One: **Number Properties**

Every number marked on this number line is an integer, and each tick mark represents a distance of 1.

Numbers such as 7, 15.000, −346, and 0 are all integers. Numbers such as 1.3, $\frac{3}{4}$, and π are not integers. Non-integers can be visualized in the spaces between integers:

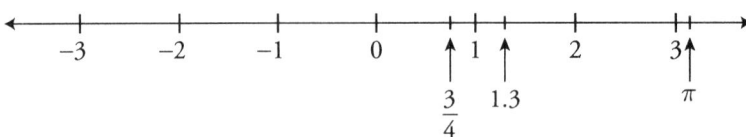

The tick marks on number lines can be spaced to illustrate integer or non-integer distances. This number line shows fractional distances, with each tick mark spaced a distance of $\frac{1}{2}$ from its neighbor on either side:

Digits

Every number is composed of **digits**. There are exactly 10 digits in our number system: 0, 1, 2, 3, 4, 5, 6, 7, 8, 9. Knowing the digits is typically not enough to determine a number. For example, a number composed of the digits 3, 5, and 6 could be 356, 536, 635, 365, 563, or 653. It may even be a decimal: 3.56, 56.3, etc.

Integers can be classified by the number of digits they contain. For example:

2, 7, and −8 are each single-digit numbers (they are each composed of one digit).
43, 63, and −14 are each double-digit numbers (composed of two digits).
500,000 and −468,024 are each six-digit numbers (composed of six digits).
789,526,622 is a nine-digit number (composed of nine digits).

A digit's location is defined as its **place value.** For example, the number 1,234 is one thousand two hundred thirty-four, meaning the 1, 2, 3, and 4 digits hold spots in the thousands, hundreds, tens, and ones (or "units") places, respectively. One way to think of a digit in a certain place value is as defining how many 1's, 10's, 100's, etc. you have. The number 1,234 has one 1,000, two 100's, three 10's, and four 1's. You can write the number as the sum of these products:

$$1{,}234 = (1 \times 1{,}000) + (2 \times 100) + (3 \times 10) + (4 \times 1)$$

In the number 452, the digit 2 is in the units place, the digit 5 is in the tens place, and the digit 4 is in the hundreds place:

$$452 = (4 \times 100) + (5 \times 10) + (2 \times 1)$$

Chapter 1: **Develop Your Number Sense**

This can also be visualized on the number line. On a number line where each tick mark represents a distance of 100, the number 452 will be somewhere between the 400 and 500:

The spaces between each 100 can be broken into tenths, with each smaller tick mark representing a distance of 10. The number 450 would be five 10's away from 400, which is very close to 452:

In fact, 452 is $\frac{2}{10}$'s of the way between 450 and 460. Putting 10 evenly spaced regions between 450 and 460 would allow you to indicate the exact position of 452:

Check Your Skills

Refer to the following evenly spaced number line for questions #1–3.

1. What is the value of *x* on the number line?

2. What is the value of *y* on the number line?

3. Place 40 on the number line.

Answers can be found on page 32.

Unit One: **Number Properties**

Non-Integers and Their Digits

Fractions

Fractions divide an integer into equal parts and express how many of those pieces are present. Fractions have two components: a **numerator** and a **denominator**. The number above the fraction bar is called the numerator and defines the number of pieces selected; the number below the fraction bar is called the denominator and defines how many parts the whole has split into:

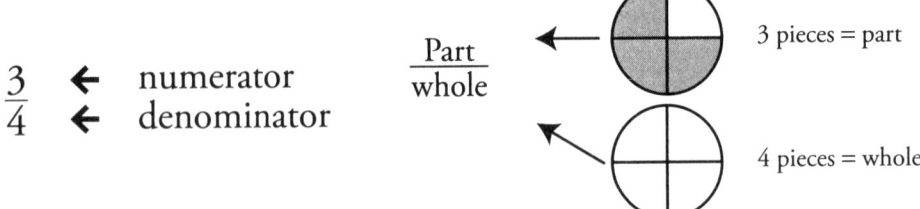

In the picture above, the circle has been divided into a total of 4 pieces, of which 3 are selected. Because 3 out of 4 are selected, the fraction is represented as $\frac{3}{4}$.

If all four pieces were selected, as illustrated below, the fraction would be $\frac{4}{4}$, which is the same as 1. Selecting all parts of a fraction turns it back into an integer:

$$\frac{4}{4} =$$

You can again visualize this on a number line. To picture $\frac{3}{4}$, break up the spaces between 0 and 1 into four equal chunks. Each tick mark represents a distance of $\frac{1}{4}$, so $\frac{3}{4}$ is 3 tick marks to the right of zero:

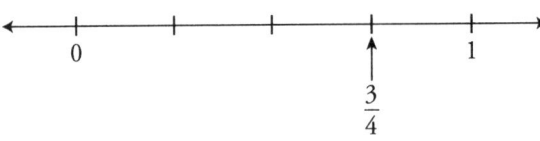

Chapter 1: **Develop Your Number Sense**

Decimals

Decimals offer another way to express the part-whole relationship. The fraction in the previous example, $\frac{3}{4}$, can also be expressed as the decimal 0.75. You can find the decimal version of a fraction by punching the fraction into the calculator: If you divide 3 by 4, then 0.75 results. Decimals and fractions express the same idea in different forms.

Digits

A deeper way to think about decimals is in terms of digits. Decimals are composed of digits, just as integers are. The number 123.456 has a 1 in the hundreds place, a 2 in the tens place, and a 3 in the units place, but what about the digits after the decimal point? Those digits represent the tenths place, the hundredths place, and the thousandths place, respectively: The tenths digit is 4, the hundredths digit is 5, and the thousandths digit is 6. The number in each place tells you *how many* tenths, hundredths, or thousandths the number has.

If you put $\frac{7}{8}$ into the calculator, you'll get 0.875 at the end, or 8 tenths, 7 hundredths, and 5 thousandths. Again, you can express this number as the sum of these products:

$$0.875 = \left(8 \times \frac{1}{10}\right) + \left(7 \times \frac{1}{100}\right) + \left(5 \times \frac{1}{1,000}\right)$$
$$= 0.8 + 0.07 + 0.005$$

You can picture this on the number line. First, picture the 0.8 (or $\frac{8}{10}$) by breaking the number line into increments of 0.1 (or $\frac{1}{10}$):

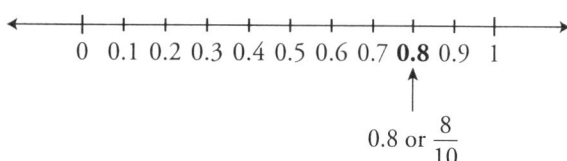

Now add the 0.07 (or $\frac{7}{100}$) to the 0.8 by splitting the distance between 0.8 and 0.9 into ten intervals:

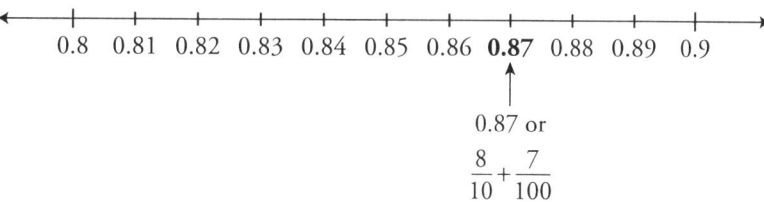

When the distance between 0.8 and 0.9 is split into ten parts, the resulting tick marks each account for a hundredth.

If you really wanted to, you could go even further and split the number line into thousandths—but thankfully the GRE is unlikely to make you go that far. It's going to be enough just to know that the value is between 0.87 and 0.88 on the number line (and it might even be enough just to know that it's between 0.8 and 0.9).

Unit One: Number Properties

Unlike integers, non-integers are not generally classified by the number of digits they contain, because you can always add any number of zeros at the end, on the right side of the decimal point, without changing the value of the number:

$$9.1 = 9.10 = 9.100$$

Here's another example:

6	9	2	5	6	7	8	9	1	0	2	3	.	8	3	4	7
HUNDRED BILLIONS	TEN BILLIONS	ONE BILLIONS	HUNDRED MILLIONS	TEN MILLIONS	ONE MILLIONS	HUNDRED THOUSANDS	TEN THOUSANDS	ONE THOUSANDS	HUNDREDS	TENS	UNITS or ONES		TENTHS	HUNDREDTHS	THOUSANDTHS	TEN THOUSANDTHS

The chart shown analyzes the place value of all the digits in the number 692,567,891,023.8347.

Consider the decimal portion of this long number: 0.8347.

The 8 is in the tenths place, giving it a value of 8 tenths, or $\frac{8}{10}$.

The 3 is in the hundredths place, giving it a value of 3 hundredths, or $\frac{3}{100}$.

The 4 is in the thousandths place, giving it a value of 4 thousandths, or $\frac{4}{1,000}$.

The 7 is in the ten-thousandths place, giving it a value of 7 ten-thousandths, or $\frac{7}{10,000}$.

You can again view 0.8347 as the sum of these products:

$$0.8375 = 8 \times \frac{1}{10} + 3 \times \frac{1}{100} + 7 \times \frac{1}{1,000} + 5 \times \frac{1}{10,000} = 0.8 + 0.03 + 0.007 + 0.0005$$

Some problems may ask you to **round** your answer to a certain place value. For example, you may be asked to round the value 12.34 to the tenths place.

The digit 3 is currently in the tenths place. In order to round to the tenths place, look at the digit that is immediately to the right of the 3. In this case, the digit 4 is immediately to the right of the tenths place. This digit, 4, is the digit that will determine how to round the tenths place.

If the value immediately to the right is 4 or less, then **round down**. When rounding down, don't do anything at all to the digit in question—leave it as is. In this case, leave the 3 as is. As a result, 12.34 rounded to the nearest tenths digit is 12.3.

What if you were asked to round 12.35 to the nearest tenths place? If the value immediately to the right of the desired place is 5 or greater, then **round up**. When rounding up, increase the digit by one—in this case, change the 3 to 4. As a result, 12.35 rounded to the nearest tenths digit is 12.4.

Rounding always depends on the single digit immediately to the right of the digit in question. Ignore any digits farther to the right. For instance, if you were to round 12.34982 to the nearest tenths place, the hundredths digit, 4, is the only digit to consider; ignore the 982. Because the digit 4 is less than 5, the tenths digit is rounded down to 12.3.

Check Your Skills

4. How many digits are in 99,999?

5. In the number 4,472.1023, in what place value is the 1?

Answers can be found on page 32.

Manipulating Integers

Addition, subtraction, or multiplication of integers always produces another integer. For example:

$3 + 2 = 5$

$5 - 3 = 2$

$2 \times 5 = 10$

Division gets funkier. Sometimes division results in an integer; sometimes it does not:

$\frac{8}{2} = 4$ You bought eight apples and want to divide them evenly between two kids. How many apples does each kid get? Four apples!

$\frac{8}{5} = 1.6$ You bought eight apples and want to divide them evenly among five kids. This time, each kid gets 1.6 apples!

In other words, the division of integers can result in integers or non-integers.

If an integer is divided by another integer and the result is an integer, then the first number is **divisible** by the second. So 8 is divisible by 2 because $8 \div 2$ equals an integer. On the other hand, 8 is *not* divisible by 5, because $8 \div 5$ is not an integer.

Unit One: **Number Properties**

Factors

Fractions and decimals result when one number doesn't divide evenly into another one. When you split 6 apples among 4 kids, the result is a decimal (1.5), not an integer. However, other integers *do* divide evenly into 6: namely, 1, 2, 3, and 6 itself. These numbers are **factors** of 6. For now, when discussing factors, we'll limit our scope to positive factors. However, negative numbers can also be factors, as you'll see later in the book.

You can confirm the factors of 6 by finding numbers that evenly divide 6:

$6 \div 1 = 6$	Any number divided by 1 equals itself, so an integer is always divisible by 1.
$6 \div 2 = 3$ $6 \div 3 = 2$	Note that 2 and 3 form a pair. They multiply to 6.
$6 \div 4 = 1.5$ $6 \div 5 = 1.2$	These results are not integers, so 6 is *not* divisible by 4 or by 5.
$6 \div 6 = 1$	Any number divided by itself equals 1, so an integer is always divisible by itself.

You can stop with 6 divided by 6 because factors are always equal to or less than the number in question. The values 7, 8, and so on cannot be factors of 6 because they are greater than 6.

So 6 is divisible by 1, 2, 3, and 6. There are a variety of ways you might see this relationship expressed on the GRE, including:

- 2 is a factor of 6
- 2 is a divisor of 6
- 2 divides 6 evenly
- 6 is a multiple of 2
- 6 is divisible by 2
- 2 goes into 6

Sometimes the GRE will ask you *what* the factors of a number are. In the case of 6, its positive factors are 1, 2, 3, and 6. Alternatively, when the GRE asks *how many* factors a number has, count the unique factors. If you're asked how many positive factors 6 has, the answer is that 6 has four positive factors. At other times, you will need to know the *prime* factors of a number. This book will explore factors, divisibility, and prime factors in greater detail in Unit 3, but for now, let's define primes in general.

Chapter 1: **Develop Your Number Sense**

Prime Numbers

What if you wanted to find the positive factors of 7? The only possibilities are the positive integers less than or equal to 7; check each one:

$7 \div 1 = 7$ — Every number is divisible by 1—no surprise there!

$7 \div 2 = 3.5$
$7 \div 3 = 2.33...$
$7 \div 4 = 1.75$ — The number 7 is not divisible by *any* integer besides 1 and itself.
$7 \div 5 = 1.4$
$7 \div 6 = 1.16...$

$7 \div 7 = 1$ — Every number is divisible by itself—boring!

Thus, 7 has only two positive factors—1 and itself. Numbers that have exactly two positive factors are **prime numbers**. Prime numbers play a very important role in answering questions about divisibility, so it's critical that you learn to identify what numbers are prime and what numbers aren't.

The prime numbers that appear most frequently on the GRE are the prime numbers less than 20. They are 2, 3, 5, 7, 11, 13, 17, and 19. Note two things about this list: First, 1 is not a prime number because it has only one distinct factor (1 itself) rather than two. Second, out of *all* the prime numbers, 2 is the *only* even prime number.

The number 2 is prime because it has exactly two factors—1 and itself. It's the only even prime number because *every* other even number is also divisible by 2 and thus has another factor besides 1 and itself. For instance, 4 is divisible by 2 (so it isn't prime), and 6 is divisible by 2 (so it isn't prime), and 12,408 isn't prime, because it is also divisible by 2. All of these even values greater than 2 have at least one additional factor besides 1 and itself: the factor 2. Therefore, the number 2 is the *only* even prime number.

Every positive integer (with one exception) can be placed into one of two categories—prime or composite:

Prime

- 2, 3, 5, 7, 11, etc.
- *exactly* two factors: 1 and itself
- e.g.: $5 = 1 \times 5$

Composite

- 4, 6, 8, 9, 10, etc.
- *more than* two factors
- e.g.: $6 = 1 \times 6$ *and* $6 = 2 \times 3$

The one exception is the number 1. It's actually neither prime nor composite. Rather, it's in its own category all by itself: the only positive integer to have exactly one factor.

Check Your Skills

6. List all the prime numbers between 20 and 50.

Answers can be found on page 32.

Unit One: **Number Properties**

Positives, Negatives, and Zero

All numbers are either positive, negative, or zero. **Positive numbers** are greater than zero, **negative numbers** are less than zero, and zero is, well, zero. Positive numbers are the numbers most people naturally think of, like the number of apples in that bowl or how much money is in your bank account. Negative numbers are a little more abstract. One way to think of them is in terms of subtraction or taking away, like how many apples you ate or how much money you owe.

Negative numbers are all to the left of 0 on the number line. Positive numbers are all to the right of 0:

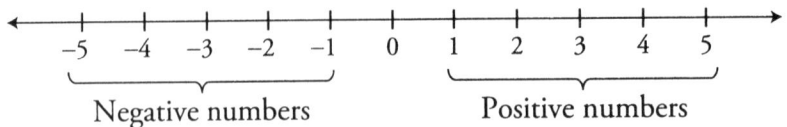

As with integers, positive and negative numbers have some predictable interactions that are helpful to memorize:

Positive + Positive = Positive

Negative + Negative = Negative

Negative + Positive = It depends! See below.

Positive × Positive = Positive

Negative × Negative = Positive

Negative × Positive = Negative

For Negative + Positive: The answer depends because the number that is farther from 0 will determine the charge of the sum. For example, $5 + (-2) = 3$. The 5 is farther from 0 than is -2, and since 5 is positive, the sum is positive. However, $-7 + 3 = -4$. The -7 is farther from 0 than is 3, and since -7 is negative, the sum is negative.

Chapter 2: Number Properties will explore positives and negatives in greater detail.

Calculator Use

On the GRE, you won't need to do all of this math on paper: The test includes an on-screen calculator. The calculator provides the four most basic operations (addition, subtraction, multiplication, and division) as well as a square root function:

The on-screen interface may be foreign to you, so take time to practice with it. You can click numbers in with your mouse or use your keyboard to input numbers when the calculator is selected. Especially if you don't have a numeric keypad on your keyboard, get comfortable completing arithmetic computations with your mouse.

The calculator is a little clunky to use, so you have a judgment call to make. When is the math so straightforward that you feel comfortable doing it in your head or on paper—without taking a lot of time or risking a mistake? And when is the math annoying enough to pull up the calculator? The GRE isn't a test of mental math; even though the calculator can be clunky, don't hesitate to pull it up when warranted. The calculator is great for turning fractions into decimals and for dividing or multiplying numbers bigger than 10. As you study, make a plan for when you will and will not pull up the calculator on screen.

There are a few things to look out for when relying on the GRE calculator. First, be aware that it respects the order of operations (a concept covered in depth in Chapter 4: Equations). For example, if you enter "$6 + 2 \times 3$" into the GRE calculator, the calculator will first multiply 2 by 3 and then will add the 6, resulting in 12. If you wanted to add the 6 and 2 first, enter $6 + 2$ into the calculator and hit enter. After the calculator produces a result (in this case, 8), prompt the calculator to multiply by 3, resulting in 24.

Second, it is easy to enter in a digit incorrectly, with no real way to check on the calculator whether you made a mistake. Therefore, it's valuable to use the calculator with an estimation in mind of what a correct answer ought to be. If you mean to compute $164 \div 2$ and the calculator returns 132, it's important to recognize that 132 can't possibly be the right answer. (In fact, 132 is $264 \div 2$.)

Third, consider when the calculator may actually cost you time. It's not typically time effective to use the calculator for every single step of a math problem. Moreover, on many problems, you can estimate—you don't actually need to calculate an exact value because the answer choices are pretty spread out or something like that.

Finally, when you do use the calculator, get into the habit of first jotting down what you're about to punch in. This is one way to minimize careless mistakes when entering in the numbers and operations.

Number Lines

The earlier number line examples were structured with evenly spaced tick marks. For example:

These number lines will almost always contain real numbers and may contain variables as well. They will usually have tick marks, not circles. In the example above, $x = 3$; solve for x by counting the number of tick marks to the right of 1.

Not all number lines will provide this level of detail. Some will display only a handful of points that are not necessarily evenly spaced. These number lines are likely to contain fewer actual numbers and will contain at least one variable. For example:

Variables are placeholders for unknown values; they will be discussed more in Chapter 2: Number Properties.

GRE number lines are always drawn to scale. As a result, you can estimate and make inferences by eye even when it's not possible to determine exact numbers. In the example above, r is closer to 0 than s is. You can also infer that r, to the left of 0, is negative, while s, to the right of 0, is positive. Put these inferences together: First, r is certainly less than s. Second, it's possible that r and s could be -2 and 5, respectively; it's also possible that they could be -13 and 24; either way, r is closer to 0 than s is.

Problems that talk about line segments or points that all lie on a line can be thought of as number lines; they will typically use points on the line, rather than tick marks. For example, a question might state that point X is the midpoint of line segment ST:

These line segments or number lines are rarely shown with any real numbers. Often, the only points on the line are designated by variables. Questions that require this type of number line may or may not provide information about the specific distance between points, although they may provide proportional information. For instance, in the previous number line, although the length of line segment ST is not given, you do know that ST is twice as long as either segment SX or segment XT (because X is the midpoint of ST).

Chapter 1: **Develop Your Number Sense**

Check Your Skills

> Refer to the following number line for questions #7 and 8.
>
>
>
> Which of the following MUST be true?

7. $v > s + t$

8. $v + s > t + r$

Answers can be found on page 32.

Unit One: **Number Properties**

Check Your Skills Answer Key

1. **10**
    The tick marks on the number line ascend from left to right by increments of 10. The variable x is on the tick mark between 0 and 20, so its value is 10.

2. **−50**
    The tick marks on the number line ascend from left to right by increments of 10. The variable y is two tick marks to the left of −30, so its value is −50.

3. **Two tick marks to the right of 20**
    The tick marks on the number line ascend from left to right by increments of 10, so 40 is placed two tick marks to the right of 20 on the number line.

4. **5**
    Although the number uses only 9's, there are five 9's total, in the ten-thousands, thousands, hundreds, tens, and ones places.

5. **Tenths place**
    The digit immediately to the right of the decimal is the tenths digit. So in the number 4,472.1023, the 1 is in the tenths place.

6. 23, 29, 31, 37, 41, 43, and 47

7. **Must be true**
    Given that v is greater than t, adding negative number s to positive number t will result in a sum that is less than t. As a result, v will still be greater than the sum $s + t$.

8. **Must be true**
    The number line defines v and t as positive, where v is greater than t. It also defines r and s as negative, where r is "more negative" than s (or r is farther away from 0 on the number line). Therefore, $v + s$ represents the greater of the two positive numbers with a closer to 0 negative number subtracted, while $t + r$ represents the lesser of the two positive numbers with a farther from 0 negative number subtracted—that is, even more is subtracted from t. As a result, $v + s$ is greater than $t + r$.

    Alternatively, try testing real values that fit the given facts: $r = -2$, $s = -1$, $t = 1$, $v = 2$.

    $v + s = 2 + (-1) = 1$

    $t + r = 1 + (-2) = -1$

Chapter 1: **Develop Your Number Sense**

Problem Set

For problems #1-4, refer to the following number line. Label each statement as **must be true**, **could be true**, or **must be false**.

1. $s + q > 0$

2. $pq > t$

3. $t - q = 2$

4. $s - p > r - q$

In problems #5-9, decide whether the expression described is **always positive**, **always negative**, or **sometimes positive**. If you answer **sometimes positive**, give numerical examples to show how the value could be either positive or negative.

5. The product of three negative numbers

6. One negative number divided by one positive number

7. $\frac{x}{y} \div z$, given that x, y, and z are negative

8. $\frac{rst}{w}$, given that $r < s < 0 < w < t$

9. $\frac{-x}{(-y)(-z)}$, given that $xyz > 0$

Unit One: **Number Properties**

> Solve problems #10–15. Use a calculator where desired. Reminder: You can only add, subtract, multiply, divide, or take a square root on the GRE calculator!

10. If $\frac{4{,}563{,}021}{100{,}000}$ is simplified and rounded to the nearest whole number, how many digits will it have?

11. What digit is in the thousandths place after simplifying the following expression: $(0.08)^2 \div 0.4$?

12. Determine the number of nonzero digits to the right of the decimal place for the following decimals:

    a. $\frac{631}{100}$ b. $\frac{13}{250}$ c. $\frac{35}{50}$

13. Which of the following must produce integers?

    Indicate all such statements.

    - [A] Integer × Integer
    - [B] Integer ÷ Integer
    - [C] Integer + Integer
    - [D] Integer − Integer
    - [E] Prime × Prime
    - [F] Prime ÷ Prime

14. How many primes are there from 10 to 41, inclusive? (Note: The term *inclusive* means to include 10 and 41 themselves in your work.)

15. Which of the following are factors of 18 ?

    Indicate all such factors.

    - [A] 2
    - [B] 3
    - [C] 6
    - [D] 12
    - [E] 18
    - [F] 36

Solutions

1. **Must be true**
   Although no specific values are given, the number line indicates that *s* is greater than 1 and that *q* is between −1 and 0. Since *s* is greater than 1 and *q* cannot be −1 (or less), *s* will always offset the negative value of *q*. Even in an extreme case, *s* would be something like 1.000001 and *q* would be something like −0.9999, so the sum of *s* and *q* would remain positive.

2. **Could be true**
   Both *p* and *q* are negative, so the product *pq* must be positive. In addition, *t* must be between 0 and 1. Test some numbers that fit these facts to see what happens.

   If $t \approx 0.75$, $q \approx -0.5$ and $p \approx -1.5$, then *pq* would be $(-1.5)(-0.5) = 0.75$, which equals *t*. In this one case, it's not true that $pq > t$. Can you tweak the numbers to make the inequality true? If *t* were 0.74 and the other numbers were left unchanged, then it would be true that $pq > t$. The inequality *could* be true, but it doesn't have to be true.

3. **Must be false**
   The value of *t* is between 0 and 1. The value of *q* is between −1 and 0. In order to reach 2, you'd need $1 - (-1) = 1 + 1 = 2$, but the first value has to be less than 1 and the second value has to be greater than −1. Even taking the most extreme possible values, $0.999999 - (-0.999999)$ cannot equal 2.

4. **Must be true**
   The value of *s* is greater than 1 and the value of *p* is less than −1. Therefore, the difference $s - p = $ (greater than 1) − (less than −1) = (greater than 1) + (greater than 1) = greater than 2. Alternatively, use real values to understand what's happening. Let $s = 1.5$ and $p = -1.5$. In this case, $s - p = 1.5 - (-1.5) = 1.5 + 1.5 = 3$. Since the second value will "turn" positive and both values have to be at least 1 point something, the answer will always be greater than 2.

   Next, *r* must be between 0 and 1 and *q* must be between −1 and 0. Let $r = 0.5$ and $q = -0.5$. In this case, the difference $r - q = 0.5 - (-0.5) = 0.5 + 0.5 = 1$. Since the second value will "turn" positive and both values have to be less than 1, the answer will always be less than 2. Finally, since $s - p$ must be greater than 2 and $r - q$ must be less than 2, it must be the case that $s - p$ is always greater than $r - q$.

5. **Always negative**
   Take this in steps. The product of the first two negative numbers is positive. This positive product times the third value, which is negative, is negative. For example:

   $(-1)(-2)(-3) = (2)(-3) = -6$

6. **Always negative**
   Two values with different signs will always produce a negative when one is divided by the other.

Unit One: **Number Properties**

7. **Always negative**

    Do this problem in two steps. First, a negative number divided by a negative number yields a positive number. Second, that positive result divided by a negative number yields a negative result.

    Alternatively, keep in mind that multiplying or dividing an odd number of negative terms will always produce a negative, while multiplying or dividing an even number of negative terms will always produce a positive. Three negative terms multiplied or divided together will be negative.

8. **Always positive**

    The inequality defines *r* and *s* as negative and *w* and *t* as positive. Therefore, *rst* is a positive value, because the two negatives multiply to a positive and the third value is already positive. A positive value (*rst*) divided by another positive value (*w*) yields a positive number.

    Alternatively, keep in mind that multiplying or dividing an odd number of negative terms will always produce a negative, while multiplying or dividing an even number of negative terms will always produce a positive. Exactly two negative terms multiplied or divided by any number of positive terms will result in a positive value.

9. **Always negative**

    Given that the product *xyz* is positive, there are two possible scenarios: (1) all of the values are positive, or (2) two of the values are negative and the third is positive. First, simplify the fraction. Then, test out both scenarios.

    Simplifying the original fraction yields $\frac{-x}{yz}$.

    If all of the values are positive, then the single negative sign will make the final value negative. If two of the numbers are negative, they will essentially cancel each other out to become positive. In this case again, the negative sign makes the end result negative.

10. **2**

    You can plug this into the calculator or you can use a shortcut (discussed more in Chapter 32: Advanced Concepts). For every zero in the denominator, shift the decimal point once to the left in the numerator to cancel out one zero. The calculator and the shortcut yield the same result: 45.63021. Regardless of whether the value is rounded up or down, there will be two digits when the value is rounded to the nearest whole number (that is, when everything after the decimal point is dropped).

    If you had instead been asked to find the actual value rounded to the nearest whole number, you would look at the place immediately to the right of the decimal—in this case, the tenths place. The digit in the tenths place, 6, is greater than 5. Therefore, round the number up, so 45 becomes 46. The value rounded to the nearest whole number is 46.

11. **6**

    To square a number in your calculator, multiply it by itself. Plug in (0.08)(0.08) to get 0.0064. Divide 0.0064 by 0.4 to get the simplified value of 0.016. The thousandths place is the third digit to the right of the decimal, which in this case is 6.

Chapter 1: **Develop Your Number Sense**

12. **(a) 2; (b) 2; (c) 1**

    Use the calculator to translate each of the fractions into decimals, and then count the number of nonzero digits to the right of the decimal:

    $\dfrac{631}{100} = 6.\underset{2}{\underline{31}}$ $\dfrac{13}{250} = 0.0\underset{2}{\underline{52}}$ $\dfrac{35}{50} = \dfrac{7}{10} = 0.\underset{1}{\underline{7}}$

13. **(A) Integer × Integer; (C) Integer + Integer; (D) Integer − Integer; (E) Prime × Prime**

    Any instance in which an integer is multiplied by, added to, or subtracted from another integer will always result in an integer. For division, however, the value of each integer determines whether the result will be an integer. Therefore, options (A), (C), and (D) must produce integers, but option (B) may not.

    Prime numbers are always integers, so they follow the same principles, with one exception: Dividing one prime by a different prime can never result in an integer. The only circumstance in which a prime divided by a prime would produce an integer is when dividing a prime number by itself. For example 3 divided by 3 equals 1, which is an integer. Therefore, option (E) must produce an integer but option (F) may not.

14. **9**

    The primes from 10 to 41, inclusive, are 11, 13, 17, 19, 23, 29, 31, 37, and 41. Note that prime numbers are *not* evenly spaced and do not follow any kind of known pattern, so you have to list them and count them manually.

15. **(A) 2; (B) 3; (C) 6; (E) 18**

    To test whether each answer choice is a factor of 18, take 18 and divide it by that choice. If the result is an integer, then that choice is a factor of 18.

Answer Choice	18 ÷ Answer Choice	Factor?
2	18 ÷ 2 = 9	Yes
3	18 ÷ 3 = 6	Yes
6	18 ÷ 6 = 3	Yes
12	18 ÷ 12 = 1.5	No
18	18 ÷ 18 = 1	Yes
36	18 ÷ 36 = 0.5	No

    There is another way to find the factors of 18, which will be taught in Chapter 9: Divisibility.

CHAPTER 2

Number Properties

In This Chapter:

- Understanding the Unknown
- Positives and Negatives
- Absolute Values
- Testing Positive and Negative Cases
- Evens and Odds
- The Sum of Two Primes
- Testing Odd and Even Cases
- Exponents
- Check Your Skills Answer Key
- Problem Set
- Solutions

CHAPTER 2 Number Properties

Why is it useful to define a number in terms of its properties—e.g., even or odd? Positive or negative? Prime? The GRE will ask you to use number properties to solve for variables, to restrict a range of numbers to test, and to simply make it through the test. In this chapter, you'll learn how to recognize and use certain properties of numbers in conjunction with the number sense concepts introduced in Chapter 1: Develop Your Number Sense. You'll also learn how to test cases, or scenarios, using real numbers and you'll learn the basics of exponents.

Understanding the Unknown

A **variable** is a letter that gets used as a stand-in for a number. Any letter can serve as a variable (x and y are probably the most commonly used), and a variable can represent any number—positive, negative, integer, decimal, or even zero. For example:

$$x, y, w^2, xy, \sqrt{x}$$

You can think of a variable as a mystery box containing a single surprise number or as a slick costume that a number wears to disguise itself. By obfuscating the numbers in a problem, variables add a layer of complexity to math. Their presence in a problem generally means that you won't be able to get to a solution using the calculator alone. (By the way, *obfuscate*—to make obscure or unclear—is a great vocabulary word for the Verbal section of the GRE. If you haven't run across that word before, pop it onto a flash card.)

The GRE will often use variables to hide whether a number is positive or negative. If the variable b shows up in a problem, for instance, any of the following could be values of b, along with infinitely more options:

$$b = 5$$
$$b = -6$$
$$b = 0$$
$$b = 3.651$$
$$b = -\frac{1}{2}$$
$$b = \sqrt{37}$$

Unit One: **Number Properties**

Positives and Negatives

The Rules

Questions testing your knowledge of the interactions between positive numbers and negative numbers are a perennial GRE favorite. Chapter 1: Develop Your Number Sense outlined some of these interactions:

Positive + positive = positive	$3 + 2 = 5$
Negative + negative = negative	$-2 + -6 = -8$
Negative + positive = it depends! Whichever has the bigger absolute value (more on this below) will win out.	$-6 + 2 = -4$ $5 + -3 = 2$ $x + y = $???

As you can see, there's uncertainty about the outcome when positives and negatives are added—you'll often need specific information about the numbers involved to know what the sign of the resulting number will be. By contrast, there is much more certainty about the outcome of multiplication and division of positives and negatives, especially when talking about multiplying or dividing two numbers:

Same sign = positive	Positive ×/ ÷ positive Negative ×/ ÷ negative	$3 \times 2 = 6$ $(-8) \div (-4) = 2$
Different signs = negative	Positive ×/ ÷ negative Negative ×/ ÷ positive	$5 \times (-6) = -30$ $-12 \div 4 = -3$

This principle can be extended to predict the results of multiplication or division involving more than two numbers. For example, if three numbers are multiplied together, the result will be positive if there are either *no* negative numbers or *two* negative numbers. The result will be negative if there are *one* or *three* negative numbers:

$$\underbrace{(-1)(-5)}_{5}(-6) = -30$$

$$\underbrace{(-2)(-4)}_{8}\underbrace{(-3)(-2)}_{6} = 48$$

> **Key Concept**
>
> When multiplying or dividing a group of nonzero numbers:
>
> - The result will be positive if you have an *even* number of negatives.
> - The result will be negative if you have an *odd* number of negatives.

Chapter 2: **Number Properties**

A Double Negative

What happens when positives and negatives are subtracted from one another? First, subtracting a negative is the same as adding a positive. For instance:

$$7 - (-3) = 7 + 3 = 10$$

This can be seen as an offshoot of the multiplication rules above: An expression such as $-(-3)$ follows the principle that two negatives multiply to make a positive, 3.

This is a very easy step to miss, especially when the double negative is more hidden. For instance:

$$\text{What is } 7 - (x - 2)?$$

Many people will make the mistake of computing this as $7 - x - 2 = 5 - x$. However, the minus sign outside the parentheses must be **distributed** to both the x and the -2, as follows:

$$7 - (x - 2)$$
$$7 - x + 2$$
$$9 - x$$

You'll learn more about order of operations and distribution in Chapter 4: Equations. For now, just know that if a negative sign is outside parentheses, every term inside the parentheses gets that negative. The expression above can be broken down into:

$$7 - (x - 2) =$$
$$7 - (x) - (-2) =$$
$$7 - x + 2 = 9 - x$$

Check Your Skills

1. What is $-(-5) + 5 - (-5)$?

2. Is the product $-12 \times -15 \times 3 \times 4 \times 5 \times -2$ positive or negative?

Answers can be found on page 60.

The first question is an example of a fill-in-the blank problem. When the GRE presents a blank box, as this problem did, you'll need to type in an answer manually. There are no answer choices, and there is no partial credit given. The answer you enter must be exactly right to receive credit.

43

Unit One: Number Properties

When signs meet variables

Remember these examples of possible values of b?

$$b = 5$$
$$b = -6$$
$$b = 0$$
$$b = 3.651$$
$$b = -\frac{1}{2}$$
$$b = \sqrt{37}$$

Variable b is not necessarily positive, which also means, perhaps counterintuitively, that $-b$ is not necessarily negative. Consider what $-b$ would imply for each of the six examples:

$b = 5$	$-b = -(5)$	$= -5$
$b = -6$	$-b = -(-6)$	$= 6$
$b = 0$	$-b = -(0)$	$= 0$
$b = 3.651$	$-b = -(3.651)$	$= -3.651$
$b = -\frac{1}{2}$	$-b = -\left(-\frac{1}{2}\right)$	$= \frac{1}{2}$
$b = \sqrt{37}$	$-b = -(\sqrt{37})$	$= -\sqrt{37}$

If b is negative, then $-b$ will be positive. It's tempting to read $-b$ as "negative b." However, it's more accurate to think of it as the **opposite** of b: Whatever the sign of the number represented by b is, $-b$ will have the opposite sign.

The GRE will often use inequalities and zero to hint at the signs of variables. For instance, to express that the variable a is positive, the GRE may say $a > 0$. Similarly, to indicate that a represents a negative number, the GRE may say $a < 0$. As such, > 0 and < 0 are GRE code for positive and negative, respectively. So if a problem tells you $x < 0$ and $y > 0$, get into the habit of reading those givens as x is negative and y is positive.

> **Strategy Tip:** Translate *greater than 0* and *less than 0* as *positive* and *negative*, respectively.

Consider the following setup:

$$\frac{a}{b} > 0$$

Chapter 2: **Number Properties**

What must be true about *a* and *b*? Translate the inequality as "*a* divided by *b* is positive." From the rules given earlier, dividing two numbers that have the same sign will produce a positive, so *a* and *b* must have the same sign to produce a positive result.

What is that sign? Are they both positive? Or are they both negative? From this inequality alone, it's impossible to know. Let's say the problem actually gave you the following:

$$\frac{a}{b} > 0$$

$$b < 0$$

If *a* and *b* have the same sign and *b* is negative, then *a* must also be negative.

Check Your Skills

> Use your number sense to determine which of these answers must be true. For the first two, note that multiple correct answers are possible.

3. If $mn < 0$, which of the following must be true?

   Indicate all such statements.

   A $\quad m > 0$
   B $\quad n < 0$
   C $\quad \frac{m}{n} < 0$

4. If $c - d > c$, which of the following must be true?

   Indicate all such statements.

   A $\quad c > 0$
   B $\quad d < 0$
   C $\quad c + d < c$

5. If $xy \neq 0$, is $(-x) \times (-y)$ definitely positive?

Answers can be found on page 60.

Unit One: **Number Properties**

Absolute Values

The **absolute value** of a number answers this question: How far away is the number from 0 on the number line? For example, the absolute value of 5 is 5 because it's a distance of 5 away from zero on a number line:

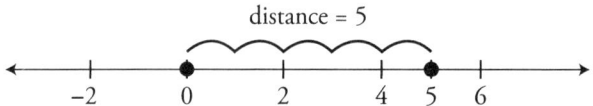

The symbol for absolute value is |number|. For instance, the absolute value of 5 is written as |5|. Interestingly, |−5| *also* equals 5:

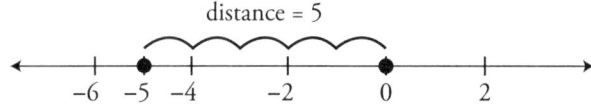

Both 5 and −5 are the same distance from 0, and so both have the same absolute value: 5. Every negative number will always have a positive absolute value:

$$|-40| = 40$$
$$|-22| = 22$$

The only exception to this rule is zero: The absolute value of 0 is 0, which is neither positive nor negative. Incidentally, zero is also the smallest possible absolute value a number can have.

A more conceptual way to think of absolute values is that they indicate the size of a number irrespective of its sign. Consider −1000 versus 3, for instance. Mathematically, 3 is greater than −1000 because 3 is positive and −1000 is negative. But imagine you receive a $1,000 fine and then find $3 lying on the ground. You probably wouldn't get much comfort from the fact that the 3 positive dollars were mathematically greater than the 1000 negative dollars. Absolute values are the symbolic way of focusing on a number's size, irrespective of its sign.

Absolute Value and Variables

What happens when variables get involved? Consider this example:

$$|p| = 7$$

Since absolute values denote a number's distance from zero on a number line, read the equation as "p is 7 points away from zero." But that still leaves out a crucial detail: 7 points in which direction? After all, 7 itself is 7 away from zero, but so is −7. So p is equal to 7 *or* −7. Absolute value equations involving variables tend to return two possible solutions rather than just one. A technical way of processing this is to replace the absolute value symbols with a +/− symbol:

$$|p| = 7$$
$$p = \pm 7$$

If it's easier to conceptualize, break plus and minus into two different equations, one for the positive scenario and the other for the negative scenario.

$$p = +7 \text{ or } p = -7$$

This works the same even when there are more complex expressions on either side of the equation. Just make sure to introduce parentheses when needed before placing the $\pm$ sign:

$$|x - 3| = -4$$
$$x - 3 = \pm(-4)$$

$x - 3 = -4$	or	$x - 3 = 4$
$x = -1$		$x = 7$

Treat the absolute value symbol like parentheses. Solve the arithmetic problem inside first, and then find the absolute value of the answer. For example, for expressions like $|4 - 7|$, first subtract 7 from 4, to get $4 - 7 = -3$, and then take the absolute value. Because -3 is three units from zero, $|4 - 7| = |-3| = 3$.

For more on handling parentheses, algebraic expressions, and equations, see Chapter 4: Equations.

Absolute Value and Positives/Negatives

Absolute values can also be used to test positives and negatives:

$$b|b| < 0$$

First, b cannot equal 0 here, since $(0)(0)$ equals 0, not less than 0. If $b \neq 0$, it follows that $|b|$ must be positive. The inequality can then be read as "b times some positive number is less than zero" or "b times some positive number yields a negative number."

The product of two numbers will be negative *only* if the two numbers have different signs. Therefore, b itself must be a negative number, since $|b|$ is positive. Generally speaking, when absolute values appear in problems along with < 0 or > 0, read the absolute values as code for "some positive number."

Check Your Skills

6. If $p|q| < pq$, which of the following must be true?

    (A) $p < 0$

    (B) $q > 0$

    (C) $pq < 0$

    (D) $|p|q > 0$

Answers can be found on page 61.

Unit One: **Number Properties**

Testing Positive and Negative Cases

Some Positives and Negatives problems deal with multiple variables, each of which can be positive or negative. As you saw on the last practice problem, it's a great idea to set up a table listing all the possible positive/negative combinations of the variables and determine what effect each combination would have on the question. Here's a more complicated problem with a full five answer choices:

If $ab > 0$, which of the following must be negative?

(A) $a + b$

(B) $|a| + b$

(C) $a - b$

(D) $\dfrac{a}{b}$

(E) $-\dfrac{a}{b}$

The product of a and b is positive, so a and b have the same sign: They are either both positive or both negative. List the possible positive/negative combinations of a and b that meet this criterion. Then, use real numbers to test the combinations in the answer choices. Keep track of your work with a chart:

	Case: +, + $a = 3$ $b = 6$	Case: −, − $a = -3$ $b = -6$
Criterion met? $ab > 0$	Y	Y
(A) $a + b$	POS	−
(B) $|a| + b$	POS	−
(C) $a - b$	NEG	POS
(D) $\dfrac{a}{b}$	POS	−
(E) $-\dfrac{a}{b}$	NEG	NEG

After testing $a = 3$ and $b = 6$, you can eliminate answers (A), (B), and (D), since they can't always be negative. When testing the second set of values, ignore the answers you've already eliminated; just test the answers that remain.

Chapter 2: **Number Properties**

What if, on your second set of values, you still can't get down to one answer? For example, here's what would have happened with the values $a = -6$ and $b = -3$:

	Case: +, + $a = 3$ $b = 6$	Case: −, − $a = -6$ $b = -3$
Criterion met? $ab > 0$	Y	Y
(A) $a + b$	POS	−
(B) $|a| + b$	POS	−
(C) $a - b$	(NEG)	(NEG)
(D) $\frac{a}{b}$	POS	−
(E) $-\frac{a}{b}$	(NEG)	(NEG)

It's still between answers (C) and (E)! Take a closer look at the two answers that remain. Try a third set of values that changes things up somehow. For example, since order matters when subtracting, try reversing the order of the numbers for one of the cases:

	+, + $a = 6$ $b = 3$
Criterion met? $ab > 0$	Y
(C) $a - b$	POS
(E) $-\frac{a}{b}$	(NEG)

Another approach to this problem is to determine what you know from the fact that $ab > 0$. The signs of a and b must be the same (both positive or both negative). Knowing that two values have the same sign isn't universally useful when adding or subtracting, but that information is really useful when multiplying or dividing. If they have the same sign, then $\frac{a}{b}$ has to be positive and $-\frac{a}{b}$ must be negative.

49

Unit One: **Number Properties**

Check Your Skills

7. If $|x| > |y|$, which of the following must be true?

    Indicate all such statements.

    ☐ A xy is positive
    ☐ B $x + y > 0$
    ☐ C $x^2 > y^2$

8. If $ab < 0$, $a > b$, and $a > -b$, which of the following must be true?

    (A) $\frac{a}{b} > 0$
    (B) $a + b < 0$
    (C) $b - (-a) > 0$
    (D) $\frac{a}{b} = 1$
    (E) $a - b < 0$

Answers can be found on pages 61–62.

Evens and Odds

All integers can be described as either **even** or **odd**. Even numbers are integers that are divisible by 2 (that is, when you divide them by 2, you get an integer result). Odd numbers are integers that are not divisible by 2.

  Evens: $-4, -2, 0, 2, 4, 6\ldots$ Odds: $-3, -1, 1, 3, 5\ldots$

Zero is even because, when you divide it by 2, the answer is 0—an integer.

Consecutive integers alternate between even and odd:

Arithmetic Rules of Evens & Odds

The GRE tests your knowledge of how even and odd numbers combine through addition, subtraction, multiplication, and, to a lesser degree, division. The outcome of these arithmetic operations can be derived by picking numbers and testing them. For instance, if a problem indicates that x is even, plug in any even number (0, 2, etc.) for x and proceed. While this is certainly a valid strategy, it also pays to memorize the rules for operations with odds and evens, as they are extremely useful for certain GRE math questions.

Addition and Subtraction

$$\text{even} \pm \text{even} = \text{even}$$
$$\text{even} \pm \text{odd} = \text{odd}$$
$$\text{odd} \pm \text{odd} = \text{even}$$

Adding or subtracting two of the same kind of number (both even or both odd) will always yield an even result.

Multiplication

$$\text{even} \times \text{even} = \text{even}$$
$$\text{even} \times \text{odd} = \text{even}$$
$$\text{odd} \times \text{odd} = \text{odd}$$

Multiplying an even number by *any* integer yields an even result. Even numbers are divisible by 2, so even numbers always have a factor of 2. When numbers with a factor of 2 are multiplied by other integers, the factor of 2 doesn't disappear—it remains in the resulting products. As a result, those products will always be even.

You may be wondering what happens when evens and odds *divide* each other. Unfortunately, there are few hard and fast rules for what the outcome will be when odds and evens divide; such cases tend to depend more on rules of **divisibility** and interactions between the numbers' factors than on properties of evens and odds themselves. In these circumstances, it will be a good idea to test specific even and odd cases. (For more on Divisibility, see Chapter 9: Divisibility, and for more on Picking Numbers to test cases, see Chapter 3: Quantitative Comparison: Pick Numbers.)

> **Key Concept**
>
> To produce an even number:
>
> - Add or subtract two evens or two odds (E − E = E and O + O = E)
> - Multiply any integer by an even number (E × O × O = E)
>
> To produce an odd number:
>
> - Add or subtract one even and one odd (E + O = O)
> - Multiply only odd integers (O × O × O × O = O)

Consecutive Integers

One common term the GRE will use to describe evens and odds is **consecutive integers**. Consecutive integers are integers in order on the number line, such as 2, 3, 4, and 5. The integers 133, 134, 135, and 136 are consecutive, as are −12, −11, −10, −9, and −8. In any list of consecutive integers, every other number is even and the remaining numbers are odd.

Unit One: **Number Properties**

Consecutive Integers	Even Integers	Odd Integers
2, 3, 4	2, 4	3
133, 134, 135, 136	134, 136	133, 135
−12, −11, −10, −9, −8	−12, −10, −8	−11, −9

The GRE could ask whether the product of two consecutive integers is odd. Or whether the sum of five consecutive integers is odd. Sometimes the problem depends on whether the number you start with is even or odd, and sometimes it doesn't.

Is the product of two consecutive integers odd? The answer is always no. Pick some numbers to test:

$$(3)(4) = 12$$
$$(4)(5) = 20$$
$$(5)(6) = 30$$

No matter what, the result is even, because one of any two consecutive integers will always be even. The other one will always be odd, but because there is at least one even integer, the product will always be even.

Is the sum of five consecutive integers odd? The answer depends on where you start. Consider these two cases:

$$1 + 2 + 3 + 4 + 5 = 15$$
$$2 + 3 + 4 + 5 + 6 = 20$$

In the first case, the sum is odd because there are three odds and two evens in the mix. The two evens add to an even value and two of the odds add to an even value. Those two pairings, even + even, also add to an even value. But there's still one more odd value to add to the mix, so the final value is even + odd = odd.

In the second case, the sum is even because there are two odds and three evens in the mix. The two odds add to an even value and two of the evens add to an even value. Those two pairings, even + even, also add to an even value. And there's still one more even value to account for, so even + even = even.

Check Your Skills

> For the following questions, indicate whether the expression will be odd or even.

9. $1{,}007{,}425 \times 305{,}313 + 2$

10. $5 \times 778 \times 3 \times 4 + 1$

11. The sum of four consecutive integers

Answers can be found on pages 62-63.

Chapter 2: **Number Properties**

The Sum of Two Primes

The GRE often uses prime numbers as a proxy to test the properties of odds and evens because all prime numbers are odd with the exception of the number 2. For example, the sum of any two primes will be even ("Add two odds …"), *unless* one of those primes is the number 2. As a result, if the problem states that the sum of two primes is odd, then one of those primes must be the number 2. Conversely, if you know that 2 *cannot* be one of the primes in the sum, then the two primes must both be odd and therefore their sum must be even.

If a and b are both prime numbers greater than 10, which of the following could be true?

Indicate all that apply.

- [A] ab is an even number.
- [B] The difference between a and b equals 37.
- [C] The sum of a and b is even.

Because a and b are both prime numbers greater than 10, they must both be odd. Therefore, ab must be an odd number, so choice (A) cannot be true. Similarly, if a and b are both odd, then their difference must be even, so $a - b$ cannot equal 37 (an odd number). Therefore, choice (B) cannot be true. Finally, because a and b are both odd, $a + b$ must be even, so choice (C) will always be true.

Before you check your skills, here's a math vocab alert: The word *distinct*, in math terms, means *different*. If a problem says that two variables are distinct, then the two variables cannot have the same value.

Check Your Skills

12. If m and n are two distinct prime numbers and $m < n$, which of the following must be true?

    (A) m is even.//
    (B) n is odd.//
    (C) $n - m$ is odd.//
    (D) mn is odd.//
    (E) mn is prime.

Answers can be found on page 63.

Unit One: **Number Properties**

Testing Odd and Even Cases

The GRE will usually bring variables into the picture when asking about evens and odds. As with positives and negatives, sometimes you will be told outright that a variable is even or odd. Usually, however, the test will only *hint* at this. Here's an example of one of the most common way the GRE hints at evens and odds:

$p = 2n$, where n is an integer

In this case, 2 times any integer produces an even result, so p must be even. This can also be extrapolated to any other even coefficient. If the test were to tell you that $p = 4n$ (where n is an integer), it would still be the case that p is even.

Here's a different example:

$q = 2n + 1$, where n is an integer

In this case, $2n$ will be even, and adding 1 (or any odd number) to an even number produces an odd result, so q must be odd. This can be extrapolated to other numbers. If the test were to tell you that $q = 6n + 3$, for instance, it would still be the case that q was odd.

The GRE will often use multiple variables to test evens and odds. For instance, a problem might state the following:

If p and q are integers such that pq is odd…

In this case, p and q are *both odd*, as the only way that two integers can multiply to an odd product is when they are both odd. On the other hand, a problem might start out as follows:

If c and d are integers and cd is even…

In this case, *at least* one of the variables is even (because an even number times any integer yields an even answer), but you would need more information about c and d in order to determine which one is even (or whether both are even).

In the most complex scenarios, multiple variables could be odd or even, and you'll need to determine the implications of each possibility. In that case, set up a table listing all the possible odd/even combinations of the variables and determine what effect that would have on the question.

If a, b, and c are integers and $ab + c$ is odd, which of the following must be true? Indicate all that apply.

[A] $a + c$ is odd.
[B] $b + c$ is odd.
[C] abc is even.

When two terms (in this case, ab and c) add to an odd number, one of the terms must be odd and the other must be even. So in this case, either ab is odd and c is even or ab is even and c is odd. Further, when ab is odd, then both a and b are odd. When ab is even, then at least one (and possibly both) of a and b are even.

54

Set up a table to keep track of the scenarios. There's only one possible scenario for the combination *ab* odd, *c* even, but there are three possible scenarios for the combination *ab* even, *c* odd:

Scenario	*a*	*b*	*c*	Check: $ab + c =$ **odd**
(1): *ab* odd, *c* even	Odd	Odd	Even	$O \times O + E = O$
(2): *ab* even, *c* odd	Odd	Even	Odd	$O \times E + O = O$
(3): *ab* even, *c* odd	Even	Odd	Odd	$E \times O + O = O$
(4): *ab* even, *c* odd	Even	Even	Odd	$E \times E + O = O$

Do check your work at the end of each row, just to make sure you didn't make a mistake.

Next, evaluate the answer choices against the four possible cases. Because the question asks what must be true, try to find a false case.

(A) $a + c$ is odd. In Scenario 2, *a* is odd and *c* is odd. Because odd + odd = even, this choice does not have to be true. Eliminate.

(B) $b + c$ is odd. In Scenario 3, *b* is odd and *c* is odd. Because odd + odd = even, this choice does not have to be true. Eliminate.

(C) *abc* is even. In all four scenarios, it is the case that *abc* is even, so this choice must be true. Therefore, the only correct answer is choice (C).

Alternatively, you can test real values rather than characteristics. As before, lay out the possible scenarios, but this time, use 1 for odd values and 2 for even values:

Scenario	*a*	*b*	*c*	Check: $ab + c =$ **odd**
(1): *ab* odd, *c* even	1	1	2	$1 \times 1 + 2 = 3$
(2): *ab* even, *c* odd	1	2	1	$1 \times 2 + 1 = 3$
(3): *ab* even, *c* odd	2	1	1	$2 \times 1 + 1 = 3$
(4): *ab* even, *c* odd	2	2	1	$2 \times 2 + 1 = 5$

Next, evaluate the three answer choices.

(A) $a + c$ is odd. In Scenario 2, *a* is 1 and *c* is 1. Since $1 + 1 = 2$, this choice does not have to be true. Eliminate.

(B) $b + c$ is odd. In Scenario 3, *b* is 1 and *c* is 1. Since $1 + 1 = 2$, this choice does not have to be true. Eliminate.

(C) *abc* is even. In all four scenarios, it is the case that *abc* is even, so this choice must be true. Therefore, the only correct answer is choice (C).

Unit One: **Number Properties**

Check Your Skills

13. If x is odd, which of the following must be true?

    Indicate all such statements.

    - [A] $x + 3$ is even.
    - [B] $2x$ is odd.
    - [C] $3x + 1$ is odd.

14. If pq is odd, which of the following must be true?

    Indicate all such statements.

    - [A] $\frac{p}{q}$ is odd.
    - [B] $p + q$ is even.
    - [C] $p - q$ is odd.

15. If x and y are integers, and $\frac{x}{y}$ is even, which of the following could be true?

    Indicate all such statements.

    - [A] xy is odd.
    - [B] xy is even.
    - [C] $x + y$ is odd.

Answers can be found on pages 63–64.

Exponents

Exponents (also known as **powers, orders,** or **indices**) are the superscript numbers that sometimes appear to the upper-right corner of larger numbers. At their most basic level, exponents are a shorthand for repeated multiplication of the number below, called the **base**. For example, taking 4 to the 5th power, or 4^5, would look like this:

$$4^1 = 4$$
$$4^2 = 4 \times 4 = 16$$
$$4^3 = 4 \times 4 \times 4 = 64$$
$$4^4 = 4 \times 4 \times 4 \times 4 = 256$$
$$4^5 = 4 \times 4 \times 4 \times 4 \times 4 = 1{,}024$$

If you've heard the phrase "exponential growth" used to describe a rapid increase, this is why: In cases involving numbers greater than 1, operations with exponents tend to produce large results, or increase exponentially.

Outcomes for numbers 1 or less than 1 are somewhat less predictable, though some outcomes are assured. For instance, for *any* number *x*:

$$x^1 = x$$
$$x^0 = 1$$
$$1^x = 1$$

The calculator will sometimes be helpful in determining the values of numbers with exponents on the GRE. However, the calculator *does not* have an exponent button. As such, it's only practical to use the calculator for relatively small exponent operations. For instance, you can use the calculator to find the value of something like 7^3 because it's not too cumbersome to punch in $7 \times 7 \times 7$ to get 343. By contrast, calculating something like 17^{10} is impossible: Even if you were inclined to put 17 into the calculator ten times, the display of the GRE calculator wouldn't be able to show all of the digits in the final product. As such, understanding the rules and properties of exponents is essential to solving these problems on the GRE.

Exponents and Evens & Odds

The GRE often uses exponents to disguise questions that test positives, negatives, evens, and odds. Consider what happens when an odd number is raised to various powers:

$$3^1 = 3$$
$$3^2 = 3 \times 3 = 9$$
$$3^3 = 3 \times 3 \times 3 = 27$$
$$3^4 = 3 \times 3 \times 3 \times 3 = 81$$

The number 3 raised to any of these powers results in an odd number. The same would be true of 5, 7, 11, 15, or any odd number raised to any positive integer power.

This occurs because the base, 3, is odd, and odd × odd always returns an odd result. The same is true for odd × odd × odd as well as odd × odd × odd × odd and so on. Similarly, raising any even base to a positive integer exponent will always result in an even outcome.

> **Key Concept**
>
> Where *n* is a positive integer:
>
> (odd)^n = odd
>
> (even)^n = even

Unit One: **Number Properties**

Exponents with Positives and Negatives

What about the *sign* of the outcome? If the base of an exponent expression is positive, the result will always be positive (even when the exponent is negative). For example, 2^2 is positive and 2^{-2} is also positive. However, when the base is negative, the sign of the outcome will depend on whether the exponent is even or odd. Consider $(-2)^4$:

$$(-2)^1 = -2$$
$$(-2)^2 = (-2) \times (-2) = 4$$
$$(-2)^3 = \underbrace{(-2) \times (-2)}_{4} \times \underbrace{(-2)}_{-2} = -8$$
$$(-2)^4 = \underbrace{(-2) \times (-2)}_{4} \times \underbrace{(-2) \times (-2)}_{4} = 16$$

When a negative number is raised to an even power, the result is positive, but when a negative number is raised to an odd power, the result is negative. This is an extension of the rules of positive/negative multiplication outlined earlier in this chapter: Multiplying two negatives results in a positive product, whereas multiplying a positive and a negative results in a negative product.

As a side note, it's important not to conflate the operation $(-2)^4$ with the operation -2^4. In the latter case, the 2^4 is processed first, and the negative sign is applied at the end: $-(2 \times 2 \times 2 \times 2) = -16$. This is a consequence of the order of operations, more information on which can be found in Chapter 4: Equations.

When the GRE tests your knowledge of interactions between positives, negatives, evens, odds, and exponents, it will often do so using variables. Consider the following:

If $x < 0$, which is greater: x^2 or x^3?

One might expect x^3 to be greater than x^2, but the problem also indicates that x is less than 0 (that is, x is negative). When x is negative, the even exponent 2 will produce a positive result, whereas the odd exponent 3 will produce a negative result. Therefore, x^2 is greater than x^3 when x is negative. In a more general sense, operations with even and odd exponents go as follows:

> **Key Concept**
>
> $x^{\text{even}} \geq 0$
>
> $x^{\text{odd}} = ?$

Raising a number to an even exponent will always result in a number 0 or greater. When raising a number to an odd exponent, the result will keep the sign of the base. In a sense, this means expressions involving even exponents have a more predictable outcome than expressions involving odd exponents. However, there's a flip side to this predictability. For instance, if $x^2 = 25$, what is the value of x?

On the surface, the solution may seem clear: $x = 5$. However, because even exponents produce a positive result even when the base is negative, it's also possible that $x = -5$. In other words, because the exponent is even, there are two possible answers to the question *What is x?* 5 and -5. By contrast, if you're told that $a^3 = -27$, then $a = -3$. Because the exponent is odd, it's not possible for *a* to equal 3.

Check your skills

16. If $ab > 0$ and $a^2b < 0$, which of the following must be positive?

    Indicate all such statements.

    - [A] a
    - [B] b
    - [C] $a + b$
    - [D] $\frac{a}{b}$
    - [E] ab^2
    - [F] a^3b

17. If *n* is an integer and $y = x^{2n}$, which of the following must be false?

    (A) $x > 0$

    (B) $y < 0$

    (C) $y > x$

    (D) x is even

    (E) y is odd

Answers can be found on page 65.

Unit One: **Number Properties**

Check Your Skills Answer Key

1. **15**
   The double negatives in front of the first term and the third term cancel each other out and make each of those terms positive: $5 + 5 + 5 = 15$.

2. **Negative**
   There are three negative numbers given. When multiplying nonzero negatives, if there are an odd number of negative values, the overall product will be negative. The product of the first two of the negative numbers will be positive, and the third negative number will make the final product negative.

3. **(C)** $\frac{m}{n} < 0$
   The fact that mn is negative indicates that m and n must have different signs, but it's impossible to know which one is positive and which is negative. Eliminate choices (A) and (B). However, $\frac{m}{n}$ must be negative, as the rules are the same for division as they are for multiplication. Answer (C) must be true.

4. **(B)** $d < 0$; **(C)** $c + d < c$
   Hmm. If you take c and subtract d...the result is *greater* than the starting point, c. What *increases* when you *subtract*? When you subtract a negative, the two negative signs create a positive, so it must be the case that d is negative. (Try some real numbers if you're not sure.) So answer (B) does have to be true: d must be negative.

   Is it possible for the starting point, c, to be negative or 0? If $c = 0$, then it's still the case that subtracting a negative will turn positive, and so $c - d$ will still be greater than c. So c does not have to be positive; eliminate answer (A).

   Finally, evaluate answer (C). If you start with c and add d—which has to be a negative value—then you will get a smaller value as a result. So it also must be true that $c + d$ is less than c itself.

   Whenever you can use logic to think through a problem, go for it. But if you're not sure, try some real numbers to prove it to yourself.

5. **No**
   Since $xy \neq 0$, neither x nor y by itself equals 0. Because the two negative signs multiply to a positive, the question can be rewritten as $(-x)(-y) = xy$. So is xy definitely positive?

   It's impossible to tell. If x and y are both positive or both negative, their product will be positive. But if x is positive and y is negative, or vice versa, the product will be negative.

Chapter 2: **Number Properties**

6. (A) $p < 0$

   The only difference between the two sides of the inequality is that one side takes the absolute value of q. Neither p nor q can be 0, because $0 < 0$ is false, so p and q have to be either positive or negative. The inequality $p|q| < pq$ must be true, so what are the possible signs of p and q?

p	q	Is $p|q| < pq$ true?
1	2	$2 < 2$ False
1	-2	$2 < -2$ False
-1	2	$-2 < -2$ False
-1	-2	$-2 < 2$ True!

   The only combination that works is one in which both p and q are negative. Answer (A) $p < 0$, then, must be true.

   Because this is a "select one choice" problem, you don't have to evaluate the other answer choices, but here's why they're incorrect. Eliminate answer (B) $q > 0$, as q is actually negative. Also eliminate answer (C) $pq < 0$, as the product pq has to be positive. Finally, eliminate answer (D) $|p|q > 0$, as a positive times a negative cannot yield a positive value.

7. (C) $x^2 > y^2$

   Test the possible situations that maintain the requirement that the absolute value of x is greater than the absolute value of y. Double-check the values you've chosen to make sure that you aren't breaking the fact given in the question stem. Then test the answer choices, but stop if you get down to just one answer:

	$x = 5$ $y = 3$	$x = -5$ $y = 3$
Criterion met? $|x| > |y|$	$|5| > |3|$ OK	$|-5| > |3|$ OK
(A) xy is positive	15	-15 Elim
(B) $x + y > 0$	8	-2 Elim
(C) $x^2 > y^2$	$25 > 9$	$25 > 9$

   At this point, stop because only choice (C) remains, so it must be true. But if you still had more than one choice remaining after testing the second case, then you'd test another case or two (perhaps $x = 3$ and $y = -5$ or $x = -3$ and $y = -5$) to see whether you could disprove any of the remaining answers.

Unit One: **Number Properties**

You could also solve this abstractly. The absolute value signs indicate that x and y could be either positive or negative. Therefore, there is no way to know whether xy is positive because x or y could be negative. And it's equally impossible to say whether $x + y$ will be positive, as nothing in the problem precludes both x and y from being negative. There always has to be at least one correct answer for any problem, so choice (C) is the only possible correct answer by process of elimination.

8. **(C) $b - (-a) > 0$**

   Though complicated, the given information here does indicate everything you need to know about a and b. Start by testing some numbers just to make sense of the given information. First, if $ab < 0$, then the two variables must have opposite signs. Pick two real values to keep track, such as -2 and 1. Second, if $a > b$, then a must be the positive number, and b the negative number, so $a = 1$ and $b = -2$. Finally, if $a > -b$, a must have a larger absolute value than b. That means the numbers initially picked won't work. Adjust them so they do fit the facts. Try $a = 2$ and $b = -1$. This keeps the signs opposite, a is positive and b is negative, and $2 > -(-1)$.

   Now, walk these values through the answer choices.

   (A) $\frac{a}{b} > 0$

   Untrue: If a and b have opposite signs, then the value will be negative: $\frac{2}{-1} = -2$.

   (B) $a + b < 0$

   Untrue: $2 + (-1) = 1$, which is not negative.

   (C) $b - (-a) > 0$

   True: $-1 - (-2) = 1$, which is greater than 0. Keep this choice in.

   (D) $\frac{a}{b} = 1$

   Untrue: $\frac{2}{-1} = -2$.

   (E) $a - b < 0$

   Untrue: $2 - (-1) = 3$, which is not negative.

9. **Odd**

   An odd multiplied by an odd is an odd. Then an even is added to that odd, which results in an odd number.

10. **Odd**

    At least one of the numbers multiplied together is even, so the product of all of the numbers will be even. Then, add an odd to that even to produce an odd number.

11. **Even**

    Because integers go back and forth between evens and odds, any four consecutive integers will consist of two evens and two odds. So the sum of any four consecutive integers can be expressed as even + odd + even + odd. The first pairing of even + odd = odd, as does the second pairing, so the simplified sum is odd + odd. Add the two odds together to produce an even.

12. **(B) n is odd**

    Testing real numbers works well for problems involving evens and odds. When primes are involved, it's important to test the number 2, since it's the only even prime number.

Answer	$m = 2$ $n = 3$	$m = 3$ $n = 5$
(A) m is even.	True	False Eliminate
(B) n is odd.	True	True
(C) $n - m$ is odd.	True	False Eliminate
(D) mn is odd.	False Eliminate	—
(E) mn is prime.	False Eliminate	—

13. **(A) $x + 3$ is even**

    The problem states only that x is odd. Test this fact against the three statements.

    (A) $x + 3$ is even. Adding 3 to an odd value will indeed always result in an even value. For example, $3 + 3 = 6$ and $7 + 3 = 10$. This choice must be true.

    (B) $2x$ is odd. Multiplying any integer by an even number will produce an even result, not an odd result. For example $2(3)$ is even. Therefore, $2x$ has to be even, not odd. Eliminate choice (B).

    (C) $3x + 1$ is odd. Multiplying an odd integer by 3 will result in an odd value; for example, $3(5) = 15$. Next, adding one to an odd value will result in an even value. Therefore, $3x + 1$ has to be even, not odd; eliminate this choice.

Unit One: **Number Properties**

14. **(B) $p + q$ is even**
    In order for pq to be odd, both p and q must be odd themselves. Choose two odd values and see what can be eliminated:

	$p = 1, q = 3$	Keep?
(A) $\frac{p}{q}$ is odd.	$\frac{p}{q} = \frac{1}{3}$, which is not odd	Eliminate
(B) $p + q$ is even.	$p + q = 4$, which is even	Keep
(C) $p - q$ is odd.	$p - q = -2$, which is not odd	Eliminate

    The only answer that remains is (B), so it must be the only correct answer.

15. **(B) xy is even; (C) $x + y$ is odd**
    If $\frac{x}{y}$ is even, then either x and y are both even, or x is even and y is odd. Also, the problem asked what *could* be true, so if you can find even one case that works for a particular answer choice, then that choice is correct. Make a chart to keep track:

	x even y even	x even y odd	Keep?
Criteria met? $\frac{x}{y}$ is even.	Y	Y	
(A) xy is odd.	No xy is even.	No xy is even.	Eliminate
(B) xy is even.	Yes	—	Keep
(C) $x + y$ is odd.	No $x + y$ is even.	Yes $x + y$ is odd.	Keep

    In the first case, both x and y are even, answer (B) results in a Yes answer, so this answer must be correct. Test answers (A) and (C) for the second case. When x is even and y is odd, answer (A) still doesn't work, so eliminate (A). Choice (C), on the other hand, does work for the second case, so choice (C) is also correct.

Chapter 2: **Number Properties**

16. **(D) $\frac{a}{b}$; (F) a^3b**

    The question asks what must be positive. First, determine what you can infer from the question stem. Since $ab > 0$, a and b must have the same sign, either both positive or both negative. Because a^2 is definitely positive, the fact that a^2b is negative indicates that b must be negative. Finally, because a and b must have the same sign, a is also negative.

	$a = $ neg, $b = $ neg	Keep?
(A) a	NEG	Eliminate
(B) b	NEG	Eliminate
(C) $a + b$	neg + neg = NEG	Eliminate
(D) $\frac{a}{b}$	$\frac{\text{neg}}{\text{neg}} = $ POS	Keep
(E) ab^2	(neg)(pos) = NEG	Eliminate
(F) a^3b	(neg)(neg) = POS	Keep

    Only answers (D) and (F) must always be positive.

17. **(B) $y < 0$**

    The question asks what must be false. Because n is an integer, it must be the case that $2n$ is even. Consequently, y is equal to x raised to an even power. Because raising a base to an even power always results in a number 0 or greater, y cannot be negative, so answer (B) must be false.

    Alternatively, test some real values. Let $n = 1$ and $x = 2$. As a result, $y = 2^2 = 4$. In this case, $x > 0$ and $y > x$, so eliminate answers (A) and (C) because they can be true. Likewise, it is also the case that x is even, so eliminate answer (D).

    The two remaining answers are (B) and (E). Try another case with different characteristics for the numbers. For example, try $n = 2$ and $x = 3$ (which changes n from odd to even and x from even to odd). In this case, $y = 3^4 = 81$. Since y is now odd, eliminate answer (E). The only answer remaining is (B).

65

Unit One: **Number Properties**

Problem Set

> In problems #1–5, decide whether the expression described is **positive**, **negative**, or **cannot be determined**. If you answer **cannot be determined**, give numerical examples to show that the expression could be either positive or negative.

1. xy, given that $x < 0$ and $y \neq 0$

2. $y^2|x|$, given that $xy \neq 0$

3. $\dfrac{|ab|}{b}$, given that $b < a < 0$

4. $-4|d|$, given that $d \neq 0$

5. $h^4 k^3 m^2$, given that $k < 0$ and $hm \neq 0$

6. If $|A| > 19$, which of the following *cannot* be equal to A?

   (A) 26
   (B) 22
   (C) 18
   (D) -20
   (E) -24

> For problems #7–20, answer each question **odd**, **even**, or **cannot be determined**. Try to explain each answer using the rules you learned in this section. All variables in problems #7–20 are assumed to be integers unless otherwise indicated.

7. If n is odd, p is even, and q is odd, what is $n + p + q$?

8. If r is a prime number greater than 2, and s is odd, what is rs?

9. If t is odd, what is t^4?

10. If u is even and w is odd, what is $u + uw$?

Chapter 2: **Number Properties**

11. If $x \div y$ yields an odd integer, what is x ?

12. If $a + b$ is even, what is ab ?

13. If c, d, and e are consecutive integers, what is cde ?

14. If f and g are prime numbers, what is $f + g$?

15. If m is odd, what is $m^2 + m$?

16. If n, p, q, and r are consecutive integers, what is their sum?

17. If $t = s - 3$, what is $s + t$?

18. If u is odd and w is even, what is $(uw)^2 + u$?

19. If xy is even and z is even, what is $x + z$?

20. If a, b, and c are consecutive integers, what is $a + b + c$?

21. Simplify: $x - (3 - x)$

22. If $x^4 = 16$, what is $|x|$?

Unit One: **Number Properties**

Solutions

1. **Cannot be determined**
   The problem indicates that *x* is negative and *y* is not equal to 0, but *y* could be either positive or negative. As a result, there is no way to determine whether the product *xy* is positive or negative. For example, if *x* = −2 and *y* = 3, then *xy* would equal −6. But if *x* = −2 and *y* = −3, then *xy* would equal 6.

2. **Positive**
   Since *xy* ≠ 0, neither *x* nor *y* can be 0. They must be either positive or negative. Therefore, the value of |*x*| is positive, because any absolute value must be either 0 or positive. Also, y^2 is positive because any nonzero value raised to an even exponent will be positive. Therefore, $y^2|x|$ is a positive number multiplied by another positive number, which will always produce a positive result.

3. **Negative**
   The inequality establishes that *a* and *b* are both negative. Therefore, the numerator is a positive number and the denominator is a negative number. A positive divided by a negative always results in a negative value.

4. **Negative**
   The value of *d* is not zero, so you can treat the expression |*d*| as a positive number. A negative number times a positive number always yields a negative number.

5. **Negative**
   Since *k* is negative, k^3 is also negative. Nonzero numbers raised to even exponents always yield positive numbers, so h^4 and m^2 are both positive. Therefore, the final product, $h^4k^3m^2$, is the product of two positives and a negative, which is always negative.

6. **(C) 18**
   Because the absolute value represents the distance from zero on the number line, the value of *A* is either greater than 19 or less than −19. The only answer choice that does not fit these parameters is choice (C), 18.

7. **Even**
   Break it into pieces. First, *n* + *p* is O + E = O. Then, that odd number plus *q* is O + O = E. If in doubt, try plugging in actual numbers: 7 + 2 + 3 = 12 (even).

8. **Odd**
   All prime numbers greater than 2 are odd. (This is one of the common indirect ways for the GRE to tell you that a number must be odd.) Multiplying odd by odd equals odd: O × O = O. If in doubt, try plugging in actual numbers: 3 × 5 = 15 (odd).

9. **Odd**
   t^4 is equal to *t* multiplied by itself four times: O × O × O × O = O. If in doubt, try plugging in actual numbers: 1 × 1 × 1 × 1 = 1 (odd).

Chapter 2: **Number Properties**

10. **Even**
    The product of an even number and an odd number will be even, so *uw* is even. Therefore, *u* + *uw* is E + E = E. If in doubt, try plugging in actual numbers: 2 + 2(3) = 2 + 6 = 8 (even).

11. **Cannot be determined**
    There are no guaranteed outcomes in division. For example, 6 ÷ 2 = 3, where *x* is even (6), but 3 ÷ 1 = 3, where *x* is odd (3). Since *x* could be even or odd, the outcome can't be determined.

12. **Cannot be determined**
    Since *a* + *b* is even, *a* and *b* are either both odd or both even. If they are both odd, then *ab* is odd. If they are both even, then *ab* is even. Therefore, it cannot be determined whether *ab* is odd or even.

13. **Even**
    Because they are consecutive, at least one of the integers *c*, *d*, or *e* must be even. Therefore, the product *cde* must be even.

14. **Cannot be determined**
    If either *f* or *g* is 2 and the other is an odd prime, then *f* + *g* will be odd. If *f* and *g* are odd primes, or if *f* and *g* are both 2, then *f* + *g* will be even. Therefore, it cannot be determined whether *f* + *g* is odd or even.

15. **Even**
    The term m^2 must be odd (O × O = O). Therefore, $m^2 + m$ must be even (O + O = E).

16. **Even**
    Since *n*, *p*, *q*, and *r* are consecutive integers, two of them must be odd and two of them must be even. Pair them up to add them: O + O = E and E + E = E. Then add the results of the pairs: E + E = E.

17. **Odd**
    Given that *t* = *s* − 3, if *s* is even, then *t* must be odd. If *s* is odd, then *t* must be even. Either way, the sum must be odd: E + O = O or O + E = O.

18. **Odd**
    Since *u* is odd and *w* is even, the product *uw* is even, so $(uw)^2$ must also be even. Therefore, E + O = O.

19. **Cannot be determined**
    Since *xy* is even, then at least one of *x* and *y* is even. Therefore, it's possible for *x* to be even or odd. Since *z* must be even, *x* + *z* could be O + E or E + E. Therefore, it cannot be determined whether *x* + *z* is odd or even.

69

Unit One: **Number Properties**

20. **Cannot be determined**

    Since *a*, *b*, and *c* are consecutive, either there are two evens and an odd or there are two odds and an even, so the sum $a + b + c$ could be O + E + O or E + O + E. In the first case, the sum is even; in the second, the sum is odd. Therefore, it cannot be determined whether $a + b + c$ is odd or even.

21. **$2x - 3$**

    Carry the negative sign through to each term inside the parentheses:

    $x - (3 - x) = x - 3 + x = 2x - 3$

22. **2**

    Because 16 is the fourth power of 2 *and* −2, the value of *x* could be either 2 or −2. However, the absolute value of both 2 and −2 is 2, making 2 the lone solution to the problem. (While it's a good idea to memorize the powers of 2 up to at least 2^4, you can also solve the original equation by finding the prime factorization of 16, a process covered in Chapter 9: Divisibility.)

CHAPTER 3

Quantitative Comparison: Pick Numbers

In This Chapter:

- QC Structure
- Simplify and Pick Numbers
- Check Your Skills Answer Key
- Problem Set
- Solutions

CHAPTER 3 Quantitative Comparison: Pick Numbers

Quantitative Comparison (QC) problems are unique to the GRE. Typically, the first 7–8 math questions in a Quant section of the exam will be QC.

As the name implies, QC questions ask you to *compare* two quantities, Quantity A and Quantity B. Your task is to determine the relationship between the two quantities: A is greater than B, or B is greater than A, or they are equal…or you weren't given enough information to be sure.

QC problems always follow the same format and always have the same answer choices. In this chapter, you will learn the baseline approach for how to solve every QC problem you'll ever see. In subsequent chapters, you'll learn how to solve more complicated QC problems.

QC Structure

The Answer Choices

QC problems will provide two quantities, labeled Quantity A and Quantity B. The four answer choices will always be written as follows:

(A) Quantity A is greater.
(B) Quantity B is greater.
(C) The two quantities are equal.
(D) The relationship cannot be determined from the information given.

The first three answer choices have an implied *always* before the words "greater" and "equal." Think of the answer choices this way:

(A) Quantity A is *always* greater.
(B) Quantity B is *always* greater.
(C) The two quantities are *always* equal.
(D) No consistent relationship exists. For example, Quantity A is usually greater, but in at least one case, Quantity B is greater.

Unit One: **Number Properties**

This implied *always* is crucially important. If one quantity is greater than the other in every single instance except one, then that quantity is not *always* greater, and the answer will be (D).

These four answers are the same on every QC problem and they are always presented in this exact order, so memorize the answers.

Check Your Skills

1.
Quantity A	Quantity B
5	12

   (A) Quantity A is greater.
   (B) Quantity B is greater.
   (C) The two quantities are equal.
   (D) The relationship cannot be determined from the information given.

2.
Quantity A	Quantity B
A number between 5 and 10	9

   (A) Quantity A is greater.
   (B) Quantity B is greater.
   (C) The two quantities are equal.
   (D) The relationship cannot be determined from the information given.

Answers can be found on page 83.

The Additional Information

QC problems may include additional information positioned in the center above the two quantities. Often, this information is pivotal to answering the question correctly. Consider this example:

x is an integer greater than 1.

Quantity A	Quantity B
x^3	1

Treat this given information as factual and apply it to the entire problem. In this case, the given information provides restrictions on the value of x, and that provides a clue about how to solve this problem. The value of x is limited to integers greater than 1, so x could be 2, 3, 4, and so on. There are an infinite number of possibilities. Try a few to get some sense of how to compare the two quantities. (This strategy will be more completely outlined in the upcoming section.)

Try a number that fits the given constraint to see what happens. For instance, if x is 2, then Quantity A is $x^3 = 2^3 = 2 \times 2 \times 2 = 8$.

What does that mean for your answer choices? Think it through for a moment before you keep reading.

Chapter 3: **Quantitative Comparison: Pick Numbers**

If Quantity A is 8 and Quantity B is 1, then in this one case, Quantity A is greater. Therefore, choice (B) is incorrect, since Quantity B cannot always be greater, and choice (C) is incorrect, since the two quantities cannot always be equal.

A B̶ C̶ D

But that doesn't mean the answer is (A)! It's true that Quantity A is greater in at least one case, but there's not enough evidence yet to conclude that Quantity A is *always* greater. You're down to either answer (A) or (D). What's next?

The current hypothesis (based on one lonely data point) is that Quantity A is always greater. To break that hypothesis, you'd need to find a *contradictory* case—a value for which Quantity B is greater or for which the two quantities are equal. Try to find such a value.

Keep track of your work systematically so that you can spot any patterns.

x	Quantity A = x^3	Analysis
2	$x^3 = 2^3 = 2 \times 2 \times 2 = 8$	A is greater
3	$x^3 = 3^3 = 3 \times 3 \times 3 = 27$	A is greater
4	$x^3 = 4^3 = 4 \times 4 \times 4 = 64$	A is greater

Quantity A is greater in all the cases tested. Is there a pattern at play? In this problem, as x increases, Quantity A increases. Since x has to be an integer greater than 1 and you then cube x, the value of x^3 will just continue to increase. It's not possible for x to equal 1 or to be less than 1. Therefore, the correct answer is (A).

What if the problem hadn't provided the given information at the beginning of the problem? How would that change things?

<u>Quantity A</u>   <u>Quantity B</u>
x^3 1

This time, x can be anything, so when testing numbers, consider trying positives, negatives, zero, and fractions. Try this yourself before you keep reading.

x	Quantity A = x^3	Analysis
2	$x^3 = 2^3 = 2 \times 2 \times 2 = 8$	A is greater
-2	$x^3 = (-2)^3 = -2 \times -2 \times -2 = -8$	B is greater

For your first case, make your task easy—try a positive integer. When $x = 2$, Quantity A is greater, so eliminate choices (B) and (C).

Next, don't try another positive integer. Try a number with different properties, such as 0 or a negative integer. If $x = -2$, then $x^3 = -8$, in which case Quantity B is bigger. Now, you can also eliminate choice (A). Therefore, the correct answer must be (D) because there isn't any consistent pattern.

Unit One: Number Properties

Bigger picture, removing the given information changed the answer entirely! When the problem provides given information, it's crucial to write that information down and figure out how it impacts the problem.

> **QC Strategy Tips**
>
> 1. Unpack and understand any given information.
> 2. When testing values, try numbers that have different characteristics, such as positives and negatives.
> 3. Try to find two conflicting cases—for example, one that makes Quantity A greater and one that makes Quantity B greater. As soon as you have two conflicting cases, you're done: The correct answer is (D).

Choice (D) is what's left when the first three are eliminated. You can think of this choice as the "sometimes" answer. Sometimes the comparison goes one way, sometimes it goes another way. You can also think of (D) as "not always" or "inconsistent answers."

The Need for a Game Plan

QC can get really complicated. The answer choices are fixed, but they don't all work the same way. And there are a lot of other potential complications that you haven't seen yet.

So, you need a QC Game Plan—a solid, straightforward, universal approach that will work for any QC problem.

You'll develop that Game Plan throughout the QC sections in this book, adding more nuances and techniques that will help you to tackle harder problems—while still using your straightforward Game Plan framework, every single time.

Simplify and Pick Numbers

Try this more complicated example:

$$x > 0$$

Quantity A	Quantity B
x^2	x

How do you approach this, *or any other*, QC problem?

At its core, the QC Game Plan has just two steps:

> **QC Gameplan, Round 1**
>
> 1. Simplify   2. Pick Numbers

Chapter 3: **Quantitative Comparison: Pick Numbers**

1. Simplify

First, simplify any givens.

Simplify means two things. First, make it simpler: Reduce the complexity, combine pieces or break them apart, and so on. Simplify also means "make sense of," in terms of both *what* it's telling you and *why* it's there. Make it more concrete and understandable.

As you consider how to simplify, take extra care to unpack the given information.

What is the significance of $x > 0$?

First, x is positive. Second, is x an integer? It might be, but it doesn't have to be. Rephrase in a way that conveys the fact that x is any positive value. Here's one way to do so:

$$x = \text{positive}$$

Quantity A	Quantity B
x^2	x

Next, is there any way to simplify the two quantities? For instance, it's a valid move to transform Quantity A into $x^2 = (x)(x)$ if that will make it easier to process, but you could also leave it as x^2 if you prefer.

On some QC problems, step 1 is enough to finish the problem. As you simplify, you pull on a thread, you keep pulling…and it's possible the whole problem unravels. You have the answer, and you're done. Be ready to stop there, enter your answer, and go on to the next problem.

But for other QC problems (such as this one!), simplifying alone won't get you to the correct answer. Next, pick numbers.

2. Pick Numbers

Pick One Case, Eliminate Two Answers

First, pick any number that seems easy and that follows the constraints (facts) given in the problem. Try $x = 2$, which fits the fact that x must be positive:

$$x = \text{positive}$$

Quantity A	Quantity B
x^2	x
$2^2 = 4$	2

If $x = 2$, then Quantity A is 4 and Quantity B is 2. In this one case, Quantity A is greater, so eliminate answer choices (B) and (C).

A ~~B~~ ~~C~~ D

77

Unit One: **Number Properties**

You can *always* eliminate two of the four answer choices by testing one case and working out what Quantities A and B are.

If...	Then...
Quantity A is greater	Eliminate answers (B) and (C)
Quantity B is greater	Eliminate answers (A) and (C)
The two are equal	Eliminate answers (A) and (B)

You can never eliminate answer (D) after testing just the first case.

In this problem, when $x = 2$, Quantity A is greater, so eliminate answers (B) and (C). But you can't know yet whether Quantity A is *always* going to be greater based on just one case.

You don't, though, want to look for a second case that also makes Quantity A greater. Instead, look for a case that gives you a *different result*. Why? You might find 100 cases in which Quantity A is greater, but it takes only one *different result* to knock out answer (A). So go find that different result, if it exists.

In other words, **try to prove (D)**. Be a skeptic about (A), (B), and (C), the "always" answer choices. For this problem, that means finding a case in which either Quantity B is greater or the two are equal.

Try to Prove (D): Weird Numbers

Many problems allow you to pick weird numbers, like zero, or fractions, or negatives. Weird numbers have weird characteristics, which can sometimes make them more challenging to test—but those same weird characteristics are also more likely to give you the different result that you're seeking.

In the current problem, if you kept going with integers, you'd keep getting the result that Quantity A is greater. Two squared is four, three squared is nine, and so on. Most numbers increase when you square them.

What kinds of numbers *don't* increase when you square them?

The value 1, for instance, does not increase when you square it: $1^2 = 1$. So, if $x = 1$, then Quantity A $= 1^2 = 1$ and Quantity B $= 1$. In this case, the two quantities are equal, so eliminate choice (A).

The only remaining answer is (D), so (D) is the correct answer.

Rather than reinventing weird numbers for each problem, use **ZONEF** to help you remember to test certain categories of numbers in addition to positive integers. ZONEF ("Zone-F") stands for **Z**ero **O**ne **N**egatives **E**xtremes **F**ractions.

Chapter 3: **Quantitative Comparison: Pick Numbers**

Here's what ZONEF looks like in **number line** form:

Negative Numbers	Negative Fractions	Positive Fractions	Positive Numbers
$x \leq -1$	$-1 < x < 0$	$0 < x < 1$	$x \geq 1$

$$-1 \qquad 0 \qquad 1$$

The best numbers to start your testing (-1, 0, and 1) are labeled on the tick marks. When the problem allows you to use these values, they're usually the easiest to try. The top of the graphic shows groupings of numbers that have specific characteristics. Depending on the problem, a negative number and a positive number could return quite different results.

As always, first check the problem to see what values it allows you to pick. When the problem indicates that $x > 0$, don't try 0 or any of the values that are to the left of 0 on the number line. But ZONEF will help you to remember to try 1 or fractions between 0 and 1.

Though you wouldn't list this out on test day, here's what each of the ZONEF categories of numbers would produce in the current problem:

Quantity A		Quantity B	
x^2		x	
$2^2 = 4$	>	2	Positive
$0^2 = 0$	=	0	Zero
$1^2 = 1$	=	1	One
$(-1)^2 = 1$	>	-1	Negative
$100^2 = 10{,}000$	>	100	Extreme
$\left(\frac{1}{2}\right)^2 = \frac{1}{4}$	<	$\frac{1}{2}$	Fraction

Unit One: **Number Properties**

Do try whatever you think is an easy value first, whether that's a positive integer or one of the ZONEF values. After that, do only as much as you need to do in order to get to an answer. (And only try values that the problem allows you to try!)

Generally speaking, try two or three—maybe four—cases. On most problems, you won't need to try more. Why? First, like this problem, many problems include constraints that will knock out some categories of numbers. Second, one single counterexample is enough to make (D) the correct answer. Third, as you learn the math and practice QC, you're going to get better at identifying which kinds of numbers will produce different results in various math scenarios, so you have a better idea of the kinds of numbers to test to give you that different result you're seeking.

There are some problems where it's either not reasonable to test weird numbers or where the weird numbers keep giving the same result. **After three cases, look for the pattern, then make a call**. Try three different numbers *that are really different*; that is, they are different *kinds* or markedly different *sizes* of numbers. If they all point to the same answer, examine the three results for a pattern that could tell you what fourth case to try to get your counterexample to prove answer (D). Coming up empty? Assume that you have found an *always* case and pick the one answer—(A), (B), or (C)—that still remains.

Try to Prove (D): Find a Pattern

In this problem, many of the weird numbers are ruled out because of the given information:

x is an integer greater than 0.

Quantity A	Quantity B
$x(10 - x)$	25

Given that x is an integer greater than 0, don't test zero, negatives, or fractions.

Try that now. (In Chapter 4: Equations, you'll get a refresher on order of operations, but for now, just remember to complete anything inside parentheses before multiplication.)

Start by rephrasing the given information at the top. You may have also simplified Quantity A by distributing the x and rewriting $x(10 - x)$ as $10x - x^2$. There's no hard and fast rule about which form is best. It's your call which seems simpler—but do pause to consider what you think will be best for you. Investing those few seconds will save you time and energy as you work through the rest of the problem.

Chapter 3: **Quantitative Comparison: Pick Numbers**

Then, pick numbers and see what happens:

x is 1, 2, 3, etc.

x	**Quantity A** $x(10 - x)$		**Quantity B** 25
1	$= 1(10 - 1)$ $= 1(9)$ $= 9$	$<$	25
2	$= 2(10 - 2)$ $= 2(8)$ $= 16$	$<$	25
3	$= 3(10 - 3)$ $= 3(7)$ $= 21$	$<$	25

In the first case, where x is 1, Quantity B is greater, so eliminate choices (A) and (C):

~~A~~ B ~~C~~ D

If you try $x = 2$ and $x = 3$ next, what's the pattern? As x gets larger, Quantity A gets *closer* to Quantity B. Based on this pattern, it's possible Quantity A will eventually reach or even pass Quantity B. So go ahead and try another case.

When $x = 4$, Quantity A is $4(10 - 4) = 4(6) = 24$, which is still less than Quantity B, but is so close! Although that was already the fourth case, given how close the result is, go ahead and try one more: $x = 5$. When x is 5, Quantity A is $5(10 - 5) = 5(5) = 25$, which is the same as Quantity B. In the case where x is 5, Quantity B equals Quantity A. Eliminate answer (B); the correct answer is (D).

Let's sum up our QC Gameplan so far:

> **QC Gameplan, Round 1**
>
> **1. Simplify**
> - Unpack givens
>
> **2. Pick Numbers**
> - Try to prove (D)
> - Easy, then weird (ZONEF, number line)
> - After 3 cases, look for the pattern, then make a call

Unit One: **Number Properties**

Try this problem:

$$y > x$$

Quantity A	**Quantity B**
x	xy

The given information states that y is greater than x, but doesn't restrict either value individually. Start again with easy numbers. If $x = 1$ and $y = 2$, then Quantity A is 1 and Quantity B is 2. In this case, Quantity B is greater. Eliminate answers (A) and (C).

A̶ B C̶ D

Now, what ZONEF case do you want to try? If $x = 0$ and $y = 2$, then Quantity A is 0 and Quantity B is also 0! Since the values of the two quantities are equal, eliminate choice (B). As there is no *always* answer, the correct answer is (D).

A̶ B̶ C̶ (D)

Whenever the problem allows you to try 0, it's usually a good number to try. Zero has weird principles that often make the math a lot easier to carry out.

Let's go back to this: "What if I can't prove (D)? What if every number I pick keeps making Quantity B greater? When do I stop?"

If you really are trying *weird* numbers and studying the results to find patterns, but you're making no progress on the goal to find a different result, stop after just a few cases. Remember, **after three cases, look for the pattern, then make a call.**

When you're reviewing the problem, if you discover that the right answer was in fact (D), then go back now to try to find the counterexample. If you can't find it, read the problem's explanation. Then examine how the problem is constructed in order to understand how you could know next time to try that type of number in order to prove answer (D). And finally, add that information to your notes, flash cards, or however you might be keeping track of your study takeaways.

Check Your Skills

3.

$$x < 0$$

Quantity A	**Quantity B**
$x - 2$	$-(x - 2)$

(A) Quantity A is greater.

(B) Quantity B is greater.

(C) The two quantities are equal.

(D) The relationship cannot be determined from the information given.

Answers can be found on page 83.

82

Chapter 3: **Quantitative Comparison: Pick Numbers**

Check Your Skills Answer Key

1. **(B)**
   This question is much easier than anything you'd really see on the GRE, but it illustrates how QC works. Quantity B, 12, is *always* greater than Quantity A.

   The correct answer is (B): Quantity B is always greater.

2. **(D)**
   Quantity A could be a range of values, including 6, 6.5, 7, 8, or 9.9. If Quantity A is 6, then it is less than Quantity B; eliminate answers (A) and (C). However, if Quantity A is 9, then it is the same as Quantity B. Eliminate answer (B).

   The correct answer is (D): The relationship can't be determined.

3. **(B)**
   First, simplify.

   The given information specifies that x is less than zero, so x is a negative number. You could also rewrite Quantity B to $-x + 2$ or $2 - x$, since both are the same as $-(x - 2)$, but note that Quantity A is in the form $x - 2$. If you leave Quantity B in the form $-(x - 2)$, then whenever you solve for Quantity A, you can just put a negative sign in front of that value to get Quantity B. For that reason, leave Quantity B in its original form.

   Second, pick numbers.

   x is negative.

	Quantity A		Quantity B
x	$x - 2$		$-(x - 2)$
-1	$-1 - 2 = -3$	<	$-(-3) = 3$
-2	$-2 - 2 = -4$	<	$-(-4) = 4$
-3	$-3 - 2 = -5$	<	$-(-5) = 5$

   What's the pattern? The absolute value is always the same, but Quantity A is always the negative version, while Quantity B is always the positive version.

   Pause to consider whether that pattern is likely to break if you were to try any weird numbers. Fractions wouldn't change the sign of the quantities—Quantity A would still be negative and, as a result, Quantity B would still be positive. Nor would extreme values matter—Quantity A will still be negative and Quantity B will be positive. This pattern is likely to hold, so it's reasonable to conclude that Quantity A will always be less than Quantity B.

   The correct answer is (B): Quantity B is always greater.

Unit One: **Number Properties**

Problem Set

> Answer each of the following questions using the Quantitative Comparison answer choices:
>
> (A) Quantity A is greater.
>
> (B) Quantity B is greater.
>
> (C) The two quantities are equal.
>
> (D) The relationship cannot be determined from the information given.
>
> One more note: Starting in Chapter 4: Equations, we're no longer going to write out the QC answer choices for you. You'll need to have them memorized. Pop them onto a flash card right now and start studying!

1.
Quantity A	**Quantity B**
x	$3x - 4$

2. x is a non-negative even integer.

Quantity A	**Quantity B**
x	1

3.

s is the midpoint of q and r.
$r = -2q$

Quantity A	**Quantity B**
s	0

4. $|x| = |y|, x \neq 0$

Quantity A	**Quantity B**
$x + y$	$2x$

5. $a > 0$

Quantity A	**Quantity B**
a^2	a^3

6.
$$x < 0$$

Quantity A	**Quantity B**
x^3	x

7.
$$a < b < 0 < c < d$$

Quantity A	**Quantity B**
abc	$c - d$

8.
$$xy > 0$$

Quantity A	**Quantity B**
$\dfrac{x}{|x|}$	$\dfrac{y}{|y|}$

Unit One: Number Properties

Solutions

1. **(D)**

    There are no constraints given, so *x* could be anything. Use ZONEF to help pick numbers to test.

    If $x = 0$, Quantity A is equal to 0 and Quantity B is equal to −4. In this case, Quantity A is greater, so eliminate answers (B) and (C).

    What could make Quantity A either equal to or less than Quantity B? Since Quantity B contains 3*x*, try a greater positive value for *x*. If $x = 10$, Quantity A is equal to 10 and Quantity B is equal to 26. Since Quantity A is now greater, eliminate answer choice (A).

    The correct answer is (D): The relationship cannot be determined.

2. **(D)**

    Note the phrasing *non-negative*. It would be much easier to say *positive*, so why didn't the problem use that language? There is one number that is not negative but also not positive: 0. So when a problem says non-negative, it's a sneaky way for the test-writer to indicate that positive values *and* 0 are allowed. ZONEF can help to remind you to test 0 when that value is allowed by the problem. If $x = 0$, then Quantity B is greater, so eliminate answers (A) and (C). However, when $x = 2$ or any other positive even integer, Quantity A is greater, so eliminate answer (B).

    The correct answer is (D): The relationship cannot be determined.

3. **(A)**

    To find the midpoint of two points, either count on the number line to halfway between the two or find the average of the two points using the equation average = $\frac{\text{Point 1} + \text{Point 2}}{2}$.

    There are no values given on the number line, so pick numbers that fit the given information. In order for *r* to equal −2*q*, one of the variables must be negative and the other must be positive. Because *r* is to the right of *q* on the number line, *q* must be the negative number and *r* must be positive. For example, if $q = -1$, then $r = -2q = 2$:

    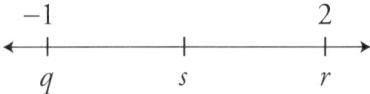

    Since *s* is the midpoint of *q* and *r*, the value of *s* is 0.5. If you feel comfortable doing so, you can also eyeball this to see that *s* will fall somewhere to the right of 0. In this case, $s > 0$, so eliminate answers (B) and (C).

    Try a few other numbers. If *q* is −10, *r* is 20, and *s* is 5. If *q* is −1,000, *r* is 2,000, and *s* is 500. In both cases, *s* is still greater than 0. What's happening with the math? Whatever the negative value chosen for *q*, it will always be the case that you reverse the sign and multiply by 2 to get *r*. As a result, it will always be the case that *r* will be farther from 0 than *q* is, so the midpoint between *q* and *r* will be something greater than 0.

    The correct answer is (A): Quantity A is greater.

4. **(D)**

Since $|x| = |y|$, the two numbers could either be equal (both positive or both negative) or opposite (one positive and one negative, but with the same magnitude). Pick numbers that test each of those possibilities. This chart shows all the possible arrangements if $|x| = |y| = 3$:

x	y	Quantity A x + y		Quantity B 2x
3	3	6	=	6
3	−3	0	<	6
−3	3	0	>	−6
−3	−3	−6	=	−6

As always, stop as soon as you're able to get down to one answer. For example, if you first try $x = 3$ and $y = 3$, then you'd eliminate answers (A) and (B). If you next try $x = 3$ and $y = -3$, you'd be able to eliminate answer (C) as well and only answer (D) would remain.

Alternatively, reason through using the characteristics. If x and y are the same sign, then $x = y$. Substitute x for y in Quantity A:

$$|x| = |y|, x \neq 0$$

Quantity A	**Quantity B**
$x + (x) = 2x$	$2x$

If x and y are the same sign, then the quantities are equal. Eliminate choices (A) and (B).

However, if x and y have opposite signs, then $-x = y$. Substitute $-x$ for y in Quantity A:

$$|x| = |y|, x \neq 0$$

Quantity A	**Quantity B**
$x + (-x) = 0$	$2x$

Since x does not equal 0, the values in the two quantities will not be equal. Eliminate choice (C).

The correct answer is (D): The relationship can't be determined.

Unit One: Number Properties

5. **(D)**

   The given information specifies that *a* is a positive number but *a* could be a fraction or an integer:

a	Quantity A a^2		Quantity B a^3
1	$1^2 = 1$	$=$	$1^3 = 1$
$\frac{1}{2}$	$\left(\frac{1}{2}\right)^2 = \frac{1}{2} \times \frac{1}{2} = \frac{1}{4}$	$>$	$\left(\frac{1}{2}\right)^3 = \frac{1}{2} \times \frac{1}{2} \times \frac{1}{2} = \frac{1}{8}$

   When *a* is 1, the quantities are the same, so eliminate choices (A) and (B). But when *a* is $\frac{1}{2}$, the two quantities are not the same, so eliminate answer (C).

   The correct answer is (D): The relationship can't be determined.

6. **(D)**

   The given information defines *x* as a negative number, but it could be either a fraction or an integer.

   If *x* is −1, then Quantity A is −1 and Quantity B is −1. In this scenario, the two quantities are equal, so eliminate choices (A) and (B). However, if *x* is −2, then Quantity A is −8 and Quantity B is −2. In this case, the two quantities are not equal, so eliminate choice (C).

   The correct answer is (D): The relationship can't be determined.

7. **(A)**

   Two of the variables, *a* and *b*, are negative, while two of them, *c* and *d* are positive. They could be fractions, but start with integers.

a	*b*	*c*	*d*	Quantity A *abc*		Quantity B *c − d*
−2	−1	1	2	$(-2)(-1)(1) = 2$	$>$	$1 - 2 = -1$

   In this case, Quantity A is greater, so eliminate choices (B) and (C). Consider what you could change to try to push Quantity B higher. If you minimize *d*, while maximizing *c*, you end up subtracting less. Test extremes to maximize *c*.

a	*b*	*c*	*d*	Quantity A *abc*		Quantity B *c − d*
−2	−1	100	101	$(-2)(-1)(100) = 200$	$>$	$100 - 101 = -1$

   Quantity A is greater again. What if you tried to minimize *a* or *b* (or both)? Because *a* and *b* are both negative, they'll multiply to a positive, so if you minimize them, that will just make the quantity *abc* even greater.

Further, since *a* and *b* are both negative while *c* is positive, the product *abc* will always be positive. And since *c* and *d* are positive and *d* is greater than *c*, the difference *c* − *d* must be negative. Trying fractions rather than integers won't change these basic relationships.

The correct answer is (A): Quantity A is greater.

8. **(C)**

    Since $xy > 0$, *x* and *y* have the same sign. Either both are positive or both are negative; test both possibilities.

x	y	Quantity A $\frac{x}{\lvert x \rvert}$		Quantity B $\frac{y}{\lvert y \rvert}$
−2	−3	$\frac{-2}{\lvert -2 \rvert} = \frac{-2}{2} = -1$	=	$\frac{-3}{\lvert -3 \rvert} = \frac{-3}{3} = -1$
2	3	$\frac{2}{\lvert 2 \rvert} = \frac{2}{2} = 1$	=	$\frac{3}{\lvert 3 \rvert} = \frac{3}{3} = 1$

    If both are negative, then the two quantities equal −1. This will be true regardless of what the values of *x* and *y* are, since the values themselves cancel out in each fraction. Likewise, if both are positive, then both quantities equal 1. In either situation, the two quantities are always equal.

    The correct answer is (C): The two quantities are equal.

UNIT TWO

Algebra

This unit covers algebra in all its various forms (and disguises) on the GRE. You will learn fundamental techniques and nuanced strategies to manipulate algebraic expressions and to solve for unknown variables of every type in equations and inequalities.

In This Unit:

- Chapter 4: Equations
- Chapter 5: Exponents and Roots
- Chapter 6: Formulas and Functions
- Chapter 7: Inequalities and Systems of Equations
- Chapter 8: QC Gameplan: Simplify

CHAPTER 4
Equations

In This Chapter:

- The Order of Operations (PEMDAS)
- Fraction Bars as Grouping Symbols
- Solving for a Variable with One Equation
- Solving Absolute Value Equations
- Check Your Skills Answer Key
- Problem Set
- Solutions

CHAPTER 4 Equations

Algebra is quite common on the GRE. In this chapter, you'll learn how to use the order of operations to simplify and solve numerical expressions and algebraic equations (with variables), including equations that contain absolute value symbols.

The Order of Operations (PEMDAS)

While it's nice that the GRE gives you a calculator, it's still possible to get in trouble if you don't follow the correct **Order of Operations**. Different mathematical operations, such as addition, multiplication, and square roots, must be performed in a specific order. Consider this expression:

$$3 + 4 \times (5 - 1) - 3^2 \times 2 = ?$$

The GRE probably won't ask you to compute something like this directly, but it's useful to practice the order of operations on numerical expressions before you move on to simplifying equations and solving for variables.

There's a standardized order to rely on any time you are simplifying an expression. In the correct order, the six operations are **P**arentheses, **E**xponents (and Roots), **M**ultiplication/**D**ivision, and **A**ddition/**S**ubtraction (or **PEMDAS**).

Depending on where you grew up, you may have learned this acronym as **BEDMAS** (**B**rackets, **E**xponents, **D**ivision/**M**ultiplication, **A**ddition/**S**ubtraction) or **BODMAS** (**B**rackets, **O**rder, **D**ivision/**M**ultiplication, **A**ddition/**S**ubtraction). All of these acronyms mean exactly the same thing: PEMDAS = BEDMAS = BODMAS.

Multiplication can be expressed with a multiplication sign ($\times$) or with parentheses: $(5)(4) = 5 \times 4 = 20$. Division can be expressed with a division sign ($\div$), a slash (/), or a fraction bar (—): $20 \div 5 = 20/5 = \frac{20}{5} = 4$. As mentioned earlier in this book, multiplying or dividing by an odd quantity of negative numbers creates a negative result:

$$4 \times (-2) = -8 \qquad \frac{-8}{-2} = 4$$

PEMDAS is a useful acronym to remember the order in which operations should be performed. Notice, however, that there are really only four levels of operations, as illustrated below. Multiplication and division are on the same level, just as addition and subtraction are.

$$P \; E \; \genfrac{}{}{0pt}{}{M}{D} \genfrac{}{}{0pt}{}{A}{S} \longrightarrow$$

Unit Two: **Algebra**

Here's a quick review of the basic operations:

Parentheses	( ) or [ ] or { }	Parentheses group terms together, isolating them from the rest of the expression. For this reason, simplify anything in parentheses first, before proceeding with the rest of the expression.
Exponents and Roots	5^2 ← these numbers $\sqrt{}$	The exponent tells you how many times to multiply the base number. For example, 5^2 ("five squared," or "five to the second power") is $5 \times 5 = 25$. Roots undo that; $\sqrt{25} = 5$. Exponents and roots have the same priority, so you can do them in either order. For instance, you can solve $\sqrt{9^2}$ as $\sqrt{81} = 9$ or as $3^2 = 9$.
Multiplication and Division	$\times$ $\div$	These operations can undo each other, so they have the same priority. Multiplication can be done in any order: $7 \times 4 = 4 \times 7 = 28$. However, division must be read from left to right: $10 \div 5 = 2$, but $5 \div 10 = \frac{1}{2}$. When multiplication and division are both present in an expression or equation, go in order from left to right. For example, to solve $10 \div 5 \times 5$, divide first to get 2, then multiply by 5 to get 10. If you multiplied first, you'd get the incorrect answer of $10 \div 25 = 0.4$.
Addition and Subtraction	$+$ $-$	These can also undo each other and have the same priority: $8 + 7 - 7 = 8$. Addition, like multiplication, is the same in any order. Subtraction is like division in that order matters, so do those parts of an expression from left to right.

Exponents were introduced in Chapter 2: Exponents, and will be covered in depth in the next chapter. For now, there are some common exponents and roots that are helpful to memorize. Feel free to use the reference below while studying this chapter, and then make flash cards for any that you haven't memorized yet.

$$
\begin{array}{rcl rcl}
1^1 &=& 1 & \sqrt{1} &=& 1 \\
2^2 &=& 4 & \sqrt{4} &=& 2 \\
2^3 &=& 8 & \sqrt[3]{8} &=& 2 \\
2^4 &=& 16 & \sqrt[4]{16} &=& 2 \\
3^2 &=& 9 & \sqrt{9} &=& 3 \\
3^3 &=& 27 & \sqrt[3]{27} &=& 3 \\
4^2 &=& 16 & \sqrt{16} &=& 4 \\
4^3 &=& 64 & \sqrt[3]{64} &=& 4 \\
5^2 &=& 25 & \sqrt{25} &=& 5 \\
5^3 &=& 125 & \sqrt[3]{125} &=& 5 \\
\end{array}
$$

Chapter 4: **Equations**

Use the order of operations and the exponents table to simplify the sample expression:

	$3 + 4 \times (5 - 1) - 3^2 \times 2$
Parentheses	$3 + 4 \times (4) - 3^2 \times 2$
Exponents	$3 + 4 \times (4) - 9 \times 2$
Multiplication and Division (left to right)	$3 + 16 - 18$
Addition and Subtraction (left to right)	$3 + 16 - 18 = 19 - 18 = 1$

Try each of the following problems first on your own, then review the explanation:

$$5 - 3 \times 4^3 \div (7 - 1)$$

	$5 - 3 \times 4^3 \div (7 - 1)$
Parentheses	$5 - 3 \times 4^3 \div 6$
Exponents	$5 - 3 \times 64 \div 6$
Multiplication and Division	$5 - 192 \div 6$ $5 - 32$
Addition and Subtraction	-27

Do take advantage of the calculator, but write out your steps and do one computation at a time. That will lessen the chance that you get the answer wrong due to a careless mistake.

Here's the second problem:

$$32 \div 2^4 \times (5 - 3^2)$$

Here's the solution in order. Notice that PEMDAS must be followed even within the parentheses: first solve 3^2, then subtract it from 5.

	$32 \div 2^4 \times (5 - 3^2)$
Parentheses	$32 \div 2^4 \times (5 - 9)$ $32 \div 2^4 \times -4$
Exponents	$32 \div 16 \times -4$
Multiplication and Division	$2 \times -4\ -8$
Addition and Subtraction	Already completed because it was inside the parentheses

Unit Two: **Algebra**

Check Your Skills

Simplify the following expressions.

1. $-4 + \frac{12}{3} = \boxed{}$

2. $(5 - 8) \times 10 - 7 = \boxed{}$

3. $-3 \times 12 \div 4 \times 8 + (4 - 6) = \boxed{}$

4. $2^4 \times \frac{(8 \div 2 - 1)}{(9 - 3)} = \boxed{}$

Answers can be found on page 107.

4. Fraction Bars as Grouping Symbols

Consider this expression:

$$\frac{5^2 - 10}{1 + 2}$$

There are no parentheses, but there's still a grouping symbol. The fraction bar not only acts to signal division, it also acts to group terms together. Even though no parentheses are written, interpret the previous expression this way:

$$\frac{(5^2 - 10)}{(1 + 2)}$$

Everything in the numerator (top of the fraction) is grouped together, and so is everything in the denominator (bottom of the fraction).

> **Key Concept**
>
> In any expression with a fraction bar, pretend that there are parentheses around the numerator and denominator of the fraction. Then simplify using PEMDAS.

$$\frac{(5^2 - 10)}{(1 + 2)} = \frac{(25 - 10)}{(1 + 2)} = \frac{(15)}{(3)} = 5$$

This may not seem to make much difference as long as the fraction bar remains in the expression, but consider this example:

$$\frac{x + 3}{2} - \frac{2x - 1}{2}$$

Because the two fractions have the same denominator, you can combine them into one big fraction—but add parentheses before you do so:

$$\frac{(x + 3) - (2x - 1)}{2}$$

98

Here's where the parentheses become important. When you simplify, distribute the subtraction sign in the middle to *both* terms inside the second set of parentheses, turning −1 into +1:

$$\frac{x + 3 - 2x + 1}{2}$$

And finally combine the like terms in the numerator:

$$\frac{-x + 4}{2}$$

Without the parentheses, it would be easy to forget to distribute the negative sign to both 2*x* and −1. This is a common source of careless errors.

Check Your Skills

5. Simplify: $\frac{a + 4}{3} - \frac{2a - 2}{3}$

Answers can be found on page 108.

Solving for a Variable with One Equation

Terms, Expressions, and Equations

So far, you've been dealing only with expressions. An **expression** is a set of numbers and/or symbols connected by at least one operator. For example, here are three expressions:

$$5(2)^3 \div 4$$

$$\frac{8}{y} + \frac{y}{8}$$

$$3x^2 - x + 5$$

Each expression is composed of at least one **term**. Each term in the expression is separated from the other terms by addition or subtraction. You can separate the expressions above into one, two, and three terms, respectively:

$5(2)^3 \div 4$	One Term:	$5(2)^3 \div 4$
$\frac{8}{y} + \frac{y}{8}$	Two Terms:	$\frac{8}{y}$ and $\frac{y}{8}$
$3x^2 - x + 5$	Three Terms:	$3x^2$, x, and 5

Recognizing distinct terms is an important part of working with **equations**. An equation is created by putting one expression equal to another expression. Another way to think of an equation is as a sentence: "Something equals something else." The somethings are each expression.

Pretty much everything you will be doing with equations is related to one basic principle: You can do anything to one side of the equation, as long as you also do the same thing to the other side of the equation.

Unit Two: Algebra

Take the equation $3 + 5 = 8$. If you want to subtract 5 from the left side of the equation, you can, but you also must subtract 5 from the right side as well:

$$\begin{array}{rcr} 3 + 5 &=& 8 \\ -5 && -5 \\ \hline 3 &=& 3 \end{array}$$

> **Key Concept**
>
> You can make a change to an equation as long as you make the same change to both sides.

In many cases you will solve for a variable by isolating it on one side of the equation:

$$\begin{array}{rcr} x + 5 &=& 8 \\ -5 && -5 \\ \hline x &=& 3 \end{array}$$

Solving Equations

What does it mean to solve an equation? What are you really doing when you manipulate algebraic equations?

Solving an equation means finding a number that, when substituted in for the variable, makes the equation *true*.

Take the equation $2x + 7 = 15$. What value of x will make this equation true? What if you plugged in 3 for x? You would get the following:

$$\begin{aligned} 2x + 7 &= 15 \\ 2(3) + 7 &= 15 \text{ ?} \\ 6 + 7 &= 15 \text{ ?} \\ 13 &= 15 \text{ ?} \end{aligned}$$

But 13 does *not* equal 15; this is false. Therefore, $x = 3$ is *not* a solution for this equation.

If, on the other hand, you tried $x = 4$, you would get $2(4) + 7 = 15$, which does simplify to the true statement $15 = 15$. Since this equation is true, $x = 4$ is a solution to the equation.

If you had to use trial and error, this process could take a very long time. The following sections will explain how to manipulate equations to find the solutions efficiently and accurately.

Isolating a Variable

You can make a change to an equation as long as you make the same change to both sides. What changes are you allowed to make? Try this problem:

$$\text{If } 5(x - 1)^3 - 30 = 10, \text{ then } x = \text{ ?}$$

100

To solve for a variable, *isolate* it—that is, get it by itself on one side of the equals sign. The good news is that all of the changes you need to make to this equation to isolate x will use what you've already learned—PEMDAS operations—but in *reverse order*.

To get x by itself, cancel every term other than x from that side of the equation. Start with Addition and Subtraction, the last step in PEMDAS. The 30 is subtracted on the left side of the equation. To move it to the other side, perform the opposite operation to cancel it out: *Add* 30 to both sides:

$$5(x-1)^3 - 30 = 10$$
$$+30 \quad +30$$
$$5(x-1)^3 = 40$$

Next, deal with Multiplication and Division. The expression in the parentheses is multiplied by 5, so divide both sides of the equation by 5 to move that value to the right side of the equation:

$$\frac{\cancel{5}(x-1)^3}{\cancel{5}} = \frac{40}{5}$$
$$(x-1)^3 = 8$$

Next, deal with Exponents. Roots are the opposite of exponents. Since the left side of the equation is raised to the third power, take the third root of both sides, also known as the cube root:

$$\sqrt[3]{(x-1)^3} = \sqrt[3]{8}$$
$$(x-1) = 2$$

Finally, deal with the parentheses. First, they can now be dropped:

$$x - 1 = 2$$

Next, add 1 to both sides, and you have $x = 3$. If you plug 3 back in for x in the original equation (a step worth doing as you're learning), you'll find that this value makes the original equation true:

$$5(x-1)^3 - 30 = 10$$
$$5(3-1)^3 - 30 = 10$$
$$5(2)^3 - 30 = 10$$
$$5(8) - 30 = 10$$
$$40 - 30 = 10$$
$$10 = 10$$

To simplify when you have only real numbers, use PEMDAS in normal order. However, when you need to isolate a variable, you can't just solve in the normal order—the variable gets in the way. Instead, use PEMDAS in reverse order to "unwind" the equation and get the variable by itself.

Unit Two: **Algebra**

Try this problem:

$$4\sqrt{x-6} + 7 = 19, \text{ then } x = ?$$

	$4\sqrt{x-6} + 7 = 19$
Addition/Subtraction *Subtract 7 from both sides*	$4\sqrt{x-6} = 12$
Multiplication/Division *Divide both sides by 4*	$\sqrt{x-6} = 3$
Exponents/Roots *Square both sides*	$(\sqrt{x-6})^2 = (3)^2$ $(x-6) = 9$
Parentheses *Add 6 to both sides*	$x = 15$

4

> **Key Concept**
>
> To isolate a variable, perform the PEMDAS operations in reverse order.
>
> 1. Addition/Subtraction
>
> 2. Multiplication/Division
>
> 3. Exponents/Roots
>
> 4. Parentheses

Check Your Skills

6. $3(x+4)^3 - 5 = 19$

    $x = $ ☐

7. $\dfrac{3x-7}{2} + 20 = 6$

    $x = $ ☐

8. $\sqrt[3]{(x+5)} - 7 = -8$

    $x = $ ☐

Answers can be found on page 108.

Equation Clean-up Moves

How would you solve for x in the following equation?

$$\frac{5x - 3(4 - x)}{2x} = 10$$

Now x appears in multiple parts of the equation. The first move is to *get variables out of the denominator*. Multiply both sides of the equation by the *entire* denominator:

$$2x \times \frac{5x - 3(4 - x)}{2x} = 10 \times 2x$$

When you multiply a fraction by its denominator, the entire denominator is canceled out, leaving you with this:

$$5x - 3(4 - x) = 20x$$

What should you do next? At some point, you're going to have to get all the terms that contain an x together. Right now, however, that x sitting inside the parentheses seems pretty tough to get to. To make that x more accessible, *simplify grouped terms* within the equation. The 3 on the outside of the parentheses can be distributed to the terms inside, so you could *distribute* it. Multiply the 3 by each term inside the parentheses, one at a time:

$$3(4 - x)$$
$$12 - 3x$$

The full equation now looks like this:

$$5x - (12 - 3x) = 20x$$

Next, subtract what's in the parentheses from $5x$ to get rid of the parentheses altogether. Just as you distributed the 3 to *both* terms inside the parentheses, distribute the subtraction sign to each term:

$$5x - (12) - (-3x) = 20x$$
$$5x - 12 + 3x = 20x$$

Because subtracting a negative number is the same as adding a positive number, the two negative signs turn into a positive.

Finally, *combine like terms*. "Like terms" are terms with the same variables and exponents (if any). For example, $3x$ and $5x$ are like terms because they both have a single power of x, so they can be added to get $8x$. Likewise, $2x^2$ and $3x^2$ are like terms, because they both contain x-squared, so they can be added to get $5x^2$.

Back to the problem. The expressions $5x$ and $3x$ are like terms and are on the same side of the equation already, so combine them:

$$8x - 12 = 20x$$

Unit Two: Algebra

Now put the 8*x* and the 20*x* on the same side of the equation. Which one should you move? The best move on this problem is to move the 8*x* to the right side of the equation, so that one side of the equation will contain only numbers (−12) and the other side will have all of the terms that contain variables (8*x* and 20*x*). It's also generally easier to subtract smaller values from larger ones:

$$8x - 12 = 20x$$
$$\text{Subtract } 8x: \quad -8x \quad\quad -8x$$
$$-12 = 12x$$
$$\text{Divide by 12:} \quad \div 12 \quad\quad \div 12$$
$$-1 = x$$

Ultimately, all of the PEMDAS operations and simplification moves have one goal: to get a variable by itself so you can determine its value. This problem began with four terms in the equation: 5*x*, −12, 3*x*, and 20*x*. The goal is to get all of the terms containing an *x* on one side of the equation and all of the terms that only contain numbers on the other side of the equation.

> **Strategy Tip:**
>
> Use these moves to simplify an equation:
>
> 1. Get variables out of the denominator by multiplying both sides by the entire denominator.
>
> 2. Simplify grouped terms by multiplying or distributing.
>
> 3. Combine like terms.

Check Your Skills

9. $\dfrac{11 + 3(x + 4)}{x - 3} = 7$

   x = ☐

10. $\dfrac{-6 - 5(3 - x)}{2 - x} = 6$

    x = ☐

11. $\dfrac{2x + 6(9 - 2x)}{x - 4} = -3$

    x = ☐

Answers can be found on page 109.

Chapter 4: **Equations**

Solving Absolute Value Equations

On the GRE, you'll sometimes see a variable inside the absolute value symbol:

$|y| = 3$

This indicates that y is 3 units away from 0, but y could be 3 or -3. Which is it? Without additional information, there's no way to know. All you can say is that y is either 3 or -3.

When there is a variable inside an absolute value, expect the variable to have two possible values. Although you will not always be able to determine which of the two is the correct value, it is important to be able to find both. Following is a step-by-step process for finding all solutions to an equation that contains a variable inside an absolute value:

Step 1: Isolate the absolute value expression on one side of the equation. In this case, the absolute value expression is already isolated.	$|y| = 3$
Step 2: Take what's inside the absolute value sign and set up two equations. The first sets the variable equal to the positive value of the other side of the equation, and the second sets the variable equal to the negative value of the other side.	$y = +3$ or $y = -3$

You may have found Step 2 familiar. It's the same as the process introduced in Chapter 2: Exponents for dealing with even exponents:

Solving Exponents	Solving Absolute Values
$(x - 2)^2 = 16$	$\|x - 2\| = 16$
$x - 2 = +4$ or $x - 2 = -4$	$x - 2 = +16$ or $x - 2 = -16$
$x = 6$ or $x = -2$	$x = 18$ or $x = -14$

In both cases, there are two possible answers. To find the answer, solve the equation for both the positive and negative solutions.

Here's a slightly more difficult problem, using the same technique:

$6 \times |2x + 4| = 30$

To solve this, use the same approach:

Step 1: Isolate the absolute value expression on one side of the equation or inequality.	$6 \times \|2x + 4\| = 30$ $\|2x + 4\| = 5$
Step 2: Set up two equations—the positive and the negative versions.	$2x + 4 = +5$ or $2x + 4 = -5$
Step 3: Solve both equations.	$2x = 1$ or $2x = -9$
As expected, there are two possible values for x.	$x = \frac{1}{2}$ or $x = -\frac{9}{2}$

Unit Two: **Algebra**

Check Your Skills

Solve the following equations with absolute values in them.

12. $|a| = 6$

13. $|x + 2| = 5$

14. $|3y - 4| = 17$

Answers can be found on page 110.

Chapter 4: **Equations**

Check Your Skills Answer Key

1. **0**

    $-4 + \dfrac{12}{3} =$

    $-4 + 4 =$ Divide first.

    $-4 + 4 = 0$ Then add the two numbers.

2. **−37**

    $(5 - 8) \times 10 - 7 =$

    $(-3) \times 10 - 7 =$ First, combine what is inside the parentheses.

    $-30 - 7 =$ Then multiply −3 by 10.

    $-30 - 7 = -37$ Subtract the two numbers.

3. **−74**

    $-3 \times 12 \div 4 \times 8 + (4 - 6) =$

    $-3 \times 12 \div 4 \times 8 + (-2) =$ First, combine what's in the parentheses.

    $-36 \div 4 \times 8 + (-2) =$ Multiply −3 by 12.

    $-9 \times 8 + (-2) =$ Divide −36 by 4.

    $-72 + (-2) =$ Multiply −9 by 8.

    $-72 - 2 = -74$ Subtract 2.

4. **8**

    $2^4 \times \dfrac{(8 \div 2 - 1)}{(9 - 3)} =$

    $2^4 \times \dfrac{(4 - 1)}{(6)} =$ Parentheses first. Division before subtraction.

    $16 \times \dfrac{(3)}{(6)} =$ Finish parentheses and move to the exponent.

    $\dfrac{48}{6} = 8$ Work multiplication/division left to right.

Unit Two: **Algebra**

5. $\dfrac{6-a}{3}$ or $\dfrac{-a+6}{3}$

   $\dfrac{a+4}{3} - \dfrac{2a-2}{3}$

   $= \dfrac{(a+4)}{3} - \dfrac{(2a-2)}{3}$ Add parentheses to group the fractional terms.

   $= \dfrac{(a+4) - (2a-2)}{3}$ Combine the two fractions into one fraction.

   $= \dfrac{a+4-2a+2}{3}$ Distribute the negative sign and drop parentheses.

   $= \dfrac{-a+6}{3} = \dfrac{6-a}{3}$ Combine like terms. Rearrange the fraction only if needed.

6. -2

   $3(x+4)^3 - 5 = 19$

   $3(x+4)^3 = 24$ Add 5 to both sides.

   $(x+4)^3 = 8$ Divide both sides by 3.

   $(x+4) = 2$ Take the cube root of both sides.

   $x = -2$ Remove the parentheses and subtract 4 from both sides.

7. -7

   Because it's part of a fraction, treat the expression $3x - 7$ as if it has parentheses around it.

   $\dfrac{3x-7}{2} + 20 = 6$

   $\dfrac{(3x-7)}{2} = -14$ Subtract 20 from both sides.

   $(3x-7) = -28$ Multiply both sides by 2.

   $3x = -21$ Drop the parentheses and add 7 to both sides.

   $x = -7$ Divide both sides by 3.

8. -6

   $\sqrt[3]{(x+5)} - 7 = -8$

   $\sqrt[3]{(x+5)} = -1$ Add 7 to both sides.

   $x + 5 = -1$ Cube both sides; remove parentheses. $(-1)^3 = -1$.

   $x = -6$ Subtract 5 from both sides.

Chapter 4: **Equations**

9. **11**

$$\frac{11 + 3(x + 4)}{x - 3} = 7$$

$11 + 3(x + 4) = 7(x - 3)$	Multiply both sides by the denominator $(x - 3)$.
$11 + 3x + 12 = 7x - 21$	Simplify grouped terms by distributing.
$23 + 3x = 7x - 21$	Combine like terms (11 and 12).
$23 = 4x - 21$	Subtract $3x$ from both sides.
$44 = 4x$	Add 21 to both sides.
$11 = x$	Divide both sides by 4.

10. **3**

$$\frac{-6 - 5(3 - x)}{2 - x} = 6$$

$-6 - 5(3 - x) = 6(2 - x)$	Multiply both sides by the denominator $(2 - x)$.
$-6 - 15 + 5x = 12 - 6x$	Simplify grouped terms by distributing.
$-21 + 5x = 12 - 6x$	Combine like terms (-6 and -15).
$-21 + 11x = 12$	Add $6x$ to both sides.
$11x = 33$	Add 21 to both sides.
$x = 3$	Divide both sides by 11.

11. **6**

$$\frac{2x + 6(9 - 2x)}{x - 4} = -3$$

$2x + 6(9 - 2x) = -3(x - 4)$	Multiply both sides by the denominator $(x - 4)$.
$2x + 54 - 12x = -3x + 12$	Simplify grouped terms by distributing.
$-10x + 54 = -3x + 12$	Combine like terms ($2x$ and $-12x$).
$54 = 7x + 12$	Add $10x$ to both sides.
$42 = 7x$	Subtract 12 from both sides.
$6 = x$	Divide both sides by 7.

Unit Two: **Algebra**

12. **6 or −6**

$|a| = 6$

$a = +6$ or $a = -6$

13. **3 or −7**

$|x + 2| = 5$

$x + 2 = +5$ or $x + 2 = -5$
$x = 3$ or $x = -7$

14. **7 or $-\frac{13}{3}$**

$|3y - 4| = 17$

$3y - 4 = +17$ or $3y - 4 = -17$
$3y = 21$ or $3y = -13$
$y = 7$ or $y = -\frac{13}{3}$

Chapter 4: **Equations**

Problem Set

> As mentioned in the Chapter 3 problem set, this problem set does not provide the answer choices for the Quantitative Comparison problems. If you aren't sure what the QC answer choice options are, check Chapter 3: QC Structure (and make yourself some flash cards to help memorize these choices).

1. Simplify: $66 \div (-33) \times |-9|$

2. Evaluate each of the five expressions, labeled (a) through (e), for both $x = 2$ and $x = -2$:

   (a) $-3x^2$ (b) $-3x^3$ (c) $3x^2$ (d) $(-3x)^2$ (e) $(-3x)^3$

3. Simplify: $(4 + 12 \div 3 - 18) - [-11 - (-4)]$

4. Simplify: $\left[\dfrac{4+8}{2-(-6)}\right] - [4 + 8 \div 2 - (-6)]$

5. Simplify: $(0.08)^2 \div 0.4$

6. Which of the parentheses in the following expressions could be removed without changing the value of the expression and are therefore unnecessary?

   (a) $- (5^2) - (12 - 7)$

   (b) $(x + y) - (w + z) - (a \times b)$

7. Simplify: $(4 - y) - 2(2y - 3)$

8. If $2(2 - 3x) - (4 + x) = 7$, what is x?

9. If $x = 2$, $y = 5$, $z = -3$, and $w = 8$, what is $2|x - y| + |z + w|$?

10. Simplify: $-\dfrac{30}{5} - \dfrac{18 - 9}{-3}$

11. Simplify: $(4.5 \times 2 + 6.6) \div 0.003$

12. Simplify: $[8 - (1.08 + 6.9)]^2$

13.
Quantity A	**Quantity B**
$\left(1 + \dfrac{2}{5}\right) \times 0.25$	0.35

14.
Quantity A	**Quantity B**
$3 \times (5 + 6) \div -1$	$3 \times 5 + 6 \div -1$

Unit Two: **Algebra**

Solutions

1. **−18**

   Multiplication and division are the same tier in the order of operations. Keep track of the changing signs. The 66 ÷ (−33) portion yields a negative number (−2). The absolute value of −9 is 9. Again, multiply a negative by a positive: −2 × 9 = −18.

2.

   When x = 2:
   - (a) $-3x^2 = -3(4) = -12$
   - (b) $-3x^3 = -3(8) = -24$
   - (c) $3x^2 = 3(4) = 12$
   - (d) $(-3x)^2 = (-6)^2 = 36$
   - (e) $(-3x)^3 = (-6)^3 = -216$

   When x = −2:
   - (a) $-3x^2 = -3(4) = -12$
   - (b) $-3x^3 = -3(-8) = 24$
   - (c) $3x^2 = 3(4) = 12$
   - (d) $(-3x)^2 = 6^2 = 36$
   - (e) $(-3x)^3 = 6^3 = 216$

   First evaluate parentheses, then exponents, then multiplication.

3. **−3**

$$(4 + 12 \div 3 - 18) - [-11 - (-4)] =$$

$$(4 + 4 - 18) - (-11 + 4) =$$

$$(-10) - (-7) =$$

$$-10 + 7 = -3$$

4. **−12.5**

   Evaluate the two parentheticals separately, then subtract the result. Here is the left half of the expression.

$$\left[\frac{4+8}{2-(-6)}\right] = \left[\frac{4+8}{2+6}\right] = \left[\frac{12}{8}\right] = \frac{3}{2} = 1.5$$

   Here is the right half of the expression, following PEMDAS:

$$[4 + 8 \div 2 - (-6)]$$

   [4 + 4 + 6]   Multiplication/Division

   14   Addition/Subtraction

   Subtract the two to get the final result: 1.5 − 14 = −12.5.

112

5. **0.016**

   Use the calculator, but write your work out as you go to minimize potential mistakes.

   $$\frac{(0.08)^2}{0.4} = \frac{0.0064}{0.4} = 0.016$$

6. **(a) (5^2)**

   The parentheses around 5^2 are *unnecessary*, because this exponent is performed before the negation and before the subtraction. The parentheses around $12 - 7$ are *necessary*. As the expression is originally written, 7 is subtracted from 12 first: $25 - (12 - 7) = 25 - 5 = 20$. If the parentheses were removed, however, then the math would be done left-to-right and the answer would change: $25 - 12 - 7 = 13 - 7 = 6$.

   (b) $(x + y)$ and $(a \times b)$

   The first and last pairs of parentheses are *unnecessary*. For $(x + y)$, the addition is performed before the neighboring subtraction by default, because addition and subtraction are performed from left to right. For $(a \times b)$, the multiplication is the first operation to be performed, so the parentheses surrounding this term are *unnecessary*. The middle parentheses, however, are *necessary* to ensure that w and z are added together before they are subtracted from $x + y$. With the parentheses, you subtract both w and z. Without them, you'd subtract w and add z.

7. **$10 - 5y$**

   The first pair of parentheses is unnecessary and can be dropped. For the second pair, distribute the -2, then combine like terms:

   $$(4 - y) - 2(2y - 3) =$$
   $$4 - y - 4y + 6 = 10 - 5y$$

8. **-1**

   Simplify the left-hand side of the equation to isolate x.

   $$2(2 - 3x) - (4 + x) = 7$$
   $$4 - 6x - 4 - x = 7$$
   $$-7x = 7$$
   $$x = -1$$

Unit Two: **Algebra**

9. **11**

   Perform the operations within the absolute value bars before taking the absolute value or performing outside operations.

   $$2|x - y| + |z + w| =$$
   $$2|2 - 5| + |-3 + 8| =$$
   $$2|-3| + |5| =$$
   $$2(3) + 5 = 11$$

   When you deal with more complicated absolute value expressions, such as $|x - y|$ in this example, *never* change the signs of the individual numbers to positive signs. For instance, in this problem $|x - y| = |2 - 5|$, not $|2 + 5|$. The absolute value occurs only after all the work within the absolute value signs has been completed.

10. **−3**

    Simplify each term before subtracting.

    $$\frac{-30}{5} - \frac{18 - 9}{-3} =$$
    $$-6 - \frac{9}{-3} =$$
    $$-6 - (-3) = -3$$

11. **5,200**

    Start with the multiplication within the parentheses.

    $$(4.5 \times 2 + 6.6) \div 0.003 =$$
    $$(9 + 6.6) \div 0.003 =$$
    $$15.6 \div 0.003 =$$

    From here, use the calculator to get 5,200.

12. **0.0004**

    Start with the interior parentheses. The sum of 1.08 and 6.9 is 7.98. Subtract that from 8 and square the result. (Feel free to use the calculator—just write out the steps as you go!)

    $$[8 - (1.08 + 6.9)]^2 =$$
    $$[8 - (7.98)]^2 =$$
    $$[0.02]^2 = 0.0004$$

13. **(C)**

    Simplify the expression in Quantity A, then compare it to Quantity B.

Quantity A	**Quantity B**
$\left(1 + \frac{2}{5}\right) \times 0.25 =$	0.35
$(1 + 0.4) \times 0.25 =$	
$1.4 \times 0.25 = 0.35$	

    Quantity A equals Quantity B.

    The correct answer is (C): The two quantities are equal.

14. **(B)**

    The only difference between the two quantities is the parentheses. Evaluate each quantity, paying special attention to order of operations.

Quantity A	**Quantity B**
$3 \times (5 + 6) \div -1 =$	$3 \times 5 + 6 \div -1 =$
$3 \times (11) \div -1 =$	$15 + 6 \div -1 =$
$33 \div -1 = -33$	$15 + (-6) = 9$

    The correct answer is (B): Quantity B is greater.

CHAPTER 5

Exponents and Roots

In This Chapter:

- Exponents and Roots Language
- Roots as Exponents
- Exponential Equations
- Same Bases
- Same Exponents
- Special Powers
- Special Bases
- Rules of Exponents
- Common Exponent Errors
- Exponents on QC
- Check Your Skills Answer Key
- Problem Set
- Solutions

CHAPTER 5 Exponents and Roots

So far, exponents have been defined as a shorthand way of expressing multiplication. For example, $5^2 = 5 \times 5 = 25$ and $\sqrt{81} = 9$ because $9^2 = 81$. For larger numbers, however, this approach could be prohibitively time consuming, and it's all but impossible when you have variables. In this chapter, you'll learn all of the exponent and root rules that will allow you to combine exponential terms and simplify complex expressions.

Exponents and Roots Language

Have you ever heard the expression, "Wow, that increased exponentially!"? This expression captures the essence of exponents. When a number greater than 1 increases exponentially, it does not merely increase; it increases a significant amount and it does so very rapidly.

In fact, the greater the exponent, the faster the rate of increase. Consider the following progression:

$5^1 = 5$	
$5^2 = 25$	Increased by 20
$5^3 = 125$	Increased by 100
$5^4 = 625$	Increased by 500

This trend holds true when positive bases greater than 1 are raised to higher and higher powers. With many other numbers, though, this trend will *not* necessarily hold true. For example, when the number 1 is raised to any exponent, it does not increase at all; it remains 1.

The expression 4^3 consists of a **base** (4) and an **exponent** (3). This expression is read as "four to the third power" or "four cubed" and means four multiplied by itself three times. Thus, four cubed is $4^3 = 4 \times 4 \times 4 = 64$.

Roots undo exponents. Asking for the cube root of 64 is the same thing as asking "What number, when cubed, gives 64?" Thus, $\sqrt[3]{64} = \sqrt[3]{4 \times 4 \times 4} = 4$. Four cubed is 64, and 64 cube rooted is 4.

Most exponents will be expressed as "the base (raised) to the power of the exponent." So 3^5 is called "three to the fifth power" (and equals 243, incidentally). To undo that, you would take the fifth root of 243, which is written as $\sqrt[5]{243}$ and which equals 3.

Something raised to the second power is called a square, and something raised to the third power is a cube. After that, use the number of the power (fourth power, fifth power, sixth power). For second and third powers, the GRE may use either the special names (square, cube) or the more traditional ones.

Unit Two: Algebra

$7^2 = 49$	7 squared is 49
$5^3 = 125$	5 cubed is 125
$2^4 = 16$	2 to the 4th power is 16
x^{12}	x to the 12th power
3^y	3 to the yth power

$\sqrt{49} = 7$	The square root of 49 is 7
$\sqrt[3]{125} = 5$	The cube root of 125 is 5
$\sqrt[4]{16} = 2$	The fourth root of 16 is 2
$\sqrt[12]{x}$	The 12th root of x
$\sqrt[y]{3}$	The yth root of 3

A root symbol like this $\sqrt{}$ represents a square root; this is the most common kind of root you'll deal with on the GRE. You may also see a little number along with the root symbol, like this: $\sqrt[3]{}$. That number represents the **power** of the root. The example shown is the cube root. If you see a 4, the symbol is telling you to take the fourth root, and so on.

The Calculator

The GRE calculator does have a square root button, but does not have the ability to do any other kind of root. It also can't directly raise something to an exponent. So to calculate 5^3, you would need to plug in $5 \times 5 \times 5$ to get 125. You could plug in $\sqrt{25}$ and get 5, but you could not plug in $\sqrt[3]{125}$.

When you get to Chapter 10: Common Factors, you'll learn how to calculate unusual roots, but for the most common roots, one of the best tools you can use is memorization. If you have memorized that the cube root of 125 is 5, you won't have to worry about testing numbers to find the solution.

Check Your Skills

> **Directions**
>
> In Chapter 4: Equations, you were given a list of commonly used powers and roots to memorize. If you haven't yet memorized them, take some time to do so before testing yourself with this quiz.

1. $1^1 =$ $\sqrt{1} =$
    $2^2 =$ $\sqrt{4} =$
    $2^3 =$ $\sqrt{9} =$
    $2^4 =$ $\sqrt{16} =$
    $3^2 =$ $\sqrt{25} =$
    $3^3 =$ $\sqrt[3]{8} =$
    $4^2 =$ $\sqrt[3]{27} =$
    $4^3 =$ $\sqrt[3]{64} =$
    $5^2 =$ $\sqrt[3]{125} =$
    $5^3 =$ $\sqrt[4]{16} =$

Answers can be found on page 141.

Chapter 5: **Exponents and Roots**

Roots as Exponents

Chapter 4: Equations explained that multiplication and division undo each other, just as exponents and roots do. More specifically, division by a number can be expressed as multiplication by the **reciprocal** of that number. The reciprocal of a number is one over that number. For example, the reciprocal of 3 is $\frac{1}{3}$ and the reciprocal of $\frac{1}{3}$ is 3.

Here's how to write division as multiplication by the reciprocal:

$$15 \div 3 = 15 \times \frac{1}{3} = 5$$

Dividing by 3 is equivalent to multiplying by the reciprocal of 3, which is $\frac{1}{3}$. Similarly, roots can be expressed as reciprocals of exponents. For example:

$$\sqrt[3]{27} = (27)^{\frac{1}{3}} = 3$$

Taking the cube root of 27 is equivalent to raising 27 to the power of $\frac{1}{3}$. This doesn't change the math required, only the way it is written. Here are a few more examples:

$$\sqrt{4} = 4^{\frac{1}{2}}$$
$$\sqrt[3]{x} = x^{\frac{1}{3}}$$
$$\sqrt[8]{32} = 32^{\frac{1}{8}}$$
$$\sqrt[y]{12} = 12^{\frac{1}{y}}$$

Exponential Equations

Unknown Base

Sometimes the base of an expression will be a variable. The key to solving algebraic expressions with an unknown base is to make use of the fact that exponents and roots are inverses. In the equation $x^3 = 8$, x is raised to the third power, so to eliminate the exponent, take the cube root of both sides of the equation:

$$x^3 = 8$$
$$\sqrt[3]{x^3} = \sqrt[3]{8}$$
$$x = 2$$

This process also works in reverse. If you are presented with the equation $\sqrt{x} = 6$, eliminate the square root by squaring both sides. Square root and squaring cancel each other out in the same way that cube root and raising something to the third power cancel each other out. Solve this equation, by squaring both sides: $(\sqrt{x})^2 = 6^2$, thus $x = 36$.

Unit Two: **Algebra**

There is one commonly tested danger. When a variable is raised to an even exponent, expect two solutions, because an even exponent hides the sign of the base. For instance, in the equation $y^2 = 100$, the value of y can be either 10 or -10. When you take a square root, consider adding a $\pm$ to the equation to remind yourself to find both solutions.

$$y^2 = 100$$
$$\sqrt{y^2} = \pm\sqrt{100}$$
$$y = 10 \quad \text{or} \quad y = -10$$

Check Your Skills

> Solve for *x* in the following equations.

2. $x^3 = 64$

3. $x^2 = 121$

Answers can be found on page 141.

Unknown Exponent

What if the variable is in the exponent? You can't make use of the relationship between exponents and roots to help solve for the variable in the equation $2^x = 8$. Instead, rewrite the equation to get the same base on both sides of the equal sign.

In this case, replace 8 with its equivalent value of 2^3 to get the equation $2^x = 2^3$. Now that the same base is on both sides of the equation, the exponents must be equal. Cancel the bases and set the exponents equal to each other: $x = 3$.

You can also use this same approach when the variable is in the base, as shown below.

> **Key Concept**
>
> To solve for an unknown exponent, transform the bases on both sides of the equation to equal one another.
>
> | Unknown Base | Unknown Exponent |
> |---|---|
> | $x^3 = 8$ | $2^y = 8$ |
> | $x^3 = 2^3$ | $2^y = 2^3$ |
> | $x = 2$ | $y = 3$ |

Chapter 5: **Exponents and Roots**

This approach can be applied to more complicated exponents as well:

Given:	$3^{x+2} = 27$
Rewrite 27 as 3^3:	$3^{x+2} = 3^3$
Drop the bases and set the exponents equal:	$x + 2 = 3$
Solve for x:	$x = 1$

Check Your Skills

4. $7^{x-2} = 49$

    $x = $ ☐

5. $5^{3x} = 125$

    $x = $ ☐

6. $2^x = 64$

    $x = $ ☐

Answers can be found on pages 141–142.

Same Bases

The GRE will often ask you to combine exponential terms. In this section you'll learn common shortcuts to combine multiple exponential terms with the same base.

Multiplication

Consider this expression:

$$a^5 \times a^3$$

Since a^5 is 5 a's all multiplied together, and a^3 is 3 a's all multiplied together, you could combine a^5 and a^3 using longhand:

$$a^5 \times a^3 = (a \times a \times a \times a \times a) \times (a \times a \times a)$$

$$= a^8$$

In other words, if you have 5 a's and 3 a's, then you have 8 a's altogether—you can add the original exponents, 5 and 3, to get 8.

Unit Two: Algebra

> **Exponent Rule 1:**
>
> $a^x \times a^y = a^{x+y}$ When asked to *multiply* exponential terms that share a common base, *add* the exponents.

More examples of this rule can be found in the table below. One note: a number written without an exponent is equal to that number raised to the first power. For example, 3 is the same thing as 3^1 or 3 to the first power.

Exponentially	Longhand
$7^3 \times 7^2 =$ $7^{3+2} =$ 7^5	$(7 \times 7 \times 7) \times (7 \times 7) =$ $7 \times 7 \times 7 \times 7 \times 7 =$ 7^5
$5 \times 5^2 \times 5^3 =$ $5^{1+2+3} =$ 5^6	$5 \times (5 \times 5) \times (5 \times 5 \times 5) =$ $5 \times 5 \times 5 \times 5 \times 5 \times 5 =$ 5^6
$f^3 \times f =$ $f^{3+1} =$ f^4	$(f \times f \times f) \times f =$ $f \times f \times f \times f =$ f^4

Because roots are another way to express exponents, they follow the same rule:

$$\sqrt{3} \times \sqrt{3} = 3^{\frac{1}{2}} \times 3^{\frac{1}{2}} = 3^{(\frac{1}{2}+\frac{1}{2})} = 3^1 = 3$$

$$\sqrt[3]{2} \times \sqrt[3]{2} \times \sqrt[3]{2} = 2^{\frac{1}{3}} \times 2^{\frac{1}{3}} \times 2^{\frac{1}{3}} = 2^{(\frac{1}{3}+\frac{1}{3}+\frac{1}{3})} = 2^1 = 2$$

$$\sqrt{5} \times \sqrt{5} \times \sqrt{5} = 5^{\frac{1}{2}} \times 5^{\frac{1}{2}} \times 5^{\frac{1}{2}} = 5^{(\frac{1}{2}+\frac{1}{2}+\frac{1}{2})} = 5^{\frac{3}{2}}$$

You'll learn more about adding fractions later, but one offshoot of Exponent Rule 1 is that **any square root times itself will equal whatever is inside the square root:**

$$\sqrt{2} \times \sqrt{2} = 2$$
$$\sqrt{8} \times \sqrt{8} = 8$$
$$\sqrt{36} \times \sqrt{36} = 36$$

This rule can be generalized as:

$$\sqrt{x} \times \sqrt{x} = x$$

Chapter 5: **Exponents and Roots**

Check Your Skills

> Simplify or solve the following expressions by combining like terms.

7. $b^5 \times b^7$

8. If $2 \times 2^x = 16$, what is x?

Answers can be found on page 142.

Division

You may also be asked, for example, to divide a^5 by a^3. Here's how that looks in longhand:

$$\frac{a^5}{a^3} = \frac{a \times a \times a \times a \times a}{a \times a \times a}$$

In Chapter 10: Common Factors, you'll see more about simplifying fractions, but for now it's sufficient to know that if a number or variable is present on both the top and bottom of the fraction, it can typically be canceled out in both places. For example:

Write out the 2's $\quad \dfrac{2^3}{2^2} = \dfrac{2 \times 2 \times 2}{2 \times 2}$

Cancel out two 2's $\quad = \dfrac{2 \times \cancel{2} \times \cancel{2}}{\cancel{2} \times \cancel{2}}$

$\quad = 2$

Use that same principle to simplify a^5 divided by a^3:

$$\frac{a^5}{a^3} = \frac{a \times a \times a \times a \times a}{a \times a \times a}$$

$$= \frac{a \times \cancel{a} \times \cancel{a} \times \cancel{a} \times a}{\cancel{a} \times \cancel{a} \times \cancel{a}}$$

$$= a \times a$$

$$= a^2$$

If you wrote this out exponentially, it would read:

$a^5 \div a^3 = a^2 \quad$ "*a* to the fifth divided by *a* cubed equals *a* squared"

In other words, if you have 5 *a*'s and you divide out 3 *a*'s, then you are left with 2 *a*'s altogether—you can subtract the original exponents, 5 − 3, to get 2.

> **Exponent Rule 2:**
>
> $a^x \div a^y = a^{x-y}$ $\quad$ When asked to *divide* exponential terms with a common base, *subtract* the exponents.

Unit Two: **Algebra**

Here are some additional examples:

Exponentially	Longhand
$7^5 \div 7^2 = 7^3$	$\dfrac{7 \times 7 \times 7 \times 7 \times 7}{7 \times 7 \times 7} = 7 \times 7 \times 7$
$5^5 \div 5^4 = 5^1$	$\dfrac{5 \times 5 \times 5 \times 5 \times 5}{5 \times 5 \times 5 \times 5} = 5$
$t^4 \div t = t^3$	$\dfrac{t \times t \times t \times t}{t} = t \times t \times t$

Since a variable or number with no exponent has an implied exponent of 1, in the final example, $t = t^1$.

This rule does work equally well for roots, but the GRE is not very likely to test roots in this way. You'll learn more about root division in the next section of this chapter.

Check Your Skills

9. Simplify $\dfrac{y^5}{y^2}$

Answers can be found on page 142.

Powers to Powers

The GRE will occasionally test what happens when a number with one exponent is raised to another power. For example:

$$(a^2)^4$$

The exponent of 4 outside the parentheses means that you'll have four groupings of whatever is *inside* the parentheses. In this case, what's inside the parentheses is *a* squared, or a pair of *a*'s. If you have four pairs of *a*'s, you will have a total of eight *a*'s:

$$(a \times a) \times (a \times a) \times (a \times a) \times (a \times a) = a \times a \times a \times a \times a \times a \times a \times a = a^8$$

This result is exactly what you would get if you multiplied the two exponents (2 and 4) to get 8, leading to the third exponent rule:

> **Exponent Rule 3:**
>
> $(a^x)^y = a^{xy}$ When a number with one exponent is *raised* to another power, *multiply* the two exponents together.

Check Your Skills

> Simplify the following expressions.

10. $(x^4)^3$

11. $(5^3)^2$

Answers can be found on page 142.

Same Exponents

In the previous section, the bases in an expression were always the same. But what happens when the bases are different? Consider these two examples:

$$\text{Example 1: } 2^2 \times 3^2$$

$$\text{Example 2: } \sqrt{3} \times \sqrt{12}$$

In both cases, different bases are multiplied together and the exponent (or root) is the same. When this is the case, group the bases together using the same exponent or root:

$$\text{Example 1: } 2^2 \times 3^2 = (2 \times 3)^2 = (6)^2 = 36$$

$$\text{Example 2: } \sqrt{3} \times \sqrt{12} = \sqrt{3 \times 12} = \sqrt{36} = 6$$

This move is allowed whenever you're asked to multiply or divide *and* the exponent (or root) is the same for all of the terms. Do *not* use this rule when you're asked to add or subtract two terms.

> **Exponent Rule 4:**
>
> $(a^x)(b^x) = (ab)^x$ When multiplying or dividing terms raised to the same
>
> $\dfrac{\sqrt[y]{c}}{\sqrt[y]{d}} = \sqrt[y]{\dfrac{c}{d}}$ power or under the same root, group the terms under a single exponent or root.

This rule works equally well for multiplication and division, even using multiple terms. Here are two examples:

$$\frac{\sqrt[3]{64}}{\sqrt[3]{8}} = \sqrt[3]{\frac{64}{8}} = \sqrt[3]{8} = 2$$

$$\frac{2^2 \times 8^2}{4^2} = \left(\frac{2 \times 8}{4}\right)^2 = (4)^2 = 16$$

Unit Two: **Algebra**

A Compound Base

A **compound base** is a base that has multiple numbers or variables. When the numbers or variables in a compound base are multiplied or divided, there are two options. Either compute the base and then raise the result to the exponent, *or* distribute the exponent to each number in the base. For example:

$$(2 \times 5)^3 = (10)^3 = 1{,}000$$

or

$$(2 \times 5)^3 = 2^3 \times 5^3 = 8 \times 125 = 1{,}000$$

> **Key Concept**
>
> Powers can be distributed among multiplied or divided terms.

You *cannot* do this with a sum or a difference, however. When addition or subtraction appears inside the parentheses, that math must be done first:

Correct	Incorrect
$(2 + 5)^3 = (7)^3 = 343$	$(2 + 5)^3 \neq 2^3 + 5^3$, which is $8 + 125 = 133$
$(5 - 2)^4 = (3)^4 = 81$	$(5 - 2)^4 \neq 5^4 - 2^4$, which is $625 - 16 = 609$
$\sqrt{25 - 16} = \sqrt{9} = 3$	$\sqrt{25 - 16} \neq \sqrt{25} - \sqrt{16}$, which is $5 - 4 = 1$

Check Your Skills

> **Directions**
>
> Where possible, solve by combining bases.

12. $20^2 \div 5^2 = $ _____

13. $\dfrac{\sqrt{384}}{\sqrt{2} \times \sqrt{3}} = $ _____

14. $\sqrt{39^2 - 36^2} = $ _____

Answers can be found on pages 142–143.

Special Powers

Consider the sequence of exponents below. You've seen examples similar to the ones in the first four rows before, but the last three are new.

$$2^4 = 2 \times 2 \times 2 \times 2 = 16$$
$$2^3 = 2 \times 2 \times 2 = 8$$
$$2^2 = 2 \times 2 = 4$$
$$2^1 = 2 = 2$$
$$2^0 = 1 = 1$$
$$2^{-1} = \frac{1}{2^1} = \frac{1}{2}$$
$$2^{-2} = \frac{1}{2^2} = \frac{1}{4}$$

What's going on with the new examples?

An Exponent of 1

Any base raised to an exponent of 1 keeps the value of the original base. This follows the rule taught earlier: The exponent represents the number of times to multiply the base by itself. For example, $3^1 = 3$, because the exponent of 1 indicates that you have just one 3.

$5^1 = 5$	$(-6)^1 = -6$	$\left(-\frac{1}{2}\right)^1 = -\frac{1}{2}$

Any number that does not have a written exponent has an exponent of 1. Here are two examples:

$$5^4 \times 5 = 5^4 \times 5^1 = 5^{(4+1)} = 5^5$$

$$\frac{6^3}{6} = \frac{6^3}{6^1} = 6^{(3-1)} = 6^2$$

Exponent Rule 5:

$a^1 = a$ Any number raised to the power of 1 is itself.

$a = a^1$ Any number without an exponent has an implicit exponent of 1.

Unit Two: **Algebra**

An Exponent of 0

By definition, any base raised to the 0 power yields 1:

| $3^0 = 1$ | $4^0 = 1$ | $(-6)^0 = 1$ | $\left(-\frac{1}{2}\right)^0 = 1$ |

To understand this fact, think of dividing a number by itself, which always results in 1:

$$\frac{3^7}{3^7} = 3^{(7-7)} = 3^0 = 1$$

When you divide 3^7 by itself, the result is 1. Also, the subtraction rule of exponents indicates that 3^7 divided by itself yields 3^0. Therefore, 3^0 *must* equal 1.

> **Exponent Rule 6:**
>
> $x^0 = 1$ Any base raised to the power of zero is equal to 1.

A Negative Exponent

An exponent can be negative. While negative exponents have all the same properties as positive ones, they can be confusing to interpret. If you start from 2^2 and divide by the base, 2, you'll move "down" one power from 2^2 to 2^1.

$$2^2 \div 2 = 2^{2-1} = 2^1 = 2$$

The below table illustrates what happens if you keep dividing by 2. The first column shows how to simplify an expression using plain math, while the second column shows how to simplify the exact same expression using exponent rules:

Plain math:	Exponent form:	Therefore:
$2^1 \div 2 = 2 \div 2 = 1$	$2^1 \div 2 = 2^{1-1} = 2^0$	$2^0 = 1$
$2^0 \div 2 = 1 \div 2 = \frac{1}{2}$	$2^0 \div 2 = 2^{0-1} = 2^{-1}$	$2^{-1} = \frac{1}{2}$

Chapter 5: **Exponents and Roots**

What happened there? When you drop below x^0 to the negative exponent x^{-1}, the value doesn't turn negative. Rather, the value turns into a fraction and the base ends up in the denominator of the fraction. This trend continues if you keep dividing by 2.

$$2^0 = 1$$

$$2^{-1} = \left(\frac{1}{2}\right)^1 = \frac{1^1}{2^1} = \frac{1}{2}$$

$$2^{-2} = \left(\frac{1}{2}\right)^2 = \frac{1^2}{2^2} = \frac{1}{4}$$

$$2^{-3} = \left(\frac{1}{2}\right)^3 = \frac{1^3}{2^3} = \frac{1}{8}$$

When you see a negative exponent, first take the reciprocal of the base. In the above examples, the base is 2, so its reciprocal is $\frac{1}{2}$.

Next, put parentheses around the entire fraction and use the positive version of the exponent you started with. In the last example shown above, the starting exponent was −3, so the positive version is 3. As a result, $2^{-3} = \left(\frac{1}{2}\right)^3$.

> **Exponent Rule 7:**
>
> $a^{-b} = \left(\frac{1}{a}\right)^b$ For any base raised to a negative power, take the reciprocal of the base and raise it to the positive power.
>
> $a^{-1} = \frac{1}{a}$ For any base raised to the −1 power, take the reciprocal of the base and you're done.

Here are three more examples of these rules:

$$5^{-1} = \left(\frac{1}{5}\right)^1 = \frac{1}{5}$$

$$\left(\frac{1}{2}\right)^{-2} = \left(\frac{2}{1}\right)^2 = \frac{4}{1} = 4$$

$$(-2)^{-3} = \left(\frac{1}{-2}\right)^3 = \frac{1^3}{(-2)^3} = -\frac{1}{8}$$

Check Your Skills

15. If $\frac{5^{y+2}}{5^3} = 1$, what is y?

16. Simplify: $(x^{-3})(x^{-4})$

Answers can be found on page 143.

Special Bases

The base of an exponent can be positive, negative, or zero. It could also be either an integer or a fraction. Chapter 2: Exponents introduced the basics of negative exponents. In this section, you'll learn more about negative bases as well as other special bases.

A Negative Base

One of the GRE's most common tricks involves negative bases with even exponents. When an integer is raised to an odd power, the answer keeps the original sign of the base. For example:

$(3)^3 = 27$	$(-3)^3 = -27$
positive base,	negative base,
positive result	negative result

However, when any nonzero base is raised to an even power, the result is always positive. For example:

$3^2 = 9$	$(-3)^2 = 9$	$(-3)^4 = 81$
positive base,	negative base,	negative base,
positive result	positive result	positive result

When a base is raised to an even exponent, the resulting answer will always be positive (or zero), never negative, and that fact makes problems with even exponents particularly dangerous. Consider this problem:

$$x^2 = 16$$

Quantity A　　　　　　　　　　　　　　　　**Quantity B**
　　x　　　　　　　　　　　　　　　　　　　　　　4

If $x = 4$, then the correct answer would be (C): The two quantities are equal. However, x may or may *not* be 4; it could also be -4. If $x = -4$, then Quantity B is greater. Therefore, the correct answer is (D): The answer cannot be determined based on the given information. Whenever you see an even exponent on the test, be wary of this trap.

Here's the source of another trap: According to the Order of Operations rules (PEMDAS), exponents have higher precedence than multiplication. What is the value of -4^2? Is that the same as the value of $(-4)^2$?

The two expressions do not have the same value. Using PEMDAS, $-(4^2) = -16$, because you must first square the value 4 and then apply the negative sign. By contrast, $(-4)^2 = 16$, because you are required to square the value -4.

Odd exponents are harmless, since they always keep the original sign of the base. For example, if you have the equation $x^3 = 64$, you can be sure that $x = 4$. It cannot equal -4 because $(-4)^3 = -64$, not 64.

Odd roots can have negative results. For example, $\sqrt[3]{64}$ is 4, while $\sqrt[3]{-64}$ is -4. On the GRE, you'll never see a negative number inside a square root sign (e.g., $\sqrt{-4}$), because that results in an imaginary number, which is thankfully way beyond the scope of this test.

Check Your Skills

17. If $x^3 = -27$, what is x ?

18. If $y^2 \times y^3 \times y = 64$, what is y ?

Answers can be found on page 143.

A Base of 0, 1, or −1

Bases of 0, 1, or −1 yield consistent results, as shown in this table:

Rule:	Examples:
The number 0 raised to any *positive** power always yields 0.	$0^2 = 0 \times 0 = 0$ $0^3 = 0 \times 0 \times 0 = 0$
The number 1 raised to any power at all yields 1.	$1^2 = 1 \times 1 = 1$ $1^3 = 1 \times 1 \times 1 = 1$
The number −1 raised to an even power yields 1.	$(-1)^2 = (-1) \times (-1) = 1$
The number −1 raised to an odd power yields −1.	$(-1)^3 = (-1) \times (-1) \times (-1) = -1$

*The GRE won't test you on 0 raised to 0 or 0 raised to a negative power.

Thus, if you are told that $x^6 = x^7 = x^{15}$, it must be the case that x is either 0 or 1. Do not try to do algebra on the equation. Instead, plug 0 and 1 into the equation to check that the equation makes sense. The values 0 and 1 are the only two numbers that stay the same when you raise them to any positive power. The value −1 does not fit the equation, since $(-1)^6 = 1$, but $(-1)^7 = -1$.

If you are told instead that $x^6 = x^8 = x^{10}$, x could be 0, 1, *or* −1. Any one of these three values fits the equation as given. (See why even exponents are so dangerous?)

Check Your Skills

19. If $x \neq 0$ and $(x^4)(x^{-4}) = y$, what is y ?

20. If $x^3 - x = 0$ and $x^2 + x^2 = 2$, what is x ?

Answers can be found on pages 143–144.

Unit Two: **Algebra**

A Fractional Base

The test makers love to test the following exponent rules:

1. Numbers greater than 1 *increase* when you raise them to successively greater positive powers:

$$2^1 < 2^2 < 2^3$$

$$2 < 4 < 8$$

2. Numbers between 0 and 1 (known as **proper fractions**) *decrease* as you raise them to successively greater positive powers:

$$\left(\frac{1}{2}\right)^1 > \left(\frac{1}{2}\right)^2 > \left(\frac{1}{2}\right)^3$$

$$\frac{1}{2} > \frac{1}{4} > \frac{1}{8}$$

Why does this happen? Multiplying any two fractions between 0 and 1 together will always produce a smaller number. You're taking a fraction of a fraction, which is tiny!

You can also calculate the result by distributing the exponent to the numerator and denominator and multiplying each part out:

$$\left(\frac{1}{2}\right)^1 = \frac{1^1}{2^1} = \frac{1}{2}$$

$$\left(\frac{1}{2}\right)^2 = \frac{1^2}{2^2} = \frac{1}{4}$$

$$\left(\frac{1}{2}\right)^3 = \frac{1^3}{2^3} = \frac{1}{8}$$

Finally, as shown earlier, raising either 0 or 1 to any positive power will do nothing—the value will remain the same.

When raising to successively greater positive powers:		
When the base is...	The value will...	Example:
greater than 1	increase	$2^2 = 4$ $2^3 = 8$ $2^4 = 16$
between 0 and 1	decrease	$\left(\frac{1}{2}\right)^1 = \frac{1}{2}$ $\left(\frac{1}{2}\right)^2 = \frac{1}{4}$
equal to 0 or 1	stay the same	$0^1 = 0$ $0^2 = 0$ $0^3 = 0$

Check Your Skills

> Try these Quantitative Comparison problems. If you need a refresher on the standard answer choices for all QC problems, check Chapter 3: QC Structure.

21.
Quantity A	**Quantity B**
0.8	$(0.8)^2$

22.
Quantity A	**Quantity B**
$\left(\frac{3}{4}\right)^2$	$(0.8)^2$

23.
Quantity A	**Quantity B**
$\frac{10}{7}$	$\left(\frac{10}{7}\right)^2$

Answers can be found on page 144.

Picking Numbers for Fractional Bases

Picking special powers, namely 0, 1, and −1, can save time when testing different cases. Try this problem:

Quantity A	**Quantity B**
$\dfrac{1}{2^t}$	2^t

Plug in 0 for t:

Quantity A	**Quantity B**
$\dfrac{1}{2^0} = \dfrac{1}{1} = 1$	$2^0 = 1$

When $t = 0$, the quantities are equal.   A̶ B̶ C D

Now plug in 1 for t:

Quantity A	**Quantity B**
$\dfrac{1}{2^1} = \dfrac{1}{2}$	$2^1 = 2$

This time, Quantity B is greater. Therefore, the correct answer is (D): The relationship cannot be determined.

Unit Two: **Algebra**

> **Strategy Tip:**
>
> When you want to plug in values for the exponents and the problem doesn't indicate that the value is not allowed to be 0 or 1, try 0 and 1 first to save yourself time.

Rules of Exponents

The exponent rules you've learned apply to negative exponents as well as to positive exponents. For instance, there are two ways to combine the expression $2^5 \times 2^{-3}$:

1. Add the exponents directly:

$$2^5 \times 2^{-3} = 2^{5+(-3)} = 2^2 = 4$$

2. Alternatively, rewrite the negative exponent as a positive exponent, and then combine:

$$2^5 \times 2^{-3} = 2^5 \times \frac{1}{2^3} = \frac{2^5}{2^3} = 2^{5-3} = 2^2 = 4$$

The first way is probably going to be the fastest way, but the second way is possible if needed.

How Can You Simplify Exponents?

Any exponential terms that are multiplied or divided can be combined as long as they have either a base or an exponent in common. Here's a summary:

Using the rules you have learned so far...		
These expressions CANNOT be simplified:	These expressions CAN be simplified:	Here's how:
$7^4 + 7^6$	$(7^4)(7^6)$	$(7^4)(7^6) = 7^{4+6} = 7^{10}$
$3^4 + 12^4$	$(3^4)(12^4)$	$(3^4)(12^4) = (3 \times 12)^4 = 36^4$
$6^5 - 6^3$	$\dfrac{6^5}{6^3}$	$\dfrac{6^5}{6^3} = 6^{5-3} = 6^2$
$12^7 - 3^7$	$\dfrac{12^7}{3^7}$	$\dfrac{12^7}{3^7} = \left(\dfrac{12}{3}\right)^7 = 4^7$

Because the terms in the middle column are all multiplied or divided, they can be simplified—and this is most commonly what the GRE will ask you to do. By contrast, because the terms in the first column are added or subtracted, they cannot be simplified *using the rules you've learned so far*. In Chapter 10: Common Factors, you'll learn more complicated rules that will cover simplification when the terms are added or subtracted.

Here's a summary of the major exponent rules in this chapter:

Exponent Rule	Examples	
$a^1 = a$ $a^0 = 1$	$13^1 = 13$ $13^0 = 1$	$(ab)^1 = ab$ $(ab)^0 = 1$
$a^x \times a^y = a^{x+y}$	$5(5^n) = (5^1)(5^n) = (5^{1+n})$	$3^5 \times 3^8 = 3^{13}$
$\dfrac{a^x}{a^y} = a^{(x-y)}$	$\dfrac{2^5}{2^{11}} = 2^{-6} = \dfrac{1}{2^6}$	$\dfrac{x^{10}}{x^3} = x^7$
$(a^x)^y = a^{xy}$	$(3^2)^4 = (3^4)^2 = 3^8$	$(5^3)^3 = 5^9$
$a^x \times b^x = (ab)^x$	$2^4 \times 3^4 = (2 \times 3)^4 = 6^4$	$6^5 = (2 \times 3)^5 = 2^5 \times 3^5$
$\left(\dfrac{a}{b}\right)^x = \dfrac{a^x}{b^x}$	$\left(\dfrac{10}{2}\right)^6 = \dfrac{10^6}{2^6} = 5^6$	$\left(\dfrac{3^5}{9^5}\right) = \left(\dfrac{3}{9}\right)^5 = \left(\dfrac{1}{3}\right)^5$
$x^{-a} = \left(\dfrac{1}{x}\right)^a$	$\left(\dfrac{3}{2}\right)^{-2} = \left(\dfrac{2}{3}\right)^2 = \dfrac{2^2}{3^2} = \dfrac{4}{9}$	$2x^{-4} = 2\left(\dfrac{1}{x^4}\right) = \dfrac{2}{x^4}$

Check Your Skills

24. Simplify each of the following expressions as far as you can, using the exponent rules from this chapter.

    (A) $x^2 \times y^2$

    (B) $\dfrac{x^3 y^2}{xy^{-2}}$

    (C) $2^n + 4^n$

Answers can be found on page 144.

Common Exponent Errors

All of the simplification processes covered in this chapter involve multiplication or division. One of the most common exponent errors is to apply these rules to addition or subtraction:

Correct!	$2^2 \times 2^2 = 2^{(2+2)} = 2^4 = 16$
INCORRECT!!	$2^2 + 2^2 \neq 2^{(2+2)}$ Don't do this!

Unit Two: **Algebra**

When can you simplify exponential expressions? For now, when:

1. The bases are multiplied or divided, and
2. Either the bases are the same or the exponents are the same

In Chapter 10: Exponents and Factors, you'll learn how to handle more complicated (and more rare) setups, including when the bases are added or subtracted.

Common Exponent Error List

Study this list of common errors carefully to help identify and avoid any mistakes you might be prone to make.

INCORRECT	CORRECT
$(x+y)^2 \ne x^2 + y^2$ $(3+2)^2 \ne 3^2 + 2^2 = 13$	$(x+y)^2 = x^2 + 2xy + y^2$ $(3+2)^2 = 5^2 = 25$
$a^x \times b^y \ne (ab)^{x+y}$ $2^4 \times 3^5 \ne (2 \times 3)^{4+5}$	Cannot be simplified further (different bases *and* different exponents)
$a^x \times a^y \ne a^{xy}$ $5^4 \times 5^3 \ne 5^{12}$	$a^x \times a^y = a^{x+y}$ $5^4 \times 5^3 = 5^7$
$(a^x)^y \ne a^{x+y}$ $(7^4)^3 \ne 7^7$	$(a^x)^y = a^{xy}$ $(7^4)^3 = 7^{12}$
$a^x + a^y \ne a^{x+y}$ $x^3 + x^2 \ne x^5$	Cannot be simplified in this way (addition **and** different exponents)
$a^x + a^x \ne a^{2x}$ $2^x + 2^x \ne 2^{2x}$	There are two a^x terms: $a^x + a^x = 2a^x$ $2^x + 2^x = 2(2^x) = 2^{x+1}$
$a \times a^x \ne a^{2x}$ $5 \times 5^z \ne 25^z$	$a^1 \times a^x = a^{x+1}$ $5^1 \times 5^z = 5^{z+1}$
$-x^2 \ne x^2$ $-4^2 \ne 16$	$-x^2$ cannot be simplified further. $-4^2 = -(4 \times 4) = -16$ $(-4)^2 = (-4 \times -4) = 16$

Chapter 5: **Exponents and Roots**

Exponents on QC

Exponent problems in Quantitative Comparisons will typically test exponents using variables. If you're picking numbers, it's particularly important to use ZONEF. Powers of zero and one, as well as negative powers, have strikingly different results than positive powers. Similarly, negative and fractional bases can produce different results than positive bases. Considering different kinds of numbers can not only avoid mistakes, but also shorten problems. For example:

x and y are positive.

Quantity A	**Quantity B**
xy	$(xy)^2$

Picking easy, positive integers could suggest that Quantity B is greater:

$x =$	$y =$	$xy =$		$(xy)^2$
2	3	$2 \times 3 = 6$	<	$(2 \times 3)^2 = 36$
4	3	$4 \times 3 = 12$	<	$(4 \times 3)^2 = 144$

As such, either of these cases will rule out (A) and (C). A̶ B C̶ D

To decide between answers (B) and (D), testing different *kinds* of numbers is key:

$x =$	$y =$	$xy =$		$(xy)^2$
1	1	$1 \times 1 = 1$	=	$(1 \times 1)^2 = 1$
$\frac{1}{2}$	$\frac{1}{3}$	$\frac{1}{2} \times \frac{1}{3} = \frac{1}{6}$	>	$\left(\frac{1}{2} \times \frac{1}{3}\right)^2 = \left(\frac{1}{6}\right)^2 = \frac{1}{36}$

As such, Quantity B can be greater than, equal to, *or* less than Quantity A. Therefore, the correct answer is (D): The relationship cannot be determined.

Be just as wary of QC questions that involve variable exponents:

Quantity A	**Quantity B**
$\left(\frac{2}{3}\right)^x$	$\left(\frac{3}{2}\right)^x$

Unit Two: **Algebra**

There are no limitations on what *x* can be, so test an easy number followed by different kinds of numbers to find the correct answer:

Quantity A		Quantity B
$\left(\frac{2}{3}\right)^x$		$\left(\frac{3}{2}\right)^x$
$\left(\frac{2}{3}\right)^1 = \frac{2}{3}$	<	$\left(\frac{3}{2}\right)^1 = \frac{3}{2}$
$\left(\frac{2}{3}\right)^0 = 1$	=	$\left(\frac{3}{2}\right)^0 = 1$
$\left(\frac{2}{3}\right)^{-1} = \frac{3}{2}$	>	$\left(\frac{3}{2}\right)^{-1} = \frac{2}{3}$

When $x = 1$, Quantity B is greater. When $x = 0$, the two quantities are equal. And when $x = -1$, Quantity A is greater. Therefore, the correct answer is (D): The relationship cannot be determined.

Strategy Tip:

On questions that involve variables and exponents, use ZONEF to prove answer (D). Consider trying 0, 1, numbers *between* 0 and 1, and negative numbers.

140

Chapter 5: **Exponents and Roots**

Check Your Skills Answer Key

1.
   $1^1 = 1$ $\sqrt{1} = 1$
   $2^2 = 4$ $\sqrt{4} = 2$
   $2^3 = 8$ $\sqrt{9} = 3$
   $2^4 = 16$ $\sqrt{16} = 4$
   $3^2 = 9$ $\sqrt{25} = 5$
   $3^3 = 27$ $\sqrt[3]{8} = 2$
   $4^2 = 16$ $\sqrt[3]{27} = 3$
   $4^3 = 64$ $\sqrt[3]{64} = 4$
   $5^2 = 25$ $\sqrt[3]{125} = 5$
   $5^3 = 125$ $\sqrt[4]{16} = 2$

2. **4**
   Because this is an odd exponent, there will be only one solution:
   $$x^3 = 64$$
   $$\sqrt[3]{x^3} = \sqrt[3]{64}$$
   $$x = 4$$

3. **11 or −11**
   Because this is an even exponent, there will be two solutions:
   $$x^2 = 121$$
   $$\sqrt{x^2} = \pm\sqrt{121}$$
   $$x = 11 \text{ or } -11$$

4. **4**
   Set the bases equal to 7 on each side:
   $$7^{x-2} = 49$$
   $$7^{x-2} = 7^2$$
   $$x - 2 = 2$$
   $$x = 4$$

Unit Two: Algebra

5. **1**

   Set the bases equal to 5 on each side:

   $$5^{3x} = 125$$
   $$5^{3x} = 5^3$$
   $$3x = 3$$
   $$x = 1$$

6. **6**

   Set the bases equal to 2 on each side:

   $$2^x = 64$$
   $$2^x = 2^6$$
   $$x = 6$$

7. b^{12}

   $b^5 \times b^7 = b^{(5+7)} = b^{12}$

8. **3**

   Combine the exponents and make the bases the same:

   $$2 \times 2^x = 16$$
   $$2^{1+x} = 2^4$$
   $$1 + x = 4$$
   $$x = 3$$

9. y^3

   $\dfrac{y^5}{y^2} = y^{(5-2)} = y^3$

10. x^{12}

    $(x^4)^3 = x^{4 \times 3} = x^{12}$

11. 5^9

    $(5^3)^3 = 5^{3 \times 3} = 5^9$

12. **16**

    $\dfrac{20^2}{5^2} = \left(\dfrac{20}{5}\right)^2 = 4^2 = 16$

Chapter 5: **Exponents and Roots**

13. **8**
    Use the calculator to divide 384 by 6.
    $$\frac{\sqrt{384}}{\sqrt{2} \times \sqrt{3}} = \sqrt{\frac{384}{2 \times 3}} = \sqrt{\frac{384}{6}} = \sqrt{64} = 8$$

14. **15**
    Use the calculator to find the squares and then to do the subtraction.
    $$\sqrt{39^2 - 36^2} = \sqrt{1521 - 1296} = \sqrt{225} = 15$$

    In this case, it's not permitted to combine the terms because they are subtracted, not multiplied or divided. Combining the terms to $(39 - 36)^2$ before performing the subtraction would lead to the wrong answer.

15. **1**
    Simplify the left side by combining the exponents. To make the base the same on the right side, use the property that anything raised to the 0 power equals 1, so $5^0 = 1$:
    $$\frac{5^{y+2}}{5^3} = 1$$
    $$5^{(y+2)-3} = 5^0$$
    $$5^{y-1} = 5^0$$
    $$y - 1 = 0$$
    $$y = 1$$

16. $\dfrac{1}{x^7}$
    $$(x^{-3})(x^{-4}) = x^{(-3+-4)} = x^{-7} = \frac{1}{x^7}$$

17. **−3**
    If a number is raised to an odd power, the result will have the same sign as the original base. In this case, x must be -3, because $(-3)^3 = -27$.

18. **2 or −2**
    Start by combining the like terms: $y^2 \times y^3 \times y = y^6 = 64$. Since the exponent is even, the base could be positive or negative, so x could be either 2 or −2.

19. **1**
    When multiplying two terms with the same base, add the exponents: $(x^4)(x^{-4}) = x^{4+(-4)} = x^0$, and $x^0 = 1$. Therefore, $y = 1$.

143

Unit Two: **Algebra**

20. **1 or −1**

    Since $x^3 - x = 0$, it's also the case that $x^3 = x$. Based on this equation alone, x can be 0, −1, or 1.

    But the problem provides a second equation, so check the values against that equation. If $x = 0$, then the second equation becomes $0 + 0 = 2$, which is false. Therefore, x cannot be 0. On the other hand, if $x = 1$ or -1, then the second equation is true, so $x = 1$ or -1.

21. **(A)**

    Every number between 0 and 1 decreases the higher you raise its power, so squaring 0.8 would create a number less than 0.8.

    Therefore, the correct answer is (A): Quantity A is greater.

22. **(B)**

    Because every number between 0 and 1 decreases the higher you raise its power, Quantities A and B will both decrease. However, the degree to which they decrease depends on the starting values. For example, $\frac{3}{4}$ is less than 0.8, so $\left(\frac{3}{4}\right)^2$ will also be less than $(0.8)^2$.

    Therefore, the correct answer is (B): Quantity B is greater.

23. **(B)**

    Although $\frac{10}{7}$ is presented in fractional form, its value is greater than 1. (Check it on the calculator to make sure.) When something greater than 1 is raised to a power greater than 1, it increases. As a result, $\left(\frac{10}{7}\right)^2 > \frac{10}{7}$.

    Therefore, the correct answer is (B): Quantity B is greater.

24. (a) $(xy)^2$

    Because the two bases are multiplied and the exponents are the same, this can be rewritten as $(xy)^2$.

    (b) $x^2 y^4$

    The x in the denominator has an implied exponent of 1. Because division is involved, subtract the exponents:

    $$\frac{x^3 y^2}{x^1 y^{-2}} = x^{(3-1)} y^{[2-(-2)]} = x^2 y^4$$

    (c) $2^n + 4^n$

    This one is a trap, sorry! Because the two terms are added together, there's nothing you can do using the rules you've learned so far. (You'll learn some other rules in Chapter 10: Exponents and Factors that could help here.)

Problem Set

1. If $y^5 > 0$, is $y < 0$?

2. If $b > a > 0$ and $c \neq 0$, is $a^2b^3c^4$ positive?

3. If $x^2 - 10 = -1$, what is the value of x ?

> For questions #4-9, simplify the exponential expression. Where possible, solve for the integer value.

4. $\dfrac{7^6}{7^4}$

5. 2^{-5}

6. $8^4(5^4)$

7. $\dfrac{9^4}{3^4} + (4^2)^3$

8. $\dfrac{y^2 \times y^5}{(y^2)^4}$

9. $\sqrt{9m^4n^3}$

10. If $G^2 < G$, which of the following could be the value of G ?

    (A) 1

    (B) $\dfrac{23}{7}$

    (C) $\dfrac{7}{23}$

    (D) -4

    (E) -2

11. For what values does $a^2 + a^4 = a^6$?

12. Are $\dfrac{\sqrt{3}}{2}$ and $\dfrac{2\sqrt{3}}{3}$ reciprocals?

13. If $r^3 + |r| = 0$, what are the possible values of r ?

14.

Quantity A	Quantity B
$\dfrac{\sqrt{6} \times \sqrt{18}}{\sqrt{9}}$	$\dfrac{\sqrt{8} \times \sqrt{12}}{\sqrt{6}}$

15. If $4\sqrt[3]{x} = -12$, what is the value of x ?

Unit Two: **Algebra**

16.
    Quantity A   **Quantity B**
    2^y $\left(\dfrac{1}{2}\right)^{-y}$

17.
         $y > 1$
    Quantity A   **Quantity B**
    $(0.99)^y$ $0.99 \times y$

18.
         $n < -1$
    Quantity A   **Quantity B**
    $(n^2)(n^4)$ $(n^2)^4$

19.
    Quantity A   **Quantity B**
    $(-101)^{102}$ $(-102)^{101}$

Chapter 5: **Exponents and Roots**

Solutions

1. **No**

   An integer raised to an odd exponent retains the original sign of the base. Therefore, if y^5 is positive, y is positive.

2. **Yes**

   Evaluate whether each of a^2, b^3, and c^4 is positive or negative. Anything raised to an even exponent will turn out positive, so a^2 and c^4 will be positive. Additionally, b is defined as positive (as is a), so any power of b will remain positive. Therefore, the product $a^2b^3c^4$ is the product of three positive numbers, which will be positive.

3. $x = -3$ **or 3**

   Isolate the x by adding 10 to both sides: $x^2 = 9$. When taking the square root, keep in mind there are two possible results: one positive and one negative. Therefore, x could be either 3 or -3.

4. **49**

   $$\frac{7^6}{7^4} = 7^{6-4} = 7^2 = 49$$

5. $\frac{1}{32}$

   A negative exponent indicates that you should find the reciprocal of the base and take it to the positive version of the exponent. Thus, $2^{-5} = \left(\frac{1}{2}\right)^5 = \frac{1^5}{2^5} = \frac{1}{32}$.

6. **40⁴ or 2,560,000**

   Because the exponents are the same, combine the bases directly: $8^4(5^4) = (8 \times 5)^4 = 40^4$.

7. **4,177**

   $$\frac{9^4}{3^4} + (4^2)^3 = 3^4 + 4^6 = 81 + 4,096 = 4,177$$

8. $\frac{1}{y}$

   $$\frac{y^2 \times y^5}{(y^2)^4} = \frac{y^7}{y^8} = y^{7-8} = y^{-1} = \frac{1}{y}$$

147

Unit Two: **Algebra**

9. **$3m^2n\sqrt{n}$**

    Roots can be written as fractional exponents and dealt with according to exponent rules. Because square roots are powers of $\frac{1}{2}$, they combine most readily with even exponents.

    $$\sqrt{9} \times \sqrt{m^4} \times \sqrt{n^3}$$
    $$3 \times (m^4)^{\frac{1}{2}} \times \sqrt{n^2 \times n}$$
    $$3 \times m^2 \times (n^2)^{\frac{1}{2}} \times \sqrt{n}$$
    $$3 \times m^2 \times n \times \sqrt{n}$$

    Because n had an odd exponent at the beginning, taking the square root of n involves separating one n out from n^3 and square rooting the n^2 that remains.

10. **(C) $\frac{7}{23}$**

    If $G^2 < G$, then G must be positive (because G^2 will never be negative), and G must be less than 1, because otherwise $G^2 > G$. Thus, $0 < G < 1$. You can eliminate choices (D) and (E) because they violate the condition that G must be positive. Then test choice (A): 1 is not less than 1, so you can eliminate (A). Choice (B) is greater than 1, so only choice (C) satisfies the inequality.

11. **0**

    Exponential expressions linked by addition can be factored (see Chapter 10: Exponents and Factors), but they cannot be combined directly. Most numbers would not work for a. For example, if a is 2, $2^2 + 2^4 \neq 2^6$ because $2^2 + 2^4 = 4 + 16 = 20$, while $2^6 = 64$.

    However, test the bases that have special properties.

a	$a^2 + a^4$	a^6
1	$1^2 + 1^4 = 1 + 1 = 2$	$1^6 = 1$
0	$0^2 + 0^4 = 0 + 0 = 0$	$0^6 = 0$
−1	$(-1)^2 + (-1)^4 = 1 + 1 = 2$	$(-1)^6 = 1$

    The only value of a for which the equation holds true is 0.

12. **Yes**

    The product of a number and its reciprocal must equal 1. To test whether two numbers are reciprocals, multiply them. If the product is not 1, they are not reciprocals.

    $$\frac{\sqrt{3}}{2} \times \frac{2\sqrt{3}}{3} = \frac{2(\sqrt{3})^2}{2(3)} = \frac{6}{6} = 1$$

    Because they multiply to 1, the numbers are indeed reciprocals.

13. **0, −1**

    If $r^3 + |r| = 0$, then $r^3 = -|r|$. But how could r^3 and $-|r|$ be equal? Higher powers of a number are only equal to lower powers of a number when the special bases (−1, 0, and 1) are involved. Test these in the equation: The only special bases that end up working here are 0 and −1.

14. **(B)**

    Simplify both quantities by combining the roots into one root.

Quantity A	**Quantity B**
$\sqrt{\dfrac{6 \times 18}{9}}$	$\sqrt{\dfrac{8 \times 12}{6}}$

    Now simplify the fractions underneath each root.

Quantity A	**Quantity B**
$\sqrt{\dfrac{6 \times \cancel{18}^{2}}{\cancel{9}_{1}}} = \sqrt{12}$	$\sqrt{\dfrac{8 \times \cancel{12}^{2}}{\cancel{6}_{1}}} = \sqrt{16}$

    $\sqrt{16}$ is larger than $\sqrt{12}$.

    Therefore, the correct answer is (B): Quantity B is greater.

15. **−27**

    First, divide both sides of the equation by 4.

    $$\dfrac{\cancel{4}\sqrt[3]{x}}{\cancel{4}} = \dfrac{\cancel{-12}^{-3}}{\cancel{4}}$$

    Now, only the cube root sign remains to be resolved. Much as exponents are canceled by roots, roots can be canceled by exponents:

    $$\sqrt[3]{x} = -3$$
    $$(\sqrt[3]{x})^3 = (-3)^3$$
    $$x = -27$$

16. **(C)**

    Recall that the negative sign in an exponent means to take the reciprocal of the base. For instance, $3^{-2} = \left(\dfrac{1}{3}\right)^2$, because $\dfrac{1}{3}$ is the reciprocal of 3. The reciprocal of $\dfrac{1}{2}$ is 2, so Quantity B can be rewritten as follows.

Quantity A	**Quantity B**
2^y	$\left(\dfrac{1}{2}\right)^{-y} = (2)^y$

    Therefore, the correct answer is (C): The two quantities are equal.

Unit Two: **Algebra**

17. **(B)**
Any number less than 1 raised to a power greater than 1 will get smaller, so even though you don't know the value of y, you do know that the value in Quantity A will be less than 0.99.

$y > 1$

Quantity A	**Quantity B**
$(0.99)^y \rightarrow$ less than 0.99	$0.99 \times y$

Conversely, any positive number multiplied by a number greater than 1 will get bigger. You don't know the value in Quantity B, but you know that it will be greater than 0.99.

$y > 1$

Quantity A	**Quantity B**
$(0.99)^y \rightarrow$ less than 0.99	$0.99 \times y \rightarrow$ greater than 0.99

Therefore, the correct answer is (B): Quantity B is greater.

18. **(B)**
Use exponent rules to simplify the expressions in each quantity.

Quantity A	**Quantity B**
$(n^2)(n^4) = n^6$	$(n^2)^4 = n^8$

In both quantities, n is raised to an even power, so both quantities will be positive. Because $n < -1$, the absolute value of n will increase as n is raised to higher powers.

Therefore, the correct answer is (B): Quantity B is greater.

19. **(A)**
Any nonzero number raised to an even exponent will be positive, while anything raised to an odd exponent will keep its original sign. In this case, that makes Quantity A positive and Quantity B negative.

Therefore, the correct answer is (A): Quantity A is greater.

CHAPTER 6
Formulas and Functions

In This Chapter:

- Plug In Formulas
- Strange Symbol Formulas
- Functions
- Check Your Skills Answer Key
- Problem Set
- Solutions

CHAPTER 6 Formulas and Functions

The GRE will attempt to make arithmetic computations harder by complicating the way they describe what you're meant to do. Rather than just give you an expression, the GRE may instead give you a **formula** or **function** and require you to determine how to plug in numbers or variables before simplifying. In this chapter, you'll learn how to recognize, simplify, and solve specific types of formulas and functions that are common on the GRE.

Plug In Formulas

Formulas define relationships between variables. The most straightforward formula problems on the GRE will provide you with a formula, define its variables, and ask you to solve for one of those variables by plugging in given values for the other variables. For example:

> The formula for determining an individual's comedic aptitude, C, on a given day is defined as $C = \frac{QL}{J}$, where Q represents the overall joke quality on a scale of 1 to 10, J represents the number of jokes told, and L represents the number of individual laughs generated. If Nicole told 12 jokes that generated 18 laughs and earned a comedic aptitude of 10.5, what was the overall quality of her jokes?

Solve this problem by plugging the given values into the formula to find Nicole's joke quality, Q:

$$C = \frac{QL}{J}$$
$$10.5 = \frac{18Q}{12}$$
$$(10.5)(12) = 18Q$$
$$\frac{(10.5)(12)}{18} = Q$$
$$7 = Q$$

The quality of Nicole's jokes is rated a 7. To get there, first plug in the values given for each of the three known variables: $C = 10.5$, $L = 18$, and $J = 12$. Then, rearrange the equation until Q is by itself on one side. At this stage, you can plug the numbers into the calculator or you can continue to simplify on paper, your choice. Generally, if the math is pretty straightforward and quick, continue on paper; otherwise, pull up the calculator.

You're not expected to come into the GRE already knowing what the formula for comedic aptitude is. The problem will always tell you what the formula is. Write it down, plug in the numbers, and solve for the

Unit Two: **Algebra**

required unknown. Alternatively, you can rearrange the original equation to isolate the unknown *before* plugging in the numbers:

$$C = \frac{QL}{J}$$
$$CJ = QL$$
$$\frac{CJ}{L} = Q$$
$$\frac{(10.5)(12)}{18} = Q$$
$$7 = Q$$

Check Your Skills

1. The baking time in minutes for a certain cake is defined as $\frac{Vk}{T}$, where *V* is the volume of the cake in inches cubed, *T* is the oven temperature in degrees Fahrenheit, and *k* is a constant. If the baking time was 30 minutes at 350 degrees Fahrenheit for a cake with a volume of 150 cubic inches, what is the value of constant *k* ?

   $k =$ ☐

Answers can be found on page 161.

Strange Symbol Formulas

Using Numbers

GRE formula problems may introduce a strange symbol that you've never seen in a math problem before, such as ❖ or ⊙. If you see something you don't recognize, don't panic! The symbol is literally made up. Keep reading: The problem will give you instructions for what to do with that symbol. It's testing you on your ability to follow directions.

When you see a weird symbol, first write down the formula or other definition they give you for that symbol. Then follow the same math steps using the given numbers. For example:

Question	Solution
If $x ♥ y = x^2 + y^2 - xy$, what is $3 ♥ 4$?	$3 ♥ 4 = 3^2 + 4^2 - (3)(4)$ $= 9 + 16 - 12$ $= 13$
If $s ○ t = (s - 2)(t + 2)$, what is $3 ○ 5$?	$3 ○ 5 = (3 - 2)(5 + 2)$ $= (1)(7)$ $= 7$

As you work, it can be helpful to refer to the variables mentally as "the first number," "the second number," and so on. Use the physical position of the numbers to keep them straight in relation to the strange symbol.

Try this problem:

$$W \psi F = (\sqrt{W})^F \text{ for all integers } W \text{ and } F. \text{ What is } 4 \psi 3 ?$$

The instructions tell you to take the square root of the first number (which is 4) and then raise that value to the power of the second number (which is 3):

$$4 \psi 3 = (\sqrt{4})^3 = 2^3 = 8$$

Watch for the exact placements of symbols and variables. Some operations will flip the order of the variables from left to right and vice versa. It is easy to automatically translate the function in a "left to right" manner even when that is *not* what the function specifies:

$$W \Phi F = (\sqrt{F})^W \text{ for all integers } W \text{ and } F. \text{ What is } 4 \Phi 9 ?$$

In this problem, the order of the operation is *reversed*—in this case, you need to take the square root of the *second* number and then raise that value to the power of the *first* number:

$$4 \Phi 9 = (\sqrt{9})^4 = 3^4 = 81$$

More challenging strange-symbol problems require you to use the given procedure more than once. For example:

$$W \Phi F = (\sqrt{F})^W \text{ for all integers } W \text{ and } F. \text{ What is } 1 \Phi 3 \Phi 16 ?$$

PEMDAS still applies. Perform the procedure inside the parentheses first:

$$3 \Phi 16 = (\sqrt{16})^3 = 4^3 = 64$$

Now that you've determined that $3 \Phi 16 = 64$, plug the value 64 into the original question: What is $1 \Phi 64$?

Perform the procedure again to get the answer:

$$1 \Phi 64 = (\sqrt{64})^1 = 8^1 = 8$$

Using Variables

The GRE might complicate things by asking you to run the function on a variable rather than a number. For example:

$$W \Phi F = (\sqrt{F})^W \text{ for all integers } W \text{ and } F. \text{ If } 3 \Phi x = 27, \text{ what is the value of } x ?$$

The definition of the function is the same as before. In this case, however, the problem tells you what the function equals (27) and asks you to solve for the second number, *x*. Treat *x* just like you would a number:

$$3 \Phi x = (\sqrt{x})^3$$

Since the problem indicates that $3 \Phi x$ *also* equals 27, set the expression above equal to 27 and solve for *x*:

$$(\sqrt{x})^3 = 27$$
$$\sqrt{x} = \sqrt[3]{27}$$
$$\sqrt{x} = 3$$
$$x = 3^2$$
$$x = 9$$

Unit Two: Algebra

Strange symbols, formulas, and functions sometimes appear in Quantitative Comparison questions. The fastest way to answer them will depend on whether the question uses numbers or variables. For example:

$$v\& = 2v - 1$$

Quantity A	Quantity B
$(v\&)\&$	$4v$

Because $v\& = 2v - 1$, rewrite Quantity A as $(2v - 1)\&$. Evaluate the formula one more time, using the entire expression $2v - 1$ in place of the v in the original formula:

$$(2v - 1)\& = 2(2v - 1) - 1$$
$$= 4v - 2 - 1$$
$$= 4v - 3$$

Now your comparison becomes:

Quantity A	Quantity B
$4v - 3$	$4v$

Since Quantity A is 3 less than whatever Quantity B is, Quantity B must always be greater, so the correct answer is (B).

Check Your Skills

2. If $A \Delta B = A^B + B$ for all integers A and B, what is the value of $-2 \Delta (3 \Delta 1)$?

    (A) -4
    (B) -2
    (C) 2
    (D) 10
    (E) 20

3. If $s \lambda t = \frac{st}{6} + \frac{3t}{2}$, for all integers s and t, what is the value of $x \lambda 6$?

    (A) $\frac{5}{2}x$
    (B) $x + 6$
    (C) $x + 9$
    (D) $3x + 6$
    (E) $5x$

Answers can be found on page 161.

Chapter 6: **Formulas and Functions**

Functions

Function problems are very similar to strange-symbol problems. Just like strange symbols, functions provide you with a definition to follow. As before, these functions are typically made up by the test-makers and are meaningful only for the question at hand. For example:

If the function $f(x) = 2x + 3$, what is $f(3)$?

The first part is the function and shows you what directions to follow. Read this as "f of x equals $2x$ plus 3." (Note: It doesn't mean f times x.) The question asks you to find $f(3)$. Read this as f of 3. Wherever you see x in the original function, substitute the value of 3:

$$f(3) = 2(3) + 3 = 6 + 3 = 9$$

Numerical Substitution

In school, you may have heard the analogy that functions are like "magic boxes." The magic box image can still be useful for conceptualizing functions. Envision this scenario:

> You put a 2 into the magic box, and a 7 comes out. You put a 3 into the magic box, and a 9 comes out. You put a 4 into the magic box, and an 11 comes out. What is the magic box doing to your number?

One possibility is that the magic box is doubling your number and adding 3:

$$2(2) + 3 = 7 \qquad 2(3) + 3 = 9 \qquad 2(4) + 3 = 11$$

Whatever number gets plugged in, its value is transformed. But this transformation isn't exactly magic. Instead, it's a specific set of defined steps: The value is doubled, then three is added. In fact, these steps match the function defined earlier, $f(x) = 2x + 3$:

What is...	$f(x) = 2x + 3$
$f(2)$	$f(2) = 2(2) + 3 = 7$
$f(3)$	$f(3) = 2(3) + 3 = 9$
$f(4)$	$f(4) = 2(4) + 3 = 11$

Here, x is the number you put in the box, the function f is the magic box itself, and the value of $2x + 3$ is the result that comes out of the box. Functions always work the same way every time, so you can think of the function f as actually representing the procedure that the magic box is using to transform your number.

The magic box analogy is a helpful way to conceptualize a function as a rule built on an independent variable, also called an input. First, you put the input into the magic box, and then a corresponding output value comes out of the box. The function is the rule that turns the input variable into the output variable.

$f(x) = 4x^2 - 11$	The output of the function f changes depending on the value of input x.
$g(t) = t^3 + \sqrt{t} - \dfrac{2t}{5}$	The output of the function g changes depending on the value of input t.

There are two pieces of vocabulary to know about functions: **domain** and **range**. The domain of a function indicates the set of possible inputs: anything that you're allowed to put into the magic box. The range of a function indicates the set of possible outputs: anything that comes out of the box based on the inputs. For instance, the function $f(x) = x^2$ can take any input, but it will never produce a negative number. So the domain of this function is all numbers, but the range is $f(x) \geq 0$.

Try this problem:

$$\text{If } f(x) = x^2 - 2, \text{ what is the value of } f(5) \text{ ?}$$

The rule for this function is to square x and then subtract 2:

$$f(5) = 5^2 - 2 = 25 - 2 = 23$$

Variable Substitution

The GRE might ask you to input a variable or even an entire expression into a function. For example:

$$\text{If } f(z) = 2z - \frac{z}{3}, \text{ what is the value of } f(w + 6) \text{ ?}$$

Input the variable expression $(w + 6)$, including parentheses, in place of the variable (z) to determine the value of the function.

$$f(w + 6) = 2(w + 6) - \frac{(w + 6)}{3}$$

Compare this equation to the equation for $f(z)$. The expression $(w + 6)$ has taken the place of every z in the original equation. Treat the expression $(w + 6)$ as one thing, as if it were a single letter or variable. Always include parentheses when substituting an expression into an equation.

Try this Quantitative Comparison example:

$$\text{The function } f \text{ is defined as } f(x) = 2x - 8$$
$$f(m) = -10$$

Quantity A	Quantity B
m	$\dfrac{m}{2}$

Instead of providing an input and asking for an output, this example provides the output, -10, and asks you to find the input, m. Read $f(m) = -10$ as "When m is plugged into the function, the output is -10." Set up an equation with the function on one side and -10 on the other:

$$f(m) = 2m - 8 = -10$$
$$2m = -2$$
$$m = -1$$

Next, plug –1 in for m and compare the two quantities. Quantity A becomes –1 and Quantity B becomes $-\dfrac{1}{2}$. Therefore, the correct answer is (B): Quantity B is greater.

Chapter 6: **Formulas and Functions**

Functions with Unknown Constants

On the GRE, you may be given a function with an unknown constant. If so, you will also be given the value of the function for a specific number. Combine these pieces of information to solve for the unknown constant:

$$\text{If } f(x) = ax^2 - x, \text{ and } f(4) = 28, \text{ what is } f(-2)\ ?$$

Solve this problem in three steps. First, use the value of the input variable, $x = 4$, and the corresponding output value of the function, 28, to solve for the unknown constant:

$$f(4) = a(4)^2 - 4 = 28$$
$$16a - 4 = 28$$
$$16a = 32$$
$$a = 2$$

Then, rewrite the original function, replacing the constant, a, with its numerical value, 2:

$$f(x) = ax^2 - x$$
$$f(x) = 2x^2 - x$$

Finally, solve the function using the new input variable, –2:

$$f(-2) = 2(-2)^2 - (-2)$$
$$= 2(4) + 2$$
$$= 10$$

Compound Functions

Imagine putting a number into one magic box, and then putting the output directly into another magic box. This is the situation you have with compound functions:

$$\text{If } f(x) = x^3 + \sqrt{x} \text{ and } g(x) = 2x + 2, \text{ what is } f(g(1))\ ?$$

You've already dealt with compound formulas when expressed as strange symbols. The process here is the same: Work from the inside out.

In this case, start with $g(1)$, the innermost part of the expression:

$$g(1) = 2(1) + 2 = 4$$

Use the result from the *inner* function, $g(1) = 4$, as the new input variable for the *outer* function f:

$$f(g(1)) = f(4) = (4)^3 + \sqrt{4} = 64 + 2 = 66$$

Try this problem—it's *almost* the same but not quite:

$$\text{If } f(x) = x^3 + \sqrt{x} \text{ and } g(x) = 2x + 2, \text{ what is } g(f(1))\ ?$$

Again, work from the inside out. This time, start with $f(1)$, which is now the inner function:

$$f(1) = (1)^3 + \sqrt{1} = 1 + 1 = 2$$

159

Use the result from the *inner* function, $f(1) = 2$, as the new input variable for the *outer* function g:

$$g(f(1)) = g(2) = 2(2) + 2 = 6$$

In general, $f(g(x))$ and $g(f(x))$ are *not* the same and will lead to different outcomes. As an analogy, think of "putting on socks" and "putting on shoes" as two separate functions: The order in which you perform these steps matters!

You may be asked to find a value of x for which $f(g(x)) = g(f(x))$. For example:

If $f(x) = x^3 + 6$ and $g(x) = 2x$, for what value of x does $f(g(x)) = g(f(x))$?

Evaluate as you did in the problems above, but this time use x itself as the input value:

$$\text{Given } f(x) = x^3 + 6 \text{ and } g(x) = 2x$$

$$f(g(x)) = g(f(x))$$

Substitute for the inner function: $\quad f(2x) = g(x^3 + 6)$

Substitute for the outer function: $\quad (2x)^3 + 6 = 2(x^3 + 6)$

Simplify: $\quad 8x^3 + 6 = 2x^3 + 12$

$$6x^3 = 6$$

$$x^3 = 1$$

$$x = \sqrt[3]{1}$$

$$x = 1$$

Check Your Skills

4. If $f(x) = \dfrac{1}{x+2} + (x-1)^2$, what is $f(-1)$?

5. If $t(u) = au^2 - 3u + 1$ and $t(3) = 37$, what is the value of a ?

6. If $f(x) = 3x - \sqrt{x}$ and $g(x) = x^2$, what is $g(f(4))$?

Answers can be found on pages 161-162.

Chapter 6: **Formulas and Functions**

Check Your Skills Answer Key

1. **70**
   Baking time in minutes $= \dfrac{Vk}{T}$

   $$30 = \dfrac{15\,\cancel{0}\,k}{35\,\cancel{0}}$$

   $$\dfrac{(30)(35)}{15} = k$$

   $$70 = k$$

   In this problem, it's useful to cancel out a zero from the top and bottom of the fraction in order to reduce both how much you have to write and how many buttons you need to push on the calculator.

2. **(E) 20**
   Deal with the portion in the parentheses first:

   $$3 \Delta 1 = 3^1 + 1 = 4$$

   Then, substitute that result for $3 \Delta 1$:

   $$-2 \Delta (3 \Delta 1) =$$
   $$-2 \Delta 4 =$$
   $$(-2)^4 + 4 =$$
   $$16 + 4 = 20$$

3. **(C) $x + 9$**
   Substitute x for s and 6 for t, then simplify:

   $$x \lambda 6 = \dfrac{(x)(6)}{6} + \dfrac{(3)(6)}{2}$$
   $$= x\ \ +\ \ 9$$

4. **5**
   Plug in (-1) for each occurrence of x in the function:

   $$f(-1) = \dfrac{1}{-1+2} + (-1-1)^2$$
   $$= \dfrac{1}{1} + (-2)^2$$
   $$= 1 + 4 = 5$$

5. **5**
   Plug in 3 for u in the definition of $t(u)$, set that equal to 37, and solve for a:

   $$t(u) = au^2 - 3u + 1$$
   $$t(3) = a(3)^2 - 3(3) + 1 = 37$$
   $$9a - 9 + 1 = 37$$
   $$9a = 45$$
   $$a = 5$$

Unit Two: **Algebra**

6. **100**

   First, find the value of the inner function:

   $$f(x) = 3x - \sqrt{x}$$
   $$f(4) = 3(4) - \sqrt{4}$$
   $$f(4) = 10$$

   Then, find $g(10)$:

   $$g(x) = x^2$$
   $$g(10) = (10)^2 = 100$$

Chapter 6: **Formulas and Functions**

Problem Set

1. If $A \diamond B = 4A - B$, what is the value of $(3 \diamond 2) \diamond 3$?

2. If 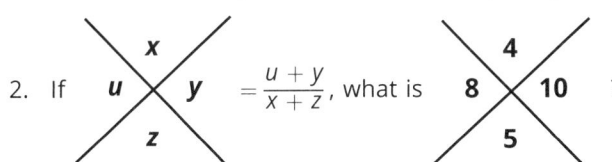 $= \frac{u+y}{x+z}$, what is [8, 4, 10, 5] ?

3. The formula for spring factor in a shoe insole is $\frac{w^2 + x}{3}$, where w is the width of the insole in centimeters and x is the grade of rubber on a scale of 1 to 9. What is the maximum spring factor for an insole that is 3 centimeters wide?

4. The cost of a certain commodity is expressed by the formula tb^4, where t and b are both greater than 0. If b is doubled, by what factor will the cost of the commodity increase?

    (A) 2

    (B) 6

    (C) 8

    (D) 16

    (E) $\frac{1}{2}$

5. The "competitive edge" of a baseball team is defined by the formula $\sqrt{\frac{W}{L}}$, where W represents the number of wins and L represents the number of losses. This year, the GRE All-Stars had twice as many wins and one-half as many losses as they had last year. By what factor did their "competitive edge" increase?

6. If $f(x) = 2x^4 - x^2$, what is the value of $f(2\sqrt{3})$?

7. If $k(x) = 4x^3 a$, and $k(3) = 54$, what is $k(2)$?

8. If $f(x) = 3x - \sqrt{x}$ and $g(x) = x^2$, what is $f(g(4))$?

9. $P \blacksquare Q = P + 2Q$ for all integers P and Q

Quantity A	**Quantity B**
$11 \blacksquare 5$	$5 \blacksquare 11$

10. $@(x) = x^2 - 4$

Quantity A	**Quantity B**
$@(10)$	$@(@(4))$

Unit Two: **Algebra**

Solutions

1. **37**

    Simplify the function inside the parentheses first.

    $$3 \diamond 2 = 4(3) - 2 = 12 - 2 = 10$$

    Then, replacing (3 ◊ 2) with its output value of 10, solve the second function.

    $$10 \diamond 3 = 4(10) - 3 = 40 - 3 = 37$$

2. **2**

    Plug the numbers in the grid into the formula, matching up the number in each section with the corresponding variable in the formula.

    $$\frac{u + y}{x + z} = \frac{8 + 10}{4 + 5} = \frac{18}{9} = 2$$

3. **6**

    Determine the maximum spring factor by setting $x = 9$.

    Let s = spring factor.

    $$s = \frac{w^2 + x}{3} \qquad s = \frac{(3)^2 + 9}{3} = \frac{18}{3} = 6$$

4. **(D) 16**

    Pick numbers to see what happens to the cost when b is doubled. If the original value of b is 1, the cost of the commodity is t. When b is doubled to 2, the new cost is $16t$. The cost has increased by a factor of 16.

5. **2**

    Let c = competitive edge.

    $$c = \sqrt{\frac{W}{L}}$$

    Pick numbers to see what happens to the competitive edge when W is doubled and L is halved. If the original value of W is 2 and the original value of L is 2, the original value of c is $\sqrt{\frac{2}{2}} = 1$. If W doubles to 4 and L is halved to 1, the new value of c is $\sqrt{\frac{4}{1}} = 2$. The competitive edge has increased from 1 to 2, so it has increased by a factor of 2.

Chapter 6: **Formulas and Functions**

6. **276**

    Substitute $2\sqrt{3}$ for x everywhere it appears in the formula, then simplify:

    $$f(x) = 2x^4 - x^2$$
    $$f(2\sqrt{3}) = 2(2\sqrt{3})^4 - (2\sqrt{3})^2$$
    $$= 2 \times 2^4 \sqrt{3}^4 - 2^2 \sqrt{3}^2$$
    $$= 2^5 \, 3^2 - 2^2 3$$
    $$= 32 \times 9 - 4 \times 3$$
    $$= 288 - 12$$
    $$f(2\sqrt{3}) = 276$$

    Note that raising a square root of a term to the fourth power is the same thing as raising that term to the second power. You can prove this by rewriting the square root as an exponent of $\frac{1}{2}$ and then combining exponents: $\sqrt{3}^4 = \left(3^{\frac{1}{2}}\right)^4 = 3^{\frac{1}{2} \times 4} = 3^2$.

7. **16**

    Use the fact that $k(3) = 54$ to solve for a, then solve for $k(2)$.

    $$k(x) = 4x^3 a$$
    $$k(3) = 4(3)^3 a = 54$$
    $$4(27)a = 54$$
    $$108a = 54$$
    $$a = \frac{1}{2}$$

    Once you've determined a, simplify and solve for $k(2)$.

    $$k(x) = 4x^3 \left(\frac{1}{2}\right) = 2x^3$$
    $$k(2) = \ 2(2)^3 \ = 16$$

8. **44**

    First, find the output value of the inner function: $g(4) = 4^2 = 16$. Substitute that output value into $f(g(4))$. If $g(4) = 16$, then $f(g(4))$ is $f(16)$. Find $f(16)$: $3(16) - \sqrt{16} = 48 - 4 = 44$.

165

Unit Two: **Algebra**

9. **(B)**
Use the given formula to solve for both quantities.

$$P \blacksquare Q = P + 2Q \text{ for all integers } P \text{ and } Q$$

Quantity A	**Quantity B**
$11 \blacksquare 5 =$	$5 \blacksquare 11 =$
$(11) + 2 \times (5) =$	$(5) + 2 \times (11) =$
$11 + 10 = \mathbf{21}$	$5 + 22 = \mathbf{27}$

Therefore, the correct answer is (B): Quantity B is greater.

10. **(B)**
Use the given formula to solve for both quantities.

$$@(x) = x^2 - 4$$

Quantity A	**Quantity B**
$@(10) =$	$@(@(4)) =$
$10^2 - 4 =$	$@(4^2 - 4) =$
$100 - 4 = \mathbf{96}$	$@(16 - 4) =$
	$@(12) =$
	$@(12^2 - 4) =$
	$144 - 4 = \mathbf{140}$

Solve for the @(4) term, then plug that solution into the formula again to determine Quantity B.

Therefore, the correct answer is (B): Quantity B is greater.

CHAPTER 7

Inequalities and Systems of Equations

In This Chapter:

- Interpreting Inequalities
- Solving Inequalities
- Manipulating Compound Inequalities
- Inequalities and Absolute Values
- Systems of Equations
- An Equation and an Inequality
- Seriously, Distribute!
- Two Inequalities
- Equations on QC
- Check Your Skills Answer Key
- Problem Set
- Solutions

CHAPTER 7: Inequalities and Systems of Equations

Now that you're more familiar with exponents and substitution, it's time to tackle inequalities and more advanced equations.

Inequalities behave similarly to equations in most ways, but with a few important distinctions. What is written on one side of the inequality has a relationship to what is on the other side, but the two sides are not defined as strictly equal. For example:

$$3x - 5 \leq 6x - 11$$

The left side, $3x - 5$, is less than *or* equal to the right side, $6x - 11$. In this chapter, you'll learn how to manipulate and solve this and more complicated inequalities, as well as how to solve when you are given an inequality alongside an absolute value equation, a regular equation, or a second inequality.

Interpreting Inequalities

Inequalities are expressions that use $<$, $>$, $\leq$, or $\geq$ to describe the relationship between two values. Each of these signs has a distinct meaning:

$<$	Less than
$>$	Greater than
$\leq$	Less than or equal to (or *at most*)
$\geq$	Greater than or equal to (or *at least*)

Translating inequalities correctly is essential. Read them from left to right:

	Read as...	or...
$5 > 4$	5 is greater than 4.	
$y \leq 7$	y is less than or equal to 7.	y is at most 7.
$x < 5$	x is less than 5.	
$2x + 3 \geq 0$	$2x + 3$ is greater than or equal to 0.	$2x + 3$ is at least 0.

You can also have two inequalities in one statement (sometimes called a **compound inequality**):

	Read as...
$9 < f < 200$	9 is less than f, and f is less than 200. Alternatively, f is between 9 and 200.
$-3 < y \leq 5$	-3 is less than y, and y is less than or equal to 5.
$7 \geq x \geq 2$	7 is greater than or equal to x, and x is greater than or equal to 2. Alternatively, x is between 2 and 7, inclusive.

Why does the last example use the word *inclusive* in the alternative reading? And why does the middle example not have an alternative form at all?

Mathematically, the word *inclusive* means *including*. If x is between 2 and 7 inclusive, then 2 and 7 are included in that range; that is, x can be 2 and x can be 7. Contrast that with: f is between 9 and 200. In this case, f must be between those two values but f cannot be either 9 or 200.

The middle example, $-3 < y \leq 5$, contains mixed inequality symbols. Using the word *inclusive* here implies that y can be -3, which is not true. Conversely, omitting the word *inclusive* implies that y cannot be 5, which also is not true. So this example can't have an alternative wording as the other two examples do.

Use the word *inclusive* when *both* symbols are "or equal to" symbols: $\leq$ or $\geq$. Otherwise, don't use the word *inclusive*.

A number line is a helpful way to visualize inequalities:

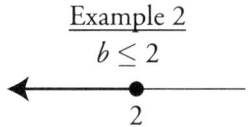

Example 1 $y > 5$	Example 2 $b \leq 2$
Example 1 indicates that any value to the right of 5—that is, greater than 5—is a possible value of y. The empty circle indicates that 5 itself is not a possible solution, since y is strictly greater than 5.	Example 2 indicates that any value to the left of *and* including 2 is a possible value of b. The closed circle indicates that b can equal 2.

Visually, any number covered by the black arrow or a closed circle will make the inequality true and is therefore a solution to the inequality. Conversely, any number not covered by the black arrow or a closed circle will make the inequality untrue and thus is not a solution.

Chapter 7: **Inequalities and Systems of Equations**

Check Your Skills

> Represent the following equations on the number line provided.

1. $x > 3$

    ← +—+—+—+—+—+—+—+—+ →
      −3 −2 −1 0 1 2 3 4 5

2. $b \geq -2$

    ← +—+—+—+—+—+—+—+—+ →
      −3 −2 −1 0 1 2 3 4 5

3. $y = 4$

    ← +—+—+—+—+—+—+—+—+ →
      −3 −2 −1 0 1 2 3 4 5

> Translate the following into inequality statements.

4. z is greater than v.

5. The total amount is at least $2,000.

Answers can be found on page 189.

Solving Inequalities

What does it mean to solve an inequality?

Essentially, the principle is the same as that for solving an equation. A solution to an equation or inequality is a number that makes that equation or inequality true. When you plug a solution back into the original equation or inequality, you get a *true statement*.

However, while equations on the GRE tend to have only one or two values as solutions, inequalities give a whole *range* of values as solutions—way too many to list individually.

Here's a comparison to illustrate:

Equation	Inequality
$x + 3 = 8$	$x + 3 < 8$
$-3 \quad -3$	$-3 \quad -3$
$x = 5$	$x < 5$

In the equation, there's just one solution: x must be 5. If you tried to substitute any number other than 5 for x into the equation you would get a nonsensical answer. For example, $2 + 3$ does not equal 8.

Unit Two: **Algebra**

However, there are many different numbers that would make the inequality true—as long as those values are less than 5. Here are just a few possible values of *x* for the inequality:

Is this true?	Check the math: $x + 3 < 8$?	Outcome
$x = 2$	$2 + 3 < 8$? $5 < 8$?	True, so 2 is a valid solution.
$x = -7$	$-7 + 3 < 8$? $-4 < 8$?	True, so -7 is a valid solution.
$x = 6$	$6 + 3 < 8$? $9 < 8$?	False, so 6 is *not* a valid solution.

Because inequalities tend to have many possible solutions, this topic is commonly tested in the Select All That Apply format.

Check Your Skills

6. Which of the following values of *x* are solutions to the inequality $x < 10$?

    Indicate <u>all</u> such values.

    A -3
    B 2.5
    C $-\frac{3}{2}$
    D 9.999

Answers can be found on page 189.

7 Simplifying Inequalities

Many of the rules you learned with respect to equations will still apply to inequalities; you'll learn about the few exceptions in this chapter.

The rules of PEMDAS apply, and whatever you do to one side of the inequality you must still do to the other side. The goal of isolating a variable remains the same:

$$2x + 6 < 12$$
Subtract 6: $\quad -6 \quad\quad -6$
$$2x < 6$$
Divide by 2: $\quad \div 2 \quad\quad \div 2$
$$x < 3$$

The inequalities $2x + 6 < 12$ and $x < 3$ provide the same information, but the second inequality is much easier to understand.

Chapter 7: Inequalities and Systems of Equations

Simplifying via Addition and Subtraction

With equations, if you add the same number to both sides, the equation is still true.

The same principle holds true for inequalities. If you add or subtract the same number from both sides, that inequality remains true:

$$\underline{\text{Example 1}}$$
$$a - 4 > 6$$
$$+4 \quad +4$$
$$a > 10$$

$$\underline{\text{Example 2}}$$
$$y + 7 < 3$$
$$-7 \quad -7$$
$$y < -4$$

You can also add or subtract variables from both sides of an inequality. There is no difference between adding/subtracting numbers and adding/subtracting variables:

$$3 - y > 0$$
$$+y \quad +y$$
$$3 > y$$

Check Your Skills

> Isolate the variable in the following inequalities.

7. $x - 6 < 13$

8. $y + 11 \geq -13$

Answers can be found on page 189.

Simplification via Multiplication and Division

You can also use multiplication and division to isolate the variables within an inequality, as long as you follow one new rule: *When you multiply or divide an inequality by a negative number, switch the direction of the inequality sign.*

For example:

$$-2x > 10$$
$$\div -2 \quad \div -2$$
$$x < -5$$

Because the two sides of the inequality are divided by a negative number, the inequality sign switches directions.

By contrast, if you multiply or divide by a positive number, the direction of the sign stays the same. You don't need to do anything special:

Example 1

$$2x > 10$$
$$\div 2 \quad \div 2$$
$$x > 5$$

Example 2

$$\frac{z}{3} \leq 2$$
$$\times 3 \quad \times 3$$
$$z \leq 6$$

> **Key Concept**
>
> When multiplying or dividing both sides of an inequality by a negative number, flip the sign.

What about multiplying or dividing an inequality by a *variable*? First, ask yourself whether you know the sign of that variable. If the problem specifies that the variable is positive, go ahead (and you won't need to flip the sign). If the problem specifies that the variable is negative, go ahead (but this time, flip the sign).

However, if the problem doesn't specify the sign of the variable, then do *not* proceed! If you don't know whether the variable represents a positive or negative number, then you can't know whether to flip the sign. Instead, try to work through the problem with the inequality as is, or simplify it in a way that doesn't involve multiplying or dividing by the variable.

If the problem is a Quantitative Comparison problem, consider whether not knowing the sign of the variable might lead to answer (D).

Check Your Skills

> Isolate the variable in each equation.

9. $2x - 4 \geq 2$

10. $-2y - 4 < 8$

11. If $ab \neq 0$ and $ab - 3 < 5$, which of the following could be true?

    Select <u>all</u> that apply.

    A. $a < \frac{8}{b}$

    B. $a > \frac{8}{b}$

    C. $ab^2 = 0$

Answers can be found on pages 189–190.

Chapter 7: **Inequalities and Systems of Equations**

Manipulating Compound Inequalities

A compound inequality has three (or more) parts, not two:

$$x + 3 < y < x + 5$$

The rules for compound inequalities are the same as for simple inequalities, including the rule to perform the same operation on both sides. In a compound inequality, though, there are three "sides" or parts to the inequality, so perform the operation on all three parts:

$$\begin{array}{ccccc} x + 3 & < & y & < & x + 5 \\ -3 & & -3 & & -3 \\ \hline x & < & y - 3 & < & x + 2 \end{array}$$

It would *not* be correct to rearrange the inequality as $x < y < x + 2$, because the 3 must be subtracted from all three parts of the inequality, not just the first and last portions. Here's another example:

$$\begin{array}{ccccc} \frac{c}{2} & \leq & b - 3 & \leq & \frac{d}{2} \\ \times 2 & & \times 2 & & \times 2 \\ \hline c & \leq & 2(b - 3) & \leq & d \end{array}$$

The 2 is multiplied across all three parts of the inequality.

Try this problem:

If $1 > 1 - ab > 0$, which of the following must be true?

Indicate all such statements.

- [A] $\frac{a}{b} > 0$
- [B] $\frac{a}{b} < 1$
- [C] $ab < 1$

The answer choices all have the variables isolated (that is, on one side by themselves), so manipulate the compound inequality given in the question stem to get the *ab* term by itself:

Given inequality:	$1 > 1 - ab > 0$
Subtract 1 from all three terms:	$0 > -ab > -1$
Multiply all three terms by -1. Flip all inequality signs:	$0 < ab < 1$

The fact that $0 < ab < 1$ indicates that *ab* must be positive, so *a* and *b* have to have the same sign. As a result, $\frac{a}{b}$ must be positive. Therefore, choice (A) must be true. The rewritten inequality also indicates that *ab* is less than 1, so answer (C) must also be true.

However, it's not possible to tell whether $\frac{a}{b} < 1$, so answer (B) is not necessarily true. Therefore, the correct answers are (A) and (C) only.

Unit Two: **Algebra**

Check Your Skills

12. If $-7 < 3 - 2x < 9$, what is the range of possible values for *x*?

Answers can be found on page 190.

Inequalities and Absolute Values

Some problems on the GRE include both inequalities and absolute values. You can solve these problems by combining everything you have learned about inequalities and about absolute value equations. For example:

$$|x| \geq 4$$

The absolute value is already isolated on one side, so set up two inequalities. The first inequality solves for the positive version, so the sign remains the same. The second inequality solves for the negative version, so the sign is flipped:

$$x \geq +(4) \qquad x \leq -(4)$$

Although it doesn't matter in this particular problem, do remember to add parentheses around whatever is on the right side of the equation. Here are the two solutions represented on a number line:

As before, any number that is covered by the black arrow, including a closed circle, will make the inequality true. Because there are two solutions, there are now two arrows instead of one, but the meaning is the same. Any number to the left of -4 and -4 itself will make the inequality true, as will 4 and any number to the right of 4.

The absolute value of a number represents its distance from 0, so you can also interpret the inequality in terms of distance: $|x| \geq 4$ means "*x* is *at least* 4 units away from zero, in either direction."

Try this problem:

$$|x + 3| < 5$$

Once again, the absolute value is already isolated on one side, so set up the two inequalities. The first inequality replaces the absolute value with the *positive* of what's inside, and the second replaces the absolute value with the *negative* of what's inside:

$$x + 3 < +(5) \qquad x + 3 > -(5)$$

Next, isolate the variable in each inequality:

$$x + 3 < 5 \qquad x + 3 > -5$$
$$x < 2 \qquad x > -8$$

Plot the result on a number line:

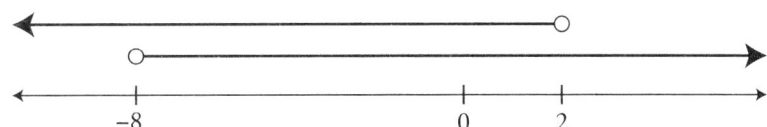

It seems like every number should be a solution to the equation However, that isn't the case. Test $x = 5$, for example. Is $|5 + 3| < 5$? No, it isn't.

As it turns out, the only numbers that make the original inequality true are those that are true for *both* inequalities. The number line should actually look like this:

In other words, the solution is $-8 < x < 2$. When the two solution ranges overlap, combine them into one compound inequality, starting with the least value (in this case, -8). You don't need to test values to see whether you need to combine them; you'll always combine when the ranges overlap. If you need to graph the solution, the graph will always be a line segment, as shown for this example.

Contrast this with the first example, for which the solution was $x \geq 4$ and $x \leq -4$. These two ranges don't overlap. When that is the case, write them in exactly this way, as two separate inequalities. If you need to graph the solution, the graph will have double arrows pointing in opposite directions, as shown for the first example.

Check Your Skills

13. Given $|x + 1| > 2$, plot x on a number line.

14. Given $|-x - 4| \geq 8$, plot x on a number line.

15. Given $|x - 7| < 9$, plot x on a number line.

Answers can be found on pages 190–191.

Systems of Equations

On the GRE, you may have to handle multiple equations or inequalities at the same time. The most common system of equations is two equations with two unknowns. These may be presented in algebraic form, hidden in word problems, or expressed as functions. The question will then ask about one variable or a relationship between the variables. For example:

If $3x + y = 10$ and $y = x - 2$, what is the value of y ?

To solve, you'll need to combine the two equations to get one equation containing one variable. There are two main ways to do so: **substitution** and **elimination**.

Unit Two: **Algebra**

Substitution

Substitution involves first isolating one variable in one of the equations and then substituting the associated expression into the other equation. For example:

Given:	$3x + y = 10$ and $y = x - 2$
1. Isolate a variable in one equation. In this case, one equation has y isolated already:	$y = x - 2$
2. Substitute $x - 2$ into the other equation for y:	$y = x - 2$ $3x + y = 10$ $3x + (x - 2) = 10$
3. Solve the new equation:	$3x + (x - 2) = 10$ $4x - 2 = 10$ $4x = 12$ $x = 3$
4. (If needed) Plug $x = 3$ into either equation to solve for y:	$y = (3) - 2 = 1$

In this case, the problem was naturally set up to solve for the value of x first, so it was necessary to use step 4 to solve for y. You can, however, take one step at the beginning to eliminate the need to have to do the extra step at the end: At step 1, try to isolate the variable for which you have *not* been asked to solve. Here's how:

Given:	$3x + y = 10$ and $y = x - 2$
1. Isolate the variable that you *don't* want. In this case, isolate x:	$y = x - 2$ $y + 2 = x$
2. Substitute $y + 2$ into the other equation for x:	$x = y + 2$ $3x + y = 10$ $3(y + 2) + y = 10$
3. Solve the new equation:	$3(y + 2) + y = 10$ $3y + 6 + y = 10$ $4y = 4$ $y = 1$
4. (If needed) Plug $y = 1$ into either equation to solve for y:	Not needed! The question asked only for the value of y.

Before you dive into the work, consider whether it's relatively easy to isolate the variable that you *don't* want to solve for. If so, isolate that variable and you'll save yourself a step at the end.

Chapter 7: **Inequalities and Systems of Equations**

> **Key Concept: Substitution**
>
> Given two variables and two equations:
>
> 1. Isolate a variable in one equation, ideally the variable that you *don't* want.
>
> 2. Substitute the result for that variable into the other equation.
>
> 3. Solve the new equation.
>
> 4. (Only if needed!) Plug that result into either equation to solve for the other variable.

Try the process yourself with this harder problem:

If $2x + 4y = 14$ and $x - y = -8$, what is the value of x?

Step 1: Isolate a variable, ideally the one you don't want

In this case, the problem asks for the value of x, so consider isolating the other variable, y. The math will work either way, so if you find it easier to isolate x instead, do so. Just remember that you'll have to do step 4 at the end. Here's how to isolate y:

$$x - y = -8$$
$$x = y - 8$$
$$x + 8 = y$$

Step 2: Substitute into the other equation

Substitute $x + 8$ into y in the other equation, the one you haven't used yet:

$$y = \underline{x + 8}$$
$$2x + 4y = 14$$
$$2x + 4(x + 8) = 14$$

Step 3: Solve the new equation

Solve the new equation for x:

$$2x + 4(x + 8) = 14$$
$$2x + 4x + 32 = 14$$
$$6x = -18$$
$$x = -3$$

179

Step 4: If needed, solve for the other variable

The question asked for x, so you're done. There's no need to find the value of y.

On math tests in school, you were almost always asked to find the values for all variables in the problem. By contrast, the GRE will usually ask you to solve for just one specific variable. Don't automatically solve for everything! Save yourself time and mental energy by setting the problem up to solve directly for the desired variable.

And there's a bonus: You'll also be saving yourself a potential careless mistake, as the GRE is likely to include the value for the other variable among the answer choices—as a trap. If you never solve for the other variable, you can't fall for that trap!

Check Your Skills

> Use substitution to solve.

16. If $x - y = 2$ and $x + 2y = 26$, what is the value of y?

17. If $x + 4y = 10$ and $y - x = -5$, what is the value of y?

18. If $6x + 15 = 3y$ and $x + y = 14$, what is the value of x?

Answers can be found on pages 192-193.

Elimination

Alternatively, elimination can be used to solve two equations. This method is sometimes called "stack and add" because you literally write one equation below the other and add vertically to make one variable cancel out. For example, you're asked to find x and given these two equations:

$$2z - 7x = -11$$
$$2x - 2z = 1$$

Rearrange so that the like variables line up, then add the equations vertically:

$$2z - 7x = -11$$
$$+ \; -2z + 2x = \;\;\; 1$$
$$\overline{0 - 5x = -10}$$

The $2z$ and $-2z$ terms add up to 0 and cancel out, leaving only x in the equation. Finally, solve for x:

$$-5x = -10$$
$$x = 2$$

Chapter 7: **Inequalities and Systems of Equations**

Here is the full process, including one step (step 2) that the prior example didn't have:

> **Key Concept: Elimination**
>
> Given two variables and two equations:
>
> 1. Arrange the equations so the variables are on the same side and in order.
>
> 2. For the variable that you *don't* want, manipulate the coefficients so that they are the same but with different signs.
>
> 3. Add vertically and solve.
>
> 4. (Only if needed!) Plug that result back into either equation to solve for the other variable.

Try this one using all four elimination steps:

$$\text{If } 3x + y = 10 \text{ and } y = x - 2, \text{ what is the value of } y?$$

Step 1: Arrange the variables in order

Subtract *x* from both sides of the second equation to put the variables on the same side. Also, put them in the same order:

$$y + 3x = 10$$
$$y - x = -2$$

Step 2: Manipulate the coefficients of the variable you don't want

This problem asked for *y*, so the undesired variable is *x*. Currently, the two x terms, $3x$ and $-x$, already have opposite signs, but they don't have the same value. Multiply every term in the second equation by 3 in order to make the second *x* term equal to $-3x$:

$$3(y - x) = 3(-2)$$
$$3y - 3x = -6$$

Step 3

Line up the two equations, add (eliminating *x*), and solve for *y*:

$$
\begin{array}{rrrcr}
 & y & + \ 3x & = & 10 \\
+ & 3y & - \ 3x & = & -6 \\
\hline
 & 4y & + \ 0 & = & 4 \\
 & y & & = & 1
\end{array}
$$

181

Unit Two: **Algebra**

Step 4: If needed, solve for the other variable

If needed, you could substitute y back into either original equation to solve for x, but since the question asks for y, don't bother.

Substitution vs. Elimination

Both solution methods are valid, so you can always choose whichever one you prefer. It's worth noticing two characteristics to help you decide.

1. If the undesired variable is already isolated or is very easy to isolate, then substitution will likely be the easier method.

2. If a variable has the same coefficient (number in front) in both equations but one is positive and one is negative, then elimination is a good path to choose.

If a particular problem has both of those characteristics—or neither of them—then use whichever solution method you prefer.

Check Your Skills

Directions

Use elimination to solve the same problems from the substitution set. Then decide which method you prefer for each problem (so that you don't have to spend much time deciding on the real test).

19. If $x - y = 2$ and $x + 2y = 26$, what is the value of y?

20. If $x + 4y = 10$ and $y - x = -5$, what is the value of y?

21. If $6x + 15 = 3y$ and $x + y = 14$, what is the value of x?

Answers can be found on pages 193-194.

An Equation and an Inequality

Substitution can also be used to combine an equation with an inequality. (But you can't use the elimination method for this.)

There is just one additional step to add to the standard substitution process: When you first isolate a variable, always do so *in the equation*, then substitute that into the inequality. For example:

If $x - 7y = 5$ and $2x - 4y < 20$, what is the range of possible values for y?

First, because the question asks for y, isolate x in the equation:

$$x - 7y = 5$$

$$x = 5 + 7y$$

Second, substitute the term $5 + 7y$ into the inequality—and don't forget the parentheses:

$$2x - 4y < 20$$
$$2(5 + 7y) - 4y < 20$$

Finally, solve for y:

$$2(5 + 7y) - 4y < 20$$
$$10 + 14y - 4y < 20$$
$$10 + 10y < 20$$
$$10y < 10$$
$$y < 1$$

Therefore, the range of all possible values of y is every number less than one.

> **Strategy Tip**
>
> When substituting for a variable, always put the substituted terms in parentheses. Then, distribute as needed.

Check Your Skills

22. If $z + 2x > 6$ and $x + 2z = 6$, what is z?

Answers can be found on page 195.

Seriously, Distribute!

By far the most common error in solving algebraic expressions is incorrectly distributing or forgetting to distribute entirely. The error most commonly occurs when there's a negative sign that needs to be distributed. Every term in the parentheses, including negative terms, needs to be multiplied by -1 when there's a negative sign outside of the parentheses. Here are three examples:

$x - (y - z) = x - y + z$	Distribute -1 to both the y and the $-z$ terms.
$x - (y + z) = x - y - z$	Distribute -1 to both the y and the z terms.
$x - 2(y - 3z) = x - 2y + 6z$	Distribute -2 to both the y and the $-3z$ terms.

Try this problem:

Simplify the expression: $5x - [y - (3x - 4y)]$

Unit Two: **Algebra**

The square brackets are just fancy parentheses, used to avoid having double parentheses right next to each other. Work from the innermost parentheses outward:

$$5x - [y - (3x - 4y)] =$$
$$5x - [y - 3x + 4y] =$$
$$5x - y + 3x - 4y = 8x - 5y$$

Try this problem:

If $2x + y = 5$, and $3x - 2y = 18$, what is $3x - y$?

Because the question stem doesn't ask for just one variable, solve for both. Use the four-step process:

Step 1: Isolate a variable (in this case, y is easiest):	$2x + y = 5$
	$y = 5 - 2x$
Step 2: Substitute $5 - 2x$ into the other equation:	$3x - 2y = 18$
	$3x - 2(5 - 2x) = 18$
Step 3: Solve for x:	$3x - 2(5 - 2x) = 18$
	$3x - 10 + 4x = 18$
	$7x - 10 = 18$
	$7x = 28$
	$x = 4$
Step 4: Plug $x = 4$ into either original equation and solve for y:	$2x + y = 5$
	$2(4) + y = 5$
	$8 + y = 5$
	$y = -3$

Now, given that $x = 4$ and $y = -3$, solve for the question: What is $3x - y$?

$$3x - y = 3(4) - (-3) = 12 + 3 = 15$$

Throughout this problem, distribution is key to arriving at the correct answer. Whenever you're substituting in an expression or even just a value, use parentheses. Then, distribute as needed from there.

Check Your Skills

23. Simplify: $3a - [2a - (3b - a)]$

Answers can be found on page 195.

Two Inequalities

While substitution is a great tool for combining equations and inequalities, don't use it to combine two inequalities. Instead, use elimination.

Elimination with two inequalities is identical to the elimination you learned with two equations, with one added caveat: The inequality signs must face the same direction in order to add inequalities to each other.

It might not be immediately clear why it's acceptable to add two inequalities. The sum of the two lesser sides will always be less than the sum of the two greater sides. For example, it is certainly true that 3 is less than 7. It is also true that 5 is less than 10. Arrange these as inequalities with the signs pointed in the same direction, then add:

$$\begin{array}{r} 3 < 7 \\ +5 < 10 \\ \hline 8 < 17 \end{array}$$

This works even when negatives are involved, as long as the inequality signs are pointed in the same direction:

$$\begin{array}{r} -6 > -10 \\ +2 > -4 \\ \hline -4 > -14 \end{array}$$

The sum of two lesser values is always going to be less than the sum of two greater values.

This method only works when adding inequalities. Never subtract inequalities! For example, try to subtract $6 > 2$ from $9 > 8$. Even though both inequalities are true, their difference is not:

$$\begin{array}{rl} 9 > 8 & \text{True} \\ -(6 > 2) & \text{True} \\ \hline 3 > 6 & \text{False!} \end{array}$$

If you try to subtract two inequalities, sometimes you'll get a true result and sometimes you won't...so just don't try this in the first place.

> **Key Concept**
>
> To combine two inequalities, arrange the inequalities so that the inequality signs are facing the *same direction*, then *add* the inequalities.

Try this problem:

If $6x + 8 > y$ and $3x + 5 < y$, what are x and y?

There are two inequalities, but the signs are pointing in opposite directions.

$$6x + 8 > y$$
$$3x + 5 < y$$

First, reframe one inequality so that the two inequality signs are facing the same direction. For example, if you multiply the second inequality by -1, it will flip the sign so the two inequality signs match:

$$3x + 5 < y \quad \rightarrow \quad -3x - 5 > -y$$

Also, the coefficients of the two y terms are the same, 1, but opposite in sign. Now add the inequalities to eliminate the y:

$$\begin{aligned} 6x + 8 &> y \\ + \quad -3x - 5 &> -y \\ \hline 3x + 3 &> 0 \end{aligned}$$

Simplify the inequality to solve for x:

$$3x + 3 > 0$$
$$3x > -3$$
$$x > -1$$

So $x > -1$. To solve for y, go back to the original inequalities and eliminate x this time. Consider what you would need to change to make the inequality signs point in the same direction and make the coefficients of x opposites:

$$6x + 8 > y$$
$$3x + 5 < y$$

Multiplying the second inequality by -2 would accomplish both tasks:

$$3x + 5 < y \quad \rightarrow \quad -6x - 10 > -2y$$

Now add the inequalities to eliminate x:

$$\begin{aligned} 6x + 8 &> y \\ + \quad -6x - 10 &> -2y \\ \hline -2 &> -y \end{aligned}$$

To solve for y, divide by -1. Don't forget to flip the sign!

$$-2 > -y \quad \rightarrow \quad 2 < y$$

The solution is $x > -1$ and $y > 2$.

Check Your Skills

24. If $2x < 1 + y$ and $1 + 3x > 2y$, what is the value of x ?

Answers can be found on page 195.

Equations on QC

The first strategy you learned for QC questions was to Simplify and Pick Numbers. If you are given an equation, it might be the case that you can pick only certain numbers and it might be the case that you don't need to pick numbers at all. Whenever you see an equation on a QC problem, simplify first. For example:

$$x - 3 = 12$$
$$y + 2x = 40$$

Quantity A	Quantity B
y	9

Given two equations and two unknowns, you may be able to solve for y and thus know the value of Quantity A definitively. Here's how to solve using substitution:

$$x - 3 = 12 \quad \text{Solve for } x.$$
$$x = 15$$
$$y + 2x = 40 \quad \text{Substitute and solve.}$$
$$y + 2(15) = 40$$
$$y + 30 = 40$$
$$y = 10$$

Since $y = 10$, the correct answer is (A): Quantity A is greater.

Try this problem:

$$\frac{x+5}{5} = \frac{y+6}{6}$$

Quantity A	Quantity B
$6x$	$5y$

In this problem, you are given one equation that contains two variables: x and y. You won't be able to solve for the value of either variable, but that doesn't mean the answer will be (D). Simplify the equation to make it more relatable to what's given in Quantities A and B:

Given:	$\frac{x+5}{5} = \frac{y+6}{6}$
Multiply both sides by 5 to get rid of the left-side fraction:	$x + 5 = \frac{5(y+6)}{6}$
Multiply both sides by 6 to get rid of the right-side fraction:	$6(x+5) = 5(y+6)$

The two steps shown above can also be done in just one step together—it's called cross-multiplying. You'll learn more about this in Chapter 11: Comparing Fractions.

Continue to simplify the equation:

$$6(x + 5) = 5(y + 6)$$
$$6x + 30 = 5y + 30$$
$$6x = 5y$$

The two sides of the equation match Quantities A and B. Therefore, the correct answer is (C): The two quantities are equal.

Chapter 7: **Inequalities and Systems of Equations**

Check Your Skills Answer Key

1. ![number line with open circle at 3, from -3 to 5]
2. ![number line with closed circle at -2, from -3 to 5]
3. ![number line with closed circle at 3, from -3 to 5]

4. $z > v$

5. If a = total amount, $a \geq 2000$

6. (A) -3; (B) 2.5; (C) $-\frac{3}{2}$; (D) 9.999

   All of the answer choice values are to the left of 10 on the number line, so all are solutions to the inequality.

   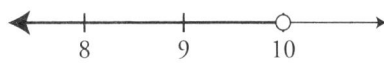

7. $x < 19$

   Add 6 to both sides of the inequality to arrive at $x < 19$.

8. $y \geq -24$

   Subtract 11 from both sides of the inequality to arrive at $y \geq -24$.

9. $x \geq 3$

   Add four to both sides, then divide by 2. Because the division is by a positive number, the sign does not change:

   $$2x - 4 \geq 2$$
   $$2x \geq 6 \quad \text{Add 4.}$$
   $$x \geq 3 \quad \text{Divide by 2.}$$

10. $y > -6$

    Add 4 to both sides and divide by -2. Because you're dividing by a negative, flip the sign:

    $$-2y - 4 < 8$$
    $$-2y < 12 \quad \text{Add 4.}$$
    $$y > -6 \quad \text{Divide by } -2 \text{ and flip the sign.}$$

Unit Two: **Algebra**

11. (A) $a < \frac{8}{b}$; (B) $a > \frac{8}{b}$

   The first step of this simplification is straightforward.

   $$ab - 3 < 5$$
   $$ab \;\;\;\;\; < 8$$

   Now, however, it gets complicated. The question stem didn't indicate whether b was positive or negative. If b is positive, then don't flip the inequality sign, but if b is negative, do flip the inequality sign:

If b is $+$	If b is $-$
$ab < 8$	$ab < 8$
$a < \frac{8}{b}$	$a > \frac{8}{b}$

   The final option, $ab^2 = 0$, cannot be true because the question stem specified that $ab \neq 0$, indicating that neither a nor b individually is equal to 0 and in turn that b^2 is not equal to 0.

12. $5 > x > -3$ or $-3 < x < 5$

   $$-7 < 3 - 2x < 9$$
   $$-10 < -2x < 6 \quad \text{Subtract 3.}$$
   $$5 > x > -3 \quad \text{Divide by } -2. \text{ Flip signs.}$$

   The answer can be written as shown or it can be written starting with the -3. To do this, reverse the order of everything, including the signs: $-3 < x < 5$.

13.

   First, solve the inequality by breaking it up into the positive and negative solutions:

   $$|x + 1| > 2$$

   $$x + 1 > (2) \quad\quad\quad x + 1 < -(2)$$
   $$x > 1 \quad\quad\quad\quad\quad x < -3$$

   Because the two ranges do not overlap, the number line consists of two arrows pointing in opposite directions. Also, because the inequality was greater than, not greater than or equal to, the two circles are open:

190

Chapter 7: **Inequalities and Systems of Equations**

14.

```
    ←●────┼──●──→
     −12  0  4
    x ≤ −12  or  x ≥ 4
```

First, solve the inequality by breaking it up into the positive and negative solutions:

$$|-x - 4| \geq 8$$

$$-x - 4 \geq +(8) \qquad\qquad -x - 4 \leq -(8)$$
$$-x \geq 12 \qquad\qquad -x \leq -4$$
$$x \leq -12 \qquad\qquad x \geq 4$$

Because the two ranges do not overlap, the number line consists of two arrows pointing in opposite directions. Also, because the inequality was greater than or equal to, the two circles are closed:

```
    ←●────┼──●──→
     −12  0  4
    x ≤ −12  or  x ≥ 4
```

15.

First, solve the inequality by breaking it up into the positive and negative solutions:

$$|x - 7| < 9$$

$$x - 7 < +(9) \qquad\qquad x - 7 > -(9)$$
$$x < 16 \qquad\qquad x > -2$$

Because the two ranges overlap, the number line consists of a line segment. The combination of $x > -2$ and $x < 16$ yields the compound inequality $-2 < x < 16$. Also, because the inequality was less than, not less than or equal to, the two circles are open:

```
    ←──○──┼──○──→
       −2 0    16
```

191

16. **y = 8**

The problem asks for y, so begin by isolating x:

$$x - y = 2 \qquad \text{Givens}$$
$$x + 2y = 26$$

$$x - y = 2 \qquad \text{Isolate } x.$$
$$x = y + 2$$

$$(y + 2) + 2y = 26 \qquad \text{Substitute into the other equation.}$$
$$3y + 2 = 26 \qquad \text{Solve for } y.$$
$$3y = 24$$
$$y = 8$$

Because the problem asks only for y, it isn't necessary to solve for x.

17. **y = 1**

The problem asks for y, so isolate x. In this case, it's easier to isolate x in the first given equation:

$$x + 4y = 10 \qquad \text{Givens}$$
$$y - x = -5$$

$$x = 10 - 4y \qquad \text{Isolate } x \text{ in the first equation.}$$

$$y - (10 - 4y) = -5 \qquad \text{Substitute into the second equation.}$$

$$y - (10 - 4y) = -5 \qquad \text{Solve for } y.$$
$$y - 10 + 4y = -5$$
$$5y - 10 = -5$$
$$5y = 5$$
$$y = 1$$

Note the importance of using parentheses when you substitute into the second equation. In this problem, the subtraction sign has to be distributed to both terms inside the parentheses. Whenever you use substitution to solve, always introduce the new expression inside parentheses, just in case, and then simplify from there.

Chapter 7: **Inequalities and Systems of Equations**

18. $x = 3$

Check out the first equation. Every term is a multiple of 3, so the entire thing can be divided by 3 to make the equation easier to work with. Do that before you start:

$$6x + 15 = 3y$$
$$2x + 5 = y \qquad \text{Divide every term by 3.}$$

Because the problem asks for x, isolate y. And it turns out that y is now isolated in the simplified equation!

$$
\begin{aligned}
2x + 5 &= y & &\text{Givens} \\
x + y &= 14 & & \\
2x + 5 &= y & &\text{Isolate } y. \\
x + (2x + 5) &= 14 & &\text{Substitute into the other equation.} \\
x + (2x + 5) &= 14 & &\text{Solve for } x. \\
3x + 5 &= 14 & & \\
3x &= 9 & & \\
x &= 3 & &
\end{aligned}
$$

Because the problem asks only for x, it's not necessary to solve for y.

19. $y = 8$

Because the problem asks for y, the undesired variable is x. Multiply one of the equations by -1 and add.

$$
\begin{array}{rrrrl}
 & x & + 2y & = & 26 \\
+ & -x & + y & = & -2 \\
\hline
 & 0 & + 3y & = & 24 \\
 & & y & = & 8
\end{array}
$$

Multiply the original equation by -1.
Add the two equations.

Because the problem asks only for y, it isn't necessary to solve for x.

20. $y = 1$

Because the problem asks for y, the undesired variable is x. The x terms in the two equations already have the same coefficient but opposite signs, so line them up and add:

$$
\begin{array}{rrrrl}
 & x & + 4y & = & 10 \\
+ & -x & + y & = & -5 \\
\hline
 & & 5y & = & 5 \\
 & & y & = & 1
\end{array}
$$

Because the problem asks only for y, it isn't necessary to solve for x.

Unit Two: **Algebra**

21. $x = 3$

This time, the undesired variable is y. In addition, the first equation does not put x and y on the same side, so start there.

$$6x + 15 = 3y$$
$$6x - 3y = -15$$

Now, the y terms in the two equations have opposite signs, but they do not have the same coefficient. There are two possible paths from here. One option is to multiply the $x + y = 14$ equation by 3:

$$x + y = 14$$
$$3(x + y) = 3(14)$$
$$3x + 3y = 42$$

Finally, stack, add, and solve for x:

$$\begin{array}{rcrcr} 6x & - & 3y & = & -15 \\ +\ 3x & + & 3y & = & 42 \\ \hline 9x & & & = & 27 \\ x & & & = & 3 \end{array}$$

Alternatively, divide every term in the $6x - 3y = -15$ equation by 3:

$$\begin{array}{rcr} (6x - 3y) & = & (-15) \\ \div\ 3 & & \div\ 3 \\ 2x - y & = & -5 \end{array}$$

And then solve from there:

$$\begin{array}{rcrcr} 2x & - & y & = & -5 \\ +\ x & + & y & = & 14 \\ \hline & & 3x & = & 9 \\ & & x & = & 3 \end{array}$$

Because the problem asks only for x, it isn't necessary to solve for y.

Chapter 7: **Inequalities and Systems of Equations**

22. $z < 2$

First isolate x in the equation:
$$x + 2z = 6$$
$$x = 6 - 2z$$

Second, substitute $6 - 2z$ into the inequality:
$$z + 2x > 6$$
$$z + 2(6 - 2z) > 6$$

Finally, solve for z. The last step divides by a negative, so the sign flips:
$$z + 2(6 - 2z) > 6$$
$$z + 12 - 4z > 6$$
$$12 - 3z > 6$$
$$-3z > -6$$
$$z < 2$$

23. $3b$

$$3a - [2a - (3b - a)] =$$
$$3a - [2a - 3b + a] = \quad \text{Distribute the interior minus sign to } 3b \text{ and } a.$$
$$3a - [3a - 3b] = \quad \text{Combine like terms } 2a \text{ and } a.$$
$$3a - 3a + 3b = \quad \text{Distribute the exterior minus sign to } 3a \text{ and } -3b.$$
$$3b \quad \text{Simplify.}$$

24. $x < 3$

To solve for x, eliminate y. Multiply the first inequality by -2 and then add the inequalities:

$$\begin{array}{r} -4x > -2 - 2y \\ + \; 1 + 3x > 2y \\ \hline 1 - x > -2 \end{array}$$

Simplify:
$$1 - x > -2$$
$$-x > -3 \quad \text{Subtract 1.}$$
$$x < 3 \quad \text{Divide by } -1.$$

Unit Two: **Algebra**

Problem Set

1. $|x - 2| > 3$

Quantity A	Quantity B
The minimum possible value of $|x - 3.5|$	The minimum possible value of $|x - 1.5|$

2. $2x + y = 10$
   $3x - 2y = 1$

Quantity A	Quantity B
x	y

3. $4x - 12 \geq x + 9$

Quantity A	Quantity B
x	6

4. Which of the following is equivalent to $-3x + 7 \leq 2x + 32$?

   (A) $x \geq -5$

   (B) $x \geq 5$

   (C) $x \leq 5$

   (D) $x \leq -5$

5. $|2x - 5| \leq 7$

Quantity A	Quantity B
x	3

6. $p < q < 0 < r$

Quantity A	Quantity B
pqr	$p - q$

7. Describe the possible values of x if $x^3 < x^2$.

Chapter 7: **Inequalities and Systems of Equations**

8. If $-13 < 3 - 2a < 10$, which of the following could be the value of a?

    Indicate all possible values

    - [A] -9
    - [B] -3
    - [C] 0
    - [D] 5
    - [E] 8
    - [F] 10

9.
$$j + 2k > 0$$
$$j - k < 3$$

Quantity A	Quantity B
k	-1

10. If $B^3 A < 0$ and $A > 0$, which of the following must be negative?

    (A) AB

    (B) $B^2 A$

    (C) B^4

    (D) $\dfrac{A}{B^2}$

    (E) $-\dfrac{B}{A}$

Unit Two: **Algebra**

Solutions

1. **(B)**
   As with all absolute value equations or inequalities, here you must solve twice.

   $$|x - 2| > 3$$
   $$x - 2 > 3 \quad \text{or} \quad x - 2 < -3$$
   $$x > 5 \quad \text{or} \quad x < -1$$

   It can then help to express the possible values of *x* on a number line.

   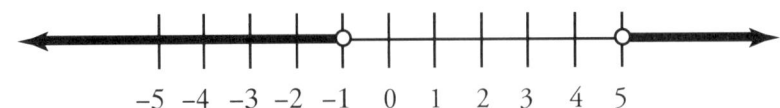

   Quantity A is equal to the minimum possible value of $|x - 3.5|$. Another way to think of $|x - 3.5|$ is the distance on a number line between *x* and 3.5. Look at 3.5 on the number line above and note that the nearest value to it is around 5 (*x* may not be exactly 5, but it could be 5.000001, for instance). Since the distance from 3.5 to 5 is 1.5, Quantity A must be just over 1.5.

   Quantity B can be conceived as the smallest distance from *x* to 1.5. Look at 1.5 on the number line—the nearest *x* value to it is just under −1, which is more than 2.5 units away. Thus, the minimum possible value of $|x - 1.5|$ is just over 2.5.

   If Quantity A's minimum is just over 1.5 and Quantity B's minimum is just over 2.5, Quantity B is larger.

   The correct answer is (B): Quantity B is always greater.

2. **(B)**
   Use substitution to solve for the values of *x* and *y*.

$2x + y = 10 \rightarrow y = 10 - 2x$	Isolate *y* in the first equation.
$3x - 2y = 1 \rightarrow 3x - 2(10 - 2x) = 1$	Substitute $(10 - 2x)$ for *y* in the second equation.
$3x - 20 + 4x = 1$	Distribute.
$7x = 21$	Group like terms (3*x* and 4*x*) and add 20 to both sides.
$x = 3$	Divide both sides by 7.
$2x + y = 10 \rightarrow 2(3) + y = 10$	Substitute 3 for *x* in the first equation.
$6 + y = 10$	
$y = 4$	

Quantity A	**Quantity B**
$x = 3$	$y = 4$

   Therefore, the correct answer is (B): Quantity B is greater.

198

Chapter 7: **Inequalities and Systems of Equations**

3. **(A)**
   Simplify the inequality.

   $$4x - 12 \geq x + 9$$
   $$3x \geq 21$$
   $$x \geq 7 \qquad \text{If } x \geq 7, \text{ then } x > 6.$$

   Therefore, the correct answer is (A): Quantity A is greater.

4. **(A)** $x \geq -5$

   $$-3x + 7 \leq 2x + 32$$
   $$-5x \leq 25 \qquad \text{When dividing by a negative value, reverse the}$$
   $$x \geq -5 \qquad \text{direction of the inequality symbol.}$$

5. **(D)**
   To evaluate the absolute value, set up two inequalities and isolate x in each.

   $$|2x - 5| < 7$$

$2x - 5 < 7$	or	$2x - 5 > -7$
$2x < 12$		$2x > -2$
$x < 6$		$x > -1$

   Combine the information from the two inequalities.

   $$|2x - 5| \leq 7$$

   | **Quantity A** | **Quantity B** |
   | $-1 \leq x \leq 6$ | 3 |

   There are possible values of x that are both greater than *and* less than 3.

   Therefore, the correct answer is (D): The relationship cannot be determined.

6. **(A)**
   Inequality problems containing 0 are often testing the rules of positives and negatives, so use the rules of signs to your advantage.

   In Quantity A, *pqr* is a negative times a negative times a positive, yielding a positive value overall.

   In Quantity B, $p - q$ is a negative minus a negative. A negative minus a negative can yield positive or negative results; therefore, as is often the case with subtraction, it will depend on the relative sizes of *p* and *q*. In this case, because *p* is more negative than *q*, it must be the case that $p - q$ results in a negative (a truth you can confirm by testing some numbers).

   Because Quantity A results in a positive number and Quantity B results in a negative number, the correct answer is (A): Quantity A is greater.

Unit Two: **Algebra**

7. **Any nonzero number less than 1**

   As positive proper fractions are multiplied together, their value decreases. For example, $\left(\frac{1}{2}\right)^3 < \left(\frac{1}{2}\right)^2$.

   Also, any negative number will make this inequality true. A negative number cubed is negative, while a negative number squared is positive. For example, $(-3)^3 < (-3)^2$. The number zero itself, however, does not work, because 0^3 is equal to 0^2.

   This could be determined algebraically.

   $$x^3 < x^2$$
   $$x^3 - x^2 < 0$$
   $$x^2(x - 1) < 0$$

   x^2 is positive for all $x \neq 0$, so $x^2(x - 1)$ is negative when $(x - 1)$ is negative, which will be whenever $x < 1$.

8. **(B) −3; (C) 0; (D) 5**

   To solve a three-part inequality, either break it down into two separate inequalities ($-13 < 3 - 2a$ and $3 - 2a < 10$) or isolate a by doing the same thing to all three parts of the inequality.

$-13 < 3 - 2a < 10$	Given.
$-16 < -2a < 7$	Subtract 3 from all parts of the inequality.
$8 > a > -\frac{7}{2}$	Divide all parts of the inequality by −2. Flip the inequality signs.

   Select all answer choices that fall within the range −3.5 to 8. Answers (B) −3, (C) 0, and (D) 5 all fall within the range.

9. **(A)**

   Setups with two variables and two inequalities can often be solved by adding the inequalities to each other. To do so, though, both inequality signs must face the same direction. Multiply everything in the second inequality by −1 to reverse the inequality, then add the two inequalities.

   $$\begin{aligned} j + 2k &> 0 \\ + \quad -j + k &> -3 \\ \hline 3k &> -3 \\ k &> -1 \end{aligned}$$

   Because k must be greater than −1, the correct answer is (A): Quantity A is always greater.

10. **(A) *AB***

    When inequalities show up with 0 on one side, the GRE is often testing the rules of positives and negatives. If A is positive and B^3A is negative, B^3 must be negative. And because numbers raised to odd exponents retain the signs of their bases, B itself must be negative. If A is positive and B is negative, the product AB must be negative.

CHAPTER 8
QC Gameplan: Simplify

In This Chapter:

- The Hidden Inequality
- Relative Order
- Pick Numbers: Part Two
- Check Your Skills Answer Key
- Problem Set
- Solutions

CHAPTER 8 QC Gameplan: Simplify

Finding quick solutions is a fairly general theme on Quantitative Comparisons, but nowhere is this theme more relevant than with algebra. If you generally associate algebra with long, complicated equations and lots of steps, then here's the good news: You will not have to do a lot of algebra on QC questions.

Things can still get tricky! But many equations that appear on QC can be simplified in just a few steps. In this chapter, you'll learn what **The Hidden Inequality** is and how to incorporate it into your QC Gameplan. You'll also learn how to use certain common problem characteristics to streamline your QC solution process.

The Hidden Inequality

Some QC problems can be simplified algebraically by imagining that a hidden inequality sign exists between Quantities A and B.

Consider this complicated-looking problem:

Quantity A	**Quantity B**
$3^{45} \times 2^{56}$	$3^{43} \times 2^{60}$

There's no reasonable way to compute these values, since the GRE calculator doesn't allow you to directly plug in exponents.

The Hidden Inequality strategy will make this problem much more manageable. Each answer choice, if it is the correct choice, implies a certain relationship between the two quantities:

	Quantity A		**Quantity B**
(A)	This	>	That
(B)	This	<	That
(C)	This	=	That
(D)	This	can't tell	That

203

Unit Two: **Algebra**

Start every QC problem with a question mark in the middle, since you don't know the relationship:

Quantity A		**Quantity B**
This	?	That

You can think of that question mark as a **Hidden Inequality**. (It might be an equals sign, too, of course.)

You can simplify both "sides" of the Hidden Inequality at the same time, using algebraic moves you're allowed to make to both sides of an inequality. The only thing to avoid is multiplying or dividing by a negative. (Since you don't know what the sign in the middle actually is, you can't know which way to flip it.)

Do the math work off to the side and keep track of the simplification of each column in the middle:

	Quantity A		**Quantity B**	
	$3^{45} \times 2^{56}$	?	$3^{43} \times 2^{60}$	
	$\div 2^{56}$	?	$\div 2^{56}$	
$3^{45} \times \frac{2^{56}}{2^{56}} \rightarrow$	3^{45}	?	$3^{43} \times 2^{4}$	$\leftarrow \frac{2^{60}}{2^{56}} = 2^{4}$
	$\div 3^{43}$	?	$\div 3^{43}$	
$\frac{3^{45}}{3^{43}} = 3^{2} \rightarrow$	3^{2}	<	2^{4}	$\leftarrow \frac{3^{45}}{3^{43}} \times 2^{4}$
	9	<	16	

First, divide both sides by 2^{56}. (Division is acceptable here because 2^{56} is positive.) In Quantity A, the 2^{56} term completely cancels out. In Quantity B, it simplifies down to a much more manageable 2^{4}.

Next, divide by sides by 3^{43}. Again, this is allowed because the value is positive. This term completely cancels in Quantity B and simplifies down to a manageable 3^{2} in Quantity A.

And now you can compare the two quantities to determine which is greater. Since $9 < 16$, the correct answer is (B): Quantity B is greater.

This approach is useful when both Quantity A and Quantity B are expressions containing numbers, variables, or both. In essence, you turn your two quantities into one big inequality (or equation). You can add or subtract anything from both sides. You can also multiply or divide by anything positive.

Do not, though, multiply or divide by a negative. Since you have no idea what the sign between the two quantities actually is, it's impossible to know which way to flip the inequality. In addition, don't divide by 0.

Be especially wary when multiplying or dividing by a variable, which might secretly be negative or zero. If the problem specifically tells you that a variable is positive, you can multiply or divide by that variable. Otherwise, avoid multiplying or dividing by variables when using the Hidden Inequality.

The Hidden Inequality is a powerful tool for peeling away complicated—looking layers of math. Often, straightforward comparisons hide beneath lengthy expressions, as in the example problem shown earlier.

This strategy is an extension of the Simplify step. Up to now, you've been simplifying *within* each column separately. But if there are common terms in the two quantities, you can simplify *across* the columns, too, as long as you respect the Hidden Inequality. Go ahead and do your algebra, both **within and across**.

Try this problem:

$$x > 1$$

Quantity A	Quantity B
$x^2 + 5x$	$x^2 + 2x + 2$

Subtract common terms to simplify across the Hidden Inequality:

Quantity A		Quantity B
$x^2 + 5x$	?	$x^2 + 2x + 2$
$-x^2$		$-x^2$
$5x$	?	$2x + 2$
$-2x$		$-2x$
$3x$	?	2

This simplification does **not** mean that $3x = 2$. Keep writing the question mark down the middle to help remember that you don't actually know the relationship.

The simplified Quantity A is $3x$, and the simplified Quantity B is 2. The question stem also specified that $x > 1$. How does this impact Quantity A?

Given $x > 1$, it must be the case that $3x > 3$. Therefore, the answer is (A): Quantity A is greater.

When the algebra is complicated, look for ways to simplify within a column or across the columns, using the Hidden Inequality strategy.

205

Unit Two: **Algebra**

Check Your Skills

> Use the Hidden Inequality strategy to solve.

1.

Quantity A	Quantity B
$3^3 \times 9^6 \times 2^4 \times 4^2$	$9^3 \times 3^6 \times 2^2 \times 4^4$

Answers can be found on page 212.

Relative Order

Inequalities can also be used to restrict the range of values allowed in a problem. In some questions, the result of that restriction is to define a relative order. For instance, the given information may indicate that $0 < p < q < r$.

This inequality indicates two crucial things:

1. p, q, and r are all positive.
2. p, q, and r are in order from least to greatest.

Questions that provide this type of information will often then use different combinations of these variables in each quantity and perform some kind of mathematical operation on them. When you see this setup, **look for the pattern**.

If there is a pattern, the answer will likely be (A), (B), or (C). If there is no pattern, the answer will be (D). Make use of the Hidden Inequality to discern the pattern, if one is present. Here are four examples, one for each of the four basic mathematical operations $(+, -, \times, \div)$.

Example 1

$$0 < p < q < r$$

Quantity A	Quantity B
$p + q$	$q + r$

Use the Hidden Inequality to simplify before picking numbers to look for a pattern. Both quantities contain a q, so subtract the q:

$$0 < p < q < r$$

Quantity A		Quantity B
$p + q$		$q + r$
$-q$	?	$-q$
p		r

The given information specified that $0 < p < q < r$, so it must be the case that r is greater than p. Therefore, the correct answer is (B): Quantity B is greater.

206

Example 2

$$0 < p < q < r$$

Quantity A		Quantity B
pq	?	qr

Once again, both sides have a q. Because q must be positive, divide both sides by q:

$$0 < p < q < r$$

Quantity A		Quantity B
$\frac{pq}{q} = p$	?	$\frac{qr}{q} = r$

Once again, from the given information, it must be the case that r is greater than p. Therefore, the correct answer is (B): Quantity B is greater.

In the first two examples, it was possible to eliminate common terms from each quantity in order to arrive at a definite conclusion.

However, take a look at the next example.

Example 3

$$0 < p < q < r$$

Quantity A		Quantity B
$q - p$	?	$r - q$

Both sides contain a q, but their signs are different. You can't actually eliminate q altogether. If you try adding q to both sides, here's what you get:

$$0 < p < q < r$$

Quantity A		Quantity B
$\begin{array}{r} q - p \\ + q \\ \hline 2q - p \end{array}$	?	$\begin{array}{r} r - q \\ + q \\ \hline r \end{array}$

Quantity A still contains q. Likewise, if you try subtracting q from both sides, you just push q into Quantity B:

$$0 < p < q < r$$

Quantity A		Quantity B
$q - p$	?	$r - q$
$-q$		$-q$
$-p$		$r - 2q$

Either way, it's not possible to arrive at a definite conclusion.

Alternatively, pick numbers to prove that there is no pattern. Remember to pick numbers satisfying $0 < p < q < r$. If $p = 1$, $q = 3$, and $r = 6$, then:

$$0 < p < q < r$$

Quantity A		Quantity B
$q - p = 3 - 1 = 2$	?	$r - q = 6 - 3 = 3$

With these numbers, Quantity B is greater. Eliminate choices (A) and (C):

~~A~~ B ~~C~~ D

Now space the numbers differently. To visualize the possibilities, imagine placing the variables p, q, and r to the right of 0 on a number line, in that order from left to right, like beads on a wire. Now slide the beads, keeping their order but changing their spacing. In the previous case, q was closer to p than to r. Try putting q closer to r instead.

If $p = 2$, $q = 7$, and $r = 8$, then:

$$0 < p < q < r$$

Quantity A		Quantity B
$q - p = 7 - 2 = 5$	?	$r - q = 8 - 7 = 1$

In this case, Quantity A is greater. Therefore, the correct answer is (D): The relationship cannot be determined.

There's a similar dilemma with the fourth example.

Example 4

$$0 < p < q < r$$

Quantity A		Quantity B
$\dfrac{q}{p}$	?	$\dfrac{r}{q}$

Because all the variables are positive, you can cross-multiply (more on this concept in Chapter 11: Comparing Fractions):

$$0 < p < q < r$$

Quantity A		Quantity B
q^2	?	pr

It's impossible to know for sure which quantity will be greater. Therefore, the correct answer is (D): The relationship cannot be determined.

For extra practice, use numbers satisfying $0 < p < q < r$ to prove the answer is (D). (Hint: Space the numbers differently, as in the third example.)

> **Strategy Tips:**
>
> Sometimes inequalities are used to order variables from least to greatest. In the previous examples, the given information $0 < p < q < r$ both:
>
> 1. Gave the sign of the variables
> 2. Gave their order from least to greatest
>
> To compare the two quantities, use the Hidden Inequality to:
>
> 1. Eliminate common terms
> 2. Try to discern a pattern, if one is present

Pick Numbers: Part Two

The strategy of picking numbers was first introduced in Chapter 3 Quantitative Comparisons. Now that you know more about how to solve equations and inequalities, it's time for another round of picking numbers strategy.

When a variable isn't a variable

$$x - 3 = 12$$
$$y + 2x = 40$$

Quantity A	Quantity B
y	9

Unit Two: **Algebra**

The first equation provides enough information to find the value of x. Once you have x, you can use the second equation to find the value of y. So, although y is presented as a variable, it has just one definite value (in this case, $y = 10$). Therefore, the correct answer is (A).

> **Strategy Tip:**
>
> Check the common information against the quantities. If it looks like you may be able to solve for the value of a variable, start there.

When a variable's range is defined

$$2 \leq z \leq 4$$

Quantity A		Quantity B
$\dfrac{2z}{5}$	?	$\dfrac{5}{2z}$

In this problem, z doesn't have one specific value, but it does have a limited range of possible values. If a variable has a specified range, examine the upper and lower bounds of z.

Start with the lower bound. Plug in 2 for z in both quantities:

$$2 \leq z \leq 4$$

Quantity A	Quantity B
$\dfrac{2(2)}{5} = \dfrac{4}{5}$	$\dfrac{5}{2(2)} = \dfrac{5}{4}$

When $z = 2$, Quantity B is greater.   A̶ B C̶ D

Now try the upper bound. Plug in 4 for z in both quantities:

$$2 \leq z \leq 4$$

Quantity A	Quantity B
$\dfrac{2(4)}{5} = \dfrac{8}{5}$	$\dfrac{5}{2(4)} = \dfrac{5}{8}$

When $z = 4$, Quantity A is greater. Therefore, the correct answer is (D).

The way in which variables are constrained (or not) can provide valuable clues about efficient ways to approach that particular problem.

When only a relationship is needed

Try this problem:

$$\frac{x+5}{5} = \frac{y+6}{6}$$

Quantity A	Quantity B
$6x$	$5y$

The common information provides an equation that contains two variables: *x* and *y*. It's not possible to solve for the value of either variable, but that doesn't necessarily mean the answer will be (D). Start by simplifying the rather complex equation:

$$\begin{aligned} 6(x+5) &= 5(y+6) \\ 6x + 30 &= 5y + 30 \\ -30 & -30 \\ 6x &= 5y \end{aligned}$$

The simplified form of the equation is a lot more useful. Compare the equation to the two quantities. They're equal, so the correct answer is (C).

The big takeaway: Always process the common or given information above the two quantities—simplify or combine information wherever possible—before you decide what to do with the quantities. It's possible that something presented as a variable will turn out to have exactly one value.

Alternatively, you might have only a narrow range of possible values, in which case, try both ends of the range, as well as any "weird" possible values in the range (such as 0 or a fraction).

Finally, it might be that you are given only the relationship between two variables...but that relationship might be enough to get you to your answer.

Unit Two: **Algebra**

Check Your Skills Answer Key

1. **(A)**
   Divide each side by the *least* power for each base. For example, Quantity A contains 3^3, while Quantity B contains 3^6. Because 3^3 is less than 3^6, divide both sides by 3^3. Figure this out for each base: Use 3^3, 9^3, 2^2, and 4^2.

   Divide both quantities by $3^3\, 9^3\, 2^2\, 4^2$:

   $$3^3\, 9^6\, 2^4\, 4^2 \qquad ? \qquad 9^3\, 3^6\, 2^2\, 4^4$$

   $$\div (3^3\, 9^3\, 2^2\, 4^2) \qquad\qquad \div (3^3\, 9^3\, 2^2\, 4^2)$$

   $$\frac{\cancel{3^3}\, 9^6\, 2^4\, \cancel{4^2}}{\cancel{3^3}\, 9^3\, 2^2\, \cancel{4^2}} \qquad ? \qquad \frac{\cancel{9^3}\, 3^6\, \cancel{2^2}\, 4^4}{3^3\, \cancel{9^3}\, \cancel{2^2}\, 4^2}$$

   The terms are not in the same order in each quantity, so be careful as you cancel. Half of the terms cancel completely, leaving only half to continue to simplify:

   $$\frac{9^6\, 2^4}{3^3\, 2^2} \qquad ? \qquad \frac{3^6\, 4^4}{3^3\, 4^2}$$

   $$9^{(6-3)}\, 2^{(4-2)} \qquad ? \qquad 3^{(6-3)}\, 4^{(4-2)}$$

   $$9^3\, 2^2 \qquad ? \qquad 3^3\, 4^2$$

   The two simplified quantities, $9^3 \times 2^2$ and $3^3 \times 4^2$, are small enough that you could plug them into the calculator. But it's still possible to simplify a bit further:

   $$9^3\, 2^2 \qquad ? \qquad 3^3\, 4^2$$

   $$9^3\, 4 \qquad\qquad 3^3\, 4^2$$
   $$\div 4 \qquad\qquad \div 4$$

   $$9^3 \qquad ? \qquad 3^3\, 4$$

   $$9^3 \qquad ? \qquad (27)(4)$$
   $$\div 9 \qquad\qquad \div 9$$

   $$9^2 \qquad > \qquad (3)(4)$$

   The value of 9^2 is 81, which is greater than $(3)(4) = 12$.

   The correct answer is (A): Quantity A is greater.

Chapter 8: **QC Gameplan: Simplify**

Problem Set

1. x is an integer.

Quantity A	**Quantity B**
$\dfrac{1}{100^x}$	$\dfrac{1}{99^x}$

2. $xyz < 0$

Quantity A	**Quantity B**
$x + y + z$	$2x + 2y + 2z$

3. $0 < a < 1 < b < c$

Quantity A	**Quantity B**
$\dfrac{c^2}{a}$	$\dfrac{bc}{ab}$

4. $6 \leq m \leq 12$

Quantity A	**Quantity B**
$9 - m$	$m - 9$

5.
Quantity A	**Quantity B**
$\dfrac{\frac{4}{3} + (-2)}{-2}$	$\dfrac{-\frac{4}{3} + 2}{2}$

6. $x + y < 0$

Quantity A	**Quantity B**
x	$-y$

7. $x \neq 0$

Quantity A	**Quantity B**
$\dfrac{1}{x^2}$	$\dfrac{1}{x}$

8.
Quantity A	**Quantity B**
$(x + 4)(x + 3)$	$(x + 5)(x + 2)$

Unit Two: **Algebra**

Solutions

1. **(D)**

   This question might be trying to trick you into picking answer (A) (the "greater looking" number). Alternatively, you might reason that a greater number under a fraction makes the fraction smaller and therefore pick answer (B). This highlights how complicated fractions can make a QC problem. Fortunately, the Hidden Inequality can be used to make this a little easier: Because 100^x and 99^x are both positive, each can be multiplied over to the other side, leaving the comparison more straightforward.

   x is an integer.

Quantity A		Quantity B
$\cancel{100^x} \times \dfrac{1}{\cancel{100^x}}$	?	$\dfrac{1}{99^x} \times 100^x$
1	?	$\dfrac{100^x}{99^x}$
$99^x \times 1$		$\dfrac{100^x}{\cancel{99^x}} \times \cancel{99^x}$
99^x		100^x

   Now, testing cases will be a bit simpler. If $x = 1$, Quantity B is greater ($99 < 100$).

   If $x = 0$, the quantities are equal (because any number to a power of 0 is equal to 1).

   Therefore, the correct answer is (D): The relationship cannot be determined.

2. **(D)**

   Both quantities have terms in common, inviting algebraic simplification. Regardless of whether we know the signs of x, y, and z, we can subtract them freely from both sides.

   $xyz < 0$

Quantity A		Quantity B
$x + y + z$		$2x + 2y + 2z$
$-\ (x + y + z)$		$-\ (x + y + z)$
0		$x + y + z$

   Now, use the information given above ($xyz < 0$) to determine the signs of the variables. There are two possible cases: (1) one is negative and the other two are positive, or (2) all three are negative. If all three are negative, Quantity B will have a negative value, and Quantity A will be larger. However, if only one variable is negative, there are scenarios in which Quantity B could be positive and therefore larger than Quantity A. (As an example, you can choose $x = -1$, $y = 2$, and $z = 3$ to get a value of 4 for Quantity B.)

   Therefore, the correct answer is (D): The relationship cannot be determined.

214

3. **(A)**

When the same variables appear in both quantities, you can often use the Hidden Inequality technique. Here, simplify inside Quantity B first, and then use the Hidden Inequality to simplify further.

$$0 < a < 1 < b < c$$

Quantity A		**Quantity B**
$\dfrac{c^2}{a}$	?	$\dfrac{\cancel{b}c}{a\cancel{b}}$
$\cancel{a} \times \dfrac{c^2}{\cancel{a}}$	?	$\dfrac{c}{\cancel{a}} \times \cancel{a}$
c^2	?	c
$c^2 \div c$	?	$c \div c$
c	?	1

The common information specifies that $1 < c$. Therefore, the correct answer is (A): Quantity A is greater.

4. **(D)**

You can use the Hidden Inequality to simplify this by adding m to both sides and 9 to both sides.

$$6 \leq m \leq 12$$

Quantity A	**Quantity B**
$\begin{array}{r} 9 - m \\ +m \\ \hline 9 \end{array}$	$\begin{array}{r} m - 9 \\ +m \\ \hline 2m - 9 \end{array}$
$\begin{array}{r} 9 \\ +9 \\ \hline 18 \end{array}$	$\begin{array}{r} 2m - 9 \\ +9 \\ \hline 2m \end{array}$
$18 \div 2$	$2m \div 2$
9	m

Now test numbers. If $m = 6$, Quantity A is greater. But if $m = 12$, Quantity B is greater.

Therefore, the correct answer is (D): The relationship cannot be determined.

Unit Two: **Algebra**

5. **(C)**
The calculator might be tempting here, but there's a faster way. These quantities can be simplified quickly if you multiply both by 2.

Quantity A	Quantity B
$\cancel{2} \times \dfrac{\frac{4}{3} + (-2)}{\frac{-2}{-1}}$	$\dfrac{-\frac{4}{3} + 2}{\cancel{2}} \times \cancel{2}$
$\dfrac{\frac{4}{3} + (-2)}{-1}$	$-\frac{4}{3} + 2$
$-\frac{4}{3} + 2$	$-\frac{4}{3} + 2$

The −1 in the denominator of Quantity A serves to change the sign of the two terms in the numerator, leaving Quantity A identical to Quantity B.

Therefore, the correct answer is (C): The two quantities are equal.

6. **(B)**
Approach this problem by simplifying the common information or by using the Hidden Inequality to reshape the quantities to better reflect the common information. In both approaches, the goal of simplification is to make the quantities resemble the common information above.

To simplify the common information, rewrite it so that it more closely resembles Quantities A and B.

$$x + y < 0$$
$$\underline{-y \quad\quad -y} \quad\quad \text{Subtract } y \text{ from both sides}$$
$$x \quad < -y$$

This rewrite reveals that Quantity A must be less than Quantity B. Choice (B) is correct. You're done!

Alternatively, add y to both quantities.

$$x + y < 0$$

Quantity A		Quantity B
$x + y$	?	$-y + y$
$x + y$	?	0

The common information makes it clear that $x + y$ is less than 0. Therefore, the correct answer is (B): Quantity B is greater.

Chapter 8: **QC Gameplan: Simplify**

7. **(D)**

    When the same variable appears in both quantities, consider whether you can combine like terms using the Hidden Inequality to simplify the comparison. In this problem, you're not told the sign of x, so multiplying both sides by x is not safe. However, since x is not equal to 0, x^2 is definitely positive. Therefore, you can multiply by quantities by x^2 to simplify.

    $$x \neq 0$$

Quantity A		Quantity B
$x^2 \times \dfrac{1}{x^2}$	?	$\dfrac{1}{x} \times x^x$
1		x

    Since you're only told that x is not equal to 0, it is impossible to say whether x is greater than 1 or not. Therefore, the correct answer is (D): The relationship cannot be determined.

8. **(A)**

    Given the presence of the same variable in both quantities, it's worth considering algebraic simplification using the Hidden Inequality. However, first each side needs to be expanded using the FOIL method (more on this in Chapter 12: Quadratic Equations).

Quantity A		Quantity B
$(x + 4)(x + 3)$	?	$(x + 5)(x + 2)$
$x^2 + 3x + 4x + 12$	?	$x^2 + 2x + 5x + 10$
$x^2 + 7x + 12$	?	$x^2 + 7x + 10$
$-(x^2 + 7x)$		$-(x^2 + 7x)$
12	?	10

    Therefore, the correct answer is (A): Quantity A is greater.

217

UNIT THREE

Factors

Factors are the building blocks of numbers and underpin many types of math, from divisibility to fraction manipulations to quadratic equations. In this unit, you will learn what factors are, how to find them, and how to use them to solve problems across the math spectrum.

In This Unit:

- Chapter 9: Divisibility
- Chapter 10: Common Factors
- Chapter 11: Fractions
- Chapter 12: Quadratic Equations
- Chapter 13: QC Gameplan: Compare

CHAPTER 9
Divisibility

In This Chapter:

- Divisibility Terms
- Divisibility Shortcuts
- Factor Pair Method
- Prime Factor Tree
- Divisibility of Unknowns
- Combining Givens
- Divisibility and Addition/Subtraction
- Divisibility and Consecutive Integers
- Remainders
- Check Your Skills Answer Key
- Problem Set
- Solutions

CHAPTER 9 Divisibility

Divisibility is one of the most commonly tested properties of numbers on the GRE.

One number is **divisible by** another number if the division results in an integer. For example, 12 is divisible by 4 because dividing 12 by 4 results in the integer 3. However, 14 is not divisible by 4 because dividing 14 by 4 results in 3.5, which is not an integer.

In this chapter, you will learn how to recognize when a question is testing divisibility, how to determine whether one number is divisible by another, and how to infer divisibility properties of variables. You will also learn how to find a number's full factor list as well as that number's prime factors.

Divisibility Terms

The GRE will test you on your conceptual understanding of divisibility. The expression 12 ÷ 4 produces the integer 3, but what makes one number divisible by another? One way to think about this is that 12 can be split evenly into 4 groups (of 3 each).

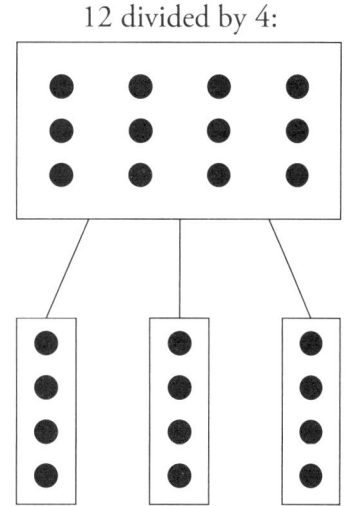

3 groups of 4 with none left over

However, when 14 is divided by 4, the result is *not* an integer. Since 14 cannot be divided evenly into 4 groups, 14 is not divisible by 4.

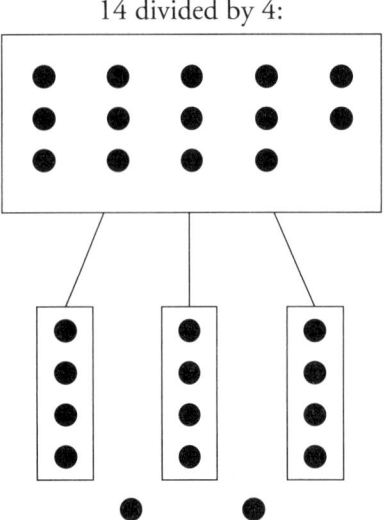

3 groups of 4 with 2 left over

The number 4 can go into 14 three times, accounting for $(4)(3) = 12$ of the dots, but there are two dots left over. Therefore, the solution to $14 \div 4$ is 3 remainder 2. You'll learn more about remainders later in this chapter, but for now, it's useful to think of remainders in terms of divisibility properties. When numbers are not evenly divisible, a remainder is left over.

The GRE will express divisibility in a variety of ways. They might look different, but they all mean the same thing. Each of the following expressions indicates that when 20 is divided by 4, the result is an integer:

- 20 is divisible by 4.
- 20 divided by 4 yields no remainder.
- 20 is a multiple of 4.
- 4 divides 20 evenly.
- 4 is a divisor of 20.
- 4 is a factor of 20.

You might want to make a flash card to study this language.

Four of the expressions use some form of the word division: *divisible*, *divided*, *divides*, and *divisor*. Divisibility can be shown with the following equation, where x is divisible by y:

$$\frac{x}{y} = \text{integer}$$

The word **divisor** can also refer to the bottom of a fraction or the number you are dividing by—that is, *divisor* can mean two different things. If the problem specifically says that a certain value is "a divisor" of another number, then the problem is indicating that one number is *divisible by* another. Otherwise, the problem is just asking you to perform division; the answer may or may not be an integer. For example:

When you see...	It means...
4 is *a divisor* of 20.	20 is divisible by 4. 20 ÷ 4 is an integer.
$\dfrac{\text{dividend}}{\text{divisor}} = \dfrac{15}{6}$	15 is the dividend and 6 is the divisor, but 6 is not *a divisor* of 15. Rather: $\dfrac{15}{6} = 2$ remainder 3 By the way, 2 is called the *quotient* and 3 is called the *remainder*.

The final two expressions in the list don't use a form of the word division, but they still convey the same meaning.

The word **factor** is interchangeable with divisor. The number 4 is a factor of 20 because 20 divided by 4 is an integer. The factors of a number are all of the integers that divide evenly into that number, including 1 and the number itself. Therefore, the positive factors of 20 are 1, 2, 4, 5, 10, and 20. The factors of a positive number are always less than or equal to that number.

The other term, **multiple**, refers to numbers that are found by multiplying that number by an integer. For example, the positive multiples of 4 are 4, 8, 12, 16, 20, and so on. The positive multiples of a number will always be greater than or equal to the number in question.

Here's one way to represent the fact that the number *x* is a multiple of the number *y*:

$$x = y \times \text{integer}$$

$$20 = 4 \times \text{integer}$$

20 is a multiple of 4 because 20 is equal to 4 times the integer 5.

This equation is a rearrangement of the equation shown earlier: $\frac{x}{y}$ = integer. The relationship holds true in both directions: Just as 20 is a multiple of 4, the value 4 is a factor of 20.

In fact, all factors and multiples are the mirror images of each other. For example, 20 is a multiple of all of its factors. Therefore, 20 is a multiple of 1, 2, 4, 5, 10, and 20.

Also, 20 is a multiple *and* a factor of itself. This is true of all positive integers! Every integer is a factor and multiple of itself.

The mnemonic "Fewer Factors, More Multiples" can help you remember the difference. Any integer has only a limited number of factors. For example, there are only four positive factors of 8, namely 1, 2, 4, and 8. By contrast, an integer has an infinite number of multiples. For example, the positive multiples of 8 are 8, 16, 24, 32, and so on to infinity.

In addition, $8 \times 0 = 0$. Because 8 multiplied by an integer gives a multiple of 8, it turns out that 0 is also a multiple of 8. In fact, 0 is a multiple of every integer! (This is the reason why 0 is even: It is divisible by 2.)

Unit Three: Factors

The GRE could ask about possible factors of a number or possible multiples of a number. Here are some ways you may be asked to find a factor of 150:

1	Which of the following is a factor of 150 ?
2	What could be a value of y if $\frac{150}{y}$ is an integer?
3	If 150 students are to be divided evenly into groups, which of the following represents a possible number of groups? (Or which represents a possible number of students in each group?)
4	150 is a multiple of which of the following? (Select all that apply.)

For all 4 questions, here are the possible answers: 1, 2, 3, 5, 6, 10, 15, 25, 30, 50, 75, and 150.

> **Key Concept**
>
> Multiples and Factors can be expressed as equations involving an integer:
>
> $$\frac{x}{y} = \frac{\text{multiple}}{\text{factor}} = \text{integer}$$
>
> $$x = y \times \text{integer}$$
>
> $$\text{multiple} = \text{factor} \times \text{integer}$$

Check Your Skills

1. Which of the following statements must be true?
   Indicate <u>all</u> such statements.

   - [A] 18 is a multiple of 12.
   - [B] 3 is a divisor of 9.
   - [C] 13 is a factor of 40.
   - [D] 80 is divisible by 20.
   - [E] 26 divided by 2 results in an integer.
   - [F] 35 divided by 70 yields no remainder.

2. What are the first 5 non-negative multiples of 3 ?

Answers can be found on page 250.

Chapter 9: Divisibility

Divisibility Shortcuts

Sometimes divisibility questions will ask for information about all of the factors of a number, and this chapter will cover how to find that information. However, sometimes all you need is to determine whether one number is divisible by another specific number. For example, is 151 divisible by 3?

You could certainly use your calculator to test divisibility, but there are a few shortcuts that can save you time. The following shortcuts allow you to determine whether an integer is divisible by 2, 3, 4, 5, 6, 9, or 10.

k	An integer is divisible by k if:	Example integers that are divisible by k	Example integers that are not divisible by k
2	The units digit of the integer is even.	12 2,345,678	13 1,234,567
3	The sum of its digits is divisible by 3.	72, because 7 + 2 = 9, which is divisible by 3.	83, because 8 + 3 = 11, which is not divisible by 3.
4	Dividing the number formed by the last two digits in half results in an even integer.	82,728, because $\frac{28}{2} = 14 =$ even 23,468, because $\frac{68}{2} = 34 =$ even	2,331, because $\frac{31}{2} =$ non-integer 25,682, because $\frac{82}{2} = 41 =$ odd
5	The integer ends in 0 or 5.	75 80	72 83
6	The integer is divisible by both 2 *and* 3.	48 is even, and 4 + 8 = 12, which is divisible by 3. 72 is even, and 7 + 2 = 9, which is divisible by 3.	51, because it is odd. 82 is even, but 8 + 2 = 10, which is not divisible by 3.
9	The sum of its digits is divisible by 9.	81, because 8 + 1 = 9. 423, because 4 + 2 + 3 = 9, which is divisible by 9.	73, because 7 + 3 = 10, which is not divisible by 9. 345, because 3 + 4 + 5 = 12, which is not divisible by 9.
10	The integer ends in 0.	670	675

227

Unit Three: Factors

There are no rules listed for divisibility by 1, 7, or 8. By definition, all integers are divisible by 1, so there is no need to test it. And while there are some neat ways to check for divisibility by 7 or 8, none of those methods are any better than just using the calculator.

Use these shortcuts to test whether 150 is divisible by 2, 3, 4, 5, 6, 9, or 10, and then check your answers below.

k	Testing $\frac{150}{k}$	$\frac{150}{k}$ = int?
2	150 is even.	Yes, 150 is divisible by 2.
3	$1 + 5 + 0 = 6$ and 6 is a multiple of 3.	Yes, 150 is divisible by 3.
4	$50 \div 2 = 25$, which is not even.	No, 150 is not divisible by 4.
5	150 ends in 0.	Yes, 150 is divisible by 5.
6	150 is divisible by both 2 and 3.	Yes, 150 is divisible by 6.
9	$1+5+0 = 6$ but 6 is not a multiple of 9.	No, 150 is not divisible by 9.
10	150 ends in 0.	Yes, 150 is divisible by 10.

So 150 is divisible by 2, 3, 5, 6, and 10, but 150 is not divisible by 4 or 9.

The GRE may also test these divisibility rules in reverse. For example, if a problem states that a number has a units digit equal to 0, you can infer that the number is divisible by 10 (and by 5 and by 2). Similarly, if a problem states that the sum of the digits of x is equal to 21, you can infer that x is divisible by 3 but *not* by 9.

Check Your Skills

3. Is 732 divisible by 3 ?
4. Is 4,578 divisible by 4 ?
5. Is 4,578 divisible by 6 ?
6. Is 603,864 divisible by 8 ?

Answers can be found on page 250.

Chapter 9: **Divisibility**

Factor Pair Method

When a problem asks you to find all of the factors of a number, use the **Factor Pair Method**.

A **factor pair** is a set of two numbers that multiply to produce the original number. For example, 4 and 9 are a factor pair of 36 because $4 \times 9 = 36$. Here are the four steps for the Factor Pair Method using the value 36:

	Process	Details	Example
Step 1	Make a table with two columns.	Label them *Small* and *Large*.	Small | Large
Step 2	List the first factor pair.	This will always be 1 and the original number.	Small | Large 1 | 36
Step 3	Find the second factor pair from the next smallest factor.	Try 2 next; if that doesn't work, try 3, and so on.	Small | Large 1 | 36 2 | 18
Step 4	Repeat step 3 until the numbers in the *Small* and the *Large* columns run into each other.	Use divisibility shortcuts whenever possible; in this case, 5 doesn't work, so skip that value.	Small | Large 1 | 36 2 | 18 3 | 12 4 | 9 6 | 6

The factor pairs of 36 are (1, 36), (2, 18), (3, 12), (4, 9), and (6, 6).

Try this problem:

How many distinct positive factors does 150 have?

Unit Three: Factors

Create a table and start with the pair 1 and 150. Next, is 2 a factor of 150? It is, and its pair is 75, because $2 \times 75 = 150$. Continue counting up to find the remaining factor pairs of 150, using divisibility rules or the calculator to help determine whether a particular number is a factor of 150:

Small	Large
1	150
2	75
3	50
5	30
6	25
10	15

Use divisibility rules or your calculator. The values 1, 2, and 3 are all factors of 150, but 4 is not, because 150 divided by 2 is not even. The values 5 and 6 are factors, but 7, 8, and 9 are not factors of 150. Finally, 10 is a factor but 11, 12, 13, and 14 are not.

Once you've tested 14, the list has now "come together" because 15 is the last factor pair figure in the right-hand column, so you can stop testing.

Count the factors listed: 150 has 12 positive factors. The word *distinct* means *different*, and all 12 of those values are different, so 150 has 12 distinct positive factors.

How many distinct positive factors does the number 36 have? In that case, though there were 5 pairs of factors, the last pairing was the same number twice: (6, 6). So the number 36 has just 9 distinct positive factors, not 10.

In general, when a problem asks for the number of positive factors, it is referring to the number of distinct factors. So it's accurate to say that 36 has 9 positive factors, not 10.

Try the process one more time. Find the factor pairs of 88:

Small	Large
1	88
2	44
4	22
8	11

9 Check Your Skills

7. What are all of the positive factors of 90 ?

8. What are all of the positive factors of 72 ?

Answers can be found on page 251.

Prime Factor Tree

The Factor Pair Method provides *every* factor of a number, but the GRE will often ask only for **prime factors**—that is, the factors that are also prime numbers. A prime number is divisible by exactly two numbers: itself and 1.

Some questions will ask how many unique or distinct prime factors a number has. For these questions, it's possible to look at all the factor pairs and count how many of those numbers are prime. Take 150 as an example:

	Small	Large	
1 is not prime.	1	150	150 is not prime.
2 is prime.	2	75	75 is not prime.
3 is prime.	3	50	50 is not prime.
5 is prime.	5	30	30 is not prime.
6 is not prime.	6	25	25 is not prime.
10 is not prime.	10	15	15 is not prime.

There are 3 unique prime factors of 150, namely, 2, 3, and 5. All of the other factors are not prime numbers.

There are three possible categorizations for all positive integers:

Category	Examples	Definition
The number 1	1	Divisible by exactly one number: 1
Prime number	2, 3, 5, 7, 11	Divisible by exactly two numbers: itself and 1
Composite number	4, 6, 8, 9, 10	Divisible by three or more numbers: itself, 1, and at least one value between itself and 1

Take a look at these three questions that have three different answers:

Question: How many positive factors does 150 have?
Answer: Twelve (1, 2, 3, 5, 6, 10, 15, 25, 30, 50, 75, and 150)

Question: How many distinct prime factors does 150 have?
Answer: Three (2, 3, and 5)

Question: How many prime factors does 150 have?
Answer: Four (2, 3, 5, and 5 again)

That last question is the focus of this section. When the GRE asks how many prime factors a number has (or what the prime factors are), it's asking for the **prime factorization** of a number: a set of prime numbers that, when multiplied together, produce the original number.

The complete list of prime factors of 150 is 2, 3, 5, and 5 because $2 \times 3 \times 5 \times 5 = 150$.

The number 8 has only one *unique* prime factor, but it has three *total* prime factors, because $2 \times 2 \times 2 = 8$.

How were you supposed to know that there was an extra 5 in the prime factorization of 150? In fact, how can you find the prime factorization of any number that has repeated primes? The Factor Pair Method isn't effective at finding repeating primes. When asked to find *all prime* factors or the prime factorization of a number, create a **prime factor tree**. A prime factor tree breaks down the original number into progressively

Unit Three: **Factors**

smaller and smaller pieces, until all you're left with are the prime factors. Here's an example of one way to write the Prime Factor Tree of 150:

The four numbers in the circles, multiplied together, will give you the starting number, 150. But how do you actually find those numbers? Let's break it down.

Start building your tree by picking any factor pair of 150 *other than* 1 and 150. For example, try 10 and 15 to start:

When 10 and 15 are multiplied together, they will produce 150. But you're not done yet because 10 and 15 are not prime numbers. Keep going until everything is broken down into primes:

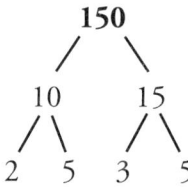

All of the values in the third row are primes, so the prime factor tree is complete. It's a good idea to circle each prime as you find it:

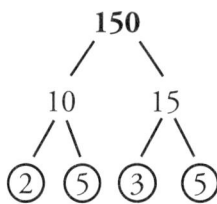

Because each factor has been broken down into its primes, you can be confident you've found *all* the prime factors of 150. Here's the proof: $2 \times 5 \times 3 \times 5 = 150$. The prime factors of 150 are 2, 3, 5, and 5.

> **Strategy Tip**
>
> Use Prime Factor Trees to list every *prime* factor of a number.
>
> Use The Factor Pair Method to list *every* factor of a number (prime and not prime).

You can break down a factor tree however you like. For example, rather than start with 10 and 15, try the pair 6 and 25:

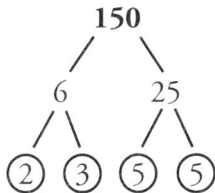

As before, 150 equals $2 \times 3 \times 5 \times 5$. Even though the prime factors are in a different order, this is the same group of prime numbers as before. In fact, *any* way you break down 150, you will end up with the same prime factors: one 2, one 3, and two 5's. Order doesn't matter for multiplication, so any ordering of $2 \times 3 \times 5 \times 5$ will always equal 150.

Prime factors are like the DNA of a number. Every number has a unique prime factorization. The only number that can be written as $2 \times 3 \times 5 \times 5$ is 150.

By the way, you may see prime factorizations written out longhand (e.g., $2 \times 3 \times 5 \times 5$) or written using exponents (e.g., $2 \times 3 \times 5^2$). Both representations mean the same thing: (one 2, one 3, and two 5's). The exponents tell you how many times that prime factor appears in the prime factorization.

Factor Trees will work to break down numbers, no matter how large. If you're not sure where to start to find factor pairs, start with smaller prime factors and work your way toward larger primes. You can use divisibility rules to test 2, 3, and 5, and your calculator to test larger primes.

For example, what is the prime factorization of 630? If possible, split off zeros—in this case, 63 and 10. But you don't need to see that shortcut to get to the prime factorization! Even if you just start with the smallest positive prime factor, 2, and test all the prime factors up from that point, you'll still get to the right prime factorization in the end.

Because 630 is even, it's divisible by 2. Break down 630 into 2 and 315:

Circle 2. It's already prime, so this branch of the tree is done. But you still need to factor 315. It's not even, so it's not divisible by 2. Because $3 + 1 + 5 = 9$ is a multiple of 3, the value 315 is divisible by 3. Specifically, $315 \div 3 = 105$. Add that pair to your factor tree:

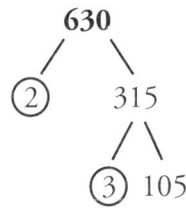

Unit Three: **Factors**

By the way, if you want to jump around in your primes, that's fine. If you see that 315 must be divisible by 5, feel free to factor out a 5 before you factor the 3. Again, in a prime factor tree, the order does not matter! Every path leads to the same result. (And use your calculator whenever you like.)

The last pair was 3 and 105. Is there another factor of 3? Yes, because $1 + 0 + 5 = 6$ is a multiple of 3. The next pairing is $105 \div 3 = 35$:

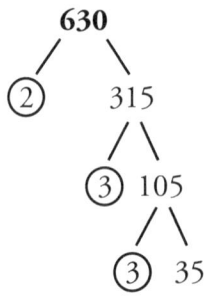

Finally, 35 is equal to 5 times 7:

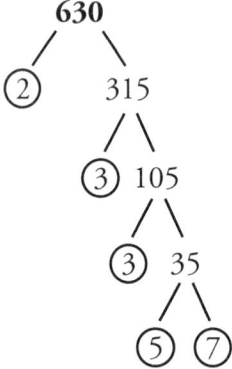

Every number on the tree has now been broken down as far as it can go. The prime factorization of 630 is $2 \times 3 \times 3 \times 5 \times 7$ or $2 \times 3^2 \times 5 \times 7$.

Use whatever factors you spot first. As mentioned earlier, for example, you could start by splitting 630 into 63 and 10 and go from there. All factor trees result in the same prime factorization in the end.

Check Your Skills

9. Find the prime factorization of 72.

10. Find the prime factorization of 105.

Answers can be found on page 251.

Divisibility of Unknowns

When the GRE uses variables rather than numbers, finding factors can be challenging, but it is still possible. All of these sentences mean the same thing:

- x is divisible by y.
- x divided by y yields no remainder.
- x is a multiple of y.
- y divides x evenly.
- y is a divisor of x.
- y is a factor of x.

The abstract logic can get confusing, so when you recognize that the problem is discussing divisibility, translate the English into one of the visual forms presented earlier. All three forms are equivalent, so use whichever form you prefer:

$\frac{x}{y}$ = integer
$x = y \times$ integer
$\begin{array}{c} x \\ / \ \backslash \\ y \quad ? \end{array}$

The factor tree shows a question mark because x may have other factors in addition to y. It's also possible that x doesn't have any additional factors and therefore x equals y. Practice each way to express these ideas in order to determine which is best for you.

Sometimes variables are used to ask for factors:

What could be a value of y if $\frac{150}{y}$ is an integer?

Indicate <u>all</u> such values.

- [A] 87
- [B] 75
- [C] 53

The question asks for a factor of 150 without explicitly using the word *factor*. Rather, the wording of the question provides the definition of a factor.

Unit Three: **Factors**

You can list out the factors of 150 using the Factor Pair Method, but this is a multiple-choice problem, so there's a faster approach: Evaluate the possible answer choices to determine which could be a factor. To test the answers, substitute them into y to see which results in an integer. If needed, plug them into your calculator:

$$\frac{150}{87} = 1.72\ldots \rightarrow \text{Eliminate}$$

$$\frac{150}{75} = 2 \quad \rightarrow \text{Correct!!}$$

$$\frac{150}{53} = 2.83\ldots \rightarrow \text{Eliminate}$$

When questions use variables to represent multiples, some interesting complexities arise:

If x is a multiple of 6, which of the following must be true about x?

Indicate all such statements.

- [A] x is divisible by 3.
- [B] x is even.
- [C] x is divisible by 12.

There are two primary ways to tackle this problem: Pick numbers or use a factor tree.

It's possible to represent the fact that x is a multiple of 6 in any of these three ways:

In all cases, 6 is a factor of x and x could have other factors (represented by the word *integer* or by the question mark). If you decide to pick numbers, either of the equation forms would be helpful. Alternatively, if you decide to use the factor tree, then the factor tree representation is most helpful.

Pick Numbers Approach

Picking numbers can help verify whether a value must be divisible by a certain number all the time or whether it might be true sometimes but not necessarily all the time. For this problem, use the equation $x = 6 \times \text{integer}$ to pick possible values for x and test each of the answer choices:

Answer	Given: $x = 6 \times$ integer	
	Case 1: integer = 1 $x = 6$	Case 2: integer = 2 $x = 12$
(A) x is divisible by 3	True	True
(B) x is even	True	True
(C) x is divisible by 12	False! Eliminate (C).	—

Set up your scratch work carefully. Test two or three cases, then examine the pattern.

The question asks what must be true. In the case of answer (C), the variable x is not divisible by 12 when $x = 6$, so eliminate this choice and don't continue to include it in future cases.

236

When $x = 6$ and when $x = 12$, answers (A) and (B) are true, but will they always be true for any value of x? Examine the math. The value of x will always equal 6 times an integer. Any even number multiplied by another integer will result in an even value, so x is always going to be even. Choice (B), then, must always be true. Further, 6 has 3 as a factor. Therefore, 6 times any integer will also continue to have 3 as a factor. Choice (A) must also always be true.

If you were to test answer choice (C) with $x = 12$, the result would be true, so answer (C) is sometimes true. But this choice is not true all the time, so it does not fit the "must be true" wording of the question.

Factor Tree Approach

Put x at the top of a factor tree. Since x is a multiple of 6, at least one of the factors of x is 6:

So, x must have both 2 and 3 as factors, at a minimum. It could also have other factors, but it might not—use the question mark to remind yourself of this fact.

Answer Choice	Analysis
(A) x is divisible by 3	Yes, this must be true: 3 is a factor of x, so x is divisible by 3.
(B) x is even	Definitely! Saying x is even is another way of saying it's divisible by 2, and the factor tree established that 2 is a factor of x.
(C) x is divisible by 12	Trickier! See below.

The first two answer choices asked directly about the prime factors 2 and 3. The third, though, is asking about 12, a composite number. Compare the factor tree of x with the factor tree of 12:

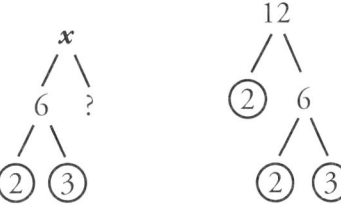

The prime factorization of 12 is $2 \times 2 \times 3$. For x to be divisible by 12, it would have to have two 2's and one 3 among its prime factors. In other words, for x to be divisible by 12, it has to be divisible by *everything* that 12 is divisible by.

But x's factor tree contains only one 2 and one 3 at a minimum. It *could* have more factors, but it doesn't absolutely have to. Because there may or may not be a second 2, it's not possible to conclude that x *must* be divisible by 12. It's only possible to conclude that x *might be* divisible by 12. Therefore, the correct answer is (A) and (B) only.

Another way to visualize this is by putting the prime factorizations into equation form. Asking whether x is divisible by 12 can be translated into this equation:

$$\text{Is } \frac{x}{12} = \text{integer?}$$

Put the prime factorization of both x and 12 into the fraction:

$$\text{Is } \frac{x}{12} = \frac{(2 \times 3 \times \text{?})}{(2 \times 2 \times 3)} = \text{integer?}$$

Simplify the fraction by canceling like terms from the top and bottom:

$$\text{Is } \frac{(\cancel{2} \times \cancel{3} \times \text{?})}{(\cancel{2} \times 2 \times \cancel{3})} = \text{integer?}$$

$$\text{Is } \frac{?}{2} = \text{integer?}$$

This changes the question to "Is some integer you know nothing about divisible by 2?" Maybe! And maybe not. There's no way to know for sure without more information. Since x may or may not be divisible by 12, choice (C) is not correct.

> **Key Concept**
>
> If x is divisible by y, then x is also divisible by everything that y is divisible by.
>
> Equivalently, if x is divisible by y, the factors of x include *all* of the factors of y, and possibly some extra ones.

Check Your Skills

> Given that x is divisible by 24, indicate whether each statement *must* be true, *could* be true, or *cannot* be true.

11. x is divisible by 6.

12. x is divisible by 9.

13. x is divisible by 8.

Answers can be found on pages 252-253.

Chapter 9: **Divisibility**

Combining Givens

When you have just a single number, creating a prime factorization is relatively straightforward. For example, given that z is a multiple of 14, then z at least shares 14's factors (2 and 7) and z might have other factors as well.

Some GRE problems, though, will tell you that a variable has multiple factors. If z is a multiple of 14 *and* 4, how do you determine z's prime factorization?

No Overlap

There are two basic scenarios to consider: overlap and no overlap. Let's start with no overlap:

If x is divisible by 3 and by 10, which of the following must be true about x?

Indicate <u>all</u> such statements.

|A| x is divisible by 2.

|B| x is divisible by 15.

|C| x is divisible by 45.

No overlap refers to the fact that the two factors, 3 and 10, don't share any prime factors. The factors don't overlap:

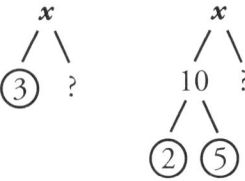

One tree contains a 3, and the other contains a 2 and a 5. None of those primes are the same. Therefore, these trees tell you that the prime factorization of x is 2 × 3 × 5 × ?. If it's helpful to rewrite that as a single tree, do so:

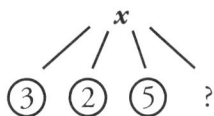

Because 2 is part of x's prime factor tree, x must be divisible by 2, so answer choice (A) is correct. But answers (B) and (C) ask about the values 15 and 45, respectively—values that are not in x's tree. Create factor trees for 15 and 45 to assess whether choices (B) or (C) are also correct. Here's 15:

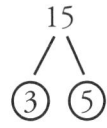

239

Unit Three: Factors

The number 15 breaks down into the prime factors 3 and 5. In order to know that *x* is divisible by 15, you would need to know that it's divisible by 3 and by 5. In this case, *x*'s factor tree does have both a 3 and a 5, so *x* is divisible by 15. Therefore, answer (B) is also correct.

Next, for *x* to be divisible by 45, you need to know that *x* has all the same prime factors as 45. Does it?

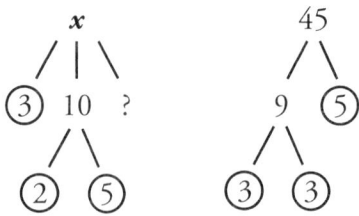

The factorization of 45 contains one 5 and two 3's. The 5 is a match, but 45 contains two 3's while *x*'s tree contains at least one 3 and a question mark. It's possible that *x* is divisible by 45, but it doesn't have to be. Answer (C) *could* be true, but the question asked what must be true, so don't include choice (C) among the correct answers. The correct answer is (A) and (B) only.

Check Your Skills

> Given that *x* is divisible by 28 and by 15, say whether each statement *must* be true, *could* be true, or *cannot* be true.

14. *x* is divisible by 14.

15. *x* is divisible by 20.

16. *x* is divisible by 24.

Answers can be found on pages 253–254.

Chapter 9: **Divisibility**

With Overlap

In all of the examples in the prior section, the two given factors had no primes in common—that is, they had no overlap. Things get more complicated when the given factors do have primes in common—that is, they do have overlap. For example:

If both 6 and 15 are factors of y, which of the following must also be factors of y?

Indicate all such factors.

- [A] 12
- [B] 24
- [C] 30

As before, start by representing the factors of y separately. First, 6 is a factor of y and, separately, 15 is a factor of y:

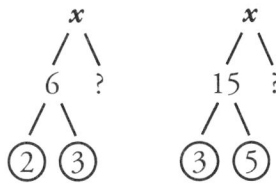

Since 6 is a factor of y, both 2 and 3 are also factors of y. And since 15 is a factor of y, both 3 and 5 are factors of y. The factor 3 appears in both trees—that is, the factor 3 overlaps in the two groups.

When you have an overlapping factor like this, you have to treat it differently. Imagine that there's a box sitting on the table and you can't see what's inside. Your friend Jaylen looks in the box and says there are two oranges, an apple, and some other pieces of fruit. Then, your friend Deniz looks and says there are two bananas, an orange, and some other pieces of fruit.

They're both telling the truth—they're just not telling you *everything* that's in the box.

What is the minimum number of apples you can be *sure* are in the box? Bananas? Oranges...?

The box contains at least one apple and at least two bananas. Deniz said there was one orange and Jaylen said there were two...so are there at least two oranges in the box or at least three?

What Deniz reported can overlap with what Jaylen reported. In other words, the one orange that Deniz reported might be the same orange as one of the two oranges that Jaylen reported. At a minimum, then, there are at least two oranges in the box. There may or may not be more than two.

This is the same situation with the prime factor 3 that is showing up in the prime trees of both 6 and 15. At the least, there is one factor of 3, because the two values 6 and 15 may be using the same instance of factor 3. There *could* be more factors of 3, but this isn't guaranteed.

You can visualize this overlap using a Venn Diagram. The left circle contains the factors of 6 (which are 2 and 3) and the right circle contains the factors of 15 (which are 3 and 5). The middle part, where the two circles overlap, contains the single 3 that is a factor of both 6 and 15:

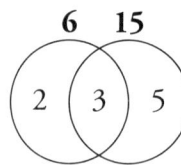

Therefore, the prime factorization of y is $2 \times 3 \times 5 \times ?$. Next, check each answer to see whether that value must also be a factor of y.

(A) Is 12 a factor of y? The prime factors of 12 are 2, 2, and 3. However, y's prime factorization has a minimum of just one 2, so 12 is not necessarily a factor of y. (It could be, but it doesn't have to be.) Eliminate choice (A).

(B) Is 24 a factor of y? The prime factors of 24 are 2, 2, 2, and 3. However, y's prime factorization contains a minimum of only one 2, so 24 is not necessarily a factor of y. Eliminate choice (B).

(C) Is 30 a factor of y? The prime factors of 30 are 2, 3, and 5. The variable y also has all of those factors, so 30 must be a factor of y.

The correct answer is (C) only.

Here's another example:

If both 6 and 9 are factors of y, which of the following must also be factors of y?

Indicate all such factors.

A 12
B 18
C 27

Start with the two factors of y individually. Since y has 6 as a factor, it must contain the factors 2 and 3. And since y has 9 as a factor, it must contain the factors 3 and 3.

What is the overlap? At a minimum, you need two 3's in order to create 9. Then, one of those threes could be reused, along with one factor of 2, to create 6. Visualize this as a Venn Diagram:

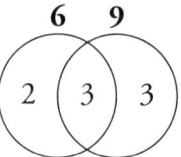

So, the prime factorization of y is $2 \times 3 \times 3 \times ?$ and the prime factorizations of the answer choices are:

(A) $12 = 2 \times 2 \times 3$

(B) $18 = 2 \times 3 \times 3$

(C) $27 = 3 \times 3 \times 3$

Answer (A) requires two 2's, but y's prime factorization shows a minimum of just one 2, so (A) could be true but does not have to be true.

The prime factors of 18 are all contained in y's prime factorization, so 18 does have to be a factor of y. Select answer (B).

Answer (C) is a trap! It requires three 3's, but y's prime factorization has a minimum of just two 3's. While it may seem that 6 and 9 have three 3's among them, one of those 3's is an overlapping factor and has to be stripped out.

The correct answer is (B) only.

Check Your Skills

> If y is divisible by 30 and by 25, say whether each statement *must* be true or merely *could* be true.

17. y is divisible by 50.
18. y is divisible by 750.

Answers can be found on pages 254–255.

Unit Three: **Factors**

Divisibility and Addition/Subtraction

Everything so far has focused on multiplication and division, because a prime factorization is a list of factors that all *multiply* to give a resulting number. To test whether something is a factor, you *divide* that factor out of the original number.

GRE problems can also ask about factors involved in addition and subtraction. To address these, there is one rule to understand: The sum or difference of two numbers with a common factor will also have that common factor. For example, if you add two multiples of 7, you get another multiple of 7:

$$\underbrace{7}_{\text{multiple of 7}} + \underbrace{14}_{\text{multiple of 7}} = \underbrace{21}_{\text{multiple of 7}}$$

This always works. For example, 14 + 21 equals a multiple of 7 and so does 21 + 35. Because each term can be individually divided by 7, the sum of the two terms will also be divisible by 7:

$$\frac{21 + 35}{7} = \frac{56}{7} = 8$$

The division results in an integer, so 21 + 35 is divisible by 7.

Likewise, if you subtract two multiples of 7, you'll get another multiple of 7. Try it: 35 − 21 = 14. Because both individually are divisible by 7, the difference between the two will also be divisible by 7.

In fact, it works no matter what multiple you try. The sum or difference of two multiples of 3 will also be a multiple of 3. The sum or difference of two multiples of 35 will also be a multiple of 35. Try this problem:

If x and y are integers, will $5x + 10y$ be divisible by 5 ?

The term $5x$ must be divisible by 5. And the term $10y$ must also be divisible by 5. Therefore, their sum will also be divisible by 5.

> **Key Concept**
>
> If x and y both share a factor n, then $x + y$ and $x - y$ will share that same factor n.
>
> For example, since 18 and 30 share the factor 6, both their sum, 48, and their difference, 12, also have 6 as a factor.

Check Your Skills

19. If a is a multiple of 18 and b is a multiple of 12, which of the following must be true? Indicate <u>all</u> such statements.

    A $a - b$ is divisible by 6.

    B $a + b$ is divisible by 12.

    C $a \times b$ is divisible by 18.

    D $a \div b$ is divisible by 6.

Answers can be found on page 255.

Chapter 9: Divisibility

Divisibility and Consecutive Integers

Consecutive integers are integers that follow one after another from a given starting point, without skipping any integers. For example, 4, 5, 6, and 7 are consecutive integers, but 4, 6, 8, and 9 are not. Consecutive integers and other evenly spaced sets can be used to disguise divisibility questions. For example:

If n is an integer, and k is the product of n, $n + 1$, $n + 2$, and $n + 3$, which of the following must be true?

Indicate <u>all</u> such statements.

- [A] k is even.
- [B] k is divisible by 3.
- [C] k is divisible by 4.
- [D] k is divisible by 6.

When you know that n is an integer, the representations $n + 1$, $n + 2$, and $n + 3$ represent the three consecutive integers following n. For example, if $n = 2$, then this list of four consecutive integers is 2, 3, 4, and 5. So the question is really saying that k is the product of four consecutive integers.

As with other divisibility problems, it's possible to solve this by picking numbers. Start by choosing values of n, then use that to solve for k (use your calculator as needed):

n	$n + 1$	$n + 2$	$n + 3$	k	even?	÷ 3?	÷ 4?	÷ 6?
1	2	3	4	24	Yes	Yes	Yes	Yes
2	3	4	5	120	Yes	Yes	Yes	Yes
3	4	5	6	360	Yes	Yes	Yes	Yes

For all these cases, all three statements are true. Therefore, select answers (A), (B), and (C). But why are they all true?

Start with this rephrased question:

If k is the product of four consecutive integers, which of the following must be true?

Since k is the *product* of the consecutive integers, each of the consecutive integers is a factor of k. Take a look at any set of consecutive integers and evaluate what patterns are present. For example:

$$12, 13, 14, 15, 16, 17, 18, 19, 20, 21, 22, 23, 24, 25$$

Every other number is even or, equivalently, divisible by 2. In fact, if you pick any two consecutive integers, one of them will be even and the other will be odd. And the product of any two consecutive integers will always be even, because it will always be an even times an odd. Therefore, since k is the product of two or more consecutive integers, it must be even, and 2 must be a factor of k. Choice (A) must be true.

It's also the case that every third number in the list (12, 15, 18, 21, and 24) is divisible by 3. In fact, for *any* set of three consecutive integers, one of them will always be divisible by 3. Try a few to prove it to yourself:

$$1, 2, \underline{3}$$

$$23, \underline{24}, 25$$

$$103, 104, \underline{105}$$

245

Unit Three: **Factors**

It doesn't matter where you start. One of the three consecutive integers will always have a factor of 3. Since k is the product of three or more consecutive integers, it will be divisible by 3.

This pattern will hold true over any size group. If there are four consecutive integers, then their product will be divisible by 4, 3, 2, and 1. If there are five consecutive integers, then their product will be divisible by 5, 4, 3, 2, and 1. A shorthand for this expression is a **factorial**:

$$5 \times 4 \times 3 \times 2 \times 1 = 5! = 120$$

$$4 \times 3 \times 2 \times 1 = 4! = 24$$

$$3 \times 2 \times 1 = 3! = 6$$

$$2 \times 1 = 2! = 2$$

$$1 = 1! = 1$$

One last thing: In the problem given earlier, there were four consecutive integers, so the product k was divisible by 4, 3, 2, and 1. Since k is divisible by both 2 and 3, it is also divisible by 6, which is answer choice (D).

> **Key Concept**
>
> If p is the product of q consecutive integers, then p is divisible by q and by all of the integers between q and 1.
>
> For example, if p is the product of 5 consecutive integers, then p is divisible by $5! = 5 \times 4 \times 3 \times 2 \times 1$.

Consecutive integers and evenly spaced sets also have some unusual properties that you'll learn about in more detail in Chapter 28: Sequences and Patterns.

Check Your Skills

20. What *must* be true about 3 consecutive positive integers?
    Indicate all such statements.

    A The product is a multiple of 3.

    B The sum is a multiple of 3.

    C The product is a multiple of 4.

    D The product is a multiple of 6.

Answers can be found on page 255.

Chapter 9: **Divisibility**

Remainders

Remainders are not that commonly tested and appear in more advanced questions. If you are aiming for a 166+ Quant score, study this section.

What happens when one number is not divisible by another? You're left with a **remainder**. For example, when 14 is divided by 4, the result is *not* an integer, so 14 is *not divisible* by 4.

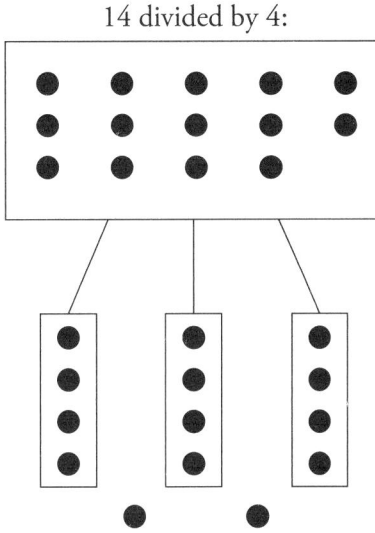

3 groups of 4 with 2 left over

Think of those dots as people for a moment. If you have 14 people and want to divide them into groups of 4 ("14 divided by 4"), you can build 3 complete groups, but 2 people will be left over. In essence, they *remain* ungrouped.

Alternatively, you could use the calculator to find the remainder when 14 is divided by 4...but it's a little more complicated than just plugging the math into the calculator.

First, 14 divided by 4 on a calculator will return the value 3.5. The fact that the result is not an integer indicates that 14 is not divisible by 4. However, the 0.5 part is *not* the remainder. Remainders are *always* integers, because a remainder is defined as the (whole) number that is left over when the division does not come out evenly.

The integer part of the 3.5 indicates the number of full groups, so you have 3 full groups of 4 and some amount left over, which is represented by the 0.5. There are two methods you could use to turn the decimal portion into the (whole number) remainder.

1. **Subtract the total grouped from the whole:** From the value 3.5, take the 3 full groups of 4 first: 3(4) = 12 people. Subtract this value from the starting total to get the reminder: 14 − 12 = 2.

2. **Find the part of the group remaining:** From the value 3.5, take just the decimal portion, 0.5. That figure indicates that you have 0.5 of a full group of 4. To find this value with your calculator, multiply: (0.5)(4) = 2. (Or recognize that half of 4 is 2.) In either case, the remainder is 2. A total of 12 people have been included in complete groups and 2 people have been left out of a group.

Unit Three: **Factors**

Try this problem:

> When the positive integer x is divided by 8, the result has a remainder of 3. What are three possible values of x?

The problem doesn't provide the starting total, but it does indicate that dividing x by 8 results in a remainder of 3. For example, if $\frac{x}{8}$ is equal to 1 remainder 3, then x contains one complete group of 8, plus it has 3 left over. In this case, $x = 8 + 3 = 11$.

According to the problem, there are always 3 left over, but the problem never specifies how many complete groups of 8 there are. Test some numbers to see what the possibilities are:

Number of groups of 8	Total from groups	Remainder	Value of x in this case
0	$0 \times 8 = 0$	3	$x = 0 + 3 = 3$
1	$1 \times 8 = 8$	3	$x = 8 + 3 = 11$
2	$2 \times 8 = 16$	3	$x = 16 + 3 = 19$
3	$3 \times 8 = 24$	3	$x = 24 + 3 = 27$

It's completely acceptable for the number of complete groups to equal zero. If you have 3 people and try to divide them into groups of 8...it's impossible! There aren't enough people to make even one full group. In this case, there are 0 groups of 8 with 3 left over.

The pattern illustrated in the table can be put into an equation based on the divisibility equation you learned earlier:

$$\text{If } x \text{ is divisible by } y: \qquad x = y \times \text{integer}$$

$$\text{If } x \text{ is not divisible by } y: \qquad x = y \times \text{integer} + \text{remainder}$$

When there is no remainder (in other words, when the remainder is 0), then x is divisible by y. For example, 32 is divisible by 8 because $32 = (8)(4) + 0$. There are four groups of 8 and nothing left over.

But 27 is *not* divisible by 8 because $27 = (8)(3) + 3$. This time, there are three groups of 8 and 3 left over or remaining.

Try this problem:

> If $\frac{x}{8} = 3.375$, what is the remainder when x is divided by 8?

The representation $\frac{x}{8} = 3.375$ indicates that there are 3 full groups of 8 and 0.375 left over. Because the problem asks only for the remainder, ignore the 3 and concentrate on the decimal portion, 0.375. The remainder is equal to this decimal times the total group size, 8, so the remainder is $0.375 \times 8 = 3$.

If the question had asked for the value of x, then you would have needed to use all of the value 3.375 to solve. The integer portion, 3, indicates that there are 3 full groups of 8, or $3 \times 8 = 24$. The decimal portion, 0.375, indicates that there are 3 left over, as shown in the prior paragraph. So, $x = 24 + 3 = 27$.

Chapter 9: **Divisibility**

Range of Possible Remainders

For any divisor (number that you divide by), the possible remainders range from zero to that divisor minus one. Take a look at this pattern:

Division	Answer
7 ÷ 7	1 remainder 0
8 ÷ 7	1 remainder 1
9 ÷ 7	1 remainder 2
10 ÷ 7	1 remainder 3
11 ÷ 7	1 remainder 4
12 ÷ 7	1 remainder 5
13 ÷ 7	1 remainder 6
14 ÷ 7	2 remainder 0

When 7 is divided by 7, there is no remainder (also written as a remainder of 0). When 8 is divided by 7, the remainder is 1. When 9 is divided by 7, the remainder is 2. In each subsequent line, the remainder increases by 1, until you reach the next multiple of 7, which is 14.

At that point, the remainder pattern resets back to 0. So, when dividing by 7, the greatest possible remainder is 6. It's not possible to have a remainder equal to or greater than 7, because then another 7 could "go into" the number.

It's also not possible to have a negative remainder. Thus, there are exactly 7 possible remainders for a number divided by 7, namely 0, 1, 2, 3, 4, 5, or 6.

You can see these remainders repeating themselves in a cycle on the Remainder Ruler, where the zeros coincide with the multiples of 7 on the number line:

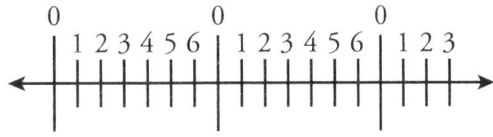

This pattern holds true for all values. If you divide by 5, the range of possible remainders is from 0 to 4. If you divide by 14, the range of possible remainders is from 0 to 13.

Chapter 32: Advanced Concepts goes through a more theoretical approach to remainders, but most remainder problems can be answered by testing numbers and/or plugging into your calculator.

Check Your Skills

21. What is the remainder when 13 is divided by 6 ?
22. What's the first double-digit number that results in a remainder of 4 when divided by 5 ?

Answers can be found on page 256.

Unit Three: **Factors**

Check Your Skills Answer Key

1. **(B) 3 is a divisor of 9; (D) 80 is divisible by 20; (E) 26 divided by 2 results in an integer**
    For each of the statements, translate the language into fractions to test:

18 is a multiple of 12.	$\frac{18}{12}$ = integer? → FALSE
3 is a divisor of 9.	$\frac{9}{3}$ = integer? → TRUE
13 is a factor of 40.	$\frac{40}{13}$ = integer? → FALSE
80 is divisible by 20.	$\frac{80}{20}$ = integer? → TRUE
26 divided by 2 results in an integer.	$\frac{26}{2}$ = integer? → TRUE
35 divided by 70 yields no remainder.	$\frac{35}{70}$ = integer? → FALSE

2. **0, 3, 6, 9, 12**
    To find the first 5 non-negative multiples of 3, multiply 3 by the first 5 non-negative integers: 0, 1, 2, 3, and 4.

    $$3 \times 0 = 0$$
    $$3 \times 1 = 3$$
    $$3 \times 2 = 6$$
    $$3 \times 3 = 9$$
    $$3 \times 4 = 12$$

    Note that 3 and 0 are both multiples of 3! There are also negative multiples of 3 (−3, −6, −9, etc.), but this problem asked only for the non-negative multiples.

3. **Yes**
    The sum of the digits is 7 + 3 + 2 = 12, which is divisible by 3, so 732 is divisible by 3.

4. **No**
    The two-digit number at the end of 4,578 is 78. Half of 78 is 39, which is odd, so 4,578 is not divisible by 4.

5. **Yes**
    Any number that is divisible by both 2 and 3 is also divisible by 6. Because the units digit (8) is an even number, 4,578 is divisible by 2. The sum of the digits of 4,578 is 24 (4 + 5 + 7 + 8 = 24), which is divisible by 3, so 4,578 is also divisible by 3. Therefore, 4,578 is divisible by 6.

6. **Yes**
    Use the calculator for this one: 603,864 ÷ 8 = 75,483, which is an integer, so 603,864 is divisible by 8.

7.

Small	Large
1	90
2	45
3	30
5	18
6	15
9	10

8.

Small	Large
1	72
2	36
3	24
4	18
6	12
8	9

9. $2^3 \times 3^2$

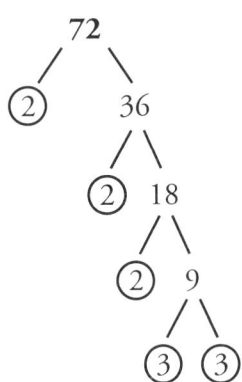

10. $3 \times 5 \times 7$

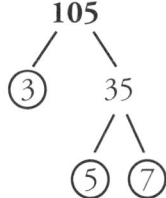

By the way, did the prime factorization of 105 feel familiar? You already found it when breaking down 630 in the chapter. That's because 105 is a factor of 630. A factor is essentially a subset of the greater number, so you already did this subset of work before.

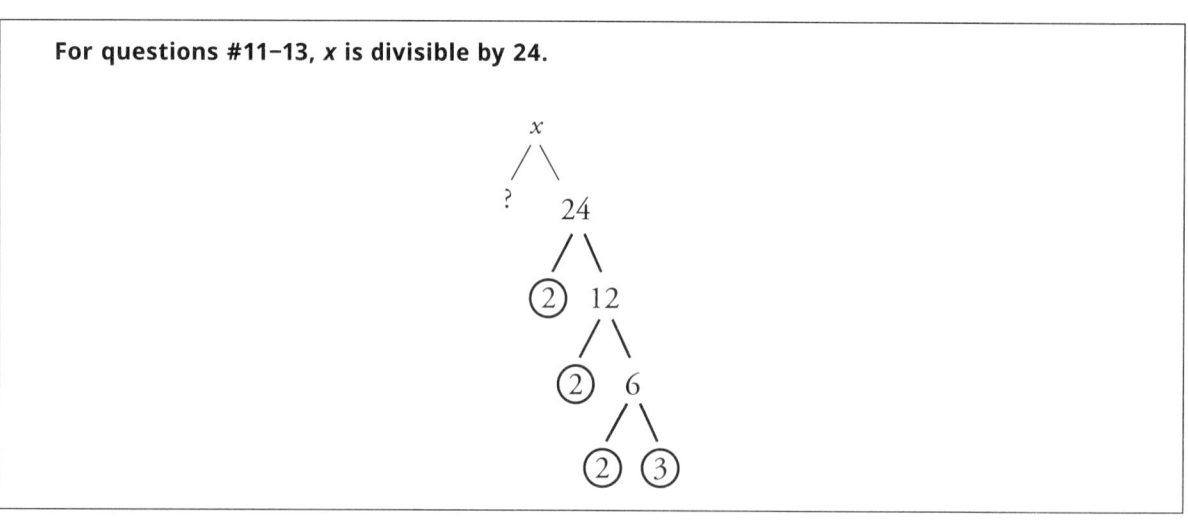

11. **Must be true**

    For x to be divisible by 6, it must be divisible by the prime factors of 6, which are one 2 and one 3. Since x is divisible by 24, x also contains a 2 and a 3. Therefore, x *must* be divisible by 6.

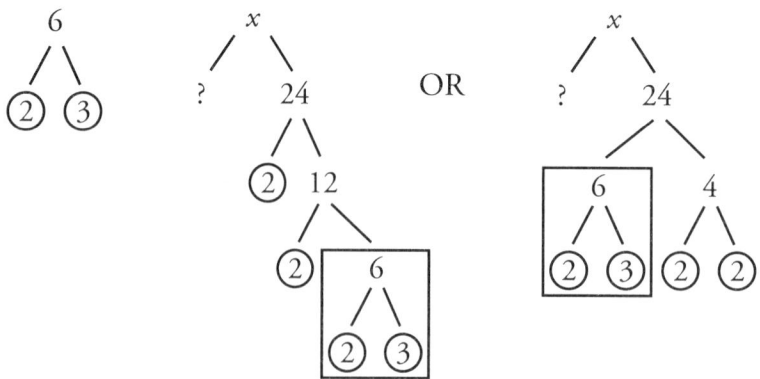

12. **Could be true**

    For x to be divisible by 9, it must be divisible by the prime factors of 9, which are 3 and 3. Since x is divisible by 24, x's prime factors are 2, 2, 2, and 3, but that provides only one 3, not two 3's. It is possible that x has additional factors, so x could be divisible by 9, but it does not have to be. For example, if x is 24 or 48, then it is not divisible by 9, but if x is 72, then it is divisible by 9.

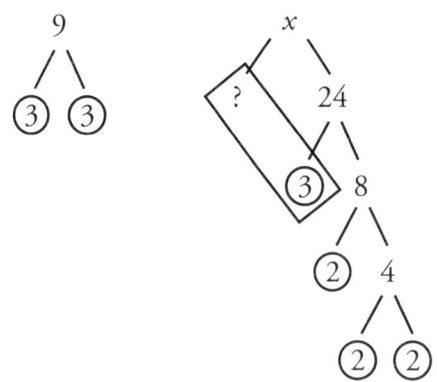

Chapter 9: **Divisibility**

13. **Must be true**
    For *x* to be divisible by 8, it must be divisible by the prime factors of 8, which are 2, 2, and 2. Since *x* is divisible by 24, *x* does contain three 2's. Therefore, *x must* be divisible by 8.

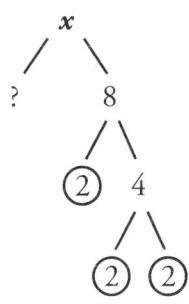

For questions #14–16, *x* is divisible by 28 and by 15.

14. **Must be true**

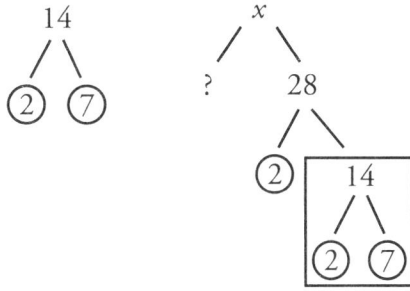

For *x* to be divisible by 14, it has to have the same prime factors as 14, which contains a 2 and a 7. Because *x* does contain a 2 and a 7, the unknown *x* must therefore be divisible by 14.

253

Unit Three: **Factors**

15. **Must be true**

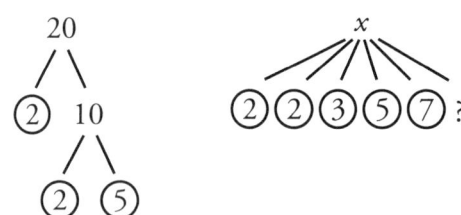

For *x* to be divisible by 20, it has to have the same prime factors as 20, which contains two 2's and one 5. Because *x* does contain two 2's and a 5, it *must* therefore be divisible by 20.

16. **Could be true**

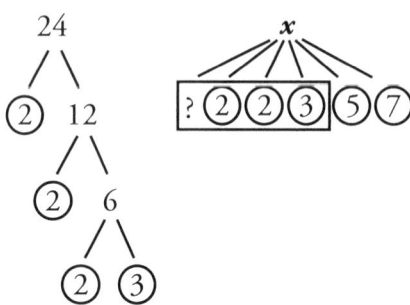

For *x* to be divisible by 24, it must have the same prime factors as 24, which contains three 2's and one 3. However, *x* contains a minimum of two 2's, not three. The question mark indicates that *x* may have other prime factors, so there could be a third factor of 2, but there may not be. So *x* could be divisible by 24, but it doesn't have to be.

For questions #17–18, *y* is divisible by 30 and by 25.

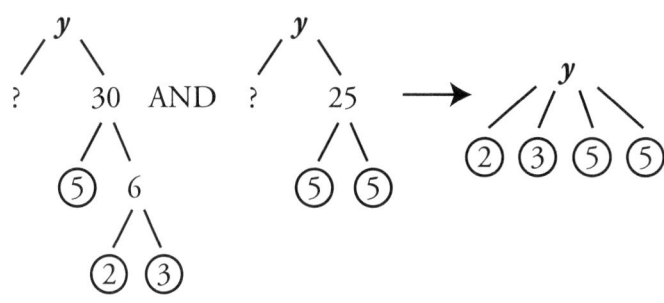

---

17. **Must be true**

For *y* to be divisible by 50, it would have to be divisible by all of 50's factors, which are 2, 5, and 5. Since *y*'s prime factorization does contain at least one 2 and two 5's, it is the case that *y* must be divisible by 50.

254

Chapter 9: **Divisibility**

18. **Could be true**

For y to be divisible by 750, it would have to be divisible by all of 750's factors, which are 2, 3, 5, 5, and 5. But y's prime factorization does not have to contain at least three 5's; rather, it just has to contain at least two 5's. Therefore, y could be divisible by 750, but it does not have to be.

19. **(A)** $a - b$ **is divisible by 6; (C)** $a \times b$ **is divisible by 18**

Create a factor tree to confirm the prime factorizations of a and b:

$$a = 18 \times ? = 3 \times 6 \times ? = 2 \times 3 \times 3 \times ?$$

$$b = 12 \times ? = 2 \times 6 \times ? = 2 \times 2 \times 3 \times ?$$

Now evaluate the answer choices. The question asks which statements *must* be true.

(A) $a - b$ is divisible by 6. The prime factors of 6 are 2 and 3. Both a and b contain the factors 2 and 3, so both a and b are divisible by 6. As a result, their difference is also divisible by 6. Select choice (A).

(B) $a + b$ is divisible by 12. The prime factors of 12 are 2, 2, and 3. The number b is a multiple of 12, but a may or may not be a multiple of 12. For example, if b is 12 and a is 18, then their sum, 30, is not a multiple of 12. Eliminate choice (B).

(C) $a \times b$ is divisible by 18. The prime factors of 18 are 2, 3, and 3. The prime factors of $a \times b$ include all of their individual prime factors:

$$a \times b = 2 \times 3 \times 3 \times 2 \times 2 \times 3 \times ?$$

This set of prime factors includes at least one 2 and at least two 3's, so $a \times b$ is definitely divisible by 18. Select choice (C).

(D) $a \div b$ is divisible by 6. Divide the prime factors of a and b:

$$\frac{a}{b} = \frac{\cancel{2} \times 2 \times \cancel{3} \times ?}{\cancel{2} \times 3 \times \cancel{3} \times ?} = \frac{2 \times ?}{3 \times ?}$$

Without more information, it's impossible to know whether the result is an integer, much less whether it's divisible by 6. Eliminate choice (D).

The correct answer is (A) and (C) only.

20. **(A) the product is a multiple of 3; (B) the sum is a multiple of 3; (D) the product is a multiple of 6**

The product of any three consecutive integers is divisible by both 3 and 2, so answer (A) must be true and so must answer (D).

Evaluate answer (C) next. The product of three consecutive integers might be divisible by 4. For example, $(2)(3)(4) = 24$ is divisible by 4. But $(1)(2)(3) = 6$ is not divisible by 4, so answer (C) does not have to be true.

Answer (B) mentions the sum, not the product. Solve algebraically or test a few cases to find the pattern.

255

Unit Three: Factors

To solve algebraically, first sum up three consecutive integers using standard consecutive integer notation.

$$n + (n + 1) + (n + 2) = 3n + 3$$

When you sum two numbers, $3n$ and 3, that are both multiples of 3, the sum itself must also be a multiple of 3. Therefore, answer (B) must be true.

Alternatively, test some numbers to see what happens.

Sum	Multiple of 3?
$1 + 2 + 3 = 6$	Yes
$2 + 3 + 4 = 9$	Yes
$3 + 4 + 5 = 12$	Yes

All three cases return a sum that is a multiple of 3. Is this a pattern that will always hold? Take the first case as the baseline: The sum is 6. The second case drops the number 1, still uses the numbers 2 and 3, and adds the number 4 in the place of the dropped 1. In other words, the second case adds a total of $4 - 1 = 3$ to the sum, and so the sum becomes 9. In the third case, the same pattern occurs: 2 is dropped and 5 is added. Again, 5 is three more than 2, so again three more is added to the sum and the sum becomes 12.

If you start from 6 (a multiple of 3) and keep adding 3, the subsequent sums will all also be multiples of 3. So, it is the case that the sum of three consecutive integers must be a multiple of 3.

The correct answer is (A), (B), and (D) only.

21. **1**

    The number 6 goes into 13 two full times, comprising $2 \times 6 = 12$ of the total and leaving $13 - 12 = 1$ as the remainder.

22. **14**

    For a number to result in a remainder of 4 when divided by 5, it has to be equal to a multiple of 5, plus 4. The first of these is 4 ($0 \times 5 + 4 = 4$), the second is 9 ($1 \times 5 + 4 = 9$), and the third is 14 ($2 \times 5 + 4 = 14$). Thus, 14 is the first double-digit number that produces the required remainder.

Problem Set

> For problems #1–10, use prime factorization, if appropriate, to answer each question **Yes**, **No**, or **Cannot Be Determined**. If your answer is **Cannot Be Determined**, use two numerical examples to show how the problem could go either way. All variables are assumed to be positive integers unless otherwise indicated.

1. If a is divided by 7 or by 18, an integer results. Is $\frac{a}{42}$ an integer?

2. If 80 is a factor of r, is 15 a factor of r ?

3. If 7 is a factor of n and 7 is a factor of p, is $n + p$ divisible by 7 ?

4. If 8 is not a factor of g, is 8 a factor of $2g$?

5. If j is divisible by 12 and 10, is j divisible by 24 ?

6. If 12 is a factor of xyz, is 12 a factor of xy ?

7. If 6 is a divisor of r and r is a factor of s, is 6 a factor of s ?

8. If 24 is a factor of h and 28 is a factor of k, must 21 be a factor of hk ?

9. If 6 is not a factor of d, is $12d$ divisible by 6 ?

10. If 60 is a factor of u, is 18 a factor of u ?

11.
Quantity A	Quantity B
The number of distinct prime factors of 40	The number of distinct prime factors of 50

12.
Quantity A	Quantity B
The product of 12 and an even prime number	The sum of the four greatest factors of 12

13. $x = 20$, $y = 32$, and $z = 12$

Quantity A	Quantity B
The remainder when x is divided by z	The remainder when y is divided by z

14. If a and b are positive integers such that the remainder is 4 when a is divided by b, what is the smallest possible value of $a + b$?

15. If x, y, and z are positive integers, x divided by y leaves a remainder of 0, and z divided by y leaves a remainder of 3, what is the remainder when xz is divided by y ?

16. 202 divided by some prime number x yields an odd number. 411 multiplied by some prime number y yields an even number.

Quantity A	Quantity B
x	y

Solutions

1. **Yes**

   If *a* is divisible by 7 and by 18, its prime factors include 2, 3, 3, and 7, as shown in the factor tree. Therefore, any integer that can be constructed as a product of any of these prime factors is also a factor of *a*. Therefore, 42 is also a factor of *a*, because $42 = 2 \times 3 \times 7$.

   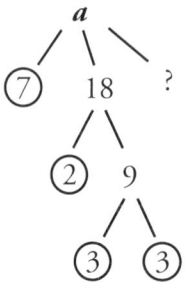

2. **Cannot be determined**

   If *r* is divisible by 80, its prime factors include 2, 2, 2, 2, and 5, as indicated by the factor tree below. Therefore, any integer that can be constructed as a product of any of these prime factors is also a factor of *r*. However, $15 = 3 \times 5$. Because the prime factor 3 is not in the factor tree, you cannot determine whether 15 is a factor of *r*. As numerical examples, you could take $r = 80$, in which case 15 is *not* a factor of *r*, or $r = 240$, in which case 15 *is* a factor of *r*.

   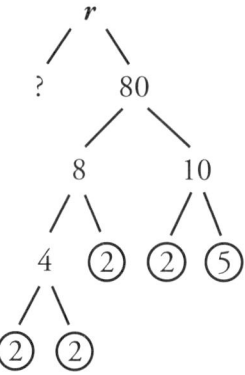

3. **Yes**

   If two numbers are both multiples of the same number, then their *sum* is also a multiple of that same number. Because *n* and *p* share the common factor 7, the sum of *n* and *p* must also be divisible by 7.

Chapter 9: **Divisibility**

4. **Cannot be determined**
   For 8 to be a factor of 2g, you would need two more 2's in the factor tree. In other words, g would need to be divisible by 4. You know that g is not divisible by 8, but there are certainly integers that are divisible by 4 and not by 8, such as 4, 12, 20, 28, and so on. However, while you cannot conclude that g is *not* divisible by 4, you cannot be certain that g *is* divisible by 4, either. For instance, you could take g = 5, in which case 8 is *not* a factor of 2g, or g = 4, in which case 8 *is* a factor of 2g.

   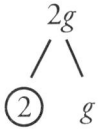

5. **Cannot be determined**
   If j is divisible by 12 and by 10, its prime factors include 2, 2, 3, and 5, as indicated by the final factor tree below. There are only two 2's that are definitely in the prime factorization of j, because the 2 in the prime factorization of 10 may be redundant—that is, it may be the same 2 as one of the 2's in the prime factorization of 12.

   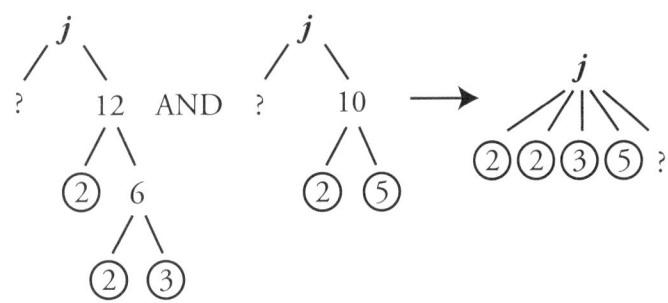

   $24 = 2 \times 2 \times 2 \times 3$. The prime factorization of 24 includes three 2's, but there are only two 2's guaranteed to be in the prime factorization of j. Therefore, 24 is not necessarily a factor of j.

6. **Cannot be determined**
   If xyz is divisible by 12, its prime factors include 2, 2, and 3, as indicated by the factor tree below. Those prime factors could all be factors of x and y, in which case 12 would be a factor of xy. For example, this is the case when x = 20, y = 3, and z = 7. However, some or all of the factors of 12 might be present only in z, in which case 12 would not be a factor of xy. For example, this is the case when x = 5, y = 11, and z = 24.

   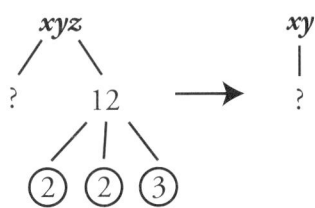

259

7. **Yes**

   If r is a factor of s, then s includes all the factors of r, including 6.

   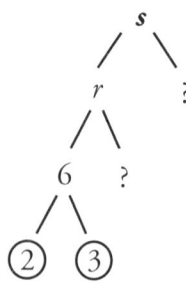

8. **Yes**

   All the factors of both h and k must be factors of the product, hk. Therefore, the factors of hk include 2, 2, 2, 2, 2, 3, and 7, as shown in the combined factor tree below. (It isn't necessary to worry about overlap here, since the factors are pulled from two different numbers.) Since $21 = 3 \times 7$ and both 3 and 7 are in the tree, 21 is a factor of hk.

   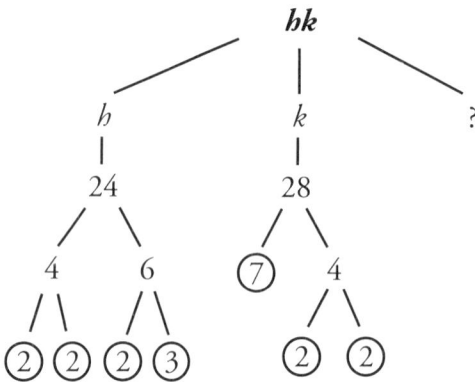

9. **Yes**

   The fact that d is not divisible by 6 is irrelevant in this case. Because 12 is divisible by 6, 12d is also divisible by 6.

   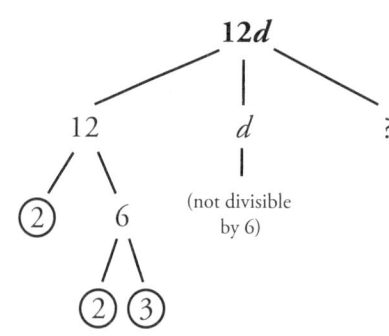

10. **Cannot be determined**

    For *u* to be a multiple of 18, it would need to include all the prime factors of 18: 2, 3, and 3. You know that *u* contains the prime factors of 60—2, 2, 3, and 5—but it may or may not contain a second 3. Therefore, 18 is not necessarily a factor of *u*.

    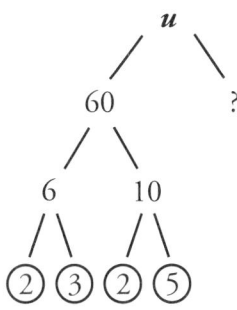

11. **(C)**

    The prime factorization of 40 is 2 × 2 × 2 × 5. So 40 has two distinct prime factors: 2 and 5. The prime factorization of 50 is 5 × 5 × 2, so 50 also has two distinct prime factors: 2 and 5.

    Therefore, the correct answer is (C): The two quantities are equal.

12. **(B)**

    Simplify Quantity A first. There is only one even prime number: 2. Therefore, Quantity A is 12 × 2 = 24.

    For Quantity B, the four greatest factors of 12 are 12, 6, 4, and 3. (Remember that every number is a factor of itself!) This yields 12 + 6 + 4 + 3 = 25.

Quantity A	**Quantity B**
The product of 12 and an even prime number =	The sum of the four greatest factors of 12 =
12 × 2 = 24	12 + 6 + 4 + 3 = 25

    Therefore, the correct answer is (B): Quantity B is greater.

Unit Three: **Factors**

13. **(C)**

    When 20 is divided by 12, the result is a quotient of 1 and a remainder of 8 ($12 \times 1 + 8 = 20$).

    When 32 is divided by 12, the result is a quotient of 2 and a remainder of 8 ($12 \times 2 + 8 = 32$).

    $$x = 20, y = 32, \text{ and } z = 12$$

Quantity A	**Quantity B**
8	8

    Therefore, the correct answer is (C): The two quantities are equal.

14. **9**

    Because $\frac{a}{b}$ has a remainder of 4, integer b must be at least 5. (Remember, the remainder must *always* be smaller than the divisor). The smallest possible value for a is 4, because $4 \div 5$ yields a quotient of 0 and a remainder of 4. (a could also be 9, 14, 19, etc.). Thus, the smallest possible value for $a + b$ is 9.

15. **0**

    Because $\frac{x}{y}$ has a remainder of 0, x is divisible by y. Therefore, xz is also divisible by y, so xz has a remainder of 0 when divided by y.

16. **(C)**

    An even divided by an odd can never yield an odd quotient. This means the prime number x must be even (because otherwise you'd have $\frac{202}{\text{odd}}$, which wouldn't yield an odd quotient). The only even prime number is 2, so $x = 2$. Similarly, an odd multiplied by an odd will always be odd, so y must be even. The only prime even number is 2, so $y = 2$.

Quantity A	**Quantity B**
$\frac{202}{x} = \text{odd} \rightarrow \frac{202}{2} = 101$	$411 \times y = \text{even} \rightarrow 411 \times 2 = 822$
$x = 2$	$y = 2$

    Therefore, the correct answer is (C): The two quantities are equal.

CHAPTER 10

Common Factors

In This Chapter:

- Distributing and Factoring
- Exponents and Factors
- Roots and Factors
- Fractions and Factors
- Check Your Skills Answer Key
- Problem Set
- Solutions

CHAPTER 10 Common Factors

Two separate terms can share factors. For example, 2 and 4 share the **common factor** 2. Likewise, 6 and 12 share the common factors 2 and 3 (they also share the common factor 6). And the expressions $7x$ and $7y$ share (at least) the common factor 7. The ability to find common factors is a frequently tested skill on the GRE.

In this chapter, you will learn how to find common factors in a variety of situations, including when working with expressions, exponents, roots, and fractions.

Distributing and Factoring

Distributing a Common Term

Here's a quick reminder on distributing, which was first introduced in Chapter 4: Equations. To simplify the expression $3(x + 2)$, distribute the 3 so that it is multiplied by both the x and the 2:

$$3(x + 2)$$
$$3(x) + 3(2)$$
$$3x + 6$$

Factoring Out a Common Term

This process can also be done in reverse. If you're given $3x + 6$, each of the two terms, $3x$ and 6, has 3 as a factor. Pull that common factor 3 out of each term, place it in front, and add parentheses around what's left:

$$3x + 6 \rightarrow 3(x + 2)$$

This can also be done with variables. In this example, each term contains one t, so pull that common t out front, leaving $t + 1$ in the parentheses:

$$t^2 + t = t(t + 1)$$

You can even pull out multiple common terms at the same time. Factor the common terms out of this expression:

$$5k^2 - 15k^3$$

The two terms both contain a 5 and a k^2, so pull $5k^2$ out of each term:

$$5k^2 - 15k^3 = 5k^2(1 - 3k)$$

Unit Three: **Factors**

The first term, $5k^2$, exactly matches the common factor that you're pulling out. When this happens, always leave a 1 inside the parentheses.

For any of these, you can check your work by distributing—multiplying everything back out. If you arrive back at your starting point, then you factored out correctly.

Check Your Skills

> Factor the following expressions.

1. $4 + 8t$
2. $5x + 25y$
3. $2x^2 + 16x^3$

Answers can be found on page 280.

Exponents and Factors

Multiplication and Division

Here's a quick review of certain exponent rules from Chapter 5: Exponents and Roots. First, when multiplying or dividing multiple terms, if the exponents are the same, you can group and perform the multiplication or division first, then apply the exponent:

$$\frac{2^3 \times 8^3}{4^3} = \left(\frac{2 \times 8}{4}\right)^3 = 4^3 = 64$$

Similarly, when multiplying or dividing terms, if the bases are the same, you can combine the exponents:

$$\frac{3^3 \times 3^4}{3^2} = 3^{(3+4-2)} = 3^5$$

But what can you do when presented with an expression such as $5^3 \times 25^2$? Neither the exponents nor the bases look the same.

Numbers that look very different might have many of the same factors. For example, 12 and 24 look different but both are made up of 2's and 3's.

The two bases from the example, 5 and 25, share a common factor: 5. The 25 can be rewritten to use 5 as the base: $25 = 5 \times 5 = 5^2$. Plug that into the original expression:

$$5^3 \times 25^2 =$$
$$5^3 \times (5^2)^2 =$$
$$5^3 \times 5^4 =$$
$$5^{(3+4)} = 5^7$$

Try another example: How would you combine the expression $2^3 \times 8^4$?

Chapter 10: **Common Factors**

The key is to recognize that $8 = 2^3$, so the two terms share a common factor of 2. Rewrite 8^4 to use the base 2, then combine the two terms:

$$2^3 \times 8^4 =$$
$$2^3 \times (2^3)^4 =$$
$$2^3 \times 2^{12} =$$
$$2^{(3+12)} = 2^{15}$$

Here are some other ways in which the GRE might ask you to do this same kind of math:

Question:	Answer
Which of the following is equivalent to $2^3 \times 8^4$?	2^{15}
How many factors of two are in the expression $2^3 \times 8^4$?	15
Is $2^3 \times 8^4$ divisible by 2^{15} ?	Yes

The process of finding common factors to combine bases works even if the prime factorization of the numbers is more complicated:

$$\frac{6^5}{2^3 \times 3^5} = \frac{(2 \times 3)^5}{2^3 \times 3^5} = \frac{2^5 \times 3^5}{2^3 \times 3^5} = \frac{2^5 \times \cancel{3^5}}{2^3 \times \cancel{3^5}} = 2^{(5-3)} = 2^2 = 4$$

> **Strategy Tip**
>
> When multiplying or dividing exponential expressions, simplify by:
>
> 1. Factoring the Bases
> 2. Combining Common Factors
> 3. Simplifying the Exponents

Check Your Skills

> Combine the following expressions.

4. $2^4 \times 16^3$

5. $7^5 \times 49^8$

6. $9^3 \times 81^3$

Answers can be found on page 280.

Unit Three: **Factors**

Addition and Subtraction

Exponential terms that are added or subtracted cannot be combined using any exponent rule discussed so far, but they can be simplified using common factors. For example:

$$7^3 + 7^4$$

Both terms share a common factor of 7. In fact, both terms have at least three factors of 7:

$$\boxed{7 \times 7 \times 7} + \boxed{7 \times 7 \times 7} \times 7$$

Factor out the 7^3 from each term to simplify the expression:

$$7^3 + 7^4 = 7^3(7^0 + 7^1) = 7^3(1 + 7) = 7^3(8)$$

When you factor 7^3 out of 7^3, a $7^0 = 1$ term is left behind. Whenever you factor out the entire starting term, leave a 1 behind in the parentheses.

As before, you can check that you've factored something out correctly by distributing to verify that you're back where you started:

$$7^3(1 + 7) = 7^3(1) + 7^3(7) = 7^3 + 7^4$$

Here are three more examples:

Given	Common factor	Simplification
$3^5 - 3^4$	3^4	$3^5 - 3^4 = 3^4(3^1 - 1) = 3^4(2)$
$x^8 + x^6$	x^6	$x^8 + x^6 = x^6(x^2 + 1)$
$8^3 + 8^4$	8^3	$8^3 + 8^4 = 8^3(1 + 8^1) = 8^3(9)$

In the three prior examples, the bases are all the same, so the common factors were contained in the exponents. However, if the bases are not the same, use prime factorization to find common factors:

$$6^3 + 3^4 = (3)^3(2)^3 + 3^4$$

When the 6 is broken down into factors of 2 and 3, both terms now have at least three 3's, so a 3^3 term can be factored out:

$$(3^3)(2^3) + 3^4$$
$$3^3(2^3 + 3^1)$$
$$3^3(8 + 3)$$
$$3^3(11)$$

In Chapter 5: Exponents and Roots, there was a list of expressions that could not be simplified using exponent rules. However, these expressions *can* be simplified using common factors. Try these problems:

$$7^4 + 7^6$$
$$3^4 + 12^4$$
$$6^5 - 6^3$$
$$12^7 - 3^7$$

Here are the solutions:

$7^4 + 7^6$	$3^4 + 12^4$	$6^5 - 6^3$	$12^7 - 3^7$
$7^4(1 + 7^2)$	$3^4 + (3 \times 4)^4$	$6^3(6^2 - 1)$	$(3 \times 4)^7 - 3^7$
$7^4(50)$	$3^4 + (3^4)(4^4)$	$6^3(35)$	$(3^7)(4^7) - 3^7$
	$3^4(1 + 4^4)$		$3^7(4^7 - 1)$

Check Your Skills

7. If $x = 4^{20} + 4^{21} + 4^{22}$, what is the greatest prime factor of *x* ?

Answers can be found on page 281.

Roots and Factors

Simplifying Roots

Prime factorization can also help to simplify roots. Earlier in this book, you were asked to memorize the fact that $\sqrt[3]{8} = 2$, because $2 \times 2 \times 2 = 8$. For standard roots like this one, memorization is the fastest path. But what if you had to simplify $\sqrt{50}$?

First, use the factor tree method to find the prime factorization of 50, which is $5 \times 5 \times 2$. The square root of 50 can be written as any of the following:

$$\sqrt{50}$$
$$\sqrt{5 \times 5 \times 2}$$
$$\sqrt{5} \times \sqrt{5} \times \sqrt{2}$$
$$\sqrt{5} \times \sqrt{5 \times 2}$$
$$\sqrt{5 \times 5} \times \sqrt{2}$$

While all of these expressions are equivalent, the final one is the most helpful. The term $\sqrt{5 \times 5}$ is equal to 5, because $\sqrt{5 \times 5} = \sqrt{25} = 5$. So, the simplified form of $\sqrt{50}$ is $5\sqrt{2}$.

Unit Three: Factors

In fact, any time you see a pair of factors under a square root sign, drop one of the pair along with the square root sign and you're done:

$$\sqrt{5 \times 5} = 5$$
$$\sqrt{10 \times 10} = 10$$
$$\sqrt{19 \times 19} = 19$$

Any pair of factors can be square rooted and simplified into an integer. Find the pairs for $\sqrt{64}$ and $\sqrt{40}$:

$$\sqrt{64} = \sqrt{2 \times 2 \times 2 \times 2 \times 2 \times 2}$$
$$= \sqrt{(2 \times 2) \times (2 \times 2) \times (2 \times 2)}$$
$$= \sqrt{(2 \times 2)} \times \sqrt{(2 \times 2)} \times \sqrt{(2 \times 2)}$$
$$= 2 \times 2 \times 2$$
$$\sqrt{64} = 8$$

The prime factorization of 64 is six 2's. Pair those into three sets and take the root of each to find the square root of 64. That produces three 2's, or 8.

$$\sqrt{40} = \sqrt{2 \times 2 \times 2 \times 5}$$
$$= \sqrt{(2 \times 2) \times 2 \times 5}$$
$$= \sqrt{(2 \times 2)} \times \sqrt{2 \times 5}$$
$$= 2 \times \sqrt{2 \times 5}$$
$$\sqrt{40} = 2\sqrt{10}$$

There's a big difference between $\sqrt{64}$ and $\sqrt{40}$. Namely, $\sqrt{64}$ can be simplified to an integer, while $\sqrt{40}$ cannot. Numbers that produce integers when they're square rooted are called **perfect squares**. For example, 4, 9, 36, and 64 are all perfect squares.

All the prime factors of perfect squares will always come as paired sets. For example, the prime factors of 4 are two 2's, the prime factors of 9 are two 3's, and the prime factors of 36 are two 2's and two 3's. You'll always be able to pair them and square root them to an integer.

However, 40 is not a perfect square. Only some of the factors can pair off and thus simplify into an integer; the rest will stay underneath the square root sign. To recognize the right answer in any form, you'll need to be able to factor $\sqrt{40}$ into $2\sqrt{10}$.

Use the properties of perfect squares to answer this question:

If x is an integer and $x^2 = 44y$, which of the following could be a value of y?

(A) 11
(B) 22
(C) 33
(D) 55
(E) 66

10

270

Because x is an integer, x^2 will be a perfect square, so its prime factors must come in pairs. Make a factor tree of x^2:

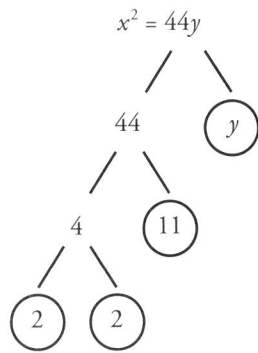

So, the prime factorization of x^2 is $2 \times 2 \times 11 \times y$. The 2's are already paired, but the 11 doesn't have a partner, so at the least, y has to contain 11 as a factor. Since 11 itself is one of the answer choices, choice (A) has to be the correct answer.

Why wouldn't 22 work? If y equaled 22, then the factors of x^2 would be $2 \times 2 \times 11 \times 11 \times 2$. But this set of factors has an extra 2 that doesn't have a partner. Since x^2 is a perfect square, all of its factors must come in pairs, so choice (B) cannot be correct.

The remaining three answers all have this same flaw. Answer (C) contains an unpaired 3, answer (D) contains an unpaired 5, and answer (E) contains an unpaired 2 and an unpaired 3.

> **Strategy Tip**
>
> | $\sqrt{a \times a \times b \times b \times c} =$ | Simplify square roots by finding pairs of factors and taking their square root. |
> |---|---|
> | $\sqrt{(a \times a)(b \times b)c} = ab\sqrt{c}$ | |
>
> Only perfect squares have perfectly paired prime factors, so only perfect squares will result in an integer when square rooted: $\sqrt{(a \times a)(b \times b)} = ab$

This system of grouping factors will work for other powers of roots as well. For a cube root, group the factors into sets of 3. For example:

$$\sqrt[3]{64} = \sqrt[3]{2 \times 2 \times 2 \times 2 \times 2 \times 2}$$
$$= \sqrt[3]{(2 \times 2 \times 2) \times (2 \times 2 \times 2)}$$
$$= \sqrt[3]{(2 \times 2 \times 2)} \times \sqrt[3]{(2 \times 2 \times 2)}$$
$$= 2 \times 2$$
$$\sqrt[3]{64} = 4$$

As before, retain just one factor from each grouping when you get rid of the root sign.

Unit Three: **Factors**

Other types of roots would work the same way, but it's unlikely that the GRE will ask you to simplify any root higher than cube roots.

Combining Roots

The GRE will typically disguise root simplification problems in equations. Try this problem:

If $x = \sqrt{2} \times \sqrt{6}$, what is x?

(A) $\sqrt{3}$
(B) $2\sqrt{3}$
(C) $3\sqrt{2}$
(D) 6
(E) 12

You could combine them and say that $x = \sqrt{2} \times \sqrt{6} = \sqrt{2 \times 6} = \sqrt{12}$. Unfortunately, $\sqrt{12}$ will never be a correct answer on the GRE because it isn't in its most simplified form.

Instead, put everything under one sign, find the prime factorization of any numbers that aren't already primes, and pull out any pairs of factors:

$$\sqrt{2} \times \sqrt{6}$$
$$\sqrt{2 \times 6}$$
$$\sqrt{2 \times 2 \times 3}$$
$$2\sqrt{3}$$

The correct answer is (B).

If any of this root logic is unfamiliar, revisit Chapter 5: Exponents and Roots for a refresher.

In general, when you take the prime factorization of any number inside a square root, any pairs of prime factors can be brought out of the square root, even if you're not dealing with a perfect square. Try this problem:

Simplify $\sqrt{360}$.

First, find the prime factorization of 360:

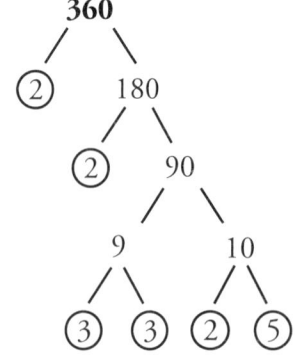

$$360 = 2 \times 2 \times 2 \times 3 \times 3 \times 5$$

10

272

Chapter 10: **Common Factors**

Find the pairs of primes and simplify:

$$\sqrt{360} = \sqrt{2 \times 2 \times 2 \times 3 \times 3 \times 5}$$
$$= \sqrt{(2 \times 2) \times 2 \times (3 \times 3) \times 5}$$
$$= (2)(3)\sqrt{2 \times 5}$$
$$= 6\sqrt{10}$$

It's possible to get to the answer via multiple paths. For example:

$$\sqrt{360} = \sqrt{36 \times 10} = \sqrt{36} \times \sqrt{10} = 6\sqrt{10}$$

This shortcut is so efficient because 36 is a perfect square. In general, take a few seconds to examine the number before you dive in to perform a full prime factorization. If you see a great shortcut, take it. But don't take a ton of time to search for such a shortcut—if you don't see something pretty quickly, go ahead and do the prime factorization.

Check Your Skills

> Simplify the following roots.

8. $\sqrt{75}$

9. $\sqrt{96}$

10. $\sqrt{441}$

Answers can be found on page 281.

Fractions and Factors

Simplifying Fractions

To master fractions (coming up in Chapter 11: Fractions), you'll need to understand how common factors play a role. For multiple choice questions, you'll need to not only compute the right answer, but also get it in a format that matches the answer choices.

Suppose that you solved a problem correctly and arrived at the answer $\frac{6}{9}$, but then saw these answer choices:

(A) $\frac{1}{3}$

(B) $\frac{4}{9}$

(C) $\frac{5}{9}$

(D) $\frac{2}{3}$

(E) $\frac{5}{6}$

273

Unit Three: **Factors**

Why isn't $\frac{6}{9}$ in the answer choices? It isn't **simplified** (also known as **reduced**). In a fully reduced fraction, the numerator (top) and denominator (bottom) will have no factors in common. To simplify, break down the numerator and denominator into prime factors:

$$\frac{6}{9} \rightarrow \frac{2 \times 3}{3 \times 3}$$

Both the numerator and the denominator have a 3 as one of their prime factors. Cancel the common factor of 3 from both the top and bottom: $\frac{6}{9} = \frac{2 \times \cancel{3}}{3 \times \cancel{3}} = \frac{2}{3}$.

> **Strategy Tip**
>
> To simplify a fraction with one term in the numerator and one term in the denominator, find and eliminate common factors in those terms.

Mathematically, this relies on the principle that you can multiply or divide the numerator by anything as long as you do the same thing to the denominator. For example, if you divide the top and bottom of the fraction by 3, the value of the fraction stays the same. So the below fractions are equivalent, even though the numerator and denominator have been divided by two at each step:

$$\frac{64}{80} = \frac{32}{40} = \frac{16}{20} = \frac{8}{10} = \frac{4}{5}$$

Here's another example of a fraction that can be reduced: $\frac{18}{60}$. Cancel out any common factors that you spot, in whatever order you spot them first. For example:

$$\frac{\cancel{18}^{3}}{\cancel{60}_{10}} \quad \text{or} \quad \frac{18}{60} = \frac{9}{30} = \frac{3}{10}$$

Alternatively, break the numbers down into their prime factors:

$$\frac{18}{60} = \frac{2 \times 3 \times 3}{2 \times 2 \times 3 \times 5}$$

Cancel out the common factors in the top and bottom, in this case one 2 and one 3, then simplify:

$$\frac{18}{60} = \frac{\cancel{2} \times \cancel{3} \times 3}{\cancel{2} \times 2 \times \cancel{3} \times 5} = \frac{3}{2 \times 5} = \frac{3}{10}$$

This simplification works with any common factor, not just prime factors. In this example, a common factor of 6 is canceled from the top and bottom:

$$\frac{18}{60} = \frac{3 \times \cancel{6}}{10 \times \cancel{6}} = \frac{3}{10}$$

It's not necessary to break the numerator and denominator all the way down into primes. Cancel out whatever common factors you see first, regardless of whether they are primes.

Chapter 10: **Common Factors**

Check Your Skills

> Simplify the following fractions.

11. $\dfrac{25}{40}$
12. $\dfrac{16}{24}$

Answers can be found on page 282.

Common Denominators

The numerator of a fraction indicates how many parts or pieces you have. In the fraction $\dfrac{1}{5}$, you have selected one part out of a total of five possible parts. For example, there are five slices of pizza and one of them is on your plate.

What if you have one slice and someone else has three slices out of the five total slices?

$$\dfrac{1}{5} + \dfrac{3}{5}$$

Your one slice and the other person's three slices add up to four out of a total of five slices of pizza:

$$\dfrac{1}{5} + \dfrac{3}{5} = \dfrac{4}{5}$$

As long as you're creating both fractions out of the same five slices of pizza—that is, as long as the denominators of the fractions are the same—go ahead and add the numerators.

As with earlier problems, reduce the final fraction as far as you can. For example, the sum of $\dfrac{3}{6}$ and $\dfrac{5}{6}$ has to be simplified further:

$$\dfrac{3}{6} + \dfrac{5}{6} = \dfrac{8}{6}$$

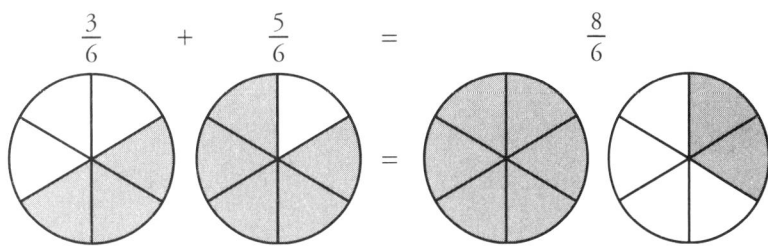

In the fraction $\frac{8}{6}$, the numerator and denominator share a common factor of 2:

$$\frac{3}{6} + \frac{5}{6} = \frac{8}{6} = \frac{4}{3}$$

The process is a little more complicated when the denominators are not the same. For example:

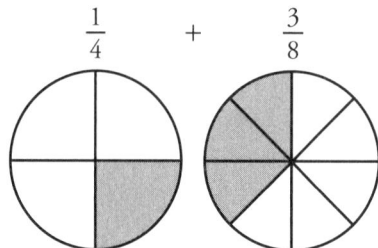

One slice of the first pizza is not the same size as one slice of the second pizza, so it doesn't make sense to add the numerators and get 4 of anything.

Make all of the slices the same size by finding a **common denominator**. Transform the $\frac{1}{4}$ into $\frac{2}{8}$:

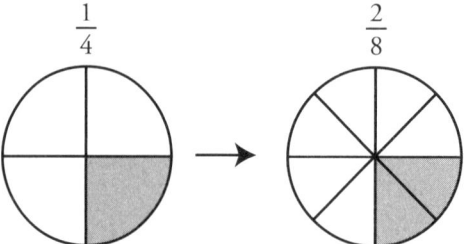

Originally, there was 1 slice out of 4. Doubling the total number of slices also doubles the number of selected slices, so there are now 2 slices out of 8. Essentially, there are twice as many slices, but each slice is half as big. The value of the fraction hasn't changed, only its form has: $\frac{1}{4} = \frac{2}{8}$.

Mathematically, this is equivalent to multiplying both the top and bottom of the fraction by a common factor:

$$\frac{1}{4} = \frac{1}{4}\left(\frac{2}{2}\right) = \frac{2}{8}$$

You've essentially *renamed* $\frac{1}{4}$ as $\frac{2}{8}$, but the value of the fraction hasn't changed. And now that the denominators are the same, you're allowed to add the two fractions:

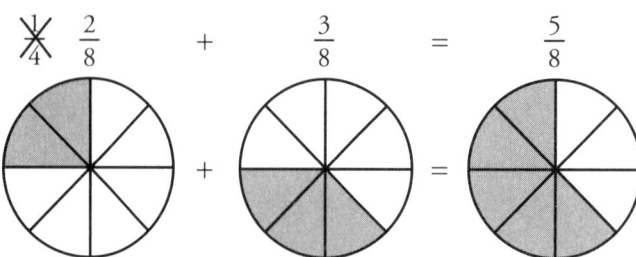

Try this problem:

$$\frac{3}{4} - \frac{5}{8} = ?$$

The two denominators are 4 and 8. In order to get them to be the same, the denominator of 4 needs to become 8. Multiply the top and bottom of that fraction by 2:

$$\frac{3}{4} = \frac{3 \times 2}{4 \times 2} = \frac{6}{8}$$

Now that there are common denominators, subtract:

$$\frac{6}{8} - \frac{5}{8} = \frac{1}{8}$$

How could you find a common denominator for a more challenging set of fractions? The answer is common factors. For example:

$$\frac{1}{30} + \frac{1}{3} = ?$$

Start by finding the prime factorization of the denominators:

$$30 = 3 \times 2 \times 5$$

$$3 = 3$$

In order for the two denominators to be the same, they have to have the exact same set of factors. The two denominators already have 3 as a common factor, but the 30 also has a 2 and a 5. Multiply the other denominator, 3, by the missing common factors, $2 \times 5 = 10$, in order to get the two denominators to match:

$$\frac{1}{30} + \frac{1}{3}\left(\frac{10}{10}\right)$$

$$\frac{1}{30} + \frac{10}{30}$$

$$\frac{11}{30}$$

In fact, you may not need to break each denominator all the way down to its primes. Look for the common factors and then whatever isn't common:

$$30 = 3 \times 10$$

$$3 = 3$$

Since they *don't* share a factor of 10, you'll need to multiply $\frac{1}{3}$ by $\frac{10}{10}$ in order to get common denominators.

Unit Three: **Factors**

> **Strategy Tip**
>
> To find common denominators:
>
> 1. Figure out what factors the denominators do and do not have in common. Use prime factorization if needed.
> 2. Multiply the numerator and denominator by those missing factors.

Here's another example to consider. This time, add $\frac{1}{4}$ and $\frac{1}{3}$:

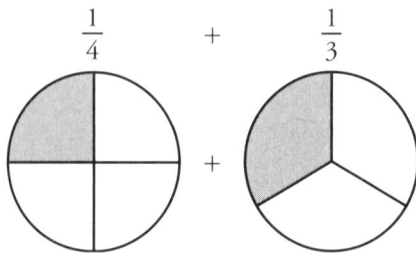

In this case, neither 3 nor 4 is a multiple of the other one, and in fact, they don't share any factors at all. Instead, look for a common *multiple* of both denominators.

When two numbers have *no* factors in common, the least common denominator between them will be their product. So the common denominator of 3 and 4 is $3 \times 4 = 12$.

You could also list out positive multiples of each denominator. Look for the least value that appears on both lists:

$$\text{Multiples of 3: 3, 6, 9, 12, 15, ...}$$

$$\text{Multiples of 4: 4, 8, 12, ...}$$

In this case, the least value that appears on both lists is 12, so 12 is the least common denominator of 3 and 4.

Next, change both fractions so that they have a denominator of 12. The first fraction, $\frac{1}{4}$, is missing a factor of 3, so multiply it by $\frac{3}{3}$. The second fraction, $\frac{1}{3}$, is missing a factor of 4, so multiply it by $\frac{4}{4}$:

$$\frac{1}{4} + \frac{1}{3} = \frac{1}{4}\left(\frac{3}{3}\right) + \frac{1}{3}\left(\frac{4}{4}\right) = \frac{3}{12} + \frac{4}{12}$$

As before, this process does not change the value of either fraction, just rewrites it to an equivalent form:

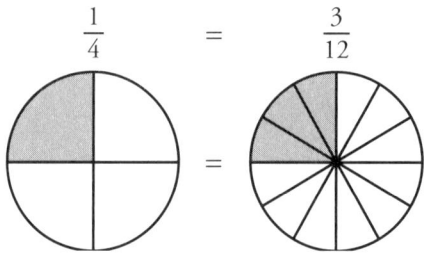

10

278

Chapter 10: **Common Factors**

Once both of the fractions have a common denominator, add:

$$\frac{3}{12} + \frac{4}{12} = \frac{7}{12}$$

Here's a recap of the fraction addition and subtraction process:

When adding (or subtracting) fractions, the denominators must be the same. When they are the same, add (or subtract) the numerators and keep the denominator the same.	$\frac{2}{9} + \frac{5}{9} = \frac{7}{9}$
If the two fractions have different denominators, first find a common multiple for the two denominators.	$\frac{1}{4} + \frac{2}{5} = ?$ Common multiple of 4 and 5 = 20
Once you know the common multiple, figure out what each fraction needs to be multiplied by to convert it to the common multiple.	Multiply the first fraction by $\frac{5}{5}$ Multiply the second fraction by $\frac{4}{4}$
Perform the multiplication to convert the fractions that need to be converted.	$\frac{1}{4}\left(\frac{5}{5}\right) = \frac{5}{20}$ $\frac{2}{5}\left(\frac{4}{4}\right) = \frac{8}{20}$
Now that the denominators are the same, add (or subtract) the fractions.	$\frac{5}{20} + \frac{8}{20} = \frac{13}{20}$

Though most of the examples so far have shown addition, the rules for subtraction are identical.

Check Your Skills

Simplify the given expressions as far as possible.

13. $\frac{3}{5} + \frac{7}{20}$

14. $\frac{5}{6} - \frac{1}{2}$

15. $\frac{5}{7} - \frac{1}{3}$

Answers can be found on page 282.

Unit Three: **Factors**

Check Your Skills Answer Key

1. **4(1 + 2t)**
   Factor a 4 out of each term.
   $$4 + 8t$$
   $$4(1 + 2t)$$

2. **5(x + 5y)**
   Factor a 5 out of each term.
   $$5x + 25y$$
   $$5(x + 5y)$$

3. **$2x^2(1 + 8x)$**
   The two terms share factors of 2 and x^2, so factor $2x^2$ out of each term.
   $$2x^2 + 16x^3$$
   $$2x^2(1 + 8x)$$

4. **2^{16}**
   $$2^4 \times 16^3$$
   $$2^4 \times (2^4)^3$$
   $$2^4 \times 2^{12} = 2^{16}$$

5. **7^{21}**
   $$7^5 \times 49^8$$
   $$7^5 \times (7^2)^8$$
   $$7^5 \times 7^{16} = 7^{21}$$

6. **3^{18} or 9^9**
   This can be broken down to a base of 3 or a base of 9. On the real test, before you start working, check the answer choices to see which base the problem wants. Here's the solution for a base of 3:
   $$9^3 \times 81^3$$
   $$(3^2)^3 \times (3^4)^3$$
   $$3^6 \times 3^{12} = 3^{18}$$

Chapter 10: **Common Factors**

And here's the solution for a base of 9:

$$9^3 \times 81^3$$
$$9^3 \times (9^2)^3$$
$$9^3 \times 9^6 = 9^9$$

7. **7**

   All three terms contain 4^{20}, so factor that out of the expression.

   $$4^{20} + 4^{21} + 4^{22}$$
   $$4^{20}(1 + 4^1 + 4^2)$$
   $$4^{20}(1 + 4 + 16)$$
   $$4^{20}(21)$$

   Since $x = 4^{20}(21)$, x's prime factors are 2, which comes from the 4^{20} term, and 3 and 7, which come from the 21 term. Of the three prime factors (2, 3, and 7), the greatest is 7.

8. **5√3**

   $$\sqrt{75} \rightarrow \sqrt{3 \times 5 \times 5} \rightarrow \sqrt{5 \times 5} \times \sqrt{3} = 5\sqrt{3}$$

9. **4√6**

   $$\sqrt{96} = \sqrt{2 \times 2 \times 2 \times 2 \times 2 \times 3}$$
   $$= \sqrt{(2 \times 2) \times (2 \times 2) \times 2 \times 3}$$
   $$= (2)(2)\sqrt{2 \times 3}$$
   $$= 4\sqrt{6}$$

10. **21**

    Use divisibility rules and your calculator to break down 441. Since the sum of the digits $(4 + 4 + 1 = 9)$ is divisible by 9, the number 441 is divisible by 9. Plug that into your calculator to get 49 and simplify from there:

    $$\sqrt{441} = \sqrt{9 \times 49}$$
    $$= \sqrt{3 \times 3 \times 7 \times 7}$$
    $$= \sqrt{(3 \times 3) \times (7 \times 7)}$$
    $$= (3)(7)$$
    $$= 21$$

Unit Three: **Factors**

11. $\dfrac{5}{8}$

Cancel out a 5 from the top and bottom.

$$\dfrac{25}{40} = \dfrac{5 \times 5}{8 \times 5} = \dfrac{5 \times \cancel{5}}{8 \times \cancel{5}} = \dfrac{5}{8}$$

12. $\dfrac{2}{3}$

Cancel out an 8 from the top and bottom.

$$\dfrac{16}{24} = \dfrac{2 \times 8}{3 \times 8} = \dfrac{2 \times \cancel{8}}{3 \times \cancel{8}} = \dfrac{2}{3}$$

13. $\dfrac{19}{20}$

The two denominators share a factor of 5, but the first fraction is missing a factor of 4.

$$\dfrac{3}{5} + \dfrac{7}{20}$$

$$\dfrac{3}{5}\left(\dfrac{4}{4}\right) + \dfrac{7}{20}$$

$$\dfrac{12}{20} + \dfrac{7}{20} = \dfrac{19}{20}$$

14. $\dfrac{1}{3}$

The two denominators share a common factor of 2, but the second fraction is missing a factor of 3.

$$\dfrac{5}{6} - \dfrac{1}{2}$$

$$\dfrac{5}{6} - \dfrac{1}{2}\left(\dfrac{3}{3}\right)$$

$$\dfrac{5}{6} - \dfrac{3}{6} = \dfrac{2}{6} = \dfrac{1}{3}$$

At the end, the fraction $\dfrac{2}{6}$ can be simplified further. The top and bottom both contain a factor of 2, so divide the top and bottom by 2 to get $\dfrac{1}{3}$.

15. $\dfrac{8}{21}$

The two denominators do not share any factors, so the least common denominator is their product: $3 \times 7 = 21$. Multiply the first fraction by $\dfrac{3}{3}$ and the second fraction by $\dfrac{7}{7}$.

$$\dfrac{5}{7} - \dfrac{1}{3}$$

$$\left(\dfrac{3}{3}\right)\dfrac{5}{7} - \dfrac{1}{3}\left(\dfrac{7}{7}\right)$$

$$\dfrac{15}{21} - \dfrac{7}{21} = \dfrac{8}{21}$$

Chapter 10: **Common Factors**

Problem Set

1. Simplify: $\dfrac{8(3)(x^2)(3)}{6x}$ (given that $x \neq 0$)

2. Simplify: $\dfrac{12ab^3 - 6a^2b}{3ab}$ (given that $ab \neq 0$)

3.
Quantity A	**Quantity B**
$\dfrac{2}{3} \times \dfrac{3}{3}$	$\dfrac{2}{3} \times \dfrac{4}{4}$

4.
Quantity A	**Quantity B**
$\dfrac{6x + 6y}{3x + y}$	8

5. Simplify: $\dfrac{2^4 \times 2^5}{2^7} - 2^4$

6.
Quantity A	**Quantity B**
$3^3 \times 9^6 \times 2^4 \times 4^2$	$9^3 \times 3^6 \times 2^2 \times 4^4$

Unit Three: **Factors**

Solutions

1. **12*x***

   First, cancel terms in both the numerator and the denominator. Then combine terms.

   $$\frac{8(3)(x^2)(3)}{6x} = \frac{8(\cancel{3})(x^2)(3)}{\cancel{6}x\,_2} = \frac{\overset{4}{\cancel{8}}(x^2)(3)}{\cancel{2}x} = \frac{4(x^{\cancel{2}})(3)}{\cancel{x}} = 4(x)(3) = 12x$$

2. **2(2*b*² − *a*) or 4*b*² − 2*a***

   First, factor out common terms in the numerator. Then, cancel terms in both the numerator and denominator.

   $$\frac{6ab(2b^2 - a)}{3ab} = 2(2b^2 - a) \text{ or } 4b^2 - 2a$$

3. **(C)**

   The fractions $\frac{3}{3}$ and $\frac{4}{4}$ are both equal to 1. Each quantity can be rewritten as $\frac{2}{3} \times 1$, which leaves you with $\frac{2}{3}$.

Quantity A	**Quantity B**
$\frac{2}{3} \times \frac{3}{3} =$	$\frac{2}{3} \times \frac{4}{4} =$
$\frac{2}{3} \times 1 = \frac{2}{3}$	$\frac{2}{3} \times 1 = \frac{2}{3}$

   Therefore, the correct answer is (C): The two quantities are equal.

4. **(D)**

   When you add fractions, you cannot split the denominator (for instance, to cancel the *x*'s and *y*'s separately and get 2 + 6 = 8). The only simplification you can perform on Quantity A, therefore, is $\frac{6(x + y)}{3x + y}$. But that isn't enough to indicate whether the value of this expression is greater than or less than 8.

   For example, if *x* = 2 and *y* = 1, then Quantity A = $\frac{6(2 + 1)}{3(2) + 1} = \frac{18}{7}$, which is less than 8.

   If, however, *x* = 1 and *y* = −8, then Quantity A = $\frac{6(1 + (-8))}{3(1) + (-8)} = \frac{6(-7)}{3 - 8} = \frac{-42}{-5} = 8.4$, which is greater than 8.

   Therefore, the correct answer is (D): The relationship cannot be determined.

5. **−12**

$$\frac{2^4 \times 2^5}{2^7} - 2^4 = 2^{(4+5-7)} - 2^4$$
$$= 2^2 - 2^4$$
$$= 2^2(1 - 2^2)$$
$$= 4(1 - 4)$$
$$= -12$$

6. **(A)**

   In multiplication, you can combine terms if you can get the same bases, the simplest versions of which will always be prime. Each quantity has the same four bases: 2, 3, 4, and 9. Because 2 and 3 are already prime, you need to manipulate 4 and 9: $4 = 2^2$ and $9 = 3^2$. Rewrite the quantities.

Quantity A	**Quantity B**
$3^3 \times 9^6 \times 2^4 \times 4^2 =$	$9^3 \times 3^6 \times 2^2 \times 4^4 =$
$3^3 \times (3^2)^6 \times 2^4 \times (2^2)^2$	$(3^2)^3 \times 3^6 \times 2^2 \times (2^2)^4$

   Now, terms can be combined using the exponent rules.

Quantity A	**Quantity B**
$3^3 \times (3^2)^6 \times 2^4 \times (2^2)^2 =$	$(3^2)^3 \times 3^6 \times 2^2 \times (2^2)^4 =$
$3^3 \times 3^{12} \times 2^4 \times 2^4 =$	$3^6 \times 3^6 \times 2^2 \times 2^8 =$
$3^{15} \times 2^8$	$3^{12} \times 2^{10}$

   Divide away common factors. Both quantities contain the product $3^{12} \times 2^8$.

Quantity A	**Quantity B**
$\frac{3^{15} \times 2^8}{3^{12} \times 2^8} = 3^3 = 27$	$\frac{3^{12} \times 2^{10}}{3^{12} \times 2^8} = 2^2 = 4$

   Therefore, the correct answer is (A): Quantity A is greater.

CHAPTER 11

Fractions

In This Chapter:

- Improper Fractions and Mixed Numbers
- Multiplying and Dividing Fractions
- Adding and Subtracting Fractions
- NEVER Split the Denominator!
- Fractions and Equations
- Comparing Fractions
- Comparing Complex Fractions
- Check Your Skills Answer Key
- Problem Set
- Solutions

CHAPTER 11 Fractions

Fractions express the relationship between a **part** and a **whole**; in other words, they express non-integer amounts. Fractions are just one possible way to express non-integers. You can also express non-integers in terms of decimals (presented in Chapter 1: Develop Your Number Sense), percents, and ratios (the latter two of which will be taught in Unit 4: Stories, Percents, Ratios, Stats, and Data).

There are two parts of any fraction: the **numerator**, which expresses the number of parts selected, and the **denominator**, which expresses the total number of parts available. For example, the fraction $\frac{3}{4}$ is used to indicate that if something is divided into 4 parts, only 3 are selected:

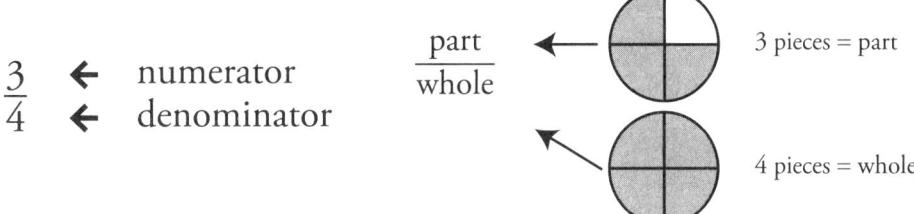

The fraction $\frac{3}{4}$ can be viewed as a decimal (0.75), a fraction (75%), or a ratio (3:4), or it can be written using a number line:

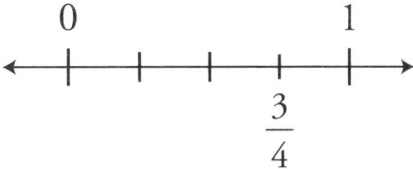

Which form you use will depend on the question at hand, as well as what you prefer to use.

In this chapter, you'll learn how to handle proper and improper fractions, how to perform certain math operations on fractions, how to solve equations containing fractions, and how to compare fractions with different denominators in order to determine which is greater.

Unit Three: **Factors**

11

Improper Fractions and Mixed Numbers

Proper fractions are fractions that are between 0 and 1, or between 0 and −1. For example, $\frac{3}{4}$ or $-\frac{2}{5}$ are proper fractions. The numerators of proper fractions have a smaller magnitude than the denominators.

Improper fractions are fractions that have a numerator with a larger magnitude than the denominator. Examples of improper fractions include:

$$\frac{8}{7}, \frac{12}{5}, -\frac{9}{2}, \frac{11}{10}, \text{ and } \frac{5}{4}$$

Mathematically, improper fractions don't behave any differently than proper fractions, but they are notable for two reasons. First, improper fractions represent a number greater than 1 or less than −1. For example, the fraction $\frac{12}{5}$ is $12 \div 5 = 2.4$.

Second, all improper fractions can be formatted as a **mixed number**: a number that includes both an integer and a fraction. The improper fraction $\frac{5}{4}$ equals the mixed number $1\frac{1}{4}$. The GRE could put the answer choice in either format, so you'll need to be comfortable converting between both forms. Here's one way to conceptualize $\frac{5}{4}$:

$$\frac{5}{4} = \frac{4}{4} + \frac{1}{4}$$

A circle is divided into fourths, then five parts are selected. That means one entire circle is selected, as well as one of the fourths from another circle. The visual looks like this in fraction form:

$$\frac{5}{4} = \frac{4+1}{4} = \frac{4}{4} + \frac{1}{4} = 1 + \frac{1}{4} = 1\frac{1}{4}$$

This manipulation is valid because it is fraction addition in reverse. If you were given the problem $1 + \frac{1}{4}$, you'd find a common denominator then add the numerators:

$$1 + \frac{1}{4} = \frac{1}{1} + \frac{1}{4} = \frac{1 \times 4}{1 \times 4} + \frac{1}{4} = \frac{4}{4} + \frac{1}{4} = \frac{5}{4}$$

> **Fraction Rule 1:**
>
> $\frac{2+3}{3} = \frac{2}{3} + \frac{3}{3}$ Splitting the numerator of a fraction into parts that are added or subtracted allows you to split one fraction into multiple fractions, each with the same denominator.

To switch from an improper fraction to a mixed number, figure out how many complete units there are. To do that, find the *greatest multiple of the denominator that is less than or equal to the numerator*. For the fraction $\frac{5}{4}$, the number 4 is the greatest multiple of 4 that is less than 5. So split the fraction into $\frac{4}{4}$ and $\frac{1}{4}$. Because $\frac{4}{4}$ equals 1, the mixed number is $1\frac{1}{4}$.

This process might seem a little familiar. You did something very similar to find remainders in Chapter 9: Divisibility. In both cases, you're answering the question "What part is left over once all the integers have been divided out?"

Try it again with the fraction $\frac{15}{4}$. This time, the greatest multiple of 4 that is less than 15 is 12, so split the numerator into $12 + 3$ and simplify from there:

$$\frac{15}{4} = \frac{12+3}{4}$$
$$= \frac{12}{4} + \frac{3}{4}$$
$$= 3 + \frac{3}{4}$$
$$= 3\frac{3}{4}$$

Try one with a different denominator: $\frac{16}{7}$. This time you need the greatest multiple of 7 that is less than or equal to 16:

$$\frac{16}{7} = \frac{14+2}{7}$$
$$= \frac{14}{7} + \frac{2}{7}$$
$$= 2 + \frac{2}{7}$$
$$= 2\frac{2}{7}$$

Check Your Skills

Change the following improper fractions to mixed numbers:

1. $\frac{11}{6}$
2. $\frac{100}{11}$

Answers can be found on page 315.

Unit Three: **Factors**

11

Changing Mixed Numbers to Improper Fractions

On the GRE, you also need to be able to do the Reverse: change a mixed number to an improper fraction. Suppose you have the mixed number $5\frac{2}{3}$.

Think of this in terms of fraction addition. The fraction $5\frac{2}{3}$ is the same thing as $5 + \frac{2}{3}$, or $\frac{5}{1} + \frac{2}{3}$.

The two fractions need common denominators in order to be added, so change $\frac{5}{1}$ to have a denominator of 3:

$$\frac{5}{1} + \frac{2}{3}$$
$$\left(\frac{3}{3}\right)\frac{5}{1} + \frac{2}{3}$$
$$\frac{15}{3} + \frac{2}{3} = \frac{17}{3}$$

If you need a refresher on finding common denominators, review Chapter 10: Common Factors.

Check Your Skills

> Change the following mixed numbers to improper fractions.

3. $3\frac{3}{4}$

4. $4\frac{5}{7}$

Answers can be found on page 315.

Multiplying and Dividing Fractions

Multiplying Fractions and Integers

The fraction $\frac{1}{2}$ represents one piece out of a total of two. Given a total, any total, split it into two equal parts, select one of them, and you will have $\frac{1}{2}$ of the original.

For example, you might be asked to find $\frac{1}{2}$ of 6. Imagine splitting 6 into two equal parts and keeping one of those two parts:

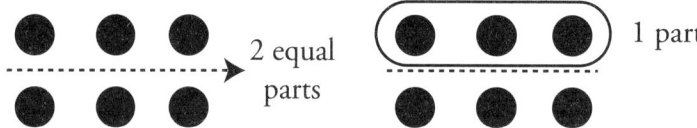

Because the denominator of the fraction $\frac{1}{2}$ is 2, divide 6 into two equal parts of 3. Then, because the numerator is 1, keep one of those two parts. So $\frac{1}{2}$ of 6 is 3.

You can also think of this problem a slightly different way. Consider each unit circle of the 6. What happens if you break each of those circles into two parts, and keep one part?

Divide every circle into two parts, and keep one out of every two parts. You end up with six halves, or $\frac{6}{2}$, written as a fraction. But $\frac{6}{2}$ is the same as 3, so $\frac{1}{2}$ of 6 is still 3:

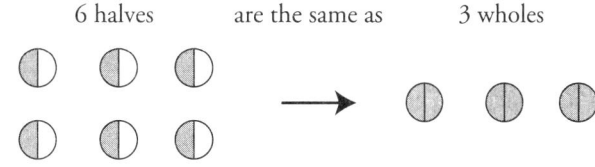

Algebraically, this is the same as multiplying $\frac{1}{2}$ by 6. Generally speaking, when the word *of* is used to relate two numbers, you can translate it to multiplication:

$$\text{What is } \frac{1}{2} \text{ of 6 ?}$$

$$n = \frac{1}{2} \times 6$$

Here are a few common English-to-math translations that will be helpful to know:

Word(s)	Math Translation	Examples	
is/was/were	equals (=)	x is 3	$x = 3$
of	multiply (×)	half of 7	$\frac{1}{2} \times 7$
what	unknown or variable (e.g., n)	3 times what is 6 ?	$3n = 6$

Solve "What is half of six?" through translation:

$$n = \frac{1}{2} \times 6$$
$$= \frac{6}{2}$$
$$= \frac{3}{1} = 3$$

293

Unit Three: Factors

11

Use any variable you like to stand for the word *what*. Also, note what happened with the multiplication:

> **Fraction Rule 2:**
>
> $\frac{1}{2} \times 6 = \frac{(1)(6)}{2} = 3$
>
> When multiplying a fraction by an integer, multiply by the numerator and divide by the denominator, in whatever order you find easiest.

You'll learn more about translations in Chapter 14: Algebraic Translations.

Try this problem:

What is $\frac{2}{3}$ of 12 ?

If you feel comfortable with why the math works the way that it does, you can skip down to the algebraic representation of the math. The visual representation is just to help you understand why the math works the way it does. (Whenever you can understand *why* the math works, it will be easier for you to remember the steps for future.)

To get $\frac{2}{3}$ of 12, first divide 12 into three equal parts because the denominator of the fraction is 3. Then, because the numerator is 2, keep two of those three parts:

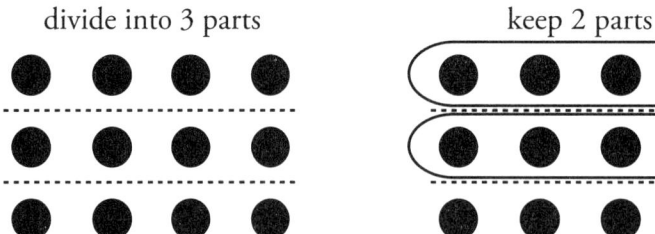

The number 12 is divided into three equal parts of 4, and two of those parts are kept, representing 8 circles:

$$\frac{2}{3} \times 12 = 8$$

Alternatively, break each unit into three pieces (because the denominator of the fraction is 3) and keep two out of every three pieces (because the numerator is 2):

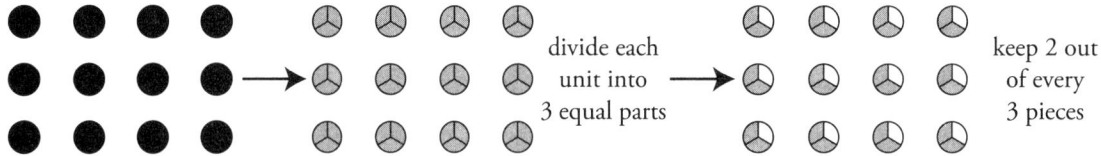

There are 24 thirds, or $\frac{24}{3}$, which simplifies to:

$$\frac{24}{3} = \frac{8 \times \cancel{3}}{\cancel{3}} = 8$$

24 thirds   are the same as   8 wholes

Here's how you would solve on test day:

$$\frac{2}{3} \times 12 = \frac{2 \times 12}{3} = \frac{2 \times \overset{4}{\cancel{12}}}{\underset{1}{\cancel{3}}} = 8$$

You could also multiply out the 2 and 12 before dividing by 3. Ideally, though, simplify before you multiply. It will save you a step.

Multiplying Fractions Together

What happens when you multiply a fraction by a fraction? The basic logic is the same. When you multiply any number by a fraction, the denominator of the fraction tells you how many parts to divide the number into, and the numerator tells you how many of those parts to keep. Now consider how that logic applies to fractions:

What is $\frac{1}{2} \times \frac{3}{4}$?

What is $\frac{1}{2}$ *of* $\frac{3}{4}$? Divide $\frac{3}{4}$ into two equal parts. Because $\frac{3}{4}$ is a fraction, the unit circle has already broken a number into four equal pieces, and three have been selected. But three pieces don't easily break into two, so break each of the bigger wedges in half again. There are now eight smaller wedges with six selected, which still represent $\frac{3}{4}$ of the pie:

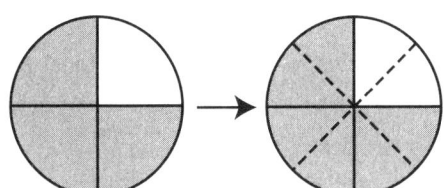

Cut each piece in half. Still keep 6 out of 8, which is the same as 3 out of 4.

Next, apply the $\frac{1}{2}$. Keep 1 out of every 2 of those smaller wedges:

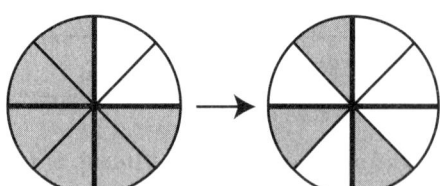

Keep one out of each of the two resulting shaded pieces.

The original number was $\frac{3}{4}$, or three out of four parts. Now the number has been broken into eight pieces, not four, and three of those eight pieces are shaded. Three represents the numerator (the *part*) and eight represents the denominator (the *whole*), so $\frac{1}{2}$ of $\frac{3}{4}$ is $\frac{3}{8}$.

Here's how to do this on test day:

$$\frac{1}{2} \times \frac{3}{4} = \frac{1 \times 3}{2 \times 4} = \frac{3}{8}$$

Fraction Rule 3:

$\frac{1}{3} \times \frac{5}{8} = \frac{(1)(5)}{(3)(8)} = \frac{5}{24}$

When multiplying fractions:

- First, simplify if possible.
- Multiply the numerators together to get the new numerator.
- Multiply the denominators together to get the new denominator.

Try one more. What is $\frac{5}{6} \times \frac{1}{2}$?

$$\frac{5}{6} \times \frac{1}{2} = \frac{5 \times 1}{6 \times 2} = \frac{5}{12}$$

Here are two more examples:

$$\frac{5}{2} \times \frac{3}{4} = \frac{5 \times 3}{2 \times 4} = \frac{15}{8} = 1\frac{7}{8}$$

$$\frac{5}{6} \times \frac{2}{3} = \frac{5 \times \overset{1}{\cancel{2}}}{\underset{3}{\cancel{6}} \times 3} = \frac{5}{9}$$

Cancel Common Factors First

Simplify before you multiply! Cancel common factors first to save time:

$$\frac{33}{7} \times \frac{14}{3} = ?$$

Look for common factors in the numerator and denominator:

$$\frac{33}{7} \times \frac{14}{3} = \frac{\overset{11}{\cancel{33}} \times \overset{2}{\cancel{14}}}{\underset{1}{\cancel{7}} \times \underset{1}{\cancel{3}}} = \frac{11 \times 2}{1 \times 1} = \frac{22}{1} = 22$$

If it's helpful to write out the prime factorization of each number before canceling, do so:

$$\frac{33}{7} \times \frac{14}{3} = \frac{(\cancel{3} \times 11) \times (2 \times \cancel{7})}{\cancel{7} \times \cancel{3}} = 11 \times 2 = 22$$

The numerator of the first fraction and the denominator of the second fraction share a factor of 3 that can be canceled. Similarly, the 7 in the denominator of the first fraction can be canceled out by the 7 in the numerator of the second fraction.

Check Your Skills

> Simplify the following expressions as far as possible.

5. $\frac{3}{10} \times \frac{6}{7}$

6. $\frac{5}{14} \times \frac{7}{20}$

Answers can be found on page 315.

Fraction Division

As discussed in Chapter 4: Equations, multiplication and division are opposite sides of the same coin. Any multiplication problem can be expressed as a division problem, and vice versa. While the mechanics for multiplication are straightforward, the mechanics for division are more complicated, so it's better to express every fraction division problem as a fraction multiplication problem instead.

How do you rephrase a division problem so that it becomes a multiplication problem? The key is **reciprocals**.

Reciprocals are numbers that, when multiplied together, equal 1. For instance, $\frac{3}{5}$ and $\frac{5}{3}$ are reciprocals:

$$\frac{3}{5} \times \frac{5}{3} = \frac{\cancel{3} \times \cancel{5}}{\cancel{5} \times \cancel{3}} = 1$$

The numbers 2 and $\frac{1}{2}$ are also reciprocals:

$$2 \times \frac{1}{2} = \frac{2}{1} \times \frac{1}{2} = \frac{2}{2} = 1$$

Unit Three: Factors

11

To find the reciprocal of a number, take the numerator and denominator and switch them around:

Fraction   Reciprocal   Fraction   Reciprocal

$$\frac{3}{5} \quad \rightleftarrows \quad \frac{5}{3} \qquad\qquad \text{Integer } 2 = \frac{2}{1} \quad \rightleftarrows \quad \frac{1}{2}$$

How are reciprocals used in fraction division? Start with this example:

Integer division:	$6 \div 2 = 3$
Same problem, but in fraction form:	$\frac{6}{2} = 3$
Same problem as multiplication:	$6 \times \frac{1}{2} = 3$

All three rows of the table show the same math, but written in three different ways. Check it out:

$$6 \div 2 = 3$$
$$6 \times \frac{1}{2} = 3$$

Dividing by 2 is the same as multiplying by $\frac{1}{2}$.

To change from division to multiplication, do two things. First, take the divisor (the number to the right of the division sign—in other words, what you are dividing *by*) and replace it with its reciprocal. In this problem, 2 is the divisor, and $\frac{1}{2}$ is the reciprocal of 2. Then, change the division sign to a multiplication sign. So $6 \div 2$ becomes $6 \times \frac{1}{2}$. Finally, do the multiplication:

$$6 \div 2 = \frac{6}{1} \times \frac{1}{2} = \frac{\overset{3}{\cancel{6}} \times 1}{1 \times \underset{1}{\cancel{2}}} = 3$$

This math is obviously overkill for $6 \div 2$, but try this one:

What is $\frac{5}{6} \div \frac{4}{7}$?

To divide by $\frac{4}{7}$, multiply by its reciprocal, $\frac{7}{4}$:

$$\frac{5}{6} \div \frac{4}{7} = \frac{5}{6} \times \frac{7}{4} = \frac{5 \times 7}{6 \times 4} = \frac{35}{24}$$

Note that the fraction bar (sometimes indicated with a slash) is another way to express division: $6 \div 2 = 6/2 = \frac{6}{2} = 3$. If you see a "double-decker" fraction, don't worry. It's just one fraction divided by another fraction.

$$\frac{\frac{5}{6}}{\frac{4}{7}} = \frac{5}{6} \div \frac{4}{7} = \frac{5}{6} \times \frac{7}{4} = \frac{35}{24}$$

> **Fraction Rule 4:**
>
> $\frac{1}{2} \div \frac{3}{4} = \frac{1}{2} \times \frac{4}{3}$ To divide by a fraction, multiply by its reciprocal.

To recap:

- When you are confronted with a division problem involving fractions, rewrite it as a multiplication problem.
- A number multiplied by its reciprocal equals 1.

$$\frac{9}{2} \times \frac{2}{9} = 1$$

- To find the reciprocal of an integer, write 1 over that integer. To find the reciprocal of a fraction, switch the numerator and denominator:

Fraction	Reciprocal
$\frac{2}{9}$ →	$\frac{9}{2}$

- To convert division to multiplication, multiply by the reciprocal:

$$\frac{\frac{3}{4}}{\frac{2}{9}} = \frac{3}{4} \div \frac{2}{9} = \frac{3}{4} \times \frac{9}{2} = \frac{27}{8}$$

Check Your Skills

> Simplify the following expressions as far as possible.

7. $\frac{1}{6} \div \frac{1}{11}$

8. $\frac{8}{5} \div \frac{4}{15}$

9. $\frac{\frac{3}{5}}{\frac{2}{3}}$

Answers can be found on pages 315–316.

Unit Three: **Factors**

11

Adding and Subtracting Fractions

In order to add or subtract fractions, the denominators must be the same.

Fraction Rule 5:

$$\frac{2}{7} + \frac{3}{7} = \frac{2+3}{7}$$

To add or subtract fractions with the same denominator, add or subtract the numerators and keep the denominator the same. Then simplify, if possible.

In Chapter 10: Common Factors, you learned how to manipulate one or both denominators in order to make them the same. (Head back to that chapter for a refresher, if needed.)

You can use the same processes even when variables are involved:

$$\frac{7}{9} + \frac{x}{9} = \frac{7+x}{9}$$

Here's another example. How would you solve for x in this equation?

$$\frac{1}{6} + \frac{x}{6} = \frac{4}{3}$$

One path is to start by adding the two fractions on the left:

$$\frac{1+x}{6} = \frac{4}{3}$$

Then, remove the fraction on the left by multiplying both sides by 6:

$$\frac{1+x}{\cancel{6}} \times \cancel{6} = \frac{4}{\cancel{3}} \times \cancel{6}^{2}$$

Finally, simplify to solve for x:

$$1 + x = 4 \times 2$$
$$1 + x = 8$$
$$x = 7$$

Here's another example. Find a common denominator to subtract:

$$\frac{x}{3} - \frac{7}{30}$$

$$\frac{x}{3}\left(\frac{10}{10}\right) - \frac{7}{30}$$

$$\frac{10x}{30} - \frac{7}{30} = \frac{10x - 7}{30}$$

This fraction is as simplified as it can be. You cannot divide out a 10 from the top and bottom of the fraction, because you would need to cancel a 10 from both of the terms in the numerator, and 7 is not divisible by 10.

For a refresher on what constitutes a separate term, see the section Solving for a Variable with One Equation in Chapter 4: Equations.

> **Fraction Rule 6:**
>
> $$\frac{1}{2} - \frac{x}{3}$$
> $$\frac{1}{2}\left(\frac{3}{3}\right) - \frac{x}{3}\left(\frac{2}{2}\right)$$
> $$\frac{3 - 2x}{6}$$
>
> To add or subtract fractions, first find a common denominator, then follow Fraction Rule 5.

Try this problem:

Solve: $\frac{1}{4} + \frac{x}{5} = \frac{13}{20}$

Here's one path to solve this problem. First, subtract $\frac{1}{4}$ from each side:

$$\frac{x}{5} = \frac{13}{20} - \frac{1}{4}$$

Second, perform the subtraction by finding the common denominator, which is 20. Simplify whenever possible:

$$\frac{x}{5} = \frac{13}{20} - \frac{1}{4}\left(\frac{5}{5}\right)$$
$$\frac{x}{5} = \frac{13}{20} - \frac{5}{20}$$
$$\frac{x}{5} = \frac{8}{20}$$
$$\frac{x}{5} = \frac{2}{5}$$

Third, because the denominators are identical, the numerators must also be the same, so $x = 2$.

Mathematically, this logic is the same as multiplying both sides of the equation by 5. If you do that, the 5 will cancel on both sides and you'll be left with $x = 2$, the equivalent of setting the numerators equal to each other.

Another way to solve this problem is to find the common denominator of all three fractions at the start. This shortcut can save work. Here's the original problem again:

Solve: $\frac{1}{4} + \frac{x}{5} = \frac{13}{20}$

The three denominators, 4, 5, and 20, have a common denominator of 20. Use that common denominator to convert the fractions:

$$\frac{1}{4}\left(\frac{5}{5}\right) + \frac{x}{5}\left(\frac{4}{4}\right) = \frac{13}{20}$$

$$\frac{5}{20} + \frac{4x}{20} = \frac{13}{20}$$

$$\frac{5 + 4x}{20} = \frac{13}{20}$$

The two fractions on each side of the equals sign have the same denominator, so the numerators must also be the same. Therefore, you can set the numerators equal to each other to solve:

$$5 + 4x = 13$$
$$4x = 8$$
$$x = 2$$

One more way may be the fastest of all, if you can find the common denominator without too much trouble. Multiply both sides of the equation by the common denominator, 20, in order to cancel out all of the denominators at once:

$$(20)\left(\frac{1}{4} + \frac{x}{5}\right) = \left(\frac{13}{20}\right)(20)$$

$$\frac{\cancel{20}^5}{\cancel{4}_1} + \frac{\cancel{20}^4 x}{\cancel{5}_1} = \left(\frac{13}{\cancel{20}}\right)(\cancel{20})$$

$$5 + 4x = 13$$

Finally, solve for x:

$$5 + 4x = 13$$
$$4x = 8$$
$$x = 2$$

Note: In the math for that problem, don't multiply both sides of the equation by $\frac{20}{20}$. Just multiply both sides by plain old 20. This is enabled by the standard equation rule that you can do anything to one side of an equation as long as you do it to the other side too.

There's one more complication to learn for finding common denominators. Sometimes, the two denominators will share some factors but also each have extra factors. For example:

$$\frac{2}{20} + \frac{y}{28} = ?$$

You could multiply the left fraction by $\frac{28}{28}$ and the right fraction by $\frac{20}{20}$. But that would be pretty cumbersome. Instead, figure out what the two values have in common and what they *don't* have in common:

$$20 = 2 \times 2 \times 5$$
$$28 = 2 \times 2 \times 7$$

Both numbers have two factors of 2, but 20 is missing a 7 and 28 is missing a 5. To create a common denominator, multiply the first fraction by $\frac{7}{7}$ and multiply the second fraction by $\frac{5}{5}$:

$$\frac{2}{20} + \frac{y}{28} = \frac{2\ (\times 7)}{20\ (\times 7)} + \frac{y\ (\times 5)}{28\ (\times 5)} = \frac{14}{140} + \frac{5y}{140} = \frac{14 + 5y}{140}$$

The denominators are the same because the prime factorization of each is the same: $2 \times 2 \times 5 \times 7$. This is the most complicated way in which you might have to find a common denominator on the GRE.

> **Strategy Tip**
>
> When the two denominators share some factors but also have extra factors, figure out what factors they do *not* share. For example, 9 and 15 already share a factor of 3, but they each have an "extra" factor not shared by the other. Create a common denominator by multiplying in the missing factors:
>
> $$\frac{1}{9} + \frac{1}{15} = \frac{1}{3\times 3} + \frac{1}{3 \times 5} = \left(\frac{5}{5}\right)\frac{1}{3 \times 3} + \frac{1}{3 \times 5}\left(\frac{3}{3}\right) = \frac{5}{45} + \frac{3}{45} = \frac{8}{45}$$

Check Your Skills

Simplify the following expressions.

10. $\frac{1}{2} + \frac{y}{4}$

11. $\frac{a}{3} - \frac{b}{8}$

12. $\frac{1}{6} + \frac{2}{9}$

13. If $\frac{x}{4} + \frac{2}{3} = \frac{11}{12}$, what is the value of x?

14. If $\frac{x}{3} - \frac{4}{9} = \frac{8}{9}$, what is the value of x?

Answers can be found on pages 316–317.

Unit Three: **Factors**

11 NEVER Split the Denominator!

When working with fractions that have more than one term in the numerator or denominator, it's crucial to know what you're allowed to split—and what you're not.

You are allowed to split up the terms of the numerator into two or more different fractions, *but you may never split the terms of the denominator.*

Here are four examples:

(1)	Numerator can be split:	$\frac{15+10}{5}$	Correct: $\frac{15}{5}+\frac{10}{5}$
(2)	Denominator *cannot* be split:	$\frac{5}{15+10}$	INCORRECT: $\frac{5}{15} + \frac{5}{10}$
(3)	Numerator can be split:	$\frac{15+10}{5+2}$	Correct: $\frac{15}{5+2}+\frac{10}{5+2}$
(4)	Denominator *cannot* be split:	$\frac{15+10}{5+2}$	INCORRECT: $\frac{15+10}{5}+\frac{15+10}{2}$

> **Fraction Rule 7:**
>
> You can split a *numerator*, but never split a fraction by separating added or subtracted terms in the *denominator*.

Often, GRE problems will involve complex fractions with variables. On these problems, it is tempting to split the denominator. *Do not fall for it!*

For example, this is incorrect:

$$\frac{5x-2y}{x-y} \neq \frac{5x}{x} - \frac{2y}{y} = 5-2 = 3 \quad \textbf{No!}$$

In fact, $\frac{5x-2y}{x-y}$ cannot be simplified further.

On the other hand, the expression $\frac{6x-15y}{10}$ can be split and then simplified, because there are two terms in the numerator, each of which shares a different factor with the denominator. For example:

$$\frac{6x-15y}{10} = \frac{6x}{10} - \frac{15y}{10} = \frac{3x}{5} - \frac{3y}{2}$$

Chapter 11: **Fractions**

Check Your Skills

Simplify the expressions. Assume that the denominators cannot equal 0.

15. $\dfrac{13 + 7}{5}$

16. $\dfrac{21 + 6}{7 + 6}$

17. $\dfrac{48a + 12b}{a + b}$

18. $\dfrac{9g - 6h}{6g - 4h}$

Answers can be found on page 318.

Fractions and Equations

When an equation contains a fraction, the math still works the same way—when you want to divide, multiply by the reciprocal. For example:

If $5x = \dfrac{7}{3}$, what is the value of x?

To isolate x, divide both sides by 5:

$$\dfrac{\cancel{5}x}{\cancel{5}} = \dfrac{7}{3} \div 5$$

$$x = \dfrac{7}{3} \times \dfrac{1}{5}$$

$$x = \dfrac{7}{15}$$

Dividing by 5 is the same thing as multiplying by the reciprocal $\dfrac{1}{5}$. Here's another way to write the math:

$$\left(\dfrac{1}{5}\right)5x = \dfrac{7}{3}\left(\dfrac{1}{5}\right)$$

$$\left(\dfrac{1}{\cancel{5}}\right)\cancel{5}x = \dfrac{7}{15}$$

$$x = \dfrac{7}{15}$$

What about when fractions appear on both sides of the equation? It may seem more complicated, but use the same process to solve. For example:

$$\dfrac{3y}{4} = \dfrac{15}{8}$$

305

Divide both sides by $\frac{3}{4}$, which is the equivalent of multiplying both sides by the reciprocal $\frac{4}{3}$:

$$\frac{3y}{4} = \frac{15}{8}$$

$$\left(\frac{\cancel{4}}{\cancel{3}}\right)\frac{\cancel{3}y}{\cancel{4}} = \frac{15}{8}\left(\frac{4}{3}\right)$$

$$y = \frac{\overset{5}{\cancel{15}} \times \overset{1}{\cancel{4}}}{\underset{2}{\cancel{8}} \times \underset{1}{\cancel{3}}}$$

$$y = \frac{5}{2}$$

Try this problem:

If $\frac{x}{7} = \frac{5}{8}$, what is the value of x?

Multiply both sides by 7 to get x by itself:

$$\frac{x}{7} = \frac{5}{8}$$

$$(7)\frac{x}{7} = \frac{5}{8}(7)$$

$$x = \frac{5}{8}\left(\frac{7}{1}\right)$$

$$x = \frac{35}{8}$$

Division is the same thing as multiplication by the reciprocal. Whenever you're dividing by something, you can always choose to multiply by the reciprocal if you prefer.

Cross-Multiplication

Cross-multiplication allows you to manipulate equations by eliminating fractions.

Consider the previous example:

$$\frac{x}{7} = \frac{5}{8}$$

In order to isolate the x, you multiplied both sides of the equation by 7. The 7's canceled on the left side, so only the right side was really multiplied by 7.

Likewise, in order to get rid of the denominator of 8 on the right side, you'd multiply both sides by 8:

$$\left(\frac{8}{1}\right)\frac{x}{7} = \frac{5}{\cancel{8}}\left(\frac{\cancel{8}}{1}\right)$$

The 8's cancel out on the right, so only the left side is really multiplied by 8.

Cross-multiplication allows you to do both of these steps simultaneously. Drop the 7 from the left side and multiply it to the right; simultaneously, drop the 8 from the right side and multiply it to the left:

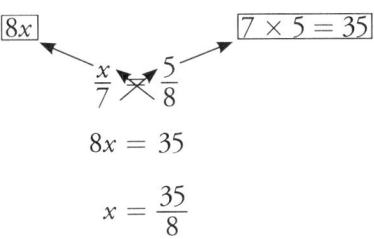

$$8x = 35$$

$$x = \frac{35}{8}$$

Once the fractions have disappeared, the equation is easier to simplify.

Try this problem:

If $\frac{6}{x} = \frac{16}{3}$, what is the value of x?

The variable in the denominator can make this problem seem harder, but you can still cross-multiply:

$$\frac{6}{x} = \frac{16}{3}$$

$$6 \times 3 = 16 \times x$$

$$18 = 16x$$

Divide by 16 to solve for x:

$$\frac{\cancel{18}^{9}}{\cancel{16}_{8}} = \frac{\cancel{16}x}{\cancel{16}}$$

$$\frac{9}{8} = x$$

Check Your Skills

> Use cross-multiplication to solve for x in the following equations.

19. $\frac{3x}{4} = \frac{3}{2}$

20. $\frac{x}{6} = \frac{5}{3}$

Answers can be found on page 318.

Unit Three: **Factors**

Comparing Fractions

Same Denominator

What's greater, $\frac{3}{4}$ or $\frac{1}{4}$? You don't need to do any fancy math to figure that out.

When comparing fractions with the same denominator, the only difference is how many parts each fraction has. That is, the only difference is in the numerators of the fractions. Three pieces are more than one, so $\frac{3}{4}$ is more than $\frac{1}{4}$.

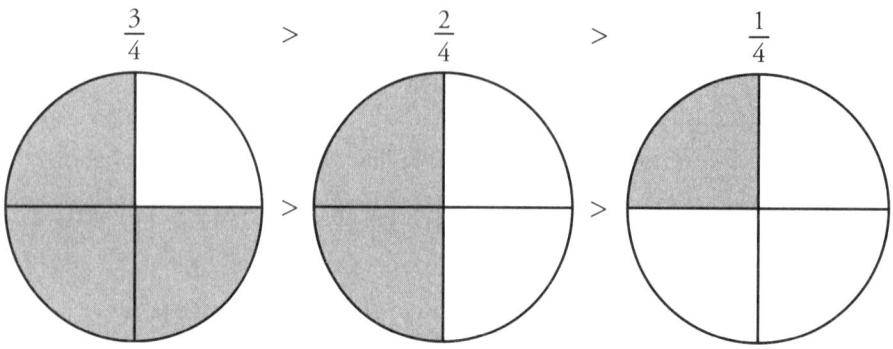

> **Fraction Rule 8:**
>
> For two positive fractions with the same denominator, the one with the *greater* numerator is the *greater* fraction.
>
> $$\frac{2}{3} > \frac{1}{3}$$

Alternatively, think about this using a number line:

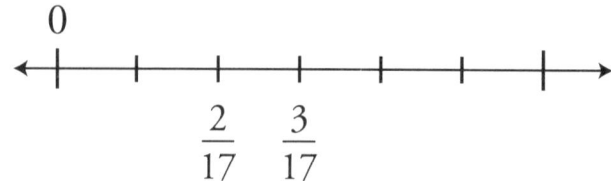

308

This trend holds true even when comparing improper fractions:

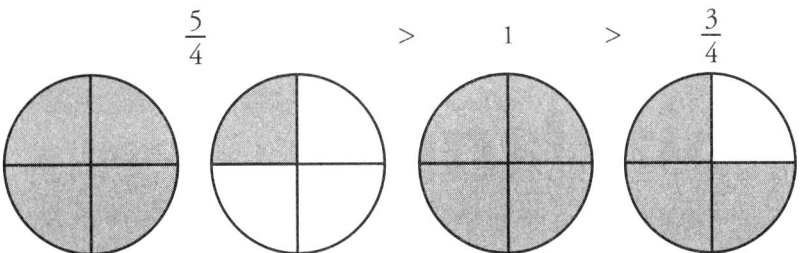

Same Numerator

What's greater, $\frac{5}{7}$ or $\frac{5}{12}$?

This time, the numerators are the same and the denominators are different. So how can the fractions be compared?

The denominator defines how many parts the total is split up into. The larger the denominator, the more pieces, and therefore the smaller each piece is. For example, three pieces of six total pieces is more than three pieces of eight total pieces:

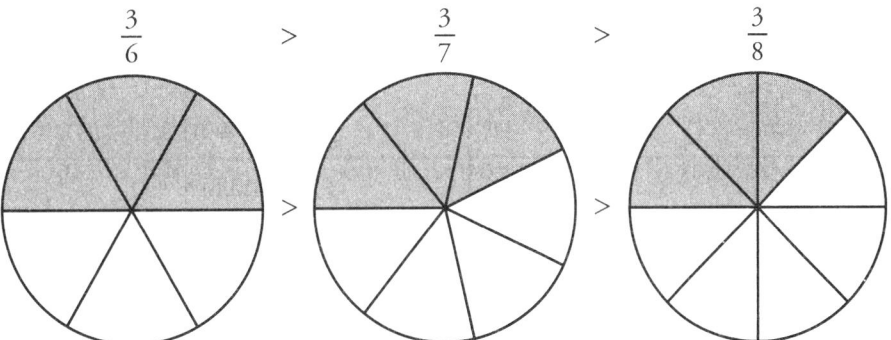

Accordingly, $\frac{5}{7}$ is greater than $\frac{5}{12}$. If you divide a circle into 7 pieces, each piece will be greater than if you divided the same circle into 12 pieces.

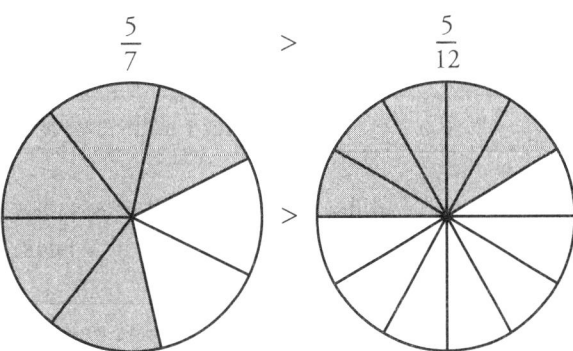

You can also eyeball the two fractions in this way: The fraction $\frac{5}{7}$ is more than one-half, while the fraction $\frac{5}{12}$ is less than one half, so $\frac{5}{7} > \frac{5}{12}$.

> **Fraction Rule 9:**
>
> For two positive fractions with the same numerator, the one with the *lesser* denominator is the *greater* fraction.
>
> $$\frac{1}{3} > \frac{1}{4}$$

Here are two more examples:

$$\frac{3}{2} > \frac{3}{4} \text{ Because } 2 < 4$$

$$\frac{8}{15} > \frac{8}{25} \text{ Because } 15 < 25$$

All of the above doesn't apply in the same way when you're dealing with negative fractions. Negative fractions flip things around because what seems to be the "smaller" fraction is actually the greater fraction. For example, $-\frac{1}{2}$ is greater than $-\frac{5}{2}$. Conceptually, if you owed someone five-halves of a dollar, you'd be more in debt to them than if you owed them only one-half of a dollar.

As a result, when comparing negative fractions with the same denominator, the one with what appears to be the "smaller" numerator is actually the greater fraction:

$$-\frac{1}{2} > -\frac{5}{2}$$

Likewise, when comparing negative fractions with the same numerator, the one with what appears to be the "bigger" denominator is actually the greater fraction. For example, $-\frac{1}{3}$ is greater than $-\frac{1}{2}$. You can also visualize this on a number line. The negative fraction that is closer to 0 is the greater of the two fractions:

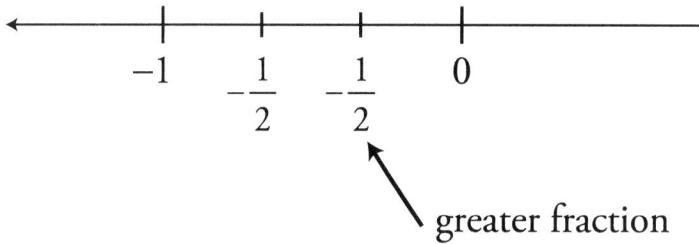

greater fraction

> **Fraction Rule 10:**
>
> When comparing *negative* fractions, rules 8 and 9 flip:
>
> For two negative fractions with the same denominator, the one with the *lesser* numerator is the *greater* fraction.
>
> $$-\frac{1}{3} > -\frac{2}{3}$$
>
> For two negative fractions with the same numerator, the one with the *greater* denominator is the *greater* fraction.
>
> $$-\frac{1}{4} > -\frac{1}{3}$$

Check Your Skills

> For each of the following sets of fractions, determine which fraction is greater.

21. $\frac{5}{7}$ vs. $\frac{3}{7}$

22. $\frac{3}{10}$ vs. $\frac{3}{13}$

Answers can be found on pages 318–319.

Different Numerator and Denominator

What if neither the numerator nor the denominator is the same across two fractions? For instance, what's greater, $\frac{7}{9}$ or $\frac{4}{5}$?

The long way to solve would be to find a common denominator—but there's a shortcut!

To find a common denominator, you'd need to do this math:

$$\frac{7}{9}\left(\frac{5}{5}\right) \quad \frac{4}{5}\left(\frac{9}{9}\right)$$

$$\frac{35}{45} \quad \frac{36}{45}$$

Once you have common denominators, all you need to compare is the numerators. That is, the denominators don't matter. So, rather than do the full math, use a modified version of cross-multiplication to find *only* the numerators:

$\frac{7}{9} \quad \frac{4}{5}$	Set up the fractions next to each other.
$\boxed{(7 \times 5)} \quad \boxed{(4 \times 9)}$ $\frac{7}{9} \quad\diagup\!\!\!\diagdown\quad \frac{4}{5}$	Multiply the denominator of one fraction with the numerator of the other fraction and put each answer by the corresponding *numerator*. (**Not** the denominator!)
$35 < 36$	The values 35 and 36 are the numerators of the full common-denominator form of the fractions. Because 35 is less than 36, the first fraction must be less than the second one.

The fraction $\frac{4}{5}$ would have the greater numerator if you wrote both fractions fully over a common denominator, so it is the greater fraction.

Check Your Skills

23. Which fraction is greater, $\frac{4}{13}$ or $\frac{1}{3}$?

24. Which fraction is lesser, $\frac{5}{9}$ or $\frac{7}{13}$?

Answers can be found on page 319.

Comparing Complex Fractions

Sometimes, the GRE wraps fractions in layers of complications, making them more challenging to compare. For example, a Quantitative Comparison problem might have a complex fraction in one or both of the quantities. A complex fraction contains a fraction within a fraction:

$$x > 0$$

Quantity A	**Quantity B**
$\dfrac{2 + \frac{2}{3x}}{2}$	$\dfrac{3 + \frac{3}{2x}}{3}$

Chapter 11: **Fractions**

Because the numerators are complex but the denominators are single terms, begin by splitting the numerator:

$$x > 0$$

Quantity A		**Quantity B**
$\dfrac{2 + \frac{2}{3x}}{2} =$	?	$\dfrac{3 + \frac{3}{2x}}{3} =$
$\dfrac{2}{2} + \dfrac{\frac{2}{3x}}{2}$	?	$\dfrac{3}{3} + \dfrac{\frac{3}{2x}}{3}$

Both $\frac{2}{2}$ and $\frac{3}{3}$ equal 1, so subtract 1 from both sides (or just cross off those two terms):

$$x > 0$$

Quantity A		**Quantity B**
$\dfrac{2}{2} + \dfrac{\frac{2}{3x}}{2} =$	?	$\dfrac{3}{3} + \dfrac{\frac{3}{2x}}{3} =$
$\dfrac{\frac{2}{3x}}{2}$	?	$\dfrac{\frac{3}{2x}}{3}$

Next, perform the division represented by the main fraction bar. To divide by the denominator, multiply by the reciprocal:

$$x > 0$$

Quantity A		**Quantity B**
$\dfrac{\frac{2}{3x}}{2}$	?	$\dfrac{\frac{3}{2x}}{3}$
$\dfrac{2}{3x} \times \dfrac{1}{2}$	?	$\dfrac{3}{2x} \times \dfrac{1}{3}$

Finally, simplify the expressions. Simplify before you multiply:

$$x > 0$$

Quantity A		**Quantity B**
$\dfrac{\cancel{2}}{3x} \times \dfrac{1}{\cancel{2}}$	?	$\dfrac{\cancel{3}}{2x} \times \dfrac{1}{\cancel{3}}$
$\dfrac{1}{3x}$	?	$\dfrac{1}{2x}$

313

Unit Three: **Factors**

11

What can you conclude? As a positive denominator increases, the fraction decreases. The problem indicates that $x > 0$, so x is positive. As a result, the denominator of $\frac{1}{3x}$ will always be greater than the denominator of $\frac{1}{2x}$. The fraction in Quantity B will always be greater, so answer (B) is correct.

> **Strategy Tip:**
>
> When simplifying complex fractions:
>
> 1. When the denominator is one term, consider whether splitting the numerator will be helpful.
>
> 2. Turn division into multiplication by the reciprocal. (e.g., $\frac{\frac{2}{2}}{3} = 2 \times \frac{3}{2}$).

Check Your Skills Answer Key

1. $1\dfrac{5}{6}$

$$\dfrac{11}{6} = \dfrac{6+5}{6} = \dfrac{6}{6} + \dfrac{5}{6} = 1 + \dfrac{5}{6} = 1\dfrac{5}{6}$$

2. $9\dfrac{1}{11}$

$$\dfrac{100}{11} = \dfrac{99+1}{11} = \dfrac{99}{11} + \dfrac{1}{11} = 9 + \dfrac{1}{11} = 9\dfrac{1}{11}$$

3. $\dfrac{15}{4}$

   Change the integer 3 to have a denominator of 4, then simplify.

$$3\dfrac{3}{4} = 3 + \dfrac{3}{4} = \dfrac{3}{1}\left(\dfrac{4}{4}\right) + \dfrac{3}{4} = \dfrac{12}{4} + \dfrac{3}{4} = \dfrac{15}{4}$$

4. $\dfrac{33}{7}$

   Change the integer 4 to have a denominator of 7, then simplify.

$$4\dfrac{5}{7} = 4 + \dfrac{5}{7} = \dfrac{4}{1}\left(\dfrac{7}{7}\right) + \dfrac{5}{7} = \dfrac{28}{7} + \dfrac{5}{7} = \dfrac{33}{7}$$

5. $\dfrac{9}{35}$

   Cancel a factor of 2 from the denominator of the first fraction and the numerator of the second fraction.

$$\dfrac{3}{10} \times \dfrac{6}{7} = \dfrac{3}{\cancel{10}} \times \dfrac{\cancel{6}^{3}}{7} = \dfrac{3 \times 3}{5 \times 7} = \dfrac{9}{35}$$

6. $\dfrac{1}{8}$

   Cancel a factor of 5 and a factor of 7 from the top and bottom.

$$\dfrac{5}{14} \times \dfrac{7}{20} = \dfrac{\cancel{5}^{1}}{\cancel{14}_{2}} \times \dfrac{\cancel{7}^{1}}{\cancel{20}_{4}} = \dfrac{1 \times 1}{2 \times 4} = \dfrac{1}{8}$$

7. $\dfrac{11}{6}$

   Multiply by the reciprocal.

$$\dfrac{1}{6} \div \dfrac{1}{11} = \dfrac{1}{6} \times \dfrac{11}{1} = \dfrac{11}{6}$$

8. 6

   Multiply by the reciprocal.

$$\dfrac{8}{5} \div \dfrac{4}{15} = \dfrac{8}{5} \times \dfrac{15}{4} = \dfrac{\cancel{8}^{2} \times \cancel{15}^{3}}{\cancel{5}_{1} \times \cancel{4}_{1}} = 6$$

Unit Three: **Factors**

9. $\dfrac{9}{10}$

   Multiply by the reciprocal.

   $$\dfrac{\frac{3}{5}}{\frac{2}{3}} = \dfrac{3}{5} \div \dfrac{2}{3} = \dfrac{3}{5} \times \dfrac{3}{2} = \dfrac{9}{10}$$

10. $\dfrac{2+y}{4}$

    Multiply the first fraction by $\dfrac{2}{2}$ to get common denominators.

    $$\dfrac{1}{2} + \dfrac{y}{4}$$
    $$\dfrac{1}{2}\left(\dfrac{2}{2}\right) + \dfrac{y}{4}$$
    $$\dfrac{2}{4} + \dfrac{y}{4} = \dfrac{2+y}{4}$$

11. $\dfrac{8a-3b}{24}$

    The two denominators do not share any common factors, so both fractions will need to be converted in order to perform the subtraction.

    $$\dfrac{a}{3} - \dfrac{b}{8}$$
    $$\dfrac{a}{3}\left(\dfrac{8}{8}\right) - \dfrac{b}{8}\left(\dfrac{3}{3}\right)$$
    $$\dfrac{8a}{24} - \dfrac{3b}{24} = \dfrac{8a-3b}{24}$$

    Note: It's not possible to simplify the final fraction any further. For example, in order to divide out an 8 from the top and bottom, you would need to take it out of each separate term: $8a$, $3b$, and 24. Both $8a$ and 24 are divisible by 8, but $3b$ is not.

12. $\dfrac{7}{18}$

    The two denominators share a common factor of 3, but they also each have different factors.

    $$6 = 2 \times 3$$
    $$9 = 3 \times 3$$

    To get the two denominators to be completely identical, the 6 will need to be multiplied by another 3 and the 9 will need to be multiplied by 2. The new denominator for both will be $2 \times 3 \times 3$, which is 18.

    $$\dfrac{1}{6} + \dfrac{2}{9}$$
    $$\dfrac{1}{6}\left(\dfrac{3}{3}\right) + \dfrac{2}{9}\left(\dfrac{2}{2}\right)$$
    $$\dfrac{3}{18} + \dfrac{4}{18} = \dfrac{7}{18}$$

Chapter 11: **Fractions**

13. 1

Move the fraction $\frac{2}{3}$ to the right side and simplify:

$$\frac{x}{4} + \frac{2}{3} = \frac{11}{12}$$

$$\frac{x}{4} = \frac{11}{12} - \frac{2}{3}$$

$$\frac{x}{4} = \frac{11}{12} - \frac{8}{12}$$

$$\frac{x}{4} = \frac{3}{12}$$

$$\frac{x}{4} = \frac{1}{4}$$

$$x = 1$$

Alternatively, multiply the entire equation by 12 in order to drop all of the fractions in the first step:

$$(12)\left(\frac{x}{4} + \frac{2}{3}\right) = \left(\frac{11}{12}\right)(12)$$

$$\frac{\overset{3}{\cancel{12}}x}{\cancel{4}} + \frac{(\overset{4}{\cancel{12}})(2)}{\cancel{3}} = 11$$

$$3x + 8 = 11$$

$$3x = 3$$

$$x = 1$$

14. 4

Combine the two fractions that do not contain variables, then simplify.

$$\frac{x}{3} - \frac{4}{9} = \frac{8}{9}$$

$$\frac{x}{3} = \frac{8}{9} + \frac{4}{9}$$

$$\frac{x}{3} = \frac{12}{9}$$

$$\frac{x}{3} = \frac{4}{3}$$

$$x = 4$$

Alternatively, multiply both sides of the equation by 9 in order to drop all of the fractions in the first step.

$$(9)\left(\frac{x}{3} - \frac{4}{9}\right) = \left(\frac{8}{\cancel{9}}\right)(\cancel{9})$$

$$\frac{9x}{3} - \frac{(\cancel{9})4}{\cancel{9}} = 8$$

$$3x - 4 = 8$$

$$3x = 12$$

$$x = 4$$

317

Unit Three: **Factors**

15. 4

    Add the numerator, then reduce the fraction:

    $$\frac{13+7}{5} = \frac{20}{5} = 4$$

16. $2\frac{1}{13}$ or $\frac{27}{13}$

    Add the numerator and the denominator. If needed (based on the answer choices), convert to a mixed number.

    $$\frac{21+6}{7+6} = \frac{27}{13} = 2\frac{1}{13}$$

17. $\frac{12(4a+b)}{a+b}$

    The only manipulation allowed is to factor 12 out of the numerator. No further simplification is possible.

    $$\frac{48a+12b}{a+b} = \frac{12(4a+b)}{a+b}$$

18. $\frac{3}{2}$

    First, factor a 3 out of the numerator and a 2 out of the denominator.

    $$\frac{9g-6h}{6g-4h} = \frac{3(3g-2h)}{2(3g-2h)}$$

    Next, cancel the $3g - 2h$ term out of the numerator and denominator:

    $$\frac{3(3g-2h)}{2(3g-2h)} = \frac{3}{2} \times \frac{3g-2h}{3g-2h} = \frac{3}{2} \times 1 = \frac{3}{2}$$

19. 2

    Cross-multiply and solve.

    $$\frac{3x}{4} = \frac{3}{2}$$
    $$2(3x) = 3(4)$$
    $$6x = 12$$
    $$x = 2$$

20. 10

    Cross-multiply and solve.

    $$\frac{x}{6} = \frac{5}{3}$$
    $$x(3) = 5(6)$$
    $$3x = 30$$
    $$x = 10$$

21. $\frac{5}{7}$

    The denominators of the two fractions are the same. The numerator of $\frac{5}{7}$ is greater, so $\frac{5}{7} > \frac{3}{7}$.

Chapter 11: **Fractions**

22. $\frac{3}{10}$

    The numerators of the two fractions are the same. The denominator of $\frac{3}{10}$ is lesser, so $\frac{3}{10} > \frac{3}{13}$.

23. $\frac{1}{3}$

    Cross-multiply to solve. Place the products next to the corresponding numerators.

    $$\boxed{3 \times 4 = 12} \qquad \boxed{13 \times 1 = 13}$$
    $$\frac{4}{13} \times \frac{1}{3} \longrightarrow \frac{1}{3}$$

    Since 13 is greater than 12, the fraction $\frac{1}{3}$ is the greater fraction.

24. $\frac{7}{13}$

    Cross-multiply, keeping the product next to its corresponding numerator.

    $$\boxed{5 \times 13 = 65} \qquad \boxed{7 \times 9 = 63}$$
    $$\frac{5}{9} \times \frac{7}{13} \longrightarrow \frac{7}{13}$$

    Since 63 is less than 65, the fraction $\frac{7}{13}$ is the lesser fraction.

Unit Three: Factors

Problem Set

11

For problems #1–5, decide whether the given operation will yield an **Increase**, a **Decrease**, or a result that will **Stay the same**.

1. Multiply the numerator of a positive, proper fraction by $\frac{3}{2}$.

2. Add 1 to the numerator of a positive, proper fraction and subtract 1 from its denominator.

3. Multiply both the numerator and denominator of a positive, proper fraction by $3\frac{1}{2}$.

4. Multiply a positive, proper fraction by $\frac{3}{8}$.

5. Divide a positive, proper fraction by $\frac{3}{13}$.

For problems #6 and 7, simplify if possible. Otherwise, indicate that the fraction cannot be simplified.

6. Simplify: $\dfrac{10x}{5+x}$

7. Simplify: $\dfrac{\frac{3}{5}+\frac{1}{3}}{\frac{2}{3}+\frac{2}{5}}$

8. Lisa spends $\frac{3}{8}$ of her monthly paycheck on rent and $\frac{5}{12}$ on food. Her roommate, Carrie, who earns twice as much as Lisa, spends $\frac{1}{4}$ of her monthly paycheck on rent and $\frac{1}{2}$ on food. If the two women decide to donate the remainder of their money to charity each month, what fraction of their combined monthly income will they donate? (Assume all income in question is after taxes.)

9. Solve for z: $\dfrac{4z-7}{3-2z} = -5$

10. Solve for x: $4\left|x+\dfrac{1}{2}\right| = 18$

11. Rob spends $\frac{1}{2}$ of his monthly paycheck, after taxes, on rent. He spends $\frac{1}{3}$ on food and $\frac{1}{8}$ on entertainment. If he donates the entire remainder, $500, to charity, what is Rob's monthly income, after taxes?

12.
$$1 < 3x < 2$$

Quantity A | **Quantity B**
x^5 | x^7

13.
$$\frac{\frac{-21}{2}m}{2} = \frac{7}{2}n$$
$$mn \neq 0$$

Quantity A | **Quantity B**
$3m$ | $-n$

14. An 18 oz. glass contains 8 oz. of orange juice. More orange juice is added so that the glass is $\frac{5}{6}$ full.

Quantity A | **Quantity B**
Number of ounces of orange juice added | 6

15.
Quantity A | **Quantity B**
$\frac{1}{3} + \frac{1}{4} + \frac{7}{12}$ | $\dfrac{1}{\frac{1}{3} + \frac{1}{4} + \frac{7}{12}}$

16.
Quantity A | **Quantity B**
$\frac{1}{6} - \left(\frac{1}{2}\right)^2 + \left(-\frac{1}{4}\right)^2$ | $\frac{1}{6}$

17.
$$x > 1$$

Quantity A | **Quantity B**
$\dfrac{x + 5}{x}$ | $\dfrac{(x - 1) + 5}{x - 1}$

18.
$$\clubsuit x = \frac{1}{x - 1}$$

Quantity A | **Quantity B**
$\clubsuit(\clubsuit x)$ | $\dfrac{x - 1}{2 - x}$

Chapter 11: **Fractions**

321

Unit Three: **Factors**

Solutions

1. **Increase**
   Multiplying the numerator of a positive fraction by a number greater than 1 increases the numerator. As the numerator of a positive fraction increases, its value increases.

2. **Increase**
   As the numerator of a positive fraction increases, the value of the fraction increases. As the denominator of a positive fraction decreases, the value of the fraction also increases. Both actions will work to increase the value of the fraction.

3. **Stay the same**
   Multiplying or dividing the numerator and denominator of a fraction by the same number will not change the value of the fraction.

4. **Decrease**
   Multiplying a positive number by a fraction between 0 and 1 decreases the number.

5. **Increase**
   Dividing a positive number by a fraction between 0 and 1 increases the number.

6. **Cannot simplify**
   There is no way to simplify this fraction; it is already in simplest form. You *cannot* split the denominator!

7. $\frac{7}{8}$

   First, add the fractions in the numerator and denominator. This results in $\frac{14}{15}$ and $\frac{16}{15}$, respectively. To save time, multiply each of the fractions by 15, which is the common denominator of all the fractions in the problem. Because you are multiplying the numerator *and* the denominator of the whole complex fraction by 15, you are not changing its value.

   $$\frac{\frac{3}{5} + \frac{1}{3}}{\frac{2}{3} + \frac{2}{5}} = \frac{\frac{9}{15} + \frac{5}{15}}{\frac{10}{15} + \frac{6}{15}} = \frac{\frac{14}{15}}{\frac{16}{15}} = \frac{\frac{14}{15} \times 15}{\frac{16}{15} \times 15} = \frac{14}{16} = \frac{7}{8}$$

8. $\frac{17}{72}$

   Pick numbers to solve this problem. The denominators in the problem are 8, 12, 4, and 2. Therefore, assign Lisa a monthly paycheck of $24, because 24 is the least common multiple of the denominators. Assign her roommate, who earns twice as much, a monthly paycheck of $48.

	Rent	Food	Remaining
Lisa	$\frac{3}{8}$ of 24 = 9	$\frac{5}{12}$ of 24 = 10	24 − (9 + 10) = 5
Carrie	$\frac{1}{4}$ of 48 = 12	$\frac{1}{2}$ of 48 = 24	48 − (12 + 24) = 12

   The women will donate a total of $17 out of their combined monthly income of $72.

Chapter 11: **Fractions**

9. $\dfrac{4}{3}$

$$\dfrac{4z-7}{3-2z} = -5$$
$$4z - 7 = -5(3 - 2z)$$
$$4z - 7 = -15 + 10z$$
$$8 = 6z$$
$$z = \dfrac{8}{6} = \dfrac{4}{3}$$

10. **4 or −5**

$$4\left|x + \dfrac{1}{2}\right| = 18$$

$4\left(x + \dfrac{1}{2}\right) = +18$ or $4\left(x + \dfrac{1}{2}\right) = -18$

$x + \dfrac{1}{2} = \dfrac{18}{4}$ or $x + \dfrac{1}{2} = -\dfrac{18}{4}$

$x = \dfrac{9}{2} - \dfrac{1}{2}$ or $x = -\dfrac{9}{2} - \dfrac{1}{2}$

$x = \dfrac{8}{2}$ or $x = -\dfrac{10}{2}$

$x = 4$ or $x = -5$

11. **$12,000**

You cannot use Smart Numbers in this problem, because an amount is specified. This means that the total is a certain number that you are being asked to find.

First, use addition to find the fraction of Rob's money that he spends on rent, food, and entertainment. You can use a common denominator of 24: $\dfrac{1}{2} + \dfrac{1}{3} + \dfrac{1}{8} = \dfrac{12}{24} + \dfrac{8}{24} + \dfrac{3}{24} = \dfrac{23}{24}$. Therefore, the $500 that he donates to charity represents the following portion of his total monthly paycheck:

$$1 - \dfrac{23}{24} = \dfrac{24-23}{24} = \dfrac{1}{24}$$

In math terms, $\$500 = \dfrac{1}{24}x$. Thus, Rob's monthly income is 500×24, or $x = \$12,000$.

12. **(A)**

Before proceeding to Quantities A and B, simplify $1 < 3x < 2$ by dividing through by 3.

$$\dfrac{1}{3} < x < \dfrac{2}{3}$$

Therefore, x is between $\dfrac{1}{3}$ and $\dfrac{2}{3}$. More importantly, x is definitely between 0 and 1, which means it decreases when multiplied by itself.

323

Unit Three: Factors

Therefore, x^5 is greater than x^7.

The correct answer is (A): Quantity A is greater.

(It would be possible to plug in a value between $\frac{1}{3}$ and $\frac{2}{3}$, such as $\frac{1}{2}$, which would make Quantity A equal to $\frac{1}{32}$ and Quantity B equal to $\frac{1}{128}$. However, a Number Properties approach is far superior here, because you know that x will behave in a certain way due to its being a fraction between 0 and 1, you are saved from having to calculate anything to the 7th power).

13. **(D)**
Never leave a complex fraction in place; that is, simplify in order to find a direct comparison. First, multiply both sides by 2.

$$\frac{\frac{-21}{2}m}{2} = \frac{7}{2}n \rightarrow \frac{-21}{2}m = 7n$$

Multiply both sides by 2 again.

$$\frac{-21}{2}m = 7n \rightarrow -21m = 14n$$

Divide by -7 in order to make the left side of the equation $3m$ (Quantity A).

$$-21m = 14n \rightarrow 3m = -2n$$

Since $3m = -2n$, you can substitute $-2n$ for $3m$ in Quantity A. The problem now reads.

$$mn \neq 0$$

Quantity A	**Quantity B**
$-2n$	$-n$

If n is positive, Quantity B is greater. If n is negative, Quantity A is greater.

The correct answer is (D): The relationship cannot be determined.

14. **(A)**
To find out how much juice was added, first calculate how much juice is needed in total for the glass to be $\frac{5}{6}$ full. Since $\frac{5}{6} \times 18 = 15$, a total of 15 ounces of orange juice are needed. There were 8 ounces of orange juice in the glass to begin with, so 7 ounces were added.

Quantity A	**Quantity B**
Number of ounces of orange juice added = 7	6

Therefore, the correct answer is (A): Quantity A is greater.

15. **(A)**

Compare, don't calculate. It is not necessary to add these fractions; just note that $\frac{1}{3} + \frac{1}{4} + \frac{7}{12}$ is greater than 1. How do you know that? Well, $\frac{7}{12}$ is more than half already, $\frac{1}{4} + \frac{1}{4}$ would be another half, and $\frac{1}{3}$ is more than $\frac{1}{4}$. Thus, $\frac{1}{3} + \frac{1}{4}$ is more than half.

In Quantity A, more than half plus more than half is more than 1.

In Quantity B, dividing 1 by more than 1 is less than 1.

The correct answer is (A): Quantity A is greater.

16. **(B)**

This is another "compare, don't calculate" problem. Because $\frac{1}{6}$ is present on both sides, subtract it.

Quantity A	Quantity B
$\frac{1}{6} - \left(\frac{1}{2}\right)^2 + \left(-\frac{1}{4}\right)^2$	$\frac{1}{6}$
$-\left(\frac{1}{2}\right)^2 + \left(-\frac{1}{4}\right)^2$	0

Now, determine whether $-\left(\frac{1}{2}\right)^2 + \left(-\frac{1}{4}\right)^2$ is negative, positive, or 0.

$$-\left(\frac{1}{2}\right)^2 + \left(-\frac{1}{4}\right)^2 = -\frac{1}{4} + \frac{1}{16}$$

$-\frac{1}{4} + \frac{1}{16}$ is negative, since the negative fraction is farther from zero than the positive one.

The correct answer is (B): Quantity B is greater.

17. **(B)**

You can simplify by splitting the numerator of each fraction.

Quantity A	$x > 1$	Quantity B
$\frac{x+5}{x} = \frac{x}{x} + \frac{5}{x}$		$\frac{(x-1)+5}{x-1} = \frac{x-1}{x-1} + \frac{5}{x-1}$

325

Unit Three: **Factors**

Because $\frac{x}{x}$ and $\frac{x-1}{x-1}$ are each equal to 1, cancel them out from both sides.

11.

Quantity A	Quantity B
$\frac{5}{x}$	$\frac{5}{x-1}$

The variable x is a positive number greater than 1. As the denominator increases, the fraction decreases. Thus, Quantity B, which has the lesser denominator, is the greater fraction.

The correct answer is (B): Quantity B is greater.

18. **(C)**
When you are given a strange symbol on the GRE, the exam will have to define that strange symbol for you, which this problem does in the given information at the top. To simplify, first evaluate the formula using the variable itself.

Quantity A asks for ♣(♣x). The question is asking you to plug the function into itself. So, plug $\frac{1}{x-1}$ in for x.

$$\frac{1}{\frac{1}{x-1} - 1}$$

Combine the two terms in the denominator.

$$\frac{1}{\frac{1}{x-1} - 1} \rightarrow \frac{1}{\frac{1}{x-1} - \frac{x-1}{x-1}} = \frac{1}{\frac{2-x}{x-1}}$$

If a fraction is under a 1, flip it over.

$$\frac{1}{\frac{2-x}{x-1}} = \frac{x-1}{2-x}$$

The correct answer is (C): The two quantities are always equal.

CHAPTER 12

Quadratic Equations

In This Chapter:

- Equivalent Forms
- Solving Quadratic Equations
- Using FOIL with Square Roots
- One-Solution Quadratics
- The Three Special Products
- Quadratics in QC
- Quadratics and Fractions
- Check Your Skills Answer Key
- Problem Set
- Solutions

CHAPTER 12 Quadratic Equations

A **quadratic equation** is any equation for which the highest power on a variable is the second power (e.g., x^2). For example:

$$x^2 = 4$$

$$x = 2 \text{ or } -2$$

Here's a more complicated example:

$$x^2 + 3x - 10 = 0$$

In this chapter, you will learn how to recognize, manipulate, and solve all forms of quadratic equations that appear on the GRE.

Equivalent Forms

Complex quadratic equations typically come in one of two equivalent forms. The example mentioned previously can be expressed in these two ways:

$$x^2 + 3x - 10 = 0 \quad \text{is equivalent to} \quad (x + 5)(x - 2) = 0$$

To differentiate, this book will refer to the first form, $x^2 + 3x - 10$, as the **distributed form** and the second form, $(x + 5)(x - 2)$, as the **factored form**.

The GRE can and does use this equivalency to complicate problems. Consider this QC question:

Quantity A	Quantity B
$x^2 + 3x - 10$	$(x + 5)(x - 2)$

How do you know whether these two forms are equivalent?

Unit Three: **Factors**

Distributing

Start with the factored form: $(x + 5)(x - 2)$

To change it to the distributed form, distribute the terms across the parentheses. You've done this before in a simpler form:

$$3(x + 2) \to 3(x) + 3(2) \to 3x + 6$$

That is, take the first term, 3, and multiply it by each individual term in the parentheses. Then, add the resulting terms together.

The quadratic $(x + 5)(x - 2)$ contains two terms in each set of parentheses. First, distribute the x from the first term into $(x - 2)$. Then, distribute the 5 from the first term into $(x - 2)$. Finally, add everything together:

Distribute the x.	$x(x - 2)$	=	$x^2 - 2x$
Distribute the 5.	$5(x - 2)$	=	$5x - 10$
Add the results.			$x^2 - 2x + 5x - 10$
$(x + 5)(x - 2) =$			$x^2 + 3x - 10$

Here are all of the steps as a single algebraic process:

$$(x + 5)(x - 2)$$
$$x(x - 2) + 5(x - 2)$$
$$x^2 - 2x + 5x - 10$$
$$x^2 + 3x - 10$$

In school, you may have learned this process under the acronym "FOIL." The letters stand for **F**irst, **O**uter, **I**nner, **L**ast, and refer to the four ways in which to multiply the various numbers and variables together to move from the factored form to the distributed form:

($\underline{x}$ + 5)($\underline{x}$ − 2)	F — multiply the **first** term in each of the parentheses	$(x)(x) = x^2$
($\underline{x}$ + 5)(x $\underline{- 2}$)	O — multiply the **outer** term in each	$(x)(-2) = -2x$
(x $\underline{+ 5}$)($\underline{x}$ − 2)	I — multiply the **inner** term in each	$(5)(x) = 5x$
(x $\underline{+ 5}$)(x $\underline{- 2}$)	L — multiply the **last** term in each	$(5)(-2) = -10$

Chapter 12: **Quadratic Equations**

> **Key Concept**
>
> To distribute the quadratic $(a + b)(x + y)$, FOIL the individual terms, then add them together:
>
> | | | |
> |---|---|---|
> | ($\underline{a}$ + b)($\underline{x}$ + y) | F – multiply the **first** term in each of the parentheses | $(a)(x) = ax$ |
> | ($\underline{a}$ + b)(x $\underline{+ y}$) | O – multiply the **outer** term in each | $(a)(y) = ay$ |
> | (a $\underline{+ b}$)($\underline{x}$ + y) | I – multiply the **inner** term in each | $(b)(x) = bx$ |
> | (a $\underline{+ b}$)(x $\underline{+ y}$) | L – multiply the **last** term in each | $(b)(y) = by$ |
>
> So, $(a + b)(x + y) = ax + ay + bx + by$.

You can verify this system with numbers. Take the expression $(3 + 4)(10 + 20)$. This is no different than multiplying $(7)(30)$, which equals 210:

(**3** + 4)(**10** + 20)	First	$3 \times 10 = 30$
(**3** + 4)(10 + **20**)	Outer	$3 \times 20 = 60$
(3 + **4**)(**10** + 20)	Inner	$4 \times 10 = 40$
(3 + **4**)(10 + **20**)	Last	$4 \times 20 = 80$

Finally, sum the four products: $30 + 60 + 40 + 80 = 210$.

Try this problem:

Distribute the expression $(x + 2)(x + 3)$.

Use FOIL to distribute:

(**x** + 2)(**x** + 3)	First	$(x)(x) = x^2$
(**x** + 2)(x + **3**)	Outer	$(x)(3) = 3x$
(x + **2**)(**x** + 3)	Inner	$(2)(x) = 2x$
(x + **2**)(x + **3**)	Last	$(2)(3) = 6$

The expression becomes $x^2 + 3x + 2x + 6$. Combine like terms to get $x^2 + 5x + 6$.

Unit Three: **Factors**

Check Your Skills

> Distribute the following expressions.

1. $(x + 4)(x + 9)$

2. $(y + 3)(y - 6)$

3. $(x + 7)(3 + x)$

Answers can be found on page 345.

Factoring

How would you go from the distributed form to the factored form? For example:

> Which of the following is equivalent to $x^2 + 3x - 10$?

(A) $(x + 5)(x - 2)$

(B) $(x + 2)(x - 5)$

(C) $(x + 1)(x - 3)$

(D) $(x + 10)(x - 1)$

(E) $(x + 1)(x - 10)$

It would take too long to completely distribute every answer choice. As you get more comfortable with quadratics, you'll learn some shortcuts to eliminate several answers without fully distributing them, but for now, the easiest way to find the right answer would be to factor the original expression.

To factor, you'll need to put things into two parentheticals, but you don't yet know what will go inside each set of parentheses:

$$(? + ?)(? + ?)$$

The equation: $x^2 + 3x - 10$ starts with an x^2 term. That's the equivalent of $(x)(x)$, so put x as the first term in each set of parentheses:

$$x^2 + 3x - 10 = (x + ?)(x + ?)$$

The last term in the distributed form is -10. Anything multiplied by an x is going to keep that variable. Because there's no x in -10, it must come from multiplying the two last terms together. So the two remaining question marks must be something that multiply together to give -10. In mathematics, that's an infinite number of possibilities (they could be -1 and 10, or 0.5 and -20, or -0.25 and $40...$) but on the GRE, those question marks are almost certainly integers. List the reasonable possibilities using the factor pair method (review Chapter 9: Divisibility if you need a reminder on how that works). For now, ignore the negative sign and just determine what positive integers multiply to 10:

Small	Large
1	10
2	5

There are only two positive factor pairs that multiply to 10. To create -10, one of the factors will have to be negative. So, the factored form of the equation is going to be one of only four possibilities:

$$(x + 1)(x - 10)$$

$$(x - 1)(x + 10)$$

$$(x + 2)(x - 5)$$

$$(x - 2)(x + 5)$$

Only one of these four is the correct form. The other three are incorrect, and some are even wrong answer choices in the problem (a common trap to watch for on quadratic problems).

To determine which one is the right one, look at the middle term in the quadratic: $3x$. The term that has a variable raised to the power of 1 (otherwise known as the variable with no exponent) comes from adding the outer and inner products when you FOIL. Consider the first listed possibility:

$$(x + 1)(x - 10) = x^2 + x - 10x - 10 = x^2 - 9x - 10$$

To arrive at $-9x$, multiply 1 and x, then add that to -10 times x. Put more directly, if you *add* the two terms with no variables together, you'll find the coefficient of the variable for that middle term with one x. Because -10 and 1 add to -9, the middle term will be $-9x$.

Unit Three: Factors

Understanding this is the key to picking the right factored form without doing a ton of extra work. Once you use the factor pair method to find the possible pairs of numbers for the two last terms in the parentheses, the pair that *adds* to the correct coefficient is the right one. The coefficient in this equation is positive 3. Consider the factor pairs for -10:

Factor Pair	Adds to $+3$?
1 and -10	Adds to a negative
-1 and 10	Positive but not 3
2 and -5	Adds to a negative
-2 and 5	$-2 + 5 = 3$, Yes!

The correct pair of factors is -2 and 5, so $x^2 + 3x - 10$ is equivalent to $(x - 2)(x + 5)$. Note that the order of the parentheticals doesn't matter. You could also write the correct answer as $(x + 5)(x - 2)$.

> **Key Concept**
>
> To factor a quadratic in the form $x^2 + bx + c$:
>
> 1. Put *x* as the first term in both parentheses: $(x + ?)(x + ?)$
> 2. List all of the factor pairs for *c*: $? \times ? = c$
> 3. Of the listed factor pairs, find the pair that adds to *b*: $? + ? = b$
> 4. Replace the question marks in the parentheses with the pair of numbers that both multiply to *c* and add to *b*.

Try this problem:

Factor the equation $x^2 - 6x + 8$.

Step 1: Put *x* as the first terms: $(x + ?)(x + ?)$

Step 2: List the factor pairs for 8, using the positive versions only:

Small	Large
1	8
2	4

Step 3: Find the pair that adds to −6. Two positives will never add to a negative, so this step indicates that you'll need the negative forms of the factors of 8:

Factor Pair	Adds to −6?
1 and 8	No (must be positive)
2 and 4	No (must be positive)
−1 and −8	$-1 + -8 = -9$, No
−2 and −4	$-2 + -4 = -6$, Yes!

Step 4: Substitute the numbers for the unknowns: $(x - 2)(x - 4)$

You can FOIL the factored form to verify your work. (But it's not a good idea to take the time to do this on the GRE unless you find yourself with extra time during the section and nothing else to do...but that's pretty unlikely!)

Check Your Skills

Factor the following expressions.

4. $x^2 - 3x + 2$

5. $x^2 + 9x + 20$

Answers can be found on page 346.

Solving Quadratic Equations

Now that you know how to express quadratics in two ways, it's time to make that final jump to solving quadratic equations.

If $7x = 0$, then x must equal 0, because the only way for the product of two or more numbers to equal 0 is for at least one of those numbers to equal 0. Clearly, 7 does not equal 0, so x must be 0.

What if you were told that $kj = 0$? Now, there are two possibilities. If $k = 0$, then $0(j) = 0$, which is true, so $k = 0$ is one solution to the equation $kj = 0$.

Likewise, if $j = 0$, then $k(0) = 0$, which is also true, so $j = 0$ is also one solution to $kj = 0$. So, the solution to the equation $kj = 0$ is that either $k = 0$ or $j = 0$...or both equal 0. At least one of k and j must be equal to 0.

Either of these scenarios make the equation true, and they are the only scenarios that make the product $kj = 0$. (Try plugging in nonzero numbers for both k and j to see what happens.)

Use this same principle to approach quadratic equations:

$$(k)(j) = 0$$
$$(x+5)(x-2) = 0$$

Either k or j or both must equal 0. Likewise, either $(x+5)$ or $(x-2)$ or both must equal 0:

$$x + 5 = 0 \quad \text{or} \quad x - 2 = 0$$
$$x = -5 \qquad\qquad x = 2$$

So, the two possible solutions for x are -5 and 2.

Before you factor a quadratic expression, you *must* make sure that the other side of the equation equals 0. For example:

$$x^2 + 10x + 7 = -14$$

The x^2 term indicates that this is a quadratic equation, but it's not set equal to 0. First, move everything to one side of the equation so that the other side equals zero. Then, you can factor:

$$x^2 + 10x + 7 = -14$$
$$x^2 + 10x + 21 = 0$$
$$(x+7)(x+3) = 0$$

Therefore, $x = -3$ or $x = -7$.

Check Your Skills

List all possible solutions to the following equations.

6. $(x-2)(x-1) = 0$

7. $(y+4)(y+5) = 0$

8. $x^2 + 2x - 35 = 0$

Answers can be found on page 346.

Using FOIL with Square Roots

Some GRE problems ask you to solve factored expressions that involve roots. For example:

What is the value of $(\sqrt{8} - \sqrt{3})(\sqrt{8} + \sqrt{3})$?

You cannot combine added or subtracted roots, so the solution is *not* $(\sqrt{5})(\sqrt{11})$ (review Chapter 5: Exponents and Roots for a refresher on this concept). Instead, use FOIL to solve:

Given:	$(\sqrt{8} - \sqrt{3})(\sqrt{8} + \sqrt{3})$
First:	$\sqrt{8} \times \sqrt{8} = 8$
Outer:	$\sqrt{8} \times \sqrt{3} = \sqrt{24}$
Inner:	$-\sqrt{3} \times \sqrt{8} = -\sqrt{24}$
Last:	$-\sqrt{3} \times \sqrt{3} = -3$

The four terms are: $8 + \sqrt{24} - \sqrt{24} - 3$.

The two middle terms cancel each other out:

$$8 + \cancel{\sqrt{24}} - \cancel{\sqrt{24}} - 3$$

$$8 \qquad\qquad -3 = 5$$

Although the problem looks complex, using FOIL reduces the entire expression to 5.

Check Your Skills

9. FOIL $(\sqrt{8} - \sqrt{2})(\sqrt{8} - \sqrt{2})$

Answers can be found on page 347.

One-Solution Quadratics

Most quadratic equations have two distinct solutions, but some have only one solution. One-solution quadratics are also called **perfect square** quadratics, because both roots are the same. For example:

$$\begin{aligned} x^2 + 8x + 16 &= 0 \\ (x+4)(x+4) &= 0 \\ (x+4)^2 &= 0 \end{aligned}$$ The one solution for x is -4.

$$\begin{aligned} x^2 - 6x + 9 &= 0 \\ (x-3)(x-3) &= 0 \\ (x-3)^2 &= 0 \end{aligned}$$ The one solution for x is 3.

Be careful not to assume that a quadratic equation always has two solutions. Always factor quadratic equations to determine their solutions. In doing so, you will see whether a quadratic equation has one or two solutions.

Unit Three: **Factors**

Check Your Skills

10. If $x^2 - 10x + 25 = 0$, what are all of the possible solutions for x?

Answers can be found on page 347.

12 The Three Special Products

There are three quadratics that are used so frequently in math that they are called *special products*. (The two perfect square quadratics in the last section are both on this list.) Put these three special products on a flash card now:

Special Product #1:	$x^2 - y^2 = (x + y)(x - y)$
Special Product #2:	$x^2 + 2xy + y^2 = (x + y)(x + y) = (x + y)^2$
Special Product #3:	$x^2 - 2xy + y^2 = (x - y)(x - y) = (x - y)^2$

Know how to identify these products when they are presented in disguised form. The GRE might change the variables, or use a mix of variables and numbers:

$$a^2 - 1 = (a + 1)(a - 1)$$

The GRE might even present things in non−standard order or use a root symbol:

$$(1 + a)^2 = 1 + 2a + a^2$$

$$(\sqrt{a} - 1)^2 = a - 2\sqrt{a} + 1$$

Avoid the following common mistakes with special products:

$(x + y)^2 \neq x^2 + y^2$	Correct:	$(x + y)^2 = x^2 + 2xy + y^2$
$(x - y)^2 \neq x^2 - y^2$	Correct:	$(x - y)^2 = x^2 - 2xy + y^2$

Try this problem:

If $x^2 - 8x + 16 = 0$, what is x?

You could factor this out using the tools taught earlier in this chapter. But you can save yourself time by recognizing that this quadratic is in the form of Special Product #3:

$$x^2 - 2xy + y^2 \quad \rightarrow \quad x^2 - 8x + 16 = 0$$
$$(x - y)(x - y) \quad \rightarrow \quad (x - 4)(x - 4) = 0$$
$$(x - 4)^2 = 0$$
$$x = 4$$

In this case, the term 16 is equivalent to y^2, so the y term is equal to 4. Because the middle term $-8x$ is negative, this quadratic is the equivalent of the third special quadratic $(x - y)^2$, not the second special quadratic $(x + y)^2$.

The GRE might also toss something like this at you:

$$9x^2 + 36x + 36 = 0$$

This time, there's a coefficient in front of the squared term. When this happens, the GRE is likely testing your understanding of the three special products. Before attempting to factor something like this, note that the first and last terms are perfect squares, so consider the special products.

The square root of $9x^2$ is $3x$ and the square root of 36 is 6. Use the second special product to distribute $(3x + 6)^2 = 0$ to see whether it matches the original equation:

$$x^2 + 2xy + y^2 = 0$$
$$(3x + 6)^2 \rightarrow (3x)^2 + 2(3x)(6) + (6)^2 = 0$$
$$9x^2 + 36x + 36 = 0$$

It does, so $(3x + 6)^2 = 0$ is indeed the correct factored form. Therefore:

$$3x + 6 = 0$$
$$3x = -6$$
$$x = -2$$

These special products are often invoked if there are two perfect squares in a quadratic. For example, both terms in the expression $9x^2 - 4y^2$ are perfect squares, so the factored form of this expression is $(3x - 2y)(3x + 2y)$.

Check Your Skills

Factor each quadratic.

11. $4a^2 + 4ab + b^2 = 0$

12. $x^2 + 22xy + 121y^2 = 0$

Answers can be found on page 348.

Unit Three: **Factors**

Quadratics in QC

On Quantitative Comparison problems, it's common to need to convert between factored and distributed forms of quadratics or to recognize that a particular quadratic will have only one solution, not two.

Pay attention to where in the problem the quadratics appear, as that will likely influence your solution strategy.

Quadratics in Quantities

If the quadratic expressions appears in the quantities, then your goal is to FOIL and use the Hidden Inequality to eliminate common terms. For example:

$$pq \neq 0$$

Quantity A	**Quantity B**
$(2p + q)(p + 2q)$	$p^2 + 5pq + q^2$

First, in order to get the two quantities in the same form, FOIL Quantity A:

First $= 2p \times p = 2p^2$

Outer $= 2p \times 2q = 4pq$

Inner $= q \times p = pq$

Last $= q \times 2q = 2q^2$

Quantity A equals $2p^2 + 5pq + 2q^2$. Use the Hidden Inequality to simplify the expressions (for a refresher on this tactic, revisit Chapter 8: QC Gameplan: Simplify):

$$pq \neq 0$$

Quantity A		**Quantity B**
$2p^2 + 5pq + 2q^2$	?	$p^2 + 5pq + q^2$
$-5pq$		$-5pq$
$2p^2 + 2q^2$	?	$p^2 + q^2$
$-p^2 - q^2$		$-p^2 - q^2$
$p^2 + q^2$	?	0

Is $p^2 + q^2$ greater than 0? The information at the top indicates that neither p nor q can be 0, so p^2 and q^2 must both be positive. Since the sum of two positive numbers is positive, the correct answer is (A): Quantity A is greater.

> **Strategy Tip:**
>
> When a quadratic expression appears in one or both quantities, express both quantities as the distributed form, eliminate common terms, and compare the quantities.

As QC questions involving quadratic expressions get more difficult, they can make either FOIL—ing or simplifying more difficult. Try this problem:

$$r > s$$

Quantity A	Quantity B
$(r+s)(r-s)$	$(s+r)(s-r)$

You can't divide out $(r+s)$ from each side, because $(r+s)$ might be negative or 0. So, this problem now requires you to FOIL two expressions, not just one. Use the special products to save time. Each of these expressions is a difference of squares:

$$r > s$$

Quantity A	Quantity B
$(r+s)(r-s) = r^2 - s^2$	$(s+r)(s-r) = s^2 - r^2$

Use the Hidden Inequality to combine like terms:

$$r > s$$

Quantity A		Quantity B
$r^2 - s^2$	?	$s^2 - r^2$
$+ s^2$		$+ s^2$
r^2	?	$2s^2 - r^2$
$+ r^2$		$+ r^2$
$2r^2$	?	$2s^2$
$\div 2$		$\div 2$
r^2	?	s^2

341

Unit Three: **Factors**

The given information indicates that *r* is greater than *s*, so it would be tempting to conclude that Quantity A is greater than Quantity B. However, the sign of *r* and *s* will impact the outcome. Test some values to see what happens:

$r > s$

r	*s*	**Quantity A**		**Quantity B**
3	2	$r^2 = 3^2 = 9$	>	$s^2 = 2^2 = 4$
−2	−3	$r^2 = (-2)^2 = 4$	<	$s^2 = (-3)^2 = 9$

In the first case, Quantity A is greater, so eliminate answers (B) and (C). In the second case, Quantity B is greater, so eliminate answer (A). The correct answer is (D): The relationship cannot be determined.

> **Strategy Tip:**
>
> When QC quantities are quadratics:
>
> 1. Convert them into similar forms.
> 2. Simplify using the Hidden Inequality.
> 3. Pick numbers if needed, making sure to consider negatives, zero, and fractions when allowed.

Quadratics in Additional Information

Questions that contain quadratic equations in the additional information before the quantities will present different challenges. For example:

$$x^2 - 6x + 8 = 0$$

Quantity A   **Quantity B**

x^2 2^x

There may be two possible values for *x*, but don't jump to conclusions to assume the relationship cannot be determined. Instead, solve for *x* and, if there are indeed two values, then plug *both* solutions into the quantities.

Factor the equation to solve for *x*:

$$x^2 - 6x + 8 = 0 \rightarrow \quad (x - 2)(x - 4) = 0$$

$x - 2 = 0$ or $x - 4 = 0$

$x = 2$ $x = 4$

Start by plugging $x = 2$ into both quantities:

Quantity A	Quantity B
$(2)^2 = 4$	$2^{(2)} = 4$

When $x = 2$, the quantities are equal.   A̷ B̷ C D

Next, try $x = 4$:

Quantity A	Quantity B
$(4)^2 = 16$	$2^{(4)} = 16$

Even though there are two possible values for x, both of these values lead to the same conclusion: The quantities are equal. Therefore, the correct answer is (C).

> **Strategy Tip:**
>
> When the common information contains a quadratic equation, solve for *both* possible values and plug them both into the quantities.

Quadratics and Fractions

One thing you *never* saw in Chapter 11: Fractions was a fraction with a denominator of zero. And you never will see it on the GRE because it is undefined! It is important to understand that the denominator of a fraction will *never* equal zero because the GRE will use that as code to restrict possible outcomes. For example, if you were given that $\frac{2y}{x} = 0$, you would be able to infer two things. First, y must equal zero and second, x *cannot* equal zero. This coding is especially prominent in quadratic questions. Consider the following:

What are the solutions to the following equation?

$$\frac{x^2 + x - 12}{x - 2} = 0$$

There is a quadratic expression in the numerator, so there may be two solutions. It is a good idea to simplify quadratic expressions by factoring, so factor this numerator as follows:

$$\frac{x^2 + x - 12}{x - 2} = 0 \rightarrow \frac{(x - 3)(x + 4)}{x - 2} = 0$$

If either of the factors in the numerator is 0, then the entire expression becomes 0. Thus, the solutions to this equation are $x = 3$ or $x = -4$.

Note that making the denominator of the fraction equal to 0 would *not* make the entire expression equal to 0. Recall that if 0 appears in the denominator, the expression becomes undefined. Thus, $x = 2$ (which would make the denominator equal to 0) is *not* a solution to this equation. In fact, because setting x equal to 2 would make the denominator 0, the value 2 is not allowed: *x cannot equal 2.*

Unit Three: **Factors**

This can become critically important in determining solutions. Solve for x in this equation:

$$\frac{x^2 + x - 12}{x - 3} = 0$$

First, factor the numerator to $(x - 3)(x + 4)$. (Remember that the order of the factors doesn't matter, so $(x + 4)(x - 3)$ is an equivalent expression.) The factored form suggests that x could be either 3 or -4, but if x is 3, the denominator is zero, and the expression is undefined. Therefore, x cannot be 3, so the only solution to this problem is $x = -4$.

Check Your Skills

13. Solve for x: $\frac{x^2 - x - 2}{x - 2} = 0$

Answers can be found on page 348.

Check Your Skills Answer Key

1. $x^2 + 13x + 36$
   FOIL, then combine like terms.

$(x + 4)(x + 9)$		
$(\boldsymbol{x} + 4)(\boldsymbol{x} + 9)$	First	$(x)(x) = x^2$
$(\boldsymbol{x} + 4)(x + \boldsymbol{9})$	Outer	$(x)(9) = 9x$
$(x + \boldsymbol{4})(\boldsymbol{x} + 9)$	Inner	$(4)(x) = 4x$
$(x + \boldsymbol{4})(x + \boldsymbol{9})$	Last	$(4)(9) = 36$

   $x^2 + 9x + 4x + 36 = x^2 + 13x + 36$

2. $y^2 - 3y - 18$
   FOIL, then combine like terms.

$(y + 3)(y - 6)$		
$(\boldsymbol{y} + 3)(\boldsymbol{y} - 6)$	First	$(y)(y) = y^2$
$(\boldsymbol{y} + 3)(y - \boldsymbol{6})$	Outer	$(y)(-6) = -6y$
$(y + \boldsymbol{3})(\boldsymbol{y} - 6)$	Inner	$(3)(y) = 3y$
$(y + \boldsymbol{3})(y - \boldsymbol{6})$	Last	$(3)(-6) = -18$

   $y^2 - 6y + 3y - 18 = y^2 - 3y - 18$

3. $x^2 + 10x + 21$
   The GRE may present things in an atypical order. The math still works the same way. FOIL, then combine like terms.

$(x + 7)(3 + x)$		
$(\boldsymbol{x} + 7)(\boldsymbol{3} + x)$	First	$(x)(3) = 3x$
$(\boldsymbol{x} + 7)(3 + \boldsymbol{x})$	Outer	$(x)(x) = x^2$
$(x + \boldsymbol{7})(\boldsymbol{3} + x)$	Inner	$(7)(3) = 21$
$(x + \boldsymbol{7})(3 + \boldsymbol{x})$	Last	$(7)(x) = 7x$

   $3x + x^2 + 21 + 7x = x^2 + 10x + 21$

Unit Three: **Factors**

4. **(x − 2)(x − 1)**
    The only factors of 2 are 1 and 2. If they are both negative, they will multiply to 2 and add to −3. Therefore, the factored form is $(x - 2)(x - 1)$.

5. **(x + 4)(x + 5)**
    Find the factor pairs of 20 and test to see which pairs sum to +9:

Factor Pair	Adds to +9?
1 and 20	No
2 and 10	No
4 and 5	4 + 5 = 9, Yes!

    Therefore, the factored form of the expression is $(x + 4)(x + 5)$.

6. **x = 2 or 1**
    Set each set of parentheses equal to 0 and solve for *x*.

    $$(x - 2)(x - 1) = 0$$

    $(x - 2) = 0$ or $(x - 1) = 0$
    $x = 2$ $x = 1$

7. **y = −4 or −5**
    Set each set of parentheses equal to 0 and solve for *y*.

    $$(y + 4)(y + 5) = 0$$

    $(y + 4) = 0$ or $(y + 5) = 0$
    $y = -4$ $y = -5$

8. **x = 5 or −7**
    First, factor the quadratic. Determine the factor pairs of +35:

Small	Large
1	35
5	7

Because the 35 is negative in the equation, one of the factors will be positive and the other will be negative. Test the factor pairs to determine which pair sums to +2:

Factor Pair	Adds to +2?
1 and −35	Negative
−1 and 35	Positive but too big
5 and −7	Negative
−5 and 7	−5 + 7 = 2, Yes!

The factored form of the equation is $(x - 5)(x + 7)$. Set each parenthetical equal to zero to solve for x:

$$(x - 5)(x + 7) = 0$$

$(x - 5) = 0$ or $(x + 7) = 0$

$x = 5$ $x = -7$

9. **2**

   First: $\sqrt{8} \times \sqrt{8} = 8$

   Outer: $\sqrt{8} \times (-\sqrt{2}) = -\sqrt{16} = -4$

   Inner: $(-\sqrt{2}) \times \sqrt{8} = -\sqrt{16} = -4$

   Last: $(-\sqrt{2}) \times (-\sqrt{2}) = 2$

   Sum of FOIL terms: $8 - 4 - 4 + 2 = 2$

10. **$x = 5$**

    Don't let the plural word *solutions* in the question trap you. In this case, the "two solutions" are just one, since this is a perfect-square quadratic.

    $$x^2 - 10x + 25 = 0$$
    $$(x - 5)(x - 5) = 0$$
    $$(x - 5)^2 = 0$$
    $$x = 5$$

Unit Three: **Factors**

11. **$(2a + b)^2 = 0$**

    Two of the terms are perfect squares, indicating this could be a special product. The square roots of the first and last terms are $2a$ and b, so test whether $(2a + b)^2$ is the correct factored form.

    $$x^2 + 2xy + y^2 = 0$$
    $$(2a + b)^2 = 0 \rightarrow (2a)^2 + 2(2a)(b) + (b)^2 = 0$$
    $$4a^2 + 4ab + b^2 = 0$$

    The math is a match to the original form, so the correct answer is indeed $(2a + b)^2 = 0$.

12. **$(x + 11y)^2 = 0$**

    Again, the first and third terms are perfect squares. The two square roots are x and $11y$, so test whether $(x + 11y)^2$ is the correct factored form.

    $$x^2 + 2xy + y^2 = 0$$
    $$(x + 11y)^2 = 0 \rightarrow (x)^2 + 2(x)(11y) + (11y)^2 = 0$$
    $$x^2 + 22xy + 121y^2 = 0$$

    The math is a match to the original form, so the correct answer is indeed $(x + 11y)^2 = 0$.

13. **$x = -1$**

    First, factor the numerator. You'll have two terms each with an x in them: $(x + ?)(x + ?)$. The unknowns could be either -1 and 2 or 1 and -2 (because they must multiply to -2). Only 1 and -2 add to the coefficient of the middle term, -1, so the factored form must be $(x + 1)(x - 2)$.

    If $x = 2$, however, then the denominator would be 0, so discard this solution. Thus, $x = -1$.

Problem Set

> Solve the following problems. Distribute and factor when needed.

1. If -4 is a solution for x in the equation $x^2 + kx + 8 = 0$, what is k?

2. If 8 and -4 are the solutions for x, which of the following could be the equation?

    (A) $x^2 - 4x - 32 = 0$

    (B) $x^2 - 4x + 32 = 0$

    (C) $x^2 + 4x - 12 = 0$

    (D) $x^2 + 4x + 32 = 0$

    (E) $x^2 + 4x + 12 = 0$

3. If $16 - y^2 = 10(4 + y)$, what are the possible values of y?

4. If $x^2 - 13x = 30$, what is x?

5. Hugo lies on top of a building, throwing pennies straight down to the street below. The formula for the height in meters, H, that a penny falls is $H = Vt + 5t^2$, where V is the original velocity of the penny (how fast Hugo throws it as it leaves his hand in meters per second) and t is equal to the time it takes to hit the ground in seconds. The building is 60 meters high, and Hugo throws the penny down at an initial speed of 20 meters per second. How long does it take for the penny to hit the ground?

6. If $f(x) = 2x^2 - 4$ and $g(x) = 2x$, for what values of x will $f(x) = g(x)$?

7. $(3 - \sqrt{7})(3 + \sqrt{7}) = ?$

8. If $x^2 - 6x - 27 = 0$ and $y^2 - 6y - 40 = 0$, what is the maximum value of $x + y$?

9. If $x^2 - 10x + 25 = 16$, what is x?

10.
$$x^2 - 2x - 15 = 0$$

Quantity A	Quantity B
x	1

Unit Three: **Factors**

11.
$$x^2 - 12x + 36 = 0$$

Quantity A	**Quantity B**
x	6

12.
$$0 < x < 1$$

Quantity A	**Quantity B**
$(x^3 - x)(4x + 3)$	$(x^2 + 1)(4x^2 + 3x)$

13.
$$x^2 + x - 42 = 0$$

Quantity A	**Quantity B**
$|x + 1|$	5

14.
$$xy > 0$$

Quantity A	**Quantity B**
$(x + y)^2$	$(x - y)^2$

Solutions

1. **6**

   If -4 is a solution, then $(x + 4)$ must be one of the factors of the quadratic equation. The other factor is $(x + ?)$. The problem indicates that the product of 4 and ? must be equal to 8; thus, the other factor is $(x + 2)$. The sum of 4 and 2 must be equal to k.
   Therefore, $k = 6$.

2. **(A) $x^2 - 4x - 32 = 0$**

   If the solutions to the equation are 8 and -4, the factored form of the equation is $(x - 8)(x + 4) = 0$.

   Distributed, this equals $x^2 - 4x - 32 = 0$.

3. **$y = -4$ or -6**

   Simplify and factor to solve.

   $$16 - y^2 = 10(4 + y)$$
   $$16 - y^2 = 40 + 10y$$
   $$y^2 + 10y + 24 = 0$$
   $$(y + 4)(y + 6) = 0$$
   $$y + 4 = 0 \quad \text{or} \quad y + 6 = 0$$
   $$y = -4 \qquad\qquad y = -6$$

   It is possible to factor the left side of the equation first: $16 - y^2 = (4 + y)(4 - y)$. However, this is likely to lead to a dead end, since your goal is to get all the terms on one side with 0 on the other. A tempting but incorrect move would be to divide both sides of the equation by $(4 + y)$. You cannot do this, because it is possible that $(4 + y)$ equals 0 (and, in fact, for one solution of the equation, it does). Because you can't divide by 0, this would be an invalid move, and you would have cut out a potential value of y. Don't divide by any unknown (a variable or an expression) unless you know it isn't equal to 0.

4. **$x = -2$ or 15**

   $$x^2 - 13x = 30$$
   $$x^2 - 13x - 30 = 0$$
   $$(x + 2)(x - 15) = 0$$
   $$x + 2 = 0 \quad \text{or} \quad x - 15 = 0$$
   $$x = -2 \quad \text{or} \quad x = 15$$

Unit Three: **Factors**

5. **2**

    To find the time, plug the known values into the given equation and solve for the possible values of *t*. You know how far the penny falls to hit the ground, and you know the initial velocity of the penny, so you end up with a quadratic equation with *t* as the only variable.

    $$H = Vt + 5t^2$$

    $$60 = 20t + 5t^2$$

    $$5t^2 + 20t - 60 = 0$$

    $$5(t^2 + 4t - 12) = 0$$

    $$5(t + 6)(t - 2) = 0$$

    $$(t + 6)(t - 2) = 0$$

    Finally, solve for the two possible values of *t*.

    $$t + 6 = 0 \quad \text{or} \quad t - 2 = 0$$

    $$t = -6 \quad \text{or} \quad t = 2$$

    But wait! Since this was a quadratic equation, you ended up with two possible values for *t* when the question only asked for one. Can the penny really have taken two different amounts of time to land at the same speed? No. One of the values is negative, so you can throw that one out. This happens fairly often with questions about real-world situations. You'll get a possible negative value for something that can't be negative, such as time, distance, units sold, etc., and you can just throw it out.

6. ***x*** = **{−1, 2}**

    To find the values for which $f(x) = g(x)$, set the functions equal to each other.

    $$2x^2 - 4 = 2x$$

    $$2x^2 - 2x - 4 = 0$$

    $$x^2 - x - 2 = 0$$

    $$(x - 2)(x + 1) = 0$$

    $$x - 2 = 0 \quad \text{or} \quad x + 1 = 0$$

    $$x = 2 \quad \text{or} \quad x = -1$$

Chapter 12: **Quadratic Equations**

7. **2**

   The most efficient solution is to recognize this as the first of the three common special products: $x^2 - y^2 = (x + y)(x - y)$.

   $$(3 - \sqrt{7})(3 + \sqrt{7}) = 3^2 - (\sqrt{7})^2 = 9 - 7 = 2$$

   Alternatively, you can use FOIL to simplify this product:

   F: $3 \times 3 = 9$

   O: $3 \times \sqrt{7} = 3\sqrt{7}$

   I: $-\sqrt{7} \times 3 = -3\sqrt{7}$

   L: $-\sqrt{7} \times \sqrt{7} = -7$

   $9 + 3\sqrt{7} - 3\sqrt{7} - 7 = 2$

8. **19**

   Factor both quadratic equations. Then use the greatest possible values of x and y to find the maximum value of the sum $x + y$.

   $$x^2 - 6x - 27 = 0 \qquad\qquad y^2 - 6y - 40 = 0$$
   $$(x + 3)(x - 9) = 0 \qquad\qquad (y + 4)(y - 10) = 0$$

   $x + 3 = 0$ or $x - 9 = 0$ $y + 4 = 0$ or $y - 10 = 0$

   $x = -3$ or $x = 9$ $y = -4$ or $y = 10$

   The maximum possible value of $x + y = 9 + 10 = 19$.

9. **$x = 1$ or 9**

   $$x^2 - 10x + 25 = 16$$
   $$x^2 - 10x + 9 = 0$$
   $$(x - 9)(x - 1) = 0$$

   $x - 9 = 0$ or $x - 1 = 0$

   $x = 9$ or $x = 1$

Unit Three: **Factors**

10. **(D)**

    First, factor the given equation.

    $x^2 - 2x - 15 = 0 \rightarrow (x - 5)(x + 3) = 0$

    $x = 5$ or $x = -3$

    $$x^2 - 2x - 15 = 0$$

Quantity A	Quantity B
$x = 5$ or -3	1

    The value of x could be greater than or less than 1.

    The correct answer is (D): The relationship cannot be determined.

11. **(C)**

    First, factor the given equation.

    $x^2 - 12x + 36 = 0 \rightarrow (x - 6)(x - 6) = 0$

    $x = 6$

    $$x^2 - 12x + 36 = 0$$

Quantity A	Quantity B
$x = 6$	6

    The correct answer is (C): The two quantities are equal.

12. **(B)**

    Notice that in each of the quantities, you can factor an x out of one of the expressions.

    $$0 < x < 1$$

Quantity A	Quantity B
$(x^3 - x)(4x + 3) =$	$(x^2 + 1)(4x^2 + 3x) =$
$x(x^2 - 1)(4x + 3)$	$(x^2 + 1)(4x + 3)x$

Because x is not 0, you can use the Invisible Inequality to divide away the common terms (x and $(4x + 3)$) from both quantities.

$$0 < x < 1$$

Quantity A	**Quantity B**
$x(x^2 - 1)(4x + 3) =$	$(x^2 + 1)(4x + 3)x =$
$x^2 - 1$	$x^2 + 1$

Now the comparison is less complicated. Because x^2 will always be positive, $(x^2 + 1)$ will always be greater than $(x^2 - 1)$.

The correct answer is (B): Quantity B is greater.

13. **(A)**

Because you're presented with a quadratic equation, you can expect two possible values for x, but that does not mean the answer will be (D). To make sure you get the right answer, solve for both values of x and plug them BOTH into the quantities.

$$x^2 + x - 42 = 0$$

$$(x + 7)(x - 6) = 0$$

$$x = -7 \text{ or } 6$$

Now the problem reads.

$$x = -7 \text{ or } 6$$

Quantity A	**Quantity B**
$|x + 1|$	5

If $x = -7$, Quantity A is equal to the absolute value of -6, which is 6.

If $x = 6$, Quantity A is equal to the absolute value of 7, which is 7.

In either case, the correct answer is (A): Quantity A is greater.

Unit Three: **Factors**

14. **(A)**
Expand the expressions in both columns.

$$xy > 0$$

Quantity A	**Quantity B**
$(x + y)^2 =$	$(x - y)^2 =$
$x^2 + 2xy + y^2$	$x^2 - 2xy + y^2$

Now subtract $x^2 + y^2$ from both columns.

$$xy > 0$$

Quantity A	**Quantity B**
$x^2 + 2xy + y^2$	$x^2 - 2xy + y^2$
$-(x^2 \;\;\;+\;\;\; y^2)$	$-(x^2 \;\;\;+\;\;\; y^2)$
$2xy$	$-2xy$

Because *xy* is positive, Quantity A will be positive, regardless of the values of *x* and *y*. Similarly, Quantity B will always be negative, regardless of the values of *x* and *y*.

The correct answer is (A): Quantity A is greater.

CHAPTER 13
QC Gameplan: Compare

In This Chapter:

- Compare, Don't Compute
- Problem Set
- Solutions

CHAPTER 13 QC Gameplan: Compare

Quantitative Comparison questions never require you to provide a numeric answer. You just need to be able to say whether a certain relationship exists between the two quantities.

In this chapter, you will learn an important strategy for avoiding unnecessary computations on QC: Compare, don't compute.

Compare, Don't Compute

Comparing with Numbers

How could you compare the quantities in this problem?

Quantity A	Quantity B
6^{20}	$(9^{10})(8^5)$

For this particular problem, the numbers can't be put into the limited GRE calculator. But even when you *can* calculate, there's often a simpler way, deliberately built into the question by the test–writers: Compare, don't compute.

How? There are no variables anywhere in the problem. Both quantities are fixed, constant numbers. There's no wiggle room in the quantities themselves, so the answer can't be (D). One quantity is always greater than the other, or they're always equal.

> **Strategy Tip**
>
> If both Quantities in a QC problem are fixed values, eliminate choice (D).

Now what?

The first step of the Game Plan is to simplify. One way to simplify the two quantities is to *make things match*. That is, rewrite the expressions to try to get the same numbers in the same positions in the two quantities. Even if the expressions look *more complicated* temporarily, you're simplifying the *problem* when you make things match.

More specifically, with exponent expressions, try rewriting them with prime bases. The base in Quantity A, which is 6, contains the same prime factors (2 and 3) as the bases in Quantity B, which are 9 and 8.

| $6 = 2 \times 3$ | $9 = 3 \times 3 = 3^2$ | $8 = 2 \times 2 \times 2 = 2^3$ |

Rewrite the quantities in terms of these bases:

Quantity A
6^{20}
$(2 \times 3)^{20}$
$2^{20} 3^{20}$

Quantity B
$9^{10} 8^5$
$(3^2)^{10} (2^3)^5$
$3^{20} 2^{15}$

Because the bases now match, the quantities are more easily comparable.

At this point, again—compare, don't compute. The 3^{20} is the same on both sides, so cancel it out:

Quantity A
$2^{20} \; \cancel{3^{20}}$

Quantity B
$\cancel{3^{20}} \; 2^{15}$

Now, Quantity A is 2^{20}, whereas Quantity B is 2^{15}. Because 2^{20} is greater than 2^{15}, Quantity A is always greater than Quantity B. The answer is (A).

> **Strategy Tip**
>
> When you encounter exponents in QC problems, make them match, then compare. You can match the bases or the powers. Finding prime bases can be a good place to start.

Try this problem:

Quantity A
$(10^3)(5^3)$

Quantity B
$(14^3)(7^3)$

First, both quantities are fixed real values, so the answer cannot be (D). Next, in this problem, the exponents already match, so compare the bases:

$$10^3 < 14^3$$

$$5^3 < 7^3$$

Since both of the terms in Quantity A are less than the corresponding terms in Quantity B, Quantity B must be greater. The correct answer is (B).

What if the problem is changed just a bit?

Quantity A	Quantity B
$(10^3)(7^3)$	$(14^3)(5^3)$

Again, the answer cannot be (D). In addition, this time, the comparison isn't as useful:

$$10^3 < 14^3$$

$$7^3 > 5^3$$

In the first comparison, Quantity B is greater, but in the second comparison, Quantity A is greater. It's tough to figure out which one will be the greater quantity overall.

Instead, break down any bases that are not already prime to their prime factors: $10 = 2 \times 5$ and $14 = 2 \times 7$. Rewrite the two quantities and distribute the exponent:

Quantity A	Quantity B
$10^3 7^3$	$14^3 5^3$
$(2 \times 5)^3 7^3$	$(2 \times 7)^3 5^3$
$2^3 5^3 7^3$	$2^3 7^3 5^3$

The two quantities are now identical, so the correct answer is (C).

There is another way to compare the two original quantities. Because the exponents are the same, you can group the bases:

Quantity A	Quantity B
$10^3 7^3$	$14^3 5^3$
$(10 \times 7)^3$	$(14 \times 5)^3$
70^3	70^3

As before, the two quantities are equal, so the correct answer is (C).

Unit Three: **Factors**

Comparing with Variables

If you know the relative values of variables, you can also compare rather than compute. For example:

$$x = -y$$
$$xy \neq 0$$

Quantity A	**Quantity B**
$\dfrac{5.5x^2}{5}$	$\dfrac{3y^2}{2.5}$

You could simplify this using the Hidden Inequality, but first consider whether you can make the two quantities match. Both are fractions, but neither the numerators nor denominators are the same. Create a common denominator by multiplying the second fraction by $\dfrac{2}{2}$:

$$x = -y$$
$$xy \neq 0$$

Quantity A	**Quantity B**
$\dfrac{5.5x^2}{5}$	$\dfrac{3y^2}{2.5}$
	$\dfrac{3y^2}{2.5}\left(\dfrac{2}{2}\right)$
	$\dfrac{6y^2}{5}$

The quantities are much more similar now, but one has an x, while the other has a y. Use the given information to relate the variables. Since $x = -y$, substitute $-y$ for x and compare:

$$x = -y$$
$$xy \neq 0$$

Quantity A	**Quantity B**
$\dfrac{5.5x^2}{5}$	$\dfrac{3y^2}{2.5}$
$\dfrac{5.5(-y)^2}{5}$	$\dfrac{3y^2}{2.5}\left(\dfrac{2}{2}\right)$
$\dfrac{5.5y^2}{5}$	$\dfrac{6y^2}{5}$

The 5 and the y^2 are the same, so all that's left to compare is 5.5 and 6. Since 6 is greater than 5.5, the answer is (B): Quantity B is greater.

Try this problem:

$$x + y < 0$$

Quantity A	Quantity B
x	$-y$

The given information that $x + y < 0$ indicates that at least one of the variables, and maybe both, are negative. (Why? Because two positive numbers cannot add up to a negative value.)

Try to rearrange the given information so that it matches the form of the variables given in the two quantities:

$$\begin{array}{rcl} x + y & < & 0 \\ -y & & -y \\ x & < & -y \end{array}$$

The given indicates directly that x is less than $-y$. Therefore, the correct answer is (B): Quantity B is greater.

Comparing with Concepts

Comparing rather than computing quantities can be particularly helpful when number properties are tested. A problem testing positives and negatives, for example, is often ideal for comparisons. If you can determine that one quantity is negative while the other is positive, you can be confident that the positive one is greater without ever needing to compute the exact numbers.

For example:

Quantity A	Quantity B
$(-a)(-a)(a)(a)$	-1

In this problem, Quantity B is negative, but Quantity A is more ambiguous. Before picking numbers, try to determine whether you can tell anything about the sign of Quantity A:

$$\underbrace{(-a)\quad(-a)}_{\text{same sign}} \quad \underbrace{a \quad a}_{\text{same sign}}$$

First, if a is 0, then Quantity A will be 0, which is greater than -1. Eliminate answers (B) and (C).

Next, if a isn't 0, then the two $-a$ terms will multiply to a positive value because they have the same sign. Likewise, the two a terms will multiply to a positive value because they have the same sign. (This is true even if a is negative—for example, if $a = -1$. Try it!)

Unit Three: Factors

Therefore, the overall product in Quantity A will be positive. Since Quantity A is either positive or 0, while Quantity B is always negative, the correct answer is (A): Quantity A is greater.

When you see signs that a problem may be testing the concept of positive and negative, think about how you might be able to benchmark the quantities around 0—that is, use negative, 0, and positive to compare the two quantities. It's always the case that a positive number is greater than 0 or a negative number, and it's always the case that 0 is greater than a negative number.

Here's another way in which a problem might test positive and negative characteristics:

n is a positive integer.

Quantity A	**Quantity B**
$(-3)^{2n}$	$(-3)^{2n+1}$

Even exponents hide the sign of the base: Anything raised to an even exponent will result in a positive number. Odd exponents, on the other hand, will not change the original sign of the base.

In this problem, the bases are negative. When negative numbers are raised to a power, they follow a pattern:

- Negative numbers raised to odd powers are negative.
- Negative numbers raised to even powers are positive.

As soon as you see that a QC has given you negative bases raised to a power, examine whether the problem might be testing positives and negatives.

Next, the exponents in this particular problem are $2n$ and $2n + 1$, where n is an integer. The term $2n$, where n is an integer, is common GRE code for an even number. And when you add 1 to an even integer, what happens? It becomes an odd integer.

Reframe the quantities to compare them:

n is a positive integer.

Quantity A	**Quantity B**
$(\text{Negative})^{\text{Even}} = \text{Positive}$	$(\text{Negative})^{\text{Odd}} = \text{Negative}$

Therefore, the correct answer is (A): Quantity A is greater.

> **Strategy Tips:**
>
> Be on the lookout for these clues that you can benchmark around 0:
>
> 1. The given information states that a variable is greater than or less than 0 (e.g., $x > 0$, $p < 0$).
> 2. The given information states that the product of two variables is greater than or less than 0 (e.g., $xy < 0$).
> 3. An expression contains a negative base raised to an exponent (e.g., $(-2)^x$).

You can also benchmark around 1. If you can determine that one quantity is greater than 1, while the other one is less than 1, you can solve the problem. (In fact, you can benchmark around any number, but 0 and 1 are the most useful on the GRE.)

Benchmarking around 1 comes up most frequently in fraction problems. For example:

Quantity A	Quantity B
$\dfrac{1}{\frac{1}{2} + \frac{1}{4} + \frac{1}{8}}$	$\dfrac{1}{2} + \dfrac{1}{4} + \dfrac{1}{8}$

This problem looks like it would take a lot of time to compute, so look to compare instead. Both quantities are greater than 0. How does each one relate to 1?

Quantity B, $\frac{1}{2} + \frac{1}{4} + \frac{1}{8}$, is less than $\frac{1}{2} + \left(\frac{1}{4} + \frac{1}{4}\right)$, and so it must be less than 1.

The numerator in Quantity A is 1 and the denominator is less than 1. When 1 is divided by a positive fraction less than 1, the resulting value is always greater than 1.

So Quantity A must be greater than 1.

Quantity A	Quantity B
$\dfrac{1}{<1}$ = a number > 1	a number < 1

Therefore, the correct answer is (A): Quantity A is greater.

In this problem, you can determine the correct answer solely by making the distinction that Quantity B is less than 1, while Quantity A is greater than 1. Whenever you can identify these kinds of distinctions, you can save time and energy spent performing long calculations. Whenever possible: *Compare, don't calculate.*

By the way, if you're not sure why 1 divided by a fraction between 0 and 1 will end up being greater than 1, try dividing 1 by $\frac{1}{2}$ to see what happens:

$$1 \div \frac{1}{2} = 1 \times 2 = 2$$

Dividing by $\frac{1}{2}$ is the same as multiplying by the reciprocal, 2.

Try one last example:

Quantity A	Quantity B
$\frac{1}{4} - \frac{1}{5} + \frac{1}{6} - \frac{1}{7} + \frac{1}{8}$	$\frac{1}{4}$

Don't do that annoying math! How can you compare, rather than calculate?

The first fraction in Quantity A is $\frac{1}{4}$, which is the same as the fraction in Quantity B. Can you compare Quantity A to $\frac{1}{4}$?

Quantity A starts with $\frac{1}{4}$, and then adds or subtracts various other fractions. Your goal is to figure out whether those other fractions will end up increasing or decreasing the starting value of $\frac{1}{4}$.

First, you need to subtract $\frac{1}{5}$, but then you add $\frac{1}{6}$. What is the *net* effect of subtracting $\frac{1}{5}$ and adding $\frac{1}{6}$? Since $\frac{1}{5}$ is greater than $\frac{1}{6}$, the net effect is negative. The value will decrease from the starting value of $\frac{1}{4}$.

Similarly, subtracting $\frac{1}{7}$ and adding $\frac{1}{8}$ will also make the value decrease. So the overall value will decrease twice from the starting value of $\frac{1}{4}$. It's not necessary to know the exact value of Quantity A. It's enough to know that it will be less than $\frac{1}{4}$. The correct answer is (B): Quantity B is greater.

The Gameplan, Slightly Bigger

Let's expand the QC Gameplan with two new tactics.

QC Gameplan, Round 3

1. **Simplify** → 2. **Pick Numbers**

- Unpack givens
- Simplify within each column
- Simplify across the Hidden Inequality
- **Compare, don't compute**
- **Make things match**

- Try to prove (D)
- Easy, then weird (ZONEF, number line)
- After 3 cases, look for the pattern, then make a call

Problem Set

1. | Quantity A | Quantity B |
    |---|---|
    | The sum of the consecutive integers from −12 to 13 | 13 |

2. | Quantity A | Quantity B |
    |---|---|
    | $\sqrt{30} \times \sqrt{5}$ | 12 |

Unit Three: **Factors**

Solutions

1. **(C)**

    If you were to write out the integers in Quantity A, you'd have −12 + −11 + −10 ... + −1 + 0 + 1 ... + 10 + 11 + 12 + 13.

    Note that for every negative there is a corresponding positive value. For instance, −12 cancels with 12, −11 cancels with 11, and so on. When all the canceling is through, you're left with 13.

    The correct answer is (C): The two quantities are always equal.

2. **(A)**

    One of the root rules is that when two individual roots are multiplied together, you can carry out that multiplication under a single root sign.

    $$\sqrt{30} \times \sqrt{5} = \sqrt{30 \times 5} = \sqrt{150}$$

    While this can be simplified ($\sqrt{150} = \sqrt{25 \times 6} = 5\sqrt{6}$,) you're actually better off leaving it as is.

Quantity A	**Quantity B**
$\sqrt{30} \times \sqrt{5} = \sqrt{150}$	12

    If you've memorized common square roots, you can compare without any further computation. The square root of 144 equals 12, so the square root of 150 is greater than 12. Alternatively, square both quantities.

Quantity A	**Quantity B**
$(\sqrt{150})^2 = 150$	$(12)^2 = 144$

    The correct answer is (A): Quantity A is greater.

UNIT FOUR

Stories, Percents, Ratios, Stats, and Data

The GRE will require you to interpret and translate complex information in everything from a story problem to a statistics problem to a chart or graph.

In this unit, you'll learn how to translate complex sentences and stories into math, especially with regard to percents and ratios (which are commonly used in stories). You'll also learn how to address questions around statistical topics, including average, median, standard deviation, and normal distributions. Finally, you'll learn how to read and interpret charts, graphs, and other diagrams that can appear on the GRE.

In This Unit:

- Chapter 14: Algebraic Translations
- Chapter 15: Percents
- Chapter 16: Ratios
- Chapter 17: Fractions, Decimals, Percents, and Ratios
- Chapter 18: Statistics
- Chapter 19: Data Interpretation

CHAPTER 14
Algebraic Translations

In This Chapter:

- Common Translations
- Complex GRE Translations
- Common Translations Errors
- Hidden Constraints
- Check Your Skills Answer Key
- Problem Set
- Solutions

CHAPTER 14 Algebraic Translations

While the GRE does sometimes present math questions in equation form, it will more frequently couch the math in words. Part of getting the questions right will involve translating the words into mathematical relationships that you can then solve. In this chapter, you will learn a framework for mathematical translations that you can then apply to a variety of GRE problems.

Common Translations

You've already seen some common translations in Chapter 11: Fractions. Here is a summary of what you've learned so far, along with a few new translations:

English Word(s)	Math Translation	Examples	
is/was/were	equals (=)	x **is** 3	$x = 3$
of	multiply (×)	half **of** 7	$\frac{1}{2} \times 7$
what	unknown (n)	3 times **what** is 6 ?	$3n = 6$
more/greater than	inequality (>)	x **is greater than** 5	$x > 5$
less/fewer than	inequality (<)	x **is less than** 5	$x < 5$
a specific value more than	addition (+)	y is **3 more than** z	$y = z + 3$
a specific value less than	subtraction (−)	y is **3 less than** z	$y = z - 3$

When describing an inequality, the words will directly compare two numbers, variables, or expressions. For example:

x plus 3 **is greater than** y minus 5:	$x + 3 > y - 5$

However, when describing addition or subtraction, there will be a description of *how much* more or less one term is than another. For example:

z **is 5 more than** $2w$:	$z = 2w + 5$

Additionally, when there is subtraction, pay attention to the order in which you translate. For example:

5 is 4 less than 9:	$5 = 9 - 4$

373

Unit Four: **Stories, Percents, Ratios, Stats, and Data**

Even though the 4 comes before the 9 in the sentence, the order is reversed in the math translation: *4 less than 9* becomes *9 minus 4*. When the words describe subtraction, move the subtracted number to the second position.

These translations will allow you to change many English phrases into mathematical ones that can then be manipulated. Try this problem:

> If y is greater than 7 more than one-third of x, which of the following could be true about x when y is 10 ?
>
> Indicate all such statements.
>
> [A] x is positive.
> [B] x is negative.
> [C] x is 12.

This problem, like many others, separates major ideas by commas. Everything before the comma is describing one equation, while everything after the comma is relating to the question itself. When translating, focus on only one major idea at a time. Start by translating the first clause:

y	is greater than	7 more than	one-third	of	x
y	$>$	$7+$	$\frac{1}{3}$	$\times$	x
$y > 7 + \frac{1}{3}x$					

The question asks what *could be true* about x when $y = 10$. Substitute 10 into the inequality to solve for x:

$$y > 7 + \frac{1}{3}x$$
$$10 > 7 + \frac{1}{3}x$$
$$-7 \quad -7$$
$$3 > \frac{1}{3}x$$
$$\times 3 \quad \times 3$$
$$9 > x$$

If y is 10, x is less than 9. As a result, x could be either positive or negative, but x could never be 12. Answers (A) and (B) are correct.

The GRE uses common phrases repeatedly throughout its math problems. Get yourself comfortable with translating these phrases to minimize the amount of concentration you'll need to use just for translation on test day.

Chapter 14: **Algebraic Translations**

Addition

Words	Math
Add, Sum, Total (of parts), More Than:	+
The sum of *x* and *y*:	$x + y$
In 50 years:	*current age* $+ 50$
Six pounds heavier than Dave:	$D + 6$
A group of ants and caterpillars:	$a + c$
The cost is increased by *x*:	$c + x$

Subtraction

Words	Math
Minus, Difference, Less Than:	−
Five less than *x*:	$x - 5$
The difference between Quentin's and Rachel's heights (if Quentin is taller):	$Q - R$
Four pounds less than expected:	$e - 4$
The profit is the revenue minus the cost:	$P = R - C$

Multiplication

Words	Math
The product of *h* and *k*:	$h \times k$
The number of reds times the number of blues:	$r \times b$
One-fifth of *y*:	$\frac{1}{5}y$
n persons have *x* beads each:	total beads $= nx$

Unit Four: **Stories, Percents, Ratios, Stats, and Data**

Ratios and Division

Words	Math
Quotient, Per, Ratio, Proportion:	÷ or /
Five dollars every two weeks:	$\frac{\$5}{2 \text{ wks}} = \$2.5$ per week
The ratio of x to y:	$\frac{x}{y}$ or $x:y$
The proportion of girls to boys:	$\frac{g}{b}$

Complex GRE Translations

When faced with a paragraph of text that must somehow solve to a single number, it's common to lose a sense of where to begin. It's also common to lose sight of what the question is asking. Use a three-step process to address complex translations:

> *Decoding a Tough Translation*
> Step 1: Define knowns and unknowns.
> Step 2: Express relationships.
> Step 3: Identify the goal and solve.

Step 1: Define Knowns and Unknowns

Decode this word problem using the three-step process:

> A steel rod 50 meters long is cut into two pieces. If one piece is 14 meters longer than the other, what is the length, in meters, of the shorter piece?

Start by defining knowns and unknowns. Write the knowns down with labels to keep track of them.

What quantities have you not been given specific values for? Create variables to represent these unknowns. Try to use letters that tell you what they are. For example, if the problem asks about the number of roses and tulips, use r and t as the variables.

Take a moment to identify those unknown quantities in the example problem. Don't worry about how the variables and knowns relate to one another; just label the unknowns.

In this question, both the *length of the shorter piece* and the *length of the longer piece* are unknown, so begin by assigning each of those values a variable. A lot of people were trained to do this in school:

x = length of shorter piece

y = length of longer piece

The danger here is that you may mix up which variable represents the shorter vs. the longer piece—and the GRE is almost certain to take advantage of that by putting both values in the answer choices.

Instead, assign variables that *inherently* indicate what they mean. Rather than using *x* and *y*, use *S* and *L* to indicate the shorter and longer pieces respectively:

$S = ?$

$L = ?$

Now, you can tell at a glance what each variable means—and you don't even have to take the time to write out the label for each one.

One more thing. You may have noticed that these variables are capitalized, while most variables used in this book are lowercase. That's intentional for two reasons. First, whenever using the variable *L*, capitalize it so you won't confuse lowercase *l* with the number 1. Second, these variables have particular meaning in the problem (shorter length and longer length) so separating them from generic *x* and *y* variables by capitalizing them makes it easier to remember that these have a specific meaning.

Only one value is given in this problem: the total length of the steel rod. Add that information to your unknowns:

$S = ?$

$L = ?$

total length $= 50$

And you're done with step 1! This may seem like a minor accomplishment in terms of the entire question, but it was an important one. Often, as soon as you start decoding a problem into math, the path forward becomes more clear.

Here's another way to think about your progress. In essence, you've asked, "What do they want?" and "What do they give me?"—and you've written down your first answers in the form of math.

> *Decoding a Tough Translation: Step 1*
> - List knowns and label them.
> - List unknowns and assign variables that tell you what they are.

Step 2: Express Relationships

Even after you've identified and labeled your variables, you still might not be sure how to continue on a particular problem. When that happens, take a deep breath, then begin examining relationships even though you're not sure yet how they will prove useful.

What distinguishes the higher-performing GRE test-takers in these moments is that they accept this uncertainty and continue forward anyway. Of course, you hope to have a clear vision right from the start, but if you don't, dive in and see what you find anyway. Ironically, it's often the roadblocks you encounter that will point the way.

Your next step is to **identify relationships** given in the problem **and create equations**.

Unit Four: **Stories, Percents, Ratios, Stats, and Data**

Go back to the problem:

> A steel rod 50 meters long is cut into two pieces. If one piece is 14 meters longer than the other, what is the length, in meters, of the shorter piece?

Look at *one piece of information at a time* and then translate that information into an equation. Try it first on your own, then read on.

> *A steel rod 50 meters long is cut into two pieces.*

The relationship expressed here is one of the two most common types of relationships found in word problems. The original length of the rod was 50 meters, and it was cut into 2 pieces. Therefore, the length of the shorter piece plus the length of the longer piece must equal 50 meters.

Use your defined variables to express this mathematically:

$S = ?$

$L = ?$

total length $= 50$

$S + L = 50$

Think of this as **Parts Add to a Sum**. When each piece is added together, it produces a given total.

Move on to the next part of the problem:

> *If one piece is 14 meters longer than the other...*

The relationship expressed here is another common type found in word problems. The longer piece of metal is 14 meters longer than the shorter piece of metal. So, if you were to add 14 meters to the *shorter* piece, it would be the same length as the *longer* piece.

This relationship is **One Part Can Be Made Equal to the Other**. Either the question will say that two values are equal, or it will tell you *how they differ*. This question told you how they were different, so your equation shows how you could make them equal: One Part + The Difference = The Other Part.

$S = ?$

$L = ?$

total length $= 50$

$S + L = 50$

$S + 14 = L$

By the way, when constructing equations in which you are making one part equal to the other, it can be very easy to express the relationship backwards. If you mistakenly wrote down $S = L + 14$, you're not alone. If you find yourself making this kind of error, get into the habit of verifying your equation with **hypothetical numbers**.

To verify, start by imagining that the shorter piece of metal is 20 meters long. If the shorter piece were 20 meters long, then the longer piece would have to be 34 meters long. Now plug those numbers into your (mistranslated) equation: $S = L + 14$. Does $20 = 14 + 34$? No!

Chapter 14: **Algebraic Translations**

So, the equation is backwards. Correct it, then check the equation again. If $S + 14 = L$, is it the case that $20 + 14 = 34$? Yes, so this equation is correct.

By the way, it doesn't matter that these made up numbers (20 and 34) aren't the correct numbers for the full problem (since they don't add up to 50). The goal here is not to guess the perfect numbers, but just to make sure that this one part of the problem—the equation $S + 14 = L$—is correct.

> *Decoding a Tough Translation: Step 2*
> - Identify relationships and express them as equations.
> - Verify relationships by plugging in hypothetical numbers to see whether the equations act as expected.
> - Watch for commonly used relationships, such as:
>
> | | |
> |---|---|
> | **Parts Add to a Sum** | One Part + The Other Part = The Total |
> | **One Part Can Be Made Equal to the Other** | The Shorter/Lesser Part + The Difference = The Longer/Greater Part |

Step 3: Identify the Goal and Solve

Finally, move on to the last part of the question to **identify the goal**:

   …what is the length, in meters, of the shorter piece?

This part of the question doesn't describe a relationship that you can use to create an equation, but it does tell you something quite useful: It tells you *what you're solving for!* Clearly denote this on your scratch paper:

$L = ?$

total length $= 50$

$S + L = 50$

$S + 14 = L$

You could put a circle or box around the S, or rewrite it again at the bottom, or put a couple of asterisks on either side. Denote it however you like, but use the same notation every single time. Make it easy for your eyes to see, every time you look at your scratch paper, that the value of S is your ultimate goal (on this problem!).

Try to solve this problem, then review the algebra below.

379

Unit Four: **Stories, Percents, Ratios, Stats, and Data**

Solve for S:

$$S + L = 50$$
$$S + 14 = L \quad \text{Use substitution to eliminate } L$$
$$S + (S + 14) = 50 \quad \text{Combine like terms}$$
$$2S + 14 = 50$$
$$2S = 36 \quad \text{Isolate } S$$
$$S = 18$$

The shorter piece is 18 meters long. Don't solve for the length of the longer piece—the question didn't ask for that. If you do solve for the length of the longer piece, you'll take more time than needed and you risk falling into the trap of accidentally selecting that unasked-for value among the answer choices.

> *Decoding a Tough Translation: Step 3*
> Identify the goal and solve.

If you want to review any of the algebra used to solve that problem, revisit Chapter 7: Systems of Equations. If you're comfortable with everything so far, then you're ready for a tougher problem.

Putting it All Together

Use the three-step process to solve this problem:

> Mirai is 13 years older than Brune. In 8 years, Mirai will be twice as old as Brune. How old is Mirai now?

» **STEP 1**

Define knowns and unknowns.

Use M and B to represent each person's current age:

$$M = ?$$
$$B = ?$$

There are no discrete ages given. The numbers 13 and 8 express relationships, so don't need to be noted in this step.

» **STEP 2**

Express relationships.

Start with the first sentence: Mirai is 13 years older than Brune. Translate:

$$M = B + 13$$

Logic check: Who is older, Mirai or Brune? Since Mirai is older, add the 13 years to Brune's age in order to make the two sides of the equation equal.

Now turn to the second sentence: In 8 years, Mirai will be twice as old as Brune. This piece is more challenging to translate. The variables M and B represent their ages now, but this statement is talking about their ages 8 years from now. As a result, you can't just write $M = 2B$. Instead, express their ages in 8 years:

$M + 8 =$ Mirai's age 8 years from now

$B + 8 =$ Brune's age 8 years from now

Use those representations to translate the second sentence:

$$(M + 8) = 2(B + 8)$$

Logic check again. Who will be older in 8 years? Still Mirai. So Brune's age in 8 years has to be multiplied by 2 in order to equal Mirai's age in 8 years.

» STEP 3

Identify the goal and solve.
Finally, circle or otherwise denote what the question asks you to find:

$$\boxed{M = ?}$$
$$B = ?$$

$$M = B + 13$$
$$(M + 8) = 2(B + 8)$$

Now, examine what you have. The second equation can be significantly simplified:

$$(M + 8) = 2(B + 8)$$
$$M + 8 = 2B + 16$$
$$M = 2B + 8$$

The unwanted variable is B, so rearrange the first equation to isolate that variable: $B = M - 13$. Then substitute into the other equation:

$$M = 2B + 8$$
$$M = 2(M - 13) + 8$$
$$M = 2M - 26 + 8$$
$$M = 2M - 18$$
$$18 = M$$

Mirai is 18 years old. If you're confident in all the previous steps, select your answer and move to the next problem. But if you're not sure of your work, use the answer to check the story.

Mirai is 13 years older than Brune, so Brune must be $18 - 13 = 5$ years old. In 8 years, Mirai will be $18 + 8 = 26$ and Brune will be $5 + 8 = 13$. And in 8 years, Mirai will be twice as old as Brune. Is that the case? Yes, in 8 years, Mirai will be 26 and Brune will be half that age, or 13. So, it is the case that Mirai is 18 years old now.

Unit Four: **Stories, Percents, Ratios, Stats, and Data**

This problem illustrates another common pattern in GRE word problems. When dealing with ages, the passage of time affects everyone. When you define M as Mirai's age, it is critical to call it *Mirai's age now*. The variable M should represent only one number—Mirai's age at one point in time. The same is true for Brune's age.

When defining relationships at times other than now, specifically write out what the ages will be at that time. For example, in four years, Mirai will be $M + 4$ and Brune will be $B + 4$.

> **Strategy Tip**
> Look for commonly used relationships, such as:
>
> | | |
> |---|---|
> | **Parts Add to a Sum** | One Part + The Other Part = The Total |
> | **One Part Can Be Made Equal to the Other** | The Shorter/Lesser Part + The Difference = The Longer/Greater Part |
> | **Ages at Different Times** | Age Now + Time Difference = Future Age |
> | | Age Now − Time Difference = Past Age |

As you use each step of the process, keep an eye on certain details.

Step 1: Define knowns and unknowns.

- Use variables that tell you what they mean (e.g., shorter piece = S).
- Be *very specific* when dealing with questions that contain two distinct but related situations (e.g., Mirai's age *now* = M versus Mirai's age in 8 years = $M + 8$).

Step 2: Express relationships.

- Look at one piece of the question at a time. Don't try to do everything at once.
- Ask "What do they give me? What do they want?" Keep asking yourself these questions until you're sure you've extracted everything from the words you're given.
- Use logic or numbers to check that you have set up your equation correctly. For example, if it says that Mirai is twice as old as Brune, which is correct: $M = 2B$ or $2M = B$? If Mirai were 40, Brune would be 20. Is it the case that $40 = 2(20)$ or $2(40) = 20$?

Step 3: Identify the goal and solve.

- Circle or denote clearly what the problem asks you to find.
- Simplify your equations before you combine them.
- Combine your equations to solve.

Common Translation Errors

One of the most frustrating feelings on the GRE is working through a word problem, doing all the math correctly, yet getting the answer wrong because you fell for a common translation error. This section goes through many common errors as well as the habits you can develop to minimize the chances of falling into these traps.

Chapter 14: **Algebraic Translations**

1. **To avoid writing a relationship backwards, check the equation you create using real numbers and/or logical reasoning.**

If You See…	Think:	Write:	Verify:
"*A* is half the size of *B*."	*A* is smaller. If *A* were 4, *B* would be 8.	$A = \frac{1}{2}B$	$4 = \frac{1}{2} \times 8$
"*A* is 5 less than *B*."	*A* is smaller. If *A* were 4, *B* would be 9.	$A = B - 5$	$4 = 9 - 5$
"*A* is less than *B*."	*A* is smaller. *A* could be 4, while *B* is 10.	$A < B$	$4 < 10$
"Jane bought twice as many apples as bananas."	Jane bought more apples. If she bought 10 apples, she bought 5 bananas.	$A = 2B$	$10 = 2 \times 5$

2. **To avoid applying relationships to terms that don't use that relationship, distinguish between terms that are being treated differently.**

   Sometimes, the math changes as the total number changes. For example, a problem may describe the cost of a shirt as $10 for the first two shirts, then $7 for every additional shirt. While it's true that everything the problem describes is the cost of a shirt, it's treating different quantities differently. Separate the first two shirts from the remaining shirts:

   $s =$ total number of shirts

   number of $10 shirts $= 2$

   number of $7 shirts $= s - 2$

   Making this distinction allows you to create individual equations:

   cost of first two shirts: $\$10 \times 2 = \$20$

   cost of remaining shirts: $\$7(s - 2) = \$7s - \$14$

   total cost of shirts: $\$20 + \$7s - \$14 = \$6 + \$7s$

3. **To maintain valid fractional relationships, distinguish between fractions *of* and fractions *more than*.**

   There is a difference in meaning between a number that is a fractional amount of another value and a number that is a fractional amount *more than* another value. Consider these two examples:

   In the United States, an elementary school teacher will make, on average, $\frac{2}{3}$ of what an MBA graduate will.

   In the United States, an MBA graduate will make, on average, $\frac{1}{2}$ more than an elementary school teacher.

   These examples describe the exact same relationship, but in different ways. The first one expresses that the average salary for one profession is $\frac{2}{3}$ **of** the other:

Unit Four: **Stories, Percents, Ratios, Stats, and Data**

$$E = \frac{2}{3} \times M$$

If the average MBA salary is $90,000, then the average elementary school teacher salary is $\frac{2}{3}$ of that, or $60,000.

The second example is written differently: M makes $\frac{1}{2}$ **more than** E. That is, M makes what E makes *plus* M makes $\frac{1}{2}$ more. That extra amount is half of what the elementary school teacher would make as a total.

$$M = E + \frac{1}{2}E$$
$$M = \frac{3}{2}E$$

If the average elementary school teacher salary is $60,000, then the average MBA salary is all of that plus half of $60,000—it's $60,000 + $30,000 = $90,000.

If you take the second equation, $M = \frac{3}{2}E$, and move the fraction to the other side, you'll get the first equation: $E = \frac{2}{3}M$. The two equations are identical; they're just written differently.

Check Your Skills

> Translate the following statements.

1. Lior is two years older than Melissa.

2. A small pizza costs $5 less than a large pizza.

3. Twice *A* is 5 more than *B*.

4. Jean has more than twice as many CDs as Kim.

Answers can be found on page 387.

Hidden Constraints

In some problems, there is a **hidden constraint** on the possible quantities. For example, Jane buys a certain number of apples and bananas. Because each fruit is a physical, countable object, Jane has a whole number of each type and that number is positive. So Jane can have 1 apple, 2 apples, 3 apples, and so on, and even 0 apples, but Jane cannot have 1.3 apples or −2 apples.

As a result of this implied whole number constraint, you often have more information than is apparent at first. For example:

> If Kanan received $\frac{1}{3}$ more votes than Micah in a student election, which of the following could have been the total number of votes cast for the two candidates?
>
> (A) 12
> (B) 13
> (C) 14
> (D) 15
> (E) 16

Let K be the number of votes cast for Kanan and M be the number cast for Micah. Kanan received however many votes Micah did, plus $\frac{1}{3}$ more:

$$K = M + \frac{1}{3}M$$
$$K = \frac{4}{3}M$$

Let T be the total number of votes. The question asks what *could* have been the total number cast for these two candidates:

$$T = K + M = ?$$

Substitute the first equation into the second one:

$$T = K + M$$
$$T = \frac{4}{3}M + M$$
$$T = \frac{7}{3}M$$

There is only one equation with two variables, so it isn't possible to solve for one definitive number of votes. The wording of the question signaled this when it asked what *could* be the number of votes. So what now?

The hidden constraint comes into play. Because M and T both represent a number of votes, they must be integers. Therefore, M must be a number that will cancel out the 3 in the denominator of $\frac{7}{3}M$. For example, it's possible for M to be 3 or 6, but not 4 or 5, because 4 or 5 would result in a non-integer number of total votes.

Just as M must be a multiple of 3 to make T an integer, so must T be a multiple of 7 to make M an integer. There are two ways to think of this.

$$T = \frac{7}{3}M$$
$$T = 7\left(\frac{M}{3}\right)$$
$$T = 7(\text{integer})$$

Since M is divisible by 3, it must be the case that $\frac{M}{3}$ is an integer. So, T is equal to 7 times some integer. Therefore, T is a multiple of 7.

385

Unit Four: **Stories, Percents, Ratios, Stats, and Data**

Alternatively, switch around the initial equation:

$$\text{If } T = \frac{7}{3}M, \text{ then } M = \frac{3}{7}T.$$

Just as M must be divisible by 3 in order to make T an integer, T must be divisible by 7 in order to make M an integer. So, the total number of votes could be any multiple of 7. Take a look at the answer choices:

(A) 12
(B) 13
(C) 14
(D) 15
(E) 16

The only multiple of 7 among the answers is 14, so the correct answer is (C).

You could also pick numbers on this problem. Based on the answer choices, the total number of votes is not that great. Since M must be a multiple of 3, pick a few small multiples of 3 to find some possible total values:

M	$K = \frac{4}{3}M$	$T = M + K$
3	4	7
6	8	14

The first case returns a vote total of 7, but that isn't in the answers. The second case returns a total of 14, which matches answer (C).

Not every unknown value related to "real-world" objects is restricted to whole numbers. Physical measurements such as weights, times, or speeds have to be positive numbers, but they do not have to be integers. Some physical measurements can even be negative (e.g., temperatures). Think about what is being measured or counted, and you will recognize whether a hidden constraint applies.

Check Your Skills

5. In a certain garden, the number of roses is $\frac{1}{4}$ more than the number of daffodils. Which of the following is a possibility for the total number of roses and daffodils in the garden?

    (A) 8
    (B) 9
    (C) 10
    (D) 11
    (E) 12

Answers can be found on page 387.

Chapter 14: **Algebraic Translations**

Check Your Skills Answer Key

1. $L = M + 2$
   Lior is older, so add 2 to Melissa.

2. $S = L - 5$
   The small pizza costs less, so subtract the $5 from the large pizza.

3. $2A = B + 5$
   If you double A, that value will be 5 more than B. For example, if $A = 10$, then twice A is 20. That value, 20, is 5 more than B, so B must be 15. Check those values in the equation:

   $$2A = B + 5$$
   $$2(10) = 15 + 5$$
   $$20 = 20$$

   The values are a match, so the equation was correctly translated.

4. $J > 2K$
   Jean has more CDs, so multiply Kim's number by 2. Also, since Jean has *more than* twice as many, use an inequality sign.

5. **(B) 9**
   First, define the variables.

   $R =$ # of roses
   $D =$ # of daffodils
   $T =$ total #

   Next, define the relationships. Both R and D must be integers. There are $\frac{1}{4}$ more roses than daffodils.

   $$R = D + \frac{1}{4}D$$
   $$R = \frac{5}{4}D$$

   Additionally, the total can be represented as the sum of the two types of flowers.

   $$T = R + D$$
   $$T = \frac{5}{4}D + D$$
   $$T = \frac{9}{4}D$$

   The goal is to solve for T. The total must be a multiple of 9, because it is equal to 9 times an integer.

   Only answer choice (B) is a multiple of 9, so it is the correct answer.

Unit Four: **Stories, Percents, Ratios, Stats, and Data**

Problem Set

> Solve the following problems using the three-step method outlined in this section.

1. Johan is 20 years older than Brian. Twelve years ago, Johan was twice as old as Brian. How old is Brian?

2. Mrs. Miller has two dogs, Jackie and Stella, who weigh a total of 75 pounds. If Stella weighs 15 pounds less than twice Jackie's weight, how much does Stella weigh?

3. Bo spent $72.50 on 50 hamburgers for the marching band. If single burgers cost $1.00 each and double burgers cost $1.50 each, how many double burgers did he buy?

4. United Telephone charges a base rate of $10.00 for service, plus an additional charge of $0.25 per minute. Atlantic Call charges a base rate of $12.00 for service, plus an additional charge of $0.20 per minute. For what number of minutes would the bills for each telephone company be the same?

5. Carla cuts a 70-inch piece of ribbon into 2 pieces. If the first piece is 5 inches more than one-fourth as long as the second piece, how long is the longer piece of ribbon?

6. Ten years ago, Bilal was twice as old as Aubrey.

Quantity A	Quantity B
Bilal's age today	Twice Aubrey's age today

7. Jaden earns a yearly base salary of $30,000, plus a commission of $500 on every car he sells above his monthly minimum of two cars. Last year, Jaden met or surpassed his minimum sales every month, and earned a total income (salary plus commission) of $60,000.

Quantity A	Quantity B
The number of cars Jaden sold last year	90

Chapter 14: **Algebraic Translations**

8. An eccentric casino owner decides that his casino should only use chips in $5 and $7 denominations. If a casino patron cashes in all of her chips for $48, which of the following could have been her total number of chips?

   Select all answers that apply.

   - [A] 7
   - [B] 8
   - [C] 9

9. Life expectancy is defined by the formula $\frac{2SB}{G}$, where S = shoe size, B = average monthly electric bill in dollars, and G = GRE score. If Melvin's GRE score is twice his monthly electric bill, and his life expectancy is 50, what is his shoe size?

Unit Four: **Stories, Percents, Ratios, Stats, and Data**

Solutions

1. **32 years old**

    Step 1: Define knowns and unknowns.
    b = Brian's age now
    j = Johan's age now

    The difference in their ages is 20 years.

    Step 2: Express relationships.
    Johan is 20 years older than Brian.

    $$j = b + 20$$

    Twelve years ago, Johan was twice as old as Brian.

    $$(j - 12) = 2(b - 12)$$
    $$j - 12 = 2b - 24$$
    $$j = 2b - 12$$

    Step 3: Identify the goal and solve.
    The problem says to solve for b, so combine the two equations by substituting the value for j from the first equation into the second equation to eliminate j and solve for b.

    $$b + 20 = 2b - 12$$
    $$20 = b - 12$$
    $$32 = b$$

2. **45 pounds**

    Step 1: Define knowns and unknowns.
    j = Jackie's weight
    s = Stella's weight

    Total weight of both dogs is 75 pounds.

    Step 2: Express relationships.
    Jackie and Stella, who weigh a total of 75 pounds.

    $$j + s = 75$$

    Stella weighs 15 pounds less than twice Jackie's weight.

    $$s = 2j - 15$$

390

Step 3: Identify the goal and solve.
The problem asks for Stella's weight. Therefore, it makes sense to get a value for j from the first equation and substitute it into the second.

$$j = 75 - s$$
$$s = 2(75 - s) - 15$$
$$s = 150 - 2s - 15$$
$$s = 135 - 2s$$
$$3s = 135$$
$$s = 45$$

As a note, it's likely mathematically simpler to substitute the value of s from the second equation into the first equation, solve for j, and then use j to get the value for s that the problem is asking for. If you choose to solve in this way, make sure that your scratchwork is clear about which value you're ultimately solving for so that you don't fall into a common trap: if the problem has answer choices, the weight of Jackie will almost certainly be among them.

3. **45**

Step 1: Define knowns and unknowns.
s = the number of single burgers purchased
d = the number of double burgers purchased

Bo bought 50 hamburgers in total and spent $72.50
Singles cost $1 each.
Doubles cost $1.50 each.

Step 2: Express relationships.
Bo bought 50 hamburgers.

$$s + d = 50$$

Bo spent $72.50 on hamburgers costing $1 each for singles and $1.50 each for doubles.

$$s + 1.50d = 72.50$$

Step 3: Identify the goal and solve.
The problem is asking for d, the number of double burgers purchased. As in the two previous problems, you can solve this system of equations by substituting a value of s from one equation into the other equation. But it can be solved more directly by elimination:

$$s + 1.5d = 72.5$$
$$-(s + d = 50)$$
$$0.5d = 22.5$$
$$d = 45$$

Unit Four: **Stories, Percents, Ratios, Stats, and Data**

4. **40 minutes**

    Step 1: Define knowns and unknowns.
    m = the number of minutes
    c_u = total cost, UT
    c_a = total cost, AC

    UT charges $10 for service.
    AC charges $12 for service.

    Step 2: Express relationships.
    A call made by United Telephone costs $10.00 plus $0.25 per minute.

    $$c_u = 10 + 0.25m$$

    A call made by Atlantic Call costs $12.00 plus $0.20 per minute.

    $$c_a = 12 + 0.20m$$

    The bills from each telephone company should be the same.

    $$c_u = c_a$$

    Step 3: Identify the goal and solve.
    The question stem asks for the number of minutes that would make both bills the same. Substitute expressions involving m in for both of the costs in the third equation above (and consider using the calculator for the final step).

    $$c_u = c_a$$
    $$10 + 0.25m = 12 + 0.2m$$
    $$0.05m = 2$$
    $$m = \frac{2}{0.05} = 40$$

5. **52 inches**

    Step 1: Define knowns and unknowns.
    f = the first piece of ribbon
    s = the second piece of ribbon

    The total ribbon is 70 inches.

    Step 2: Express relationships.
    Carla cuts a 70-inch piece of ribbon into 2 pieces.

    $$f + s = 70$$

    If the first piece is 5 inches more than one-fourth as long as the second piece.

    $$f = \frac{1}{4}s + 5$$

Chapter 14: **Algebraic Translations**

Step 3: Identify the goal and solve.
The problem asks for the longer piece of ribbon; however, it only provides relationships in terms of a first and second piece of ribbon (rather than a longer and shorter piece of ribbon). While there is good reason to suspect from the second relationship that *f* is the shorter piece of ribbon and *s* is the longer piece, it's safer to solve for both pieces and reread the question before finalizing an answer. As such, you can use substitution or elimination to solve. One option is shown below.

$$4 \times \left(f - \frac{1}{4}s = 5\right)$$
$$4f - s = 20$$
$$+ \quad f + s = 70$$
$$\overline{5f = 90}$$
$$f = 18$$
$$18 + s = 70$$
$$s = 52$$

Reread the question: It asks for the longer piece. Therefore, the answer is 52.

6. **(B)**

Step 1: Define knowns and unknowns.
A = Aubrey's age today
B = Bilal's age today

Step 2: Express relationships.
Ten years ago, Bilal was twice as old as Aubrey.

$$B - 10 = 2(A - 10)$$
$$B - 10 = 2A - 20$$
$$B = 2A - 10$$

Step 3: Identify the goal and solve.
Unlike a Discrete Quant problem, a QC problem won't necessarily require you to solve for unknowns. Therefore, any algebra you do in this problem should serve to make the two quantities easier to compare. As they're written, the two quantities focus on two different variables: Bilal's age today (B) and twice Aubrey's age today ($2A$). Using the relationship given in the problem, however, Quantity A can be rewritten in terms of A:

Ten years ago, Bilal was twice as old as Aubrey.

Quantity A	**Quantity B**
Bilal's age today	Twice Aubrey's age today
$2A - 10$	$2A$

Because $2A - 10$ is less than $2A$ itself, the answer is (B): Quantity B is greater.

Unit Four: **Stories, Percents, Ratios, Stats, and Data**

7. **(B)**
The simplest method for solving a problem like this is to work backward from the value in Quantity B. Suppose Jaden sold exactly 90 cars. Then, because he met or surpassed his two-car minimum each month (which adds up to 24 cars in the entire year), he would have sold another 90 − 24, which equals 66 cars above the minimum.

The commission he earned on those cars is calculated as follows:

$$\$500 \times 66 = \$33{,}000$$

This would put his total yearly income at $30,000 (base salary) + $33,000 (commission), which sums to $63,000. However, you know that Jaden actually earned less than that; therefore, he must have sold fewer than 90 cars.

Quantity A	Quantity B
The number of cars Jaden sold last year = less than 90	90

Therefore, the correct answer is (B): Quantity B is greater.

The alternative approach is, of course, to translate Jaden's total earnings into an algebraic equation and solve.

Step 1: Define knowns and unknowns.
c = cars sold

Jaden earned $60,000.
His base salary was $30,000.

Step 2: Express relationships.
Jaden earned $60,000 last year, comprising a base salary of $30,000 and a commission of $500 for each car above the minimum of 24 cars (2 per month × 12 months).

$$60{,}000 = 30{,}000 + 500(c - 24)$$

Step 3: Identify the goal and solve.
Quantity A asks for the number of cars Jaden sold, which is the variable c in this equation, so solve for c.

$$30{,}000 = 500(c - 24)$$
$$60 = c - 24$$
$$84 = c$$

Quantity A	Quantity B
The number of cars Jaden sold last year = 84	90

Again, the answer is (B): Quantity B is greater.

Chapter 14: **Algebraic Translations**

8. **(B) 8**

   This problem is a grouping problem with a hidden constraint: You have some *integer* number of 5's and some *integer* number of 7's. Therefore, while it can be set up as an algebraic equation, algebra alone is unlikely to be sufficient to solve the problem, as algebra doesn't account well for integer constraints.

   If you define the unknowns as f for the number of $5 chips and s for the number of $7 chips, then the relationship in the problem can be expressed as $5f + 7s = 48$. But unlike many of the problems above, this problem doesn't provide a second relationship between f and s. Functionally, this means you can't get a second equation to use substitution or elimination, leading to an algebraic dead end because as a general rule it takes two equations to solve for two variables.

   Instead, you can leverage the hidden integer constraint by testing numbers. Start with 1 chip of either kind and count up from there to see which combinations of chips work to get $48.

Number of $5 chips ($f$)	Portion of the $48 remaining	Number of $7 chips ($s$) needed
1	$48 − $5 = $43	non-integer
2	$48 − $10 = $38	non-integer
3	$48 − $15 = $33	non-integer
4	$48 − $20 = $28	4
5	$48 − $25 = $23	non-integer
6	$48 − $30 = $18	non-integer
7	$48 − $35 = $13	non-integer
8	$48 − $40 = $8	non-integer
9	$48 − $45 = $3	non-integer

   Notice that the hidden integer constraint rules out almost every possibility for the total number of chips. The only combination that works is $f = 4$ and $s = 4$, a total of 8 chips.

9. **50**

   Like other formula problems, this problem defines the knowns and unknowns for you and then asks you to apply the formula. However, as this particular problem also provides a relationship between two unknowns (rather than providing numbers for all the unknowns), it offers an opportunity to use translation skills.

   Step 2: Express relationships.

   If Melvin's GRE score is twice his monthly electric bill:

   $$G = 2B$$

Unit Four: **Stories, Percents, Ratios, Stats, and Data**

Step 3: Identify the goal and solve.
The goal is to solve for *S*. Since this is a formula problem, plug in everything you know. Life expectancy is 50, so set the entire formula equal to that value. Substitute 2*B* for *G* in the formula. Because the term 2*B* appears in both the numerator and denominator, they cancel out.

$$\frac{2S\cancel{B}}{2\cancel{B}} = 50$$
$$S = 50$$

CHAPTER 15

Percents

In This Chapter:

- Percents as Fractions
- Percents as Word Problems
- Percent Change
- Percent of Original
- Successive Percents
- Pick 100 for Unspecified Amounts
- Check Your Skills Answer Key
- Problem Set
- Solutions

CHAPTER 15 Percents

In addition to decimals and fractions, percents are another way to express a part-whole relationship. In this chapter, you will learn how percents relate to fractions and decimals, and you'll also learn how to solve common percent-related math problems, such as percent change and successive percents.

Percent literally means "per one hundred." You can conceive of percents as a special type of fraction or decimal that involves the number 100. For example:

75% of the students like chocolate ice cream.

Out of every 100 students, 75 like chocolate ice cream. In fraction form, this is written as $\frac{75}{100}$, which simplifies to $\frac{3}{4}$.

In decimal form, this is written as 0.75, or seventy-five hundredths. The units digit of the percent is in the *hundredths* place value. For example, 3% can be written as 0.03, putting the 3 in the hundredths place. Be careful when making this conversion! It's easy to mistranslate percents into decimals, for example by expressing 3% incorrectly as 0.3. When converting from percents to decimals, always move the decimal point *two* places to the left: $3.0\% \to 0.03$.

It's also common for people to mistake 100% for 100. In fact, $100\% = \frac{100}{100} = 1$. Make a flash card for this concept.

Finally, be extra careful when entering a percent into the GRE calculator, which does not have a percent button. For example, 7% must be entered as 0.07, which is $\frac{7}{100}$. This is not the same as 0.7, which is $\frac{7}{10} = \frac{70}{100} = 70\%$. Practice some fractions math by hand to help develop your number sense and avoid these kinds of mistakes.

Percents as Fractions

Relating percents to fractions can be really helpful on the GRE. Just as a fraction expresses how many pieces of a total are selected, a percent expresses how many parts of a whole are selected. Percents, however, *always* use 100 as the total.

For example:

$$\frac{7}{20} = \text{what percent?}$$

Since percents always use 100 as the total, one way to convert this fraction into a percent is to consider what you would need to do to both the numerator and the denominator in order to get the denominator to equal 100. In this case, multiply the top and bottom by 5:

$$\frac{7}{20} = \frac{7 \times 5}{20 \times 5} = \frac{35}{100}$$

Unit Four: **Stories, Percents, Ratios, Stats, and Data**

Therefore, the fraction $\frac{7}{20}$ is equivalent to the fraction $\frac{35}{100}$, which is equivalent to 35%.

When the denominator is 100, the percent is equal to the number that appears as the numerator:

$$\frac{\text{Part}}{\text{Whole}} = \frac{n}{100} = n\%$$

Using this formula enables you to solve for the percent, the part, or the whole. Try this problem:

What is 30% of 80?

The percent figure has a % sign as the giveaway, but how can you tell whether the 80 is the whole or the part? The question asks you to take 30% of (or out of) 80, so it's asking you to find a part (30%, to be exact) of the whole 80.

In future, when a problem asks you to take a percentage *of something*, the word *of* is your clue that this is the whole. You're always taking a percentage *of a whole*. Beware, however, that what gets treated as the whole can change within a problem. It's always important to carefully read what comes after the word *of*.

This question gives the *whole* amount and the *percent* and asks for the *part*. Substitute the known values into the equation and choose a variable for the unknown value:

$$\frac{\text{Part}}{\text{Whole}} = \frac{\text{Percent}}{100}$$

$$\frac{x}{80} = \frac{30}{100}$$

Multiply both sides by 80 and simplify:

$$80 \times \frac{x}{80} = \frac{30}{100} \times 80$$

$$x = \frac{3}{10} \times 80$$

$$x = \frac{3}{1} \times 8$$

$$x = 24$$

Try another one:

75% of what number is 21?

The % sign gives away the percent figure, but is that other value the part or the whole? The question is asking you to take 75% *of* some unknown value in order to get 21—that is, take 75% *of the whole* in order to get the part 21. As before, the word *of* signals the *whole*.

So, this time, the problem gives the *part* and the *percent* and asks for the *whole* amount:

$$\frac{21}{y} = \frac{75}{100}$$

Cross-multiply to get *y* out of the denominator:

$$21 \times 100 = 75y$$

Divide both sides by 75 to solve for *y*:

$$\frac{21 \times \overset{4}{\cancel{100}}}{\underset{3}{\cancel{75}}} = y$$

$$\frac{\overset{7}{\cancel{21}} \times 4}{\underset{1}{\cancel{3}}} = y$$

$$28 = y$$

Finally, try this problem:

   90 is what percent of 40 ?

This time, the word *what* is before the word *percent*—so this problem is asking you to find the percent. Assign a variable for the percent. Next, of the two values given in the problem, which one is the part and which one is the whole?

Be careful with this problem! It's a mistake to say that the greater number, 90, is the whole. The word *of* goes with the 40, so the 40 is the whole and goes on the denominator of the fraction:

$$\frac{90}{40} = \frac{x}{100}$$

Again, isolate the *x* and solve:

$$100 \times \frac{9\cancel{0}}{4\cancel{0}} = x$$

$$\overset{25}{\cancel{100}} \times \frac{9}{\underset{1}{\cancel{4}}} = x$$

$$225 = x$$

The answer is 225%. You can indeed have percents greater than 100%. In fact, expect this result whenever the part is greater than the whole.

One more note: When the GRE asks you to calculate a percent, it will typically include the percent sign in the answer choices. So you will see 225% listed as the correct answer, as opposed to 225.

Check Your Skills

1. Translate this sentence: *R* is 45 percent of *Q*.

2. 84 is 70% of what number?

3. 30 is what percent of 50 ?

Answers can be found on page 411.

Unit Four: **Stories, Percents, Ratios, Stats, and Data**

Percents as Word Problems

Add the direct translation of percent as divided by 100 to your table of commonly used translations.

English Word(s)	Math Translation	Example	
is/was/were	equals ($=$)	x is 3	$x = 3$
of	multiply ($\times$)	half of 7	$\frac{1}{2} \times 7$
what	unknown (n)	3 times what is 6?	$3n = 6$
more/greater than	inequality ($>$)	x is greater than 5	$x > 5$
less/fewer than	inequality ($<$)	x is less than 5	$x < 5$
a specific value more than	addition ($+$)	y is 3 more than z	$y = z + 3$
a specific value less than	subtraction ($-$)	y is 3 less than z	$y = z - 3$
percent	**divided by 100**	25%	$\frac{25}{100}$

When you see "% of n," there are two ways to translate the text. You can use the method taught in the previous section (setting up the part-to-whole equation) or you can perform a direct translation. Translate the same three problems from the last section, but this time don't use that percent formula. Instead, directly translate each word, using the guidelines in the table:

What is 30% of 80 ?

75% of what number is 21 ?

90 is what percent of 40 ?

Here's the direct translation of each:

What is 30% of 80 ? $\qquad x = \frac{30}{100} \times 80$

75% of what number is 21 ? $\qquad \frac{75}{100} \times n = 21$

90 is what percent of 40 ? $\qquad 90 = \frac{y}{100} \times 40$

These equations look different from the ones in the prior section, but they're actually identical. They're just arranged differently. If you solve each equation, you'll arrive at the same answers.

It's your call which way you want to translate equations—using the percent equation introduced in the last section or using the direct-translation method shown in this section. Use whatever method your brain finds easier to process.

Chapter 15: **Percents**

Check Your Skills

> Solve each of these problems using direct translation.

4. 12 is 40% of what number?

5. 100 is what percent of 50 ?

Answers can be found on pages 411–412.

Percent Change

Some percent problems involve the concept of percent change. For example:

The price of a cup of coffee increased from 80 cents to 84 cents. By what percent did the price change?

Percent change problems can be solved using the percent equation, with a small adjustment. Here's the original percent equation:

$$\frac{\text{Part}}{\text{Whole}} = \frac{\text{Percent}}{100}$$

The right side of the equation will stay the same. And the Whole will essentially stay the same, but the name will change to Original. The *whole* is the original or starting whole value.

The *part*, however, is now going to represent the *change* from the original value to the new value:

$$\frac{\text{Change}}{\text{Original}} = \frac{\text{Percent}}{100}$$

Identify the knowns and unknowns in this problem:

Original = 80 cents

Change = 84 cents − 80 cents = 4 cents

Percent = x

Plug in the values and solve:

$$\frac{4}{80} = \frac{x}{100}$$

$$\frac{\cancel{4}^{1}}{\cancel{80}_{20}} = \frac{x}{100}$$

$$\cancel{100} \times \frac{1}{\cancel{20}} = \frac{x}{\cancel{100}} \times \cancel{100}$$

$$10 \times \frac{1}{2} = x$$

$$5 = x$$

The price of a cup of coffee increased by 5%.

403

The most common mistake is to divide by 84, the new value, rather than by 80, the original value. The formula specifies the *original* to help you keep this straight. Always divide by the original value. In some cases, the GRE will attempt to disguise this original value, so it's worth knowing that the "original" value can be denoted in three different ways:

- It can come earlier in time.
- It can come after the word *from*.
- It can come after the word *than*.

Alternatively, a percent change question might be phrased as follows:

If the price of a $30 shirt decreased by 20%, what was the new price of the shirt?

The *original* is the starting price of the shirt, $30. The *percent change* is 20%. To find the answer, you must first find the *change*, which is the amount of the decrease:

$$\frac{x}{30} = \frac{20}{100}$$

$$\frac{x}{30} = \frac{\overset{1}{\cancel{20}}}{\underset{5}{\cancel{100}}}$$

$$\overset{}{\cancel{30}} \times \frac{x}{\cancel{30}} = \frac{1}{\underset{1}{\cancel{5}}} \times \overset{6}{\cancel{30}}$$

$$x = 6$$

Therefore, the price of the shirt *decreased* by $6. But the question asked what the *new* price was, so there's one more step: The new price of the shirt was $30 − $6 = $24.

As on all problems, clearly denote on your scratch paper what the question asks you to find. The GRE would likely include $6 among the answer choices—but that value answers a question that this problem didn't ask.

Check Your Skills

6. If a student successfully lobbied a professor to change her score on a certain exam to 1,600, then her new score was what percent greater than her original score of 1,250 ?

7. One day after a 30-gallon drum of water was completely filled, 15% of the water had evaporated. How much water was remaining at that point?

Answers can be found on page 412.

Percent of Original

The last section had this percent change problem about a cup of coffee:

The price of a cup of coffee increased from 80 cents to 84 cents. By what percent did the price change?

Here's the same scenario but with a different question:

> The price of a cup of coffee increased from 80 cents to 84 cents. The new price is what percent of the original price?

This question is not asking what the percent *change* is. Instead, this question is asking what the new price represents as a *percent of* the original price. So the original price is the whole and the new price is the part:

$$\frac{84}{80} = \frac{x}{100}$$

Pause for a second before continuing to solve. Because the new price is greater than the original price, the new price represents something greater than 100% of the original price. So, expect the answer to be greater than 100%:

$$100 \times \frac{\overset{21}{\cancel{84}}}{\underset{20}{\cancel{80}}} = \frac{x}{\cancel{100}} \times \cancel{100}$$

$$\cancel{100} \times \frac{21}{\cancel{20}} = x$$

$$\overset{5}{\cancel{10}} \times \frac{21}{\underset{1}{\cancel{2}}} = x$$

$$105 = x$$

Thus, the new price is 105% of the original price. (As always, simplify in the order that works best for you.)

You could also solve this problem using direct translation:

> The new price is what percent of the original price?

$$84 = \frac{x}{100} \times 80$$

Solve to arrive at the same answer:

$$x = 84 \times \frac{100}{80} = 105$$

Again, the new price is 105% of the original price.

The original price is always equivalent to 100%. Therefore, the new price is 105% **of** the original, and the new price is 5% **greater than** the original price.

There is a fundamental relationship between these numbers, resulting from the fact that the *Change* equals the *New* value minus the *Original* value, or equivalently, *Original* + *Change* = *New*.

> ### Key Concept
>
> If a quantity is **increased** by x percent, then the new quantity is $(100 + x)\%$ **of** the original. For example:
>
> A 15% increase produces a quantity that is 115% of the original.
>
> The new price is 115% of the original price.
>
> The new price is 15% greater than the original price.

Unit Four: **Stories, Percents, Ratios, Stats, and Data**

Likewise, in the shirt problem, the $30 cost decreased by 20%, resulting in a new price of $24.

The new price is some percent of the old price. Calculate that percent:

$$\frac{24}{30} = \frac{x}{100}$$

$$100 \times \frac{24}{30} = \frac{x}{100} \times 100$$

$$100 \times \frac{4}{5} = x$$

$$80 = x$$

The new price is 80% of the original price.

The original price is always equivalent to 100%. The new price is 80% **of** the original price, and the new price is 20% **less than** the original price.

> *Key Concept*
>
> If a quantity is decreased by x percent, then the new quantity is $(100 - x)\%$ of the original. For example:
>
> A 15% decrease produces a quantity that is 85% of the original.
>
> The new price is 85% of the original price.
>
> The new price is 15% less than the original price.

These formulas are all just another way of saying:

$$\text{Original} \pm \text{Change} = \text{New}$$

Try this problem:

What number is 50% greater than 60 ?

One way to solve is to find the 50% change, then add that change to the original to arrive at the new number:

$$\frac{\text{Change}}{60} = \frac{50}{100}$$

$$60 \times \frac{x}{60} = \frac{50}{100} \times 60$$

$$x = \frac{1}{2} \times 60$$

$$x = 30$$

The original was 60 and the change is 30, so the new value is $60 + 30 = 90$. The value 90 is 50% greater than 60.

Chapter 15: **Percents**

There's also a more direct way to solve. A 50% increase is the same thing as 100% (the original) + 50% (the increase) and therefore equals 150% **of** the original number. Reframe the question as "What number is 150% of 60?":

What number is 150% of 60 ?

$$x = \frac{150}{100} \times 60$$

$$x = \frac{15\cancel{0}}{10\cancel{0}} \times 6\cancel{0}$$

$$x = 90$$

Compare that question with this next problem, which will *not* have the same answer:

What number is 150% greater than 60 ?

The setup 150% *of* 60 and the setup 150% *greater than* 60 are related, but they are not the same thing.

The answer to the second problem will be 150% *more than* 60, or 100% + 150% of 60, or 250% of 60. Reframe the question as "What number is 250% of 60?" and use direct translation to solve:

What number is 150% greater than 60 ?

$$y = \frac{250}{100} \times 60$$

$$y = \frac{25\cancel{0}}{10\cancel{0}} \times 6\cancel{0}$$

$$y = 150$$

Pay particular attention to whether the problem says *of* or *greater than*:

Question wording	What to do	For example
20% *of* 50	Percent × Original	20% × 50
20% *greater than* 50	Original + (Percent × Original) Shortcut: Original × (100% + Percent)	50 + (20% × 50) 50 × 120%

Check Your Skills

8. A plant originally cost $35. The price is increased by 20%. What is the new price?

9. 70 is 250% greater than what number?

Answers can be found on page 413.

Unit Four: **Stories, Percents, Ratios, Stats, and Data**

Successive Percents

One of the GRE's favorite tricks involves successive percents. For example:

> If a ticket increased in price by 20%, and then increased again by 5%, by what percent did the ticket price increase in total?

Although it may seem counterintuitive, the answer is *not* 25%.

To understand why, consider a concrete example. Say that the ticket initially cost $100. If the total percent increase were 25%, then the new price would be $125…but that's not how the math plays out.

Rather, the first increase is 20%, so the ticket price goes up to $120, because $20 is 20% of $100.

Next, the ticket price goes up again by 5%. However, it increases by 5% of the *new price* of $120, not 5% of the *original* $100 price.

Since 5% of $120 is 0.05 × 120 = $6, the final price of the ticket is $120 + $6, or $126.

These two successive percent increases, the first of 20% and the second of 5%, *do not* result in a combined 25% increase. In fact, they result in a combined 26% increase (because the ticket price increased from $100 to $126).

Successive percents *cannot* simply be added together. This holds for successive increases, successive decreases, and for combinations of increases and decreases. If a ticket goes up in price by 30% and then goes down by 10%, the price has *not* in fact gone up a net of 20%. Likewise, if an index increases by 15% and then falls by 15%, it does *not* return to its original value! (Try it—you will see that the index is actually *down* 2.25% overall.)

A great way to solve successive percent problems is to choose real numbers and see what happens. The preceding example used the real value of $100 for the initial price of the ticket, since 100 usually works well with percents.

As with all percent problems you could also solve by converting to decimals. Increasing a price by 20% is the same as multiplying the price by 120%, which is the same as multiplying by the decimal 1.20. Increasing the new price by 5% is the same as multiplying that new price by 105% or by the decimal 1.05.

So, you can also write the relationship this way:

$$\text{Original} \times 1.20 \times 1.05 = \text{final price}$$

Try plugging 1.20 × 1.05 into your calculator. What do you get?

It turns out that 1.20 × 1.05 = 1.26, indicating that the price increased by 26% overall.

This approach works well for problems that involve many successive steps (e.g., compound interest, which will be addressed later). If you have just one or two steps, it's often better to pick 100 and work out the math from there.

Check Your Skills

10. If your stock portfolio increased by 25% and then decreased by 20%, what percent of the original value would your new stock portfolio have?

Answers can be found on page 414.

Pick 100 for Unspecified Amounts

As seen in the previous section, when a GRE problem discusses a value but never gives you a real number for that value, you can pick your own number for the problem. For example:

> A shirt that initially cost d dollars was on sale for 20% off. If s represents the sale price of the shirt, then d is what percent of s?

The problem never specifies a real value for the initial *or* final cost of the shirt, so pick 100 for the initial cost (just as you did when solving successive percents).

If the shirt initially cost $100, then $d = 100$. If the shirt was on sale for 20% off, then the new price of the shirt is 20% less than 100, or $80. Thus, $s = 80$.

Next, d is what percent of s? Plug in the values you have:

$$d \text{ is what percent of } s?$$

$$100 = \frac{x}{100} \times 80$$

Isolate x to solve:

$$100 = \frac{x}{\cancel{100}_{5}} \times \cancel{80}^{4}$$

$$100 = \frac{4x}{5}$$

$$\left(\frac{5}{4}\right) \times 100 = \frac{\cancel{4}x}{\cancel{5}} \times \left(\frac{\cancel{5}}{\cancel{4}}\right)$$

$$\left(\frac{5}{\cancel{4}_1}\right) \times \cancel{100}^{25} = x$$

$$125 = x$$

Therefore, d is 125% of s.

Like successive percent problems and other problems that include unspecified amounts, this example is most easily solved by plugging in a real value. For percent problems, 100 is generally a good number to choose. (Note that if *any* amounts are specified, you cannot pick your own numbers—you must solve the problem using the specified numbers.)

Try this QC problem:

> The price of an item is discounted by 20%, and then the price of the item is increased by 20%.

Quantity A	**Quantity B**
The price after the discount and increase	The original price

Unit Four: **Stories, Percents, Ratios, Stats, and Data**

The problem doesn't specify any real numbers for the price of this item, so pick a total number and solve for each quantity. Since this is a percent problem, try 100.

In the first step, the $100 item is discounted by 20%. You can either find 20% of 100 and then subtract that value from 100, or you can shortcut the work by finding 80% of 100:

$$\text{Step 1:} \quad 20\% \text{ discount} \quad \$100\left(\frac{80}{100}\right) = \$80$$

Next, the new price is increased by 20%:

$$\text{Step 2:} \quad 20\% \text{ increase} \quad \$80\left(\frac{120}{100}\right) = \$96$$

The original price ($100) is greater than the final price after the discount and increase ($96). Therefore, the correct answer is (B): Quantity B is greater.

Check Your Skills

11. If your stock portfolio decreased by 25% and then increased by 20%, what percent of the original value would your new stock portfolio have?

Answers can be found on page 414.

Chapter 15: **Percents**

Check Your Skills Answer Key

1. $\dfrac{R}{Q} = \dfrac{45}{100}$

   The *of* signals that Q is the whole.

2. **120**

   Of what number is the whole. Cross-multiply to solve (use the calculator for that last step).

   $$\dfrac{84}{x} = \dfrac{7\cancel{0}}{10\cancel{0}}$$

   $$\dfrac{84(10)}{7} = x$$

   $$120 = x$$

3. **60%**

   Of 50 indicates that 50 is the whole.

   $$\dfrac{x}{100} = \dfrac{3\cancel{0}}{5\cancel{0}}$$

   $$x = \dfrac{3}{\cancel{5}}(\cancel{100})^{20}$$

   $$x = 60$$

4. **30**

   There are several valid ways to simplify the math; do so however you like.

   $$12 \text{ is } 40\% \text{ of what number?}$$

   $$12 = \dfrac{4\cancel{0}}{10\cancel{0}} \times x$$

   $$12 = \dfrac{4}{10}x$$

   $$\cancel{12}^{3}\left(\dfrac{10}{\cancel{4}_{1}}\right) = x$$

   $$30 = x$$

Unit Four: **Stories, Percents, Ratios, Stats, and Data**

5. **200%**
   Careful! It would be easy to set up this problem backwards. This is another example of a percent greater than 100.

   $$100 \text{ is what percent of } 50 ?$$

   $$100 = \frac{x}{100} \times \overset{1}{\cancel{50}}_{2}$$

   $$100 = x\left(\frac{1}{2}\right)$$

   $$100(2) = x$$

   $$200 = x$$

6. **28%**
   The original is 1,250. The change is 1600 − 1250 = 350. Use the percent change equation to solve:

   $$\frac{350}{1250} = \frac{x}{100}$$

   $$100 \times \frac{35}{125} = \frac{x}{100} \times \cancel{100}$$

   $$28 = x$$

   Use the calculator to do the last line of math. The score increased by 28%.

7. **25.5**
   The original is 30 and the change is unknown. Start by determining that change (how much water evaporated):

   $$\frac{x}{30} = \frac{15}{100}$$

   $$\frac{x}{30} = \frac{\overset{3}{\cancel{15}}}{\underset{20}{\cancel{100}}}$$

   $$\cancel{30} \times \frac{x}{\cancel{30}} = \frac{3}{\cancel{20}} \times \cancel{30}$$

   $$x = \frac{3}{2} \times 3$$

   $$x = \frac{9}{2} = 4.5$$

   The question asks how much water *remains* in the drum. Because 4.5 gallons have evaporated, there are 30 − 4.5 = 25.5 gallons remaining.

Chapter 15: **Percents**

8. **$42**

    You could find the change and add it back to the original:

    $$\frac{\text{change}}{35} = \frac{20}{100}$$

    $$\cancel{35} \times \frac{x}{\cancel{35}} = \frac{\cancel{20}^{1}}{\cancel{100}_{5}} \times 35$$

    $$x = \frac{1}{\cancel{5}_{1}} \times \cancel{35}^{7}$$

    $$x = 7$$

    The price increased by $7 so the new price is $35 + $7 = $42.

    If you spot the shortcut, though, use it. The original (100%) plus the price increase (20%) translates to a new price that is 120% of the original:

    $$\frac{\text{new price}}{35} = \frac{120}{100}$$

    $$\cancel{35} \times \frac{y}{\cancel{35}} = \frac{\cancel{120}^{6}}{\cancel{100}_{5}} \times 35$$

    $$y = \frac{6}{\cancel{5}_{1}} \times \cancel{35}^{7}$$

    $$y = 42$$

    The new price is $42.

9. **20**

    The question uses *greater than*. Rephrase it: *250% greater than* is the same as *350% of*.

    $$70 \text{ is } 350\% \text{ of what number?}$$

    $$70 = \frac{350}{100} \times x$$

    $$\frac{\cancel{100}}{\cancel{350}} \times 70 = x$$

    $$\frac{700}{35} = x$$

    $$20 = x$$

413

Unit Four: **Stories, Percents, Ratios, Stats, and Data**

10. **100%**

    Pick $100 for the original value of the portfolio. If it increases by 25%, then it increases by $25 to a new value of $125.

    Next, the $125 value decreases by 20%. A decrease of 20% is the same thing as taking 100% − 20% = 80%, so multiply 125 by 0.8 on the calculator. You end up back at $100, so the value of your portfolio has stayed the same. The new value is 100% of the original value.

    Alternatively, set the math up algebraically to solve.

    $$100\left(1 + \frac{25}{100}\right) = 100(1.25) = 125$$

    Next, calculate a 20% decrease from the new value of 125.

    $$125\left(1 - \frac{20}{100}\right) = 125(0.8) = 100$$

    The final value is 100. Because the starting value was also 100, the portfolio is 100% of its original value.

    You can also solve algebraically by representing the change as Original × 1.25 × 0.80 = New. Multiplying the two successive percents results in 1.25 × 0.80 = 1. As a result, the new value is 100% of the original value.

11. **90%**

    Pick $100 for the original value of the portfolio. First, the value decreases by 25%. A 25% decrease is the equivalent of taking 75% of the original number, so the new value of the portfolio is $75.

    Next, the new value increases by 20%. A 20% increase is the equivalent of taking 120% of the new value:

    $$75(120\%) = 75(1.2) = 90$$

    The final value is $90 and the original value was $100. Thus, the new value of the portfolio is $\frac{90}{100}$ = 90% of the original value.

Chapter 15: **Percents**

Problem Set

> Solve the following problems using the relevant percent formula or algebraic translation. Pick 100 when dealing with unspecified amounts, and use the calculator when appropriate.

1. If x% of y is 10, and y% of 120 is 48, what is x?

2. A stereo was marked down by 30% and sold for $84. What was the presale price of the stereo?

3. From 1980 to 1990, the population of Mitannia increased by 6%. From 1990 to 2000, the population decreased by 3%. What was the overall percentage change in the population of Mitannia from 1980 to 2000?

4. If y is decreased by 20% and then increased by 60%, what is the new number, expressed in terms of y?

5. A bowl was half full of water. Next, 4 cups of water were added to the bowl, filling the bowl to 70% of its capacity. How many cups of water are now in the bowl?

6. A large tub is filled with 920 liters of water and 1,800 liters of alcohol. If 40% of the alcohol evaporates, what percent of the remaining liquid is water?

7. If x is 40% of y and 50% of y is 40, then 16 is what percent of x?

8. What number is yielded when 800 is increased by 50% and then decreased by 30%?

9. If 1,600 is increased by 20%, and then reduced by y%, yielding 1,536, what is y?

10. Steve uses a certain copy machine that reduces an image by 13%.

Quantity A	Quantity B
The percent of the original if Steve reduces the image by another 13%	75%

11. x and y are positive numbers, and y is 50% of x% of x.

Quantity A	Quantity B
y	x

Unit Four: **Stories, Percents, Ratios, Stats, and Data**

12.
Quantity A
10% of 643.38

Quantity B
20% of 321.69

13. From 2003 to 2004, the rent on a certain property increased by x%.
From 2004 to 2005, the rent then decreased by x%.
x is a positive integer.

Quantity A
The difference between 2004's rent and 2003's rent, in dollars

Quantity B
The difference between 2004's rent and 2005's rent, in dollars

14. A town's population rose 40% from 2006 to 2007.
The 2007 population was 10,080.

Quantity A
The 2006 population

Quantity B
7,000

Chapter 15: **Percents**

Solutions

1. **25**

   Use two percent equations to solve this problem. Begin with the fact that y% of 120 is 48.

   $$\frac{48}{120} = \frac{y}{100}$$

   $$100 \times \frac{48}{120} = y$$

   $$40 = y$$

   Then, set up a percent equation for the fact that x% of 40 is 10.

   $$\frac{10}{40} = \frac{x}{100}$$

   $$100 \times \frac{\cancel{10}}{\cancel{40}} = x$$

   $$25 = x$$

   You could also set up algebraic equations with decimal equivalents to solve: $(0.01y)(120) = 48$, so $1.2y = 48$ or $y = 40$. Therefore, because you know that $(0.01x)(y) = 10$, you have.

   $$(0.01x)(40) = 10 \qquad 40x = 1{,}000 \qquad x = 25$$

2. **$120**

   Use the percent change formula to solve this problem. Remember that the stereo was marked down 30% from the original, so you have to solve for the original price.

   $$\frac{\text{change}}{\text{original}} = \frac{30}{100}$$

   $$\frac{\text{original} - 84}{\text{original}} = \frac{30}{100}$$

   $$\text{original} - 84 = 0.3(\text{original})$$

   $$0.7(\text{original}) = 84$$

   $$\text{original} = 120$$

   You could also solve this problem using the algebraic translation. Let p be the original price of the stereo.

   $$\text{original} \pm (\text{percent})(\text{original}) = \text{new}$$

   $$p - 0.3p = 84$$

   $$0.7p = 84$$

   $$p = 120$$

Unit Four: **Stories, Percents, Ratios, Stats, and Data**

3. **2.82% increase**

   For percent problems with no specified value, pick 100 as your Smart Number. In this case, use the 100 for the original (1980) population of Mitannia. Then, apply the successive percents procedure to find the overall percent change.

From 1980–1990, there was a 6% increase:	$100(1 + 0.06) = 100(1.06) = 106$
From 1990–2000, there was a 3% decrease:	$106(1 - 0.03) = 106(0.97) = 102.82$

   Overall, the population increased from 100 to 102.82, representing a 2.82% increase.

4. **1.28y**

   Because there is no concrete value specified, assign y a value of 100. Then, apply the successive percents procedure to find the overall percentage change.

(1) y is decreased by 20%:	$100(1 - 0.20) = 100(0.8) = 80$
(2) Then, it is increased by 60%:	$80(1 + 0.60) = 80(1.6) = 128$

   Overall, there was a 28% increase. If the original value of y is 100, the new value is 1.28y. On the test, you could confirm that this answer was correct by replacing y with 100 and calculating: It would come out to a value of 128.

5. **14**

   For some percent problems, you cannot use Smart Numbers, because the presence of a concrete value (in this case, the 4 cups) means that the total amount can be calculated. In these cases, find out the percent represented by the concrete value and use the percent formula. Here, for instance, because the addition of 4 cups of water raised the water level in the bowl from half full to 70% full, those 4 cups must represent 20% of the bowl's capacity, and the following equation can be set up.

   $$\frac{4}{b} = \frac{20}{100}$$

   $$100 \times \frac{4}{b} = \frac{20}{\cancel{100}} \times \cancel{100}$$

   $$\cancel{b} \times \frac{400}{\cancel{b}} = 20 \times b$$

   $$400 = 20b$$

   $$20 = b$$

   The capacity of the bowl is 20 cups. Because the bowl is 70% full, the amount of water in the bowl can now be calculated as $0.70(20) = 14$ cups.

6. **46%**
   When percents appear in any problem, the important things to ascertain are whether the situation calls for a percent **of** setup or a percent **change** setup and what *whole* the percent is part of. In this case, the fact that 40% of the alcohol *evaporates* entails a percent decrease, as that percentage of the alcohol in the tub will disappear entirely in the evaporation process. Use any of the percent change setups from this chapter to find the new amount of alcohol in the tub. Here's one version of the formula that will work:

   $$\text{Original} \times \left(1 - \frac{\text{Percent Decrease}}{100}\right) = \text{New}$$

   Using the information in this problem, the formula would be applied as follows.

   $$1{,}800 \times \left(1 - \frac{40}{100}\right) = \text{new alcohol}$$

   $$1{,}800 \times (0.6) = \text{new alcohol}$$

   $$1{,}080 = \text{new alcohol}$$

   With the new amount of alcohol in the mixture, it's possible to calculate the *remaining liquid* in the tub and answer the question. Water will be $\frac{920}{920 + 1{,}080} = \frac{920}{2{,}000} = 46\%$ of the total.

7. **50%**
   Because percents appear three times in this problem (40%, 50%, and *what percent*), expect to set up three percent equations in order to solve. Start from the part of the problem that provides the most concrete information (*50% of y is 40*) and set it up using fractions or the algebraic translation. The algebraic translation is shown.

   $$\frac{50}{100} \times y = 40$$

   $$0.5y = 40$$

   $$y = \frac{40}{0.5} = 80$$

   Now that you have a value for *y*, the first part of the problem (*x is 40% of y*) has the most concrete information, so set up an equation to solve for *x*.

   $$x = \frac{40}{100} \times y$$

   $$x = 0.4(80) = 32$$

Unit Four: **Stories, Percents, Ratios, Stats, and Data**

With a value of *x* in hand, move on to the question stem. Read 32 in place of *x* and you may be able to answer the question intuitively (*16 is what percent of 32?*); however, the question can also be translated into an equation and solved.

$$16 = \frac{?}{100} \times x$$

$$16 = \frac{?}{100} \times 32$$

$$\frac{16}{32} = \frac{?}{100}$$

$$100 \times 0.5 = \frac{?}{\cancel{100}} \times \cancel{100}$$

$$50 = ?$$

The answer is 50.

8. **840**

   Apply the successive percents procedure.

   (1) 800 is increased by 50%: $800 \times 1.5 = 1{,}200$

   (2) The result is decreased by 30%: $1{,}200 \times 0.7 = 840$

9. **20%**

   This is a successive percents problem with a twist. In this case, there is no value for the second percent change. Solve for the first percent change, and set up an algebraic formula for the second percent change.

   $$1{,}600 \times \left(1 + \frac{20}{100}\right) = \text{new}$$

   $$1{,}600 \times 1.2 = \text{new}$$

   $$1{,}920 = \text{new}$$

   then, use the same setup for the next part of the problem with a different unknown.

   $$1{,}920 \times \left(1 - \frac{y}{100}\right) = 1{,}536$$

   $$1{,}920 - 19.2y = 1{,}536$$

   $$-19.2y = -384$$

   $$y = 20$$

Alternatively, you could use the percent change formula to solve that part of the question, as you know the change and the original number.

$$\frac{1{,}920 - 1{,}536}{1{,}920} = \frac{y}{100}$$

$$\frac{384}{1{,}920} = \frac{y}{100}$$

$$0.2 = \frac{y}{100}$$

$$20 = y$$

In either case, use your calculator!

10. **(A)**
In dealing with percents problems in which no concrete value is provided, choose 100 as your starting number. In this case, think of the original size of the image as 100 inches (or centimeters—whatever feels easiest to relate to). The question tells you that Steve reduces the image by 13%, which can be processed as shown.

$$100 - 0.13(100) = 100 - 13 = 87$$

So after the 13% reduction described in the given information above, the image is at 87 inches. Quantity A calls for a further 13% reduction of the image size, which can be processed in the same way as above.

$$87 - 0.13(87) = 87 - 11.31 = 75.69 \text{ inches}$$

Because the original image was 100 inches, the new size of 75.69 inches also serves as the new *percent of the original* in Quantity A.

Quantity A	Quantity B
The percent of the original if Steve reduces the image by another 13% = 75.69%	75%

Therefore, the correct answer is (A): Quantity A is greater.

11. **(D)**
First translate the statement in the question stem into an equation.

$$y = \frac{50}{100} \times \frac{x}{100} \times x$$

$$y = \frac{1}{2} \times \frac{x^2}{100}$$

$$y = \frac{x^2}{200}$$

Unit Four: **Stories, Percents, Ratios, Stats, and Data**

At this point, you can try to pick some numbers to compare the quantities. If $x = 10$, then $y = 0.5$, making Quantity B larger.

Quantity A	Quantity B
$y = 0.5$	$x = 10$

However, if $x = 200$, then y must also equal 200, making both quantities equal.

Quantity A	Quantity B
$y = 200$	$x = 200$

Thus the relationship cannot be determined, as y can be less than x, but y can also be *equal* to x.

Alternatively, after simplifying the relationship between x and y, the two quantities can be further processed using the Hidden Inequality.

Quantity A	Quantity B
y	x
$\cancel{200} \times \dfrac{x^2}{\cancel{200}}$	$x \times 200$
$x^2 \div x$	$200x \div x$
x	200

Note that the two sides can only be divided by x because the common information tells you that x is positive. However, there's no way to know whether x is greater than 200, so the answer is (D): The relationship cannot be determined.

12. **(C)**
To calculate 10% of 643.38, move the decimal to the left one place: 643.38 → 64.338.

Quantity A	Quantity B
10% of $643.38 = 64.338$	20% of 321.69

To calculate 20% of 321.69, multiply 321.69 by 0.2 using the calculator.

Quantity A	Quantity B
64.338	20% of $321.69 = 64.338$

Therefore, the correct answer is (C): The two quantities are equal.

15

13. **(B)**

    An important consideration in dealing with percents is the size of the total. You don't know 2003's rent price, but you do know that 2004's—after the increase—is higher.

    When the rent increases from 2003 to 2004, it goes up *x percent of 2003's price.*

    When the rent decreases from 2004 to 2005, it goes down *x percent of 2004's price.*

    Because 2004's rent is higher than 2003's rent, the second change is a greater dollar figure. That is, although both changes are *x* percent, the second change is *x* percent of a larger whole and hence represents a larger change in dollars. Quantity B's figure is greater.

    You could also demonstrate this with numbers. Say 2003's rent is $100 and $x = 10$. Thus,

    $$2003 = \$100$$
    $$2004 = \$110$$
    $$2005 = \$99$$

    The difference between 2004 and 2005 is $11, greater than the $10 difference between 2003 and 2004.

    The correct answer is (B): Quantity B is greater.

14. **(A)**

    The common information tells you that the 2006 population rose by 40 percent to a population of 10,080. Let *p* be the population in 2006. The common information translates to $p(1 + 0.40) = 10,080$, which can then be solved thus:

    $$p = \frac{10,080}{1.4} = 7,200$$

    This is greater than Quantity B.

    Trap alert: You may **not** simply take away 40 percent of 10,080. This will yield an incorrect answer. Why? The 40-percent increase is 40 percent *of the 2006 population,* not 40 percent of the 2007 population. The GRE will take almost any opportunity to exploit this potential confusion, making it one of the GRE's most common traps. Stick to the formula or careful algebraic translations when dealing with percent changes.

    Alternatively, you could find the answer by using Quantity B as a benchmark.

    What if the original population had been 7,000? Raise *that* by 40 percent:

    $$7,000 \times 1.4 = 9,800$$

    That is, if the 2006 population had been 7,000, the 2007 population would have been 9,800. Because the 2007 population was actually 10,080, you know that the original population must have been higher than 7,000.

    The correct answer is (A): Quantity A is greater.

CHAPTER 16

Ratios

In This Chapter:

- Label A Ratio with Units
- Ratios and Fractions
- Proportions
- The Unknown Multiplier
- Multiple Ratios: Make a Common Term
- Ratios in QC
- Check Your Skills Answer Key
- Problem Set
- Solutions

CHAPTER 16 Ratios

A **ratio** expresses a particular relationship between two or more quantities, but it's not exactly the same relationship you've seen so far with fractions, percents, and decimals. In this chapter, you will learn what ratios represent, how they relate to fractions and proportions, and how to solve both single and multiple ratios.

A standard ratio expresses a **part-to-part** relationship. For example:

In this recipe, use 2 cups of sugar for every 3 cups of flour.

The ratio defines the number of *parts* of sugar and the number of *parts* of flour to use in the recipe:

$$\text{Part} : \text{Part}$$
$$\text{Sugar} : \text{Flour}$$
$$2 : 3$$

The ratio indicates a *relative* relationship, but not an exact given amount you must use. For example, If you use 2 cups of sugar, then you'll need 3 cups of flour. If you use 4 cups of sugar, then you'll need 6 cups of flour, and so on.

If you use 2 cups of sugar and 3 cups of flour, then you'll use a total of 5 cups of ingredients:

$$\text{Part} : \text{Part} : \text{Whole}$$
$$\text{Sugar} : \text{Flour} : \text{Total}$$
$$2 : 3 : 2 + 3 = 5$$

So it is possible for a ratio to convey information about the whole, as well as the parts:

Part to Part:	There are 2 cups of sugar for every 3 cups of flour in the recipe.	S : F : Total 2 : 3 :
Part to Whole:	There are 2 cups of sugar for every 5 cups of ingredients in the recipe.	S : Other : Total 2 : : 5

In the part-to-part example, the sugar is *not* a subset of the flour; rather, the sugar and the flour are two completely separate ingredients. So, their relationship is a part-to-part relationship. Given those two pieces of information, it is also possible to calculate the total for sugar and flour together: $2 + 3 = 5$.

In the part-to-whole example, by contrast, the sugar *is* a subset of all of the ingredients in the recipe. This time, the given information provides one part (the sugar), as well as the total (all ingredients). Given those two pieces of information, it is possible to calculate the other unknown part of the recipe: $5 - 2 = 3$.

Unit Four: **Stories, Percents, Ratios, Stats, and Data**

Part to Part:	There are 2 cups of sugar for every 3 cups of flour in the recipe.	S : F : Total 2 : 3 : 2 + 3
Part to Whole:	There are 2 cups of sugar for every 5 cups of ingredients in the recipe.	S : Other : Total 2 : 5 − 2 : 5

A ratio can be expressed in various ways:

Wording	Example
the ratio of (item 1) to (item 2) is (number) to (number)	The ratio of bananas to apples is 3 to 4.
for every	For every 3 bananas, there are 4 apples.
colon (:)	Bananas : Apples 3 : 4
fraction (for ratios with exactly 2 quantities)	$\dfrac{3 \text{ bananas}}{4 \text{ apples}}$

That last example is tricky. Fractions typically express part-to-whole relationships, not part-to-part relationships. You can write a ratio in the form of a fraction, but when you do, it's crucial to label the information carefully, as a part-to-part relationship.

Label A Ratio with Units

The order in which a ratio is given is vital. For example, these two representations are not the same:

The ratio of dogs to cats is 2 to 3. Dogs : Cats 2 : 3	The ratio of dogs to cats is 3 to 2. Dogs : Cats 3 : 2

It is very easy to accidentally reverse the order of a ratio—especially on a timed test like the GRE. To avoid this type of mistake, always include labels or units when you write down a ratio.

You can also choose whether to write the information with a colon or as a part-to-part fraction:

There are 2 dogs for every 3 cats.	
With a colon:	Dogs : Cats 2 : 3
As a part-to-part fraction with labels:	$\dfrac{2 \text{ dogs}}{3 \text{ cats}}$
As a part-to-part fraction, assigning variables:	$\dfrac{D}{C} = \dfrac{2}{3}$

If you use the last option, assigning variables, make sure that you choose variables that tell you what they are. If you use generic variables such as x and y instead, it will be much more difficult to keep track of which value represents dogs and which value represents cats.

Also, *don't* write $\frac{2D}{3C}$. It's easy to mistake this for 2 times *D* and 3 times *C*. The ratio doesn't convey that 2 times the variable *D* equals something; it implies that the number of dogs (*D*) divided by the number of cats (*C*) would reduce to the fraction $\frac{2}{3}$.

> **Strategy Tip**
> When labeling variables, never use a single letter next to a number. You risk mistaking the label for a multiplied variable.

Ratios and Fractions

Although both ratios and fractions can be written in fraction form, they are conveying slightly different information.

If you are given the ratio 3 bananas to 4 apples and the fact that there are no other types of fruit, then you can represent the information using a ratio. You can also calculate the ratio total: $3 + 4 = 7$. That ratio total is the equivalent of the Whole in a fraction, so you can also write part-to-whole fractions. For example:

Ratio: Part to Part	
3 bananas to 4 apple	$\frac{3 \text{ bananas}}{4 \text{ apples}}$
Fraction: Part to Whole	
3 bananas to 7 pieces of fruit	$\frac{3 \text{ bananas}}{7 \text{ total}}$
4 apples to 7 pieces of fruit	$\frac{4 \text{ apples}}{7 \text{ total}}$

You can also do this in reverse. If the problem tells you that there are nine animals, exactly two of whom are cats, you can infer that the other seven animals are not cats, so the ratio is:

Cats : Other : Total
2 : 7 : 9

It's also the case that $\frac{2}{9}$ of all of the animals are cats and that $\frac{7}{9}$ of all of the animals are not cats.

Finally, it's possible that there are 2 cats and 7 other animals, but it's also possible that there are 4 cats and 14 other animals... or maybe 6 cats and 21 other animals. The ratio does not convey the definite amount of each group; it just conveys the *relative* relationship between the groups.

You can also have a three- or four-part ratio (or more!). Here's an example of a three-part ratio:

Three friends invest in a certain stock in the ratio of 2 to 3 to 8. (For every $2 the first friend invests, the second friend invests $3, and the third friend invests $8.)

In this scenario, the part-to-part-to-part ratio is 2 : 3 : 8. It's not possible to write this entire ratio in fraction form because there are three parts.

Unit Four: **Stories, Percents, Ratios, Stats, and Data**

The ratio total is 2 + 3 + 8 = 13. It is possible to write each individual part of the ratio as a fraction: The first friend invests $\frac{2}{13}$ of the total amount invested collectively by all three friends, the second friend invests $\frac{3}{8}$ as much as the third friend, etc.

Data Interpretation questions often contain charts that show part–to–part and part–to–whole relationships. It will be important to examine the given information to determine whether something is part-to-part or part-to-whole. You'll see more of this in Chapter 19: Data Interpretation.

Check Your Skills

> Convey the given information in both part-to-part form and part-to-whole form. For part-to-part form, you decide whether to use colon or fraction form.

1. In a garden containing only tulips and lilies, there are 3 tulips and 7 lilies.
2. On a certain sports team, 4 of the players are left-handed, and 7 of the players are right-handed. (And nobody is ambidextrous or cross-handed!)

Answers can be found on page 438.

Proportions

When two quantities have a constant ratio, they are **directly proportional** to each other. For example:

> If the ratio of apples to oranges in the basket is 3 : 4, then $\frac{\text{\# of apples}}{\text{\# of oranges}} = \frac{3}{4}$.

The number of apples divided by the number of oranges is always the same—in this case, it is always $\frac{3}{4}$ or 0.75. There could be 3 apples and 4 oranges, 9 apples and 12 oranges, or even 600 apples and 800 oranges, but there could not be 4 apples and 3 oranges because then the number of apples divided by the number of oranges would *not* equal $\frac{3}{4}$.

Try this problem:

> The ratio of business majors to economics majors in the class is 4 to 7. If there are 35 economics majors in the class, how many business majors are there?

Step 1: Set up a labeled proportion. The ratio in fraction form equals the actual number of things in fraction form:

$$\frac{4 \text{ Bus Maj}}{7 \text{ Eco Maj}} = \frac{b \text{ Bus Maj}}{35 \text{ Eco Maj}}$$

Step 2: Cross-multiply to solve:

$$\frac{4}{7} = \frac{b}{35}$$

$$(35)4 = b(7)$$

$$\frac{(35)4}{7} = b$$

$$20 = b$$

You can use the calculator or you can cancel on paper. If you cancel on paper, simplify before you multiply.

Check Your Skills

3. The ratio of apples to mangos in a fruit basket is 3 : 5. If there are 15 apples, how many mangos are there?

4. In a certain musical collection, there are 7 jazz songs for every 12 classical songs. If there are 60 classical songs, how many jazz songs are in the collection?

Answers can be found on page 438.

The Unknown Multiplier

For more complicated Ratio problems, use the **Unknown Multiplier** to solve. For example:

> The ratio of scientists to artists in a room is 3 : 4. If there are 56 people in the room, and all are either scientists or artists, how many of the people are scientists?

The number of scientists will be some multiple of 3. It could be 3, 6, 9, 30, or 300 scientists. Similarly, the number of artists will be a multiple of 4—perhaps 4, 8, 12, 400. . .but which exact pairing of a multiple of 3 and a multiple of 4 will add up to 56 people in the room?

Go back to the ratio. If there are exactly 3 scientists, there must be exactly 4 artists. If there are 6 scientists, then there are 8 artists. Whatever you multiply the 3 by to get to the real number of scientists, you will also multiply the 4 by that same value to get the number of artists. This is the **Unknown Multiplier**.

The unknown multiplier is always the same for all parts within one ratio. You can think of the number of scientists as $3x$ and the number of artists as $4x$ where you just don't know what x, the multiplier, is yet:

Unknown Multiplier	Number of Scientists ($3x$)	Number of Artists ($4x$)
1	$3 \times 1 = 3$	$4 \times 1 = 4$
2	$3 \times 2 = 6$	$4 \times 2 = 8$
3	$3 \times 3 = 9$	$4 \times 3 = 12$
10	$3 \times 10 = 30$	$4 \times 10 = 40$

Unit Four: **Stories, Percents, Ratios, Stats, and Data**

Express the unknowns and givens using the unknown multiplier:

Scientists $= 3x$

Artists $= 4x$

Total $= 56$

The sum of the parts equals the total:

$$\begin{array}{rcl} \text{Scientists} + \text{Artists} &=& 56 \\ 3x + 4x &=& 56 \\ 7x &=& 56 \\ x &=& 8 \end{array}$$

Since the unknown multiplier is 8, then the number of scientists is $3x = 3(8) = 24$ and the number of artists is $4x = 4(8) = 32$.

> **Strategy Tip**
>
> Use the unknown multiplier to create an algebraic expression for the real number of any component of a ratio. The unknown multiplier is always the same for all parts of one ratio.

The unknown multiplier is particularly useful with three-part ratios:

A recipe calls for amounts of lemon juice, wine, and water in the ratio of 2 : 5 : 7. If all three combined yield 35 milliliters of liquid, how much wine was included?

Define your givens and unknowns using the unknown multiplier:

Lemon Juice $= 2x$

Wine $= 5x$

Water $= 7x$

Total $= 35$

One way to solve this is to express the total in terms of the unknown multiplier. The parts sum to the whole:

$$\begin{array}{rcl} \text{Lemon Juice} + \text{Wine} + \text{Water} &=& \text{Total} \\ 2x + 5x + 7x &=& 14x \end{array}$$

Now set the ratio total equal to the actual number of milliliters of liquid and solve:

$$14x = 35$$
$$x = 2.5$$

Finally, the question asked for the number of milliliters of wine, so the wine was $5x = 5(2.5) = 12.5$ milliliters of the mixture. (Don't solve for the other two values unless they ask you to!)

In this problem, the unknown multiplier turns out to be a non-integer, which is acceptable because the problem deals with continuous quantities (milliliters of liquids).

Some problems, such as the one about scientists and artists, will have the hidden constraint that the unknown multiplier must be a positive integer. You can't have 1.5 people. But for scenarios in which decimal values are acceptable, such as an amount of liquid, it's okay for the unknown multiplier to be a non-integer.

Check Your Skills

5. The ratio of apples to oranges in a fruit basket is 3 to 5. If there are a total of 48 pieces of fruit, how many oranges are there?

6. A toolbox contains only nuts, bolts, and screws in the ratio 5 : 4 : 6. If there are a total of 180 pieces of hardware, how many bolts are in the toolbox?

7. A dry mixture consists of 3 cups of flour for every 2 cups of sugar. How much sugar is in 4 total cups of the mixture?

Answers can be found on pages 438–439.

Multiple Ratios: Make a Common Term

You may encounter two separate ratios that share a common element. For example, one basket of fruit may contain pears and bananas in the ratio 2 to 3, while another basket of fruit contains bananas and cherries in the ratio 4 to 5.

It's possible to combine these separate ratios into one three-part ratio, using a process similar to creating a common denominator for fractions.

Because ratios act like fractions, you can multiply both sides of a ratio (or all sides, if there are more than two) by the same number, just as you can multiply the numerator and denominator of a fraction by the same number. You can change *fractions* to have common *denominators*. Likewise, you can change *ratios* to have common *terms* corresponding to the same quantity. For example:

> In a box containing action figures of the three Fates from Greek mythology, there are three figures of Clotho for every two figures of Atropos, and five figures of Clotho for every four figures of Lachesis.
>
> (A) What is the least number of action figures that could be in the box?
> (B) What is the ratio of Lachesis figures to Atropos figures?

Because there are two separate ratios, you can't use the unknown multiplier to represent total quantities across both ratios. When faced with a problem that asks you to combine multiple ratios together, represent your knowns and unknowns as one long ratio with different rows for each separate ratio:

	C	:	A	:	L
first ratio	3	:	2	:	?
second ratio	5	:	?	:	4

The first row shows the overall ratio you want to create: *C* to *A* to *L*. The next row represents the ratio of *C* to *A*, leaving *L* unknown, while the final row shows the ratio of *C* to *L*, leaving *A* unknown.

Unit Four: **Stories, Percents, Ratios, Stats, and Data**

Both ratios have a value for C, but that value is different. Use common multiples to get that value to be the same for both ratios. Multiply all parts of a single ratio by the same value:

C	:	A	:	L				C	:	A	:	L
3	:	2	:	?	→	Multiply by 5	→	15	:	10	:	?
5	:	?	:	4	→	Multiply by 3	→	15	:	?	:	12

Now that the values for C are identical in the two separate ratios, you're allowed to combine them into one three-part ratio:

$$C : A : L$$
$$15 : 10 : 12$$

And now you can actually answer the questions.

(a) What is the least number of action figures possible? The actual *numbers* of action figures are these three numbers times an unknown multiplier, which must be a positive integer. To find the least possible number of action figures, use the smallest possible multiplier, which is 1. There are $15 + 10 + 12 = 37$ action figures at a minimum.

(b) What is the ratio of L to A? Pull the desired parts from the combined ratio:

$$L : A$$
$$12 : 10$$
$$6 : 5$$

One last thing! As with fractions, simplify ratios as far as you can. In this problem, 12 : 10 can be simplified to 6 : 5.

Try this four-part ratio problem:

In a certain pet store, there are twice as many cats as dogs. For every cat, there are three birds. The ratio of hamsters to birds is four to five. What is the ratio of dogs to total number of animals?

Start by defining the knowns and representing the given ratios:

	C	:	D	:	B	:	H
first ratio	2	:	1	:	?	:	?
second ratio	1	:	?	:	3	:	?
third ratio	?	:	?	:	5	:	4

Chapter 16: **Ratios**

The first two ratios both have a value for cats, so find a common term for this column and combine:

C	:	D	:	B	:	H		C	:	D	:	B	:	H
2	:	1	:	?	:	?		2	:	1	:	?	:	?
1	:	?	:	3	:	?	→ Multiply by 2 →	2	:	?	:	6	:	?
?	:	?	:	5	:	4								

The first two ratios combine into this ratio:

$$C : D : B$$
$$2 : 1 : 6$$

Next, connect this newly created ratio with the third ratio given in the problem. They both have a value for birds:

C	:	D	:	B	:	H		C	:	D	:	B	:	H
2	:	1	:	6	:	?	→ ×5 →	10	:	5	:	30	:	?
?	:	?	:	5	:	4	→ ×6 →	?	:	?	:	30	:	24

Here is the fully combined ratio:

$$C : D : B : H$$
$$10 : 5 : 30 : 24$$

The question asks for the ratio of dogs to total number of animals, so add up the parts to find the ratio total:

$$10 + 5 + 30 + 24 = 69$$

The ratio of dogs to total animals is 5 to 69.

Check Your Skills

> Solve the following problem using a combination of the strategies taught in this section and the prior section of the chapter.

8. A school has 3 first-year students for every 4 second-year students, and 5 second-year students for every 4 third-year students. If there are 240 third-year students in the school, how many first-year students are there?

Answers can be found on page 439.

Ratios in QC

With ratio problems, one of the most important things to keep straight is the difference between ratios and real numbers.

When you are using the ratio, you know the relationship between the values, but you don't know the real values. If you know the unknown multiplier, you can then calculate the real values from the parts of the ratio.

For instance, if a store carries red shirts and white shirts in a 2 to 3 ratio, you can express the relationship as $\frac{R}{W} = \frac{2}{3}$, or the real number of red shirts as $2x$ and the real number of white shirts as $3x$. But there's no way to tell how many shirts there actually are. There may be 5 total shirts (2 red and 3 white), 10 total shirts (4 red and 6 white), 500 total shirts (200 red and 300 white), and so on.

This is a critical distinction because questions will sometimes expect you to add or remove items based on an original ratio. If the store with the $\frac{R}{W} = \frac{2}{3}$ relationship added 3 more red shirts, it would be incorrect to change the ratio to $\frac{R}{W} = \frac{5}{3}$.

Instead, add the 3 new red shirts to the algebraic representation of red shirts:

Original: $2x$ red shirts

New: $2x + 3$ red shirts

The way in which the addition of 3 red shirts will impact the ratio depends upon how many shirts there are to begin with. For example, if the store had 5 total shirts originally (2 red and 3 white), adding 3 red shirts changes the ratio to 5 to 3 (5 red and 3 white). But if the store started with 500 total shirts (200 red and 300 white), adding 3 red shirts doesn't change the ratio very much at all; it's now 203 to 300.

Try this problem:

A university has French majors
and Spanish majors in a 5 to 7 ratio.

Quantity A	Quantity B
The number of French majors if 10 French majors transfer into the university and no other students join, leave, or change majors	The number of French majors if $\frac{3}{7}$ of the Spanish majors switch to French

Define your knowns and unknowns:

$F = 5x$

$S = 7x$

To evaluate the impact of the changes described in each quantity, either pick numbers for the unknown multiplier or work algebraically.

If you decide to pick numbers, focus on extremes (since zero, negatives, and fractions don't make sense here). Start with an easier positive integer.

If the unknown multiplier is 1, then the university begins with 5 French majors and 7 Spanish majors. Evaluate how each quantity changes those numbers:

Initially 5 French majors
and 7 Spanish majors

Quantity A	Quantity B
10 more French majors	3 more French majors $\left(\frac{3}{7} \times 7 = 3\right)$
Total of 15 French majors >	Total of 8 French majors

In this scenario, Quantity A is greater. Eliminate choices (B) and (C).

Next try an extreme unknown multiplier, such as 100:

Initially 500 French majors
and 700 Spanish majors

Quantity A	Quantity B
10 more French majors	300 more French majors $\left(\frac{3}{7} \times 700 = 300\right)$
Total of 510 French majors <	Total of 800 French majors

In this scenario, Quantity B is greater. Therefore, the correct answer is (D): The relationship cannot be determined.

> **Strategy Tip**
>
> Ratios provide *no* information about actual values. The problem will need to provide additional information beyond a ratio in order for you to know anything definitive about actual values.
>
> To try to prove answer (D) on a ratios problem, choose one scenario in which the unknown multiplier is one (or another easy positive integer) and a second scenario in which the unknown multiplier is much greater (but still pick numbers that are easy to work with, such as 10 or 100).

Unit Four: **Stories, Percents, Ratios, Stats, and Data**

Check Your Skills Answer Key

1.

Part-to-Part	$T:L$ $3:7$ or $\frac{3 \text{ tulips}}{7 \text{ lilies}}$
Part-to-Whole	$\frac{3}{10}$ tulips and $\frac{7}{10}$ lilies

The ratio is 3 parts tulips to 7 parts lilies, so the total is $3 + 7 = 10$. Therefore, 3 out of a total 10 flowers are tulips, and 7 out of a total 10 flowers are lilies.

2.

Part-to-Part	$L:R$ $4:7$ or $\frac{4 \text{ left}}{7 \text{ right}}$
Part-to-Whole	$\frac{4}{11}$ left-handed and $\frac{7}{11}$ right-handed

The ratio is 4 parts left to 7 parts right, so the total is $4 + 7 = 11$. Therefore, 4 out of a total 11 players are left-handed, and 7 out of a total 11 players are right-handed.

3. **25**

Set up a proportion.

$$\frac{3 \text{ apples}}{5 \text{ mangos}} = \frac{15 \text{ apples}}{m \text{ mangos}}$$

Cross-multiply to solve.

$$3m = 15(5)$$

$$m = \frac{\cancel{15}^{5}(5)}{\cancel{3}_{1}}$$

$$m = 25$$

4. **35**

Set up a proportion.

$$\frac{7 \text{ jazz}}{12 \text{ classical}} = \frac{j \text{ jazz}}{60 \text{ classical}}$$

Cross-multiply to solve. (As always, use the calculator whenever you prefer.)

$$(60)7 = 12j$$

$$\frac{(\cancel{60})^{5} 7}{\cancel{12}_{1}} = j$$

$$35 = j$$

5. **30**

Call the number of apples $3x$ and the number of oranges $5x$, where x is the unknown multiplier. Sum the parts to get the total: $3x + 5x = 8x$. The total is equal to $8x$, and there are 48 total pieces of fruit.

$$8x = 48$$

$$x = 6$$

Therefore, the number of oranges is $5x = 5(6) = 30$.

6. **48**

   Call the number of nuts $5x$, the number of bolts $4x$, and the number of screws $6x$, where x is the unknown multiplier.

   $$\begin{array}{ccc} N & B & S \end{array}$$
   $$5x + 4x + 6x = 15x \rightarrow 15x = 180$$
   $$x = 12$$

   There are $4x$ bolts, or $4(12) = 48$ bolts.

7. $\dfrac{8}{5}$

   Call the amount of flour $3x$ and the amount of sugar $2x$, where x is the unknown multiplier. The total amount of mixture is $3x + 2x = 5x$.

   $$5x = 4 \text{ cups}$$
   $$x = \dfrac{4}{5}$$

   The amount of sugar in the mixture is is $2\left(\dfrac{4}{5}\right)$, which equals $\dfrac{8}{5}$ cups.

8. **225**

   First, organize the different ratios.

	F	:	S	:	T
first ratio	3	:	4	:	?
second ratio	?	:	5	:	4

   The two ratios overlap in column S. To combine the ratios, multiply the first ratio by 5 and the second ratio by 4.

F	:	S	:	T
15	:	20	:	?
?	:	20	:	16
15	:	20	:	16

   Finally, use the unknown multiplier to solve. There are $15x$ first-years, $20x$ second-years, and $16x$ third-years, where x is the unknown multiplier. There are 240 third-years so 240 equals $16x$. Find x.

   $$16x = 240$$
   $$x = 15$$

   There are $15x$ first-years; apply the unknown multiplier to find the actual number of first years.

   $$15x = 15(15) = 225$$

Unit Four: **Stories, Percents, Ratios, Stats, and Data**

Problem Set

> Solve the following problems using the strategies you have learned in this section. Use proportions and the Unknown Multiplier to organize ratios.
>
> For problems #1–5, assume that none of the quantities is equal to 0.

1. 48 : 2x is equivalent to 144 : 600. What is x?

2. x : 15 is equivalent to y to x. If $y = 3x$, what is x?

3. Brody's marbles have a red to yellow ratio of 2 : 1. If Brody has 22 red marbles, how many yellow marbles does Brody have?

4. Initially, the dogs and cats in a room were in the ratio of 5 : 7. Six cats then leave the room. If there are 35 dogs in the room, how many cats are left in the room?

5. It is currently raining cats and dogs in the ratio of 5 : 6. If there are 18 fewer cats than dogs, how many dogs are raining?

6. The amount of time that three people worked on a special project was in the ratio of 2 to 3 to 5. If the project took 110 hours, how many more hours did the person who worked the most hours work than the person who worked the least hours?

7. On a certain field trip, the ratio of students to teachers is 8 to 1. The total number of people on the field trip is between 60 and 70.

Quantity A	Quantity B
The number of teachers on the field trip	6

8. The ratio of roses to tulips in a bouquet was 3 to 4 before one tulip was replaced by one rose.

Quantity A	Quantity B
The number of roses in the bouquet	The number of tulips in the bouquet

9. A bracelet contains rubies, emeralds, and sapphires, such that there are 2 rubies for every 1 emerald and 5 sapphires for every 3 rubies.

Quantity A	Quantity B
The minimum possible number of gemstones on the bracelet	20

Chapter 16: **Ratios**

10. Bag A contains red and black marbles in a 3 to 4 ratio.
Bag B contains red and black marbles in a 4 to 3 ratio.

Quantity A	Quantity B
The total number of red marbles in both bags combined	The total number of black marbles in both bags combined

11. At a certain fruit stand, there is a 2 to 5 ratio of pomelos to quinces and a 2 to 7 ratio of quinces to raspberries. Which of the following could be the number of pomelos at the stand?

    Select all that apply.

    - [A] 2
    - [B] 4
    - [C] 6
    - [D] 8
    - [E] 10

12. A, B, C, and D all lie on a number line. C is the midpoint of $\overline{AB}$ and D is the midpoint of $\overline{AC}$.

Quantity A	Quantity B
The ratio of $\overline{AD}$ to $\overline{CB}$	The ratio of $\overline{AC}$ to $\overline{AB}$

Unit Four: **Stories, Percents, Ratios, Stats, and Data**

Solutions

1. **100**

   First set up a proportion and then cross-multiply.

   $$\frac{48}{2x} = \frac{144}{600}$$

   $$2x \times 144 = 48 \times 600$$

   Isolate x and use the calculator to solve.

   $$x = \frac{48 \times 600}{2 \times 144} = 100$$

2. **45**

   $$\frac{x}{15} = \frac{y}{x}$$

   First substitute $3x$ for y.

   $$\frac{x}{15} = \frac{3x}{x} = 3$$

   Then solve for x: $x = 3 \times 15 = 45$.

3. **11**

   Write a proportion to solve this problem.

   $$\frac{\text{red}}{\text{yellow}} = \frac{2}{1} = \frac{22}{y}$$

   Cross-multiply to solve.

   $$2y = 22$$

   $$y = 11$$

4. **43**

   First, establish the starting number of dogs and cats with a proportion, and simplify.

   $$\frac{5 \text{ dogs}}{7 \text{ cats}} = \frac{35 \text{ dogs}}{C \text{ cats}}$$

   Cross-multiply.

   $$5C = 7 \times 35$$

   Isolate C and simplify.

   $$C = \frac{7 \times \cancel{35}^{7}}{\cancel{5}} = 49$$

   Since 6 cats leave the room, there are $49 - 6 = 43$ cats left.

Chapter 16: **Ratios**

5. **108**

    For ratio problems involving real-number changes, the Unknown Multiplier approach is the most useful. Since the ratio of cats to dogs is 5 : 6, there are 5*x* cats and 6*x* dogs. Express the fact that there are 18 fewer cats than dogs with an equation.

    $$6x - 5x = 18$$

    $$x = 18$$

    Therefore, there are 6(18) = 108 dogs.

6. **33**

    Use an equation with the unknown multiplier to represent the total hours put in by the three people.

    $$2x + 3x + 5x = 110$$

    $$10x = 110$$

    $$x = 11$$

    Therefore, the person who worked the most hours put in 5(11) = 55 hours, and the person who worked the least hours put in 2(11) = 22 hours. This represents a difference of 55 − 22 = 33 hours.

7. **(A)**

    You can use the unknown multiplier *x* to help express the number of students and teachers. In light of the given ratio, there would be *x* teachers and 8*x* students, and the total number of people on the field trip would therefore be *x* + 8*x* = 9*x*. Note that *x* in this case must be a positive integer, because you cannot have fractional people.

    The total number of people must therefore be a multiple of 9. The only multiple of 9 between 60 and 70 is 63. Therefore, *x* must be $\frac{63}{9}$ which equals 7. Rewrite the quantities.

Quantity A	**Quantity B**
The number of teachers on the field trip = 7	6

    Therefore, the correct answer is (A): Quantity A is greater.

Unit Four: **Stories, Percents, Ratios, Stats, and Data**

8. **(D)**
While you know the ratio of roses to tulips, you do not know the actual number of roses and tulips. The following Before and After charts illustrate two of many possibilities.

Case 1	Roses	Tulips
Before	3	4
After	4	3

Case 2	Roses	Tulips
Before	300	400
After	301	399

These charts illustrate that the number of roses may or may not be greater than the number of tulips after the change.

Therefore, the correct answer is (D): The relationship cannot be determined.

9. **(B)**
This Multiple Ratio problem is complicated by the fact that the number of rubies is not consistent between the two given ratios, appearing as 2 in one and 3 in the other. You can use the least common multiple of 2 and 3 to make the number of rubies the same in both ratios.

```
E  :  R  :  S                  E  :  R  :  S
1  :  2  :  ?   →   ×3   →    3  :  6  :  ?
?  :  3  :  5   →   ×2   →    ?  :  6  :  10
```

Combining the two ratios into a single ratio yields.

E : R : S : Total

3 : 6 : 10 : 19

The smallest possible total number of gemstones is 19.

Therefore, the correct answer is (B): Quantity B is greater.

10. **(D)**

    While you have the red-to-black ratios for each of the two bags, you don't have any real numbers of marbles anywhere or any relationship between the marbles in the two bags, so it's impossible to combine the two ratios. Therefore, try to prove answer (D). For instance, say that the Unknown Multiplier for each bag is 1. In such a case, Bag A would have 3 red and 4 black marbles, and Bag B would have 3 black and 4 red marbles. Quantity A and Quantity B would then each be equal to 7. Eliminate answers (A) and (B).

    However, what if the unknown multiplier for Bag A is 1 but the unknown multiplier for Bag B is 100? In this case, Bag A would have 3 red and 4 black marbles, and Bag B would have 400 red and 300 black marbles. In such a case, Quantity A would be equal to 403 and Quantity B would be equal to 304.

    Therefore, the correct answer is (D): The relationship cannot be determined.

11. **(B) 4; (D) 8**

    The first thing to do in this Multiple Ratio problem is to find a common number of quinces using least common multiples. Multiply the values in the first ratio by 2 and those in the second ratio by 5 to get the following ratio.

    $$P : Q : R$$
    $$4 : 10 : 35$$

    The actual number of pomelos must therefore be a multiple of 4, making the correct answers (B) 4 and (D) 8.

12. **(C)**

    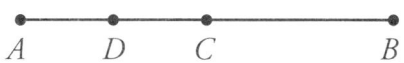

    Visualizing the preceding number line, the ratio of $\overline{AD}$ to $\overline{CB}$ is $\frac{1}{2}$. Similarly, the ratio of $\overline{AC}$ to $\overline{AB}$ is $\frac{1}{2}$.

    Therefore, the correct answer is (C): The two quantities are equal.

CHAPTER 17

Fractions, Decimals, Percents, and Ratios

In This Chapter:

- Converting Forms
- Powers of 10: Shifting the Decimal
- Common FDP Equivalents
- When to Use Which Form
- Pull It All Together
- Check Your Skills Answer Key
- Problem Set
- Solutions

CHAPTER 17 Fractions, Decimals, Percents, and Ratios

Fractions, decimals, percents, and ratios are all ways of representing parts of a whole. For example:

Fraction:	$\frac{1}{3}$ of the team members
Decimal:	2.5 times the distance
Percent:	110% of the sales
Ratio:	5 dogs for every 3 cats

Each of these examples conveys some part of a whole—a portion of the whole time, the whole distance, the whole sales figure, or the whole number of animals. In fact, any of these forms could be used to convey the exact same piece of information:

Fraction:	$\frac{1}{5}$ of the mixture is honey
Decimal:	0.2 of the mixture is honey
Percent:	20% of the mixture is honey
Ratio:	The mixture contains 1 part honey to 4 parts something else.

Fractions, decimals, and percents show a part-to-whole relationship:

	Fraction	Decimal	Percent
Part = 1 Whole = 4	$\frac{1}{4}$	0.25	25%
Part = 1 Whole = 2	$\frac{1}{2}$	0.5	50%
Part = 3 Whole = 2	$\frac{3}{2}$	1.5	150%

Unit Four: **Stories, Percents, Ratios, Stats, and Data**

Ratios usually show a part-to-part relationship, even when written in fraction form. You can also transform a ratio into a standard fraction by writing it in part-to-whole form:

	Ratio in colon form	Ratio in fraction form (part to part)	Standard Fraction (part to whole)
Part = 1 Part = 3 Whole = 4	1 : 3	$\dfrac{1 \text{ part}}{3 \text{ parts}}$	$\dfrac{1}{4}$ and $\dfrac{3}{4}$
Cat = 1 Dog = 3 Total = 4	$C : D$ 1 : 3	$\dfrac{1 \text{ cat}}{3 \text{ dogs}}$	$\dfrac{1}{4}$ are cats $\dfrac{3}{4}$ are dogs

As you solve GRE problems, you can use whichever form is most convenient to solve a particular problem. In this chapter, you will learn how to convert between all of these forms, and you'll learn which form is typically most convenient to use for certain types of math operations.

Converting Forms

In Chapter 16: Ratios, you learned how to convert between ratios and fractions. It's also possible to convert among fractions, decimals, and percents—and you're about to learn how.

Later in this chapter, you'll find a list of common fraction-decimal-percent conversions that you're likely to need to use on test day. Memorize these common conversions. For conversions of values that are not on the common conversions list, use the processes described in this section.

From Percents to Fractions or Decimals

To convert from a percent to a fraction, put the percent figure over one hundred and simplify if needed:

$$45\% = \frac{45}{100} = \frac{\cancel{45}^{9}}{\cancel{100}_{20}} = \frac{9}{20}$$

$$8\% = \frac{8}{100} = \frac{\cancel{8}^{2}}{\cancel{100}_{25}} = \frac{2}{25}$$

To convert from a percent to a decimal, do one of two things. Either remove the percent sign and move the decimal two places to the left, or write the percent as a fraction and use the calculator to divide:

$$53\% = \frac{53}{100} = 0.53$$

$$40.57\% = \frac{40.57}{100} = 0.4057$$

$$0.3\% = \frac{0.3}{100} = 0.003$$

If the percent is a straightforward one, go ahead and use the first method (move the decimal). If the percent is confusing in any way—like that last example—don't hesitate to use the calculator to make sure.

Chapter 17: **Fractions, Decimals, Percents, and Ratios**

Check Your Skills

1. Change 87% to a decimal.

2. Change 30% to a fraction.

Answers can be found on page 465.

From Decimals to Percents or Fractions

To convert from a decimal to a percent, multiply the decimal by 100, effectively moving the decimal point two spots to the right, and add a percent symbol:

0.53 becomes 53%.

0.4057 becomes 40.57%.

0.003 becomes 0.3%.

Converting a decimal to a fraction can be one of the more powerful conversions you make. Every number can be expressed as that number over one. So 3 is also $\frac{3}{1}$, and 2.48 is also $\frac{2.48}{1}$.

A fraction, though, doesn't typically have decimal points in it. Multiply the top and bottom of the fraction by multiples of 10 to get rid of the decimal in the numerator:

$$2.3 = \frac{2.3 \times 10}{1 \times 10} = \frac{23}{10}$$

For every decimal place movement to the right in the numerator, put another zero after the one in the denominator:

$3.1 = \frac{3.1}{1} = \frac{31}{10}$ Move the decimal 1 place to the right. Add 1 zero to the denominator.

$0.578 = \frac{0.578}{1} = \frac{578}{1,000}$ Move the decimal 3 places to the right. Add 3 zeros to the denominator.

$0.0047 = \frac{0.0047}{1} = \frac{47}{10,000}$ Move the decimal 4 places to the right. Add 4 zeros to the denominator.

There's also a verbal way to convert decimals to fractions. As discussed in Chapter 1: Integers and Their Digits, the first digit to the right of the decimal point is the tenths digit, next is the hundredth-digit, next is the thousandth-digit, and so on.

4	5	7	.	1	2	3	5
Hundreds	Tens	Units		Tenths	Hundredths	Thousandths	Ten-Thousandths

These digit names can be helpful in converting decimals to fractions. For example, the decimal 0.1 is read as "one-tenth," or $\frac{1}{10}$. The digit name corresponds to the denominator when it's converted into a decimal.

Unit Four: **Stories, Percents, Ratios, Stats, and Data**

Check Your Skills

3. Change 0.37 to a percent.

4. Change 0.25 to a fraction.

Answers can be found on page 465.

From Fractions to Decimals or Percents

To convert from a fraction to a decimal, use the calculator to divide the numerator by the denominator:

$$\frac{3}{8} = 3 \div 8 = 0.375$$

$$\frac{1}{4} = 1 \div 4 = 0.25$$

To convert from a fraction to a percent, first convert from fraction to decimal, and then convert that decimal to a percent.

Step 1 (use calculator): $\quad \frac{3}{8} = 0.375$

Step 2: $\quad 0.375 = 37.5\%$

Chapter 17: **Fractions, Decimals, Percents, and Ratios**

FDPR Conversions

The following chart reviews the ways to convert from fractions to decimals, from decimals to fractions, from fractions to percents, from percents to fractions, from decimals to percents, and from percents to decimals.

To → From ↓	Fraction $\frac{3}{8}$	Decimal 0.375	Percent 37.5%
Fraction $\frac{3}{8}$		Divide the numerator by the denominator: $3 \div 8 = 0.375$	Convert to decimal then move the decimal two places to the right, adding a percent symbol: $3 \div 8 = 0.375$ $0.375 = 37.5\%$
Decimal 0.375	Write the decimal as a fraction over 1, and then add zeros after the 1 for every decimal movement to the right. Simplify as needed: $\frac{0.375}{1} = \frac{375}{1,000} = \frac{3}{8}$		Move the decimal point two places to the right and add a percent symbol: $0.375 = 37.5\%$
Percent 37.5%	Put the percent over 100. Then simplify: $\frac{37.5}{100} = \frac{375}{1,000} = \frac{3}{8}$	Move the decimal point two places to the left and remove the percent symbol: $37.5\% \rightarrow 0.375$ $37.5\% = 0.375$	

Check Your Skills

5. Convert $\frac{3}{5}$ to a decimal.

6. Change $\frac{5}{8}$ to a percent.

Answers can be found on page 465.

Unit Four: **Stories, Percents, Ratios, Stats, and Data**

Powers of 10: Shifting the Decimal

As the prior section explained, you can convert decimals into fractions by moving the decimal places, which is the same as multiplying by powers of 10. There are a few other times that powers of 10 come into play on the GRE.

Scientific Notation

You will sometimes see a number multiplied by an actual power of 10. For example, all of the following numbers equal 110,700:

$$110.7000 \times 10^3 \text{ is the same as } 110.7000 \times 1{,}000$$
$$11.0700 \times 10^4 \text{ is the same as } 11.0700 \times 10{,}000$$
$$1.1070 \times 10^5 \text{ is the same as } 1.1070 \times 100{,}000$$
$$0.1107 \times 10^6 \text{ is the same as } 0.1107 \times 1{,}000{,}000$$

The numbers on the left side are written in scientific notation. As the baseline value appears to decrease (for example, from 110.7 to 11.07), the exponent increases by 1 to compensate, so all of the rows do still represent the same value: 110,700.

What about when you do want to change the value of a number? If you *multiply* any number by a *positive* power of 10, move the decimal one place to the *right* for every power of 10. Multiplying a number by a power of 10 increases the value of positive numbers:

When asked to	Do this
Multiply by 10	Move the decimal one place to the right: $89.507 \times 10 = 895.07$
Multiply by 10^3	There are 3 powers of 10, so move the decimal three places to the right: $3.9742 \times 10^3 = 3{,}974.2$

Division reverses multiplication. When you *divide* any number by a positive power of 10, move the decimal to the *left* the specified number of places. This action decreases the value of positive numbers:

When asked to	Do this
Divide by 10	Move the decimal one place to the left: $83.708 \div 10 = 8.3708$
Divide by 10^2	Move the decimal two places to the left: $4{,}169.2 \div 10^2 = 41.692$

Chapter 17: **Fractions, Decimals, Percents, and Ratios**

Add zeros as needed in order to shift a decimal:

When asked to	Do this
Multiply by 10^6 when there aren't six places available	Move the decimal six places to the right and add four zeros at the end: $2.57 \times 10^6 = 2,570,000$
Divide by 10^5 when there aren't 5 places available	Move the decimal five places to the left and add three zeros just after the decimal point: $14.29 \div 10^5 = 0.0001429$

Finally, negative powers of 10 work by the same rule but will move the decimal in the *opposite* direction. A power of 4 shifts the decimal four places to the right, but a *negative* power of 4 shifts the decimal four places to the left:

When asked to	Do this
Multiply by 10^{-3}	Multiplying by a negative power will decrease the value. Move the decimal three places to the left: $6,782.01 \times 10^{-3} = 6.78201$
Divide by 10^{-2}	Dividing by a negative power will increase the value. Move the decimal two places to the right: $53.0447 \div 10^{-2} = 5,304.47$

This reversal of direction is a result of the properties of exponents. A negative exponent is the same as the reciprocal, or one over the positive version. For example, 10^{-4} is equivalent to $\frac{1}{10^4}$.

Another way to think about this is that multiplying by a negative power of 10 is equivalent to dividing by a positive power of ten, resulting in a leftward shift of the decimal:

$$3,540 \times 10^{-2} = 3,540 \times \frac{1}{10^2} = \frac{3,540}{10^2} = 3,540 \div 10^2 = 35.4$$

Removing Decimals from Fractions

When presented with a fraction that involves decimals, you can use powers of 10 to remove the decimals, while keeping the overall number unchanged. Before computing this fraction, use powers of ten to turn the numerator and denominator into integers:

$$\frac{0.0028}{0.0007}$$

Whatever you do to the top of the fraction, do the same thing to the bottom. Both numbers have four digits to the right of the decimal. If you multiplied them by 10^4, then, they would both become integers:

$$\frac{0.0028 \times 10^4}{0.0007 \times 10^4} = \frac{28}{7} = 4$$

Unit Four: **Stories, Percents, Ratios, Stats, and Data**

When do you take the time to do this math on your scratch paper and when do you just pull up the calculator? Consider these two examples:

$$\frac{4.5}{0.09} = \frac{4.5 \times 10^2}{0.09 \times 10^2} = \frac{450}{9} = 50$$

$$\frac{2.35}{24.5} = \frac{2.35 \times 10^2}{24.5 \times 10^2} = \frac{235}{2450} = \frac{47}{490}$$

First, note that even when the numerator and denominator have a different number of decimals, you still need to multiply them by the same power of ten. Whatever you do to the top, do the exact same thing to the bottom.

Second, note the form of the answers. If they're in decimal or whole-number form, use the calculator to handle the fractions. If the answers are in fraction form, however, go through with shifting the decimal places in the numerator and denominator, and expect to simplify. In these cases, it helps to eyeball the fractions initially and consider the scale of the outcome. For instance, $\frac{2.35}{24.5}$ should yield a result that's smaller than 1 and probably close to one-tenth.

Finally, if you are trying to reach an answer in fraction form, you don't actually have to write out the powers of ten. Save time by counting the decimal places and moving them:

$$\frac{4.5}{0.09} \rightarrow \text{move 2 places to right} \rightarrow \frac{450}{9}$$

$$\frac{2.35}{24.5} \rightarrow \text{move 2 places to right} \rightarrow \frac{235}{2,450}$$

Check Your Skills

7. $0.0652 \times 10^{-2} = ?$

8. $\frac{264}{10^{-6}} = ?$

9. Put these numbers in order from least to greatest:
   a. 234×10^{-2}
   b. 2.34×10^4
   c. 0.234×10^2

10. Which of the following is equivalent to $\frac{3.568}{2.42}$?
    a. $\frac{344}{715}$
    b. $\frac{688}{573}$
    c. $\frac{892}{605}$

Answers can be found on pages 465–466.

Chapter 17: **Fractions, Decimals, Percents, and Ratios**

Common FDP Equivalents

To save time on the test, memorize the following common equivalents (make flash cards for any you don't already know!):

Fraction	Decimal	Percent
$1/100$	0.01	1%
$1/50$	0.02	2%
$1/25$	0.04	4%
$1/20$	0.05	5%
$1/10$	0.10	10%
$1/9$	$0.\overline{11} \approx 0.111$	$\approx 11.1\%$
$1/8$	0.125	12.5%
$1/6$	$0.1\overline{6} \approx 0.167$	$\approx 16.7\%$
$1/5$	0.2	20%
$1/4$	0.25	25%
$3/10$	0.3	30%
$1/3$	$0.\overline{3} \approx 0.333$	$\approx 33.3\%$
$3/8$	0.375	37.5%
$2/5$	0.4	40%
$1/2$	0.5	50%
$3/5$	0.6	60%
$5/8$	0.625	62.5%
$2/3$	$0.\overline{6} \approx 0.667$	$\approx 66.7\%$
$7/10$	0.7	70%
$3/4$	0.75	75%
$4/5$	0.8	80%
$5/6$	$0.8\overline{3} \approx 0.833$	$\approx 83.3\%$
$7/8$	0.875	87.5%
$9/10$	0.9	90%
$1/1$	1	100%
$5/4$	1.25	125%
$4/3$	$1.\overline{3} \approx 1.33$	133%
$3/2$	1.5	150%
$7/4$	1.75	175%

Unit Four: **Stories, Percents, Ratios, Stats, and Data**

When to Use Which Form

Fractions are great for multiplication and division because you can cancel common factors. They are also the best way to express proportions that do not have clean decimal equivalents, such as $\frac{1}{7}$. Switch to fractions if there is a handy fractional equivalent of the decimal or percent and/or you think you can cancel a lot of factors. For example:

> The price of a dress is increased by $16\frac{2}{3}\%$ to a final price of $140. What is the original price of the dress?

It would be easy to make a mistake when trying to plug $16\frac{2}{3}\%$ into a calculator. But this fraction is on the list of common equivalents to memorize: $16\frac{2}{3}\% = \frac{1}{6}$.

The price is increased by $\frac{1}{6}$ of the original price. The new price will be the original price plus $\frac{1}{6}$ more, or $1 + \frac{1}{6} = \frac{7}{6}$:

$$\frac{7}{6}x = 140$$
$$x = 140\left(\frac{6}{7}\right)$$
$$x = \overset{20}{\cancel{140}}\left(\frac{6}{\cancel{7}_1}\right)$$
$$x = 120$$

The original price was $120.

Fractions are not great when you need to add or subtract, since it takes more effort to find a common denominator. If you need to add or subtract, consider converting the fractions to decimals or percents (especially if the given fractions are on the common conversions list to memorize).

Decimals and percents are also good for estimating results or for comparing sizes, because you don't have to worry about the possibility of different denominators. For example, it's immediately clear that 0.8 is greater than 0.79 and that 45% is less than 47%.

Convert fractions into decimals to compare them more easily. For example, compare the fractions $\frac{17}{25}$ and $\frac{16}{23}$:

$$\frac{17}{25} = 0.68 \text{ vs. } \frac{16}{23} = 0.696\ldots$$

458

Chapter 17: **Fractions, Decimals, Percents, and Ratios**

Even though $\frac{16}{23}$ isn't a **terminating decimal** (more on this in a moment), using the calculator to convert it into a decimal makes it easier to compare and see that it's greater than $\frac{17}{25}$.

> **Strategy Tip**
>
> In general:
> - Prefer fractions for multiplication and division.
> - Prefer decimals for addition and subtraction.
> - Prefer decimals or percents for estimation and comparison.
>
> There is no mathematical difference between fractions, decimals, and percents. Before committing to one format, consider which form fits the problem and the answer choices best.

A **terminating decimal** is one that does not continue on infinitely. By contrast, a non-terminating decimal continues forever. For example:

Terminating decimals	Non-terminating decimals
$\frac{2}{10} = 0.2$	$\frac{2}{9} = 0.2222\ldots = 0.\overline{2}$
$\frac{1}{10} = 0.1$	$\frac{1}{11} = 0.0909\ldots = 0.\overline{09}$
$\frac{6}{5} = 1.2$	$\frac{6}{7} = 0.\overline{857142}$
$\frac{9}{20} = 0.45$	$\sqrt{2} = 1.41421\ldots$

There are a few things to note about non-terminating decimals. First, there is no way to put a non-terminating decimal (in decimal form) into a calculator without rounding. That might be okay if the problem asks for an estimated answer, but if the problem requires an exact answer, then turn the decimal into a fraction before plugging the fraction into the calculator.

Second, some decimals go on forever without repeating their digits, while others fall into a special category called **repeating decimal**. A repeating decimal is one that has decimal values that cycle over and over. The first three examples of non-terminating decimals in the table are all repeating decimals. For $\frac{2}{9}$, the "2" repeats over and over in decimal form. For $\frac{6}{7}$, the sequence of digits "857142" repeats over and over. Repeating decimals are represented by putting a bar over the numbers that are repeated.

Other decimals are non-terminating, but do not repeat, such as $\sqrt{2}$ (1.414213…) or π (3.1415926…). They go on forever, but there isn't a pattern to their decimals. These numbers are referred to as **irrational numbers**. You may not be able to rewrite irrational numbers in fraction form, but if you do have to use them in calculations, the GRE will specify that you only need approximations for these decimals (e.g., $\sqrt{2} \approx 1.4$, $\sqrt{3} \approx 1.7$, and $\pi \approx 3.14$). For numbers such as these, you can often find an estimate of the decimal using your GRE on-screen calculator.

Unit Four: **Stories, Percents, Ratios, Stats, and Data**

> **Strategy Tip**
>
> If a problem specifies directions for rounding (for example, "round to the nearest tenth"), work in whichever form you prefer: fraction or decimal.
>
> If a problem does not specify directions for rounding and there's a non-terminating decimal, then work in fraction form.

Check Your Skills

11. Which of the following is a terminating decimal?

    (A) $\frac{11}{250}$

    (B) $\frac{393}{7}$

    (C) $\frac{1,283}{741}$

    (D) $\frac{\sqrt{3}}{\sqrt{2}}$

Answers can be found on page 467.

Put It All Together

Try these four problems to practice everything you just learned.

The Big Game

A school play premiered at the same time as the big school game. Twenty percent of the students attended the play, while $\frac{1}{3}$ of the remaining students attended the game. If there are 300 total students at the school, and none of those who attended the play also attended the game, how many of the students attended the game?

Because this is a complex problem, implement the three step process for word problems introduced in Chapter 14: Algebraic Translations.

Step 1: Define Knowns and Unknowns

Write down any knowns. Assign the unknowns variables that indicate what they mean. Circle what the question is asking for:

Total = 300

$P = ?$

$(G = ?)$

Chapter 17: **Fractions, Decimals, Percents, and Ratios**

Step 2: Express Relationships

Decide what form you want to use to describe relationships. Because $\frac{1}{3}$ is a fraction that's not expressible as a terminating decimal, convert everything to fractions.

The first given relationship is that 20% of the total students attended the play:

$$20\% = \frac{20}{100} = \frac{1}{5}$$

Since 20% is on the list of common conversions, if you have it memorized, you can go straight to the simplified fraction $\frac{1}{5}$.

The problem indicated that there are 300 students total, so you have a choice: Solve now for the number of students who attended the play or wait until you've written everything else down. If you solve now, the problem may feel more approachable. If you wait, you may be able to reduce the number of computations you have to perform. Try problems both ways to see what you prefer.

The problem also indicates that $\frac{1}{3}$ of the *remaining* students attended the game:

Total = 300

$P = \frac{1}{5} \times 300$

$G = \frac{1}{3} \times$ Remaining

Now, examine everything before you do any math. If $\frac{1}{5}$ attended the play, then the remaining $\frac{4}{5}$ did not. So that *remaining* figure is equal to $\frac{4}{5}$ of the total number of students:

Total = 300

$P = \frac{1}{5} \times 300$

$G = \frac{1}{3} \times \frac{4}{5} \times 300$

Identify the Goal and Solve

It turns out that you don't have to solve for *P* first in order to find *G*. If you wait to solve, then you can save yourself that step. However, you might find that waiting to solve slows you down so much that you'd prefer to go ahead and solve each step as you write it down. Do what works best for you.

The problem asks for the number who attended the game, so solve for *G*. Simplify before you multiply:

$$G = \frac{1}{\cancel{3}} \times \frac{4}{5} \times \cancel{300}^{100}$$
$$G = 1 \times \frac{4}{\cancel{3}} \times \cancel{100}^{20}$$
$$G = 80$$

Therefore, 80 students attended the game.

Unit Four: **Stories, Percents, Ratios, Stats, and Data**

> **Strategy Tip**
>
> To simplify the work required for any problem, use one consistent format: all fractions, all decimals, or all percents.

The Pet Store

If 20% of the animals in a pet store are cats, 30% of the animals are dogs, and $\frac{1}{2}$ of the remaining animals are rabbits, what is the ratio of cats to rabbits?

This question asks for a ratio, but the given values are a mix of percents and fractions. Because the fraction is easy to convert to a percent, do this problem in percent form, then convert it to a ratio at the end.

First, define variables. The first two are based on the total number of animals, but the third one is based on only a subset:

$C = 20\%$ of Total

$D = 30\%$ of Total

$R = 50\%$ of Remaining

$(C : R = ?)$

Next, this problem doesn't provide any actual numbers. It provides several relationships and asks for a relationship as well. To simplify this problem, pick a number for the total. Any number that makes the math easier will work, but since this is a percent problem, choose 100 for the total number of animals:

$C = 20\%$ of $100 = 20$

$D = 30\%$ of $100 = 30$

$R = 50\%$ of Remaining

$(C : R = ?)$

There are 50 total cats and dogs, leaving 50 animals remaining. Take 50% of the *remaining* 50 animals to determine the number of rabbits:

$R = 50\%$ of $50 = 25$

The ratio of cats to rabbits is 20 : 25. Reduce the values to the most simplified form. The ratio of cats to rabbits is 4 : 5.

The Water Drum

A water drum is currently filled to 25% of its capacity. If another 20 gallons of water were added, then the drum would be filled to $\frac{3}{4}$ of its capacity. How many gallons of water does the drum currently contain?

First, define unknowns. It's not clear yet how the math is going to work, so you may not yet be able to decide whether to use percents or fractions to solve. In this story, $c =$ capacity currently, $h =$ the hypothetical scenario, and $t =$ the total capacity of the drum:

$c = 25\%$ of capacity

$h = \dfrac{3}{4}$ of capacity

$t =$ total capacity

Next, express the overall relationship—and use this step to decide whether to use percents or fractions:

$c + 20 = h$

Since the problem requires addition, use percents, not fractions. Update your scratch paper accordingly:

$c = 25 + \%$ of capacity $= 25\%$ of t

$h = 75\%$ of capacity $= 75\%$ of t

$t =$ total capacity

$c + 20 = h$

The problem does provide a real number of gallons of water for one of the steps, so you can't just pick your own number to solve. Instead, set up an equation with a variable:

$$25\%T + 20 = 75\%T$$

Convert those percentages to decimals to solve:

$$0.25T + 20 = 0.75T$$
$$20 = 0.5T$$
$$40 = T$$

The total capacity of the drum is 40 gallons. The question asks how much water is currently in the drum, so find 25% of 40. Since this is multiplication, use the fraction form of 25%:

$$\dfrac{1}{\cancel{4}}(\cancel{40}^{10}) = 10$$

There are currently 10 gallons of water in the drum.

If you feel really comfortable with these kinds of story problems, there is a shortcut you can use to solve this problem.

The drum is currently filled to 25% capacity. If you were to add another 20 gallons, then the drum would be filled to 75% capacity.

That additional 20 gallons takes the drum from 25% full to 75% full. In other words, the 20 gallons represent $75\% - 25\% = 50\%$ of the drum's capacity.

You can set up a proportion to find the number of gallons at 25% capacity:

$$\dfrac{25\%}{50\%} = \dfrac{?\text{ gallons}}{20\text{ gallons}}$$

Alternatively, logic it out. If 50% capacity represents 20 gallons, then 25% capacity (half of 50%) must represent half the number of gallons, or 10 gallons.

Unit Four: **Stories, Percents, Ratios, Stats, and Data**

QC and FDP

Quantity A	Quantity B
$33\frac{1}{3}\%$ of $\frac{3}{4}$ of 100	75% of $\frac{1}{3}$ of 100

Since $33\frac{1}{3}\%$ can be converted to $\frac{1}{3}$ (and vice versa), and since 75% can be converted to $\frac{3}{4}$ (and vice versa), the problem can be rewritten as:

Quantity A	Quantity B
$\frac{1}{3}$ of $\frac{3}{4}$ of 100	$\frac{3}{4}$ of $\frac{1}{3}$ of 100

OR

Quantity A	Quantity B
$33\frac{1}{3}\%$ of 75% of 100	75% of $33\frac{1}{3}\%$ of 100

The order in which multiplication is performed doesn't matter: The value of 2(3) is the same as the value of 3(2). The same is true when the numbers are in fraction or percent form: The order for multiplication doesn't matter. Therefore, the correct answer is (C): The two quantities are equal.

17

Chapter 17: **Fractions, Decimals, Percents, and Ratios**

Check Your Skills Answer Key

1. **0.87**
   Shift the decimal two places to the left and remove the percent symbol: 87% becomes 0.87. Alternatively, convert 87% to a fraction, then use the calculator.
   $$87\% = \frac{87}{100} = 0.87$$

2. $\frac{3}{10}$
   Divide the percent figure by 100, then simplify.
   $$30\% = \frac{30}{100} = \frac{3}{10}$$

3. **37%**
   Shift the decimal two places to the right and add a percent sign: 0.37 becomes 37%.

4. $\frac{1}{4}$
   The decimal has two digits to the right of the decimal place, so multiply the top and bottom by 100 (or move the decimal two places to the right and add two zeros to the bottom), then simplify.
   $$0.25 = \frac{0.25}{1} \times \frac{100}{100} = \frac{25}{100} = \frac{1}{4}$$

5. **0.6**
   Use the calculator to divide the numerator by the denominator.
   $$\frac{3}{5} = 3 \div 5 = 0.6$$

6. **62.5%**
   Use the calculator to divide the numerator by the denominator. Then, shift the decimal two places to the right, and add a percent sign.
   $$\frac{5}{8} = 5 \div 8 = 0.625 = 62.5\%$$

7. **0.000652**
   When multiplying by a negative power of ten, move the decimal to the left. In this case, move the decimal to the left two places, adding two more zeros after the decimal.
   $$0.0652 \times 10^{-2} = 0.000652$$

Unit Four: **Stories, Percents, Ratios, Stats, and Data**

8. 264,000,000

    Dividing by 10 raised to a negative power has exactly the same effect as multiplying by 10 raised to the positive version of that power. Here, it results in a rightward shift of the implicit decimal at the end of 264.

    $$\frac{264}{10^{-6}} = 264 \times 10^6 = 264,000,000$$

9. a, c, b

    Convert all the numbers into decimal form to compare them.

    $a = 2.34$

    $b = 23,400$

    $c = 23.4$

10. (C) $\frac{892}{605}$

    The answers are in fraction form, often an indication to solve on paper. Use powers of 10 to remove the decimals from the numerator and denominator, then simplify. In this case, because the numerator has three digits to the right of the decimal, move the decimal three places in both the top and bottom.

    $$\frac{3.568}{2.42} = \frac{3,568}{2,420}$$

    None of the answer choices match this form, so simplify by canceling common factors. (Use the calculator to divide out the common factors.) Glance at the answers after each simplification step, just in case!

    $$\frac{3,568}{2,420} = \frac{1,784}{1,210} = \frac{892}{605}$$

    Answer choice (C) is correct.

    Alternatively, use the calculator to convert both the original fraction and all the answers into their decimal equivalents. The complex nature of the fractions in this question makes this approach likely to be the more efficient option.

    $$\text{Question: } \frac{3.568}{2.42} = 1.474\ldots$$

    $$\text{(A) } \frac{344}{715} = 0.481\ldots$$

    $$\text{(B) } \frac{688}{573} = 1.200\ldots$$

    $$\text{(C) } \frac{892}{605} = 1.474\ldots$$

    The decimal version of the question is the same as that of answer choice (C).

11. **(A)** $\frac{11}{250}$

Use a calculator to determine that the fraction $\frac{11}{250}$ equals 0.044. The decimal ends, so it is a terminating decimal. The other fractions do not terminate for at least as long as what can be shown on the calculator's display. In Chapter 32: Advanced Concepts, you'll learn how to prove they don't terminate, but for most questions, just keep the problem in fraction form when the decimal doesn't terminate and the problem is asking for a precise answer.

Unit Four: **Stories, Percents, Ratios, Stats, and Data**

Problem Set

1. Express the following as fractions:
   (a) 2.45
   (b) 0.008

2. Express the following as fractions:
   (a) 420%
   (b) 8%

3. Express the following as decimals:
   (a) $\dfrac{9}{2}$
   (b) $\dfrac{3,000}{10,000}$

4. Express the following as decimals:
   (a) $1\dfrac{4}{25}$
   (b) $12\dfrac{3}{8}$

5. Express the following as percents:
   (a) $\dfrac{1,000}{10}$
   (b) $\dfrac{25}{9}$

6. Express the following as percents:
   (a) 80.4
   (b) 0.0007

7. Order from least to greatest:
   (a) $\dfrac{8}{18}$
   (b) 0.8
   (c) 40%

8. Order from least to greatest:
   (a) 1.19
   (b) $\dfrac{120}{84}$
   (c) 131.44%

9. Order from least to greatest:
   (a) $2\dfrac{4}{7}$
   (b) 2,400%
   (c) 2.401

Chapter 17: **Fractions, Decimals, Percents, and Ratios**

10. Order from least to greatest ($x \neq 0$):
    (a) $\frac{50}{17}x^2$
    (b) $2.9x^2$
    (c) $(x^2)(3.10\%)$

11. What number is 62.5% of 192?

12. 200 is 16% of what number?

For problems #13–14, express your answer in terms of the variables given.

---

13. What is X percent of Y?

14. X is what percent of Y?

15. For every 1,000,000 toys sold, 337,000 are action figures.

Quantity A	Quantity B
Percent of toys sold that are action figures	33.7%

16.
Quantity A	Quantity B
$10^{-3} \times \left(\frac{0.002}{10^{-3}}\right)$	0.02

17. Tae Yang has a stack of $20 bills totaling $1,600 and a stack of $10 bills totaling $1,050. (Assume that all bills have the same thickness.)

Quantity A	Quantity B
The percent by which the height of the stack of $10 bills is greater than that of the stack of $20 bills	33.5%

18.
Quantity A	Quantity B
$(0.\overline{7})(0.8)(35)$	$(1.8)(15)(0.\overline{7})$

19. *m* is 120 percent of *n*

Quantity A	Quantity B
$\frac{6}{5}n$	$\frac{5}{6}m$

20.
Quantity A	Quantity B
$0.125 + \frac{4}{5} + \frac{2}{3} + 1.2$	$0.8 + 0.\overline{6} + \frac{6}{5} + \frac{1}{8}$

469

Unit Four: **Stories, Percents, Ratios, Stats, and Data**

Solutions

1. (a) $\dfrac{49}{20}$; (b) $\dfrac{1}{125}$

    To convert a decimal to a fraction, write it over the appropriate power of 10 and simplify.

    $$2.45 = 2\dfrac{45}{100} = 2\dfrac{9}{20} \text{ (improper)} = \dfrac{49}{20} \text{ (mixed)}$$

    $$0.008 = \dfrac{8}{1{,}000} = \dfrac{1}{125}$$

2. (a) $4\dfrac{1}{5}$; (b) $\dfrac{2}{25}$

    To convert a percent to a fraction, write it over a denominator of 100 and simplify.

    $$420\% = \dfrac{420}{100} = \dfrac{21}{5} \text{ (improper)} = 4\dfrac{1}{5} \text{ (mixed)}$$

    $$8\% = \dfrac{8}{100} = \dfrac{2}{25}$$

3. (a) 4.5; (b) 0.3

    To convert a fraction to a decimal, divide the numerator by the denominator.

    $$\dfrac{9}{2} = 9 \div 2 = 4.5$$

    When the numbers are small enough to be plugged into the calculator, doing so is often the safest way to handle this conversion. However, you can also simplify the fraction *before* you divide.

    $$\dfrac{3{,}000}{10{,}000} = \dfrac{3}{10} = 0.3$$

    This can prove particularly helpful in cases involving numbers too large to plug into the calculator, such as fractions with large powers of 10 in the numerator and denominator.

4. (a) 1.16; (b) 12.375

    To convert a mixed number to a decimal, rewrite it as addition between the whole number and the fraction and convert the fraction component to a decimal.

    $$1\dfrac{4}{25} = 1 + \dfrac{4}{25} = 1 + 0.16 = 1.16$$

    $$12\dfrac{3}{8} = 12 + \dfrac{3}{8} = 12 + 0.375 = 12.375$$

5. (a) 10,000%; (b) $277.\overline{7}\%$

    To convert a fraction to a percent, rewrite the fraction with a denominator of 100.

    $$\dfrac{1{,}000}{10} = \dfrac{10{,}000}{100} = 10{,}000\%$$

    Alternatively, you can convert the fraction to a decimal using the calculator, shift the decimal point two places to the right, and add a percent symbol.

    $$\dfrac{25}{9} = 25 \div 9 = 2.7777\ldots = 2.\overline{7} = 277.\overline{7}\%$$

Chapter 17: **Fractions, Decimals, Percents, and Ratios**

6. **(a) 8,040%; (b) 0.07%**
   To convert a decimal to a percent, shift the decimal point two places to the right and add a percent symbol.

   $$80.4 = 8,040\%$$
   $$0.0007 = 0.07\%$$

7. $40\% < \dfrac{8}{18} < 0.8$

   To order from least to greatest, express all the terms in the same form. Decimal form usually works best, as the calculator makes it easier to convert fractions to decimals than vice versa.

   $$\dfrac{8}{18} = 0.4444\ldots$$
   $$0.8 = 0.8$$
   $$40\% = 0.4$$
   $$0.4 < 0.4444\ldots < 0.8$$

8. $1.19 < 131.44\% < \dfrac{120}{84}$

   To order from least to greatest, first express all the terms in the same form.

   $$1.19 = 1.19$$
   $$\dfrac{120}{84} \approx 1.4286$$
   $$131.44\% = 1.3144$$

   Finally, put the original terms in order according to the decimal equivalents:
   $1.19 < 1.3144 < 1.4286$.

9. $2.401 < 2\dfrac{4}{7} < 2400\%$

   To order from least to greatest, first express all the terms in the same form.

   $$2\dfrac{4}{7} \approx 2.5714$$
   $$2,400\% = 24$$
   $$2.401 = 2.401$$

   Finally, put the original terms in order according to the decimal equivalents: $2.401 < 2.5714 < 24$.

10. $(x^2)(3.10\%) < 2.9\,x^2 < \dfrac{50}{17}x^2$

    To order from least to greatest, express all the terms in the same form. Because x^2 is a positive term common to all the terms you are comparing, you can ignore its presence completely and just compare the numbers.

    $$\dfrac{50}{17} \approx 2.94$$
    $$2.9 = 2.9$$
    $$3.10\% = 0.031$$

    Finally, put the original terms in order according to the decimal equivalents: $0.031 < 2.9 < 2.94$.

Unit Four: **Stories, Percents, Ratios, Stats, and Data**

11. **120**

    This is best handled as a percent-to-decimal conversion problem. Convert 62.5% to the decimal 0.625 and use the calculator to finish: $0.625 \times 192 = 120$.

12. **1,250**

    This is best handled with algebraic translation and decimal conversion. Use n to represent the number in question.

    $$200 = 0.16n$$
    $$\frac{200}{0.16} = n$$

    Use the calculator to finish the problem: $200 \div 0.16 = 1{,}250$.

13. $\dfrac{XY}{100}$

    Given the variables in this problem, algebraic translation is a good approach.

    $$n = \frac{X}{100} \times Y$$
    $$n = \frac{XY}{100}$$

14. $\dfrac{100X}{Y}$

    Use the variable n to represent the number the problem is asking for (represented by the word *what* in the question) and solve for n.

    $$X = \frac{n}{100} \times Y$$
    $$\frac{X}{Y} = \frac{n}{100}$$
    $$\frac{100X}{Y} = n$$

15. **(C)**

    Simplify Quantity A. Divide the number of action figures by the total number of toys to find the percentage of action figures.

Quantity A	Quantity B
Percent of toys sold that are action figures = $\dfrac{337{,}000}{1{,}000{,}000}$	33.7%

    You can use the calculator to find the value of Quantity A. Alternatively, you can use a fraction-to-percent conversion. A percentage is defined as being out of 100, so reduce the fraction until the denominator is 100.

Chapter 17: **Fractions, Decimals, Percents, and Ratios**

Quantity A	Quantity B
$\dfrac{337,000}{1,000,000} = \dfrac{337,\cancel{000}}{1,000,\cancel{000}}$	33.7%
$\dfrac{337}{1,000} = \dfrac{33.7}{100}$	

Once the denominator is 100, the number in the numerator is effectively the percent. So action figures constitute 33.7% of the total number of toys sold.

Therefore, the correct answer is (C): The two quantities are equal.

16. **(B)**
    Take a close look at the expression in Quantity A: 0.002 is first divided by 10^{-3}, and then multiplied by 10^{-3}. Because these two 10^{-3} terms cancel each other out, the net effect is the same as multiplying by 1.

Quantity A	Quantity B
$10^{-3} \times \left(\dfrac{0.002}{10^{-3}}\right) = 0.002 \times \dfrac{10^{-3}}{10^{-3}} =$	0.02
$0.002 \times 1 = 0.002$	

Therefore, the correct answer is (B): Quantity B is greater.

17. **(B)**
    Because all bills have the same thickness, you can compare the number of bills in each stack to determine the percent difference in height. There are $1,600 worth of $20 bills, so the number of $20 bills in the stack is $\dfrac{1,600}{20} = 80$. There are $1,050 worth of $10 bills, so the number of $10 bills is $\dfrac{1,050}{10} = 105$. Plug these values into the percent change formula to evaluate Quantity A.

Quantity A	Quantity B
The percent by which the height of the stack of $10 bills is greater than that of the stack of $20	33.5%
$\dfrac{105 - 80}{80} = \dfrac{25}{80} = 0.3125$	

Now compare the two quantities. Since 0.3125 converts to 31.25%, Quantity A is less than Quantity B.

Therefore, the correct answer is (B): Quantity B is greater.

Unit Four: **Stories, Percents, Ratios, Stats, and Data**

18. **(A)**
First, divide the common element ($0.\overline{7}$) out from each side.

Quantity A	Quantity B
(0.8)(35)	(1.8)(15)

From there, it's a calculator workout.

Quantity A	Quantity B
(0.8)(35) = 28	(1.8)(15) = 27

Therefore, the correct answer is (A): Quantity A is greater.

19. **(D)**
Converting 120% to fraction form will help simplify. The equivalent of 120% is $\frac{6}{5}$. Rewrite the common information as $m = \frac{6}{5}n$. Then substitute m for $\frac{6}{5}n$ in Quantity A.

Quantity A	Quantity B
m	$\frac{5}{6}m$

Initially, it might seem that Quantity A is greater—a whole m is usually greater than a fraction of m. However, what if m is a negative number? For example, if m is −6, Quantity A would be −6 and Quantity B would be −5, making Quantity B greater.

Therefore, the correct answer is (D): The relationship cannot be determined.

20. **(C)**
Use fraction-to-decimal equivalencies to make the quantities look more alike, and then use the hidden inequality to cancel terms from both sides.

The decimal 0.125 is equal to the fraction $\frac{1}{8}$, so cancel 0.125 from Quantity A and $\frac{1}{8}$ from Quantity B.

Next, $\frac{4}{5} = 0.8$, so cancel $\frac{4}{5}$ from Quantity A and 0.8 from Quantity B.

Then, $\frac{2}{3} = 0.\overline{6}$, so cancel $\frac{2}{3}$ from Quantity A and $0.\overline{6}$ from Quantity B.

The last remaining quantities, 1.2 and $\frac{6}{5}$, are also equal to each other.

Therefore, the correct answer is (C): The two quantities are equal.

CHAPTER 18
Statistics

In This Chapter:

- Averages
- Using the Average Formula
- Special Cases: Weighted Averages
- Median: The Middle Number
- Range
- Quartiles and Percentiles
- Standard Deviation
- The Normal Distribution
- Check Your Skills Answer Key
- Problem Set
- Solutions

CHAPTER 18 Statistics

On the GRE, most statistics questions revolve around describing a list of numbers. That list can be stated directly, it can be described in terms of variables, or it can be largely unknown, with only limited or general information provided.

In this chapter, you will learn the common properties of these lists, including average, median, range, quartiles, percentiles, and standard deviation. You'll also learn how to analyze a list of values and derive certain properties, as well as how to derive part of a list when given certain properties of that list.

Averages

The **average** (or the **arithmetic mean**) of a list of numbers is given by the average formula:

$$\text{Average} = \frac{\text{Sum}}{\text{\# of Terms}}$$
$$A = \frac{S}{n}$$

The language in an average problem will often explicitly use the terms *average* or *arithmetic mean*, but not always. For example, "The cost per employee, if equally shared, is $20" is another way of saying that the *average* cost per employee is $20.

If you're given any two parts of the average formula, you can find the third. On the GRE, it's not uncommon to be told the average and the number of terms, in which case you can find the sum. In many GRE average problems, all that matters is the *sum* of the terms—which often can be found even when the individual terms in the list cannot be determined.

> *Average Formulas*
>
> $\text{Average} = \dfrac{\text{sum}}{\text{number of terms}} \qquad A = \dfrac{S}{n}$
>
> $\text{Average} \times \text{number of terms} = \text{sum} \qquad A \times n = S$

Unit Four: **Stories, Percents, Ratios, Stats, and Data**

Using the Average Formula

As soon as you're aware that a GRE problem is asking about an average, write down the average formula. Then, see which two of the three variables are given in the problem:

The sum of 6 numbers is 90. What is the average (arithmetic mean) of the terms?

The sum, S, is 90. The number of terms, n, is 6.

$$A = \frac{S}{n}$$ Solve for the average: $\frac{90}{6} = 15$.

You do not need to know the value of each individual term to find the average. Knowing the sum of the terms is enough.

Sometimes, you will need to pay attention to the individual values in the list. For example:

If the average of the list {2, 5, 5, 7, 8, 9, x} is 6.1, what is the value of x?

Plug the given information into the average formula, then use your calculator to solve for x:

$$A \times n = S \quad (6.1)(7) = 2 + 5 + 5 + 7 + 8 + 9 + x$$
$$42.7 = 36 + x$$
$$6.7 = x$$

More complex average problems can involve setting up two average formulas. For example:

Sam earned a $2,000 commission on a big sale, raising her average commission by $100. If Sam's new average commission is $900, how many sales has she made?

To keep track of two average formulas in the same problem, set up a table. Use *Average* × *number* = *Sum* as the column headers and the different stages of the story for each row. Since Sam's new average commission of $900 is $100 higher than her old average, her old average must have been $800:

	Average	×	Number	=	Sum
Original scenario	800	×		=	
Big sale	2,000	×	1	=	2,000
Original + big sale	900	×	◯	=	

Put a circle or other signal in the cell for which you're trying to solve.

Because you don't know how many sales Sam made prior to the $2,000 commission, label that cell n and calculate the sum before the newest commission:

	Average	×	Number	=	Sum
Original scenario	800	×	n	=	$800n$
Big sale	2,000	×	1	=	2,000
Original + big sale	900	×	◯	=	

478

Here's the key to using this table: The *Number* column adds up. The original number of sales plus the one big sale add up to the final number of sales in the "original + big sale" column. The same is true for the *Sum* column:

	Average	×	Number	=	Sum
Old total	800	×	n	=	$800n$
This sale	2,000	×	1	=	2,000
New total	900	×	$(n+1)$	=	$800n + 2000$

One note: The *Average* column does *not* add up. Only the *Number* and *Sum* columns will add up.

The bottom row of the table creates an equation. Use it to solve for n:

$$900(n+1) = 800n + 2000$$
$$900n + 900 = 800n + 2000$$
$$100n = 1100$$
$$n = 11$$

The original number of sales is 11. The question asks for the *new* number of sales, which is $n + 1$, so Sam has made a total of 12 sales. Watch out for 11 as a trap answer!

In even more complicated problems, you'll need to make certain inferences about the list before you can use the average formula to find the answer. Often these problems involve finding a maximum or minimum value in the list. For example:

> In a certain course, the overall grade is calculated by averaging the scores of the 6 exams in the course, each graded on a scale of 0 to 100. If Issy's overall grade for the course was 94, what is the minimum score Issy could have received on one of the exams?

To start, use the average formula to calculate the sum of all of Issy's exam scores:

$$\frac{sum}{6} = 94$$
$$sum = 94 \times 6 = 564$$

Issy must have earned 564 points total across all 6 exams, but it's not immediately clear what this means for individual exam scores.

To find the *minimum* possible score on one test, *maximize* Issy's scores on the other 5 exams. This will ensure that as many as possible of the 564 total points are allocated to the other 5 exams, leaving as few points as possible for the one exam with the lowest score.

The maximum score on any exam was 100 points and there's no restriction on choosing the same score for those 5 exams, so say that Issy scored 100 points on each of those exams:

	Average	×	Number	=	Sum
5 exams	100	×	5	=	500
Lowest exam		×	1	=	
Total	94	×	6	=	564

The 5 exams would then account for 500 of the 564 total points that Issy scored, leaving 64 points unaccounted for. Thus, the minimum score Issy could have received on one exam was 64 points.

This is an example of an Optimization problem, which will be covered in more depth in Chapter 31: Optimization.

Check Your Skills

1. The sum of 6 integers is 45. What is the average of the 6 integers?

2. The average price per item in a shopping basket is $2.40. If there are a total of 30 items in the basket, what is the total cost of the items in the basket?

3. The average price per item in a shopping basket was $2.40. Then, an item costing $9 is added to the basket, increasing the average price per item in the basket to $3. How many items are now in the basket?

Answers can be found on page 489.

Special Cases: Weighted Averages

Weighted-average problems involve situations in which populations, substances, or other things are mixed together. The basic idea is this: If you mix two things together in unequal amounts, the resulting mixture will look more like whichever you added more of. For example, if you were to mix one gallon of yellow paint with one gallon of blue paint, you would end up with green paint. However, if you were to mix one gallon of yellow paint with *three* gallons of blue paint, the paint, though still *greenish*, would be considerably more blue. If you've ever taken a course in which test scores, homework scores, and participation scores all accounted for different percentages of your overall grade (that is, they were *weighted* differently), then you've encountered a weighted average.

Although weighted averages can differ from traditional averages in how the math is set up, they are still averages, so they can still be solved using the average formula. Moreover, weighted averages will still fall somewhere in the middle of the values being averaged (or between the highest and lowest of those values, if there are more than two). For example:

> A certain drink is made by combining three shots of liquor A with two shots of liquor B. Liquor A is 20% alcohol, while liquor B is 30% alcohol. What percent alcohol is the resulting drink?

First, one type of liquor is 20% alcohol and the other type is 30% alcohol, so the mixture will be somewhere between 20% and 30% alcohol.

Second, because the mixture contains more of liquor A, the mixture will be closer to liquor A's percentage (that is, closer to 20% than 30%). It may help to visualize the average as the fulcrum balancing the two components on a scale. One side holds liquor A and the other holds liquor B. If the two sides are equally weighted, the fulcrum will be in the middle, but if one side has more weight, then the fulcrum will shift closer to that side:

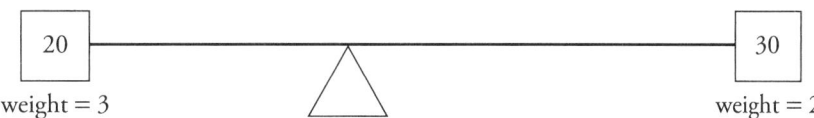

You could figure out the exact position of the weighted average using this diagram and considering the ratio of the two endpoints, but on the GRE, it's often more straightforward to use the weighted average formula, which consists of the weighted sum divided by the weights. In the formula, a and b are the individual components of the average. The other variables in the formula—n_a and n_b—are the weights (or amounts) of those components:

$$\text{Weighted average} = \frac{a(n_a) + b(n_b)}{n_a + n_b}$$

This question stem asks for a percent of alcohol, so here a and b are the individual alcohol percentages.

To find the percentage of alcohol in the mixed drink, define each of the unknowns as follows:

a = 20% alcohol
b = 30% alcohol
n_a = 3 shots
n_b = 2 shots

Plug the values into the formula:

$$\frac{a(n_a) + b(n_b)}{n_a + n_b} = \frac{0.2(3) + 0.3(2)}{2 + 3} = \frac{1.2}{5} = 0.24 = 24\%$$

The resulting drink mixture will be 24% alcohol. Does this answer make sense given the details in the story? Yes, 24% is closer to 20% than 30%, so this answer makes sense.

The weighted average formula can be expanded to include as many components (c, d, etc.) as the problem requires. If the drink also included one shot of 40% alcohol and two shots of 10% alcohol, the overall alcohol percent would be found using the weighted–average formula:

$$\frac{a(n_a) + b(n_b) + c(n_c) + d(n_d)}{n_a + n_b + n_c + n_d} = \text{Weighted average}$$

$$\frac{0.2(3) + 0.3(2) + 0.4(1) + 0.1(2)}{2 + 3 + 1 + 2} = \frac{1.8}{8} = 0.225 = 22.5\%$$

Unit Four: **Stories, Percents, Ratios, Stats, and Data**

Check Your Skills

4. A stock portfolio comprised of Stock *A* and Stock *B* gained 14% last year. Stock *A*'s annual gain last year was 20%, and Stock *B*'s annual gain last year was 10%.

Quantity A	Quantity B
The number of shares of Stock *A* in the portfolio	The number of shares of Stock *B* in the portfolio

5. On Planet *X*, $\frac{2}{3}$ of the aliens are Zorgs, whose average IQ is 120. The rest are Weebs, whose average IQ is 180. What is the average IQ of all the aliens on Planet *X* ?

Answers can be found on pages 489-490.

Median: The Middle Number

Some GRE problems feature another type of measure: the **median**, or "middle value." The median is calculated in one of two ways, depending on the number of data points in the list.

For lists containing an *odd* number of values, the median is the middle value when the data are arranged in increasing (or decreasing) order. For instance, the median of the set {5, 17, 24, 25, 28} is the unique middle number 24.

However, for lists containing an *even* number of values, the median is the average (arithmetic mean) of the two middle values when the data are arranged in increasing (or decreasing) order. For example, the median of the list {3, 4, 9, 17} is found by averaging the two middles values, 4 and 9. The median is 6.5.

> *Median*
>
> If the list has an odd number of values, the median is the value in the exact center of the ordered list.
>
> If the list has an even number of values, the median is the average of the two values in the center of the ordered list.

The median of a list containing an odd number of values must be a value in the list. However, the median of a list containing an even number of values does not have to be in the list—and indeed will not be in the list unless the two middle values in the list are equal.

Medians of Lists Containing Unknown Values

Unlike the arithmetic mean, the median of a list depends only on the one or two values in the middle of the ordered list. Therefore, you may be able to determine a specific value for the median of a list even if one or more numbers in the list are unknown. For instance, consider the unordered list of integers {*x*, 2, 5, 11, 11, 12, 33}. No matter whether *x* is less than 11, equal to 11, or greater than 11, the median of the resulting set will be 11. (Try substituting different integer values of *x* to see that the median does not change.)

By contrast, the median of the unordered list {x, 2, 5, 11, 12, 12, 33} depends on x. If x is 11 or less, then the median is 11. If x is 12 or greater, the median is 12. When a list in a median problem contains an unknown value, write the rest of the numbers in order and test a low, middle, and high number for the unknown to see if you can pin down the list's median.

Check Your Skills

6. What is the median of the set {1, 2, x, 8}, if 2 < x < 8 ?

7. Set S contains the 6 distinct integers {−1, 4, 2, 6, 0, x}. Which of the following could be the median of Set S ?

   Indicate all such numbers.

   A. 1
   B. 1.5
   C. 2
   D. 2.5
   E. 3
   F. 3.5
   G. 4

Answers can be found on page 490.

Range

The **range** of a list of numbers is one way to measure the dispersion of the numbers in the list. The range is defined as the difference between the greatest number in the list and the least number in the list. As such, range is always expressed as a single number. For example, in the list {3, 6, −1, 4, 12, 8}, the greatest number is 12 and the least number is −1. Therefore, the range is $12 - (-1) = 13$.

Check Your Skills

8. The list {2, −1, x, 5, 3} has a range of 13. What are the possible values of x ?

Answers can be found on page 490.

Quartiles and Percentiles

Lists of numbers can be described by **quartiles**, and for larger datasets (another word that the GRE will use for lists), by **percentiles**. For example, the dataset of the 16 numbers {0, 1, 2, 2, 3, 4, 5, 5, 5, 6, 7, 8, 10, 11, 13, 14} can be divided up into four subsets or quartiles:

$$\left\{ \underbrace{0, 1, 2, 2}_{\text{Quartile 1}} \mid \underbrace{3, 4, 5, 5}_{\text{Quartile 2}} \mid \underbrace{5, 6, 7, 8}_{\text{Quartile 3}} \mid \underbrace{10, 11, 13, 14}_{\text{Quartile 4}} \right\}$$

Q_1 Q_2 Q_3

Unit Four: **Stories, Percents, Ratios, Stats, and Data**

The list is placed in increasing order before it is separated into quartiles. Each quartile denotes one quarter of the list, so dividing the number of members in the list by 4 will tell you how many members are in each quartile. There are 16 members in the list above, and since 16 divided by 4 is 4, each quartile contains 4 members. These quartiles are separated by "Quartile Markers," shown as Q values with dashed lines above. You can calculate each Q value by averaging the two numbers immediately adjacent to it. Thus, Q_1 is the average of the greatest item in Quartile 1 and the least item in Quartile 2, and so on from there:

$$Q_1 = \frac{2+3}{2} = 2.5$$
$$Q_2 = \frac{5+5}{2} = 5$$
$$Q_3 = \frac{8+10}{2} = 9$$

Interestingly, Q_2 will always equal the median of the list because Q_2 is equal to the average of the two middle numbers in the list.

For a larger dataset, percentiles are often used instead of quartiles. Percentile rankings range from 1st percentile to 99th percentile.

To know how many of a dataset's members will be assigned to each percentile ranking, divide the number of members in the dataset by 100. For instance, in a dataset of 1,000 numbers, each percentile will contain 10 members. The 10 least items will be in the 1st percentile, the next 10 least items will be in the 2nd percentile, and so on.

As with quartiles, you can calculate the cutoff value for each percentile by averaging the two adjacent values in the dataset. If there are 1,000 numbers, P_1 will be the average of the 10th and 11th items (in increasing order).

Quartiles and percentiles overlap: $P_{25} = Q_1$, $P_{50} = Q_2 =$ median, and $P_{75} = Q_3$. Percentiles just offer a more granular grouping of the members of a dataset.

Check Your Skills

9. In the list {2, 3, 0, 8, 11, 1, 4, 7, 8, 2, 1, 3}, what is $Q_3 - Q_1$?

Answers can be found on page 490.

18 Standard Deviation

The mean and median both give "average" or "representative" values for a list, but they do not tell the whole story. It is possible for two lists to have the same average but to differ widely in how spread out their values are. To describe the spread, or variation, of the data in a list, use a different measure: the **standard deviation**.

Standard deviation (SD) is a measure of how far the members of a list are from the average (mean) of the list.

- A lesser SD indicates that the members of the list are clustered closely around the average (mean) value.
- A greater SD indicates that the members of the list are spread more widely, with some points appearing far from the mean.

Take a look at these three lists:

$$\text{List 1:} \quad \{5, 5, 5, 5\}$$
$$\text{List 2:} \quad \{2, 4, 6, 8\}$$
$$\text{List 3:} \quad \{0, 0, 10, 10\}$$

All three lists have the same mean value of 5. You can see at a glance, though, that the lists are very different. The SD reflects these differences. List 1 has an SD of 0 (no spread at all) because all of the values are the same. List 2 is more spread out than list 1, and list 3 is even more spread out than list 2. List 3 has the greatest SD, while list 2's SD is somewhere between 0 and list 3's SD.

The formula for calculating SD is cumbersome—so cumbersome that you won't be asked to calculate an SD from scratch on the GRE. Most GRE SD problems involve either (1) comparisons of the SDs of two or more lists, or (2) changes in the SD resulting from an alteration to the list. For case (1), you just need to know that the more spread out the numbers in a list, the greater the list's SD.

Case (2) is a bit more complicated. If you see a problem focusing on changes in the SD, ask yourself whether the changes to the list move the data closer together, farther apart, or neither.

For example:

(a) Which list has the greater standard deviation: {1, 2, 3, 4, 5} or {442, 442, 443, 444, 445} ?

(b) If each data point in a list is increased by 7, does the list's SD increase, decrease, or remain constant?

(c) If each data point in a list is increased by a factor of 7, does the list's SD increase, decrease, or remain constant?

(d) If the number 100 is removed from the list {20, 40, 60, 80, 100}, does the list's SD increase, decrease, or remain constant?

In (a), the list {1, 2, 3, 4, 5} has the greater SD. Examine the gaps between the numbers. The first list ranges from 1 to 5, while the second list ranges from 442 to 445. The second list would need to be changed to {*441*, 442, 443, 444, 445} in order to have the same spread (and therefore the same SD) as the first list.

Only the *spread* matters. The numbers in the second list are greater and more "consistent" in one sense—they are all within about 1 percent of each other, while the greatest numbers in the first list are several times greater than the smallest ones. However, this "percent variation" idea is irrelevant to the SD—only the actual distance between the numbers in a list matters.

For this reason, in (b), if all values of a list are increased by 7, the SD will not change. If you add 7 to every data point in the list, then the spread of the numbers relative to each other will not change. Try it. If the original list were {1, 2, 3, 4, 5}, then the transformed list would be {8, 9, 10, 11, 12}. The values have changed, but the spread or distance between the numbers has not changed.

In (c), if all data points in a list are increased by a *factor* of 7, then the SD will *usually* increase. "Increased by a *factor* of 7" means that each data point is multiplied by 7. For example, if the original list were {1, 2, 3, 4, 5}, then the transformed list would be {7, 14, 21, 28, 35}. The values are more spread out, so the SD will increase. In fact, the SD will increase by a factor of 7, since that's the factor by which all of the individual values increased.

Unit Four: **Stories, Percents, Ratios, Stats, and Data**

There is one exception to this rule: lists whose members are all equal. The lists {10, 10, 10} and {70, 70, 70}, for instance, both have the same standard deviation, 0, so in this case, the standard deviation stays the same.

In (d), if the value 100 is removed from the list {20, 40, 60, 80, 100}, then the SD will decrease. Because 100 is one of the farthest members from the mean, it is contributing to a greater spread—that is, a greater SD. Removing such numbers will decrease the SD by leaving the remaining numbers relatively closer to the mean. Conversely, removing the middle number 60 from the set would cause the SD to increase, as this value is equal to the mean.

As a final note, you may see the term variance on the GRE. The variance is the *square* of the standard deviation. As such, problems that mention variance are essentially the same as SD problems.

Check Your Skills

10.   **Quantity A**   **Quantity B**

The standard deviation of the   The standard deviation of the
set {3, 4, 5, 6, 7}   set {3, 3, 5, 7, 7}

Answers can be found on page 491.

The Normal Distribution

One of the most important distributions for random variables is the Normal Distribution (also known as the Gaussian Distribution). A normal distribution looks like the classic "bell curve" with a high and rounded middle section, long and low tails on either side, and symmetry around the mean (which is equal to the median or P_{50}, the 50th percentile marker).

Imagine that a game has a scoring range of −5 to +25 points. The scores that people earn as they play this game fall into the normal distribution as shown:

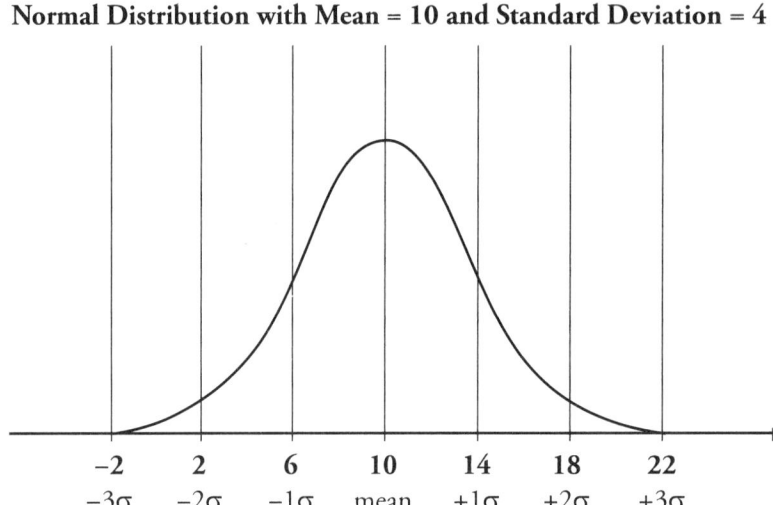

Normal Distribution with Mean = 10 and Standard Deviation = 4

The GRE tests distributions that are both *normal* and *approximately normal*. These distributions have the following characteristics:

For all normal distributions	Example (based on chart for game shown)
The *mean* and *median* are equal, or *almost exactly* equal. The mean or median can be represented as P_{50}, or the 50th percentile.	The mean score earned in this game is 10. If you earn a score of 10, you have scored better than 50% of the people who play the game.
The data is exactly, or *almost exactly*, symmetric around the mean/median.	In this game, one standard deviation *below* the mean is 6, which is 4 less than 10; one standard deviation *above* the mean is 14, which is 4 greater than 10. The spacing is symmetrical.
About 34% of the sample falls between the mean and 1 standard deviation below it. One standard deviation below the mean represents the 16th percentile, because 50% − 34% = 16%.	In this game, 34% of players earn a score between 6 (one standard deviation below the mean) and 10 (the mean). A player who earns a score of 6 does better than 16% of all the people who played the game.
Likewise, 34% of the sample falls between the mean and 1 standard deviation above it. One standard deviation above the mean represents the 84th percentile, because 50% + 34% = 84%.	In this game, 34% of players earn a score between 10 (the mean) and 14 (one standard deviation above the mean). If you earned a score of 14, you performed better than 84% of the people who played the game.
Collectively, approximately 34% + 34% = 68% of the sample falls within one standard deviation of the mean (in either direction).	In this game, 68% of players earn a score between 6 (one standard deviation below the mean) and 14 (one standard deviation above the mean).
Roughly 96% of the total sample falls within 2 standard deviations of the mean (in either direction). Roughly 48 percent of the sample falls between the mean and 2 standard deviations below the mean, for a percentile ranking of 50% − 48% = 2%. Roughly 48 percent of the sample falls between the mean and 2 standard deviations above the mean, for a percentile ranking of 50% + 48% = 98%.	In this game, 96% of all scores fall between 2 and 18. About 48% of the scores fall between 2 and 10 and 48% of the scores fall between 10 and 18. Someone who receives a score of 2 has done better than 2% of all players and someone who receives a score of 18 has done better than 98% of all players.
Only about $\frac{1}{1{,}000}$ or 0.1% of the scores are 3 or more standard deviations below the mean. The same is true at the high end: About 0.1% of the scores are 3 or more standard deviations above the mean.	In this game, only about 0.1% of players score below −2 and only about 0.1% of players score above 22. These scores are very rare!

You may see a question that says a particular distribution is *nearly* normal or *nearly* normally distributed. Treat these the same as normal distributions.

Unit Four: Stories, Percents, Ratios, Stats, and Data

Though the GRE will typically only test these concepts in a general way, it is important to memorize the percentages associated with certain SDs above and below the mean:

A measurement that is...	...is equal to...
two SDs below the mean	the 2nd percentile
one SD below the mean	the 16th percentile
equal to the mean	the 50th percentile
one SD above the mean	the 84th percentile
two SDs above the mean	the 98th percentile

The GRE might also give you information in a less precise form. Memorize these values, too:

A measurement that is...	...is...
within one SD of the mean	between the 34th and 86th percentiles
within two SDs below the mean	between the 2nd and 50th percentiles
within two SDs above the mean	between the 50th and 98th percentiles

If a problem does *not* specify that the distribution is normal or nearly normal, then do not use the above values. Instead, in this case, the problem will present you with the data to use for that particular problem.

Check Your Skills

For questions #11–15, variable X is nearly normally distributed, with a mean of 6 and a standard deviation of 2.

11. Approximately what percent of the observations in X will be less than 4 ?

12. Approximately what percent of the observations in X will be greater than 12 ?

13. For variable X, approximately what percentile corresponds to a value of 2 ?

14. For variable X, which of the following values is closest to the 70th percentile?

    (A) 5
    (B) 6
    (C) 7
    (D) 8
    (E) 9

15. Would the answers to questions #12–15 be the same if variable X were not normally or nearly normally distributed?

Answers can be found on page 491.

Chapter 18: **Statistics**

Check Your Skills Answer Key

1. **7.5**
   Use the average equation to solve:
   $$A = \frac{S}{n}$$
   $$A = \frac{45}{6} = 7.5$$

2. **$72**
   Use the average formula to solve:
   $$A = \frac{S}{n}$$
   $$2.40 = \frac{S}{30}$$
   $$S = 2.40(30) = 72$$

3. **11**
   As this problem involves two averages ($2.40 and $3), set up an average table:

	Average	×	Number	=	Sum
Old total	$2.40	×	n	=	$2.4n$
This sale	$9	×	1	=	9
New total	$3	×	$(n+1)$	=	$2.4n+9$

   Solve for n using the equation from the last row:
   $$3(n+1) = 2.4n + 9$$
   $$3n + 3 = 2.4n + 9$$
   $$0.6n = 6$$
   $$n = 10$$

   The question is asking how many items are in the basket after the new item was added, so there are $n + 1 = 11$ items.

4. **(B)**
   Because the overall gain of 14% is closer to 10% than to 20%, the portfolio must be weighted more heavily towards Stock *B* (i.e., contain more shares of Stock *B*).

   The correct answer is (B): Quantity B is greater.

Unit Four: **Stories, Percents, Ratios, Stats, and Data**

5. 140

   Two-thirds of the total population is Zorgs, so their IQ will have a weight of $\frac{2}{3}$. Similarly, Weebs account for $\frac{1}{3}$ of the population, so their IQ is weighted accordingly. Plug everything into the weighted average formula:

   $$\text{Weighted Average} = \frac{(120)\frac{2}{3} + (180)\frac{1}{3}}{\frac{2}{3} + \frac{1}{3}}$$

   $$= \frac{80 + 60}{1}$$

   $$= 140$$

6. $\frac{2+x}{2}$ or $1 + \frac{x}{2}$

   Because the number of terms is even, the median is the average of the two middle terms. Because $2 < x < 8$, the two middle terms are 2 and x. Therefore, the median is $\frac{2+x}{2}$, or equivalently $1 + \frac{x}{2}$.

7. (A) 1; (B) 1.5; (D) 2.5; (E) 3

   Because the question asks for a median, put the known values in order and test low, middle, and high values for x, calculating the median in each case. Note that the question stem indicates that the 6 integers are distinct, so integer x cannot have the same value as any of the other integers in the list.

low:	x_{-2}	−1	0	2	4	6	→	median = 1
middle:	−1	0	x_1	2	4	6	→	median = 1.5
middle:	−1	0	2	x_3	4	6	→	median = 2.5
high:	−1	0	2	4	6	x_7	→	median = 3

   For the last case, you could also have tested $x = 5$. The median would still be 3, because whether $x = 5$ or $x = 7$, the two middle numbers are still 2 and 4.

8. 12 and −8

   Because the known values in this list are relatively close (and therefore wouldn't account for a range of 13), x is either the least number or the greatest number in the list. If x is the least number, then 5 is the greatest number and $5 - x = 13$, so x is −8. If x is the greatest number, then −1 is the least number and $x - (-1) = 13$, so x is 12.

9. 6

   First, write out the members of the list in increasing order. There are 12 values total, so each quartile contains three members of the list:

   $$\{0, 1, 1, | 2, 2, 3, | 3, 4, 7, | 8, 8, 11\}$$
   $$\quad\quad\quad\; Q_1 \quad\quad Q_2 \quad\quad Q_3$$

   Calculate Q_1 and Q_3:

   $$Q_3 = \frac{7+8}{2} = 7.5$$

   $$Q_1 = \frac{1+2}{2} = 1.5$$

   Therefore, $Q_3 - Q_1 = 6$.

10. **(B)**
Each dataset has a mean of 5. The dataset whose members are farther away from the mean will have the higher standard deviation. To compare them, focus on the differences between the datasets. The numbers that the datasets have in common are **bolded**:

  Dataset A: {**3**, 4, **5**, 6, **7**} Dataset B: {**3**, 3, **5**, 7, **7**}

Compare the numbers that are not the same. The numbers 4 and 6 in Dataset A are closer to the mean (5) than are the 3 and 7 in Dataset B. The values in Dataset B are more spread out. Therefore, the numbers in Dataset B are farther away from the mean, so Dataset B has a greater standard deviation.

The correct answer is (B): Quantity B is greater.

11. **16%**
The question asks for the percent of observations that fall below 4. If the mean is 6 and the standard deviation is 2, then a measurement of 4 (i.e., 6 − 2) represents exactly 1 standard deviation below the mean.

In a normal or near-normal distribution, approximately half of all measurements fall below the mean (in this case, 6). In addition, approximately 34% of measurements fall between the mean and one standard deviation below it (in this case, between 4 and 6). So the percentage of measurements that fall below 4 can be represented by the difference: 50 − 34% = 16% of the measurements are less than 4.

12. **0.1%**
Because the mean of X is 6 and each standard deviation is 2, a value of 12 represents 3 standard deviations above the mean, since $12 = 6 + 2 + 2 + 2$. Roughly 1 in 1,000 observations in a normal distribution will be at or more than 3 standard deviations above the mean, a fraction that corresponds to 0.1%.

13. **2nd Percentile**
Because the mean of X is 6 and each SD is 2, a value of 2 is $6 − 2 − 2 = 2$ standard deviations below the mean. Two SDs below the mean is the 2nd percentile.

14. **(C) 7**
Sometimes, normal distribution problems ask about values or percentiles that do *not* correspond to the exact standard deviations for the distribution. The 70th percentile, for instance, will fall somewhere between the mean of variable X (at 6, the 50th percentile) and 1 standard deviation above (at 8, the 84th percentile). Therefore, the answer must fall between 6 and 8. Only answer (C) qualifies.

15. **No, not necessarily**
If a distribution is not normal or near-normal, then you cannot necessarily use the standard values. The problem would have to provide you with the values to use if the distribution is not normal or near-normal.

Unit Four: **Stories, Percents, Ratios, Stats, and Data**

Problem Set

1. The average of 11 numbers is 10. When one number is eliminated, the average of the remaining numbers is 9.3. What is the eliminated number?

2. The average of 9, 11, and 16 is equal to the average of 21, 4.6, and what number?

3. For the list of numbers {4, 5, 5, 6, 7, 8, 21}, how much greater is the mean than the median?

4. The sum of 8 numbers is 168. If one of the numbers is 28, what is the average of the other 7 numbers?

5. If the average of the list {5, 6, 6, 8, 9, x, y} is 6, then what is the average of $x + y$?

6. Will the average of six consecutive integers be an integer?

7. On 4 sales, Ayesha received commissions of $300, $40, x, and $140. Without the x commission, her average commission would be $50 lower. What is x ?

8. The class mean score on a test was 60, and the standard deviation was 15. If Elena's score was within 2 standard deviations of the mean, what is the lowest score she could have received?

9. Milo gets a $1,000 commission on a big sale. This commission alone raises his average commission by $150. If Milo's new average commission is $400, how many sales has Milo made?

10. Grace's average bowling score over the past 6 games is 150. If she wants to raise her average score by 10%, and she has two more games remaining in the season, what must her average score on the last two games be?

11. If the average of x and y is 50, and the average of y and z is 80, what is the value of $z - x$?

12. If $x > 0$ and the range of 1, 2, x, 5, and x^2 equals 8, what is the average (arithmetic mean) of the list?

13. In the list {1, 2, 3, 4, 7, 7, 10, 10, 11, 14, 19, 19, 23, 24, 25, 26}, what is the ratio of the greatest item in Quartile 2 to the average value in Quartile 4 ?

14. N is a normally distributed set with a mean of 0. If 2% of the observations in N are −10 or less, approximately what fraction of the observations are between 0 and 5 ?

15. A college class is attended by Poets and Bards in the ratio of 3 Poets for every 2 Bards. On a midterm, the average score of the Poets is 60 and the average score of the Bards is 80.

Quantity A	Quantity B
The overall average score for the class	70

16. $x > 2$

Quantity A	Quantity B
The median of $x - 4$, $x + 1$, and $4x$	The mean of $x - 4$, $x + 1$, and $4x$

17.   A is the set of the first five positive odd integers. B is the set of the first five positive even integers.

Quantity A	Quantity B
The standard deviation of A	The standard deviation of B

18. If the sum of a sequence of 10 consecutive integers is 195, what is the smallest term of the sequence?

19.   Abe's quiz scores are 62, 68, 74, and 68.
      Ben's quiz scores are 66 and 70.

Quantity A	Quantity B
The score Abe needs on his fifth quiz to raise his average to 70	The score Ben needs on his third quiz to raise his average to 70

20.   Set $S = \{2, 3, 5, 2, 11, 1\}$

Quantity A	Quantity B
The average of Set S	The mode of Set S if every number in the set were doubled

21.   Silky Dark Chocolate is 80% cocoa.
      Rich Milk Chocolate is 50% cocoa.
      Smooth White Chocolate is 0% cocoa.

Quantity A	Quantity B
Percent cocoa of a mixture of 3 parts Silky Dark Chocolate and 1 part Smooth White Chocolate	Percent cocoa of a mixture of 2 parts Rich Milk Chocolate and 1 part Silky Dark Chocolate

22.   The average of six numbers is 44.
      The average of two of those numbers is 11.

Quantity A	Quantity B
The average of the other 4 numbers	77

Unit Four: **Stories, Percents, Ratios, Stats, and Data**

Solutions

1. **17**

   If the average of 11 numbers is 10, their sum is 11 × 10, which is 110. After one number is eliminated, the average is 9.3, so the sum of the 10 remaining numbers is 10 × 9.3, which is 93. The number eliminated is the difference between these sums, 110 − 93 = 17.

2. **10.4**

   $$\frac{9 + 11 + 16}{3} = \frac{21 + 4.6 + x}{3}$$
   $$9 + 11 + 16 = 21 + 4.6 + x$$
   $$x = 10.4$$

3. **2**

   The mean of the listed terms is the sum of the numbers divided by the number of terms, 56 ÷ 7 = 8. The median is the middle number: 6. Thus, 8 is 2 greater than 6.

4. **20**

   The sum of the other 7 numbers is 140 × (168 − 28). So, the average of the numbers is 140 ÷ 7 = 20.

5. **4**

   If the average of seven terms is 6, then the sum of the terms is 7 × 6, which is 42. The listed terms have a sum of 34. Therefore, the remaining terms, *x* and *y*, must have a sum of 42 − 34, which is 8. Finally, because the problem asks for the average of *x* and *y*, divide the sum by the number of terms: 8 ÷ 2 = 4.

6. **No**

   For any sequence of consecutive integers with an *even* number of items, the average is *never* an integer. For example, if you pick 4, 5, 6, 7, 8, and 9.

   $$\frac{4 + 5 + 6 + 7 + 8 + 9}{6} = \frac{39}{6} = 6.5$$

   Since any set of consecutive integers is evenly spaced, the average is equal to the median. And if the set also has an even number of terms, the median is equal to the average of the two middle terms (i.e., exactly in between two consecutive integers). In the example above, the two middle terms are 6 and 7, giving you a median of 6.5, which is also the average of this evenly spaced set.

7. **$360**

   Without *x*, Ayesha's average commission can be calculated as $\frac{300 + 40 + 140}{3} = 160$. With *x*, Ayesha's average is $50 more, or $210. Using this average, the sum of the four original commissions can be obtained as 210 × 4 = 840. Since the sum of the known commissions is 300 + 40 + 140 = 480, the difference 840 − 480 = 360 must be the value of the unknown commission *x*.

8. **30**

   Elena's score was within 2 standard deviations of the mean. The standard deviation is 15, so her score is no more than 30 points from the mean. The lowest possible score she could have received, then, is 60 − 30, or 30.

9. **5**

   Before the $1,000 commission, Milo's average commission was $250; this is expressed algebraically by the equation $S = 250n$.

   After the sale, the sum of Milo's sales increased by $1,000, the number of sales made increased by 1, and his average commission was $400. You can set this up in an average table.

	Average	×	Number	=	Sum
Original scenario	250	×	n	=	$250n$
Big sale	1,000	×	1	=	1,000
Original + big sale	400	×	$(n+1)$	=	$250n + 1,000$

   Now, use the relationship in the last row of the table to solve.

   $$400(n+1) = 250n + 1,000$$
   $$400n + 400 = 250n + 1,000$$
   $$150n = 600$$
   $$n = 4$$

   Be careful. This result means that *before* the big sale, Milo had made 4 sales. Including the big sale, Milo has made 5 sales.

10. **210**

    After 6 games, Grace wants to raise her average score by 10 percent over the final 2 games of the season. Because 10 percent of 150 is 15, her target average for the 8 games is 165. Set up an average table to organize the information.

	Average	×	Number	=	Sum
Original scenario	150	×	6	=	900
Two final games	(A)	×	2	=	$2A$
Targeted outcome	165	×	8	=	$900 + 2A$

    Now, solve for A using the last row of the table:

    $$165 \times 8 = 900 + 2A$$
    $$1320 = 900 + 2A$$
    $$420 = 2A$$
    $$210 = A$$

Unit Four: **Stories, Percents, Ratios, Stats, and Data**

11. **60**
    The sum of two numbers is twice their average. Therefore,
    $$x + y = 100 \qquad y + z = 160$$
    $$x = 100 - y \qquad z = 160 - y$$

    Substitute these expressions for z and x.
    $$z - x = (160 - y) - (100 - y) = 160 - y - 100 + y = 160 - 100 = 60$$

    Alternatively, pick Smart Numbers for x and y. Let $x = 50$ and $y = 50$ (this is an easy way to make their average equal 50). Because the average of y and z must be 80, the sum of y and z must be 160 and z must be $160 - 50 = 110$. Therefore, $z - x = 110 - 50 = 60$.

12. **4**
    If the range of the list is 8 and $x > 0$, then x^2 has to be the greatest number in the list and $x^2 - 1 = 8$. Therefore, $x^2 = 9$ and $x = 3$. The average can then be obtained.
    $$\frac{1 + 2 + 3 + 5 + 9}{5} = \frac{20}{5} = 4$$

13. $\dfrac{20}{49}$
    The list is given in order and contains 16 members. Therefore, the greatest item in Quartile 2 is the eighth item in the list, which is 10. The items in Quartile 4 are 23, 24, 25, and 26, and their average is $\dfrac{23 + 24 + 25 + 26}{4} = 24.5$. (Note that these numbers are an evenly spaced list, so the average equals the median or middle number.)

    Thus, the ratio is $\dfrac{10}{24.5} = \dfrac{20}{49}$.

14. $\dfrac{1}{3}$
    If 2 percent of the observations are less than -10, then -10 must be approximately 2 standard deviations from the mean. Thus the standard deviation is approximately $\dfrac{|-10|}{2} = 5$. This question is asking for the fraction of the observations that fall between 0 (the mean of the set) and 5 (one standard deviation above the mean). Because 34% of the members of a normally distributed set will fall between the mean and one standard deviation above the mean, the answer is approximately $\dfrac{1}{3}$.

15. **(B)**
    This is a Weighted Average problem. The overall average score can be computed by assigning weights to the average scores of Poets and Bards that reflect the number of people in each subgroup. Because the ratio of Poets to Bards is 3 to 2, and collectively the two groups account for all students, the multiple ratio may be written as $P : B : Total = 3 : 2 : 5$.

    This means that Poets constitute $\dfrac{3}{5}$ of the students and Bards the remaining $\dfrac{2}{5}$. Therefore, the overall average score is given by the weighted average formula.
    $$\frac{3}{5} \times 60 + \frac{2}{5} \times 80 = 68$$

Chapter 18: **Statistics**

Alternatively, you could reason as follows: If there were the same number of Poets as there were Bards, the overall average score would be 70. However, there are actually more Poets than Bards, so the overall average score will be closer to 60 than to 80 (i.e., less than 70).

The correct answer is (B): Quantity B is always greater.

16. **(B)**

Begin with the median. In a set with an odd number of terms, the median will be the middle term when the terms are put in ascending order. It is clear that $x + 1 > x - 4$. Moreover, because $x > 2$, $4x$ must be greater than $x + 1$. Therefore, the median is $x + 1$. Rewrite Quantity A.

Quantity A	Quantity B
The median of $x - 4$, $x + 1$, and $4x = x + 1$	The mean of $x - 4$, $x + 1$, and $4x$

To compute the mean, add all three terms and divide by 3.

$$\text{mean} = \frac{(x - 4) + (x + 1) + 4x}{3} = \frac{6x - 3}{3} = 2x - 1$$

Rewrite Quantity B.

Quantity A	Quantity B
The median of $x - 4$, $x + 1$, and $4x = x + 1$	The mean of $x - 4$, $x + 1$, and $4x = 2x - 1$

The comparison thus boils down to which is greater between $x + 1$ and $2x - 1$. The answer is not immediately clear. Take advantage of the hidden inequality by subtracting x from both quantities to try and isolate x.

Quantity A	Quantity B
$x + 1$	$2x + 1$
$-x$	$-x$
1	$x - 1$

Now add 1 to both sides to isolate x.

Quantity A	Quantity B
$1 + 1 = 2$	$(x - 1) + 1 = x$

The question stem states that x must be greater than 2.

Therefore, the correct answer is (B): Quantity B is always greater.

Unit Four: **Stories, Percents, Ratios, Stats, and Data**

17. **(C)**

    The sets in question are $A = \{1, 3, 5, 7, 9\}$ and $B = \{2, 4, 6, 8, 10\}$. Each is a set of evenly spaced integers with an odd number of terms, such that the mean is the middle number. The deviations between the elements of the set and the mean of the set in each case are the same: $-4, -2, 0, 2,$ and 4. Thus, the standard deviations of the sets must also be the same.

    The correct answer is (C): The two quantities are always equal.

18. **15**

    First, find the average of the terms in the sequence, as for any consecutive set of integers the average will be exactly in the middle of the integers (and thus will always be equal to the median of the set). In this problem, the average is $\frac{195}{10} = 19.5$. Because the average is in the middle of the 10 consecutive terms, you can now list out the 10 terms around it (5 below and 5 above):

    $$\underbrace{15\ 16\ 17\ 18\ 19}_{5\ integers\ less} \xleftarrow[19.5]{avg} \underbrace{20\ 21\ 22\ 23\ 24}_{5\ integers\ greater}$$

    Once the 10 numbers are arrayed around the average, it is easy to find the smallest term: 15.

19. **(A)**

    This is an excellent example of a word problem for which no real calculation is needed if the idea of weighted averages is understood. Abe's current average is 68 (for a quick average, note that two scores *are* 68, and of the other two scores, one is six points over 68 and one is six points under 68, keeping the overall average at 68). Ben's average is also 68 (halfway between 66 and 70).

    For Abe to get a 70 overall, his fifth score will have to compensate for four too-low scores. For Ben to get a 70 overall, his third score will only have to compensate for two too-low scores. So Abe will need a higher score to raise his average to 70 than Ben will. (This is the same as the more bad grades you have, the higher you have to get on the next quiz to pull your average back up.)

    Actually doing this problem mathematically would take too much time, but for the curious, Abe's fifth score could be calculated as such:

    $$\frac{62 + 68 + 74 + 68 + x}{5} = 70$$

    As it turns out, Abe needs a 78.

    Ben's third score could be calculated as such.

    $$\frac{66 + 70 + x}{3} = 70$$

    Ben needs a 74.

    Therefore, the correct answer is (A): Quantity A is always greater.

20. **(C)**

    There's no shortcut to find the average here. Simply add $2 + 3 + 5 + 2 + 11 + 1$ to get 24 and divide by 6 to get 4. Quantity A is therefore equal to 4.

    Finding the mode is much easier (the mode is simply the number that occurs most often in the list). The current mode is 2. When you double everything in the list, the mode will then be 4. (The other numbers in the list are irrelevant—don't bother to double them).

    The correct answer is (C): The two quantities are always equal.

21. **(C)**

    Problems involving mixtures can usually be solved using the average formula, and as in most problems with only percents and ratios (no concrete values), you can make up concrete values in accordance with the ratios set out in the problem to find that average. Quantity A calls for the percentage of cocoa of a mix that is three parts dark and one part smooth white, so think of it as the average between 3 cups of the former and 1 cup of the latter.

    $$\frac{80 + 80 + 80 + 0}{4} = 60$$

    Quantity A's mix will be 60 percent cocoa. Create a similar weighted average for Quantity B (2 parts milk, 1 part dark).

    $$\frac{50 + 50 + 80}{3} = 60$$

    Quantity B's mix will also be 60 percent cocoa.

    The correct answer is (C): The two quantities are always equal.

22. **(B)**

    No actual calculation is required here. Six numbers average to 44 and two of them average to 11. That is, two of the numbers have an average that is 33 points below the overall average. Therefore, the other four numbers must bring the average up 33 points. However, because there are *four* numbers bringing the average up (versus *two* bringing the average down), each of the individual numbers doesn't have to "compensate" as much—they will not have to be as high as 77, which is 33 points above 44.

    Put another way, there are only two numbers dragging the average down, so they have to be pretty extreme. But because there are four numbers dragging the average up, they get to share the burden—they don't have to be as extreme.

    The correct answer is (B): Quantity B is always greater.

    If you can master that logic, you can solve problems like this one very fast. However, as with all average problems, you can also opt for a more mathematical approach.

    If six numbers average to 44, their sum is $6 \times 44 = 264$.

    If two of the numbers average to 11, their sum is $2 \times 11 = 22$.

    Thus, the other four numbers must sum to $264 - 22 = 242$.

    $242 \div 4 = 60.5$

    Thus, the average of the other four numbers referred to in Quantity A is 60.5, well under 77.

    The correct answer is (B): Quantity B is always greater.

CHAPTER 19

Data Interpretation

In This Chapter:

- The Basic DI Process
- Types of Charts
- Pie Charts
- Column Charts
- Line Charts
- Bar Charts
- Tables
- Other Diagrams
- Check Your Skills Answer Key
- Problem Set
- Solutions

CHAPTER 19 Data Interpretation

Data Interpretation (DI) problems appear as sets of problems that refer to the same group of one to three related graphs or charts. On the GRE, you will see an average of two DI sets per exam, each with two or three associated problems. In this chapter, you will learn a standard process for solving any DI problem. You will also learn how to analyze various kinds of charts that appear frequently within DI problems, including pie, column, line, and bar charts.

In general, DI problems can take a lot of time to solve. You'll also learn how to tackle them efficiently, using the on-screen calculator when appropriate.

The Basic DI Process

1. Scan the graph(s). (15–20 seconds)
   - What type of graph is it?
   - Is the data displayed in percentages or absolute quantities?
   - Does the graph provide any overall total value?

2. Figure out what the question is asking you to do.
   - Calculate a value?
   - Establish how many data points meet a criterion?

3. Find the graph(s) with the needed information.
   - Look for key words in the question that reference labels in the graph(s).

4. *If* you need to establish how many data points meet a criterion, keep track on your scratch paper as you count.

5. *If* you need to perform a computation, translate the question stem into a mathematical expression *before* you try to find the information to solve it.

6. *If* one of the answer choices is "cannot be determined," check that you have *all* the information you need before performing any calculations.

7. Use the calculator when needed, but keep your eye out for opportunities to use time-saving estimation techniques:
   - Does the question use the word "approximate"?
   - Are the numbers in the answer choices sufficiently far apart?
   - Can you get a sense of the median, mean, ratio, or percent change in question *visually* before using the appropriate formula?

Unit Four: **Stories, Percents, Ratios, Stats, and Data**

Use this list of steps as a high-level process checklist, to help you remember what to look for and do as you solve. Some of these steps are relevant only to some types of problems. The examples in this chapter show how to tailor this process to various types of problems.

Types of Charts

Most GRE Data Interpretation questions focus on data in five standard formats: **Pie Charts**, **Column Charts**, **Line Charts**, **Bar Charts**, and **Tables**. You will be much faster at extracting the data if you are already familiar with interpreting these types of formats.

GRE DI charts always tell a data story, and the questions you will be answering are about that story. The examples in this chapter use a story about a produce (fruit and vegetable) stand. The owner of this stand has some general sales figures over a one-year period, as well as some detailed data for one particular month of that one-year period. The different sections of this chapter will present that data in various different formats and show you how to answer the questions that might be asked.

Many DI problems also involve calculations using fractions, decimals, and percents, and you will find that you will be much faster at those calculations if you already know various standard formulas, such as the percentage increase/decrease formula, as well as computation shortcuts, such as estimating fractions, that were taught in prior chapters.

The solutions shown in this chapter will also point out various computation shortcuts. Use the calculator when it's easy to, but also work on developing estimation techniques. This will ultimately save you time.

As you study the solutions, go one step at a time, trying to anticipate the next step before reading it. Although there are many ways to solve these problems, time is critical on the GRE, and learning to follow a standard process and use computation shortcuts will ultimately save you a great deal of time and stress.

Pie Charts

Understanding Pie Charts

A pie chart is used to show the relative sizes of parts of a whole. The size of each pie slice is proportional to the percentage of the whole that the component accounts for. In other words, a smaller slice of pie corresponds to a smaller piece of the whole. Here's an example of a pie chart for the produce stand:

Chapter 19: **Data Interpretation**

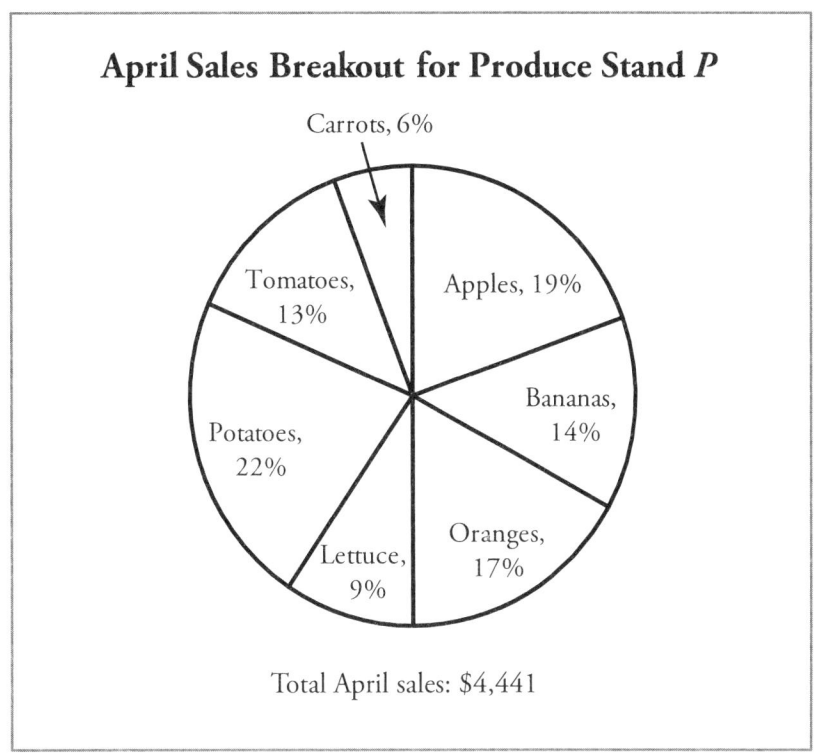

This pie chart shows the total dollar amount of April sales for Produce Stand P ($4,441), as well as what percentage of sales were attributable to various types of produce (for example, apples were 19% of total sales).

Pie charts are similar to the circles used in Chapter 11: Fractions, with one important difference: The sizes of the slices of a pie chart are usually not the same. So one slice could represent $\frac{1}{4}$ of the circle, while another slice represents $\frac{1}{3}$, and several more represent larger or smaller portions.

Most frequently, the slices are noted with percents, as shown in the above example, but they could also be labeled with fractions. The pie chart is always drawn to scale, so if one slice is visually bigger than another, the quantity it's describing is greater than the other.

Sometimes a pie chart shows amounts instead of percentages. The example pie chart could have omitted the percents, instead just labeling the pie slices as Carrots $266.46, Apples $843.79, Bananas $621.74, and so on. Even in this case, the point of a pie chart is to offer a visual representation of percentages (or relative quantities), so you'll know that they are still important to the story. Given the amounts, you can still infer that apples constitute a higher percentage of total sales than bananas. If you see data in a pie chart on the GRE, anticipate one or more questions about percentages or proportions.

Many pie charts include a total amount annotated on or around the chart, often placed in a relatively inconspicuous location. When a pie chart shows up, look carefully for a total; if you see one, you can be almost certain that the GRE will ask you to calculate the actual numbers represented by specific slices of the pie.

To find the real values, multiply the total by the percentages of the relevant slices of the pie. Given that carrots are 6% of a $4,441 total, the carrots accounted for $266.46 in sales, because $4,441 × 0.06 = $266.46.

Unit Four: **Stories, Percents, Ratios, Stats, and Data**

Alternatively, if the pie chart didn't list percentages but instead indicated that carrot sales were $266.46, you could infer that carrots represented 6% of the total, because $\frac{\$266.46}{\$4,441} = 0.06 = 6\%$.

A pie chart can only show components of one specific total, so if you see two pie charts in a Data Interpretation section, assume that they represent two different totals. In this case, anticipate that one or more of the questions will ask you to compare components from each of the two different pies.

Be careful in these cases. If one pie's actual total is greater than the other's, the percentages for the two pies will probably not be directly comparable. To put it another way, 15% of a larger pie represents more than 15% of a smaller pie. As such, use the relevant percentages and the total for each pie to calculate the actual quantities represented by each of the percentages and then compare those actual quantities to each other.

> *Pie Chart Tips*
> - Pie charts are used to show relative quantities, most often as percentages.
> - Pie charts are always drawn to scale.
> - Pie charts may be labeled with a total amount. In these cases, you will usually have to convert percents to numbers or numbers to percents.

Try these problems:

506

1. In April, what was the total sale value of tomatoes at Produce Stand P?

   13% of $\$4{,}441 = 0.13 \times \$4{,}441 = \$577.33$

2. In April, what was the total sales amount from both lettuce and tomatoes at Produce Stand P?

   9% of $\$4{,}441 + $ 13% of $\$4{,}441 = $ 22% of $\$4{,}441$

   $0.22 \times \$4{,}441 = \$977.02$

Because the two percentages are part of the same pie chart, it's valid to add the two percents before multiplying by the total. If they were percents from two different pie charts or of two different totals, each percent would need to be calculated individually.

Pie Charts and Geometry

Because pie charts are circles, some questions may ask you to bring in geometry knowledge. Chapter 23: Circles and Cylinders will cover circle geometry in depth, but the geometry in pie charts tends to be relatively straightforward.

For pie charts, the main thing to know about circles is that there are 360° from any point on the circle all the way around to that same point. The GRE may ask you to calculate the degree measure of any **sector** in a circle:

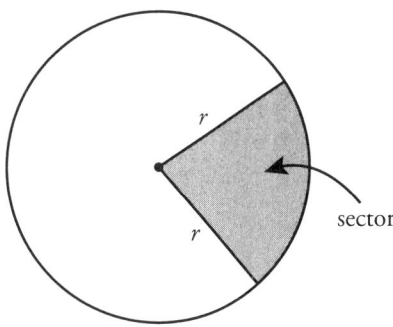

For the April sales pie chart, you could be asked to compute the angle of the sector represented by the sales of bananas. Given that bananas are 14% of the circle, you can infer that the angle is 14% of the entire angle measure of the circle. Therefore, the angle of that sector is 14% of 360°:

$0.14 \times 360° = 50.4°$

The sector represented by banana sales has an angle of 50.4°.

Unit Four: **Stories, Percents, Ratios, Stats, and Data**

Check Your Skills

Use the April Sales Pie Chart to answer the following questions:

Total April sales: $4,441

1. In April, approximately what amount of Produce Stand *P*'s total sales came from sales of apples, bananas, and tomatoes combined?

    (A) $2,043
    (B) $2,221
    (C) $2,362
    (D) $2,495
    (E) $2,571

2. If sales of potatoes were to increase by $173 in May, while sales of all other items remained the same, approximately what would be the ratio of sales of potatoes to total sales in May?

    (A) 1 : 5
    (B) 1 : 4
    (C) 7 : 20
    (D) 2 : 5
    (E) 3 : 7

3. If the areas of the sectors in the circle graph are drawn in proportion to the percentages shown, what is the approximate measure, in degrees, of the sector representing the percent of total April sales due to lettuce?

   (A) 24°
   (B) 28°
   (C) 32°
   (D) 36°
   (E) 40°

Answers can be found on pages 523–524.

Column Charts

A column chart shows amounts as heights. Often, the *x*-axis is time (e.g., months, years), and column charts are used to show trends over time.

The hardest thing about a column chart is often just reading the exact values. The GRE never makes an exact reading of the value necessary unless numeric values are explicitly given (and even then you can usually just round), so just raise your index finger up near the computer monitor, draw an imaginary line across the chart from the column in question to the *y*-axis, and find the approximate quantity represented by the column.

Single Series Column Charts

A single data series chart doesn't usually have a legend because you can understand it by reading the labels on the *x*- and *y*-axes. For example:

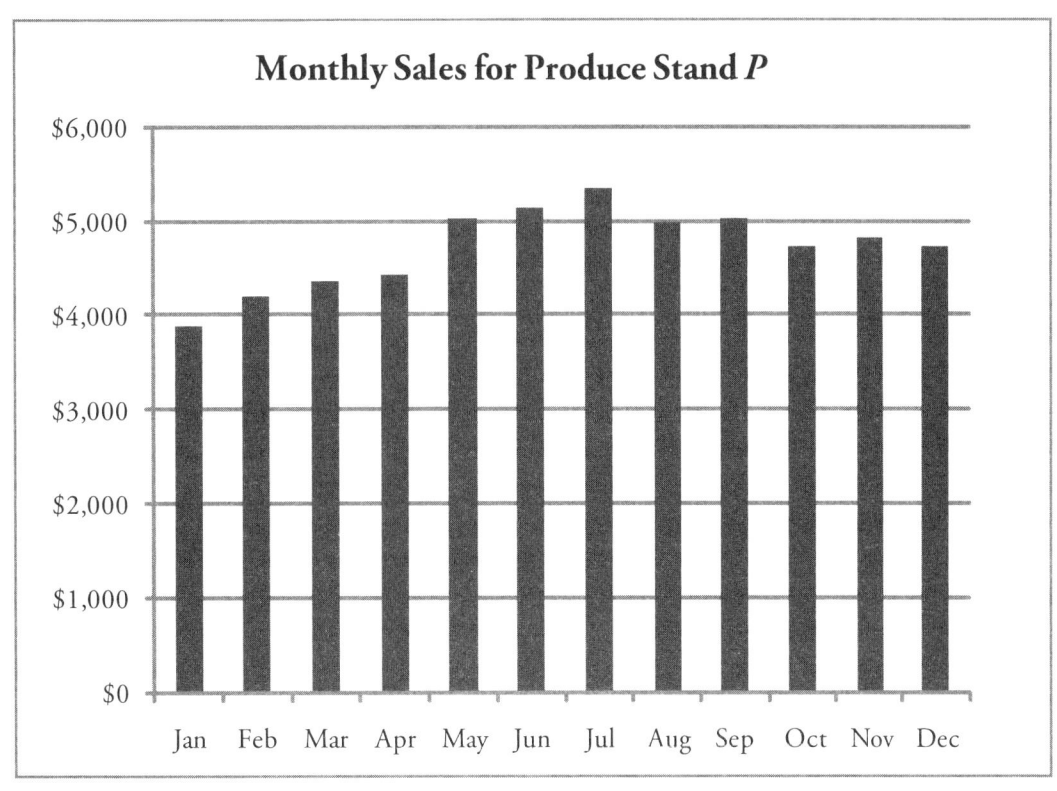

Unit Four: **Stories, Percents, Ratios, Stats, and Data**

This chart indicates the total monthly sales, in dollars, for a period of 12 months. You might be asked to calculate the percentage increase or decrease from one time period to the next, or to find the median in the chart, or even to count the number of periods when data values were above or below a particular value. For example:

1. By approximately what percentage did the monthly sales dollar amount increase from April to May?

$$\frac{\text{May sales} - \text{April sales}}{\text{April sales}} \approx \frac{5{,}000 - 4{,}400}{4{,}400} = \frac{600}{4{,}400} \approx 14\%$$

2. Approximately what was the median dollar amount of monthly sales for the year shown?

    $4,750: The median of 12 values will be the average of the 6th and 7th greatest values. Start counting in order of size from the least value (January) upwards until you find the 6th and 7th greatest values. The 6th greatest sales figure was in October or December (which are about equal at $4,700), while the 7th greatest was in November (about $4,800). The median, then is about halfway between these two figures, or about $4,750. Note that the GRE would likely only give you one answer choice in the $4,700 to $4,800 range, so there's no need to be more precise.

3. For how many of the 12 months recorded in the graph is the total sale dollar amount lower than it was in February?

    1: Only January earned less than February did.

Check Your Skills

> Use the single series column chart from this section to answer the following question.

4. In how many of the months shown were total produce sales greater than $4,600 ?
    - (A) 5
    - (B) 8
    - (C) 10
    - (D) 11
    - (E) 12

Answers can be found on page 524.

Stacked Column Charts

The GRE is especially fond of stacked column charts because they can be used to show two or more data series as differently shaded parts of one column. For instance, in the chart below, "vegetable sales" and "fruit sales" sum to "total sales." Charts that show multiple data series have legends, so you can tell which part of the bar represents which category:

Chapter 19: **Data Interpretation**

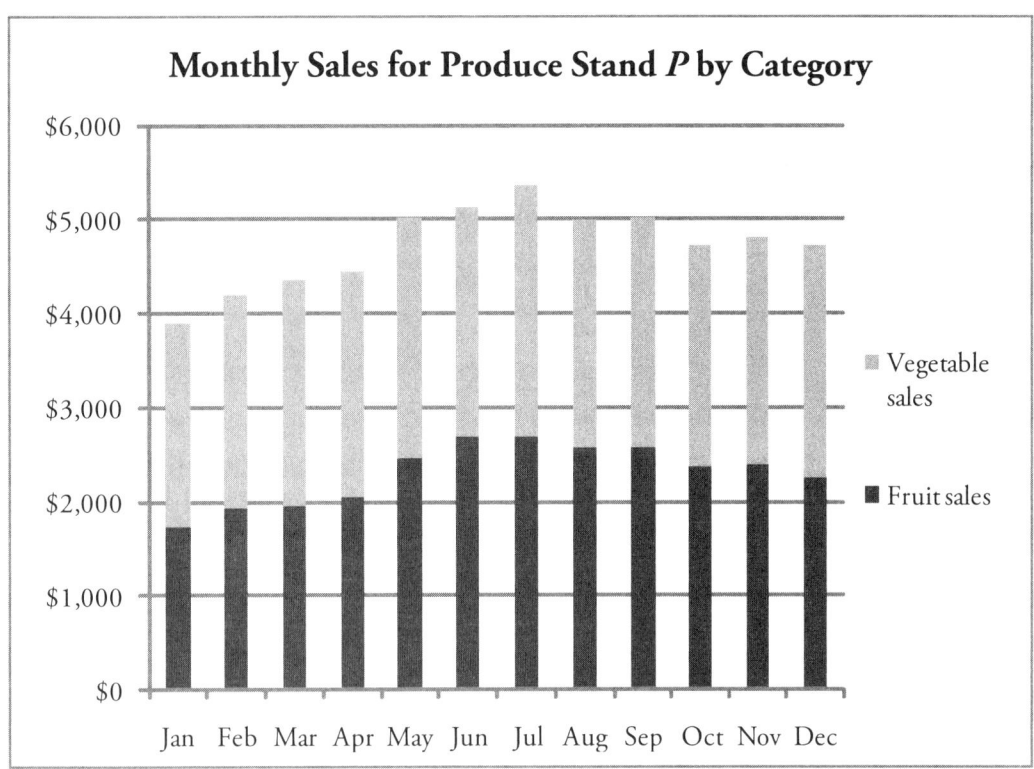

While total sales and fruit sales are both fairly straightforward to read off the chart, it is a little harder to read vegetable sales. To get those values, you'll have to determine the total sales, then subtract the fruit sales. For example, in January, fruit sales made up approximately $1,800 of the total $3,900 monthly sales. That means vegetable sales must have made up the remaining $2,100.

Because vegetable sales require a bit more work to figure out in this particular chart, you can be almost certain that you will see a question about vegetables. Furthermore, given that there are now three sales values accounted for by each of the 12 columns, it is essential that you read the question carefully, both before you go to the chart and before you choose your final answer. In a question that asks something about vegetable sales in March, for instance, there will almost certainly be a trap answer that you could get to by accidentally using the value for fruit sales in March.

> **Strategy Tip**
>
> To calculate the upper values shown in stacked column charts, subtract the other individual values in the column from the total value for that column.

Unit Four: **Stories, Percents, Ratios, Stats, and Data**

Check Your Skills

> Use the stacked column chart shown in this section to answer the following question.

5. Approximately what were the total vegetable sales in September?

   (A) $5,000
   (B) $4,000
   (C) $3,500
   (D) $2,500
   (E) $1,500

Answers can be found on page 524.

Clustered Column Charts

Another variation on column charts has clustered columns instead of stacked columns. The following example shows exactly the same data as the previous stacked column chart, except in the clustered column format:

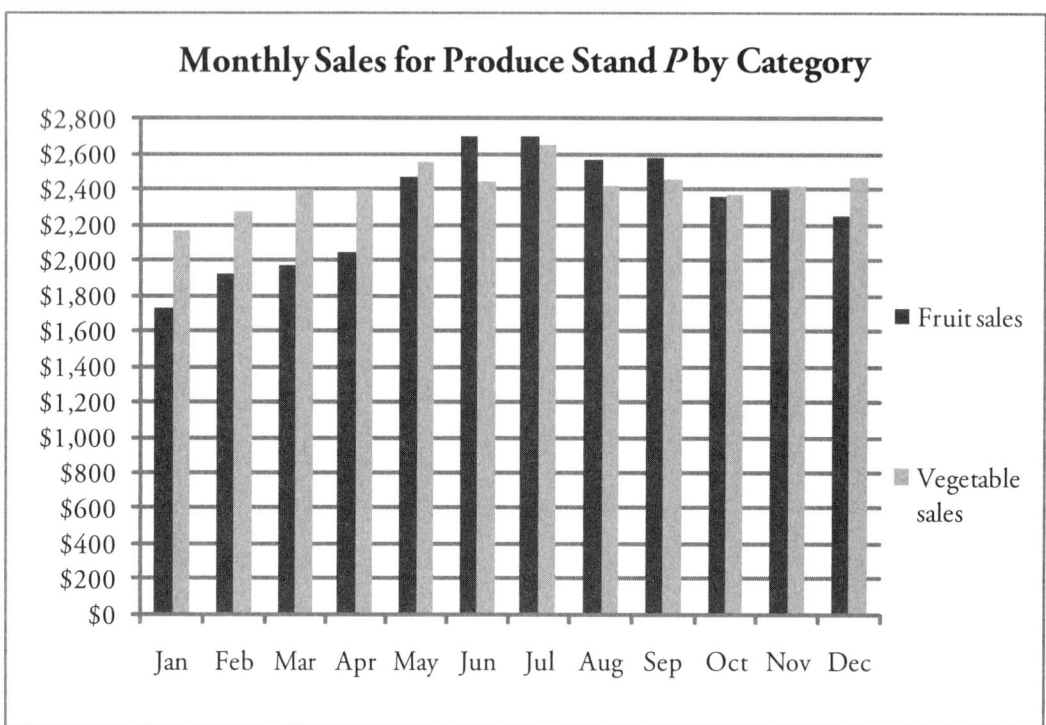

Clustered column charts make it easier to compare the parts of the total, but more difficult to determine the actual total because you have to sum the columns. You would now have to sum the two pieces to find the total, but you could more easily compare the fruit sales directly to the vegetable sales.

The types of questions typically asked about a clustered column chart are the same as those typically asked about a stacked column chart.

Check Your Skills

> Use the clustered column chart given in this section to answer the following question.

6. Which month had the greatest percentage of vegetable sales relative to total sales?

   Ⓐ Jan
   Ⓑ Mar
   Ⓒ Jun
   Ⓓ Oct
   Ⓔ Nov

Answers can be found on page 524.

Percentage Column Charts

Occasionally, the GRE uses column charts to show percentages directly. For example:

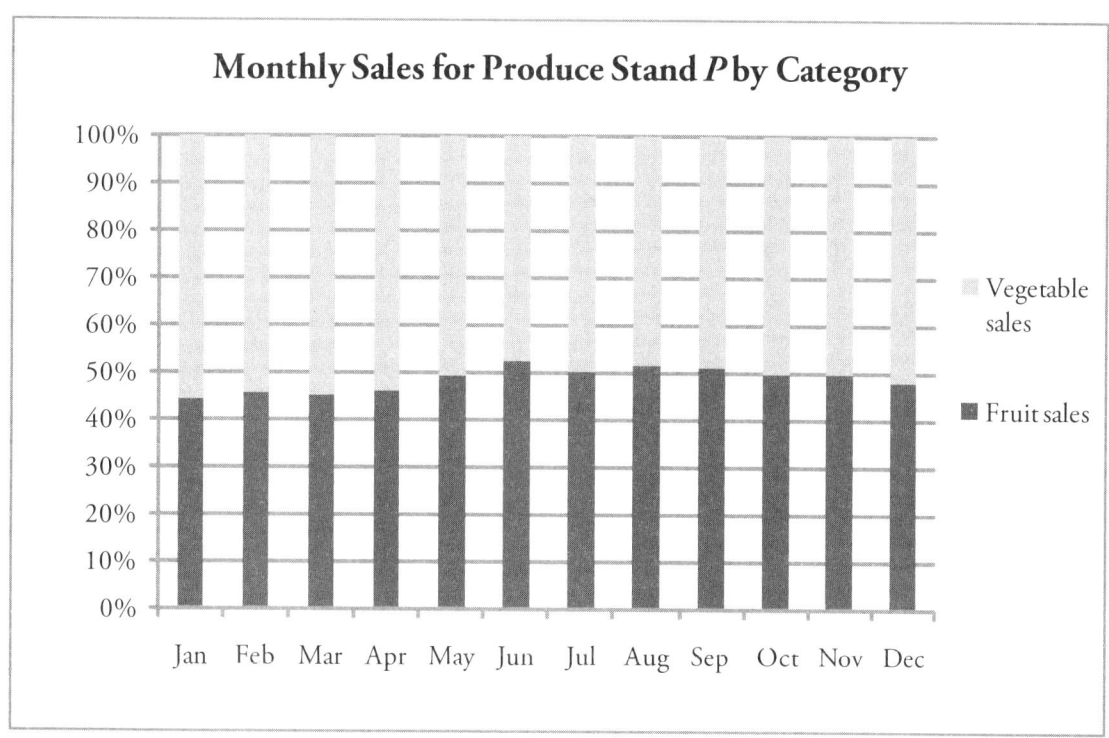

If you're given this type of chart and asked a question that requires quantity information, the test will need to provide you with some information about quantities. This will usually happen either in a second chart or in the question itself.

Otherwise, the types of questions typically asked about a percentage column chart are the same as those for stacked column charts.

Unit Four: **Stories, Percents, Ratios, Stats, and Data**

Be very cautious when you interpret this kind of graph. The total amount of sales each month are not necessarily equivalent. The columns only indicate percent based on the total for *that* month, not overall. So while all the columns have the same height, they do not necessarily represent the same absolute total. For example, February and April look about the same because they have the same percentages. However, it's possible that there were half as many sales in February, so April had a higher quantity of both fruits and vegetables sold. The sales just happened to be in the same ratio as the fruits and vegetables sold in February.

> **Strategy Tip**
> Differentiate between charts that show percentages and charts that show actual quantities. Without a total quantity given, the charts do not display the same information.

Check Your Skills

> Use the percentage column chart shown in this section to answer the following question.

7. If the total produce sales in July at Produce Stand *P* were $4,500, what were the approximate total fruit sales in December at Produce Stand *P* ?

    (A) $2,100
    (B) $2,200
    (C) $2,300
    (D) $2,400
    (E) Cannot be determined

Answers can be found on page 525.

Line Charts

Line charts are very similar to column charts, but each amount is shown as a floating dot instead of as a column, and the dots are connected by lines. Often, the *x*-axis is time (e.g., months, years), and the lines show trends over time. Because of the continuous nature of lines, data series that are shown in line charts are usually continuous values for something. For example:

Chapter 19: **Data Interpretation**

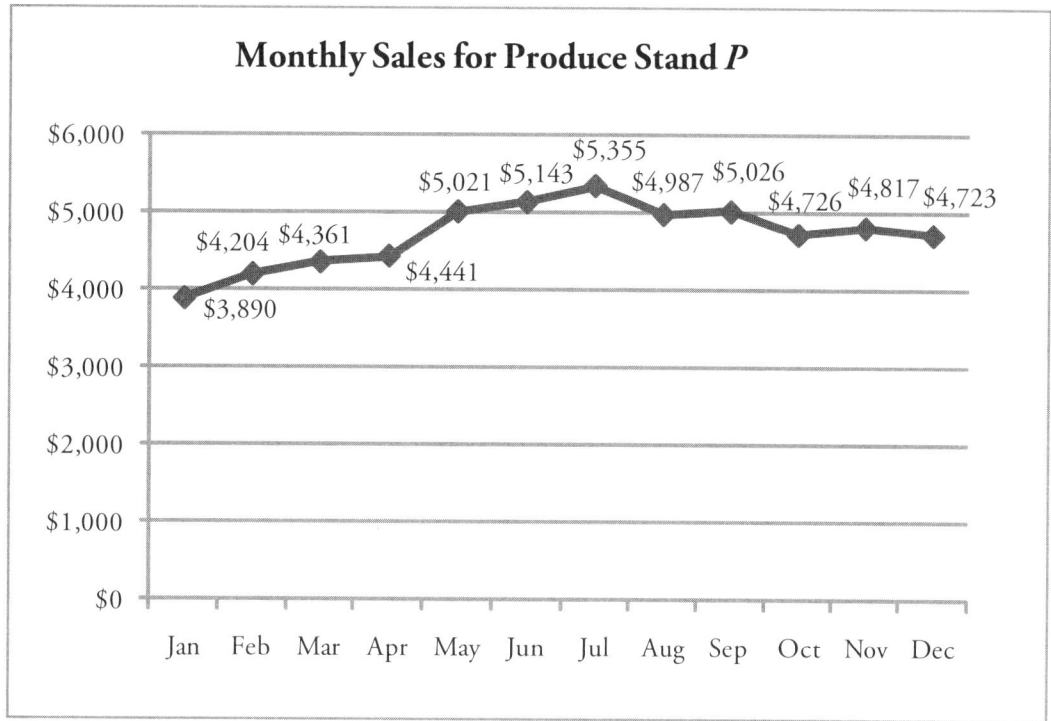

You might be asked to calculate percentage increase or decrease from one time period to the next, operations involving the average or median of the overall set, or even more simply, a count of the number of periods when data values were above or below a particular level. For example:

1. What was the approximate percentage increase in sales from April to May?

$$\frac{\text{May sales} - \text{April sales}}{\text{April sales}} \approx \frac{5{,}021 - 4{,}441}{4{,}441} \approx 13\%$$

2. For how many of the months shown were the sales less than those in July?

11: July sales were the greatest, so the sales volume in all 11 other months was less than that of July.

Check Your Skills

Use the line chart given in this section to answer the following questions.

8. For the time period given, the average sales per month at Produce Stand *P* were $4,725, rounded to the nearest dollar. If it were then discovered that the sales in January were actually $4,072, what would the approximate correct average sales per month be?

   (A) $4,740
   (B) $4,762
   (C) $4,769
   (D) $4,775
   (E) Cannot be determined

Unit Four: **Stories, Percents, Ratios, Stats, and Data**

9. At Produce Stand *P*, by what approximate percent did total sales increase in June compared to January?

   A) 19%
   B) 24%
   C) 28%
   D) 32%
   E) 38%

Answers can be found on pages 525–526.

Multi-Line Charts

The GRE is especially fond of multi-line charts because they can be used to show two or more data series at a time. Multi-line charts, like stacked and clustered column charts, have legends to show what each line represents. For example:

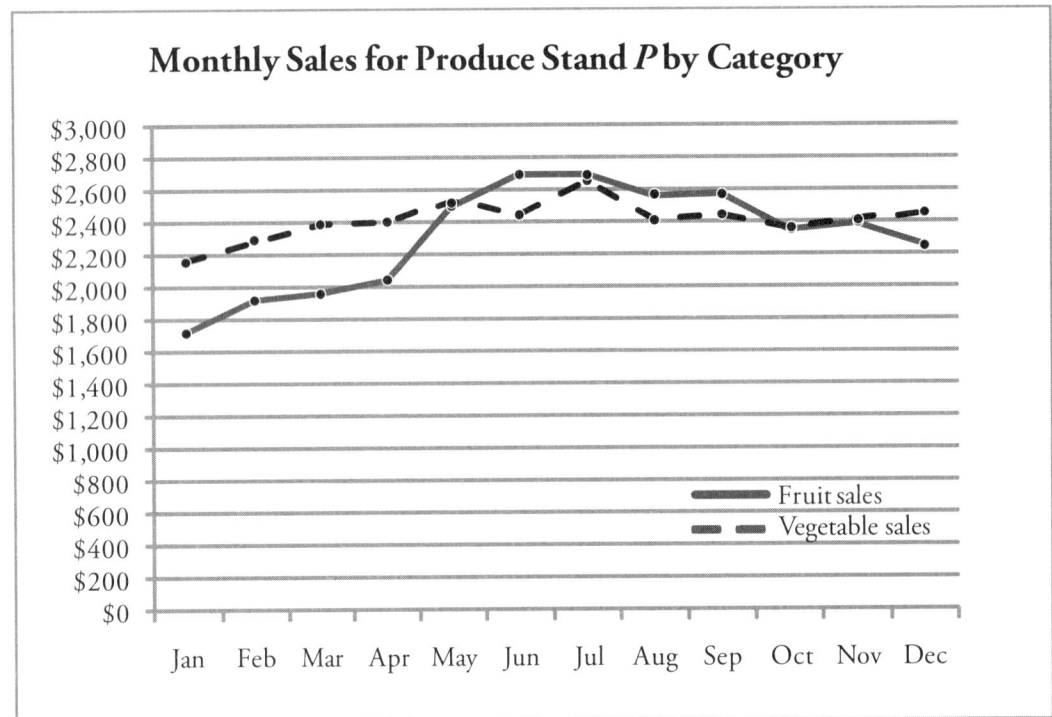

With line charts, you have to sum data points to calculate a total, because a total line is seldom shown. In this way, line charts are similar to clustered column charts.

Questions will often require you to pick out data points from one of the data lines. It's also common to be asked to either combine or compare the data that make up one line to the data that make up the other. For example:

1. What was the approximate percent change in fruit sales in the month of May compared to the month of January?

$$\frac{\text{May sales} - \text{Jan sales}}{\text{Jan sales}} \approx \frac{2{,}500 - 1{,}700}{1{,}700} \approx 47\%$$

516

2. For how many of the months shown were vegetable sales more than $100 greater than fruit sales?

In certain months, vegetable sales were less than fruit sales; ignore those months on the chart. For the rest, look for the months in which the difference between the lines is greater than half of the distance between two tick marks.

Five months had vegetables sales that were more than $100 greater than fruit sales: Jan, Feb, Mar, Apr, and Dec.

Check Your Skills

> Use the multi-line chart given in this section to answer the following questions.

10. Over which of the following pairs of consecutive months did total sales decline the most?
    - (A) Feb–Mar
    - (B) Mar–Apr
    - (C) Jun–Jul
    - (D) Aug–Sep
    - (E) Sep–Oct

11. In May, Produce Stand *P* bought fruit for an average cost of 25 cents per pound and sold that fruit for an average price of 80 cents per pound. Assuming there was no spoilage, approximately how much was Produce Stand *P*'s gross profit on the sale of fruit in May?
    - (A) $1,600
    - (B) $1,630
    - (C) $1,680
    - (D) $1,720
    - (E) Cannot be determined

Answers can be found pages 526–527.

Bar Charts

Bar charts, which are essentially column charts on their sides, are fairly uncommon on the GRE. They usually display a single data series, and, like pie charts, some bar charts include information about the total amount represented.

The length of each bar represents either an absolute number or, more rarely, a percentage. In this example, the bars represent an absolute numbers:

Unit Four: **Stories, Percents, Ratios, Stats, and Data**

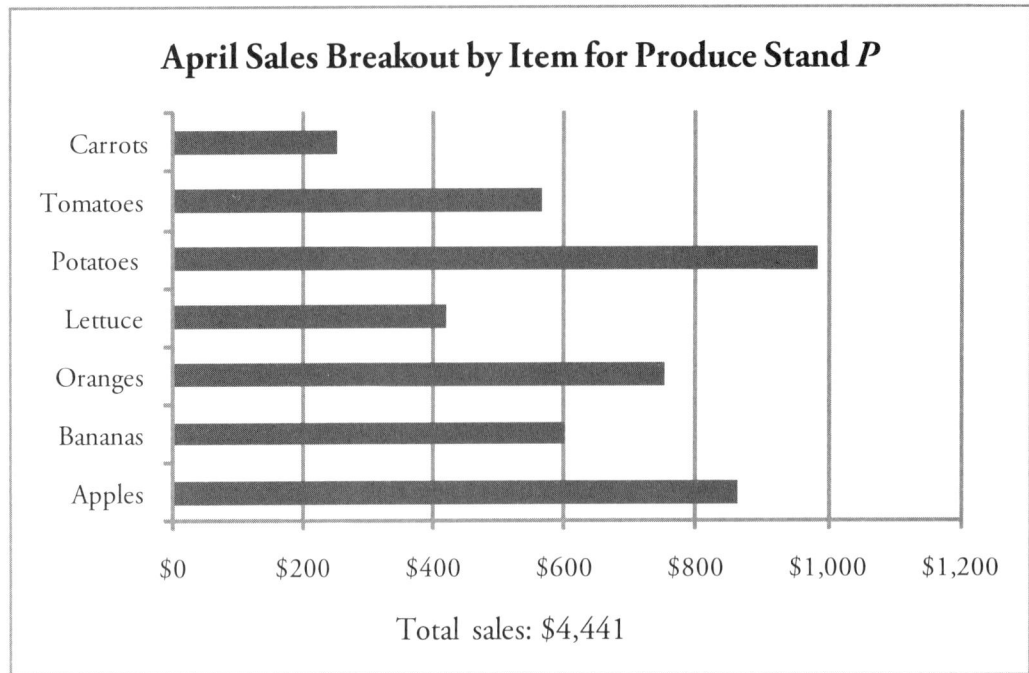

This chart presents the same information as the pie chart earlier in this chapter but shows dollar amounts rather than percents for each type of produce.

It's possible to convert each of these dollar amounts to percents using the total sales figure given at the bottom of the chart, just as it was possible to convert the percents in the pie chart to actual dollar amounts.

The GRE will often pair a bar chart with another, more general chart in a Data Interpretation section. This bar chart, for instance, is essentially a detailed breakout of Produce Stand P's sales in April, one of the twelve months shown by the column charts and line charts earlier in this chapter. In these cases, the bar chart will usually *not* provide a total, as the total can be found on the accompanying column or line chart.

> **Strategy Tip**
> Use a finger or a piece of paper to create a vertical line to help read bar chart values.

Check Your Skills

> Use the bar chart given in this section to answer the following questions.

12. Which item generated the third greatest sales revenue in April for Produce Stand *P* ?

    (A) tomatoes
    (B) lettuce
    (C) oranges
    (D) bananas
    (E) apples

13. Which of the following ratios is closest to the ratio of carrot sales to potato sales at Produce Stand *P* in the month of April?

   (A) 1 : 4
   (B) 2 : 9
   (C) 1 : 5
   (D) 1 : 6
   (E) 3 : 20

Answers can be found on page 528.

Tables

With tables, there is no need to estimate numbers; you'll be given the exact figures. The tradeoff for this precision, though, is that a table does not allow you to see trends as easily or estimate using visual techniques. It can also be easy to accidentally look at the wrong data.

When a table appears alone (that is, without an accompanying chart), it will often contain a mix of absolute quantities and percentage data. Be careful not to confuse the two. The GRE does not always label individual percentages with a percent sign. Rather, the entire row or column is generally labeled as such in the row or column header, so on first glance this information can easily be mistaken for absolute quantities. Read all of the column and row headers. For example:

Monthly Sales Breakout for Produce Stand *P*

Month	Total (in Dollars)	% Fruit	% Vegetable
Jan	3,890	44.29	55.71
Feb	4,204	45.74	54.26
Mar	4,361	45.10	54.90
Apr	4,441	45.96	54.04
May	5,021	49.17	50.83
Jun	5,143	52.40	47.60
Jul	5,355	50.38	49.62
Aug	4,987	51.41	48.59
Sep	5,026	51.21	48.79
Oct	4,726	49.89	50.11
Nov	4,817	49.78	50.22
Dec	4,723	47.77	52.23

The Total (in Dollars) column contains absolute numbers, while the Fruit and Vegetable columns contain percentages. Also, the table has 36 separate cells with values! Read the question and the table carefully. Don't hesitate to put your finger on the screen to track the correct cell and pull the figures that you need.

Unit Four: **Stories, Percents, Ratios, Stats, and Data**

Check Your Skills

> Use the table given in this section to answer the following question.

14. What was the approximate total revenue from vegetable sales at Produce Stand *P* for September, October, and November combined?

    Ⓐ $5,724
    Ⓑ $6,230
    Ⓒ $6,621
    Ⓓ $7,239
    Ⓔ $7,685

Answers can be found on page 528.

Other Diagrams

Other Common Types of Diagrams

Occasionally, other common types of diagrams, such as floor plans or outline maps, may appear on the GRE. When you do see an atypical diagram, the questions that go with them tend to be a little bit easier. There are questions that ask you to calculate surface area of walls and volume of rooms, but unusual diagrams will have far fewer of the more challenging percent change and "how many points satisfy this complicated set of criteria" questions.

Questions That Typically Require Input from More Than One Graph to Solve

The GRE can complicate things by asking questions that require you to look up and integrate information from multiple charts. This type of multi-chart question is not mathematically harder than a single-chart question, but since it requires using data from two different graphs, it can be more challenging to find the necessary information.

Efficient solving techniques and good scrap paper organization become even more valuable with multiple charts, because more charts mean more opportunities to accidentally look at the wrong values or to do more calculations than needed. For example:

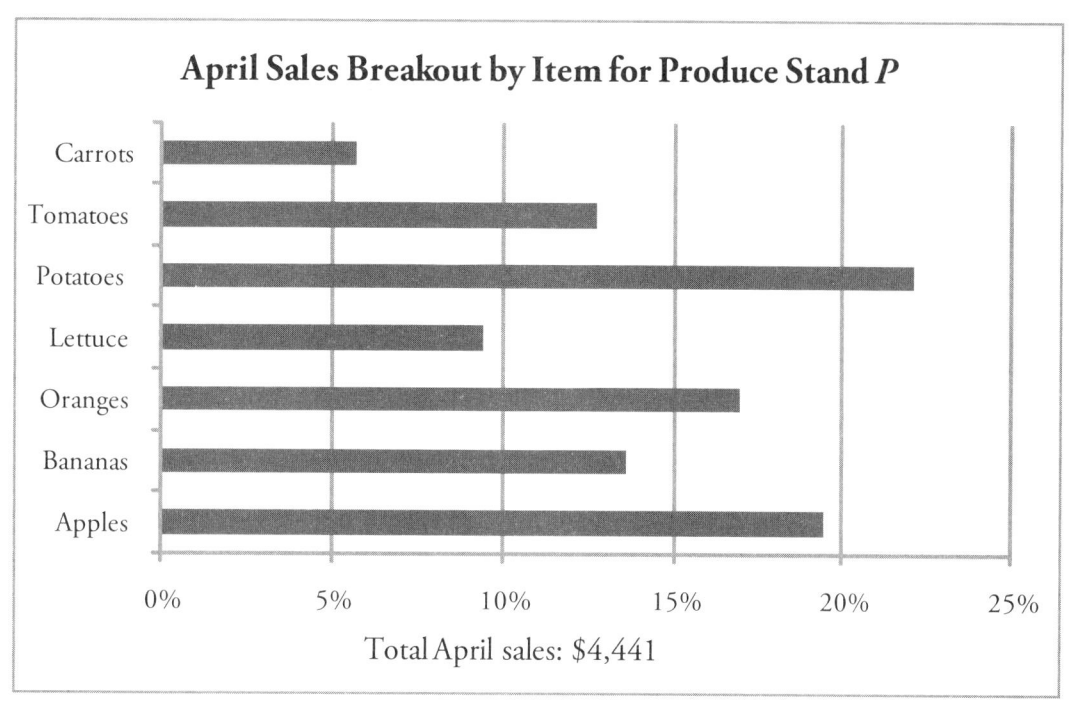

Vitamin Content of Produce Items Sold at Produce Stand *P* in April

	Vitamin A Content	Vitamin C Content
Apples	low	low
Bananas	medium	low
Oranges	high	medium
Lettuce	high	low
Potatoes	medium	low
Tomatoes	high	high
Carrots	low	high

Unit Four: **Stories, Percents, Ratios, Stats, and Data**

Check Your Skills

> Use the two charts given in this section to answer the following questions.

15. Of the produce sold in April at Produce Stand *P*, what was the approximate sales total of items that were high in both vitamin A and vitamin C?

    (A) $451
    (B) $488
    (C) $577
    (D) $624
    (E) $683

16. Approximately what dollar amount of the produce sold by Produce Stand *P* in April had medium or high amounts of either vitamin A or vitamin C?

    (A) $3,120
    (B) $3,600
    (C) $4,000
    (D) $4,600
    (E) Cannot be determined

Answers can be found on page 529.

Check Your Skills Answer Key

1. **(A) $2,043**

   The question asks for the sum of the absolute dollar amount of total sales of apples, bananas, and tomatoes.

   There is just one pie chart showing percentages, so you can combine the three percentages into one figure and then multiply by the total sales to get the portion of sales attributable just to apples, bananas, and tomatoes.

   First, make sure you're looking at the right components—the GRE will often test your attention to detail by asking for non-adjacent components of the pie. Apples are 19%, bananas are 14%, and tomatoes are 13%, so collectively they account for 46% of sales. The total sales were $4,441.

   $$46\% \times \$4{,}441 = 0.46 \times \$4{,}441 = \$2{,}043$$

   Notice there are several points where you could estimate. Pie charts often afford you the opportunity to visually estimate, especially when questions ask about adjacent components (such as apples, bananas, and oranges). Other times, you can estimate in a more numerical way. Here, for instance, apples, bananas, and tomatoes account for a little less than 50% of the total. Because answer choice (A) is the only one that is less than half of $4,441, it must be the correct answer.

2. **(B) 1 : 4**

   The question asks for the new ratio of potato sales to total sales, after adding $173 in potato sales and keeping the rest of the sales the same.

   In April, potatoes were 22% of sales, but the chart doesn't directly indicate the dollar amount. It shows only that total sales were $4,441 in April.

   Because this question involves an actual quantity ($173), calculate the April dollar amount of potato sales and add the $173 to it:

   $$0.22 \times \$4{,}441 = \$977.02$$

   In May, if potato sales were $173 higher, then potato sales would be $1,150.02. Watch out, though: The total sales will *also* increase by $173 to $4,614 (there is almost always a trap answer waiting for test takers who miss this subtle detail). Next, write out the ratio of potato sales to total sales in May:

   $$\text{potato sales} : \text{total sales} = \$1{,}150.02 : \$4{,}614$$

   The answers don't look anything like this. To simplify the ratio, use the calculator to divide both parts of the ratio by the lesser value:

   $$\begin{array}{ccc} P & : & T \\ \dfrac{1{,}150.02}{1{,}150.02} & : & \dfrac{4{,}614}{1{,}150.02} \\ 1 & : & \sim 4.012 \end{array}$$

Unit Four: **Stories, Percents, Ratios, Stats, and Data**

The first fraction doesn't actually have to be plugged into the calculator, since a number divided by itself will always equal 1. The second fraction simplifies to approximately 4. The simplified ratio is 1 : 4. However, because of the spread in the answer choices, you could also estimate here: Rounding $1,150 down to 11 and $4,614 down to 46 shows that the ratio is around 1 to 4 (and makes it easy to eliminate the other answers).

3. **(C) 32°**
The first clause is establishing that the pie chart is drawn to scale. Since that's something you can assume to be true, it doesn't impact how you would answer this question. The question itself asks for the degree measure of the lettuce wedge on the chart.

Lettuce represents 9% of total sales, so lettuce represents 9% of the 360-degree circle.

$$0.09 \times 360° = 32.4°$$

4. **(B) 8**
The question asks you to count the number of months shown that were greater than $4,600.

To find the $4,600 cutoff, start at the horizontal lines for $4,000 and $5,000. Next, imagine a line halfway between those two. This imaginary line will represent $4,500, and anything above it will likely also be above $4,600 (because again, the GRE will not require you to be very precise in these situations). Most months appear to have sales greater than $4,600; therefore, count the number that were less than $4,600. January, February, March, and April were all less than $4,500, so therefore were less than $4,600.

Glance at the answers. Because at least four months were less than $4,600, the answer can't be 10, 11, or 12; eliminate (C), (D), and (E). But there were also at least 6 months with sales of more than $4,600, so the answer also can't be 5; eliminate (A). Only answer (B) is possible. The test writers will adjust the answers such that you don't have to make a judgment call about whether something that looks pretty close to $4,600 is actually above or below that line.

5. **(D) $2,500**
The question asks for vegetable sales in September.

To get vegetable sales, find total sales minus fruit sales. For September, that is equal to about $5,000 − $2,500, or $2,500.

Also, be careful! The question intentionally refers to the vegetable sales for September as *total vegetable sales* because it can be easy to misread this as *total sales* and choose trap answer (A). Remember to read the question one last time before you finalize your answer to make sure that you've looked at the right part of the chart.

6. **(A) Jan**
Though it uses the word *percentage*, the question asks for the relative amount of vegetable sales *to* total sales, so use ratios to evaluate this question. The month with the greatest percentage of vegetable sales relative to the total will be the month in which the ratio of vegetable sales to fruit sales is the greatest.

First, glance at the answer choices. Only five months are possible. In January and March, vegetable sales were higher than fruit sales, so vegetables accounted for more than half of total sales.

In June, by contrast, fruit sales were higher than vegetable sales, so vegetable sales were less than half of total sales. Eliminate answer choice (C). In October and November, sales of fruits and vegetables were about equal, so these can't be the correct month; either January or March will be the one with the greatest relative percentage of vegetable sales. Eliminate choices (D) and (E).

January and March are close enough that you'll need to look more closely at the math.

In January, vegetable sales were about $2,200 and fruit sales were about $1,700. In March, vegetable sales were about $2,400 and fruit sales were about $2,000.

Total sales were less in January than in March. In January, vegetable sales were about $500 greater, while in March, vegetable sales were about $400 greater. If you're comfortable with comparing this conceptually, it must be the case that vegetable sales in January represent a greater percentage of the total, because the January differential between the two was greater *and* the overall total was less for this month.

Alternatively, use the calculator to check the figures:

$$\frac{\text{Jan veg sales}}{\text{Jan veg sales} + \text{Jan fruit sales}} \approx \frac{2{,}200}{1{,}700 + 2{,}200} \approx 0.56$$

$$\frac{\text{Mar veg sales}}{\text{Mar veg sales} + \text{Mar fruit sales}} \approx \frac{2{,}400}{2{,}000 + 2{,}400} \approx 0.55$$

January vegetable sales represented a slightly greater percentage of total sales than did March vegetable sales.

7. **(E) Cannot be determined**
The question asks you to determine the fruit sales in December.

This chart shows the percentage of sales from fruit and vegetables for each month. In order to calculate the dollar amount of the December fruit sales, you'd have to use an equation like this:

Fruit sales in December = % fruit sales × total sales in December

The chart does indicate that fruit accounted for about 48% of December's total sales. However, the chart provides no information on total sales in December. Further, the information provided about July has no clear relationship to December. You cannot, for instance, assume that total sales in December are the same as in July. The problem did not provide the data necessary to calculate a value for December's fruit sales, so this value cannot be determined.

8. **(A) $4,740**
The average sales per month is the sum of all the monthly sales divided by the number of months (12).

Unit Four: **Stories, Percents, Ratios, Stats, and Data**

The old amount for January was $3,890. The new value for January ($4,072) is $182 greater than the original value. Use this along with the average formula to solve.

$$\text{old average} = 4{,}725 = \frac{\text{old sum}}{12}$$
$$56{,}700 = \text{old sum}$$
$$56{,}700 + 182 = \text{new sum}$$
$$\text{new average} = \frac{56{,}882}{12} \approx 4{,}740$$

The correct answer is (A). (For a refresher on solving average problems, revisit Chapter 18: Statistics.)

You can also solve this problem using the principles of weighted averages. The amount for one month increased by $182, but that doesn't mean the average will increase by $182. Instead, because that increase only happened in one out of twelve months, it will have a one-twelfth impact. This is shown algebraically below:

$$\text{new average} = \frac{\text{old sum} + 182}{12}$$
$$= \frac{\text{old sum}}{12} + \frac{182}{12}$$
$$= \text{old average} + \sim 15$$
$$\approx 4{,}725 + 15$$
$$\approx 4{,}740$$

Since you already know the old average, the math is more efficient than recalculating the entire average.

9. **(D) 32%**
To calculate the percent increase from January to June, find the total sales in January ($3,890) and in June ($5,143).

$$\frac{\text{new} - \text{old}}{\text{old}} = \frac{\text{June sales} - \text{Jan sales}}{\text{Jan sales}} = \frac{5{,}143 - 3{,}890}{3{,}890} \approx 0.32$$

The increase was approximately 32%.

10. **(E) Sep–Oct**
Total sales are the sum of fruit and vegetable sales. A decline in total sales would mean that sales in at least one of the two categories would have to go down, and that drop would have to be greater than any increase in the other category.

Use the answer choices to limit which pairs to examine. From Feb–Mar and Mar–Apr, both fruit and vegetable sales increased, so there was no decline. Eliminate answers (A) and (B). From Jun–Jul, vegetable sales increased, but fruit sales stayed flat, so still no decline. Eliminate answer (C). Aug–Sep also looks about the same for both fruit and vegetable sales. However, from Sep–Oct, both fruit and vegetable sales declined, so the correct answer must be (E).

The long way to do this problem is to read both fruit and vegetable sales and calculate approximate total sales for each month. Don't do that—it will take way too long!

> **Strategy Tip**
>
> Many Data Interpretation problems can be solved by visual estimation. Only perform precise calculations for close calls.

11. **(D) $1,720**

    Gross profit is equal to the revenue minus the costs. If you can determine values for fruit sales revenue and fruit cost, you can answer this question.

    The chart shows the monthly fruit sales revenue in May. Unfortunately, the answer choices are too close together to estimate, so you'll have to calculate.

    In May, fruit sale revenue was about $2,500. The produce stand charged an average of $0.80 per pound for this fruit. Calculate the number of pounds of fruit sold.

    $$\text{Rev per lb of fruit} \times \text{\# of lb} = \text{total fruit rev}$$
    $$\$0.80 \times \text{\# of lb} = \$2,500$$
    $$\text{\# of lb} = \frac{\$2,500}{\$0.80}$$
    $$\text{\# of lb} = 3,125$$

    The produce stand bought the 3,125 pounds of fruit for an average cost of $0.25 per pound. Calculate how much it cost the produce stand to acquire the 3,125 pounds of fruit.

    $$\text{Cost per lb of fruit} \times \text{\# of lb} = \text{total fruit cost}$$
    $$\$0.25 \times 3,125 = \text{total fruit cost}$$
    $$\$781.25 = \text{total fruit cost}$$

    Finally, find the approximate gross profit on fruit sales:

    $$\text{gross profit} = \text{revenue} - \text{cost}$$
    $$\text{gross profit} = \$2,500 - \$780$$
    $$\text{gross profit} = \$1,720$$

    > **Strategy Tip**
    >
    > When you need a quantity (such as number of pounds of fruit sold) that is not directly shown in a graph, try writing out equations for it in terms of quantities you do know.

Unit Four: **Stories, Percents, Ratios, Stats, and Data**

12. **(C) oranges**

    The question asks for the item that generated the third highest sales amount in the month of April.

    Scan the chart, starting from the longest bar and working your way back. Potatoes had the greatest revenue, followed by apples and then oranges. So, oranges generated the third-greatest revenue.

13. **(A) 1 : 4**

    To calculate the ratio of carrot sales to potato sales in April, find the sales amounts for each. Carrot sales were about $250 and potato sales were about $980. Find the ratio by dividing the two totals:

    $$\frac{\text{carrot sales}}{\text{potato sales}} \approx \frac{25\cancel{0}}{98\cancel{0}} \approx \frac{25}{100} \approx \frac{1}{4}$$

    The ratio is approximately 1 to 4.

14. **(D) $7,239**

    The question asks you to calculate the approximate total revenue from vegetable sales in September, October, and November.

    In September, vegetable sales were 48.79% of $5,026. In October, vegetable sales were 50.11% of $4,726. In November, vegetable sales were 50.22% of $4,817. The question asks for an approximation, so glance at the answers. They are far enough apart that you can round these values to reduce the number of clicks needed to use the calculator:

    $$\underbrace{0.49 \times 5,000}_{\text{Sep veg sales}} + \underbrace{0.5 \times 4,700}_{\text{Oct veg sales}} + \underbrace{0.5 \times 4,800}_{\text{Nov veg sales}} =$$

    $$2,450 \quad + \quad 2,350 \quad + \quad 2,400 \quad = 7,200$$

    Total vegetable sales in this period were approximately $7,200. Most of the calculations were rounded down slightly, so the actual value should be a bit more than $7,200. Only answer choice (D) is close.

15. **(C) $577**

First, figure out which produce items were high in both vitamin A and vitamin C. Then, calculate the total sales of those items. The table shows that only tomatoes are high in both vitamins, so calculate total tomato sales.

Note that the while bar chart provides information on the same fruits and vegetables as the table, they are listed in a different order. Take care to make sure that you're looking at the correct bar! Tomatoes account for about 13% of April's sales. Since total April sales are given as $4,441, calculate 13% of $4,441:

$$0.13 \times \$4,441 = \$577.33$$

> **Strategy Tip**
>
> Don't assume that information that appears on two charts or tables will appear in the same order.

16. **(B) $3,600**

Determine which produce items have *either* medium or high amounts of in *either* vitamin A or vitamin C. Then, calculate the total sales of those items.

That direction is pretty complex. Rephrase it: Which items have at least one label of medium or high? All of them except for apples.

It's pretty annoying to calculate all but one—so switch it around. Total sales were $4,441. Calculate apples, then subtract from $4,441 to find sales for all of the other items.

The bar graph shows that apples accounted for about 19 percent of total sales:

$$0.19 \times \$4,441 = \$843.79$$

Round both figures down (by almost the same amount—so you're not introducing much error at all!), then subtract to determine revenue from all of the other items:

$$\$4,400 - \$800 = \$3,600$$

The long way to do this problem is to sum up the percentages of each type of produce that has a medium or high level of vitamin A or vitamin C. That can be done…it's just going to take longer.

> **Strategy Tip**
>
> Sometimes, it's easier to calculate the percentage that does *not* satisfy a condition rather than to calculate the percentage that does satisfy the condition.

Unit Four: **Stories, Percents, Ratios, Stats, and Data**

Problem Set

Directions: Each set of charts is accompanied by several questions. Note that the number of questions here is more than you would expect to see for Data Interpretation on the GRE. Typically, a set of charts is followed by no more than three associated questions. More are presented here for additional practice.

The first question for each set asks for your initial reflections on the charts. This is not a question you will find on the GRE, but it is an important step to complete before moving on to the actual questions.

Problem Set A

Questions #1–6 refer to the following charts.

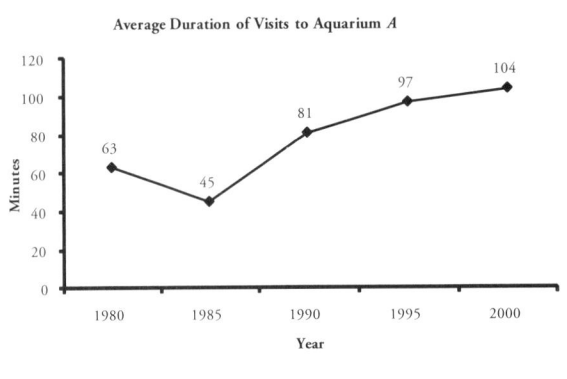

Chapter 19: **Data Interpretation**

1. Take 30 seconds to scan the graphs. What seems important?

2. In how many of the time periods shown was the average duration of visits to Aquarium A more than twice as much as the average in 1985 ?

    (A) Four
    (B) Three
    (C) Two
    (D) One
    (E) Zero

3. In 1980, if a full-price ticket cost $4.70, what was the average daily revenue, in thousands of dollars, from the sale of full-price tickets?

    ☐ thousands of dollars

4. In 2000, the total number of dollars of gift shop revenue was how many times as great as the average daily number of full-price tickets sold?

    (A) 400
    (B) 200
    (C) 80
    (D) 40
    (E) 20

5. What was the approximate percent increase in average daily full-price ticket sales from 1990 to 1995 ?

    (A) 10%
    (B) 20%
    (C) 33%
    (D) 48%
    (E) 66%

6. Which of the following statements can be inferred from the data?

    Indicate all such statements.

    ☐ A In each of the time periods shown in which yearly gift shop revenue decreased from the previous time period, average daily full-price ticket sales also decreased.
    ☐ B The greatest increase in total yearly gift shop revenue between any two consecutive time periods shown was $2.7 million.
    ☐ C From 1995 to 2000, the average duration of visits to the museum increased by 12 minutes.

531

Unit Four: **Stories, Percents, Ratios, Stats, and Data**

Problem Set B

Questions #7–11 refer to the following charts.

Total conveyances: 785,000

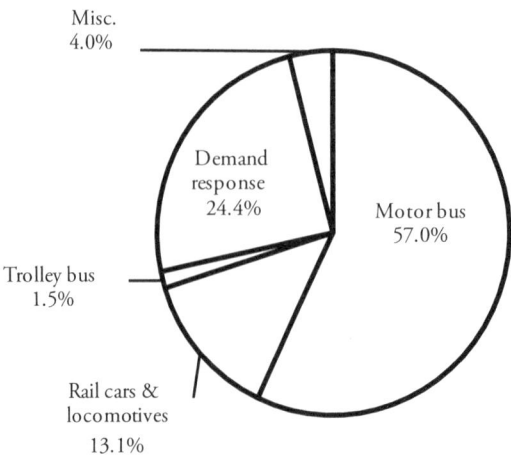

Chapter 19: **Data Interpretation**

7. Take 30 seconds to scan the graphs. What seems important?

8. Approximately what was the ratio of trucks to passenger cars?

    (A) 1 to 20
    (B) 1 to 18
    (C) 1 to 17
    (D) 1 to 15
    (E) 1 to 12

9. Approximately how many more miscellaneous public transit vehicles than public transit trolley buses were there in 2000 ?

    (A) 1,000
    (B) 1,500
    (C) 2,000
    (D) 2,500
    (E) 3,000

10. If the number of aircraft, vehicles, and other conveyances was 572,000 in 1995, what was the approximate percentage increase from 1995 to 2000 ?

    (A) 37%
    (B) 32%
    (C) 27%
    (D) 20%
    (E) 15%

11. In 2000, if an equal percentage of passenger cars and demand-response vehicles experienced mechanical problems, and the number of passenger cars that experienced such problems was 13,436, approximately how many demand-response vehicles experienced mechanical problems?

    (A) 1,352
    (B) 2,928
    (C) 4,099
    (D) 7,263
    (E) 9,221

Unit Four: **Stories, Percents, Ratios, Stats, and Data**

Problem Set C

Questions #12–15 refer to the following charts.

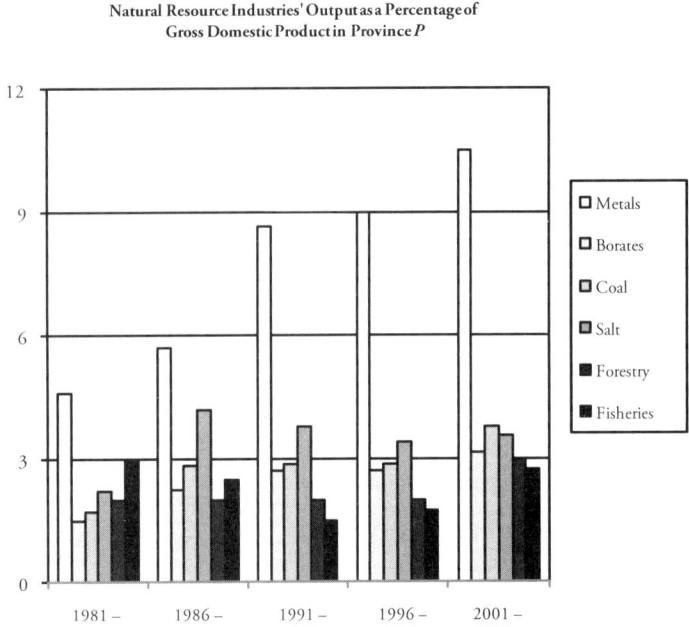

Natural Resource Industries' Output as a Percentage of Gross Domestic Product in Province *P*

	Mining Industries' Average Annual Production							
		Percentage of Mining Industries' Production					
	Mining Industries' Average Annual Production, in millions of 2005 dollars	Metals			Other Mined Products		
Years		Uranium, Titanium, & Aluminum	Gold & Silver	Copper	Borates	Coal	Salt
1981–1985	$342.5	10%	20%	16%	15%	17%	22%
1986–1990	$326.8	12	17	9	15	19	28
1991–1995	$310.0	16	20	12	15	16	21
1996–2000	$257.9	12	22	16	15	16	19
2001–2005	$205.0	14	24	12	15	18	17

12. Take 30 seconds to scan the graphs. What seems important?

13. Approximately what percent of the mining industries' average annual production from 1991–1995 came from production of aluminum?

    Ⓐ 4%
    Ⓑ 7%
    Ⓒ 11%
    Ⓓ 22%
    Ⓔ Cannot be determined

14. Approximately what percent of average annual GDP of Province *P* from 1996–2000 came from copper production?

    Ⓐ 3%
    Ⓑ 6%
    Ⓒ 9%
    Ⓓ 14%
    Ⓔ 18%

15. Which of the following statements can be inferred from the information given?

    Indicate all such statements.

    ☐ A For all the time periods shown, borate production, in millions of 2005 dollars, was the same.
    ☐ B Of the time periods shown, 1981–1985 was the one in which the mining industries produced the greatest value of gold and silver, measured in 2005 dollars.
    ☐ C Of the time periods shown, 2001–2005 had the highest average annual GDP, measured in 2005 dollars.

Unit Four: **Stories, Percents, Ratios, Stats, and Data**

Solutions

1. All three graphs illustrate the same time period. The topmost displays average ticket sales, the middle displays gift shop revenue, and the bottom displays duration of visits. Notice that units change for each graph. Ticket sales are in thousands, gift shop revenue is in millions, and duration of visits is in minutes. Now, you're ready for the questions!

2. **(C) Two**
   First, identify the chart that gives information about the average duration of visits: the bottom one. Next, find the relevant figure—the average duration of a visit in 1985—and double it to determine the cutoff duration. The average visit duration in 1985 was 45 minutes, so look for the years that had an average visit duration greater than 90 minutes. Only 1995 and 2000 fit this constraint, so the correct answer is choice (C).

3. **235**
   The average daily revenue for the aquarium can be found using the following equation:

   $$\text{average daily revenue} = \$ \text{ per ticket} \times \text{average \# of tickets}$$

   The price per ticket is given in the question ($4.70), and the top graph gives the average daily number of tickets sold. In 1980, the average daily number of tickets sold was 50,000, so the average daily revenue is 50,000 × $4.70 = $235,000. The question asks for the revenue in thousands, so the answer is 235.

4. **(D) 40**
   To answer this question, you'll need information about both gift shop revenue and the average number of full-price tickets sold. The former can be found in the middle graph, and the latter can be found in the top graph.

   In 2000, total gift shop revenue was $3,600,000 and the average daily number of full-price tickets sold was 90,000. The question asks how many times greater 3,600,000 is than 90,000. To find out, divide 3,600,000 by 90,000 using the calculator. The answer is 40, choice (D).

5. **(D) 48%**
   The average daily full-price ticket sales are shown in the top graph. Percent increase is defined as the change divided by the original value. In this question then, the percent increase can be found using the following formula (let *x* stand for the average daily full-price ticket sales).

   $$\frac{(x \text{ in } 1995) - (x \text{ in } 1990)}{(x \text{ in } 1990)}$$

   The average number in 1990 was 220, and in 1995 it was 325.

   $$\frac{325 - 220}{220} = \frac{105}{220} = 0.477$$

   Remember that the question asks you to approximate. The answer is closest to choice (D).

Chapter 19: **Data Interpretation**

6. **(B) The greatest increase in total yearly gift shop revenue between any two consecutive time periods shown was $2.7 million.**

   This question asks which statements can be inferred from the data; therefore, you have to use the process of elimination and treat each statement as its own mini question.

   For answer (A), identify the five-year periods in which gift shop revenue (middle graph) decreased: 1990–1995 and 1995–2000. Next, locate the graph for average ticket sales, which is the top graph. Ticket sales did *not* decrease in 1990–1995, so answer (A) is false.

   For answer (B), the graph for gift shop revenue is the middle one. Locate the biggest jump—it is from 2.3 to 5. Compute the size of this jump: $5 - 2.3 = 2.7$, so answer (B) is true.

   For answer (C), the graph for duration of visits is the bottom one. The increase from 1995–2000 was from 97 to 104, which equals 7 minutes, not 12 minutes, so answer (C) is false.

   Only the box for answer (B) should be selected.

7. The first chart displays absolute quantity data, while the second and third display percentages. This is a common combination on the GRE. All of the graphs are from the same year. The bar chart shows total quantities of a variety of vehicles, along with a total conveyances line at the bottom. The pie charts give additional information on the percentages of two varieties of vehicles: public transit and private highway vehicles.

8. **(D) 1 to 15**

   Trucks and passenger cars are both listed as subsets of private highway vehicles in the middle graph. Though the pie chart does not give specific information about the number of trucks or the number of cars, it does tell you what percent of the total number of private vehicles each represents. Because each of the percents is out of the same total, you can compare the percents directly to find the ratio of trucks to cars.

   Note: You could also use the information in the top graph in conjunction with the information in the pie chart to calculate the actual numbers of trucks and cars, but that would be time-consuming and unnecessary.

   Remember that the question asks you to approximate. The ratio of 4% to 59.5% is approximately the ratio of 4 to 60. Reduce the ratio to get the correct answer, 1 : 15. The correct answer is (D).

9. **(E) 3,000**

   To find the total numbers of miscellaneous public transit vehicles and public transit trolley buses, you will need to combine information from the top and bottom graphs.

   According to the top graph, there were roughly 120,000 public transit vehicles in 2000 (remember the question asks you to approximate). Of those 120,000 public transit vehicles, 4% were miscellaneous vehicles and 1.5% were trolley buses.

   The difference in the number of miscellaneous and trolley bus vehicles is:

   $$\left(\frac{4}{100} \times 120{,}000\right) - \left(\frac{1.5}{100} \times 120{,}000\right)$$

   Either calculate both numbers and subtract, or realize that the difference will be $\left(\frac{4}{100} - \frac{1.5}{100}\right) \times 120{,}000$. However you perform the calculation, the difference is 3,000. The correct answer is (E).

Unit Four: **Stories, Percents, Ratios, Stats, and Data**

10. **(A) 37%**

    Percent increase is defined as change divided by original value. In this question, the percent increase can be found using the following equation (let x stand for the total number of U.S. aircraft, vehicles, and other conveyances).

    $$\frac{(x \text{ in } 2000) - (x \text{ in } 1995)}{(x \text{ in } 1995)}$$

    The question says that the total number in 1995 was 572,000. The total number in 2000 can be found in the top graph. Fortunately, the question doesn't require you to add the values in every column together! At the bottom, the graph states that the total number of conveyances was 785,000. Plug this total along with the total from the question into the formula to find the approximate percent increase.

    $$\frac{785{,}000 - 572{,}000}{572{,}000} = 0.372 \approx 37\%$$

    Answer choice (A) is the closest to the actual value.

11. **(B) 2,928**

    The question asks for a number of demand-response vehicles that experienced mechanical problems. It provides a number of passenger cars that experienced such problems as well as a percentage relationship between passenger cars with mechanical problems and demand-response vehicles with mechanical problems. Now formulate a plan. You can use the *number* of passenger cars with mechanical problems given in the question along with information in the graphs to calculate the *percentage* of passenger cars with mechanical problems. Then, you can use that same percentage on the total number of demand-response vehicles (which can also be found in the graphs) to find out how many of those vehicles had mechanical problems.

    $$\% \text{ of cars with problems} = \frac{\# \text{ of cars with problems}}{\text{total \# of cars}}$$

    You know from the second pie that passenger cars make up 59.5% of all private highway vehicles, and from the top chart you know that there are about 225,000 private highway vehicles, so the total number of passenger cars will be $0.595 \times 225{,}000 = 133{,}875$. Plug that into the formula above.

    $$\% \text{ of cars with problems} = \frac{13{,}436}{133{,}875} \approx 0.10, \text{ or } 10\%$$

    Now, find the total number of demand-response vehicles in much the same way as you found the number of cars, and you can apply the same percentage to that total. From the bottom pie, demand-response vehicles make up 24.4% of all public transit vehicles, and from the top chart, there are roughly 120,000 public transit vehicles, so the total number of demand-response vehicles is $0.244 \times 120{,}000 = 29{,}280$. Apply the 10% calculated before to that total number of demand-response vehicles to find the approximate number of these vehicles with mechanical problems: $0.10 \times 29{,}280 = 2{,}928$, or answer (B).

12. The clustered column chart displays percents in five-year chunks. The table uses the same five-year chunks to show production of several of the categories represented in the clustered column chart. The column chart is about output relative to GDP, while the table is solely about production. Both use percents, but while the chart shows percents of the GDP, the table shows percents of total production.

Chapter 19: **Data Interpretation**

It's worth noting that this is a particularly tricky set. The graphs and the questions that follow are at the more complicated end of the range for the GRE. (Because the GRE is a section-level adaptive test, only those who have performed at a high level on their first Quant section would ever see a Data Interpretation set this difficult.)

13. **(E) Cannot be determined**

    One of the answer choices is "cannot be determined," so check exact wording and be sure you have enough information to solve it before doing any math.

    Locate the relevant column within the table on the bottom: "Uranium, Titanium, & Aluminum." The figures in this column represent uranium + titanium + aluminum, but do not tell you the level of aluminum *alone*. Because the question is asking *only* about aluminum, you do not have enough information.

    The correct answer is (E).

    > **Strategy Tip**
    >
    > You can save yourself a lot of time by first checking whether you have enough information to answer the question—before making any calculations.

14. **(A) 3%**

    Rephrase the question. Expressing the desired percentage as a fraction is a good way to abbreviate the question:

    $$\text{In 1996-2000, } \frac{\text{Copper}}{\text{GDP}} = ?$$

    The chart that mentions copper is on the bottom and tells you that from 1996–2000, copper accounted for 16% of Province *P*'s mining industries' production. As an equation, this can be written as follows:

    $$\text{Copper} = 0.16 \times \text{Mining}$$

    However, mining itself accounts for only a part of the province's total GDP. To find out how the copper production relates to the overall GDP, you'll have to know how mining relates to the GDP. This is when the first chart comes into play. The first chart shows various sectors as a percent of Province *P*'s GDP. Take care with this: Not all of the columns shown in each cluster are relevant to mining. Pay attention only to those sectors that are mentioned in the mining table; ignore Forestry and Fisheries. From 1996–2000, mining production (that is, metals, borates, coal, and salt) accounted for roughly 18% of Province *P*'s GDP.

    $$\text{Mining} = 0.18 \times \text{GDP}$$

    Using substitution, we can now manipulate the two equations above to find the relationship between copper production and total GDP.

    $$\text{Copper} = 0.16 \times \underbrace{\text{Mining}}_{0.18 \times \text{GDP}}$$

    $$\text{Copper} = 0.16 \times (0.18 \times \text{GDP})$$

    $$\text{Copper} = 0.0288 \times \text{GDP}$$

    Translated back to English, the last line of the equation contains our answer: Copper production accounted for 2.9% of Province *P*'s GDP from 1996–2000. The correct answer is (A).

Unit Four: **Stories, Percents, Ratios, Stats, and Data**

> **Strategy Tip**
>
> Higher-level Data Interpretation questions will usually make you work harder to find needed values and will benefit from careful algebraic translation.

15. **(B) Of the time periods shown, 1981–1985 was the one in which the mining industries produced the greatest value of gold and silver, measured in 2005 dollars.**

    Answer (A): For each time period, the production of borates (as shown in the table) is given as 15% of that period's mining industries' production. However, each period has a *different* dollar figure for the mining industries' total production, meaning that the 15% figure for borate production will translate to different dollar amounts for each time period. For example, from 1981–1985, borate production was 15% × $342.5, whereas from 1986–1990, borate production was 15% × $326.8. Answer (A) is therefore false.

    Answer (B): To test whether this is true, notice that the dollar values of Gold & Silver production were as follows:

    1981–1985: 20% × $342.5
    1986–1990: 17% × $326.8
    1991–1995: 20% × $310
    1996–2000: 22% × $257.9
    2001–2005: 24% × $205

    While you *could* plug all of these into your calculator, this may take unnecessary time—time that's all the more precious in the harder Quant sections in which Data Interpretation sets as difficult as this one will appear. Rather than go straight to the calculator, you can eliminate two of these five choices without doing any arithmetic at all. The figure for 1986–1990 is clearly lower than that for 1981–1985, because 1986–1990 has a lower percentage (17% as opposed to 20%) *and* a lower dollar amount ($326.8 as opposed to $342.5). Likewise, you can see that 1991–1995 is lower than 1981–1985: The percentage is the same for both periods (20%), but for 1991–1995 that percentage is multiplied by a smaller dollar amount ($310 as opposed to $342.5). For the three remaining periods, you can estimate or use the calculator:

    1981–1985: 20% × $342.5 = $68.50
    1996–2000: 22% × $257.9 = $56.74
    2001–2005: 24% × $205 = $49.20

    These calculations show that 1981–1985 had the highest gold & silver production, so answer (B) is true.

    Answer (C): This statement asks you about Gross Domestic Product (GDP) measured in dollars. To decide whether it is true, you must use both sets of data (GDP is only mentioned in the column chart, whereas dollar figures are only provided in the table) and find a way to mathematically link them.

    There are many ways to use the data in both sets to calculate total GDP, but one of the more straightforward ways is to use an approach similar to the approach used in the previous question to tie the dollar figures for total mining production in Province *P* to the percentages of GDP that mining production accounted for. For the 2001–2005 time period, the columns representing mining in the first chart account for about 21% of total GDP. The table shows that the dollar figure for mining in the same period was $205 million. These can be related as follows:

540

$$\text{Mining}_{(2001\text{-}2005)} \approx \frac{21}{100} \times \text{GDP}$$

$$\$205 \text{ million} \approx \frac{21}{100} \times \text{GDP}$$

$$\frac{\$205 \text{ million}}{0.21} \approx \text{GDP}$$

$$\$976 \text{ million} \approx \text{GDP}$$

To determine whether this is the highest GDP dollar figure for any of the periods shown, you would have to calculate the GDP for the other time periods. While it may prove necessary to do so for each of the other time periods, it will likely be best to go all the way to the other extreme. Visually, you can see that the columns for mining in the 2001–2005 time period on the first chart are the tallest of all. By contrast, the columns for the 1981–1985 time period are collectively the shortest, accounting altogether for about 10% of total GDP. Test this other extreme to see whether answer (C) is valid:

$$\text{Mining}_{(1981\text{-}1985)} \approx \frac{10}{100} \times \text{GDP}$$

$$\$342.5 \text{ million} \approx \frac{10}{100} \times \text{GDP}$$

$$\frac{\$342.5 \text{ million}}{0.10} \approx \text{GDP}$$

$$\$3{,}425 \text{ million} \approx \text{GDP}$$

This is enough to show conclusively that 2001–2005 did *not* have the highest dollar amount for GDP for the time periods shown. Eliminate answer (C).

Only the box for answer (B) should be checked.

> **Strategy Tip**
>
> On problems this difficult, it is essential to *avoid hard math* even with a calculator, and rely on approximation, algebraic translation, and bounding (using extreme values) instead. The calculator can be helpful, but setting up efficient mathematical relationships is essential in order to save time.

UNIT FIVE

Geometry

In this unit, you'll learn about the shapes, planes, lines, angles, and objects that are tested on the GRE. You'll also learn how to use the necessary geometric principles, rules, and formulas to solve geometry problems on the GRE.

In This Unit:

- Chapter 20: Geometry on the GRE
- Chapter 21: Triangles and Diagonals
- Chapter 22: Polygons
- Chapter 23: Circles and Cylinders
- Chapter 24: Lines and Angles
- Chapter 25: The Coordinate Plane
- Chapter 26: QC Geometry

CHAPTER 20
Geometry on the GRE

In This Chapter:

- Geometry Formulas
- Using Geometry Equations
- Check Your Skills Answer Key
- Problem Set
- Solutions

CHAPTER 20 Geometry on the GRE

Geometry on the GRE involves not just memorizing formulas, but also applying those formulas appropriately and recognizing when different geometric properties are relevant. In this chapter, you will learn how to use common geometry formulas, as well as a standard process for solving any problems involving geometry. The rest of the geometry unit will dive deeper into individual shapes to provide a more complete understanding.

Unit Five: Geometry

Geometry Formulas

Use this cheat sheet as you go through the following chapters. You do need to memorize these equations, but don't stop there. Keep pushing to acquire a deep understanding so you can apply these formulas effectively.

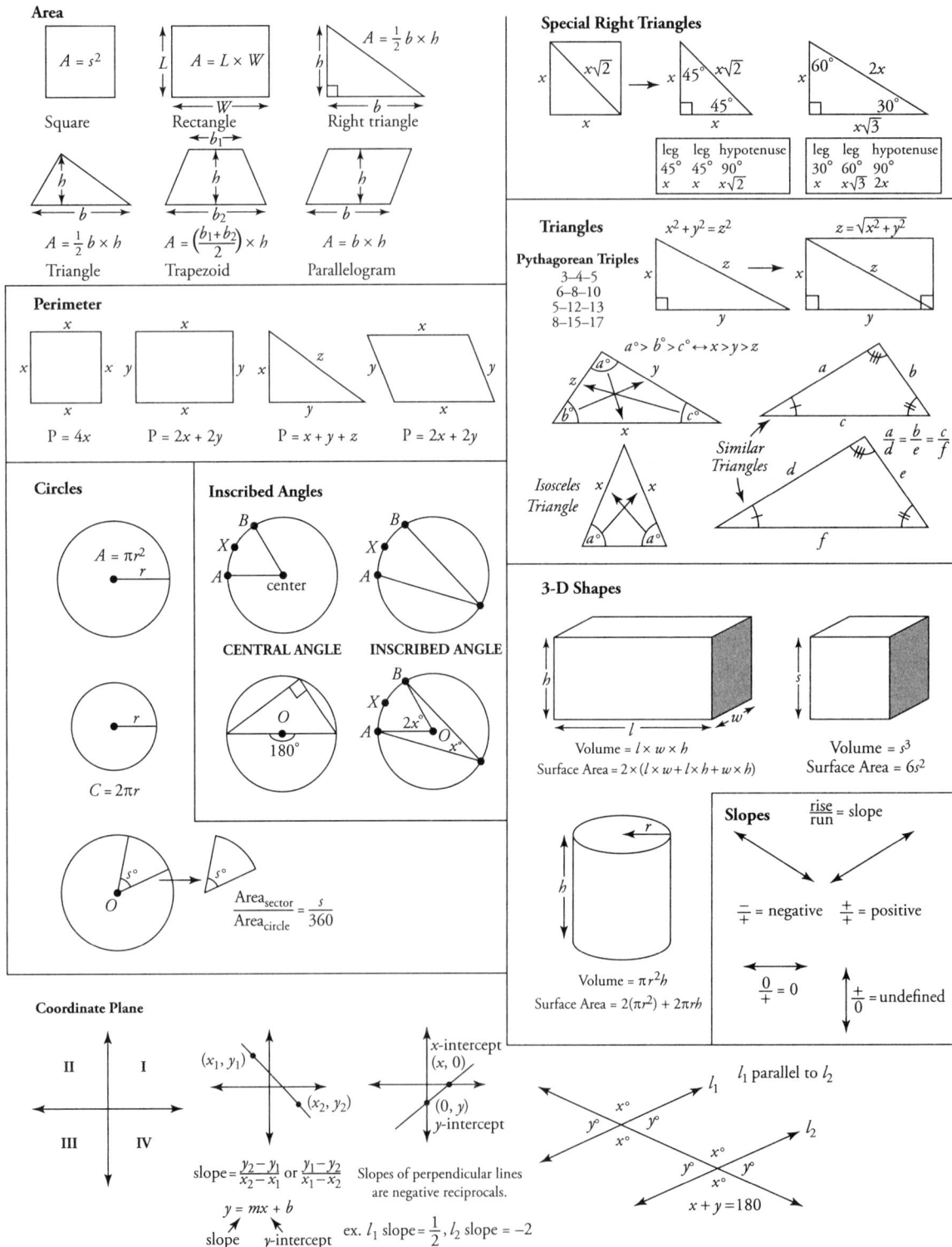

Chapter 20: **Geometry on the GRE**

Using Geometry Equations

The GRE complicates geometry problems by presenting them in English rather than in algebraic terms. It's important to know how to translate the information presented in questions into math. To start, try the following problem:

> Rectangles *ABCD* and *EFGH*, shown below, have equal areas. The length of side *AB* is 5. What is the length of diagonal *AC*?

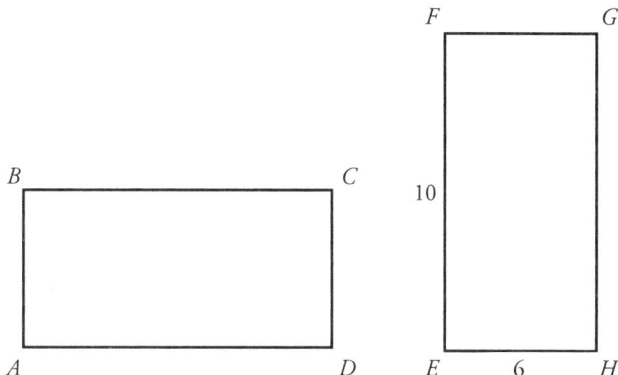

The first step: Draw your own copies of the shapes on your scratch paper and fill in everything you know. In this problem, redraw both rectangles and add the given information that side *AB* has a length of 5. Also, make note of what you're looking for—in this case, the length of diagonal *AC*. For example:

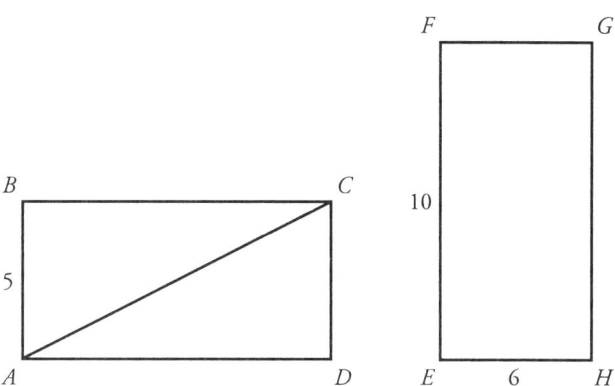

Has the problem provided you any information that can be expressed mathematically? In other words, can you create equations? It did indicate that the two rectangles have equal areas. The formula for the area of a rectangle is length times width:

$$(l_{ABCD})(w_{ABCD}) = (l_{EFGH})(w_{EFGH})$$

Unit Five: **Geometry**

The length and width of rectangle *EFGH* are 6 and 10, and the length of *AB* is 5. Substitute those values into the equation:

$$(l_{ABCD}) \times (w_{ABCD}) = (l_{EFGH}) \times (w_{EFGH})$$
$$5 \times (w_{ABCD}) = 6 \times 10$$
$$5w = 60$$
$$w = 12$$

Within one rectangle, it doesn't matter which dimension you call length and which you call width, since the two values will be multiplied together.

Every time you figure out a new piece of information (in this case the width of rectangle *ABCD*), add that information to your diagram:

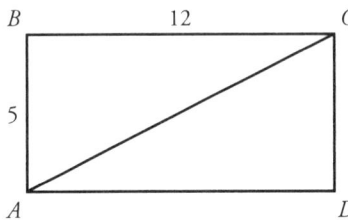

Here's the general process for the three steps taken so far:

> ### Geometry Process (Steps 1–3)
>
> Step 1: **Draw or redraw figures and fill in all given information.**
> Fill in all known angles and lengths and make note of any equal sides or angles.
>
> Step 2: **Identify relationships and create equations.**
> Often, these relationships will be explicitly stated in the question. Add these values to your diagram.
>
> Step 3: **Solve the equations for the missing value(s).**
> If you can solve for a value, you will often need that value to answer the question.
> Add these values to your diagram.

These first three steps set up the problem. But even with all of that work, you still don't have the asked-for value, the length of diagonal *AC*.

Even if you're not sure yet how calculating the width of rectangle *ABCD* will help, go ahead and calculate it anyway. If you're given three values for a four-variable equation on a geometry problem, the chances are excellent that you're going to need that fourth value to get to the eventual answer.

What can you do now that you know the width of rectangle *ABCD* that you couldn't do before? To answer that, take another look at the value you're looking for: the length of *AC*.

The length AC is the diagonal of rectangle ABCD, yes, but it's also the hypotenuse of a right triangle (because all four interior angles of a rectangle are right angles):

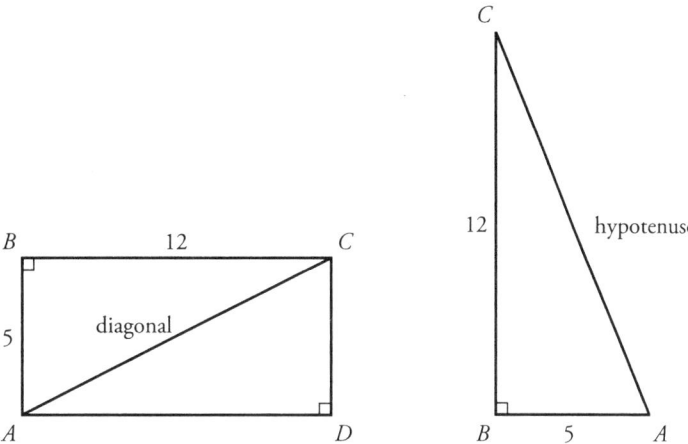

Since AC is the hypotenuse of a right triangle, you can use the Pythagorean theorem to find the length of the hypotenuse using the two side lengths.

Pythagorean Theorem: $a^2 + b^2 = c^2$

The Pythagorean theorem is true for all right triangles, where a and b are the two legs (shorter sides) of the triangle and c is the hypotenuse (longest side) of the triangle.

Sides BC and BA are the legs of the triangle, and AC is the hypotenuse, so:

$$(BC)^2 + (BA)^2 = (AC)^2$$
$$(12)^2 + (5)^2 = (AC)^2$$
$$144 + 25 = (AC)^2$$
$$169 = (AC)^2$$
$$13 = AC$$

The length of diagonal AC is 13.

It turns out that this particular right triangle is a common Pythagorean triple: a 5–12–13 triangle. Memorize this and you won't have to calculate it on the test. When you see that there are two legs of 5 and 12, the hypotenuse will always be 13. Alternatively, if you know the hypotenuse is 13 and one leg is 5, then the other leg must be 12. (You'll learn more Pythagorean triples in Chapter 21: Triangles and Diagonals.)

Unit Five: **Geometry**

Here's the full process, including the final step:

> *Geometry Problem Solving Process*
>
> Step 1: **Draw or redraw figures and fill in all given information.**
> Fill in all known angles and lengths and make note of any equal sides or angles.
>
> Step 2: **Identify relationships and create equations.**
> Often, these relationships will be explicitly stated in the question. Add these values to your diagram.
>
> Step 3: **Solve the equations for the missing value(s).**
> If you can solve for a value, you will often need that value to answer the question. Add these values to your diagram.
>
> Step 4: **Make inferences from the figures.**
> Make use of the given information and the new information calculated in steps 2 and 3.

Geometry questions can feel particularly intimidating, because it won't always be clear at first how to get to step 4. Get yourself to step 3 and see what you can infer. Then, ask yourself how to get to the final answer from there.

Try this problem:

> Rectangle $PQRS$ is inscribed in circle O pictured below. If the circumference of circle O is 5π, what is the area of rectangle $PQRS$?

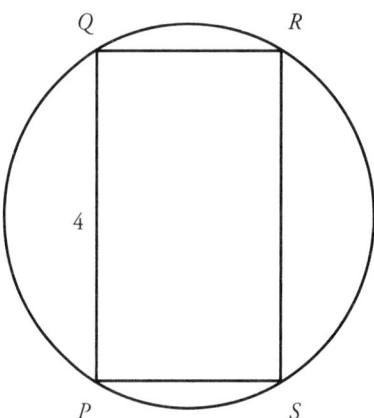

Step 1: Draw or redraw figures and fill in all given information.

The question didn't explicitly provide the value of any side lengths or angles, but it did say that *PQRS* is a rectangle, so all four internal angles are right angles. Add that info to your diagram:

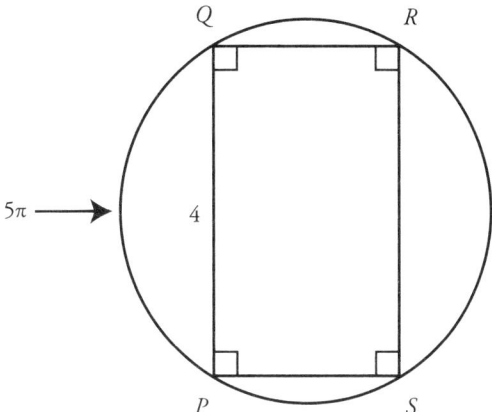

Step 2: Identify relationships and create equations.

The question stated that the circumference of circle *O* is 5π. The formula for circumference is $C = 2\pi r$, so $5\pi = 2\pi r$.

Step 3: Solve the equations for the missing value(s).

Solve for *r*:

$$5\pi = 2\pi r$$
$$5 = 2r$$
$$2.5 = r$$

Since the radius is 2.5, the diameter of circle *O* is 5.

Step 4: Make inferences from the figures.

How do the radius and diameter help? You were able to solve for them, which is a very good clue that you need at least one of them to answer the question.

This question asked for the area of rectangle *PQRS*. To find the area, you need the length and width of the rectangle. The question stem provided the length of *QP*. Can you find the length of the other side of the rectangle?

Unit Five: **Geometry**

Look for a connection between the rectangle and the radius or diameter. Put a diameter into the circle:

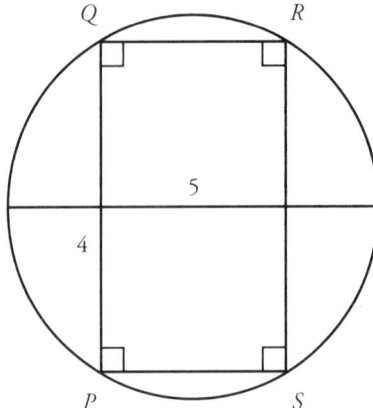

That doesn't connect the circle and the rectangle. But what if you drew the diameter so that it touched the circle at points *P* and *R*? This is still a diameter of the circle . . . *and* it's the diagonal of the rectangle:

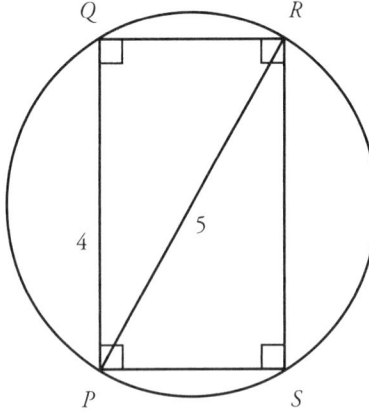

The circle and the rectangle have a common element. The diameter is 5, so the diagonal of the rectangle is also 5.

> **Strategy Tip**
>
> When there are overlapping shapes, draw new elements such that they relate one shape to another.
>
> (If you're unsure where to start, look for triangles, since so much can be inferred given only a small amount of information.)

Now what? You still need the length of either *QR* or *PS*. Look at the angles in the figure—*PQR* is a right triangle and you know the lengths of two of the sides: *PQ* and *PR*. Use the Pythagorean theorem to find the length of the third side, *QR*:

$$(QR)^2 + (PQ)^2 = (PR)^2$$
$$(QR)^2 + (4)^2 = (5)^2$$
$$(QR)^2 + 16 = 25$$
$$(QR)^2 = 9$$
$$QR = 3$$

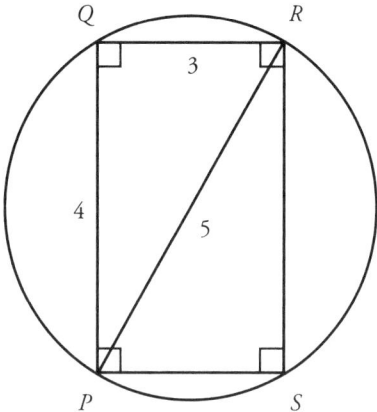

This is another Pythagorean triple, by the way: Triangle *PQR* is a 3–4–5 triangle. This is the most common triple—definitely memorize this one.

Now, find the area of rectangle *PQRS*:

$$\text{Area} = \text{length} \times \text{width} = 3 \times 4 = 12$$

It probably wasn't clear at the beginning exactly what steps you'd need to take to finally calculate that the area is 12. A lot of geometry problems will feel this way. Just start calculating what you can calculate and see where that information takes you.

At every step, keep adding your new inferences to your diagram. The key insight in this problem was that a diameter of the circle could also act as the diagonal of the rectangle. These kinds of insights are going to be crucial to success on GRE geometry—recognizing shapes when they're presented in an unfamiliar format and finding connections between different shapes.

Unit Five: **Geometry**

Check Your Skills

1. In rectangle *ABCD*, the distance between *B* and *D* is 10. What is the area of the circle inside the rectangle, if the circle is tangent to both *AD* and *BC*?

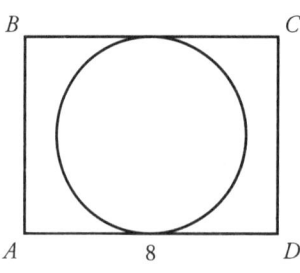

Area = ☐ π

Answers can be found on page 558.

This page intentionally left blank

Unit Five: **Geometry**

Check Your Skills Answer Key

1. 9

    Consider only the rectangle for a moment. Diagonal *BD* cuts the rectangle into two right triangles:

    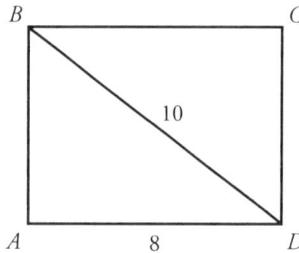

    Now look at right triangle *ABD*. The line segment *BD* functions not only as the diagonal of rectangle *ABCD* but also as the hypotenuse of right triangle *ABD*. Find the third side of triangle *ABD*, either using the Pythagorean theorem or recognizing a Pythagorean triple (6–8–10).

    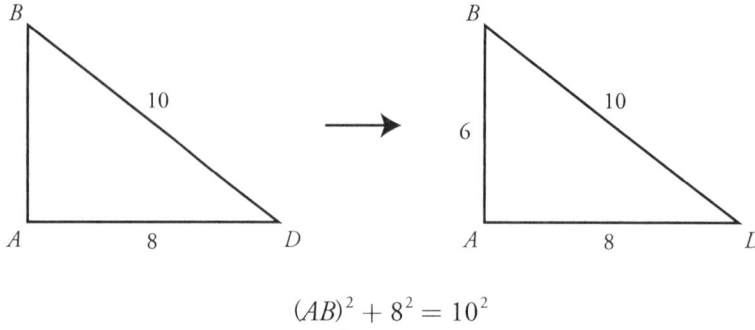

    $$(AB)^2 + 8^2 = 10^2$$
    $$(AB)^2 + 64 = 100$$
    $$(AB)^2 = 36$$
    $$AB = 6$$

    Now consider the circle within this 6 by 8 rectangle:

    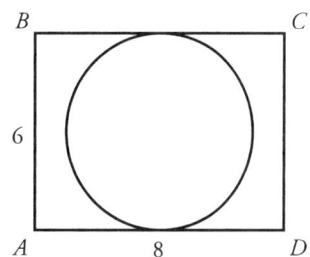 Since the circle touches both *AD* and *BC*, its diameter must be 6.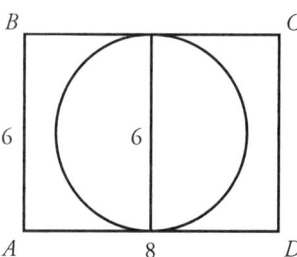

Finally, find the radius and compute the area:

$$d = 6 = 2r \qquad \text{Area} = \pi r^2$$
$$3 = r \qquad \text{Area} = \pi(3)^2$$
$$\text{Area} = 9\pi$$

This is a fill-in-the-blank problem. The area is 9π, but take a look at the blank provided at the end of the problem. The blank is followed by a π. Enter "9" into the blank.

This is common for fill-in-the-blank geometry problems, because the GRE won't expect you to type π from your keyboard. Whenever completing a fill-in-the-blank problem, consider anything preceding or trailing the blank, as that may affect what you need to put into the box.

Unit Five: **Geometry**

Problem Set

1. Ten 8-foot-long poles will be arranged in a rectangle to surround a flower bed.

Quantity A	Quantity B
The area in square feet of the flower bed	300

2.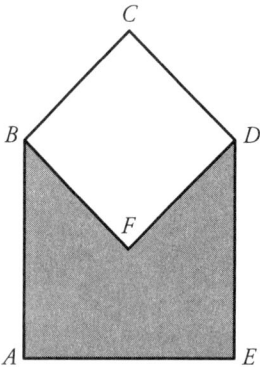

   BCDF and ABDE are squares.

Quantity A	Quantity B
Twice the area of the shaded region	Three times the area of BCDF

3. Challenge problem!

   The "aspect ratio" of a rectangular TV screen is the ratio of its width to its height.

Quantity A	Quantity B
The area of a rectangular TV screen with an aspect ratio of 4 : 3 and a diagonal of 25"	The area of a rectangular TV screen with an aspect ratio of 16 : 9 and a diagonal of 25"

Unit Five: **Geometry**

Solutions

1. **(D)**
   First, draw the figure and fill in all given information. The flower bed might look like this:

   Or like this:

   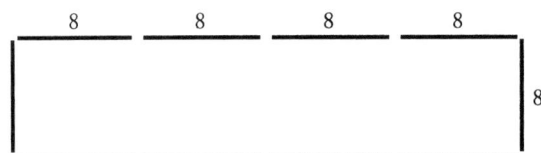

   Next, make inferences from the figures. The area of a rectangle equals the width times the height.

   The top flower bed has a width of 24 and a length of 16, giving it an area of $24 \times 16 = 384$, which is greater than 300. Eliminate choices (B) and (C): A ~~B~~ ~~C~~ D

   The bottom flower bed has a width of 32 and a length of 8, giving it an area of $32 \times 8 = 256$, which is less than 300. Eliminate choice (A).

   Therefore, the correct answer is (D): The relationship cannot be determined.

2. **(C)**

    Draw the figure and fill in all given information. Label each of the sides of the small square *x* and the sides of the other square *y*.

    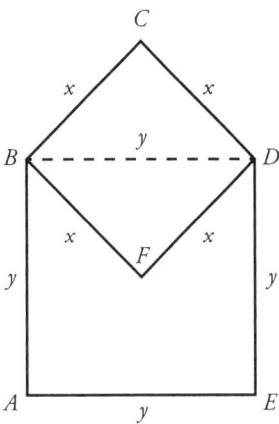

    The area of *BCDF* is x^2. Quantity B is therefore 3 times x^2.

Quantity A	Quantity B
Twice the area of the shaded region	$3x^2$

    Next, identify relationships to relate the shaded region to *x*, and thus to Quantity B. The dashed line *BD* is both an edge of square *ABDE* and the diagonal of square *BCDF*, so *BD* is the hypotenuse of equal right triangles *BCD* and *BDF*. Use the Pythagorean theorem on one of the triangles to find the length of the hypotenuse, *BD*.

    $$c^2 = a^2 + b^2$$
    $$BD^2 = x^2 + x^2$$
    $$BD^2 = 2x^2$$
    $$BD = \sqrt{2x^2}$$
    $$BD = x\sqrt{2}$$

    Thus, the area of square *ABDE* is $\left(x\sqrt{2}\right)^2 = 2x^2$. Add that information to your diagram.

Unit Five: **Geometry**

The shaded area is equal to the area of square *ABDE* minus half the area of square *BCDF*.

$$\text{Area}_{ABDE} - \frac{1}{2}\text{Area}_{BCDF} = \text{Shaded area}$$

$$2x^2 - \frac{1}{2}x^2 = \frac{3}{2}x^2$$

Quantity A is twice the area of the shaded region.

Quantity A	Quantity B
$2\left(\frac{3}{2}x^2\right) = 3x^2$	$3x^2$

Therefore, the correct answer is (C): The two quantities are equal.

3. **(A)**
An aspect ratio of 4 : 3 means that the width of the TV is 4*x* and the height is 3*x*, where *x* is some unknown multiplier. Calculate the unknown multiplier of the TV via the Pythagorean theorem:

$$c = \sqrt{a^2 + b^2}$$
$$25 = \sqrt{(4x)^2 + (3x)^2}$$
$$25 = \sqrt{16x^2 + 9x^2}$$
$$25 = \sqrt{25x^2}$$
$$25 = 5x$$
$$5 = x$$

Alternatively, use the 3–4–5 Pythagorean triple as a shortcut. If the two legs are 3*x* and 4*x*, then the hypotenuse must be 5*x*. Set 5*x* equal to 25 to find *x*.

Since *x* = 5, the width of this TV, 4*x*, is equal to 20 and the height, 3*x*, is equal to 15. The area is *wh* = (20)(15) = 300. Note the value of Quantity A on your scratch paper.

Quantity A	Quantity B
300	The area of a rectangular TV screen with an aspect ratio of 16 : 9 and a diagonal of 25"

For the TV in Quantity B, the aspect ratio of 16 : 9 means the width is 16y and the height is 9y, where y is some unknown multiplier. Use the Pythagorean theorem to find y:

$$c = \sqrt{a^2 + b^2}$$
$$25 = \sqrt{(16y)^2 + (9y)^2}$$
$$25 = \sqrt{256y^2 + 81y^2}$$
$$25 = \sqrt{337y^2}$$
$$25 = \approx 18.3576y$$
$$1.36 \approx y$$

Use the calculator for the last couple of steps of that math. Since y ≈ 1.36, the width of the TV, 16y, is approximately 21.76, and the height, 9y, is approximately 12.24. The area is (width)(height) = (21.76)(12.24), which equals approximately 266.

Since Quantity A is 300 and Quantity B is about 266, the correct answer is (A): Quantity A is greater.

That was a lot of work. You will learn a shortcut for this problem in Chapter 31: Optimization. For a rectangle with either a fixed perimeter or a fixed diagonal, the area is maximized when the aspect ratio is 1. Because the aspect ratio 4 : 3 (equivalent to $\frac{4}{3} = 1.\overline{3}$) is closer to 1 than the aspect ratio 16 : 9 (equivalent to $\frac{16}{9} = 1.\overline{7}$), the TV with the 4 : 3 aspect ratio has the greater area.

CHAPTER 21

Triangles and Diagonals

In This Chapter:

- The Basic Properties of a Triangle
- Perimeter and Area
- Right Triangles
- Pythagorean Triples
- Isosceles Triangles and the 45–45–90 Triangle
- Equilateral Triangles and the 30–60–90 Triangle
- Diagonals of Other Polygons
- Check Your Skills Answer Key
- Problem Set
- Solutions

CHAPTER 21 Triangles and Diagonals

Triangles are one of the most common geometry shapes on the GRE. Of the basic shapes, triangles are perhaps the most challenging to master both because multiple different properties of triangles can be tested and because triangles can be hidden inside other shapes. In this chapter, you will learn all of the general properties of triangles and diagonals, providing the foundation you'll use to solve both triangle problems and more advanced problems that combine triangles with other shapes.

The Basic Properties of a Triangle

Side Length

Triangles have three sides. If you know information about two of those side lengths, you can make some inferences about the third side. Take a look:

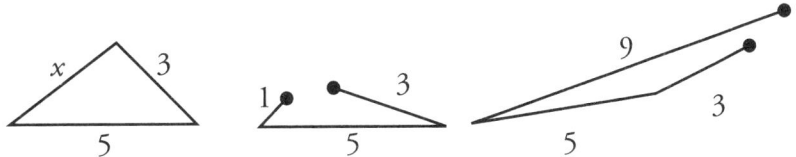

The length of a side will always be greater than the difference between the other two sides. If it were shorter, then it wouldn't be able to reach, as illustrated in the middle image. If $x = 1$, then that side is too short to reach the side labeled 3. So, x has to be greater than $5 - 3 = 2$.

The length of a side will also always be less than the sum of the other two sides. If it were longer, then it would be too long to connect the other two sides, as illustrated in the right-hand image. If $x = 9$, then the side labeled 3 can't reach the side labeled x. So, x also has to be less than $5 + 3 = 8$.

The length of any side of a triangle must be:

- greater than the *difference* between the other two sides
- less than the *sum* of the other two sides

So, the possible range of values for x is:

$$\text{difference} < x < \text{sum}$$
$$5 - 3 < x < 5 + 3$$
$$2 < x < 8$$

Unit Five: **Geometry**

Check Your Skills

1. Two sides of a triangle have lengths of 5 and 19. Can the third side have a length of 13 ?
2. Two sides of a triangle have lengths of 8 and 17. What is the range of possible values of the length of the third side?

Answers can be found on page 587.

Angles

A triangle has three internal angles. The **internal angles** of a triangle must add up to 180°. If you know the measures of two angles of the triangle, you can determine the measure of the third angle:

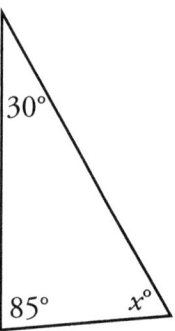

The three internal angles must add up to 180°, so $30 + 85 + x = 180$. Solve for x: The third angle is 65°. The GRE can also test your knowledge of this rule in more complicated ways. For example:

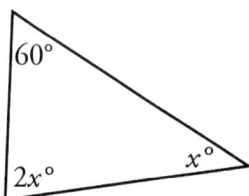

One angle is 60°, but the other two are given in terms of x. Even though you only know one angle, you can still determine the other two. The three angles will still add up to 180°:

$$60 + x + 2x = 180$$
$$60 + 3x = 180$$
$$3x = 120$$
$$x = 40$$

The GRE will not always draw triangles to scale, so don't try to guess angles from the picture, which could be distorted. Instead, solve for angles mathematically.

Chapter 21: **Triangles and Diagonals**

Check Your Skills

Find the missing angle(s).

3.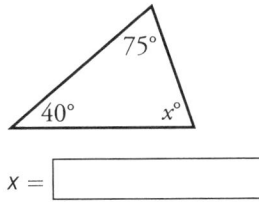

X = [   ]

4.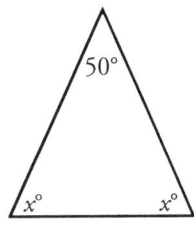

X = [   ]

Answers can be found on page 587.

Internal angles of a triangle are important on the GRE for another reason. Sides correspond to their opposite angles. The longest side is always opposite the greatest angle, and the shortest side is opposite the least angle. Think about an alligator opening its mouth, bigger and bigger . . . as the angle between its upper and lower jaws increases, the distance between the front teeth on the bottom and top would get greater and greater:

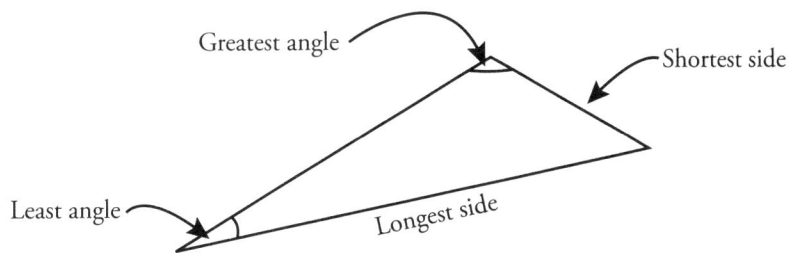

One important thing to remember about this relationship is that it works both ways. If you know the sides of the triangle, you can make inferences about the angles. If you know the angles, you can make inferences about the sides, as shown here.

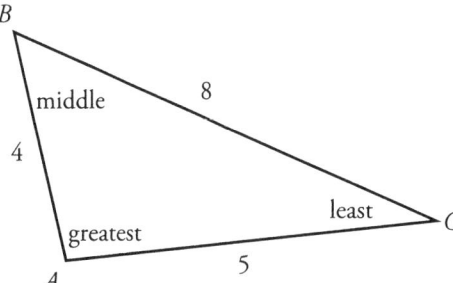

571

Unit Five: **Geometry**

21

Although you can determine from the angle measures which sides are longer or shorter, you cannot determine how *much* longer or shorter. For instance, in the triangle above on the left, ∠BAC is twice as large as ∠ABC, but that does *not* mean that side BC is twice as long as side AC.

Things get interesting when a triangle has sides that are the same length or has angles that have the same measure. You can classify triangles by the number of equal sides that they have:

- A triangle that has two equal angles and two equal sides (opposite the equal angles) is an **isosceles triangle**.
- A triangle that has three equal angles (all 60°) and three equal sides is an **equilateral triangle**.

This relationship between equal angles and equal sides works in both directions. Take a look at these isosceles triangles:

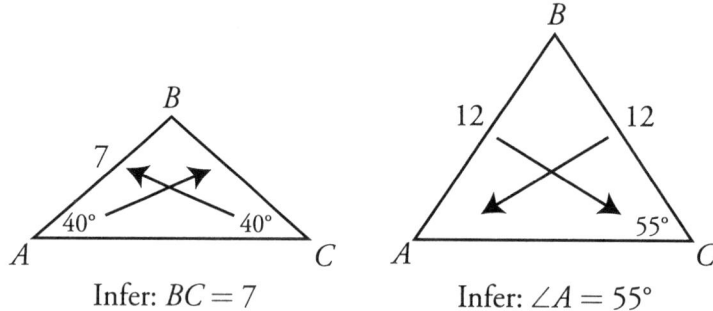

The GRE uses isosceles triangles in a variety of ways. The following is a more challenging application of the equal sides/equal angles rule:

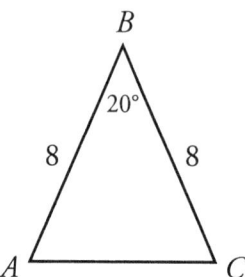

What other information can you fill in?

Chapter 21: **Triangles and Diagonals**

Because side *AB* is the same length as side *BC*, it must be the case that ∠*BAC* has the same degree measure as ∠*ACB*. Label each of those angles as *x*° on your diagram:

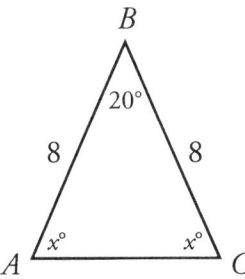

The three internal angles will add up to 180°, so 20 + *x* + *x* = 180. Thus, 2*x* = 160, and *x* = 80. So, ∠*BAC* and ∠*ACB* each equal 80°. You can't find the side length *AC* without more advanced math, and the GRE wouldn't ask you for the length of *AC* for that very reason.

Check Your Skills

Find the value of *x*.

5.

x =

6.

x =

7.

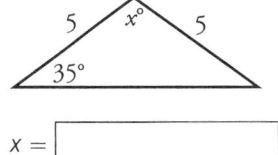

x =

Answers can be found on page 588.

Triangle Properties

- The sum of any two side lengths of a triangle will always be greater than the third side length.
- The positive difference between any two side lengths of a triangle will always be less than the length of the third side.
- The internal angles of a triangle must add up to 180°.
- Sides correspond to their opposite angles: The longest side is opposite the greatest angle, and the shortest side is opposite the least angle.

Unit Five: **Geometry**

21

Perimeter and Area

The **perimeter** of a triangle is equal to the sum of the lengths of all three sides:

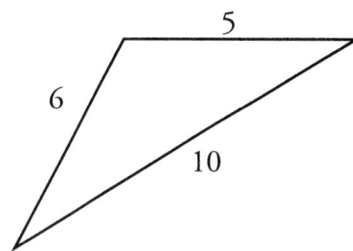

In this triangle, the perimeter is $5 + 6 + 10 = 21$. This is a relatively simple property of a triangle, so often it will be used in combination with another property. For example:

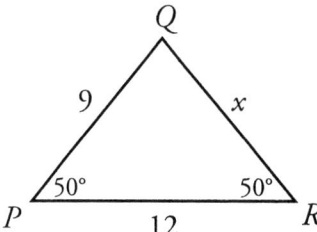

To solve for the perimeter, it's necessary to determine the value of x. Because angles QPR and PRQ are both $50°$, their opposite sides will have equal lengths.

Since side $PQ = 9$, side QR also has a length of 9. Therefore, the perimeter of triangle PQR is $9 + 9 + 12 = 30$.

Chapter 21: **Triangles and Diagonals**

Check Your Skills

Find the perimeter of each triangle.

8.

9.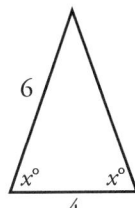

Note: Figure not drawn to scale.

Answers can be found on pages 588–589.

You may also be asked to find the area of a triangle. Memorize this formula:

> **Area of a Triangle**
>
> Area = $\frac{1}{2}$(base × height)

The area of a triangle is based on the relationship between the base and the height. The base and the height *must* be perpendicular to each other. In a triangle, one side of the triangle is the base, and the height is formed by dropping a line from the opposite point of the triangle straight down toward the base, so that the line forms a 90° angle with the base:

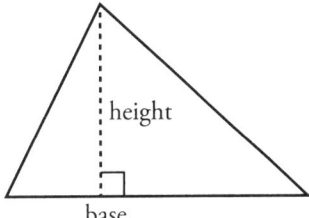

You can picture this as dropping a straight line from the "roof" of the shape to the "floor." The small square located where the height and base meet is used to denote a right angle.

Unit Five: **Geometry**

21

The GRE is likely to present shapes in orientations you are not accustomed to. Most people think of the base of the triangle as the bottom side of the triangle, but, in reality, any side of the triangle could act as a base. The following three triangles are all the same triangle, but each one uses a different side as the base, and the corresponding height is drawn in.

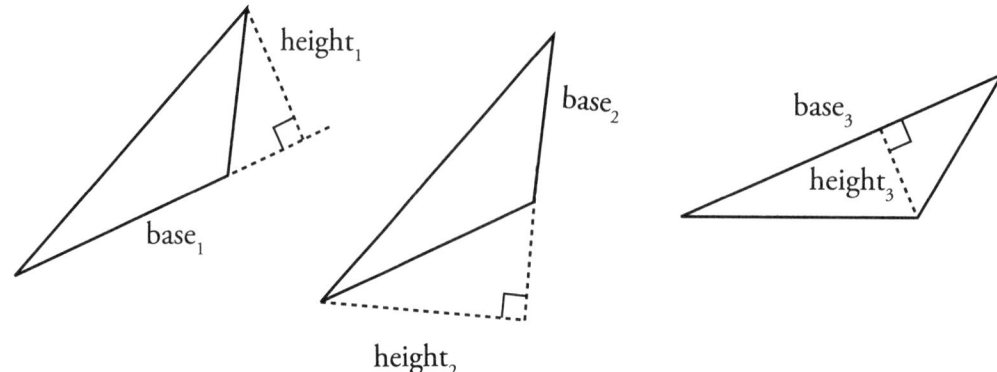

As it turns out, not only can any side be the base, but the height might have to be drawn outside the triangle! The only requirement is that the base and the height are perpendicular to each other.

Check Your Skills

Determine the areas of the following triangles.

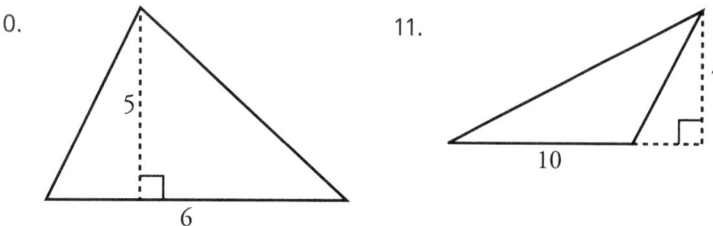

10.

11.

Answers can be found on page 589.

Chapter 21: **Triangles and Diagonals**

Right Triangles

There is one more class of triangle that is very common on the GRE: the **right triangle**. A right triangle is any triangle in which one of the angles is a right angle. For example:

What is the perimeter of triangle *ABC* ?

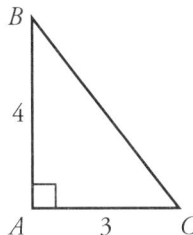

The GRE likes to make use of a special property of triangles: There is a consistent relationship among the lengths of their sides. For right triangles, this relationship is known as the **Pythagorean theorem**. For *any* right triangle, the relationship is $a^2 + b^2 = c^2$, where *a* and *b* are the lengths of the sides forming the right angle, also known as **legs**, and *c* is the length of the side opposite the right angle, also known as the **hypotenuse**.

In the given triangle, sides *AB* and *AC* are *a* and *b* (it doesn't matter which is which) and side *BC* is *c*:

$$a^2 + b^2 = c^2$$
$$3^2 + 4^2 = (BC)^2$$
$$9 + 16 = (BC)^2$$
$$25 = (BC)^2$$
$$5 = BC$$

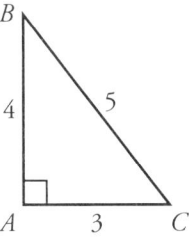

The perimeter of the triangle is $3 + 4 + 5 = 12$.

> **Pythagorean Theorem**
>
> $a^2 + b^2 = c^2$ For a right triangle, the sum of the squares of the two legs
> (*a* and *b*) equals the square of the hypotenuse (*c*).

577

Here are two more examples:

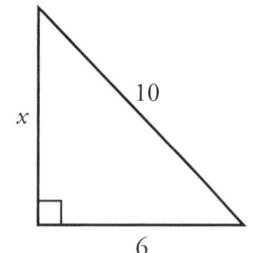

What is x?

$a^2 + b^2 = c^2$

$x^2 + 6^2 = 10^2$

$x^2 + 36 = 100$

$x^2 = 64$

$x = 8$

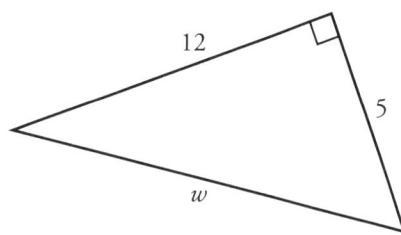

What is w?

$a^2 + b^2 = c^2$

$5^2 + 12^2 = w^2$

$25 + 144 = w^2$

$169 = w^2$

$13 = w$

Pythagorean Triples

Right triangles show up in many problems on the GRE, and many of these problems require the Pythagorean theorem to solve. However, there is a shortcut that you can use in some situations to avoid extra calculations.

The GRE favors a certain subset of right triangles in which all three sides have lengths that are integer values. The previous section had three such special right triangles. In the first, the lengths of the sides were 3, 4, and 5—all integers. This group of side lengths is a **Pythagorean triple**—in this case a 3–4–5 triangle. For each triple, the first two numbers are the lengths of the sides that *form the right angle*, and the third (and greatest) number is the *length of the hypotenuse*. Memorize at least the three triples in bold in this table:

Common Combinations	Key Multiples
3–4–5 The most popular of all right triangles: $3^2 + 4^2 = 5^2$	**6–8–10** 9–12–15 12–16–20
5–12–13 Also quite popular on the GRE: $5^2 + 12^2 = 13^2$	10–24–26
8–15–17 This one appears less frequently: $8^2 + 15^2 = 17^2$	None

If you are going for an especially high score, also memorize the non-bold triples in the table.

Warning: Don't assume that all triangles fall into these categories. When using common combinations to solve a problem, be sure that the triangle is a right triangle, and that the longest side (hypotenuse) corresponds to the greatest number in the triple. For example, if you have a right triangle with one side measuring 3 and the *hypotenuse* measuring 4, it is *not* the case that the remaining side is 5.

Try this problem:

In the figure below, what is the area of triangle *DEF*?

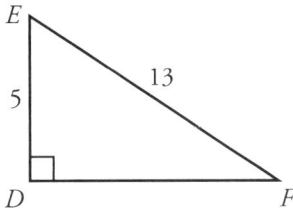

Step 1: Draw or redraw figures and fill in all given information.

Copy the figure, including all the side lengths and the right angle.

Step 2: Identify relationships and create equations.

Use the formula for area of a triangle:

$$A = \frac{1}{2}bh$$

Step 3: Solve the equations for the missing value(s).

This is a right triangle, so sides *DE* and *DF* are perpendicular to each other, which means the two legs of the triangle are the base and height. Plug in what you already know:

$$A = \frac{1}{2}b(5) = \frac{5}{2}b$$

Step 4: Make inferences from the figures.

The base of the triangle is side *DF*. If you have a right triangle and know the lengths of two sides, you can *always* use the Pythagorean theorem to find the length of the third side. Just check first whether this is one of the common triples you've memorized. In this case, it is: It's a 5–12–13 triangle, so the length of *DF* is 12.

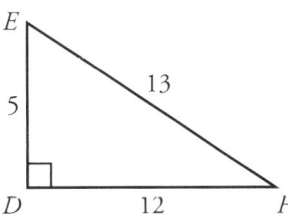

Now you have what you need to find the area of triangle *DEF*: $\frac{1}{2}(12)(5) = 6 \times 5 = 30$.

Unit Five: **Geometry**

Check Your Skills

12. What is the length of the third side of the triangle?

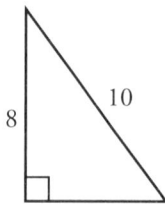

13. What is the length of the third side of the triangle?

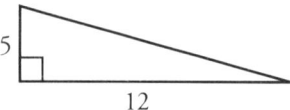

14. What is the area of the triangle?

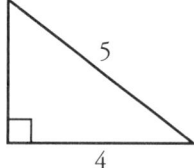

15. What is the length of hypotenuse *C* ?

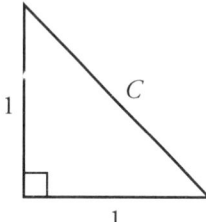

16. What is the length of leg *B* ?

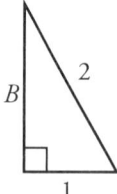

17. Triangle *ABC* is isosceles. If side *AB* = 3, and side *BC* = 4, what are the possible lengths of side *AC* ?

Answers can be found on pages 589–590.

Isosceles Triangles and the 45–45–90 Triangle

An isosceles triangle is one in which exactly two of the sides are equal. The two angles opposite those two sides will also be equal. The most important isosceles triangle on the GRE is the isosceles right triangle.

An isosceles right triangle has one 90° angle (opposite the hypotenuse) and two 45° angles (opposite the two equal legs). This triangle is called the 45–45–90 triangle.

The lengths of the legs of every 45–45–90 triangle have a specific ratio, which is helpful to memorize:

45°	:	45°	:	90°
leg	:	leg	:	hypotenuse
1	:	1	:	$\sqrt{2}$
x	:	x	:	$x\sqrt{2}$

The sides are some multiple of $1:1:\sqrt{2}$. For instance, they could actually be 1, 1, and $\sqrt{2}$, or they could be 2, 2, and $2\sqrt{2}$, or 5.5, 5.5, and $5.5\sqrt{2}$. In each of these cases, you multiply the ratio by a consistent multiplier, like the unknown multiplier.

Try this problem:

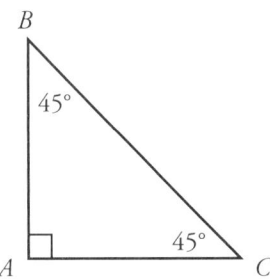

If the length of side AB is 5, what are the lengths of sides BC and AC?

Because this is a right isosceles triangle, the sides of the triangle are in ratio $1:1:\sqrt{2}$. Further, because the length of one of the sides is 5, which corresponds to one of the 1's in the ratio, the multiplier is 5.

Therefore, the sides of the triangle have lengths $5:5:5\sqrt{2}$. The length of side $AC = 5$, and the length of side $BC = 5\sqrt{2}$. Using the same figure, though without the information from the previous question, review the following problem:

In a 45–45–90 triangle, if the length of the hypotenuse is $3\sqrt{2}$, what are the lengths of the two legs?

The hypotenuse is represented by $x\sqrt{2}$ in the ratio, so for this triangle, $3\sqrt{2} = x\sqrt{2}$, and therefore x must be 3.

The two legs of the triangle are represented by x in the ratio, so the two legs are both 3:

leg	:	leg	:	hypotenuse
x	:	x	:	$x\sqrt{2}$
3	:	3	:	$3\sqrt{2}$

581

The 45–45–90 triangle is so important because this triangle is exactly half of a square! That is, two 45–45–90 triangles put together make up a square. If you are given the diagonal of a square, you can use the 45–45–90 ratio to find the length of one side of the square:

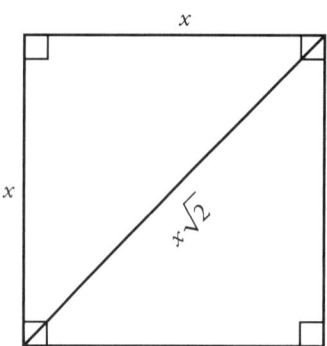

Similar to a rectangle, the area of a square is equal to its length times its width. Since the length and width of a square are the same, the area of a square is (side)^2.

Check Your Skills

18. What is the area of a square with diagonal of 6 ?

19. What is the diagonal of a square with an area of 25 ?

Answers can be found on pages 590–591.

Equilateral Triangles and the 30–60–90 Triangle

An equilateral triangle is one in which all three sides (and all three angles) are equal. Each angle of an equilateral triangle is 60° (because all three angles must sum to 180°). A close relative of the equilateral triangle is the 30–60–90 triangle, because two 30–60–90 triangles form an equilateral triangle:

Equilateral Triangle

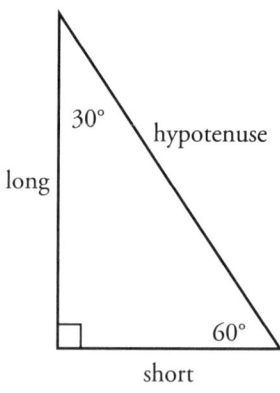

30–60–90 Triangle

Chapter 21: **Triangles and Diagonals**

The lengths of the legs of every 30–60–90 triangle have the following ratio, which you'll definitely want to memorize for the GRE:

$$30° : 60° : 90°$$
$$\text{shorter leg} : \text{longer leg} : \text{hypotenuse}$$
$$1 : \sqrt{3} : 2$$
$$x : x\sqrt{3} : 2x$$

For example:

> If the shorter leg of a 30–60–90 triangle has a length of 6, what are the lengths of the longer leg and the hypotenuse?

The shorter leg, which is opposite the 30° angle, is 6:

$$30° : 60° : 90°$$
$$x : x\sqrt{3} : 2x$$
$$6 : ? : ?$$

Therefore, $x = 6$, so the longer leg is $6\sqrt{3}$ and the hypotenuse is 12.

Try this problem:

> If an equilateral triangle has a side of length 10, what is its height?

Examine the earlier diagram of an equilateral triangle. The side of an equilateral triangle is the same as the hypotenuse of a 30–60–90 triangle. Additionally, the height of an equilateral triangle is the same as the longer leg of a 30–60–90 triangle.

$$30° : 60° : 90°$$
$$x : x\sqrt{3} : 2x$$
$$: ? : 10$$

Because the hypotenuse is 10, the value of x is 5. The height is the longer leg, so the height is $5\sqrt{3}$.

If you get tangled up on a 30–60–90 triangle, try to find the length of the short leg. The other legs will then be easier to figure out.

Unit Five: **Geometry**

Check Your Skills

20. Quadrilateral *ABCD*, below, is composed of four identical 30-60-90 triangles. If the length of line $BD = 10\sqrt{3}$, what is the perimeter of *ABCD*?

21. The length of each side of the equilateral triangle shown is 2. What is the height *h* of the triangle?

Answers can be found on page 591.

Diagonals of Other Polygons

Right triangles are useful for more than just triangle problems. They are also helpful for finding the diagonals of other polygons, including squares, cubes, rectangles, and rectangular solids.

The diagonal of a square can be found using the formula $d = s\sqrt{2}$, where *s* is a side of the square. (By the way, this is also the diagonal of any one face of a cube.)

Where did this formula come from? Any square can be divided into two identical 45–45–90 triangles. The hypotenuse of the triangle is equivalent to the diagonal of the square and the leg of the triangle is equivalent to the side of the square:

$$
\begin{array}{ccccccc}
\text{Triangle:} & \text{leg} & : & \text{leg} & : & \text{hypotenuse} \\
& 45 & : & 45 & : & 90 \\
& x & : & x & : & x\sqrt{2} \\
\text{Square:} & \text{side} & : & \text{side} & : & \text{diagonal}
\end{array}
$$

So, when the side of a square is *s*, the diagonal of that square is $s\sqrt{2}$.

Try this problem:

If a square has a side of length 7, what is the length of the diagonal of the square?

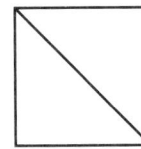

Since $d = s\sqrt{2}$, the length of the diagonal of the square is $7\sqrt{2}$.

What if the shape is not a square but a rectangle? To find the diagonal of a rectangle, you must know or be able to find the length and the width of the rectangle. For example:

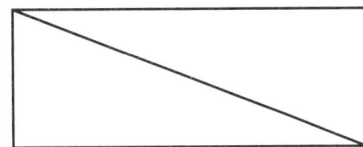

If the rectangle has a length of 12 and a width of 5, what is the length of the diagonal?

The diagonal creates a right triangle with legs 5 and 12. This is the 5–12–13 Pythagorean triple, so the length of the hypotenuse (which is also the diagonal of the rectangle) is 13. If you forget the triple, plug the values into the Pythagorean theorem to solve.

Try this problem:

If a rectangle has a width of 6, and the ratio of the width to the length is 3 : 4, what is the diagonal?

Use the ratio to find the value of the length:

$$\begin{array}{ccc} w & : & l \\ 3 & : & 4 \\ 6 & : & ? \end{array}$$

The unknown multiplier is 2, so the length is 8. The two legs are 6 and 8, so this is a 6–8–10 right triangle. Therefore, the diagonal must be 10.

Unit Five: **Geometry**

Check Your Skills

22. What is the diagonal of the rectangle shown?

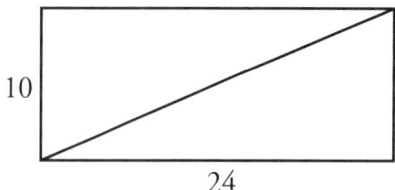

23. If the rectangle shown has a perimeter of 6, what is its diagonal?

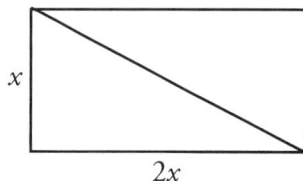

Answers can be found on pages 591–592.

Chapter 21: **Triangles and Diagonals**

Check Your Skills Answer Key

1. **No**
   If the two known sides of the triangle are 5 and 19, then the third side of the triangle must be between $19 - 5 = 14$ and $19 + 5 = 24$. The side length 13 does not fit in this range.

   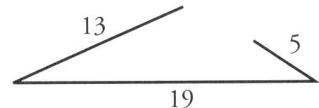 No possible triangle with these lengths.

2. **$9 <$ third side < 25**
   If the two known sides of the triangle are 8 and 17, then the third side must be less than the sum of the other two sides, which is $8 + 17 = 25$, and greater than the difference of the other two sides, which is $17 - 8 = 9$. The range of possible values is $9 <$ third side < 25.

3. **65°**
   The internal angles of a triangle must add up to 180°, so $40 + 75 + x = 180$. Therefore, $x = 65°$.

   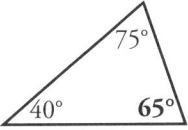

4. **65°**
   The three internal angles of the triangle must add up to 180°.

   $$50 + x + x = 180$$
   $$2x = 130$$
   $$x = 65$$

   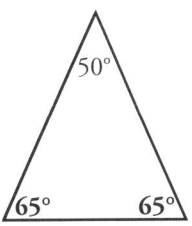

Unit Five: **Geometry**

21

5. **80°**
In this triangle, two sides have the same length, which means this triangle is isosceles. The two angles opposite the two equal sides will also be equal, so *x* must be 80.

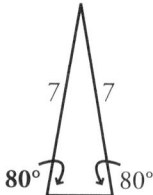

6. **4**
In this triangle, two angles are equal, so this triangle is isosceles. The two sides opposite the equal angles must also be equal, so *x* must equal 4.

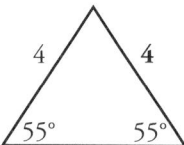

7. **110°**
This triangle is isosceles, because two sides have the same length. The angles opposite the equal sides must also be equal. That means the triangle really looks like this:

The three angles must add to 180.

$$35 + 35 + x = 180$$
$$70 + x = 180$$
$$x = 110$$

8. **25**
To find the perimeter of the triangle, add up all three sides: $5 + 8 + 12 = 25$.

9. **16**

Two angles are equal, so the sides opposite the equal angles must also be equal. So the triangle looks like this:

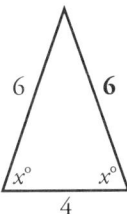

The perimeter is 6 + 6 + 4, which equals 16.

10. **15**

The area of a triangle is $\frac{1}{2}bh$. In the triangle shown, the base is 6 and the height is 5, so the area is $\frac{1}{2}(6)(5) = 15$.

11. **35**

In this triangle, the base is 10 and the height is 7. The height must be perpendicular to the base, but it doesn't need to lie within the triangle. Thus, the area is $\frac{1}{2}(10)(7) = 35$.

12. **6**

This is a right triangle, so you can use the Pythagorean theorem to solve for the length of the third side—or you can recognize the triple. This is a 6–8–10 triple (which is a multiple of the 3–4–5 triple), so the missing side has a length of 6. If you forget the triple, use the Pythagorean theorem to solve:

$$a^2 + b^2 = c^2$$
$$a^2 + 8^2 = 10^2$$
$$a^2 + 64 = 100$$
$$a^2 = 36$$
$$a = 6$$

13. **13**

This is a right triangle, so you can use the Pythagorean theorem to solve for the length of the third side—or you can recognize the triple. This is a 5–12–13 triple, so the missing side has a length of 13. If you forget the triple, use the Pythagorean theorem to solve:

$$5^2 + 12^2 = c^2$$
$$25 + 144 = c^2$$
$$169 = c^2$$
$$13 = c$$

Unit Five: **Geometry**

14. 6

    This is a right triangle, so use the triple—this is a 3–4–5 triangle— or use the Pythagorean theorem to solve for the third side. The length of the third side is 3.

    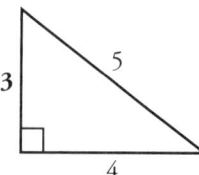

    The area of a triangle is $\frac{1}{2}bh$, so the area of this triangle is $\frac{1}{2}(3)(4) = 6$.

15. $\sqrt{2}$

    This is not a triple, so solve using the Pythagorean theorem.

    $$1^2 + 1^2 = C^2$$
    $$2 = C^2$$
    $$C = \sqrt{2}$$

16. $\sqrt{3}$

    This is not a triple, so solve using the Pythagorean theorem.

    $$1^2 + B^2 = 2^2$$
    $$1 + B^2 = 4$$
    $$B^2 = 3$$
    $$B = \sqrt{3}$$

17. 3 or 4

    Because an isosceles triangle has two equal sides, the third side must be equal to one of the two named sides. So the third side is either 3 or 4.

18. 18

    Call the side length of the square x. Half of the square is a 45–45–90 triangle and can be represented using the standard ratio of the sides.

    $$x \ : \ x \ : \ x\sqrt{2}$$
    $$? \ : \ ? \ : \ 6$$

    Set the $x\sqrt{2}$ and 6 equal to each other and solve for x.

    $$x\sqrt{2} = 6$$
    $$x = \frac{6}{\sqrt{2}}$$

    The area of a square is equal to the side times the side, or x^2.

    $$\left(\frac{6}{\sqrt{2}}\right)^2 = \frac{36}{2} = 18$$

Chapter 21: **Triangles and Diagonals**

19. $5\sqrt{2}$

If the area is 25, then the length of one side is 5. In the standard 45–45–90 ratio, $x = 5$, so the diagonal is $x\sqrt{2} = 5\sqrt{2}$.

20. 40

The perimeter of the quadrilateral is equal to the hypotenuse of one triangle times four.

The long diagonal BD is the sum of two longer legs of the 30–60–90 triangle, so each longer leg is $5\sqrt{3}$.

$$30° \ : \ 60° \ : \ 90°$$
$$x \ : \ x\sqrt{3} \ : \ 2x$$
$$\ : \ 5\sqrt{3} \ : \ ?$$

The value of x is 5, so the length of one hypotenuse is $2(5) = 10$. The perimeter is $4(10) = 40$.

21. $\sqrt{3}$

The line along which the height is measured in the figure bisects (or cuts in half) the equilateral triangle, creating two identical 30–60–90 triangles, each with a base of 1. The base of each of these triangles is the shorter leg of a 30–60–90 triangle and the height of each triangle is the longer leg.

$$x \ : \ x\sqrt{3} \ : \ 2x$$
$$\ : \ ? \ : \ 2$$

Since the hypotenuse is 2, the value of x is 1 and the length of the longer leg is $x\sqrt{3} = 1\sqrt{3} = \sqrt{3}$.

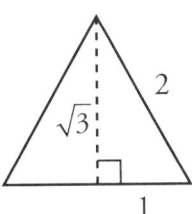

22. 26

The legs of the right triangle are 10 and 24. This is a multiple of the 5–12–13 triple: The triple is 10–24–26, so the diagonal is 26. If you don't spot it (it is well hidden!), plug the leg lengths into the Pythagorean theorem and use the calculator to solve.

$$a^2 + b^2 = c^2$$
$$10^2 + 24^2 = c^2$$
$$100 + 576 = c^2$$
$$676 = c^2$$
$$26 = c$$

Unit Five: Geometry

23. $\sqrt{5}$

    The perimeter of a rectangle is equal to the four sides added together

    $$x + 2x + x + 2x = 6$$
    $$6x = 6$$
    $$x = 1$$

    Therefore, the width is 1 and the length is 2. Plug these values into the Pythagorean theorem and solve for the hypotenuse (otherwise known as the diagonal of the rectangle).

    $$a^2 + b^2 = c^2$$
    $$1^2 + 2^2 = c^2$$
    $$5 = c^2$$
    $$\sqrt{5} = c$$

Problem Set

> Note: Figures are not drawn to scale.

1. A square is bisected into two equal triangles, as shown. If the length of BD is 16 $\sqrt{2}$ inches, what is the area of the square?

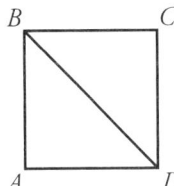

2. Starting from Town A, Bob rode his bike 10 miles west, 3 miles north, 5 miles east, and then 9 miles north to Town B. How far apart are Town A and Town B ? (Assume perfectly flat terrain.)

3. From Town B, Bob walked 10 miles due west, and then straight north to Town C. If Town B and Town C are 26 miles apart, how many miles north did Bob go? (Assume perfectly flat terrain.)

4. The longest side of an isosceles right triangle measures $20\sqrt{2}$. What is the area of the triangle?

5. A square field has an area of 400 square meters. Four posts are set at the four corners of the field. What is the greatest distance between any two posts?

6. In triangle ABC, AD = BD = DC, as shown. What is the measure of angle x ?

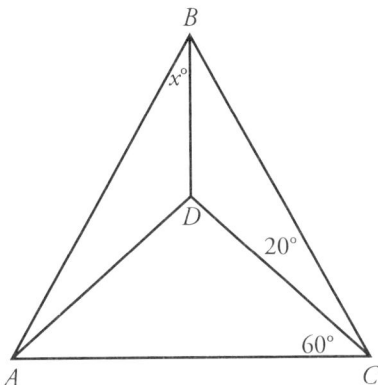

7. Two sides of a triangle are 4 and 10. If the third side is an integer x, how many possible values are there for x ?

8. What is the area of an equilateral triangle whose sides measure 8 cm long?

Unit Five: **Geometry**

9. What is x in the following figure?

10.

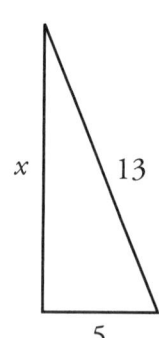

Quantity A	Quantity B
x	12

11.

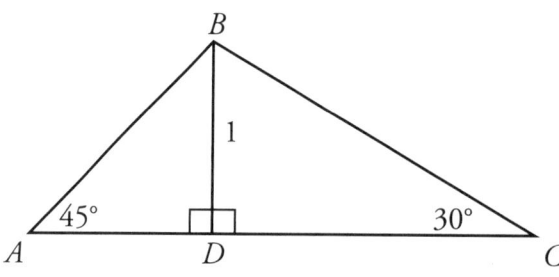

Quantity A	Quantity B
The perimeter of triangle ABC	5

12.

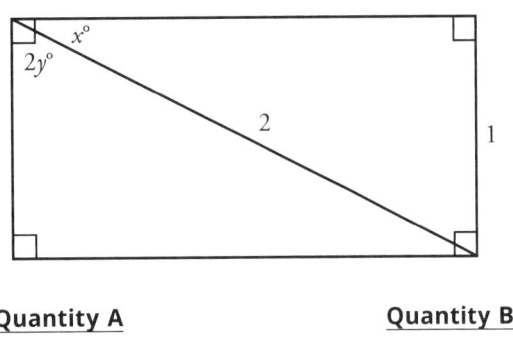

Quantity A	Quantity B
x	y

13. In the figure, triangle *ABC* has a base of 2*y*, a height of *y*, and an area of 49. What is *y*?

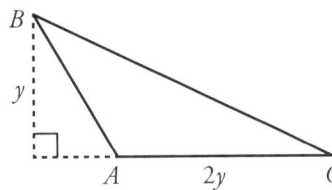

14. Challenge problem! The points of a six-pointed star consist of six identical equilateral triangles, with a side length of 4 cm, as shown. What is the area of the entire six-pointed star, including the center?

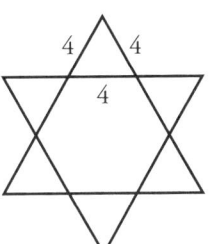

Unit Five: **Geometry**

Solutions

1. **256 inches²**

   The diagonal of a square is $s\sqrt{2}$. Since the diagonal of this square is $16\sqrt{2}$, the length of one side of this square is 16. The area of the square is s^2, or 16^2, which is 256.

2. **13 miles**

   Draw a rough sketch of the path Bob takes. The direct distance from *A* to *B* forms the hypotenuse of a right triangle. The shorter leg (horizontal) is $10 - 5 = 5$ miles, and the longer leg (vertical) is $9 + 3 = 12$ miles.

   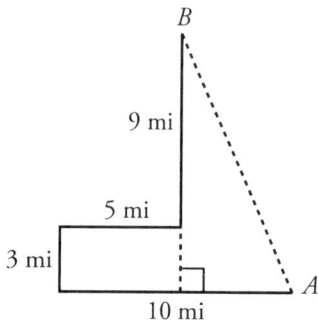

   This is the Pythagorean triple 5–12–13, so the distance from Town *A* to Town *B* is 13 miles. If you forget the triple, use the Pythagorean theorem to solve.

   $$5^2 + 12^2 = c^2$$
   $$25 + 144 = c^2$$
   $$169 = c^2$$
   $$13 = c$$

3. **24 miles**
   Draw a rough sketch of the path Bob takes. The direct distance from B to C forms the hypotenuse of a right triangle.

   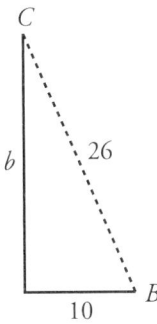

   The right triangle has the dimensions 10–b–26. This is a multiple of the 5-12-13 triple, so b is equal to 24. If you don't spot the triple, use the Pythagorean theorem to find b.

   $$10^2 + b^2 = 26^2$$
   $$100 + b^2 = 676$$
   $$b^2 = 576$$
   $$b = 24$$

4. **200**
   An isosceles right triangle is a 45–45–90 triangle, with sides in the ratio of $1 : 1 : \sqrt{2}$. If the longest side, the hypotenuse, measures $20\sqrt{2}$, the two other sides each measure 20. The two legs are the base and height, so plug them into the formula for the area of a triangle and solve.

   $$A = \frac{1}{2}(b \times h) = \frac{20 \times 20}{2} = 200$$

5. **$20\sqrt{2}$ meters**
   The greatest distance between any two posts is the diagonal of the field. If the area of the square field is 400 square meters, then each side must measure $\sqrt{400} = 20$ meters. The diagonal is $d = s\sqrt{2}$, so d is $20\sqrt{2}$.

Unit Five: **Geometry**

6. **10**

   If $AD = BD = DC$, then the three triangular regions in this figure are all isosceles triangles. Therefore, you can fill in some of the missing angle measurements.

   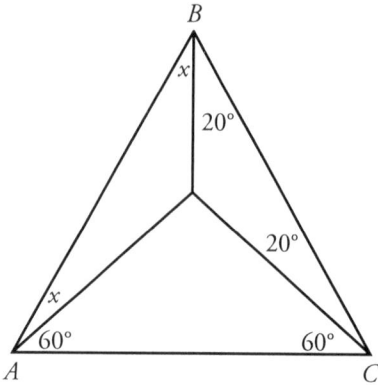

   There are 180° in the large triangle *ABC*, so fill in the known measurements and solve for *x*.

   $$x + x + 20 + 20 + 60 + 60 = 180$$
   $$2x + 160 = 180$$
   $$x = 10$$

7. **7**

   If two sides of a triangle are 4 and 10, the third side must be greater than $10 - 4 = 6$ and less than $10 + 4 = 14$. Therefore, there are seven possible integer values for *x*: {7, 8, 9, 10, 11, 12, and 13}. Here's a visual representation.

8. **$16\sqrt{3}$ cm³**

   Draw a diagram. Label the sides 8 and add in the height of the triangle. Since the triangle is equilateral, the height divides into two identical, smaller triangles that are 30–60–90 triangles. The sides of the smaller triangles are in the ratio of $1 : \sqrt{3} : 2$. If the hypotenuse is 8, then the shorter leg is 4, and the longer leg is $4\sqrt{3}$. The longer leg is the height of the triangle.

   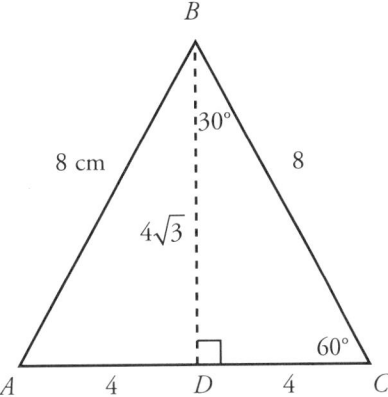

   Use the base of 8 and the height of $4\sqrt{3}$ to find the area of the triangle.

   $$A = \frac{b \times h}{2} = \frac{8 \times 4\sqrt{3}}{2} = 16\sqrt{3}$$

9. **$\dfrac{36}{7}$**

   The diagram shows two base-and-height pairs: A base of 12 with a height of 3 and a base of 7 with a height of x. First, calculate the area of the triangle using the first pair.

   $$\frac{1}{2}(12)(3) = 18$$

   Next, use that area to find x in the other base-and-height pair.

   $$\frac{1}{2}(7x) = 18$$
   $$7x = 36$$
   $$x = \frac{36}{7}$$

Unit Five: **Geometry**

10. **(D)**
Although this appears to be a 5–12–13 triangle, the diagram does *not* indicate that it is a right triangle. There are any number of possibilities for the triangle. For example:

The correct answer is (D): The relationship cannot be determined.

11. **(A)**
First, fill in the additional angles in the diagram.

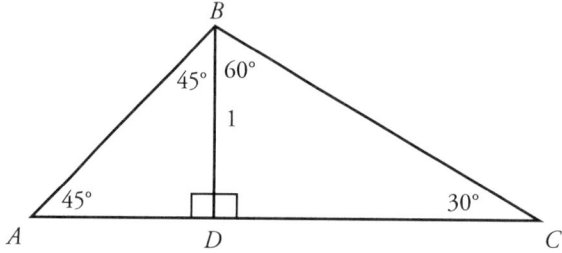

The two smaller triangles are special right triangles: A 45–45–90 triangle and a 30–60–90 triangle. For a 45–45–90 triangle, the ratio is $x : x : x\sqrt{2}$. In this diagram, the value of x is 1 (side *BD*), so *AD* is also 1 and *AB* is $\sqrt{2}$.

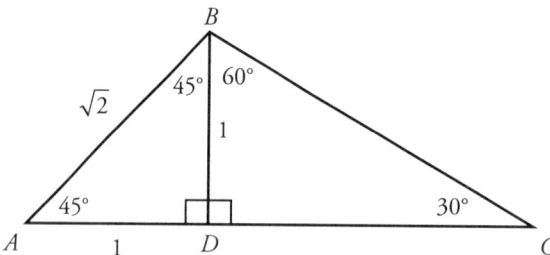

For a 30-60-90 triangle, the ratio is $x : x\sqrt{3} : 2x$. In this diagram, x is 1 (side BD), so DC is $\sqrt{3}$ and BC is 2.

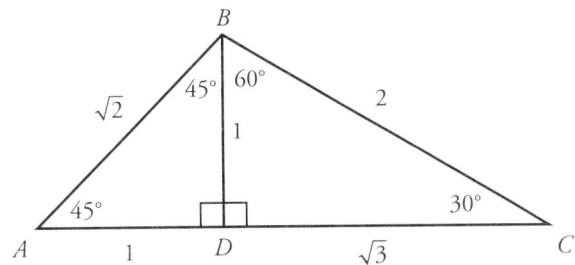

Now calculate the perimeter of triangle ABC.

Quantity A	Quantity B
The perimeter of triangle $ABC = 1 + 2 + \sqrt{2} + \sqrt{3}$	5

A good approximation of $\sqrt{2}$ is 1.4 and a good approximation of $\sqrt{3}$ is 1.7:

Quantity A	Quantity B
$1 + 2 + \sqrt{2} + \sqrt{3} \approx$ $1 + 2 + 1.4 + 1.7 = 6.1$	5

Alternatively, each square root is a value greater than 1, so Quantity A equals $1 + 2 + {>}1 + {>}1$, which is something greater than 5.

The correct answer is (A): Quantity A is always greater.

12. **(C)**

The diagonal of the rectangle is the hypotenuse of a right triangle whose legs are the length and width of the rectangle. Plug the width and diagonal into the Pythagorean theorem to determine the length of the rectangle.

$$a^2 + b^2 = c^2$$
$$1^2 + b^2 = 2^2$$
$$1 + b^2 = 4$$
$$b^2 = 3$$
$$b = \sqrt{3}$$

Label this value on the diagram.

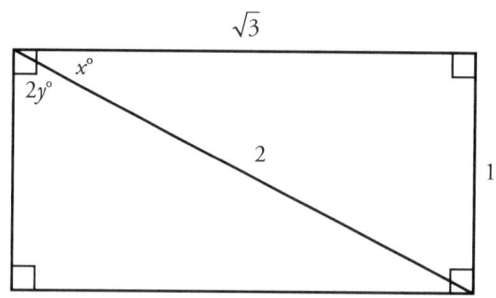

The labeled triangles sides are in the ratio $1 : \sqrt{3} : 2$, so this triangle is a 30–60–90 triangle. Any time you see a right triangle and one of the sides has a length of $\sqrt{3}$ or a multiple of $\sqrt{3}$, check whether it is a 30–60–90 triangle. Angle x is opposite the shorter leg, so x has a degree measure of 30.

The other triangle is identical to the labeled triangle, so it is also a 30–60–90 triangle. In this triangle, $2y$ is opposite the longer leg, so it has a degree measure of 60. Since $2y = 60$, the value of y is 30.

Quantity A	Quantity B
$x = 30$	$y = 30$

The correct answer is (C): The two quantities are always equal.

13. **7**

Write the formula for the area of a triangle and plug in the given values.

$$\frac{bh}{2} = A$$
$$\frac{2y(y)}{2} = 49$$
$$y^2 = 49$$
$$y = 7$$

14. **$48\sqrt{3}$ cm²**

The problem doesn't appear to provide any information about the center of the six-pointed star, but take another look. It could also be viewed as two large equilateral triangles, one on top of the other.

Using the area of both large triangles wouldn't work, though, since the overlapping area would be counted twice. Instead, think of it as one large equilateral triangle with sides of 12, and three small equilateral triangles with sides of 4, as shown in the below diagram. The height of the larger equilateral triangle is $6\sqrt{3}$, and the height of the smaller equilateral triangle is $2\sqrt{3}$.

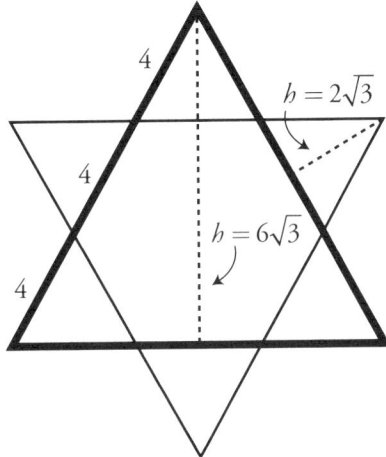

Calculate the area of the large triangle and the area of one small triangle.

Large triangle: $A = \dfrac{b \times h}{2} = \dfrac{12 \times 6\sqrt{3}}{2} = 36\sqrt{3}$

Each small triangle: $A = \dfrac{b \times h}{2} = \dfrac{4 \times 2\sqrt{3}}{2} = 4\sqrt{3}$

Finally, find the total area of one large triangle plus three small triangles.

$$36\sqrt{3} + 3(4\sqrt{3}) = 48\sqrt{3} \text{ cm}^2$$

CHAPTER 22

Polygons

In This Chapter:

- Polygons and Interior Angles
- Polygons and Perimeter
- Polygons and Area
- 3 Dimensions: Surface Area
- 3 Dimensions: Volume
- 3 Dimensions: Diagonal of Cube
- Quadrilaterals: An Overview
- Quadrilaterals
- Check Your Skills Answer Key
- Problem Set
- Solutions

CHAPTER 22 Polygons

A **polygon** is a closed, two-dimensional shape formed entirely by line segments. The polygons tested on the GRE include:

- Three-sided shapes (triangles)
- Four-sided shapes (quadrilaterals)
- Other polygons with n sides (where n is five or more)

Many questions about triangles will often involve other polygons, most notably quadrilaterals, or four-sided polygons. To master polygons, you'll need to understand the basic properties of polygons, such as perimeter and area, and be able to distinguish certain polygons from other shapes within the context of a larger diagram.

In this chapter, you'll learn rules and formulas associated with polygons of four or more sides. The most commonly tested polygons on the GRE are four-sided polygons—especially squares, rectangles, parallelograms, and trapezoids.

The GRE also tests your knowledge of three-dimensional shapes formed from polygons, particularly rectangular solids and cubes. In this chapter, you'll learn how to calculate the surface area and volume of polygons.

Polygons and Interior Angles

The sum of the interior angles of a given polygon depends on the number of sides in the polygon:

Polygon	# of Sides	Sum of Interior Angles
Triangle	3	180°
Quadrilateral	4	360°
Pentagon	5	540°
Hexagon	6	720°

This sum follows a specific pattern that depends on n, the number of sides of the polygon:

> ### Interior Angles of a Polygon
>
> $(n - 2)180$ = the sum of interior angles of a polygon, where n is the number of sides.

Each time *n* increases by 1, the number of degrees increases by 180. A triangle has 180°, a rectangle has 360°, a five-sided figure has 360° + 180°, a six-sided figure has 360° + 180° + 180°, and so on.

Take a look at this diagram:

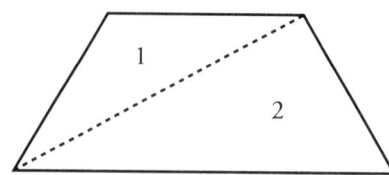

Because this polygon has four sides, the sum of its interior angles is (4 − 2)180° = 2 × 180° = 360°. Alternatively, note that a quadrilateral can be cut into two triangles by a line connecting opposite corners. A four-sided figure can always be cut into two triangles, so the sum of the angles is 2(180°), which equals 360°.

If a polygon has six sides, the sum of its interior angles is (6 − 2)180° = 4 × 180° = 720°:

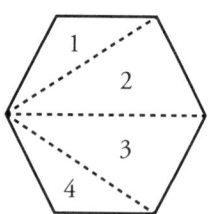

Alternatively, a hexagon can be cut into four triangles by three lines connecting corners. Thus, the sum of the angles is 4(180°), which is 720°.

By the way, the corners of polygons are also known as **vertices** (singular: vertex).

Check Your Skills

1. What is the sum of the interior angles of an octagon (eight-sided polygon)?

   ☐ degrees

2. A regular polygon is a polygon in which every side is of equal length and all interior angles are equal. What is the degree measure of each interior angle in a regular hexagon (six-sided polygon)?

   ☐ degrees

Answers can be found on page 618.

Polygons and Perimeter

The perimeter refers to the distance around a polygon, or the sum of the lengths of all the sides. The amount of fencing needed to surround a yard would be equivalent to the perimeter of that yard (the sum of all the sides). For example:

What is the perimeter of the pentagon?

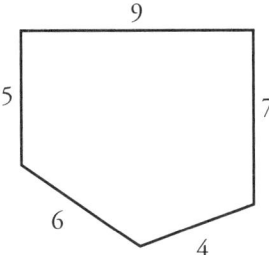

Add up the sides to find the perimeter: $9 + 7 + 4 + 6 + 5 = 31$.

Check Your Skills

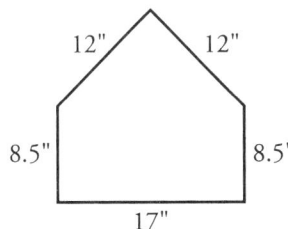

3. The figure shown represents a standard baseball home plate. What is the perimeter of a standard baseball home plate?

Answers can be found on page 618.

Polygons and Area

The area of a polygon refers to the space inside the polygon. For example, the amount of space that a garden occupies is the area of that garden. Area is measured in square units, such as cm² (square centimeters), m² (square meters), or ft² (square feet).

The first two area formulas shown below, for a triangle and a rectangle, were first taught in Chapter 21: Triangles and Diagonals. You will definitely need to use these on the GRE. You may or may not see problems testing the third and fourth area formulas, for trapezoids and parallelograms.

Unit Five: **Geometry**

1. Area of a Triangle = $\dfrac{\text{Base} \times \text{Height}}{2}$

The height *always* refers to a line that is perpendicular (at a 90° angle) to the base. The area of this triangle is:

$$\text{Area}_\triangle = \dfrac{6 \times 8}{2} = 24$$

2. Area of a Rectangle = Length × Width

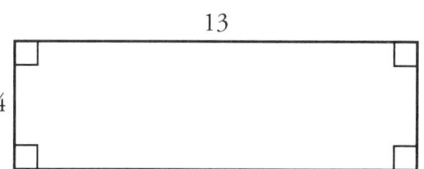

The length of this rectangle is 13, and the width is 4. Therefore, the area is 13 × 4 = 52.

3. Area of a Trapezoid = $\dfrac{(\text{Base}_1 + \text{Base}_2)}{2} \times \text{Height}$

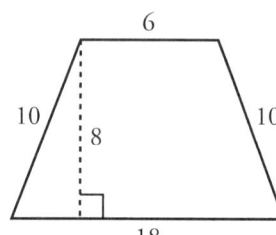

The two bases are always the two lines that are parallel. The height always refers to a line drawn perpendicular to the two bases. (You often have to draw in the height, as in this case.)

In the trapezoid shown, the two bases are 6 and 18 and the height is 8. The trapezoid formula first takes the average of the two bases, then multiplies by the height:

$$\dfrac{18 + 6}{2} \times 8 = 96$$

4. Area of any Parallelogram = Base × Height

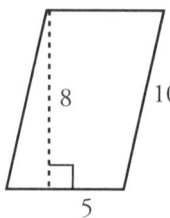

610

The height refers to a line drawn perpendicular to the base. (As with the trapezoid, you often have to draw in the height.) In the parallelogram shown, the base is 5 and the height is 8. Therefore, the area is $5 \times 8 = 40$.

Strange polygons can generally be divided into some combination of rectangles and right triangles on the GRE. If you need the area of a strange polygon, or if you forget the trapezoid formula, cut the shape into rectangles and right triangles, and then find the areas of these individual pieces. For example:

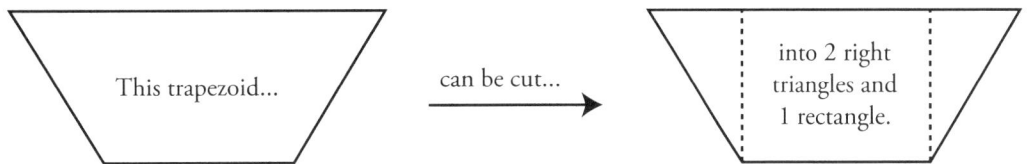

3 Dimensions: Surface Area

The GRE tests two particular three-dimensional shapes formed from polygons: the **rectangular solid** and the **cube**. A cube is just a special type of rectangular solid in which all the sides are equal:

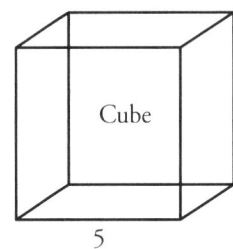

The **surface area** of a three-dimensional shape is the amount of space on the surface of that particular object. For example, the amount of paint that it would take to fully cover a rectangular box could be determined by finding the surface area of that box. As with simple area, surface area is measured in square units, such as in² (square inches) or ft² (square feet).

A **face** is a single side of a 3D figure. Both a rectangular solid and a cube have six faces.

> ### Surface Area of 3D Shapes
> Surface Area = the sum of the areas of all of the faces

To determine the surface area of a rectangular solid, find the area of each face. In a rectangular solid, the front and back faces have the same area, the top and bottom faces have the same area, and the two side faces have the same area.

In the rectangular solid shown earlier, the area of the front face is equal to $12 \times 4 = 48$. Thus, the back face also has an area of 48. The area of the bottom face is equal to $12 \times 3 = 36$. Thus, the top face also has an area of 36. Finally, each side face has an area of $3 \times 4 = 12$. Therefore, the surface area, or the sum of the areas of all six faces, is: $48(2) + 36(2) + 12(2) = 192$.

A cube is made of six identical square surfaces, so to determine the surface area of a cube, you need only the length of one side. First, find the area of one face: 5 × 5 = 25. Then, multiply the area of a single face by 6 to find the surface area of all of the faces: 25 × 6 = 150.

Check Your Skills

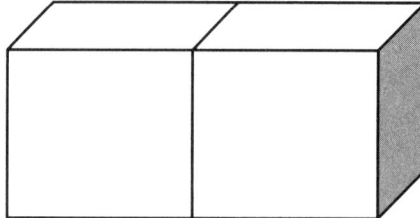

4. The figure here shows two wooden cubes joined to form a rectangular solid. If each cube has a surface area of 24 in², what is the surface area of the resulting rectangular solid?

 in²

Answers can be found on page 618.

3 Dimensions: Volume

The volume of a three-dimensional shape is the amount of "stuff" it can hold. For example, the amount of liquid that a rectangular milk carton holds can be determined by finding the volume of the carton. Volume is measured in cubic units, such as in³ (cubic inches) or ft³ (cubic feet).

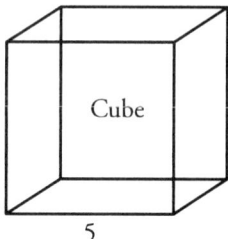

> ### Volume of 3D Figures
> Volume = Length × Width × Height

The length of the rectangular figure is 12, the width is 3, and the height is 4. Therefore, the volume is 12 × 3 × 4, which is 144.

In a cube, all three of the dimensions—length, width, and height—are identical. Therefore, knowing the measurement of just one side of the cube is sufficient to find the volume. In the cube shown, the volume is 5 × 5 × 5, which equals 125.

Chapter 22: **Polygons**

Check Your Skills

5. The volume of a rectangular solid with length 8, width 6, and height 4 is how many times the volume of a rectangular solid with length 4, width 3, and height 2?

Answers can be found on page 618.

3 Dimensions: Diagonal of Cube

The main diagonal of a cube can be found using the formula $d = s\sqrt{3}$, where s is an edge of the cube. For example:

What is the measure of an edge of a cube with a main diagonal of length $\sqrt{60}$?

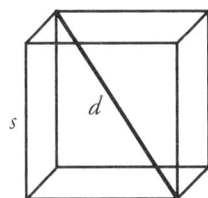

Use the formula $d = s\sqrt{3}$ to solve:

$$\sqrt{60} = s\sqrt{3}$$
$$\frac{\sqrt{60}}{\sqrt{3}} = s$$
$$\sqrt{20} = s$$

Thus, the length of the edge of the cube is $\sqrt{20} = 2\sqrt{5}$.

Check Your Skills

6. What is the edge length of a cube that has a diagonal of $\sqrt{192}$?

Answers can be found on page 619.

Unit Five: **Geometry**

Quadrilaterals: An Overview

Aside from the triangle, the most common polygon tested on the GRE is the quadrilateral (any four-sided polygon). Almost all GRE polygon problems involve the special types of quadrilaterals shown in this diagram:

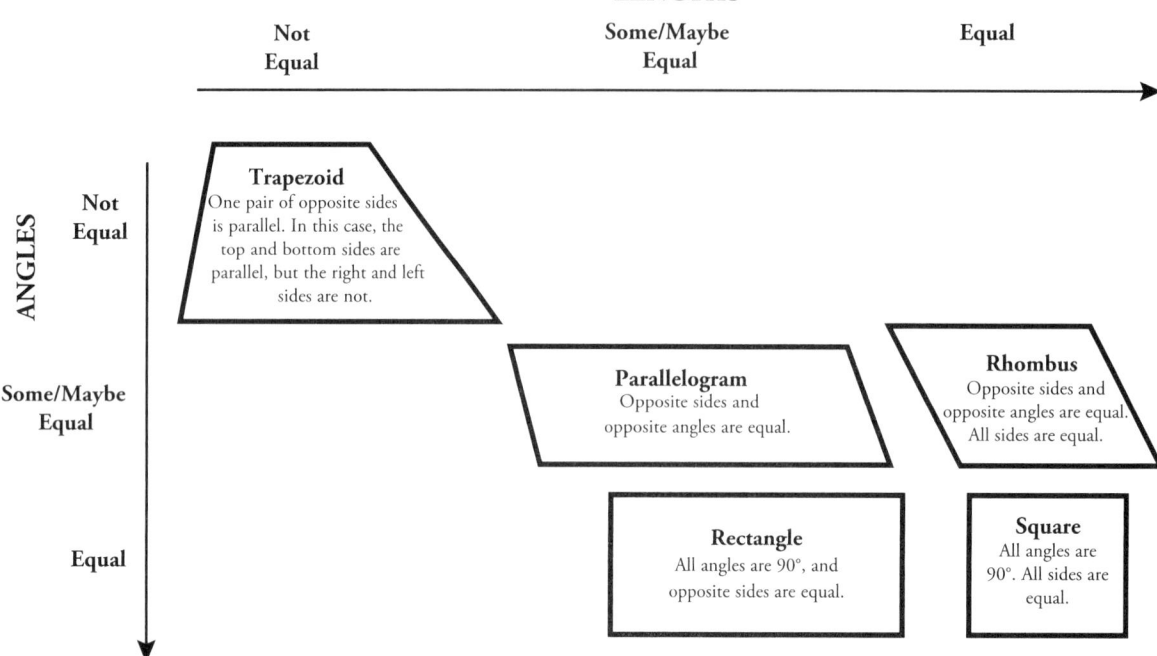

Quadrilaterals

A quadrilateral is any figure with four sides. The GRE largely deals with one class of quadrilaterals known as **parallelograms**. A parallelogram is any four-sided figure in which the opposite sides are parallel and equal and in which opposite angles are equal. This is an example of a parallelogram:

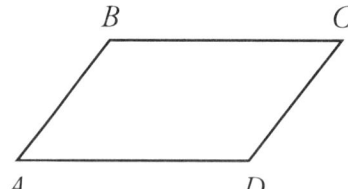

Chapter 22: **Polygons**

In this figure, sides *AB* and *CD* are parallel and have equal lengths, sides *AD* and *BC* are parallel and have equal lengths, angles *ADC* and *ABC* are equal, and angles *BAD* and *BCD* are equal:

 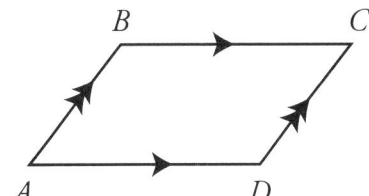

Use hash marks to indicate equal lengths or equal angles.

Use arrows to indicate parallel lines.

Any quadrilateral that has two sets of opposite and equal sides is a parallelogram, as is any quadrilateral with two sets of opposite and equal angles.

In any parallelogram, the diagonal will divide the parallelogram into two identical triangles:

  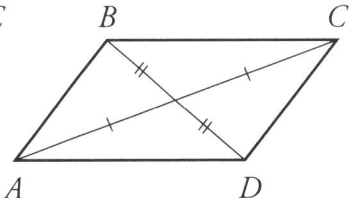

Triangle *ABC* = Triangle *ACD*

Triangle *ABD* = Triangle *BCD*

The diagonals also cut each other in half (bisect each other)

For any parallelogram, the perimeter is the sum of the lengths of all the sides and the area is equal to (base) × (height). With parallelograms, as with triangles, the base and the height *must* be perpendicular to one another.

What is the perimeter and what is the area in this parallelogram?

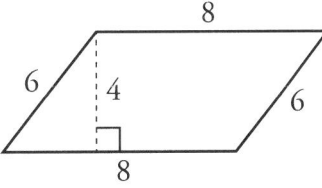

The perimeter is the sum of the sides, so the perimeter is 6 + 8 + 6 + 8, which is 28. Alternatively, parallelograms have two sets of equal sides. In this parallelogram, two of the sides have a length of 6, and two of the sides have a length of 8, so the perimeter equals (2)(6) + (2)(8). You can even factor out a 2 to save time: The perimeter is 2(6 + 8), which equals 28.

To calculate the area, find the base and height. It might be tempting to say that the area is 8 × 6 = 48. But the two sides of this parallelogram are not perpendicular to each other, whereas a base and a height must *always* be perpendicular to one another. The dotted line drawn into the figure, however, is perpendicular to the base. The area of the parallelogram is therefore 8 × 4 = 32.

Unit Five: **Geometry**

Check Your Skills

7. What is the perimeter of the parallelogram?

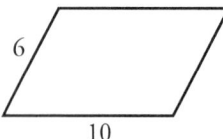

8. What is the area of the parallelogram?

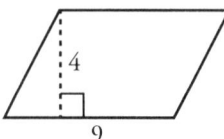

Answers can be found on page 619.

Rectangles

Rectangles are a specific type of parallelogram. Rectangles have all the same properties as parallelograms, with one additional property: All four internal angles of a rectangle are right angles. Additionally, with rectangles, one pair of sides is referred to as the length and one pair of sides as the width.

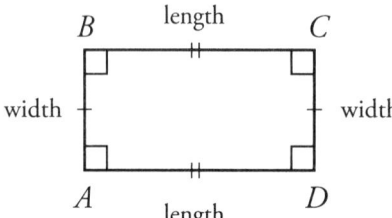

It's common to call the longer side the length and the shorter side the width, but it actually doesn't matter. The math will work the same way regardless of which pair of sides you call the length and which you call the width.

The formula for the perimeter of a rectangle is the same as for the perimeter of a parallelogram—either sum the lengths of the four sides or add the length and the width, then multiply by 2.

The formula for the area of a rectangle is also the same as for the area of a parallelogram, but for any rectangle, the length and width are by definition perpendicular to each other, so you don't need to find the height separately. For this reason, the area of a rectangle is commonly expressed as length × width.

What are the perimeter and area of this rectangle?

Start with the perimeter. There are two sides of length 5 and two sides of length 7, so the perimeter is 2(5 + 7), which equals 24.

The formula for area is length × width, so the area is 5 × 7 = 35.

Check Your Skills

Find the area and perimeter of each rectangle.

9.

10.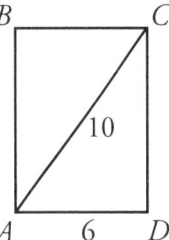

Answers can be found on pages 619–620.

Squares

A square is a parallelogram and a square is a rectangle. Everything that is true of parallelograms and rectangles is true of squares as well. A square has one additional characteristic: The lengths of all four sides are equal. As long as you know the length of one side, you can calculate anything for a square.

If you have a square, and you know that the length of one of its sides is 3, you know that all four sides have a length of 3:

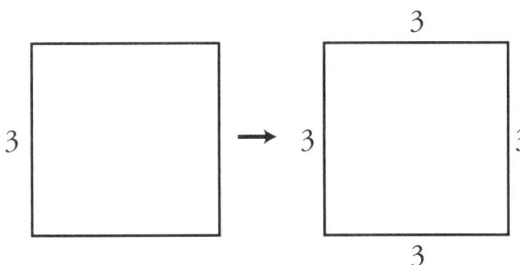

The perimeter of a square is four times the length of one side, or 4(3) = 12.

To find the area, use the same formula as for a rectangle: Area = length × width. But, because the shape is a square, the length and the width are equal. Therefore, the area of a square is Area = (side)². In this case, Area = (3)² = 9.

Unit Five: **Geometry**

Check Your Skills Answer Key

1. **1,080**

   An octagon has 8 sides, so plug $n = 8$ into the formula for the sum of interior angles.

   $$\text{Sum of the interior angles} = (8 - 2)180$$
   $$= (6)180$$
   $$= 1,080$$

2. **120**

   Each interior angle is the same, so divide the sum of the interior angles by 6 (the number of interior angles) in order to find the measure of one interior angle. First, find the sum of all of the interior angles of a six-sided figure.

   $$(6 - 2)180 = 4(180) = 720$$

   Then, divide 720 by 6 to find the value for one angle.

   $$\frac{720}{6} = 120$$

3. **58"**

   Add the side lengths together: $12 + 12 + 17 + 8.5 + 8.5 = 58$.

4. **40**

   The surface area of a cube is 6 times the area of one face. Since the surface area of one cube is 24 in², each square face of each cube must have an area of 4 in². When the two cubes are joined together, one face of each cube is lost, so the total surface area of the figure will be the sum of the surface areas of both cubes minus the surface areas of the two covered faces.

   Each cube has a surface area of 24, so the total surface area before the two cubes are joined is 48. Subtract the surface area of each of the two touching (and thus non-exterior) faces: $48 - 2(4) = 40$.

   Alternatively, because the surface area of one side of each cube is 4, the side length of each cube is 2. Thus, the length of the overall rectangular solid is 4, while its width is 2 and its height is 2. The surface area will now be equal to the sum of all six faces of the rectangular solid: $2(2 \times 4) + 2(2 \times 4) + 2(2 \times 2) = 40$.

5. **8**

   The volume of a rectangular solid is the product of its length, width, and height.

First rectangular solid:	$V = 8 \times 6 \times 4 = 192$
Second rectangular solid:	$V = 4 \times 3 \times 2 = 24$

The volume of the first one is how many times the second one? Divide to find out: $\frac{192}{24} = 8$, so the volume of the larger solid is 8 times the volume of the smaller solid.

Alternatively, note that each dimension of the larger solid is 2 times the corresponding dimension of the smaller solid. The volume will be $2 \times 2 \times 2 = 8$ times greater.

6. **8**

   Use the formula $d = s\sqrt{3}$, where s is an edge of the cube and d is $\sqrt{192}$.

   $$\sqrt{192} = s\sqrt{3}$$
   $$\frac{\sqrt{192}}{\sqrt{3}} = s$$
   $$\sqrt{\frac{192}{3}} = s$$
   $$\sqrt{64} = s$$
   $$8 = s$$

7. **32**

   In parallelograms, opposite sides have equal lengths.

   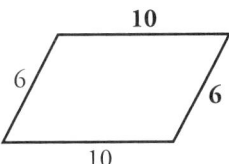

   Thus, the perimeter is $6 + 10 + 6 + 10$, which equals 32. Alternatively, $2(6 + 10) = 32$.

8. **36**

   The area of a parallelogram is bh. In this parallelogram, the base is 9 and the height is 4, so the area is 9×4, which equals 36.

9. **Area = 21, Perimeter = 20**

   There are two sides of 3 and two sides of 7.

   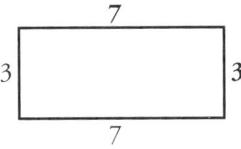

   The perimeter is $2(3 + 7)$, which equals 20. The area is 7×3, which equals 21. The area is 21, and the perimeter is 20.

Unit Five: **Geometry**

10. **Area = 48, Perimeter = 28**

To find the area and perimeter of the rectangle, you need to know the length of either side *AB* or side *CD*. The diagonal of the rectangle creates a right triangle, and the two lengths given indicate that triangle *ACD* is a 6–8–10 triangle. Therefore, the length of side *CD* is 8.

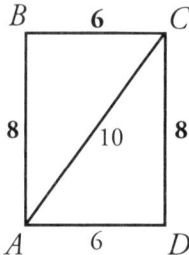

Thus, the perimeter of the rectangle is 2(6 + 8), which equals 28, and the area is 6 × 8, which equals 48.

Problem Set

1. The length of a rectangle increased by a factor of 2, and at the same time its area increased by a factor of 6.

Quantity A	Quantity B
The factor by which the width of the rectangle increased	3

2. Frances completely fences in a rectangular plot of land, except for one 40-foot side of the plot. The plot has an area of 280 square feet. How many feet of fencing is needed for the job?

3. A pentagon has three sides with length x, and two sides with length $3x$. If x is $\frac{2}{3}$ of an inch, what is the perimeter of the pentagon, in inches?

4. In the figure, ABCD is a quadrilateral, with AD parallel to BC. Line BE represents the height of ABCD and Point E is the midpoint of AD. If the area of triangle ABE is 12.5 square inches, what is the area of ABCD, in square inches?

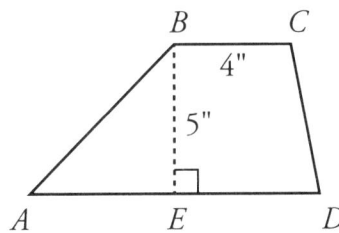

5. The surface of a rectangular tank needs to be coated with insulation. The tank has dimensions of 4 feet, 5 feet, and 2.5 feet. Each square foot of insulation costs $20. How much will it cost to cover the surface of the tank with insulation?

6. Forty percent of Arya's living room floor is covered by a carpet that measures 4 feet by 9 feet. What is the area of Arya's living room floor, in square feet?

7. The scale model of a cube sculpture is 0.5 cm per every 1 m of the real sculpture. What is the volume of the model if the volume of the real sculpture is 64 m³ ?

8. If the perimeter of a rectangular flower bed is 30 feet and its area is 44 square feet, what is the length of each of its shorter sides, in feet?

9. A rectangular parking lot has a length of $2x$ and a width of x. What is the ratio of the perimeter of the parking lot to the area of the parking lot, in terms of x ?

10. A box is in the shape of a cube, the inside edges of which are 4 inches long. What is the longest object that could fit inside the box (i.e., what is the diagonal of the cube), in inches?

11. A rectangular solid has a square base, with each side of the base measuring 4 meters. If the volume of the solid is 112 cubic meters, what is the surface area of the solid, in square meters?

Unit Five: Geometry

12. A solid cube has an edge length of 5. What is the ratio of the cube's surface area to its volume?

13. If the length of an edge of cube *A* is one-third the length of an edge of cube *B*, what is the ratio of the volume of cube *A* to the volume of cube *B* ?

14. In the figure, *ABCD* denotes a square picture frame with a cutout in the middle. *EFGH* is a square centered within *ABCD* as a space for a picture. The area of *EFGH* is equal to the area of the picture frame (the area of *ABCD* minus the area of *EFGH*). If $AB = 6$, what is the length of *EF* ?

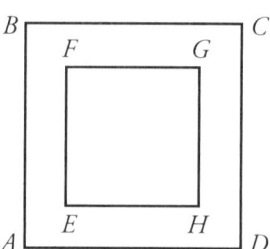

15.
Quantity A	Quantity B
The surface area, in square inches, of a cube with edges of length 6	The volume, in cubic inches, of a cube with edges of length 6

16.
Quantity A	Quantity B
The total volume of 3 cubes with edges of length 2	The total volume of 2 cubes with edges of length 3

17.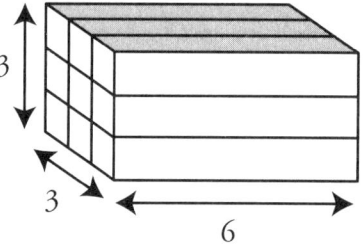

A large rectangular solid is formed by binding together nine identical rectangular rods, as shown.

Quantity A	Quantity B
Four times the surface area of just one of the identical rectangular rods	The surface area of the large rectangular solid shown in the figure

18. If the area of a certain square (expressed in square meters) is added to its perimeter (expressed in meters), the sum is 77. What is the length of one side of the square?

Chapter 22: **Polygons**

Solutions

1. **(C)**
   Plug in numbers to answer this question. Use a table to organize the information.

	Old	New
Length	2	$2 \times 2 = 4$
Width	1	W
Area (l × w)	2	$2 \times 6 = 12$

   $$4 \times W = 12$$
   $$W = 3$$

   Compare the new width to the original: $\frac{\text{New}}{\text{Old}} = \frac{3}{1} = 3$. The width increased by a factor of 3.

   The correct answer is (C): The two quantities are equal.

2. **54**
   One side of the yard is 40 feet long, so call this the length. The area of the yard is 280 square feet. To determine the perimeter, find the width of the yard.

   $$A = l \times w$$
   $$280 = 40 \times w$$
   $$7 = w$$

   The two 7-foot sides and one of the 40-foot sides are fenced in, so $40 + 2(7) = 54$ feet of fence are needed.

3. **6**
   The perimeter of a pentagon is the sum of its five sides: $x + x + x + 3x + 3x = 9x$. If x is $\frac{2}{3}$ of an inch, the perimeter is $9 \times \frac{2}{3}$, or 6 inches.

4. **35**
   If E is the midpoint of AD, then $AE = ED$. Set x as the length of each of AE and ED. Use the area of the triangle to determine the length of x:

   $$\text{Area} = \frac{b \times h}{2}$$
   $$12.5 = \frac{(x)(5)}{2}$$
   $$25 = 5x$$
   $$5 = x$$

   Therefore, the length AD is $2x = 10$.

623

Unit Five: **Geometry**

Because *AD* is parallel to *BC*, the shape *ABCD* is a trapezoid.

$$A_{trap} = \frac{b_1 + b_2}{2} \times h$$

$$= \frac{4 + 10}{2} \times 5$$

$$= 35 \text{ in}^2$$

5. **$1,700**

   To find the surface area of a rectangular solid, sum the individual areas of all six faces.

	One	Both
Top and Bottom:	$5 \times 4 = 20$	$2(20) = 40$
Front and Back:	$5 \times 2.5 = 12.5$	$2(12.5) = 25$
Left and Right:	$4 \times 2.5 = 10$	$2(10) = 20$

   The sum of the areas is $40 + 25 + 20 = 85$, so covering the entire tank will cost $85 \times \$20$, which equals $1,700.

6. **90**

   The area of the carpet is equal to $l \times w$, or 36 ft². Set up a percent table or a proportion to find the area of the whole living room floor.

   $$\frac{40\%}{100\%} = \frac{36}{A}$$

   $$\frac{2}{5} = \frac{36}{A}$$

   $$A = \frac{(\overset{18}{\cancel{36}})(5)}{\underset{1}{\cancel{2}}}$$

   $$A = 90$$

7. **8 cm³**

   $V = s^3 \rightarrow 64 = s^3 \rightarrow s = 4$ The length of a side on the real sculpture is 4 m.

   $\dfrac{0.5 \text{ cm}}{1 \text{ m}} = \dfrac{x \text{ cm}}{4 \text{ m}} \rightarrow x = 2$ The length of a side on the model is 2 cm.

   $V = s^3 = (2)^3 = 8$ The volume of the model is 8.

Chapter 22: **Polygons**

8. **4**

    Set up equations to represent the area and perimeter of the flower bed.

    $$A = l \times w \qquad P = 2(l + w)$$

    Then, substitute the known values for the variables A and P.

    $$44 = l \times w \qquad 30 = 2(l + w)$$

    Solve the two equations using the substitution method.

$l = \frac{44}{w}$	Isolate *l* and substitute into the other equation.
$30 = 2\left(\frac{44}{w} + w\right)$	
$30 = \frac{88}{w} + 2w$	
$15w = 44 + w^2$	Multiply everything by *w* to get rid of the fraction, then solve the quadratic.
$0 = w^2 - 15w + 44$	
$0 = (w - 11)(w - 4)$	
$w = \{4, 11\}$	

    The shorter side is 4 feet and the longer side is 11 feet.

    Alternatively, if you feel comfortable doing so, you can arrive at the correct solution by picking numbers. What length and width add up to 15 (half of the perimeter) and multiply to produce 44 (the area)? The integers that multiply to 44 are (1, 44), (2, 22), and (4, 11). Only the last pair, 4 and 11, add up to 15.

9. **3 : x or $\frac{3}{x}$**

    Using the length of the parking lot 2*x* and the width *x*, set up a fraction to represent the ratio of the perimeter to the area as follows.

    $$\frac{\text{perimeter}}{\text{area}} = \frac{2(2x + x)}{(2x)(x)} = \frac{6x}{2x^2} = \frac{3}{x}$$

    Check the answers. The ratio can be presented in fraction form or written as 3 : *x*.

10. **4√3**

    The diagonal of a cube with side *s* is $s\sqrt{3}$. Therefore, the longest object that could fit inside the box would be $4\sqrt{3}$ inches long.

Unit Five: **Geometry**

11. **144**

    The volume of a rectangular solid equals length × width × height. Since the length and width are both 4 meters long, solve for the height.

    $$112 = 4 \times 4 \times h$$
    $$7 = h$$

    To find the surface area of a rectangular solid, sum the individual areas of all six faces.

	One	Both
Top and Bottom:	$4 \times 4 = 16$	$2(16) = 32$
Front and Back:	$4 \times 7 = 28$	$2(28) = 56$
Left and Right:	$4 \times 7 = 28$	$2(28) = 56$

    The sum of the faces is $32 + 56 + 56 = 144$ square meters.

12. $\dfrac{6}{5}$

    To find the surface area of a cube, find the area of one face, and multiply that by 6 faces, $6(5^2) = 150$.

    To find the volume of a cube, take the cube of its edge length: $5^3 = 125$.

    Therefore, the ratio of the cube's surface area to its volume is $\dfrac{150}{125}$, which simplifies to $\dfrac{6}{5}$.

13. **1 : 27 or $\dfrac{1}{27}$**

    Assign the variable x to the length of one side of cube A. Then, the length of one side of cube B is $3x$. The volume of cube A is x^3. The volume of cube B is $(3x)^3$, or $27x^3$.

    Therefore, the ratio of the volume of cube A to cube B is $\dfrac{x^3}{27x^3}$, which simplifies to $\dfrac{1}{27}$. This can also be written 1 : 27.

    Alternatively, pick a value for the length of a side of cube A and solve accordingly. For example, if one side of cube A is 2, then one side of cube B is 6. The area of cube A is $2^3 = 8$ and the area of cube B is $6^3 = 216$. The ratio of cube A's area to cube B's area is therefore $\dfrac{8}{216} = \dfrac{1}{27}$.

14. **$3\sqrt{2}$**

    Since $AB = 6$, the total area of the picture and picture frame is $6^2 = 36$. The area of the frame and the area of the picture sum to 36. Therefore, the area of the frame and the area of the picture are each equal to half of 36, or 18. EFGH is a square, so use the area to solve for the length of one side.

    $$A = s^2$$
    $$18 = s^2$$
    $$\sqrt{18} = s$$
    $$3\sqrt{2} = s$$

Chapter 22: **Polygons**

15. **(C)**
    The surface area of a cube is equal to the area of one face times 6.

Quantity A	Quantity B
The surface area, in square inches, of a cube with edges of length $6 = 6 \times (6 \times 6)$	The volume, in cubic inches, of a cube with edges of length 6

    The volume of a cube is equal to the cube of one side.

Quantity A	Quantity B
$6 \times (6 \times 6)$	The volume, in cubic inches, of a cube with edges of length $6 = 6 \times 6 \times 6$

    The correct answer is (C): The two quantities are equal.

    It is not usually the case that the volume of a cube in cubic units is equal to the surface area of the cube in square inches. They are only equal when the edge of the cube is of length 6, as in this problem.

16. **(B)**
    The volume of a cube is e^3, where e is the length of each edge.

Quantity A	Quantity B
The total volume of 3 cubes with edges of length 2 $3 \times 2^3 = 24$	The total volume of 2 cubes with edges of length 3 $2 \times 3^3 = 54$

    The correct answer is (B): Quantity B is greater.

17. **(A)**
    A rectangular solid has three pairs of opposing equal faces, each pair representing two of the dimensions of the solid (length × width; length × height; height × width). The total surface area of a rectangular solid is the sum of the surface areas of those three pairs of opposing sides.

627

Unit Five: **Geometry**

22.

According to the diagram, the dimensions of one rod must be 1 × 1 × 6. Find the surface area of one rod.

$$2(1 \times 1) + 2(1 \times 6) + 2(1 \times 6) =$$
$$2 + 12 + 12 = 26$$

Since one rod has a total surface area of 26, four rods have a total surface area of $4 \times 26 = 104$.

The large rectangular solid has dimensions 3 by 3 by 6. Find the surface area of the large solid.

$$2(3 \times 3) + 2(3 \times 6) + 2(3 \times 6) =$$
$$18 + 36 + 36 = 90$$

Quantity A	Quantity B
Four times the surface area of just one of the identical rectangular rods	The surface area of the large rectangular solid above
104	90

Therefore, the correct answer is (A): Quantity A is greater.

18. **7**

The area of the square = s^2. The perimeter of the square = $4s$. The sum equals 77.

$$\text{Area} + \text{Perimeter} = \text{Sum}$$
$$s^2 + 4s = 77 \quad \rightarrow \quad s^2 + 4s - 77 = 0$$
$$(s + 11)(s - 7) = 0$$

Solve for the two possible values of s.

$$s + 11 = 0 \quad \text{or} \quad s - 7 = 0$$
$$s = -11 \qquad\qquad s = 7$$

The length of the side of a cube must be positive, so discard the negative answer. The length of one side equals 7.

CHAPTER 23

Circles and Cylinders

In This Chapter:

- The Basic Elements of a Circle
- Sectors
- Inscribed vs. Central Angles
- Inscribed Triangles
- Cylinders and Surface Area
- Cylinders and Volume
- Check Your Skills Answer Key
- Problem Set
- Solutions

CHAPTER 23 Circles and Cylinders

Circles and their properties are tested on their own on the GRE, but circles are also often tested in conjunction with other shapes. Cylinders are less commonly tested but may still appear on the GRE.

In this chapter, you will learn all of the standard properties and formulas for circles and cylinders, as well as how to approach problems that combine circles with other shapes.

The Basic Elements of a Circle

A **circle** is a set of points that are all the same distance from a central point. By definition, every circle has a **center**. Although the center is not itself a point on the circle, it is nevertheless an important component of the circle. The **radius** of a circle is defined as the distance between the center of the circle and any point on the circle. The first thing to know about radii is that *any* line segment connecting the center of the circle (usually labeled O) and *any* point on the circle is a radius (usually labeled r). All radii in the same circle have the same length:

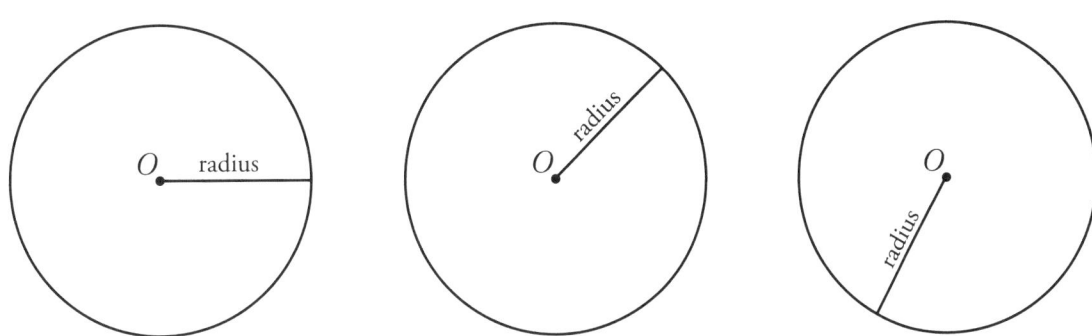

Once you know the radius of a circle, you can infer almost anything you need to know about a circle. For example:

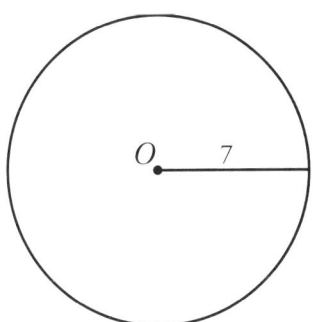

631

Once you know the radius, the next easiest piece to figure out is the **diameter**. The diameter passes through the center of a circle and connects two opposite points on the circle:

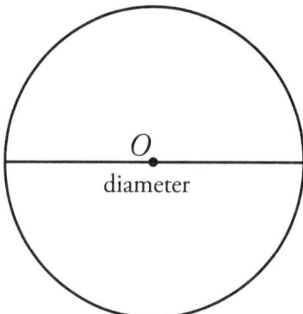

The diameter (usually referred to as d) is 2 radii laid end to end, so the diameter will always be exactly twice the length of the radius. This relationship can be expressed as $d = 2r$. The circle with radius 7 has a diameter of 14.

The **circumference** (usually referred to as C) is a measure of the distance around a circle. The circumference is essentially the perimeter of a circle:

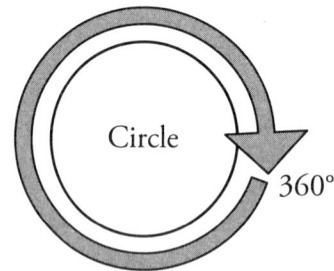

There is a consistent relationship between the circumference and the diameter of any circle. If you were to divide the circumference by the diameter, you would always get the same number—3.14159.... This value, **pi** (or the Greek letter π), is a non-terminating decimal, so it's usually rounded to the hundredths place: 3.14. If you multiply pi by the diameter, you'll get the circumference:

$$\frac{\text{circumference}}{\text{diameter}} = \pi \qquad \text{OR} \qquad \pi d = C$$

In the circle with a diameter of 14, the circumference is $\pi(14) = 14\pi$.

The vast majority of questions that involve circles and π will use the Greek letter rather than the decimal approximation for π. For example, the correct answer on the GRE would almost certainly read 14π, rather than 43.96 (which is 14×3.14).

One more note: The circumference can also be expressed in terms of the radius, since the diameter is exactly twice the radius:

$$C = \pi d = 2\pi r$$

The **area** of a circle (usually referred to as A) is the space inside the circle:

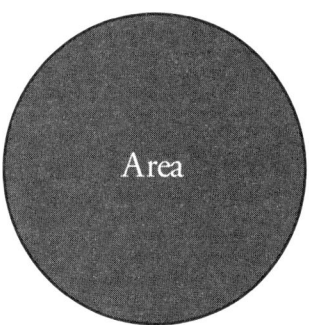

The formula for the area of a circle is $A = \pi r^2$. For a circle of radius 7, the area is $\pi(7)^2 = 49\pi$.

Once you know the radius, you are able to determine the diameter, the circumference, and the area:

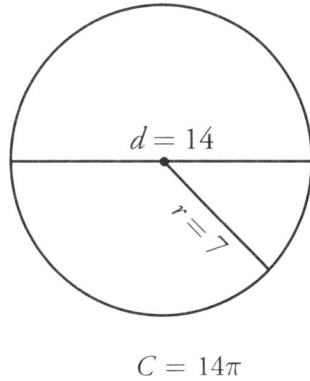

$C = 14\pi$
$A = 49\pi$

These relationships are true of any circle. What's more, if you know *any* one of these values, you can determine the rest. In fact, the ability to use one element of a circle to determine any of the other elements is one of the most important skills for answering questions about circles. To review:

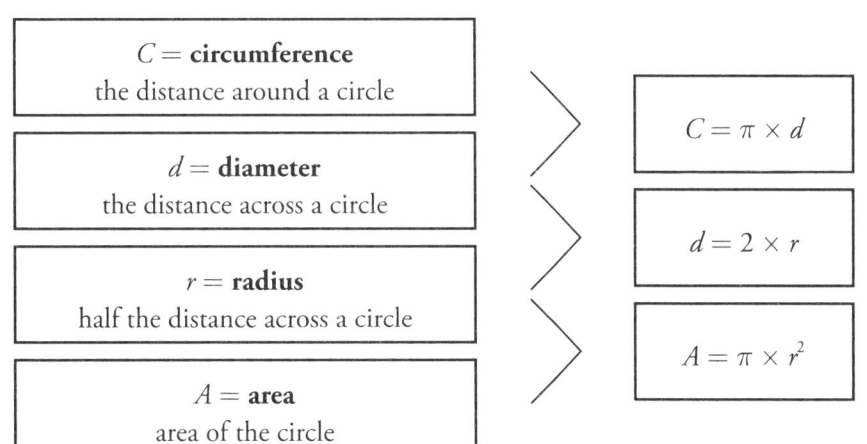

Unit Five: **Geometry**

Try this problem:

Given a circle with area 36π, what else can you determine about the circle's measurements?

First, set up the area formula and solve for the radius by isolating r:

Divide both sides by π: $36π = πr^2$
Take the square root of both sides: $36 = r^2$
     $6 = r$

Since the radius is 2, the diameter is 6 × 2, which is 12. Finally, to find the circumference, multiply the diameter by π. The circumference is 12π.

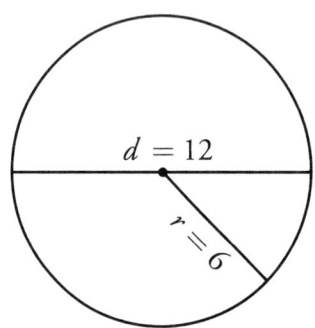

A final basic element of the circle pertains to sectors of circles and the interior angle, which was touched on in Chapter 19: Data Interpretation. The degree rotation around any circle is 360°. Imagine a light rotating from the center of the circle around the edges of the circle. By the time the light travels back to where it started, it has turned 360 degrees.

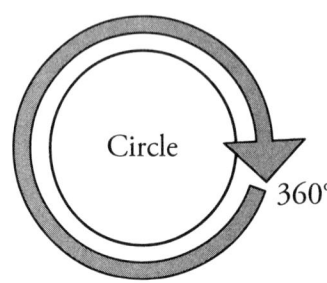

Check Your Skills

1. The radius of a circle is 5. What is the area?

   ☐ π

2. The circumference of a circle is 17π. What is the diameter?

   ☐

3. The area of a circle is 64π. What is the circumference?

   ☐ π

Answers can be found on page 641.

Sectors

The GRE will also expect you to be able to work with parts of a circle. If you cut a circle in half, it will be a semicircle. Any time you have a fractional portion of a circle, it's known as a **sector**:

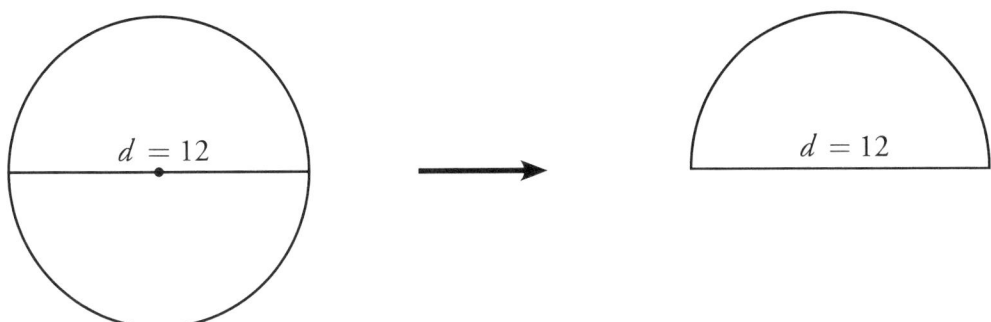

What effect does cutting the circle in half have on the basic elements of the circle? The diameter stays the same, as does the radius. But the area and the circumference are also cut in half. The area of the full circle is $A = \pi r^2 = 36\pi$ and the circumference is 12π. So the area of this semicircle is 18π and the circumference of this semicircle is 6π. When dealing with sectors, the portion of the circumference that remains is called the **arc length**. So the arc length of this sector is 6π.

The arc length is *not* equivalent to the perimeter of the semicircle. The arc length is a measure of only the curved portion. By contrast, the perimeter includes both the arc length and the flat portion—in this case, the full diameter. The perimeter of a semicircle with a radius of 6 is $6\pi + 12$.

What happens if, instead of cutting the circle in half, you cut it into quarters? In that case, each piece of the circle would have $\frac{1}{4}$ of the area of the entire circle and $\frac{1}{4}$ the circumference (for the curved portion):

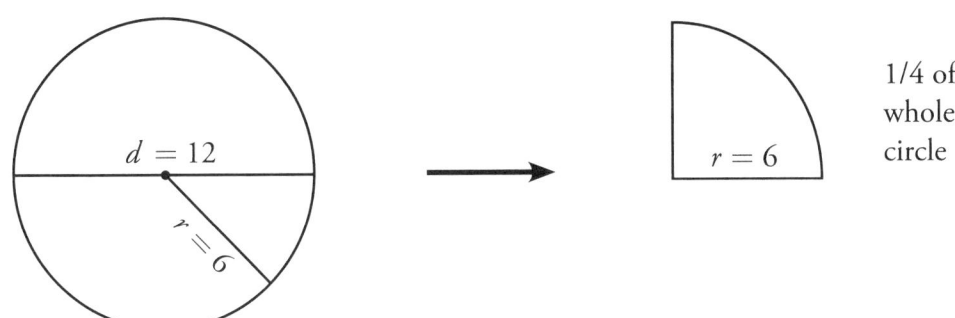

On the GRE, you're unlikely to be told that you have one-quarter of a circle. Instead, the test will likely tell you the **central angle** of a sector. The central angle of a sector is the degree measure between the two radii that cut off that sector.

There are 360° in a full circle. What is the central angle of one-quarter of a circle? The same thing that happens to area and circumference happens to the central angle. It is now $\frac{1}{4}$ of 360°, which is 90°:

$$\frac{90°}{360°} = \frac{1}{4}$$

How can you use the central angle to determine sector area and arc length? A circle has an area of 36π and a circumference of 12π. If the central angle of a sector of that circle is 60°, here's how to find the sector's area and arc length:

Since 360° is the full degree measure, and 60° is the part, then $\frac{60}{360}$ is the portion of the circle remaining and $\frac{60}{360}$ reduces to $\frac{1}{6}$. This sector with a central angle of 60° is $\frac{1}{6}$ of the entire circle. Use that fraction to calculate the sector's area and arc length:

$$\text{Sector Area} = \frac{1}{6} \times (36\pi) = 6\pi$$

$$\text{Arc Length} = \frac{1}{6} \times (12\pi) = 2\pi$$

$$\frac{1}{6} = \frac{60°}{360°} = \frac{\text{Sector Area}}{\text{Circle Area}} = \frac{\text{Arc Length}}{\text{Circumference}}$$

Determining what fraction of the original circle remains is a key part of computations involving sectors. Review Chapter 11: Fractions for a refresher on part to whole analysis.

Any of the three properties of a sector (central angle, arc length, and area) can be used to find the central angle. For example:

A sector has a radius of 9 and an area of 27π. What is the central angle of the sector?

This time, the problem provides the area of just the sector, as well as the radius of the circle. Since the radius is 9, the area of the whole circle is Area $= \pi(9)^2 = 81\pi$. Use $\frac{\text{sector area}}{\text{circle area}}$ to find the fraction for the sector.

Because $\frac{27\pi}{81\pi} = \frac{1}{3}$, the sector is $\frac{1}{3}$ of the circle. The full circle has a central angle of 360°, so the central angle of the sector is 120°:

$$\frac{1}{3} = \frac{120°}{360°}$$

$$\frac{1}{3} = \frac{27\pi \text{ (sector area)}}{81\pi \text{ (circle area)}}$$

Every question about sectors involves determining what fraction of the circle that sector represents. As a result, every question about sectors will provide you with enough information to calculate one of the following fractions:

$$\frac{\text{central angle}}{360} = \frac{\text{sector area}}{\text{circle area}} = \frac{\text{arc length}}{\text{circumference}}$$

Once you know any of those fractions, you know them all, and, if you know any specific value, you can find the value of any piece of the sector or the original circle.

Check Your Skills

4. A sector has a central angle of 270° and a radius of 2. What is the area of the sector?

   ☐ π

5. A sector has an arc length of 4π and a radius of 3. What is the central angle of the sector?

   ☐ °

6. A sector has an area of 40π and a radius of 10. What is the arc length of the sector?

   ☐ π

Answers can be found on page 641.

Inscribed vs. Central Angles

A central angle is an angle whose vertex lies at the center point of a circle. A central angle defines both an arc and a sector of a circle.

Another type of angle is termed an **inscribed angle**. An inscribed angle has its vertex on the circle itself (rather than on the center of the circle). Here is the difference between a central angle and an inscribed angle:

Central Angle

Inscribed Angle

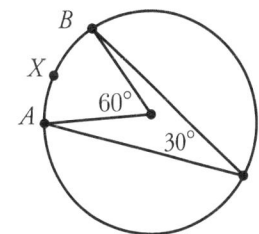

The far right-hand circle shows both a central angle and an inscribed angle, both of which intercept arc *AXB*. The central angle defines the arc. **An inscribed angle is equal to half of the central angle of the arc it intercepts,** in degrees. In this example, the arc is 60°. As a result, the inscribed angle is 30°, which is half of 60°.

Inscribed Triangles

A triangle is said to be **inscribed** in a circle if all of the vertices of the triangle are points on the circle. That triangle is called an **inscribed triangle**.

Here's an example of a right triangle inscribed in a circle. In this case, the right angle (90°) lies opposite a semicircle, which is an arc that measures 180°. The hypotenuse of the triangle is also the diameter of the circle:

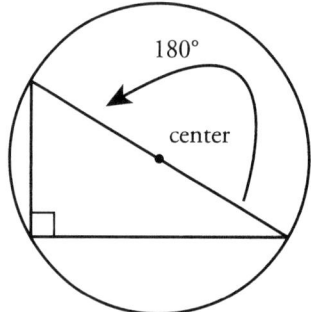

If one of the sides of an inscribed triangle is a *diameter* of the circle, then the triangle *must* be a right triangle. Why? When this occurs, the central angle is 180° and so the inscribed angle must be half of that, or 90°.

It's also the case that any right triangle inscribed in a circle must have the diameter of the circle as its hypotenuse (thereby splitting the circle in half). So if you are told that a right triangle is inscribed in the circle, then the hypotenuse is the same as the circle's diameter.

Here's a third variation of the same rule:

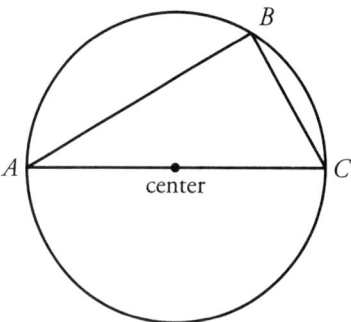

The inscribed triangle *ABC* must be a right triangle, because *AC* runs through the center of the circle. Any line across a circle that runs through the center of the circle is a diameter of the circle.

Chapter 23: **Circles and Cylinders**

Cylinders and Surface Area

Two circles and a rectangle combine to form a three-dimensional shape called a right circular cylinder (referred to from now on simply as a **cylinder**). The top and bottom of the cylinder are circles, while the middle of the cylinder is formed from a rolled-up rectangle, as shown in the diagram.

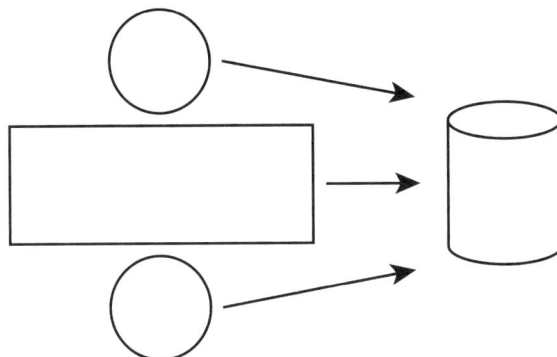

To determine the surface area of a cylinder, sum the areas of the three surfaces: The area of each circle is πr^2, while the area of the rectangle is length × width.

The length of the rectangle is equal to the circumference of the circle ($2\pi r$), and the width of the rectangle is equal to the height of the cylinder (h). Therefore, the area of the rectangle is $2\pi r \times h$. To find the total surface area (SA) of a cylinder, add the area of the circular top and bottom, as well as the area of the rectangle that wraps around the outside:

> *Surface Area of a Cylinder*
>
> SA = 2 circles + rectangle = $2(\pi r^2) + 2\pi rh$

In order to find the surface area of a cylinder, then, you need two pieces of information: the radius of the cylinder and the height of the cylinder.

Cylinders and Volume

The volume of a cylinder measures how much "stuff" it can hold inside. In order to find the volume of a cylinder, use the following formula, where V is the volume, r is the radius of the cylinder, and h is the height of the cylinder:

> *Volume of a Cylinder*
>
> $V = \pi r^2 h$

As with surface area, the formula for the volume of a cylinder requires two pieces of information: the radius of the cylinder and the height of the cylinder.

To help remember this formula, think of a cylinder as a stack of circles, each with an area of πr^2. Multiply πr^2 by the height (h) of the stack of circles to find the area.

639

Two cylinders can have the same volume but different shapes:

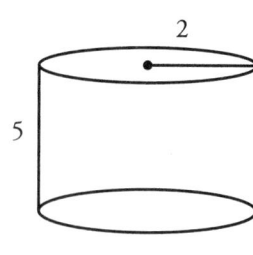

$V = \pi r^2 h$
$= \pi(1^2)20$
$= 20\pi$

$V = \pi r^2 h$
$= \pi(2^2)5$
$= 20\pi$

These two cylinders can hold the same volume of water, but they would not both be able to fit the same way into a larger object. For example, if the dimensions on the cylinders are in inches, then the cylinder on the left could fit inside a box that is 3 inches wide on each side and 21 inches tall, but the cylinder on the right would be too wide to fit into such a box. Likewise, the cylinder on the right could fit completely inside a box that is 5 inches wide and 6 inches tall, but the cylinder on the left would be too tall to fit completely inside such a box.

Chapter 23: **Circles and Cylinders**

Check Your Skills Answer Key

1. **25**

   The formula for area is $A = \pi r^2$. The radius is 5, so the area is $\pi(5)^2 = 25\pi$. Because the symbol for π is already included after the numeric entry box, do not incorporate it into your entry. The value to enter is 25, not 25π.

2. **17**

   The circumference of a circle is either $C = 2\pi r$ or $C = \pi d$. The question asks for the diameter, so use the latter formula: $17\pi = \pi d$. Divide by π to get $17 = d$.

3. **16**

   The link between the area and the circumference of a circle is the radius.

   $$A = \pi r^2$$
   $$64\pi = \pi r^2 \qquad C = 2\pi r$$
   $$64 = r^2 \qquad C = 2\pi(8)$$
   $$8 = r \qquad C = 16\pi$$

   The answer already includes π, so enter only the number 16 in the box.

4. **3**

   Since the central angle of the sector is 270°, the sector is $\frac{3}{4}$ of the full circle, because $\frac{270°}{360°} = \frac{3}{4}$. Since the radius is 2, the area of the full circle is $\pi(2)^2$, which equals 4π. If the area of the full circle is 4π, then the area of the sector will be $\frac{3}{4} \times 4\pi$, which equals 3π. The π is already positioned after the numeric entry box, so enter only 3 into the box.

5. **240**

   To find the central angle of the sector, first figure out the fraction that the arc length represents of the full circumference. The radius is 3, so the circumference of the circle is $2\pi(3) = 6\pi$. The sector is $\frac{2}{3}$ of the circle, because $\frac{4\pi}{6\pi} = \frac{2}{3}$. Therefore, the central angle of the sector is $\frac{2}{3} \times 360°$, which equals 240°.

6. **8**

   Since the area of the sector was given, find the area of the whole circle.

   $$\text{Area of circle: } \pi r^2 = 100\pi$$
   $$\frac{\text{Sector Area}}{\text{Circle Area}} : \frac{40\pi}{100\pi} = \frac{2}{5}$$

   Next, find the circumference, then use the fraction to find the arc length of the sector.

   $$\text{Circumference: } 2\pi r = 20\pi$$
   $$\text{Arc length: } \frac{2}{5}(20\pi) = 8\pi$$

Unit Five: **Geometry**

Problem Set

1. If the radius of a circle is tripled, what is the ratio of the area of half the original circle to the area of the whole new circle?

2. In the figure, triangle *ABC* is inscribed in a circle, such that *AC* is a diameter of the circle. What is the circumference of the circle?

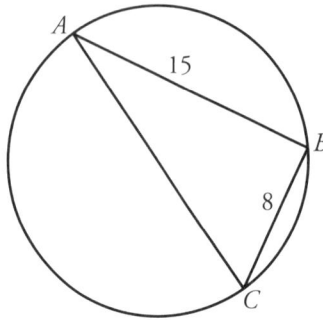

3. A cylinder has a surface area of 360π and height of 3. What is the diameter of the cylinder's circular base?

4. In the figure, a circular lawn with a radius of 5 meters is surrounded by a circular walkway that is 4 meters wide. What is the area of the walkway, in meters squared?

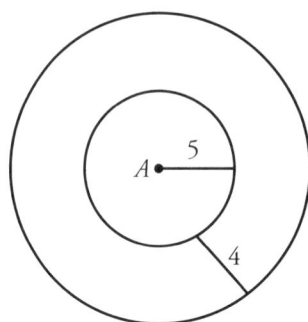

5. In the figure, *AC* and *DE* are both diameters of the circle. If the area of the circle is 180, what is the total area of the shaded sectors?

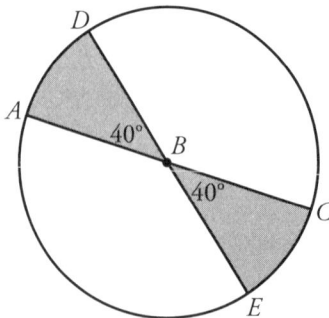

642

Chapter 23: **Circles and Cylinders**

6. Jana has to paint a cylindrical column that is 14 feet high and that has a circular base with a radius of 3 feet. If one bucket of paint will cover 10π square feet, how many whole buckets of paint does Jana need to buy in order to paint the entire column, including the top and bottom?

7. A circular flower bed takes up half the area of a square lawn. If an edge of the lawn is 200 feet long, what is the radius of the flower bed, in feet? (Express the answer in terms of π.)

8. In the figure, angle *ABC* is 40 degrees, and the area of the circle is 81π. What is the length of arc *AXC* ?

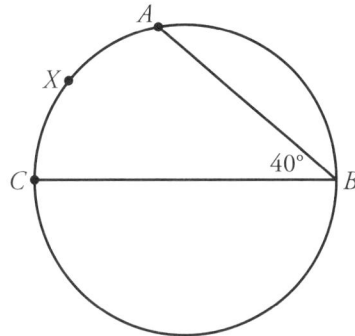

9. In the figure, triangle *ABD* is inscribed in a circle, such that *AD* is a diameter of the circle and angle *BAD* is 45°. If the area of triangle *ABD* is 72, how much greater is the area of the circle than the area of triangle *ABD* ?

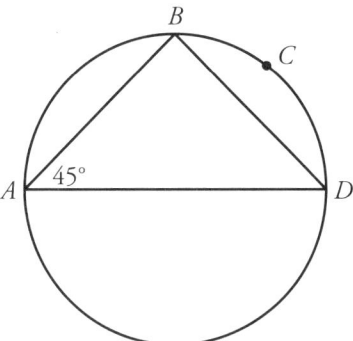

10. Challenge problem! In the figure, triangle *ABD* is inscribed in a circle, such that *AD* is a diameter of the circle and angle *BAD* is 45°. If the area of triangle *ABD* is 84.5, what is the length of arc *BCD* ?

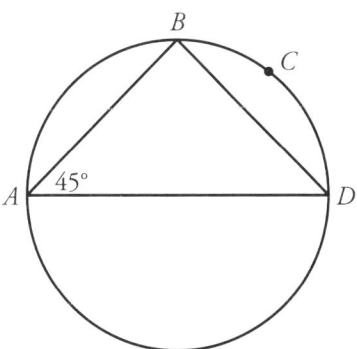

643

Unit Five: **Geometry**

11.

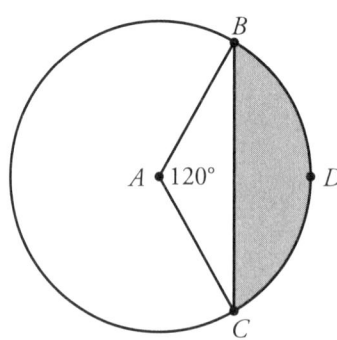

In the figure, A is the center of the circle.

Quantity A	**Quantity B**
The perimeter of triangle ABC	The perimeter of the shaded region

12.

In the figure, a circle with area π is inscribed in a square.

Quantity A	**Quantity B**
The combined area of the shaded regions	1

13.

Quantity A	**Quantity B**
The combined area of four circles, each with radius 1	The area of a circle with radius 2

Chapter 23: **Circles and Cylinders**

Solutions

1. **1:18 or $\frac{1}{18}$**

   Pick real numbers to solve this problem. Set the radius of the original circle equal to 2. Therefore, the radius of the new circle is equal to 6. Calculate the areas of both circles to find the ratio.

   $$\frac{\text{Area of half the original circle}}{\text{Area of the new circle}} = \frac{2\pi}{36\pi} = \frac{1}{18}$$

2. **17π**

   If AC is a diameter of the circle, then inscribed triangle ABC is a right triangle, with AC as the hypotenuse. Since one leg is 15 and one leg is 8, the triangle is an 8–15–17 triple and the hypotenuse AC is 17.

   AC is also the diameter of the circle, so $d = 17$. The circumference of the circle is πd, or 17π.

3. **24**

   The surface area of a cylinder is the area of the circular top and bottom, plus the area of its wrapped-around rectangular third face. Substitute the known values into this formula to find the radius of the circular base.

   $$SA = 2(\pi r^2) + 2\pi rh$$
   $$360\pi = 2(\pi r^2) + 2\pi r(3)$$
   $$0 = 2\pi r^2 + 6\pi r - 360\pi$$
   $$0 = r^2 + 3r - 180$$
   $$0 = (r+15)(r-12)$$

   The two possible values of r are −15 and 12. Use only the positive value of r. Since the radius of the cylinder's base is 12, the diameter is 24.

4. **56π**

   The area of the walkway is the area of the entire image (walkway + lawn, or larger circle) minus the area of the lawn (smaller circle).

Large Circle	−	Small Circle		
πr^2	−	πr^2		
$\pi(9)^2$	−	$\pi(5)^2$		
81π	−	25π	=	56π

5. **40**

   The two central angles of the shaded sectors add up to 80°. Calculate the fraction of the circle represented by the shaded sectors, then multiply that fraction by the total area to find the area of the shaded sectors.

   $$\frac{80}{360} = \frac{2}{9} \rightarrow \frac{2}{9}(180) = 40$$

Unit Five: **Geometry**

6. **11**

    The surface area of a cylinder is the area of the circular top and bottom, plus the area of its wrapped-around rectangular third face.

    $$SA = 2\pi r^2 + 2\pi rh$$
    $$SA = 2\pi(3)^2 + 2\pi(3)(14)$$
    $$SA = 18\pi + 84\pi$$
    $$SA = 102\pi$$

    Since one bucket of paint will cover 10π ft², Jana will need 10.2 buckets to paint the entire column. Because the question asked for the total number of whole buckets, Jana will need to purchase 11 buckets.

7. $\sqrt{\dfrac{20{,}000}{\pi}}$

    The area of the lawn is $(200)^2 = 40{,}000$ ft².

    The area of the flower bed is half of that, or 20,000 ft². Use the formula for the area of a circle to find the radius.

    $$A = \pi r^2$$
    $$20{,}000 = \pi r^2$$
    $$\frac{20{,}000}{\pi} = r^2$$
    $$\sqrt{\frac{20{,}000}{\pi}} = r$$

    The question said to "express the answer in terms of π," which is a fancy way of saying "leave the pi symbol in the final answer."

8. **4π**

    Since the area of the circle is 81π, the radius of the circle is 9 (from $A = \pi r^2$). Therefore, the total circumference of the circle is 18π (from $C = 2\pi r$). Angle ABC, an inscribed angle of 40°, corresponds to a central angle of 80°.

    Use that degree measure to find the fraction that arc AXC represents of the entire circle, then multiply by the total circumference to find the length of arc AXC.

    $$\frac{80}{360} = \frac{2}{9} \rightarrow \frac{2}{\cancel{9}_1}(\cancel{18}^{2}\pi) = 4\pi$$

646

9. **72π − 72**

   Since AD is a diameter of the circle, angle ABD is a right angle. Therefore, triangle ABD is a 45–45–90 triangle, and the base and height are equal. Assign the variable y to represent both the base and height of the triangle.

   The area of the triangle is 72 and the base and height are each y. Solve for the value of y.

   $$A = \frac{bh}{2}$$
   $$72 = \frac{y^2}{2}$$
   $$144 = y^2$$
   $$12 = y$$

   Because the triangle is a 45–45–90 triangle, the hypotenuse is equal to $12\sqrt{2}$. The hypotenuse is also the diameter of the circle, so the radius of the circle is equal to $6\sqrt{2}$. Use the radius to find the area of the circle.

   $$A = \pi r^2$$
   $$A = \pi \left(6\sqrt{2}\right)^2$$
   $$A = 72\pi$$

   Finally, subtract the area of the triangle from the area of the circle. The area of the circle is $72\pi - 72$ greater than the area of triangle ABD.

10. $\dfrac{13\pi\sqrt{2}}{4}$

    Since AD is a diameter of the circle, angle ABD is a right angle. Therefore, triangle ABD is a 45–45–90 triangle, and the base and height are equal. The area of triangle ABD is 84.5 square units. Assign the same variable to the base and height and use the area to solve.

    $$A = \frac{bh}{2}$$
    $$84.5 = \frac{x^2}{2}$$
    $$169 = x^2$$
    $$13 = x$$

    The base and height of the 45–45–90 triangle are equal to 13, so the hypotenuse is equal to $13\sqrt{2}$. The hypotenuse is equal to the diameter. circumference ($C = \pi d$) is equal to $13\sqrt{2} \times \pi$. The labeled 45° angle, which is the inscribed angle for arc BCD corresponds to a central angle of 90°. Thus, arc BCD = $\dfrac{90}{360} = \dfrac{1}{4}$ of the total circumference.

    $$C = \pi d$$
    $$C = \pi(13\sqrt{2})$$

Finally, the 45° angle, which is the inscribed angle for arc BCD, corresponds to a central angle of 90°. Find the fraction of the circle represented by arc BCD, then solve for the arc length.

$$\frac{90}{360} = \frac{1}{4} \rightarrow \frac{1}{4}(13\sqrt{2})\pi = \frac{13\pi\sqrt{2}}{4}$$

When a term combines a root value and a pi symbol, it's a good idea to place pi before the root symbol so that you don't mistakenly include pi under the square root.

11. **(B)**
The two perimeters share the line BC, so rephrase the question:

Quantity A	Quantity B
The combined length of two radii (AB and AC)	The length of arc BDC

Pick values to solve. If the radius of the circle is 2, then Quantity A is 4.

For Quantity B, first find the total circumference: $C = 2\pi(2) = 4\pi$. Then find the fraction the arc length represents of the total circumference and use that to solve for the arc length.

$$\frac{120°}{360°} = \frac{1}{3} \rightarrow \frac{1}{3}(4\pi) = \frac{4\pi}{3}$$

Quantity A	Quantity B
The combined length of two radii (AB and AC)	The length of arc BDC
4	$\frac{4\pi}{3}$

Since π is greater than 3, the value of $\frac{4\pi}{3}$ is slightly greater than 4. Alternatively, plug the fraction into your calculator (use 3.14 to approximate pi).

The correct answer is (B): Quantity B is greater.

12. **(B)**
Use the area of the circle to determine the area of the square, then subtract the area of the circle from the area of the square to determine the shaded region.

$$A = \pi r^2$$
$$\pi = \pi r^2$$
$$1 = r^2$$
$$1 = r$$

The radius of the circle is 1, so the diameter of the circle is 2, as is each side of the square. The area of the square is 4.

Quantity A	Quantity B
The combined area of the shaded regions = $\text{Area}_{Square} - \text{Area}_{Circle} = 4 - \pi$	1

The value of π is about 3.14, so $4 - \pi$ is a bit less than 1.

The correct answer is (B): Quantity B is greater.

13. **(C)**

Start with Quantity A. Find the area of one circle.

$$A = \pi r^2$$
$$A = \pi (1)^2$$
$$A = \pi$$

Each circle in Quantity A has an area of π, so all four circles together have an area of 4π.

For Quantity B, use the radius 2 to find the area.

$$A = \pi r^2$$
$$A = \pi (2)^2$$
$$A = 4\pi$$

Quantity A	Quantity B
The combined area of four circles, each with radius 1	The area of a circle with radius 2
4π	4π

The correct answer is (C): The two quantities are always equal.

CHAPTER 24
Lines and Angles

In This Chapter:

- Line Segments
- Intersecting Lines
- Exterior Angles
- Parallel Lines
- Check Your Skills Answer Key
- Problem Set
- Solutions

CHAPTER 24 Lines and Angles

A straight line is 180°. Think of a line as half of a circle:

Parallel lines are lines that lie in a plane and never intersect. No matter how far you extend the lines, they never meet:

Perpendicular lines are lines that intersect at a 90° angle:

In this chapter, you'll learn how to handle the three major line-angle relationships that appear on the GRE:

1. The angles formed by any intersecting lines
2. The exterior angles formed by shapes
3. The angles formed by parallel lines cut by a transversal

Line Segments

Some questions on the GRE will describe either several points that lie on one line or line segments that all lie together on one line. Use a number line to set up these problems.

Position

When a question mentions a line segment but doesn't draw a picture for you, there are two possible versions of that segment. For example, if a question indicates that the length of line segment $\overline{BD}$ is 4, then there are two possible versions of $\overline{BD}$:

653

This can be taken even further. Suppose there are three points on a line: *A, B,* and *C*. Without more information, you can't know the order of the three points. Here are some of the possible arrangements:

When questions provide incomplete information about the relative positions of points, be suspicious! Account for the lack of information by drawing multiple number lines.

Distance

If you have incomplete information about the positions of points on the line, calculating distance can get complicated.

Suppose that *A, B,* and *C* all lie on a number line. Further, suppose that $\overline{AB} = 3$ and $\overline{BC} = 7$. There are multiple ways to draw this information:

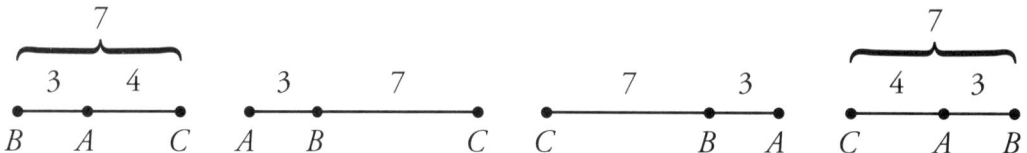

To construct number lines efficiently and accurately, while remembering to keep track of different possible scenarios, start with the most restrictive pieces of information. For example:

> On a line, point *E* is the midpoint of $\overline{DF}$, and $\overline{DE}$ has a length of 6. Point *G* does not lie on the line and $\overline{EG} = 4$. What is the range of possible values of $\overline{FG}$?

In this problem, the most restrictive piece of information is the fact that point *E* has to be the midpoint of $\overline{DF}$. Start by drawing $\overline{DF}$ with point *E* exactly in the middle. There are two possible versions:

Since *E* is the midpoint of $\overline{DF}$, the length of $\overline{EF}$ must also be 6:

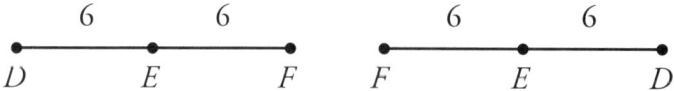

What about point *G*? The problem indicates that it is not on the line with the other points and that it is 4 away from point *E*. The set of all points that are equidistant from a fixed point is actually a circle—in other words, to represent the possible positions of *G*, draw a circle around point *E* with a radius of 4.

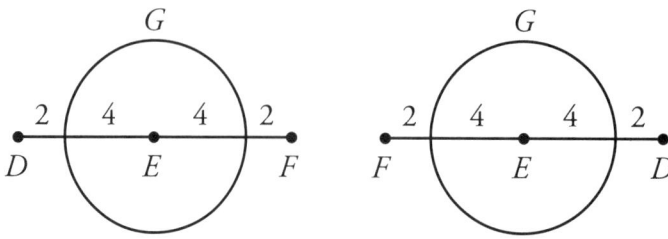

As it turns out, the two representations are symmetrical, so from here, you can ignore one and use the other to solve.

The circle represents all of the possible points of point G, with the exception of the two points exactly on the line, since the problem stated that G does not lie on the line.

If point G could be on the line, it would be closest to F where the circle crosses the line 2 units away from F. Similarly, point G would be farthest away from F where the circle crosses the line between points D and E. That point is 10 away from F.

If G could be on the line, the range of possible values of $\overline{FG}$ would be $2 \leq \overline{FG} \leq 10$. Because G can't be on the line, the range is instead all of the values between 2 and 10, but not including 2 and 10: $2 < \overline{FG} < 10$.

Check Your Skills

1. X, Y, and Z all lie on a number line. Segment $\overline{XY}$ has a length of 5 and $\overline{YZ}$ has a length of 7. If point U is the midpoint of $\overline{XZ}$, and $\overline{UZ} > 2$, what is the length of $\overline{UZ}$?

Answers can be found on page 659.

Intersecting Lines

Intersecting lines have three important properties.

First, the interior angles formed by intersecting lines form a circle, so the sum of these angles is 360°. In the diagram shown, $a + b + c + d = 360$.

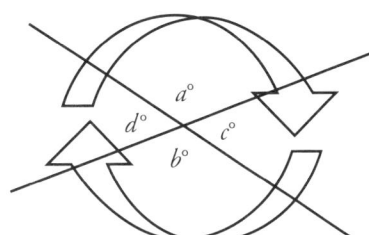

Second, interior angles that combine to form a line sum to 180°. These are termed **supplementary angles**. Thus, in the same diagram shown, $a + d = 180$, because angles a and d form a line together. Other supplementary angles are $b + c = 180$, $a + c = 180$, and $d + b = 180$.

Third, where two lines intersect, the opposite angles are equal. These are called **vertical angles**. Thus, in the previous diagram, $a = b$, because these angles are opposite one another. Additionally, $c = d$ for the same reason.

These rules apply to more than two lines that intersect at a point, as shown in the following image. In this diagram, $a + b + c + d + e + f = 360$, because these angles combine to form a circle. In addition, $a + b + c = 180$, because these three angles combine to form a line. Finally, $a = d$, $b = e$, and $c = f$, because they are pairs of vertical angles.

Unit Five: Geometry

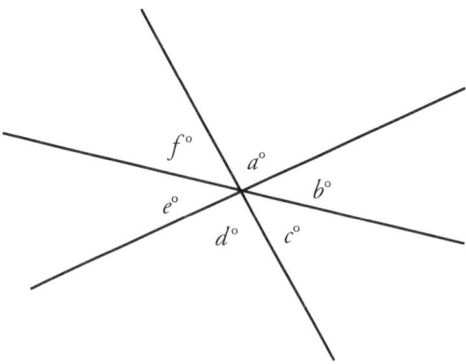

Check Your Skills

2. If $b + f = 150$, what is d?

3. What is $x - y$?

Answers can be found on page 659.

Exterior Angles

An **exterior angle** of a triangle is formed by extending one of the sides of the triangle straight past a vertex. In the diagram below, x is an exterior angle. An exterior angle is equal in measure to the sum of the two non-adjacent (opposite) **interior angles** of the triangle:

$a + b + c = 180$ (sum of angles in a triangle)
$b + x = 180$ (supplementary angles)
Therefore, $x = a + c$.

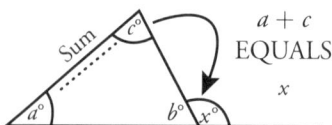

This property is frequently tested on the GRE. In particular, look for exterior angles within more complicated diagrams. You might even redraw the diagram with certain lines removed to isolate the triangle and exterior angle you need:

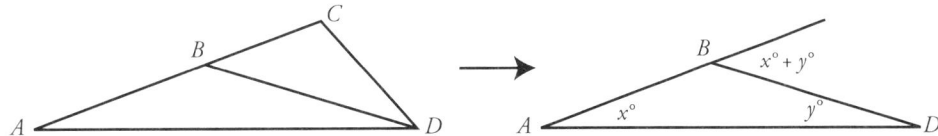

Check Your Skills

4. If $c + d = 200$, what is $a + b$?

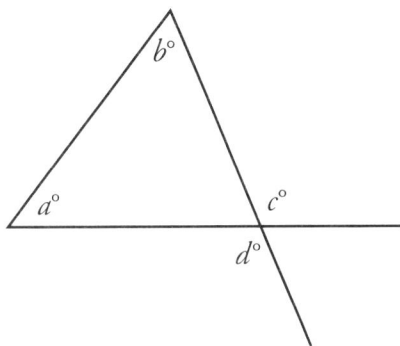

Answers can be found on page 659.

Parallel Lines

The GRE makes frequent use of diagrams that include parallel lines cut by a **transversal**. A transversal is a line that cuts across two (or more) other lines at two different points, as in the following diagram:

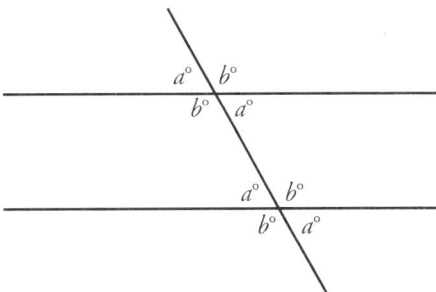

Eight angles are formed by this construction, but there are only two *different* angle measures (*a* and *b*). All the **acute** angles (less than 90°) in this diagram are equal. Likewise, all the **obtuse** angles (more than 90° but less than 180°) are equal. The acute angles are supplementary to the obtuse angles. Thus, $a + b = 180°$.

In shorthand: The four "small" angles are equal, the four "big" angles are equal, and any small angle plus any big angle equals 180°.

Unit Five: **Geometry**

When you see a third line intersecting two lines that you know to be parallel, fill in all the *a* (acute) and *b* (obtuse) angles, just as in the diagram here.

Sometimes the GRE disguises the parallel lines and the transversal so that they are not readily apparent, as in the diagram below, in which the top and bottom lines are parallel:

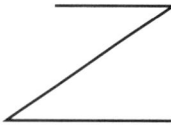

In these disguised cases, extend the lines so that you can see the parallel lines and the transversal. You might also mark the parallel lines with arrows:

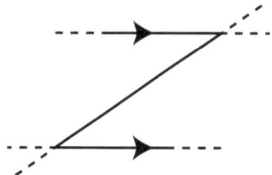

Check Your Skills

Refer to the following diagram for questions #5–6.

Lines *p* and *q* are parallel.

5. If $g = 120$, what is a?

6. If $g = 120$, what is $a + b + c$?

Answers can be found on page 659.

Chapter 24: **Lines and Angles**

Check Your Skills Answer Key

1. **6**

   Start either with the fact that U is the midpoint or with the specific given lengths. Both givens are restrictive. This explanation starts with the lengths between X, Y, and Z. There are two possible starting arrangements.

   Next, place U on each number line.

   On the right-hand number line, $\overline{UZ} = 1$, but the question stated that $\overline{UZ} > 2$, so discard that number line. Use the left-hand number line to answer the question: $\overline{UZ}$ must equal 6.

2. **30°**

   Because a and d are vertical angles, angle a is equal to angle d.

   Because a, b, and f add to form a straight line, $a + b + f = 180$. Since $b + f = 150$, it is the case that $a = 30$.

   Therefore, $d = 30$.

3. **140°**

   Because $x°$ and $20°$ are supplementary angles, $x = 180 - 20 = 160$. Because $y°$ and $20°$ are vertical angles, $y = 20$. So $x - y = 160 - 20 = 140$.

4. **100°**

   The angles c and d are vertical angles, so they are equal. Because they sum to 200, each must be 100. Additionally, $a + b = c$, because c is an exterior angle of the triangle shown, and a and b are the two non-adjacent interior angles. Thus, $a + b = c = 100$.

5. **120°**

   Both g and a are big angles, so $g = a = 120$.

6. **300°**

   Any small angle plus any big angle is 180, so $a + b = 180$. Because c and g are both "big" angles, $c = g$. So $a + b + c = 180 + 120 = 300$.

Unit Five: **Geometry**

Problem Set

Problems #1–4 refer to the following diagram, in which line AB is parallel to line CD. Note: Figures are not drawn to scale.

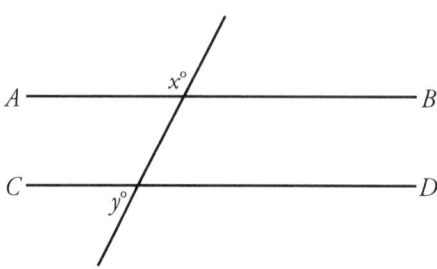

1. If $x - y = 10$, what is x?

2. If the ratio of x to y is 3 : 2, what is y?

3. If $x + (x + y) = 320$, what is x?

4. If $\dfrac{x}{x - y} = 2$, what is x?

Problems #5–8 refer to the following diagram.

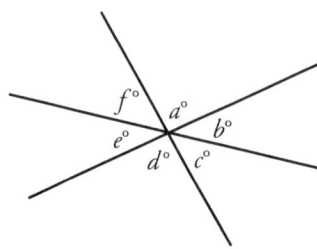

5. If $a = 95$, what is $b + d - e$?

6. If $c + f = 70$, and $d = 80$, what is b?

7. If a and b are **complementary angles** (they sum to 90°), name three other pairs of complementary angles.

8. If $e = 45$, what is the sum of all the other angles?

Chapter 24: **Lines and Angles**

Problems #9–12 refer to the following diagram, where line XY is parallel to line QU.

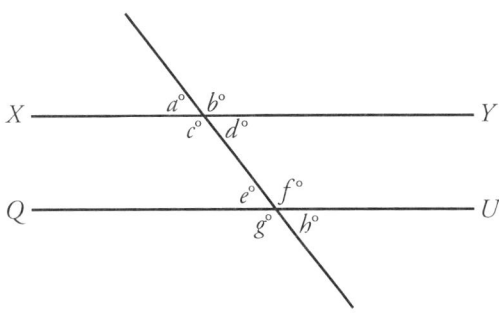

9. If $a + e = 150$, what is f?

10. If $a = y$, $g = 3y + 20$, and $f = 2x$, what is x?

11. If $g = 11y$, $a = 4x - y$, and $d = 5y + 2x - 20$, what is h?

12. If $b = 4x$, $e = x + 2y$, and $d = 3y + 8$, what is h?

Problems #13–15 refer to the following diagram.

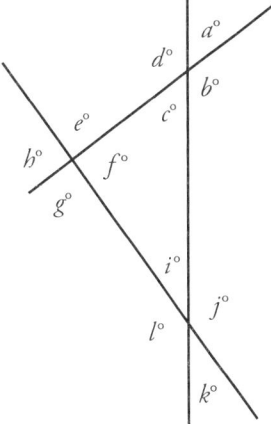

13. If $c + f = 140$, what is k?

14. If $f = 90$, what is $a + k$?

15. If $f + k = 150$, what is b?

661

Unit Five: **Geometry**

16.

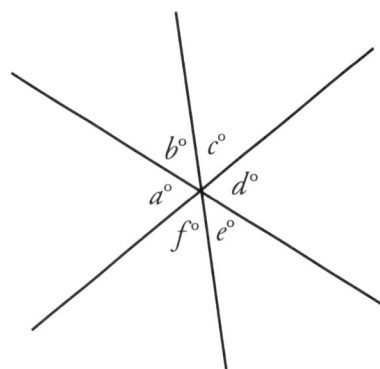

Quantity A	Quantity B
$a + f + b$	$c + d + e$

17.

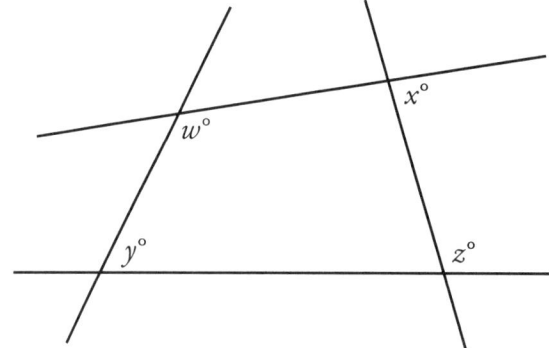

Quantity A	Quantity B
$w + y$	$x + z$

18.

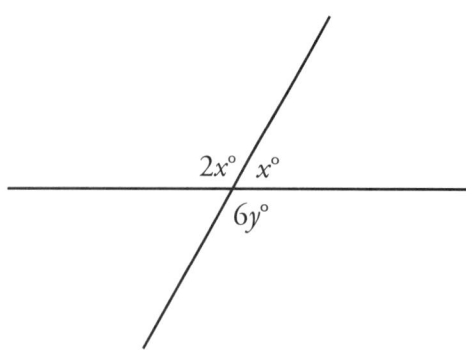

Quantity A	Quantity B
y	10

19. Points *A*, *B*, and *C* lie on a line. Point *D* is the midpoint of $\overline{AB}$, point *E* is the midpoint of $\overline{BC}$, $\overline{AB} = 4$, and $\overline{BC} = 10$. Which of the following could be the length of $\overline{AE}$?

    (A) 1
    (B) 2
    (C) 3
    (D) 4
    (E) 5

Unit Five: **Geometry**

Solutions

1. **95°**
   Any small angle and any big angle add up to 180, so $x + y = 180$. Use the information given to set up a system of two equations with two variables and add the equations to solve for x.

   $$x + y = 180$$
   $$x - y = 10$$
   $$\overline{}$$
   $$2x = 190$$
   $$x = 95$$

2. **72°**
   Any small angle and any big angle add up to 180, so $x + y = 180$. Since the ratio of $x : y$ is 3 : 2, use the unknown multiplier a to represent the actual values of x and y. Set $x = 3a$ and $y = 2a$.

   $$x + y = 180 = 2a + 3a$$
   $$180 = 5a$$
   $$36 = a$$

   Since $a = 36$, $y = 2a = 72$.

3. **140°**
   Use the fact that $x + y = 180$ to substitute into the given equation and solve for x.

   $$x + (x + y) = 320$$
   $$x + y = 180 \rightarrow \quad x + 180 = 320$$
   $$x = 140$$

4. **120°**
   First, simplify the given equation.

   $$\frac{x}{(x - y)} = 2$$
   $$x = 2(x - y)$$
   $$x = 2x - 2y$$
   $$0 = x - 2y$$

   Next, use the fact that $x + y = 180$ to set up a system of two equations with two variables. Isolate the unwanted variable, y, in one equation and substitute into the other.

   $$x + y = 180 \qquad 0 = x - 2y$$
   $$y = 180 - x \rightarrow \quad 0 = x - 2(180 - x)$$
   $$0 = x - 360 + 2x$$
   $$360 = 3x$$
   $$120 = x$$

5. **95°**
   Because a and d are vertical angles, they have the same measure: $a = d = 95$. Likewise, because b and e are vertical angles, they have the same measure: $b = e$. Therefore, $b - e = 0$, so $b + d - e = d = 95$.

Chapter 24: **Lines and Angles**

6. **65°**

    Because c and f are vertical angles, they have the same measure: $c + f = 70$, so $c = f = 35$. Next, b, c, and d form a straight line: $b + c + d = 180$. Substitute the known values of c and d to solve for b.

    $$b + 35 + 80 = 180$$
    $$b + 115 = 180$$
    $$b = 65$$

7. **b and d, a and e, d and e**

    If a is complementary to b, then d (which is equal to a, since they are vertical angles), is also complementary to b. Likewise, if a is complementary to b, then a is also complementary to e (which is equal to b, since they are vertical angles). Finally, d and e must be complementary, since $d = a$ and $e = b$. You do not need to know the term *complementary* for the GRE, but do be able to work with the concept (two angles adding up to 90°).

8. **315°**

    Since $e = 45$, the sum of all the other angles is $360 - 45 = 315$.

9. **105°**

    Since the lines are parallel, all of the small angles are equal and all of the big angles are equal. Both a and e are small angles and $a + e = 150$. Therefore, $a = e = 75$. Any small angle plus any big angle equals 180, so $75 + f = 180$, and $f = 105$.

10. **70°**

    Angles a and g are supplementary; their measures sum to 180. Use this fact to solve for y.

    $$a + g = 180$$
    $$y + 3y + 20 = 180$$
    $$4y = 160$$
    $$y = 40$$

    Angle f is equal to angle g, so its measure is also $3y + 20$.

    Therefore, $f = 3(40) + 20 = 140$. Finally, $f = 2x$, so $140 = 2x$ and, therefore, $x = 70$.

11. **70°**

    The question asks for h, which is one of the smaller angles. Angles a and d are both smaller angles as well, so solve for one of those. Angle a and angle g sum to 180.

    $$a + g = 180$$
    $$4x - y + 11y = 180$$
    $$4x + 10y = 180$$
    $$2x + 5y = 90$$

    Further, angle a and angle d are equal.

    $$a = d$$
    $$4x - y = 5y + 2x - 20$$
    $$2x = 6y - 20$$
    $$x = 3y - 10$$

665

Unit Five: **Geometry**

Substitute $x = 3y - 10$ into the first equation and solve for y.

$$2(3y - 10) + 5y = 90$$
$$6y - 20 + 5y = 90$$
$$11y = 110$$
$$y = 10$$

There are two paths forward from here. In order to solve directly for *a*, you need the values of both *x* and *y*, so you could solve for *x* next, then plug into the formula for *a*. Alternatively, use *y* alone to find the value of *g*. Since $g = 11y = 11(10)$, the value of *g* is 110. And since *g* is a big angle, the measure of a small angle is $180 - g = 180 - 110 = 70$.

12. **68°**

    Both *d* and *e* are small angles and *b* is a big angle. The question asks for *h*, which is a small angle.

    $$b + d = 180 \qquad d = e$$
    $$4x + 3y + 8 = 180 \qquad 3y + 8 = x + 2y$$
    $$4x + 3y = 172 \qquad y + 8 = x$$

    Substitute $x = y + 8$ into the other equation and solve for *y*.

    $$4(y + 8) + 3y = 172$$
    $$4y + 32 + 3y = 172$$
    $$7y = 140$$
    $$y = 20$$

    Glance at the original equations for *d* and *e*, both of which are small angles, like *h*. The equation for *e* requires both *x* and *y*, but the equation for *d* requires only *y*, so use that one to solve for the value of a small angle.

    $$d = 3y + 8$$
    $$d = 3(20) + 8$$
    $$d = 68$$

13. **40°**

    If $c + f = 140$, then $i = 40$, because there are 180° in a triangle. Because *k* is vertical to *i*, the value of *k* is also 40.

    Alternatively, if $c + f = 140$, then $l = 140$, since *l* is an exterior angle of the triangle and is therefore equal to the sum of the two remote interior angles. Because *k* is supplementary to *l*, the value of *k* is $180 - 140 = 40$.

14. **90°**

    Since $f = 90$, the other two angles in the triangle, *c* and *i*, sum to 90. The angles *a* and *k* are vertical angles to *c* and *i*, respectively, so angles *c* and *i* sum to 90 as well.

15. **150°**

    Angles *k* and *i* are vertical angles, so they are equal. Since $f + k = 150$, it's also the case that $f + i = 150$. Angle *b*, an exterior angle of the triangle, must be equal to the sum of the two remote interior angles, *f* and *i*. Therefore, $b = 150$.

16. **(C)**

    The angles measured by *a, f,* and *b* together form a straight line. So, $a + f + b$ must be 180. Likewise, $c + d + e$ must be 180, because the corresponding angles form a straight line. Therefore, the two quantities are equal.

    If you don't spot that shortcut, substitute each of the values in Quantity A for a corresponding value in Quantity B: $a = d$, $c = f$, and $b = e$, in each case because the equal angles are vertical angles.

Quantity A	Quantity B
$a + f + b = d + c + e$	$c + d + e$

    The correct answer is (C): The two quantities are always equal.

17. **(C)**

    Label the remaining two interior angles of the quadrilateral according to the rules for supplementary angles.

    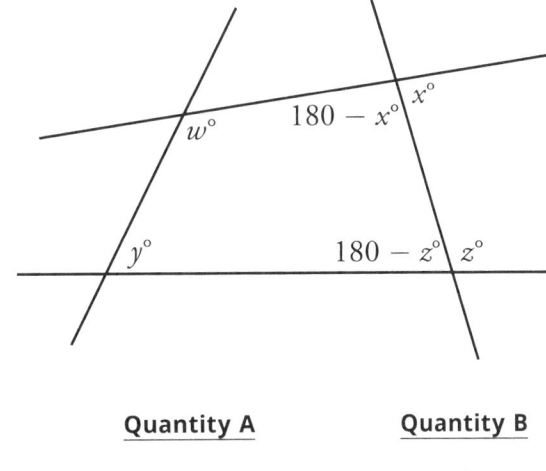

Quantity A	Quantity B
$w + y$	$x + z$

    There are several relationships that can be described based on the diagram. For instance, the sum of the four internal angles of the quadrilateral is 360.

    $$w + y + (180 - x) + (180 - z) = 360$$
    $$w + y - x - z = 0$$
    $$w + y = x + z$$

    The correct answer is (C): The two quantities are always equal.

Unit Five: **Geometry**

18. **(A)**
    First solve for *x*. The two angles *x* and 2*x* add up to 180.

    $$x + 2x = 180$$
    $$3x = 180$$
    $$x = 60$$

    Next, 2*x* = 6*y*, because 2*x* and 6*y* are vertical angles. Plug in 60 for *x* and solve for *y*.

    $$2(60) = 6y$$
    $$120 = 6y$$
    $$20 = y$$

Quantity A	Quantity B
y = 20	10

    The correct answer is (A): Quantity A is greater.

19. **(A)** 1
    The "could be" language in the question signals that there are multiple possible arrangements for the points on the number line. Because $\overline{BC}$ is longer than $\overline{AB}$, it might be the case that *A* is to one side of *B* and *C* or that *A* is between *B* and *C*.

    Using the information about the midpoints (*D* and *E*) and the lengths of the line segments, fill in all of the remaining information for the two number lines.

    The diagrams show that $\overline{AE}$ has two possible lengths, 1 and 9, however, only 1 appears in the answer choices, so (A) is the correct answer.

CHAPTER 25

The Coordinate Plane

In This Chapter:

- Creating the Coordinate Plane
- Knowing Just One Coordinate
- Knowing Ranges
- Reading a Graph
- Plotting a Relationship
- Lines in the Plane
- The Intercepts of a Line
- The Intersection of Two Lines
- The Distance Between Two Points
- Check Your Skills Answer Key
- Problem Set
- Solutions

CHAPTER 25 The Coordinate Plane

The coordinate plane is used to describe points and lines. In this chapter, you'll learn how to solve a variety of coordinate-plane problems, including identifying and plotting points, differentiating kinds of lines, finding distances, and manipulating equations of lines.

Creating the Coordinate Plane

The coordinate plane is a more complex version of the number line introduced in Chapter 1: Number Lines:

The number line is a measuring stick that goes as far as you want in two directions. The number line links a position with a number:

Position	Number	Number Line
Two units right of 0	2	
One and a half units left of 0	−1.5	

A number line represents both positive and negative numbers, because it can indicate positions both left and right of 0.

A number represented on a number line is called a **point**, which is just a dot:

→ The point is at −2.

→ The point is at 0.

This works even if you have only partial information about a point. If you're told *something* about where the point is, you can say *something* about the number, and vice versa.

Unit Five: **Geometry**

For instance, if you're told that the number is positive, then you know that the point lies somewhere to the right of 0 on the number line:

The number is positive.
In other words, the number is greater than (>) 0.

Therefore,

The open circle indicates that 0 is not included in the range of possible values.

This also works in reverse. If you see a range of potential positions on a number line, you can indicate the range for the number:

 Therefore, the number is less than (<) 0.

What if you want to be able to locate a point that's not on a straight line, but on a page?

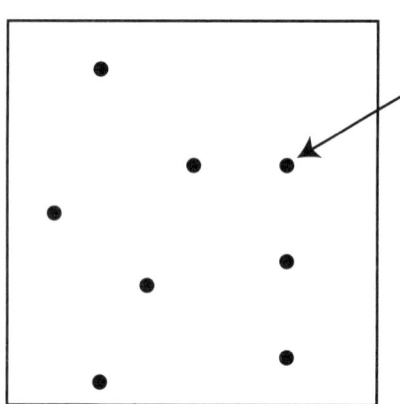

The point you want.

Now one number line won't be enough to tell you where the point is.

One number line can help to determine how far to the right or left of 0 the point is:

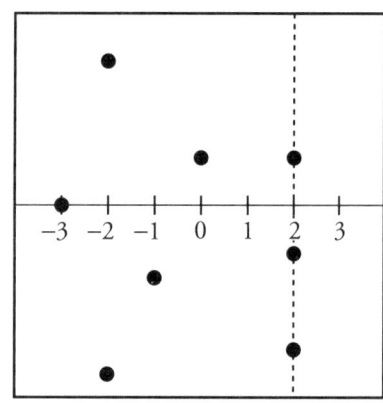

The point is 2 units to the right of 0.

But all three points that touch the dotted line are 2 units to the right of 0. There's not enough information to determine the unique location of each point.

Chapter 25: **The Coordinate Plane**

A vertical number line can address the vertical dimension:

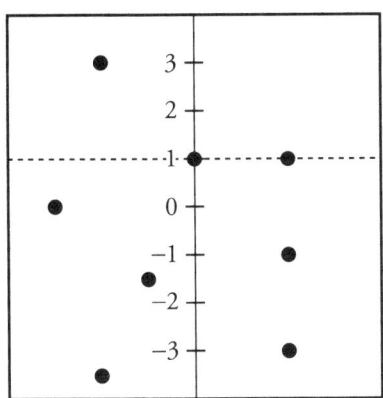

The point is 1 unit above 0.

A **coordinate plane** combines two number lines, one horizontal and one vertical:

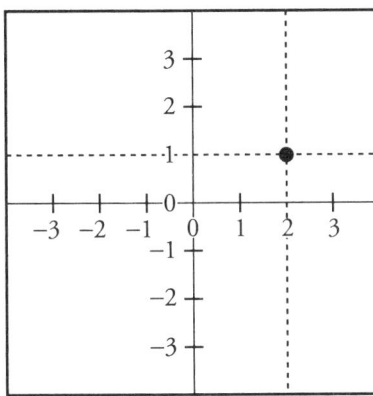

The point is 2 units to the right of 0.

AND

The point is 1 unit above 0.

There is now a unique description of the point's position. There is only one point on this plane that is *both* 2 units to the right of 0 *and* 1 unit above 0.

Given the location of the point, you can draw it yourself on the coordinate plane. In this example, the point is negative in both dimensions:

The point is 3 units to the left of 0.

AND

The point is 2 units below 0.

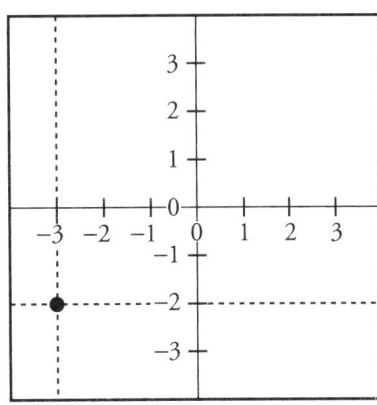

673

Unit Five: **Geometry**

The point could also be positive in one dimension and negative in the other:

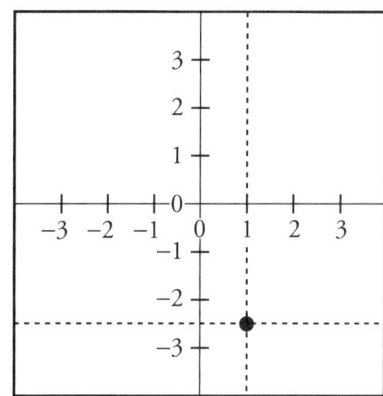

The point is 1 unit to the right of 0.
AND
The point is 2.5 units below 0.

The *x*-coordinate is always the left-right number:

Numbers to the right of 0 are positive.
Numbers to the left of 0 are negative.

This number line is the *x*-axis.

The *y*-coordinate is the up-down number:

Numbers above 0 are positive.
Numbers below 0 are negative.

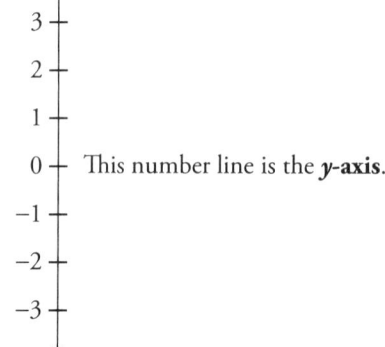

This number line is the *y*-axis.

Here is the technical description of a point in a coordinate plane:

The *x*-coordinate of the point is 1 and the *y*-coordinate of the point is 0.

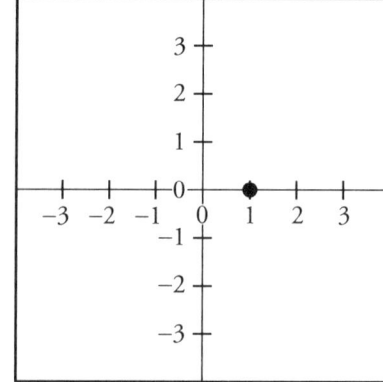

Chapter 25: **The Coordinate Plane**

You can condense this to $x = 1$ and $y = 0$. In fact, you can go even further: The point is at (1, 0). This **ordered pair** always has the same basic layout. The first number in the parentheses is the *x*-coordinate, and the second number is the *y*-coordinate: (*x*, *y*). For example:

The point is at $(-3, -1)$.

OR

The point has an *x*-coordinate of -3 and a *y*-coordinate of -1.

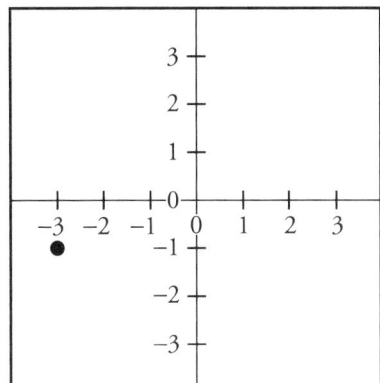

To help remember the order of an ordered pair: *x* always comes before *y* in the alphabet, and *x* always comes before *y* in the ordered pair.

By the way, the pair (0, 0) has a special name: It's called the **origin**. The GRE may use this word rather than tell you explicitly that a point is at (0, 0). If a question says that a line passes through the origin, it's telling you that (0, 0) is a point on this line.

The coordinate plane allows you to determine the unique position of any point on a **plane** (essentially, a flat sheet of paper).

And in case you were ever curious about what one-dimensional and two- dimensional mean, now you know. A line is one-dimensional, because you only need *one* number to identify a point's location. A plane is two-dimensional, because you need *two* numbers to identify a point's location.

Check Your Skills

1. Draw a coordinate plane and plot the following points:

    1. (3, 1)   2. (−2, 3.5)   3. (0, −4.5)   4. (1, 0)

2. Match each point on the coordinate plane with its coordinates.

    1. (2, −1)   2. (−1.5, −3)   3. (−1, 2)   4. (3, 2)   5. (2, 3)

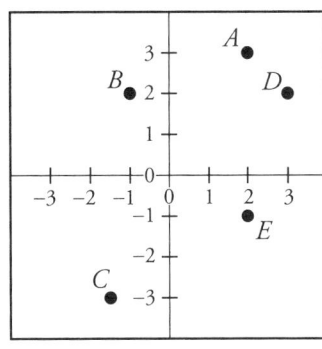

Answers can be found on page 695.

675

Unit Five: **Geometry**

Knowing Just One Coordinate

You need to know both the *x*-coordinate and the *y*-coordinate to plot a point exactly on the coordinate plane. If you know only one coordinate, you can't tell precisely where the point is, but you can narrow down the possibilities.

For example, if you know the point is 4 units to the right of 0:

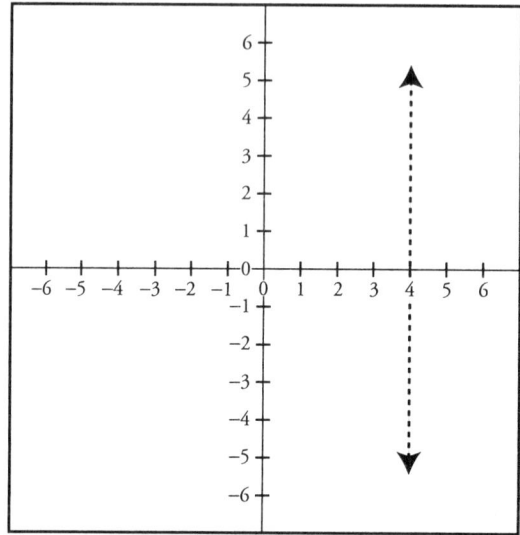

Any point along the vertical dotted line is 4 units to the right of 0. In other words, every point on the dotted line has an *x*-coordinate of 4. You could shorten that and say $x = 4$. The *y*-coordinate could be any number. All the points along the dotted line have different *y*-coordinates but the same *x*-coordinate, which equals 4.

So, if you know that $x = 4$, then your point can be anywhere along a vertical line that crosses the *x*-axis at (4, 0).

Try another one. If you know that $x = -3$:

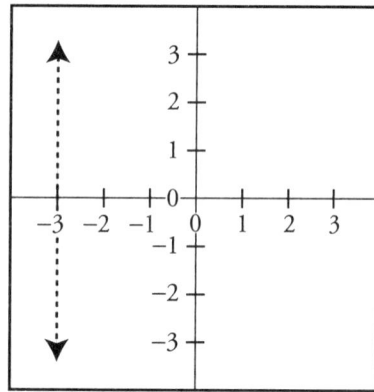

Every point on the dotted line has an *x*-coordinate of -3. Points on the dotted line include $(-3, 1)$, $(-3, -7)$, $(-3, 100)$, and so on.

Chapter 25: **The Coordinate Plane**

What if you're given the *y*-coordinate of a number but not the *x*-coordinate? For example, say $y = -2$:

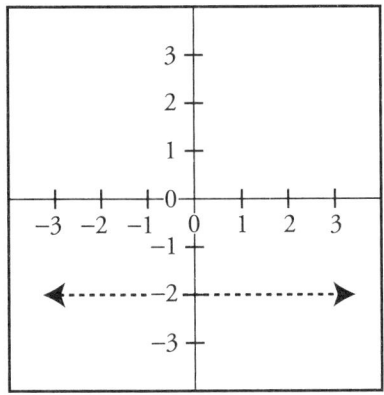

Every point 2 units below 0 falls along a horizontal line. The *x*-coordinate could be any number. All the points along the horizontal dotted line have different *x*-coordinates but the same *y*-coordinate, which equals -2. For instance, $(-3, -2)$, $(-2, -2)$, and $(50, -2)$ are all on the line.

Try another example. If you know that $y = 1$:

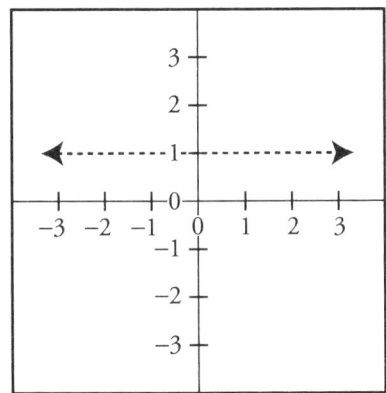

Every point on the dotted line has a *y*-coordinate of 1.

In general, if you know the *x*-coordinate of a point and not the *y*-coordinate, then you can say the point lies somewhere along the *vertical* line that corresponds to the *x*-coordinate.

And if you know the *y*-coordinate but not the *x*-coordinate, then you know the point lies somewhere along the *horizontal* line that corresponds to that *y*-coordinate.

Check Your Skills

> Draw a coordinate plane and plot the following lines.

3. $x = 6$

4. $y = -2$

5. $x = 0$

Answers can be found on pages 695–696.

Unit Five: **Geometry**

Knowing Ranges

What happens if all you know is a range of possible values for x? For example, what if all you know is that $x > 0$? To answer that question, return to the number line for a moment. If $x > 0$, then the target is anywhere to the right of 0:

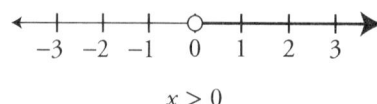

$x > 0$

Now look at the coordinate plane. All you know is that x is greater than 0. And you don't know *anything* about y, which could be any number.

Shade in the part of the coordinate plane that corresponds to this information:

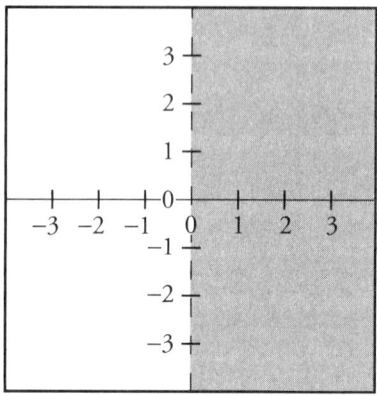

Every point in the shaded region has an x-coordinate greater than 0. The dashed line indicates that x cannot equal 0 itself.

Now say that all you know is $y < 0$. The x-coordinate can be anything. Shade in the bottom half of the coordinate plane:

Then you know . . .

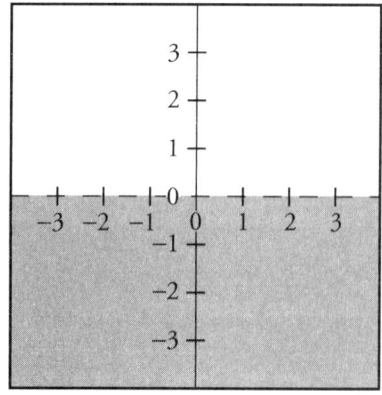

Every point in the shaded region has a y-coordinate less than 0. The dashed line indicates that y cannot equal 0 itself.

678

Finally, if you know information about both *x* and *y*, then you can narrow down the shaded region. For example, if $x > 0$ and $y < 0$:

The only place where *x* is greater than 0 and *y* is less than 0 is in the bottom right quarter, or **quadrant**, of the plane. So, the point lies somewhere in the bottom-right quadrant of the coordinate plane.

There are four quadrants in a coordinate plate and each one corresponds to a different combination of signs of *x* and *y*. The quadrants are always numbered I through IV, as shown in the figure below, starting with the top right quadrant and moving counterclockwise:

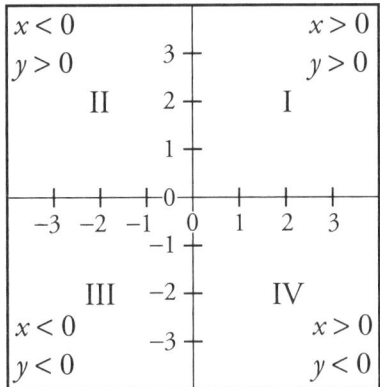

In quadrant I, both *x* and *y* are positive. In quadrant II, *x* is negative and *y* is positive. In quadrant III, both *x* and *y* are negative. In quadrant IV, *x* is negative and *y* is positive.

Check Your Skills

6. In which quadrant do each of the following points lie?

    1. (1, −2)
    2. (−4.6, 7)
    3. (−1, −2.5)
    4. (3, 3)

7. Which quadrant or quadrants are indicated by the following?

    1. $x < 0, y > 0$
    2. $x < 0, y < 0$
    3. $y > 0$
    4. $x < 0$

Answers can be found on page 696.

Unit Five: **Geometry**

Reading a Graph

If you see a point on a coordinate plane, you can read off its coordinates as follows. To find an *x*-coordinate, drop an imaginary line to the *x*-axis and read off the number. For example:

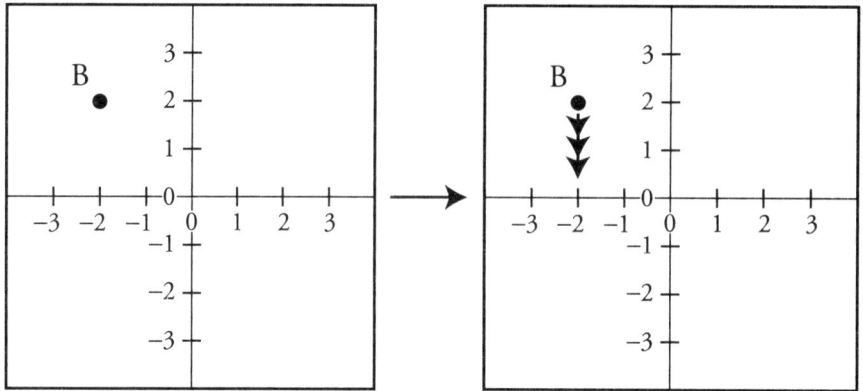

The line hits the *x*-axis at −2, so the *x*-coordinate of the point is −2. To find the *y*-coordinate, employ a similar technique, but this time draw a horizontal line to the *y*-axis:

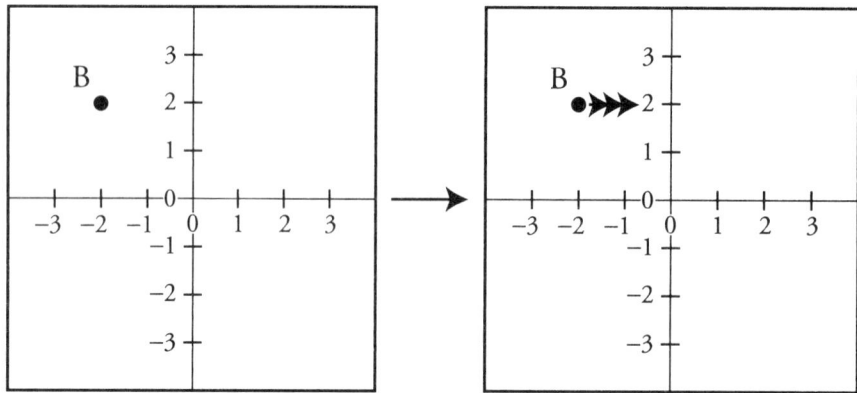

The line touches the *y*-axis at 2, so the *y*-coordinate of the point is 2. Thus, the coordinates of point B are (−2, 2).

Try this problem:

On the line shown, what is the *y*-coordinate of the point that has an *x*-coordinate of −4 ?

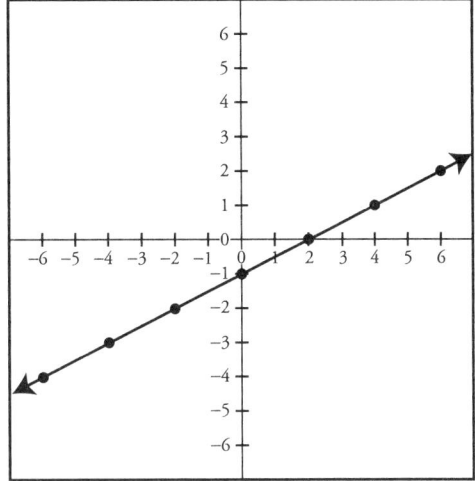

To find the point that has an *x*-coordinate of −4, find the tick mark −4 on the *x*-axis. Then, find the point that lies directly above or below that tick mark. Finally, draw a horizontal line from that point to the *y*–axis to determine the *y*-coordinate of that point:

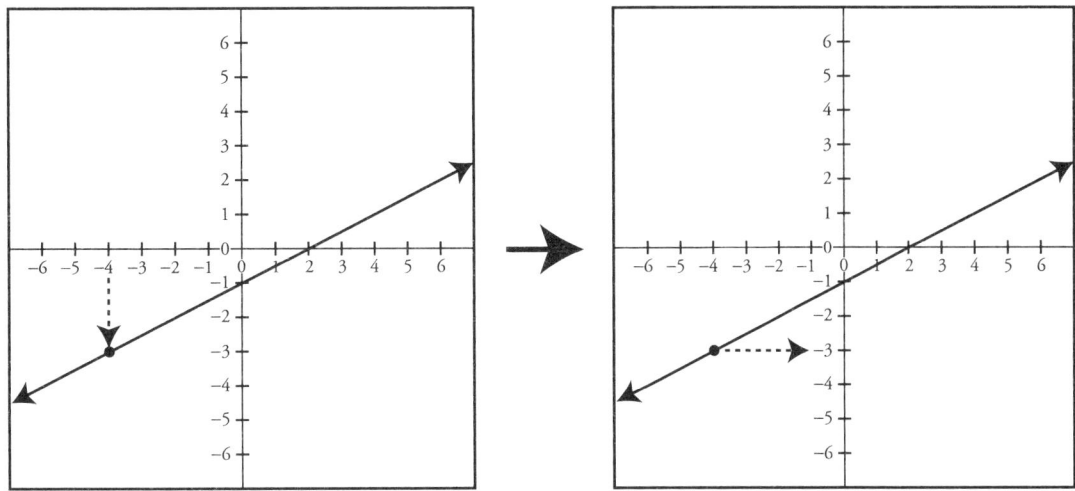

The point on the line that has an *x*-coordinate of −4 has a *y*-coordinate of −3. The ordered pair is (−4, −3).

This method of locating points applies equally well to any shape or curve you may encounter on a coordinate plane. For example:

On the curve shown, what is the value of y when $x = 2$?

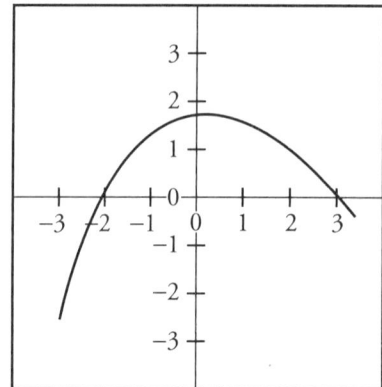

It doesn't matter that the line is curved. Draw a line from the tick mark 2 on the x-axis to the curve, and then draw a line to the y-axis:

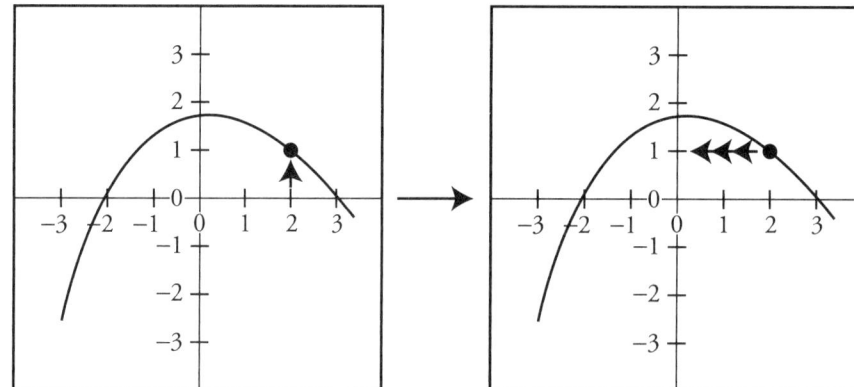

On the curve shown, the point that has an x-coordinate of 2 has a y-coordinate of 1. The ordered pair is (2, 1).

The GRE may mathematically define lines or curves, allowing for more precision in determining where a point falls. Later in this chapter, you'll learn how to work with the mathematical definitions.

Check Your Skills

8. On the following graph, what is the *y*-coordinate of the point on the line that has an *x*-coordinate of –3 ?

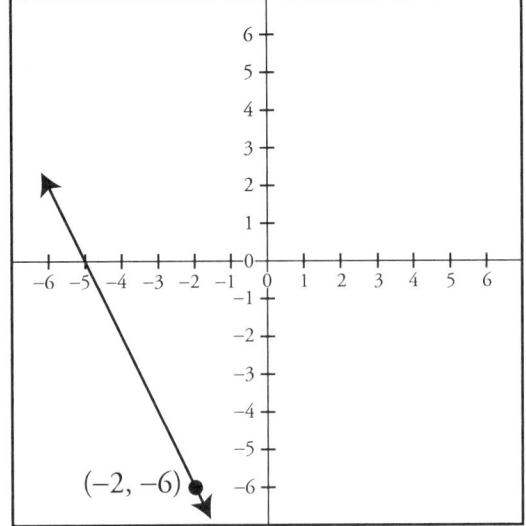

Answers can be found on page 697.

Plotting a Relationship

The most frequent use of the coordinate plane is to display a relationship between *x* and *y*.

As an equation, this sort of relationship looks like this:

$y =$ some expression involving x

Examples:
$y = 2x + 1$
$y = x^2 - 3x + 2$
$y = \dfrac{x}{x + 2}$

Another way of saying this is "*y* in terms of *x*."

If you plug a number for *x* into any of these equations, you can calculate a value for *y*.

Take $y = 2x + 1$. You can generate a set of values for *y* by plugging in various values of *x*. Start by making a table:

x	$y = 2x + 1$
–1	$y = 2(-1) + 1 = -1$
0	$y = 2(0) + 1 = 1$
1	$y = 2(1) + 1 = 3$
2	$y = 2(2) + 1 = 5$

Unit Five: Geometry

When x equals 0, the value of y is 1. These two values form the ordered pair (0, 1). You express this connection by plotting the point (0, 1) on the coordinate plane. Similarly, you can plot all the other points from the table:

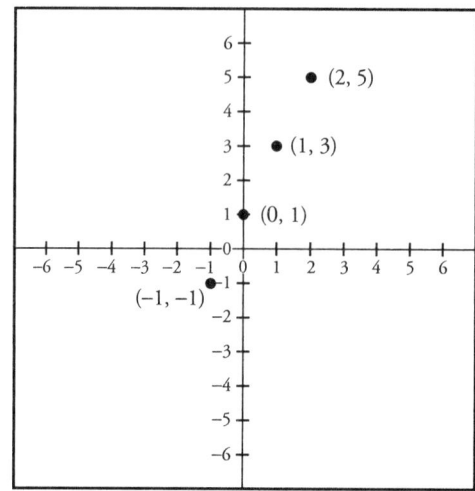

These four points lie on a straight line. In fact, any point that you can generate using the relationship $y = 2x + 1$ will also lie on the same line:

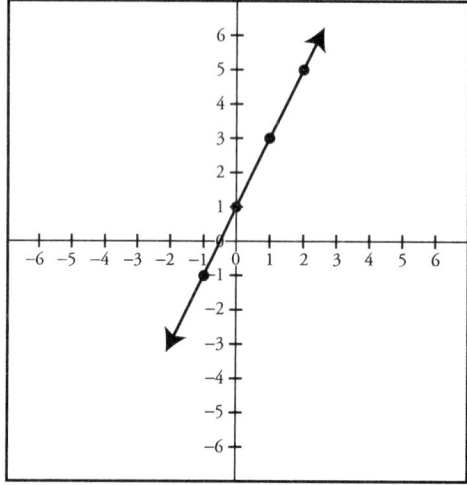

This line is the graphical representation of $y = 2x + 1$. Each point that falls on this line will, when plugged into the equation, make this equation true.

So, now you can talk about equations in visual terms. In fact, that's what lines and curves on the coordinate plane are—they visually represent all the (x, y) pairs that make an equation true. For example:

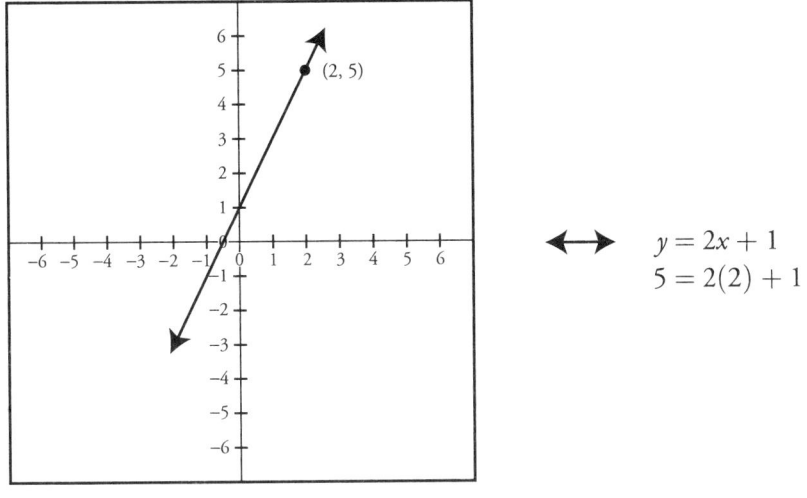

The point (2, 5) lies on the line $y = 2x + 1$. ⟷ If you plug 2 for x into the equation, you get 5 for y.

All of the points, or ordered pairs, that lie on this line will make the equation true. Plugging a point that does not lie on this line into the equation will result in a false outcome. For example, does the point (3, 1) lie on this line?

$$y = 2x + 1$$
$$1 = 2(3) + 1$$
$$1 = 5 + 1$$
$$1 = 6 \quad \text{FALSE}$$

Because the outcome is false, the point (3, 1) does not fall on this line.

You can even write points in terms of variables:

$y = 2x + 1$
$b = 2(a) + 1$

The point (a, b) lies on the line $y = 2x + 1$. ⟷ If you plug a for x into the equation, you get b for y.

Check Your Skills

9. True or False? The point (9, 21) is on the line $y = 2x + 1$.

10. True or False? The point (4, 14) is on the curve $y = x^2 - 2$.

Answers can be found on page 697.

Lines in the Plane

The relationship $y = 2x + 1$ forms a line. You can actually generalize this relationship. *Any* relationship of the following form represents a line:

$$y = mx + b$$

Here are some examples of equations that form straight lines, as well as equations that do not form straight lines:

Lines, aka linear equations	Not Lines
$y = 3x - 2$	$y = x^2$
$y + x = 4 \rightarrow y = -x + 4$	$y = \frac{1}{x}$

If the equation you are given doesn't initially appear to match $y = mx + b$ form, consider whether the equation can be rearranged to the proper form, as in the second example in the above table. If it can be rearranged to the proper form, then it is still a linear equation.

Chapter 25: **The Coordinate Plane**

The form $y = mx + b$ is called the **slope-intercept** form of the equation of a line. Here are the parts of the slope-intercept form:

		Example:
	$y = mx + b$	$y = 2x + 1$
The coordinate pair:	x and y (x, y)	$\boldsymbol{y} = 2\boldsymbol{x} + 1$
The slope:	m	$y = \boldsymbol{2}x + 1$
The y-intercept:	b	$y = 2x + \boldsymbol{1}$

The numbers m and b have special meanings when you are dealing with linear equations. First, m is the **slope**. The slope indicates how steep the line is and whether the line is rising or falling:

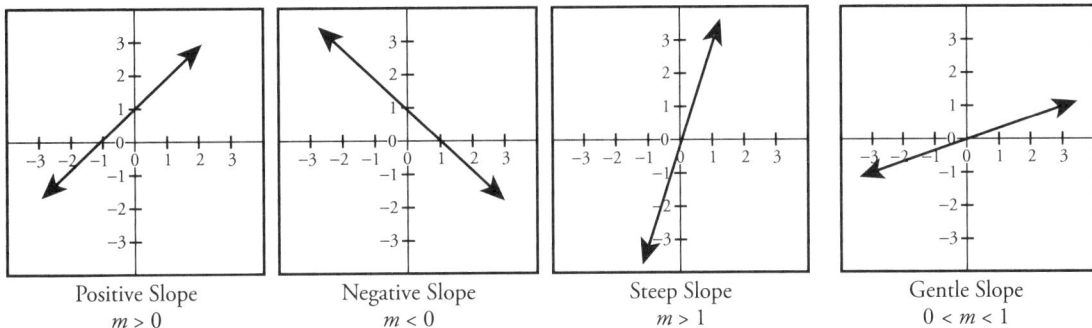

Positive Slope
$m > 0$

Negative Slope
$m < 0$

Steep Slope
$m > 1$

Gentle Slope
$0 < m < 1$

Next, b is the **y-intercept**. The y-intercept indicates where the line crosses the y-axis and is always where $x = 0$. It can always be written as $(0, y)$, where y is the point at which the line crosses the y-axis. In the left-hand graph, the y-intercept is 2 and in the right-hand graph, the y-intercept is -1.

 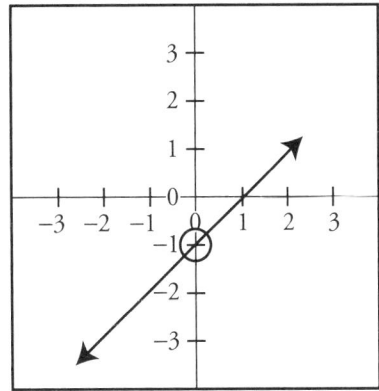

Any line or curve crosses the y-axis when $x = 0$. If you know the equation and are asked to find the y-intercept, substitute $x = 0$ into the equation and solve for y:

$$y = 3x - 2$$
$$y = 3(0) - 2$$
$$y = -2$$

Substituting 0 for x has the effect of erasing the entire mx term in the equation, leaving only b on the right-hand side. Therefore, b is the y-intercept, or the value when $x = 0$.

Unit Five: **Geometry**

Check Your Skills

> Find the slope and *y*-intercept of the following lines.

11. $y = 3x + 4$

12. $2y = 5x - 12$

Answers can be found on page 697.

You can use *m* and *b* to sketch the line on a coordinate plane. For example:

$$y = \frac{1}{2}x - 2$$

Begin with the *y*-intercept, which in this case is −2. Place a dot where −2 crosses the *y*-axis:

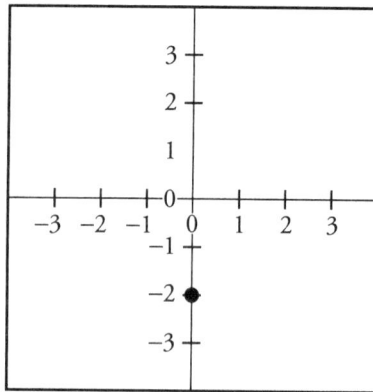

Next, use the slope to finish drawing your line. In this equation, *m* is $\frac{1}{2}$. Here's what the parts of the fraction indicate about the slope:

$$\frac{1}{2} \begin{array}{l} \rightarrow \\ \rightarrow \end{array} \frac{\text{Numerator}}{\text{Denominator}} \begin{array}{l} \rightarrow \\ \rightarrow \end{array} \frac{\text{Rise}}{\text{Run}} \begin{array}{l} \rightarrow \\ \rightarrow \end{array} \frac{\text{Change in } y}{\text{Change in } x}$$

The numerator indicates how many units to move in the *y* direction—in other words, how far up or down to move. The denominator indicates how many units to move in the *x* direction—in other words, how far left or right to move. For this particular equation, the slope is positive $\frac{1}{2}$, so move up 1 unit and right 2 units:

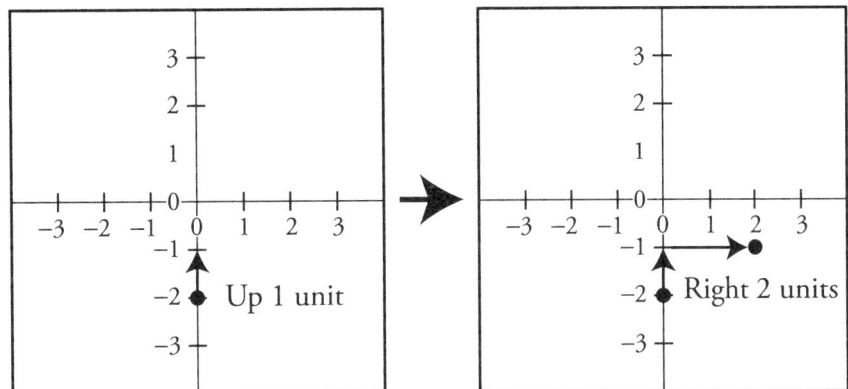

Draw a second point at this new spot, which in this problem is at the point $(2, -1)$. The point $(2, -1)$ also lies on the line of the equation $y = \frac{1}{2}x - 2$. If you plug the point into the equation, the outcome will be true:

$$y = \frac{1}{2}x - 2$$
$$-1 = \frac{1}{2}(2) - 2$$
$$-1 = -1 \quad \text{TRUE}$$

If, from the point $(2, -1)$, you go up another 1 unit and right another 2 units, you will end up with another point that appears on the line. You could keep doing this indefinitely, but don't bother. As soon as you have two points, connect the dots and you have a line:

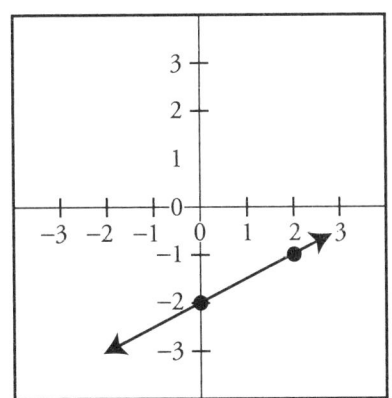

$y = \frac{1}{2}x - 2$

Unit Five: **Geometry**

Try another one. Graph the equation $y = \left(-\frac{3}{2}\right)x + 4$.

Start with the *y*-intercept. Since $b = 4$, the line crosses the *y*-axis at the point (0, 4):

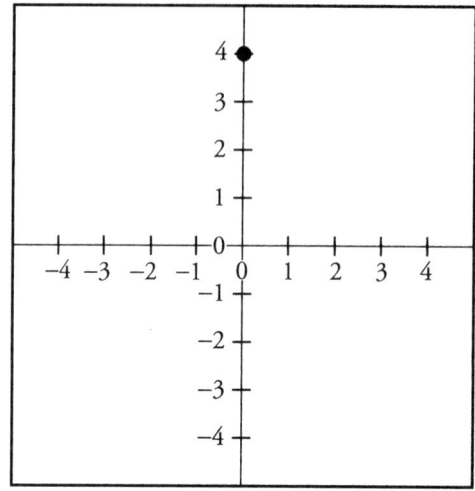

Use the slope to find a second point. This time, the slope is $-\frac{3}{2}$.

Positive slopes go up and to the right, but negative slopes go *down* and still to the right. Since the "rise" is negative, it's really a fall. On the coordinate plane, go *down* 3 units and right 2 units:

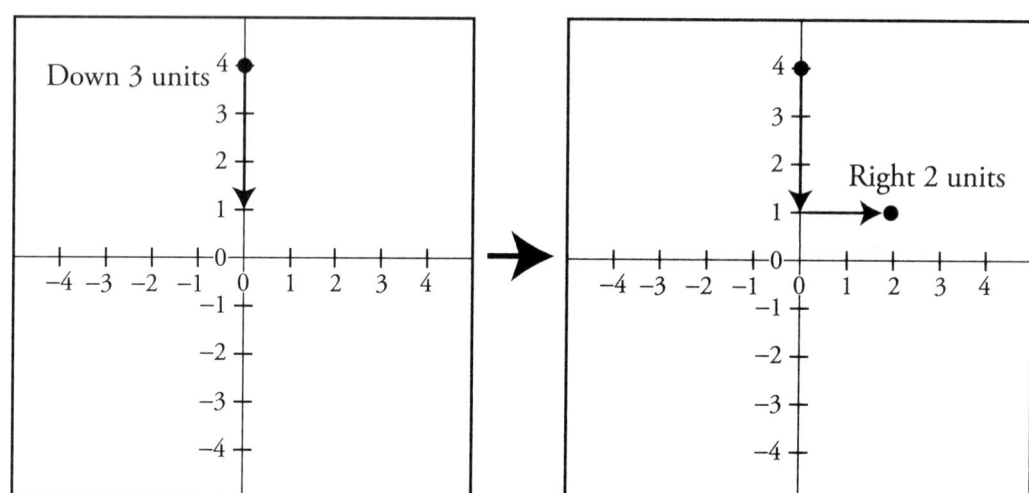

The new point (2, 1) also falls on the line. Now that you have two points, draw the line:

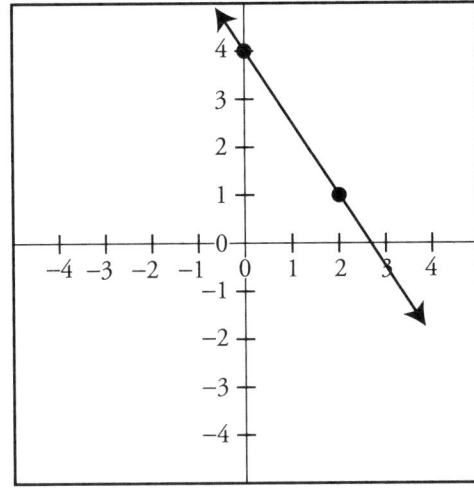

$y = \left(-\frac{3}{2}\right)x + 4$

In both of these examples, the slope was a fraction. If you're given an integer slope, rewrite it as a fraction by putting it over a denominator of 1. For example, write the slope $m = 5$ as $\frac{5}{1}$.

When given two points (x_1, y_1) and (x_2, y_2) on a line, you can also calculate the slope algebraically, using this equation:

$$\text{slope} = \frac{\text{rise}}{\text{run}} = \frac{y_2 - y_1}{(x_2 - x_1)}$$

If you're also given a diagram, however, or you need to sketch out the coordinate plane yourself, it's usually better to just count it out on the coordinate plane. It's very easy to make a mistake with the algebraic approach and it often takes longer to solve.

Check Your Skills

13. Draw a coordinate plane and graph the line $y = 2x - 4$. Identify the slope and the y-intercept.

Answers can be found on page 698.

Unit Five: **Geometry**

The Intercepts of a Line

There are two **intercepts** in a coordinate plane: the *y*-intercept, where the line crosses the *y*-axis, and the *x*-**intercept**, where the line crosses the *x*-axis.

The *x*-intercept is expressed using the ordered pair (*x*, 0), where *x* is the point where the line intersects the *x*-axis. The *x*-intercept is the point on the line at which *y* = 0. In this diagram, the *x*-intercept is −4, as expressed by the ordered pair (−4, 0):

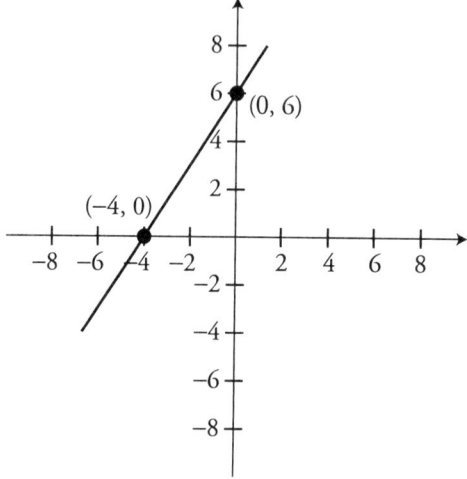

As discussed in the prior section of this chapter, the *y*-intercept is expressed using the ordered pair (0, *y*), where *y* is the point at which the line intersects the *y*-axis. The *y*-intercept is the point on the line at which *x* = 0. In this diagram, the *y*-intercept is 6, as expressed by the ordered pair (0, 6).

You may be given an equation and asked to find either the *x*- or *y*-intercept (or both!). To find the *x*-intercept, plug in 0 for *y*. To find the *y*-intercept, plug in 0 for *x*.

Check Your Skills

14. What are the *x*- and *y*-intercepts of the equation $x - 2y = 8$?

Answers can be found on page 698.

The Intersection of Two Lines

If a point (*x*, *y*) lies on a line, then those values of *x* and *y* satisfy the equation or make the equation true. For instance, the point (3, 2) lies on the line defined by the equation $y = 4x - 10$, because the equation is true when you plug in *x* = 3 and *y* = 2:

$$y = 4x - 10$$
$$2 = 4(3) - 10$$
$$2 = 12 - 10$$
$$2 = 2 \quad \text{TRUE}$$

On the other hand, the point (7, 5) does *not* lie on that line, because the equation is false when you plug in $x = 7$ and $y = 5$:

$$y = 4x - 10$$
$$5 = 4(7) - 10$$
$$5 = 28 - 10$$
$$5 = 18 \quad \text{FALSE}$$

When *two* lines intersect in the coordinate plane, then at the point of intersection, *both* equations representing the lines are true. That is, the pair of numbers (x, y) that represents the point of intersection solves *both* equations.

Finding this point of intersection is equivalent to solving a system of two linear equations. Often, solving via algebra is more efficient than trying to graph the two lines. For example:

At what point does the line represented by $y = 4x - 10$ intersect the line represented by $2x + 3y = 26$?

Because $y = 4x - 10$, replace y in the second equation with $4x - 10$ and solve for x:

$$2x + 3y = 26$$
$$2x + 3(4x - 10) = 26$$
$$2x + 12x - 30 = 26$$
$$14x = 56$$
$$x = 4$$

Now solve for y. Use whichever equation seems easier to you:

$$y = 4x - 10$$
$$y = 4(4) - 10$$
$$y = 6$$

Therefore, the point of intersection of the two lines is (4, 6).

If two lines in a plane do *not* intersect, then the lines are parallel. In this case, there is *no* pair of numbers (x, y) that satisfies both equations at the same time.

Two linear equations can represent two lines that intersect at a single point, or they can represent parallel lines that never intersect. There is one other possibility: The two equations might represent the exact same line. In this case, infinitely many points (x, y) along the line satisfy the two equations. For example:

$$y = x + 3 \qquad 2y = 2x + 6$$

The second equation is just the first equation multiplied by 2. In other words, these are the exact same equation, so they represent the exact same line and have infinitely many points in common.

Unit Five: **Geometry**

The Distance Between Two Points

The distance between any two points in the coordinate plane can be calculated by using the Pythagorean theorem. For example:

What is the distance between the points (1, 3) and (7, −5)?

First, draw a right triangle connecting the points:

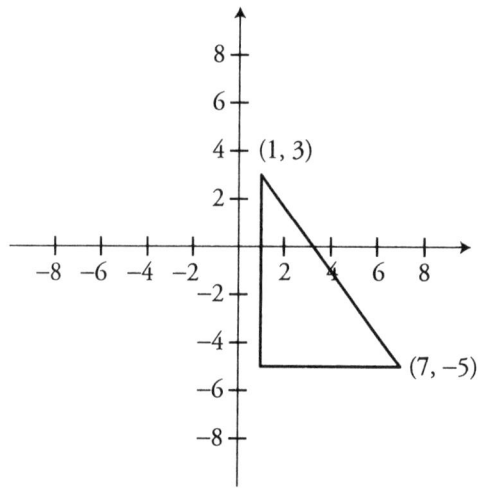

Second, find the lengths of the two legs of the triangle by calculating the rise and the run:

The *y*-coordinate changes from 3 to −5, a vertical difference of 8. This value corresponds to the vertical leg of the triangle.

The *x*-coordinate changes from 1 to 7, a horizontal difference of 6. This value corresponds to the horizontal leg of the triangle.

Third, use the Pythagorean theorem (or recognize the triple!) to find the length of the diagonal, which is the distance between the points:

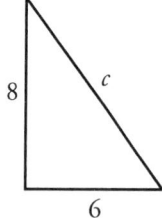

This is a 6–8–10 triple.

$$6^2 + 8^2 = c^2$$
$$c = 10 \qquad 36 + 64 = c^2$$
$$100 = c^2$$
$$10 = c$$

The distance between the two points is 10 units.

Check Your Skills

15. What is the distance between (−2, −4) and (3, 8)?

Answers can be found on page 699.

Check Your Skills Answer Key

1.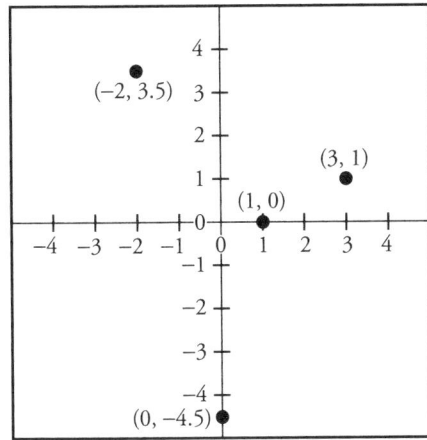

2. 1. $(2, -1)$: **E**
   2. $(-1.5, -3)$: **C**
   3. $(-1, 2)$: **B**
   4. $(3, 2)$: **D**
   5. $(2, 3)$: **A**

3.

Unit Five: **Geometry**

4. $y = -2$

5. 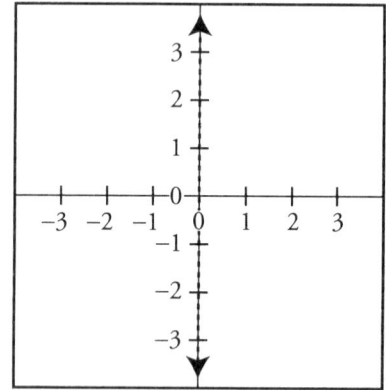 $x = 0$ is equivalent to the y-axis.

6. You can draw a coordinate plane but you don't have to. If you have the dimensions of each quadrant memorized, use those to answer.

   1. $(1, -2)$ is in Quadrant IV
   2. $(-4.6, 7)$ is in Quadrant II
   3. $(-1, -2.5)$ is in Quadrant III
   4. $(3, 3)$ is in Quadrant I

7. 1. $x < 0, y > 0$ indicates Quadrant II
   2. $x < 0, y < 0$ indicates Quadrant III
   3. $y > 0$ indicates Quadrants I and II
   4. $x < 0$ indicates Quadrants II and III

Chapter 25: **The Coordinate Plane**

8. **−4**

   From $x = -3$, draw a vertical line down to find the y-coordinate:

   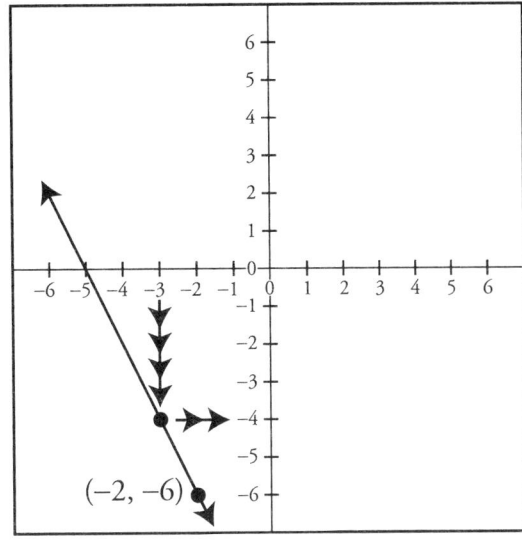

9. **False**

   If (9, 21) does fall on the line $y = 2x + 1$, then plugging the point into the equation will result in a true outcome. Plug the point (9, 21) into the equation to see what happens.

   $$y = 2x + 1$$
   $$21 = 2(9) + 1$$
   $$21 = 18 + 1$$
   $$21 = 19 \quad \text{FALSE}$$

   The outcome is false, so point (9, 21) does not fall on this line.

10. **True**

    If (4, 14) does fall on the curve $y = x^2 - 2$, then plugging the point into the equation will result in a true outcome. Plug the point (4, 14) into the equation to see what happens.

    $$y = x^2 - 2$$
    $$14 = (4)^2 - 2$$
    $$14 = 16 - 2$$
    $$14 = 14 \quad \text{TRUE}$$

    The outcome is true, so point (4, 14) does fall on this curve.

11. **Slope = 3; y-intercept = 4**

    The equation $y = 3x + 4$ is already in $y = mx + b$ form. The slope is 3, and the y-intercept is 4.

12. **Slope = 2.5; y-intercept = −6**

    First, put the equation in $y = mx + b$ form.

    $$2y = 5x - 12$$
    $$y = \frac{5}{2}x - 6$$

    The slope is $\frac{5}{2}$ or 2.5 and the y-intercept is −6.

13. **Slope = 2; y-intercept = −4**

Place the first point at (0, −4). Then count up two and over 1 to place a second point and draw your line. (This figure also shows a third point, but it's not necessary to draw three points.)

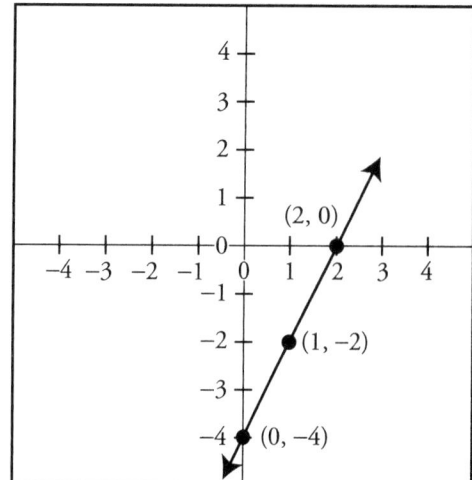

$y = 2x - 4$

14. **x-intercept = 8; y-intercept = −4**

There are two ways to find the y-intercept. Either plug $x = 0$ into the original equation, or rearrange the equation to fit the standard $y = mx + b$ format.

If $x = 0$, then $x - 2y = 8$ becomes $0 - 2y = 8$, and $y = -4$.

Here's the equation rearranged into $y = mx + b$ format.

$$x - 2y = 8$$
$$-2y = -x + 8$$
$$y = \frac{1}{2}x - 4$$

The y-intercept is −4.

To find the x-intercept, plug $y = 0$ into either form of the equation, whichever you think is easier, and solve for x.

$$x - 2y = 8$$
$$x - 2(0) = 8$$
$$x = 8$$

The x-intercept is 8.

Here's what the equation looks like on the coordinate plane:

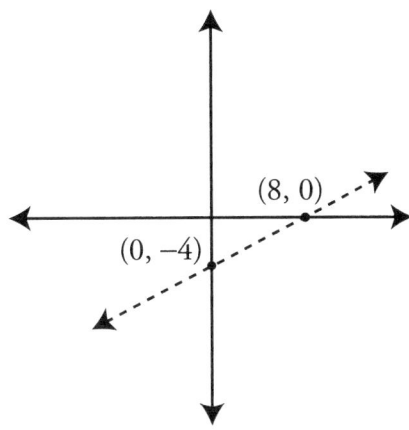

15. **13**

    First, plot the two given points and draw a triangle. Then, calculate the lengths of the two legs of the triangle. Finally, use the Pythagorean theorem or recognize the triple to find the hypotenuse.

    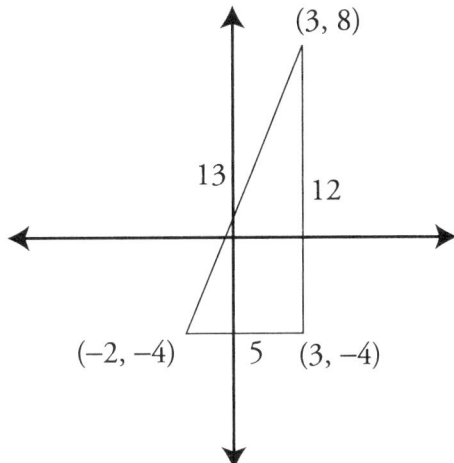

    The right triangle has legs of 5 (the change from −2 to 3) and 12 (the change from −4 to 8). The two legs are 5 and 12, so this is a 5–12–13 triple. The hypotenuse, which is also the distance between the two points, is 13.

Unit Five: **Geometry**

Problem Set

1. A line has the equation $y = 3x + 7$. At which point will this line intersect the y-axis?

2. A line has the equation $x = \frac{y}{80} - 20$. At which point will this line intersect the x-axis?

3. A line has the equation $x = -2y + z$. If (3, 2) is a point on the line, what is z?

4. A line is represented by the equation $y = zx + 18$. If this line intersects the x-axis at (−3, 0), what is z?

5. A line has a slope of $\frac{1}{6}$ and intersects the x-axis at (−24, 0). Where does this line intersect the y-axis?

6. Which quadrants, if any, do not contain any points on the line represented by $x - y = 18$?

7. Which quadrants, if any, do not contain any points on the line represented by $x = 10y$?

8. Challenge problem! Which quadrants contain points on the line $y = \frac{x}{1,000} + 1,000,000$?

9. Which quadrants contain points on the line represented by $x + 18 = 2y$?

Problems #10–11 refer to the following diagram.

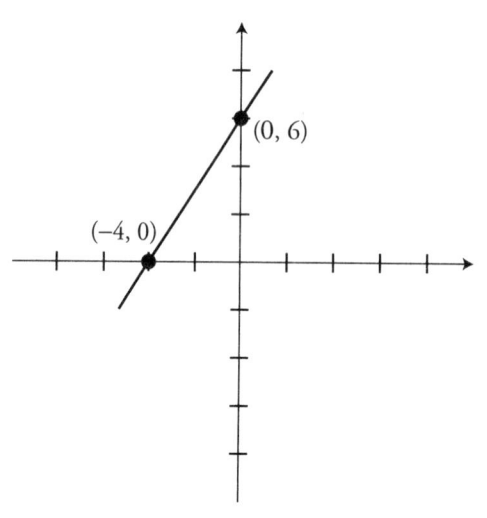

10. What is the equation of the line shown?

11. What is the intersection point of the lines defined by the equations $2x + y = 7$ and $3x - 2y = 21$?

12.

Quantity A	Quantity B
The y-intercept of the line $y = \frac{3}{2}x - 2$	The x-intercept of the line $y = \frac{3}{2}x - 2$

13.

Quantity A	Quantity B
The slope of the line $2x + 5y = 10$	The slope of the line $5x + 2y = 10$

14.

Quantity A	Quantity B
The distance between points $(0, 9)$ and $(-2, 0)$	The distance between points $(3, 9)$ and $(10, 3)$

Unit Five: **Geometry**

Solutions

1. **(0, 7)**
   A line intersects the y-axis at the y-intercept, where $x = 0$. When an equation is in the form $y = mx + b$, the b represents the y-intercept. Thus, the line $y = 3x + 7$ intersects the y-axis at the point (0, 7).

2. **(−20, 0)**
   A line intersects the x-axis at the x-intercept, or when the y-coordinate is equal to 0. Substitute 0 for y and solve for x.

   $$x = \frac{0}{80} - 20$$
   $$x = -20$$

   Therefore, the point at which the line crosses the x-axis is (−20, 0).

3. **7**
   Substitute the coordinates (3, 2) for x and y and solve for z.

   $$x = -2y + z$$
   $$3 = -2(2) + z$$
   $$3 = -4 + z$$
   $$7 = z$$

4. **6**
   Substitute the coordinates (−3, 0) for x and y and solve for z.

   $$y = zx + 18$$
   $$0 = z(-3) + 18$$
   $$3z = 18$$
   $$z = 6$$

5. **(0, 4)**
   Use the information given to find the equation of the line.

   $$y = \frac{1}{6}x + b$$
   $$0 = \frac{1}{6}(-24) + b$$
   $$0 = -4 + b$$
   $$4 = b$$

   The variable b represents the y-intercept. Therefore, the line intersects the y-axis at (0, 4).

6. **Quadrant II**

   First, rewrite the equation in slope-intercept form.

   $y = x - 18$

   Next, find the intercepts by setting $x = 0$ and $y = 0$.

y-intercept	x-intercept
$y = 0 - 18$	$0 = x - 18$
$y = -18$	$18 = x$
Point: (0, −18)	Point: (18, 0)

   Plot the points (0, −18), and (18, 0) and draw a line.

   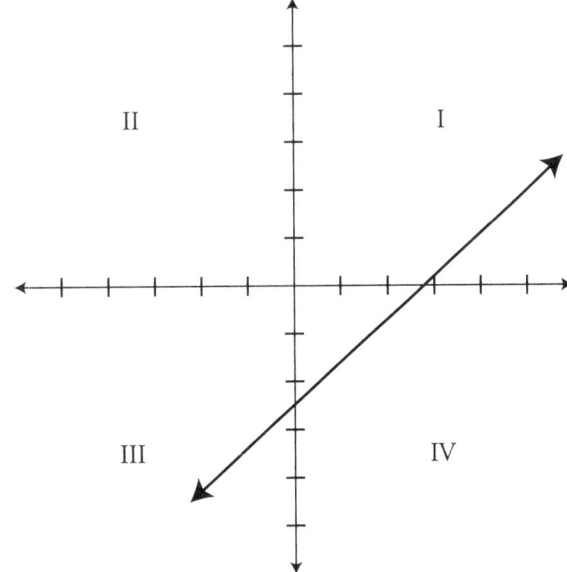

   The line does not pass through quadrant II.

Unit Five: Geometry

7. **Quadrants II and IV**

   First, rewrite the line in slope-intercept form.

   $$y = \frac{x}{10}$$

   A slope-intercept equation in the form $y = mx$ is the same as $y = mx + 0$. As a result, the y-intercept of the line is (0, 0), or the origin. Whenever a line passes through the origin, (0, 0) represents both the x-intercept and the y-intercept.

   To find another point on the line, substitute any convenient number for x. Given the equation, 10 would be a smart number to use for x.

   $$y = \frac{10}{10} = 1 \qquad \text{The point (10, 1) is on the line.}$$

   Plot the points (0, 0) and (10, 1) and draw a line.

   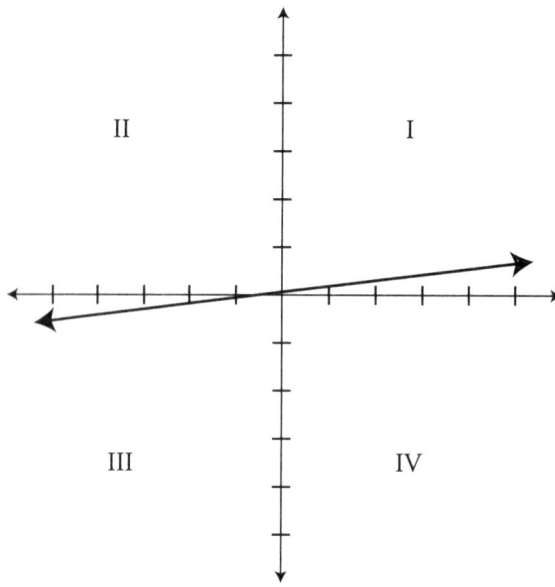

   The line does not pass through quadrants II and IV.

8. **Quadrants I, II, and III**

   The line is already written in slope-intercept form.

   $$y = \frac{x}{1{,}000} + 1{,}000{,}000$$

   Find the intercepts by setting $x = 0$ and $y = 0$.

   $$y = \frac{0}{1{,}000} + 1{,}000{,}000 \qquad 0 = \frac{x}{1{,}000} + 1{,}000{,}000$$
   $$y = 1{,}000{,}000 \qquad\qquad\qquad x = -1{,}000{,}000{,}000$$

   Given what the question is asking, it's enough to solve these equations as "When $x = 0$, then y is positive and really big and when $y = 0$, then x is negative and really small." Plot the points and draw the line.

   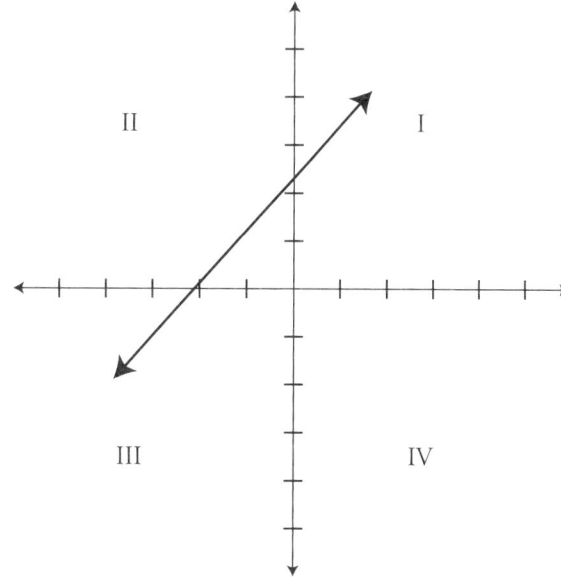

   From the sketch, which is definitely not to scale, the line passes through quadrants I, II, and III.

Unit Five: **Geometry**

9. **Quadrants I, II, and III**
   First, rewrite the line in slope-intercept form.

   $$y = \frac{x}{2} + 9$$

   Find the intercepts by setting $x = 0$ and $y = 0$.

   $$y = \frac{0}{2} + 9 \qquad 0 = \frac{x}{2} + 9$$
   $$y = 9 \qquad x = -18$$

   Plot the points $(-18, 0)$ and $(0, 9)$ and sketch the line.

   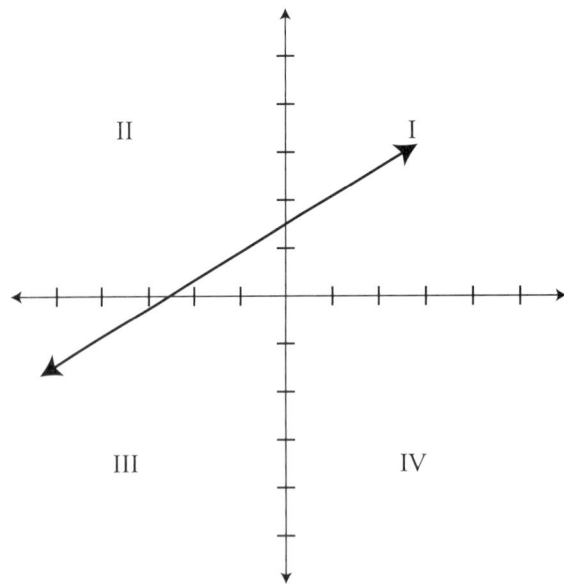

   The line passes through quadrants I, II, and III.

10. $y = \frac{3}{2}x + 6$

    First, calculate the slope m of the line. You can use the formula or just count it out on the figure (which is probably safer!).

    $$\text{slope} = \frac{\text{rise}}{\text{run}} = \frac{6-0}{0-(-4)} = \frac{6}{4} = \frac{3}{2}$$

    The line crosses the y-axis at (0, 6), so $b = 6$. Plug the values for m and b into the slope-intercept form of the equation.

    $$y = \frac{3}{2}x + 6$$

11. **(5, −3)**

    To find the coordinates of the point of intersection, solve the system of two linear equations. Multiply the first equation by 2 and then add that to the second equation.

    $$\begin{array}{ll} 2x + y = 7 & 3x - 2y = 21 \\ 4x + 2y = 14 \rightarrow & + 4x + 2y = 14 \\ & \overline{7x = 35} \\ & x = 5 \end{array}$$

    Now plug $x = 5$ into either equation to find y.

    $$2x + y = 7$$
    $$2(5) + y = 7$$
    $$y = -3$$

    Therefore, the point (5, −3) is the point of intersection.

Unit Five: **Geometry**

12. **(B)**

The equation is already in slope-intercept form, so the *y*-intercept is −2. To find the *x*-intercept, either sketch out the graph or plug *y* = 0 into the equation to find *x*, your choice.

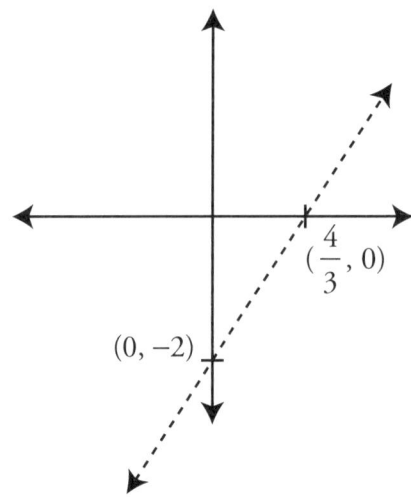

Because this is a QC problem, you don't need to determine the exact value of the *x*-intercept; you just need to know whether it is greater or less than −2. Plot the *y*-intercept at (0, −2) and look at the slope. Since the slope is positive, the line will run up and to the right, so it will cross the *x*-axis at some positive value. A positive value is always greater than a negative value, so Quantity B is greater.

Alternatively, to determine the *x*-intercept, set *y* = 0, then solve for *x*.

$$y = \frac{3}{2}x - 2$$
$$0 = \frac{3}{2}x - 2$$
$$2 = \frac{3}{2}x$$
$$\frac{4}{3} = x$$

A positive value is always greater than a negative value.

The correct answer is (B): Quantity B is greater.

13. **(A)**

    Put each equation into slope-intercept form ($y = mx + b$) and compare the values for m, which represents the slope. Start with the equation in Quantity A.

    $$2x + 5y = 10$$
    $$5y = -2x + 10$$
    $$y = -\frac{2}{5}x + 2$$

Next, rearrange the equation in Quantity B.

$$5x + 2y = 10$$
$$2y = -5x + 10$$
$$y = -\frac{5}{2}x + 5$$

Quantity A	Quantity B
$-\frac{2}{5}$	$-\frac{5}{2}$

Be careful with negative fractions, $-\frac{2}{5} > -\frac{5}{2}$.

The correct answer is (A): Quantity A is greater.

Unit Five: **Geometry**

14. **(C)**

Sketch out two triangles for each set of points and find the hypotenuse for each.

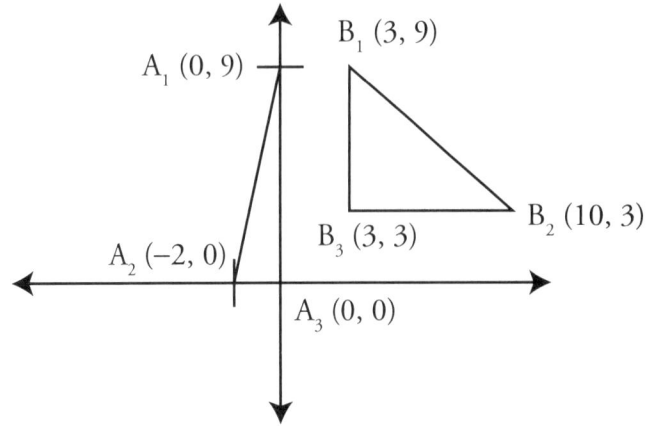

The illustration shows the two points from Quantity A, here labeled A_1 and A_2, and the two points from Quantity B, here labeled B_1 and B_2. Quantity A's right triangle has legs of 2 (the change from −2 to 0) and 9 (the change from 0 to 9). Use the Pythagorean theorem to solve for the hypotenuse.

$$a^2 + b^2 = c^2$$
$$(2)^2 + (9)^2 = c^2$$
$$4 + 81 = c^2$$
$$85 = c^2$$

Because the calculation to be performed is the same for both quantities, just find c^2 for Quantity B as well and compare from there.

Quantity B's right triangle has legs of 7 (the change from 3 to 10) and 6 (the change from 3 to 9). Use the Pythagorean theorem to solve for the hypotenuse.

$$a^2 + b^2 = c^2$$
$$(7)^2 + (6)^2 = c^2$$
$$49 + 36 = c^2$$
$$85 = c^2$$

The two values are the same!

The correct answer is (C): The two quantities are always equal.

CHAPTER 26
QC Geometry

In This Chapter:

- Shape Geometry
- Variable Creation
- Word Geometry
- Pick Numbers
- Problem Set
- Solutions

CHAPTER 26 QC Geometry

Quantitative Comparison questions that focus on geometry will use the rules and formulas you've already learned, but these problems can often be solved using strategies that don't work for non-QC problems. In this chapter, you'll learn a practical approach that will save you time and effort on QC geometry problems, specifically.

This chapter is broken down as follows:

1. How to deal with **Shape Geometry** questions that include a diagram:

   A. What to do when Quantity B contains a number

   B. What to do when Quantity B contains an unknown, such as a variable or an angle shown in the diagram

2. How to deal with **Word Geometry** questions that do *not* include a diagram.

The following three-step process for tackling Geometry QC questions will be emphasized:

1. Establish what you **need to know**.

2. Establish what you **know**.

3. Establish what you **don't know**.

Shape Geometry

Quantity B is a Number

In some Geometry Quantitative Comparison problems, Quantity B is a number. You can attack these with the three-step process of establishing what you **need to know**, what you **know**, and what you **don't know**.

If you are given a diagram, redraw and label it. Avoid the temptation simply to look at the diagram and solve the problem in your head; you risk falling into a trap. Taking the time to redraw and label the diagram is worthwhile.

On Geometry QCs, as on all QCs, there is always the possibility that you will not have enough information, resulting in a correct answer of (D).

Unit Five: Geometry

However, to arrive at the correct answer consistently, *act as though there is enough information, while accepting that the answer may ultimately be (D)*. For example:

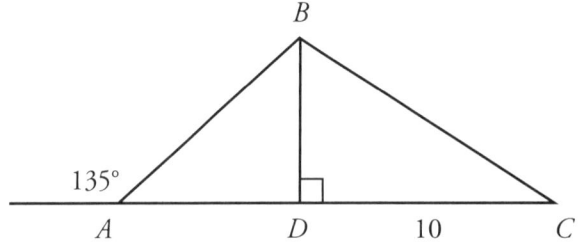

The area of $\triangle DBC$ is 30.

Quantity A	Quantity B
Area of $\triangle ABD$	18

For any Geometry QC problem, the first step is the same: Establish what you **need to know**.

Quantity B is a number, so no calculations are necessary.

Quantity A is the area of triangle *ABD*. To answer this question correctly, you need to know whether the area of triangle *ABD* is greater than, equal to, or less than 18. For any value you need to know, there are three possible scenarios:

1. You can find an exact value.
2. You can find a range of possible values.
3. You do not have enough information to find any value or range of values.

Once you've determined what you need to know, write it down, along with any equations you believe will be relevant. For example:

$$\text{Area}_{\triangle ABD} = \frac{1}{2}bh$$

Next, establish what you **know**. It will be more than what is directly stated in the question. Use the given information to find values for previously unknown lengths and angles.

Keywords such as *area*, *perimeter*, and *circumference* are good indications that you can set up equations to solve for a previously unknown length. In this example, the area of triangle *DBC* is given as 30, and line segment *DC* = 10 is the base of the triangle:

$$\text{Area}_{\triangle DBC} = 30 = \frac{1}{2}(10)(h)$$

Solve for the height of the triangle:

$$30 = \frac{1}{2}(10)(h)$$
$$30 = 5h$$
$$6 = h$$

Add any new information to your diagram:

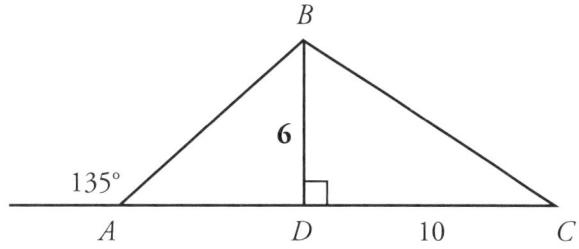

The area of △DBC is 30.

Quantity A	**Quantity B**
Area of △ABD	18

Next, you *could* use the Pythagorean theorem to calculate the length of *BC*. However, *keep the end in mind as you work*. Knowing the length of *BC* won't tell you anything about triangle *ABD*, so save time by focusing on that part of the diagram relevant to what you **need to know**. In this case, line segment *BD* is the height of triangle *ABD*. Plug that value in:

Quantity A	**Quantity B**
Area$_{\triangle ABD} = \frac{1}{2}b(6)$	18
Area$_{\triangle ABD} = 3b$	

At this point, you don't know the *b*. The ultimate goal is to determine whether Quantity A is greater than, equal to, or less than Quantity B. If *b* is 6, then the two quantities are equal. If *b* is less than 6, the answer is (B), and if *b* is more than 6, the answer is (A). Reframe the question to "How does the base of triangle *ABD* compare to 6?"

The figure contains another piece of information you haven't used yet: The exterior angle measure of 135°.

26

715

Unit Five: Geometry

Key features of diagrams include intersecting lines with one known angle, parallel lines with a transversal and one known angle, and triangles with two known angles:

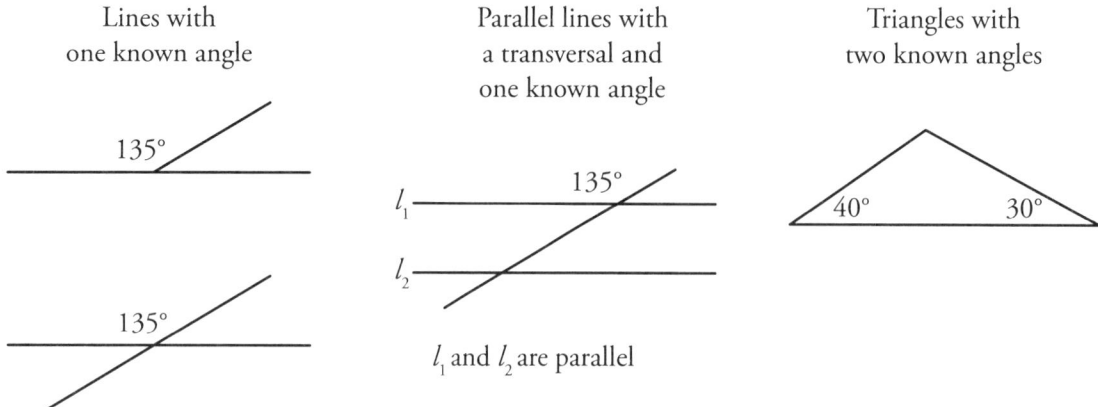

In this diagram, you have lines with a known angle. Line segment AB divides the horizontal line into two parts. Straight lines have a degree measure of 180°, so set up an equation:

$$135° + \angle BAD = 180°$$

$$\angle BAD = 45°$$

By the same logic, angle ADB is 90°. Label both angles on your copy of the diagram:

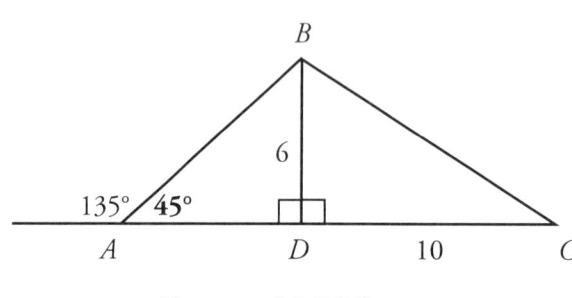

The area of △DBC is 30.

Quantity A	Quantity B
3b	18

Now, solve for the third angle. In this case, since the two known angles are 45 and 90, this must be a 45–45–90 triangle:

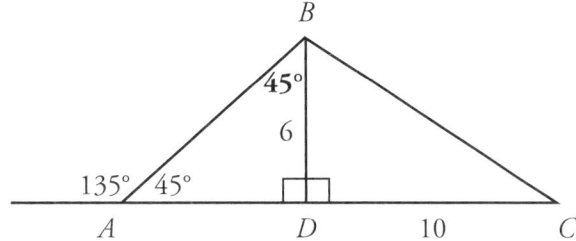

The area of △DBC is 30.

Quantity A   **Quantity B**

$3b$ 18

In this diagram, ∠BAD and ∠ABD both lie in triangle ABD and have a degree measure of 45°. So, triangle ABD is isosceles and the sides opposite ∠BAD and ∠ABD are equal. Since side BD has a length of 6, side AD also has a length of 6:

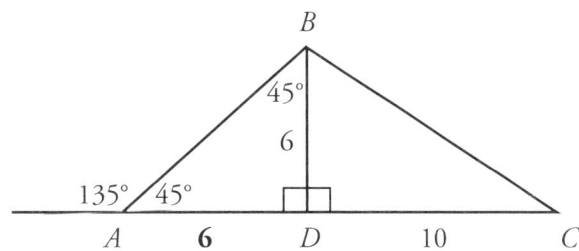

The area of △DBC is 30.

Quantity A   **Quantity B**

$3b$ 18

The base, b, is 6, so Quantity A is equal to 18.

The answer is (C): The two quantities are always equal.

Unit Five: Geometry

> **Strategy Tip**
>
> Many QCs will provide enough information to reach a definite conclusion. To solve for the value you **need to know**:
>
> **Establish What You Know**
>
> 1. *Set up equations* to find the values of previously unknown *lines* and *angles*.
> 2. *Make inferences* to find additional information.
> 3. Keep your eye on what you *need to know*; if a particular step takes you away from what you need to know, look for another path.
>
> **Establish What You Don't Know**
>
> While many questions provide you enough information, you will not always be able to find an exact number for the value you need. For these questions, an additional step will be required: Establish what you don't know.

Even though you will not always be able to find the exact value of something you need to know, implicit constraints within a diagram will often provide you a range of possible values. For example:

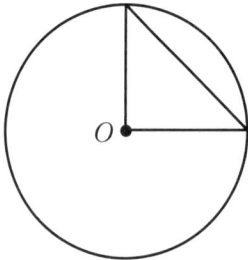

The circle with center O has an area of 4π.

Quantity A	Quantity B
Area of the triangle	1.5

First, establish what you **need to know**. To find the area of the triangle, you will need the base and the height. Write the equation:

$$\text{Area} = \frac{1}{2}bh$$

Two sides of the triangle are equal to the radius. However, those two sides are only the base and height if the triangle is a right triangle. Hold off on equating the base and height to the radius until you establish what you **know**.

The area of the circle is 4π, so:

$$4\pi = \pi r^2$$
$$4 = r^2$$
$$2 = r$$

Chapter 26: **QC Geometry**

The radius equals 2. Two lines in the diagram are radii. Label these radii:

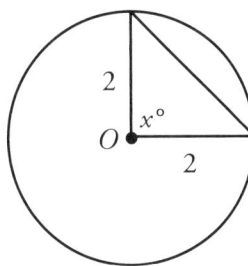

The circle with center O has an area of 4π.

Quantity A	**Quantity B**
$\frac{1}{2}bh$	1.5

Is there enough information to find the area of the triangle?

Be careful! *There's no indication of the value of central angle* x. The triangle in the diagram *appears* to be a right triangle. If that were the case, then the radii could act as the base and the height of the triangle, and you could use the area formula to solve.

But there is one problem—the diagram does not actually indicate that angle x is a right angle.

You do know a few things about the angle. Because x is one angle in a triangle, it has an implicit range: It must be greater than 0° and less than 180°.

Angle x is a value you **don't know**. The question now becomes, "How do changes to x affect the area of the triangle?" To find out, take the unknown value (x) to extremes.

If $x = 90°$, the area would be $\frac{1}{2}(2)(2) = 2$. What happens to the area as x increases?

  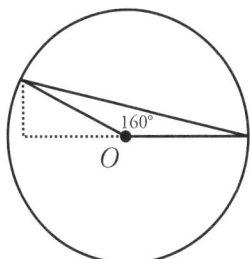

As x increases, the base stays the same and the height of the triangle decreases. Therefore, the area of the triangle decreases as well. In fact, as x gets closer and closer to its maximum value, the height gets closer and closer to 0. As the height gets closer to 0, so does the area of the triangle.

The same is true if the angle gets smaller: The base will stay the same and the height will decrease. In other words, the maximum value of the area of this triangle is 2 and the minimum value is something very close to 0.

719

Compare this range to Quantity B, which is 1.5. The area of the triangle can be either greater than or less than 1.5, so the correct answer is (D): The relationship can't be determined.

Remember the strategy of **Proving D** on Quantitative Comparison questions? For Geometry QC, Proving D means stretching and squishing shapes to test cases. When you have unknown angles, lengths, or other values, take them to extremes and see how these changes affect the relationship between Quantities A and B.

It may seem counterintuitive to squish shapes so that they no longer look like the given diagram. However, the GRE is testing you on your ability to make inferences from given information, and to recognize when you *lack* the required information to make an inference. When stretching and squishing geometry diagrams, it's crucial to know when to trust your eyes and when not to trust your eyes:

> ### Trusting the Picture
> **Trust the Picture for things like...**
> - straight lines
> - relative position
> - intersections
>
> **Doubt the Picture and Test Extremes for...**
> - unlabeled lengths
> - unlabeled angles
>
> The GRE will often provide diagrams with things that look like right angles, but in fact could be a range of angles! Stretch and squish the angle to see how it impacts your answer.

Quantity B Is an Unknown Value

What if both quantities contain *unknown values*?

The basic process remains the same:

1. Establish what you **need to know**.
2. Establish what you **know**.
3. Establish what you **don't know**.

For example:

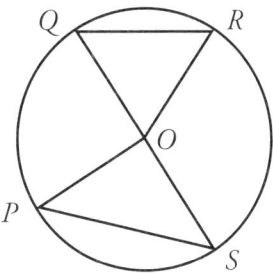

O is the center of the circle.
∠QOR > ∠POS

Quantity A	**Quantity B**
minor arc *QR*	minor arc *PS*

Note that a **minor arc** is the smaller of two arc lengths made by two points on a circle. Consider the points *P* and *S*. To get from *P* to *S* by traveling around the circle, you could either go clockwise from *P*, all the way around the top of the circle and across Q and R, before finally reaching *S*. Or you could go counterclockwise from *P*, making the small jump to *S*. The shorter distance is the minor arc, while the longer one is the major arc. The minor arc will always be less than half the circumference of the circle.

First, establish what you **need to know**. There are two unknown values: Quantity A and Quantity B. When both quantities contain an unknown, you need to know *either* the values in both quantities *or*, more likely, the relative size of the two values. For this problem, you will need to either solve for minor arcs *QR* and *PS* or determine their relative size.

Now, establish what you **know**. Be skeptical of the picture! The way the diagram is drawn, minor arc *PS* appears greater than minor arc *QR*. However, none of the angles are defined, so you could redraw the picture with wildly different angles.

Actually, there is not a whole lot to know—no actual numbers have been given. Infer relationships instead: *OP, OQ, OR,* and *OS* are radii, and thus have equal lengths. Other than that, the only thing you know is that ∠QOR > ∠POS. With no numbers provided in the question, finding exact values for either quantity is impossible. But you may still be able to say something definite about their *relative size*.

Now, establish what you **don't know**. What values in the diagram are unknown and can affect the lengths of minor arcs *QR* and *PS*? ∠QOR and ∠POS fulfill both criteria. Take the values of ∠QOR and ∠POS to extremes.

Unit Five: **Geometry**

How do changes to ∠QOR and ∠POS affect the lengths of minor arcs QR and PS?

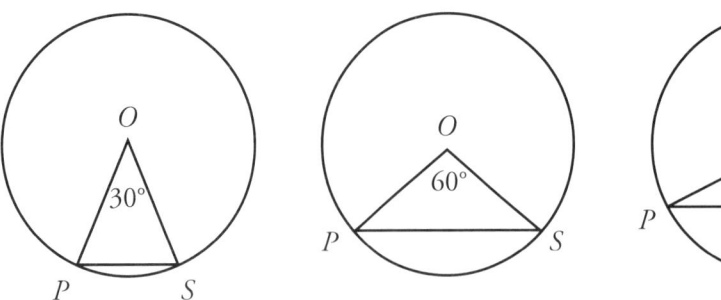

As ∠POS gets bigger, so does minor arc PS. The same relationship is true in triangle QOR. Note that you do not need specific angle measures in these examples—rough sketches will do.

Since ∠QOR > ∠POS, no matter what the values of ∠QOR and ∠POS actually are, minor arc QR is definitely greater than minor arc PS. Therefore, the correct answer is (A): Quantity A is greater.

> **Strategy Tip**
>
> When QC questions include a diagram, there are two possibilities for Quantity B:
>
> 1. Quantity B is a number, or
> 2. Quantity B is an unknown value.
>
> For both situations, the process is the same: Establish what you **need to know**.
>
> 1. Establish what you **know**:
>   a. *Set up equations* to solve for previously unknown lines and angles.
>   b. *Make inferences* based on the properties of shapes.
>   c. Keep your eye on what you *need to know*.
>
> 2. Establish what you **don't know**:
>   a. Take unknown values to extremes.
>   b. If both quantities contain unknown values, look to gauge *relative* size.
>
> And, no matter what, *don't trust the unlabeled lengths and angles*.

Variable Creation

Take a look at another example of a Geometry QC in which both quantities are unknown values:

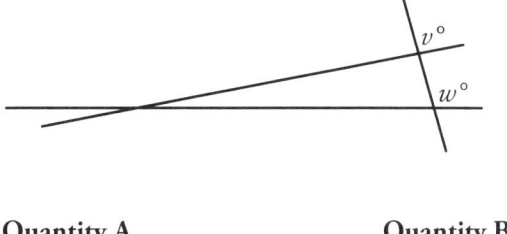

Quantity A	Quantity B
v	w

As in the preceding example, there are no numbers given, so an exact value for any of these angles is impossible to determine. This does not, however, mean that the answer is necessarily (D).

What you **need to know** is the relative size of v and w. As this type of problem gets more difficult, it becomes more difficult to establish what you **know**. In this figure, the intersection of the three lines creates a triangle. Triangles, when they appear, are often very important parts of diagrams, because there are many rules related to triangles that test makers can make use of.

This question appears to be about angles. After all, the values in both quantities are angles. *Create variables* to represent the three angles of the triangle:

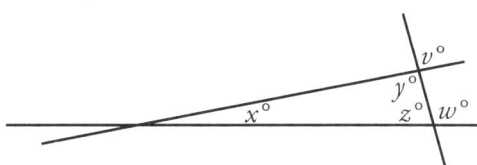

Part of the challenge is the fact that there are actually many relationships, and thus many equations you could create. For instance:

$$x + y + z = 180$$
$$w + z = 180$$

But not all of the possible relationships will directly help determine the relative size of v and w. Look for relationships that will allow you to directly compare v and w. Begin with v. Angles v and y are vertical angles, and thus equal:

Quantity A	Quantity B
$v = y$	w

Unit Five: **Geometry**

If you can also express w in terms of y, then you may be able to determine the relative size of v and w. Start with the fact that w and z are related:

Quantity A	Quantity B
$v = y$	$w = 180 - z$

Next, try to find an equation that links y and z. There's a great shortcut on this problem…if you spot it. That solution is a bit farther down. First, here's the relationship that more people are likely to notice first: $x + y + z = 180$. Isolate z:

$$x + y + z = 180$$
$$z = 180 - x - y$$

Now, substitute $(180 - x - y)$ for z in Quantity B:

Quantity A	Quantity B
$v = y$	$w = 180 - z = 180 - (180 - x - y)$ $= x + y$

Since x represents an angle, it must be positive, so $x + y$ must be greater than y by itself. Therefore, the correct answer is (B): Quantity B is greater.

Here's the great shortcut: Angle w is an exterior angle, so it's equal to the sum of the two remote interior angles, which are x and y. If you spot that, you can go directly to the fact that $w = x + y$.

> **Strategy Tip**
>
> If a diagram presents a common shape, such as a triangle or a quadrilateral, it is often helpful to create variables to represent unknown angles or lengths. Once you've created variables, try to:
> 1. Create equations, based on the properties of the shape
> 2. Compare the relative size of both quantities using common variables

Word Geometry

Some QC geometry questions don't provide a picture. For example:

4 points, P, Q, R, and T lie in a plane. PQ is parallel to RT and $PR = QT$.

Quantity A	Quantity B
PQ	RT

The basic process remains the same, but you'll need a little more time to consider how to draw your diagram.

First, establish what you **need to know**. Both quantities contain unknown values, so you need to determine the relative size of each one. Next, establish what you **know**. For *any* Word Geometry question, start by drawing the picture. Be reasonably accurate but don't be so accurate that it slows you down.

This question mentions parallel lines, so draw those first:

Because *PQ* is parallel to *RT*, points *P* and *Q* lie on one line and points *R* and *T* lie on the other. Start by creating a simple relationship. In this case, arranging them as a rectangle also addresses the final given *PR* = *QT*:

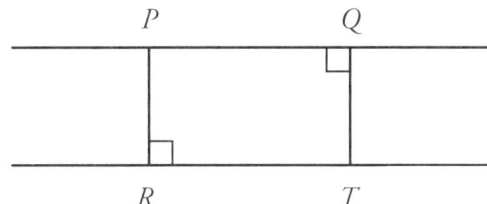

This is one possible diagram because it reflects all the information provided, but keep in mind that it is not the only possible diagram. Consider this diagram as if it is one specific case you're testing.

Quantity A	Quantity B
PQ	RT

When *PQRT* is a rectangle, *PQ* = *RT*.   A̶ B̶ C D

But are there other possible cases? To figure that out, establish what you **don't know**.

In the previous diagram, *PQ* and *RT* were drawn perpendicular to the two parallel lines. But the angle can change. Redraw the diagram with *PR* and *QT* slanted:

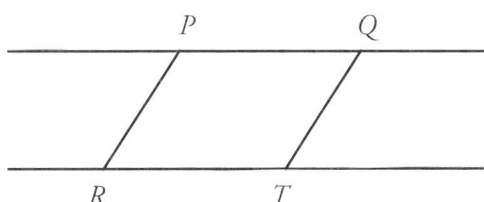

This diagram represents another possible configuration of the four points. Now how does *PQ* compare to *RT*? Although it may not be immediately obvious, *PQ* is still equal to *RT*. Whereas the first diagram created a rectangle, this diagram has created a parallelogram.

Try again. Is there anything else you can change in the diagram that will change the relative lengths of *PQ* and *RT*, yet still leave *PR* and *QT* equal?

Unit Five: Geometry

The two preceding cases share a common feature that is not required by the common information: *PR* and *QT* are parallel. Redraw the figure so that *PR* and *QT* are NOT parallel, but still equal in length:

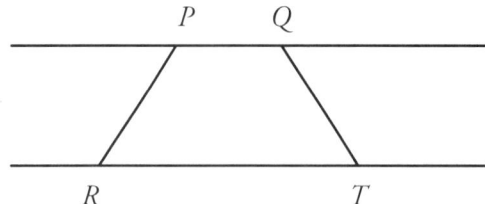

In this version of the diagram, *RT* is clearly longer than *PQ*. Therefore, the correct answer is (D): The relationship cannot be determined.

> **Strategy Tip**
>
> Word Geometry problems follow the same basic process:
>
> 1. Establish what you **need to know**.
> 2. Establish what you **know**.
>   a. Draw the picture.
>   b. If you're trying to prove answer (D), you may need to redraw the picture at least once.
> 3. Establish what you **don't know**.
>   a. Ask yourself, "What changes to the picture would affect the *relative size* of the quantities?"

Pick Numbers

For many geometry Quantitative Comparison questions, picking numbers is an effective technique. It is most effective when the question references specific dimensions of a shape (e.g., length, width, radius) but provides no actual numbers. For example:

Rectangles *R* and *S* have equal areas. Rectangle *R*'s length is greater than Rectangle *S*'s width.

Quantity A	**Quantity B**
The area of Rectangle *R* if its length increases 30%	The area of Rectangle *S* if its width increases 30%

First, establish what you **need to know**. Both quantities have an unknown value, so you will have to judge their relative size. The best way to judge the relative size of each quantity in this cases is to pick real numbers.

Next, what do you **know**? The common information states that the rectangles have equal areas. Assign any number that will be easy to work with for the areas. The numbers chosen in this example are only one set of possibilities, but they were chosen because they are easy to use for the details of this problem. Try 10:

$$\text{Area}_R = \text{Area}_S = 10$$

Next, draw the picture. Make sure you include the numbers you chose. Each rectangle has an area of 10, but the length of R is greater than the width of S:

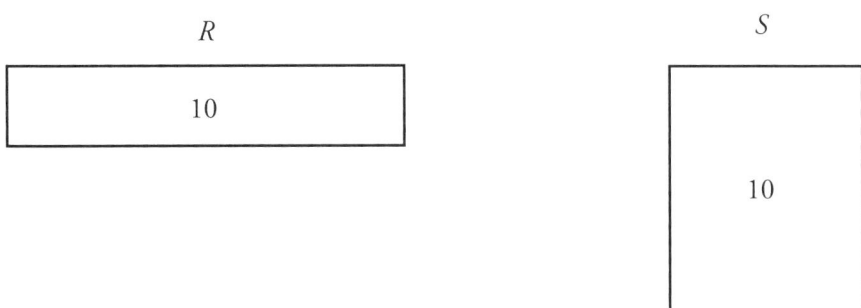

Quantity A mentions the length of R and Quantity B mentions the width of S. Test cases by picking values for the length and width of R and S. For R, set length = 10 and width = 1. For S, set length = 2 and width = 5:

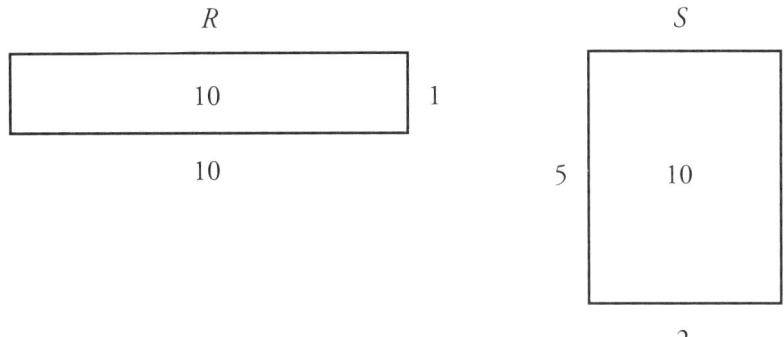

Quantity A	Quantity B
The area of Rectangle R if the length increases 30%	The area of Rectangle S if the width increases 30%

Now, evaluate the quantities. For Quantity A, increase the length of R by 30 percent:

$$130\% \text{ of } 10 = (1.3)(10) = 13$$

The new area of R is $l \times w = (13)(1) = 13$.

For Quantity B, increase the width of S by 30 percent:

$$130\% \text{ of } 5 = (1.3)(5) = 6.5$$

Unit Five: **Geometry**

Use the calculator for this computation. The new area of S is $l \times w = (2)(6.5) = 13$.

Quantity A	Quantity B
R	S
rectangle: 13 wide, 1 tall, area 13	rectangle: 6.5 wide, 2 tall, area 13

The new areas are equal. Eliminate answers (A) and (B).

Next, you can pick another set of values to see what happens, but take a moment first to examine how the math worked:

Original:

$\text{Area}_R = l_R \times w_R = 10$

$\text{Area}_S = l_S \times w_S = 10$

New:

$\text{Area}_R = (l_R \times 1.3) \times w_R = 10(1.3)$

$\text{Area}_S = l_S \times (w_S \times 1.3) = 10(1.3)$

The starting area for each is 10, and then each area is multiplied by the same number, 1.3. The order of multiplication doesn't change the outcome, so the new area is always going to be equal regardless of what number you pick for the area. Therefore, the correct answer is (C): The two quantities are equal.

> **Strategy Tip**
>
> When a QC Geometry question references specific dimensions (e.g., length, width, radius) but does not provide actual numbers, pick numbers.
>
> To successfully pick numbers, remember the following:
>
> 1. Pick numbers that match any restrictions in the common information or statements.
> 2. Try to prove answer (D) by testing several valid cases or by testing one case and examining how the math plays out.
> 3. Look for patterns that suggest the answer is (A), (B), or (C).

Problem Set

1. The length of a rectangular room is 8 feet greater than its width. The total area of the room is 240 square feet.

Quantity A	Quantity B
The width of the room in feet	12

2. l_1 and l_2 are parallel lines, and none of the lines in the figure are perpendicular.

   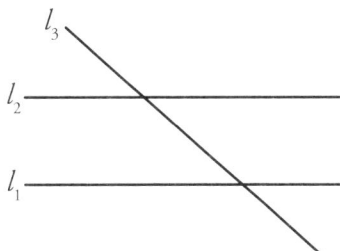

Quantity A	Quantity B
The slope of line l_1 minus the slope of line l_3	The slope of line l_2 minus the slope of line l_3

3.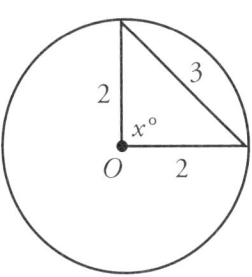

   O is the center of the circle.

Quantity A	Quantity B
x	90

4.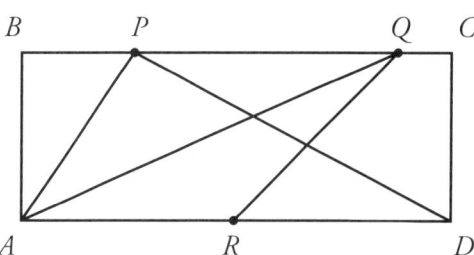

ABCD is a rectangle.
R is the midpoint of AD.

Quantity A	Quantity B
The area of Triangle APD	Twice the area of Triangle AQR

5. The circumference of Circle A is twice the circumference of Circle B.

Quantity A	Quantity B
The area of Circle A	Twice the area of Circle B

6. 1,600 feet of fencing is used to enclose a square plot.

Quantity A	Quantity B
The plot's new area if the length were reduced by 4 feet and the width increased by 4 feet	The plot's new area if the length were equal to 398 feet and the width were equal to 402 feet

7.

Quantity A	Quantity B
The third side of an isosceles triangle with sides of 3 and 9	The third side of an isosceles triangle with sides of 6 and 8

8.

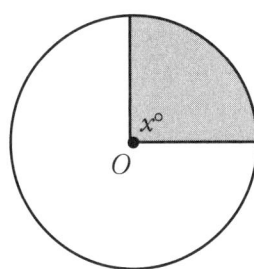

O is the center of the circle.
The area of the circle is 16π.
The area of the shaded region is less than 4π.

Quantity A	**Quantity B**
x	90

9. A circle with radius $\frac{4}{\sqrt{\pi}}$ has the same area as a particular square.

Quantity A	**Quantity B**
9π	The area of the square if each side were increased by 1

10.

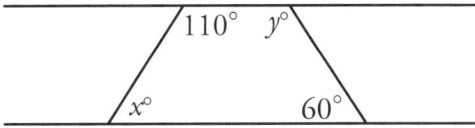

Quantity A	**Quantity B**
y − x	50

11. Rectangle A has twice the area of Rectangle B. The width of Rectangle A is less than $\frac{1}{2}$ the width of Rectangle B.

Quantity A	**Quantity B**
The area of Rectangle A	The area of Rectangle B if its width is increased by more than 2

Unit Five: **Geometry**

Solutions

1. **(C)**

   Let *L* and *W* stand for the length and width of the room in feet. Turn the two pieces of information into equations.

   $$L = W + 8 \qquad LW = 240$$

   Isolate the known variable, *L*. In fact, it's already isolated. Substitute $W + 8$ into the other equation, then solve.

   $$W(W + 8) = 240$$
   $$W^2 + 8W = 240$$
   $$W^2 + 8W - 240 = 0$$
   $$(W + 20)(W - 12) = 0$$

   The two solutions are $W = -20$ and $W = 12$. A negative width is impossible, so *W* must equal 12 feet.

   Alternatively, test the value in Quantity B as the width of the room. Plug in 12 for *W* in the first equation.

   $$L = 12 + 8 = 20 \text{ feet}$$

   If $W = 12$ and $L = 20$, then the area is (20)(12), which equals 240 square feet. So, 12 feet is indeed the width of the room.

   The correct answer is (C): The two quantities are always equal.

2. **(C)**

   Parallel lines have equal slopes. Therefore, the slope of line l_1 and the slope of line l_2 are identical, and Quantities A and B are equal, regardless of the slope of line l_3.

   The correct answer is (C): The two quantities are always equal.

3. **(A)**

   Use Quantity B as a benchmark by trying to make *x* equal to 90. Mark the angle as 90 degrees and use the Pythagorean theorem to find the hypotenuse, using the two legs of 2.

   $$c^2 = 2^2 + 2^2$$
   $$c^2 = 8$$
   $$c = \sqrt{8}$$
   $$c = 2\sqrt{2} \approx 2(1.4) = 2.8$$

   The figure indicates that the hypotenuse is actually 3, not 2.8. If angle *x* were 90 degrees, the hypotenuse would be about 2.8. However, the length of that side is actually 3, so angle *x* must be greater than 90 degrees.

   The correct answer is (A): Quantity A is greater.

Chapter 26: **QC Geometry**

4. **(C)**

   There are no numbers mentioned anywhere in the problem, but that doesn't mean the answer is (D). Some important observations: Both of the triangles mentioned in the quantities have the same height (both are equal to the side of the rectangle AB). Also, since R is the midpoint of AD, the base of triangle APD is exactly twice the base of triangle AQR.

Quantity A	**Quantity B**
The area of triangle	Twice the area of triangle
$APD = \frac{1}{2}(AD)(AB)$	$AQR = 2 \times \frac{1}{2}(AR)(AB)$
	$= (AR)(AB)$
	$= \frac{1}{2}(AD)(AB)$

   You could use numbers to make the comparison easier. Note that if this is the only approach you take, you should try to prove (D) by testing several cases and confirming whether any emerging pattern makes sense. Let the height of each triangle (also the height of the rectangle) be 5. Let AD be 8, so $AR = RD = 4$.

Quantity A	**Quantity B**
The area of triangle	Twice the area of triangle
$APD = \frac{1}{2}(8)(5) = 20$	$AQR = 2 \times \frac{1}{2}(4)(5) = 20$

   Thus, the two quantities are equal. If you tried different numbers, you would continue to get this result, a pattern that makes sense based on the way equivalent values are input into both quantities.

   The correct answer is (C): The two quantities are always equal.

5. **(A)**

   The formula for circumference is $C = 2\pi r$; therefore, doubling the radius will double the circumference. But this is *not* true for the area formula, which involves *squaring* the radius. Since the circumference of Circle A is twice the circumference of Circle B, it must be the case that the radius of A is twice that of B.

   If A's radius is 2 and B's radius is 1, then the area of Circle A is 4π, so Quantity A = 4π. The area of Circle B is π, so Quantity B = 2π. Quantity A is greater, so eliminate choices (B) and (C).

   This will still be the case for any numbers you pick. If a circle's radius is double another circle's radius, its area will always be four times the other's area, because the double-radius is then squared.

   The correct answer is (A): Quantity A is greater.

Unit Five: **Geometry**

6. **(B)**

    A square has a perimeter of 1,600 feet. To find the length of each side of the square, divide 1,600 by 4, because each side has the same length. The length of each side of the square is 400.

    Quantity A describes a 396 by 404 rectangle, and Quantity B describes a 398 by 402 rectangle. Use the calculator to find the area for these dimensions: Quantity A is 396 × 404 = 159,984 and Quantity B is 398 × 402 = 159,996.

    The answer is (B): Quantity B is greater.

    If two numbers have a finite sum (396 + 404 = 800 and 398 + 402 = 800), their product will increase as the two numbers get closer together. For example, 4 × 4 is greater than 3 × 5, and 10 × 10 is greater than 9 × 11.

    In geometry, for a finite perimeter, the area of a shape is maximized by making the shape as regular as possible. That is, the more equilateral the shape, the greater the area. Thus, a square has greater area than any other quadrilateral with the same perimeter. The rectangle in Quantity B is closer to square than the rectangle in Quantity A, so it has the greater area. (And the original shape, which was a square, has the greatest area of the three: 400 × 400 = 160,000.)

    The correct answer is (B): Quantity B is greater.

7. **(A)**

    In any isosceles triangle, two of the sides are equal. Both triangles in the problem are isosceles, so Quantity A's third side must be either 3 or 9 and Quantity B's third side must be either 6 or 8.

    But that's not all! In any triangle, the third side must be less than the sum of the other two sides and greater than their difference. Quantity A's third side must be between 9 − 3 = 6 and 9 + 3 = 12. Only the value of 9 fits this restriction, so Quantity A's third side has a length of 9.

    Quantity B's third side must be between 8 − 6 = 2 and 8 + 6 = 14. Both 6 and 8 fit into this range. However, whether Quantity B is 6 or 8, it is definitely less than Quantity A's 9.

    The correct answer is (A): Quantity A is greater.

8. **(B)**

    Use Quantity B as a benchmark. If x were equal to 90, the shaded region would have an area equal to $\frac{1}{4}$ that of the entire circle (since 90 is $\frac{1}{4}$ of 360). Thus, if the angle were equal to 90, the shaded region would have an area of 4π (or $\frac{1}{4}$ of the entire circle's area). Since the area of the shaded region is actually less than 4π, it must be the case that x is less than 90.

    The correct answer is (B): Quantity B is greater.

9. **(A)**

   The radius of the circle is $\frac{4}{\sqrt{\pi}}$ and its area equals the area of the square. Find the area of the circle.

   $$A = \pi\left(\frac{4}{\sqrt{\pi}}\right)^2$$
   $$A = \pi\left(\frac{16}{\pi}\right)$$
   $$A = 16$$

   The area of the square is also 16 and, therefore, each side of the square is 4.

   Quantity B is the area of the square if each side were increased by 1—that is, if each side were now equal to 5. Thus, Quantity B = 25. Quantity A is equal to 9π. Since π is more than 3, Quantity A is more than 27.

   The correct answer is (A): Quantity A is greater.

10. **(D)**

    The figure does *not* indicate that the two horizontal-seeming lines in the figure are actually parallel, so do *not* assume this. It is the case that all four angles of the quadrilateral must sum to 360°, so $x + y$ must equal 190°.

    However, without knowing that you have parallel lines, you have no way of knowing how to split up the 190 between x and y, and therefore no way of knowing whether $y - x$ is greater than 50. For instance, if the lines were parallel, then y would equal 120 and x would equal 70, so $y - x$ would be exactly 50. But if y is 130 and x is 60, then $y - x$ would be 70.

    The correct answer is (D): The relationship cannot be determined.

11. **(D)**

    Rectangle A has twice the area of Rectangle B and less than $\frac{1}{2}$ the width. Start by drawing one scenario of how this could be.

    Rectangle A   Rectangle B
       40   5
    ┌────────┐   ┌────────┐
   1│   │   4│   │
    └────────┘   └────────┘

    In this scenario, Quantity A equals 40.

Unit Five: **Geometry**

In Quantity B, Rectangle *B*'s width is increased by "more than 2." (Because you were not given any real numbers so far, it's likely that you could come up with a scenario in which this increase of "more than 2" yields a larger Quantity B, and another scenario in which it does not—answer (D) is probably a good guess at this point.)

Thus, Rectangle *B* now has a width of more than 6. Its area is now more than 30. But more than 30 could still be less than 40, or it could be more than 40.

The correct answer is (D): The relationship cannot be determined.

UNIT SIX

Advanced Topics

Are you aiming for an extra-high Quant score? In this unit, you'll learn how to interpret, translate, and solve the most complicated GRE problems, including rates, sequences, patterns, combinatorics & probability, optimization, and other advanced topics.

In This Unit:

- Chapter 27: Rates
- Chapter 28: Sequences and Patterns
- Chapter 29: Combinatorics
- Chapter 30: Probability
- Chapter 31: Optimization
- Chapter 32: Advanced Concepts

CHAPTER 27
Rates

In This Chapter:

- Rate Formula
- Basic Motion: The RTD Chart
- Matching Units in the RTD Chart
- Multiple Rates
- Average Rate: Don't Just Add and Divide
- Working Together: Add the Rates
- Population Problems
- Check Your Skills Answer Key
- Problem Set
- Solutions

CHAPTER 27 Rates

Rate problems come in a variety of forms on the GRE, but all are marked by three primary components: *rate*, *time*, and *distance* or *work*. These questions may ask when two cars will meet or how much production can be completed in a certain time. In this chapter, you will learn how to recognize and deconstruct rate problems, organize your work, and solve efficiently. You'll also learn specific strategies for finding average rates, solving when two entities are working together, and approaching population problems.

Rate Formula

All basic motion problems involve three elements: rate, time, and distance (or work).

Rate is expressed as a ratio of distance and time, with two corresponding units. Some examples of rates include 30 miles per hour, 10 meters/second, and 15 units every day. Note that *per*, the slash symbol, and *every* all serve the same function in those labels.

Time describes how long it takes an event to occur, expressed using a unit of time. For rate problems, it doesn't refer to the time of day, though time of day can be included to complicate the problem. (For example, if they start at 2:00, and it takes 2.5 hours, when do they arrive?) Some examples of times include 6 hours, 23 seconds, and 5 months.

Distance or **Work** is an expression of the distance covered or the work completed. The units can be distance units or units of production. Some examples of distances include 18 miles, 20 meters, and 100 kilometers. Some examples of work include 5 units, 3 widgets, and 7 baskets.

These three elements are related by the following equations:

$$\text{Rate} \times \text{Time} = \text{Distance} \quad \text{OR} \quad \text{Rate} \times \text{Time} = \text{Work}$$

These equations can be abbreviated as $RT = D$ or as $RT = W$. Basic Rate problems involve simple manipulation of these equations. To help remember the equations, reverse the order and use the mnemonics *dert* and *wert*. The *e* stands for the equals sign:

$$D = RT \qquad W = RT$$

$$DeRT \qquad WeRT$$

The word *per* equates to division, so 60 miles per hour and 130 kilometers per hour can be represented as follows:

$$60 \, \frac{\text{miles}}{\text{hour}} = 60 \, \frac{\text{mi}}{\text{hr}}$$

$$130 \, \frac{\text{kilometers}}{\text{hour}} = 130 \, \frac{\text{km}}{\text{hr}}$$

Unit Six: Advanced Topics

If you were told that one car drove for two hours at 60 miles per hour, you can calculate how far it went. The **units** (miles and hours) illustrate why the multiplication works:

$$R \times T = D$$
$$60\,\frac{mi}{hr} \times 2\,hr = D$$
$$60\,\frac{mi}{\cancel{hr}} \times 2\,\cancel{hr} = D$$
$$120\,mi = D$$

The hours units cancel out, leaving only miles for the distance. Units can be canceled out just as effectively as factors.

A rate is typically "per unit time"—for example, 60 miles per hour is really 60 miles per 1 hour—so, to cancel the time unit out, multiply by the time and you'll be left with distance. Here's the same process with another example:

$$R \times T = D$$
$$130\,\frac{km}{hr} \times 3\,hr = D$$
$$130\,\frac{km}{\cancel{hr}} \times 3\,\cancel{hr} = D$$
$$390\,km = D$$

If you ever forget the rate formula, test the process with a familiar rate to recreate the formula. (Or think about driving on a *dirt* road … DeRT is the formula!)

Basic Motion: The RTD Chart

With easier rate problems, plugging into the rate formula will likely be sufficient. However, to prepare for the more complicated questions, make it a habit to create an **RTD (Rate, Time, Distance) chart** (or an RTW chart) to solve a rate problem. Use the formula $R \times T = D$ or $R \times T = W$ as the headers of the chart, then fill in the given information in the appropriate columns. For example:

If a car is traveling at 30 miles per hour, how long does it take to travel 75 miles?

Set up an RTD chart:

Rate	×	*Time*	=	*Distance*
30 mi/hr	×	t	=	75 mi

Use the equation created in the RTD chart to solve for t:

$$30 \frac{\text{mi}}{\text{hr}} \times t = 75 \text{ mi}$$
$$t = 75 \text{ mi} \div 30 \frac{\text{mi}}{\text{hr}}$$
$$t = 75 \text{ mi} \times \frac{\text{hr}}{30 \text{ mi}}$$
$$t = 75 \cancel{\text{mi}} \times \frac{\text{hr}}{30 \cancel{\text{mi}}}$$
$$t = \frac{75}{30} \text{ hr}$$
$$t = 2.5 \text{ hr}$$

The miles units cancel out this time, leaving just hours for the time. As you get better with this problem type, you won't always have to write out and explicitly cancel the units—but it's a good idea as you're getting comfortable with this math.

The math without the units is less complicated:

$$30t = 75$$
$$t = \frac{75}{30} = 2.5$$

The next section will explore when units become more important in these problems. Throughout this chapter and in your work, use standard shorthand for common units:

Longhand Unit	Shorthand Unit
second	sec
minute	min
hour	hr
feet	ft
yards	yd
meters	m
miles	mi
kilometers	km

It's not uncommon for a problem to have both meters and minutes or both miles and minutes, so be careful that you're not using just m for all of these. For less common units, create your own shorthand to keep track of what each number is describing.

Unit Six: **Advanced Topics**

Check Your Skills

1. Shams can address 20 envelopes in one hour. How many hours will it take Shams to address 50 envelopes?

2. If a steel mill can produce 1,500 feet of I-beams every 20 minutes, how many feet of I-beams can it produce in 50 minutes?

Answers can be found on page 758.

Matching Units in the RTD Chart

Comparing Rates

Comparing rates is easiest when the unit of time is the same. For example:

Meade can core 12 apples in 10 minutes and peel 17 potatoes in 15 minutes.

Quantity A	**Quantity B**
The rate at which Meade can core apples	The rate at which Meade can peel potatoes

The rate of apple coring is given per 10 minutes, while the rate of potato peeling is given per 15 minutes, making it hard to assess which is greater. Convert the rate to the same unit of time. You could determine how much work was done per hour or per minute—your choice. Here's how much was done per hour:

$$\text{Core Apples:} \quad \frac{12}{10 \text{ min}} = \frac{12 \times 6}{60 \text{ min}} = \frac{72}{1 \text{ hr}}$$

$$\text{Peel Potatoes:} \quad \frac{17}{15 \text{ min}} = \frac{17 \times 4}{60 \text{ min}} = \frac{68}{1 \text{ hr}}$$

Meade can core 72 apples in the same time it takes to peel 68 potatoes, so Meade is faster at coring apples. Therefore, the correct answer is (A): Quantity A is greater.

Alternatively, calculate Meade's rate per minute:

$$\text{Core Apples:} \quad \frac{12}{10 \text{ min}} = \frac{1.2}{1 \text{ min}}$$

$$\text{Peel Potatoes:} \quad \frac{17}{15 \text{ min}} = \frac{1.133\ldots}{1 \text{ min}}$$

Meade can core 1.2 apples per minute compared to 1.13 potatoes per minute, so Meade is faster at coring apples. As long as the rates are measured in the same unit of time, the two rates can be directly compared.

However, comparing rates is different than comparing total outputs. Consider this variation on the previous example:

Chapter 27: **Rates**

Meade can core 12 apples in 10 minutes and peel 17 potatoes in 15 minutes.

Quantity A	**Quantity B**
The number of apples Meade has cored	The number of potatoes Meade has peeled

Meade is capable of coring 72 apples in an hour and peeling 68 potatoes in an hour. However, how many has Meade actually cored and peeled? Maybe Meade has been coring apples for an hour, but peeling potatoes for three hours. Maybe the reverse is true. Therefore, the correct answer is (D): The relationship cannot be determined.

Consistent Units

Before you start solving a rate problem, ensure that all the units in your RTD chart match up with one another. The two units in the rate should match up with the unit of time and the unit of distance. For example:

> An elevator can descend at a rate of 15 floors each minute. How many floors can the elevator descend in 40 seconds?

Start by creating an RTD chart:

	Rate	×	*Time*	=	*Distance*
Car	15 floors/min	×	40 sec	=	F

Treating this like an accurate equation would result in a nonsensical answer because the units aren't the same. The rate column uses minutes, while the time column uses seconds. Those units must match in order to cancel out. Before starting to solve, convert either the rate to floors/second or the time to minutes. It's typically simpler to convert the time, even if that results in a fraction or decimal.

Keep the conversion "direction" in mind as you work, so that you can do a quick check to see whether your answer makes sense. If it doesn't, you might have accidentally converted in the wrong direction. When converting from seconds into minutes, you'll arrive at a lesser number: For example, 60 seconds equals just 1 minute.

Given 40 seconds total and 60 seconds per minute, set up an equation to convert:

$$40 \text{ sec} \times \frac{1 \text{ min}}{60 \text{ sec}} =$$

$$40 \; \cancel{\text{sec}} \times \frac{1 \text{ min}}{60 \; \cancel{\text{sec}}} =$$

$$40 \times \frac{1 \text{ min}}{60} =$$

$$\frac{40}{60} \text{ min} = \frac{2}{3} \text{ min}$$

Unit Six: Advanced Topics

Update your RTD chart so that the units are consistent:

	Rate	×	Time	=	Distance
Car	15 floors/min	×	40 sec = $\frac{2}{3}$ min	=	F

Finally, solve for the number of floors:

$$15 \frac{\text{floors}}{\text{min}} \times \frac{2}{3} \text{min} = F$$

$$15 \frac{\text{floors}}{\cancel{\text{min}}} \times \frac{2}{3} \cancel{\text{min}} = F$$

$$15 \text{ floors} \times \frac{2}{3} = F$$

$$10 \text{ floors} = F$$

In 40 seconds, the elevator will descend 10 floors.

> **Key Concept**
>
> The units in a rate problem must be internally consistent. The units in the rate must match the units in the time and the units in the distance (or work).

Try this problem:

A train travels 90 kilometers per hour. How many hours does it take the train to travel 450,000 meters? (1 kilometer = 1,000 meters)

It's up to you whether you first put all the information in an RTD chart as it is, then convert as needed, or you first convert everything to appropriate units, then use the RTD chart. This solution does the conversions before using the RTD chart.

Divide 450,000 meters by 1,000 to convert this distance to 450 km. Now, the distance unit (kilometers) and the rate unit (kilometers per hour) match. If you're unsure whether to multiply or divide, set up the conversion both ways to see which will cancel the appropriate units:

$$\text{m} \times \frac{1 \text{ km}}{1,000 \text{ m}} = \cancel{\text{m}} \times \frac{1 \text{ km}}{1,000 \cancel{\text{m}}}$$

or

$$\text{m} \times \frac{1,000 \text{ m}}{1 \text{ km}} = ???$$

Only the first equation correctly cancels out the meters, leaving kilometers. Alternatively, use logic: Meters are shorter than kilometers, so going from a measurement in meters to one in kilometers should result in a lesser number—therefore, divide. However you get there, insert the converted values into the RTD chart:

	R	×	T	=	D
Train	90 km/hr	×	t	=	450 km

Now, solve for the time: $90t = 450$. Thus, t is 5 hours. Here's the math with all the units carried through:

$$90 \frac{\text{km}}{\text{hr}} \times t = 450 \text{ km}$$

$$t = 450 \text{ km} \div 90 \frac{\text{km}}{\text{hr}}$$

$$t = 450 \text{ km} \times \frac{1 \text{ hr}}{90 \text{ km}}$$

$$t = 450 \text{ k\cancel{m}} \times \frac{1 \text{ hr}}{90 \text{ \cancel{km}}}$$

$$t = \frac{450}{90} \text{ hr}$$

$$t = 5 \text{ hr}$$

Note that 5 hours is the "stopwatch" time: If you started a stopwatch at the beginning of the trip, what would the stopwatch read at the end of the trip? A GRE problem might tell you that the train started its trip at 1pm and ask when the train finished its trip. In that case, the answer would be 1pm plus 5 hours, which is 6pm.

The RTD chart may seem like overkill for relatively easier problems such as these. If you are comfortable doing so, just set up the equation $RT = D$ or $RT = W$ and then substitute. However, the RTD chart can be very valuable when you have more complicated scenarios that contain more than one RTD relationship, as you'll see in the next section.

Check Your Skills

3. Convert 10 meters per second to meters per hour.

4. It takes an inlet pipe 2 minutes to supply 30 gallons of water to a pool. How many hours will it take to fill a 27,000 gallon pool that starts out empty?

Answers can be found on page 759.

Multiple Rates

Some rate questions on the GRE will involve *more than one trip or traveler*. To deal with this, you will need to multiple $RT = D$ relationships. This is where the RTD chart shines because you can add more information by adding more rows.

For example:

> Hani runs a 30-mile course at a constant rate of 4 miles per hour. If Cam runs the same track at a constant rate and completes the course in 90 fewer minutes, how fast did Cam run?

Create a chart with two rows, one for Hani and one for Cam:

	R	×	T	=	D
H					
C					

Unit Six: **Advanced Topics**

Start by filling in the information about Hani:

	R	×	T	=	D
H	4 mi/hr				30 mi
C					

Cam runs the same track as Hani. In other words, Cam also ran 30 miles. This is a common method the GRE uses to obscure rate information—defining one entity's total in terms of the other's:

	R	×	T	=	D
H	4 mi/hr				30 mi
C					30 mi

Cam ran for 90 fewer minutes than Hani. Again, this is defining one piece of information in terms of another, but this time, the problem didn't explicitly provide Hani's time:

	R	×	T	=	D
H	4 mi/hr	×	t	=	30 mi
C			$t-90$ min		30 mi

First, you can calculate Hani's time, since the problem provides Hani's rate and distance.

Second, the units don't match! Hani's rate is in hours, but Cam's time is in minutes. Make a note that you'll have to deal with that. First, though, calculate Hani's time.

$$4t = 30$$
$$t = 7.5$$

It takes Hani 7.5 hours to complete the course. Next, to make the units match, convert 90 minutes to 1.5 hours. So, Cam takes 6 hours:

	R	×	T	=	D
H	4 mi/hr	×	$t = 7.5$ hr	=	30 mi
C			$t - 1.5$ hr = 6 hr		30 mi

Before solving, define what you're looking for. The question asks how fast Cam ran—in other words, Cam's rate:

	R	×	T	=	D
H	4 mi/hr	×	$t = 7.5$ hr	=	30 mi
C	$r = ?$	×	$t - 1.5$ hr = 6 hr	=	30 mi

From here, it's justified to ignore the units because the units are now consistent across the table. The miles will cancel out, and the time will be in terms of hours:

$$r \times 6 = 30$$

$$r = 5$$

Cam ran at a rate of 5 miles per hour. For questions that involve multiple rates, set up multiple $RT = D$ rows and look for relationships between the rows. These relationships will help you reduce the number of variables you need and allow you to solve for the desired value.

> **Strategy Tip**
> Watch for common relationships the GRE uses in rate problems:
>
> | What they say | What to infer |
> |---|---|
> | Two people travel the same route. | They both go the same distance. |
> | A travels for x minutes less than B. | If B travels for t minutes, then A travels for $t - x$ minutes. |

Check Your Skills

5. One hour after Adrienne started walking the 60 miles from Town *X* to Town *Y*, James started walking on the same path from *X* to *Y* as well. Adrienne walks 3 miles per hour, and James walks 1 mile per hour faster than Adrienne. How far will James have walked when he catches up with Adrienne?

    (A) 8 miles
    (B) 9 miles
    (C) 10 miles
    (D) 11 miles
    (E) 12 miles

6. Nicky and Cristina are running a 1,000-meter race. Because Cristina is faster than Nicky, she gives him a 12-second head start. If Cristina runs at a pace of 5 meters per second and Nicky runs at a pace of 3 meters per second, how many seconds will Nicky have run before Cristina catches up to him?

    (A) 15 seconds
    (B) 18 seconds
    (C) 25 seconds
    (D) 30 seconds
    (E) 45 seconds

Answers can be found on pages 759–760.

Average Rate: Don't Just Add and Divide

Finding an average rate is a bit complicated. For example:

> If Lucia walks to work at a rate of 4 miles per hour and walks home by the same route at a rate of 6 miles per hour, what is Lucia's average walking rate for the round trip?

It is very tempting to find an average rate using the direct average formula: Add up the two rates, divide by two, and arrive at an average rate of 5 miles per hour.

However, this is *incorrect*! An average rate is actually a *weighted* average (review Chapter 18: Statistics for a refresher), not a regular average, so you can't just add up the two rates and divide by two.

For example, imagine that the distance from Lucia's home to her work is 6 miles.

	R	×	T	=	D
to work	4 mi/hr	×	t	=	6

If she walks a distance of 6 miles at a rate of 4 miles per hour, it will take her $\frac{6 \text{ miles}}{4 \text{ mi/hr}} = 1.5$ hours to get to work. On the way home, though, she walks at a rate of 6 miles per hour, so it takes her just 1 hour to walk the 6 miles home.

Her total distance traveled is 12 miles, and her total time spent is 2.5 hours, so her average rate is $\frac{12 \text{ mi}}{2.5 \text{ hr}} = 4.8$ miles per hour.

> **Key Concept**
>
> To find average rate, find the total distance and the total time, then plug into the formula:
>
> $$R = \frac{D}{T}$$
> $$\text{average rate} = \frac{\text{total distance}}{\text{total time}}$$

The weighted average of 4.8 miles per hour is less than the "regular" (and incorrect) average of 5 miles per hour because Lucia spent more time walking at the slower rate. As a result, the weighted average is more heavily weighted towards the slower rate of 4 miles per hour.

In fact, when an object moves the same distance twice but at different rates, then that object will *always* spend more time traveling at the slower rate and less time traveling at the faster rate. If you drive to work one day at 30 miles per hour, that will take you more time than driving to work at 40 miles per hour the next day (assuming you take the same route and your trip doesn't get interrupted by something else). So, when the distance is the same, the weighted average will *always* be more heavily weighted towards the slower rate.

Chapter 27: **Rates**

> **Key Concept**
>
> For two trips of the *same* distance, the average rate will always be weighted more heavily towards the *slower* rate, because more time is spent traveling at the slower rate to cover the same distance.

The original problem didn't provide the distance. It just said that Lucia walks to and from work by the *same route*. Infer from this that the distances are the same, and assign a single variable, *d*. However, the rates are different for the two trips, so the times will also be different. Assign two separate variables for time:

	R	×	T	=	D
to work	4 mi/hr	×	t_1	=	d
to home	6 mi/hr	×	t_2	=	d

There is one more row to consider adding. To find the average rate, you'll need the total time and total distance. Either write that below the original table or add another row for the totals:

	R	×	T	=	D
to work	4 mi/hr	×	t_1	=	d
to home	6 mi/hr	×	t_2	=	d
total	$(r = ?)$	×	$t_1 + t_2$	=	$2d$

Note: The two times add up and the two distances add up, but the two rates never add up.

From here, there are two primary routes you can use to solve this problem: algebra or picking numbers. Picking numbers is usually the easier and more efficient path—you'll see why as you review both solutions below.

Picking Numbers Solution Path

Here's the problem again:

> If Lucia walks to work at a rate of 4 miles per hour and walks home by the same route at a rate of 6 miles per hour, what is Lucia's average walking rate for the round trip?

The question asks for average rate. The rates in these problems are constant. She travels at a constant rate of 4 miles per hour to work and a constant rate of 6 miles per hour to her home. Her average rate, whatever it is, is also constant. The distance she travels will impact the time—a 100-mile trip will take longer than a 5-mile trip at the same rate—but the rate itself will still be one constant rate.

Why is that helpful? It means you can choose any distance you want, and you can solve the problem accurately for the rate. Alternatively, you could choose any time you want, and then solve for the rest to find the average rate. The caveat is that the numbers you pick need to be internally consistent. So if Lucia walks 3 miles to work, she must also walk 3 miles home, since the problem says that the distance is the same.

Unit Six: Advanced Topics

You can't make up *both* a distance and a time. If Lucia walks 3 miles to work, it's not reasonable to say t_1 is 5 hours, because it will take her less than an hour to walk 3 miles at a rate of 4 miles per hour. Because the problem tells you Lucia's rates, once you choose a value for either time or distance, you'll calculate the rest based on the given rates.

In this case, because *d* is the same for both trips, pick a value for *d*. Any number will work, but some numbers will make the math easier than others. Consider what happens if you select $d = 3$:

	R	×	T	=	D
to work	4 mi/hr	×	t_1	=	3
to home	6 mi/hr	×	t_2	=	3
total	$r = ?$	×	$t_1 + t_2$	=	6

The next step would be to solve for t_1 and t_2 by dividing 3 by the rates, but both times would be fractions. It's more annoying to use fractions than integers, so instead, pick a number that will produce an integer when divided by the rates, 4 and 6. In other words, pick a common multiple of 4 and 6. (Revisit Chapter 10: Common Factors for a refresher on how to do this.)

The smallest common multiple of 4 and 6 is 12, so define the distance as 12. (Any other multiple of 4 and 6 would also work well in the problem, but smaller is better—the math is less complicated.)

	R	×	T	=	D
to work	4 mi/hr	×	t_1	=	12
to home	6 mi/hr	×	t_2	=	12
total	$r = ?$	×	$t_1 + t_2$	=	24

Use the RTD equation to find the two individual times, then add them up to get the total time:

	R	×	T	=	D
to work	4 mi/hr	×	3	=	12
to home	6 mi/hr	×	2	=	12
total	$r = ?$	×	5	=	24

Finally, use the relationship in the final row to find the average rate:

$$r(5) = 24$$
$$r = 4.8 \text{ mi/hr}$$

The average rate is 4.8 miles per hour when the distance is 12 miles, just as the average rate was 4.8 miles per hour when the distance was 6 miles.

If you're driving at a constant rate, it doesn't matter whether you drive for one hour or two hours, or whether you drive for 5 miles or 100 miles. You're still maintaining that constant rate the whole time. An average rate, by definition, is always a constant rate.

Algebraic Solution Path

The algebraic solution path is messier ... but here it is. Start by writing the equations from the table:

$$\text{to work:} \qquad 4t_1 = d$$
$$t_1 = \frac{d}{4}$$
$$\text{to home:} \qquad 6t_2 = d$$
$$t_2 = \frac{d}{6}$$

Also, plug your variables into the average rate formula:

$$\text{average rate} = \frac{2d}{t_1 + t_2}$$

Substitute from the first two equations into the third in order to get down to a single variable:

$$\text{average rate} = \frac{2d}{t_1 + t_2}$$
$$= \frac{2d}{\frac{d}{4} + \frac{d}{6}}$$

That's a pretty ugly fraction. It's solvable—but this is one reason why picking real numbers is often much easier.

To simplify the fractions, combine the two fractions in the denominator into a single fraction:

$$\text{Average rate} = \frac{2d}{\frac{d}{4} + \frac{d}{6}} \qquad \text{Find common denominators.}$$

$$= \frac{2d}{\frac{3d}{12} + \frac{2d}{12}} \qquad \text{Add the two fractions.}$$

$$= \frac{2d}{\frac{5d}{12}} \qquad \text{Multiply by the reciprocal.}$$

$$= 2d \times \frac{12}{5d}$$

$$= \frac{24\cancel{d}}{5\cancel{d}}$$

$$\text{Average rate} = 4.8$$

The average rate is (still) 4.8 miles per hour. The algebraic path is completely valid. It's just more annoying than working with real numbers.

Check Your Skills

7. Juan bikes halfway to school at 9 miles per hour, and walks the rest of the distance at 3 miles per hour. What is Juan's average speed for the whole trip, in miles per hour?

Answers can be found on page 761.

Working Together: Add the Rates

The previous problems dealt with a single person traveling at different rates. The GRE may also give you problems involving more than one entity, especially when it's framed as workers performing a task.

When two or more workers are performing the same task, their rates can be added together. For instance, if Machine A can make 5 boxes in an hour, and Machine B can make 12 boxes in an hour, then working together, the two machines can make $5 + 12 = 17$ boxes per hour. Likewise, if Panya can complete $\frac{1}{3}$ of a task in an hour and Ranee can complete $\frac{1}{2}$ of that task in an hour, then working together they can complete $\frac{1}{3} + \frac{1}{2} = \frac{5}{6}$ of the task every hour.

If, on the other hand, one worker is undoing the work of the other, subtract the rates. For instance, if one hose is filling a pool at a rate of 3 gallons per minute, and another hose is draining the pool at a rate of 1 gallon per minute, the pool is being filled at a rate of $3 - 1 = 2$ gallons per minute.

Try this problem:

> Machine C fills soda bottles at a constant rate of 60 bottles every 12 minutes, and Machine D fills soda bottles at a constant rate of 120 bottles every 8 minutes. Working together at their respective rates, how many bottles can the two machines fill in 25 minutes?

Create the RTW chart, filling in the known information and assigning a variable for what you're trying to find:

	R	×	T	=	W
C	$\frac{60 \text{ bot}}{12 \text{ min}}$				
D	$\frac{120 \text{ bot}}{8 \text{ min}}$				
Total			25 min		$b = ?$

It is a good idea to simplify rates so they express a measurement per one unit time—in this case, per minute rather than per 12 minutes or per 8 minutes:

$$\text{Rate}_C = \frac{60 \text{ bot}}{12 \text{ min}} = 5 \text{ bot/min}$$

$$\text{Rate}_D = \frac{120 \text{ bot}}{8 \text{ min}} = 15 \text{ bot/min}$$

Working together, they fill $5 + 15 = 20$ bottles every minute. Fill in the final row of the chart:

	R	×	T	=	W
C	$\frac{60 \text{ bot}}{12 \text{ min}}$				
D	$\frac{120 \text{ bot}}{12 \text{ min}}$				
Total	$\frac{20 \text{ bot}}{\text{min}}$	×	25 min	=	$b = ?$

Now solve for b:

$b = 20 \times 25 = 500$ bottles

The two machines, working together, can fill 500 bottles in 25 minutes.

Try another problem:

> Amal, working alone, can build a doghouse in 4 hours. Betty can build the same doghouse in 3 hours. If Betty and Carmelo, working together, can build the doghouse twice as fast as Amal can, how long would it take Carmelo, working alone, to build the doghouse?

Establish the givens and unknowns in the RTW chart. Because some of the information is about Betty and Carmelo working together, include a Betty and Carmelo row. Since those two together are twice as fast as Amal alone, they must take 2 hours because Amal takes 4 hours:

	R	×	T	=	W
A			4 hrs		1 dh
B			3 hrs		1 dh
C			$t = ?$		1 dh
B and C			2 hrs		1 dh

All three people are working to accomplish the same task: building a doghouse. As such, you can add their rates. However, rates are the *only* thing you can add. Don't add the time or the work as you did when it was one person working at different rates.

When there are multiple people working at different rates, divide the work by the time to find the rate for each row. Use the header row to keep track of the labels:

	$R \left(\frac{dh}{hr}\right)$	×	T (hr)	=	W (dh)
A	$\frac{1}{4}$	×	4	=	1
B	$\frac{1}{3}$	×	3	=	1
C	$\frac{1}{t}$	×	$t = ?$	=	1
B and C	$\frac{1}{2}$	×	2	=	1

Unit Six: **Advanced Topics**

The rate of Betty and Carmelo working together equals the sum of Betty's individual rate and Carmelo's individual rate. Set up an equation to solve for t:

$$\frac{1}{3} + \frac{1}{t} = \frac{1}{2}$$
$$\frac{1}{t} = \frac{1}{2} - \frac{1}{3}$$
$$\frac{1}{t} = \frac{1}{6}$$
$$t = 6$$

Carmelo can build a doghouse in 6 hours.

When the work involves completing a task, treat completing the task as doing one "unit" of work. For example, if someone can paint a house in 20 hours or change the oil in a car in 30 minutes, that person has completed 1 job in that length of time.

Take a look at the table with the rates again. Amal can build a doghouse in 4 hours and Amal's rate is $\frac{1}{4}$. Similarly, Betty can build a doghouse in 3 hours and Betty's rate is $\frac{1}{3}$. It isn't a coincidence that the denominator equals the time that it takes the person to do the job. When you are told that it takes a person or a machine a certain amount of time to complete one entire job, you can always write the rate as 1 over that time:

$$\frac{1 \text{ job}}{4 \text{ hours}} = \frac{1}{4} \text{ job/hr}$$

One job in four hours is one-quarter of the job per hour.

When dealing with multiple rates, be careful to express the rates in equivalent units. For example, if one rate is in hours and another is in minutes, convert one of the rates so that they are using the same time unit.

Once you know the rates of every worker, add the rates of workers who work together on a task.

Finally, you may get to the point where you can solve rate problems by translating the pieces you need and writing equations without first having to set up a table. Feel free to do so—as long as you feel comfortable enough with the math that you aren't introducing careless mistakes.

Check Your Skills

8. Tarik can complete a job in 12 minutes. If Andy helps Tarik, they can complete the job in 4 minutes. How long would it take, in minutes, for Andy to complete the job on his own?

Answers can be found on page 761.

Population Problems

GRE population problems will describe a population that increases or decreases by a defined factor every time period. For example:

> The population of a certain colony of bacterium triples every 10 minutes. Twenty minutes ago, the population size was 100. Approximately how many minutes from now will the population reach 24,000 ?

Use a population chart to sketch out the growth pattern described. Make a table with rows labeled to show the passage of time in chronological order, based on the time increment given in the problem (in this case, every 10 minutes):

Time	Population
20 min ago	100
10 min ago	
NOW	
in 10 min	
in 20 min	

To start, you won't know how far forward in the future to go. Just leave yourself enough space to add rows as needed. Work forward, backward, or both (as necessary in the problem), obeying any conditions given in the problem statement about the rate of growth or decay. In this case, the population triples every 10 minutes:

Time	Population
20 min ago	100
10 min ago	$100 \times 3 = 300$
NOW	$300 \times 3 = 900$
in 10 min	$900 \times 3 = 2{,}700$
in 20 min	$2{,}700 \times 3 = 8{,}100$
in 30 min	$8{,}100 \times 3 \approx 24{,}000$

The population chart shows that the bacterial population will reach 24,000 approximately 30 minutes from now. Because the question asks for an approximation, it's enough to notice that 8,000 times 3 is approximately 24,000. It isn't necessary to calculate the exact value.

In this problem, the population increases by a constant *multiple*. The rate of growth keeps accelerating because, each time, the new number is multiplied by three. In other problems, the increase may be a constant *amount* per time period (for example, there are 5 new bunnies every day). In that case, you would add five each day, not multiply by five.

Check Your Skills

9. The population of amoebas in a colony doubles every two days. If there were 200 amoebas in the colony six days ago, how many amoebas will there be four days from now?

Answers can be found on page 762.

Unit Six: **Advanced Topics**

Check Your Skills Answer Key

1. **2.5**

   Given a rate of 20 envelopes per hour and 50 envelopes made, set up an RTW chart to find the time.

	Rate	×	Time	=	Work
Shams	20 env/hr	×	t	=	50 env

   $$20t = 50$$
   $$t = \frac{50}{20} = \frac{5}{2} = 2.5$$

   It will take 2.5 hours to address 50 envelopes.

   Alternatively, "logic out" the story, hour by hour. In one hour, Shams addresses 20 envelopes, so in two hours, Shams addresses 40 envelopes. At this point, there are only 10 more envelopes to be addresses, and that will take an additional half an hour. Total, Shams needs 2.5 hours to address all 50 envelopes. You can use this "write it out" approach when the numbers aren't too cumbersome.

2. **3,750 feet**

   Set up an RTW chart and solve for w.

   When a rate is given in a non-unit increment of time (here, the time increment is 20 minutes), it's often useful to simplify the rate before putting it in the RTW chart.

   $$\frac{1500}{20} = 75 \text{ ft/min}$$

	Rate	×	Time	=	Work
Steel Mill	75 ft/min	×	50 min	=	w

   Set up the equation and solve for w.

   $$\frac{75 \text{ ft}}{1 \text{ min}} \times 50 \text{ min} = w$$
   $$3{,}750 \text{ ft} = w$$

   You can also logic this out on paper. If the company can produce 1,500 feet in 20 minutes, then it can produce 3,000 feet in 40 minutes. In 10 minutes more, it can produce half as many as 1,500 feet, or another 750 feet, for a total of 3,750 feet of I-beams.

3. **36,000 meters/hour**

   First convert seconds to minutes. There are 60 seconds in a minute.

   $$10\frac{m}{s} \times \frac{60s}{min} = 600 \text{ m/min}$$

   Now convert minutes to hours. There are 60 minutes in 1 hour.

   $$600\frac{m}{min} \times \frac{60 min}{hr} = 36,000 \text{ m/hr}$$

4. **30 hours**

   First, simplify the rate: $R = \frac{30 \text{ gal}}{2 \text{ min}} = \frac{15 \text{ gal}}{1 \text{ min}}$, which is the same as 15 gal/min.

   The question asks for the number of hours it will take to fill the pool, so convert minutes to hours. There are 60 minutes in an hour, so the rate is 15 gal/min $\times$ 60 = 900 gal/hr. Let t be the time it takes to fill the pool.

	R (gal/hr)	$\times$	T (hr)	$=$	W (gal)
inlet pipe	900	$\times$	t	$=$	27,000

   Solve for t:

   $$900t = 27,000$$
   $$t = 30 \text{ hours}$$

5. **(E) 12 miles**

   Adrienne walks at a rate of 3 miles an hour and James walks 1 mile per hour faster, so James walks 4 miles per hour. Adrienne walks for one hour longer than James, so call James' time t and Adrienne's time $t + 1$.

   The distance is interesting. They both start from Town X and walk towards Town Y, but they don't make it all the way to Town Y. James catches up to Adrienne before that. The question asks how far James walked at the moment that he catches up to Adrienne—so, wherever that is, they have both walked the same distance to get there.

	R (mi/hr)	$\times$	T (hr)	$=$	D (mi)
A	3	$\times$	$t+1$	$=$	d
J	4	$\times$	t	$=$	d

   Set up equations from the table.

   Adrienne: $3(t+1) = d$
   James: $4t = d$

Unit Six: Advanced Topics

The two equations are both equal to d, so set the left-hand sides equal to each other and solve for t.

$$3(t + 1) = 4t$$
$$3t + 3 = 4t$$
$$3 = t$$

James walked for 3 hours at a rate of 4 miles per hour, so James walked for 12 miles before catching up with Adrienne.

6. **(D) 30 seconds**

Set up an RTD chart. Nicky starts 12 seconds before Cristina, so Nicky runs for 12 seconds longer. Set Cristina's time to t and Nicky's time to $t + 12$. The question asks about the moment when Cristina catches up to Nicky, so they both travel the same distance to get to that point. Finally, the rate and time both use seconds, so it's not necessary to convert anything before solving.

	R (m/s)	×	T (s)	=	D (m)
C	5	×	t	=	d
N	3	×	$t + 12$	=	d

Use the two equations created by each row to solve for t:

$$5t = d$$
$$3(t + 12) = d$$

Both equations equal d, so set the left-hand sides equal to each other and solve for t.

$$5t = 3(t + 12)$$
$$5t = 3t + 36$$
$$2t = 36$$
$$t = 18$$

Therefore, Nicky will have run for $18 + 12 = 30$ seconds before Cristina catches up. Watch out for trap answer (B)! That's how long Cristina runs, not how long Nicky runs.

Chapter 27: **Rates**

7. **4.5**

   Solve this either algebraically or by picking numbers (recommended). Start by creating an RTD chart to represent the knowns and unknowns. The distance Juan walks equals the distance he bikes, because both are halfway to school. Pick a value for this distance, ideally something that is divisible by both 3 and 9, the two rates given in the problem. This solution uses $d = 9$.

	R	×	T	=	D
bikes	9 mi/hr	×	t_1	=	9
walks	3 mi/hr	×	t_2	=	9
total	$r = ?$	×	$t_1 + t_2$	=	18

   Solve for the times.

	R	×	T	=	D
bikes	9 mi/hr	×	1	=	9
walks	3 mi/hr	×	3	=	9
total	$r = ?$	×	4	=	18

   Finally, solve for the average rate.

   $$\text{average rate} = \frac{\text{total distance}}{\text{total time}} = \frac{18}{4} = 4.5$$

   The average rate is 4.5 miles per hour.

8. **6**

   Start by setting up a chart.

	R	×	T	=	W
T		×	12 min	=	1 job
A		×	$t = ?$	=	1 job
T + A		×	4 min	=	1 job

   Fill in the rate column by dividing the work by the time:

	R	×	T	=	W
T	$\frac{1}{12}$ job/min	×	12 min	=	1 job
A	$\frac{1}{t}$ job/min	×	$t = ?$	=	1 job
T + A	$\frac{1}{4}$ job/min	×	4 min	=	1 job

Andy's rate plus Tarik's rate equals their combined rate. Set up an equation to solve for t.

$$\frac{1}{12} + \frac{1}{t} = \frac{1}{4}$$

$$\frac{1}{t} = \frac{1}{4} - \frac{1}{12}$$

$$\frac{1}{t} = \frac{3}{12} - \frac{1}{12}$$

$$\frac{1}{t} = \frac{1}{6}$$

$$t = 6$$

It will take 6 minutes for Andy to complete the job on his own.

9. **6,400**

Set up a table to find the pattern. The colony doubles every two days.

Time	Population
6 days ago	200
4 days ago (Careful! Count by two days.)	400
2 days ago	800
NOW	1,600
2 days from now	3,200
4 days from now	6,400

Chapter 27: **Rates**

Problem Set

> Solve the following problems using the strategies you have learned in this section. As needed, use RTD or RTW tables to organize more complex problems.

1. A cat travels at a speed of 60 inches/second. How long will it take this cat, in seconds, to travel 300 feet? (12 inches = 1 foot)

2. Water is being poured into a tank at the rate of approximately 4 cubic feet per hour. If the tank is 6 feet long, 4 feet wide, and 8 feet deep, how many hours will it take to fill up the tank?

3. The population of grasshoppers in a particular field doubles every year. Approximately how many years, rounded to the nearest year, will it take the population to grow from 2,000 grasshoppers to at least 1,000,000 ?

4. A machine fills buckets with paint at a constant rate. It takes 6 minutes to fill a bucket to $\frac{3}{5}$ of its capacity. How much time does it take to fill an empty bucket to capacity?

5. The Technotronic can produce 5 bad songs per hour. Wanting to produce bad songs more quickly, the record label also buys a Wonder Wheel, which works as fast as the Technotronic. Working together, how many bad songs can the two devices produce in 72 minutes?

6. Four years from now, the population of a colony of bees will reach 1.6×10^8. If the population of the colony doubles every 2 years, what was the population 4 years ago?

    (A) 4×10^7
    (B) 2×10^7
    (C) 1×10^7
    (D) 5×10^6
    (E) 1×10^6

7. Jack spends one hour putting together gift boxes at a rate of 3 boxes per hour. Then Jill comes over and yells, "Work faster!" Jack, now nervous, works at the rate of only 2 gift boxes per hour for the next two hours. Then Alexandra comes to Jack and whispers, "The steadiest hand is capable of the divine." Jack, calmer, then puts together 5 gift boxes in the fourth hour. What is the average rate at which Jack puts together gift boxes over the entire period?

Unit Six: **Advanced Topics**

8. At 12 noon, a train leaves Kyoto for Tokyo traveling at a constant rate of 240 miles per hour. Ten minutes later, another train leaves Tokyo for Kyoto traveling at a constant rate of 150 miles per hour. If Tokyo and Kyoto are 300 miles apart, at what time will the trains pass each other?

    (A) 12:30pm
    (B) 12:40pm
    (C) 12:50pm
    (D) 1:00pm
    (E) 1:10pm

9. A car travels from Town *A* to Town *B* at an average speed of 40 miles per hour, and returns along the same route at an average speed of 50 miles per hour. What is the approximate average speed in miles per hour for the entire trip?

10. Alde drove from *A* to *B* at 60 miles per hour, then returned on the same route from *B* to *A* at 80 miles per hour. Alde then drove on the same route from *A* back to *B* at 90 mph. What was Alde's approximate average speed in miles per hour for the entire trip, rounded to the nearest tenth?

11. A hose, working alone, is capable of filling up an empty pool in 6 hours. A second hose, working alone, is capable of filling up the empty pool in 4 hours. How long would it take for both hoses together to fill two-thirds of the pool?

12. Aala takes 6 minutes to pack a box and Berhane takes 5 minutes to pack a box. Working together, how many hours will it take them to pack 110 boxes?

13. Hector can solve one word problem every 4 minutes before noon, and one word problem every 10 minutes after noon.

Quantity A	Quantity B
The number of word problems Hector can solve between 11:40am and noon	The number of word problems Hector can solve between noon and 12:40pm

14. The number of users (nonzero) of a social networking website doubles every 4 months.

Quantity A	Quantity B
Ten times the number of users one year ago	The number of users today

15. A high-speed train can cover the 420 kilometers between Xenia and York at a rate of 240 kilometers per hour.

Quantity A	Quantity B
The number of minutes it will take the train to travel from Xenia to York	110

16. A swimming pool has a length of 30 meters, a width of 10 meters, and an average depth of 2 meters. If a hose can fill the pool at a rate of 0.5 cubic meters per minute, how many hours will it take the hose to fill the pool?

17. Riku can run π meters every 2 seconds. If a circular track has a radius of 75 meters, how many minutes does it take Riku to run twice around the track?

18. Yesterday, Riku ran 8 laps on a circular track with a radius of 75 meters. Today, Riku is running on a circular track with a radius of 200 meters. How many laps does Riku have to run in order to run the same distance today as yesterday?

19. A cylindrical water tank has a diameter of 14 meters and a height of 20 meters. A water truck can fill π cubic meters of the tank every minute. How long in hours and minutes will it take the water truck to fill the water tank from empty to half full?

20. June can run 6 laps in x minutes and Marijn can run 11 laps in $2x$ minutes.

Quantity A	Quantity B
The number of minutes it takes June to run 24 laps	The number of minutes it takes Marijn to run 22 laps

21. Tavi drives 113 miles at 50 miles per hour and returns via the same route at 60 miles per hour.

Quantity A	Quantity B
Tavi's average speed for the entire round trip	55 mph

22. Preeti can make 100 sandwiches in 1 hour and 15 minutes, and Mariska can make 50 sandwiches in 30 minutes.

Quantity A	Quantity B
The time it would take Preeti and Mariska to make a total of 180 sandwiches, each working at her own independent rate	The time it would take to make 110 sandwiches if Mariska worked alone for 30 minutes and then Mariska and Preeti worked together to finish the job

23. A train travels from Town A to Town B at x miles per hour, and then from Town B to Town C at $1.2x$ miles per hour.

Quantity A	Quantity B
The train's travel time from Town A to Town B	The train's travel time from Town B to Town C

Unit Six: **Advanced Topics**

Solutions

1. **60 seconds**

   Because the question asks about a distance of 300 feet, first convert the rate, 60 inches per second, into feet per second.

   $$\frac{60 \text{ in}}{\text{sec}} \times \frac{1 \text{ ft}}{12 \text{ in}} = 5 \text{ ft/sec}$$

   Now that everything is expressed in feet and seconds, plug the rate and distance into the RTD formula to solve.

   $$R \times T = D$$
   $$5 \times t = 300$$
   $$t = \frac{300}{5} = 60$$

2. **48 hours**

   The capacity of the tank is $6 \times 4 \times 8$, or 192 cubic feet. This is the work being done. The problem states that the rate is 4 cubic feet per hour.

   $$R \times T = W$$
   $$4 \times t = 192$$
   $$t = \frac{192}{4} = 48$$

3. **9 years**

   Organize the given information in a population chart.

Time Elapsed	Population
NOW	2,000
1 year	4,000
2 years	8,000
3 years	16,000
4 years	32,000
5 years	64,000
6 years	128,000
7 years	256,000
8 years	512,000
9 years	1,024,000

4. **10 minutes**

   The rate is not given, but the time needed to do $\frac{3}{5}$ of the job is given, so use this information to find the constant rate.

   $$R \times T = W$$
   $$R \times 6 = \frac{3}{5}$$
   $$R = \frac{\cancel{3}^1}{5} \times \frac{1}{\cancel{6}_2} = \frac{1}{10}$$

   The bucket is being filled at a rate of $\frac{1}{10}$ of the job per minute. From here, use the rate formula again or logic it out. If $\frac{1}{10}$ of the job is done every minute, then it will take a total of 10 minutes to do $\frac{10}{10}$ of the job (also known as the whole job).

   $$R \times T = W$$
   $$\frac{1}{10} \times t = 1$$
   $$t = 10$$

5. **12 songs**

   This is a "working together" problem, so add the individual rates: $5 + 5 = 10$ songs per hour.

   Convert the given 72 minutes into hours:

   $$(72 \text{ min})\left(\frac{1 \text{ hr}}{60 \text{ min}}\right) = \frac{72}{60} = 1.2 \text{ hr}$$

   Use the $RT = W$ equation to find the total work done in 1.2 hours.

   $$R \times T = W$$
   $$10 \times 1.2 = 12$$

6. **(C) 1×10^7**

   Organize the information given in a population chart. The doubling rate is once every *two* years, not every year. Work backward from the population four years from now to the population four years ago, halving every two years.

Time	Population
in 4 years	1.6×10^8
in 2 years	0.8×10^8
NOW	0.4×10^8
2 years ago	0.2×10^8
4 years ago	0.1×10^8

Unit Six: **Advanced Topics**

Then convert to eliminate the decimal.

$$0.1 \times 10^8 = 1 \times 10^7$$

7. **3 boxes per hour**

   The average rate is equal to the total work done divided by the total time in which the work was done. To find the total work, add up the boxes Jack put together in each hour: $3 + 2 + 2 + 5 = 12$. Then, divide by the total time of 4 hours. The average rate is $\frac{12}{4}$, or 3 boxes per hour.

8. **(C) 12:50pm**

   This is a variation on a "working together" problem in which the two trains are working together at the goal of approaching each other. They start 300 miles apart. At the moment they pass each other, they have collectively traveled the 300 miles separating them at the start.

   You can either use logic to estimate or solve algebraically.

   The two trains are approaching each other at a rate of $240 + 150 = 390$ miles per hour. That is, for every hour they both are moving, they collectively cover a bit less than 400 miles. However, the slower train doesn't start to move until 10 minutes later, so in the first hour after the first train starts, they're collectively covering something close to, but definitely less than, 400 miles ... maybe 375-ish miles.

   They start out only 300 miles apart, so it will take less than a full hour before they pass each other; eliminate answers (D) and (E). But it will take them more than three-quarters of an hour to cover 300 miles, since 300 is more than three-quarters of 375-ish. Eliminate answers (A) and (B). The only answer remaining is (C).

   Alternatively, solve algebraically. Set up the RTD chart for the two trains. Since you want to find how much time has passed since noon, set t to represent the time for the first train. That makes the time for the second train $t - 10$ minutes. Once you've solved for t, add that to the 12:00 noon start time to find the time the two trains pass.

   But wait! The rate is in miles per *hour*, while the time differential is in minutes, so one of these needs to be converted. Because most of the answer choices represent minutes, not full hours, convert the rate to miles per minute by dividing by 60.

	R (mi/min)	×	T (min)	=	D (mi)
K to T	4	×	t	=	$4t$
T to K	2.5	×	$t - 10$	=	$2.5(t - 10)$
Total	—		—		300

Because the trains start out 300 miles apart, the collective distance traveled at the point that they pass each other is equal to 300 miles. Add up the two distance representations for each train, set that equal to 300, and solve for t.

$$4t + 2.5(t - 10) = 300$$
$$4t + 2.5t - 25 = 300$$
$$6.5t = 325$$
$$t = 50$$

The first train leaves at 12:00 noon and passes the second train 50 minutes later, at 12:50pm.

9. **44.4 miles per hour**
On average rate problems, find the total distance and divide by the total time. Start by selecting a Smart Number for d, such as 200 miles. (This is a common multiple of the two rates in the problem, 40 and 50.) Then, find the time for each trip.

$$t_1 = \frac{200}{40} = 5 \text{ hr}$$
$$t_2 = \frac{200}{50} = 4 \text{ hr}$$

The total time for the two trips is 5 + 4 = 9 hours. The total distance for the two trips is 400 miles.

$$\text{Average speed} = \frac{\text{Total } d}{\text{Total } t} = \frac{400}{9} \approx 44.4$$

When the distances are the same, as they are in this problem, the average rate will always be weighted toward the slower rate, since more time is spent at that rate.

10. **Approximately 74.5 mph**
To find average speed, calculate the total distance and divide by the total time, regardless of the number of trips taken. The distance, d, for each of the three trips is the same. Start by selecting a Smart Number for d, such as 720 miles. (This is a common multiple of the 3 rates given in the problem. Use 6, 8, and 9 to find the common multiple of 72, then add a 0.) Use the distance and rate to find the time for each trip.

$$\text{time} = \frac{\text{distance}}{\text{rate}}$$
$$t_1 = \frac{720}{60} = 12 \text{ hr}$$
$$t_2 = \frac{720}{80} = 9 \text{ hr}$$
$$t_3 = \frac{720}{90} = 8 \text{ hr}$$

Alde's total time for the three trips was 12 + 9 + 8 = 29 hours. The total distance was 3(720) = 2,160 miles.

$$\text{Average speed} = \frac{\text{Total } d}{\text{Total } t} = \frac{2,160}{29} \approx 74.5$$

Unit Six: Advanced Topics

11. $\frac{8}{5}$ of an hour

    Since Hose 1 can fill the pool in 6 hours, its rate is $\frac{1}{6}$ pool per hour. Likewise, since Hose 2 can fill the pool in 4 hours, its rate is $\frac{1}{4}$ pool per hour. Add the two rates to find the combined rate.

    $$\frac{1}{6} + \frac{1}{4} = \frac{2}{12} + \frac{3}{12} = \frac{5}{12}$$

    In the question, the pool is filled to two-thirds of its capacity. Use the rate and work to find the time.

    $$\text{Rate} \times \text{Time} = \text{Work}$$

    $$\frac{5}{12} \times t = \frac{2}{3}$$

    $$t = \frac{2}{3}\left(\frac{12}{5}\right)$$

    $$t = \frac{8}{5}$$

    It will take $\frac{8}{5}$ of an hour. The real test could also put the answer choice in the form 1 hour 36 minutes or $1\frac{3}{5}$ of an hour.

12. **5 hours**

    Aala's rate is $\frac{1}{6}$ of a box per minute and Berhane's rate is $\frac{1}{5}$ of a box per minute. Working together, Aala and Berhane pack $\frac{1}{6} + \frac{1}{5} = \frac{11}{30}$ boxes per minute. Next, determine how many minutes it will take them to pack 110 boxes.

    $$R \times T = W$$

    $$\frac{11}{30} \times t = 110$$

    $$t = 110\left(\frac{30}{11}\right)$$

    $$t = 300$$

    It will take 300 minutes, but the question asks for the time in hours, so divide by 60 to convert. It will take 5 hours for the two of them to pack 110 boxes.

13. **(A)**

    Hector's work rate is different for the two time periods. Quantity A asks for the number of problems Hector can solve between 11:40am and noon, a period of 20 minutes. Before noon, Hector works at a rate of one problem every 4 minutes, so in 20 minutes, Hector solves 5 problems.

    Quantity B asks for the number of problems Hector can solve between noon and 12:40pm, a period of 40 minutes. After noon, Hector works at a rate of one problem every 10 minutes, so in 40 minutes, Hector solves 4 problems.

    The correct answer is (A): Quantity A is greater.

14. **(A)**

    Set up a Population chart, letting X denote the number of users one year ago:

Time	Number of Users
12 months ago	X
8 months ago	$2X$
4 months ago	$4X$
NOW	$8X$

    Quantity A is ten times the number of users one year ago, or $10X$, while Quantity B is the number of users today, which is $8X$. The given information stated that X is not zero and there can't be a negative number of people, so X must be positive. Therefore, $10X$ must be greater than $8X$.

    The correct answer is (A): Quantity A is greater.

15. **(B)**

    Use the rate equation to solve for the time it will take the train to cover the distance.

    $$R \times T = D$$
    $$240 \times t = 420$$
    $$t = \frac{420}{240} = \frac{42}{24} = \frac{7}{4}$$

    Finally, convert the time from hours into minutes:

    $$\frac{7}{4} \times 60 = \frac{7}{\cancel{4}_1} \times \cancel{60}^{15} = 105 \text{ minutes}$$

    The correct answer is (B): Quantity B is greater.

16. **20 hours**

    The volume of the pool is (length) × (width) × (height), or $30 \times 10 \times 2 = 600$ cubic meters. The rate is given in meters per minute, but the question asks for hours, so make a note that you'll need to convert the answer to hours before you're done.

    $$R \times T = W$$
    $$\frac{1}{2} \times t = 600$$
    $$t = 600 \times 2 = 1{,}200 \text{ min}$$

    To convert from minutes to hours, divide 1,200 by 60 to get 20 hours.

Unit Six: Advanced Topics

17. **10 minutes**

    The distance around the track is equal to the circumference of the circle. The radius of the circle is 75 meters. Make a note that the rate is given in meters per second, but the question asks for the answer in minutes.

    $$C = 2\pi r$$
    $$C = 150\pi$$

    Running twice around the circle would equal a distance of 300π meters. Riku runs at a rate of π meters every 2 seconds, so it will take 600 seconds to run 300π meters. To convert seconds to minutes, divide 600 by 60 to get 10 minutes.

18. **3 laps**

    The distance around a circular track is equal to the circumference of the circle. One lap around the track with a radius of 75 meters is equal to $2\pi r = 150\pi$ meters. Eight laps around this track is therefore a distance of $1{,}200\pi$ meters.

    The track with a radius of 200 meters has a circumference of $2\pi r = 400\pi$ meters. Riku will have to run 3 laps around this track to cover a distance of $1{,}200\pi$ meters.

19. **8 hours and 10 minutes**

    Make a note that the question asked how long it will take to fill half of the tank, not the whole tank. First, find the volume of the cylindrical tank. The radius is 7 and the height is 20.

    $$V = \pi r^2 h$$
    $$V = \pi (7^2)(20)$$
    $$V = 980\pi$$

    Since the water truck can fill π cubic meters of the tank every minute, it will take 980 minutes to fill the tank completely. Therefore, it will take $980 \div 2 = 490$ minutes, or 8 hours and 10 minutes, to fill the tank halfway.

20. **(C)**

    June can run 6 laps in x minutes. If Marijn were equally fast, Marijn could run 12 laps in $2x$ minutes (twice the laps in twice the time). However, Marijn can run only 11 laps in $2x$ minutes, so Marijn is slightly slower than June. If the quantities then asked for June and Marijn's times to run the *same* number of laps, you would not have to do any calculating: June is faster, so Marijn would take longer.

    However, June (the slightly faster person) is being asked to run slightly more laps, so it's pretty hard to estimate. Although that didn't work out for this problem, it's still worth checking when you see a similar problem. Instead, since x is never specified, pick a number for that value. If $x = 3$, then June can run 6 laps in 3 minutes and Marijn can run 11 laps in 6 minutes.

Quantity A asks for the number of minutes it takes Jane to run 24 laps. If she can run 6 laps in 3 minutes, then to run 4 times as many laps, it will take her 4 times as long, or 12 minutes. Alternatively, set up a proportion:

$$\frac{6 \text{ laps}}{3 \text{ min}} = \frac{24 \text{ laps}}{y \text{ min}}$$

$$6y = 72$$

$$y = 12$$

Quantity B asks for the number of minutes it takes Marijn to run 22 laps. If she can run 11 laps in 6 minutes, then it will take her twice as long, or 12 minutes, to run twice as many laps.

Since the two quantities are both 12, the correct answer is (C): The two quantities are always equal.

21. **(B)**

    These calculations would be a little messy, but no actual calculation is required here. When the distance is the same for two trips, the average speed is never the "regular" average of the two values. It is always a weighted average skewed towards the slower of the two speeds.

    In this case, the two speeds are 50 and 60, so the weighted average has to be closer to 50, or somewhat less than the "regular" average of 55.

    The correct answer is (B): Quantity B is greater.

22. **(A)**

    Convert Preeti's and Mariska's sandwich speeds into standard rate format—that is, figure out how many sandwiches they each make per one hour. Preeti can make 100 sandwiches in 1 hour 15 minutes (or 75 minutes).

    $$\frac{100 \text{ sand}}{75 \text{ min}} = \frac{x \text{ sand}}{60 \text{ min}}$$

    $$6{,}000 = 75x$$

    $$80 = x$$

    Therefore, Preeti makes 80 sandwiches per hour.

    Mariska can make 50 sandwiches in 30 minutes, so she can make 100 sandwiches in 1 hour.

    Working together, they make $80 + 100 = 180$ sandwiches in an hour. Fortunately, Quantity A asks for their time to make 180 sandwiches working together, so Quantity A is 1 hour.

    Quantity B asks for the time it would take to make 110 sandwiches if Mariska worked alone for 30 minutes and then they finished the job together. Working alone for 30 minutes, Mariska will make 50 sandwiches. That leaves 60 sandwiches for the two of them to make together. They work at a combined rate of 180 sandwiches per hour, and 60 is one-third of 180, so it will take them $\frac{1}{3}$ of an hour to make the remaining 60 sandwiches together.

    Quantity B is equal to the 30 minutes Mariska works alone, plus the 20 minutes the two work together, for a total of 50 minutes to do the job.

    The correct answer is (A): Quantity A is greater.

Unit Six: **Advanced Topics**

23. **(D)**

    Whenever you see a story problem on Quantitative Comparisons, *make sure you have the information you need before doing any computation.*

    Unlike earlier problems, the train does not travel back across the same distance for the second trip. Rather, it travels from Town *A* to Town *B* and then from Town *B* to Town *C*. No information is given about the exact or even the relative distances between the towns. Town *A* could be 1 mile from Town *B*, while Town *B* is 1,000 miles from Town *C*, or vice versa.

    Quantities A and B ask about travel time. If the two distances are not necessarily the same, then you need to know something about both distance and rate in order to calculate time. However, you are given only the relative rates (*x* and 1.2*x*). Without any information about the distances—even just the relative relationship between them—it's impossible to figure out anything about the time.

    The correct answer is (D): The relationship cannot be determined.

CHAPTER 28

Sequences and Patterns

In This Chapter:

- Sequence Formulas
- Logical Sequencing
- Properties of Terms
- Digit Problems
- Evenly Spaced Sequences
- Defining Evenly Spaced Sequences
- Visualizing Evenly Spaced Sets
- Properties of Evenly Spaced Sequences
- Evenly Spaced Sets on QC
- Check Your Skills Answer Key
- Problem Set
- Solutions

CHAPTER 28 Sequences and Patterns

The GRE will sometimes ask questions revolving around numbers or unknowns in a **sequence**. Consecutive integers are examples of sequences. Alternatively, the GRE might define an unusual sequence using a formula. In this chapter, you will learn how to:

- Determine which answer choice corresponds to the correct *definition* (or *rule*) for a sequence
- Determine the value of a particular *item* in a sequence
- Determine the sum, difference, or product of a *set of items* in a sequence

A problem could even ask for something that would seem to take hours to figure out. For example, it could ask for the sum of 100 different numbers or the 71st number in a list of 150. The GRE doesn't give you enough time to calculate such values manually, so you'll also learn certain shortcuts that will allow you to solve these problems much more efficiently.

Sequence Formulas

In Chapter 6: Formulas and Functions, you learned about formulas that produced one output for a given input. For example, the function $f(x) = 9x + 3$ allows you to plug in a value for x and return an output. If x is 2, then $f(2) = 9(2) + 3 = 21$.

The GRE will also use formulas to describe entire sequences—that is, there will be many outputs, not just one. For example:

$$A_n = 9n + 3$$

The first step is identical to what you learned for functions. For example, when n is 2, replace n with 2 everywhere in the rule and calculate the output:

$$A_n = 9n + 3$$
$$A_2 = 9(2) + 3$$
$$A_2 = 21$$

The difference between sequence rules and ordinary functions is that a sequence problem isn't talking about just one input and one output. Instead, a sequence describes an entire set of numbers, where n indicates which value in the set you're describing. Think about it as creating a list of n numbers. You start with just blanks:

$$A_n: \underline{} \quad \underline{} \quad \underline{} \quad \underline{} \quad \underline{} \quad \ldots$$
$$n = \quad 1 \quad 2 \quad 3 \quad 4 \quad 5 \quad \ldots$$

Unit Six: Advanced Topics

The blanks are where to put the first five numbers in the sequence. To determine what those numbers are, plug the value of n in for each position in the sequence. For example, the second position is when n is 2, and that value is 21:

$$A_n: \quad \underline{} \quad \underline{21} \quad \underline{} \quad \underline{} \quad \underline{} \quad \ldots$$
$$n = \quad 1 \quad\quad 2 \quad\quad 3 \quad\quad 4 \quad\quad 5 \quad \ldots$$

Solve for the first position by plugging in 1 for n:

$$A_1 = 9(1) + 3 = 12$$

The first number in the sequence is 12:

$$A_n: \quad \underline{12} \quad \underline{21} \quad \underline{} \quad \underline{} \quad \underline{} \quad \ldots$$
$$n = \quad 1 \quad\quad 2 \quad\quad 3 \quad\quad 4 \quad\quad 5 \quad \ldots$$

Solve for the remaining terms in the sequence before reading on.

You've just found the first five terms in the sequence $A_n = 9n + 3$:

$$A_3 = 9(3) + 3 = 30$$
$$A_4 = 9(4) + 3 = 39$$
$$A_5 = 9(5) + 3 = 48$$

$$A_n: \quad \underline{12} \quad \underline{21} \quad \underline{30} \quad \underline{39} \quad \underline{48} \quad \ldots$$
$$n = \quad 1 \quad\quad 2 \quad\quad 3 \quad\quad 4 \quad\quad 5 \quad \ldots$$

Examine the sequence and look for a pattern. In this case, the sequence starts at 12 and then adds 9 each time. Once you calculate the three, if the pattern is something straightforward like adding the same value each time, you can just start writing out the later values, adding 9 each time. If the pattern isn't straightforward, solve for another couple of terms. (If the pattern still isn't straightforward, find another way to solve or make a guess and move on.)

You could technically continue to expand this sequence infinitely. Luckily, the GRE will not require you to list outrageously long sequences. It may, however, ask for a specific term in a sequence. Try this problem:

If $n \geq 1$, what is the 73rd term in the sequence defined by $A_n = 9n + 3$?

When n is 73, what is A_{73}? Plug in 73 for n:

$$A_{73} = 9(73) + 3 = 657 + 3 = 660$$

So, the 73rd term is 660.

These cases are all known as **direct sequences**. In a direct sequence, each term can be individually calculated as long as you know that term's place in sequence. In the previous example, the value of A_{73} can be calculated simply because it is the 73rd term in the sequence.

Most sequences on the GRE are defined for integers $n \geq 1$. That is, sequence Sn almost always starts at S_1. Occasionally, the GRE may define a sequence as starting at S_0, but in that case, you will be told that n could equal 0.

Check Your Skills

1. List the terms of the sequence defined as $Qn = n^2 + 4$ from $n = 1$ to $n = 5$. Also find $n = 10$.

2. $S_n = 2n - 5$ for all integers $n \geq 1$. What is the 11th term of the sequence?

Answers can be found on page 793.

Recursive Sequences

The GRE also uses **recursive** formulas to define sequences. In a recursive formula, each term in a sequence is defined by the value of other terms in the sequence. A recursive formula could look like this:

$$A_n = A_{n-1} + 9$$

This formula translates to "This term (A_n) equals the previous term (A_{n-1}) plus 9." It is shorthand for a series of specific relationships between successive terms:

$$A_2 = A_1 + 9$$
$$A_3 = A_2 + 9$$
$$A_4 = A_3 + 9, \text{ and so on}$$

Whenever you look at a recursive formula, in your mind, *articulate its meaning in words*. If necessary, also write out one or two specific relationships that the recursive formula stands for. Think of a recursive formula as a "domino" relationship: If you know A_1, then you can find A_2, and then you can find A_3, then A_4, and so on for all the terms. You can also work back to front: If you know A_4, then you can find A_3, A_2, and A_1. However, if you do not know the value of any one term, then you cannot calculate the value of any other. You need one domino to fall, so to speak, to knock down all the others.

Thus, to solve for the values of a recursive sequence, you need to be given the recursive rule *and* the value of at least one of the items in the sequence. For example:

> The first number in the sequence defined by $A_n = A_{n-1} + 9$ is 12. What is the fourth number in that sequence?

This problem defines the first term, or A_1, as 12. Given that, you can find the other terms in the sequence:

$$A_2 = A_1 + 9 = 12 + 9 = 21$$
$$A_3 = A_2 + 9 = 21 + 9 = 30$$
$$A_4 = A_3 + 9 = 30 + 9 = 39$$

A_n:	12	21	30	39	__	__	...
$n =$	1	2	3	4	5	6	...

The fourth number in the sequence is 39. Try another example:

> $F_n = F_{n-1} + F_{n-2}$ for all integers $n \geq 3$. If $F_1 = 1$ and $F_2 = 1$, what is F_5?

Unit Six: Advanced Topics

In this example, F_n is defined in terms of both the previous item, F_{n-1}, and the item before that, F_{n-2}. This recursive formula means "This term equals the previous term plus the term before that." You need to be given two terms to start solving for F_5:

$$F_1 = 1$$
$$F_2 = 1$$
$$F_3 = F_2 + F_1 = 1 + 1 = 2$$
$$F_4 = F_3 + F_2 = 2 + 1 = 3$$
$$F_5 = F_4 + F_3 = 3 + 2 = 5$$

F_n:	1	1	2	3	5	—	…
$n =$	1	2	3	4	5	6	…

By the way, if you've ever heard of the Fibonacci sequence, this is it. Every term is the sum of the previous two terms. (The GRE won't expect you to recognize a sequence by name.)

Check Your Skills

3. $B_n = (-1)^n \times n + 3$ for all integers $n \geq 1$. What is the 9th term of the sequence?

4. If $A_n = 2A_{n-1} + 3$ for all $n \geq 1$, and $A_4 = 45$, what is A_1?

Answers can be found on pages 793–794.

Logical Sequencing

Sometimes the sequence will not be defined algebraically. You will need to either derive the formula based on the information given or logically determine what the answer will be based on a pattern. For example:

> If each number in a sequence is three more than the previous number, and the 6th number is 32, what is the 100th number?

Imagine this sequence as little jumps of 3 from one number to the next:

A_n:	—	$\xrightarrow{+3}$	—	$\xrightarrow{+3}$	—	$\xrightarrow{+3}$	—	$\xrightarrow{+3}$	—	$\xrightarrow{+3}$	32	…
$n =$	1		2		3		4		5		6	…

To find the 100th term, reason through the pattern. From the 6th term to the 100th term, there are 94 "jumps" of 3. Each jump will increase the term by 3. Because $94 \times 3 = 282$, there is an increase of 282 from the 6th term to the 100th term, so the 100th term is $32 + 282 = 314$.

A problem could ask you to write the formula that represents the relationship described. First, pick a starting point, called A_n. Then relate it to the term before or after it. The next number up would be A_{n+1} and would be 3 more than A_n. So the relationship between these two numbers is:

$$A_{n+1} = A_n + 3$$

If you need to find the formula in the answers, that process is helpful, but it's not directly helpful in finding the 100th term. You would still need to count how many jumps there are between the 6th term and the 100th term and infer that each jump adds another 3. When you're asked to do something that would take much longer than a couple of minutes to solve step by step, look for patterns instead.

Check Your Skills

5. If each number of a sequence is 4 more than the previous number, and the 3rd number in the sequence is 13, what is the 114th number in the sequence?

Answers can be found on page 794.

Properties of Terms

The GRE could also ask for a *property* of a particular value. For example, will the 57th term be even or will the 68th term be divisible by 3? If you can solve for that term, answering these questions requires just one additional step:

In the sequence $S_n = 4n + n^2$, the 8th term is NOT divisible by which of the following values?

(A) 2
(B) 3
(C) 4
(D) 5
(E) 6

First, solve for the 8th term in the sequence by plugging in 8 for *n*:

$$S_8 = 4(8) + 8^2$$
$$S_8 = 32 + 64$$
$$S_8 = 96$$

Second, use divisibility rules to determine which answer choices are factors of 96 and which one is not. (Review Chapter 9: Divisibility for a refresher on divisibility rules.) The value 96 is divisible by 2, 3, 4, and 6, but it is not divisible by 5. The correct answer is (D).

However, GRE problems that ask about properties of terms aren't typically this straightforward. The most common twist? You won't be able to solve for the term in question. For example:

If $S_n = 3^n$, what is the units digit of S_{65}?

Unit Six: Advanced Topics

Technically, you do know that $S_{65} = 3^{65}$, but you cannot reasonably multiply out 3^{65} on the GRE, even with a calculator. When a question seems to be asking for something that would take an unreasonable number of calculations, look for a pattern. List out the first several terms in the sequence. Pay attention to the units digit since that's what the question is asking about:

			Units Digit
3^1	=	3	3
3^2	=	9	9
3^3	=	27	7
3^4	=	81	1
3^5	=	243	3
3^6	=	729	9
3^7	=	2,187	7
3^8	=	6,561	1

The units digits of powers of 3 follow the pattern "3, 9, 7, 1" before repeating. After the 4th term, the pattern starts over. In fact, after every 4th term, the pattern will start over. So, the 4th, 8th, 12th, 16th, and all the way up to the 64th term will have a units digit of 1 (the fourth value in the pattern). The next term after each of those will begin the cycle again, and be a 3. Thus, the units digit of 3^{65} will be 3.

> **Strategy Tip**
> 1. Any time the direct calculation is unreasonable or impossible, look for a pattern.
> 2. For a units digit question, base your prediction on the pattern of the units digit alone.

The units digit repeats in a predictable way for all digits 0 through 9. The maximum number of terms in any one list is four before the pattern repeats.

Digit n	Power sequence $n, n^2, (n^3, n^4)$	Unit's digit pattern
0	0, 0	0
1	1, 1	1
2	2, 4, 8, 16	2, 4, 8, 6
3	3, 9, 27, 81	3, 9, 7, 1
4	4, 16	4, 6
5	5, 25	5
6	6, 36	6
7	7, 49, 343, 2,401	7, 9, 3, 1
8	8, 64, 512, 4,096	8, 4, 2, 6
9	9, 81	9, 1

Only digits 2, 3, 7, and 8 have a four-term pattern. All of the rest have either a one- or two-term pattern. Memorize the patterns for 2, 3, 7, and 8. For the others, if needed, recreate the pattern on test day—all you need is n and n^2 to know the pattern. (And if you forget the pattern for 2, 3, 7, or 8, you can also recreate that pattern on test day. Use the calculator as needed.)

Check Your Skills

6. If $A_n = 7^n - 1$, what is the units digit of A_{33}?

Answers can be found on page 794.

Digit Problems

Patterns in repeating digits are frequent enough on the GRE that they deserve special attention. The test could ask you to determine a specific digit based on a sequence (as shown in the previous section) or based on a large product.

The previous example was a units digit problem. Raising an integer to an increasing exponent will always create a repeating pattern in the units digit, so this is the digit that a question is most likely to ask you about. However, that request may be disguised. For instance, these two questions are actually the same question:

> What is the units digit of 193?
> What is the remainder when 193 is divided by 10?

The units digit of 193 is 3, since the units digit is the final digit before the decimal.

What about the second question? When you divide 193 by 10, you get 19.3, or $19\frac{3}{10}$. The 19 part is still an integer; the only thing that gets "left over" is whatever started out in the units digit. And, since you're dividing by 10, that exact units digit will turn into the remainder. So 193 divided by 10 is 19 with a remainder of 3. (Revisit Chapter 9: Remainders for a refresher on remainders.)

In addition or multiplication, the units digit of a number will only be impacted by other units digits. For example, the units digit of 568 × 742 will be 6, because the units digit of 8 multiplied by the units digit of 2 will produce 8 × 2 = 1<u>6</u>, which has a units digit of 6.

In some cases, the GRE may ask about other digits, like the tens digit. If that happens, ignore everything to the left of that digit. You can find the tens digit of a product by looking only at the tens and units digits. For example:

$$325{,}846 \times 54{,}748 = (\ldots 46)(\ldots 48) = (\ldots 08)$$

The values 46 and 48 multiply to 2,208. The tens digit is 0 (and the units digit is 8).

> **Strategy Tip**
>
> To find the units digit of a product or a sum of integers, *only pay attention to the units digits of the numbers you are working with*. Ignore any other digits.

Use this tip when you're asked to find a large product:

> What is the remainder when $(8)^2(9)^2(3)^3$ is divided by 10?

Find the units digits of each of the exponential terms, then multiply those units digits together, ignoring all the other digits. This shortcut works because only units digits contribute to the units digit of the product:

$8 \times 8 = 6\underline{4}$	Drop the tens digit and keep only the units digit: 4.
$9 \times 9 = 8\underline{1}$	Drop the tens digit and keep only the units digit: 1.
$3 \times 3 \times 3 = 2\underline{7}$	Drop the tens digit and keep only the units digit: 7.
$4 \times 1 \times 7 = 2\underline{8}$	Multiply the units digits of each of the prior values. Take only the units digit of this outcome.

The units digit of the final product is 8. (You can verify this by plugging the product into your calculator: $(8)^2(9)^2(3)^3 = 139{,}968$.) When a number is divided by 10, the remainder is equal to the units digit, so the remainder is 8.

The answer wouldn't change if the 8, 9, and 3 were changed into much greater numbers with the same units digits:

What is the remainder when $(238)^2(59)^2(743)^3$ is divided by 10?

Use only the units digits to determine the resulting unit digit:

$$(238)^2 = (\ldots 8)^2 = (\ldots 4)$$
$$(59)^2 = (\ldots 9)^2 = (\ldots 1)$$
$$(743)^3 = (\ldots 3)^3 = (\ldots 7)$$
$$(238)^2(59)^2(743)^3 = (\ldots 4)(\ldots 1)(\ldots 7) = (\ldots 8)$$

The final units digit is still 8, and so the remainder when divided by 10 is also still 8.

Other digit problems can focus on different kinds of patterns. For example:

What is the 50th digit after the decimal in the decimal representation of $\frac{3}{11}$?

This computation is unreasonable, so look for a pattern. When you plug $3 \div 11$ into the GRE calculator, you'll see 0.2727273 result. This is a repeating decimal with the digits 2 and 7 repeating infinitely: $\frac{3}{11} = 0.\overline{27}$. The final 3 on the calculator appears because the last digit rounded up from 2 to 3.

Use the pattern to find the value of the 50th digit. The 1st, 3rd, 5th and so on digits are 2. The 2nd, 4th, 6th, and so on up to the 50th digit are 7.

Check Your Skills

7. What is the units digit of $4^3 \times 7^2 \times 8$?

8. What is the units digit of 13^3?

Answers can be found on page 794.

Evenly Spaced Sequences

Some sequences fall into a special category called **evenly spaced sequences**. These are sequences of numbers whose values go up or down by the same amount, or **increment**, from one item in the sequence to the next. In fact, the first sequence formula in this chapter, $A_n = 9n + 3$, is an evenly spaced sequence because every number in the sequence is exactly 9 greater than the previous number:

$$A_n: \quad \underline{12} \xrightarrow{+9} \underline{21} \xrightarrow{+9} \underline{30} \xrightarrow{+9} \underline{39} \xrightarrow{+9} \underline{48} \xrightarrow{+9} \underline{57} \quad ...$$
$$n = \quad 1 \qquad 2 \qquad 3 \qquad 4 \qquad 5 \qquad 6 \quad ...$$

On the GRE, evenly spaced sequences are rarely described using a formula. More often, the test will describe a set of numbers, and it will be up to you to determine that those numbers are evenly spaced.

Consecutive multiples are special cases of evenly spaced sequences: All of the values in the sequence are multiples of the increment. For example, {12, 16, 20, 24} is a sequence of consecutive multiples because each element is a multiple of 4 (and, as a result, each number increases by 4 from the prior number). Sequences of consecutive multiples *must* be composed of integers.

Consecutive integers are special cases of consecutive multiples: All of the values in the sequence are integers that increase by 1. For example, {12, 13, 14, 15, 16} is a sequence of consecutive integers because the values increase from one to the next by 1, and each element is an integer.

Evenly spaced sequences represent the broadest category. Consecutive multiples are a type of evenly spaced sequence, and consecutive integers are a type of consecutive multiples:

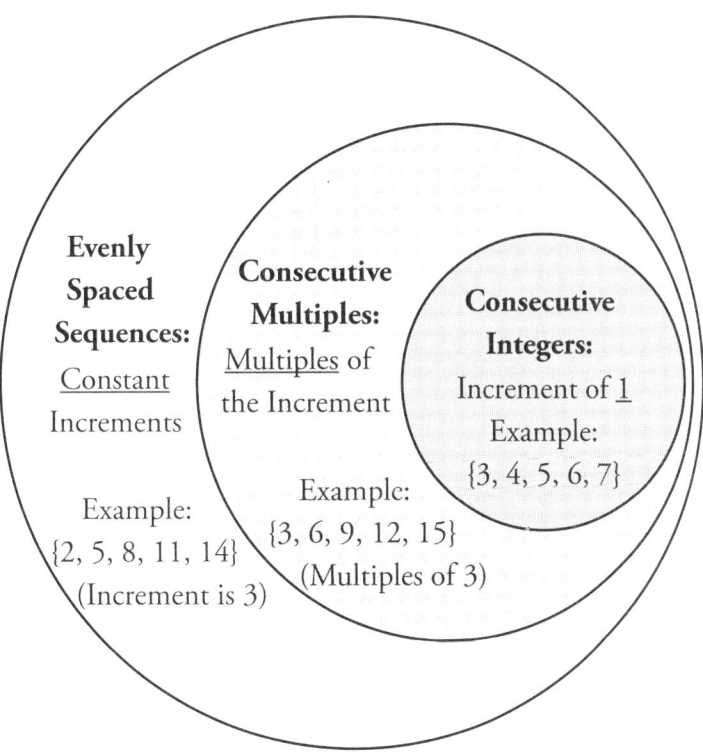

Unit Six: **Advanced Topics**

Check Your Skills

9. Which of the following are evenly spaced sequences?

   Select <u>all</u> that apply.

   ☐ A $\sqrt{1}, \sqrt{2}, \sqrt{3}, \sqrt{4}, \sqrt{5}$
   ☐ B $x, x - 4, x - 8, x - 12, x - 16$
   ☐ C $\sqrt{4}, \sqrt{9}, \sqrt{16}, \sqrt{25}, \sqrt{36}$
   ☐ D $5^1, 5^2, 5^3, 5^4, 5^5$
   ☐ E $y, 2y, 3y, 4y, 5y$

Answers can be found on page 794.

Defining Evenly Spaced Sequences

Identifying evenly spaced sequences is important because they have special properties. In order to use those properties, you'll need to know three parameters about the evenly spaced sequence:

1. The least (**first**) *or* greatest (**last**) number in the sequence

   and

2. The **increment** (always 1 for consecutive integers)

   and

3. The **number of items** in the sequence

The GRE can give you this information in a variety of ways. For example:

- The first 50 positive multiples of 4
- Every integer from 100 to 200, inclusive
- The multiples of 3 between 400 and 500

All of these phrasings provide the three essential parameters for using evenly spaced sequences. The first example is the most direct:

The first 50 positive multiples of 4

1. The least number in the set is 4.
2. The increment is 4.
3. There are 50 items in the sequence.

It will take a little more work to extract the necessary information from the second example: every integer from 100 to 200, inclusive.

First, the word *inclusive* indicates that you need to include the two numbers named as endpoints. So the first integer in the sequence *from 100 to 200* would be 100, not 101. The sequence ends at 200, not 199.

Next, the increment is 1, because it includes every integer.

What about the number of items? When you're given both the start and endpoint of the sequence, along with the increment, use this formula to solve for the number of items in the sequence:

$$\# \text{ of terms} = \frac{\text{last} - \text{first}}{\text{increment}} + 1$$

Last minus first is also known as the **range** of numbers:

$$\# \text{ of terms} = \frac{\text{range}}{\text{increment}} + 1$$

Use whichever form of this equation is easier for you. Here is the number of terms for the second example:

$$\# \text{ of terms} = \frac{200 - 100}{1} + 1 = 100 + 1 = 101$$

This formula accounts for the fact that in a list of numbers, you have to count both endpoints. Typically, subtraction will remove one of the endpoints, so you need to add that one back in before finalizing your count. For example, how many integers are there from 6 to 10? Subtraction suggests only 4 (because $10 - 6$ is 4). But count it out on your fingers!

There are actually five integers: 6, 7, 8, 9, 10. The plus-one in the formula will account for subtracting out the 6, since the 6 should be included in the final count:

$$\# \text{ of terms} = \frac{10 - 6}{1} + 1 = 4 + 1 = 5$$

In short, when using this formula to count the number of terms, **add 1 before you are done**.

The second example is defined as follows:

Every integer from 100 to 200, inclusive

1. The least number in the set is 100 and the greatest is 200.
2. The increment is 1.
3. There are 101 items in the sequence.

For consecutive integers the interval will always be one. The third example, however, is a consecutive multiple sequence, not a consecutive integer sequence: the multiples of 3 between 400 and 500.

The least and greatest numbers are not necessarily 400 and 500, because numbers are only included if they are multiples of 3. Is 400 a multiple of 3? It is not, because the digits 4, 0, and 0 do not add up to a multiple of 3. Neither do the digits of 401. The digits of 402, however, add up properly: $4 + 0 + 2 = 6$. So, 402 is the least number in this sequence.

Do the same to find the greatest number in the sequence. It's not 500, nor 499, but 498 is divisible by 3.

And there's one last complication: This sequence is in multiples of 3, so the increment is 3. Use that fact when calculating the number of items in the sequence.

The multiples of 3 between 400 and 500

1. The least number in the set is 402 and the greatest is 498.
2. The increment is 3.
3. There are 33 items in the sequence $\left(\frac{498 - 402}{3} + 1 = \frac{96}{3} + 1 = 33\right)$.

The greater the increment, the fewer numbers will be in the list, since you have to divide by the increment. If the sequence is a shorter one, it may be easier to write out the terms and count them. For example:

How many multiples of 5 are there between 101 and 143 ?

Unit Six: Advanced Topics

The first value is 105, and multiples of 5 are relatively easy to list out: 105, 110, 115, 120, 125, 130, 135, and 140. There are 8 items in the sequence.

Alternatively, you could note that 105 is the first number, 140 is the last number, and 5 is the increment:

$$\text{\# of terms} = \frac{\text{range}}{\text{increment}} + 1 = \frac{140 - 105}{5} + 1 = 8$$

Check Your Skills

10. How many integers are there from 1,002 to 10,001, inclusive?

11. How many multiples of 11 are there between 55 and 144, inclusive?

Answers can be found on page 795.

Visualizing Evenly Spaced Sets

The GRE sometimes uses number lines to define evenly spaced sets. On an evenly spaced number line, each tick mark represents a specific number, and the intervals between tick marks are constant. For example:

You could be given a n4umber line with missing values, and asked to infer what a value is, based on the regular spacing of the number line:

First, determine the interval spacing between each tick mark. Each interval in this diagram represents a distance of 1, so the value of x is 3.

However, intervals on number lines are not required to be 1, nor do they need to be integers. Use the number of intervals (spaces between the tick marks) between two endpoints to determine what the interval is. For example:

The range contains six tick marks and five intervals:

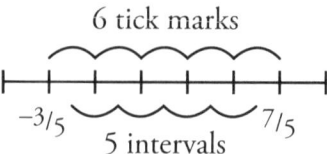

788

Chapter 28: **Sequences and Patterns**

There are five intervals spanning the distance between $\frac{7}{5}$ and $-\frac{3}{5}$:

$$\frac{7}{5} - \left(-\frac{3}{5}\right) = 5 \text{ intervals}$$
$$\frac{10}{5} = 5 \text{ intervals}$$
$$2 = 5 \text{ intervals}$$
$$\frac{2}{5} = 1 \text{ interval}$$

Here's another way to write the math:

$$\text{length of interval} = \frac{\text{range}}{\text{\# of intervals}}$$

$$\text{length of interval} = \frac{\text{range}}{\text{\# of intervals}} = \frac{\frac{7}{5} - \left(-\frac{3}{5}\right)}{5} = \frac{2}{5}$$

Use whichever approach works better for you; the math is the same. The distance from one tick mark to the next is $\frac{2}{5}$. It's now possible to determine the value of any tick mark on this number line using the interval measure:

Check Your Skills

12. On the given number line, what is the value of point *x* ?

Answers can be found on page 795.

Properties of Evenly Spaced Sequences

Once you've determined that you're dealing with an evenly spaced sequence, you can use some crucial shortcuts to answer challenging questions about them. The following three properties apply to *all* evenly spaced sequences.

1. The average (arithmetic mean) equals the median.
2. The average equals the average of the first and last terms (this is a specific application of the next point).
3. The average equals the average of any two terms equidistant from the median.

Caveat: Just because a sequence has these properties does not necessarily mean that the sequence is evenly spaced. All squares are rectangles but not all rectangles are squares. In the same way, all evenly spaced sets have these properties, but not all sets that have these properties are evenly spaced.

There are several different shortcuts for how to find the average. Here's how, given these two sets of evenly spaced integers: Set 1 = {4, 8, 12, 16, and 20} and Set 2 = {2, 4, 6, 8, 10, and 12}.

789

Unit Six: **Advanced Topics**

Because these are short sequences, it's reasonable to find the averages directly by adding the terms and dividing by the number of terms:

$$\text{Set 1 Average: } \frac{4 + 8 + 12 + 16 + 20}{5} = 12$$

$$\text{Set 2 Average: } \frac{2 + 4 + 6 + 8 + 10 + 12}{6} = 7$$

Compare those computed averages with what you would find using the three properties listed above:

1. *The average (arithmetic mean) equals the median.* Find the median to verify that it is equal to the average. The median is the middle number or the average of the two middle numbers:

   Set 1 Median: 4   8   ⑫   16   20   = 12

   Set 2 Median: 2   4   6 ⟨?⟩ 8   10   12 $= \frac{6+8}{2} = 7$

   Because there are an odd number of terms in the first set, the middle number is the median. Because there are an even number of terms in the second set, the average of the two middle terms is the median. Either way, the median of each set equals the average of that set.

2. *The average equals the average of the first and last terms.* Use the first and last term to solve for the average:

   $$\text{Set 1 Average: } \frac{4 + 20}{2} = 12$$

   $$\text{Set 2 Average: } \frac{2 + 12}{2} = 7$$

   This shortcut is one of the most useful, because it's common to be given the first and last term of an evenly spaced set.

3. *The average equals the average of any two terms equidistant from the median.* Use any two terms equidistant (or the same distance) from the median to solve for the average. In the first set, 8 and 16 are on either side of the median, and in the second set, 4 and 10 are on either side of the two middle terms:

   $$\text{Set 1 Average: } \frac{8 + 16}{2} = 12$$

   $$\text{Set 2 Average: } \frac{4 + 10}{2} = 7$$

   This property comes up more rarely, but can be useful. You don't necessarily need the first and last term to find the average if you have the second term and the second to last or the third term and third to last.

Finally, when you are asked to calculate the average of just two numbers and the numbers are relatively easy to work with, use this super-shortcut: The average lies halfway between the two values. The average of 4 and 10 is 7, because 7 is halfway between the original two values. The average of 8 and 16 is 12, because 12 is halfway between the original two values.

Chapter 28: **Sequences and Patterns**

> *Key Concept*
>
> For any evenly spaced set:
>
> $$\text{average} = \text{median} = \frac{\text{first} + \text{last}}{2} = \text{halfway between}$$
>
> and
>
> $$\text{\# of terms} = \frac{\text{last} - \text{first}}{\text{increment}} + 1$$

You'll be expected to find the sum of terms in an evenly spaced set using the average, just as you did in Chapter 18: Statistics:

$$\text{sum} = \text{average} \times \text{number of terms}$$

Try this problem:

What is the sum of the multiples of 3 between 400 and 500 ?

In asking for the sum, the question is really asking for the average multiplied by the number of terms. First, find the number of terms:

$$\text{number of terms} = \frac{\text{last} - \text{first}}{\text{increment}} + 1 = \frac{498 - 402}{3} + 1 = 33$$

Find the average using the first and last term, which are 402 and 498:

$$\frac{\text{first} + \text{last}}{2} = \frac{402 + 498}{2} = \frac{900}{2} = 450$$

Multiply them together to find the sum:

$$\text{sum} = \text{average} \times \text{number of terms} = 450 \times 33 = 14{,}850$$

Throughout this process, identifying the first and last numbers in the sequence is critical to solving this correctly. Using the numbers 400 and 500 as the terms would result in a wrong answer because they are not multiples of 3.

Check Your Skills

13. What is the average of the set {2, 5, 8, 11, 14} ?

14. What is the average of the set {−1, 3, 7, 11, 15, 19, 23, 27} ?

15. What is the sum of the numbers 130, 140, 150, and 160 ?

16. If $x = 3$, what is the sum of $2x$, $(2x + 1)$, $(2x + 2)$, $(2x + 3)$, and $(2x + 4)$?

17. What is the sum of the first 50 positive multiples of 4 ?

Answers can be found on pages 795–796.

Unit Six: **Advanced Topics**

Evenly Spaced Sets on QC

QC questions will sometimes ask you to compare the sum or product of sets of consecutive integers. Comparing rather than computing can save significant time. Consecutive integer problems allow you to make full use of this tactic by *eliminating overlap*:

Quantity A	Quantity B
The product of all the integers from 2 to 23, inclusive	The product of all the integers from 5 to 24, inclusive

You could solve for both products and then compare. But save time by comparing and canceling as much as you can.

In this problem, the numbers 5 through 23 appear in both sets. Rewrite the products:

Quantity A	Quantity B
$2 \times 3 \times 4 \times (5 \times 6 \times \ldots 22 \times 23)$	$(5 \times 6 \times \ldots 22 \times 23) \times 24$

The product of the numbers 5 through 23 is positive, and has the same value in each quantity. Cancel out $(5 \times 6 \times \ldots 22 \times 23)$, and focus on what is left:

Quantity A	Quantity B
$2 \times 3 \times 4 = 24$	24

The correct answer is (C): The two quantities are equal.

> **Strategy Tip**
>
> To compare the sums or products of evenly spaced sets, eliminate overlap in order to make a direct comparison.

Chapter 28: **Sequences and Patterns**

Check Your Skills Answer Key

1. **5, 8, 13, 20, 29, 104**
   To solve, plug in the values 1 through 5 and the value 10 for *n*.

   $$Q_n = n^2 + 4$$
   $$Q_1 = 1^2 + 4 = 5$$
   $$Q_2 = 2^2 + 4 = 8$$
   $$Q_3 = 3^2 + 4 = 13$$
   $$Q_4 = 4^2 + 4 = 20$$
   $$Q_5 = 5^2 + 4 = 29$$
   $$Q_{10} = 10^2 + 4 = 104$$

   There is a pattern here, but it's not as straightforward as the earlier example. The first value is 5. For the second value, 3 is added. For the third value, 5 is added. For the fourth value, 7 is added, and for the fifth value, 9 is added.

Q_n:	5	8	13	20	29	...	104
$n =$	1	2	3	4	5	...	10

2. **17**
   Plug 11 directly into the formula to solve.

   $$S_n = 2n - 5$$
   $$S_{11} = 2(11) - 5$$
   $$S_{11} = 22 - 5$$
   $$S_{11} = 17$$

   The 11th term in the sequence is 17.

3. **−6**
   This is a direct sequence, so plug 9 directly into the formula and use order of operations to solve:

   $$B_n = (-1)^n \times n + 3$$
   $$B_9 = (-1)^9 \times 9 + 3$$
   $$B_9 = -1 \times 9 + 3$$
   $$B_9 = -9 + 3$$
   $$B_9 = -6$$

   The 9th term in the sequence is −6.

Unit Six: **Advanced Topics**

4. 3

   This is a recursive sequence. Since the value of A_4 is given, solve for A_3, then A_2, and finally A_1.

   $$A_4 = 2A_3 + 3 \rightarrow 45 = 2A_3 + 3 \rightarrow A_3 = 21$$
   $$A_3 = 2A_2 + 3 \rightarrow 21 = 2A_2 + 3 \rightarrow A_2 = 9$$
   $$A_2 = 2A_1 + 3 \rightarrow 9 = 2A_1 + 3 \rightarrow A_1 = 3$$

A_n:	3	9	21	45
$n =$	1	2	3	4

5. 457

   There are $114 - 3 = 111$ "jumps" of 4 between the 3rd and the 114th terms. Each jump is 4, so the total increase is $111 \times 4 = 444$. The value of the 114th term is $13 + 444 = 457$.

6. 6

   The units digits of the powers of 7 follow a repeating pattern: **7**, 4**9**, 34**3**, 2,40**1**, etc. Pattern = {7, 9, 3, 1}. Every 4th term ends the pattern. So, every term that is a multiple of 4 will end the pattern: 4th, 8th, 12th, continuing up to the 32nd term. The pattern begins again for the 33rd term, so A_{33} has the same units digit as A_1, which is 7. The units digit of 7^{33} is 7, and $7 - 1 = 6$.

7. 8

   Focus only on the units digit of each step of the problem.

   $$4^3 = 4 \times 4 \times 4 = 6\underline{4}$$
   $$7^2 = 7 \times 7 = 4\underline{9}$$
   $$8 = \underline{8}$$
   $$(\ldots 4)(\ldots 9)(\ldots 8) = (\ldots 8)$$

8. 7

   Because the problem asks for the units digit of the product, ignore the tens digit and focus only on 3^3.

   $$3 \times 3 \times 3 = 27$$

   The units digit is 7.

9. (B) $x, x - 4, x - 8, x - 12, x - 16$;
   (C) $\sqrt{4}, \sqrt{9}, \sqrt{16}, \sqrt{25}, \sqrt{36}$;
   (E) $y, 2y, 3y, 4y, 5y$

   The terms in answer (A) are not evenly spaced. The terms are irrational, so the increments shown below are all rounded to the tenths place. Stop after you have confirmed that any two of the jumps are not equal; don't calculate all of them.

   $$\sqrt{1} \xrightarrow{+0.4} \sqrt{2} \xrightarrow{+0.3} \sqrt{3} \xrightarrow{+0.3} \sqrt{4} \xrightarrow{+0.2} \sqrt{5}$$

The terms in answer (B) are evenly spaced. Each term is four less than the prior term.

$$\underline{x} \xrightarrow{-4} \underline{x-4} \xrightarrow{-4} \underline{x-8} \xrightarrow{-4} \underline{x-12} \xrightarrow{-4} \underline{x-16}$$

The terms in answer (C) are evenly spaced. Simplify them; each term is one greater than the prior term.

$$\underline{2} \xrightarrow{+1} \underline{3} \xrightarrow{+1} \underline{4} \xrightarrow{+1} \underline{5} \xrightarrow{+1} \underline{6}$$

The terms in answer (D) are not evenly spaced. Stop after you have confirmed that any two of the jumps are not equal; don't calculate all of them.

$$\underline{5} \xrightarrow{+20} \underline{25} \xrightarrow{+100} \underline{125} \xrightarrow{+500} \underline{625} \xrightarrow{+2500} \underline{3{,}125}$$

The terms in answer (E) are evenly spaced. The increment is a variable, but it is a consistent change each time.

$$\underline{y} \xrightarrow{+y} \underline{2y} \xrightarrow{+y} \underline{3y} \xrightarrow{+y} \underline{4y} \xrightarrow{+y} \underline{5y}$$

10. **9,000**

Use the formula for number of terms in an evenly spaced sequence.

$$\text{\# of terms} = \frac{10{,}001 - 1{,}002}{1} + 1 = 8{,}999 + 1 = 9{,}000$$

11. **9**

First, find the least and greatest numbers in the set. The least multiple of 11 is 55, and the greatest is 143. If needed, use your calculator to show 144 is not divisible by 11, but 143 is. You can solve either by counting or by using the equation.

Counting: 55, 66, 77, 88, 99, 110, 121, 132, 143 = 9 terms

Equation:

$$\text{\# of terms} = \frac{143 - 55}{11} + 1 = \frac{88}{11} + 1 = 9$$

12. $\dfrac{5}{4}$

To find *x*, first figure out the interval between tick marks. You'll need to find a common denominator to define the range.

$$\frac{\text{range}}{\text{\# of intervals}} = \frac{\frac{1}{2} - \left(-\frac{13}{4}\right)}{5} = \frac{\frac{2}{4} + \frac{13}{4}}{5} = \frac{\frac{15}{4}}{5} = \frac{3}{4}$$

The distance between tick marks is $\dfrac{3}{4}$, so *x* is: $\dfrac{1}{2} + \dfrac{3}{4} = \dfrac{5}{4}$.

13. **8**

This is an evenly spaced set because each term is 3 more than the last. Because this set is evenly spaced, the median and the average will be the same. The median is 8, and so the average is also 8.

Unit Six: **Advanced Topics**

14. **13**

    This is an evenly spaced set because each term is 4 more than the last. Because this set is evenly spaced, the median and the average will be the same. The number of terms in the set is even, so the median of the set is the average of the two middle terms, 11 and 15: halfway between is 13. Alternatively, use the average formula:

    $$A = \frac{11 + 15}{2} = 13$$

    You can also find the average from the first and last terms:

    $$A = \frac{(-1 + 27)}{2} = 13$$

15. **580**

    While you could use the calculator to add up these numbers, try using the properties of evenly spaced sequences. The average is halfway between 140 and 150, or 145. Multiply this by the number of terms: $4 \times 145 = 580$.

16. **40**

    While you could plug 3 in for x everywhere, it's faster to notice that this is an evenly spaced sequence. Each term is one more than the previous. There are five terms, so the middle term $(2x + 2)$ is the average. Plug x into that term to find the average: $2(3) + 2 = 8$. Then, multiply the average by the number of terms: $8 \times 5 = 40$.

17. **5,100**

    There are 50 terms in this sequence. The first term is 4. The final term is $4 \times 50 = 200$. If it's helpful, you can verify this by finding the pattern in the sequence as if this were presented as a formula:

    $$A_1 = 4 = 4 \times 1$$
    $$A_2 = 8 = 4 \times 2$$
    $$A_3 = 12 = 4 \times 3$$
    $$A_n = 4n$$
    $$A_{50} = 200 = 4 \times 50$$

    Find the average using the first and last terms in the set: $\frac{4 + 200}{2} = 102$. Multiply 50 by 102 to find the sum of the terms in the sequence: $50 \times 102 = 5{,}100$.

Chapter 28: **Sequences and Patterns**

Problem Set

1.
Quantity A	**Quantity B**
The sum of the consecutive integers from 2 to 15	34 less than the sum of the consecutive integers from 1 to 17

   For problems #2–3, use the following sequence definition: $A_n = 3 - 8n$.

2. What is A_1?

3. What is $A_{11} - A_9$?

4. A sequence S is defined as follows: $S_n = \dfrac{S_{n+1} + S_{n-1}}{2}$ for all $n \geq 2$. If $S_1 = 15$ and $S_4 = 10.5$, what is S_2?

5. $$A_n = 2^n - 1 \text{ for all integers } n \geq 1$$

Quantity A	**Quantity B**
The units digit of A_{26}	The units digit of A_{34}

6. What is the units digit of $16^4 \times 27^3$?

7.

   If the tick marks on the number line above are evenly spaced, what is the distance between Y and Z?

8. How many terms are there in the sequence of consecutive integers from −18 to 33, inclusive?

9. Set A is comprised of all the even numbers between 0 and 20, inclusive.

Quantity A	**Quantity B**
The sum of all the numbers in Set A	150

10.
Quantity A	**Quantity B**
The number of multiples of 7 between 50 and 100, inclusive	The number of multiples of 9 between 30 and 90, inclusive

Unit Six: **Advanced Topics**

11. Set A is comprised of the following terms: (3x), (3x − 4), (3x − 8), (3x − 12), (3x − 16), and (3x − 20).

Quantity A	Quantity B
The sum of all the terms in Set A	18x − 70

12.

Quantity A	Quantity B
A × B	−1

Chapter 28: **Sequences and Patterns**

Solutions

1. **(C)**

   To compare the sums or products of sets of consecutive integers, eliminate overlap to make a direct comparison. You can abbreviate "the sum of the consecutive integers from 2 to 15" as $(2 + 3 + \ldots + 15)$:

Quantity A	Quantity B
$(2 + 3 + \ldots + 15)$	$1 + (2 + 3 + \ldots + 15) + 16 + 17 - 34$

   Cancel $(2 + 3 + \ldots + 15)$ from both sides, leaving Quantity A equal to 0 and Quantity B equal to $1 + 16 + 17 - 34 = 0$.

   The correct answer is (C): The two quantities are always equal.

2. **−5**

   $A_n = 3 - 8n$

   $A_1 = 3 - 8(1) = 3 - 8 = -5$

3. **−16**

   $A_n = 3 - 8n$

   $A_{11} = 3 - 8(11) = 3 - 88 = -85$

   $A_9 = 3 - 8(9) = 3 - 72 = -69$

   $A_{11} - A_9 = -85 - (-69) = -16$

4. **13.5**

   It can help to start by interpreting what the rule is saying in plain language. Each term after the first is the average of the term directly before it and the term directly after it. Using this definition, write equations for S_2 and S_3 in terms of the other items in the sequence and solve for S_2:

   $$S_2 = \frac{S_3 + S_1}{2} \rightarrow S_2 = \frac{S_3 + 15}{2}$$

   $$S_3 = \frac{S_4 + S_2}{2} \rightarrow S_3 = \frac{10.5 + S_2}{2}$$

   Now substitute the expression for S_3 into the first equation and solve:

   $$S_2 = \frac{\left(\frac{10.5 + S_2}{2}\right) + 15}{2}$$

   $$2S_2 = \frac{10.5 + S_2}{2} + 15$$

   $$4S_2 = 10.5 + S_2 + 30$$

   $$3S_2 = 40.5$$

   $$S_2 = 13.5$$

Unit Six: Advanced Topics

5. **(C)**

   The powers of 2 have a repeating pattern of four terms for their units digits: {2, 4, 8, 6}. Every fourth term, the pattern repeats. For instance, the fifth term has the same units as the first term. So terms that are four terms apart, or a multiple of four terms apart, will have the same units digit.

   The 34th term and the 26th term are 34 − 26 = 8 terms apart. Because 8 is a multiple of 4, the terms will have the same units digit.

   Incidentally, the units digit of both A_{26} and A_{34} is 3. Both 26 and 34 are 2 more than a multiple of 4, so the pattern will be on its second term: 4. The rule for the sequence An then requires you to subtract 1, so the units digit of each of these terms is 3. But you don't need to figure this out! It's enough to figure out that the power of two for each quantity must have the same units digit.

   The correct answer is (C): The two quantities are always equal.

6. **8**

   In integer multiplication, the units digit of the product is only affected by the units digits of the factors, so you can focus on those digits and ignore the rest: $16^4 \times 27^3 \rightarrow 6^4 \times 7^3$

   $$6^4 \rightarrow 6^2 \times 6^2 \rightarrow 3\underline{6} \times 3\underline{6} \rightarrow 3\underline{6} \rightarrow 6$$

   $$7^3 \rightarrow 7^2 \times 7 \rightarrow 4\underline{9} \times 7 \rightarrow 6\underline{3} \rightarrow 3$$

   Alternatively, memorize the patterns for each digit. When 6 is raised to any power, the units digit will always be 6. When 7 is raised to a power, the units digit repeats in the pattern 7, 9, 3, 1. This question asks for 7 to the 3rd power, so the units digit is 3.

   Finally, multiply the two units digits and take the units digit of the result: $6 \times 3 = 1\underline{8}$.

7. **2.5**

   First, figure out the distance between tick marks. Use the two numbered points on the number line $\left(\frac{3}{4} \text{ and } \frac{41}{8}\right)$ to find the distance. There are 7 intervals (spaces) between these two points:

   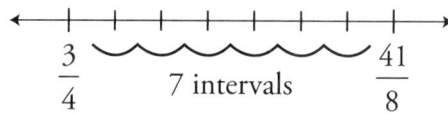

   Divide the distance by the number of intervals:

   $$\frac{\frac{41}{8} - \frac{3}{4}}{7} = \frac{\frac{41}{8} - \frac{6}{8}}{7} = \frac{\frac{35}{8}}{7} = \frac{5}{8}$$

   It's not necessary to find the values of Y and Z in order to find the distance between them. There are 4 intervals between Y and Z, so the distance is:

   $$4 \times \frac{5}{8} = \frac{20}{8} = 2.5$$

8. **52**

   Calculate 33 − (−18) = 51. Then add 1 before you are done: 51 + 1 = 52.

9. **(B)**

   There are two ways to solve this problem: estimation or direct calculation. To estimate, first find the number of terms by finding the range, dividing by the increment (in this case, 2) and adding 1 before you're done: $\frac{20 - 0}{2} = 10$, and 10 + 1 = 11 terms.

Chapter 28: **Sequences and Patterns**

There will be 11 terms in Set A, and one of them is 0. Even if every term in the set were 20, the sum would only be 220 (11 × 20 = 220). But half of the terms are less than 10, so it is unlikely that Quantity A will be greater than or equal to 150.

If you aren't confident in that estimation, finish solving mathematically. Use the equation for the sum of an evenly spaced sequence. Add up the first and last terms and divide by 2 to find the average:

$$\frac{0 + 20}{2} = 10$$

The sum of the terms will be the average value of the terms multiplied the number of terms: 10 × 11 = 110.

The correct answer is (B): Quantity B is greater.

10. **(C)**

The first multiple of 7 between 50 and 100 is 56, and the last is 98. Take this range, divide by the increment (7), and add 1: $\frac{98 - 56}{7} + 1 = 7$. There are 7 multiples of 7 between 50 and 100.

Similarly, the first multiple of 9 between 30 and 90 is 36, and the last is 90: $\frac{90 - 36}{9} + 1 = 7$. There are 7 multiples of 9 between 30 and 90.

The correct answer is (C): The two quantities are always equal.

11. **(A)**

The key is that Set A is an evenly spaced sequence. The median will be equal to $\frac{\text{first term} + \text{last term}}{2}$:

$$\frac{(3x) + (3x - 20)}{2} = \frac{6x - 20}{2} = 3x - 10$$

Count the number of terms listed: There are six terms in the set.

The sum of the terms in the set is the average value of the terms (3x − 10) multiplied by the number of terms (6):

$$(3x - 10) \times 6 = 18x - 60$$

Quantity A is subtracting a smaller number (60) than is Quantity B (70), and so will have a greater value, regardless of the value of x. In fact, you could go further and cancel 18x from both quantities, leaving the final quantities as −60 and −70.

The correct answer is (A): Quantity A is greater.

12. **(D)**

With only one actual number displayed on the number line, there is no way of knowing the distance between tick marks. Because A and B are on opposite sides of 0, you can determine that their product will be negative. However, that product may or may not be greater than −1. If the tick marks are a small fractional distance away from each other, then A × B will be greater than −1. For instance, if the distance between tick marks is $\frac{1}{8}$, then A is $-\frac{1}{4}$, B is $\frac{1}{2}$ and A × B is $-\frac{1}{8}$, which is greater than −1. Alternatively, if the distance between tick marks is 1, then A is −2, B is 4, and A × B is −8, which is less than −1.

The correct answer is (D): The relationship cannot be determined.

CHAPTER 29
Combinatorics

In This Chapter:

- The Fundamental Counting Principle
- Distinct Labels
- Repeated Labels
- Multiple Arrangements
- Overlapping Sets
- Check Your Skills Answer Key
- Problem Set
- Solutions

CHAPTER 29 Combinatorics

Many GRE problems are, ultimately, just about counting things. Although counting may seem to be a simple concept, problems about counting can be complex. In fact, counting problems are a whole subfield of mathematics: **combinatorics**, which is essentially advanced counting. In combinatorics, you are often counting the **number of possibilities.** In this chapter, you will learn the fundamentals of combinatorics as tested on the GRE.

You'll also learn how to tackle more advanced counting problems. Here are some examples of the kinds of questions you may see:

- A restaurant menu features 5 appetizers, 6 main dishes, and 3 desserts. If a dinner special consists of 1 appetizer, 1 main dish, and 1 dessert, how many different dinner specials are possible?
- Four people sit down in 4 fixed chairs lined up in a row. How many different seating arrangements are possible?
- If there are 7 people in a room, but only 3 chairs in a row, how many different seating arrangements are possible?
- If a group of 3 people is to be chosen from 7 people in a room, how many different groups are possible?

The Fundamental Counting Principle

Counting problems commonly feature multiple separate choices. Whether such choices are made simultaneously (e.g., choosing types of bread and filling for a sandwich) or sequentially (e.g., choosing among routes between successive towns on a road trip), the rule for counting the number of options is the same.

> *Key Concept*
>
> Fundamental Counting Principle: When making a number of *separate* decisions, *multiply* the numbers of ways to make each individual decision to find the total number of ways to make all the decisions.

Imagine that you are making a sandwich. You'll choose one type of bread out of 2 types (rye or whole wheat) and one type of filling out of 3 types (chicken salad, peanut butter, or tuna fish). How many different kinds of sandwich can you make?

Unit Six: Advanced Topics

One option is to list all the possibilities:

- Rye + Chicken salad
- Rye + Peanut butter
- Rye + Tuna fish
- Whole wheat + Chicken salad
- Whole wheat + Peanut butter
- Whole wheat + Tuna fish

There are six possible sandwiches overall in this table. Instead of listing all the sandwiches, however, you can *multiply* the number of bread choices by the number of filling choices, as dictated by the Fundamental Counting Principle:

$$2 \text{ breads} \times 3 \text{ fillings} = 6 \text{ possible sandwiches}$$

You're still counting all of the possibilities. You're just doing so more efficiently. Multiplication is just high-speed addition.

As its name implies, the Fundamental Counting Principle is essential to solving combinatorics problems. It is the basis of many other techniques that appear later in this chapter.

You can also apply the Fundamental Counting Principle visually, using slots and labels.

- Slot = a blank line for every decision
- Label = a description of the kind of thing that goes in the slot

For the sandwich problem, first draw the following:

$$\underline{} \quad \underline{}$$
$$\text{Br} \quad\quad \text{Fill}$$

These two slots represent the two decisions you have to make. One decision is about the bread. You can label that slot "Bread" or "Br" or even just "B." The other decision is about the filling, so label the other slot accordingly ("Filling" or "Fill" or just "F").

Next, fill in each slot with the number of choices for each decision:

$$\underline{2} \quad \underline{3}$$
$$\text{Br} \quad\quad \text{Fill}$$

Finally, multiply the choices to get your answer:

$$\underline{2} \times \underline{3} = 6 \text{ possible sandwiches}$$
$$\text{Br} \quad\quad\quad \text{Fill}$$

Here's a more complicated example:

> A restaurant menu features 5 appetizers, 6 main dishes, and 3 desserts. If a dinner special consists of 1 appetizer, 1 main dish, and 1 dessert, how many different dinner specials are possible?

This problem features three decisions: an appetizer (which can be chosen in 5 different ways), a main dish (6 ways), and a dessert (3 ways).

Set up your slots and labels:

$$\underline{} \quad \underline{} \quad \underline{}$$
$$A M D$$

Fill in the slots with the number of choices you have at each stage:

$$\underline{5} \quad \underline{6} \quad \underline{3}$$
$$A M D$$

Finally, multiply across:

$$\underline{5} \times \underline{6} \times \underline{3} = 90 \text{ possible dinner specials}$$
$$A M D$$

In theory, you could list all 90 dinner specials. In practice, that is the last thing you would ever want to do. It would take far too long, and it is likely that you would miss at least one combination. Multiplying is *much* faster—and more accurate.

Check Your Skills

1. How many ways are there of getting from Alphaville to Gammerburg via Betancourt, if there are 3 roads between Alphaville and Betancourt and 4 roads between Betancourt and Gammerburg?

2. Kanan's outfit each day consists of one pair of pants (blue, black, or brown), one shirt (white, yellow, or pink), and possibly a hat (optional). How many days can Kanan go without wearing the same combination twice?

Answers can be found on page 817.

Distinct Labels

The GRE may ask you to count the possible arrangements of a set of distinct objects (e.g., "Four people sit down in four fixed chairs lined up in a row. How many different seating arrangements are possible?") To count these arrangements, use **factorials**.

The term "*n* factorial" (*n*!) refers to the product of all of the positive integers from *n* down to 1, inclusive:

$$n! = (n)(n-1)(n-2)\ldots(1)$$
$$7! = (7)(6)(5)(4)(3)(2)(1)$$

It's annoying to plug so many values into the calculator, so it is helpful to memorize the factorials through 5! or 6! If you remember the first few, you can build on them as needed by using the calculator to multiply in the final few numbers.

- $1! = 1$
- $2! = 2 \times 1 = 2$
- $3! = 3 \times 2 \times 1 = 6$
- $4! = 4 \times 3 \times 2 \times 1 = 24$
- $5! = 5 \times 4 \times 3 \times 2 \times 1 = 120$
- $6! = 6 \times 5 \times 4 \times 3 \times 2 \times 1 = 720$

Unit Six: **Advanced Topics**

Equal numbers of Slots and Elements

The factorial expression $n!$ counts the arrangements of n distinct objects as a special, but very common, application of slots and labels. In this scenario, you have n distinct objects, n slots, and n different labels for those slots. The number of objects, the number of slots, and the number of different labels are all the same.

For example, consider the case of 4 people assigned to 4 distinct positions. Each slot represents a position:

$$\underline{} \quad \underline{} \quad \underline{} \quad \underline{}$$
$$\text{First} \quad\quad \text{Second} \quad\quad \text{Third} \quad\quad \text{Fourth}$$

In deciding who will go in the first position, there are four options, and you could place any one of the 4 people in the first slot:

$$\underline{4} \quad \underline{} \quad \underline{} \quad \underline{}$$
$$\text{First} \quad\quad \text{Second} \quad\quad \text{Third} \quad\quad \text{Fourth}$$

Now, you have only 3 choices for the person in the second position, because one of your people is already in the first slot:

$$\underline{4} \quad \underline{3} \quad \underline{} \quad \underline{}$$
$$\text{First} \quad\quad \text{Second} \quad\quad \text{Third} \quad\quad \text{Fourth}$$

Next, you have 2 choices for the third position, which leaves whomever is left for the final position:

$$\underline{4} \quad \underline{3} \quad \underline{2} \quad \underline{1}$$
$$\text{First} \quad\quad \text{Second} \quad\quad \text{Third} \quad\quad \text{Fourth}$$

Finally, multiply together all those separate choices:

$$\underline{4} \times \underline{3} \times \underline{2} \times \underline{1} = 24$$
$$\text{First} \quad\quad \text{Second} \quad\quad \text{Third} \quad\quad \text{Fourth}$$

Notice this is exactly the same result as if you defined n as 4 (because there were four people put into four different positions) and solved for $n!$:

$$4! = 4 \times 3 \times 2 \times 1 = 24$$

This example illustrates why you can use a shortcut and solve for $n!$ in order to count the number of arrangements. When you put n different people or things in n distinct slots or positions, you have n choices for the first slot, $n - 1$ choices for the second slot, $n - 2$ choices for the third slot, and so on down the line until you reach the last slot, where you have just 1 choice (there's just 1 person or thing left to pick).

$$\underline{n} \times \underline{n-1} \times \underline{n-2} \times \ldots \times \underline{1} = n!$$
$$\text{First} \quad\quad \text{Second} \quad\quad\quad \text{Third} \quad\quad\quad \ldots \quad\quad \text{Last}$$

Chapter 29: **Combinatorics**

> *Key Concept*
>
> The number of ways of putting *n* distinct objects in order, if there are no restrictions, is *n*! (which is read as *n* factorial).

Here's another example:

Six different books are placed on a bookshelf. In how many different orders can the books be arranged?

Using the Fundamental Counting Principle, you have 6 choices for the book that goes first, 5 choices for the book that goes next, and so forth. Draw out all 6 slots or recognize that the number of different orders will equal 6 factorial:

$$6! = \underline{6} \times \underline{5} \times \underline{4} \times \underline{3} \times \underline{2} \times \underline{1} = 720 \text{ different orders}$$

If you *don't* place all the people or things into slotted positions, then the answer won't be a direct factorial. The factorial formula assumes that you place *everyone* or *everything* into position.

More Elements than Slots

Sometimes you only pick *some* of the people or things, and the rest are left out. In this case, draw slots—and stop before you get all the way down to 1.

For example:

If there are 7 people in a room, but only 3 chairs in a row, how many different seating arrangements are possible? (Assume that exactly 3 of the 7 will actually take the seats.)

The 3 different seats are your 3 different slots:

$$\underline{} \quad \underline{} \quad \underline{}$$
$$\text{First} \qquad \text{Second} \qquad \text{Third}$$

Fill in the slots with the number of choices you have at each stage. You can pick from all 7 people for the first slot. Once you've made that pick, there are only 6 people to choose from for the second slot. Then, there are 5 people to choose from for the third slot:

$$\underline{7} \quad \underline{6} \quad \underline{5}$$
$$\text{First} \qquad \text{Second} \qquad \text{Third}$$

Finally, multiply across:

$$\underline{7} \times \underline{6} \times \underline{5} = 210 \text{ possible seating arrangements}$$
$$\text{First} \qquad \text{Second} \qquad \text{Third}$$

Unit Six: **Advanced Topics**

Check Your Skills

3. A jeweler is creating a pattern that consists of 5 colored gemstones in a row. If one each of black, red, green, yellow, and blue will be used, how many different patterns can the jeweler make?

4. In how many different ways can the letters of the word DEPOSIT be arranged (meaningful or nonsense)?

Answers can be found on page 817.

Repeated Labels

Up to this point, you've dealt only with labels that are all different from each other.

But what if more than one slot is labeled the same way? In other words, what if some of the labels are *repeated*? For example:

> If a group of 3 people is to be chosen from 7 people in a room, how many different groups are possible?

At first, this problem may seem the same as one from the previous section, because it also involves selecting three people out of a pool of seven.

However, there is a crucial difference. In the earlier problem, the three slots (the seats) were labeled *differently*:

$$\underline{} \quad \underline{} \quad \underline{}$$
$$\text{First} \quad\quad \text{Second} \quad\quad \text{Third}$$

The three chosen people each got something different: a different seat.

But in this case, the three chosen people are all getting the same thing. They're just getting chosen for a group. So the three slots should be labeled the *same* way:

$$\underline{} \quad \underline{} \quad \underline{}$$
$$\text{In Group} \quad \text{In Group} \quad \text{In Group}$$

This makes a dramatic difference in the number of possible outcomes. Fortunately, you start the problem the same way. Fill in the numbers to represent the choices you have at each step. These numbers are the same as before. You pick from 7 people first, then from 6 people, and finally from 5 people:

$$\underline{}\ 7 \quad \underline{}\ 6 \quad \underline{}\ 5$$
$$\text{In Group} \quad \text{In Group} \quad \text{In Group}$$

Again, multiply these numbers: $7 \times 6 \times 5 = 210$.

Now comes the different, but essential, final step. For this problem, you've actually *overcounted*. If you listed out all the possibilities, you'd find that there aren't 210 different possible subgroups of 3 people chosen from 7 people. In fact, there are only 35 different subgroups. If the people are named A, B, C, D, E, F, and G, then here are those 35 different subgroups of 3 people:

A B C	A C D	A D F	B C D	B D F	C D E	C F G
A B D	A C E	A D G	B C E	B D G	C D F	D E F
A B E	A C F	A E F	B C F	B E F	C D G	D E G
A B F	A C G	A E G	B C G	B E G	C E F	D F G
A B G	A D E	A F G	B D E	B F G	C E G	E F G

Why is there such a big difference between 210 and 35? Take the subgroup ABC. Nowhere on the list is there any *other arrangement* of those three letters (ACB, BCA, BAC, CAB, or CBA). The subgroup ABC accounts for *all* of the 6 possible arrangements of those three letters, because in this problem, you are *not distinguishing between those arrangements*. The order in which the elements of the group are chosen does not matter.

All you care about is *who* out of the 7 people is chosen. So here, the subgroup ABC means that you've picked those three particular people named A, B, and C. It doesn't matter whether you choose A first, then B, and then C, or whether you choose C first, then A, and then B. In the end, these three are the three who are in the group.

So how do you get from 210 to 35, the right answer? Divide by the number of arrangements you don't care about. In this case, there are 3 slots that are all equivalent; you don't care about the possible arrangement within those three slots. So to remove them, divide 210 by 3!, or the factorial of the number of repeated labels.

> **Key Concept**
>
> When you have a label used more than once, divide by the factorial of the number of repeated labels.

Here's the full calculation for the problem above: picking 3 people from a pool of 7 people. You have $7 \times 6 \times 5$ for the 3 slots, then you divide by 3! because the three slots were all labeled the same:

$$\frac{7 \times 6 \times 5}{3!} = \frac{7 \times 6 \times 5}{6} = \frac{7 \times \cancel{6} \times 5}{\cancel{6}} = 35$$

Try one with only some of the labels repeated:

> An animal shelter has five dogs available. Samina plans to adopt two dogs, while Zuri and Navita will each adopt one. In how many ways can the dogs be distributed among the three people?

Start by creating slots for the adopted dogs:

$$\underline{} \quad \underline{} \quad \underline{} \quad \underline{}$$
$$\ \ \text{S} \qquad\ \ \text{S} \qquad\ \ \text{Z} \qquad\ \ \text{N}$$

Fill in the slots based on having 5 dogs initially:

$$\underset{S}{5} \quad \underset{S}{4} \quad \underset{Z}{3} \quad \underset{N}{2}$$

Since Samina plans to adopt two dogs, two slots repeat. Divide the product of the slots by 2! :

$$\frac{5 \times 4 \times 3 \times 2}{2!} = \frac{5 \times 4 \times 3 \times \cancel{2}}{\cancel{2}} = 60$$

There are 60 different combinations of dogs for the three people. It doesn't matter what order the slots start in. If Navita was in the first position while Samina was in the final two, the numbers (and thus the math) would be the same. All that matters is how many of the slots are identical to one another.

It's possible to have two different sets of repeated labels. If this happens, the process is the same, but you'll divide by the factorial of *each* set of repeats. For example:

> An animal shelter has five dogs available. Samina plans to adopt two dogs, while Zuri will adopt the remaining three. In how many ways can the dogs be distributed between the two people?

Draw the slots and fill in with the number of options:

$$\underset{S}{5} \quad \underset{S}{4} \quad \underset{Z}{3} \quad \underset{Z}{2} \quad \underset{Z}{1}$$

Samina repeats twice, while Zuri repeats three times, so divide the product by both 2! and 3! to get to the correct answer:

$$\frac{5 \times 4 \times 3 \times 2 \times 1}{2! \times 3!} = \frac{5 \times 4 \times 3 \times 2 \times 1}{(2 \times 1) \times (3 \times 2 \times 1)} = \frac{5 \times \cancel{4} \times \cancel{3} \times 2}{\cancel{(2)} \times \cancel{(3 \times 2)}} = 10$$

There are 10 ways to distribute the 5 dogs between Samina and Zuri. Whenever possible, cancel out common factors to make the math less computation-heavy.

In general, when there are more repeats of labels, you'll divide more out, so there will be fewer combinations.

Elsewhere in your life, you may have encountered the formula for "combinations." If you're more comfortable using the formula, that's an equally valid way to solve combination problems.

Imagine that you are picking k people from a larger pool of n people. All k people are picked for a team and labeled identically. The order in which the people are picked does not matter, and they are not assigned to different positions. All that matters is who is on the team and who isn't.

Use this formula to count the combinations:

$$\frac{n!}{k!(n-k)!} = \frac{\text{Pool!}}{\text{Team!}(\text{Not on team})!}$$

Here's how this formula would work when you're picking 3 group members from a pool of 7 people.

$$\frac{n!}{k!(n-k)!} = \frac{7!}{3!4!} = \frac{7 \times \cancel{6} \times 5 \times \cancel{4!}}{\cancel{3} \times \cancel{2} \times 1 \times \cancel{4!}} = 7 \times 5 = 35$$

This is the same as creating 3 identical slots with 7, 6, and 5 options to choose from, then dividing that product by the factorial of number of repeated slots, 3. Use whichever method you prefer.

Check Your Skills

5. Peggy will choose 5 of her 8 friends to join her for a volleyball match. In how many ways can she do so?

Answers can be found on page 818.

Multiple Arrangements

Sometimes, the GRE will combine smaller combinatorics problems into one larger problem. In this case, you'll need to deal with successive or *multiple arrangements*. Fortunately, you do the same thing you've been doing all along: multiply!

> **Key Concept**
>
> If a GRE problem requires you to choose two or more sets of items from separate pools, count the arrangements *separately*. Then multiply the numbers of possibilities for each step.

Distinguish these problems—which require choices from *separate pools*—from complex problems that are still single arrangements (all items chosen from the *same pool*), for which you create a single set of slots.

For instance, say you have to choose 1 president, 1 treasurer, and 3 representatives from *one* class of 20 students. This requires just one set of slots. Set up 5 slots, labeled T, S, R, R, and R:

$$\underline{} \quad \underline{} \quad \underline{} \quad \underline{} \quad \underline{}$$
$$P T R R R$$

Fill in the slots. You can pick from all 20 students for the first slot, 19 for the second slot, and so on:

$$\underline{20} \quad \underline{19} \quad \underline{18} \quad \underline{17} \quad \underline{16}$$
$$P T R R R$$

Finally, use the calculator to multiply those numbers together and divide by $3! = 6$, the factorial of the number of repeated labels:

$$20 \times 19 \times 18 \times 17 \times 16 = 1{,}860{,}480 \div 6 = 310{,}080$$

Here's a different scenario:

> The I Eta Pi student organization must choose a delegation of 3 senior members and 2 junior members for an annual conference. If I Eta Pi has 12 senior members and 11 junior members, how many different delegations are possible?

Unit Six: **Advanced Topics**

This problem involves two genuinely different arrangements: 3 seniors chosen from a pool of 12 seniors, and 2 juniors chosen from a *separate* pool of 11 juniors. Calculate the number of combinations for each arrangement separately, then multiply together to find the total number of possible delegations.

First, choose the 3 senior delegates from a pool of 12 seniors. The 3 slots are the same, so there are $\frac{12 \times 11 \times 10}{3!} = 220$ different possible senior delegations.

Next, choose the 2 junior delegates from a pool of 11 juniors. Again, the 2 slots are the same, so there are $\frac{11 \times 10}{2!} = 55$ different possible junior delegations.

Finally, for each of the 220 senior delegation combinations, there are 55 different junior delegation combinations available. Therefore, multiply the results from each little sub-problem:

$$220 \times 55 = 12{,}100 \text{ different delegations are possible}$$

This brings us all the way back to the sandwich problem at the start of this chapter. For each of the 2 choices of bread, you had all 3 fillings available. So you multiply the 2 and the 3 to get 6 possible sandwiches. Ultimately, multiple arrangements work the same way.

Check Your Skills

6. Three managers (out of 7 managers) and 3 engineers (out of 6 engineers) will be chosen to serve on a committee. In how many ways can the committee be formed?

Answers can be found on page 818.

Overlapping Sets

The GRE can ask one other, fundamentally different kind of counting problem. Rather than having you count the number of arrangements or number of possibilities, it will ask you to count how many items fall into a group.

For example, consider a group of 20 items that fall into Set *A*, Set *B*, both, or neither. If all of them fall into at least one set and exactly 14 of them fall into Set *A*, how many fall into Set *B*?

To get to the right answer, you'll need to consider *overlap* between the sets. For starters, exactly 14 are in Set *A*, and every item has to be in at least one set, so the remaining 6 must be in Set *B*. But it's possible that some are in both sets—for example, imagine that 7 items are in both Set *A* and Set *B*. In that case, a total of $6 + 7 = 13$ items are in Set *B*.

Here's that example with specific numbers:

List *X*: {4, 6, 8, 9, 12, 14, 15, 16, 18, 21, 22, 24, 27, 30, 32, 33, 36, 38, 39, 42}

Let Set *A* be the set of all even numbers in List *X*, and Set *B* be the set of all multiples of 3 in List *X*.

Set *A* contains 14 numbers: {4, 6, 8, 12, 14, 16, 18, 22, 24, 30, 32, 36, 38, 42}. Set *B* has 13 numbers: {6, 9, 12, 15, 18, 21, 24, 27, 30, 33, 36, 39, 42}. There are still just 20 total numbers across the two sets, because 7 of the numbers appear in both Set *A* and Set *B*: {6, 12, 18, 24, 30, 36, 42}.

If these questions were presented as long lists of numbers on the GRE, they might be tedious. However, the GRE is much more likely to present these as groups of people or items. Consider this more typical question:

> At Factory X, there are 400 total workers. Of these workers, 240 are salaried, and 220 work in Operations. If 100 of the workers are non-salaried and do not work in Operations, how many are both salaried and work in Operations?

This question specifically asks what the overlap between the two sets of workers is. One way to process this information is by using a **Venn Diagram**, in which you represent the groups as overlapping circles:

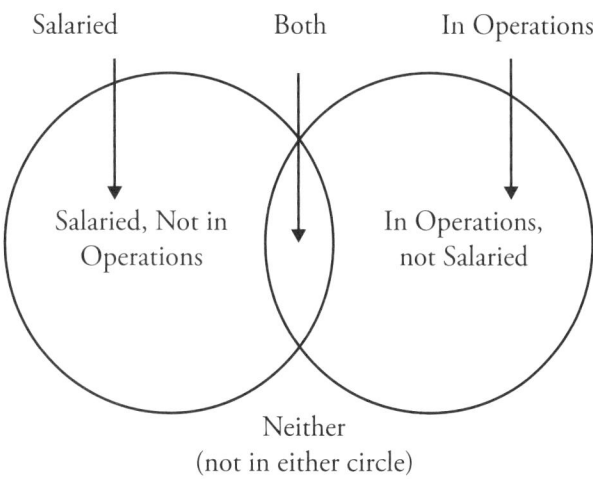

The two key points to note are the following:

1. The workers will *always* fall into one of four classifications:
   (a) Salaried and in an Operations role (i.e., "both A and B")
   (b) Salaried and NOT in an Operations role (i.e., "just A")
   (c) NOT salaried and in an Operations role (i.e., "just B")
   (d) NOT salaried and NOT in an Operations role (i.e., "neither A nor B")

Therefore, there are four unknowns in this type of problem (although the question itself may only require that you work with two or three of them, and some of the classifications may have zero members).

2. The problem will often give you total amounts for the groups, and you will have to use logic to figure out whichever unknown the question is asking about.

The trick for these problems is not to overcount or undercount. The problem indicated that 240 workers are salaried, but that 240 figure includes people who are salaried but don't work in Operations as well as people who are salaried and also work in Operations.

If you add just the two groups, you'll have left out anyone who's in neither group, so you need to add in the number of Neithers. But if there are people in *both* groups, you will have counted them twice, so you need to subtract the number of Boths. This yields a formula you can memorize:

Total = Group 1 + Group 2 − Both + Neither

The subtraction step removes the overcounting for anyone who appears in both groups. Plug the values into the formula to solve:

$$\text{Total} = \text{Group 1} + \text{Group 2} - \text{Both} + \text{Neither}$$
$$400 = 240 + 220 - B + 100$$
$$400 = 560 - B$$
$$B = 160$$

Therefore, there are 160 workers who are both salaried and in Operations.

How many workers are salaried but don't work in Operations?

The question stated that there are 240 salaried workers. Because there are 160 who are salaried and do work in Operations, there must be $240 - 160 = 80$ workers who are salaried but do not work in Operations. Once you have all four components of the original equation, you can calculate any possible subgroup.

Check Your Skills

7. Of 320 consumers, 200 eat strawberries and 300 eat oranges. If all 320 eat at least one of the fruits, how many eat both?

Answers can be found on page 819.

Chapter 29: **Combinatorics**

Check Your Skills Answer Key

1. **12**

   Use slots and labels. Put 3 in the first slot (maybe labeled "A to B"), and 4 in the second slot (maybe labeled "B to G"). Then, multiply the number of choices for each leg of the trip: $3 \times 4 = 12$.

2. **18**

   Kanan has 3 choices of pants, 3 choices of shirts, and 2 choices involving a hat (yes or no). Label the first slot "P," the second slot "S," and the third slot "H." Finally, multiply: $3 \times 3 \times 2 = 18$.

3. **120**

   This question is asking for the number of ways to order 5 differently colored stones with no other restrictions. So, compute (or remember) 5 factorial.

   $$5! = \underline{5} \times \underline{4} \times \underline{3} \times \underline{2} \times \underline{1} = 120$$

4. **5,040**

   The 7 letters in a word with all distinct letters (such as DEPOSIT) are distinct objects. There are 7 slots they can go into: the first position in the word, the second position in the word, and so on.

   So the letters can be arranged in $7! = \underline{7} \times \underline{6} \times \underline{5} \times \underline{4} \times \underline{3} \times \underline{2} \times \underline{1} = 5{,}040$ different ways. (These rearrangements are called anagrams.)

   Even though 7! isn't on the list of factorials to memorize, you don't have to plug all seven numbers into the calculator to compute it. The value of 6! is embedded into 7! (so are 5!, 4!, 3!, 2!, and 1!, but focus on the greatest factorial you know).

   $$7! = 7 \times \underbrace{6 \times 5 \times 4 \times 3 \times 2 \times 1}_{6!} = 7 \times 6! = 7 \times 720 = 5{,}040$$

   Memorizing the smaller factorials will help when it's time to compute a larger factorial.

Unit Six: **Advanced Topics**

5. **56**

   Write down 5 slots for the 5 people Peggy chooses for her team, all labeled the same.

   $$\underline{} \quad \underline{} \quad \underline{} \quad \underline{} \quad \underline{}$$
   $$\text{On Team} \quad \text{On Team} \quad \text{On Team} \quad \text{On Team} \quad \text{On Team}$$

   Next, fill in the slots. Peggy has 8 friends to choose from for the first slot, then 7 for the second, and on down the line.

   $$\underline{8} \quad \underline{7} \quad \underline{6} \quad \underline{5} \quad \underline{4}$$
   $$\text{On Team} \quad \text{On Team} \quad \text{On Team} \quad \text{On Team} \quad \text{On Team}$$

   Finally, multiply those numbers together and divide by 5!, the factorial of the number of repeated labels.

   $$\frac{8 \times 7 \times 6 \times 5 \times 4}{5!} = \frac{8 \times 7 \times \cancel{6} \times \cancel{5} \times \cancel{4}}{\cancel{5} \times \cancel{4} \times \cancel{3} \times \cancel{2} \times 1} = 8 \times 7 = 56$$

6. **700**

   For the 7 managers, there are 3 identical slots.

   $$\frac{7 \times 6 \times 5}{3!} = \frac{7 \times \cancel{6} \times 5}{\cancel{3} \times \cancel{2} \times 1} = 35$$

   For the 6 engineers, there is a separate set of 3 identical slots.

   $$\frac{6 \times 5 \times 4}{3!} = \frac{\cancel{6} \times 5 \times \cancel{4}}{\cancel{3} \times \cancel{2} \times 1} = 20$$

   Finally, multiply the choices to get the total: $35 \times 20 = 700$ different ways to form the committee.

   By the way, this is considerably fewer than the number of ways to choose 6 out of 13 people without regard to role. Specifying the number of managers and engineers that can be selected limits the total number of possibilities.

7. **180**

The total equals the first group plus the second group minus Both plus Neither. Because all of the consumers eat at least one of the fruits, Neither is equal to 0.

$$320 = 200 + 300 - B + 0$$
$$320 = 500 - B$$
$$B = 180$$

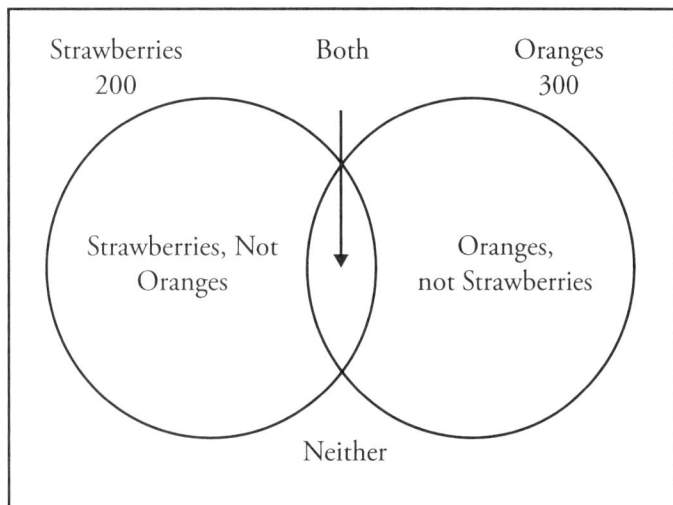

Unit Six: **Advanced Topics**

Problem Set

> Solve the following problems using the strategies you have learned in this section.

1. You have a team of 5 people and 3 tasks to assign. Task A needs two people, Task B needs two people, and Task C needs one person. You are only going to assign one task to each person. In how many different ways can you assign the tasks?

2. A worker is making boxes of truffles. There is an unlimited supply of 5 different types of truffles. If each box holds truffles of 2 different types, how many different boxes can be made?

3. A basketball league assigns every player a two-digit number for the back of their jersey. If the league uses only the digits 1–5, what is the maximum number of players that can join the league such that no player has a number with a repeated digit (e.g., 22), and no two players have the same number?

4. A pod of 6 dolphins always swims single file, with 3 females at the front and 3 males in the rear. In how many different arrangements can the dolphins swim?

5. If the mayor of a town chooses 3 members of the 7-person city council to serve on a special committee, how many different 3-person combinations are possible?

6. A pizza restaurant has 2 choices of crust: deep dish crust or thin crust. The restaurant also has a choice of 5 toppings: tomatoes, sausage, peppers, onions, and pepperoni. The order of the toppings doesn't matter. Finally, the restaurant offers every pizza in extra cheese as well as regular. If someone orders a pizza with 4 unique toppings, how many different combinations are possible for the toppings?

7. Country X has a four-digit postal code assigned to each town The first digit is nonzero, and none of the digits are repeated.

Quantity A	Quantity B
The number of possible postal codes in Country X	4,500

8. Eight athletes compete in a race in which a gold, a silver, and a bronze medal will be awarded to the top three finishers, in that order.

Quantity A	Quantity B
The number of ways in which the medals can be awarded	$8 \times 3!$

9. Lothar has 6 stamps from Utopia and 4 stamps from Cornucopia in his collection. He will give two stamps of each type to his friend Peggy Sue.

Quantity A	Quantity B
The number of ways Lothar can give 4 stamps (two of each type) to Peggy Sue	100

10. All of the concert tickets sold at a particular venue offer premium seating, backstage access after the event, or both. The venue sold 1,200 premium-seating tickets and 500 backstage-access tickets for a certain concert. If at least 150 of the tickets offered both premium seating and backstage access, what is the greatest total number of tickets the venue could have sold for this concert?

11. A jar contains four 1-cent coins, one 5-cent coin, and one 10-cent coin.

Quantity A	Quantity B
The number of different cent values that can be created using one or more of the coins in the jar	20

12. A farmer sold vegetables to 180 different customers. Of these, 90 purchased zucchini and 115 purchased cauliflower.

Quantity A	Quantity B
The number of customers who purchased both zucchini and cauliflower	The number of customers who purchased neither zucchini nor cauliflower

Unit Six: **Advanced Topics**

Solutions

1. **30**

    Set up 5 slots, because you have five tasks to assign. Label two of the slots A, two other slots B, and the last slot C. You have 5 choices for the first slot, 4 for the second, on down to 1 choice for the last slot:

    $$\frac{5}{A} \quad \frac{4}{A} \quad \frac{3}{B} \quad \frac{2}{B} \quad \frac{1}{C}$$

    There are two sets of 2 repeated labels each, so divide by 2! *twice* to account for these two sets of repeats.

    There are $\frac{5 \times \cancel{4} \times 3 \times 2 \times 1}{\cancel{2!} \times 2!} = 30$ possible task assignments.

2. **10**

    In every combination, 2 types of truffles will be in the box. Set up two slots, both labeled "In Box."

    $$\frac{}{\text{In Box}} \quad \frac{}{\text{In Box}}$$

    There are 5 options for the first slot and 4 for the second (because the boxes have to contain *different* types of truffles).

    $$\frac{5}{\text{In Box}} \quad \frac{4}{\text{In Box}}$$

    Multiply 5 by 4 and then divide by 2! because there are 2 repeated labels. (The problem doesn't ask you to make a distinction between, say, "espresso and raspberry" and "raspberry and espresso." The truffles are either in the box or not.)

    $$(5 \times 4) \div 2 = 10 \text{ possible boxes of truffles}$$

    This problem can also be solved with the formula for combinations, because it is a combination of 2 items chosen from a set of 5 and order does not matter. Therefore, there are $\frac{5!}{2! \times 3!} = 10$ possible boxes.

Chapter 29: **Combinatorics**

3. **20**

    In this problem, each of the digits 1–5 can be either the tens digit, the units digit, or not a digit in the jersey number. What you're really counting is the number of unique jersey numbers.

    Make two slots, one for the tens digit and one for the units digit. You have 5 choices for the tens digit and 4 choices for the units digit (since you cannot use the same digit again), resulting in $5 \times 4 = 20$ possibilities. The slot labels are different (Tens and Units), so don't divide 20 by anything.

    You could also list out the jersey numbers, since the number of possibilities is relatively limited.

    $$12, 13, 14, 15$$
    $$21, 23, 24, 25$$
    $$31, 32, 34, 35$$
    $$41, 42, 43, 45$$
    $$51, 52, 53, 54$$

    There are 5 groups of 4 each for 20 total possibilities. If you notice partway through your list that each of the 5 possible tens digits will have 4 possibilities (any of the available units digits other than the same), use the pattern to solve more quickly.

4. **36**

    There are 3! ways in which the 3 females can swim. There are 3! ways in which the 3 males can swim. Therefore, there are $3! \times 3!$ ways in which the entire pod can swim:

    $$3! \times 3! = 6 \times 6 = 36$$

    This is a multiple arrangements problem in which you have two separate pools (females and males).

5. **35**

    In this problem, 3 people are chosen for the committee from a larger pool of 7 people.

    Set up 3 slots, all labeled "C" for committee. Fill the slots in: 7 for the first slot, then 6 and 5.

    $$\frac{7}{C} \quad \frac{6}{C} \quad \frac{5}{C}$$

    Divide by 3!, because the three slots are labeled identically.

    $$\frac{7 \times \cancel{6} \times 5}{\cancel{3} \times \cancel{2} \times 1} = 35$$

    Alternatively, use the textbook combinations formula:

    $$\frac{n!}{k!(n-k)!} = \frac{7!}{3!4!} = \frac{7 \times \cancel{6} \times 5 \times \cancel{4!}}{\cancel{3} \times \cancel{2} \times 1 \times \cancel{4!}} = 35$$

823

Unit Six: **Advanced Topics**

6. **20**

   Set up 4 slots for the toppings and label all the slots the same, since order doesn't matter. Fill in the numbers from 5 on down, because the person orders 4 *unique* toppings.

   $$\frac{5}{T} \quad \frac{4}{T} \quad \frac{3}{T} \quad \frac{2}{T}$$

   Now multiply the numbers and divide by 4! because the labels are all the same.

   $$\frac{5 \times 4 \times 3 \times 2}{4!} = 5$$

   Alternatively, use the combinations formula to count the combinations of toppings:

   $$\frac{5!}{4! \times 1!} = 5$$

   Or use an intuitive approach: choosing 4 toppings out of 5 is equivalent to choosing the 1 topping that will not be on the pizza. There are only 5 ways to reject a single topping.

   Next, since each of these pizzas can also be offered in 2 choices of crust, there are $5 \times 2 = 10$ possible pizzas with 4 unique toppings and one of the two crusts.

   The same logic applies for extra cheese and regular. The number of pizzas with 4 toppings, one crust, and one version of cheese is $5 \times 2 \times 2 = 20$.

7. **(A)**

   Use slots to solve this problem. The first slot can be filled by any one of the digits from 1 through 9, since 0 isn't allowed. The second digit has no restriction involving 0; however, the digit that was used in the first slot may not be reused. Thus, the second slot also has 9 possibilities. The third and fourth slots may not be filled with previously used digits, so they may be filled with 8 and 7 different digits, respectively.

   The total number of possible postal codes is $9 \times 9 \times 8 \times 7 = 4,536$. Therefore, the correct answer is (A): Quantity A is greater.

8. **(A)**

   Set up three slots, labeled *G*, *S*, and *B*, to indicate the 3 different medals. You have 8 choices of athlete for the gold, 7 choices for the silver, and 6 choices for the bronze. Therefore, the number of ways to award the medals is $8 \times 7 \times 6$.

   Compare this number to $8 \times 3!$:

   $$8 \times 3! = 8 \times 3 \times 2 \times 1 = 8 \times 6$$

   It must be the case that $8 \times 7 \times 6$ is greater than 8×6. The correct answer is (A): Quantity A is greater.

9. **(B)**

This exercise can be regarded as two successive "pick a group" problems. Lothar picks 2 out of 6 Utopian stamps, and then 2 out of 4 Cornucopian stamps. Each selection may be computed by using the combinations formula to compute the number of groups of size 2 of each type of stamp. To get the total number of ways, multiply the Utopian result and the Cornucopian result. Lothar can choose the Utopian stamps in $\frac{6 \times 5}{2!} = 15$ ways and the Cornucopian stamps in $\frac{4 \times 3}{2!} = 6$ ways, so together, there are $15 \times 6 = 90$ possible ways for Lothar to give Peggy Sue two stamps of each type.

Alternatively, use the textbook formula.

$$\text{Total number of ways} = \left(\frac{6!}{2!4!}\right) \times \left(\frac{4!}{2!2!}\right)$$
$$= \left(\frac{6 \times 5}{2 \times 1}\right) \times \left(\frac{4 \times 3}{2 \times 1}\right) = 15 \times 6 = 90$$

The correct answer is (B): Quantity B is greater.

10. **1,550**

Use the formula Total $= G_1 + G_2 - B + N$. The values for group 1 and group 2 are given in the question. Because all of the tickets will offer premium seating, backstage access, or both, the *neither* category will equal 0.

However, the value of the *both* category less certain: It is *at least* 150 but could be more. The question asks you to maximize the total value. Because B is subtracted from the other numbers in the formula, the total will be maximized when the value of B is minimized. Therefore, use $B = 150$ to solve.

$$\text{Total} = 1{,}200 + 500 - 150 + 0$$
$$\text{Total} = 1{,}550$$

11. **(B)**

Any amount from 1 cent to 19 cents can be created. Write out the possibilities.

Value:	Using:
1 to 4 cents	The four one-cent coins
5 cents	The five-cent coin
6 to 9 cents	The five-cent coin plus the four one-cent coins
10 cents	The 10-cent coin
11 to 14 cents	The ten-cent coin plus the four one-cent coins
15 cents	The 10-cent coin plus the five-cent coin
16 to 19 cents	The 10-cent coin plus the five-cent coin plus the four one-cent coins

The 19 cent value requires every coin in the jar, so 19 is the greatest possible value.

Therefore, the correct answer is (B): Quantity B is greater.

Unit Six: **Advanced Topics**

12. **(A)**

    Use the formula Total = $G_1 + G_2 - B + N$. The total is 180, and the two groups are 90 and 115. No information is given about B or N, so find the relationship between the two variables.

    $$180 = 90 + 115 - B + N$$
    $$180 = 205 - B + N$$
    $$B - N = 25$$

    The relationship indicates that 25 *more* customers purchased both zucchini and cauliflower than purchased neither.

    Therefore, the correct answer is (A): Quantity A is greater.

CHAPTER 30
Probability

In This Chapter:

- Probability Outcomes
- The Range of Probabilities
- Combining Probabilities
- The "$1 - x$" Probability Shortcut
- Overlapping Sets and Probability
- Check Your Skills Answer Key.
- Problem Set
- Solutions

CHAPTER 30 **Probability**

Probability is a quantity that expresses the chance, or likelihood, that an event will occur in a series of repeated trials.

For events with countable outcomes, probability is defined by the following fraction:

$$\text{Probability} = \frac{\text{Number of } desired \text{ or } successful \text{ outcomes}}{\text{Total number of } possible \text{ outcomes}}$$

This fraction assumes *all outcomes are equally likely*. If not, the math can be more complicated. In this chapter, you will learn how to handle both types of scenarios.

This fraction also assumes that you know the number of outcomes, both desired and total. Sometimes you'll be able to count the outcomes directly. At other times, you'll need to use combinatorics (see Chapter 29: Combinatorics). In this chapter, you'll learn how to make use of counting skills to determine probability in a variety of scenarios.

Probability Outcomes

With rare exception, every probability question you come across on the GRE will define all individual outcomes as equally likely. If you pull a marble out of a mixed jar, there is nothing that makes it more likely for you to pull out one marble than another. Often, these questions will use gaming items, like coins or dice, because they are designed to be "fair," meaning every outcome is equally likely.

If you have a fair die (the word *die* is singular for dice) with 6 faces and the numbers 1, 2, 3, 4, 5, and 6, then you have an equal likelihood of rolling each of those numbers when you roll that die.

The probability of rolling a 5 on a fair die is $\frac{1}{6}$, because there is only one desired outcome out of a total of 6 possible outcomes. However, the probability of rolling a prime number is $\frac{3}{6}$, which simplifies to $\frac{1}{2}$, because in that case, three of the six possible outcomes—2, 3, and 5—are considered successes.

Again, all the individual outcomes must be equally likely. For instance, you could say that the lottery has only two "outcomes"—win or lose—but that does not mean the probability of winning the lottery is $\frac{1}{2}$. To calculate the correct probability of winning the lottery, you must find *all of the possible* equally likely outcomes. Losing with one particular set of numbers is one outcome. Losing with a different set of numbers is another, different outcome. In other words, you have to count up all the specific combinations of different outcomes to figure out the total possibilities. Only one of those many outcomes will make you a winner.

Unit Six: **Advanced Topics**

In some problems, you will have to think carefully about how to break a situation down into equally likely outcomes. Consider the following problem:

> If a fair coin with heads on one side and tails on the other is tossed three times, what is the probability that it will turn up heads exactly twice?

You may be tempted to say that there are four outcomes—no heads, 1 head, 2 heads, and 3 heads—and that the probability of 2 heads is thus $\frac{1}{4}$. This would be wrong, though, because those four outcomes are not equally likely. You are much more likely to get 1 or 2 heads than to get all heads or all tails. Here are the eight possible outcomes of three flips of a coin:

HHH	TTT
HHT	TTH
HTH	THT
HTT	THH

From here, count the number of successful outcomes and the number of total outcomes. Three of the listed scenarios have exactly two heads, and there are eight total scenarios. The probability of getting exactly two heads is $\frac{3}{8}$.

You can use any method that works for you to write out the possible outcomes. One way to draw this list from scratch is using a counting tree, which breaks down possible outcomes step by step, with only one decision at each branch of the tree:

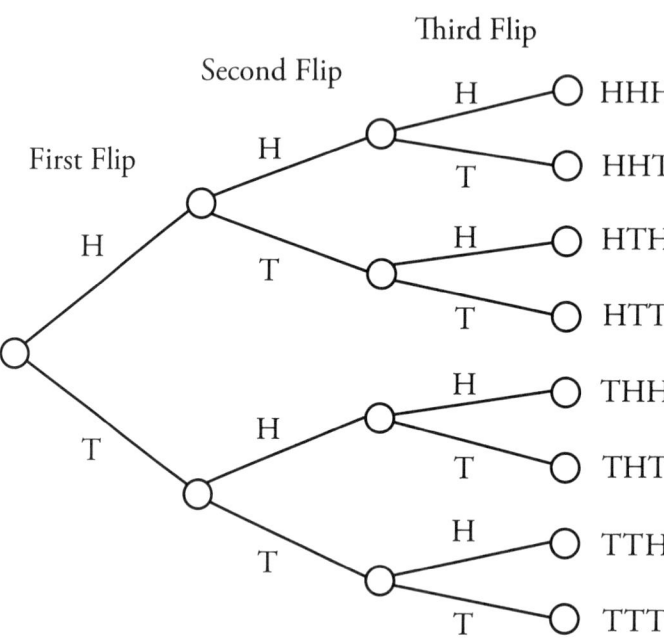

30

830

For problems in which drawing out all possible outcomes would take too much time, use the combinatorics methods you learned in Chapter 29: Combinatorics to count more efficiently:

$$\underset{\text{1st Flip}}{2} \quad \underset{\text{2nd Flip}}{2} \quad \underset{\text{3rd Flip}}{2}$$

In each of the three flips, there are two possible options: heads or tails. Multiply the individual options together to get the total number of outcomes $2 \times 2 \times 2 = 8$.

Of these outcomes, how many will have exactly 2 heads? The one tails result can be first, second, or third: THH, HTH, HHT. Therefore, the probability of getting heads exactly twice when a coin is flipped 3 times is $\frac{3}{8}$.

This result can also be written using probability notation:

$$P(\text{exactly 2 heads}) = \frac{3}{8}$$

The Range of Probabilities

The greatest probability—the *certainty* that an event will occur—is 1. This applies when all possible outcomes are successful. For example, if you roll a die numbered one through six once, the probability that it lands on a number less than seven, is certain, or 1:

$$\frac{\text{Number of } successful \text{ outcomes}}{\text{Total number of possible outcomes}} = \frac{6}{6} = 1$$

As a percent, this certainty is expressed as 100%.

The least probability—the *impossibility* that an event will occur—is 0. This applies when no successful outcome is possible. For example, if you roll a die numbered one through six once, the probability that it lands on the number nine is impossible—a probability of 0:

$$\frac{\text{Number of } successful \text{ outcomes}}{\text{Total number of possible outcomes}} = \frac{0}{6} = 0$$

As a percent, this impossibility is expressed as 0%.

Thus, probabilities can also be expressed as percents from 0 percent to 100 percent, inclusive, or fractions from 0 to 1, inclusive.

Combining Probabilities

In most GRE probability problems, you will be dealing with multiple events. You could flip a coin three times (three flips are three events), as discussed in the previous example. Or you could select five people from a group of 12 (five selections are five events). To deal with these problems, you must be confident in two things: (1) whether the events are independent or dependent, and (2) whether to multiply or add the individual probabilities.

Unit Six: Advanced Topics

Independent vs. Dependent Events

An **independent event** is one that is unchanged by the outcome of other events. Successive coin flips are examples of independent events, because the outcome of the first flip doesn't impact later flips. Even if you've flipped a coin and it's come up heads three times in a row, on the fourth flip, there's still a 50% probability it will come up heads again. Regardless of how many flips there are, you can be confident that the probabilities for any individual flip are unchanged.

A **dependent event** is one whose probabilities change depending on the events that came before it. Imagine standing in a group of 10 people waiting to be selected for a team. The first person who was picked had a 1 in 10 chance of being selected. However, now that the first person is already on the team, there are only 9 people still waiting, so the probability of being selected at that point is 1 in 9. As more people are selected, the odds continue to change because the total group shrinks. The GRE often describes dependent events as selecting something "without replacement." One item is selected, but not replaced, so the total group is smaller for the next selection.

Solving "And" Problems: Multiply

Once you've decided whether the events are dependent or independent, you must decide what constitutes a successful outcome. If multiple outcomes all have to turn out a certain way, that's more restrictive, and thus less probable, than if any one of several possible outcomes could be successful. Consider these two very different questions:

> If two fair dice are rolled (with faces 1, 2, 3, 4, 5, and 6), what is the probability that two 3's will be rolled?

> If two fair dice are rolled (with faces 1, 2, 3, 4, 5, and 6), what is the probability that at least one 3 will be rolled?

The first question is an "and" question. It asks for the probability that a 3 is rolled on the first die AND that a 3 is rolled on the second die. The second question is an "or" question. It asks for the probability that a 3 is rolled on the first die OR on the second die. (The second problem will be solved later in this chapter.)

"And" probability questions tend to be much more straightforward than "or" probability questions, because there are typically fewer options to consider. Everything has to line up exactly right to be considered a success. To solve an "and" problem, find each of the individual event probabilities and multiply them together to get the overall probability.

In this case, there are 6 possible numbers on a die, so the probability that the first die will be a 3 is one of out six, or $\frac{1}{6}$. Because the two rolls are independent, the probability that the second die will be a 3 is also $\frac{1}{6}$. To find the probability that the first die AND the second die are both 3's, multiply the individual probabilities together:

$$P(\text{die 1} = 3) \times P(\text{die 2} = 3) = P(\text{die 1 and 2} = 3)$$
$$\frac{1}{6} \times \frac{1}{6} = \frac{1}{36}$$

The probability that both dice will be 3 is $\frac{1}{36}$.

Try this problem:

> What is the probability that a fair coin (with heads and tails) flipped twice will land on heads the first time and tails the second time?

One coin flip doesn't impact the result of the other flip, so the two flips are independent of each other. The question asks for the probability of heads the first time and tails the second time, so this is an "and" problem. Find the individual probabilities, then multiply them together.

There's a *sequence* of events here: The first flip happens, *then* the second flip happens. Fortunately, many "and" problems involve a sequence like this one, or you can pretend that there is such a sequence. For instance, if you are asked about a coin flip and a roll of a die that occur simultaneously, you can pretend that the coin flip comes before the die roll, or vice versa. When results are independent, the order in which you look at them doesn't change the result.

In the case of the two coin flips, the first flip has two options, and the desired result is heads. The second flip also has two options, and the desired result is tails.

The probability that the coin will land on heads on the first flip is $\frac{1}{2}$. The probability that the coin will land on tails on the second flip is also $\frac{1}{2}$. Multiply the individual probabilities together to determine the probability that both will happen:

$$P(1 \text{ head and } 1 \text{ tail}) = \frac{1}{2} \times \frac{1}{2} = \frac{1}{4}$$

There is a $\frac{1}{4}$, or 25%, probability that two coin flips will result in heads the first time and tails the second time.

This process works with dependent events too. For example:

> In a box with 10 blocks, 3 of which are red, what is the probability of picking out a red block at random on each of your first two tries? Assume that you do NOT replace the first block after you have picked it.

Because this is an "and" problem, find the probabilities of selecting a red block on the first try and on the second try, then multiply them together. The two events are *dependent*, because after removing the first block, there are only 9 total blocks left to pick from and only 2 of those remaining blocks will be red (the third was just taken out!).

The probability of picking a red block on your first pick is $\frac{3}{10}$.

The probability of picking a red block on your second pick, *given that you already picked a red block on your first pick*, is $\frac{2}{9}$. There are two red blocks at this point, and you're choosing at random out of a set of nine.

Therefore, the probability of picking a red block on both picks is $\frac{\cancel{3}^1}{\cancel{10}_5} \times \frac{\cancel{2}^1}{\cancel{9}_3} = \frac{1}{15}$.

When solving probability problems, consider whether one event affects subsequent events. The first roll of a die or flip of a coin has no effect on any subsequent rolls or flips. However, if you are selecting certain items from a group and you actually pull the selected items out of the group, then the first pick of an item *does* affect subsequent picks. In such a scenario, always adjust the subsequent probabilities.

Unit Six: **Advanced Topics**

If you *are* supposed to replace the object or leave it with the group, then the problem will clearly tell you so. In that sort of scenario (called "with replacement"), the first pick does not affect the second pick because the full group is still available for the second pick.

For coin flips and rolls of a die, you can always assume independence. For instance, if you roll a 6, that number doesn't disappear and nothing will stop you from rolling 6 again. With each flip or roll, you're starting fresh, so the chance of getting any particular number on the die on a subsequent roll is still $\frac{1}{6}$, with no adjustment.

Solving "Or" Problems: Add

Some problems will ask about the probability that one thing or another will happen. For example:

> What is the probability that a fair die rolled once will land on either 4 or 5?

In "or" probability questions, there are multiple different outcomes that all could constitute a success. To find the desired probability, calculate the probability for each successful outcome and *add* them together. This is the essence of what makes "or" questions different than "and" questions. Multiply for "and." Add for "or."

To find the probabilities for an "or" problem, you must first understand the concept of **mutual exclusivity**. Two events are said to be mutually exclusive if they cannot both occur at the same time. For example, when you roll a single die one time, you will either get a 4 or not get a 4. It's not possible to roll both a 4 and another number *at the same time*.

Because it's impossible to roll both a 4 and a 5 on a single roll, these are mutually exclusive outcomes. The probability that the die will land on 4 is $\frac{1}{6}$. The probability that the die will land on 5 is also $\frac{1}{6}$. To find the probability that the die will land on either 4 or 5, add the individual probabilities: $\frac{1}{6} + \frac{1}{6} = \frac{2}{6} = \frac{1}{3}$.

Note that the probability of having the die come up either 4 or 5 $\left(\frac{1}{3}\right)$ is greater than the probability of a 4 by itself $\left(\frac{1}{6}\right)$ or of a 5 by itself $\left(\frac{1}{6}\right)$. When success is defined in a less constrained way (e.g., "I can win *either* this way *or* that way"), then the probability of success will be greater. When you add together two fractions, you get a *greater* result, which means a greater probability.

Remember this question?

> If two fair dice are rolled (with faces 1, 2, 3, 4, 5, and 6), what is the probability that at least one 3 will be rolled?

There are three possible successful outcomes: Just the first die could be a 3, just the second die could be a 3, or both could be 3.

When you roll one die, you have a one-in-six chance of rolling a 3, so the probability of rolling a 3 is $\frac{1}{6}$. If you don't roll a 3, then you will roll a 1, 2, 4, 5, or 6. The probability of *not* rolling a 3 is $\frac{5}{6}$.

Those two scenarios—rolling a 3 or not rolling a 3—constitute all of the possible outcomes when you roll this one die, so those two probabilities add up to 100%, or 1. For any scenario, it's always the case that the probabilities of *all* of the possible outcomes will add up to 100%, or 1.

If you are going to roll two dice, what are the possible outcomes relative to a 3 being rolled? There are four mutually exclusive outcomes:

1. The first die is a 3 and the second die is a 3.
2. The first die is a 3 and the second die is not a 3.
3. The first die is not a 3 and the second die is a 3.
4. The first die is not a 3 and the second die is not a 3.

The question asks for the probability that *at least one* 3 will be rolled. Compute the probabilities of the three mutually exclusive successful outcomes:

P(both are 3's)	$\frac{1}{6} \times \frac{1}{6} = \frac{1}{36}$
P(first die is 3 and second die is not)	$\frac{1}{6} \times \frac{5}{6} = \frac{5}{36}$
P(first die is not 3 and second die is)	$\frac{5}{6} \times \frac{1}{6} = \frac{5}{36}$

Once you have the probabilities for each individual successful outcome, add them to arrive at the overall probability that at least one 3 is rolled:

$$\frac{5}{36} + \frac{5}{36} + \frac{1}{36} = \frac{11}{36}$$

There is an 11 in 36 probability that at least one of the dice will be a 3.

This solution was more complex than that for the earlier "and" questions because you had to find multiple probabilities and then add them together.

One more note on mutual exclusivity. Imagine that there is a 60% probability that it will rain today and an independent 70% probability that you will drink coffee today. It either rains (60% chance) or does not rain (40% chance), so those two outcomes are mutually exclusive. And you either drink coffee (70% chance) or you don't (30% chance), so those two outcomes are also mutually exclusive.

However, raining and drinking coffee are not mutually exclusive—you may drink coffee whether it does or does not rain. So, it would be nonsensical to say that the probability either that it rains or that you drink coffee (but *not* both) is 60% + 70% = 130%. There can't be a more than 100% chance that something will happen.

Instead, consider the four outcomes that are possible:

1. It rains and you drink coffee.
2. It rains and you don't drink coffee.
3. It doesn't rain and you drink coffee
4. It doesn't rain and you don't drink coffee.

To find the probability that either it rains or you drink coffee (but *not* both), find the probability of each of the successful outcomes. If the probability of rain is 60%, the probability of no rain must be 40%, and if the probability of drinking coffee is 70%, the probability of no coffee must be 30%:

| It rains and you don't drink coffee. | P(rains) × P(no coffee) | 0.60 × 0.30 = 0.18 |
| It doesn't rain and you drink coffee. | P(no rain) × P(coffee) | 0.40 × 0.70 = 0.28 |

Finally, add the probability of each mutually exclusive event together: 0.18 + 0.28 = 0.46. Therefore, there is a 46% chance that either it will rain or you will drink coffee (but not both).

> **Strategy Tip**
>
> To find the overall probability of an "and" problem, multiply the individual probabilities of each successful outcome.
>
> To find the overall probability of an "or" problem, add the individual probabilities of each mutually exclusive successful outcome.
>
> In both cases, take into account whether the events are independent or dependent when determining the individual probabilities.

All that said, the majority of probability questions on the GRE are of the "and" variety. When in doubt, *multiply*. Most GRE probability problems just want you to multiply two or three fractions together.

Advanced Note

If you're interested, it's also possible to compute "or" probabilities using an equation. When adding events where you want one option or the other but *not both*, subtract the instances of overlap, as you did with overlapping sets in Chapter 29: Combinatorics.

If events *X* and *Y* are not mutually exclusive, then $P(X \text{ OR } Y) = P(X) + P(Y) - P(X \text{ AND } Y)$. For example:

> A box contains 20 balls. Ten balls are white and marked with the integers 1–10. The other 10 balls are red and marked with the integers 11–20. If one ball is selected, what is the probability that the ball will be white OR will be marked with an even number?

Because half the balls are white and half are marked with an even number, P(white) + P(even) alone would give you $\frac{1}{2} + \frac{1}{2}$, which equals 1 . . . and that doesn't make sense, since some balls are obviously not white and not even. This calculation is incorrect because some of the counted balls are both white and even, so they've been counted twice, once in each group.

To correct for this overcount, add up the two individual probabilities but also subtract out the probability that the ball is both white AND marked with an even number. There are 5 such balls out of 20:

$$P(X) + P(Y) - P(X \text{ and } Y)$$
$$P(\text{White}) + P(\text{even}) - P(\text{White and even})$$
$$\frac{1}{2} + \frac{1}{2} - \frac{5}{20} = \frac{15}{20} = \frac{3}{4}$$

Check Your Skills

1. A drawer contains 7 white shirts and 3 red shirts. What is the probability of picking a white shirt and then a red shirt, if the first shirt is not put back into the drawer?
2. If a 6-sided fair die with sides 1, 2, 3, 4, 5, and 6 is rolled twice, what is the probability that it will land on an even number both times?
3. Eight runners in a race are equally likely to win the race. What is the probability that the race will be won either by the runner in lane 1 or by the runner in lane 8 ? (Assume a tie is impossible.)
4. A fair die, numbered 1 through 6, is rolled, and a fair coin (heads and tails) is flipped. What is the probability that either the die will roll a 2 or 3, or the coin will land heads up, or both?

Answers can be found on page 841.

The "$1 - x$" Probability Shortcut

Sometimes a question asks for a probability that will take a significant number of computations to figure out. For example:

> A fair coin is flipped four times. What is the probability that at least one of the flips will result in tails?

The phrase "at least" adds a layer of complexity. To answer this question directly, you would need to calculate the probability of the coin flips producing exactly one tails, exactly two tails, exactly three tails, and exactly four tails, then add those individual probabilities together to get the final probability of at least one of those mutually exclusive results occurring. That's a lot of work.

There is, fortunately, a shortcut. Here are all of the possible scenarios when flipping the coin four times:

1. No tails
2. Exactly 1 tails
3. Exactly 2 tails
4. Exactly 3 tails
5. Exactly 4 tails

The collective probability of all of those scenarios is 1, because it is certain that one of those outcomes will occur when you flip a coin four times.

In this case, the problem asks about scenarios two through five: at least one tails. That's the desired outcome. The first scenario—no tails—is the undesired outcome. You can generalize the idea this way:

$$P(\text{desired result}) + P(\text{undesired result}) = 1$$

In this problem, solving for the desired result is cumbersome because there are four possible scenarios. However, solving for the undesired result is a lot more straightforward because there's only one possible way to have no tails: when you have all heads.

What's the probability that you'll get no tails when you flip a coin four times?

837

Unit Six: **Advanced Topics**

For each individual coin flip, there is a $\frac{1}{2}$ probability that it will not be tails. Each flip is independent of the previous flips, so multiply the four probabilities together to find the probability that none of them are tails:

$$\frac{1}{2} \times \frac{1}{2} \times \frac{1}{2} \times \frac{1}{2} = \frac{1}{16}$$

The probability that none of the four coin flips will be tails is $\frac{1}{16}$. The question asks for the probability that *at least one* of the flips will be tails. Subtract the undesired result from 1 to find the desired result:

$$P(\text{desired result}) + \frac{1}{16} = 1$$

$$P(\text{desired result}) = 1 - \frac{1}{16}$$

$$P(\text{desired result}) = \frac{15}{16}$$

Because there is a $\frac{1}{16}$ chance that there will be *no* tails, there is a $\frac{15}{16}$ chance that there will be *at least one* tail.

> **Strategy Tip**
>
> When it's cumbersome to find the probability of a certain desired outcome, check whether it would be easier to find the probability of the *undesired* outcome instead. If so, subtract the undesired outcome from 1 to find the probability of the desired outcome.
>
> $P(\text{desired outcome}) = 1 - P(\text{undesired outcome})$

Another way to understand this concept is in terms of success and failure. Say that a salesperson makes five sales calls, and you want to find the likelihood that at least one of the calls results in a sale. If you try to calculate this probability directly, you will have to confront five separate possibilities that constitute "success": exactly one sale, exactly two sales, exactly three sales, exactly four sales, or exactly five sales.

However, consider the probability of *failure*—that is, the salesperson *does not* make at least one sale. Now you have only one possibility to consider: 0 sales.

Probability of SUCCESS + Probability of FAILURE = 1
(the event happens)   (it does *not* happen)

What is the probability that, on three rolls of a single fair die, at least one of the rolls will be a 6 ?

Don't try to compute all the different ways to achieve success! Instead, reverse the question:

Failure: What is the probability that NONE of the rolls will yield a 6 ?

On each roll, there is a $\frac{5}{6}$ probability that the die will NOT yield a 6. Thus, the probability that on all three rolls the die will *not* yield a 6 is: $\frac{5}{6} \times \frac{5}{6} \times \frac{5}{6} = \frac{125}{216}$.

Subtract this probability from 1 to find the probability that at least one 6 will be rolled:

$$1 - \frac{125}{216} = \frac{91}{216}$$

Chapter 30: Probability

> **Strategy Tip**
>
> If the wording contains phrases such as "at least" and "at most," then consider finding the probability that success does *not* happen. If you can find this "failure" probability more easily (call it *x*), then solve for the probability of success as 1 minus the probability of failure, or 1 − *x*.

Glance back through the prior section of this chapter, Combining Probabilities. Where could the 1 − *x* shortcut save you time and effort?

Really: Go back and look before you keep reading. Found something that you think might work? Try it out.

The problem that asked for the probability that at least one 3 would be rolled can be solved much more efficiently using the 1 − *x* shortcut. Why?

There are four total scenarios possible when rolling the pair of dice:

1. The first die is a 3 and the second die is a 3.
2. The first die is a 3 and the second die is not a 3.
3. The first die is not a 3 and the second die is a 3.
4. The first die is not a 3 and the second die is not a 3.

The first, second, and third scenarios are all successful outcomes. Only the fourth scenario is unsuccessful, so it's possible to calculate the probability of that lone failure and subtract it from 1 in order to find the probability of the successful outcomes. First, calculate the probability that neither die is a 3:

$$P(\text{not } 3) \times P(\text{not } 3)$$
$$\frac{5}{6} \times \frac{5}{6} = \frac{25}{36}$$

Then, subtract from 1:

$$1 - \frac{25}{36} = \frac{11}{36}$$

When you're asked to find the probability of multiple scenarios and there's just one lone scenario that is not included in the successful outcomes, use the 1 − *x* shortcut to save yourself time and effort.

Check Your Skills

5. If a die is rolled twice, what is the probability that it will land on an even number at least once?

Answers can be found on page 842.

Unit Six: **Advanced Topics**

Overlapping Sets and Probability

The GRE may ask to you answer an overlapping sets question in the form of a probability. Consider this variation of the problem presented in Chapter 29: Combinatorics:

> At Factory X, there are 400 total workers. Of these workers, 240 are salaried, and 220 work in Operations. If 100 of the workers are non-salaried and do not work in Operations, what's the probability that Malak, a worker at Factory X, is both salaried and works in Operations?

The previous chapter used a Venn Diagram to determine that 160 workers are both salaried and in Operations. To answer this new question, you would still need to calculate the 160 figure, and you would then need to go one step further to find the probability that Malak falls into that subgroup.

Because the question is asking for the probability that Malak is both salaried and works in Operations, consider that group to be the "desired" group. You know that Malak is one of 400 workers, so 400 is the total pool. Use the probability formula to find the probability Malak is salaried and in Operations:

$$\frac{\text{desired outcomes}}{\text{total outcomes}} = \frac{\text{\# salaried and Ops}}{\text{\# total workers}} = \frac{160}{400} = 0.4$$

There is a 0.4 or 40% probability that Malak is both salaried and works in Operations.

Check Your Skills

6. Of 320 consumers, 200 eat strawberries and 300 eat oranges. If all 320 eat at least one of the fruits, what is the probability that Evie, one of the 320 consumers, ate both?

Answers can be found on page 843.

Chapter 30: **Probability**

Check Your Skills Answer Key

1. $\frac{7}{30}$

    This is an "and" problem with two dependent events. There are 10 shirts total, with seven white shirts and three red shirts.

    Probability of picking a white shirt first: $\frac{7}{10}$.

    Probability of picking a red shirt next, given that a white shirt was chosen first and removed: $\frac{3}{9} = \frac{1}{3}$.

    Probability of picking white first, and then red: $\frac{7}{10} \times \frac{1}{3} = \frac{7}{30}$.

2. $\frac{1}{4}$ or 25%

    This is an "and" problem with two independent events. For each roll of the die, the probability of an even number is $\frac{3}{6}$, which simplifies to $\frac{1}{2}$. Multiply the individual probabilities because the two outcomes are independent: $\frac{1}{2} \times \frac{1}{2} = \frac{1}{4}$.

3. $\frac{1}{4}$

    This is an "or" problem with only one event: One person wins the race. The probability that the runner in lane 1 will win is $\frac{1}{8}$, which is the same as the probability that the runner in lane 8 will win. The two events are mutually exclusive because ties are impossible, so add the individual probabilities: $\frac{1}{8} + \frac{1}{8} = \frac{1}{4}$.

4. $\frac{2}{3}$

    There are two independent events: the die roll and the coin flip.

    Because the outcomes of the events in this question are not mutually exclusive, you have two options to solve. Option 1 is to compute each mutually exclusive event before adding them. Option 2 is to add up the probabilities of the two events as though they were independent, and then subtract the overlap.

    To use either option, first calculate the probability that the die will come up 2 or 3. Those are mutually exclusive and each has a probability of $\frac{1}{6}$, so the probability that one or the other will occur is $\frac{1}{6} + \frac{1}{6} = \frac{1}{3}$. The probability that you will get neither a 2 nor a 3 is therefore $\frac{2}{3}$.

    Next, the probability of flipping heads is $\frac{1}{2}$ and the probability of not getting heads is also $\frac{1}{2}$.

Unit Six: Advanced Topics

Option 1: List out every mutually exclusive successful scenario and calculate its probability.

$$P(2 \text{ or } 3 \text{ and not heads}) \quad \frac{1}{3} \times \frac{1}{2} = \frac{1}{6}$$

$$P(\text{not } 2 \text{ or } 3 \text{ and heads}) \quad \frac{2}{3} \times \frac{1}{2} = \frac{1}{3}$$

$$P(2 \text{ or } 3 \text{ and heads}) \quad \frac{1}{3} \times \frac{1}{2} = \frac{1}{6}$$

Add the individual probabilities to get the overall probability of success: $\frac{1}{6} + \frac{1}{3} + \frac{1}{6} = \frac{2}{3}$.

Option 2: Add up the overall probabilities of getting a 2 or 3 and flipping a heads, then subtract the overlap.

$$P(2 \text{ or } 3) + P(\text{heads}) - P(2 \text{ or } 3 \text{ AND heads})$$

$$\frac{1}{3} + \frac{1}{2} - \frac{1}{6}$$

$$\frac{2}{6} + \frac{3}{6} - \frac{1}{6}$$

The answer is $\frac{4}{6}$, which simplifies to $\frac{2}{3}$.

If you arrived at an answer of $\frac{5}{6}$ by adding $\frac{1}{3}$ and $\frac{1}{2}$, you were accidentally double-counting. Using this method, when the die lands on a 2 or 3 AND the coin lands on heads, you will have counted that outcome twice. It's necessary to subtract out one of the two double-counted items.

5. $\frac{3}{4}$ or 75%

Calculate the probability of failure. If the die does not land on an even number at least once, then it must have landed on an odd number both times. For each throw, the probability of an odd number is $\frac{1}{2}$. Multiply the individual probabilities to get the probability of two odd numbers in a row: $\frac{1}{2} \times \frac{1}{2} = \frac{1}{4}$. Therefore, the probability of at least one even number is 1 − the probability of failure, which is $1 - \frac{1}{4}$, or $\frac{3}{4}$.

842

6. **56.25%**

Graphically:

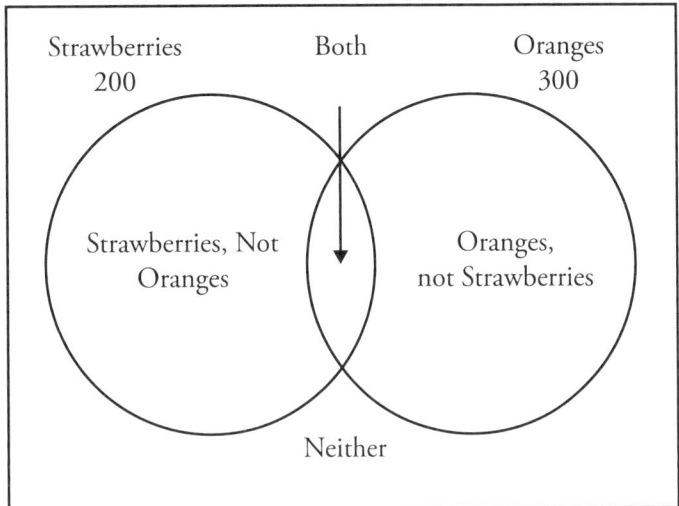

Mathematically, you can use Total = Group 1 + Group 2 − Both + Neither.

Because all of the consumers eat at least one of the fruits, $f = 0$. So:

$$320 = 200 + 300 - e + 0$$
$$320 = 500 - e$$
$$e = 180$$

The probability that Evie will be one of those 180 out of the 320 total consumers is $\frac{180}{320} = 0.5625$ or 56.25%.

Unit Six: **Advanced Topics**

Problem Set

> Solve the following problems. Assume all coins and die are fair unless otherwise described. Express probabilities as fractions or percentages unless otherwise instructed.

1. What is the probability that the sum of two dice rolls will yield a 4 OR 6 ?

2. What is the probability that the sum of two dice rolls will yield anything but an 8 ?

3. What is the probability that the sum of two dice rolls will yield a 7, and then when both are thrown again, their sum will again yield a 7 ?

4. What is the probability that the sum of two dice rolls will yield a 5, and then when both are thrown again, their sum will yield a 9 ?

5. At a certain pizzeria, $\frac{1}{6}$ of the pizzas sold in a week were mushroom, and $\frac{1}{5}$ of the OTHER pizzas sold were pepperoni. If Brandon bought a randomly chosen pizza from the pizzeria that week, what is the probability that Brandon ordered a pepperoni pizza?

6. There are 12 guests at a dinner party: 6 doctors and 6 writers. Exactly one doctor and one writer are bringing desserts. If one person from this group is selected at random, what is the probability that the person selected is a doctor who is not bringing a dessert OR that the person selected is a writer?

7. A coin is flipped 5 times.

Quantity A	Quantity B
The probability of getting more heads than tails	$\frac{1}{2}$

8. A jar contains three red and two white marbles. Two marbles are picked without replacement.

Quantity A	Quantity B
The probability of picking two red marbles	The probability of picking exactly one red and one white marble

9. A die is rolled *n* times, where *n* is at least 3.

Quantity A	Quantity B
The probability that at least one of the throws yields a 6	$\frac{1}{2}$

30

10. A bag contains 5 red, 4 blue, and 8 orange jellybeans. 3 jellybeans are randomly selected from this bag.

Quantity A	**Quantity B**
The probability of selecting a red, then a blue, then an orange jellybean	The probability of selecting a red, then another red, then an orange jellybean

Unit Six: **Advanced Topics**

Solutions

1. $\frac{2}{9}$

   There are 36 ways in which 2 dice can be thrown (6 × 6 = 36). The combinations that yield sums of 4 and 6 are 1 + 3, 2 + 2, 3 + 1, 1 + 5, 2 + 4, 3 + 3, 4 + 2, and 5 + 1, for a total of 8 different combinations. Therefore, the probability is $\frac{8}{36}$, which simplifies to $\frac{2}{9}$.

2. $\frac{31}{36}$

   Solve this problem by calculating the probability that the sum *will* yield a sum of 8, and then subtract the result from 1. There are 5 combinations of 2 dice that yield a sum of 8: 2 + 6, 3 + 5, 4 + 4, 5 + 3, and 6 + 2. (7 + 1 is not a valid combination, as there is no 7 on a standard die.) Therefore, the probability that the sum will be 8 is $\frac{5}{36}$, and the probability that the sum will *not* be 8 is $1 - \frac{5}{36}$, which equals $\frac{31}{36}$.

3. $\frac{1}{36}$

   There are 36 ways in which 2 dice can be thrown (6 × 6 = 36). The combinations that yield a sum of 7 are 1 + 6, 2 + 5, 3 + 4, 4 + 3, 5 + 2, and 6 + 1, for a total of 6 different combinations. Therefore, the probability of rolling a 7 is $\frac{6}{36}$, which simplifies to $\frac{1}{6}$. To find the probability that this will happen twice in a row, multiply $\frac{1}{6}$ by $\frac{1}{6}$ to get $\frac{1}{36}$.

4. $\frac{1}{81}$

   First, find the individual probability of each event. The probability of rolling a 5 is $\frac{4}{36}$, or $\frac{1}{9}$, since there are 4 ways to roll a sum of 5 (1 + 4, 2 + 3, 3 + 2, and 4 + 1). The probability of rolling a 9 is also $\frac{4}{36}$, or $\frac{1}{9}$, since there are 4 ways to roll a sum of 9 (3 + 6, 4 + 5, 5 + 4, and 6 + 3). To find the probability that both events will happen in succession, multiply: $\frac{1}{9} \times \frac{1}{9} = \frac{1}{81}$.

5. $\frac{1}{6}$

   If $\frac{1}{6}$ of the pizzas were mushroom, $\frac{5}{6}$ of the pizzas were not. Because $\frac{1}{5}$ of these $\frac{5}{6}$ were pepperoni, multiply to find the total portion: $\frac{1}{5} \times \frac{5}{6} = \frac{1}{\cancel{5}} \times \frac{\cancel{5}}{6} = \frac{1}{6}$. Since $\frac{1}{6}$ of the pizzas sold were pepperoni, there is a $\frac{1}{6}$ chance that Brandon bought a pepperoni pizza.

6. $\frac{11}{12}$

   The question asks about either a doctor who is not bringing a dessert or a writer (who may or may not be bringing a dessert). Five doctors *who are not bringing a dessert* are invited and 6 writers are invited. Thus, 11 of the 12 guests would fit the description.

   Alternatively, you could ask who does *not* fit the description. Only the one doctor who is bringing a dessert would be excluded. The chance of selecting that person at random is $\frac{1}{12}$, so the chance of selecting someone else is $1 - \frac{1}{12} = \frac{11}{12}$.

7. **(C)**

    Because heads and tails are equally likely, it follows that the probability of getting more heads than tails should be exactly the same as the probability of getting more tails than heads. The only remaining option is that you might get equally as many heads and tails. However, because the total number of coin flips is an odd number, the latter is impossible. Therefore, the probability of getting more heads than tails must be exactly $\frac{1}{2}$. (It is, of course, also possible to compute this probability directly by considering the cases of getting 5, 4, or 3 heads separately. However, this approach would be very time-consuming.)

    Another way of thinking about it is that, for every set of flips that has more heads than tails, there is a corresponding set of flips, in which every flip gets the opposite result, yielding more tails than heads. For instance, the sequence of throws *HHHHH* is balanced by the sequence *TTTTT*. The sequence *HHHHT* is balanced by the sequence *TTTTH*.

    Therefore, the correct answer is (C): The two quantities are equal.

8. **(B)**

    First, compute the probability of picking two red marbles without replacement. This is given by:

    $$P(RR) = \frac{3}{5} \times \frac{2}{4} = \frac{3}{10}$$

    Next, consider the probability of picking a red marble followed by a white marble:

    $$P(RW) = \frac{3}{5} \times \frac{2}{4} = \frac{3}{10}$$

    However, this is not the only way to pick one red *and* one white marble; you could have picked the white one first, followed by the red one:

    $$P(WR) = \frac{2}{5} \times \frac{3}{4} = \frac{3}{10}$$

    This event is mutually exclusive from picking a red marble followed by a white marble. Thus, the total probability of picking one red *and* one white marble is the sum of the probabilities of *RW* and *WR*, yielding an answer of:

    $$P(RW \text{ OR } WR) = \frac{3}{10} + \frac{3}{10} = 2 \times \left(\frac{3}{10}\right) = \frac{3}{5}$$

    This is a greater probability than the one for the Quantity A scenario. Therefore, the correct answer is (B): Quantity B is greater.

Unit Six: **Advanced Topics**

9. **(D)**

    The easiest way to compute the probability in question is through the "1 − x" shortcut. To do so, imagine the opposite of the event of interest, namely, that *none* of the *n* throws yields a 6. The probability of a single throw not yielding a 6 is $\frac{5}{6}$, and because each throw is independent, the cumulative probability of none of the *n* throws yielding a 6 is found by multiplication:

    $$P(\text{No 6 in } n \text{ throws}) = \left(\frac{5}{6}\right)^n$$

    Powers of fractions less than one decrease as the exponent increases, so this probability will become very small for large values of *n*, such that the probability of getting at least one 6 (which is $1 - \left(\frac{5}{6}\right)^n$) will come closer and closer to 1. Thus, as *n* increases, it becomes more and more likely that a 6 will be thrown. The question now is, what is the least possible probability of getting at least one six? To answer that question, set *n* to its lowest possible value, which is 3. In that case, the probability of never getting a 6 is given by:

    $$P(\text{No 6 in three throws}) = \left(\frac{5}{6}\right)^3 = \frac{125}{216}$$

    Use the calculator to compute the numerator and denominator separately.

    The probability of getting at least one 6 in three throws is given by:

    $$P(\text{At least one 6 in three throws}) = 1 - \frac{125}{216} = \frac{91}{216}$$

    This value is less than $\frac{1}{2}$. As explained earlier, however, as *n* grows, it becomes ever more likely that at least one throw will yield a 6, so the probability will eventually surpass $\frac{1}{2}$.

    Thus, Quantity A can be less than or greater than $\frac{1}{2}$.

    The correct answer is (D): The relationship cannot be determined.

    You may have figured intuitively that given three throws, the chance of getting at least one 6 would be $\frac{3}{6} = \frac{1}{2}$. But if you extend this reasoning, it soon breaks down. If you had six throws, you couldn't say that you had a 100% chance of rolling a 6, and if you had more than six throws, you certainly wouldn't want to say the chance was now *more* than 1. Since a die can keep turning up the same number each time, the events are completely independent, and you can't just add up the chances.

10. **(C)**
    Set up the probabilities in both quantities before calculating either value. The bag contains 5 red, 4 blue, and 8 orange jellybeans, and thus 17 total jellybeans.

    In Quantity A, the probability of picking a red is $\frac{5}{17}$. Once the red is selected, there are only 16 jellybeans left in the bag, so the probability of then picking a blue is $\frac{4}{16}$, and then the probability of picking an orange is $\frac{8}{15}$. Thus, Quantity A is equal to $\frac{5}{17} \times \frac{4}{16} \times \frac{8}{15}$.

    In Quantity B, the probability of picking a red first is still $\frac{5}{17}$. Notice that *once a red is picked first, there are now equal numbers of blues and reds left in the bag* (4 each). Thus, the probability of now picking another red is $\frac{4}{16}$ (equal to the probability in Quantity A of picking a blue at this point), and then the probability of picking an orange is still $\frac{8}{15}$. Thus, Quantity B is also equal to $\frac{5}{17} \times \frac{4}{16} \times \frac{8}{15}$.

    The correct answer is (C): The two quantities are equal.

    One note: Don't do math unless or until you have to. In this case, it wasn't necessary to actually multiply out the values.

CHAPTER 31
Optimization

In This Chapter:

- Optimization Constraints
- Algebraic Optimization
- Optimization in QC
- Optimizing Groups
- Overlapping Sets
- Geometry Optimization
- Check Your Skills Answer Key
- Problem Set
- Solutions

CHAPTER 31 Optimization

The GRE can make problems more challenging by asking for a maximum or minimum possible value. In this chapter, you will learn how to handle **optimization** problems, in which you're expected to balance the given criteria to find the optimal values of related quantities. The general principle is this: To maximize one value, you'll have to minimize others (and vice versa).

Optimization Constraints

If you have 12 oranges, what is the maximum number of people who could eat at least one entire orange?

Since you can't split oranges, a maximum of 12 people could each get one orange. The GRE, of course, will not make things this simple. Here's a more realistic example of what you might see on the test:

> If there are 12 oranges and every person must eat a different number of whole oranges, what is the maximum number of people who could eat at least one orange?

This problem has an additional constraint regarding how the oranges can be distributed. In order to answer optimization questions, focus on **extreme scenarios** that fit the given constraints.

Since you're asked to maximize the number of people who can eat an orange, assign each person the *least* number of oranges possible. This will ensure that you find the *greatest* possible number of orange eaters:

Person 1 eats 1 orange (leaves 11 remaining)

Person 2 eats 2 oranges (leaves 9 remaining)

Person 3 eats 3 oranges (leaves 6 remaining)

Person 4 eats 4 oranges (leaves 2 remaining)

Person 5 cannot eat any oranges: 1 and 2 have already been used.

The maximum number of people who could eat at least 1 orange is 4.

Unit Six: Advanced Topics

31

> **Strategy Tip**
>
> For optimization problems:
>
> 1. Watch out for **explicit constraints** (restrictions directly stated in the problem, such as the "different number of oranges" constraint in the example above).
> 2. Consider **hidden constraints** (restrictions implied by the real-world aspects of a problem, such as the implied integer constraint in a problem asking you to count the number of people—no fractional parts of people allowed!).
> 3. Consider what other values can be manipulated and whether those values should be maximized or minimized.
> 4. Test extreme values for the numbers that you are allowed to manipulate.

Try this problem:

> The guests at a banquet consumed a total of 401 pounds of food. If no individual guest consumed more than 2.5 pounds of food, what is the minimum number of guests that could have attended the banquet?

Here's one way to write out the information:

Pounds of food per guest	×	Guests	=	Total pounds food
At MOST		At LEAST		EXACTLY
2.5	×	???	=	401
		minimize		constant

The 401 figure is an exact figure—so it is a constant in the problem. You're not allowed to change it. The pounds of food per guest, on the other hand, is not an exact figure: Each person consumed at most 2.5 pounds. So this value can be manipulated as you solve.

The question asks for the *minimum* value of the number of guests. What's the best way to manipulate the 2.5 figure in order to minimize the number of guests?

Because the two quantities multiply to a constant, to minimize one quantity, maximize the other. This sort of inversion (i.e., maximizing one thing to minimize another) is typical in optimization problems.

If each guest eats as much food as possible, or 2.5 pounds apiece, then there are 401 ÷ 2.5 = 160.4 guests at the banquet.

However, you cannot have a fractional number of people at the banquet. The number of people must be an integer. Thus, the answer must be rounded. The *minimum* number of guests is 160.4 (if guests could be fractional), so the minimum *whole* number of guests is 161. If you set the number of guests at 160, then you wouldn't reach the fractional required minimum of 160.4.

If you're not sure, try multiplying it back out:

$$\text{Guests} \times \text{\# Food per guest} = \text{\# Food}$$
$$160 \quad \times \quad 2.5 \quad = \quad 400 \quad \text{Not enough food!}$$

The problem specified that 401 pounds of food were consumed. If 160 guests consume at most 2.5 pounds each, only 400 pounds of food would have been consumed. So, there must be at least 161 guests.

If you're unsure which way to round in a problem, plug the options in to see which one violates the parameters of the question.

Check Your Skills

1. A group of friends purchases a TV for $1,100. If no single person in the group contributes more than $75, what is the least number of people who could be in the group?

Answers can be found on page 864.

Algebraic Optimization

A common hidden constraint in word problems is that everything must be positive. Often, the thing must be a positive integer, specifically.

By contrast, optimization problems presented directly as equations, inequalities, or algebraic expressions frequently don't have those hidden constraints. When dealing with given variables, continue to focus on the extreme possible values for each of the variables, as some combination of them will usually lead to the maximum or minimum possible result. For example:

If $-7 \leq a \leq 6$ and $-7 \leq b \leq 8$, what is the maximum possible value for ab?

Test the extreme values for a and for b to determine which combinations of extreme values will maximize the product ab:

Extreme Values for a	Extreme Values for b
The least value for a is -7.	The least value for b is -7.
The greatest value for a is 6.	The greatest value for b is 8.

Next, combine the extreme values of a and b to determine what happens to ab:

$$a_{min} \times b_{min} = (-7)(-7) = 49$$
$$a_{min} \times b_{max} = (-7)(8) = \text{negative!}$$
$$a_{max} \times b_{min} = (6)(-7) = \text{negative!}$$
$$a_{max} \times b_{max} = (6)(8) = 48$$

Interestingly, ab is maximized when you take the *negative* extreme values for both a and b, resulting in $ab = 49$.

Unit Six: Advanced Topics

Only do as much work as you need in order to tell that something will *not* be the value you want. For example, the middle two cases are both a positive multiplied by a negative, which will result in a negative number. Since the first case already returned a positive number, don't bother to multiply out the second and third cases.

Try this problem with a twist:

If $-4 \leq m \leq 7$ and $-3 < n < 10$, what is the maximum possible integer value for $m - n$?

The second inequality presents a complication. The variable n is between -3 and 10, but cannot be -3 or 10. It could be -2.99999 or $9.99999\ldots$ but it would be cumbersome to test -2.99999.

Still test using the integer values, but note the restriction by putting an arrow next to -3 and 10 to indicate whether n must be above or below those extremes:

Extreme Values for m	**Extreme Values for n**
The least value for m is -4.	The least value for n is greater than -3: $-3 \uparrow$.
The greatest value for m is 7.	The greatest value for n is less than 10: $10 \downarrow$.

Next, consider the different extreme value scenarios for $m - n$. Here's the first one:

$$m_{min} - n_{min} = -4 - (-3 \uparrow) = -1 \downarrow$$

First, when you subtract something negative, the two negatives turn into one positive sign: $-(-3) = +3$. But the starting value is *not* really -3. Rather, it's something *greater* than -3, such as -2.

$$-4 - (-3) = -4 + 3 = -1$$
$$-4 - (-2) = -4 + 2 = -2$$

What happens? When you subtract something that is *greater* than -3, you end up adding something that is *less* than $+3$, so the result ends up being *more* negative. That's why the arrow flips directions when doing this subtraction:

$$m_{min} - n_{min} = -4 - (-3 \uparrow) = -1 \downarrow$$
$$m_{min} - n_{max} = -4 - (10 \downarrow) = -14 \uparrow$$
$$m_{max} - n_{min} = 7 - (-3 \uparrow) = 10 \downarrow$$
$$m_{max} - n_{max} = 7 - (10 \downarrow) = -3 \uparrow$$

Three of the four possible combinations result in negative values, but the third scenario results in a positive, so the maximum possible value is a bit less than 10. The problem asked for the maximum possible *integer* value, so the answer is 9, because 9 is the greatest integer that is still less than 10.

If you feel comfortable with this kind of math, you can shortcut this process via logic. To maximize the value of $m - n$, choose the greatest possible value of m and the least possible value of n. The greatest possible value of m is 7 and the least possible value of n is -2.999, but the problem asks for an *integer* value. The least possible integer value of n is -2, so the maximum value of $m - n$ is $7 - (-2) = 9$.

Chapter 31: **Optimization**

Try this problem:

If $x \geq 4 + (z+1)^2$, what is the minimum possible value for x?

To minimize x, you also need to minimize z (since x is greater than or equal to the expression that includes z). When you need to minimize something where a variable has an even exponent, the key is to recognize that the squared term will be minimized when it is set equal to 0.

So, figure out what value for z will make $(z+1)^2$ equal to 0:

$$x \geq 4 + (-1+1)^2$$
$$x \geq 4 + (0)^2$$

Therefore, 4 is the minimum possible value for x.

Check Your Skills

2. If $-1 \leq a \leq 4$ and $-6 \leq b \leq -2$, what is the minimum value for $b - a$?

3. If $(x+2)^2 \leq 2 - y$, what is the maximum possible value for y?

Answers can be found on pages 864–865.

Optimization in QC

QC problems can also ask for the maximum or minimum possible value of an expression. For example:

$$-2 \leq x \leq 3$$
$$-3 \leq y \leq 2$$

Quantity A	**Quantity B**
The maximum value of x^2	The maximum value of y^2

Both quantities ask for the maximum value, but don't test just the positive extremes for x and y. Instead, test both the maximum and minimum values for x and y to see how they impact x^2 and y^2:

$$(x_{min})^2 = (-2)^2 = 4$$
$$(x_{max})^2 = (3)^2 = 9$$
$$(y_{min})^2 = (-3)^2 = 9$$
$$(y_{max})^2 = (2)^2 = 4$$

Even though the maximum value of x is 3, while the maximum value of y is only 2, the minimum value of y makes the difference. The maximum value of x and the minimum value of y transform into squared values that are equal. Therefore, the correct answer is (C): The two quantities are equal.

Unit Six: Advanced Topics

Optimization is also relevant to problems involving absolute values. For example:

$$-2 \leq x \leq 3$$
$$-3 \leq y \leq 2$$

Quantity A	**Quantity B**
The maximum value of $\|x - 4\|$	The maximum value of $\|y + 4\|$

The extremes of *x* and *y* are the same as they were in the previous problem, but now there's the added twist of absolute values. The least possible value of any absolute value will be 0.

> **Key Concept**
>
> The minimum possible value of $|x|$ or *x* raised to an even exponent is 0. Absolute values and even exponents cannot produce negative results.

Test the extremes to find the maximum possible value of each quantity:

$$|x_{min} - 4| = |-2 - 4| = |-6| = 6$$
$$|x_{max} - 4| = |3 - 4| = |-1| = 1$$
$$|y_{min} + 4| = |-3 + 4| = |1| = 1$$
$$|y_{max} + 4| = |2 + 4| = |6| = 6$$

The maximum value of each quantity is 6. Therefore, the correct answer is (C): The two quantities are equal.

> **Strategy Tip**
>
> When absolute values contain variables, **maximize** the absolute value by making the expression *inside* the absolute value symbols as far away from 0 as possible—even if that "inside" value is negative.

Optimizing Groups

In grouping problems, you make complete groups of items, drawing these items out of a larger pool. The goal is usually to maximize or minimize some quantity, such as the number of complete groups or the number of leftover items that do not fit into complete groups.

For example, a recipe calls for 3 cups of flour, 1 teaspoon of salt, $\frac{1}{2}$ teaspoon of yeast, and 1.5 cups of water. If you've got a full bag of flour, a new package of salt, and all the water you could use, but only 1 teaspoon of yeast, you can't make more than two batches of this recipe.

Why? Because the yeast is the first thing that will run out—it's the **limiting factor** on the number of complete groups. Use the limiting factor by first figuring out how many groups you can make with each item, ignoring the other items (as though you had unlimited quantities of those other items), and then comparing your results. For example:

Orange Computers is breaking up its conference attendees into groups. Each group must have exactly one person from Division A, two people from Division B, and three people from Division C. There are 20 people from Division A, 30 people from Division B, and 40 people from Division C at the conference. What is the least number of people who will NOT be able to be assigned to a group?

This question asks you to optimize the group creation by minimizing the number of people not assigned to a group, thus maximizing the number of groups created. First, figure out the maximum number of groups possible with the people from each division separately, ignoring the other divisions.

There are enough Division A people for 20 groups, but only enough Division B people for 15 groups (30 people ÷ 2 people per group). As for Division C, there are only enough people for 13 groups (40 people ÷ 3 people per group, with one person left over). So the limiting factor is Division C: Only 13 complete groups can be formed. These 13 groups will include 13 Division A people (leaving $20 - 13 = 7$ Division A people unassigned) and 26 Division B people (leaving $30 - 26 = 4$ Division B people unassigned). Together with the 1 Division C person left over, there are $7 + 4 + 1 = 12$ people who are unassigned.

For some grouping problems, think about the **most or least evenly distributed** arrangements of the items. That is, assign items to groups as evenly (or unevenly) as possible to create extreme cases.

Check Your Skills

4. A salad dressing requires oil, vinegar, and water in the ratio 2 : 1 : 3. Given 1 cup of oil, $\frac{1}{3}$ cup of vinegar, and 2 cups of water, what is the maximum number of cups of dressing that can be made?

Answers can be found on page 865.

Overlapping Sets

Some problems will take a group of something (often people) and divide them into subsets, then ask questions about how many people fall into one particular subcategory. For example, out of a group of 100 people, 40 play hockey and 70 play tennis. If everyone plays at least one of the two sports, how many play both?

The two subgroups, 40 and 70, add up to 110, which is more than the total group (100). So 10 people must play *both* hockey and tennis—and are therefore counted twice, once in each subgroup. That's why the total is 110 rather than 100.

Some of the hardest overlapping sets problems won't tell you exactly how many people are in each group or subgroup. Instead, they'll provide minimums or maximums and ask you to find the same. For example:

At a factory, there are 400 total workers. Of these workers, 240 are salaried, and 220 work in Operations. If at least 100 of the workers are non-salaried and do not work in Operations, what is the minimum number of workers who both are salaried and work in Operations?

In Chapter 29: Combinatorics and Chapter 30: Probability, you answered variations of this problem in which there were exactly 100 workers who fit neither category. In the version of the problem given above, the information is a little different: There could be *more than* 100 workers who fit neither category. Keep track of that as you attempt to find the minimum who are salaried and in Operations.

Here's a graphical way to display this information:

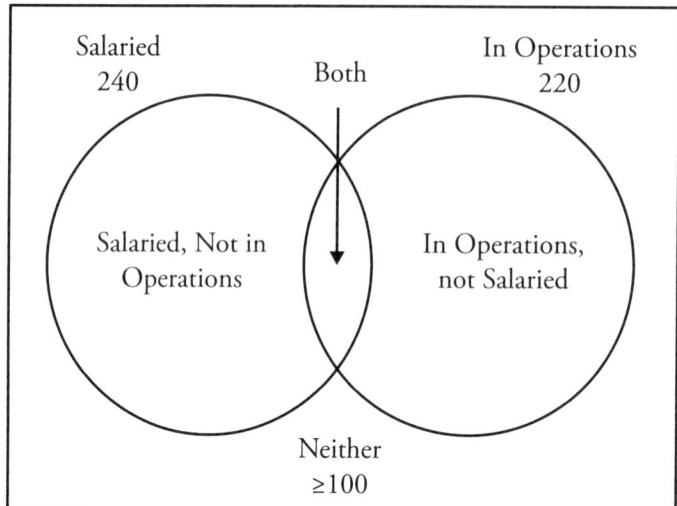

In your own picture, abbreviate where possible (for example, use *S* for Salaried and *O* for In Operations).

Use this formula to solve:

Total = Group 1 + Group 2 − Both + Neither

To remember the formula: Everything is added together except for the Both group, because the Both group is double-counted. As such, subtract out the Both group to remove the double-count. Leave the inequality sign in the ≥ 100 figure intact while solving:

$$T = G1 + G2 - B + N$$
$$400 = 240 + 220 - B + (\geq 100)$$
$$400 = \geq 560 \quad - B$$
$$B = \geq 160$$

Therefore, at *least* 160 workers are salaried and work in operations.

Chapter 31: **Optimization**

Check Your Skills

5. Of 320 consumers, 200 eat strawberries and 300 eat oranges. How many people could eat both fruits?

    Select all that apply.

    - [A] 140
    - [B] 150
    - [C] 170
    - [D] 180
    - [E] 190
    - [F] 210

Answers can be found on page 866.

Geometry Optimization

In Geometry, area and perimeter are related. Given a certain perimeter, there is a limit to how large the area can be. For example, if the perimeter of something is 4 feet, there's no shape you can make that would encompass an area of miles.

In some problems, the GRE may require you to determine the maximum or minimum area of a given figure, especially on QC problems. Take advantage of a few shortcuts to help solve these problems quickly.

Maximum Area of a Quadrilateral

Perhaps the best-known maximum area problem is one that asks you to maximize the area of a *quadrilateral* (usually a rectangle) with a *fixed perimeter*. If a quadrilateral has a fixed perimeter, say, 36 inches, it can take a variety of shapes:

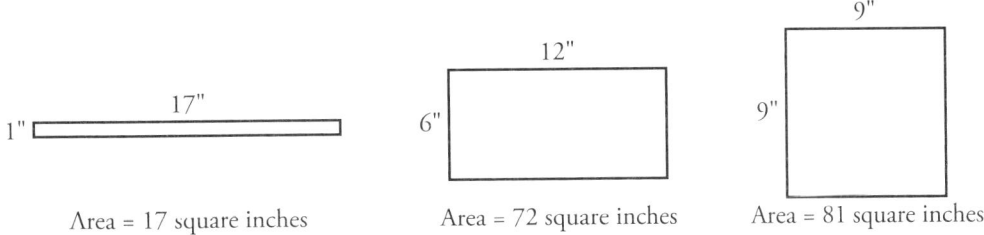

For a given perimeter, the more **regular** a polygon is—that is, the closer the polygon is to having all sides and angles the same—the greater the area. The quadrilateral with the maximum area will be the one with four equal sides and four equal angles: that is, a square.

Imagine you have a length of string. The shape with the biggest area that you can make with that string is a circle. With the circle, the string is completely stretched out. It's even and symmetrical; the string is pushing outwards instead of backwards or inwards. Every time you add a dent in that circle to turn it into a different shape, you are shrinking the area a little bit.

861

Unit Six: Advanced Topics

This principle can be applied to maximizing and minimizing any polygon. The more even and regular a given polygon is, the more its area is maximized. You could even say that the closer to a circle the polygon is, the more its area is maximized.

In addition, the area gets bigger as more sides are added (a regular twelve-sided polygon, for instance, is closer to a circle than is a regular square).

To maximize the area of a quadrilateral, make it most circle-like by forming it into a square. This is true even in cases involving non-integer lengths. For instance, of all quadrilaterals with a perimeter of 25 feet, the one with the greatest area is a square with $25 \div 4 = 6.25$ feet per side.

This principle can also be turned around to yield the following corollary: Of all quadrilaterals with a given area, the square has the *minimum* perimeter.

Maximum Area of a Parallelogram

Another common optimization problem involves maximizing the area of a parallelogram with given side lengths.

There are many parallelograms with two sides 3 and 4 units long. For example:

The maximum area for this perimeter is achieved when the angles are regular—in other words, when they are all 90°. The formula for area of a parallelogram is base × height. As the angles change from 90°, the height of the parallelogram will decrease, thus decreasing the area. If the sides are not perpendicular, then the figure is squished, so to speak.

If you are given two sides of a parallelogram, maximize the area by placing those two sides *perpendicular* to each other.

Minimum Area of a Quadrilateral

The minimum area of any quadrilateral is infinitely close to zero. Think of flattening a box to ready it for recycling: The box can become almost entirely flat. Any shape can be "squished" to be very, very tiny. On the GRE, you don't typically need to calculate minimum areas, but it can be helpful to know that shapes *can* be very small.

Maximum Area of Triangles

When a triangle has a fixed perimeter, maximize the triangle's area by making all its sides and angles the same. That is, given a fixed perimeter, make a triangle *equilateral* to maximize its area.

However, when given the lengths of just two legs of a triangle, maximize the area of the triangle by making it a right triangle. For example, given a triangle with two sides 3 and 4 units long, you can draw multiple possible triangles:

Chapter 31: **Optimization**

  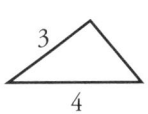

The area of a triangle is given by $A = \frac{1}{2}bh$. Because this formula involves the perpendicular height h, the maximum area occurs when the height is at its maximum—which is when one leg is perpendicular to the other, as shown in the middle triangle. The other two figures have lesser heights, so their areas are not as great.

> *Maximizing and Minimizing Areas*
>
> - For any polygon with a given perimeter, a regular polygon (all sides and all angles equal) has the maximum area. For example, a square has the maximum area for any four-sided figure. For triangles, an equilateral triangle has the maximum area.
> - For any polygon with a given area, a regular polygon (all sides and all angles equal) has the minimum perimeter. For example, a square has the minimum perimeter for any four-sided figure. For triangles, an equilateral triangle has the minimum perimeter.
> - When given a triangle with exactly *two* fixed leg lengths, a right triangle has the maximum area.

Practice manipulating geometric figures by squishing and stretching unknown angles. This will help you to maximize and minimize different lengths and areas.

Unit Six: **Advanced Topics**

Check Your Skills Answer Key

1. **15**

   To minimize the number of people in the group, maximize how much each person contributes. The most anyone can contribute is $75, so assume that everyone contributes $75.

Contribution	×	Friends	=	TV Price
At MOST		At LEAST		EXACTLY
$75	×	???	=	$1,100
maximize		*minimize*		*constant*

   $$1{,}100 \div 75 = 14.666\ldots$$

   If 14 people contribute $75 each, they'd only have $1,050, so they couldn't afford the TV. Therefore, round up. The least number of people that could be in the group is 15.

2. **−10**

   Test the extreme values for *a* and *b*.

a	b	$b - a$
−1	−6	$-6 - (-1) = -5$
−1	−2	$-2 - (-1) = -1$
4	−6	$-6 - 4 = -10$
4	−2	$-2 - 4 = -6$

3. **2**

   First, rearrange the inequality to isolate *y*.

   $$(x+2)^2 \leq 2 - y$$

   $$y + (x+2)^2 \leq 2 \qquad \text{Add } y \text{ to both sides.}$$

   $$y \leq 2 - (x+2)^2 \qquad \text{Subtract } (x+2)^2 \text{ from both sides.}$$

   Because *y* is less than or equal to 2 minus something squared, it's not possible for *y* to be greater than 2. (In order for that to happen, you'd have to have 2 minus a negative, but the squared term can't be negative. A squared term has to be at least 0.)

Therefore, the greatest possible value for *y* occurs when the squared term is minimized. Choose a value for *x* that makes the squared term 0.

$$y \leq 2 - (x+2)^2$$
$$y \leq 2 - (-2+2)^2$$
$$y \leq 2 - 0$$
$$y \leq 2$$

The maximum possible value for *y* is 2.

4. **2 cups**

   Test the recipe using the real value for one of the given ingredients to find the limiting factor. For example, given 1 cup of oil, figure out how much vinegar and water you would need.

	o	:	*v*	:	*w*	
ratio	2	:	1	:	3	
real	1	:	$\frac{1}{2}$	:	$\frac{3}{2}$	Not enough *v*

   To use the full 1 cup of oil, you'd need a half-cup of vinegar, but only one-third of a cup of vinegar is available, so vinegar is the limiting factor. Figure out how much dressing can be made using one-third of a cup of vinegar.

	o	:	*v*	:	*w*
ratio	2	:	1	:	3
real		:	$\frac{1}{3}$	:	
real	$\frac{2}{3}$	:	$\frac{1}{3}$	:	1

   A total of $\frac{2}{3} + \frac{1}{3} + 1 = 2$ cups of dressing can be made. All of the vinegar will be used, but there will be oil and water left over.

Unit Six: **Advanced Topics**

5. **(D) 180; (E) 190**

The question asks how many people could eat both types of fruit. Graphically:

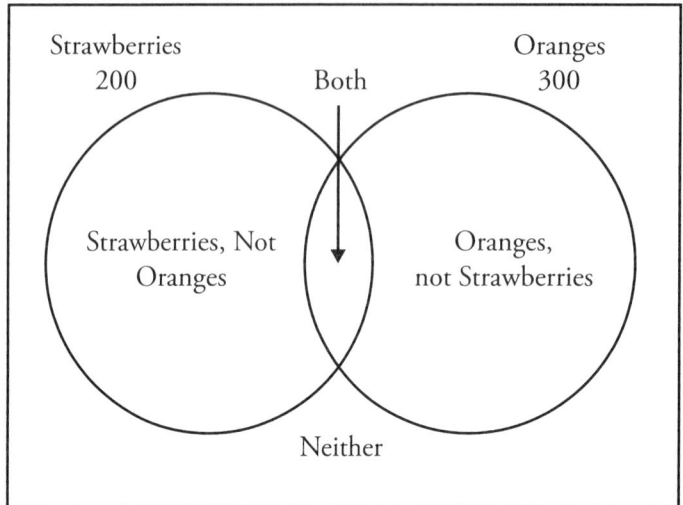

Mathematically, you can use the formula Total = Group 1 + Group 2 − Both + Neither. The complication, however, is that you're given no information about either the Both or Neither groups. Are there any hidden constraints? At the very least, 300 people must be eating some kind of fruit, because there are 300 people who eat oranges.

There are 320 total in the group; of the remaining 20 people (who don't eat oranges), anywhere from 0 to all 20 people could eat no fruit at all.

$$320 = 200 + 300 - \text{Both} + 0$$

Neither = 0 $320 = 500 - \text{Both}$

$180 = \text{Both}$

$$320 = 200 + 300 - \text{Both} + 20$$

Neither = 20 $320 = 520 - \text{Both}$

$200 = \text{Both}$

Therefore, the number of people who could eat both fruits is 180 at a minimum and 200 at a maximum. Any value that falls between these two bounds is valid. The correct answers are 180 and 190.

Problem Set

1.
$$98 < x < 102$$
$$103 < y < 107$$

Quantity A	**Quantity B**
$y - x$	$|y - x|$

2. Huey's Hip Pizza sells two sizes of square pizzas: a small pizza that measures 10 inches on a side and costs $10, and a large pizza that measures 15 inches on a side and costs $20. If two friends go to Huey's with $30 apiece, how many more square inches of pizza can they buy if they pool their money than if they each purchase pizza alone?

3. At age 18, Taylor started babysitting. Whenever Taylor babysat for a child, that child was no more than half Taylor's age at the time. Taylor is currently 32 years old and stopped babysitting 10 years ago. What is the current age of the oldest person for whom Taylor could have babysat?

4. What is the maximum possible area of a quadrilateral with a perimeter of 80 centimeters?

5. What is the minimum possible perimeter of a quadrilateral with an area of 1,600 square feet?

6. What is the maximum possible area of a parallelogram with one side of length 2 meters and a perimeter of 24 meters?

7. What is the maximum possible area of a triangle with one side of length 7 units and another side of length 8 units?

8. The lengths of the two shorter legs of a right triangle add up to 40 units. What is the maximum possible area of the triangle?

9. As of Sunday, Velma has exactly seven days to learn all 71 Japanese hiragana characters. If she can learn at most a dozen characters on any one day and will only have time to learn four characters on Friday, what is the least number of hiragana characters that Velma will have to learn on Saturday?

10.
$$1 \leq x \leq 5 \text{ and } 1 \geq y \geq -2$$

Quantity A	**Quantity B**
xy	-10

Unit Six: Advanced Topics

11. A "Collector's Coin Set" contains a one-dollar coin, a fifty-cent coin, a 25-cent coin, a 10-cent coin, a 5-cent coin, and a 1-cent coin. The coin sets are sold for the combined face price of the currency. If Casey buys as many coin sets as possible with $25, how much money will Casey have left over?

12. Shea is writing a novel that will be 950 pages long when finished. Shea can write 10 pages per day on weekdays and 20 pages per day on weekends.

Quantity A	Quantity B
The least number of consecutive days it will take Shea to finish the novel	Twice the area of Circle B

13. A ribbon 40-inches long is to be cut into three pieces, each of whose lengths is a different integer number of inches.

Quantity A	Quantity B
The least possible length, in inches, of the longest piece	15

14. $36 < x < 49$

Quantity A	Quantity B
$2^{\sqrt{x}}$	4^3

Chapter 31: **Optimization**

Solutions

1. **(C)**

   Examine the range for each variable: *y* has to be greater than *x*. Therefore, the value of $y - x$ must be positive. A positive number is the same as its own absolute value.

   Therefore, the correct answer is (C): The two quantities are always equal.

2. **25 square inches**

   First, understand the story. It asks you to maximize how much pizza they can buy. The large pizza has a 50% greater side length in each direction, yielding a pizza that is $1.5 \times 1.5 = 2.25$ times the area, but the price "only" doubles—so they can get more pizza per dollar by buying more large pizzas.

   Alone, they could each buy 1 small and 1 large pizza, for a total of 2 small and 2 large pizzas. But if they pool their money, they can buy a total of 3 large pizzas. The difference between the two scenarios is the difference in area between 1 large pizza and 2 small pizzas. The area of one large pizza is $15^2 = 225$ square inches. The area of one small pizza is $10^2 = 100$ square inches, so the area of two small pizzas is 200 square inches. If they pool their money to buy an extra-large pizza rather than two small ones, they will get an additional 25 square inches of pizza.

3. **23**

   You are given actual ages for Taylor. Therefore, think about the extremes: the youngest and oldest ages at which Taylor babysat. At one extreme, 18-year-old Taylor could have babysat a child of age 9. Taylor is now 32, so 14 years have passed, and that child would now be 23. At the other extreme, 22-year-old Taylor could have babysat a child of age 11. Taylor is now 32, so 10 years have passed, and that child would now be 21. Therefore, the first scenario yields the oldest possible current age, 23, of a child that Taylor babysat.

4. **400 cm²**

   The quadrilateral with the maximum area for a given perimeter is a square, which has four equal sides. A square with a perimeter of 80 centimeters has sides of length 20 centimeters each. Because the area of a square is the side length squared, the area is $(20)(20) = 400$.

5. **160 feet**

   The quadrilateral with minimum perimeter for a given area is a square. The area of a square is the side length squared: $s^2 = 1{,}600$ ft², yielding $s = 40$ ft. The perimeter, which is four times the side length, is $(4)(40) = 160$ ft.

   If you accidentally tried to solve for the *maximum* perimeter, it's worth noting that there is actually no maximum perimeter, as long as the sides don't have to be integers. You could make the dimensions $1{,}600 \times 1$, or $3{,}200 \times 0.5$, etc., yielding ever-longer perimeters as the quadrilateral got closer and closer to being a flat line.

Unit Six: **Advanced Topics**

6. **20 m²**

   If one side of the parallelogram is 2 meters long, then the opposite side must also be 2 meters long. You can solve for the unknown sides, which are equal in length, by writing an equation for the perimeter: $24 = 2(2) + 2x$, with x as the unknown side. Therefore, $x = 10$ meters. The parallelogram with these dimensions and maximum area is a *rectangle* with 2-meter and 10-meter sides. Thus, the maximum possible area of the figure is $(2)(10) = 20$ m².

7. **28 square units**

   To maximize a triangle with two given sides, create a right triangle. For this triangle, one of the given sides can be considered the base, and the other side can be considered the height (because they meet at a right angle). The triangle's area is $A = \frac{1}{2}(7)(8) = 28$.

8. **200 square units**

   You can think of a right triangle as half of a rectangle. Constructing this right triangle with legs adding to 40 is equivalent to constructing a rectangle with a perimeter of 80. Because the area of the triangle is half that of the rectangle, you can use the previously mentioned technique for maximizing the area of a rectangle: Of all rectangles with a given perimeter, the *square* has the greatest area. Likewise, of all right triangles with a given perimeter, the isosceles right triangle (a 45–45–90 triangle) has the greatest area. The desired rectangle is thus a 20 by 20 square, and the right triangle has an area of $\frac{1}{2}(20)(20) = 200$ units.

   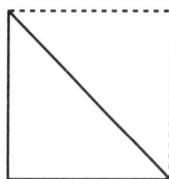

9. **7**

   To minimize the number of hiragana that Velma will have to learn on Saturday, consider the extreme case in which she learns *as many* hiragana characters *as possible* on the other days. She learns 4 on Friday, leaving $71 - 4 = 67$ to learn. If Velma learns the maximum of 12 hiragana on the other five days (besides Saturday), then she will have $67 - 5(12) = 7$ left to learn on Saturday.

10. **(D)**

    Because Quantity B is a fixed value, first figure out whether xy can equal -10. If $x = 5$ and $y = -2$, then $xy = -10$. In this case, the two quantities are equal, so eliminate answers (A) and (B).

    Next, is there any other possible value for xy (regardless of whether that value is more or less than -10)? Yes, there must be, since there is a range of possible values for both x and y. It's enough to recognize this in order to eliminate answer (C), but if you're not completely confident, try another case. For example, if $x = 1$ and $y = 1$, then $xy = 1$, in which case (C) cannot be the correct answer.

    Therefore, the correct answer is (D): The relationship cannot be determined.

Chapter 31: Optimization

11. **17 cents**

    The first step is to compute the value of a complete "Collector's Coin Set":
    $1.00 + $0.50 + $0.25 + $0.10 + $0.05 + $0.01 = $1.91. Next, determine how many sets of $1.91 Casey can buy for $25. First, multiply by 10: for $19.10, Casey can buy 10 complete sets. Now add $1.91 successively. Casey can buy 11 sets for $21.01, 12 sets for $22.92, and 13 sets for $24.83. There are 17 cents left over.

    Alternatively, use your calculator. Divide 25 by 1.91 to get 13 plus a long decimal. Multiply 13 by 1.91 to get 24.83 and then subtract from $25. There are 17 cents left over.

12. **(B)**

    In five weekdays, Shea will write $5 \times 10 = 50$ pages and in two weekend days, Shea will write $2 \times 20 = 40$ pages, so in one week, Shea will write 90 pages.

    Therefore, in 10 consecutive full weeks (i.e., 70 consecutive days), Shea can write 900 pages of the novel, leaving another 50 pages to be written. The least number of days it would take Shea to write 50 pages is 3 days: 2 weekend days at 20 pages per day and 1 weekday at 10 pages per day. Thus, it is possible for Shea to finish the novel in 73 days. (This assumes that Shea optimizes the start day to take advantage of as many weekends as possible.)

    Therefore, the correct answer is (B): Quantity B is greater.

13. **(C)**

    To minimize the length of the longest piece, maximize the lengths of the remaining pieces, subject to the constraints that they be shorter than the longest piece and different from each other. Suppose that the longest piece were 14 inches long (the largest possible length that is still less than the 15 in Quantity B). That would leave $40 - 14 = 26$ inches to be accounted for by the other two pieces.

    Because each piece must be a different number of inches long, those pieces cannot each be 13 inches long. This, in turn, implies that one of the two remaining pieces would have to be more than 13 inches long—but then, that piece would be 14 inches long, again violating the constraint that each piece be of a different length. Thus, it's not possible for the longest piece to be 14 inches or shorter. The longest piece must be at least 15 inches long. In the case that the longest piece is exactly 15 inches long, the shorter pieces could then be 12 and 13 inches long, for a total of 40 inches.

    Therefore, the correct answer is (C): The two quantities are always equal.

Unit Six: **Advanced Topics**

14. **(A)**

The value of *x* is between 36 and 49, so the square root of *x* must be between 6 and 7. Rewrite Quantity A.

Quantity A	Quantity B
$2^6 < 2^{\sqrt{x}} < 2^7$	4^3

Now rewrite Quantity B so that it has a base of 2 to match the base in quantity A: $4^3 = (2^2)^3 = 2^6$.

The value in Quantity A must be greater than 2^6, and so must be greater than the value in Quantity B.

Therefore, the correct answer is (A): Quantity A is greater.

CHAPTER 32

Advanced Concepts

In This Chapter:

- Making Up Numbers
- Substituting Properties
- Benchmarking
- Benchmarking Around B
- Interest Formulas: Simple and Compound
- Division Theory
- Sequencing
- Geometry
- Check Your Skills Answer Key
- Problem Set
- Solutions

CHAPTER 32 Advanced Concepts

Picking numbers and doing problems more mechanically will be sufficient for most GRE problems and for most GRE test-takers. If, however, you are interested in some of the most advanced techniques for getting an exceptionally high score on the GRE, this chapter is for you. In it, you will learn some of the most nuanced techniques for getting through a challenging problem efficiently. You'll also learn some concepts that are rarely tested, but could show up—so, if you're aiming for a perfect or near-perfect math score, you'll need to be prepared.

This chapter will also revisit some questions that you've already seen and that *could* be done with what you already know, but this time you'll tackle them using abstract reasoning to solve more definitively and efficiently. Finally, this chapter will show you how to predict the answer to some questions before you've done a single computation.

Making Up Numbers

That's right, this is the section where you learn how to make up numbers on the test and yet still arrive at the right answer. Obviously, there will have to be some restrictions on this process. You can't just say "I feel like this value should be 16" and expect to select the correct answer choice. However, with careful application, making up numbers can make abstract questions much more manageable.

You've already practiced a version of this. On QC questions, you tested numbers of different kinds using the mnemonic ZONEF. The point of that was to test different possible cases so you could eliminate answer choices. You made up numbers, but tested a wide enough variety of numbers to be confident that the answer would be consistent.

To take that concept to the next level, this section discusses problems on which you can pick a single number and still be confident you'll get a consistent answer. Consider this problem:

> A hot tub is halfway filled. An adjacent swimming pool, which has a capacity four times that of the hot tub, is filled to four-fifths of its capacity. If the hot tub is drained into the swimming pool, then the swimming pool will be filled to what fraction of its capacity?

As written, this is an incredibly abstract problem. You do already have the tools to solve it, but picking a number will make it much simpler, and you'll be much less likely to make a mistake. There are two properties of this problem that allow you to make up a number:

1. Everything is expressed as a relationship.
2. There are no specific quantities.

Unit Six: Advanced Topics

A specific quantity is a number that has a measurable meaning. For example, if the problem said the hot tub held 700 liters of water, that would be a specific quantity and it would likely stop you from picking a number. However, as the problem is actually written, there are no specific quantities.

Consider what you know. You know how filled the hot tub is relative to its total capacity. You know how big the swimming pool is relative to the size of the hot tub. You need to know how much the swimming pool will be filled relative to its total capacity after the hot tub drains into the pool. Every component is about a relationship, so you can make up a number and solve as if your made-up value were a given.

In this problem, it would make sense to make up a number for the total capacity of the pool or the hot tub, then solve based on the given relationships. It doesn't matter what number you use, because every number will still have to function under the same relationships, so the final result, a relationship, will be the same.

Imagine that the total capacity of the hot tub is 20 liters. This is a lot smaller than a real one would be, but that's irrelevant. Choose a number that isn't too hard to work with. Consider what else you could solve for based on the relationships in the problem.

The hot tub is currently halfway filled, so it has 10 liters of something, probably water, in it. The swimming pool is four times the size of the hot tub, so it has a capacity of $20 \times 4 = 80$ liters. It is currently filled to four-fifths of its capacity, so it contains $80 \times \frac{4}{5} = 64$ liters of water.

If the hot tub were drained into the swimming pool, that would add another 10 liters, so the pool would contain 74 liters. The question asks how full the pool would be at that point. The answer is $\frac{74}{80} = \frac{37}{40}$ or 92.5%. If you try this problem again with a different number for the capacity of the hot tub, you'll arrive at the same fraction or percentage.

Try another problem:

> The employees of an event planning business each specialize in one of four fields: food, beverages, venues, or music. Twice as many people specialize in food as music. There are 25% more people who specialize in venue planning than in music. If the music specialists make up 20% of this company's employees, what percentage of this company's employees specialize in beverages?

Pick a number of employees that seems easy to work with given the percentages involved and start solving for the different specialties. If 100 employees work at the business, then 20%, or 20, of them specialize in music. Twice as many specialize in food, so that's 40. To compute the venue planners, find 25% more than the 20 music coordinators: 125% of 20 is 25. Keep track of everything on your scratch paper:

Total = 100
M = 20
F = 40
V = 25
B = ?

The four specialties must sum to the total, so $20 + 40 + 25 = 85$ people are accounted for. Therefore, the remaining 15 people must be the beverage coordinators. The answer to this question is $\frac{15}{100}$, or 15%, of the employees specialize in beverages.

Because geometry problems are based on geometric relationships, they will frequently exclude given values and instead offer you the opportunity to pick numbers:

> If the length of the side of a cube decreases by two-thirds of its original value, by what percent will the volume of the cube decrease?

The volume of a cube is defined by the formula $V = s^3$, where s represents the length of a side. Pick a number for the length of the side of the cube.

The question stem talks about taking two-thirds of something, so say the cube has a side of 3 units, because 3 will work nicely in a calculation involving two-thirds.

If $s = 3$, the cube's volume equals $s^3 = 3^3 = 27$.

If the cube's side length decreases by two-thirds, its new length is $3 - \frac{2}{3}(3) = 1$. (Watch out for a trap here: The problem does *not* say that the new length is two-thirds *of* the old length. If that were the case, the new length would have been 2.)

The cube's new volume equals $s^3 = 1^3 = 1$.

Finally, determine the percent decrease:

$$\frac{\text{change}}{\text{original}} = \frac{27 - 1}{27} = \frac{26}{27} \approx 0.963 = 96.3\% \text{ decrease}$$

(Revisit Chapter 15: Percents for a refresher on percent change.)

When Not to Pick Numbers

In some problems, even though an amount might be unknown to you, it is actually specified in the problem in another way—specifically, because some other related quantity *is* given. In these cases, you *cannot make up numbers*. For example:

> A comic book collection contains $\frac{1}{3}$ Killer Fish comics and $\frac{3}{8}$ Shazaam Woman comics. The remainder of this collection consists of Boom comics. If there are 70 Boom comic books, how many comic books are in the entire collection?

Even though you do not know the number of Killer Fish and Shazaam Woman comics, one real piece of the total is given: There are 70 Boom comics. *Do not pick numbers here.* Instead, solve problems like this one by figuring out how big the known piece is. Then, use that knowledge to find the size of the *whole*:

$$\begin{array}{ccc} KF & SW & B \\ \frac{1}{3} + \frac{3}{8} & + & 70 = \text{Total} \end{array}$$

$$\frac{8}{24} + \frac{9}{24} + 70 = \text{Total}$$

$$\frac{17}{24} + 70 = \text{Total}$$

All of the books have to add up to $\frac{24}{24}$, so $\frac{24}{24} - \frac{17}{24} = \frac{7}{24}$ of the books are Boom comic books. Set up an equation to solve for the total number, x, of books. The fraction $\frac{7}{24}$ of the total books equals the 70 Boom books:

$$\frac{7}{24}x = 70$$

$$x = \overset{10}{\cancel{70}} \times \frac{24}{\underset{1}{\cancel{7}}}$$

$$x = 240$$

Unit Six: **Advanced Topics**

The collection contains 240 comics.

In summary, **do** pick numbers when *no real amounts* are given in the problem, but **do not** pick numbers when *any real amount or total* is given.

Check Your Skills

> **32** If possible, pick numbers to solve.

1. Mili's first-generation uHear is filled to $\frac{1}{2}$ capacity with songs. Her second-generation uHear, which has 3 times the capacity of her first-generation uHear, is filled to $\frac{4}{5}$ capacity. Will Mili be able to transfer all of her music from her first-generation uHear to her second-generation uHear?

2. John spends $\frac{1}{3}$ of his waking hours working, $\frac{1}{5}$ of his waking hours eating meals, $\frac{3}{10}$ of his waking hours at the gym, and 3 hours going to and from work. He engages in no other activities while awake. How many hours is John awake?

3.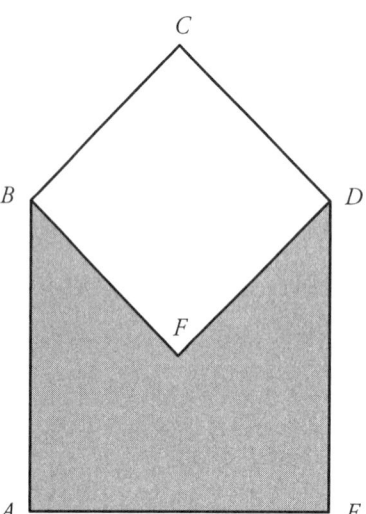

   BCDF and ABDE are squares.

Quantity A	**Quantity B**
Twice the area of the shaded region	Three times the area of BCDF

Answers can be found on page 900.

Chapter 32: **Advanced Concepts**

Substituting Properties

You can substitute a number for a variable, but you can also substitute a more abstract concept like "positive" or "even" into an equation to evaluate what happens to the result. For example:

n is an integer.

Quantity A	**Quantity B**
$(-3)^{2n}$	$(-3)^{2n+1}$

Rewrite the quantities, substituting *int* or *integer* for *n*:

n is an integer.

Quantity A	**Quantity B**
$(-3)^{2(int)}$	$(-3)^{2(int)+1}$

Any integer multiplied by 2 will produce an even number:

n is an integer.

Quantity A	**Quantity B**
$(-3)^{even}$	$(-3)^{even+1}$

An even number plus 1 will produce an odd number:

n is an integer.

Quantity A	**Quantity B**
$(-3)^{even}$	$(-3)^{odd}$

When negative numbers are raised to a power, they follow a pattern:

1. Negative numbers raised to odd powers are negative.
2. Negative numbers raised to even powers are positive.

Rewrite the quantities one last time to reflect these rules:

n is an integer.

Quantity A	**Quantity B**
$(neg)^{even} = pos$	$(neg)^{odd} = neg$

Unit Six: Advanced Topics

Any positive number is greater than any negative number, so the correct answer is (A): Quantity A is greater.

Try this problem:

$$x < 0$$

Quantity A	**Quantity B**
$x - 2$	$-(x - 2)$

If x is negative, then $x - 2$ must also be negative, because a negative minus a positive will always be negative. Rewrite the two quantities:

$$x < 0$$

Quantity A	**Quantity B**
Negative	−(Negative)

A negative multiplied by a negative becomes positive:

$$x < 0$$

Quantity A	**Quantity B**
Negative	Positive

Therefore, the correct answer is (B): Quantity B is greater.

> **Strategy Tip**
> If you are told a property of a variable, consider substituting that property to make inferences.

If there are multiple possible properties for variables, you can test multiple cases using abstract concepts. In the next problem, it's not clear whether x and y are positive or negative, but use the fact that there are limited options to test all the possibilities:

$$xy > 0$$

Quantity A	**Quantity B**
$x + y$	0

The given information indicates that there are two possible scenarios:

1. x and y are *both* positive.
2. x and y are *both* negative.

Chapter 32: **Advanced Concepts**

To find the answer, test both scenarios. First, test the scenario in which x and y are both positive:

$$xy > 0$$

Quantity A	**Quantity B**	
$x + y =$ Pos + Pos = Pos	0	Eliminate (B) and (C).
$x + y =$ Neg + Neg = Neg	0	Eliminate (A).

Therefore, the correct answer is (D): The relationship cannot be determined.

> **Strategy Tip**
>
> When the product of more than one variable is either greater than or less than 0, consider all possible signs and test all possible scenarios.
>
> If $xy > 0$, the scenarios are:
>
>   1. x and y are *both* positive.
>   2. x and y are *both* negative.
>
> If $xy < 0$, the scenarios are:
>
>   1. x is positive and y is negative.
>   2. x is negative and y is positive.
>
> If $xyz > 0$, the scenarios are:
>
>   1. All three are positive.
>   2. Any two are negative and the third is positive.
>
> If $xyz < 0$, the scenarios are:
>
>   1. All three are negative.
>   2. Any one is negative and the other two are positive.

Check Your Skills

4.
$$x > y$$
$$xy < 0$$

Quantity A	**Quantity B**
3^x	3^y

Answers can be found on page 901.

Unit Six: **Advanced Topics**

Benchmarking

Comparing complex ideas to simpler ones will help you to work faster. You first learned a version of this in Chapter 13: QC Gameplan: Compare, where you practiced comparing the two quantities in a QC problem to each other.

In this section, you'll learn how to compare complex values to **benchmarks**. A benchmark is a comfortable number you can use for comparison.

Benchmark Around Fractions

Here are some fractions that are commonly known and used:

$$\frac{1}{10}, \frac{1}{5}, \frac{1}{4}, \frac{1}{3}, \frac{1}{2}, \frac{2}{3}, \text{ and } \frac{3}{4}$$

Compare more complex fractions to these common ones to more quickly compare or estimate an answer. For example:

Quantity A	Quantity B
$\frac{123}{250}$	$\frac{162}{320}$

In Quantity A, 123 is *less* than half of 250, while in Quantity B, 162 is *more* than half of 320:

Quantity A	Quantity B
$\frac{123}{250} < \frac{1}{2}$	$\frac{162}{320} > \frac{1}{2}$

The correct answer is (B): Quantity B is greater.

You can also use Benchmark Values to estimate computations involving fractions:

Approximately what is $\frac{10}{22}$ of $\frac{5}{18}$ of 2,000 ?

(A) 150
(B) 250
(C) 500
(D) 1,000
(E) 1,500

The question uses the word "approximately," indicating that estimation will likely be sufficient. Glance at the answers to confirm. The answers are pretty spread out, so it's safe to estimate:

$$\text{Compare } \frac{10}{22} \text{ to } \frac{11}{22}: \frac{10}{22} \approx \frac{1}{2}$$

Note that this one is rounded *up* a little, as the fraction is really a little less than one-half. Next, tackle the second fraction:

$$\frac{5}{18} \text{ is between } \frac{5}{15} \text{ and } \frac{5}{20}$$

$$\frac{1}{3} \text{ and } \frac{1}{4}$$

This one is a little more complex, but it falls between one-third and one-quarter. The fraction $\frac{5}{18}$ is a little closer to $\frac{5}{20}$, and this direction is rounding *down* as the real value is a bit greater, so call the second fraction $\frac{1}{4}$.

When you're estimating, try to round in a way that compensates for the estimates that you're making. If one value is rounded up, try to round the other one down, and vice versa.

Finally, solve:

$$\frac{1}{2} \times \frac{1}{4} \times 2{,}000 = 250$$

Therefore, the correct answer is (B).

If, for the second fraction, you had rounded up a second time to $\frac{1}{3}$, this would lead to a *slight* but *systematic* overestimation:

$$\frac{1}{2} \times \frac{1}{3} \times 2000 \approx 333$$

Given the answer choices in this problem, you would have still gotten to the correct answer—but on a different problem, this could lead to an error. If you want to estimate, first glance at the answers to confirm that they are pretty spread out. In addition, whenever possible, estimate in a way that balances out by the end of the problem.

Benchmarking Around Percents

You can also use Benchmark Values to estimate percents. For example:

> A television set originally priced at $690 was sold for a $67 discount. Approximately what was the percent discount of the television set?
>
> (A) 5%
> (B) 10%
> (C) 15%
> (D) 20%
> (E) 25%

The most useful percent benchmarks are 50%, 10%, and 1%, because they are all pretty easy to find.

In this case, the original price was $690 and the discount was $67, so start with 10% of $690, which is $69. Since the actual discount was $67, the discount was a little bit less than 10% but definitely more than 5% (which is half of 10%). The correct answer must be (B).

Unit Six: **Advanced Topics**

Benchmarking Around 1

Some comparisons are best made relative to the number 1. For example:

$$n > 0$$

Quantity A	Quantity B
$\dfrac{n}{n+1}$	$\dfrac{n+1}{n}$

Since n is positive, so is $n + 1$. Both fractions have positive numerators and denominators, so it is not helpful to benchmark around 0. But is $\dfrac{n}{n+1}$ greater than or less than 1?

Because $n + 1$ is greater than n, it must be the case that $\dfrac{n}{n+1}$ is less than 1. If you're not sure, try a real number to confirm. If $n = 2$, then $\dfrac{2}{3}$ is less than 1.

Likewise, $\dfrac{n+1}{n}$ represents a greater value divided by a lesser value, so it must be greater than 1. Therefore, the correct answer is (B): Quantity B is greater.

> **Strategy Tip**
>
> Use Benchmarking to make approximations. Compare complex fractions or percentages to common fractions or percentages. Alternatively, compare values to common integers such as 1 and 0.

Check Your Skills

5. Which is greater: $\dfrac{123}{250}$ or $\dfrac{171}{340}$?

6. Approximate $\left(\dfrac{15}{58}\right)\left(\dfrac{9}{19}\right) 403$.

Answers can be found on page 901.

Benchmarking Around B

Benchmarking on QC has another, very specialized use. In the case where Quantity B is a number, it's often possible to Benchmark around B. To finish the problem, you may not need to compute whatever complicated scenario was presented in Quantity A. For example:

The cost of a suit was reduced by 30% to $99.

Quantity A	Quantity B
The original selling price of the suit	$150

You can absolutely solve this algebraically. Name a variable for the original selling price of the suit, say P. Set up an equation to represent the given information: $P - 0.3P = 99$. Solve for P.

It is, however, much faster to use Quantity B as a benchmark. To do so, assume that the two quantities are equal. That is, assume the original price *was* $150, the value of Quantity B. Determine whether the given information makes sense with that assumption.

If the original price was $150, and it was reduced 30%, then the discount was $0.3 \times 150 = \$45$. Therefore, the discounted price was $150 − \$45 = \$105$.

An original price of $150 with a 30% discount would make the new price $105. But the actual new price is only $99, so the original price must have been *less* than $150. Therefore, the correct answer is (B): Quantity B is greater.

> **Strategy Tip**
>
> Benchmark against Quantity B by testing whether the two quantities could reasonably be equal.

Even in a problem without given information, Quantity B can help. Try this problem:

Quantity A	Quantity B
The perimeter of Triangle *ABC*, an isosceles triangle whose longest side is equal to 11	22

The triangle is isosceles and has one side equal to 11. One possibility is that the two equal-length sides are both 11, in which case, the perimeter must be greater than 22—the value of Quantity B. Eliminate answers (B) and (C).

In that first case, the perimeter of the triangle is greater than 22. To prove (D), try to find a triangle that has a perimeter of 22 or less. Start with the *equality:* Make Quantity A equal to 22. This value gives you a goal, so that you do not have to create random isosceles triangles that may or may not get you closer to an answer.

One of the sides is 11. The remaining two sides must have a combined length of 11 to achieve a perimeter of 22. For the triangle to be isosceles, the two unknown sides must be equal. The only way they could be equal is when they each have a length of 5.5.

Careful! There is a trap here. Any two sides of a triangle must add up to *greater* than the length of the third side. If the sides are 11, 5.5, and 5.5, you can't make a triangle. The two shorter sides are together the same length as the longer one, so they collapse down and you're left with a straight line rather than a triangle.

So this triangle can't exist. And you can't make the lengths shorter than 5.5, because they still won't be able to connect to the 11 to make a triangle.

So, the perimeter of Triangle *ABC* will be greater than 22. Therefore, the correct answer is (A): Quantity A is greater.

By specifically trying to make the two values equal, you can prove that Quantity A will always be greater. Using Quantity B as a Benchmark and trying to prove answer (C) broke open the problem.

Unit Six: **Advanced Topics**

Try this problem:

A company has two divisions.
Division A has 105 employees and an average salary of $60,000.
Division B has 93 employees and an average salary of $70,000.

Quantity A	**Quantity B**
The average salary of all the employees at the company	$65,000

A lot of unnecessary computation could go into answering this QC question. The key to answering efficiently is the fact that the benchmark value in Quantity B is exactly halfway between the average salaries of the two divisions. Use the principle of weighted averages to solve.

A weighted average will be skewed toward the side that has more elements (see Chapter 18: Statistics for a refresher on this topic). Given that there are more employees making $60,000 than $70,000, the weighted average will be closer to $60,000 than $70,000—that is, the weighted average will be less than $65,000. Therefore, the correct answer is (B): Quantity B is greater.

> **Strategy Tip**
>
> In any question that involves two groups that have some kind of average value, use the principles of weighted averages.

Add this advanced move to your QC Gameplan:

> *QC Gameplan, Final*
>
> 1. **Simplify** → 2. **Pick Numbers**
>
> - Unpack givens
> - Simplify within each column
> - Simplify across the Hidden Inequality
> - Compare, don't compute
> - Make things match
>
> - Try to prove (D)
> - Easy, then weird (ZONEF, number line)
> - After 3 cases, look for the pattern, then make a call
> - **Use B as a Benchmark**

Keep in mind you will almost never need to use all of these tools on a single problem. This is your toolbox—pull out the tools you need when you need them.

Chapter 32: Advanced Concepts

Interest Formulas: Simple and Compound

Compound interest problems are an especially complex type of successive-percent problem. Be prepared to use the GRE on-screen calculator to help with the math involved.

Each of the formulas in this section defines how to calculate interest using the following abbreviations:

- P = Principal, or the initial amount invested
- r = Rate, or the rate at which interest accrues
- t = Time, in years, for which the investment accrues interest
- n = Number of times the interest is compounded annually

	Formula	Example
Simple Interest	$(P)(r)(t)$	$5,000 invested for 6 months at an annual rate of 7% will earn how much in simple interest? Principal = $5,000, Rate = 7% or 0.07, Time = 0.5 years $Prt = \$5{,}000(0.07)(0.5) = \$175$ in interest earned
Compound Interest	$P\left(1 + \dfrac{r}{n}\right)^{nt}$	$5,000 invested for 1 year at a rate of 8% compounded quarterly will earn approximately how much in interest? Principal = $5,000, Rate = 8% or 0.08, Time = 1 year, Number = 4 (compounded quarterly) $\$5{,}000\left(1 + \dfrac{0.08}{4}\right)^{4(1)} = \$5{,}412$ The original $5,000 investment is now worth $5,412, so the amount of interest earned is $412.

Determining the amount of simple interest earned uses a single percent equation. If you invest $2,000 at 3% simple interest over 2 years, then the interest earned in one year is determined by the first formula in the table, where P is $2,000, r is 3% $= \dfrac{3}{100}$, and t is 2 years:

$$\text{Interest} = Prt = (2{,}000)\left(\dfrac{3}{100}\right)(2) = 120$$

So the interest on this 2-year investment is $120. The simple interest formula returns only the interest earned; the value does not include the amount of the original investment.

Contrast this with the scenario in which the interest in an investment is compounded. If you invest $1,000 at 3% compounded annually and you invest the money for 2 years, then you are essentially making a series of investments. After the first year, you'll earn 3% on your 1,000 principal investment, or $30. For the second year, though, that interest is included in your principal—you're now investing $1,030 and earning 3% on this new figure.

$$P\left(1 + \dfrac{r}{n}\right)^{nt} = 1{,}000\left(1 + \dfrac{0.03}{1}\right)^{1 \times 2} = 1{,}060.90$$

The original investment was $1,000, so the compound interest earned is $60.90.

887

Unit Six: Advanced Topics

Simple interest of 3% per year over two years would return 6% over the two-year period, or $60. Compound interest pays more than simple interest over the same time period, and the more frequently the interest compounds, the more you'll earn in the end.

Check Your Skills

7. An auto loan is made in the amount of $12,000. The loan carries an interest charge of 14% per year. What is the amount of interest owed in the first three years of the loan, assuming there are no payments on the loan, and there is <u>no</u> compounding?

8. For the same loan, what is the loan balance after 3 years assuming no payments on the loan and <u>annual</u> compounding?

Answers can be found on page 902.

Division Theory

Understanding the theory behind certain scenarios is sometimes necessary to solve the hardest division problems.

When a Decimal Terminates

Consider this problem you first encountered in Chapter 17: When to Use Which Form:

Which of the following is a terminating decimal?

Ⓐ $\frac{11}{250}$

Ⓑ $\frac{393}{7}$

Ⓒ $\frac{1,283}{741}$

Ⓓ $\frac{\sqrt{3}}{\sqrt{2}}$

A decimal will always terminate if it meets a very specific criterion:

> **Key Concept**
>
> A fraction can be written as a terminating decimal if, in its simplest form, the denominator has only 2's and/or 5's as prime factors.

Therefore, choice (A) will terminate because 250's prime factorization contains only 2's and 5's (specifically, it is $2 \times 5 \times 5 \times 5$).

Using this rule, determine whether each of the following fractions is or is not a terminating decimal:

$$\frac{6}{7}, \frac{27}{225}, \frac{9}{26}, \frac{39}{50}$$

The fraction $\frac{6}{7}$ has a seven in the denominator and that denominator cannot be simplified with the numerator, so this fraction will not terminate.

Simplify $\frac{27}{225}$ before factoring the denominator: $\frac{27}{225} = \frac{3}{25}$. The simplified denominator 25 is 5 × 5, so $\frac{27}{225}$ will terminate. Alternatively, since this one needs to be simplified first, plug this one into the calculator.

The fraction $\frac{9}{26}$ cannot be simplified further and the denominator factors to 2 × 13, so this fraction will not terminate.

The fraction $\frac{39}{50}$ cannot be simplified further and 50 factors to 2 × 5 × 5, so $\frac{39}{50}$ will terminate.

You can also plug each answer into the calculator. During the test, evaluate each choice individually to decide whether you can already tell that it will or won't terminate or whether you want to pull up the calculator.

Remainder Theory

Remainders were first introduced in Chapter 9: Divisibility. For the hardest problems, use this remainder formula:

Dividend ⟶ $x = QN + R$ ⟵ Remainder
Quotient ⟶ ⟵ Divisor

Example: $23 = (5)(4) + 3$

This formula comes with new terminology. The GRE could still talk about multiples and factors, but for remainder problems, there are two more terms that could be used: **dividend** and **quotient**.

The dividend is the total, the thing that gets divided. The quotient is the integer part of the formula: The number of whole groups created after the dividend is divided. You've used the word divisor before to mean factor, but this word has also has a second meaning. Here, the divisor is not a factor, but it's the thing doing the division, so it's still called the divisor. For example, given 23 divided by 4:

Dividend = (Quotient)(Divisor) + Remainder
23 = (Q) (4) + R

The divisor 4 goes into 20 a total of 5 times, so the quotient is 5. Then, there are 3 left over, so the remainder is 3:

$$23 = (5)(4) + 3$$

All of x, Q, N, and R must be integers. In addition, R must be between 0 and $N - 1$, inclusive. For a refresher on this concept, revisit the Remainders section of Chapter 9: Divisibility.

Try this problem:

The remainder when x is divided by 8 is 6. What is the remainder when $x + 7$ is divided by 8 ?

The problem never specifies a real value for x, just relative values, so pick your own value.

If the divisor is 8 and the remainder is 6, then that value is equal to Q(8) + 6. For example, if Q is 1, then the value of this number is 8 + 6 = 14. (Check the math: Does this make sense? Yes, 14 divided by 8 is equal to 1 remainder 6.)

Unit Six: Advanced Topics

So x could be 14. In that case, $x + 7$ is 21. When 21 is divided by 8, what is the remainder?

$$21 = Q(8) + R$$

Find the maximum value for Q. In this case, Q is 2, so $8Q$ is 16. Therefore, R must be 5 in order for the total to be 21. When $x + 7$ is divided by 8, the remainder is 5.

You can also do this work algebraically if you keep in mind a few restrictions:

1. **You can add and subtract remainders directly, as long as you correct excess or negative remainders.** "Excess remainders" are remainders greater than or equal to the divisor. To correct excess or negative remainders, subtract or add the divisor, such that the resulting remainder is one of the possible remainders. For example:
   - If x leaves a remainder of 4 after division by 7, and y leaves a remainder of 2 after division by 7, then $x + y$ leaves a remainder of $4 + 2 = 6$ after division by 7. You do not need to pick numbers or write algebraic expressions for x and y. Just write R4 + R2 = R6.
   - If x leaves a remainder of 4 after division by 7, and z leaves a remainder of 5 after division by 7, then adding the remainders together yields 9—but this can't be the remainder. For division by 7, the remainder must be between 0 and 6, inclusive. Therefore, take a 7 out of the remainder, because 7 is the *excess* portion. The correct remainder is R4 + R5 = R9 = R2 (subtracting a 7 at the last step).
   - If x leaves a remainder of 4 after division by 7, and z leaves a remainder of 5 after division by 7, then the remainder for $x - z$ is R4 – R5 = R–1, which is also an unacceptable remainder (it must be between 0 and 6, inclusive). In this case, add 7 to the initial result: R4 – R5 = R(–1) = R6 (adding a 7 at the last step).

2. **You can multiply remainders, as long as you correct excess remainders at the end.**
   - If x has a remainder of 4 upon division by 7, and z has a remainder of 5 upon division by 7, then 4×5 gives 20. Two additional 7's can be taken out of this remainder, so xz has a remainder 6 upon division by 7. In other words, (R4)(R5) = R20 = R6 (subtracting out two 7's). You can prove this by again picking $x = 25$ and $z = 12$ (try the calculator method on your own!):

$$25 \times 12 = 300 = 42 \times 7 + 6 \leftarrow \text{Remainder}$$

Quotient ⏐ ⏐ Divisor

The Heavy Division Shortcut

Some division problems involving decimals can be challenging to plug into the calculator. In these cases, simplify the setup using the Heavy Division Shortcut: Move the decimals in the same direction and round to whole numbers. For example:

What is $1{,}530{,}794 \div (31.49 \times 10^4)$ to the nearest whole number?

Step 1:
Set up the division problem in fraction form: $\dfrac{1{,}530{,}794}{31.49 \times 10^4}$

Step 2:
Rewrite the problem, eliminating powers of 10: $\dfrac{1{,}530{,}794}{314{,}900}$

Step 3:
Move the decimal the same number of places on top and bottom to make the math a lot easier:

$$\frac{153.0794}{31.4900}$$

In step 3, the goal is to get just two digits to the left of the decimal in the denominator. In this problem, move the decimal point backward five spaces on both the top and bottom:

$$\frac{1{,}530{,}794}{314{,}900} = \frac{153.0794}{31.4900}$$

Plug just 153 divided by 31 into the calculator. The answer is approximately 5.

Note: On some problems, it's possible to move the decimal place one more over and divide 15 by 3. But, depending on the mix of answer choices, this could introduce a large enough error to get you to the wrong answer. Hold it to two decimal places in the denominator, just in case.

Check Your Skills

9. If x has a remainder of 4 when divided by 9 and y has a remainder of 3 when divided by 9, what is the remainder when $x + y$ is divided by 9?

10. If x has a remainder of 4 when divided by 9 and y has a remainder of 3 when divided by 9, what is the remainder when xy is divided by 9?

11. The circumference of the Earth is 131,479,714 feet. If someone travels 1,643,849 feet per day, approximately how many days would it take them to travel around the circumference of the Earth?

    (A) 50
    (B) 70
    (C) 80
    (D) 100
    (E) 150

Answers can be found on pages 902–903.

Sequencing

The evenly spaced sequences you tackled in Chapter 28: Sequences and Patterns were **linear sequences**. Each number in the set was a constant value greater than or less than the previous term. Linear sequences are the most commonly used type of pattern on the GRE, but there are a few other, rarer kinds of sequences that you may encounter.

Unit Six: **Advanced Topics**

Exponential Sequences

Exponential sequences are created when a base is raised to an increasing exponent. For example, $S_n = 3^n$ represents an exponential sequence:

$$S_n: \quad \underline{3} \xrightarrow{+6} \underline{9} \xrightarrow{+18} \underline{27} \xrightarrow{+54} \underline{81} \xrightarrow{+162} \underline{243} \xrightarrow{+486} \underline{729}$$
$$n = \quad 1 \qquad 2 \qquad 3 \qquad 4 \qquad 5 \qquad 6$$

Notice a few things about exponential sequences. First, they are not evenly spaced (except for 1^x and 0^x). Instead, the spacing between terms changes as the exponent increases, so the terms will get very large or very small (depending on whether the base is an integer or a fraction) much more quickly than they would in a linear sequence.

Second, if the base is an integer, the units digits repeat. That's why questions involving patterns and digit prediction often involve exponential sequences. Any exponential sequence for an integer base will have repeating units digits. See Chapter 28: Sequences and Patterns for a refresher on units digit patterns.

Geometric Sequences

A **geometric sequence** is one in which each subsequent value is found by multiplying the previous number by a constant. For example, given $T_n = 2 T_{n-1}$ and $T_1 = 5$:

$$T: \quad \underline{5} \xrightarrow{+5} \underline{10} \xrightarrow{+10} \underline{20} \xrightarrow{+20} \underline{40} \xrightarrow{+40} \underline{80} \xrightarrow{+80} \underline{160}$$
$$n = \quad 1 \qquad 2 \qquad 3 \qquad 4 \qquad 5 \qquad 6$$

This type of sequence is not evenly spaced, but there are still patterns that the GRE can test. In the T_n example, the spacing between successive terms doubles each time.

Geometric patterns are often associated with successive percents. If an item is 20% off and the store then gives an additional 20% off, the price will decrease geometrically. For example, if the initial price were $100, the first discount would make the item $0.80 \times 100 = \$80$, a decrease of $20, and the next discount would decrease the price to $0.8 \times 80 = \$64$, a decrease of only $16 this time.

The full geometric sequence is $0.8 \times 0.8 \times 80$. The 0.8 multiplier is used twice for the two discounts of 20% each.

Deriving a Linear Formula

The GRE might present a geometric sequence, but then ask you to find a term you can't solve for directly. For example:

> If $T_n = 2 T_{n-1}$, and T_1 is 5, what is T_{20}?
>
> (A) 2^{20}
> (B) 10^{20}
> (C) $2(5^{19})$
> (D) $5(2^{19})$
> (E) 10^{19}

To solve this manually, you'd first have to find T_2, and then T_3, and then T_4... all the way up to T_{20}. This would take way too long on the GRE.

Glance at the answers—they contain an important clue. The question isn't expecting you to calculate out the "long-form" value! Instead, it wants you to find the pattern.

Start by writing two equations for the first several terms using the recursive formula:

$$T_2 = 2T_1$$
$$T_3 = 2T_2$$

Next, rewrite the second equation in terms of T_1 using substitution:

$$T_3 = 2T_2 = 2(2T_1) = 2^2(T_1)$$

It's helpful to express the two 2's (or anything that will be multiplied together) exponentially rather than in longhand, because each additional term will likely impose additional 2's, and it's easier to keep track of them with exponents.

Do this one more time, this time for T_4:

$$T_2 = 2T_1$$
$$T_3 = 2^2 T_1$$
$$T_4 = 2T_3 = 2(2^2 T_1) = 2^3 T_1$$

What's the pattern? Each subsequent term can be defined as the first term multiplied by an additional power of two.

In fact, the power of two is consistently one less than the term for that line of math. For example, T_3 has 2^2 and T_4 has 2^3.

Given that pattern, T_{20} will use 2^{19} for the power of 2 term. Solve for T_{20}:

$$T_{20} = 2^{19} T_1$$
$$T_{20} = 2^{19}(5) \text{ or } 5(2^{19})$$

Therefore, the correct answer is (D).

Geometry

Benchmarking and picking numbers can be extraordinarily useful, but there are a few more concepts that geometry GRE questions can test that require a deeper understanding.

If geometry is not a strength, consider not studying these topics and guessing if you see a question like this on the test. (There's a good chance you won't; these topics are not commonly tested.)

Unit Six: **Advanced Topics**

Graphing Multiple Solutions

Some equations, like quadratics, have multiple solutions. You're most likely to see those in algebraic form on the GRE. However, it's possible to see them represented graphically:

Which equation would best represent the curve shown?

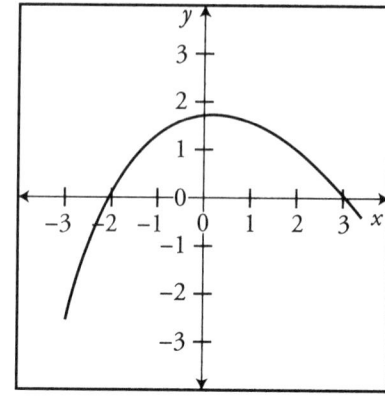

Ⓐ $y = -0.25(x + 2)(x - 3)$
Ⓑ $y = 0.25(x + 2)(x - 3)$
Ⓒ $y = 0.25(x - 2)(x + 3)$
Ⓓ $y = -0.25(x - 2)(x + 3)$
Ⓔ $y = 1.25(x + 2)(x - 3)$

The graph is a parabola illustrating a quadratic equation. Because the graph crosses the x axis in two places, there are two possible solutions for x.

To find the solutions to a quadratic algebraically, first set the quadratic equal to 0, then solve. For example, if you were given the equation for the graph $y = (x + 4)(x - 5)$, you'd change the y to a 0 and then solve for x:

$$y = (x + 4)(x - 5)$$
$$0 = (x + 4)(x - 5)$$

In other words, the algebraic solution involves evaluating what x is when y equals 0. When $y = 0$ in a coordinate plane, you're solving for the x-intercepts.

Go back to the graph for this problem. Where does the parabola cross the x axis? It crosses the x-axis at $(-2, 0)$ and $(3, 0)$. These x-intercepts are the graphical representations of the algebraic solutions, so x equals -2 and 3. The equation must therefore include $(x + 2)$ and $(x - 3)$. Choices (C) and (D) are incorrect.

Next, a parabola will open upwards (or look like a ∪) if the coefficient on the quadratic term is positive. The parabola will open downwards (or look like a ∩) if that coefficient is negative. This graph opens down, so the quadratic term in the equation must be negative. Choice (A)'s coefficient is negative, while choices (B) and (E) are positive. Only choice (A) fits all of the necessary criteria for this graph.

Quadratic equations will always appear as parabolas on a coordinate plane graph. The solutions to a graph are the points at which the line intersects the *x*-axis. If the parabola intersects the *x*-axis twice, there are two real solutions. If the parabola intersects it only once, there is one real solution, and if the parabola doesn't intersect the *x*-axis at all, there is no real solution.

(Note: If you research this topic using another source, for example a popular online open-source encyclopedia, you will likely see discussion of complex numbers. The GRE does not test this concept.)

You might see a similar-looking graph but with straight lines rather than curved lines:

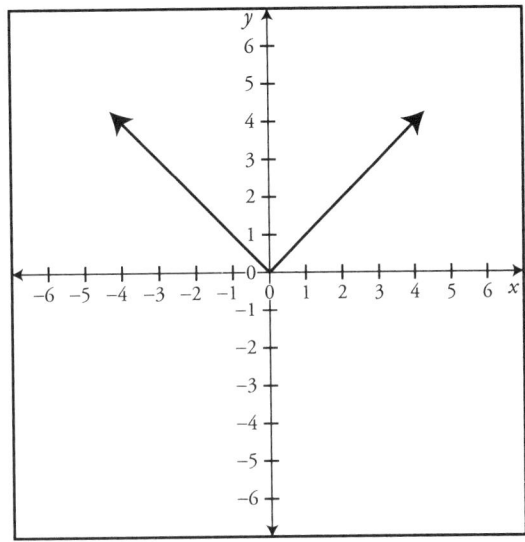

When the lines are straight and make a V like this, the graph represents an absolute value function, specifically $y = |x|$. It's not common to see this type of graph on the GRE, but it's possible.

Adapting a Graph

Changing the equations that define a graph will change how a graph looks and possibly what the solutions are. Often, thinking critically about the component parts of the slope-intercept equation will be sufficient to anticipate the changes. For example:

When the slope of a straight line is doubled, which of the following could be true about the value of *x* at $y = 2$?

Indicate all such statements:

[A] It increases.
[B] It decreases.
[C] It stays the same.

The slope is the *m* term in the slope-intercept equation $y = mx + b$. This problem specifies that $y = 2$, so write the equation as $2 = mx + b$.

If the slope is positive, then doubling the slope will *increase* that value. In order for the left-hand side of the equation to still be 2, the value of *x* will have to *decrease* to compensate. You can visualize that by comparing these two lines:

Unit Six: **Advanced Topics**

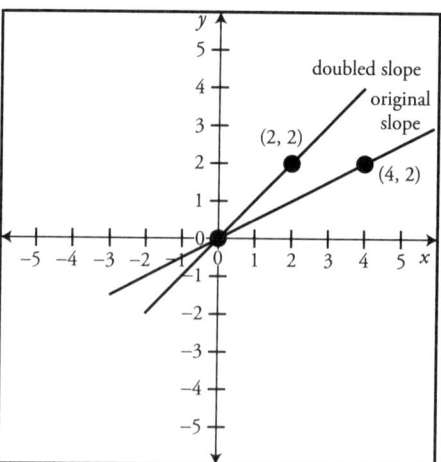

At $y = 2$, the value of x decreases from 4 to 2. Therefore, (B) is a correct answer: The value of x could decrease.

If, however, the slope is negative, doubling it will end up *decreasing* the slope, so x will need to *increase* to compensate. Again, you can visualize this graphically:

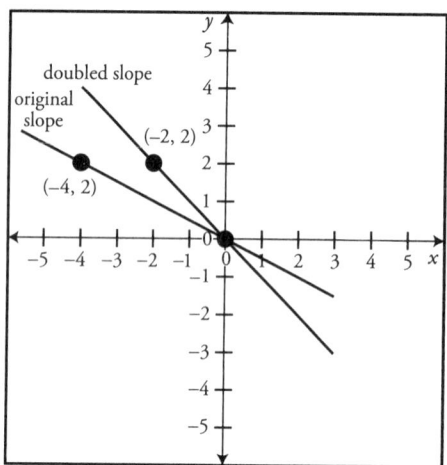

At $y = 2$, the value of x increases from -4 to -2. Therefore, (A) is a correct answer: The value of x could increase.

Finally, consider what would happen if the slope were 0. Doubling the slope would still leave the slope equal to 0, so the slope would not change. Therefore, the line itself would not change, and neither would the value of x when $y = 2$:

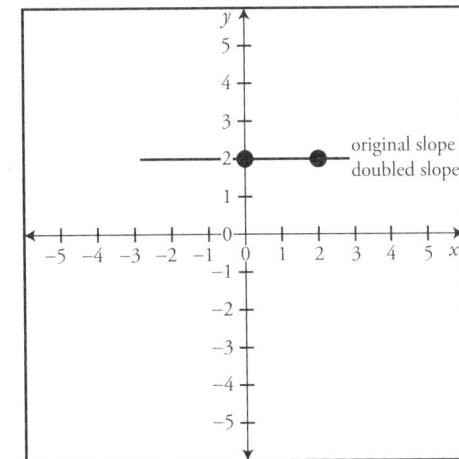

Since *x* could stay the same, answer (C) is also possible. The correct answers to the above problem are (A), (B), and (C).

Changing only the *b* value of a graph will shift a line up or down, but the line will retain the same slope. For example:

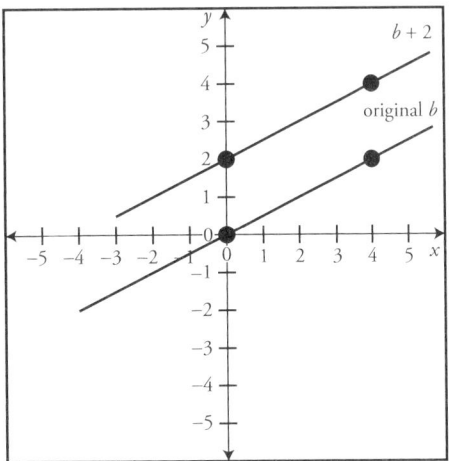

Right Angles

Every line segment drawn on a coordinate plane can be re-visualized as a side of a right triangle. Add a horizontal line from one endpoint, and a vertical line from the other endpoint, and you now have a right triangle. This principle underpins the line length calculation taught in Chapter 24: Lines and Angles.

Creating right angles can also be used in more advanced problems to find areas. Given an unusual shape in a coordinate plane, look for right angles to define it.

What is the area of the quadrilateral defined by the vertices $(-5, 9)$, $(-9, 6)$, $(6, 3)$, and $(1, -1)$?

First, draw the described shape on a coordinate plane:

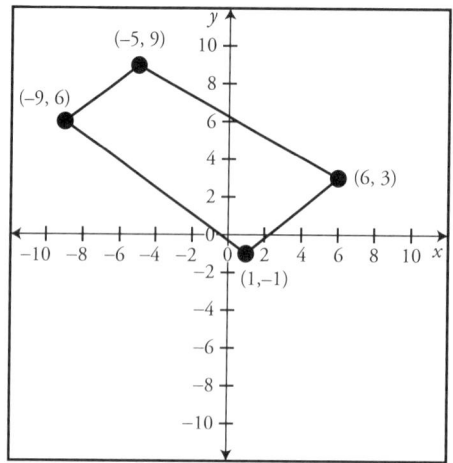

There is no formula for the area of an irregular shape like this one. Create right triangles to inscribe this shape in a rectangle, noting all the side lengths:

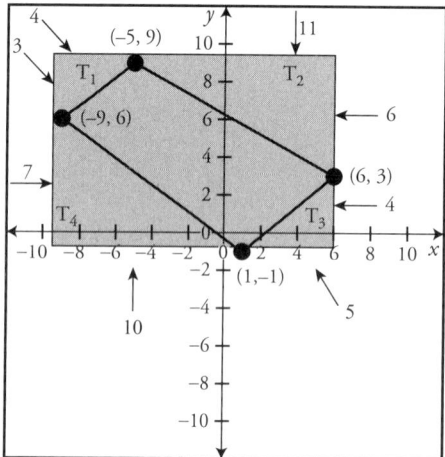

Find the area of the overall rectangle, then subtract the areas of each of the triangles that are outside of the quadrilateral:

Area of rectangle = $(4 + 11)(3 + 7) = 150$

Area of Triangle 1 = $\frac{1}{2}(3)(4) = 6$

Area of Triangle 2 = $\frac{1}{2}(11)(6) = 33$

Area of Triangle 3 = $\frac{1}{2}(5)(4) = 10$

Area of Triangle 4 = $\frac{1}{2}(7)(10) = 35$

Area of Rectangle − areas of all triangles = $150 - 6 - 33 - 10 - 35 = 66$

The overall area of this irregular shape is 66.

Similar Triangles

Two triangles are defined as similar if their angles are identical and their sides are proportional. You first learned about similar triangles when learning the properties of 45–45–90 and 30–60–90 triangles in Chapter 21: Triangles and Diagonals.

In fact, any triangles that have identical angles will have proportional side lengths, not just the special triangles. For example:

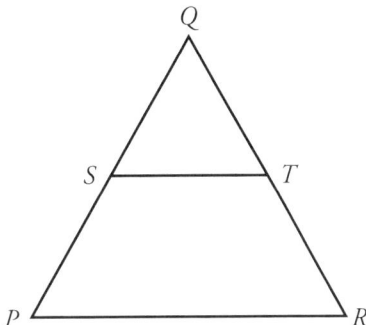

> Line segment *ST* is parallel to line segment *PR* and *S* is the midpoint of *PQ*. If *PR* is 10, what is the length of line segment *ST*?

Angle *Q* is the same for both triangles *PQR* and *SQT*. Because *ST* and *PR* are parallel, the other two angles in the triangles are also equivalent (for a refresher on the properties of parallel lines cut by a transversal, see Chapter 24: Lines and Angles). So, the smaller triangle *SQT* is similar to the larger triangle *PQR*.

Finally, because the problem indicates that *S* is the midpoint of *PQ*, the side length of the smaller triangle is half that of the larger triangle. Since these are similar triangles, all the side lengths must be proportional. If *PR* in the larger triangle has a side length of 10, then line *ST* in the smaller triangle must be half that, or 5. Therefore, the length of *ST* is 5.

Unit Six: **Advanced Topics**

Check Your Skills Answer Key

1. **Yes**

    Because you are given only relationships, pick a number. The number 10 is a good option because it is the common denominator of the fractions $\frac{1}{2}$ and $\frac{4}{5}$. Define Mili's first generation uHear as having a capacity of 10 gigabytes. Her second-generation uHear has three times the capacity, so it has a capacity of 30 gigabytes.

    Next, determine how filled each device is. Her first-generation uHear contains $\frac{1}{2} \times 10 = 5$ gigabytes and her second-generation uHear contains $\frac{4}{5} \times 30 = 24$ gigabytes. If Mili transferred the songs on the first uHear to the second, she would be using 29 total gigabytes out of a 30 gigabyte capacity, so there is enough room for the transfer.

2. **18 hours**

    This problem provides a real number (3 hours going to and from work), so don't pick numbers on this one. Figure out what portion of the total waking time that 3 hours represents.

    $$\frac{1}{3} + \frac{1}{5} + \frac{3}{10} = \frac{10}{30} + \frac{6}{30} + \frac{9}{30} = \frac{25}{30}$$

    The other three activities take up a total of $\frac{25}{30}$ of John's waking hours, so the 3 hours spent traveling back and forth to work represent the remaining $\frac{5}{30}$ of his time. That fraction of his total waking time equals 3 hours.

    $$\frac{5}{30} y = 3$$
    $$y = 3 \left(\frac{30}{5} \right)$$
    $$y = 18$$

    John is awake for 18 total hours.

3. **(C)**

    No lengths are given, therefore, you are free to pick some easy numbers to work with. Draw the figure and fill in all given information: The figures are squares. For the sides of the small square, 1 is an easy number, as it makes the area of square *BCDF* equal to (1)(1) = 1.

    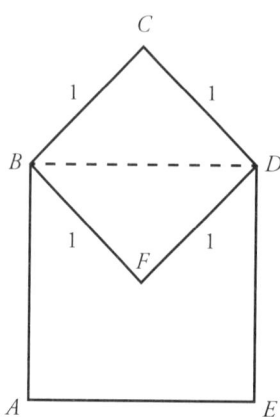

Next, identify relationships. The figure implies that the dashed line *BD* is both an edge of square *ABDE* and the diagonal of square *BCDF*, so line *BD* is the hypotenuse of equal right triangles *BCD* and *BDF*. Use the Pythagorean theorem on right triangle *BCD* to find the length of *BD*.

$$c^2 = a^2 + b^2$$
$$BD^2 = 1^2 + 1^2$$
$$BD^2 = 2$$
$$BD = \sqrt{2}$$

Thus, the area of square *ABDE* is $\sqrt{2} \times \sqrt{2} = 2$.

The shaded area is equal to the area of square *ABDE* minus half the area of square *BCDF*. The shaded area is $2 - \frac{1}{2} = \frac{3}{2}$.

Quantity A is 2 times the shaded area, or $2 \times \frac{3}{2} = 3$.

Quantity B is 3 times the area of *BCDF*, or $3 \times 1 = 3$.

The correct answer is (C): The two quantities are always equal.

You may recognize this problem—it was in the problem set for Chapter 20: Geometry on the GRE. Revisit that solution to see how much more complex it is to use variables. Assigning real, definitive numbers makes the solution much easier.

4. **(A)**

Since the product of *x* and *y* is negative, one variable is positive and the other is negative. And since *x* is greater than *y*, the variable *x* must be the positive one, while *y* must be negative. Next, compare the quantities: 3 raised to a positive value will be greater than 3 raised to a negative value.

The correct answer is (A): Quantity A is greater.

5. $\frac{171}{340}$

Compare the fractions to benchmarks.

$$\frac{123}{250} < \frac{125}{250} \rightarrow \frac{123}{250} < \frac{1}{2}$$
$$\frac{171}{340} > \frac{170}{340} \rightarrow \frac{171}{340} > \frac{1}{2}$$

Therefore, the second fraction must be greater.

6. **50**

Approximate each term. Try to cancel out the rounding errors, if possible.

$$\frac{15}{58} \approx \frac{15}{60} = \frac{1}{4} \text{ (rounded down)}$$
$$\frac{9}{19} \approx \frac{9}{18} = \frac{1}{2} \text{ (rounded up)}$$

Unit Six: **Advanced Topics**

The two estimations so far are rounded in opposite directions. Round the final value to 400 and solve.

$$\frac{1}{2} \times \frac{1}{4} \times 400 = 50$$

7. **$5,040**

    Use the simple interest formula to solve.

    $$Prt = (12,000)(0.14)(3)$$
    $$= 5,040$$

8. **$17,778.53**

    Use the compound interest formula (and the calculator!) to solve. $P = \$12,000$, $r = 14\%$, $n = 1$ (annual compounding), and $t = 3$ years.

    $$12,000\left(1 + \frac{0.14}{1}\right)^{1 \times 3}$$
    $$12,000 \times (1.14)^3$$
    $$17,778.53$$

    First, simplify what's in the parentheses, then find the cube of 1.14 on the calculator, and finally, multiply by 12,000. The total owed at the end of the three years is $17,778.53: the original loan of $12,000 and interest of $5,778.53.

9. **7**

    No real values are given for x and y, so choose your own. Since x has a remainder of 4 when divided by 9, start with the first multiple of 9 (which is 9 itself) and add 4. Make $x = 13$.

    Since y has a remainder of 3 when divided by 9, again start with the first multiple of 9 and add 3. Make $y = 12$.

    Therefore, $x + y = 13 + 12 = 25$. Finally, 9 goes into 25 two whole times $(2)(9) = 18$, leaving 7 left over to add up to 25.

    Alternatively, add the remainders directly, compensating for any excess remainders.
    R4 + R3 = R7, which is less than the divisor, 9, so there are no excess remainders to remove. The remainder is 7.

10. **3**

    No real values are given for x and y, so choose your own. Since x has a remainder of 4 when divided by 9, start with the first multiple of 9 (which is 9 itself) and add 4. Make $x = 13$.

    Since y has a remainder of 3 when divided by 9, again start with the first multiple of 9 and add 3. Make $y = 12$.

    Therefore, $(12)(13) = 156$. Next, use the calculator to find the quotient, which is the integer portion of the decimal result returned by a calculator.

    $$\frac{156}{9} = 17.333$$

So, the 9 goes evenly into 156 a total of 17 times, or $(17)(9) = 153$, leaving 3 for the remainder.

Alternatively, multiply the remainders directly, compensating for any excess remainders. $(R4)(R3) = R12$, which is more than the divisor, 9, so subtract 9 to correct for the excess remainder. $R12 - R9 = R3$, so the remainder is 3.

11. **(C) 80**

    Use the $r \times t = d$ equation to solve for time.

    $$1{,}643{,}849 \times t = 131{,}479{,}714$$

    Use the heavy division shortcut to simplify before plugging into the calculator.

    $$\frac{131{,}479{,}714}{1{,}643{,}849} = \frac{1{,}314.79714}{16.43849} \approx \frac{1{,}314}{16} \approx 82$$

Unit Six: Advanced Topics

Problem Set

1.
Quantity A	Quantity B
The tenths digit of the product of two even integers divided by 4	The tenths digit of the product of an even and an odd integer divided by 4

2. $$\frac{x}{y} < 0$$
   $$y > x$$

Quantity A	Quantity B
$y - x$	xy

3. Estimate to the closest integer: What is $\frac{11}{40}$ of $\frac{5}{16}$ of 120 ?

4. Put these fractions in order from least to greatest: $\frac{9}{17}, \frac{3}{16}, \frac{19}{20}, \frac{7}{15}$

5. Put these fractions in order from least to greatest: $\frac{2}{3}, \frac{3}{13}, \frac{5}{7}, \frac{2}{9}$

6. Lori deposits $100 in a savings account at 2% interest, compounded annually. After three years, what is the balance on the account? (Assume Lori makes no withdrawals or deposits and that the balance is rounded to the hundreds digit.)

7. A loan is provided at 7% interest, compounded annually. If the interest after the first year is $210, what was the initial principal on the loan?

8. If k is an integer, and if 0.02468×10^k is greater than 10,000, what is the least possible value of k ?

9. Estimate to the nearest 10,000: $\frac{4{,}509{,}982{,}344}{5.042 \times 10^4}$

10. Simplify: $(4 \times 10^{-2}) - (2.5 \times 10^{-3})$

11. Which integer values of j would give the number $-37{,}129 \times 10^j$ a value between -100 and -1 ?

12. Which integer values of b would give the number $2002 \div 10^{-b}$ a value between 1 and 100 ?

13. Simplify: $\frac{0.00081}{0.09}$

14.
Quantity A	Quantity B
$\frac{573}{10^{-2}}$	0.573×10^5

15.
Quantity A	Quantity B
$\frac{603{,}789{,}420}{13.3 \times 10^7}$	5

16.
$$a < b < 0 < c < d$$

Quantity A	**Quantity B**
abc	$c - d$

17.
n is an integer.

Quantity A	**Quantity B**
$(-1)^{2n+1} \times (-1)^n$	$(1)^n$

18. When is $|x - 4|$ equal to $4 - x$?

19. Which of the following graphs is the graph of function $g(x) = |x - 1| - 1$?

Ⓐ

Ⓑ
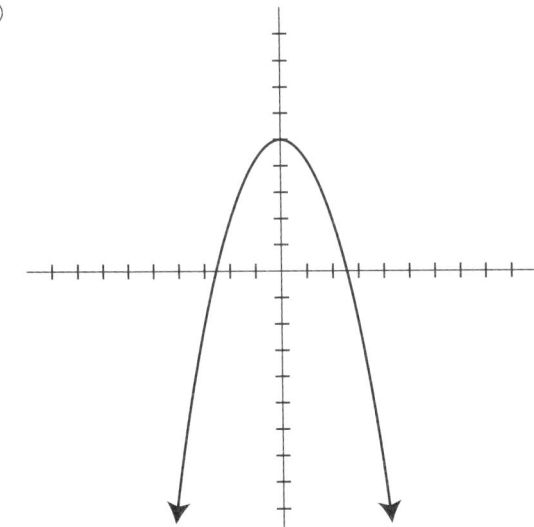

Unit Six: **Advanced Topics**

C

D

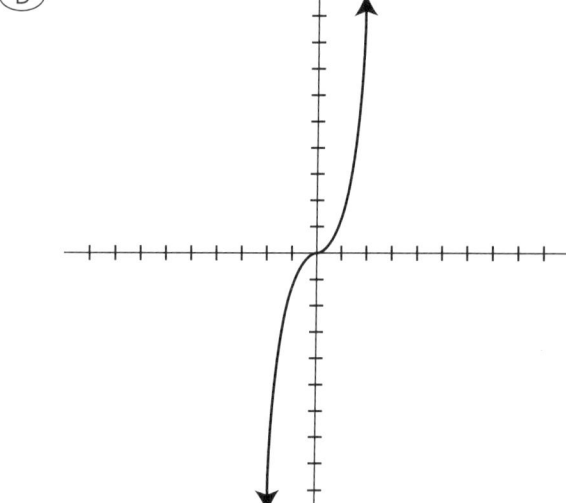

Chapter 32: **Advanced Concepts**

Solutions

1. **(D)**

   For Quantity A, the product of two even integers will always divide evenly by 4 because each even number has a 2 in its prime tree. For instance, 2 × 2 = 4, 2 × 4 = 8, and 2 × 6 = 12. All of these numbers are divisible by 4, and the integer that results after dividing by 4 will always have a zero in the tenths digit.

   $$\frac{4}{4} = 1.0$$
   $$\frac{8}{4} = 2.0$$

   For Quantity B, the product will be an even integer, because even × odd = even. That even value will be divisible by 4 is the even number is a multiple of 4, but it will not be divisible by 4 if the even number is only a multiple of 2.

   $$\frac{2 \times 1}{4} = \frac{1}{2} = 0.5$$
   $$\frac{4 \times 1}{4} = 1.0$$

   Quantity A must be 0, but Quantity B could be 5 or 0, so it could be equal to or greater than Quantity A.

   The correct answer is (D): The relationship cannot be determined.

2. **(A)**

   The first inequality indicates that this is a Positive/Negative question. If $\frac{x}{y}$ is negative, then x and y have different signs. If $y > x$, then y must be positive and x negative. In Quantity A, you have a positive minus a negative—this will create a greater positive. In Quantity B, you have a negative times a positive, which is always negative.

   The correct answer is (A): Quantity A is greater.

3. **Approximately 10**

   Use Benchmark Values to estimate: $\frac{11}{40}$ is slightly more than $\frac{1}{4}$, whereas $\frac{5}{16}$ is slightly less than $\frac{1}{3}$. Therefore, $\frac{11}{40}$ of $\frac{5}{16}$ of 120 is approximately $\frac{1}{4}$ of $\frac{1}{3}$ of 120, or $\frac{120}{12} = 10$. In this process, you rounded one fraction up and the other down, reducing the error you introduced by rounding.

   According to a calculator, the exact result is 10.3125. You can, of course, pull up the calculator, but it can be cumbersome to use. It's a good idea to get into the habit of checking whether the problem can be estimated quickly without having to bother with the calculator.

4. $\frac{3}{16} < \frac{7}{15} < \frac{9}{17} < \frac{19}{20}$

   Use Benchmark Values to compare these fractions:

$\frac{9}{17}$ is slightly more than $\frac{1}{2}$.	$\frac{3}{16}$ is slightly less than $\frac{1}{4}$.
$\frac{19}{20}$ is slightly less than 1.	$\frac{7}{15}$ is slightly less than $\frac{1}{2}$.

   This is the order of the fractions from least to greatest:

   $$\frac{3}{16} < \frac{7}{15} < \frac{9}{17} < \frac{19}{20}.$$

Unit Six: **Advanced Topics**

All four of these fractions are spread out in such a way that you don't have to use the calculator. If, on a different problem, two values are too close to estimate easily, use the calculator to compare—but save time whenever you can by estimating.

5. $\frac{2}{9} < \frac{3}{13} < \frac{2}{3} < \frac{5}{7}$

Using Benchmark Values, you can determine that $\frac{3}{13}$ and $\frac{2}{9}$ are both less than $\frac{1}{2}$, and $\frac{2}{3}$ and $\frac{5}{7}$ are both more than $\frac{1}{2}$. Use cross-multiplication to compare each pair of fractions:

| $3 \times 9 = 27$ | $\frac{3}{13} \times \frac{2}{9}$ | $2 \times 13 = 26$ | Thus, $\frac{3}{13} > \frac{2}{9}$. |
| $2 \times 7 = 24$ | $\frac{2}{3} \times \frac{5}{7}$ | $5 \times 3 = 15$ | Thus, $\frac{2}{3} < \frac{5}{7}$. |

Alternatively, use the calculator to compare the two pairs. If you already know the decimal equivalent of $\frac{2}{3}$, no need to plug that one in.

This is the order of the fractions from least to greatest: $\frac{2}{9} < \frac{3}{13} < \frac{2}{3} < \frac{5}{7}$.

6. **$106.12**

Interest compounded annually is a series of successive percent increases. Use the calculator for the second and third years.

(1) 100.00 is increased by 2%:	$100(1.02) = 102$
(2) 102.00 is increased by 2%:	$102(1.02) = 104.04$
(3) 104.04 is increased by 2%:	$104.04(1.02) \cong 106.12$

7. **$3,000**

$210 represents 7% of the original loan. Use a proportion to find 100% of the loan value.

PART	210	7
WHOLE	x	100

$\frac{210}{x} = \frac{7}{100}$

$21,000 = 7x$

$3,000 = x$

8. **6**

Multiplying 0.02468 by a positive power of 10 will shift the decimal point to the right. Shift the decimal point to the right until the result is greater than 10,000. Shifting the decimal point five times results in 2,468. This is still less than 10,000. Shifting one more place yields 24,680, which is greater than 10,000.

9. **90,000**

Use the Heavy Division Shortcut to estimate.

$$\frac{4,509,982,344}{50,420} = \frac{4,509,982,344}{50,420} = \frac{4,500,000}{50} \approx 90,000$$

908

Because the denominator in this case has a zero in the units digit, you can simplify this fraction all the way down to just one digit on the bottom—that is, cross off an extra zero on the top and bottom so that you're dividing by 5. If the units digit is not a 0, though, then keep two digits in the denominator, as the chapter explained.

10. **0.0375**
    First, rewrite the numbers in standard notation by shifting the decimal point. Then add zeros, line up the decimal points, and subtract—or use the calculator.

    $$\begin{array}{r} 0.0400 \\ -0.0025 \\ \hline 0.0375 \end{array}$$

    If you write it out, ignore the decimals and zeros to the left of the numbers for a moment: At heart, the problem is 400 minus 25. So the answer contains the numbers 375; you just need to adjust for the decimal point.

11. **{−3, −4}**
    To give −37,129 a value between −100 and −1, you must shift the decimal point to change the number to −37.129 or −3.7129. This requires a shift of either three or four places to the left. Multiplication by a positive exponent shifts the decimal point to the right. To shift the decimal point three places to the *left*, multiply by 10^{-3}. To shift it four places to the left, multiply by 10^{-4}. Therefore, the exponent $j = \{-3, -4\}$.

12. **{−2, −3}**
    To give 2002 a value between 1 and 100 when dividing by a power of 10, you must shift the decimal point to change the number to 2.002 or 20.02. This requires a shift of either two or three places to the left. Multiplication shifts the decimal point to the right, and division shifts it to the left. To shift the decimal point two places to the left, divide by 10^2. To shift it three places to the left, divide by 10^3. Therefore, the exponent $-b = \{2, 3\}$, and $b = \{-2, -3\}$.

13. **0.009**
    You can plug this directly into your calculator, but there are so many zeros that you might want to simplify first in order to reduce the chances of making a mistake while punching the keys. Move the decimal two places over on the top and bottom.

    $$\frac{0.00081}{0.09} = \frac{0.081}{9}$$

    Then divide to get 0.009.

14. **(C)**
    In Quantity A, dividing by 10 raised to a negative power is the same as multiplying by 10 raised to a positive power. Move the decimal two places to the right, so that 573 becomes 57,300.

    In Quantity B, multiplying by 10 raised to a positive power moves the decimal five places to the right, so that 0.573 becomes 57,300.

    The correct answer is (C): The two quantities are always equal.

Unit Six: **Advanced Topics**

15. **(B)**

    Quantity A looks pretty intimidating at first. The trap here is to try to find an exact value for the expression in Quantity A. Estimate instead:

    $603{,}789{,}420 \approx 600{,}000{,}000$

    $13.3 \times 10^7 \approx 133{,}000{,}000$, or even better, $130{,}000{,}000$

    $$\frac{600{,}000{,}000}{130{,}000{,}00} = \frac{60}{13}$$

    Plug that into your calculator or glance at Quantity B—can you estimate whether this fraction is greater or less than 5?

    5×13 is 65, not 60. So $\frac{60}{13}$ is going to be something less than 5.

    The correct answer is (B): Quantity B is greater.

16. **(A)**

    When variables are ordered from least to greatest, look for the pattern. Variables *a* and *b* are negative, while *c* and *d* are positive. Try working only with positives and negatives first, before considering more specific numbers.

    In Quantity A, *abc* is a negative times a negative times a positive—that is, Quantity A is a positive value.

    In Quantity B, *c* − *d* is a positive minus a positive. A positive minus a positive can yield either a positive or a negative value (for instance 10 minus 1 is positive while 1 minus 10 is negative). So look back up at the initial information: *d* is greater than *c*. Thus, *c* − *d* is an instance of subtracting a larger positive from a smaller positive, which yields a negative.

    Quantity A is positive and Quantity B is negative.

    The correct answer is (A): Quantity A is greater.

17. **(D)**

    The values −1 and 1, when raised to an integer power, have very limited possibilities. Negative 1 raised to an even power is 1, and −1 raised to an odd power is −1, whereas 1 raised to any power is always 1. Therefore, this is really a problem about odds and evens.

    Start with Quantity B, as it's less complicated. It is always equal to 1. For Quantity A, try an even and an odd value for *n* to see what happens.

    If $n = 2$, Quantity A is equal to $(-1)^5 \times (-1)^2 = (-1) \times (1) = -1$.

    If $n = 3$, Quantity A is equal to $(-1)^7 \times (-1)^3 = (-1) \times (-1) = 1$.

    Alternatively, examine Quantity A theoretically. The value $(-1)^{2n+1}$ is equal to −1 raised to an odd power, because 2*n* must be even, so 2*n* + 1 must be odd. So $-1^{(odd)}$ will always be −1. By contrast, in the term $(-1)^n$, the exponent could be odd or even, so this value may be either 1 or −1. The full expression $(-1)^{2n+1} \times (-1)^n$ could therefore be equal to $(-1)(1) = -1$ or $(-1)(-1) = 1$.

    The correct answer is (D): The relationship cannot be determined.

910

18. **x ≤ 4**

There are two ways to interpret absolute value, depending on whether the expression inside the absolute value is negative or not. If $x - 4$ is 0 or greater, the absolute value sign does nothing. But if the value of $x - 4$ is negative, then the absolute value flips the sign. Test both cases for $|x - 4| = 4 - x$.

$$\text{If } (x - 4) \geq 0:$$
$$|x - 4| = 4 - x$$
$$x - 4 = 4 - x$$
$$2x = 8$$
$$x = 4$$

$$\text{If } (x - 4) < 0:$$
$$|x - 4| = 4 - x$$
$$x - 4 = -(4 - x)$$
$$x - 4 = -4 + x$$
$$x = x$$

So what does all this mean? The left column indicates that the two sides will be equal when $x = 4$. The result in the right column may not seem to mean much, since x is always equal to x. But that means that this result will work for *any* value of x that fits the initial condition: $(x - 4) < 0$. This simplifies to $x < 4$. So $|x - 4|$ is also equal to $4 - x$ when x is less than 4. Put the two results together: $x \leq 4$.

19. **(C)**

$g(x) = |x - 1| - 1$. This function is built on an absolute value, which typically has a V-shape. You can identify the correct graph by trying $x = 0$, which yields $g(0) = 0$, the origin. Then, try $x = 1$, which yields $g(1) = -1$ and the point $(1, -1)$. Next, try $x = 2$: $g(2) = |2 - 1| - 1 = 1 - 1 = 0$. These three points fall on the V-shape.

You can also arrive at the answer by process of elimination. First, all of the other answers include an infinite range of negative y-values, so they can't be built on an absolute value function. Second, they all represent graphs of other common functions:

(A) is a standard linear equation of the form $y = mx + b$.

(B) is a quadratic equation. The equation would need to include x^2.

(D) is a cubic equation (something with an x^3).

APPENDIX

GRE Math Glossary

absolute value: The distance from zero on the number line for a particular term (e.g., the absolute value of -7 is written as $|-7|$ and equals 7).

arc length: A section of a circle's circumference.

area: The space enclosed by a given closed shape on a plane; the formula depends on the specific shape (e.g., the area of a rectangle equals $length \times width$).

axis: One of the two number lines (x-axis or y-axis) used to indicate position on a coordinate plane. (See figure.)

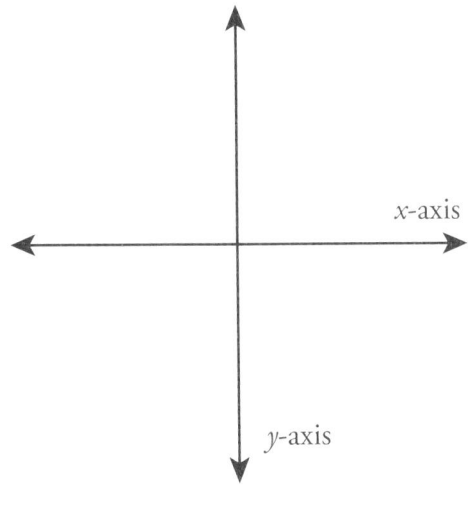

base: In the expression b^n, the variable b represents the base. This is the number that you multiply by itself n times. Also can refer to the horizontal side of a triangle.

center (circle): The point from which any point on a circle's radius is equidistant.

central angle: The angle created by any two radii of a circle. (See figure.)

circle: A set of points in a plane that are equidistant from a fixed center point.

circumference: The measure of the perimeter of a circle. The circumference of a circle can be found with this formula: $C = 2\pi r$, where C is the circumference and r is the radius.

coefficient: A number being multiplied by a variable. In the equation $y = 2x + 5$, the coefficient of the x term is 2.

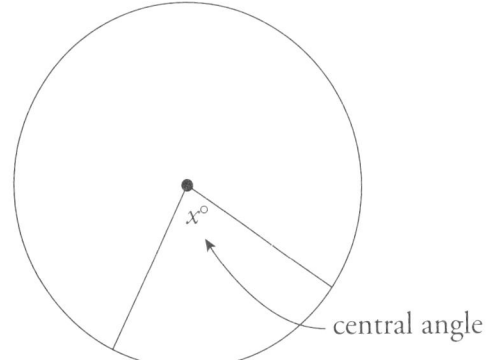

common denominator: When adding or subtracting fractions, you first must find a common denominator, generally the least common multiple of both numbers.

Example:

Given $\left(\frac{3}{5}\right) + \left(\frac{1}{2}\right)$, the two denominators are 5 and 2. The least multiple that works for both numbers is 10. The common denominator, therefore, is 10.

Appendix: GRE Math Glossary

composite number: Any number that has more than two factors. Thus, composite numbers are not prime. For example, 4 is a composite number because it has three factors: 1, 2, and 4.

constant: A number that doesn't change in an equation or expression. You may not know its value, but the number is "constant," in contrast to a variable, which varies. In the equation $y = 3x + 2$, the values 3 and 2 are constants. In the equation of a line, $y = mx + b$, both m and b are constants, even if you have not been told what the values are.

coordinate plane: Consists of a horizontal axis (typically labeled "x") and a vertical axis (typically labeled "y"), crossing at the number zero on both axes.

decimal: Numbers that fall in between integers. A decimal can express a part-to-whole relationship, just as a percent or fraction can.

Example:

The number 1.2 is a decimal. The integers 1 and 2 are not decimals. An integer written as 1.0, however, is considered a decimal. The decimal 0.2 is equivalent to 20% or to $\frac{2}{10} \left(= \frac{1}{5}\right)$.

denominator: The bottom of a fraction. In the fraction $\frac{7}{2}$, the denominator is 2.

diameter: A line segment that passes through the center of a circle and whose endpoints lie on the circle.

difference: When one number is subtracted from another, the difference is what is left over. The difference of 7 and 5 is 2, because $7 - 5 = 2$.

digit: The ten numbers 0, 1, 2, 3, 4, 5, 6, 7, 8, and 9. Used in combination to represent other numbers (e.g., 12 or 0.38).

distributed form: Presenting an expression as a sum or difference. In distributed form, terms are added or subtracted. For example, $x^2 - 1$ is in distributed form, as is $x^2 + 2x + 1$. In contrast, $(x + 1)(x - 1)$ is not in distributed form; it is in factored form.

divisible: If an integer x divided by another integer y yields an integer, then x is said to be divisible by y.

Example:

The number 12 divided by 3 yields the integer 4. Therefore, 12 is divisible by 3. However, 12 divided by 5 does not yield an integer. Therefore, 12 is not divisible by 5.

divisor: The part of a division operation that comes after the division sign. In the operation $22 \div 4$ (or $\frac{22}{4}$), 4 is the divisor. Divisor is also a synonym for factor. (See *factor*.)

equation: A combination of mathematical expressions and symbols that contains an equals sign. For example, $3 + 7 = 10$ is an equation, as is $x + y = 3$. An equation makes a statement: The left side equals the right side.

equilateral triangle: A triangle in which all three angles are equal (and since the three angles in a triangle always add to 180°, each angle is equal to 60°). In addition, all three sides are of equal length.

even: An integer is even if it is divisible by 2. For example, 14 is even because $\frac{14}{2}$ equals the integer 7.

Appendix: **GRE Math Glossary**

exponent: In the expression b^n, the variable n represents the exponent. The exponent indicates how many times to multiply the base, b, by itself. For example, $4^3 = 4 \times 4 \times 4$, or 4 multiplied by itself three times.

expression: A combination of numbers and mathematical symbols that does not contain an equals sign. For example, xy is an expression, as is $x + 3$. An expression represents a quantity.

factor: Positive integers that divide evenly into an integer. Factors are equal to or less than the integer in question. For example, 12 is a factor of 12, as are 1, 2, 3, 4, and 6.

factored form: Presenting an expression as a product. In factored form, expressions are multiplied together. The expression $(x + 1)(x - 1)$ is in factored form: $(x + 1)$ and $(x - 1)$ are the factors. In contrast, $x^2 - 1$ is not in factored form; it is in distributed form.

factor foundation rule: If a is a factor of b, and b is a factor of c, then a is also a factor of c. For example, 2 is a factor of 10 and 10 is a factor of 60. Therefore, 2 is also a factor of 60.

factor tree: Use the "factor tree" to break any number down into its prime factors. (See figure.)

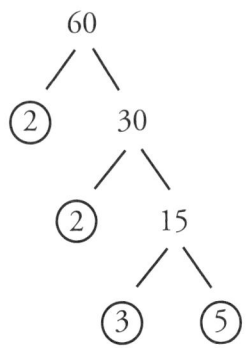

FOIL: First, Outside, Inside, Last; an acronym to remember the method for converting from factored to distributed form in a quadratic equation or expression. For example, $(y + 2)(y - 3)$ is a quadratic expression in factored form. Multiply the First, Outside, Inside, and Last terms to get the distributed form: $y \times y = y^2$, $y \times -3 = -3y$, $2 \times y = 2y$, and $2 \times -3 = -6$. The full distributed form is $y^2 - 3y + 2y - 6$. This can be simplified to $y^2 - y - 6$.

fraction: A way to express numbers that fall in between integers. A fraction expresses a part-to-whole relationship in terms of a numerator (the part) and a denominator (the whole); for example, $\frac{3}{4}$ is a fraction. Integers can also be expressed in fractional form; for example, the integer 1 can be expressed as $\frac{4}{4}$.

hypotenuse: The longest side of a right triangle. The hypotenuse is always the side opposite the right angle.

improper fraction: Fractions that are greater than 1. An improper fraction can also be written as a mixed number. For example, $\frac{7}{2}$ is an improper fraction. This can also be written as a mixed number: $3\frac{1}{2}$.

inequality: A comparison of quantities that have different values. There are four ways to express inequalities: less than ($<$); less than or equal to ($\leq$); greater than ($>$); greater than or equal to ($\geq$). Can be manipulated in the same way as equations with one exception: When multiplying or dividing by a negative number, the inequality sign flips.

integers: Numbers, such as $-1, 0, 1, 2,$ and 3, that have no fractional part. Integers include the counting numbers $(1, 2, 3, \ldots)$, their negative counterparts $(-1, -2, -3, \ldots)$, and 0.

interior angles: The angles that appear in the interior of a closed shape.

isosceles triangle: A triangle in which exactly two of the three angles are equal; in addition, the sides opposite the two equal angles are equal in length.

line: A set of points that extend infinitely in one direction without curving. On the GRE, lines are by definition perfectly straight.

Appendix: **GRE Math Glossary**

line segment: A continuous, finite section of a line. For example, the sides of a triangle or of a rectangle are line segments.

linear equation: An equation that does not contain exponents or multiple variables multiplied together. For example, $x + y = 3$ is a linear equation; $xy = 3$ and $y = x^2$ are not. When plotted on a coordinate plane, linear equations create lines.

mixed number: An integer combined with a proper fraction. A mixed number can also be written as an improper fraction: $3\frac{1}{2}$ is a mixed number. This can also be written as an improper fraction, $\frac{7}{2}$.

multiple: Multiples are integers formed by multiplying some integer by any other integer. For example, 12 is a multiple of 12 ($= 12 \times 1$), as are 24 ($= 12 \times 2$), 36 ($= 12 \times 3$), 48 ($= 12 \times 4$), and 60 ($= 12 \times 5$). (Negative multiples are possible in mathematics but are not typically tested on the GRE.)

negative: Any number to the left of zero on a number line; can be an integer or non-integer.

negative exponent: Any exponent less than zero. To find a value for a term with a negative exponent, put the term containing the exponent in the denominator of a fraction and make the exponent positive.

Examples:

$$4^{-2} = \frac{1}{4^2}$$

$$\frac{1}{3^{-2}} = \frac{1}{\left(\frac{1}{3}\right)^2} = \frac{1}{\frac{1}{9}} = 9$$

number line: A straight line that represents all the numbers from negative infinity to infinity.

numerator: The top of a fraction. In the fraction $\frac{7}{2}$, the numerator is 7.

odd: An integer that is not divisible by 2. For example, 15 is odd because $\frac{15}{2}$ is not an integer; it equals 7.5.

order of operations: The order in which mathematical operations must be carried out in order to simplify an expression. (See *PEMDAS*.)

the origin: The coordinate pair (0, 0) represents the origin of a coordinate plane.

parallelogram: A four-sided, closed shape composed of straight lines in which the opposite sides are equal and the opposite angles are equal. (See figure.)

PEMDAS: An acronym that stands for Parentheses, Exponents, Multiplication, Division, Addition, Subtraction; used to remember the order of operations.

percent: Literally, "per one hundred"; expresses a special part-to-whole relationship between a number (the part) and one hundred (the whole). A special type of fraction or decimal that involves the number 100 (e.g., 50% = 50 out of 100).

perimeter: In a polygon, the sum of the lengths of the sides.

perpendicular: Lines that intersect at a 90° angle.

plane: A flat, two-dimensional surface that extends infinitely in every direction.

point: An object that exists in a single location on the coordinate plane. Each point has a unique *x*-coordinate and *y*-coordinate that together describe its location. For example, $(1, -2)$ is a point.

polygon: A two-dimensional, closed shape made of line segments. For example, a triangle is a polygon, as is a rectangle. A circle is a closed shape, but it is not a polygon because it does not contain line segments.

positive: Any number to the right of zero on a number line; can be an integer or non-integer.

prime factorization: A number expressed as a product of prime numbers. For example, the prime factorization of 60 is $2 \times 2 \times 3 \times 5$.

prime number: A positive integer with exactly two factors: 1 and itself. The number 1 does not qualify as prime because it has only one factor, not two. The number 2 is the least prime number; it is also the only even prime number. The numbers 2, 3, 5, 7, 11, 13, etc. are prime.

product: The end result when two numbers are multiplied together (e.g., the product of 4 and 5 is 20).

Pythagorean theorem: A formula used to calculate the sides of a right triangle: $a^2 + b^2 = c^2$, where *a* and *b* are the lengths of the two legs of the triangle and *c* is the length of the hypotenuse of the triangle.

Pythagorean triplet: A set of three numbers that describes the lengths of the three sides of a right triangle in which all three sides have integer lengths. Common Pythagorean triplets are 3–4–5, 6–8–10, and 5–12–13.

quadrant: One quarter of the coordinate plane. Bounded on two sides by the *x*-axis and *y*-axis. Often labeled I, II, III, and IV. (See figure.)

quadratic expression: An expression including a variable raised to the second power (and no higher powers). Commonly of the form $ax^2 + bx + c$, where *a*, *b*, and *c* are constants.

quotient: The result of dividing one number by another. The quotient of $10 \div 5$ is 2.

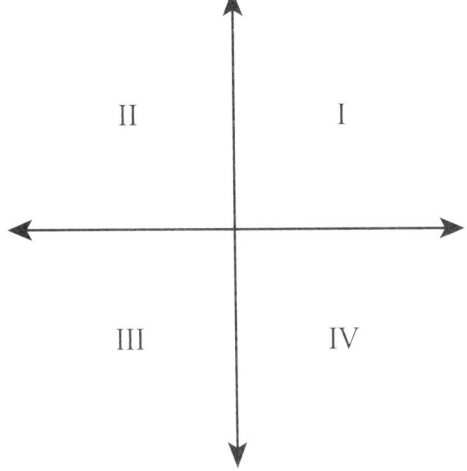

radius: A line segment that connects the center of a circle with any point on that circle's circumference. Plural: radii.

reciprocal: The product of a number and its reciprocal is always 1. To get the reciprocal of a number, divide 1 by that number. For example, the reciprocal of 2 is $\frac{1}{2}$ and the reciprocal of $\frac{2}{3}$ is $\frac{1}{\left(\frac{2}{3}\right)} = \frac{3}{2}$. This works even when the number is a decimal; for example, the reciprocal of 0.25 is $\frac{1}{0.25} = 4$.

rectangle: A four-sided closed shape in which all of the angles equal $90°$ and in which the lengths of the opposite sides are equal. Rectangles are also parallelograms.

right triangle: A triangle that includes a $90°$, or right, angle.

Appendix: **GRE Math Glossary**

root: The opposite of an exponent (in a sense). The square root of 16 (written $\sqrt{16}$) is the number (or numbers) that, when multiplied by itself, will yield 16. In this case, both 4 and -4 would multiply to 16 mathematically. However, when the GRE provides the root sign for an even root, such as a square root, then the only accepted answer is the positive root, 4. That is, $\sqrt{16} = 4$, *not* $+4$ or -4. In contrast, the equation $x^2 = 16$ has *two* solutions, $+4$ and -4.

sector: A wedge of a circle, composed of the area enclosed by two radii and the arc connecting those two radii. (See figure.)

simplify: Reduce numerators and denominators to the least form by taking out common factors. Dividing the numerator and denominator by the same number does not change the value of the fraction.

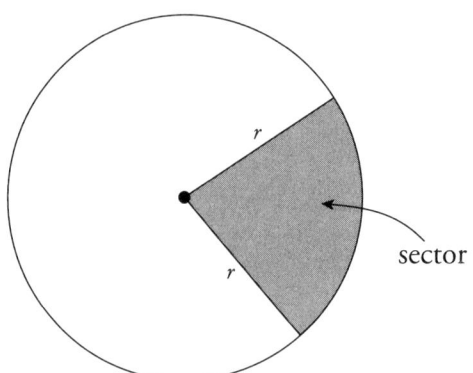

Example:

Given $\frac{21}{6}$, simplify by dividing both the numerator and the denominator by 3. The simplified fraction is $\frac{7}{2}$.

slope: Rise over run, or the distance the line runs vertically divided by the distance the line runs horizontally. The slope of any given line is constant over the length of that line. In the example shown, the slope of the line is 2, because from the leftmost labeled point to the rightmost labeled point, the line goes up 2 units and over 1 unit, and $\frac{2}{1} = 2$. (See figure.)

square: A four-sided, closed shape in which all of the angles equal 90° and the lengths of all of the sides are equal. Squares are also rectangles and parallelograms.

sum: The result when two numbers are added together. The sum of 4 and 7 is 11.

term: Parts within an expression or equation that are separated by either a plus sign or a minus sign (e.g., in the expression $x + 3$, the two terms are x and 3).

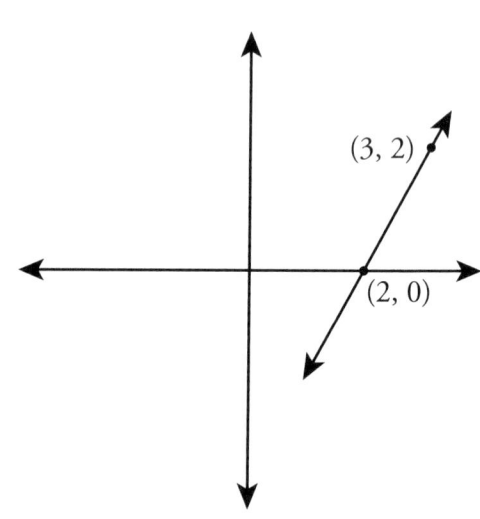

triangle: A three-sided, closed shape composed of straight lines; the interior angles add up to 180°.

two-dimensional: A shape containing a length and a width.

variable: A letter used as a substitute for an unknown value, or number. Common letters for variables are x, y, z, and t. In contrast to a constant, you can generally think of a variable as a value that can change (hence the term variable). In the equation $y = 3x + 2$, both y and x are variables.

***x*-axis:** A horizontal number line that indicates left–right position on a coordinate plane.

***x*-coordinate:** The number that indicates where a point lies along the *x*-axis. Always written first in a coordinate pair. For example, the *x*-coordinate of $(2, -1)$ is 2.

x-intercept: The point where a line crosses the x-axis (that is, when $y = 0$). (See figure.)

y-axis: A vertical number line that indicates up–down position on a coordinate plane.

y-coordinate: The number that indicates where a point lies along the y-axis. Always written second in a coordinate pair. The y-coordinate of $(2, -1)$ is -1.

y-intercept: The point where a line crosses the y-axis (that is, when $x = 0$). In the equation of a line $y = mx + b$, the y-intercept equals b. Technically, the coordinates of the y-intercept are $(0, b)$. (See figure.)

NEED MORE THAN BOOKS? TRY INTERACT™ FOR GRE®!

Interact for GRE is an on-demand, adaptive learning experience made by Manhattan Prep's 99th-percentile GRE instructors. It's like having a GRE teacher with you anywhere you are. Interact adapts to your performance by providing you with prompts and delivering customized feedback based on your responses. This branching video technology makes Interact personalized to your skill level, so you'll never feel left behind.